SHIRAK'S

English-Armenian
Dictionary with Transliteration

OHANNES HANNESSIAN

ISBN: 1-58253-035-1

First edition Year: 1999
Published & distributed by: **Shirak Publishing House**

Library of Congress CIP: 99-70905

Printed by:
Shirak Printing & Bookstore
4960 Hollywood Blvd.,
Los Angeles, CA 90027 U.S.A.
Phone: (323) 667-1128
Fax: (323) 667-1126
e-mail: SHIRAKUSA@AOL.COM

AN INVITATION TO THE ARMENIAN LANGUAGE

The function of a dictionary is to bring together its literal and figurative words, defining objects and concepts that describe the cutting edge of modern life, as well as those terms which transmit the rich legacy of a historic past. All these are accessible and in a understandable format.

The difficulties of compiling such a dictionary under the most ideal circumstances seems challenging enough. Hovhannes Hannessian has taken on and brought to fruition a daunting lexicographic endeavor of love, a manifestation of his faith commitment to the spirit of linguistic education and enrichment for his Armenian people.

Procrastination is a rationalization for seeking to produce the perfect, most comprehensive dictionary is not the course Mr. Hannessian has chosen. Rather, he has opted to compile a useful, practical tool for an audience of readers perhaps familiar with the spoken Armenian language but unfamiliar with the Armenian script, created in the 5th century AD by the missionary monk, Mesrob Mashtots.

The compiler has taken great sacrifices to correct errata that have been passed down from one generation of dictionaries to another. Usefulness is dependent not only upon the words contained, but also of those omitted. Obsolete or obsolescent words have been replaced by the more useful contemporary, technical and commercial terms.

Historical events, breakthroughs in science and technology, new trends in music, culinary tastes and leisure activities, all produce their own vocabulary at a startling. Some of these new words, like the phenomena themselves, will be outmoded and soon forgotten. A good dictionary reflects such linguistic developments, that includes new terms, contains an extensive business list, a geographical list which takes into account the dramatic upheavals of the past few years, examples taken from contemporary usage and vocabulary, and the latest terms used in such ever-changing fields as ecology, computer science, and medicine.

Meticulous observation of the way language has been evolving has been incorporated into the existing text to give an accurate picture of the way English and Armenian are being spoken and written as we approach the millenium.

The present work embodies a fresh approach to bilingual lexicography with its emphasis on the current living language of everyday communication enlightenment and appreciation of all who use it. It demonstrates to the young generation of Armenians in the Diaspora that they can use their knowledge of English to look and find the meaning and pronunciation of its Armenian equivalent, not only in the script of our forefathers, but also in Romanized phonetic form. It confirms for the Armenophone newcomers the value of their knowledge of the mother tongue, which is helping them develop proficiency in the English language.

This dictionary is a true key for the student of language, regardless of his or her cultural background, who wishes to master the Mesrobian tongue as a new idiom, for *"To know wisdom and counsel is to understand the words of genius."*

SYLVA NATALIE MANOOGIAN
Northeast Area Manager, Los Angeles Public Library

ԱՅՍ ԲԱՌԱՐԱՆԸ

Կեանքի սրընթաց վազքն ու արագ թաւալումը պատճառ կը հանդիսանան ծնունդ տալու նոր կարիքներու բոլոր բնագաւառներէ ներս:

Նորայայտ ամէն իր ու երեւոյթ, որ հանրային սեփականութեան վերածուի, զայն պէտք է կնքել անունով մը, որ կը կոչուի ԲԱՌ:

Յատկապէս բառարաններուն վիճակուած է իր բովանդակութեան մէջ համախմբելու նոր բառերը, անոնց իմաստն ու արժէքը՝ փոխանցելու համար ժողովուրդին, ենթահող ունենալով հինէն ժառանգ եկած բառերու հարստութիւնը:

Այս ոգիէն մեկնած, սոյն հատորին մէջ կը գտնէք բոլոր բնագաւառներու նորաստեղծ բառերը՝ որպէս յաւելում հին բառացանկին:

Հայ մարդուն համար, ժամանակակից անգլիերէն լեզուին նորակերտ բառերու աշխարհին մէջ մուտք գործելը կենսական անհրաժեշտութիւն է. առ այդ, իրաւ ուղին ա՛յս բառարանն է:

* * *

Հայ ազգի զաւակները մի՛շտ ենթակայ եղած են տեղափոխութեանց, հեռացած հայրենիքէն ու հայ կեանքէն: 20րդ դարու վերջաւորութեան՝ առաւել ուժգնութեամբ:

Երէկ, Հայաստանի ու Միջին Արեւելքի հայաշատ շրջաններու մէջ ծնած ու մեծցած բազմահազար հայեր ցրուած են աշխարհի տարածքին, ինչպէս՝ Եւրոպա, Աւստրալիա, Գանատա, եւ յատկապէս՝ Միացեալ Նահանգներ:

Տասնամեակ մը բաւեց, որ ուսանողական տարիքի հայ երախաներու փոքրաքանակ թիւ մը միայն կարենան յաճախել ազգային վարժարաններ, որոնք ի վիճակի կ՚ըլլան հայերէն խօսիլ ու կարդալ առանց խորացումի: Ալ չենք խօսիր հայ վարժարանի դուռ չտեսնող նոր սերունդին մասին:

Լոս Անճելըսի «ՇԻՐԱԿ» հրատարակչատունէն լոյս ընծայուած այս բառարանը ցոյց կու տայ ճիշդ ուղին սփիւռքահայ նորահաս այս սերունդին, որ իր գիտցած անգլիերէնով փնտռէ ու գտնէ հայերէն բառին իմաստն ու հնչումը,

- նախ՝ անգլիերէն տառադարձութեամբ,
- ապա՝ հայերէն ուղղագրութեամբ:

Այսպէս՝

way – jampa, oughi, antsk, michots (ճամբայ, ուղի, անցք, միջոց)

Այս բառարանը նաեւ վստահելի բանալի մըն է օտարին՝ տիրանալու համար հայ լեզուին ու բառամթերքին:

ՅՈՎՀ. ՀԱՆՆԷՍԵԱՆ

TRANSLITERATION TABLE
ՏԱՌԱՓՈԽՈՒՄԻ ՑԱՆԿ

Key to effective use of this dictionary
How to pronounce - ի՞նչպէս հնչել

English letters	Corresponding In Armenian	Pronunciations as in
a	ա	arm
b	պ	baby
c	գ-ք	key, cat
d	տ	dear
e	է	egg
f	ֆ	fire
g	կ	go
h	հ	home
i	ի	ill
j	ճ	joke
k	գ-ք	key, cat, quick
l	լ	love
m	մ	my
n	ն	nice
o	օ	open
p	բ-փ	paint
q	գ-ք	quick, key, cat
r	ր-ռ	red
s	ս	say
t	դ-թ	tea
u	ը	until
v	վ	voice
w	ուէ, ուի, ուու	way, we, wood
x	քս	fax
y	ի	ready
z	զ	zoo

English letters	Corresponding In Armenian	Pronunciations as in
ch	չ	church
dz	ծ	dzov
gh	ղ	Afghan
kh	խ	Khan
ou	ու	tourist, tour, too
ouy	ույ	ouyster, wye
sh	շ	shop
tiun	թիւն	tune
ts	ձ-ց	tsar
zh	յ	jabot (in French - jour, joli)

Table of Abbreviations

Համառօտագրութիւններ

a - adjective - ածական
n - noun - գոյական
v - verb - բայ
pl - plural - յոգնակի

A

a, an - *mu, mun* (մը, մըն)
a b c - *aypoupen* (այբուբեն)
aback - *tebi yed, yedevu* (դէպի ետ, ետեւը)
abacus - *aghiusag* (աղիւսակ)
abandon - *lukel, toghoul* (լքել, թողուլ)
abandoned - *lukvads, tzukvads* (լքուած, ձգուած)
abase - *nuvasdatsunel, tsadztsunel, ichetsunel* (նուաստացնել, ցածցնել, իջեցնել)
abasement - *nuvasdatsoum* (նուաստացում)
abash - *shupotetsunel, amuchtsunel* (շփոթեցնել, ամչցնել)
abate - *nuvazetsunel, ichetsunel, nuvazil* (նուազեցնել, իջեցնել, նուազիլ)
abatement - *nuvazoum* (նուազում)
abattoir - *usbantanots* (սպանդանոց)
abba - *vanagan, guronavor* (վանական, կրօնաւոր)
abbe - *guronagan* (կրօնական)
abbey - *vank* (վանք)
abbreviate - *gurjadel, ampopel* (կրճատել, ամփոփել)
abbreviation - *gurjadoum, habavoum* (կրճատում, յապաւում)
abdicate - *hurazharil* (Հրաժարիլ)
abdication - *hurazharoum* (Հրաժարում)
abdomen - *vorovayn, por* (որովայն, փոր)
abduce - *vudarel, darakurel* (վտարել, տարագրել)
abduct - *hapushdagel, gorzel* (յափշտակել, կորզել)
abduction - *hapushdagoum, gorzoum* (յափշտակում, կորզում)
abductor - *hapushdagogh, gorzogh* (յափշտակող, կորզող)
aberrance - *see: aberration* (տե՛ս՝ *aberration*)
aberrate - *moloril, khodoril* (մոլորիլ, խոտորիլ)
aberration - *khodoroum, moloroum* (խոտորում, մոլորում)
abet - *kachalerel, kurkurel* (քաջալերել, գրգռել)
abettor - *kurkurogh* (գրգռող)
abhor - *adel, zuzvil* (ատել, զզուիլ)
abhorrence - *zuzvank, kanoum* (զզուանք, քանում)
abhorrible - *zuzveli* (զզուելի)
abide - *punagil, munal, garchil* (բնակիլ, մնալ, կառչիլ)
ability - *garoghoutiun* (կարողութիւն)
abject - *anarzhek, kutsouts* (անարժէք, գձուձ)
abjuration - *ouratsoum, herkoum* (ուրացում, Հերքում)
abjure - *turzhel, ouranal* (դրժել, ուրանալ)
abjurer - *ouratsogh, herkogh* (ուրացող, Հերքող)
able - *garogh, untounag, khelatsi* (կարող, ընդունակ, խելացի)
ablution - *luvatsoum, lokank* (լուացում, լոգանք)
abnegate - *ouranal, lukel* (ուրանալ, լքել)
abnormal - *anpunagan* (անբնական)
aboard - *navou mech, navou vura, yergaynkov* (նաւու մէջ, նաւու վրայ, երկայնքով)
abolish - *vochunchatsunel, chunchel, gordzanel* (ոչնչացնել, ջնջել, կործանել)
abolition - *gordzanoum, chunchoum* (կործանում, ջնջում)
abominable - *zuzveli* (զզուելի)
abominate - *zuzvil, kanil* (զզուիլ, գանիլ)

abomination - zuzvank, kanoum (զզուանք, գանում)
abort - vizhil, tsakhoghil (վիժիլ, ձախողիլ)
aborted - vizhadz (վիժած)
abortion - vizhoum (վիժում)
abound - hortil, aradanal (յորդիլ, առատանալ)
about - shourch, modavorabes, masin, chap (շուրջ, մօտաւորապէս, մասին, չափ)
above - modavorabes, mod, ver, aveli ver, verev (մօտաւորապէս, մօտ, վեր, աւելի վեր, վերեւ)
abrade - mashel, kerel (մաշել, քերել)
abrase - hughgel, kerel (յղկել, քերել)
abrasive - hughgich (յղկիչ)
abridge - gurjadel (կրճատել)
abridgment - gurjadoum, ampopoum (կրճատում, ամփոփում)
abroad - ardasahman, herou, spiurk (արտասահման, հեռու, սփիւռք)
abrogate - chunchel, tatretsunel (ջնջել, դադրեցնել)
abrogation - khapanoum, chounchoum (խափանում, ջնջում)
abscess - balar, tarakhagouyd (պալար, թարախակոյտ)
abscind - anchadel, gudrel (անջատել, կտրել)
abscission - anchadoum (անջատում)
abscond - bahvudil, pakhchil, khousapil (պահուըտիլ, փախչիլ, խուսափիլ)
absence - patsagayoutiun (բացակայութիւն)
absent - patsaga, patsagayil (բացակայ, բացակայիլ)
absentee - patsagan, patsaga antsu (բացական, բացակայ անձը)
absent-minded - mudazpagh, anoushatir, mudatsir (մտազբաղ, անուշադիր, մտացիր)
absinth - oshintur (օշինդր)
absistence - hurazharoum (հրաժարում)
absolute - patsartsag, ampoghchagan (բացարձակ, ամբողջական)
absolutely - patsartsagabes (բացարձակապէս)
absolutiun - arzhagoum, toghoutiun (արձակում, թողութիւն)
absolve - nerel, artsagel, toghoutiun dal (ներել, արձակել, թողութիւն տալ)
absonant - annertashnag, hagarag (աններդաշնակ, հակառակ)
absorb - dzudzel, gulanel, usbarel (ծծել, կլանել, սպառել)
absorbent - dzudzogh, nerdzudzogh, gulanogh (ծծող, ներծծող, կլանող)
absorption - dzudzoum, kuravoum (ծծում, գրաւում)
absract - veratzagan, veratsunel, hamarodakurel (վերացական, վերացնել, համառօտագրել)
abstain - yed genal, uzkoushanal, hurazharil (ետ կենալ, զգուշանալ, հրաժարիլ)
abstention - hurazharoum, tserunbahoutiun (հրաժարում, ձեռնպահութիւն)
absterge - makrel (մաքրել)
abstinence - bahk, zhouzhgaloutiun (պահք, ժուժկալութիւն
abstract - veratsunel, hanel, veratsoum, ampopoum (վերացնել, հանել, վերացում, ամփոփում)
abstraction - anchadoum, veratsoum (անջատում, վերացում)
absurd - animasd, ardarots, dzidzagheli (անիմաստ, արտառոց, ծիծաղելի)
absurdness - anhetetoutiun (անհեթեթութիւն)
abundance - aradoutiun, shadoutiun (առատութիւն, շատութիւն)
abundant - arad, letsoun, li (առատ, լեցուն, լի)
abuse - yeghdzel, charashahel, vunasel, charashahoum (եղծել, չարաշահել, վնասել, չարաշահում)
abut - verchanal, hankil, sahmanagtsil (վերջանալ, յանգիլ, սահմանակցիլ)
abyss - antount, khorkhorad, tuzhokhk (անդունդ, խորխորատ, դժոխք)

acacia - murpeni, akasia (մրփենի, ագասիա)
academic - agatemagan (ակադեմական)
academy - agatemia, gajar (ակադեմիա, կաճառ)
acantha - poush, pushatev tsoug (փուշ, փշաթեւ ձուկ)
accectable - untouneli (ընդունելի)
accede - hamatsaynil, miyanal, hajil, partsuranal (համաձայնիլ, միանալ, հաճիլ, բարձրանալ)
accelaration - arakatsoum (արագացում)
accelerate - arakatsunel, poutatsunel (արագացնել, փութացնել)
accelerator - arakatsoutsich, arakatsunogh (արագացուցիչ, արագացնող)
accend - purungetsunel (բռնկեցնել)
accension - purungoum (բռնկում)
accensor - lousarar (լուսարար)
accent - sheshd, shehsdel (շեշտ, շեշտել)
accentuate - sheshdel, untkudzel (շեշտել, ընդգծել)
accept - untounil, havanil (ընդունիլ, հաւանիլ)
acceptance, acceptation - untouneloutiun (ընդունելութիւն)
acceptilate - bardke artsagel (պարտքէ արձակել)
access - madchoum, zhamanoum, moudk (մատչում, ժամանում, մուտք)
accessible - madcheli (մատչելի)
accession - haveloum, kahagaloum (յաւելում, գահակալում)
accessive - havelvadzagan (յաւելուածական)
accessory - kordzik, gudor, meghsagits (գործիք, կտոր, մեղսակից)
accident - argadz, tibvadz, tebk (արկած, դիպուած, դէպք)
accidental - badahagan (պատահական)
accidie - toulamortoutiun, tantaghoutiun (թուլամորթութիւն, դանդաղութիւն)
acclaim - dzapaharel, voghchounel, dzap (ծափահարել, ողջունել, ծափ)
acclaimer - dzapaharogh (ծափահարող)
acclamation - dzapaharoutiun, tsuntsoutiun (ծափահարութիւն, ցնծութիւն)
acclivity - zariver (զառիվեր)
accoast - yezerken tiavarel, modenal (եզերքէն թիավարել, մօտենալ)
accoil - havakel, miadeghel (հաւաքել, միատեղել)
accomodate - harmartsunel, garkaturel, badshajil (յարմարցնել, կարգադրել, պատշաճիլ)
accomodation - harmaroutiun, hamatsaynoutiun (յարմարութիւն, համաձայնութիւն)
accompanier - ungeratsogh (ընկերացող)
accompaniment - nuvakagtsoum, zoukerkoutiun, ungeragtsoum (նուագակցում, զուգերգութիւն, ընկերակցում)
accompany - ungeragtsil, ungeranal (ընկերակցիլ, ընկերանալ)
accomplice - meghsagits (մեղսակից)
accomplish - gadarel, avardel, luratsunel, iragasnatsunel (կատարել, աւարտել, լրացնել, իրականացնել)
accomplishment - gadaroum, ampoghchatsoum (կատարում, ամբողջացում)
accord - hamatsaynoutiun, hamatsaynetsunel (համաձայնութիւն, համաձայնեցնել)
accordance - hamatsaynoutiun, nertashnagoutiun (համաձայնութիւն, ներդաշնակութիւն)
according - hamatsayn (համաձայն)
accordingly - hedevapar (հետեւաբար)
accordion - tsernatashnag (ձեռնադաշնակ)
accordionist - tsernatashnagahar, tashnonahar (ձեռնադաշնակահար, դաշնօնահար)
accorporate - miayatsunel, shaghgabel (միացնել, շաղկապել)

accost - modenal, yezerel, madchil, ap hasnil, voghchiun (մօտենալ, եզերել, մատչիլ, ափ հասնիլ, ողջիւն)
accouchement - dzununtaperoutiun (ծննդաբերութիւն)
account - hashiv, hashvel, hashiv dal (հաշիւ, հաշուել, հաշիւ տալ)
account book - domar, hashvekirk (տոմար, հաշուեգիրք)
accountable - hamaradou, badaskhanadou (համարատու, պատասխանատու)
accountant - hashvagal, hashvabah, domaragal (հաշուակալ, հաշուապահ, տոմարակալ)
accountantship - hashvagaloutiun (հաշուակալութիւն)
accounting - hashvaroum, hashvoum (հաշուառում, հաշւում)
accouple - miatsunel, zoukortel (միացնել, զուգորդել)
accourage - kachalerel (քաջալերել)
accouter, accoutre - hakvetsunel (հագուեցնել)
accoutrements - hantertsank (հանդերձանք)
accoy - hantardetsunel, undelatsunel (հանդարտեցնել, ընտելացնել)
accredit - varg dal, vargavorel, hasdadel, hantsunararel (վարկ տալ, վարկաւորել, հաստատել, յանձնարարել)
accredited - vargavor, harki, vusdahoutiun vayelogh (վարկաւոր, յարգի, վստահութիւն վայելող)
accrete - miadegh medznal, avelnal, aveltsunel (միատեղ մեծնալ, աւելնալ, աւելցնել)
accretion - ajoum, ourjatzoum (աճում, ուռճացում)
accroach - hapushdagel, purni arnel (յափշտակել, բռնի առնել)
accroachment - hapushdagoutiun (յափշտակութիւն)
accrual - ajoum (աճում)
accumb - ungoghmanil, pazmil, bargil (ընկողմանիլ, բազմիլ, պառկիլ)
accumulate - tizel, goudagel, amparel (դիզել, կուտակել, ամբարել)
accumulation - goudagoum, muteroum, amparoum (կուտակում, մթերում, ամբարում)
accumulator - goudagich (կուտակիչ)
accuracy - jushtoutiun (ճշդութիւն)
accurse - anidzel (անիծել)
accursed - anidzial (անիծեալ)
accusation - ampasdanoutiun (ամբաստանութիւն)
accuse - ampasdanel, meghaturel (ամբաստանել, մեղադրել)
accustom - varzhetsunel, sorvetsunel (վարժեցնել, սորվեցնել)
ace - miavor, masnaked otanavort, shahadz ged (միաւոր, մասնագէտ օդանաւորդ, շահած կէտ)
acedia - dzouloutiun, melamaghdzodoutiun (ծուլութիւն, մելամաղձոտութիւն)
acer - tsakh (ձախ)
acerb - tutou, gudzou (թթու, կծու)
acerbate - tutvetsunel (թթուեցնել)
acerbitude - tazhanoutiun (դաժանութիւն)
acetize - tutvil (թթուիլ)
acetone - katsakhon (քացախոն)
acharnement - gadaghoutiun (կատաղութիւն)
ache - tsav, tsavil (ցաւ, ցաւիլ)
achieve - gadarel, irakordzel, hachoghil (կատարել, իրագործել, յաջողիլ)
achievement - iraganatsoum, gadaroum (իրագործում, կատարում)
acid - tutou, tutvayin (թթու, թթուային)
acidify - tutvetsunel (թթուեցնել)
acknowledge - janchunal, hasdadel, khosdovanil (ճանչնալ, հաստատել, խոստովանիլ)
acknowlegement - janachoum, hasdadoum (ճանաչում, հաստատում)
acolyte - tubir (դպիր)
acoustic - lusoghagan (լսողական)
acoustics - tsaynapanoutiun (ձայնաբանութիւն)
acquaint - dzanotatsunel, endelatsunel (ծանօթացնել, ընտելացնել)
acquaintance - dzanotoutiun, unda-

noutiun (ծանօթութիւն, ընտանութիւն)
acquiet - hantardel (հանդարտել)
acquire - usdanal, tserk perel (ստանալ, ձեռք բերել)
acquisition - usdatsoum, diratsoum (ստացում, տիրացում)
acquisitor - usdatsogh (ստացող)
acquit - artsagel, vujarel, artsagial (արձակել, վճարել, արձակեալ)
acre - ardavar (արտավար)
acrobat - larakhaghats (լարախաղաց)
acropolis - michnapert (միջնաբերդ)
act - arark, kordz, gadarel, kordzel, nergayatsunel (արարք, գործ, կատարել, գործել, ներկայացնել)
action - sharzhoum, kordz, guriv, tadavaroutiun (շարժում, գործ, կռիւ, դատավարութիւն)
activate - mughel, kordzon tartsunel, poutatsunel (մղել, գործօն դարձնել, փութացնել)
active - kordzounia, yerantoun (գործունեայ, եռանդուն)
acto - tad (դատ)
actor - terasan (դերասան)
actress - terasanouhi (դերասանուհի)
actual - arti, ayzhmeagan, iragan (արդի, այժմէական, իրական)
actualist - irabashd, turabashd (իրապաշտ, դրապաշտ)
actuality - iraganoutioun (իրականութիւն)
actualize - iraganatsunel (իրականացնել)
actuate - aztel, turtel, ashkhadtsunel (ազդել, դրդել, աշխատցնել)
actuation - sharzhoum, turtoum (շարժում, դրդում)
acupuncture - aseghnapouzhoutiun (ասեղնաբուժութիւն)
acute - sour, sasdig, suradzayr, surtsunel (սուր, սաստիկ, սրածայր, սրցնել)
ad, ads - see - տե՛ս (advertisement)
adage - asatsvadzk, aradz (ասացուածք, առած)
adagio - hamur, hamrerk (յամր, յամրերգ)
adamant - atamant (ադամանդ)
adapt - harmartsunel (յարմարցնել)
adaptation - harmaretsoum (յարմարեցում)
adapter - harmaretsnogh, harmarogh (յարմարեցնող, յարմարող)
add - aveltsunel, gutsel, koumarel (աւելցնել, կցել, գումարել)
adder - koumarogh, khoumarogh mekena (գումարող, գումարող մեքենայ)
addict - hedabuntel, yedevel iynal, moli (հետապնդել, ետեւէն իյնալ, մոլի)
addicted - moli tartsadz, nouirial (մոլի դարձած, նուիրեալ)
addition - koumaroum (գումարում)
addle - abaganel, nekhel, nekhadz (ապականել, նեխել, նեխած)
address - hastse, ougherts, jar, ghurgel, khosil (հասցէ, ուղերձ, ճառ, ղրկել, խօսիլ)
addressee - hastseader (հասցէատէր)
adduce - arach perel, hasdadel, vugayel (առաջ բերել, հաստատել, վկայել)
adept - kidag, jardar, masnaked, humoud (գիտակ, ճարտար, մասնագէտ, հմուտ)
adequate - hamarzhek, adag, garogh, havasaril (համարժէք, ատակ, կարող, հաւասարիլ)
adhere - haril, gutsvil, pagil (յարիլ, կցուիլ, փակիլ)
adherence - haroum, mioutiun (յարում, միութիւն)
adherent - miatsopgh, harogh, gousagits (միացող, յարող, կուսակից)
adhesion - haroum, mioutiun (յարում, միութիւն)
adhesive - gubchoun (կպչուն)
adhibit - untounil, gutsel, kordzadzel (ընդունիլ, կցել, գործածել)
adieu - tsudesoutiun, munak parov (ցտեսութիւն, մնաք բարով)
adjacence - modigoutiun (մօտիկութիւն)

adjacent - haragits, modig (յարակից, մօտիկ)
adject - gutsel, miatsunel (կցել, միացնել)
adjection - gutsoum, miatsoum (կցում, միացում)
adjective - adzagan (ածական)
adjoin - gutsel, miatsunel (կցել, միացնել)
adjoint - havelvadz, ozhantag, gutsial (յաւելուած, օժանդակ, կցեալ)
adjourn - hedatsukel, habaghel, argakhel (յետաձգել, յապաղել, առկախել)
adjudge - vujrel, voroshel (վճռել, որոշել)
adjudgment - tadoum, tadogoutiun, vujir (դատում, դատողութիւն, վճիռ)
adjunct - hedevogh, haragitz, kordzagits, gutsort (հետեւող, յարակից, գործակից, կցորդ)
adjure - yertouentsunel, yertoum unel dal (երդուընցնել, երդում ընել տալ)
adjust - jushtel, shudgel, hartarel, garki tunel (ճշդել, շտկել, յարդարել, կարգի դնել)
adjustment - gakavoroum, hartaroum, harmaretsoum (կագաւորում, յարդարում, յարմարեցում)
adjutant - oknagan, usbayi asdijan mu (օգնական, սպայի աստիճան մը)
adjutator - khurovarar, kharnagich (խռովարար, խառնակիչ)
administer - dunorinel, varel, dal, pashkhel, varich (տնօրինել, վարել, տալ, բաշխել, վարիչ)
administration - varjoutiun, khunamagaloutiun (վարչութիւն, խնամակալութիւն)
administrative - varchagan, madagararagan (վարչական, մատակարարական)
administrator - varich, ghegavar (վարիչ, ղեկավար)
admirable - hianali, hurashali, uskancheli (հիանալի, հրաշալի, ըսքանչելի)
admiral - dzovagal (ծովակալ)
admiration - hiatsoum, uskanchatsoum (հիացում, սքանչացում)
admiraton - hiatsoum (հիացում)
admire - hianal, uskanchanal, zarmanal (հիանալ, սքանչանալ, զարմանալ)
admissible - untouneli, touyladureli (ընդունելի, թոյլատրելի)
admission - untouneloutiun, touyldoutiun, moudk (ընդունելութիւն, թոյլտուութիւն, մուտք)
admit - untounil, toghoul (ընդունիլ, թողուլ)
admittance - untouneloutiun, moudki ardonoutiun (ընդունելութիւն, մուտքի արտօնութիւն)
admix - kharnel (խառնել)
admixture - kharnourt (խառնուրդ)
admonish - khuradel, hantimanel, uzkoushatsunel (խրատել, յանդիմանել, զգուշացնել)
admonitor - aztarar, uzkoushatsunogh (ազդարար, զգուշացնող)
adobe - aghius (աղիւս)
adopt - vortekurel, undurel, untounil (որդեգրել, ընտրել, ընդունիլ)
adoption - vortekuroum (որդեգրում)
adoptive - vortekir zavag (որդեգիր զաւակ)
adorable - bashdeli (պաշտելի)
adoration - bashdoum (պաշտում)
adore - bashdel (պաշտել)
adorn - zartarel (զարդարել)
adornment - zartaroum, bujnoum (զարդարում, պճնում)
adrift - jarbig, tsernerets (ճարպիկ, ձեռներէց)
adulate - shoghokortel (շողոքորթել)
adulation - shoghokortoutiun (շողոքորթութիւն)
adult - chapahas, yerets (չափահաս, երէց)
adultery - amousnagan anhavadarmoutiun, shunoutiun (ամուսնական անհաւատարմութիւն, շնութիւն)
adultness - chapahasoutiun (չափահասութիւն)
advance (n) - harachatsoum, harach-

timoutiun, gankhavujar (յառաջացում, յառաջդիմութիւն, կանխավճառ)
advance (v) - harachanal, zarkanal, partsuratsunel (յառաջանալ, զարգանալ, բարձրացնել)
advance payment - gankhavujar (կախավճար)
advanced - harachatsadz (յառաջացած)
advancement - harachatsoum (յառաջացում)
advantage - araveloutiun, okoud (առաւելութիւն, օգուտ)
Advent - kalousd, yergurort kalousdu hisousi (Գալուստ, Բ.Գալուստը Յիսուսի)
adventist - kalusdagan (գալստական)
adventure - argadzakhunturoutiun (արկածախնդրութիւն)
adverb - magpay (մակբայ)
adversary - hagaragort (Հակառակորդ)
adverse - hagarag (Հակառակ)
adversity - tsakhortoutiun, hagaragoutiun (ձախորդութիւն, Հակառակութիւն)
advert - agnargel, oushatroutiun kuravel (ակնարկել, ուշադրութիւն գրաւել)
advertise - dzanoutsanel (ծանուցանել)
advertisement - dzanoutsoum, haydararoutiun, kovazt (ծանուցում, յայտարարութիւն, գովազդ)
advertiser - dzanoutsogh, nergayatsunogh (ծանուցող, ներկայացնող)
advice - khorhourt, khurad (խորհուրդ, խրատ)
advisable - harmar, telatreli (յարմար, թելադրելի)
advise - khuradel, telaturel (խրատել, թելադրել)
adviser - khorhurtadou, khuradadou (խորհրդատու, խրատատու)
adviser, advisor - khorhurtadou (խորհրդատու)
advocate - pasdapan, iravapan, bashdubanel, chadakovel (փաստաբան, իրաւաբան, պաշտպանել, ջատագովել)
advocation - pasdapanoutiun (փաստաբանութիւն)
aerate - otasoun unel, otu makrel (օդասուն ընել, օդը մաքրել)
aerobatics - varbed otachou (վարպետ օդաչու)
aerodrome - otagayan (օդակայան)
aerometer - otachap (օդաչափ)
aeronaut - otanavort (օդանաւորդ)
aeroplane - otanav, savarnag, inknatir (օդանաւ, սաւառնակ, ինքնադիր)
aeroscope - otatidag, otalhouyz (օդադիտակ, օդախոյզ)
aerospace - anchurbed (անջրպետ)
aesthetic - keghakidagan virahadoutiun (գեղագիտական վիրաՀատութիւն)
aesthetics - kekhakidoutiun (գեղագիտութիւն)
afar - herou (Հեռու)
affable - azniv, hez, kaghakavar (ազնիւ, Հեզ, քաղաքավար)
affair - kordz, kordzarnoutiun (գործ, գործառնութիւն)
affear - vakhtsunel (վախցնել)
affect - aztel, hagaztel, ser, korov (ազդել, Հակազդել, սէր, գորով)
affectation - geghdzik, arvesdaganoutiun (կեղծիք, արուեստականութիւն)
affected - shindzou, tsevatsunogh, varagial, siretsial (շինծու, ձեւացնող, վարակեալ, սիրեցեալ)
affection - aztetsoutiun, khantaghadant, korov (ազդեցութիւն, խանդաղատանք, գորով)
affiance - nushandouk, vusdahoutiun, nushanel (նշանտուք, վստաՀութիւն, նշանել)
affidavit - vugayakir, vugayatought (վկայագիր, վկայաթուղթ)
affiliate - vortekurel (որդեգրել)
affiliation - vortekuroutiun, dzununtian artsanakuroutiun (որդեգրութիւն, ծննդեան արձանագրութիւն)
affinity - khunamioutiun (խնամիութիւն)
affirm - hasdadel, vugayel, buntel

(հաստատել, վկայել, պնդել)
affirmation - hasdadoum (հաստատում)
affirmative - hasdadagan, turagan (հաստատական, դրական)
affirmer - hasdadogh (հաստատող)
affix - gutsel, amratsunel, hedatas masnig (կցել, ամրացնել, յետադաս մասնիկ)
afflation - nerhunchoum, adrashunchoum, puchoum (ներշնչում, արտաշնչում, փչում)
afflict - vushdatsunel, darabetsunel (վշտացնել, տառապեցնել)
affliction - tarnoutiun, tsav (դառնութիւն, ցաւ)
affluence - hosank, aradoutiun (հոսանք, առատութիւն)
affluent - arad, hortahos (առատ, յորդահոս)
afflux - hosoum, hortoutiun (հոսում, յորդութիւն)
afforce - zoratsunel (զօրացնել)
afford - danil, garenal, haytaytel (տանիլ, կարենալ, հայթայթել)
affordable - gareli, haitaiteli (կարելի, հայթայթելի)
affranchise - azadel, artsagel, azadakurel (ազատել, արձակել, ազատագրել)
affray - sosgatsunel, guriv, sosgoum (սոսկացում, կռիւ, սոսկում)
affriction - shupoum (շփում)
affright - sosgatsunel, sosgoum, ahapegoum (սոսկացնել, սոսկում, ահաբեկում)
affront - jagadil, nakhadel, viravorel (ճակատիլ, նախատել, վիրաւորել)
afield - tashdi mech, heroun (դաշտի մէջ, հեռուն)
afire - purungadz (բռնկած)
aflame - potsavar (բոցավառ)
afloat - aledzadzan, dzupatsogh (ալեծածան, ծփացող)
afoot - ganknadz, vodki vura (կանգնած, ոտքի վրայ)
afore - nakhabes (նախապէս)
aforesaid - nakhabes usvadz (նախապէս ըսուած)
afraid - vakhtsadz (վախցած)
afresh - gurgin, noren, verusdin (կրկին, նորէն, վերստին)
Africa - aprige (Ափրիկէ)
african - aprigetsi, aprigian (ափրիկեցի, ափրիկեան)
after - yedevu, yedku, hachortogh (ետեւը, ետքը, յաջորդող)
after all - verjabes, i verjo (վերջապէս, ի վերջոյ)
after glow - verjalouys (վերջալոյս)
after guard - hedsabah (յետսապահ)
afternoon - gesore yedk (կէսօրէ ետք)
aftershock - yergurasharzhe yedk nor tsuntsoum (երկրաշարժէ ետք նոր ցնցում)
again - noren, tartsial, gurgin (նորէն, դարձեալ, կրկին)
against - tem, hagarag (դէմ, հակառակ)
agate - agad (ակատ)
age - darik, giank, darikodil, dzeranal (տարիք, կեանք, տարիքոտիլ, ծերանալ)
aged - darets, dzer, darikod (տարեց, ծեր, տարիքոտ)
agency - kordzagaloutiun (գործակալութիւն)
agenda - houshadedur, haydakir (յուշատետր, յայտագիր)
agent - kordzagadar, kordzagal, kordzich, aztag (գործակատար, գործակալ, գործիչ, ազդակ)
agglomarate - tizel, goudagel, hamakhumpel (դիզել, կուտակել, համախմբել)
agglomaration - goudagoum (կուտակում)
agglomerate - tizel, goudagel, goudagil, tez (դիզել, կուտակել, կուտակիլ, դէզ)
agglomeration - goudagoum (կուտակում)
agglutinate - pagtsunel, pagadz (փակցնել, փակած)
aggrandize - medztsunel (մեծցնել)
aggrandizement - medzatsoum (մեծացում)
aggravate - dzanratsunel, khusda-

tsunel (ծանրացնել, խստացնել)
aggravation - sasdgatsoum, vadatsoum (սաստկացում, վատացում)
aggregate - havakel, koumarel, hamakhoump, ampoghchoutiun (հաւաքել, գումարել, համախումբ, ամբողջութիւն)
aggregation - hamakhumpoum (համախմբում)
aggrege - dzanratsunel (ծանրացնել)
aggress - hartsagil, gurivi usgusil (յարձակիլ, կռիւի սկսիլ)
aggressive - hartsagoghagan (յարձակողական)
aggressor - nakhahartsag (նախայարձակ)
aggrieve - vushdatsunel, vushdanal, harusdaharel (վշտացնել, վշտանալ, հարստահարել)
aggrieved - vushdatsadz, ungjuvadz (վշտացած, ընկճուած)
aghast - ahapegvadz, sosgatsadz (ահաբեկուած, սոսկացած)
agile - jugoun, arakasharzh (ճկուն, արագաշարժ)
agitate - sharzhel, kharnel, houzel (շարժել, խառնել, յուզել)
agitation - sharzhoum, houzoum, vej (շարժում, յուզում, վէճ)
agitator - khurovarar (խռովարար)
aglow - gasgarmir (կասկարմիր)
agnize - janchunal (ճանչնալ)
agnominate - anvanel (անուանել)
ago - arach, antsial (առաջ, անցեալ)
agog - antsgalits (անձկալից)
agonize - hokevarel, daknabel, charcharel (հոգեւարել, տագնապել, չարչարել)
agony - hokevark, daknab (հոգեվարք, տագնապ)
agrarian - hoghayin (հողային)
agree - hamatsaynil, havanil, akhorzhil (համաձայնիլ, հաւանիլ, ախորժիլ)
agreeable - hajeli, nubasdavor (հաճելի,նպաստաւոր)
agreement - hamatsaynoutiun (համաձայնութիւն)
agricultor - hoghakordz (հողագործ)
agriculture - hoghakordzoutiun (հողագործութիւն)
agrise - sarsurel, sarsour dal (սարսռել, սարսուռ տալ)
agronomy - kiughadundesoutiun (գիւղատնտեսութիւն)
agroupment - khumpoum, havakoum (խմբում, հաւաքում)
agrufe - kunkhivayr (գլխիվայր)
ague - cherm, togh (ջերմ, դող)
aguise - hakvetsunel, zartarel, hakousd (հագուեցնել, զարդարել, հագուստ)
ahead - archeven, archev (առջեւէն, առջեւ)
ahoy - hey (հէյ)
aid - oknel, hadgatsunel, oknoutiun (օգնել, յատկացնել, օգնութիւն)
aider - oknogh (օգնող)
aiel - nakhahayr (նախահայր)
aigre - tutou (թթու)
aiguille - asegh (ասեղ)
ail - danchel, neghel, anhankusdoutiun (տանջել, նեղել, անհանգստութիւն)
aim - nushan arnel, tsukdil, nushan, nubadag (նշան առնել, ձգտիլ, նման, նպատակ)
aims - voghormoutiun (ողորմութիւն)
air - ot, mutnolord (օդ, մթնոլորտ)
air condition - otapokhel, otapokhich zedeghel (օդափոխել, օդափոխիչ զետեղել)
air conditioned - zovatsvadz ot, otapokhvadz (զովացուած օդ, օդափոխուած)
air conditioner - otapokhich, baghoutsich mekena (օդափոխիչ, պաղուցիչ մեքենայ)
air conditioning - zovatsvadz ot (զովացուած օդ)
air filter - otazudich (օդազտիչ)
air freight - otaper (օդաբեռ)
air jacket - purgapajgon (փրկաբաճկոն)
air mail - otadar, otayin arakoum (օդատար, օդային առաքում)
airbag - otabarg (օդապարկ)
aircraft - otanav, savarnag, otadormigh (օդանաւ, սաւառնակ, օդա-

տորմիղ)
airline - atoughi (օդուղի)
airplane - otanav, inknatir, savarnag (օդանաւ, ինքնաթիռ, սաւառնակ)
airport - otagayan (օդակայան)
airport shuttle - otagayani pokhatragark (օդակայանի փոխադրակառք)
airway - otoughi (օդուղի)
airy - otaved, tetev (օդաւէտ, թեթեւ)
aisle - antsk (անցք)
ajar - gisapats (կիսաբաց)
akin - numan, azkagan (նման, ազգական)
alabaster - kaj (գաճ)
alarm - ahazank, irarantsoum, khoujab, zartoutsich (ահազանգ, իրարանցում, խուճապ, զարթուցիչ)
alarming - sosgatsunogh (սոսկացնող)
alarmist - borchudan, ahazantogh (պոռչտան, ահազանգող)
alas - avagh (աւաղ)
albatross - tsugungoul, tsoug vorsatsogh turchoun (ձկնկուլ, ձուկ որսացող թռչուն)
albeit - teyev (թէեւ)
album - badgeradedur, nugaradedur (պատկերատետր, նկարատետր)
albumen - usbidagouts, havgiti jermugouts (սպիտակուց, հաւկիթի ճերմկուց)
albumin - punasbid (բնասպիտ)
alcohol - alkol, voki (ալքոլ, ոգի)
alcoholic - alkolamol, khumichki moli (ալքոլամոլ, խմիչքի մոլի)
alcove - angoghini khorsh (անկողինի խորշ)
alder - lasdeni (լաստենի՝ ծառ մը)
alderman - taghabed (թաղապետ)
aleatory - anorosh, usd pakhdi (անորոշ, ըստ բախտի)
Aleppo - haleb (Հալէպ)
alert - ahazank, ashkhouzh, artoun (ահազանգ, աշխոյժ, արթուն)
alertness - jugounoutiun (ճկունութիւն)
algebra - kurahashiv (գրահաշիւ)
alias - dzadzganoun (ծածկանուն)
alibi - chukmeghank, inknartaratsoum, aylouroutiun (չքմեղանք, ինքնարդարացում, այլուրութիւն)
alien - odar, aylaseradz, odaratsunel (օտար, այլասերած, օտարացնել)
alienate - odaratsadz, odaratsunel (օտարացած, օտարացնել)
alienation - odaratsoum, heratsoum (օտարացում, հեռացում)
alight - ichnel tsien (իջնել՝ձիէն)
align - doghakurel (տողագրել)
alignement - doghatroum, sharoum, tasavoroum (տողադրում, շարում, դասաւորում)
alignment - doghakuroutiun, gark (տողագրութիւն, կարգ)
alike - numan, numanabes (նման, նմանապէս)
aliment - sunount, sunount dal (սնունդ, սնունդ տալ)
alimentation - sununtaroutiun, sunount (սննդառութիւն, սնունդ)
alimony - sununtakin, abrelamichots (սննդագին, ապրելամիջոց)
aline - doghakurel, tasavorel (տողագրել, դասաւորել)
alive - voghch, abrogh (ողջ, ապրող)
all - ampoghch, polor (ամբողջ, բոլոր)
Allah - asduvadz (Աստուած)
allay - meghmel, meghmanal, amokel, meghmoum (մեղմել, մեղմանալ, ամոքել, մեղմում)
allegation - mechperoum, vugayoutiun (մէջբերում, վկայութիւն)
allege - hasdadel, vugayel, tetevtsunel (հաստատել, վկայել, թեթեւցնել)
allegiance - havadarmoutiun (հաւատարմութիւն)
allegory - aylapanoutiun, arag (այլաբանութիւն, առակ)
allegresse - tsundzoutiun (ցնծութիւն)
allegretto - ashkhouyzh, zuvartakin (աշխոյժ, զուարթագին)
allegro - ourakh yeghanag, zuvart (ուրախ եղանակ, զուարթ)

allergy - keruzkaynoutiun (գերզգայնութիւն)
alleviate - meghmel (մեղմել)
alley - nurpantsk, dzaroughi (նրբանցք, ծառուղի)
allheal - amenapouyzh (ամենաբոյժ)
alliance - zinagtsoutiun, tashnagtsil (զինակցութիւն, դաշնակցիլ)
alliant - tashnagits (դաշնակից)
allied - zinagits, tashnagits (զինակից, դաշնակից)
alligate - gabel, garel, miatsunel (կապել, կարել, միացնել)
alligation - zoukortoutiun, paghaturoutiun (զուգորդութիւն, բաղադրութիւն)
alligator - gogortilos, mushdatiter (կոկորդիլոս, մշտաթիթեռ)
allision - untharoum, pakhoum (ընդհարում, բախում)
allocate - pashkhel, pazhnel, hadgatsunel (բաշխել, բաժնել, յատկացնել)
allocation - hadgatsoum, shunorhoum (յատկացում, շնորհում)
allot - pazhnel, phazhin hanel, shunorhel (բաժնել, բաժին հանել, շնորհել)
allotment - pazhin, pashkhoum (բաժին, բաշխում)
allow - touyladurel, toghoul, untounil (թոյլատրել, թողուլ, ընդունիլ)
allowance - ardonoutiun (արտօնութիւն)
alloy - kharnourt-medaghnerou, medaghatsoulel (խառնուրդ՝ մետաղներու, մետաղաձուլել)
allude - agnargel (ակնարկել)
allumette - loutsgi (լուցկի)
allurance - hurabouyr (հրապոյր)
allure - hurabourel, kravchoutiun, untatsk (հրապուրել, գրաւչութիւն, ընթացք)
allusion - agnargoutiun (ակնարկութիւն)
allwhere - amenourek, amen degh (ամենուրեք, ամէն տեղ)
ally -
almanac - daretsouyts, darekirk, domar (տարեցոյց, տարեգիրք, տոմար)
almighty - amenagarogh (ամենակարող)
almond - noush (նուշ)
almost - kurete (գրեթէ)
alms - voghormoutiun (ողորմութիւն)
aloft - partsru (բարձրը)
alone - arantsin, miaynag (առանձին, միայնակ)
along - yergaynkin (երկայնքին)
aloof - herou, arantsin (հեռու, առանձին)
aloud - partsuratsayn (բարձրաձայն)
Alp - albian ler (Ալպեան լեռ)
alp - partsounk, partsur ler (բարձունք, բարձր լեռ)
alpha - alfa-hounaren arachin kiru, usgizp (ալֆա-յունարէն առաջին գիրը, սկիզբ)
alphabet - aypoupen (այբուբեն)
alphabetic - ayppenagan (այբբենական)
already - arten isg (արդէն իսկ)
also - nayev, nouynbes (նաեւ, նոյնպէս)
altar - khoran, zohaseghan (խորան, զոհասեղան)
alter - pokhel, pokvil (փոխել, փոխուիլ)
alterable - popokheli (փոփոխելի)
alteration - popokhoutiun, tsevapokhoutiun (փոփոխութիւն, ձեւափոխութիւն)
altercate - vijil (վիճիլ)
altercation - vej, guriv (վէճ, կռիւ)
altern - pokhnipokh (փոխնիփոխ)
alternate - aylapokhel, popokhagi (այլափոխել, փոփոխակի)
alternately - pokhnipokh (փոխն ի փոխ)
alternation - pokhagarkoutiun (փոխակարգութիւն)
alternative - pokhunduroutiun, aylundurank (փոխընտրութիւն, այլընտրանք)
alternator - yelekdurapokhich (ելեքտրափոխիչ)
although - teyev (թէեւ)
altitude - partsuroutiun (բարձրու-

թիւն)
alto - vernapamp, partsuranuvak (վերնաբամբ, բարձրանուագ)
altogheter - ampoghchovin, miasnapar (ամբողջովին, միասնաբար)
altruism - aylasiroutiun (այլասիրութիւն)
altruist - aylaser (այլասէր)
aluminium - bagh leghadzin (պաղ լեղածին)
alumna - sanouhi (սանուհի)
alumni - saner (սաներ)
alumnus - shurchanavard, san (շրջանաւարտ, սան)
alure - kunatsk (գնացք)
alway, always - mishd, devabes (միշտ, տեւապէս)
am - yem (եմ)
amability - sirelioutiun (սիրելիութիւն)
amalgam - kharnourt medaghi (խառնուրդ մետաղի)
amalgamate - miatsoulel (միաձուլել)
amand - doukank (տուգանք)
amanuensis - kurakir (գրագիր)
amass - havakel, tizel (հաւաքել, դիզել)
amassment - havakoum, gouyd (հաւաքում, կոյտ)
amate - vakhtsunel, surdapegel (վախցնել, սրտաբեկել)
amateur - arvesdaser, sirogh (արուեստասէր, սիրող)
amatory - siroghagan (սիրողական)
amaze - abshetsunel, abshil, zarmank (ապշեցնել, ապշիլ, զարմանք)
amazement - zarmatsoum, abshoutiun (զարմացում, ապշութիւն)
amazing - abshetsoutsich (ապշեցուցիչ)
ambassador - tesban, badkamavor (դեսպան, պատգամաւոր)
ambassy - tesbanoutiun (դեսպանութիւն)
amber - sat (սաթ)
ambidexter - yergeres, khartakh (երկերես, խարդախ)
ambiguity - dardam, yergtimoutiun (տարտամ, երկդիմութիւն)
ambiguous - yergtimi (երկդիմի)
ambit - shurchabad (շրջապատ)
ambition - parasiroutiun, paramoloutiun (փառասիրութիւն, փառամոլութիւն)
ambry - maran (մառան)
ambulance - hivantagark (հիւանդակառք)
ambulate - sharzhil (շարժիլ)
ambulatory - sharzhoun (շարժուն)
ambuscade - vorokayt, dzoughag (որոգայթ, ծուղակ)
ambush - taran, bahelou degh (դարան, պահելու տեղ)
ameliorate - parelavel (բարելաւել)
amelioration - parelavoum, parvokoum (բարելաւում, բարւոքում)
amen - amen (ամէն)
amenable - badizhi arzhani (պատիժի արժանի)
amenage - shudgel, garkavorel, ghegavarel (շտկել, կարգաւորել, ղեկավարել)
amend - parepokhel, shudgel, shudguvil (բարեփոխել, շտկել, շտկուիլ)
amendment - parepokhoum (բարեփոխում)
amends - hadoutsoum, doukank (հատուցում, տուգանք)
amenity - hajelioutiun (հաճելիութիւն)
America - ameriga (Ամերիկա)
american - amerigatsi, amerigian (ամերիկացի, ամերիկեան)
amiable - siroun, shunorhali (սիրուն, շնորհալի)
amicable - paregamagan (բարեկամական)
amicably - paregamoren (բարեկամօրէն)
amid, amidst - mechdegh (մէջտեղ)
amiss - sukhal, kesh (սխալ, գէշ)
amity - paregamoutiun (բարեկամութիւն)
amma - mayrabed (մայրապետ)
ammunition - razmamuterk (ռազմամթերք)
amnesia - anhishoghoutiun (անյիշողութիւն)
amnesty - kaghakagan neroum, han-

tsaneroum (քաղաքական ներում, յանցանքներում)
Amnesty International - michazkayin neroum (Միջազգային Ներում)
among, amongst - mechu (մէջը)
amoral - paroyagane zourg (բարոյականէ զուրկ)
amorous - sirahar, darpalits (սիրահար, տարփալից)
amorphous - antsev (անձեւ)
amortization - meghmatsoum, nuvazetsoum, bardachunchoum (մեղմացում, նուազեցում, պարտաջնջում)
amortize - bardachunchel, nuvazetsunel, meghmel (պարտաջնջել, նուազեցնել, մեղմել)
amount - hasnil, havasaril, koumar, arjek (հասնիլ, հաւասարիլ, գումար, արժէք)
amour - ser, darpank (սէր, տարփանք)
amove - vudarel, vudarvil, kurkurel (վտարել, վտարուիլ, գրգռել)
ample - layn, arad (լայն, առատ)
amplifier - untlaynogh (ընդլայնող)
amplify - untlaynel, untlaynil (ընդլայնել, ընդլայնիլ)
amplitude - laynoutiun, daradzk (լայնութիւն, տարածք)
amputate - antamahadel (անդամահատել)
amputation - antamahadoutiun (անդամահատութիւն)
ampyx - mazagal, kulkhagab (մազակալ, գլխակապ)
amuck - vayrak, vayrakapar (վայրագ, վայրագաբար)
amuse - zuvarjatsunel (զուարճացնել)
amusement - zuvarjoutiun (զուարճութիւն)
amy - paregam (բարեկամ)
an - mu, mun (մը, մըն)
anabolism - verapokhoutiun (վերափոխութիւն)
anachronism - zhamanagavureb, zhamanagakuragan sukhal (ժամանակավրէպ, ժամանակագրական սխալ)
anaemia, anemia - arian bagasoutiun (արեան պակասութիւն)
anaesthetize -
analectic - hadundir (հատընտիր)
analogue - numan, hamazor (նման, համազօր)
analogy - numanoutiun (նմանութիւն)
analphabet - ankuraked (անգրագէտ)
analysis - verloudzoum, kunnoutiun (վերլուծում, քննութիւն)
analyst - verloudzogh (վերլուծող)
analytic - verloudzagan (վերլուծական)
analyze - verloudzel (վերլուծել)
anarchy - anishkhanoutiun (անիշխանութիւն)
anatomy - martagazmoutiun, gazmakhosoutiun (մարդակազմութիւն, կազմախօսութիւն)
ancestor - nakhahayr (նախահայր)
anchor - khariskh, kharuskhel (խարիսխ, խարսխել)
anchorage - navagayk (նաւակայք)
ancient - hin, nakhgin, vaghemi (հին, նախկին, վաղեմի)
and - yev (եւ)
andante - chapavor arakoutiamp yeghanag, untatsig (չափաւոր արագութեամբ եղանակ, ընթացիկ)
androgyne - vortsevek (որձեւէգ)
anecdote - manraveb (մանրավէպ)
anele - odzel (օծել)
anemia - anariunoutiun (անարիւնութիւն)
anes - adenok, ankam mu (ատենօք, անգամ մը)
anesthesia - uzkayazurgoutiun, anuzkayatsoum (զգայազրկութիւն, անզգայացում)
anesthesiology - kunaperoutiun kidoutiun (քնաբերութեան գիտութիւն)
anesthetist - uzkayazurgogh (զգայազրկող)
anew - noren (նորէն)
angel - hureshdag (հրեշտակ)
anger - pargoutiun, zayrouyt, pargatsunel (բարկութիւն, զայրոյթ, բարկացնել)

angina - gogortatsav (կոկորդացաւ)
angina pectoris - lanchatsav (լանջացաւ)
angiopathy - anotakhd, anotnerou hivantoutiun (անօթախտ, անօթնեբու հիւանդութիւն)
angle - angiun, gart, gartel (անկիւն, կարթ, կարթել)
anglican - ankliagan, anglican yegeghetsi (անգլիական, անկլիգան եկեղեցի)
angry - pargatsadz, zayratsadz (բարկացած, զայրացած)
anguish - antsgoutiun, vushdatsunel (անձկութիւն, վշտացնել)
angular - angiunavor, angiunayin (անկիւնաւոր, անկիւնային)
angulate - anguinavorel (անկիւնաւորել)
angulometer - anguinachap (անկիւնաչափ)
anharmonic - annertashnag (աններդաշնակ)
anhele - heval (Հեւալ)
anight - kisherants (գիշերանց)
animadvert - kunnatadel (քննադատել)
animal - gentani (կենդանի)
animate - gentanatsunel, vokovorel, voghch (կենդանցնել, ոգեւորել, ողջ)
animation - gentanoutiun, vokevoroutiun (կենդանութիւն, ոգեւորութիւն)
animator - vokevorogh, vokevorich (ոգեւորող, ոգեւորիչ)
animosity - adeloutiun, gadaghoutiun (ատելութիւն, կատաղութիւն)
anise - anison (անիսոն)
ankle - hot, poump, bujegh (յօդ, (բումբ, պճեղ)
annals - darekirk, darekuroutiun (տարեգիրք, տարեգրութիւն)
annex - miatsunel, gutsel, gutsort, havelvavadz (միացնել, կցել, կցորդ, յաւելուած)
annexation - gutsoum (կցում)
annihilate - punachunchel, gordzanel (բնաջնջել, կործանել)
annihilation - punachunchoum, gordzanoum (բնաջնջում, կործանում)
annihilator - punachunchogh (բնաջնջող)
anniversary - daretarts (տարեդարձ)
annotate - dzanotakrel (ծանօթագրել)
annotation - dzanotakuroutiun (ծանօթագրութիւն)
announce - dzanoutsanel, haydnel, hurchagel (ծանուցանել, յայտնել, Հռչակել)
announcement - dzanoutsoum, azt (ծանուցում, ազդ)
annoy - tsantsuratsunel, neghatsunel (ձանձրացնել, նեղացնել)
annoyance - tsantsurouyt (ձանձրոյթ)
annual - daregan (տարեկան)
annuary - darekirk, daregan (տարեգիրք, տարեկան)
annuity - darevujar (տարեվճար)
annul - chunchel (ջնջել)
annular - oghagatsev (օղակաձեւ)
annulate - oghagavorel (օղակաւորել)
annunciate - avedel, haydararel (աւետել, յայտարարել)
annunciation - avedoum, haydararoutiun (Աւետում – Ս. Կոյսի, յայտարարութիւն)
anoint - odzel, yiughodel (օծել, իւղոտել)
anointment - odzoum (օծում)
anomaly - anpunaganoutiun, zardoughoutiun (անբնականութիւն, զարտուղութիւն)
anonym - ananoun (անանուն)
anonymous - andzanot (անծանօթ)
anorexia, anorexy - anakhorzhoutiun (անախորժութիւն)
anormal - anpunagan (անբնական)
anosmia - anhodaroutiun (անՀոտառութիւն)
another - ourish, darper (ուրիշ, տարբեր)
answer - badaskhan, badaskhanel (պատասխան, պատասխանել)
ant - murchiun (մրջիւն)
antacid - hagatutou (Հակաթթու)
antagonism - hagaragoutiun (Հակառակութիւն)

antagonist - hagaragort, vosokh, nerhag (հակառակորդ, ոսոխ, ներհակ)
antagonize - hagaragil, unttimanal (հակառակիլ, ընդդիմանալ)
antecede - gankhel (կանխել)
antecedent - nakhuntats, nakhortogh (նախընթաց, նախորդող)
antedate - nakhashurchan (նախաշրջան)
antenna - alehavak, tsaynungalouch, ungalouch, tsogh (ալեհաւաք, ձայնընկալուչ, ընկալուչ, ձող)
antepast - nakhajashag (նախաճաշակ)
anteport - nakhatour (նախադուռ)
anteroom - nakhaseniag (նախասենեակ)
antetype - nakhadib (նախատիպ)
anthem - saghmoserkoutiun, saghmoserkich (սաղմոսերգութիւն, սաղմոսերգիչ)
anthology - dzaghgakagh, havakadzo (ծաղկաքաղ, հաւաքածոյ)
anthropology - martapanoutiun (մարդաբանութիւն)
anti - haga (հակա-)
antibiotic - manreasban (մանրէասպան)
antibody - hagamarmin (հակամարմին)
antic - hin (հին)
anticipate - gankhel, agungalel (կանխել, ակնկալել)
anticipation - agungaloutiun, nakhadesoutiun (ակնկալութիւն, նախատեսութիւն)
anticoagulant - haga-magartogh (հակա-մակարդող)
antidote - teghtap (դեղթափ)
antilogy - unttimakhosoutiun (ընդդիմախօսութիւն)
antipathy - hagaguroutiun, khorshank (հակակրութիւն, խորշանք)
antiquarian - hunaked, hunakidagan (հնագէտ, հնագիտական)
antiquary - hunoutiun havakogh (հնութիւն հաւաքող)
antique - hin, hunatarian (հին, հնադարեան)
antiquity - hunoutiunner, hin tar (հնութիւններ, հին դար)
antiseptic - haganekhich (հականեխիչ)
antithesis - hagaturoutiun, hagaturouyt (հակադրութիւն, հակադրոյթ)
antonym - haganish (հականիշ)
anus - surpan, nusdadeghi (սրբան, նստատեղի)
anvil - sal (սալ)
anxiety - antsgoutiun, hok (անձկութիւն, հոգ)
anxious - mudahok (մտահոգ)
any - voryeve (որեւէ)
anybody, anyone - voyeve megu (ոեւէ մէկը)
anyhow - voryeve gerbov (որեւէ կերպով)
anymore - aylevus (այլեւս)
anyone - voyeve megu (ոեւէ մէկը)
anything - voryeve pan (որեւէ բան)
anytime - voryeve aden (որեւէ ատեն)
anywhere - voryeve degh (որեւէ տեղ)
aorta - mayrerag, surdi medz shuncherag (մայրերակ, սրտի մեծ շնչերակ)
apart - zad, anchad, megti (զատ, անջատ, մէկդի)
apartment - hargapazhin, punagaran (յարկաբաժին, բնակարան)
apathetic - andarper, anuzka (անտարբեր, անզգայ)
apathy - andarperoutiun, anuzkayoutiun (անտարբերութիւն, անզգայութիւն)
ape - gabig, gabgel (կապիկ, կապկել)
aper - gabgogh, mimos (կապկող, միմոս)
aperitive - akhorzhaper (ախորժաբեր)
apert - pats, hayduni, haydunabes (բաց, յայտնի, յայտնապէս)
aperture - patsvadzk, dzag (բացուածք, ծակ)
apex - kakatu, dzayru (գագաթը, ծայրը)

aphorism - aradz, asatsvadzk (առած, ասացուածք)
apiary - petag, meghvanots (փեթակ, մեղուանոց)
apiculture - meghvapoudzoutiun (մեղուաբուծութիւն)
apiece - iurakanchiurin (իւրաքանչիւրին)
apieces - gudor gudor (կտոր կտոր)
apogee - heraged, dzayrakouyn (հեռակէտ, ծայրագոյն)
apologize - chadakovel, bashdubanel, neroghoutiun khunturel (ջատագովել, պաշտպանել, ներողութիւն խնդրել)
apologue - arag (առակ)
apology - chukmeghank (չքմեղանք)
apostasy - ouratsoum (ուրացում)
apostate - tasalik (դասալիք)
apostle - arakyal (առաքեալ)
apostolic - arakelagan (առաքելական)
Apostolicism - arakelaganoutiun (Առաքելականութիւն)
apostrophe - abatarts (ապաթարց)
appal, appall - vakhtsunel, vakhnal, sarsapil, vakh (վախցնել, վախնալ, սարսափիլ, վախ)
appalling - vuhadoutiun (վհատութիւն)
apparatus - kordzikner (գործիքներ)
apparel - hakousdeghen, hantertsel (հագուստեղէն, հանդերձել)
apparent - desaneli, haydni (տեսանելի, յայտնի)
apparition - yerevoum, voki (երեւում, ոգի)
appeal - verakunnoutian timel, verakunnoutiun (վերաքննութեան դիմել, վերաքննութիւն)
appear - yerevnal, haydnuvil (երեւնալ, յայտնուիլ)
appearance - yerevouyt, yerevoum, desk (երեւոյթ, երեւում, տեսք)
appease - khaghaghetsunel, hantardetsunel (խաղաղեցնել, հանդարտեցնել)
appelate - verakunnich (վերաքննիչ)
appellant - khunturargou (խնդրարկու)
appellation - anoun, gochoum, poghok (անուն, կոչում, բողոք)
appellee - ampasdanial (ամբաստանեալ)
append - gakhel, gutsel, aveltsunel (կախել, կցել, աւելցնել)
appendage - havelvadz (յաւելուած)
appendix - gouraghi (կուրաղի)
apperceive - nushmarel, umpurnel (նշմարել, ըմբռնել)
appertain - badganil (պատկանիլ)
appetite - akhorzhag (ախորժակ)
appetizer - akhorzhaper (ախորժաբեր)
applaud - dzapaharel (ծափահարել)
applause - dzapaharoutiun (ծափահարութիւն)
apple - khuntsor (խնձոր)
appliance - garasi, kordzik, kordzaturoum, giraroutiun (կարասի, գործիք, գործածութիւն, կիրարութիւն)
applicable - kordzatureli, girargeli (գործածելի, կիրարկելի)
applicant - timogh, khunturargou (դիմող, խնդրարկու)
application - kordzatroutiun, girargoutiun, timoum (գործադրութիւն, կիրարկութիւն, դիմում)
applier - timogh, girarogh (դիմող, կիրարող)
apply - timel, kordzaturel (դիմել, գործադրել)
appoint - hasdadel, nushanagel, garkel (հաստատել, նշանակել, կարգել)
appointment - zhamatroutiun, garkaturoum (ժամադրութիւն, կարգադրում)
apporter - neradzogh (ներածող)
apportion - pazhnel (բաժնել)
apposite - vayelouch, harmar (վայելուչ, յարմար)
appraisal - kunahadoum, arzhevoroum (գնահատում, արժեւորում)
appraise - kunahadel (գնահատել)
appraiser - kunahadogh (գնահատող)
apprecation - maghtank (մաղթանք)
appreciable - kunahadeli (գնահա-

տելի)
appreciate - kunahadel (գնահատել)
appreciation - kunahadoum (գնահատում)
apprehend - purnel, tserpagalel, umpurnel, vakhnal (բռնել, ձերբակալել, ըմբռնել, վախնալ)
apprehension - umpurnoum, ungaloum, vakh, gasgadz (ըմբռնում, ընկալում, վախ, կասկած)
apprentice - ashgerd, usgusnag (աշկերտ, սկսնակ)
apprise - haydnel, imatsunel, deghegoutiun (յայտնել, իմացնել, տեղեկութիւն)
apprize - kunahadel (գնահատել)
approach - modenal, modetsunel, modetsoum (մօտենալ, մօտեցնել, մօտեցում)
approbate - hasdadel, havanil, vaveratsunel (հաստատել, հաւանիլ, վաւերացնել)
approbation - vaveratsoum, havanoutiun (վաւերացում, հաւանութիւն)
appropriate - sepaganatsunel, antsnagan, sepagan (սեփականացնել, անձնական, սեփական)
approval - vaveratsoum, havanoutiun (վաւերացում, հաւանութիւն)
approve - vaveratsunel, hasdadel, untounil (վաւերացնել, հաստատել, ընդունիլ)
approximate - modenal, modig (մօտենալ, մօտիկ)
approximately - modavorabes (մօտաւորապէս)
appurtenance - haragits mas (յարակից մաս)
appurtenant - haragits (յարակից)
apricot - dziran (ծիրան)
April - abril (Ապրիլ)
apriori - arachouts, gankhav (առաջուց, կանխաւ)
apron - koknots (գոգնոց)
apropos - masin, i teb (մասին, ի դէպ)
apt - harmar, untounag (յարմար, ընդունակ)
aptitude - untounagoutiun (ընդունակութիւն)
aqua - chour (ջուր)
aquamarine - dzovagun (ծովակն)
aquarium - churavazan, tsugnaman (ջրաւազան, ձկնաման)
aquatic - churayin (ջրային)
aqueduc - churamough, churoughi (ջրամուղ, ջրուղի)
aqueous - churod, churayin (ջրոտ, ջրային)
aquiferous - churadar, churaper (ջրատար, ջրաբեր)
aquiline - ardzvayin (արծուային)
arab - arap (արաբ)
arabesque - arapagan, arapagan kantag (արաբական, արաբական քանդակ)
arabic - araperen (արաբերէն)
arabism - arapaganoutiun (արաբականութիւն)
arable - hergeli (հերկելի)
arace - armadakhulel, khulel (արմատախլել, խլել)
Ararat - ararad (Արարատ)
arbiter - iravarar, iravararel (իրաւարար, իրաւարարել)
arbitrament - iravararoutiun (իրաւարարութիւն)
arbitrary - gamayagan (կամայական)
arbitrate - tadel, voroshel (դատել, որոշել)
arbitration - iravararoutiun (իրաւարարութիւն)
arbor - sarpina, dzar (սարփինայ, ծառ)
arc - gamar, aghegh (կամար, աղեղ)
arcade - gamaragab, gamarashar (կամարակապ, կամարաշար)
arch - gamar, charajuji, gamarel (կամար, չարաճճի, կամարել)
arch prest - avak kahana (աւագ քահանայ)
archaeologist - hunaked (հնագէտ)
archaeology - hunakidoutiun (հնագիտութիւն)
archaic - hunakidagan, hunaturoshm, hin, ankordzadzeli (հնագիտական, հնադրոշմ, հին, անգործածելի)
archangel - hureshdagabed (հրեշտակապետ)

archbishop - *arkebisgobos* (արքեպիսկոպոս)
archer - *agheghnatsik* (աղեղնաձիգ)
archipelago - *gughzekhoump* (կղզեխումբ)
architect - *jardarabed* (ճարտարապետ)
architecture - *jardarabedoutiun* (ճարտարապետութիւն)
archive - *tivan, hunataran* (դիւան, Հնադարան)
archives - *arkhiv, tivan, hishadagaran, tivanatoughter* (արխիւ, դիւան, յիշատակարան, դիւանաթուղթեր)
archivist - *tivanabah* (դիւանապահ)
archway - *gamaroughi* (կամարուղի)
arctic - *archayin* (արջային)
ardent - *yerantoun, pourun* (եռանդուն, բուռն)
ardor - *chermoutiun, yerant* (ջերմութիւն, եռանդ)
arduous - *dazhaneli, tuzhvar* (տաժանելի, դժուար)
are - *yen* (են)
area - *mageres, shurchan, michots, daradzoutiun* (մակերես, շրջան, միջոց, տարածութիւն)
area code - *nakhativ- heratsayni* (նախաթիւ՝ Հեռաձայնի)
arefy - *chortsunel* (չորցնել)
arena - *gurges, murtsaran* (կրկէս, մրցարան)
arenose - *avazoud* (աւազուտ)
aren't, are not - *chen* (չեն)
argent - *ardzat* (արծաթ)
argue - *vijil, arargel* (վիճիլ, առարկել)
argument - *arargoutiun, pasd, vijapanoutiun, vijil* (առարկութիւն, փաստ, վիճաբանութիւն, վիճիլ)
aria - *megheti, yeghanagh, yerk* (մեղեդի, եղանակ, երգ)
arid - *chor, anchurti* (չոր, անջրդի)
aridity - *choroutiun* (չորութիւն)
aright - *shidag, oughigh* (շիտակ, ուղիղ)
arise - *yellel, partsuranal, dzakil* (ելլել, բարձրանալ, ծագիլ)
aristocracy - *aznuvaganoutiun* (ազնուականութիւն)
aristocrat - *aznuvagan* (ազնուական)
arithmetic - *tuvapanoutiun* (թուաբանութիւն)
ark - *daban* (տապան)
arm - *pazoug, tev, zinel, zinvil* (բազուկ, թեւ, զինել, զինուիլ)
armada - *navadormigh* (նաւատորմիղ)
armament - *razmouzh, usbarazinoutiun, zork* (ռազմուժ, սպառազինութիւն, զօրք)
armchair - *pazgator* (բազկաթոռ)
armed - *zinvadz* (զինուած)
Armenia - *hayasdan* (Հայաստան)
armenian - *hay, hayeren, haygagan* (Հայ, Հայերէն, Հայկական)
armenology - *hayakidoutiun* (Հայագիտութիւն)
armistice - *zinatatar* (զինադադար)
armless - *anzen, antev* (անզէն, անթեւ)
armlet - *pazgig, dzovakhorsh* (բազկիկ, ծովախորշ)
armor - *zurah, bashdbanag* (զրահ, պաշտպանակ)
armory - *zinaran, zenk, zinanushan* (զինարան, զէնք, զինանշան)
armpit - *anout* (անութ)
arms - *zenk* (զէնք)
army - *panag* (բանակ)
aroma - *khoung, pouyr* (խունկ, բոյր)
aromatize - *hamemel* (Համեմել)
around - *shourchu, moderu* (շուրջը, մօտերը)
arousal - *zartnoum, gentanatsoum, ustapoum* (զարթնում, կենդանացում, սթափում)
arouse - *artuntsunel, vokevorel* (արթնցնել, ոգեւորել)
arrack - *oghi* (օղի)
arraign - *ampasdanel, ampasdanoutiun* (ամբաստանել, ամբաստանութիւն)
arrange - *garkaturel, shudgel* (կարգադրել, շտկել)
arrangement - *zartarank, garkaturoutiun* (զարդարանք, կարգադրութիւն)

arrant - vad, dukhrahurchag (վատ, տխրահռչակ)
array - hakvetsunel, tasavorel, hakousd, shark (հագուեցնել, դասաւորել, հագուստ, շարք)
arrear - bardk, yed munalu, hedamunats (պարտք, ետ մնալը, յետամնաց)
arrearage - hedamunats, hedatem (յետամնաց, յետադէմ)
arrest - getsunel, tserpagalel, tserpagaloutiun, tatar (կեցնել, ձերբակալել, ձերբակալութիւն, դադար)
arrestment - tserpagaloum, arkiloum (ձերբակալում, արգիլում)
arret - verakurel, vujir, kuravoum, hurovardag (վերագրել, վճիռ, գրաւում, հրովարտակ)
arrival - zhamanoum (ժամանում)
arrive - hasnil, zhamanel (հասնիլ, ժամանել)
arrogance - hokhordank, ampardavanoutiun (յոխորտանք, ամբարտաւանութիւն)
arrogant - ampardavan (ամբարտաւան)
arrogate - bahanchel, iuratsunel, shortel (պահանջել, իւրացնել, շորթել)
arrogation - anirav bahanch (անիրաւ պահանջ)
arrose - turchel, churel (թրջել, ջրել)
arrow - ned (նետ)
arrowhead - nedakuloukh (նետագլուխ)
arse - hedouyk, hadag (յետոյք, յատակ)
arsenal - zinaran (զինարան)
arson - hurtsikoutiun (հրձիգութիւն)
art - arvesd, jardaroutiun (արուեստ, ճարտարութիւն)
arteriosclerosis - bunteragoutiun (պնդերակութիւն)
artery - shuncherag, zaregerag (շնչերակ, զարկերակ)
artful - khoramang (խորամանկ)
artheritis - hotatsav, hotadab (յօդացաւ, յօդատապ)
arthritis - hotatsav (յօդացաւ)
artichoke - gangar (կանկառ)
article - hotvadz, niut (յօդուած, նիւթ)
articulate - hotavorel, ardasanel, husdag (յօդաւորել, արտասանել, յստակ)
artifice - hunark, varbedoutiun, jardaroutiun (հնարք, վարպետութիւն, ճարտարութիւն)
artificial - arvesdagan, geghdz (արուեստական, կեղծ)
artillery - huredani, tuntanot (հրետանի, թնդանօթ)
artisan - arhesdavor (արհեստաւոր)
artist - arvesdaket, terasan (արուեստագէտ, դերասան)
artless - anarvesd, punagan (անարուեստ, բնական)
as - kani vor, numan, inchbes (քանի որ, նման, ինչպէս)
ascend - makultsil, partsuranal (մաքլցիլ, բարձրանալ)
ascendancy - ishkhanoutiun, verelk, keratasoutiun, nakhnik (իշխանութիւն, վերելք, գերադասութիւն, նախնիք)
ascendant - ver yellogh, veramparts, zarkatsogh, nakhnik (վեր ելլող, վերամբարձ, զարգացող, նախնիք)
ascending - partsuratsogh (բարձրացող)
ascension - verelk, partsuratsoum, hampartsoum (վերելք, բարձրացում, համբարձում)
ascertain - hasdadel, usdoukel (հաստատել, ստուգել)
ascetic - juknavor, khusdagiats (ճգնաւոր, խստակեաց)
ascribe - verakurel (վերագրել)
asexual - anserayin (անսեռային)
ash - mokhrel (մոխրել)
ashame - amuchtsunel (ամչցնել)
ashamed - amotahar, amotalits (ամօթահար, ամօթալից)
ashes - mokhir, ajiunner (մոխիր, աճիւններ)
ashtray - mokhraman (մոխրաման)
Asia - asia (Ասիա)
asian - asiagan, asiatsi (ասիական, ասիացի)

aside - megti, megousi (մէկդի, մեկուսի)
asinine - ishavari (իշավարի)
ask - hartsunel, khunturel (Հարցնել, խնդրել)
askance - gasgadzankov, goghmunagi (կասկածանքով, կողմնակի)
askew - goghmunagi, dzour (կողմնակի, ծուռ)
asleep - kunatsadz (քնացած)
aspect - yerevouyt, desk (երեւոյթ, տեսք)
asper - goshd, pird, tazhan (կոշտ, բիրտ, դաժան)
asperity - khusdoutiun, tazhanoutiun (խստութիւն, դաժանութիւն)
asperse - surusgel, zurbardel (սրսկել, զրպարտել)
aspersion - zurbardoutiun (զրպարտութիւն)
asphalt - goubur, asfalt (կուպր, ասֆալթ)
asphyxia - shunchaheghtsoutiun (շնչահեղձութիւն)
asphyxiate - shunchaheghtsel, anshunchatsunel (շնչահեղձել, անշնչացնել)
aspirant - tsukdogh, hedamoud, tegnadzou (ձգտող, հետամուտ, թեկնածու)
aspiration - tsukdoum, denchank, ot kashel (ձգտում, տենչանք, օդը քաշել)
aspirator - otadzudzich, poshedzudzich (օդածծիչ, փոշեծծիչ)
aspire - denchal, ughtsal, partsuranal, ughtsank (տենչալ, ըղձալ, բարձրանալ, ըղձանք)
asquint - shil, shegh (շիլ, շեղ)
ass - esh, avanag (էշ, աւանակ)
assail - hartsagil (յարձակիլ)
assailant - hartsagogh (յարձակող)
assassin - martasban, vojrakordz (մարդասպան, ոճրագործ)
assassinate - usbannel (սպաննել)
assassination - usbanoutiun (սպանութիւն)
assault - hartsagoum (յարձակում)
assay - portsel, chanal, ports, kunnoutiun (փորձել, ջանալ, փորձ, քննութիւն)
assemblage - havakoum (հաւաքում)
assemble - havakel, khumpel (հաւաքել, խմբել)
assembly - havakouyt, zhoghov, hamakhumpoum (հաւաքոյթ, ժողով, համախմբում)
assemblyman - zhoghovagan (ժողովական)
assent - untounil, hamatsaynil, havanoutiun (ընդունիլ, համաձայնիլ, հաւանութիւն)
assert - haydararel, buntel (յայտարարել, պնդել)
assertion - hasdadoum (հաստատում)
assess - doukankel, hargel, kunahadel (տուգանքել, հարկել, գնահատել)
assessment - kunahadoum, hargaturoutiun (գնահատում, հարկադրութիւն)
assessor - dourk - doukank voroshogh (տուրք – տուգանք որոշող)
asset - galvadzamas, inchk, ounetsvadzk (կալուածամաս, ինչք, ունեցուածք)
assets - bardki tem ounetsvadzk (պարտքի դէմ ունեցուածք)
assiduate - haradev (յարատեւ)
assiduity - haradevoutiun (յարատեւութիւն)
assiduous - haradevogh (յարատեւող)
assiege - basharel, basharoum (պաշարել, պաշարում)
assign - nushanagel, dal (նշանակել, տալ)
assignation - gochnakir, sahmanoum, voroshoum, nushanagoum (կոչնագիր, սահմանում, որոշում, նշանակում)
assimilable - iuranali, tsouleli (իւրանալի, ձուլելի)
assimilate - tsoulel, tsoulvil, marsel, iuratsunel (ձուլել, ձուլուիլ, մարսել, իւրացնել)
assimilation - tsouloum, pokhagerboum (ձուլում, փոխակերպում)
assist - oknel, ozhantagel, nerga

ullal (օգնել, օժանդակել, ներկայ ըլլալ)
assistance - oknoutiun (օգնութիւն)
assistant - oknagan (օգնական)
assize - nisd, zhoghov, huramanakir (նիստ, ժողով, Հրամանագիր)
associate - ungeragtsil, mianal, pazhnegits (ընկերակցիլ, միանալ, բաժնեկից)
association - ungeragtsoutiun, miuoutiun (ընկերակցութիւն, միութիւն)
assort - tasavorel, shudgel (դասաւորել, շտկել)
assorted - undurvadz, zadvadz, darper (ընտրուած, զատուած, տարբեր)
assortment - tasavoroum, desagavoroum, numoushner (դասաւորում, տեսակաւորում, նմոյշներ)
assuage - meghmel, nuvazil (մեղմել, նուազիլ)
assuager - meghmatsunogh (մեղմացնող)
assume - usdantsnel, geghdsel (ստանձնել, կեղծել)
assumer - yentaturogh, geghdz (ենթադրող, կեղծ)
assumpt - usdatsunel, yentaturel, yentaturoutiun (ստանձնել, ենթադրել, ենթադրութիւն)
assumption - usdantsnoum, yentaturoutiun, verapokhoum (ստանձնում, ենթադրութիւն, վերափոխում)
assurance - abahovakroutiun (ապաՀովագրութիւն)
assure - vusdahetsunel, abahovakurel, hasdadel (վստաՀեցնել, ապաՀովագրել, Հաստատել)
assurer - abahovogh (ապաՀովող)
assyrian - asori, asoreren, asoragan (ասորի, ասորերէն, ասորական)
asterisk - asdghanish (աստղանիշ)
asthma - shuncharkeloutiun (շնչարգելութիւն)
astigmatism - aghodadesoutiun (աղօտատեսութիւն)
astir - sharzhoun (շարժուն)
astonish - zarmatsunel (զարմացնել)
astonishment - hiatsoum (Հիացում)
astound - abshetsunel (ապշեցնել)
astray - moloradz (մոլորած)
astrict - seghmel, seghm, ampop (սեղմել, սեղմ, ամփոփ)
astringe - gabel, ampopel (կապել, ամփոփել)
astrologer - asdghaked (աստղագէտ)
astrology - asdghapashkhoutiun, asdghakoushagoutiun (աստղաբաշխութիւն, աստղագուշակութիւն)
astronaut - asdghanavort (աստղանաւորդ)
astronomer - asdghaked, asdghapashkh (աստղագէտ, աստղաբաշխ)
astronomic - asdghapanagan, asdghapashkhagan (աստղաբանական, աստղաբաշխական)
astronomical - asdghakidagan (աստղագիտական)
astronomy - asdghakidoutiun (աստղագիտութիւն)
astute - khoraked, suramid (խորագէտ, սրամիտ)
asunder - anchad, yergou mas (անջատ, երկու մաս)
aswewe - abshetsunel (ապշեցնել)
asylum - abasdanaran, himaranots (ապաստանարան, յիմարանոց)
at - mechu, modu, kovu (մէջը, մօտը, քովը)
atake - vura hasnil (վրայ Հասնիլ)
atavism - zharankaganoutiun, arhavoutiun (ժառանգականութիւն, առՀաւութիւն)
ate - gerav (կերաւ)
atelier - arhesdanots (արՀեստանոց)
atheism - anasdvadzoutiun (անաստուածութիւն)
atheist - anasdvadz (անաստուած)
atheous - amparishd (ամբարիշտ)
atherosclerosis - yeragakhutsoum (երակախցում)
athetize - merzhel (մերժել)
athist - dzarav (ծարաւ)
athlete - marzig, umpish (մարզիկ, ըմբիշ)
athletic - marzagan (մարզական)
athletism - marzarvesd (մարզարուեստ)
Atlantic - adlandian (Ատլանտեան)

atlas - kardesakirk, adlas (քարտէսագիրք, ատլաս)
atmosphere - mutnolord (մթնոլորտ)
atom - hiule (հիւլէ)
atomic bomb - hiuleagan roump (հիւլէական ռումբ)
atone - hamatsaynil, kavel (համաձայնիլ, քաւել)
atrocious - vayrak, kazanayin (վայրագ, գազանային)
atrocity - vayrakoutiun (վայրագութիւն)
atrophy - hiudzakhd, hiudzoum (հիւծախտ, հիւծում)
attach - gubtsunel, gabel, gutsil, amratsunel (կպցնել, կապել, կցիլ, ամրացնել)
attache - gutsort tesbanadan (կցորդ դեսպանատան)
attachement - gab, haroum (կապ, յարում)
attack - hartsagil, hartsagoum (յարձակիլ, յարձակում)
attain - hasnil, hachoghil (հասնիլ, յաջողիլ)
attaint - shunorazurgel, harvadzel, harvadz (շնորհազրկել, հարուածել, հարուած)
attaminate - varagel, abaganel (վարակել, ապականել)
attar - vartachour (վարդաջուր)
attask - khudzpudzel (խծբծել)
attemper - meghmel, parekharnel (մեղմել, բարեխառնել)
attempt - mahaports, tav, portsel, tavel, hartsagil (մահափորձ, դաւ, փորձել, դաւել, յարձակիլ)
attend - hajakhel, ungeragtsil, usbasel, khunamel (յաճախել, ընկերակցիլ, սպասել, խնամել)
attendance - hajakhoum, nergayoutiun, dzarayoutiun (յաճախում, ներկայութիւն, ծառայութիւն)
attendant - usbasogh, oughegtsogh, usbasargogh, oknagan (սպասող, ուղեկցող, սպասարկող, օգնական)
attent - oushatir, mudaturoutiun (ուշադիր, մտադրութիւն)
attention - oushatroutiun (ուշադրութիւն)
attentive - oushatir (ուշադիր)
attenuate - meghmel, nurpatsunel, nuvazetsunel (մեղմել, նրբացնել, նուազեցնել)
attenuation - meghmoum (մեղմում)
attest - vugayel (վկայել)
attestation - vugayoutiun (վկայութիւն)
attestor - vuga, vugayogh (վկայ, վկայող)
attire - haktzunel, zartarel (հագցնել, զարդարել)
attitude - tirk, verapermounk (դիրք, վերաբերմունք)
attorney - pasdapan, pokhanort, tadakhaz, deghagal (փաստաբան, փոխանորդ, դատախազ, տեղակալ)
attract - kashel, hurabourel (քաշել, հրապուրել)
attraction - kashoghoutiun, hurabouyr, tsukoghoutiun (քաշողութիւն, հրապոյր, ձգողութիւն)
attractive - kashoghagan, hurabourich (քաշողական, հրապուրիչ)
attribute - verakurel, hamarel (վերագրել, համարել)
attribution - verakuroum, shunorhoum (վերագրում, շնորհում)
attrition - shupoum, mashoum (շփում, մաշում)
attune - tashnavorel, nertashnagel (դաշնաւորել, ներդաշնակել)
au revoir - tsudesoutiun (ցտեսութիւն)
aubade - aykerk (այգերգ)
aube - arshalouys (արշալոյս)
aubergine - sumpoug (սմբուկ)
auburn - shakanagakouyn (շագանակագոյն)
auction - ajourt, ajourtov dzaghel (աճուրդ, աճուրդով ծախել)
audacious - hantoukun (յանդուգն)
audacity - khizakhoutiun, hantuknoutiun (խիզախութիւն, յանդգնութիւն)
audible - luseli (լսելի)
audience - oungunturoutiun, ounguntirner, hantisadesner (ունկնդրութիւն, ունկնդիրներ, հանդիսատեսներ)

audient - ounguntir (ունկնդիր)
audio - tsaynayin (ձայնային)
audiotape - tsaynakurvadz yeriz (ձայնագրուած երիզ)
audiovisual - lusa-desoghagan (լսա-տեսողական)
audio-visual - desa-lusoghagan (տեսա-լսողական)
audit - tadakunnoutiun, lusoum, hashvekunnel (դատաքննութիւն, լսում, հաշուեքննել)
audition - oungunturoutiun, lusoum (ունկնդրութիւն, լսում)
auditor - ounguntir, hashvekunnich (ունկնդիր, հաշուեքննիչ)
auditorium - lusaran (լսարան)
aught - voryeve pan, vochinch (որեւէ բան, ոչինչ)
augment - aveltsunel (աւելցնել)
augmentation - haveloum (յաւելում)
augur - koushag, koushagel, humayel (գուշակ, գուշակել, հմայել)
August - okosdos (Օգոստոս)
aunt - horakouyr, morakouyr (հօրաքոյր, մօրաքոյր)
aural - lusoghagan (լսողական)
aureola, aureole - lousabusag (լուսապսակ)
auricle - pultag, luselapogh, surdi khorsh (բլթակ, լսելափող, սրտի խորշ)
auriferous - vosgeper (ոսկեբեր)
auspices - hovanavoroutiun (հովանաւորութիւն)
auspicious - parekoushag (բարեգուշակ)
austere - khisd, khozhor (խիստ, խոժոռ)
austerity - khusdoutiun, khozhoroutiun (խստութիւն, խոժոռութիւն)
Australia - avusduralia (Աւստրալիա)
Austria - avusduria (Աւստրիա)
authentic - vaveragan (վաւերական)
authenticity - vaveraganoutiun (վաւերականութիւն)
author - heghinag, kurogh, heghinagel (հեղինակ, գրող, հեղինակել)
authoress - heghinagouhi (հեղինակուհի)
authority - ishkhanoutiun, heghinagoutiun (իշխանութիւն, հեղինակութիւն)
authorization - ardonoutiun (արտօնութիւն)
authorize - ardonel, vaveratsunel (արտօնել, վաւերացնել)
authorship - heghinagoutiun (հեղինակութիւն)
auto - inkna-, inknasharzh (ինքնա-, ինքնաշարժ)
autobiography - inknagensakroutiun (ինքնակենսագրութիւն)
autobus - pokhaturagark, hanragark (փոխադրակառք, հանրակառք)
autocar, automobile - inknasharzh (ինքնաշարժ)
autocracy - inknagaloutiun (ինքնակալութիւն)
autograph - inknakir, heghinagi tserakir (ինքնագիր, հեղինակի ձեռագիր)
automate - inknakordz, inknakordzi veradzel (ինքնագործ, ինքնագործի վերածել)
automatic - inknakordz, mekenagan (ինքնագործ, մեքենական)
automobile - inknasharzh, gark (ինքնաշարժ, կառք)
autonomy - inknavaroutiun (ինքնավարութիւն)
autopsy - tiazunnoutiun, tiahertsoutiun (դիազննութիւն, դիահերձութիւն)
autumn - ashoun (աշուն)
auxiliary - ozhantag, oknagan (օժանդակ, օգնական)
avail - okduvil, okdakordzel (օգտուիլ, օգտագործել)
available - okdakordseli, dramatreli (օգտագործելի, տրամադրելի)
avalanche - tsiunagouyd (ձիւնակոյտ)
avant-garde - harachabah (յառաջապահ)
avarice - akahoutiun (ագահութիւն)
avaricious - akah, gudzdzi (ագահ, կծծի)
ave - voghchiun (ողջոյն)
avenge - vurezh arnel (վրէժ առնել)
avengeance - vurezhkhunturoutiun (վրէժխնդրութիւն)

avenger - vurizharou (վրիժառու)
avenue - boghoda (պողոտայ)
aver - hasdadel, sheshdel (հաստատել, շեշտել)
average - michin, michini veradzel, vunas (միջին, միջինի վերածել, վնաս)
averse - khorshogh, anhozhar (խորշող, անյօժար)
aversion - khorshank, zuzvank (խորշանք, զզուանք)
avert - megti tartsunel (մէկդի դարձնել)
aviary - turchnaran, pouyn (թռչնարան, բոյն)
aviation - otanavortoutiun, savarnoum (օդանաւորդութիւն, սաւառնում)
aviator - savarnort, otanavort (սաւառնորդ, օդանաւորդ)
avid - anhak, denchatsogh (անյագ, տենչացող)
avidity - anhakoutiun, gudzdzioutiun (անյագութիւն, կծծիութիւն)
avocado - avgad (աւկատ)
avocation - nuviroum, nakhasiroutiun (նուիրում, նախասիրութիւն)
avoid - uzkoushanal, khousapil, pakhchil, kashvil (զգուշանալ, խուսափիլ, փախչիլ, քաշուիլ)
avoider - khousapogh, vakhtsunogh (խուսափող, վախցնող)
avouch - hasdadel, khosdovanil, untounil, pasd (հաստատել, խոստովանիլ, ընդունիլ, փաստ)
avow - khosdovanil, haydnel (խոստովանիլ, յայտնել)
avulse - khulel, gorzel (խլել, կորզել)
avulsion - khuloum, gorzoum, badaroum (խլում, կորզում, պատառում)
await - usbasel (սպասել)
awake - artuntsunel, artunnal, vokevorel (արթնցնել, արթննալ, ոգեւորել)
award (n) - murtzanag, tapni, kunahadoum, tadoum (մրցանակ, դափնի, գնահատում, դատում)
award (v) - murtzanag dal, shunorhel, voroshel, sahmanel (մրցանակ տալ, շնորհել, որոշել, սահմանել)
awarder - vujrogh, voroshogh (վճռող, որոշող)
aware - uzkouysh, artoun, deghiag (զգոյշ, արթուն, տեղեակ)
awarn - aztararel, uzkoushatsunel (ազդարարել, զգուշացնել)
away - patsaga, megti (բացակայ, մէկդի)
awe - yergiugh, badgarank (երկիւղ, պատկառանք)
awful - ahreli, badgareli (ահռելի, պատկառելի)
awhape - shuvaretsunel, sosgatsunel (շուարեցնել, սոսկացնել)
awhile - kich mu aden, zhananag nu (քիչ մը ատեն, ժամանակ մը)
awkward - anjarag, putamid, anharmar (անճարակ, բթամիտ, անյարմար)
awkwardness - anjaragoutiun (անճարակութիւն)
awless - anamot, anbadgar (անամօթ, անպատկառ)
awning - dzadzgots, vuranag (ծածկոց, վրանակ)
awry - dzour, goghmnagi (ծուռ, կողմնակի)
ax, axe - gatsin (կացին)
axiom - aradz, usguzpounk, arachargoutiun (առած, սկզբունք, առաջարկութիւն)
axis - arantsk (առանցք)
axle - arantsk, surnag (առանցք, սռնակ)
ay - ah, apsos (ահ, ափսոս)
aye - mishd, sharounag (միշտ, շարունակ)
azote - porogadzin (բորոկածին)
azure - yergnagabouyd, yergnakouyn (երկնակապոյտ, երկնագոյն)

B

babble - murtmurtal, totovel (մրթմրթալ, թոթովել)
babe - mangig, pokrig, dugheg (մանկիկ, փոքրիկ, տղեկ)
babel - papelon, aghmoug, kharnagoutiun (Բաբելոն, աղմուկ, խառնակութիւն)
baby - mangig, noradzin (մանկիկ, նորածին)
babyhood - mangoutiun (մանկութիւն)
baby-sitter - mangabah (մանկապահ)
baccalaureate - busagavoroutiun (պսակաւորութիւն)
bachelor - amouri, busagavor (ամուրի, պսակաւոր)
bachelorship - amourioutiun (ամուրիութիւն)
back - gurnag, yed, tartsial, netsoug genal (կռնակ, ետ, դարձեալ, նեցուկ կենալ)
back pain - gurnagi tsav (կռնակի ցաւ)
backache - gurnagi tsav (կռնակի ցաւ)
backbite - pampasel (բամբասել)
backbiter - pampasogh (բամբասող)
backbone - voghnahar (ողնահար)
backcast - tsakhortoutiun (ձախորդութիւն)
backed - amratsadz, gurnag ounetsogh (ամրացած, կռնակ ունեցող)
backer - zoravik (զօրավիգ)
background - yentahogh, himk, portsaroutiun (ենթահող, հիմք, փորձառութիւն)
backing - netsoug, bashdbanoutiun, yedevi masu (նեցուկ, պաշտպանութիւն, ետեւի մասը)
backside - hedouyk, yedevu (յետոյք, ետեւը)
backslider - havadourats (հաւատուրաց)
backstair - dzadzoug, gurnagen, tavatragan (ծածուկ, կռնակէն, դաւադրական)
backster - hatsakordz (հացագործ)
backup - gurnag genal, zoratsunel, henaran, netsoug (կռնակ կենալ, զօրացնել, յենարան, նեցուկ)
backward - hedatem, varanod (յետադէմ, վարանոտ)
bacon - khozaboukhd (խոզապուխտ)
bacteria - manre (մանրէ)
bacteria-bacterium - manre (մանրէ)
bacteriologist - manreapan (մանրէաբան)
bacteriology - manreapanoutiun (մանրէաբանութիւն)
bad - kesh, char (գէշ, չար)
badge - shukanushan, shukanushanel (շքանշան, շքանշանել)
badly - kesh gerbov (գէշ կերպով)
badness - keshoutiun (գէշութիւն)
baffle - dzaghrel, arkilel, khapanel, chunchel (ծաղրել, արգիլել, խափանել, ջնջել)
baffler - khapanogh, arkilogh (խափանող, արգիլող)
bag - bayousag, dobrag, amparel (պայուսակ, տոպրակ, ամբարել)
bagage - oughekouyk, abrank (ուղեգոյք, ապրանք)
bagatelle - sin, barab pan (սին, պարապ բան)
bail (n) - yerashkhavoroutiun, yerashkhakir, got, shurchapag (երաշխաւորութիւն, երաշխագիր, կոթ, շրջափակ)
bail (v) - yerashkhavoroutiamp artsagel, chouru barbel (երաշխաւորութեամբ արձակել, ջուրը պարպել)
bail-bond - yerashkhakir (երաշխա-

գիր)
bait - khaydz (խայծ)
bake - yepel (եփել)
baker - hatsakordz (հացագործ)
bakery - pour, hatsakordzoutiun (փուռ, հացագործութիւն)
baking - yep, yepoum (եփ, եփում)
balance - gushirk, gushrel, havasaragushrel (կշիռք, կշռել, հաւասարակշռել)
balcony - badushkam (պատշգամ)
bald - jaghad, anmaz, aneres (ճաղատ, անմազ, աներես)
baldness - jaghadoutiun (ճաղատութիւն)
bale - tushvaroutiun, aghed, chouru barbel (թշուառութիւն, աղէտ, ջուրը պարպել)
baleful - aghidali, tsavalits (աղիտալի, ցաւալից)
ball - kuntag, barahantes (գնդակ, պարահանդէս)
ballad - barek, dagh, keghon (պարերգ, տաղ, գեղօն)
ballerina - barouhi (պարուհի)
ballet - taderabar, barakhagh (թատերապար, պարախաղ)
balloon - otabarig, puchig (օդապարիկ, փչիկ)
ballot - kaghduni kuve, kuveatought (գաղտնի քուէ, քուէաթուղթ)
ballot box - kuveadoup (քուէատուփ)
ballotage - hamemadagan kuve, kuveargel (համեմատական քուէ, քուէարկել)
ballottement - yereroum (երերում)
ballroom - barasurah (պարասրահ)
balm - odzanelik, palasan (օծանելիք, բալասան)
balsa - lasd (լաստ)
balsam - palasan (բալասան)
baltic - baltian (պալթեան)
baluster - vantagasiun (վանդակասիւն)
balustrade - vantagabad (վանդակապատ)
bamboo - huntgagan yeghek (հնդկական եղէգ)
ban - arkilel, nuzovel, arkiloum, nuzovk, panatrank (արգիլել, նզովել, արգիլում, նզովք, բանադրանք)
banal - hasarag, kurehig, sovoragan (հասարակ, գռեհիկ, սովորական)
banana - banan (պանան)
band - gab, yeriz, nuvakakhoump (կապ, երիզ, նուագախումբ)
bandage - viragab, viragabel (վիրակապ, վիրակապել)
banderole - pokur troshag, khachgab (փոքր դրօշակ, խաչկապ)
bandit - avazag, hurosag, yelouzag (աւազակ, հրոսակ, ելուզակ)
bane - touyn, aver, gordzanel (թոյն, աւեր, կործանել)
baneful - tounalits (թունալից)
bang - dzedzel, harvadzel (ծեծել, հարուածել)
bangle - abaranchan (ապարանջան)
banish - aksorel, vudarel (աքսորել, վտարել)
banishment - aksor (աքսոր)
banister - santukhamad (սանդղխամատ)
banjo - panzho, yerazhushdagan kordzik mu (պանժօ, երաժշտական գործիք մը)
bank - turamadoun, nusdaran, toump, kedag (դրամատուն, նստարան, թումբ, գետակ)
bank transfer - turamadunayin pokhantsoum (դրամատնային փոխանցում)
banker - turamader (դրամատէր)
banking - turamadunayin kordzouneoutiun (դրամատնային գործունէութիւն)
banknote - turamanish, tughtaturam (դրամանիշ, թղթադրամ)
bankrupt - sunang, sunangatsunel (սնանկ, սնանկացնել)
bankruptcy - sunangoutiun (սնանկութիւն)
banner - basdar, turoshag, turosh (պաստառ, դրօշակ, դրօշ)
banns - busagi dzanoutsoum (պսակի ծանուցում)
banquet - khunjouyk, gochounk, hatsgerouyt (խնճոյք, կոչունք, հացկերոյթ)
banter - gadagel, zuvarjanal,

dzaghrel (կատակել, զուարճանալ, ծաղրել)
banterer - zuvarjakhos (զուարճախօս)
baptism - mugerdoutiun (մկրտութիւն)
baptist - mugurdchagan (մկրտչական)
baptization - mugurdoutiun (մկրտութիւն)
baptize - mugurdel, anvanel, orhnel (մկրտել, անուանել, օրհնել)
bar - tsogh, toump, adian, kinedoun, kidz, khapanel (ձող, թումբ, ատեան, գինետուն, գիծ, խափանել)
barb - morouk, morouku gudrel-hartarel (մօրուք, մօրուք կտրել-յարդարել)
barbarian - parparos, tazhan (բարբարոս, դաժան)
barbarism - parparosoutiun (բարբարոսութիւն)
barbarity - vayrenoutium (վայրենութիւն)
barbarous - parparos, vayreni (բարբարոս, վայրենի)
barbecue - khorovel, garmuradz gentani (խորովել, կարմրած կենդանի)
barber - saprich, varsahartar (սափրիչ, վարսայարդար)
barcon - magouyg (մակոյկ)
bare - merg, pats, mergatsunel (մերկ, բաց, մերկացնել)
barefaced - barzeres (պարզերես)
barefoot - pobig (բոպիկ)
bareheaded - kulkhapats (գլխաբաց)
barely - barzabes, haziv te (պարզապէս, հազիւ թէ)
bareness - mergoutiun (մերկութիւն)
bargain - sagargoutiun, sagargel (սակարկութիւն, սակարկել)
bargainer - sagargogh (սակարկող)
barge - uzposanav (զբօսանաւ)
baritone, barytone - arnatsayn, pamp tsayn (առնաձայն, բամբ ձայն)
bark - dzari geghev, hachots, geghevel, hachel (ծառի կեղեւ, հաչոց, կեղեւել, հաչել)
barker - geghevogh, hachogh (կեղեւող, հաչող)
barley - kari (գարի)
barm - khumor, perpour (խմոր, փրփուր)
barn - marak (մարագ)
barometer - otachap (օդաչափ)
baron - baron, erig mart, amousin (պարոն, էրիկ մարդ, ամուսին)
baroscope - dzanratsouyts (ծանրացոյց)
barque - arakasdanav (առագաստանաւ)
barrack - zoranots, zoranots punagil (զօրանոց, զօրանոց բնակիլ)
barrage - badnesh, toump, ampardag, churarkel (պատնէշ, թումբ, ամբարտակ, ջրարգել)
barrel - dagar (տակառ)
barren - amoul, anbudough (ամուլ, անպտուղ)
barrenness - amloutiun (ամլութիւն)
barricade - badnesh, amrapagel, badneshel (պատնէշ, ամրափակել, պատնէշել)
barrier - arkelk, badvar, badnesh, sahman (արգելք, պատուար, պատնէշ, սահման)
barrow - tsernagark (ձեռնակառք)
barter - pokhanagel, pokhanagoum (փոխանակել, փոխանակում)
basa - khariskh, him (խարիսխ, հիմ)
base - him, khariskh, tsadz, kurehig, himnel (հիմ, խարիսխ, ցած, գռեհիկ, հիմնել)
baseball - kuntakhagh (գնդախաղ)
basement - kednaharg, negough (գետնայարկ, նկուղ)
baseness - tsadzoutiun (ցածութիւն)
bash - amuchtsunel, dzanur harvadz (ամչցնել, ծանր հարուած)
bashful - amuchgod, vakhgod (ամչկոտ, վախկոտ)
bashfulness - amotkhadzoutiun (ամօթխածութիւն)
basic - himnagan (հիմնական)
basin - avazan, navagayk, dashd, gonk, hovid (աւազան, նաւակայք, դաշտ, կոնք, հովիտ)

basis - himk, khariskh, nakhadar (հիմք, խարիսխ, նախատարր)
bask - arevu bargil, daknal (արեւը պառկիլ, տաքնալ)
basket - goghov, sagar (կողով, սակառ)
basketball - basketbol (պասքէթպոլ)
bass - tamp, tav tsayn, dzovakayl (թամբ, թաւ ձայն, ծովագայլ)
bastard - bornugorti (պոռնկորդի)
baste - telagarel, kanagodzel, surusgel (թելակարել, գանակոծել, սրսկել)
bat - chughchig (ջղջիկ)
bate - bagsetsunel, hartsagil, pakhel -teveru, chank (պակսեցնել, յարձակիլ, բախել–թեւերը, ջանք)
batement - nuvazoum (նուազում)
bath - paghnik, lokank (բաղնիք, լոգանք)
bathe - loghal, loktsunel, turchel (լողալ, լոգցնել, թրջել)
bathing suit - loghazkesd (լողազգեստ)
bathometer - khorachap (խորաչափ)
bathroom - paghnik (բաղնիք)
bathtub - lokaran (լոգարան)
baton - kavazan (գաւազան)
battalion - vashd, koumardag (վաշտ, գումարտակ)
batten - kirtsunel, kirnal, nourp dakhdag (գիրցնել, գիրնալ, նուրբ տախտակ)
batter - zarnel, harvadzel, por dal, goroutiun (զարնել, հարուածել, եոր տալ, կորութիւն)
battery - huredani, part, yelegduramardgots (հրետանի, բարդ, ելեկտրամարտկոց)
battle - guriv, baderazm (կռիւ, պատերազմ)
battleground - razmatashd (ռազմադաշտ)
battleship - razmanav (ռազմանաւ)
batty - khent, aboush (խենդ, ապուշ)
bauble - khaghalik, ouloungk (խաղալիք, ուլունք)
bawd - gavad, pozaradz, gavadoutiun unel (կաւատ, բոզարած, կաւատութիւն ընել)
bawdy - anparo, poz, lugdi (անբարոյ, բոզ, լկտի)
bawl - juchal, boral, jich (ճչալ, պոռալ, ճիչ)
baxter - hatsakordzouhi (հացագործուհի)
bay - dzots, dzovakhorsh (ծոց, ծովախորշ)
bayonet - suvin, suvinel (սուին, սուինել)
bazaar, bazar - shouga (շուկայ)
be - ullal, kudnuvil (ըլլալ, գտնուիլ)
beach - dzovezur, dzovezerk, avazoud ap (ծովեզր, ծովեզերք, աւազուտ ափ)
beachy - avazoud (աւազուտ)
beacon - uzkoushanish (զգուշանիշ)
bead - hamrichi hadig, vartaran, shit (համրիչի հատիկ, վարդարան, շիթ)
beadle - nuvirag, zhamgoch, paraban (նուիրակ, ժամկոչ, բարապան)
beak - gudouts (կտուց)
beaker - pazhag, kavat (բաժակ, գաւաթ)
beal - balar, girj, balaril (պալար, կիրճ, պալարիլ)
beam - keran (գերան)
bean - loupia, pagla (լուբիա, բակլայ)
bear (n) - arch, takagh (արջ, դագաղ)
bear (v) - gurel, dogal, dzunanil (կրել, տոկալ, ծնանիլ)
beard - morouk (մօրուք)
beardless - anmorous (անմօրուս)
bearer - gurogh, perogh (կրող, բերող)
bearing - varmounk (վարմունք)
beast - kazan, anasoun (գազան, անասուն)
beasty - kazanayin (գազանային)
beat - dzedzel, zarnel (ծեծել, զարնել)
beaten - dzedzvadz (ծեծուած)
beater - zarnogh, haghtogh (զարնող, յաղթող)
beath - chortsunel, daktsunel, lok-

tsunel (չորցնել, տաքցնել, լոգցնել)
beatify - yerchangatsunel, yeraneli hurchagel (երջանկացնել, երանելի հռչակել)
beating - dzedz, harvadz, hovou tem navargoum (ծեծ, հարուած, հովու դէմ նաւարկում)
beatitude - surpaznoutiun (սրբազնութիւն)
beau - bujnaser, sirahar (պճնասէր, սիրահար)
beauteous - chuknagh (չքնաղ)
beautifier - keghetsgatsnogh (գեղեցկացնող)
beautiful - keghetsig, aghvor (գեղեցիկ, աղուոր)
beautify - keghetsgatsunel, keghetsganal (գեղեցկացնել, գեղեցկանալ)
beauty - keghetsgoutiun (գեղեցկութիւն)
bebleed - ariunel, ariunodel (արիւնել, արիւնոտել)
beblot - pudzavorel (բծաւորել)
becalm - hantardetsunel (հանդարտեցնել)
because - vorovhedev (որովհետեւ)
becharm - tiutel (դիւթել)
beck - gudouts, nushan unel (կտուց, նշան ընել)
beclip - voghchakourel, shurchabadel (ողջագուրել, շրջապատել)
become - ullal, usgusil, tarnal (ըլլալ, սկսիլ, դառնալ)
becoming - vayelouch, badshaj (վայելուչ, պատշաճ)
bed - angoghin (անկողին)
bedable - turchel, surusgel (թրջել, սրսկել)
bedding - dzadzgotsner (ծածկոցներ)
bedeek - zartarel (զարդարել)
bedgown - kisheranots (գիշերանոց)
bedlam - himaranots (յիմարանոց)
bedmaker - mahjagalakordz (մահճակալագործ)
bedquiet - vermag (վերմակ)
bedroom - nunchaseniag, nuncharan (ննջասենեակ, ննջարան)
bedspread - angoghini dzadzgots (անկողինի ծածկոց)
bedstead - mahjagal (մահճակալ)
bedtime - nunchazham, angoghini zham (ննջաժամ, անկողինի ժամ)
bee - meghou (մեղու)
beef - yez, govou mis (եզ, կովու միս)
beehive - petag (փեթակ)
been - yeghadz (եղած)
beeper - tsayn-aztanushan heratsayni (ձայն-ազդանշան հեռաձայնի)
beer - karechour (գարեջուր)
beeswax - meghramom (մեղրամոմ)
beet, beetrave - jaguntegh (ճակնդեղ)
beetle - tag, tagel, puzez (թակ, թակել, բզէզ)
befall - badahil (պատահիլ)
befit - harmaril, badshajil (յարմարիլ, պատշաճիլ)
beflatter - shoghokortel (շողոքորթել)
befool - khapel, khentetsunel (խաբել, խենդեցնել)
before - nakhabes, arach (նախապէս, առաջ)
beforehand - arachouts, gankhav (առաջուց, կանխաւ)
beg - khunturel, aghachel (խնդրել, աղաչել)
beget - dzunanil, ardaturel (ծնանիլ, արտադրել)
beggar - mouratsgan (մուրացկան)
beggary - mouratsganoutiun (մուրացկանութիւն)
begild, begilt - vosgezodzel (ոսկեզօծել)
begin - usgusil (սկսիլ)
beginner - usgusnag, usgusogh (սկսնակ, սկսող)
beginning - usgizpu, usguzpunavoroutiun (սկիզբը, սկզբնաւորութիւն)
begone - gorsuve, kuna (կորսուէ, գնա)
begore - tsekhodel (ցեխոտել)
begrease - youghodel (իւղոտել)
begrime - aghdodel, murodel (աղտոտել, մրոտել)
beguile - nenkel, hurabourel (նենգ-

գել, Հրապուրել)
beguilement - badrank (պատրանք)
beguiler - khapogh (խաբող)
behalf - okoud, shah, nubasd (օգուտ, շահ, նպաստ)
behave - varvil (վարուիլ)
behavior - verapermounk (վերաբերմունք)
behead - kulkhadel (գլխատել)
beheading - kulkhadoum (գլխատում)
behest - huraman, oukhd (Հրաման, ուխտ)
behind - yedevu, mius goghmu (ետեւը, միւս կողմը)
behold - tidel, nushmarel (դիտել, նշմարել)
behoof - garik, bedk (կարիք, պէտք)
behoove - anhurazheshd ullal (անՀրաժեշտ ըլլալ)
beige - surjakiun-teghin (սրճագոյն-դեղին)
being - ullalov, eag (ըլլալով, էակ)
bejade - hoknetsunel (յոգնեցնել)
bejape - dzaghrel, khapel (ծաղրել, խաբել)
belabor - beghel, dzedzel (պեղել, ծեծել)
belate - oushatsunel (ուշացնել)
belated - oushatsadz (ուշացած)
belaud - kovapanel (գովաբանել)
belay - amratsunel, gabel (ամրացնել, կապել)
belch - uzkayrel, puskhel (զգայրել, փսխել)
belfry - zankagadoun (զանգակատուն)
belie - herkel, zurbardel (Հերքել, զրպարտել)
belief - havadk, hamozoum (Հաւատք, Համոզում)
bell - zankag (զանգակ)
bellow - parachel (բառաչել)
bellows - pukots (փքոց)
belly - por, vorovayn (փոր, որովայն)
belly-dancer - bordabarouhi (պորտապարուհի)
bell-tower - zankagadoun (զանգակատուն)
belong - badganil (պատկանիլ)
belonging - veraperial (վերաբերեալ)
belongings - inchk, ounetsvadzk (ինչք, ունեցուածք)
beloved - sireli (սիրելի)
below - dagu, var, nerkev (տակը, վար, ներքեւ)
belt - kodi, kodevorel, kodi gabel (գօտի, գօտեւորել, գօտի կապել)
belted - kodegabvadz, kodebuntuvadz (գօտեկապուած, գօտեպնդուած)
belvedere - vernadoun (վերնատուն)
bemask - timagadzadzgel (դիմակածածկել)
bemaster - youratsunel (իւրացնել)
bemoan - voghpal, hedzedzel (ողբալ, Հեծեծել)
bemuse - kinovtsunel (գինովցնել)
bench - nusdaran, adian (նստարան, ատեան)
bend - dzuril, hagil, sheghil, tartsuvadzk (ծռիլ, Հակիլ, շեղիլ, դարձուածք)
beneath - dagu, varu, usdorev (տակը, վարը, ստորեւ)
benediction - orhnoutiun (օրՀնութիւն)
benefaction - pareraroutiun (բարերարութիւն)
benefactor - parerar (բարերար)
benefactress - parerarouhi (բարերարուՀի)
benefic - nubasdavor (նպաստաւոր)
benefice - shunorh, shah, okoud (շնորՀ, շաՀ, օգուտ)
beneficence - parekordzoutiun (բարեգործութիւն)
beneficent - parerar (բարերար)
beneficial - shahaved, parerar (շաՀաւէտ, բարերար)
beneficiary - nubasdungal, parerarvogh (նպաստընկալ, բարերարուող)
benefit - shah, parik, okduvil (շաՀ, բարիք, օգտուիլ)
benevolence - paresiroutiun (բարեսիրութիւն)
benevolent - paresiragan (բարեսիրական)

benight - mutuntsunel (մթնցնել)
benign - pareser, azniv (բարեսէր, ազնիւ)
benignity - martasiroutiun (մարդասիրութիւն)
benignly - aznuvoren (ազնուօրէն)
benigrant - azniv, martaser (ազնիւ, մարդասէր)
benison - orhnoutiun (օրհնութիւն)
bent - dzuradz, hagoum (ծռած, հակում)
benzine - gunturid (կնդրիտ)
bequeath - gudagel, avantel (կտակել, աւանդել)
bequeather - gudagarar (կտակարար)
bequest - gudag, avant, gudagel (կտակ, աւանդ, կտակել)
berate - hantimanel (յանդիմանել)
beray - aghdodel (աղտոտել)
bereave - hapushdagel, zurgel (յափշտակել, զրկել)
beret - kulkharg, kutag (գլխարկ, գդակ)
bergh - pulour (բլուր)
berry - hadabudough, pulrag, budghanal (հատապտուղ, բլրակ, պտղանալ)
berth - navagayk (նաւակայք)
beryl - piuregh (բիւրեղ)
besaint - surpatsunel (սրբացնել)
bescreen - dzadzgel (ծածկել)
beseech - baghadil, aghachel (պաղատիլ, աղաչել)
beset - deghavorel, sharel (տեղաւորել, շարել)
besetment - basharoum (պաշարում)
beshrew - anidzel, nuzovel (անիծել, նզովել)
beside - kovu, goghmu, megti (քովը, կողմը, մէկդի)
besides - patsi, avelin (բացի, աւելին)
besiege - basharel (պաշարել)
beslave - kerel (գերել)
besmirch - aghdodel (աղտոտել)
besom - avel, avlel (աւել, աւլել)
bespeak - hantsnararel (յանձնարարել)
best - lavakouyn (լաւագոյն)
bestial - anasnagan (անասնական)
bestir - houzel, tsuntsel (յուզել, ցնցել)
bestorm - potorgel (փոթորկել)
bestow - amparel, muterel, dal, shunorhel (ամբարել, մթերել, տալ, շնորհել)
bestower - madagarar, pashkhogh (մատակարար, բաշխող)
bestowment - pashkhoum, endzayoum, muteroum (բաշխում, ընծայում, մթերում)
bestrew - surusgel, daradzel (սրսկել, տարածել)
bestseller - shad dzakhvogh, kerusbarogh (շատ ծախուող, գերսպառող)
bet - kurav, kurav tunel (գրաւ, գրաւ դնել)
betake - timel, yertal (դիմել, երթալ)
beteem - shunorhel, touyladurel, hamatsaynil (շնորհել, թոյլատրել, համաձայնիլ)
betide - badahil (պատահիլ)
betoken - nushanagel (նշանակել)
betray - madnel, tavajanel (մատնել, դաւաճանել)
betroth - nushanel (նշանել)
betrothal - nushandouk, khosgab (նշանտուք, խօսկապ)
betrothed - nushanats (նշանած)
betrothment - nushandouk, nushanakhosoutiun (նշանտուք, նշանախօսութիւն)
better - aveli lav (աւելի լաւ)
between - mechdegh, michev (մէջտեղ, միջեւ)
bevel - angiunachap (անկիւնաչափ)
beverage - khumichk (խմիչք)
bevy - havakouyt, khoump, yeram (հաւաքոյթ, խումբ, երամ)
bewail - voghpal, sukal (ողբալ, սգալ)
bewailer - voghpatsogh (ողբացող)
bewailing - voghp, godz (ողբ, կոծ)
beware - uzkoushanal, khousapil (զգուշանալ, խուսափիլ)
bewhore - pozatsunel (բոզացնել)
bewilder - moloretsunel, shupotetsunel (մոլորեցնել, շփոթեցնել)

bewildering - shupotoutiun (շփոթութիւն)
bewitch - tiutel, gakhartel (դիւթել, կախարդել)
bewitchery, ment - gakhartoutiun (կախարդութիւն)
beyond - antin, herou (անդին, Հեռու)
biannual - gisamia (կիսամեայ)
bias - sheghoum, khodoroum, sheghetsunel (շեղում, խոտորում, շեղեցնել)
bib - gurdzgal (կրծկալ)
bibber - gondzogh (կոնծող)
Bible - asdvadzashounch, sourp kirk (Աստուածաշունչ, Սուրբ Գիրք)
bibler - khumogh (խմող)
biblical - asdvadzashunchagan (աստուածաշնչական)
bibliograph, bibliographer - madenakir (մատենագիր)
bibliographic - madenakidagan (մատենագիտական)
bibliography - madenakidoutiun (մատենագիտութիւն)
bibliophile - kurkaser (գրքասէր)
bibliopolist - kuravajar-hin kirkerou (գրավաճառ՝ Հին գիրքերու)
bibliothec - kurkahavak, kuratarana-bed, madenataran (գրքաՀաւաք, գրադարանապետ, մատենադարան)
bibliotheke - madenataran (մատենադարան)
bicentennial - yerg-hariuramiag (երկՀարիւրամեակ)
biceps - tunter, yergdzayr, yergkuloukh (դնդեր, երկծայր, երկգլուխ)
bicker - vijil, gurvil (վիճիլ, կռուիլ)
bicycle - hedzaniv, yerganiv (Հեծանիւ, երկանիւ)
bid - kin arachargel, usel, huramayel (գին առաջարկել, ըսել, Հրամայել)
biddable - hunazant, hulou (Հնազանդ, Հլու)
bide - punagil, munal (բնակիլ, մնալ)
biennial - yergamia, yergou darvan (երկամեայ, երկու տարուան)
bier - takagh (դագաղ)
big - medz, khoshor (մեծ, խոշոր)
bigamy - yergamousnoutiun, gurgnamousnoutiun (երկամուսնութիւն, կրկնամուսնութիւն)
biggest - amenamedz (ամենամեծ)
bight - angiun, khorsh (անկիւն, խորշ)
bigot - molerant, geghdzavor (մոլեռանդ, կեղծաւոր)
bijou - kohar (գոՀար)
bijoutry - kohareghen (գոՀարեղէն)
bike - hedzig, petag (Հեծիկ, փեթակ)
bikini - yerggudor ganatsi dzova-uzkesd (երկկտոր կանացի ծովազգեստ)
bilateral - yerggoghmani (երկկողմանի)
bile - maghts, leghouts (մաղձ, լեղուց)
bilingual - yerglezou (երկլեզու)
bilinguist - yerglezvaked (երկլեզուագէտ)
bilious - maghtsod (մաղձոտ)
bilk - khapel, nenkel (խաբել, նենգել)
bill - hashvetsouyts, mourhag, dzanoutsakir, gudouts (Հաշուեցոյց, մուրՀակ, ծանուցագիր, կտուց)
billboard - tsoutsadakhdag (ցուցատախտակ)
billet - doms, yergdogh, huramanakir, payd, otevanel (տոմս, երկտող, Հրամանագիր, փայտ, օթեւանել)
billiards - kuntamough (գնդամուղ)
billing - hashvakuroum, kukvogh (Հաշուագրում, գգուող)
billion - yergilion (երկիլիոն)
billionaire - yergilionader (երկիլիոնատէր)
billow - gohag, alik (կոՀակ, ալիք)
bimonthly - yergamsia (երկամսեայ)
bin - ampar, sundoug, amparel (ամբար, սնտուկ, ամբարել)
binary - gurgnag, yergiag (կրկնակ, երկեակ)
bind - gabel, seghmel, gazmel, yerashkhavorel (կապել, սեղմել,

կազմել, երաշխաւորել)
binder - gazmarar, gazmogh (կազմարար, կազմող)
bindery - gazmadoun (կազմատուն)
binding - gazm, gab (կազմ, կապ)
bing - tez (դէզ)
bingo - pakhdakhagh mu, bingo (բախտախաղ մը, պինկօ)
binoculars - heratidag (Հեռադիտակ)
biochemistry - gensadarrapanoutiun (կենսատարրաբանութիւն)
biographer - gensakir (կենսագիր)
biography - gensakroutiun (կենսագրութիւն)
biologist - gensapan (կենսաբան)
biology - gensapanoutiun (կենսաբանութիւն)
biped - yergodani (երկոտանի)
bird - turchoun (Թռչուն)
birth - dzunount, dzakoum (ծնունդ, ծագում)
birth certificate - dzununtian vugayakir (ծննդեան վկայագիր)
birth control - khousapoum hughoutene (խուսափում յղութենէ)
birthday - daretarts, dzununtyan or (տարեդարձ, ծննդեան օր)
birthplace - dzununtavayr (ծննդավայր)
bis - gurgin (կրկին)
biscuit - gurgnep (կրկնեփ)
bisect - yerghadel (երկՀատել)
bisexual - yergser, vortsevek (երկսեռ, որձեւէգ)
bishop - yebisgobos (եպիսկոպոս)
bishopdom - yebisgobosoutiun (եպիսկոպոսութիւն)
bishopic - yebisgobosoutiun, arachnortoutiun (եպիսկոպոսութիւն, առաջնորդութիւն)
bissextile - nahanch dari (ՆաՀանջ տարի)
bit - gudor, mas (կտոր, մաս)
bitch - poz, kadz, ek shoun gam gadou (բոզ, քած, էգ շուն կամ կատու)
bite - khadznel, tsavtsunel, khapel (խածնել, ցաւցնել, խաբել)
biter - khadzan, tsavtsunogh (խածան, ցաւցնող)
biting - khadzan, gudzou (խածան, կծու)
bitter - leghi, gudzou, tarun (լեղի, կծու, դառն)
bitterness - tarnoutiun (դառնութիւն)
bitumen - asfalt, goubur (ասֆալԹ, կուպր)
biweekly - yergshapatia, yergshapatatert (երկշաբաԹեայ, երկշաբաԹաԹերԹ)
bizarre - ardarots, darorinag, dzidzagheli (արտառոց, տարօրինակ, ծիծաղելի)
blab - shaghagradel (շաղակրատել)
black - sev, mout, sevtsunel (սեւ, մուԹ, սեւցնել)
blackberry - mormeni (մորմենի)
blackboard - kuradakhdag (գրատախտակ)
blacken - sevtsunel, sevnal (սեւցնել, սեւնալ)
blackish - sevoug, sevoulig, sevorag (սեւուկ, սեւուլիկ, սեւորակ)
blacklist - sev tsang (սեւ ցանկ)
blackmail - purnadourk, usbanalikov goghoboud (բռնատուրք, սպառնալիքով կողոպուտ)
blackout - guragmar (կրակմար)
blacksmith - yergatakordz (երկաԹագործ)
bladder - mizabarg, ouretsunel (միզապարկ, ուռեցնել)
blade - sheghp, derev, sheghpel (շեղբ, տերեւ, շեղբել)
blamable - meghatreli (մեղադրելի)
blame - meghatrel, barsavel (մեղադրել, պարսաւել)
blanch - jermugtsunel, makrel, jermugil, jermag (ճերմկցնել, մաքրել, ճերմկիլ, ճերմակ)
bland - meghm, kaghtsur (մեղմ, քաղցր)
blandish - shoghokortel, kudznil (շողոքորթել, քծնիլ)
blank - jermag, barab (ճերմակ, պարապ)
blanket - dzadzgots, vermag (ծածկոց, վերմակ)
blare - aghaghagel, koral, kochel,

kochiun (աղաղակել, գոռալ, գոչել, գոչիւն)
blarney - shoghokortoutiun (շողոքորթութիւն)
blaspheme - hayhoyel, nakhadel (Հայհոյել, Նախատել)
blast - murrig, potorig, baytoum (մրրիկ, փոթորիկ, պայթում)
blasting - baytetsunoum, averoum (պայթեցնում, աւերում)
blastus - dzil (ծիլ)
blat - mayel (մայել)
blatant - aghmugarar (աղմկարար)
blatter - shadakhosel, dzaghrel (շատախօսել, ծաղրել)
blaze - pots, tsolk, louys, potsavaril (բոց, ցոլք, լոյս, բոցավառիլ)
blazing - potsavar (բոցավառ)
blazon - dohmanushan (տոհմանշան)
bleach - jermugtsunel, jermugnal, kounadil (ճերմկցնել, ճերմկնալ, գունատիլ)
bleacher - luvatsarar (լուացարար)
bleak - ankouyn, kounad, amayi, tsourd (անգոյն, գունատ, ամայի, ցուրտ)
blear - churod, jubrod achk (ջրոտ, ճպռոտ աչք)
bleat - mayel (մայել)
bleating - mayiun (մայիւն)
bleb - pushdig, bughbuchag (փշտիկ, պղպջակ)
bleed - ariunel, ariun arnel, goghobdel (արիւնել, արիւն առնել, կողոպտել)
bleeding - ariunahosoutiun (արիւնաՀոսութիւն)
blemish - avrel, khankarel (աւրել, խանգարել)
blench - kashvil, ungurgil (քաշուիլ, ընկրկիլ)
blend - kharnel, kharnourt (խառնել, խառնուրդ)
blenk - achk kuttel (աչք քթթել)
bless - orhnel, parapanel (օրՀնել, փառաբանել)
blessed - orhnial, yerchanig (օրՀնեալ, երջանիկ)
blesser - orhnogh (օրՀնող)
blessing - orhnoutiun (օրՀնութիւն)
blight - khamretsunel, housakhapel, vuhadoutiun (խամրեցնել, յուսախաբել, վՀատութիւն)
blind - gouyr, gourtsunel (կոյր, կուրցնել)
blindness - gouroutiun (կուրութիւն)
blink - achk kuttel, tartel, bulbulal, hayadzk, agnarg (աչք քթթել, թարթել, պլպլալ, Հայեացք, ակնարկ)
bliss - yeranoutiun (երանութիւն)
blissful - yeraneli (երանելի)
blissom - tsangal, durpal, durpamol (ցանկալ, տռփալ, տռփամոլ)
blister - pushdig, balar, ouril (բշտիկ, պալար, ուռիլ)
blithe - zuvart, ourakh (զուարթ, ուրախ)
blithesome - yerchanig (երջանիկ)
bloat - ouretsunel, ouril (ուռեցնել, ուռիլ)
bloc - khoump, zankuvadz (խումբ, զանգուած)
block - gojgh, poun (կոճղ, բուն)
blockade - basharoum, shurchapagoum, shurchapagel (պաշարում, շրջափակում, շրջափակել)
blockhead - putamid, aboush (բթամիտ, ապուշ)
blond - khardiash, teghtsan (խարտեաշ, դեղձան)
blood - ariun (արիւն)
blood pressure - arian kerjunshoum (արեան գերճնշում)
bloodless - anariun, duzhkouyn (անարիւն, տժգոյն)
bloodshed - ariunaheghoutiun (արիւնաՀեղութիւն)
bloodsucker - duzroug (տզրուկ)
bloody - ariunod (արիւնոտ)
bloom - gogon, dzaghgil (կոկոն, ծաղկիլ)
blooming - dzaghgaputit (ծաղկափթիթ)
bloomy - dzaghgalits (ծաղկալից)
blossom - dzaghig, dzaghgil (ծաղիկ, ծաղկիլ)
blot - pidz, pudzavorel, aradavorel, avrel (բիծ, բծաւորել, արատաւորել, աւրել)

blotch - arad, pushdig (արատ, բշտիկ)
blothing paper - dzudzoun tought (ծծուն թուղթ)
blouse - pajgon (բաճկոն)
blow - puchel, ouretsunel, dzaghgetsunel, harvadz (փչել, ուռեցնել, ծաղկեցնել, հարուած)
blow out - puchel, marel (փչել, մարել)
blow up - baytetsunel (պայթեցնել)
blub - ouril (ուռիլ)
blubber - bughbuchag (պղպջակ)
blue - gabouyd (կապոյտ)
bluff - zhayroud, hokhordank, hokhordal, khapel (ժայռուտ, յոխորտանք, յոխորտալ, խաբել)
bluish - gabdorag (կապտորակ)
blume - dzaghgil (ծաղկիլ)
blunder - sukhalil, saytakil (սխալիլ, սայթաքիլ)
blunge - shaghakhel (շաղախել)
blunging - shaghakhoum (շաղախում)
blunt - putatsunel, putamid (բթացնել, բթամիտ)
blur - aradavorel, arad (արատաւորել, արատ)
blurt - tsapurdel (ձաբռտել)
blush - garmuril, shignil, amuchnal (կարմրիլ, շիկնիլ, ամչնալ)
bluster - puchel, sharachel, aghmoug (փչել, շառաչել, աղմուկ)
boa - vishabots (վիշապօձ)
boar - varaz (վարազ)
board - dakhdag, khavakard, seghan, hantsunakhoump (տախտակ, խաւաքարտ, սեղան, յանձնախումբ)
boarder - kisherotig (գիշերօթիկ)
boast - bardzenal, bardzank (պարծենալ, պարծանք)
boaster - medzamid, havagnod (մեծամիտ, յաւակնոտ)
boat - navargel, navag (նաւարկել, նաւակ)
boatman - navavar (նաւավար)
bob - jojvil, jojanag (ճօճուիլ, ճօճանակ)
bode - koushagel, koushagoum (գուշակել, գուշակում)
bodice - seghmiran (սեղմիրան)
body - marmin, iran, ants (մարմին, իրան, անձ)
bodycare - marmunapouyzh (մարմնաբոյժ)
bodyguard - tignabah (թիկնապահ)
bog - jahij (ճահիճ)
boggle - sosgal, varanil (սոսկալ, վարանիլ)
boggy - jakhjakhoud (ճախճախուտ)
bogle, bogy - ourvagan, huresh (ուրուական, հրէշ)
boil - yeral, yepil, yeratsunel, yerk, ouretsk (եռալ, եփիլ, եռացնել, եռք, ուռեցք)
boisterous - potorgalits (թոփորկալից)
bold - hantoukun, desaneli, hamartsag, hamartsagil (յանդուգն, տեսանելի, համարձակ, համարձակիլ)
bolden - kachalerich (քաջալերիչ)
bolster - parts, ozhantagel (բարձ, օժանդակել)
bolt (n) - soghnag, nik, ned, sulak, shant, pakhousd panden (սողնակ, նիգ, նետ, սլաք, շանթ, փախուստ բանտէն)
bolt (v) - pakhchil, artsagel, nikel, gullel oudeliku, usel (փախչիլ, արձակել, նիգել, կլլել ուտելիքը, ըսել)
bomb - roump (ռումբ)
bombard - rumpagodzel (ռմբակոծել)
bombardier - rumpatsik - zinvor (ռմբաձիգ՝ զինուոր)
bombardment - rumpagodzoum (ռմբակոծում)
bomber - rumpatsik otanav (ռմբաձիգ օդանաւ)
bonbon - shakareghen (շաքարեղէն)
bond - gab, chuvan, mourhag, arzhetought (կապ, չուան, մուրհակ, արժեթուղթ)
bone - vosgor, gumakhk (ոսկոր, կմախք)
bone marrow - vosguradzoudz (ոսկրածուծ)
boneless - anosgur, noghnahar, anchikh, dugar (անոսկր, անողնահար, անջիղ, տկար)

bonfire - hurakhagh, kharougahantes (հրախաղ, խարուկահանդէս)
bonify - parvokel (բարւոքել)
bonnet - kudag, kulkharg (գտակ, գլխարկ)
bonus - tseratsir, kunahadanuver, shah (ձեռաձիր, գնահատանուէր, շահ)
book - kirk, madian, domar, hashvakurel (գիրք, մատեան, տոմար, հաշուագրել)
bookbinder - gazmarar (կազմարար)
bookbinding - gazmararoutiun (կազմարարութիւն)
bookbindry - gazmadoun (կազմատուն)
bookish - kurkounag, sopesd (գրքունակ, սոփեստ)
bookkeeper - domaragal (տոմարակալ)
bookkeeping - domaragaloutiun, hashvagaloutiun (տոմարակալութիւն, հաշուակալութիւն)
booklet - kurkouyg (գրքոյկ)
bookmate - tasunger (դասընկեր)
bookmonger - kuravajar (գրավաճառ)
bookseller - kuravajar (գրավաճառ)
bookshop, bookstore - kuradoun, kurakhanout, kuravajaradoun (գրատուն, գրախանութ, գրավաճառատուն)
boom - tuntiun, arzhetsunel, partsunel (թնդիւն, արժեցնել, բարձրացնել)
boon - parereroutiun, aghotk, shunorhk (բարերարութիւն, աղօթք, շնորհք)
boor - mimos, kiughatsi (միմոս, գիւղացի)
boorish - goshd, keghchgagan (կոշտ, գեղջկական)
boost - harach kushel, mughoum (յառաջ քշել, մղում)
boot - goshig, ghoshig haknil, shah, tarman, dzarayel (կօշիկ, կօշիկ հագնիլ, շահ, դարման, ծառայել)
booth - gurbag, hiughag (կրպակ, հիւղակ)
booty - avar, goghoboud (աւար, կողոպուտ)
booze - kinovnal, kinarpoum (գինովնալ, գինարբում)
boozer - kinovtsogh, arpetsogh (գինովցող, արբեցող)
bordel - pozanots, hanradoun (բոզանոց, հանրատուն)
border - sahman, yezerk (սահման, եզերք)
bordering - sahmanagits (սահմանակից)
bore - dzagel, panal, neghel, tsantsuratsunel (ծակել, բանալ, նեղել, ձանձրացնել)
borer - dzagogh, neghogh (ծակող, նեղող)
boring - dzagoum, dzag (ծակում, ծակ)
born - dzunadz (ծնած)
borough - avan, medz kiugh (աւան, մեծ գիւղ)
borrow - pokh arnel (փոխ առնել)
borrower - pokharou, pokh arnogh (փոխառու, փոխ առնող)
borrowing - pokharoutiun (փոխառութիւն)
bosom - gourdzk, kirg (կուրծք, գիրկ)
boss - veragatsou, varbed (վերակացու, վարպետ)
botanist - pousapan (բուսաբան)
botany - pousapanoutiun (բուսաբանութիւն)
botch - gargudan, gargudel (կարկտան, կարկտել)
botcher - gargudnogh (կարկտնող)
both - yergouku, yergoukun al (երկուքը, երկուքն ալ)
bother - tsantsuratsunel, neghel (ձանձրացնել, նեղել)
bothersome - tsantsuratsoutsich (ձանձրացուցիչ)
boton - gojag, hankouyts (կոճակ, հանգոյց)
bottle - shish, survag, dzudzag (շիշ, սրուակ, ծծակ)
bottom - hadag, himnuvil (յատակ, հիմնուիլ)
bottom line - himnagan gedu, eaganu (հիմնական կէտը, էականը)

bottomless - anhadag (անհատակ)
bough - jiugh, vosd (ճիւղ, ոստ)
boulevard - boghoda, dzaroughi (պողոտայ, ծառուղի)
bounce - tsaydetsunel, tsadgel, harvadz (ցայտեցնել, ցատկել, հարուած)
bounced - merzhuvadz (մերժուած)
bound - sahman, vosdoum (սահման, ոստում)
boundary - sahman (սահման)
boundless - ansahman (անսահման)
bounteous - aradatserun (առատաձեռն)
bounty - aradatsernoutiun (առատաձեռնութիւն)
bouquet - dzaghgepounch (ծաղկեփունջ)
bourg - avan, kiughakaghak (աւան, գիւղաքաղաք)
bourgeois - kaghkeni, kaghakatsi, sepaganader (քաղքենի, քաղաքացի, սեփականատէր)
bourgeoisie - kaghkenioutiun, sepaganadiroutiun (քաղքենիութիւն, սեփականատիրութիւն)
bout - harvadz, murtsoum, ports, ankam (հարուած, մրցում, փորձ, անգամ)
bow (n) - aghegh, jubod, oghagab, hagoum, khonarhoum (աղեղ, ճպոտ, օղակապ, հակում, խոնարհում)
bow (v) - dzurel, hagil, khonarhil, dzuril, parevel (ծռել, հակիլ, խոնարհիլ, ծռիլ, բարեւել)
bowel - aghik, kout, zavag, porodik makrel (աղիք, գութ, զաւակ, փորոտիք մաքրել)
bowels - porodik (փորոտիք)
bower - zartaseniag, hagogh (զարդասենեակ, հակող)
bowl - pazhag, aman (բաժակ, աման)
bowling - kuntagakhagh (գնդակախաղ)
bowssen - tatkhel, mukhurchel (թաթխել, մխրճել)
box - doup, sundoug, puruntskamard, gurpamardil (տուփ, սնտուկ, բռնցքամարտ, կռփամարտիլ)
boxer - gurpamardig (կռփամարտիկ)
boxing - grpamard (կռփամարտ)
boy - manch, dugha (մանչ, տղայ)
boy friend - ayrunger, dugha unger, nakhasiradz unger (այրընկեր, տղայ ընկեր, նախասիրած ընկեր)
boycott - arkiloum, arkilel (արգիլում, արգիլել)
boyhood - mangoutiun, dughayoutiun (մանկութիւն, տղայութիւն)
brace - gab, kodi, netsoug, amratsunel, burgel (կապ, գօտի, նեցուկ, ամրացնել, պրկել)
bracelet - abaranchan (ապարանջան)
brack - dzag, jeghk (ծակ, ճեղք)
bracket - pagakidz, dzorag (փակագիծ, ծորակ)
brad - ankuloukh kam (անգլուխ գամ)
brag - bardzenal, hokhordal (պարծենալ, յոխորտալ)
braggart, bragger - bardzengod, sunabardz (պարծենկոտ, սնապարծ)
bragger - hubardatsogh, hokhordatsogh (հպարտացող, յոխորտացող)
braid - yeriz, hiusk, hiusel (երիզ, հիւսք, հիւսել)
braille - gouyrerou aypoupen (կոյրերու այբուբեն)
brain - oughegh, midk (ուղեղ, միտք)
brainstorm - khelakaroutiun (խելագարութիւն)
brainwash - muda junshoum (մտաճնշում)
brake - arkelag, bourag, arkelagel (արգելակ, պուրակ, արգելակել)
bramble - momeni (մորենի)
bran - tep tsoreni (թեփ ցորենի)
brancard - badkarag (պատգարակ)
branch - jiugh, masnajiugh, sharavigh, jiughavoril (ճիւղ, մասնաճիւղ, շառաւիղ, ճիւղաւորիլ)
brand - ayrogh payd, vajaranish, turoshm, turoshmel (այրող փայտ, վաճառանիշ, դրոշմ, դրոշմել)
brandish - jojel, shoghatsunel, jojoum (ճօճել, շողացնել, ճօճում)

brandnew - norakouyn, amenanor, polorovin nor (նորագոյն, ամենանոր, բոլորովին նոր)
brandy - oghi (օղի)
brangle - vej, guriv, gurvil (վէճ, կռիւ, կռուիլ)
brangler - gurvazan (կռուազան)
brasier, brazier - bughuntsakordz, guragaman (պղնձագործ, կրակաման)
brass - arouyr, kharun bughints (արոյր, խառն պղինձ)
brattle - tuntal, tuntiun, zhukhor (թնդալ, թնդիւն, ժխոր)
bravado - hokhordank (յոխորտանք)
brave - kach (քաջ)
bravo - getstses, avazag, helouzag (կեցցես, աւազակ, յելուզակ)
brawl - boral, vijil, gurvil (պոռալ, վիճիլ, կռուիլ)
brawler - gurvaser (կռուասէր)
brawn - tunter, tunteri ouzh (դնդեր, դնդերի ուժ)
brawny - muganoud, marmunegh, zoravor (մկանուտ, մարմնեղ, զօրաւոր)
bray - zural, zurots (զրալ, զրոց)
brayer - zuratsogh (զրացող)
braze - zotel, buntatsunel (զօդել, պնդացնել)
Brazil - burazilia (Պրազիլիա)
breach - khuzoum, pegoum (խզում, բեկում)
bread - hats (Հաց)
breadth - laynk, daradzoutiun (լայնք, տարածութիւն)
break - godrel, khordagel, getsunel, avrel, chunchel (կոտրել, խորտակել, կեցնել, աւրել, ջնջել)
break up - pokratsunel, tsurvel, tsurvil, loudzel (փոքրացնել, ցրուել, ցրուիլ, լուծել)
breakdown - angoum, tsakhoghoutiun, housalukoum (անկում, ձախողութիւն, յուսալքում)
breaker - godrogh, turzhogh (կոտրող, դրժող)
breakfast - nakhajash (նախաճաշ)
breast - gourdzk, dzidz, dzots (կուրծք, ծիծ, ծոց)
breath - shounch (շունչ)
breathe - shunchel, abril (շնչել, ապրիլ)
breather - shunchogh, hevatsogh (շնչող, Հեւացող)
breathful - pouroumnalits (բուրումնալից)
breathless - shunchasbar (շնչասպառ)
breavement - hapushdagoum (յափշտակում)
breeches - dapad, vardik (տաբատ, վարտիք)
breed - hughanal, dzunanil, ardaturel (յղանալ, ծնանիլ, արտադրել)
breeder - ardaturogh, dzunogh (արտադրող, ծնող)
breeding - ardaturoutiun (արտադրութիւն)
breeze - zepiur, vej, mokhir, puchel (զեփիւռ, վէճ, մոխիր, փչել)
breezy - hovasoun (Հովասուն)
brethren - hokevor yeghpayrner (Հոգեւոր եղբայրներ)
brevet - ardonakir (արտօնագիր)
breviary - hamarodoutiun, zhamakirk (Համառօտութիւն, ժամագիրք)
breviate - ampopel, hamarodel, ampopoum (ամփոփել, Համառօտել, ամփոփում)
brevity - garjoutiun (կարճութիւն)
brew - gasgel, niutel, yepel, gasgachour (կասկել, նիւթել, եփել, կասկաջուր)
bribe - gashark, gasharel (կաշառք, կաշառել)
brick - gughminder, aghius (կղմինտր, աղիւս)
bricklayer - vormunatir (որմնադիր)
bridal - harsanegan, harsnik (Հարսանեկան, Հարսնիք)
bride - hars, harsnatsou (Հարս, Հարսնացու)
bridegroom - pesa, pesatsou (փեսայ, փեսացու)
bridesmaid - harsnakouyr (Հարսնաքոյր)
bridge - gamourch (կամուրջ)
bridle - sants, santsel, zusbel

(սանձ, սանձել, զսպել)
brief - garj, seghm, hamarodel (կարճ, սեղմ, Համառօտել)
briefcase - gashebanag (կաշեպանակ)
brier - mormeni (մորմենի)
brigade - vashd, koumardag (վաշտ, գումարտակ)
brigadier - kuntabed, (գնդապետ)
brigand - avazag (աւազակ)
bright - payloun, baydzar (փայլուն, պայծառ)
brighten - payletsunel, paylil (փայլեցնել, փայլիլ)
brightness - paylounoutiun (փայլունութիւն)
brillant - payloun, atamant (փայլուն, ադամանդ)
brilliance - baydzaroutiun (պայծառութիւն)
brilliantine - anoushahod yiugh, suntous (անուշահոտ իւղ, սնդուս)
brim - yezerk, dzayr, yeriz (եզերք, ծայր, երիզ)
brimstone - dzudzoump (ծծումբ)
brindle - pudzavoroutiun, khaydapughed (բծաւորութիւն, խայտաբղէտ)
brindled - pudzavor (բծաւոր)
brine - aghchour, artsounk (աղջուր, արցունք)
bring - perel (բերել)
brink - yezur, dzayr (եզր, ծայր)
brisk - ashkhouyzh, gaydar, varvuroun, vokevorel (աշխոյժ, կայտառ, վառվռուն, ոգեւորել)
bristle - usdev, maz, tsutsvil (ստեւ, մազ, ցցուիլ)
Britania - medzun puridania (Մեծն Բրիտանիա)
british - puridanagan, puridanatsi, ankliatsi (բրիտանական, բրիտանացի, անգլիացի)
brittle - tiurapeg (դիւրաբեկ)
broach - shampour, jagh, gopel, shampurel (շամփուր, ճաղ, կոփել, շամփրել)
broad - layn, untartsag (լայն, ընդարձակ)
broadcast - tsaynasuprel, tsaynasuproum, haghortashar (ձայնասփռել, ձայնասփռում, Հաղորդաշար)
broadcaster - tsaynasuprogh (ձայնասփռող)
broadcasting - tsaynasuproum (ձայնասփռում)
brob - sulak (սլաք)
broccoli - untagaghamp (ընդակաղամբ)
brochure - kurkouyg (գրքոյկ)
broid - hiusel (Հիւսել)
broider - aseghnakordzel (ասեղնագործել)
broiderer - aseghnakordz (ասեղնագործ)
broidery - aseghnakordzoutiun (ասեղնագործութիւն)
broil - khorovel, khorovil, aghmoug (խորովել, խորովիլ, աղմուկ)
broiler - khorovogh, aghmugarar (խորովող, աղմկարար)
broke - michnortel (միջնորդել)
broken - godradz, ungjuvadz (կոտրած, ընկճուած)
broker - michnort (միջնորդ)
brokerage - michnortoutiun, michnortchek (միջնորդութիւն, միջնորդչէք)
bronchitis - tsuntsghadab (ցնցղատապ)
bronze - bughints, anakabughints (պղինձ, անագապղինձ)
brooch - zartasegh (զարդասեղ)
brood - toukhs, tukhsel (Թուխս, Թխսել)
brook - kedag, vudag, hantourzhel (գետակ, վտակ, Հանդուրժել)
broom - avel, tsakh (աւել, ցախ)
brose - varsagov abour (վարսակով ապուր)
broth - arkanag, musachouri abour (արգանակ, մսաջուրի ապուր)
brothel - pozanots, (բոզանոց)
brothelry - tsopoutiun, pozanots (ցոփութիւն, բոզանոց)
brother - yeghpayr (եղբայր)
brother in law - kerayr, dakur (քերայր, տագր)
brotherhood - yeghpayroutiun (եղբայրութիւն)

brotherly - yeghpayrapar, yeghpayragan (եղբայրաբար, եղբայրական)
brow - honk, jagad (յօնք, ճակատ)
browless - aneres (աներես)
brown - toukh (թուխ)
brownie - voki, gurdser usgaoudouhi (ոգի, կրտսեր սկաուտուհի)
browse - aradzil, jaragel, achke antsunel, dzil (արածիլ, ճարակել, աչքէ անցընել, ծիլ)
browsing - jaragoum, matsark, hayetsoum (ճարակում, մացառք, հայեցում)
bruise - juzmel, pushrel (ճզմել, փշրել)
bruit - daratsaynoutiun, zhukhor, hampav (տարածայնութիւն, ժխոր, համբաւ)
brume - mushoush, shoki (մշուշ, շոգի)
brunt - harvadz, tap, zoroutiun (հարուած, թափ, զօրութիւն)
brush - khozanag, vurtsin, khozanagel (խոզանակ, վրձին, խոզանակել)
brusk, brusque - hangardzagan (յանկարծական)
brutal - kazanayin, vayrak (գազանային, վայրագ)
brutalism - vayrakoutiun (վայրագութիւն)
brute - kazan, anasoun, gadaghi (գազան, անասուն, կատաղի)
brutify - anpanatsunel, kazanatsunel (անբանացնել, գազանացնել)
bubble - bughbuchag, badrank, bughbuchal (պղպջակ, պատրանք, պղպջալ)
buccaneer - helouzag (յելուզակ)
buck - mokhrachour, aydziam, luvadzk, mokhrachurel (մոխրաջուր, այծեամ, լուացք, մոխրաջրել)
bucket - touyl, dashd (դոյլ, տաշտ)
buckle - jarmant, oghagel (ճարմանդ, օղակել)
buckler - vahan (վահան)
bucolic - kiughagan (գիւղական)
bud - dzil, gogon, poghpoch, dzaghgil (ծիլ, կոկոն, բողբոջ, ծաղկիլ)
Buddhism - bouddayaganoutiun (Պուտտայականութիւն)
buddhism - bouddayaganoutiun (պուտտայականութիւն)
buddhist - bouddayagan (պուտտայական)
budding - poghpochoum, badvasdoum (բողբոջում, պատուաստում)
budge - sharzhil, khulurdil (շարժիլ, խլրտիլ)
budget - hashvetsouyts, yelevmudatsouyts, yelevmoud (հաշուեցոյց, ելեւմտացոյց, ելեւմուտ)
buffalo - komesh (գոմէշ)
buffer - arkelag (արգելակ)
buffet - usbasagal, jasharan vodki oudelou, abdagel (սպասակալ, ճաշարան ոտքի ուտելու, ապտակել)
buffoon - mimos, kheghgadag, mimosel, kheghgadagel (միմոս, խեղկատակ, միմոսել, խեղկատակել)
bug - muloug, michad (մլուկ, միջատ)
buggy - vochlod (ոջլոտ)
bugle - tsoul, ouloung, shepor (ցուլ, ուլունք, շեփոր)
build - shinel, garoutsel (շինել, կառուցել)
builder - shinarar (շինարար)
building - shenk (շէնք)
built - tsev, gerduvadzk, gerduvadz (ձեւ, կերտուածք, կերտուած)
bulbul - pulpoul, sokhag (բլբուլ, սոխակ)
Bulgaria - boulgaria (Պուլկարիա)
bulge - por, hadag, ouril (փոր, յատակ, ուռիլ)
bulk - dzaval, zankuvadz, medzamasnoutiun (ծաւալ, զանգուած, մեծամասնութիւն)
bulk mail - medzakanag tantagh tughtadaroutiun (մեծաքանակ դանդաղ թղթատարութիւն)
bull - tsoul (ցուլ)
bulldog - kampur, tsulashoun (գամփռ, ցլաշուն)
bulldoz - vakhtsunel, mudragel (վախցնել, մտրակել)
bulldozer - hoghaparts, hoghu her-

gogh mekena (Հողաբարձ, Հողը Հերկող մեքենայ)
bullet - pampoushd, kuntag, roump (փամփուշտ, գնդակ, ռումբ)
bulletin - deghegakir, zegouyts (տեղեկագիր, զեկոյց)
bullfeast - tsulamard (ցլամարտ)
bullirag - khurchetsunel, vakhtsunel (խրտչեցնել, վախցնել)
bullition - yeratsoum (եռացում)
bullock - hort, yez (Հորթ, եզ)
bully - ampardavan, hokhordatsogh, usbarnal, hokhordal (ամբարտաւան, յոխորտացող, սպառնալ, յոխորտալ)
bultel - magh (մաղ)
bulwark - amroutiun, badnesh, badvar, bashdbanel (ամրութիւն, պատնէշ, պատուար, պաշտպանել)
bum - hedouyk, murmounch, murmunchel (յետոյք, մրմունջ, մրմնջել)
bummer - bunagalez, dzouyl mart (պնակալէզ, ծոյլ մարդ)
bump - zarnel, harvadz (զարնել, Հարուած)
bumper - taparkel, vutaragankhich, letsoun pazhan (Թափարգել, վԹարականխիչ, լեցուն բաժակ)
bumptious - inknahavan (ինքնաՀաւան)
bunch - voghgouyz, pounch, durtsag, khourts (ողկոյզ, փունջ, տրցակ, խուրձ)
bundle - durtsag, khourts, dzurarel (տրցակ, խուրձ, ծրարել)
bungalow - huntgagan miaharg doun (Հնդկական միայարկ տուն)
bungle - gargudnel, avrel, anjarag kordz (կարկտնել, աւրել, անճարակ գործ)
bungler - anjarag, taptupadz (անճարակ, ԹափԹփած)
bunn - pulit (բլիԹ)
buoy - kharuskhanushan, dzadzanel, dzupatsunel (խարսխանշան, ծածանել, ծփացնել)
burden - per, dzanroutiun, imasd, pernavorel (բեռ, ծանրուԹիւն, իմաստ, բեռնաւորել)
bureau - kuraseniag, kuraseghan (գրասենեակ, գրասեղան)
bureaucracy - tivanagaloutiun, bashdonagaloutiun (դիւանակալուԹիւն, պաշտօնակալուԹիւն)
burg - avan, kiughakaghak (աւան, գիւղաքաղաք)
burgeois - kaghkeni (քաղքենի)
burgeon - puttil (փԹԹիլ)
burglar - kogh, avazag (գող, աւազակ)
burglary - koghoutiun, avazagoutiun (գողուԹիւն, աւազակուԹիւն)
burial - taghoum (Թաղում)
burier - merelatagh (մեռելաԹաղ)
burlap - gudav (կտաւ)
burlesque - dzaghragan, kheghgadag, heknel (ծաղրական, խեղկատակ, Հեգնել)
burly - ker, marmunegh (գեր, մարմնեղ)
burn - ayrel, gizel, hurtehel (այրել, կիզել, ՀրդեՀել)
burner - ayrogh, gizogh (այրող, կիզող)
burning - ayroum, gizoum (այրում, կիզում)
burnish - payletsunel, hughgel (փայլեցնել, յղկել)
burrito - khozatsoug (խոզաձուկ)
bursar - kantsabah (գանձապաՀ)
burst - baytil, jatil, badril (պայԹիլ, ճաԹիլ, պատռիլ)
bury - taghel, dzadzgel (Թաղել, ծածկել)
bus - hanragark (Հանրակառք)
bush - matsar, tavoud (մացառ, Թաւուտ)
bushy - matsaroud (մացառուտ)
business - kordz, uzpaghoum, arevdour (գործ, զբաղում, առեւտուր)
business card - aytsekard, arevdurakard (այցեքարտ, առեւտրաքարտ)
businessman - arevduragan, vajaragan, kordzarar (առեւտրական, վաճառական, գործարար)
buss - hampouyr, hampourel (Համբոյր, Համբուրել)
bust - gisantri (կիսանդրի)
bustle - aghmoug, yerant, aghmugel

(աղմուկ, եռանդ, աղմկել)
busy - uzpaghadz, pazmaspagh, kordzounia (զբաղած, բազմազբաղ, գործունեայ)
but - payts, patsi, miayn (բայց, բացի, միայն)
butcher - musakordz, tahij, mortel, usbannel (մսագործ, դահիճ, մորթել, սպաննել)
butler - madagarar, maranabed (մատակարար, մառանապետ)
butt - vakhjan, nushanaged (վախճան, նշանակէտ)
butter - garak (կարագ)
butterfly - titernig (թիթեռնիկ)
buttery - maran, ushdemaran (մառան, շտեմարան)
butthinge - dzughni (ծխնի)
buttock - hedouyk, nusdadeghi (յետոյք, նստատեղի)
button - gojag, gogon, gojguvil (կոճակ, կոկոն, կոճկուիլ)
buttress - henaran (յենարան)
buxon - gaydar, gensalits (կայտառ, կենսալից)
buy - kunel (գնել)
buyer - kunogh, hajakhort (գնող, յաճախորդ)
buzz - puzzal, puzziun (բզզալ, բզզիւն)
by - modu, kovu, mod, megti, vura (մօտը, քովը, մօտ, մէկդի, վրայ)
bye - angarevor, yergurortagan khuntir (անկարեւոր, երկրորդական խնդիր)
bygone - antsial (անցեալ)
byland - teragughzi (թերակղզի)
bylaw, byelaw - masnavor orenk, nerkin ganonakir (մասնաւոր օրէնք, ներքին կանոնագիր)
bypass - goghmnagi antsk, goghmunagi antsnil (կողմնակի անցք, կողմնակի անցնիլ)
bypass operation - surdi yeragneri virahadoutiun (սրտի երակների վիրահատութիւն)
bystander - hantisades, nerga (հանդիսատես, ներկայ)
byword - aradz, asatsvadzk (առած, ասացուածք)
byzantian, tine - puizantagan, puizantatsi (բիւզանդական, բիւզանդացի)

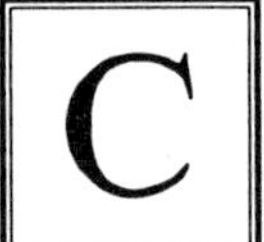

cab - vartsou inknasharzh, gark (վարձու ինքնաշարժ, կառք)
cabaret - gabela (կապելայ)
cabas - sagar (սակառ)
cabbage - gaghamp (կաղամբ)
cabin - dunag, hiugh, khurjit (տնակ, հիւղ, խրճիթ)
cabinet - tahlij, kuraseniag, peghgataran, baharan (դահլիճ, գրասենեակ, փեղկադարան, պահարան)
cable - herakir, herakralar, yelegduratel (հեռագիր, հեռագրալար, ելեկտրաթել)
cable TV - yelegduratelov heradesil (ելեկտրաթելով հեռատեսիլ)
cablecasting - yelegduratelov haghortoum (ելեկտրաթելով հաղորդում)
cablegram - herakir, baranakir (հեռագիր, պարանագիր)
cabman - garaban (կառապան)
cacao - durmeni (տրմենի)
cache - takusdots, dzadzgaran (թաքստոց, ծածկարան)
cachet - gunik, turoshm (կնիք, դրոշմ)
cackle - garachel, kekevel, shaghagradel, borchudouk (կառաչել, քեքեւել, շաղակրատել, պոռչտուք)
cacophony - annertashnagoutiun, kharnatsaynoutiun (աններդաշնակութիւն, խառնաձայնութիւն)

cactus - pushadzar (փշածառ)
cad - usdahag, tadargabord (ստահակ, դատարկապորտ)
cadastre - galvadzakir, galvadzadomar (կալուածագիր, կալուածատոմար)
cadaver - tiag (դիակ)
cadaverous - mereladib (մեռելատիպ)
cadence - gushrouyt, amanag, verchanuvak, tashnavorel (կշռոյթ, ամանակ, վերջանուագ, դաշնաւորել)
cadet - gurdser, pokur (կրտսեր, փոքր)
cafe - sourj, surjaran (սուրճ, սրճարան)
cafeteria - surjaran (սրճարան)
caffeine - punasourj (բնասուրճ)
cage - vantag, vantagel (վանդակ, վանդակել)
Cairo - kahire (Գահիրէ)
cajole - paghakushel, shoghomel (փաղաքշել, շողոմել)
cajoler - kudznogh (քծնող)
cajolery - paghakushank, kudznank (փաղաքշանք, քծնանք)
cake - gargantag, pulit (կարկանդակ, բլիթ)
calamity - aghed, portsank (աղէտ, փորձանք)
calcify - guratsunel, guranal (կրացնել, կրանալ)
calcination - guratsoum (կրացում)
calcite - gurakar (կրաքար)
calcium - guradzin, punagir (կրածին, բնակիր)
calculate - hashvel, hamrel, mudadzel (հաշուել, համրել, մտածել)
calculation - hashvoum, hashiv (հաշուում, հաշիւ)
calculator - hashvich, hashvogh mekena (հաշուիչ, հաշուող մեքենայ)
calcule - hashvel, hashiv (հաշուել, հաշիւ)
caldron - gatsa (կաթսայ)
calefy - cheroutsanel, daknal (ջեռուցանել, տաքնալ)
calembour - parakhagh (բառախաղ)
calendar - oratsouyts, domar (օրացոյց, տոմար)
calf - hort, aboush (հորթ, ապուշ)
caliber - duramakidz, garoghoutiun (տրամագիծ, կարողութիւն)
calico - dubadzo (տպածոյ)
call - ganchel, anvanel, heratsaynel (կանչել, անուանել, հեռաձայնել)
calligrapher, caligraphist - keghakurogh, keghakir (գեղագրող, գեղագիր)
calligraphy - keghakuroutiun (գեղագրութիւն)
calling - goch, uzpaghoum, arhesd, huraver (կոչ, զբաղում, արհեստ, հրաւէր)
calm - hantard, khaghagh, hantardetsunel (հանդարտ, խաղաղ, հանդարտեցնել)
calmer - khaghagharar, hantardetsunogh (խաղաղարար, հանդարտեցնող)
calorie - chermouyzh (ջերմոյժ)
calorie, calory - chermouyzh, chermasdijan (ջերմոյժ, ջերմաստիճան)
calumniate - zurbardel (զրպարտել)
calumniator - zurbardogh (զրպարտող)
calumny - zurbardoutiun (զրպարտութիւն)
calvary - koghkota, darabanki jampa (գողգոթա, տառապանքի ճամբայ)
calvities - jaghadoutiun, arants mazi (ճաղատութիւն, առանց մազի)
camaraderie - paregamoutiun (բարեկամութիւն)
camber - gor, goratsev, goril, goratsevel (կոր, կորաձեւ, կորիլ, կորաձեւել)
cambist - loumayapokh, seghanavor (լումայափոխ, սեղանաւոր)
camel - oughd (ուղտ)
camera - lousanugari mekena (լուսանկարի մեքենայ)
camouflage - dzubdoum (ծպտում)
camp - vuranatashd, panagadegh, panagetsnel (վրանադաշտ, բանակատեղ, բանակեցնել)
campaign - ard, tashd, arshavank,

panagoum, undurabaykar (արտ, դաշտ, արշաւանք, բանակում, ընտրապայքար)
campus - tubrotsatashd, tubrotsapag (դպրոցադաշտ, դպրոցաբակ)
can - garenal, titeghadoup (կարենալ, թիթեղատուփ)
Canada - kanada (Գանատա)
canadian - kanadatsi, kanaderen, kanadagan (գանատացի, գանատերէն, գանատական)
canal - churantsk, tsuntsough (ջրանցք, ցնցուղ)
canalize - churantsk panal, oughghoutiun dal (ջրանցք բանալ, ուղղութիւն տալ)
canard - pat (բադ)
canary - teghtsanig (դեղձանիկ)
cancan - fransagan bar mu (ֆրանսական պար մը)
cancel - chunchel, avrel (ջնջել, աւրել)
cancellation - chunchoum (ջնջում)
cancer - kaghtsgegh, khulirt (քաղցկեղ, խլիրդ)
candescent - lousavar (լուսավառ)
candid - angeghdz, anpidz, barz, miamid (անկեղծ, անբիծ, պարզ, միամիտ)
candidacy - tegnadzoutiun (թեկնածութիւն)
candidate - tegnadzou, undureli (թեկնածու, ընտրելի)
candidature - tegnadzoutiun (թեկնածութիւն)
candle - mom, jurak (մոմ, ճրագ)
candle holder - comagal (մոմակալ)
candle stick - varelamom (վառելամոմ)
candour, candor - barzoutiun, anacharoutiun (պարզութիւն, անաչառութիւն)
candy - kaghtsureghen, shakarov yepel (քաղցրեղէն, շաքարով եփել)
cane - yeghek, shakareghek (եղէգ, շաքարեղէգ)
canine - shunagan, shunadam (շնական, շնատամ)
canister - doup, goghov, teyadoup (տուփ, կողով, թէյատուփ)
canker - pudoutiun, pudil, mashil (փտութիւն, փտիլ, մաշիլ)
cannibal - martager (մարդակեր)
cannon - tuntanot (թնդանօթ)
cannonade - rumpagodzel, rumpagodzoum (ռմբակոծել, ռմբակոծում)
cannoning - tuntanotatsukoutiun (թնդանօթաձգութիւն)
cannot, can't - chugarenal (չկարենալ)
canoe - navag, uzposanav, navavarel (նաւակ, զբօսանաւ, նաւավարել)
canon - ganon, ganonakirk (կանոն, կանոնագիրք)
canonical - ganonagan (կանոնական)
canonics - ganonakidoutiun (կանոնագիտութիւն)
canonist - ganonaked (կանոնագէտ)
canonization - surpatsoum (սրբացում)
canonize - surpatsunel (սրբացնել)
canopy - ambhovani, vuran, dzadzk, hovanavorel, dzadzgel (ամպհովանի, վրան, ծածք, հովանաւորել, ծածկել)
cant (I) - khorsh, anguin, mughoum, hagoum (խորշ, անկիւն, մղում, հակում)
cant (II) - geghdzavoroutiun, parpar, geghdzapanel (կեղծաւորութիւն, բարբառ, կեղծաբանել)
cant (III) - ajourt, ajourtov dzaghel (աճուրդ, աճուրդով ծախել)
cantata - dagh, nuvak, yerki vodanavor, yerkotsoghoutiun (տաղ, նուագ, երգի ոտանաւոր, երգեցողութիւն)
canteen - jasharan, panagi khumichki khanout, churaman (ճաշարան, բանակի խմիչքի խանութ, ջրաման)
canterbury - kuragal, tertagal (գրակալ, թերթակալ)
canticle - saghmoserkoutiun (սաղմոսերգութիւն)
canto - dagh, yerk (տաղ, երգ)
canton - kavar (գաւառ)
canvas - ganepagudav (կանեփակտաւ)
canvass - houzel, kunnel, vijil

(յուզել, քննել, վիճիլ)
cany - *yegheknoud* (եղէգնուտ)
canyon - *tsor* (ձոր)
canzone - *yerk, yeghanag* (երգ, եղանակ)
canzonet - *manrerk, pokur yerk* (մանրերգ, փոքր երգ)
caoutchouc - *tsukakhezh* (ձգախէժ)
cap - *kutag, kulkharg, kuloukhu dzadzgel, busagel* (գդակ, գլխարկ, գլուխը ծածկել, պսակել)
capable - *garogh, untounag* (կարող, ընդունակ)
capacious - *layn, untartsag* (լայն, ընդարձակ)
capacity - *barounagoutiun, garoghoutiun, daroghoutiun* (պարունակութիւն, կարողութիւն, տարողութիւն)
cape - *kuloukh, hurvantan, otsik* (գլուխ, հրուանդան, օձիք)
caper - *vosdosdel, tsadgurdel, barel* (ոստոստել, ցատկռտել, պարել)
capital - *turamakuloukh, mayrakaghak, kulkhakir, khoyag* (դրամագլուխ, մայրաքաղաք, գլխագիր, խոյակ)
capitalism - *turamadiroutiun* (դրամատիրութիւն)
capitalist - *turamader, medzaharousd* (դրամատէր, մեծահարուստ)
capitol - *bedagan doun, bashdonadoun, balad* (պետական տուն, պաշտօնատուն, պալատ)
capitulate - *antsnadour ullal tashinkov* (անձնատուր ըլլալ դաշինքով)
capitulation - *antsnadououtiun, hashdoutiun* (անձնատուութիւն, հաշտութիւն)
capon - *vortsad, vortsadel, gudrel* (որձատ, որձատել, կտրել)
caprice - *kumahajouyk, kumayk, gamayaganoutiun* (քմահաճոյք, քմայք, կամայականութիւն)
capricious - *kumaykod, gamayagan* (քմայքոտ, կամայական)
capricorn - *aydzeghchiur* (այծեղջիւր)
capsize - *shurchel, tartsunel, shurchoum* (շրջել, դարձնել, շրջում)
capsule - *badian, teghabadij, gaydz huratsani, anot* (պատեան, դեղապատիճ, կայծ հրացանի, անօթ)
captain - *hariurabed, navabed, huramanadar* (հարիւրապետ, նաւապետ, հրամանատար)
caption - *khorakir, vernakir, tserpagaloutiun* (խորագիր, վերնագիր, ձերբակալութիւն)
captious - *khudzpudzogh, imasdag, tuzhvarahaj* (խծբծող, իմաստակ, դժուարահաճ)
captivate - *kerel, kuravel, hurabourel* (գերել, գրաւել, հրապուրել)
captivation - *keroutiun, galank, hapushdagoutiun* (գերութիւն, կալանք, յափշտակութիւն)
captive - *keri, kerel* (գերի, գերել)
captivity - *keroutiun* (գերութիւն)
capture - *galank, kuravoum, kuravel, purnel* (կալանք, գրաւում, գրաւել, բռնել)
car - *inknasharzh, gark* (ինքնաշարժ, կառք)
car rental - *vartsou inknasharzh* (վարձու ինքնաշարժ)
carafe - *gouzh, shish, churaman* (կուժ, շիշ, ջրաման)
caramel - *ayradz shakar, shakareghen* (այրած շաքար, շաքարեղէն)
carat - *gushrachap* (կշռաչափ)
caravan - *garavan, garakhoump* (կարաւան, կառախումբ)
carbohydrate - *adzkhachuradzin* (ածխաջրածին)
carbon - *adzoukh, punadzoukh* (ածուխ, բնածուխ)
carbon paper - *badjenahan, punadzkhatought* (պատճէնահան, բնածխաթուղթ)
carbonize - *adzkhatsunel* (ածխացնել)
carburater, carburator - *adzkhatsoutzich, inknasharzhi vareladegh* (ածխացուցիչ, ինքնաշարժի վառելատեղ)
carcasse, carcass - *tiag, gumakhk, vosgurodi, munatsortats* (դիակ, կմախք, ոսկրոտի, մնացորդաց)
card - *khavakard, kard, aitsekard,*

khaghatought (խաւաքարտ, քարտ, այցեքարտ, խաղաթուղթ)
cardboard - khavakard, usduvaratought (խաւաքարտ, ստուարաթուղթ)
cardholder - vargakardader (վարկաքարտատէր)
cardiac - surdayin, surdi veraperogh (սրտային, սրտի վերաբերող)
cardiac, cardiacal - surdayin (սրտային)
cardinal - gardinal, kulkhavor (կարտինալ, գլխաւոր)
cardiogram - surdakir, surdakidz (սրտագիր, սրտագիծ)
cardiography - surdakuroutiun (սրտագրութիւն)
cardiometer - surdachap (սրտաչափ)
cardiovascular surgery - sird-anotayin virahadoutiun (սիրտ-անօթային վիրահատութիւն)
care - khunamk, tarmanoum, hok, hokal (խնամք, դարմանում, հոգ, հոգալ)
career - asbarez, arshav, untatsk, arak untanal (ասպարէզ, արշաւ, ընթացք, արագ ընթանալ)
careful - uzkouysh, oushatir (զգոյշ, ուշադիր)
carefully - uzkoushoutiamp (զգուշութեամբ)
careless - anhok, anpouyt (անհոգ, անփոյթ)
caress - kukvank, kukvel (գգուանք, գգուել)
cargo - pernanav, pernadar nav (բեռնանաւ, բեռնատար նաւ)
caricature - yerkidzanugar (երգիծանկար)
caricaturist - yerkidzanugarich (երգիծանկարիչ)
caries - vosgurapudoutiun (ոսկրափտութիւն)
carjacker - inknasharzh purnakuravogh (ինքնաշարժ բռնագրաւող)
carjacking - inknasharzhi purnakuravoum (ինքնաշարժի բռնագրաւում)
carmine - vortan garmir (որդան կարմիր)
carnage - godoradz, usbant (կոտորած, սպանդ)
carnal - marmunagan, heshdaser, vavash (մարմնական, հեշտասէր, վաւաշ)
carnalism - tsopoutiun (ցոփութիւն)
carnalist - vavashod (վաւաշոտ)
carnality - durpank, tsangoutiun, darpank (տռփանք, ցանկութիւն, տարփանք)
carnalize - tsopatsunel (ցոփացնել)
carnation - vartakouyn, mekhag (վարդագոյն, մեխակ)
carnival - paregentan, timagahantes (Բարեկենդան, դիմակահանդէս)
carniverous - musager, kishager (մսակեր, գիշակեր)
carob - yeghchiur, yeghchereni (եղջիւր, եղջերենի)
carol - barerkoutiun, yerk, koverkel (պարերգութիւն, երգ, գովերգել)
carousal - khurakhjank, kinarpouk (խրախճանք, գինարբուք)
carouse - geroukhoum, arpetsoutiun, arpenal (կերուխում, արբեցութիւն, արբենալ)
carp - khudzpudzel, barsavel (խծբծել, պարսաւել)
carpenter - adaghtsakordz (ատաղձագործ)
carpentry - adaghtsakordzoutiun, hiusnoutiun (ատաղձագործութիւն, հիւսնութիւն)
carpet - kork, gaberd, korkabadel (գորգ, կապերտ, գորգապատել)
carriage - gark, sayl, pokhaturoutiun, pernaguroutiun (կառք, սայլ, փոխադրութիւն, բեռնակրութիւն)
carrier - arakogh, danogh, pokhaturogh (առաքող, տանող, փոխադրող)
carrot - usdebghin (ստեպղին)
carry - danil, pokhaturel, shalgel (տանիլ, փոխադրել, շալկել)
cart - pernagark, sayl (բեռնակառք, սայլ)
cartage - pokhatrakin (փոխադրագին)
carte - jashatsoutsag (ճաշացուցակ)
cartel - mardagoch, keri pokhatrogh

nav, asbarez gartal (մարտակոչ, գերի փոխադրող նաւ, ասպարէզ կարդալ)
carter - garaban, saylort (կառապան, սայլորդ)
cartilage - gurjig, ajar (կռճիկ, աճառ)
carton - khavakard (խաւաքարտ)
cartoon - yerkidzanugar (երգիծանկար)
cartoonist - yerkidzanugarich (երգիծանկարիչ)
cartridge - pampushdagal, yerizadoup (փամփշտակալ, երիզատուփ)
carve - kantagel, porakurel (քանդակել, փորագրել)
carver - kantagogh, mis gudrogh tanag, mis gudrogh ants (քանդակող, միս կտրող դանակ, միս կտրող անձ)
carving - kantagoum (քանդակում)
cascade - churvezh, sahank (ջրվէժ, սահանք)
case - doup, sundoug, argugh, baraka (տուփ, սնտուկ, արկղ, պարագայ)
casern - zoranots (զօրանոց)
cash - gankhig, kantsel, vujarel, turamargugh (կանխիկ, գանձել, վճարել, դրամարկղ)
cash and carry - vujare ou dar (վճարէ ու տար)
cash flow - turamahosk (դրամահոսք)
cash register - hashvekir mekena (հաշուեգիր մեքենայ)
cashier - kantsich, kantsabah, vujarogh, bashdonazurgel (գանձիչ, գանձապահ, վճարող, պաշտօնազրկել)
casino - khaghasurah, khaghadoun, pakhdasurah (խաղասրահ, խաղատուն, բախտասրահ)
cask - dagar (տակառ)
casket - koharadoup, kuzrots (գոհարատուփ, գզրոց)
cassation - pegoum, chunchoum (բեկում, ջնջում)
casserole - san, gatsa (սան, կաթսայ)
cassette - yerizadoup, argughig (երիզատուփ, արկղիկ)
cassock - pilon, shourchar (փիլոն, շուրջառ)
cast (I) - nedel, mughel, badnesh shinel, tsoulel, pazhnel (նետել, մղել, պատնէշ շինել, ձուլել, բաժնել)
cast (II) - gartu nedel, khorhil, chapel, hashvel, tsevel (կարթը նետել, խորհիլ, չափել, հաշուել, ձեւել)
cast (III) - mughoum, nedvadzk, tsouloum, gerbarank, desk (մղում, նետուածք, ձուլում, կերպարանք, տեսք)
castaway - anarag, anbidan, ungetsig, nedvadz (անառակ, անպիտան, ընկեցիկ, նետուած)
castigate - badzhel, oughghel (պատժել, ուղղել)
castle - tughlag, pert, amrots (դղեակ, բերդ, ամրոց)
castrate - nerkinatsunel, gudrel (ներքինացնել, կտրել)
casual - badahagan, zhamanagavor (պատահական, ժամանակաւոր)
casualty - tibvadz, badahar, mah, gorousd (դիպուած, պատահար, մահ, կորուստ)
cat - gadou, khariskhu ver arnel (կատու, խարիսխը վեր առնել)
cataclysm - badouhas, churheghegh, voghoghoum, gordzanoum (պատուհաս, ջրհեղեղ, ողողում, կործանում)
catacomb - kednatampan (գետնադամբան)
catafalque - tiagark, mahapem (դիակառք, մահաբեմ)
catalogue - tsoutsag, tsang, tsoutsagakurel (ցուցակ, ցանկ, ցուցակագրել)
catalysis - neraztetsoutiun, kimiagan aylapokhoum (ներազդեցութիւն, քիմիական այլափոխում)
catamenia - tashdan (դաշտան)
cataplasm - usbeghani, khius (սպեղանի, խիւս)
cataract - churvezh, deghadarap,

achki varakouyr (ջրվէժ, տեղատարափ, աչքի վարագոյր)
catarrh - harpoukh (Հարբուխ)
catastrophe - aghed, argadz (աղէտ, արկած)
catch - purnel, kuravel, umpurnel, umpurnoum (բռնել, գրաւել, ըմբռնել, ըմբռնում)
catechism - guronakidoutiun, guronagan ousoutsoum (կրօնագիտութիւն, կրօնական ուսուցում)
catechist - guronapan (կրօնաբան)
categorical - patsartsag, gudroug, huramayagan (բացարձակ, կտրուկ, Հրամայական)
category - desag, tasagark, khoump, gark (տեսակ, դասակարգ, խումբ, կարգ)
catenate - shughtayel, gabel (շղթայել, կապել)
catenation - shughtayoum (շղթայում)
cater - madagararel (մատակարարել)
caterer - madagarar (մատակարար)
catering - madagararoum (մատակարարում)
cathedral - dajar, mayr yegeghetsi (տաճար, մայր եկեղեցի)
catherization - khorasouzoum (խորասուզում)
catherize - khorasouzel (խորասուզել)
catheter - khorasouyz, marmunin khoru mudnogh kordzik (մարմնին խորը մտնող գործիք)
catholic - gatoghige (կաթողիկէ)
Catholicism - gatoghigeoutiun (Կաթողիկէութիւն)
catholicism - gatoligoutiun (կաթոլիկութիւն)
catholicos - gatoghigos, hayrabed (կաթողիկոս, Հայրապետ)
cattle - archar, nakhir (արջառ, նախիր)
caucasian - govgasian (կովկասեան)
caul - kogh, kulkhazart ganants (քօղ, գլխազարդ կանանց)
cauma - mahakoun, khor koun, gizacherm (մաՀաքուն, խոր քուն, կիզաջերմ)
cause - badjar, tad, iravounk, badjarel (պատճառ, դատ, իրաւունք, պատճառել)
causer - badjarogh (պատճառող)
causerie - khosagtsoutiun, asoulis (խօսակցութիւն, ասուլիս)
caustic - ayrogh, hadou, gudzou, yerkidzagan (այրող, Հատու, կծու, երգիծական)
cauterize - kharazanel, daghel (խարազանել, տաղել)
caution - uzkoushoutiun, aztararoutiun, aztararel (զգուշութիւն, ազդարարութիւն, ազդարարել)
cautious - uzkoushavor, shurchahayats, khohagan (զգուշաւոր, շրջաՀայեաց, խոՀական)
cautiously - uzkoushoutiamp (զգուշութեամբ)
cavalcade - hedzelahantes (ՀեծելաՀանդէս)
cavalier - tsiavor, hedzial, asbed, barunger (ձիաւոր, Հեծեալ, ասպետ, պարընկեր)
cavalry - hedzelazork, hedzelakount, ayroutsi (Հեծելազօրք, Հեծելագունդ, այրուձի)
cavate - porel, posatsadz (փորել, փոսացած)
cave - karayr, nugough (քարայր, նկուղ)
cavern - karantsav, karayr, khoroch (քարանձաւ, քարայր, խոռոչ)
caviar - tsugungit, aghgit (ձկնկիթ, աղկիթ)
cavil - khudzpudzel, imasdagel, khudzpudzank (խծբծել, իմաստակել, խծբծանք)
cavity - pos, khoroch, dzag (փոս, խոռոչ, ծակ)
caw - gurunchel, gurinch (կռնչել, կռինչ)
cease - tatril, genal, tatar (դադրիլ, կենալ, դադար)
ceasefire - zinatarar, huratatar, guragi tataretsoum (զինադադար, Հրադադար, կրակի դադարեցում)
ceaseless - antatar (անդադար)
cecity - gouroutiun (կուրութիւն)

cedar - yeghevin, mayri (եղեւին, մայրի)
cede - dal, hantsunel, toghoul, tsukel (տալ, յանձնել, Թողուլ, ձգել)
ceil - dzepel, badel (ծեփել, պատել)
ceiling - arasdagh, tseghoun (առաստաղ, ձեղուն)
celebrant - badarakich (պատարագիչ)
celebrate - hurchagel, donel, donakhumpel (Հռչակել, տօնել, տօնախմբել)
celebration - donakhumpoutiun, hantes (տօնախմբութիւն, Հանդէս)
celebrity - hampav, hurchag, hampavavor ants (Համբաւ, Հռչակ, Համբաւաւոր անձ)
celerity - arakoutiun, pouyt (արագութիւն, փոյթ)
celestial - yergnavor (երկնաւոր)
celibacy - amourioutiun (ամուրիութիւն)
cell - khouts, dzag, menaran (խուց, ծակ, մենարան)
cellar - maran, ushdemaran (մառան, շտեմարան)
cello - tavchoutag (Թաւջութակ)
cellular - puchichayin (բջիջային)
cellular telephone - sharzhoun heratsayn (շարժուն Հեռաձայն)
cement - guraposhi (կրափոշի)
cemetery - kerezmanadoun (գերեզմանատուն)
cenoby - miapanoutiun (միաբանութիւն)
cense - khungel (խնկել)
censer - pourvar (բուրվառ)
censor - kurakunnich, kurakunnel (գրաքննիչ, գրաքննել)
censorship - kurakunnoutiun (գրաքննութիւն)
censure - meghaturel, meghaturank (մեղադրել, մեղադրանք)
censurer - barsavogh, khudzpudzogh (պարսաւող, խծբծող)
census - martahamar (մարդաՀամար)
census bureau - vijagakuragan kuraseniag (վիճակագրական գրասենեակ)
cent - hariurerort (Հարիւրերորդ)
centaur - houshgabarig (յուշկապարիկ)
centenary - hariuramiag, hariuramia (Հարիւրամեակ, Հարիւրամեայ)
center - getron, mechdeghu (կեդրոն, մէջտեղը)
central - getronagan (կեդրոնական)
Central America - getronagan ameriga (Կեդրոնական Ամերիկա)
centralization - getronatsoum (կեդրոնացում)
centralize - getronatsunel (կեդրոնացնել)
centrifugal - getronakhouys (կեդրոնախոյս)
centripetal - getronatsik (կեդրոնաձիգ)
century - tar, hariur dari (դար, Հարիւր տարի)
cephalic - kulkhayin, kulkhategh (գլխային, գլխադեղ)
ceramic - proudakordzagan (բրուտագործական)
ceramics - puroudakordzoutiun, khetsekordzoutiun (բրուտագործութիւն, խեցեգործութիւն)
cereal - armudik, hatsahadig (արմտիք, ՀացաՀատիկ)
cerebral - ougheghayin (ուղեղային)
ceremony - araroghoutiun (արարողութիւն)
cerise - gerasakouyn (կեռասագոյն)
certain - vorosh, usdouyk, abahov, havasdi (որոշ, ստոյգ, ապաՀով, Հաւաստի)
certainly - angasgadz, anshoushd, abahovapar (անկասկած, անշուշտ, ապաՀովաբար)
certificate - vugayagan, vugayatought, hasdadakir (վկայական, վկայաԹուղԹ, Հաստատագիր)
certify - hasdadel, vugayel, havasdel (Հաստատել, վկայել, Հաւաստել)
certitude - abahovoutiun, havasdik, usdoukoutiun (ապաՀովութիւն, Հաւաստիք, ստուգութիւն)
cess - harg, chap, dourk tunel, tatril, lukel (Հարկ, չափ, տուրք

դնել, լքել)
cessation - tatar, unthadoum (դադար, ընդհատում)
cession - hantsunoum, pokhantsoum, zichoum (յանձնում, փոխանցում, զիջում)
cesspool - goyoughi, goyanots, aghpanots (կոյուղի, կոյանոց, աղբանոց)
chafe - shupel, zayratsunel, mashoum (շփել, զայրացնել, մաշում)
chaff - hart, anbedk (յարդ, անպէտք)
chaffer - sagargel, kunel, sagargoutiun (սակարկել, գնել, սակարկութիւն)
chafing - mashoum, shupoum (մաշում, շփում)
chagrin - vishd, vushdatsunel (վիշտ, վշտացնել)
chain - shughtayel, shughta, gabank (շղթայել, շղթայ, կապանք)
chair - ator, kah (աթոռ, գահ)
chairman - adenabed, nakhakah (ատենապետ, նախագահ)
chalet - hiughag, tarbas (հիւղակ, դարպաս)
chalice - sugih, pazhag (սկիհ, բաժակ)
chalk - gavij (կաւիճ)
challenge - mardahuraver, murtsahuraver, asbarez gartal (մարտահրաւէր, մրցահրաւէր, ասպարէզ կարդալ)
challenger - mardahuravirogh (մարտահրաւիրող)
cham - dzamel (ծամել)
chamber - seniag (սենեակ)
chamber of commerce - arevduragan kuraseniag (առեւտրական գրասենեակ)
chambermaid - usbasouhi (սպասուհի)
chameleon - kednariudz (գետնաւիւծ)
chamois - karaydz (քարայծ)
champ - dzamel, dzamdzumel (ծամել, ծամծմել)
champagne - purpurag, jermag kini (փրփրակ, ճերմակ գինի)
champaign - tashdakedin (դաշտագետին)
champe - dzamdzumel (ծամծմել)
champer - khadznogh, gurdzogh (խածնող, կրծող)
champignon - soung (սունկ)
champion - akhoyan, umpish, ara chamardig, haghtel (ախոյեան, ախոյեան, ըմբիշ, առաջամարտիկ, յաղթել)
championship - akhoyanoutiun (ախոյանութիւն)
chance - pakhd, badehoutiun, badahil (բախտ, պատեհութիւն, պատահիլ)
chancellor - varchabed, tivanabed (վարչապետ, դիւանապետ)
chancer - artaratadel (արդարադատել)
chancery - adian, tivanadoun (ատեան, դիւանատուն)
chandelier - chah, jurakaran, ashdanag (ջահ, ճրագարան, աշտանակ)
chandler - momavajar (մոմավաճառ)
change - pokhel, manrel, pokhanagel (փոխել, մանրել, փոխանակել)
changeability - popokelioutiun (փոփոխելիութիւն)
channel - churantsk, neghouts, antsk, heradesili gayan (ջրանցք, նեղուց, անցք, հեռատեսիլի կայան)
chant - megheti, yerk, yerkel (մեղեդի, երգ, երգել)
chantage - usbarnalikov shortoum (սպառնալիքով շորթում)
chanting - dagherkoutiun, saghmoserkoutiun (տաղերգութիւն, սաղմոսերգութիւն)
chaos - kaos, vih, antount, shupotoutiun (քաոս, վիհ, անդունդ, շփոթութիւն)
chap - jeghkel, zarnel, zarnuvil, jekhk, zarnuvadzk (ճեղքել, զարնել, զարնուիլ, ճեղք, զարնուածք)
chapel - madour, khoran (մատուռ, խորան)
chaperon - khunamagalouhi, hokadar, hokadarel (խնամակալուհի, հոգատար, հոգատարել)

chaplain - madranabed, danerets (մատռանապետ, տանէրէց)
chaplet - busag, hamrich (պսակ, համրիչ)
chapman - perezag, shurchoun manravajar (փերեզակ, շրջուն մանրավաճառ)
chapter - kirki kuloukh, masnajiugh, zhoghov yegeghetsagan (գիրքի գլուխ, մասնաճիւղ, ժողով եկեղեցական)
char - adzkhatsnel (ածխացնել)
character - nugarakir, punavoroutiun, kir, daradesag (նկարագիր, բնաւորութիւն, գիր, տառատեսակ)
characteristic - hadganushagan, voroshich (յատկանշական, որոշիչ)
characterize - hadganushel, nugarakurel (յատկանշել, նկարագրել)
charcoal - paydadzoukh (փայտածուխ)
chard - jaguntegh (ճակնդեղ)
charge - pernavorel, pertsunel, letsunel, per, dzakhs (բեռնաւորել, բեռցնել, լեցնել, բեռ, ծախս)
chariot - gark, sayl, garkov pokhaturel (կառք, սայլ, կառքով փոխադրել)
charitable - parekordz, voghormadz, martaser (բարեգործ, ողորմած, մարդասէր)
charity - kout, garegtsoutiun, voghormoutiun, ser (գութ, կարեկցութիւն, ողորմութիւն, սէր)
charlatan - khapepa, shaghagrad, soud puzhishg (խաբեբայ, շաղակրատ, սուտ բժիշկ)
charm - humayk, hurabouyr, tiutel, humayel (հմայք, հրապոյր, դիւթել, հմայել)
charmful - humaykod, uzmayleli, kuravich (հմայքոտ, զմայլելի, գրաւիչ)
charming - uzmayleli, tiutich, keghetsig (զմայլելի, դիւթիչ, գեղեցիկ)
chart - kardes, ashkharhatsouyts, tashnakir (քարտէս, աշխարհացոյց, դաշնագիր)
charter - hurovardag, vartsoum, hadoug pokhatroum, arantsnayert (հրովարտակ, վարձում, յատուկ փոխադրում)
chary - uzkouysh, khohagan, khunayogh (զգոյշ, խոհական, խնայող)
chase - haladzel, hedabuntel, vorsal, vors (հալածել, հետապնդել, որսալ, որս)
chaser - vorsort, haladzich (որսորդ, հալածիչ)
chasm - antount, vih, antsk (անդունդ, վիհ, անցք)
chasse - nushkhar, masounk (նշխար, մասունք)
chassis - garagumakhk (կառակմախք)
chaste - anarad, makour, gouys, bargeshd (անարատ, մաքուր, կոյս, պարկեշտ)
chat - shadakhosel, shaghagradel, shadakhosoutiun (շատախօսել, շաղակրատել, շատախօսութիւն)
chateau - tughiag (դղեակ)
chatter - gurgural, shadakhosel, totovel, parpanchel (կռկռալ, շատախօսել, թոթովել, բարբանջել)
chatterer - shadakhos (շատախօս)
chatty - zuroutsaser, khosoun (զրուցասէր, խօսուն)
chauffeur - sharzhavar, mekenavar (շարժավար, մեքենավար)
chauvinist - molerant, azkaynamol (մոլեռանդ, ազգայնամոլ)
chaw - dzamel, vorojal midkov, guzag, badar (ծամել, որոճալ միտքով, կզակ, պատառ)
chawdrom - unterk, porodik (ընդերք, փորոտիք)
cheap - azhan, nuvazakin, sagargel (աժան, նուազագին, սակարկել)
cheapen - azhantsunel (աժանցնել)
cheapener - azhantsunogh (աժանցնող)
cheapness - azhanoutiun (աժանութիւն)
cheat - khapel, khapeoutiun (խաբել, խաբէութիւն)
cheater - khapepa, khapogh (խաբեբայ, խաբող)
check (n) - vujarakir, pokhkir, arkelk, usdoukoum (վճարագիր,

փոխգիր, արգելք, ստուգում)
check (v) - usdoukel, kunnel, arkilel, khapanel (ստուգել, քննել, արգիլել, խափանել)
checkbook - vujaradedur (վճարատետր)
checkpoint - gankar inknasharzhu kunnelou (կանգառ՝ ինքնաշարժը քննելու)
checkup - fizikagan kunnoum (ֆիզիքական քննում)
cheek - ayd, dzunod (այտ, ծնօտ)
cheeky - angirt, aneres (անկիրթ, աներես)
cheep - jurvoghel, jurvoghiun (ճռուողել, ճռուողիւն)
cheer - ourakhoutiun, zuvartoutiun, zuvartatsnel (ուրախութիւն, զուարթութիւն, զուարթացնել)
cheerful - zuvart, yerchanig (զուարթ, երջանիկ)
cheese - banir (պանիր)
cheesecake - banradzagh (պանրածաղ)
chef - bed, arachnort, ghegavar, khohararabed (պետ, առաջնորդ, ղեկավար, խոհարարապետ)
chef d'oeuvre - kuloukh kordzots (գլուխ գործոց)
chemical - kimiagan (քիմիական)
chemise - shabig (շապիկ)
chemist - kimiaked (քիմիագէտ)
chemistry - kimiapanoutiun (քիմիաբանութիւն)
chemotherapy - kimiagan pouzhoum (քիմիական բուժում)
cheque -
cherish - sirel, kukvel, kourkoural (սիրել, գգուել, գուրգուրալ)
cherry - geras, geraseni (կեռաս, կեռասենի)
chess - jadrag, shakhmad (ճատրակ, շախմատ)
chest - sundoug, gourdzk, arghughel (սնտուկ, կուրծք, արկղել)
chestnut - shakanag (շագանակ)
cheval - tsi, netsoug, henag (ձի, նեցուկ, յենակ)
chevalier - tsiavor, asbed (ձիաւոր, ասպետ)
chew - dzamel, dzamon (ծամել, ծամոն)
chic - tsevavor, paretsev (ձեւաւոր, բարեձեւ)
chicane - vejer hanel, kashkushel, khapeoutiun (վէճեր հանել, քաշքշել, խաբէութիւն)
chicaner - vijogh, kashkushogh (վիճող, քաշքշող)
chicanery - kashkushouk, nenkoutiun (քաշքշուք, նենգութիւն)
chich - siser, poghpochil (սիսեռ, բողբոջիլ)
chick - joudig, variag (ճուտիկ, վառեակ)
chick pea - siser (սիսեռ)
chicken - hav, variag (հաւ, վառեակ)
chickenpox - churdzaghig (ջրծաղիկ)
chide - hantimanel, sasdel (յանդիմանել, սաստել)
chief - arachnort, bed, kuloukh, huramanadar (առաջնորդ, պետ, գլուխ, հրամանատար)
chief justice - kulkhavor tadavor (գլխաւոր դատաւոր)
chiefless - ankuloukh, anbed (անգլուխ, անպետ)
chieftain - arachnort, bed, hohmabed, ishkhan (առաջնորդ, պետ, տոհմապետ, իշխան)
child - manoug, zavag, dugha, yerekha (մանուկ, զաւակ, տղայ, երեխայ)
childish - dughayagan, mangagan (տղայական, մանկական)
children - zavagner, yerekhaner (զաւակներ, երեխաներ)
childship - mangoutiun (մանկութիւն)
chili - gudzou bughbegh (կծու պղպեղ)
chill - tsourd, bagh, togh, baghil (ցուրտ, պաղ, դող, պաղիլ)
chilly - musgod, tsurdakin (մսկոտ, ցրտագին)
chimney - dzukhnelouyz (ծխնելոյզ)
chin - guzag, dzunod, tounch (կզակ, ծնօտ, դունչ)
China - chinasdan, hakhjabagi (Չինաստան, յախճապակի)

chinar - sosi dzar (սօսի ծառ)
chine - tigounk, gurnag, tsor (թիկունք, կռնակ, ձոր)
chinese - chinagan, chinaren, chinatsi (չինական, չինարէն, չինացի)
chink - dzag, jeghk, hunchiun turram, jeghkel (ծակ, ճեղք, հնչիւն դրամ, ճեղքել)
chip - dashegh, manrouk, geghev, (տաշել, մանրուք, կեղեւ)
chipper - jurvoghel, zuvart, gaydar (ճռուողել, զուարթ, կայտառ)
chiropodist - vodnapouyh (ոտնաբոյժ)
chiropractic - marmunapouzhoutiun, antegh puzhushgoutiun (մարմնաբուժութիւն, անդեղ բժշկութիւն)
chiropractor - voghnapouyzh, marmunapouyzh (ողնաբոյժ, մարմնաբոյժ)
chirp - jurvoghiun, jurvoghel (ճռուողիւն, ճռուողել)
chirurgeon - virapouyzh (վիրաբոյժ)
chirurgery - virapouzhoutiun (վիրաբուժութիւն)
chit - manoug, dugheg, yergdogh, untsiughil (մանուկ, տղեկ, երկտող, ընձիւղիլ)
chlorophyll - pousaganach (բուսականաչ)
chock - khutsel, letsvil, khets, seb (խցել, լեցուիլ, խեց, սեպ)
chocolate - dourm (տուրմ)
choice - unduroutiun (ընտրութիւն)
choir - yerkchakhoump (երգչախումբ)
choke - kheghtel, kheghtuvil, kotsel (խեղդել, խեղդուիլ, գոցել)
choler - pargoutiun, zayrouyt (բարկութիւն, զայրոյթ)
cholera - zhandakhd (ժանտախտ)
cholesterol - maghtsajarb, maghtsid (մաղձաճարպ, մաղձիտ)
chomage - kortsatoul, ashkhadatatar (գործադուլ, աշխատադադար)
choose - undurel, zadel, nakhundurel (ընտրել, զատել, նախընտրել)
chop - godurdel, jeghkel, pokhel, pokhanagel, godroum (կոտրտել, ճեղքել, փոխել, փոխանակել, կոտրում)
choral - khumperkagan (խմբերգական)
chord - lar choutagi, tashnavorel (լար ջութակի, դաշնաւորել)
choreograph - barakir (պարագիր)
choreographer - barakir (պարագիր)
choreography - barakuroutiun, bararvesd (պարագրութիւն, պարարուեստ)
chorus - yerkchakhoump (երգչախումբ)
chosen - undurvadz, undurial (ընտրուած, ընտրեալ)
chrism - miuron (միւռոն)
Christ - krisdos (Քրիստոս)
christen - krisdoneatsunel, mugurdel (քրիստոնէացնել, մկրտել)
christening - mugurdoutiun (մկրտութիւն)
christian - kurisdonia (քրիստոնեայ)
christianity - kurisdoneoutiun (քրիստոնէութիւն)
Christmas - Sourp dzunount (Սուրբ Ծնունդ)
Christmas tree - donadzar, gaghanti dzar (տօնածառ, կաղանդի ծառ)
chrome - kurom, zhahin (քրոմ, ժահին)
chronic - yergaradev, oralour (երկարատեւ, օրալուր)
chronic, -al - zhamanagakuragan, yergaradev, deghegadou (ժամանակագրական, երկարատեւ, տեղեկատու)
chronicle - zhamanagakroutiun, zhamanagakir (ժամանակագրութիւն, ժամանակագիր)
chronicler - zhamanagakir (ժամանակագիր)
chronologer, chronologist - zhamanagakir (ժամանակագիր)
chronology - zhamanagakroutiun (ժամանակագրութիւն)
chronometer - zhamanagachap (ժամանակաչափ)
chubby - kiroug, medzayd (գիրուկ, մեծայտ)
chuck - kukvel, khuntal, kurtkurtel, kutrkurtots havi (գգուել, խնդալ,

գրդգրդել, գրդգրդոց հաւի)
chuckle - *khuntouk, dzidzagh, kekevel* (խնդուք, ծիծաղ, քեքեւել)
chud - *khadznel, dzamdzumel* (խածնել, ծամծմել)
chuff - *aboush* (ապուշ)
chum - *senegagits, unger, senegagtsil* (սենեկակից, ընկեր, սենեկակցիլ)
church - *yegeghetsi* (եկեղեցի)
churchman - *yegeghetsagan* (եկեղեցական)
churl - *shinagan, keghchoug, kiughagan, goshd* (շինական, գեղջուկ, գիւղական, կոշտ)
chute - *sahank, kuloroum, angoum* (սահանք, գլորում, անկում)
cicada - *jubour* (ճպուռ)
cicatrice, cicatrix - *usbi* (սպի)
cicatrize - *usbiatsunel, usbianal* (սպիացնել, սպիանալ)
cicilian - *giligetsi, giligian* (կիլիկեցի, կիլիկեան)
cider - *khuntsoroghi* (խնձորօղի)
cigar - *dzukhaklan* (ծխագլան)
cigarette - *kulanig, sigaret* (գլանիկ, սիկարէթ)
cil - *him* (հիմ)
cilia - *ardevanounk, tartich* (արտեւանունք, թարթիչ)
Cilicia - *giligia* (Կիլիկիա)
cilium - *tartich* (թարթիչ)
cima - *dzunod* (ծնօտ)
cimex - *muloug* (մլուկ)
cincture - *kodi, gamar* (գօտի, կամար)
cinema - *sharzhanugar, sharzhabadger* (շարժանկար, շարժապատկեր)
cinematograph - *sharzhanugarogh, sharzhanugarayin* (շարժանկարող, շարժանկարային)
cinematographer - *sharzhanugarahanogh* (շարժանկարահանող)
cinematography - *sharzhanugarchoutiun* (շարժանկարչութիւն)
cinephile - *sharzhanugaraser, sharzhanugaramol* (շարժանկարասէր, շարժանկարամոլ)
cinnamon - *tarajeni* (դարաճենի)
cipher - *zero, vochinch* (զէրօյ, ոչինչ)
circa - *shourch, mod* (շուրջ, մօտ)
circle - *polorag, shurchanag, shurchanagel* (բոլորակ, շրջանակ, շրջանակել)
circuit - *shurchan, shurchanag, shurchakayil* (շրջան, շրջանակ, շրջագայիլ)
circular - *poloratsev, shurchaperagan* (բոլորաձեւ, շրջաբերական)
circulary - *manvadzabad* (մանուածապատ)
circulate - *shurchaperel, shurchan unel* (շրջաբերել, շրջան ընել)
circulation - *shurchakayoutiun, shurchanaroutiun* (շրջագայութիւն, շրջանառութիւն)
circumcise - *tulpadel* (թլփատել)
circumcision - *tulpadoum* (թլփատում)
circumference - *shurchakidz, shurchabad, shurchabadel* (շրջագիծ, շրջապատ, շրջապատել)
circumscribe - *shurchapagel, barpagel* (շրջափակել, պարփակել)
circumspect - *shurchahayats, oushatir* (շրջահայեաց, ուշադիր)
circumstance - *baraka, hankamank, vijag* (պարագայ, հանգամանք, վիճակ)
circumvent - *khapel, dzadzgel, nenkel, tagartel* (խաբել, ծածկել, նենգել, թակարդել)
circumvention - *khapeoutiun* (խաբէութիւն)
circus - *gurges* (կրկէս)
cirque - *gurges, shurchapag, lernahovid* (կրկէս, շրջափակ, լեռնահովիտ)
cistern - *churampar, avazan* (ջրամբար, աւազան)
citadel - *amrots, michnapert* (ամրոց, միջնաբերդ)
citation - *vugayoutiun, gochnakir, hishadagoutiun* (վկայութիւն, կոչնագիր, յիշատակութիւն)
cite - *hishadagel, mechperel, tadaran ganchel* (յիշատակել, մէջբերել, դատարան կանչել)
citizen - *kaghakatsi* (քաղաքացի)

citizenship - kaghakatsioutiun (քաղաքացիութիւն)
citron - gidron (կիտրոն)
city - kaghak (քաղաք)
civic - kaghakayin (քաղաքային)
civil - kaghakayin, kaghakatsiagan (քաղաքային, քաղաքացիական)
civil engineer - yergurachap (երկրաչափ)
civil engineering - yergurachapoutiun (երկրաչափութիւն)
civilization - kaghakagurtoutiun (քաղաքակրթութիւն)
civilize - kaghakagurtel (քաղաքակրթել)
cizar - mugradel (մկրատել)
clack - sharachel, shachel, shaghagradel, sharachiun (շառաչել, շաչել, շաղակրատել, շառաչիւն)
clad - hakvadz, gogvadz (Հագուած, կոկուած)
claim - bahanch, bahanchel, poghokel (պաՀանջ, պաՀանջել, բողոքել)
claimant - bahanchogh, bahanchader (պաՀանջող, պաՀանջատէր)
clairvoyant - husdagades (յստակատես)
clamber - makultsil (մաքլցիլ)
clammy - tats, gubchoun (Թաց, կպչուն)
clamor - aghaghag, borchudouk, aghmugel (աղաղակ, պոռչտուք, աղմկել)
clamp - jiran, jang, hotagab, akoutsel (ճիրան, ճանկ, յօղակապ, ագուցել)
clan - dohm, tseghakhoump, khumpag (տոՀմ, ցեղախումբ, խմբակ)
clandestine - kaghdni, dzadzoug (գաղտնի, ծածուկ)
clang, clank - medaghatsayn, sharachetsunel, hunchetsunel (մետաղաձայն, շառաչեցնել, Հնչեցնել)
clannish - dohmig (տոՀմիկ)
clap - dzapel, zarnel, mukhel, dzap, harvadz, paghkhiun (ծափել, զարնել, մխել, ծափ, Հարուած, բաղխիւն)
clapper - dzapaharogh (ծափաՀարող)
clarification - husdagatsoum, barzoum (յստակացում, պարզում)
clarify - husdagatsnel, barzel (յստակացնել, պարզել)
clart - aghdodel (աղտոտել)
clash - pakhoum, pakhil, untharil (բախում, բախիլ, ընդՀարիլ)
clasp - voghchakouroum, seghmoum, seghmel (ողջագուրում, սեղմում, սեղմել)
class - tasaran, gark, tas, tasagark, tasagarkel (դասարան, կարգ, դաս, դասակարգ, դասակարգել)
classic - tasagan (դասական)
classification - tasavoroum (դասաւորում)
classified adds - tasavorvadz dzanoutsoumner (դասաւորուած ծանուցումներ)
classify - tasavorel (դասաւորել)
classmate - tasunger (դասընկեր)
class-room - tasaran (դասարան)
clatch - gouyd (կոյտ)
clatter - aghmoug, aghmugel, jarjadil (աղմուկ, աղմկել, ճարճատիլ)
clause - barperoutiun, bayman, hadvadz, mas (պարբերութիւն, պայման, Հատուած, մաս)
claustral - vanagan (վանական)
clavier - usdeghnashar (ստեղնաշար)
claw - jang, jangel (ճանկ, ճանկել)
clay - gav, tsekh (կաւ, ցեխ)
clean - makour, makrel (մաքուր, մաքրել)
cleaner - makrogh (մաքրող)
cleaning - makroum (մաքրում)
cleanness - makroutiun (մաքրութիւն)
cleanse - makrel, luval, surpel (մաքրել, լուալ, սրբել)
cleanser - surpich, makrich (սրբիչ, մաքրիչ)
clear - husdag, makour, husdagatsunel (յստակ, մաքուր, յստակացնել)
clearance - makrakordzoum, hashvehartar, loudzark (մաքրագործում, Հաշուեյարդար, լուծարք)
clearer - husdagatsunogh, zudogh, barzogh (յստակացնող, զտող, պարզող)
clearing - makroum, hashveharta-

roum, patsasdan (մաքրում, Հաշուեյարդարում, բացատան)
clearness - husdagoutiun (յստակութիւն)
cleave - pagchil, haril (փակչիլ, յարիլ)
clef - panali (բանալի)
cleft - patsvadzk (բացուածք)
clemency - kout, meghmoutiun (գութ, մեղմութիւն)
clergy - gugher, gugheraganoutiun (կղեր, կղերականութիւն)
clergyman - gugheragan (կղերական)
clerk - kurakir, tubir, diratsou (գրագիր, դպիր, տիրացու)
cleve - vayrechk, kahavezh (վայրէջք, գահավէժ)
clever - oushim, hachoghag, jarbig (ուշիմ, յաջողակ, ճարպիկ)
clew - gudzig, baran (կծիկ, պարան)
click - shachel, chukhgel, shachiun, chukhgots (շաչել, չխկել, շաչիւն, չխկոց)
client - hajakhort, bashdbanial (յաճախորդ, պաշտպանեալ)
cliff - kharag, tsits (խարակ, ցից)
climate - gulima, punagil (կլիմայ, բնակիլ)
climax - partsuraged, verelk, asdijanavoroum (բարձրակէտ, վերելք, աստիճանաւորում)
climb - makultsil, yellel, partsuranal (մագլցիլ, ելլել, բարձրանալ)
clime - shurchan, yergir, gulima (շրջան, երկիր, կլիմայ)
climp - makultsoum (մագլցում)
clinch - seghmel, burgel, garchil, garchoum (սեղմել, պրկել, կառչիլ, կառչում)
cling - garchil, paril, haril (կառչիլ, փարիլ, յարիլ)
clinic - tarmanadoun, pouzharan (դարմանատուն, բուժարան)
clink - hunchel, hunchetsunel (Հնչել, Հնչեցնել)
clip - amratsunel, gabel (ամրացնել, կապել)
clipper - khouzich, gudrich mekena, arakanav (խուզիչ, կտրիչ մեքենայ, արագանաւ)
clique - khumpag (խմբակ)
clitoris - dzulig (ծլիկ)
cloak - timag, dzadzgel (դիմակ, ծածկել)
clock - medz zhamatsouyts (մեծ ժամացոյց)
cloister - menasdan, vank (մենաստան, վանք)
close - pagel, kotsel, pag (փակել, գոցել, փակ)
close out - zeghchuvadz kinov dzakhel (զեղչուած գինով ծախել)
closen - modetsunel, pagel (մօտեցնել, փակել)
closet - baharan, taran (պահարան, դարան)
closing - pagoum, verch (փակում, վերջ)
closure - pagoum, arkelapag, verch (փակում, արգելափակ, վերջ)
clot - magart, tontogh (մակարդ, դոնդող)
cloth - hakousd, gudav, gerbas (Հագուստ, կտաւ, կերպաս)
clothe - hakvetsunel (Հագուեցնել)
clothes - hakousdner (Հագուստներ)
clothes stand - gakhich (կախիչ)
clothing - hakousdeghen, uzkesd (Հագուստեղէն, զգեստ)
clothing store - hakousdi khanout (Հագուստի խանութ)
cloud - amb, ambodil (ամպ, ամպոտիլ)
cloudbirst - deghadarap (տեղատարափ)
cloudiness - ambodoutiun (ամպոտութիւն)
cloudy - ambod, dukhour (ամպոտ, տխուր)
clout - tsuntsodi, kourch, gargudel (ցնցոտի, քուրջ, կարկտել)
clove - mekhag, mekhagi desag (մեխակ, մեխակի տեսակ)
clown - mimos, kheghgadag, dzaghradzou (միմոս, խեղկատակ, ծաղրածու)
cloy - haketsunel, gushdatsunel, tukhmel (յագեցնել, կշտացնել, թխմել)
club - agoump, lakhd, antamavujar

(ակումբ, լախտ, անդամավճար)
cluck - kurkal-vahi, kurkank (գրգալ՝Հաւի, գրգանք)
clue - gudzig, tel, hedk (կծիկ, թել, Հետք)
clump - bourag, khourts (պուրակ, խուրձ)
clumsy - anshunorh, anjarag (անշնորՀ, անճարակ)
cluster - voghgouyz, havakvil (ողկոյզ, Հաւաքուիլ)
clutch - purnel, khulel, akoutsich, gorzoum, jang (բռնել, խլել, ագուցիչ, կործում, ճանկ)
clutter - kharnagouyd, angarkoutiun (խառնակոյտ, անկարգութիւն)
coach - marzich, tsiagark, marzel megu gam khoumpu (մարզիչ, ձիակառք, մարզել մէկը խումբը)
coagulate - tantsuratsunel, magartel, tantsuranal, magartil (թանձրացընել, մակարդել, թանձրանալ, մակարդիլ)
coagulation - tantsuratsoum, magartoum (թանձրացում, մակարդում)
coal - adzoukh, karadzoukh, adzkhatsunel (ածուխ, քարածուխ, ածխացնել)
coalesce - mianal, tashnagtsil (միանալ, դաշնակցիլ)
coalition - zinagtsoutiun, tashnagtsoutiun (զինակցութիւն, դաշնակցութիւն)
coarse - goshd, anoghorg, hasd (կոշտ, անողորկ, Հաստ)
coast - dzovap, dzovezerk (ծովափ, ծովեզերք)
coast guard - yezerabah (եզերապաՀ)
coat - verargou, geghev, dzadzgel, dzepel (վերարկու, կեղեւ, ծածկել, ծեփել)
coat hanger - uzkesdagal (զգեստակալ)
coax - tapantsel, hamozel, paypayel (թափանցել, Համոզել, փայփայել)
cobbler - hunagargad (Հնակարկատ)
cobblestone - khujakar (խճաքար)
cobweb - sartosdayn (սարդոստայն)
cock (n) - aklor, dzorak, pultag, sulak, hoghmatsouyts (աքլոր, ծորակ, ըլթակ, սլաք, Հողմացոյց)
cock (v) - sudgel, dungel, larel, shinel, khurokhdanal (շտկել, տնկել, լարել, շինել, խրոխտանալ)
cockboat - magouyg (մակոյկ)
cocker - kourkoural, kukvel, akaghagh gurvetsunogh (գուրգուրալ, գգուել, աքաղաղ կռուեցնող)
cockeye - shil achk (շիլ աչք)
cocking - akloramard (աքլորամարտ)
cocktail - kharunkhumichk, untouneloutiun (խառնխմիչք, ընդունելութիւն)
cocoa - cacao (քաքաոյ)
coconut - huntgungouyz (Հնդկընկոյզ)
code - orinakirk, ganonakirk, dzadzgakir, nushan (օրինագիրք, կանոնագիրք, ծածկագիր, նշան)
codification - neshanakuroum (նշանագրում)
codify - ganonakurel, orenkneru tasavorel (կանոնագրել, օրէնքները դասաւորել)
coerce - purnatadel, usdibel, nuvajel (բռնադատել, ստիպել, նուաճել)
coeval - daregits, zhamanagagits (տարեկից, ժամանակակից)
coexistence - hamagetsoutiun (Համակեցութիւն)
coffee - sourj (սուրճ)
coffer - sundoug, argugh, turamargugh (սնտուկ, արկղ, դրամարկղ)
coffin - takagh (դագաղ)
cog - paghakushel, hurabourel, nenkel (փաղաքշել, Հրապուրել, նենգել)
cogitation - khorhurtadzoutiun, umpurnoghoutiun (խորՀրդածութիւն, ըմբռնողութիւն)
cognac - coniac, kinoghi (քոնեաք, գինօղի)
cognate - ariunagits, azkagan (արիւնակից, ազգական)
cognation - azkaganoutiun (ազգականութիւն)
cognition - janachoum, dzanotoutiun (ճանաչում, ծանօթութիւն)

cognize - janjunal (ճանչնալ)
cohabit - punagagtsil (բնակակցիլ)
cohabitation - punagagtsoutioun, genagtsoutiun (բնակակցութիւն, կենակցութիւն)
coheir - zharankagits (ժառանգակից)
cohere - haril, harmaril (յարիլ, յարմարիլ)
coherent - haragits, gutsort (յարակից, կցորդ)
cohesion - haragtsoutiun, shaghgaboum (յարակցութիւն, շաղկապում)
cohibit - zusbel, arkilel (զսպել, արգիլել)
coiffeur - saprich, varsahartar (սափրիչ, վարսայարդար)
coil - bullel, pattel (պլլել, փաթթել)
coin - medaghaturam, usdag, turam tarpunel (մետաղադրամ, ստակ, դրամ դարբնել)
coincide - zoukatibil, hamungnil (զուգադիպիլ, համընկնիլ)
coincidence - zoukatiboutiun (զուգադիպութիւն)
coiner - turamahad (դրամահատ)
coition - zoukavoroutiun, genagtsoutiun (զուգաւորութիւն, կենակցութիւն)
coitus - genagtsoutiun, zoukagtsoutiun (կենակցութիւն, զուգակցութիւն)
coke - hankadzoukh, karadzoukh (հանգածուխ, քարածուխ)
colander - kamots, souzag (քամոց, սուզակ)
cold - tzourd, bagh, bagharoutiun (ցուրտ, պաղ, պաղառութիւն)
cold blooded - baghariun, hantard (պաղարիւն, հանդարտ)
cole - gaghamp (կաղամբ)
collaborate - kordzagtsil, hamakordzagtsil (գործակցիլ, համագործակցիլ)
collaboration - kordzagtsoutiun, ashkhadagtsoutiun (գործակցութիւն, աշխատակցութիւն)
collage - sosuntsoum, sosuntsel, pagtsunel (սոսնձում, սոսնձել, փակցնել)
collapse - gukil, pulil, dabalil, sunangoutiun, gukoum (կքիլ, փլիլ, տապալիլ, սնանկութիւն, կքում)
collar - otsik, maniag, koghnal, arnel (օձիք, մանեակ, գողնալ, առնել)
collate - hamemadel, paghtadel (համեմատել, բաղդատել)
collateral - zoukaheragan, goghk goghki, yerashkhik (զուգահեռական, կողք կողքի, երաշխիք)
colleague - bashdonagits, bashdonagtsil (պաշտօնակից, պաշտօնակցիլ)
collect - havakel, kantsel, zhoghvel, mudaghotk (հաւաքել, գանձել, ժողվել, մտաղօթք)
collection - havakoum, kantsoum, havakadzo, gouyd (հաւաքում, գանձում, հաւաքածոյ, կոյտ)
collective - havakagan, miazankuvadz (հաւաքական, միազանգուած)
collector - havakogh, hargahavak (հաւաքող, հարկահաւաք)
college - colej, ousoumnaran, hamalusaran, zhoghov (գոլէճ, ուսումնարան, համալսարան, ժողով)
collide - pakhil, zarnuvil (բախիլ, զարնուիլ)
collie - kampur (գամփռ)
collier - adzkhahan, adzkhakordz (ածխահան, ածխագործ)
colliery - adzkhahank (ածխահանք)
colline - pulour, pulrag (բլուր, բլրակ)
collision - pakhoum, untharoum (բախում, ընդհարում)
collocate - zedeghel, deghavorel, tasavorel (զետեղել, տեղաւորել, դասաւորել)
collocation - tasavoroum, deghavoroum (դասաւորում, տեղաւորում)
colloquial - khosagtsagan, undani, lezvagits (խօսակցական, ընտանի, լեզուակից)
collusion - tavatroutiun, satrank (դաւադրութիւն, սադրանք)
colly - murodel, mour (մրոտել,մուր)
colo(u)r - kouyn, nerg (գոյն, ներկ)

colon - michaged, siunag, hasd aghik (միջակէտ, սիւնակ, հաստ աղիք)
colonel - kuntabed (գնդապետ)
colonial - kaghtavayri, kaghoutayin (գաղթավայրի, գաղութային)
colonisation - kaghtararoutiun (գաղթարարութիւն)
colonist - kaghtagan, kaghtapunag (գաղթական, գաղթաբնակ)
colonize - kaghout hasdadel (գաղութ հաստատել)
colonnade - siunashark (սիւնաշարք)
colony - kaghout, kaghtavayr, kaghtaganoutiun (գաղութ, գաղթավայր, գաղթականութիւն)
color, colour - kouyn, kounavorel, nergel (գոյն, գունաւորել, ներկել)
coloratura - pazmerank tsayn, kounakegh (բազմերանգ ձայն, գունագեղ)
colorful - kounavor (գունաւոր)
colosal - vitkhari, huga (վիթխարի, հսկայ)
colossal - husga, vitkhari (հսկայ, վիթխարի)
colporter, teur - shurchoun vajaragan (շրջուն վաճառական)
column - siun, siunag, shark (սիւն, սիւնակ, շարք)
columnist - siunagakir, tughtagits (սիւնակագիր, թղթակից)
coma - mahakoun, tumpir, kunadoutiun (մահաքուն, թմբիր, քնատութիւն)
comb - sandur, kerich, sandurvil (սանտր, քերիչ, սանտրուիլ)
combat - gurvil, baderazmil, baderazm, guriv (կռուիլ, պատերազմիլ, պատերազմ, կռիւ)
combattant - razmig, gurvogh, mardig (ռազմիկ, կռուող, մարտիկ)
comber - sandurogh, kuzogh, kuzich (սանտրող, գզող, գզիչ)
combination - paghatroutiun, miakhumpoutiun (բաղադրութիւն, միախմբութիւն)
combine - miatsunel, paghaturel, mianal (միացնել, բաղադրել, միանալ)
combution - gizoum, ayroum (կիզում, այրում)
come - kal, zhamanel, hasnil, hachoghtsunel (գալ, ժամանել, հասնիլ, յաջողցնել)
comeback - veratarts, veratarnal (վերադարձ, վերադառնալ)
comedian - gadagerkag, terasan (կատակերգակ, դերասան)
comedy - gadagerkoutiun (կատակերգութիւն)
comely - vayelouch, shunorhali (վայելուչ, շնորհալի)
comestible - oudelik, geragour (ուտելիք, կերակուր)
comet - kisavor, kisasdgh (գիսաւոր, գիսաստղ)
comfort - hankusdatsunel, hankusdoutiun, hankisd (հանգստացնել, հանգստութիւն, հանգիստ)
comfortable - hankusdaved, hankisd (հանգստաւէտ, հանգիստ)
comic - dzidzaghasharzh, khuntalik, gadagerkag (ծիծաղաշարժ, խնդալիք, կատակերգակ)
coming - kalik, zhamanoum, kalousd (գալիք, ժամանում, գալուստ)
coming in - hasouyt, yegamoud, moudk (հասոյթ, եկամուտ, մուտք)
coming out - nakhakayl, nakhaports (նախաքայլ, նախափորձ)
coming up - hachort, hedaka, kalik (յաջորդ, հետագայ, գալիք)
comity - paregurtoutiun, kaghakavaroutiun (բարեկրթութիւն, քաղաքավարութիւն)
comma - usdoraged (ստորակէտ)
command - huramayel, varel, huramanadaroutiun (հրամայել, վարել հրամանատարութիւն)
commemorable - hishadageli, nushanavor (յիշատակելի, նշանաւոր)
commemorate - hishadagel, donakhumpel (յիշատակել, տօնախմբել)
commemoration - hishadagoutiun, hishadag (յիշատակութիւն, յիշատակ)
commend - hantsunel, hantsunararel, kovel, parev unel (յանձնել, յանձնարարել, գովել, բարեւ ընել)

comment - megnel, patsadrel, megnapanoutiun (մեկնել, բացատրել, մեկնաբանութիւն)
commentary - megnoutiun, dzanotakroutiun (մեկնութիւն, ծանօթագրութիւն)
commentation - kuratadoutiun (գրադատութիւն)
commenter - megnapan, dzanotakir (մեկնաբան, ծանօթագիր)
commerce - arevdour, vajaraganoutiun, arevdour unel (առեւտուր, վաճառականութիւն, առեւտուր ընել)
commercial - arevduragan, vajaraganagan, vajarashah (առեւտրական, վաճառականական, վաճառաշահ)
commercialization - arevduraganatsoum (առեւտրականացում)
commercialize - arevduraganatsunel (առեւտրականացնել)
comminate - panaturel (բանադրել)
commination - panaturank (բանադրանք)
commiserate - kutal, garegtsil, tsavil (գթալ, կարեկցիլ, ցաւիլ)
commiseration - kutoutiun, garegtsoutiun, vushdagtsoutiun (գթութիւն, կարեկցութիւն, վշտակցութիւն)
commissary - hantsnagadar, kordzagal, vosdiganabed (յանձնակատար, գործակալ, ոստիկանապետ)
commission - michnortchek, hantsnaraoutiun, hantsnakhoump (միջնորդչէք, յանձնարարութիւն, յանձնախումբ)
commit - gadarel, hantsunel, pandargel, unel (կատարել, յանձնել, բանտարկել, ընել)
commitment - hantsnaroutiun, yentargoum, pandargoum (յանձնառութիւն, ենթարկում, բանտարկում)
committee - gomide, hantsnazhoghov (կոմիտէ, յանձնաժողով)
commmentate - kuratadel, megnapanel (գրադատել, մեկնաբանել)
commodious - hankusdaved, harmar (հանգստաւէտ, յարմար)
commodity - harmaroutiun, abrank, ardaturank (յարմարութիւն, ապրանք, արտադրանք)
commodore - avak navabed, hazarabed (աւագ նաւապետ, հազարապետ)
common - hasarag, sovoragan, unthanour (հասարակ, սովորական, ընդհանուր)
commons - hamaynk, khorhurtaran, seghanagits, seghanagtsil (համայնք, խորհրդարան, սեղանակից, սեղանակցիլ)
commonwealth - hasaragabedoutiun (հասարակապետութիւն)
commotion - khurovoutiun, angarkoutiun, houzoum (խռովութիւն, անկարգութիւն, յուզում)
communal - hamaynkayin, taghayin (համայնքային, թաղային)
commune - haghortagtsoutiun, tem, vijag, hoghortagtsil (հաղորդակցութիւն, թեմ, վիճակ, հաղորդակցիլ)
communicate - haghortagtsil (հաղորդակցիլ)
communication - haghortagtsoutiun (հաղորդակցութիւն)
communion - haghortoutiun, masnagtsoutiun, masnagtsil (հաղորդութիւն, մասնակցութիւն, մասնակցիլ)
communism - hamaynavaroutiun (համայնավարութիւն)
communist - hamaynavar (համայնավար)
community - hamaynk, hasaragoutiun (համայնք, հասարակութիւն)
commutation - pokhanagoutiun, popokhoutiun (փոխանակութիւն, փոփոխութիւն)
commute - pokhanagel, pokhargel (փոխանակել, փոխարկել)
compact - khid, seghm, gour, khudatsunel, seghmel (խիտ, սեղմ, կուռ, խտացնել, սեղմել)
compact disc (CD) - seghmeriz, seghm tsayneriz (սեղմերիզ, սեղմ ձայներիզ)
compaction - khudoutiun, khudatsoum

(խտութիւն, խտացում)
companion - unger, oughegits (ընկեր, ուղեկից)
company - ungeroutiun, ungeragtsoutiun, ungeragtsil (ընկերութիւն, ընկերակցութիւն, ընկերակցիլ)
comparable - paghtadeli (բաղդատելի)
compare - paghtadel, hamemadel (բաղդատել, համեմատել)
comparison - paghtadoutiun, numanoutiun (բաղդատութիւն, նմանութիւն)
compart - pazhnel (բաժնել)
compartment - pazhanoum, masnapazhin (բաժանում, մասնաբաժին)
compass - gargin, shurchan, shurchabadel (կարկին, շրջան, շրջապատել)
compassion - garegtsoutiun, kout (կարեկցութիւն, գութ)
compassionate - garegtsil, kutal, kutasird (կարեկցիլ, գթալ, գթասիրտ)
compatibility - harmaroutiun, miapanoutiun (յարմարութիւն, միաբանութիւն)
compatible - harmarogh, hamamid, miapan (յարմարող, համամիտ, միաբան)
compatriot - hayrenagits, yergratsi (հայրենակից, երկրացի)
compear - nergayanal, yerevnal (ներկայանալ, երեւնալ)
compeer - havasar, unger, havasaril (հաւասար, ընկեր, հաւասարիլ)
compel - bardatrel, usdibel (պարտադրել, ստիպել)
compensate - hadoutsanel, pokharinel, vartsadurel (հատուցանել, փոխարինել, վարձատրել)
compensation - hadoutsoum, vartsaduroutiun, pokharinoum (հատուցում, վարձատրութիւն, փոխարինում)
compete - murtsil (մրցիլ)
competence - tserunhasoutiun, garoghoutiun (ձեռնհասութիւն, կարողութիւն)
competency - garoghoutiun (կարողութիւն)
competent - tserunhas, garogh, iravasou (ձեռնհաս, կարող, իրաւասու)
competition - murtsoum, murtsagtsoutiun (մրցում, մրցակցութիւն)
competitive - murtsagtsagan, murtsounag (մրցակցական, մրցունակ)
competitor - murtsagits (մրցակից)
compilation - dzaghgakagh, kurakaghoutiun (ծաղկաքաղ, գրաքաղութիւն)
compile - dzaghgakagh unel, havakel, khumpakurel (ծաղկաքաղ ընել, հաւաքել, խմբագրել)
complacence - kohounagoutiun, inknakohoutiun (գոհունակութիւն, ինքնագոհութիւն)
complacent - tiurahaj, kaghakavar (դիւրահաճ, քաղաքավար)
complain - kankadil, durdunchal (գանգատիլ, տրտնջալ)
complaint - kankad, durdounch (գանգատ, տրտունջ)
complaisance - kohounagoutiun, hajoyagadaroutiun (գոհունակութիւն, հաճոյակատարութիւն)
complaisant - hajoyagadar, kaghakavar (հաճոյակատար, քաղաքավար)
complement - luratsoutsich, ampoghchoutiun, medzarel (լրացուցիչ, ամբողջութիւն, մեծարել)
complementary - luratsoutsich, havelvadzagan (լրացուցիչ, յաւելուածական)
complete - luratsunel, ampoghchatsunel, gadarial (լրացնել, ամբողջացնել, կատարեալ)
completion - gadareloutiun, ampoghchoutiun (կատարելութիւն, ամբողջութիւն)
complex - part, kharun, paghatroutiun, hamalir (բարդ, խառն, բաղադրութիւն, համալիր)
complexion - kharnuvadzk, gazmuvadzk, gazmoutiun, punoutiun (խառնուածք, կազմուածք, կազմութիւն, բնութիւն)
complexity - partoutiun (բարդութիւն)

compliance - zichoum, havanoutiun (զիջում, հաւանութիւն)
complicate - partatsunel, kharnel, part, gunjurod (բարդացնել, խառնել, բարդ, կնճռոտ)
complicity - meghsagtsoutiun (մեղսակցութիւն)
compliment - harkank, medzarank, medzarel, shunorhavorel (յարգանք, մեծարանք, մեծարել, շնորհաւորել)
comply - hamatsaynil, yentarguvil (համաձայնիլ, ենթարկուիլ)
compone - garkaturtel, gazmel (կարգադրել, կազմել)
component - paghgatsoutsich, eagan, himnagan (բաղկացուցիչ, էական, հիմնական)
comport - varvil, hamatsaynil, harmaril (վարուիլ, համաձայնիլ, յարմարիլ)
compose - gazmel, paghatrel, khumpakrel, horinel (կազմել, բաղադրել, խմբագրել, յօրինել)
composer - yerkahan (երգահան)
composite - kharnourt, kharun, paghatrial (խառնուրդ, խառն, բաղադրեալ)
composition - sharatroutiun, gazmoutiun, kurasharoutiun (շարադրութիւն, կազմութիւն, գրաշարութիւն)
compositor - yerkanah, horinogh, kurashar, gazmogh (երգահան, յօրինող, գրաշար, կազմող)
compost - kharnourt, barardatsunel, aghpakharnel (խառնուրդ, պարարտացնել, աղբախառնել)
composture - barardaniut, aghp (պարարտանիւթ, աղբ)
compote - mukanouysh (մրգանոյշ)
compound - paghatrel, kharnel, paghaturoutiun, shurchapag (բաղադրել, խառնել, բաղադրութիւն, շրջափակ)
comprador - madagarar (մատակարար)
comprehend - hasgunal, imanal, umpurnel, barpagel (հասկնալ, իմանալ, ըմբռնել, պարփակել)
comprehensible - hasgunali, imanali, umperneli (հասկնալի, իմանալի, ըմբռնելի)
comprehension - umpernoum, umpernoghoutiun (ըմբռնում, ըմբռնողութիւն)
comprehensive - umperneli, hasgunali (ըմբռնելի, հասկնալի)
compress - junshel, seghmel, viragab (ճնշել, սեղմել, վիրակապ)
compression - seghmoum, junshoum (սեղմում, ճնշում)
compressor - junshag, junshogh mekena (ճնշակ, ճնշող մեքենայ)
comprise - barounagel, povantagel (պարունակել, բովանդակել)
compromise - hamakhohoutiun, zichoum, hamatsaynil (համախոհութիւն, զիջում, համաձայնիլ)
compromit - vudankel, khosdanal (վտանգել, խոստանալ)
comptograph - hashvemekena (հաշուեմեքենայ)
comptroller - hashvekunnich (հաշուեքննիչ)
compulsion - usdiboum, purnatadoum (ստիպում, բռնադատում)
compunction - khughjaharoutiun, zughchoum (խղճահարութիւն, զղջում)
computation - hashvarg, hashiv (հաշուարկ, հաշիւ)
compute - hashvel, tuvel (հաշուել, թուել)
computer - hamagarkich, hashvich mekana (համակարգիչ, հաշուիչ մեքենայ)
comrade - paregam, unger (բարեկամ, ընկեր)
con - kots sorvil, serdel (գոց սորվիլ, սերտել)
concave - kokavor, pos, tadarg, porel (գոգաւոր, փոս, դատարկ, փորել)
concavity - kokavoroutiun (գոգաւորութիւն)
conceal - dzadzgel, bahel (ծածկել, պահել)
concede - touyladrel, untounil, deghi dal (թոյլատրել, ընդունիլ, տեղի

տալ)
conceit - inknahamaroum, inknakoh, sin, hughanal (ինքնահամարում, ինքնագոհ, սին, յղանալ)
conceivable - umperneli, imanali (ըմբռնելի, իմանալի)
conceive - hughanal, umpernel, yerevagayel (յղանալ, ըմբռնել, երեւակայել)
conceiver - hughatsogh (յղացող)
concenter - getronatsnel, getronanal, ampopvil (կեդրոնացնել, կեդրոնանալ, ամփոփուիլ)
concentrate - getronatsnel, hamakhumpel, khudanal (կեդրոնացնել, համախմբել, խտանալ)
concentration - getronatsoum, hamakhumpoum, tantsuratsoum (կեդրոնացում, համախմբում, թանձրացում)
concentric - hamagetron (համակեդրոն)
concept - mudabadger, mudahughatsoum, hughatsk (մտապատկեր, մտայղացում, յղացք)
conception - hughoutiun, hughatsoum, umpurnoum, hayetsaged (յղութիւն, յղացում, ըմբռնում, հայեցակէտ)
concern - veraperil, badganil, vajaradoun (վերաբերիլ, պատկանիլ, վաճառատուն)
concert - hamerk, nevakahantes, yerkahantes, hamatsaynil (համերգ, նուագահանդէս, երգահանդէս, համաձայնիլ)
concertation - jik, baykar (ճիգ, պայքար)
concerted - nertashnag, hamatsaynuvadz (ներդաշնակ, համաձայնուած)
concertion - hamatsaynoum, garkatu routiun (համաձայնում, կարգադրութիւն)
concerto - menanuvak (մենանուագ)
concession - zichoum, ardonoutiun (զիջում, արտօնութիւն)
concierge - turnaban, bahag, dunabah (դռնապան, պահակ, տնապահ)
conciliate - hashdetsunel, hamatsaynetsunel (հաշտեցնել, համաձայնեցնել)
conciliation - hashdoutiun, hamatsaynoutiun (հաշտութիւն, համաձայնութիւն)
conciliator - hashdarar (հաշտարար)
concinnate - haramaretsunel (յարմարեցնել)
concionate - karozel (քարոզել)
concionator - karozich (քարոզիչ)
concise - garj, hagirj (կարճ, հակիրճ)
concision - gurjadoum, hertsuvadz (կրճատում, հերձուած)
conclave - babundir zhoghov, zhoghovadeghi (պապընտիր ժողով, ժողովատեղի)
conclude - yezragatsunel, hedevtsunel, avardel (եզրակացնել, հետեւցնել, աւարտել)
conclusion - yezragatsoutiun, hedevant, avard, voroshoum (եզրակացութիւն, հետեւանք, աւարտ, որոշում)
concoct - badrasdel, dzurakurel, khorhil (պատրաստել, ծրագրել, խորհիլ)
concomitant - zoukuntats, hamuntats (զուգընթաց, համընթաց)
concord - hamatsaynoutiun, tashink, hamatsaynil (համաձայնութիւն, դաշինք, համաձայնիլ)
concordance - hamatsaynoutiun, hamabadaskhan ullalu (համաձայնութիւն, համապատասխան ըլլալը)
concourse - hamakhumpoum, hamakoumar, murtsank (համախմբում, համագումար, մրցանք)
concrete (I) - hasdadoun, miatsouyl, khudatsial, turdzashaghakh (հաստատուն, միաձոյլ, խտացեալ, թրծաշաղախ)
concrete (II) - tantsuranal (թանձրանալ)
concretion - tantsuratsoum, magartoum (թանձրացում, մակարդում)
concupiscence - vavashodoutiun, heshdasiroutiun (վաւաշոտութիւն, հեշտասիրութիւն)
concupy - tsangasiroutiun (ցանկասիրութիւն)
concur - kordsagtsil, hamatsaynil

(գործակցիլ, համաձայնիլ)
concusion - tsuntsoum, harvadz, dugaratsoum (ցնցում, հարուած, տկարացում)
concuss - khankarel, tsuntsel (խանգարել, ցնցել)
condemn - tadabardel, meghaturel (դատապարտել, մեղադրել)
condemnation - tadabardoutiun (դատապարտութիւն)
condemner - tadabardogh (դատապարտող)
condensate - khudatsunel, khudatsadz (խտացնել, խտացած)
condensation - khudatsoum, khudatsnoum (խտացում, խտացնում)
condense - khudatsunel, tantsuratsunel (խտացնել, թանձրացնել)
condenser - khudatsoutsich, khudarar (խտացուցիչ, խտարար)
condescend - zichanil, khonarhil (զիջանիլ, խոնարհիլ)
condescension - khonarhoum, parehajoutiun (խոնարհում, բարեհաճութիւն)
condign - arzhani, arzhanavor, harmar (արժանի, արժանաւոր, յարմար)
condiment - hamem, tatsan (համեմ, թացան)
condition - bayman, vijag, gatsoutiun, hankamank (պայման, վիճակ, կացութիւն, հանգամանք)
conditional - baymanagan, teagan (պայմանական, թէական)
conditionate - baymanavorel, baymanaturel (պայմանաւորել, պայմանադրել)
conditioner - parelavogh, baymanavorogh (բարելաւող, պայմանաւորող)
conditioning - zovatsvadz, baymanavorvadz (զովացուած, պայմանաւորուած)
condole - tsavagtsil, vushdagtsil, voghpal (ցաւակցիլ, վշտակցիլ, ողբալ)
condolence - tsavagtsoutiun, vushdagtsoutiun (ցաւակցութիւն, վշտակցութիւն)
condom - abahovich, bahbanag hughoutian tem (ապահովիչ, պահպանակ յղութեան դէմ)
condominium - hamadirabedoum, diragtsoutiun (համատիրութիւն, տիրակցութիւն)
condonation - neroum (ներում)
conduce - badjarel, nubasdel, arachnortel (պատճառել, նպաստել, առաջնորդել)
conducible - nubasdavor (նպաստաւոր)
conduct - arachnortel, oughghel, varel, untatsk, vark (առաջնորդել, ուղղել, վարել, ընթացք, վարք)
conductor - khumpavar, arachnort, ghegavar, varich (խմբավար, առաջնորդ, ղեկավար, վարիչ)
confect - anoushepel, kharnel, gazmel (անուշեփել, խառնել, կազմել)
confection - kaghtsureghen, shakareghen (քաղցրեղէն, շաքարեղէն)
confectioner - shakarakordz, dzagharar (շաքարագործ, ծաղարար)
confeder - tashnagtsil (դաշնակցիլ)
confederate - tashnagits, zinagits, tashnagtsil (դաշնակից, զինակից, դաշնակցիլ)
confederation - tashnagtsoutiun, hamatashnagtsoutiun (դաշնակցութիւն, համադաշնակցութիւն)
confer - khorhurtagtsil, shunorhel, badvel (խորհրդակցիլ, շնորհել, պատուել)
conferee - khorhurtagtsogh, khorhurtagan, untounogh (խորհրդակցող, խորհրդական, ընդունող)
conference - khorhurtagtsoutiun, khorhurtazhoghov (խորհրդակցութիւն, խորհրդաժողով)
confess - khosdovanil, untounil (խոստովանիլ, ընդունիլ)
confession - khosdovanoutiun, khosdovanank (խոստովանութիւն, խոստովանանք)
confessor - khosdovanogh, khosdovanahayr (խոստովանող, խոստովանահայր)
confide - havadal, vusdahil (հաւատալ, վստահիլ)

confidence - vusdahoutiun, havadk, havasdik (վստահութիւն, հաւատք, հաւաստիք)
confident - muderim, khorhurtagits, vusdah (մտերիմ, խորհրդակից, վստահ)
confidential - mudermagan, kaghduni, khorhurtabahagan (մտերմական, գաղտնի, խորհրդապահական)
configuration - gerbarank, ardakin tsev (կերպարանք, արտաքին ձեւ)
configure - tsevapokhel, tsevel (ձեւափոխել, ձեւել)
confine - sahman, yezur, sahmanel, voroshel, pagel (սահման, եզր, սահմանել, որոշել, փակել)
confirm - hasdadel, abahovel (հաստատել, ապահովել)
confirmation - hasdadoum, vaveratsoum, azkaturoshm, gunik (հաստատում, վաւերացում, ազգադրոշմ, կնիք)
confiscate - purnakuravel, arnel (բռնագրաւել, առնել)
confiscation - purnakuravoum (բռնագրաւում)
confiture - anousheghen (անուշեղէն)
conflict - pakhoum, guriv, vej, untharoum (բախում, կռիւ, վէճ, ընդհարում)
conform - hamanuman, hamagerbil, badshajil (համանման, համակերպիլ, պատշաճիլ)
conformer - hamagerbogh (համակերպող)
confortable - hankusdaved, hankisd (հանգստաւէտ, հանգիստ)
confound - shupotel, kharnagel, shupot, kharun (շփոթել, խառնակել, շփոթ, խառն)
confront - jagadil, unttimatrel (ճակատիլ, ընդդիմադրել)
confrontation - jagadoum, unttimoutiun (ճակատում, ընդդիմութիւն)
confuse - shupotel, khankarel (շփոթել, խանգարել)
confusion - shupotoutiun, khoujab (շփոթութիւն, խուճապ)
confutation - herkoum (հերքում)
confute - herkel, churel (հերքել, ջրել)
conge - artsagourt, hurazheshd, hurazheshd arnel (արձակուրդ, հրաժեշտ, հրաժեշտ առնել)
congeal - saretsunel, baghetsunel (սառեցնել, պաղեցնել)
congelation - saroum (սառում)
congenital - punadzin, i dzune, untodzin (բնածին, ի ծնէ, ընդոծին)
congest - goudagel, tizel, khujoghel (կուտակել, դիզել, խճողել)
congestion - ariunakhurnoum, goudagoum (արիւնախռնում, կուտակում)
congratulate - shunorhavorel (շնորհաւորել)
congratulation - shunorhavoroutiun (շնորհաւորութիւն)
congregate - havakvil, havakel, koumarel, havakvadz (հաւաքուիլ, հաւաքել, գումարել, հաւաքուած)
congregation - hamakhumpoum, zhoghov (համախմբում, ժողով)
congress - hamazhoghov, hamakoumar, khorhurtaran (համաժողով, համագումար, խորհրդարան)
congressman - yerespokhan (երեսփոխան)
congrue - badshajil, hamatsaynil (պատշաճիլ, համաձայնիլ)
congruence, cy - harmaroutiun, badshajoutiun (յարմարութիւն, պատշաճութիւն)
congruent - harmar, badshaj (յարմար, պատշաճ)
conic - gonatsev (կոնաձեւ)
conject - yentaturel, nedel, chapchupel (ենթադրել, նետել, չափչըփել)
conjecture - gardzik, yentaturoutiun, vargadz (կարծիք, ենթադրութիւն, վարկած)
conjoin - miatsunel, mianal, ludzagtsil (միացնել, միանալ, լծակցիլ)
conjugal - amousnagan, ludzagtsagan (ամուսնական, լծակցական)
conjugate - amousnatsunel, khonarhel, ludzort (ամուսնացնել, խոնարհել, լծորդ)
conjunction - shaghgab, miatsoum (շաղկապ, միացում)

conjuncture - gabagtsoutiun, hankamank (կապակցութիւն, համգամանք)
conjure - yertvetsunel, aghersel, tavaturel (երդուեցնել, աղերսել, դաւադրել)
conjurer, conjuror - ajbarar, gakhart (աճպարար, կախարդ)
connect - gabel, miatsunel (կապել, միացնել)
connection - gab, gabagtsoutiun, haraperoutiun (կապ, կապակցութիւն, յարաբերութիւն)
connoisseur - janchtsogh, kidtsogh, hasgutsogh, humoud (ճանչցող, գիտցող, հասկցող, հմուտ)
conquer - haghtel, nuvajel, direl (յաղթել, նուաճել, տիրել)
conqueror - haghtogh, ashkharhagal (յաղթող, աշխարհակալ)
consanguin - ariunagits (արիւնակից)
conscience - khighj, khughjmudank (խիղճ, խղճմտանք)
conscious - kidagits, irazeg (գիտակից, իրազեկ)
conscript - zinvorakurel, norazen (զինուորագրել, նորազէն)
conscription - zinvorakuroutiun (զինուորագրութիւն)
consecrate - nuvirakordzel, undzayel, orhnial (նուիրագործել, ընծայել, օրհնեալ)
consecration - nouirakordzoutiun, odzoum (նուիրագործութիւն, օծում)
consecute - hedevil, hedabuntel (հետեւիլ, հետապնդել)
consecutive - hachortagan, ananunthad (յաջորդական, անընդհատ)
consent - hamagerbil, havanil, untounil (համակերպիլ, հաւանիլ, ընդունիլ)
consequence - hedevank, artiunk (հետեւանք, արդիւնք)
consequently - hedevapar (հետեւաբար)
conservation - bahbanoum, bahbanoutiun (պահպանում, պահպանութիւն)
conservative - bahogh, bahbanoghagan (պահող, պահպանողական)
conservatory - yerazhushdanots, bahbanoghagan (երաժշտանոց, պահպանողական)
conserve - bahel, bahbanel, bahadzo (պահել, պահպանել, պահածոյ)
consider - nugadel, tidel, kunnel, harkel (նկատել, դիտել, քննել, յարգել)
considerable - nugadeli, garevor (նկատելի, կարեւոր)
considerate - papganugad, uzkouysh, khohagan (փափկանկատ, զգոյշ, խոհական)
consideration - nugadaroum, nugadoum, garevoroutiun (նկատարում, նկատում, կարեւորութիւն)
consign - hantsunel, avantel, vusdahil, ghurgel (յանձնել, աւանդել, վստահիլ, ղրկել)
consignee - hantsnarou, hantsnagadar, untounogh (յանձնառու, յանձնակատար, ընդունող)
consigner - hantsunogh, ghurgogh (յանձնող, ղրկող)
consignment - avant, bahesd, hantsnoum, bahavajar (աւանդ, պահեստ, յանձնում, պահավաճառ)
consist - gayanal, paghganal (կայանալ, բաղկանալ)
consistence, cy - dogounoutiun, serdoutiun, buntoutiun (տոկունութիւն, սերտութիւն, պնդութիւն)
consistent - hasdad, dogoun, bint (հաստատ, տոկուն, պինդ)
consolate - mukhitarel (մխիթարել)
consolation - mukhitaroutiun, uspopoum (մխիթարութիւն, սփոփում)
console - mukhitarel, uspopel, henaran, gahagal (մխիթարել, սփոփել, յենարան, կահակալ)
consolidate - amratsunel, hasdadel, amrabuntel, buntel (ամրացնել, հաստատել, ամրապնդել, պնդել)
consonant - paghatsayn, nouynatsayn (բաղաձայն, նոյնաձայն)
conspectus - ourvakidz (ուրուագիծ)
conspicuous - desaneli, agnerev (տեսանելի, ակներեւ)
conspiracy - tavatroutiun, mekena-

youtiun (դաւադրութիւն, մեքենայութիւն)
conspiration - tavaturoutiun (դաւադրութիւն)
conspirator - tavatir (դաւադիր)
conspire - tavaturel, dzurakurel (դաւադրել, ծրագրել)
conspirer - tavaturogh (դաւադրող)
constant - hasdad, gayoun, anpopokh (հաստատ, կայուն, անփոփոխ)
constate - hasdadel, usdoukel, abatsoutsel (հաստատել, ստուգել, ապացուցել)
constellation - hamasdeghoutiun (համաստեղութիւն)
consternation - sarsap, ahapegoutiun, arhavirk (սարսափ, ահաբեկութիւն, արհաւիրք)
constipate - buntatsunel (պնդացնել)
constipation - buntoutiun, khurnoum (պնդութիւն, խռնում)
constituent - paghgatsoutsich, kuveargogh (բաղկացուցիչ, քուէարկող)
constitute - gazmel, hasdadel, himnel (կազմել, հաստատել, հիմնել)
constitution - sahmanaturoutiun, gazm (սահմանադրութիւն, կազմ)
constitutional - sahmanaturagan (սահմանադրական)
constrain - usdibel, purnatadel, usdiboum (ստիպել, բռնադատել, ստիպում)
constrict - seghmel, burgel, buntel (սեղմել, պրկել, պնդել)
constriction - usdiboum, arkilapagoum (ստիպում, արգիլափակում)
construct - shinel, garoutsanel, gazmel (շինել, կառուցանել, կազմել)
construction - shinoutiun, garoutsoum (շինութիւն, կառուցում)
constructive - shinich, garoutsoghagan (շինիչ, կառուցողական)
constructure - shenk, garoutsvadzk, horinvadzk (շէնք, կառուցուածք, յօրինուածք)
construe - megnel, loudzel, patsadurel (մեկնել, լուծել, բացատրել)
consul - hiubados (հիւպատոս)
consulate - hiubadosoutiun, hiubadosaran (հիւպատոսութիւն, հիւպատոսարան)
consult - khorhurtagtsil, kunnel (խորհրդակցիլ, քննել)
consultation - khorhurtagtsoutiun, khorhourt (խորհրդակցութիւն, խորհուրդ)
consumate - gadarelakordzel, avardel (կատարելագործել, աւարտել)
consume - usbarel, vadnel (սպառել, վատնել)
consumer - usbarogh, vadnogh (սպառող, վատնող)
consumption - usbaroum, mashoum, hiudzoum (սպառում, մաշում, հիւծում)
contact - shupoum, huboum, gab (շփում, հպում, կապ)
contagion - varagoum, pokhantsoum (վարակում, փոխանցում)
contagious - varagich, pokhantsig (վարակիչ, փոխանցիկ)
contain - povantagel, barounagel (բովանդակել, պարունակել)
container - pernasundoug, pokhatrampar, barounagogh (բեռնասնտուկ, փոխադրամբար, պարունակող)
contaminate - varagel, abaganel, bighdz, abaganial (վարակել, ապականել, պիղծ, ապականեալ)
contamination - abaganoutiun, nekhoum (ապականութիւն, նեխում)
contemn - arhamarhel, andesel (արհամարհել, անտեսել)
contemplate - tidel, zunnel, khogal, hianal (դիտել, զննել, խոկալ, հիանալ)
contemplation - khogoum, nugadoum, hiatsoum (խոկում, նկատում, հիացում)
contemporary - zhamanagagits (ժամանակակից)
contempt - arhamarhank, andesoum (արհամարհանք, անտեսում)
contemptible - arhamarheli, anark (արհամարհելի, անարգ)
contemptuous - arhamarhod, koroz (արհամարհոտ, գոռոզ)
contend - gurvil, hagaragil, vijil

(կռուիլ, Հակառակիլ, վիճիլ)
contender - vijogh, baykarogh (վիճող, պայքարող)
content - barounagoutiun, dzaval, koh, kohatsunel (պարունակութիւն, ծաւալ, գոհ, գոհացնել)
contentation - kohounagoutiun (գոհունակութիւն)
contention - vej, baykar, hagaragoutiun (վէճ, պայքար, Հակառակութիւն)
contentious - vijeli, vijaser, gurvaser (վիճելի, վիճասէր, կռուասէր)
contentment - kohounagoutiun, kohatsoum (գոհունակութիւն, գոհացում)
contents - povantagoutiun (բովանդակութիւն)
contest (n) - hagaragoutiun, baykar, guriv, murtsoum, vej (Հակառակութիւն, պայքար, կռիւ, մրցում, վէճ)
contest (v) - hagaragil, baykaril, gurvil, vijil, ouranal (Հակառակիլ, պայքարիլ, կռուիլ, վիճիլ, ուրանալ)
contex - hiusel, miatsunel, gabagtsoutiun (Հիւսել, միացնել, կապակցութիւն)
context - punakidz, kuradzir (բնագիծ, գրածիր)
contexture - panahiusoutiun, hiusvadzk, gabagtsoutiun (բանաՀիւսութիւն, Հիւսուածք, կապակցութիւն)
contiguity - haragtsoutiun, mertsagtsoutiun (յարակցութիւն, մերձակցութիւն)
continence - zhouzhgaloutiun, uzkasdoutiun (ժուժկալութիւն, զգաստութիւն)
continent - tsamakamas, yergir, zhouzhgal (ցամաքամաս, երկիր, ժուժկալ)
continental - tsamakayin, yevrobagan (ցամաքային, եւրոպական)
contingent - badahagan, pazhin, mas (պատաՀական, բաժին, մաս)
continiuous - anunthad, sharounag, irerahachort (անընդՀատ, շարունակ, իրերայաջորդ)
continuation - sharounagoutiun (շարունակութիւն)
continue - sharounagel, yergarel, devel (շարունակել, երկարել, տեւել)
continuity - sharounagoutiun, devaganoutiun (շարունակութիւն, տեւականութիւն)
contort - volorel, kalarel (ոլորել, գալարել)
contortion - voloroum, kalaroum, kheghatiuroum (ոլորում, գալարում, խեղաթիւրում)
contour - shurchakidz, shurchabad, dzir (շրջագիծ, շրջապատ, ծիր)
contra - haga, hagarag, tem (Հակա, Հակառակ, դէմ)
contraband - maksanenkoutiun (մաքսանենգութիւն)
contraception - hughoutian arvesdagan arkiloum (յղութեան արուեստական արգիլում)
contract - ampopel, hamatsaynil, baymanakir (ամփոփել, Համաձայնիլ, պայմանագիր)
contraction - gudzgoum, ampopoum, gurjadoum (կծկում, ամփոփում, կրճատում)
contractor - hantsnarou, gabalarou (յանձնառու, կապալառու)
contradict - hagasel, zhukhdel, ouranal (Հակասել, ժխտել, ուրանալ)
contradiction - hagasoutiun (Հակասութիւն)
contrary - hagarag, nerhag (Հակառակ, ներՀակ)
contrast - hagaturel, hagabadger, hagaturoutiun (Հակադրել, Հակապատկեր, Հակադրութիւն)
contravene - hagaragil, hagasel, avrel (Հակառակիլ, Հակասել, աւրել)
contravention - unttimoutiun, orinazantsoutiun (ընդդիմութիւն, օրինազանցութիւն)
contribute - sadarel, nubasdel, oknel (սատարել, նպաստել, օգնել)
contribution - nubasd, hankanagoutiun, pazhin, purnaharg (նպաստ, Հանգանակութիւն, բաժին, բռնա-

Հարկ)
contributor - nubasdogh, oknogh, kordzagits (Նպաստող, օգնող, գործակից)
contrition - zughchoum, vushdagtsoutiun (զղջում, վշտակցութիւն)
contrivance - hunark, kiud, tav (Հնարք, գիւտ, դաւ)
contrive - hunarel, dzurakurel, tsevatsunel (Հնարել, ծրագրել, ձեւացնել)
control - kunnel, hagagushrel, kunnoutiun, hagagushir (քննել, Հակակշռել, քննութիւն, Հակակշիռ)
controller - verahusgich, hamararou (վերաՀսկիչ, Համարարու)
controverse - vijil (վիճիլ)
controversial - vijeli, hagajareli, hagamard (վիճելի, Հակաճառելի, Հակամարտ)
controversy - vej, vijapanoutiun, hagajaroutiun (վէճ, վիճաբանութիւն, Հակաճառութիւն)
controvert - hagajarel, vijapanil, ouranal (Հակաճառել, վիճաբանիլ, ուրանալ)
contumacious - hamar, anhunazant, umposd (յամառ, անՀնազանդ, ըմբոստ)
contumacy - hamaroutiun, orinazantsoutiun (յամառութիւն, օրինազանցութիւն)
contumely - tushnamank, lurpoutiun (Թշնամանք, լրբութիւն)
contuse - jumlel, pushrel (ճմլել, փշրել)
contusion - jumloum (ճմլում)
conundrum - haneloug, areghdzuvadz (Հանելուկ, առեղծուած)
convalesce - aroghchanal, abakinil, pouzhvil (առողջանալ, ապաքինիլ, բուժուիլ)
convalescence - abakinoum, pouzhoum (ապաքինում, բուժում)
convection - pokhantsoum (փոխանցում)
convene - havakvil, havakel, tadi ganchel (Հաւաքուիլ, Հաւաքել, դատի կանչել)
convenience - harmaroutiun, badshajoutiun (յարմարութիւն, պատշաճութիւն)
convenient - harmar, badshaj, vayelouch (յարմար, պատշաճ, վայելուչ)
convent - vank, vanadoun, menasdan (վանք, վանատուն, մենաստան)
convention - hamakoumar, hamatsaynoutiun, tashink (Համագումար, Համաձայնութիւն, դաշինք)
converge - nouyn gedin tsukdil (նոյն կէտին ձգտիլ)
conversation - khosagtsoutiun, zurouyts (խօսակցութիւն, զրոյց)
converse - khosagtsil, haraperil (խօսակցիլ, յարաբերիլ)
conversion - shurchoum, popokhoum, tarts (շրջում, փոփոխում, դարձ)
convert - pokhel, tartsunel, tarnal, veradzel, guronapokh (փոխել, դարձնել, դառնալ, վերածել, կրօնափոխ)
converter - tartsunogh, pokhogh, pokhargich (դարձնող, փոխող, փոխարկիչ)
convertibility - pokhargelioutiun (փոխարկելիութիւն)
convertion - guronapokhoutiun, shurchoum, tarts (կրօնափոխութիւն, շրջում, դարձ)
convey - gurel, danil, pokhaturel (կրել, տանիլ, փոխադրել)
conveyance - pokhaturoutiun, pokhantsoum (փոխադրութիւն, փոխանցում)
convict - tadabardel, hantsavor (դատապարտել, յանցաւոր)
conviction - tadabardoutiun, hamozoum, abatsouyts (դատապարտութիւն, Համոզում, ապացոյց)
convince - hamozel, abatsoutsel (Համոզել, ապացուցել)
convincible - hamozich (Համոզիչ)
convocation - huraver, khumpoum, zhoghov (Հրաւէր, խմբում, ժողով)
convoke - koumarel, zhoghovi ganchel, huravirel (գումարել, ժողովի կանչել, Հրաւիրել)
convolution - kalaroum, voloroum (գալարում, ոլորում)

convolve - kalarel, volorel (գալարել, ոլորել)
convoy - shukakhoump, garashar, tapor, oughegtsil (շքախումբ, կառաշար, Թափոր, ուղեկցիլ)
convulse - tsuntsel, burgel, gudzgel (ցնցել, պրկել, կծկել)
convulsion - tsuntsoum, kalaroum, chughatsukoutiun (ցնցում, գալարում, ջղաձգութիւն)
cony - nabasdag, jakar (նապաստակ, ճագար)
cook - yepel, khoharar (եփել, խոհարար)
cookbook - jashakirk (ճաշագիրք)
cookery - khohararoutiun (խոհարարութիւն)
cooky - pulit (բլիթ)
cool - bagh, zov, hantard, baghil, baghetsunel (պաղ, զով, հանդարտ, պաղիլ, պաղեցնել)
cooper - dagarakordz (տակառագործ)
cooperate - kordzagtsil, oknel (գործակցիլ, օգնել)
cooperation - kordzagtsoutiun, nertashnagoutiun (գործակցութիւն, ներդաշնակութիւն)
cooperative - hamakordzagtsagan, kordzagtsagan ungeroutiun (համագործակցական, գործակցական ընկերութիւն)
cooperator - kordzagtsogh (գործակցող)
coordinate - hamagarkel, nertashnagel, tasavorel, hamagark (համակարգել, ներդաշնակել, դասաւորել, համակարգ)
coordination - hamagarkoutiun, nertashnagoutiun (համակարգութիւն, ներդաշնակութիւն)
coordinator - hamagarkogh, garkavorogh (համակարգող, կարգաւորող)
copier - untorinagogh, numanadubogh (ընդօրինակող, նմանատպող)
copious - arad, hort (առատ, յորդ)
copper - bighints, bughuntsia (պղինձ, պղնձեայ)
coppice - bourag, bouragel (պուրակ, պուրակել)
copy - badjenahanel, orinag, badjen (պատճենահանել, օրինակ, պատճէն)
copybook - keghakradedur, keghakroutiun (գեղագրատետր, գեղագրութիւն)
copyguard - ardatrarkel (արտադրարգել)
copying machine - badjenahan, lousadib mekena (պատճէնահան, լուսատիպ մեքենայ)
copyright - heghinagi iravounk, dubelou iravasoutiun (հեղինակի իրաւունք, տպելու իրաւասութիւն)
coquet - buchril, chanal havnuvil, kudznil (պչրիլ, ջանալ հաւնուիլ, քծնիլ)
coquette - buchrouhi (պչրուհի)
cord - baran, chuvan (պարան, չուան)
cordial - siralir, surdakin (սիրալիր, սրտագին)
cordless phone - antel heratsayn (անթել հեռաձայն)
cordon - chuvan, lar, yeriz, gab, zorashughta (չուան, լար, երիզ, կապ, զօրաշղթայ)
core - michoug, goriz, geghvel, panal (միջուկ, կորիզ, կեղուել, բանալ)
Corea - korea (Քորէա)
cork - khits, khutsan, soung, khutsel (խից, խցան, սունկ, խցել)
corkscrew - khutsahan (խցահան)
corn - yekibdatsoren, tsoren, armudik, vodki goshd (եգիպտացորեն, ցորեն, արմտիք, ոտքի կոշտ)
corner - angiun, tartsuvadzk (անկիւն, դարձուածք)
corner stone - angiunakar (անկիւնաքար)
cornerstone - anguinakar (անկիւնաքար)
cornet - pogh, yegchiur, godosh, turoshagir, kudag (փող, եղջիւր, կոտոշ, դրօշակիր, գտակ)
cornice - kiv (քիւ)
corol - busag (պսակ)
corollary - hedevoutiun, hedevank

(հետեւութիւն, հետեւանք)
coronary - busagatsev (պսակաձեւ)
coronation - takaturoutiun (թագադրութիւն)
corporal - marmunagan, dasnabed (մարմնական, տասնապետ)
corporate - ungeroutiun gazmel, miatsial (ընկերութիւն կազմել, միացեալ)
corporation - ungeragtsoutiun, ungeroutiun (ընկերակցութիւն, ընկերութիւն)
corps - panag, khoump, marmin (բանակ, խումբ, մարմին)
corpse - tiag, marmin (դիակ, մարմին)
corpsecandle - merelamom (մեռելամոմ)
corpulence - musodoutiun, kiroutiun, khudoutiun (մսոտութիւն, գիրութիւն, խտութիւն)
corpulent - musod, ker, marmunegh (մսոտ, գէր, մարմնեղ)
corral - tsangabad, shurchapagel (ցանկապատ, շրջափակել)
correct - jishd, oughigh, surpakurel, shudgel (ճիշդ, ուղիղ, սրբագրել, շտկել)
correction - surpakuroutiun, shudgoum (սրբագրութիւն, շտկում)
correctness - jushtoutiun, shidagoutiun (ճշդութիւն, շիտակութիւն)
correlate - gabagtsil, arunchuvil (կապակցիլ, առնչուիլ)
correlation - gabagtsoutiun, arunchoutiun (կապակցութիւն, առնչութիւն)
correspond - tughtagtsil, hamabadaskhanel (թղթակցիլ, համապատասխանել)
correspondence - tughtagtsoutiun, gab, namagagtsoutiun (թղթակցութիւն, կապ, նամակակցութիւն)
correspondent - tughtagits, hamabadaskhan (թղթակից, համապատասխան)
corridor - nurpantsk (նրբանցք)
corrigible - shudgeli, oughgheli (ճշկելի, ուղղելի)
corroborate - havasdel, hasdadel, zoratsunel (հաւաստել, հաստատել, զօրացնել)
corrode - gurdzel, halel, mashel, mashil (կրծել, հալել, մաշել, մաշիլ)
corrosion - gurdzoum, mashoum, haloum (կրծում, մաշում, հալում)
corrugate - gunjurel, khorshomel, khorshomial (կնճռել, խորշոմել, խորշոմեալ)
corrupt - avruvadz, pudadz, abaganil (աւրուած, փտած, ապականիլ)
corruption - abaganoutiun, nekhoum, gashark (ապականութիւն, նեխում, կաշառք)
corruptness - pudoutiun, gasharasiroutiun (փտութիւն, կաշառասիրութիւն)
corsage - seghmiran, lanchazkesd (սեղմիրան, լանջազգեստ)
corsair - dzovahen, avazag, asbadaganav (ծովահէն, աւազակ, ասպատականաւ)
corse - marmin, tiag (մարմին, դիակ)
corset - seghmiran, lanchagal, seghmiranel (սեղմիրան, լանջակալ, սեղմիրանել)
cortege - tapor, shukakhoump (թափօր, շքախումբ)
coruscate - paylil, shoghal (փայլիլ, շողալ)
cosmetic - keghakidagan, keghategh (գեղագիտական, գեղադեղ)
cosmetic surgery - keghakidagan kordzoghoutiun (գեղագիտական գործողութիւն)
cosmetics - odzanelik (օծանելիք)
cosmic - diyezeragan (տիեզերական)
cosmic rays - diyezeragan jarakaytner (տիեզերական ճառագայթներ)
cosmology - diyezarakidoutiun (տիեզերագիտութիւն)
cosmopolitan - ashkharhakaghakatsiagan, pazmakaghakatsigan (աշխարհաքաղաքացիական, բազմաքաղաքացիական)
cosmopolite - ashkharhakaghakatsi (աշխարհաքաղաքացի)

cosmos - *diyezerk, ashkhar, hamagarkoutiun (տիեզերք, աշխարհ, համակարգութիւն)*
cost - *kin, arzhek, dzakhk, arzhel (գին, արժէք, ծախք, արժել)*
cost price - *arzhekin (արժէգին)*
costly - *sough, medzadzakhs (սուղ, մեծածախս)*
costume - *daraz, hamazkesd, hakousd (տարազ, համազգեստ, հագուստ)*
cosy - *hankusdaved, gogig (հանգստաւէտ, կոկիկ)*
cottage - *dunag, khurjit (տնակ, խրճիթ)*
cotton - *pambag (բամպակ)*
couch - *bargetsunel, daradzel, angoghnel (պառկեցնել, տարածել, անկողնել)*
coucher - *bargetsunogh, daradzogh (պառկեցնող, տարածող)*
cough - *hazal, haz (հազալ, հազ)*
council - *khorhourt, adian, khorhurtagtsoutiun (խորհուրդ, ատեան, խորհրդակցութիւն)*
councillor, councilman - *khourhurti antam (խորհուրդի անդամ)*
councilman - *khorhourti antam (խորհուրդի անդամ)*
counsel - *khorhurtagtsoutiun, khurad, khuradel (խորհրդակցութիւն, խրատ, խրատել)*
counselor, counsellor - *khorhurtadou, orenusked (խորհրդատու, օրէնսգէտ)*
count - *hamrel, hashvel, tuvel (համրել, հաշուել, թուել)*
countenance - *gerbarank, temk, ardahaydoutiun (կերպարանք, դէմք, արտայայտութիւն)*
counter - *hashvogh, hashveseghan, unttem (հաշուող, հաշուեսեղան, ընդդէմ)*
counteract - *hagaztel (հակազդել)*
counterattack - *hagahartsagoum (հակայարձակում)*
counterfeit - *geghdz, shindzou, geghdzel (կեղծ, շինծու, կեղծել)*
countess - *gomsouhi (կոմսուհի)*
country - *yergir, hayrenik, kiugh, kiughagan (երկիր, հայրենիք, գիւղ, գիւղական)*
county - *gomsoutiun, nahank, kavar (կոմսութիւն, նահանգ, գաւառ)*
coup - *harvadz (հարուած)*
couple - *zouyk, amol, amousnatsunel (զոյգ, ամոլ, ամուսնացնել)*
coupon - *gudron (կտրօն)*
courage - *kachoutiun, arioutiun (քաջութիւն, արիութիւն)*
courageous - *kach, ari, gudrij (քաջ, արի, կտրիճ)*
courb - *goranal, goratsadz (կորանալ, կորացած)*
courrier - *sourhantag, namagadar, namagaper, oratert (սուրհանդակ, նամակատար, նամակաբեր, օրաթերթ)*
course - *vazk, arshav, tasuntatsk, shurchan, vazel (վազք, արշաւ, դասընթացք, շրջան, վազել)*
court (n) - *tadaran, balad, pag (դատարան, պալատ, բակ)*
court (v) - *tarbasel, sirapanil, hurabourel, kudznil (դարպասել, սիրաբանիլ, հրապուրել, գծնիլ)*
courteous - *paregirt, kaghakavar (բարեկիրթ, քաղաքավար)*
courtesy - *kaghakavaroutiun, harkank, voghchounel (քաղաքավարութիւն, յարգանք, ողջունել)*
courthouse - *tadaran (դատարան)*
courtier - *baladagan, shoghokort (պալատական, շողոքորթ)*
courtlike - *kaghakavar, shunorhali (քաղաքավար, շնորհալի)*
courtling - *bunagalez (պնակալէզ)*
courtroom - *tadaseniag (դատասենեակ)*
courtyard - *pag, kavit (բակ, գաւիթ)*
cousin - *zarmig, zarmouhi (զարմիկ, զարմուհի)*
cove - *dzotsig, khorshig, gamarel (ծոցիկ, խորշիկ, կամարել)*
covenant - *tashink, oukhd, tashink gunkel, oukhdel (դաշինք, ուխտ, դաշինք կնքել, ուխտել)*
cover - *dzadzgel, bahel, goghk, dzadzgots (ծածկել, պահել, կողք,

ծածկոց)
cover girl - goghki aghchig, goghkaghchig (կողքի աղջիկ, կողքաղջիկ)
covert - dzadzoug, dzadzguvadz, bashdbanvadz, badusbaran (ծածուկ, ծածկուած, պաշտպանուած, պատսպարան)
coverture - takusdots, dzadzgaran, bashdbanoutiun (Թագստոց, ծածկարան, պաշտպանուԹիւն)
covet - tsangal, denchal, achk dungel (ցանկալ, տենչալ, աչք տնկել)
cow - gov (կով)
coward - vad, vakhgod, yergchod (վատ, վախկոտ, երկչոտ)
cowboy - govaradz (կովարած)
cower - gudzgil, toghal, kourkoural (կծկիլ, դողալ, գուրգուրալ)
cox - aboush, dukhmar, tiavar (ապուշ, տխմար, Թիավար)
coxcomb - tsoutsamol, ounaynamid, himar (ցուցամոլ, ունայնամիտ, յիմար)
coxy - inknahavan, ampardavan (ինքնահաւան, ամբարտաւան)
coy - amuchgod, varanod, shoyel, amuchnal (ամչկոտ, վարանոտ, շոյել, ամչնալ)
cozy - hankusdaved, hantardig, kunkouysh (հանգստաւէտ, հանդարտիկ, քնքոյշ)
co-author - hamaheghinag, heghinagagits (համահեղինակ, հեղինակակից)
crab - khechapar, charakhosel, jangel (խեչափառ, չարախօսել, ճանկել)
crack - jeghkel, godrel, jeghk, jaytiun (ճեղքել, կոտրել, ճեղք, ճայԹիւն)
cracker - peganogh, baytoug, jarjadiun, jarjadil (բեկանող, պայԹուկ, ճարճատիւն, ճարճատիլ)
crackle - jarjadiun, jarjadil (ճարճատիւն, ճարճատիլ)
cradle - ororel, ororots (օրօրել, օրօրոց
craft - jardaroutiun, arhesdner, naver, otanav (ճարտարուԹիւն, արհեստներ, նաւեր, օդանաւ)
craftman - arhesdavor, varbed (արհեստաւոր, վարպետ)
crafty - khoramang, jardar, nenkamid (խորամանկ, ճարտար, նենգամիտ)
crag - zhayr, sebazhayr (ժայռ, սեպաժայռ)
crake - juchel, hokhordal, hokhordank (ճչել, յոխորտալ, յոխորտանք)
cram - tukhel, khujoghel, khurnel khujoghoum (Թխել, խճողել, խռնել, խճողում)
cramp - seghmel, neghel, chughaburgoum, gudzgoum (սեղմել, նեղել, ջղապրկում, կծկում)
crane - pernaparts, guroung, verhan (բեռնաբարձ, կռունկ, վերհան)
cranium - kang (գանկ)
crank - purnadegh, got, hamar, ashkhouzh (բռնատեղ, կոԹ, յամառ, աշխոյժ)
crape - shugharsh, kankurel (շղարշ, գանգրել)
crapple - jang (ճանկ)
crase - khordagel (խորտակել)
crash - chakhchakhel, iynal, khordagel, chakhchakhoum (ջախջախել, իյնալ, խորտակել, ջախջախում)
crass - goshd, pird, tantsur, putamid (կոշտ, բիրտ, Թանձր, բԹամիտ)
cratch - musour (մսուր)
crater - kharnaran, huraperan (խառնարան, հրաբերան)
cravat - poghgab (փողկապ)
crave - khunturel, aghersel, haytsel (խնդրել, աղերսել, հայցել)
craven - vakhgod, vadasird, vad (վախկոտ, վատասիրտ, վատ)
crawl - soghal, soghosgil, marminu pushodil, soghosgoum (սողալ, սողոսկիլ, մարմինը փշոտիլ, սողոսկում)
crayon - madid, adzkhatsubig (մատիտ, ածխացպիկ)
craze - khentatsnel, khentanal, pushrel, himaroutiun (խենԹացնել, խենԹանալ, փշրել, յիմարուԹիւն)

crazy - khent, himar, khelakar (խենթ, յիմար, խելագար)
creak - jurinch, jurunchel (ճռինչ, ճռնչել)
cream - ser, keghategh, lavakouyn masu (սեր, գեղադեղ, լաւագոյն մասը)
crease - dzalk, pot, sahman, dzalel, sahmanakudzel (ծալք, փոթ, սահման, ծալել, սահմանագծել)
create - usdeghdzel, hunarel, badjarel (ստեղծել, հնարել, պատճառել)
creation - usdeghdzakordzoutiun, usdeghdzoum (ստեղծագործութիւն, ստեղծում)
Creator - ararich (Արարիչ)
creature - araradz, eag (արարած, էակ)
credence - havadk, vusdahoutiun (հաւատք, վստահութիւն)
credential - hantsnararagan (յանձնարարական)
credentials - vugayakir, hantsnarakir (վկայագիր, յանձնարագիր)
credibility - vusdahelioutiun (վստահելիութիւն)
credible - vusdaheli, havadali (վստահելի, հաւատալի)
credit - varg, varganish, vusdahoutiun, varg panal (վարկ, վարկանիշ, վստահութիւն, վարկ բանալ)
credit card - vargakard (վարկաքարտ)
creditor - bahanchader, vargadou (պահանջատէր, վարկատու)
credulity - tiurahavadoutiun (դիւրահաւատութիւն)
credulous - tiurahavad (դիւրահաւատ)
creed - hankanag, havadamk (հանգանակ, հաւատամք)
creek - khorsh, antsk, kedag (խորշ, անցք, գետակ)
creep - soghal, sahil, soghosgil (սողալ, սահիլ, սողոսկիլ)
creeper - soghatsogh, soghoun, makultsogh (սողացող, սողուն, մագլցող)
creeping - asdijanagan, kayl ar kayl (աստիճանական, քայլ առ քայլ)
creepy - vakhaztetsig (վախազդեցիկ)
crepitate - jarjadil (ճարճատիլ)
crescent - mahig, gisalousin (մահիկ, կիսալուսին)
cress - godem (կոտեմ)
cresset - chah, labder (ջահ, լապտեր)
crest - gadar, kakat, pupoug (կատար, գագաթ, բբուկ)
crestfallen - kulkhigor, nevasd (գլխիկոր, նուաստ)
cretin - tantsuramid (թանձրամիտ)
crib - musour, kom, dunag (մսուր, գոմ, տնակ)
cricket - dzughrit, marakh, atorag (ծղրիթ, մարախ, աթոռակ)
crier - mounedig, ganchogh (մունետիկ, կանչող)
crime - vojir, yeghern, vojrakordzoutiun (ոճիր, եղեռն, ոճրագործութիւն)
criminal - vojrakordz, vojrayin (ոճրագործ, ոճրային)
criminate - vojrabardel, vojirov ampasdanel (ոճրապարտել, ոճիրով ամբաստանել)
crimination - ampasdanoutiun (ամբաստանութիւն)
crimp - vedvidel, potel, pukhroun, zinvortsou (վէտվիտել, փոթել, փխրուն, զինուորցու)
cringe - kudznil, dzekdzekil, kudznank (քծնիլ, ծեքծեքիլ, քծնանք)
crinkle - kalarel, dzurmurgel, pot (գալարել, ծռմռկել, փոթ)
cripple - hashmantam, gagh, gaghal, hashmel (հաշմանդամ, կաղ, կաղալ, հաշմել)
crisis - daknab, juknazham (տագնապ, ճգնաժամ)
crisp - kankurel, volorel, hiusel, kankour, pukhroun (գանգրել, ոլորել, հիւսել, գանգուր, փխրուն)
critic - kunnatad, kunnatadoutiun (քննադատ, քննադատութիւն)
critical - jagadakragan, juknazhamayin (ճակատագրական, ճգնաժա-

մային)
critique - kunnatadoutiun (քննադատութիւն)
croak - gurgural, durdunchal, gurgurots (կռկռալ, տրտնջալ, կռկռոց)
crochet - ger, jang, gerasegh (կեռ, ճանկ, կեռասեղ)
crocodile - gogortilos (կոկորդիլոս)
croft - pokur akarag, dunard (փոքր ագարակ, տնարտ)
crofter - akaragaban, manur yergurakordz (ագարակապան, մանր երկրագործ)
crony - muderim, hin paregam (մտերիմ, հին բարեկամ)
crook - goroutiun, dzuroutiun (կորութիւն, ծռութիւն)
croon - murmunchel, murmounch (մրմնջել, մրմունջ)
crop - huntsel, hountsk, perk (հնձել, հունձք, բերք)
croquis - ourvakidz (ուրուագիծ)
cross - khach, khachatsev, khachatsevel, mechdeghen (խաչ, խաչաձեւ, խաչաձեւել, մէջտեղէն)
crossing - khachmeroug, khachoughi, khachagunkoum (խաչմերուկ, խաչուղի, խաչակնքում)
crossword - kaghdunapar, kaghdunakir (գաղտնաբառ, գաղտնագիր)
crouch - kudznil, khonarhil, dzuril (քծնիլ, խոնարհիլ, ծռիլ)
crow - akaghaghi ganch, akrav, aktsan, borodal (աքաղաղի կանչ, ագռաւ, աքցան, պոռոտալ)
crowd - junshel, khujoghel, ampokh, khouzhan (ճնշել, խճողել, ամբոխ, խուժան)
crown (n) - tak, busag, murtzanag, gadar, takavor (թագ, պսակ, մրցանակ, կատար, թագաւոր)
crown (v) - takavorel, busagel, gadarelakordzel, zartarel (թագաւորել, պսակել, կատարելագործել, զարդարել)
crucial - khachatsev, khisd, vujragan (խաչաձեւ, խիստ, վճռական)
crucible - halots, tsoularan (հալոց, ձուլարան)
crucifixion - khacheloutiun, darabank (խաչելութիւն, տառապանք)
crucify - khachel, charcharel (խաչել, չարչարել)
crude - houm, khag, duhas (հում, խակ, տհաս)
cruel - ankout, tazhan, khisd (անգութ, դաժան, խիստ)
cruet - yiughaman (իւղաման)
cruise - dzovabudouyd, dzovakunatsoutiun (ծովապտոյտ, ծովագնացութիւն)
cruise control - jebagayounarar, arakahusgich (ճեպակայունարար, արագահսկիչ)
cruiser - hadzanav (հածանաւ)
crumb - pushrank, gudor, vochil (փշրանք, կտոր, ոչիլ)
crumble - manrel, pushrel, manruvil (մանրել, փշրել, մանրուիլ)
crumple - jumurtgel, khorshomil (ճմրթկել, խորշոմիլ)
crunch - jarjadil, sharachil, tsaynov dzamel (ճարճատիլ, շառաչիլ, ձայնով ծամել)
crusade - khachaguroutiun (խաչակրութիւն)
crusader - khachagir (խաչակիր)
crush - chakhchakhel, khordagel, juzmel, khordagoum (ջախջախել, խորտակել, ճզմել, խորտակում)
crust - geghev, khav, geghev gabel (կեղեւ, խաւ, կեղեւ կապել)
crutch - antatsoub, gurtnil, henoul (անթացուպ, կռթնիլ, յենուլ)
cry - lal, boral, aghaghagel, jich, lats, aghaghag (լալ, պոռալ, աղաղակել, ճիչ, լաց, աղաղակ)
crying - aghaghagogh, patsahayd (աղաղակող, բացայայտ)
crystal - piuregh (բիւրեղ)
cubboard - baharan (պահարան)
cube - khoranart (խորանարդ)
cucumber - varounk (վարունգ)
cuddle - pattuvil, paypayel, gudzgil (փաթթուիլ, փայփայել, կծկիլ)
cue - dzam, mazi hiusk, telatrank, kuntatsogh (ծամ, մազի հիւսք, թելադրանք, գնդաձող)
cuff - abdagel, dzedzel, abdag, tevnots (ապտակել, ծեծել, ապտակ,

թեւնոց)
cuirass - zurah, badian (զրահ, պատեան)
cuirassier - zurahavor (զրահաւոր)
cuisine - khohanots, khohararoutiun (խոհանոց, խոհարարութիւն)
culinary - khohanotsayin (խոհանոցային)
cullender - kamots (քամոց)
culminant - kakatnaged, partsurakouyn asdijan (գագաթնակէտ, բարձրագոյն աստիճան)
culminate - kakatnagedin hasnil (գագաթնակէտին հասնիլ)
culpable - hantsavor, meghabard (յանցաւոր, մեղապարտ)
culprit - charakordz, hantsabard (չարագործ, յանցապարտ)
cult - bashdamounk, yergurbakoutiun (պաշտամունք, երկրպագութիւն)
cultivable - mushageli (մշակելի)
cultivate - mushagel, gurtel, varel (մշակել, կրթել, վարել)
cultivator - mushagogh, hoghakordz (մշակող, հողագործ)
cultural - mushagoutayin, mushagayin (մշակութային, մշակային)
culture - mushagouyt, mushagoum, hoghakordzoutiun, mushagel (մշակոյթ, մշակում, հողագործութիւն, մշակել)
cumber - neghel, junshel, khapanel, neghoutiun (նեղել, ճնշել, խափանել, նեղութիւն)
cumbrance - per, dzanroutiun (բեռ, ծանրութիւն)
cumin - chaman (չաման)
cumulate - tizel, muterel, goudagel (դիզել, մթերել, կուտակել)
cumulation - tizoum, tez (դիզում, դէզ)
cuneiform - sebatsev, sebakir (սեպաձեւ, սեպագիր)
cunning - khoramang, nenk, khapogh (խորամանկ, նենգ, խաբող)
cup - kavat, pazhag, survag (գաւաթ, բաժակ, սրուակ)
cupboard - baharan (պահարան)
cupidity - unchakaghtsoutiun, ardzatasiroutiun (ընչաքաղցութիւն, արծաթասիրութիւն)
cupola - kumpet (գմբէթ)
curable - pouzheli (բուժելի)
curate - zhoghovurtabed, dzukhader (ժողովրդապետ, ծխատէր)
curative - pouzhich, tarmanagan (բուժիչ, դարմանական)
curator - khunamagal, hokapartsou (խնամակալ, հոգաբարձու)
curb - santsel, zusbel, hagagushrel (սանձել, զսպել, հակակշռել)
curd - magart, madzoun, magartel (մակարդ, մածուն, մակարդել)
cure - tarmanel, pouzhel, khunamel, pouzhoum, yerets (դարմանել, բուժել, խնամել, բուժում, երէց)
curfew - guragmar, lousarkel (կրակմար, լուսարգել)
curiosity - hedakurkuroutiun, darorinagoutiun (հետաքրքրութիւն, տարօրինակութիւն)
curious - hedakurkir, hartsaser (հետաքրքիր, հարցասէր)
curl - kankour, khobob, volorel (գանգուր, խոպոպ, ոլորել)
curlew - tsugungoul, aror (ձկնկուլ, արօր)
currency - shurchaperoutiun, turam (շրջաբերութիւն, դրամ)
current - hosank, untatsig, untatsk (հոսանք, ընթացիկ, ընթացք)
curriculum - tasuntatsk (դասընթացք)
curse - anidzel, nuzovel, hayhoyel (անիծել, նզովել, հայհոյել)
curt - gudroug, pird, ankaghakavar (կտրուկ, բիրտ, անքաղաքավար)
curtail - gurjadel, habavel, mugradel (կրճատել, յապաւել, մկրատել)
curtain - varakouyr, varakourel (վարագոյր, վարագուրել)
curvation - goroutiun, dzuroutiun (կորութիւն, ծռութիւն)
curve - tartsuvadzk, gor, goroutiun, dzurel (դարձուածք, կոր, կորութիւն, ծռել)
cushion - parts (բարձ)
custody - bahbanoutiun, bahesd, khunamk, galank (պահպանութիւն, պահեստ, խնամք, կալանք)

custom - sovoroutiun, hajakhortoutiun, orenk (սովորութիւն, յաճախորդութիւն, օրէնք)
custom house - maksadoun (մաքսատուն)
custom jewelry - geghdz kohareghen (կեղծ գոհարեղէն)
customer - hajakhort (յաճախորդ)
customs - maks (մաքս)
cut - gudrel, tsevel, jeghkel, gudurvadz, jekhk, verk (կտրել, ձեւել, ճեղքել, կտրուած, ճեղք, վէրք)
cutter - gudrogh, dashogh, gopogh (կտրող, տաշող, կոփող)
cutting - hadoum, gudrogh, sour (հատում, կտրող, սուր)
cycle - shurchanag, dzir, hedzaniv, shurchanunel (շրջանակ, ծիր, հեծանիւ, շրջան ընել)
cyclic - shurchanayin (շրջանային)
cyclist - hedzanvort, hedzelanvort (հեծանուորդ, հեծելանուորդ)
cylinder - kulan (գլան)
cylindric - kulanatsev (գլանաձեւ)
cymbal - dzundzgha, pampir (ծնծղայ, բամբիռ)
cynic - shunagan, lugdi, anamot (շնական, լկտի, անամօթ)
cynicism - shunaganoutiun, lurpoutiun (շնականութիւն, լրբութիւն)
cypress - noji (նոճի)
cyst - otapampoushd, barg (օդափամփուշտ, պարկ)
czar, tsar, tzar - tsar (ձար)

dab - jardar tserk, varbed, huboum, tetev zarnel (ճարտար ձեռք, վարպետ, հպում, թեթեւ զարնել)
dabble - turchudel, tsoghel (թրջտել, ցօղել)
dacker - dzadzanil, dadanil, pundurel (ծածանիլ, տատանիլ, փնտռել)
dad - hayrig, dadi, harvadz (հայրիկ, տատի, հարուած)
daddy - dadig, hayrig (տատիկ, հայրիկ)
daft - aboush, tetevsolig, megti nedel, vakhtsunel (ապուշ, թեթեւսոլիկ, մէկդի նետել, վախցնել)
dagger - tashouyn, khachanish (դաշոյն, խաչանիշ)
daggle - turchel, turchil, tsekhodil (թրջել, թրջիլ, ցեխոտիլ)
daily - amenoria, aroria, oratert (ամէնօրեայ, առօրեայ, օրաթերթ)
daintiness - nurpoutiun, papgoutiun (նրբութիւն, փափկութիւն)
dainty - papganugadoutiun, nourp, sirounoutiun, hamegh (փափկանկատութիւն, նուրբ, սիրունութիւն, համեղ)
dairy - gatnadoun, gatnaran (կաթնատուն, կաթնարան)
dairyman - gatnavajar (կաթնավաճառ)
daisy - markardadzaghig (մարգարտածաղիկ)
dale - hovid, tsor (հովիտ, ձոր)
dally - dundunal, habaghil, zuvarjanal (տնտնալ, յապաղիլ, զուարճանալ)
dam - churampar, ampardag, toump, arkilel (ջրամբար, ամբարտակ, թումբ, արգիլել)
damage - vunas, gorousd, doukank, hadoutsoum (վնաս, կորուստ, տուգանք, հատուցում)
Damascus - tamasgos (Դամասկոս)
dame - digin, takouhi (տիկին, թագուհի)
damn - tadabardel, anidzel, hayhoyel (դատապարտել, անիծել, հայհոյել)
damnable - tadabardeli, anark (դատապարտելի, անարգ)
damnation - anedzk, tadabardoutiun

(անէծք, դատապարտութիւն)

damned - anidzial, tadabardial (անիծեալ, դատապարտեալ)

damp - khonavoutiun, mushoush, vuhadetsunel (խոնաւութիւն, մշուշ, վհատեցնել)

dampen - khonavtsunel, khonavnal, vuhadil (խոնաւցնել, խանաւնալ, վհատիլ)

dance - barel, khaghal, bar (պարել, խաղալ, պար)

dancer - barogh (պարող)

dancing - barogh, barelu (պարող, պարելը)

dancing room - barasurah (պարասրահ)

dandle - paypayel, kukvel, ororel (փայփայել, գգուել, օրօրել)

dandy - bujnaser, zartaser, tetevsolig (պճնասէր, զարդասէր, թեթեւսոլիկ)

danger - vudank (վտանգ)

dangerous - vudankavor (վտանգաւոր)

dangle - dadanil, jojil, gakhvil, jojel, gakhel (տատանիլ, ճօճիլ, կախուիլ, ճօճել, կախել)

dank - tats, khonav, khonavoutioun (թաց, խոնաւ, խոնաւութիւն)

daphne - tapni (դափնի)

dapper - varvuroun, gogig, artnamid, kordzounia (վառվռուն, կոկիկ, արթնամիտ, գործունեայ)

dapple - khadoudig, bisagavor, bisagel (խատուտիկ, պիսակաւոր, պիսակել)

darbies - tsernagab (ձեռնակապ)

dare - hantuknil, hamartsagil, ahapegel, arhamarhank (յանդգնիլ, համարձակիլ, ահաբեկել, արհամարհանք)

daredevil - hantoukn, hamartsag (յանդուգն, համարձակ)

dark - mout, khavar, kaghdni, char, mutuntsunel (մութ, խաւար, գաղտնի, չար, մթնցնել)

darken - mutuntsunel, aradavorel (մթնցնել, արատաւորել)

darkness - mutoutiun, khavar, dukidoutiun (մթութիւն, խաւար, տգիտութիւն)

darkroom - mout seniag (մութ սենեակ)

darksome - mout, khavar, aghod, dukhour, nusem (մութ, խաւար, աղօտ, տխուր, նսեմ)

darky - sevamort (սեւամորթ)

darling - siragan, siregan, sireli (սիրական, սիրեկան, սիրելի)

darn - gargudel, norokel, gargudan (կարկտել, նորոգել, կարկտան)

dart - nizag, ned, sulak, khoyanal (նիզակ, նետ, սլաք, խոյանալ)

dash - nedel, khordagel, chunchel, kudzig (նետել, խորտակել, ջնջել, գծիկ)

dashing - guragod, yerantoun (կրակոտ, եռանդուն)

dashy - tsoutsamol (ցուցամոլ)

dastard - vad, vakhgod, yergchod (վատ, վախկոտ, երկչոտ)

data - noter, deghegoutiunner, duvyalner, pasd (նօթեր, տեղեկութիւններ, տուեալներ, փաստ)

database - deghegank, deghegatsang (տեղեկանք, տեղեկացանկ)

date (n) - tuvagan, siro zhamatrouriun, armav (թուական, սիրոյ ժամադրութիւն, արմաւ)

date (v) - tuvagan kurel, zhamaturvil hagarag serin hed (թուական գրել, ժամադրուիլ հակառակ սեռին հետ)

dateless - antuvagir, anverch, anhishadag (անթուակիր, անվերջ, անյիշատակ)

dateline - avardazham, sahmanakidz, zhamazants (աւարտաժամ, սահմանագիծ, ժամազանց)

dating - zouykerou zhaturoutiun (զոյգերու ժամադրութիւն)

datum - himnaged, him, devyal (հիմնակէտ, հիմ, տուեալ)

daub - dzepel, kusel, dzep (ծեփել, քսել, ծեփ)

daughter - tousder, aghchig (դուստր, աղջիկ)

daughter-in-law - hars, dughoun ginu (հարս, տղուն կինը)

daunt - junshel, vuhadetsunel, vakh-

tsunel, ahapegel (ճնշել, վհատեցնել, վախցնել, ահաբեկել)
daunter - junshogh, vakhtsunogh (ճնշող, վախցնող)
dawdle - tantaghil, dundunal (դանդաղիլ, տնտնալ)
dawdler - zhamavajar (ժամավաճառ)
dawk - badrel, khoroung jeghkel, viravorel (պատռել, խորունկ ճեղքել, վիրաւորել)
dawn - dzakil, yerevnal, arshalouys (ծագիլ, երեւնալ, արշալոյս)
day - or, tsereg (օր, ցերեկ)
daybook - oradedur (օրատետր)
daydream - yerazank, tzangoutiun, yerazel (երազանք, ցանկութիւն, երազել)
daylight - tsereg, louys, or tseregov (ցերեկ, լոյս, օր ցերեկով)
daytime - tsereg, ashkadanki zham (ցերեկ, աշխատանքի ժամ)
day-long - orun i poun, ampoghch oru (օրն ի բուն, ամբողջ օրը)
daze - shulatsunel, shulatsoum (շլացնել, շլացում)
dazzle - hurabourel, abshetsunel, shoghshoghal, shulatsoum (հրապուրել, ապշեցնել, շողշողալ, շլացում)
dazzling - shulatsoum, hurabouroum (շլացում, հրապուրում)
deacon - sargavak (սարկաւագ)
dead - meradz, merial, tiag, angentan (մեռած, մեռեալ, դիակ, անկենդան)
dead end - ougheverch, oughevakhjan, anel, pagoughi (ուղեվերջ, ուղեվախճան, անել, փակուղի)
deadbeat - charakhos, khapepa, mashadz, chartuvadz (չարախօս, խաբեբայ, մաշած, ջարդուած)
deaden - hamatsuenl, ouzhadel (մահացնել, ուժատել)
deadline - zhamged, mahakidz (ժամկէտ, մահագիծ)
deadly - mahatsou, ahreli (մահացու, ահռելի)
deaf - khoul, anuzka, khoultsunel (խուլ, անզգայ, խուլցնել)
deafen - khulatsunel, khoultsunel (խլացնել, խուլցնել)
deafness - khuloutiun (խլութիւն)
deal - mas, kanag, kordzarnoutiun, michnortel, dal (մաս, քանակ, գործառնութիւն, միջնորդել, տալ)
dealbate - jermugtsunel (ճերմկցնել)
dealer - vajarogh, arevduragan, panagtsogh, tughtapashkh (վաճառող, առեւտրական, բանակցող, թղթաբաշխ)
dealing - arevdour, untatsk, kordzarnoutiun (առեւտուր, ընթացք, գործառնութիւն)
dean - ousoutschabed, dunoren, yeritsabed (ուսուցչապետ, տնօրէն, երիցապետ)
dear - sireli, siregan, sough, tangakin, kourkoural (սիրելի, սիրական, սուղ, թանկագին, գուրգուրալ)
dearth - sov, sughoutiun (սով, սղութիւն)
death - mah, tiag, vakhjan (մահ, դիակ, վախճան)
deathbed - mahvan angoghin (մահուան անկողին)
deathless - anmah (անմահ)
debar - arkilel, pagel, kotsel (արգիլել, փակել, գոցել)
debark - tsamakahanoum (ցամաքահանում)
debase - arzhezurgel, usdornatsnel (արժեզրկել, ստորնացնել)
debate - vijil, vijapanil, kunnel (վիճիլ, վիճաբանիլ, քննել)
debauch - abaganel, moloretsunel, tsopatsunel, shuvaydank (ապականել, մոլորեցնել, ցոփացնել, շուայտանք)
debauchee - tsop, poz, anbadiv (ցոփ, բոզ, անպատիւ)
debenture - mourhag, maksadoms (մուրհակ, մաքսատոմս)
debilitate - dugaratsunel (տկարացնել)
debit - bardk, yelk, bardki antsunel (պարտք, ելք, պարտքի անցընել)
debris - pegor, munatsort, nushkhar (բեկոր, մնացորդ, նշխար)
debt - bardk, bardavoroutiun

(պարտք, պարտաւորութիւն)
debtee - bahanchader, bardader (պահանջատէր, պարտատէր)
debtor - bardagan, bardaban (պարտական, պարտապան)
debut - nakhaports, usgizp, usguzpnakhagh (նախափորձ, սկիզբ, սկզբնախաղ)
debutant - usgusnag, noravarzh (սկսնակ, նորավարժ)
decade - dasnamiag (տասնամեակ)
decadence, decadency - angoum, gordzamoum, vadtaratsoum (անկում, կործանում, վատթարացում)
decalcomania - verahanoum, nugari pokhaturoum (վերահանում, նկարի փոխադրում)
decapitate - kulkhadel (գլխատել)
decapitation - kulkhadoum (գլխատում)
decay - avruvil, puddil, gordzanil (աւրուիլ, փտտիլ, կործանիլ)
decease - mernil, vakhjanil, mah (մեռնիլ, վախճանիլ, մահ)
deceive - housakhapel, khapel, nenkel (յուսախաբել, խաբել, նենգել)
December - tegdemper (Դեկտեմբեր)
decency - badshajoutiun, bargeshdoutiun (պատշաճութիւն, պարկեշտութիւն)
decennial - dasnamia (տասնամեայ)
decent - vayelouch, harmar, badshaj (վայելուչ, յարմար, պատշաճ)
decentralise - abagetronatsunel (ապակեդրոնացնել)
deception - housakhapoutiun, khapeoutiun, nenkoutiun (յուսախաբութիւն, խաբէութիւն, նենգութիւն)
decide - voroshel, vujrel (որոշել, վճռել)
decision - voroshoum, vujir (որոշում, վճիռ)
decisive - vujragan (վճռական)
deck - dzadzg, dakhdagamadz, dzadzgel (ծածկ, տախտակամած, ծածկել)
declaim - jarakhosel, ardasanel (ճառախօսել, արտասանել)
declaration - haydararoutiun, dzanoutsoum, hurchagoum (յայտարարութիւն, ծանուցում, հռչակում)
declare - haydararel, hasdadel, haydnel (յայտարարել, հաստատել, յայտնել)
declension - angoum, khonarhoum, holovoum (անկում, խոնարհում, հոլովում)
declination - hagoum, hurazharoum, holovoum (հակում, հրաժարում, հոլովում)
decline - khonarhil, hagil, nuvaghil, dugaranal, holovel (խոնարհիլ, հակիլ, նուաղիլ, տկարանալ, հոլովել)
decolor - kounatapel (գունաթափել)
decolorize - kounadel (գունատել)
decompose - gazmaloudzel, loudzel, avrel, avruvil (կազմալուծել, լուծել, աւրել, աւրուիլ)
decomposition - gazmaloudzoum, kaykayoum, darpaghatroum (կազմալուծում, քայքայում, տարբաղադրում)
decor - pemazart, pemahartaroum (բեմազարդ, բեմայարդարում)
decorate - zartarel, keghetsgatsunel (զարդարել, գեղեցկացնել)
decoration - zartaroum, shukanushan, zart (զարդարում, շքանշան, զարդ)
decorative - zartarich, zartagan (զարդարիչ, զարդական)
decorator - zartarich, keghazartogh, pemahartar (զարդարիչ, գեղազարդող, բեմայարդար)
decoy - hurabourel, tagartel, dzoughag, tagart (հրապուրել, թակարդել, ծուղակ, թակարդ)
decrease - nuvazil, bagsil, nuvazoum, angoum (նուազիլ, պակսիլ, նուազում, անկում)
decree - vujir, huramanakir, hurovardag, vujrel (վճիռ, հրամանագիր, հրովարտակ, վճռել)
decrepitate - jarjadel (ճարճատել)
decrew - nuvazil (նուազիլ)
decry - anvanargel, vadapanel (անուանարկել, վատաբանել)
dedicate - nuvirel, undzayel, tsonel (նուիրել, ընծայել, ձօնել)

dedication - *nuviroum, undzayoum, tson* (նուիրում, ընծայում, ձօն)
deduce - *hedevtsunel, yezragatsunel, hanel* (հետեւցնել, եզրակացնել, հանել)
deduct - *bagsetsunel, hanel, veradzel, yezragatsunel* (պակսեցնել, հանել, վերածել, եզրակացնել)
deductible - *bagsetsunelik, hanelik* (պակսեցնելիք, հանելիք)
deduction - *hedevoutiun, yezragatsoutiun, hanoum, zeghch* (հետեւութիւն, եզրակացութիւն, հանում, զեղչ)
deed - *kordz, arark, artiunk* (գործ, արարք, արդիւնք)
deedful - *kordzounia* (գործունեայ)
deem - *hamarel, gardzel, yentaturel* (համարել, կարծել, ենթադրել)
deep - *khor, khoroung, khorimasd, khork, antount* (խոր, խորունկ, խորիմաստ, խորք, անդունդ)
deepen - *khoranal, khoratsunel* (խորանալ, խորացնել)
deer - *yeghnig, yeghcherou* (եղնիկ, եղջերու)
deess - *asdvadzouhi* (աստուածուհի)
deface - *aylantagel, avrel, gerbaranapokhel* (այլանդակել, աւրել, կերպարանափոխել)
defacto - *pasdoren, iragan* (փաստօրէն, իրական)
defalcate - *nuvazetsunel, bagsetsunel* (նուազեցնել, պակսեցնել)
defalcation - *turamashortoutiun* (դրամաշորթութիւն)
defalcator - *turamashort* (դրամաշորթ)
defalk - *shortel* (շորթել)
defame - *zurbardel, anarkel, anvanargel* (զրպարտել, անարգել, անուանարկել)
default - *teroutiun, bagas, vuribag, hantsank* (թերութիւն, պակաս, վրիպակ, յանցանք)
defeat - *bardoutiun, gordzanoum, barduvil* (պարտութիւն, կործանում, պարտուիլ)
defeatist - *barduvoghagan* (պարտուողական)
defecate - *gughgughel, usdamoksi aveltsouku hanel* (կղկղել, ստամոքսի աւելցուքը հանել)
defecation - *zudoum, barzoum, barboum* (զտում, պարզում, պարպում)
defect - *bagasoutiun, teroutiun, arad, teranal* (պակասութիւն, թերութիւն, արատ, թերանալ)
defection - *oudzatsoum* (ուծացում)
defective - *teri, angadar, bagasavor* (թերի, անկատար, պակասաւոր)
defend - *bashdbanel, chadakovel, arkilel* (պաշտպանել, ջատագովել, արգիլել)
defense - *bashdbanoutiun* (պաշտպանութիւն)
defensive - *bashdbanoghagan* (պաշտպանողական)
defer - *hedatsukel, habaghel, zichil* (յետաձգել, յապաղել, զիջիլ)
deference - *zichoghoutiun, agnadzank* (զիջողութիւն, ակնածանք)
defiance - *arhamarhoum, merzhoum, mardahuraver* (արհամարհում, մերժում, մարտահրաւէր)
defiant - *anvakh, hantoukun, arhamarhogh* (անվախ, յանդուգն, արհամարհող)
deficiency - *anpavararoutiun, bagasoutiun* (անբաւարարութիւն, պակասութիւն)
deficient - *anpavarar, bagas, hashivi bagasort, garikavor* (անբաւարար, պակաս, հաշիւի պակասորդ, կարիքաւոր)
deficit - *bagas, pats, bagasort* (պակաս, բաց, պակասորդ)
defile - *aghdodel, anbadvel, doghantsel, doghantsk, girj* (աղտոտել, անպատուել, տողանցել, տողանցք, կիրճ)
define - *sahmanel, voroshel* (սահմանել, որոշել)
definite - *vorosh, voroshial, husdag, hasdad* (որոշ, որոշեալ, յստակ, հաստատ)
definition - *sahmanoum, voroshoum, husdagoutiun* (սահմանում, որոշում, յստակութիւն)

definitive - verchnagan, verchin, vorosh (վերջնական, վերջին, որոշ)
defix - hasdadel (Հաստատել)
deflagate - potsagizil, potsagizel (բոցակիզիլ, բոցակիզել)
deflect - sheghel, sheghil, khodorel khodoretsunel (շեղել, շեղիլ, խոտորել, խոտորեցնել)
deforce - purnakuravel, purnatadel (բռնագրաւել, բռնադատել)
deform - tsevapokhel, aylapokhel (ձեւափոխել, այլափոխել)
deformation - tsevapokhoum, tsevazeghdzoum (ձեւափոխում, ձեւազեղծում)
defraud - aniravel, gorzel, khapel (անիրաւել, կորզել, խաբել)
defray - vujarel, hokal, hadoutsanel (վճարել, Հոգալ, Հատուցանել)
defrost - sarazerdzel (սառազերծել)
deft - jarbig, jardar, gogig (ճարպիկ, ճարտար, կոկիկ)
defunct - meradz, hankhoutsial, nunchetsial (մեռած, Հանգուցեալ, ննջեցեալ)
defy - mardahuraver, kurkuroutiun (մարտաՀրաւէր, գրգռութիւն)
deg - surusgel (սրսկել)
degenarate (v) - aylaseril, vadtaranal, khortanal, odaranal (այլասերիլ, վատթարանալ, խորթանալ, օտարանալ)
degenerate (a) - aylaseradz, vadtaratsadz, oudzatsadz (այլասերած, վատթարացած, ուծացած)
degeneration - aylaseroum, khortatsoum, odaratsoum (այլասերում, խորթացում, օտարացում)
degradation - asdijanazurgoum, garkazurgoum, nevasdatsoum (աստիճանազրկում, կարգազրկում, նուաստացում)
degrade - vadtaratsunel, asdijanazurgel, shunorhazurgel (վատթարացնել, աստիճանազրկել, շնորՀազըրկել)
degree - asdijan, gark, chap (աստիճան, կարգ, չափ)
degustation - hamdesoutiun, hamaroutiun (Համտեսութիւն, Համառութիւն)
dehydrate - chour gorsuntsunel - marminen (ջուր կորսնցնել՝ մարմինէն)
dehydration - churazurgoum, anchutiun (ջրազրկում, անջրութիւն)
deify - asdvadzatsunel, bashdel (աստուածացնել, պաշտել)
deign - shunorhel, parehajil, arzhanatsunel (շնորՀել, բարեՀաճիլ, արժանացնել)
deintegrate - kaykayel, puchatsunel (քայքայել, բջացնել)
deity - asdvadzoutiun (աստուածութիւն)
deject - vuhadetsunel, junshel, lukel (վՀատեցնել, ճնշել, լքել)
dejection - vuhadoutiun, lukoum, gughgughank (վՀատութիւն, լքում, կղկղանք)
dejeratation - yertnoum (երդնում)
dejerate - yertnoul (երդնուլ)
delay - habaghoum, hedatsukoum, hedatsukel, oushatsunel (յապաղում, յետաձգում, յետաձգել, ուշացնել)
delegate - badvirag, badkamavor, nuvirag, pokhanort (պատուիրակ, պատգամաւոր, նուիրակ, փոխանորդ)
delegation - badviragoutiun, badkamavoroutiun (պատուիրակութիւն, պատգամաւորութիւն)
delete - chunchel, hanel, avrel (ջնջել, Հանել, աւրել)
deletion - chunchoum, gordzanoum (ջնջում, կործանում)
delf - pos, karahank (փոս, քարաՀանք)
deli - hamatam oudelik (Համադամ ուտելիք)
deliberate - kunnargel, khorhil, khohagan, uzkoushavor (քննարկել, խորՀիլ, խոՀական, զգուշաւոր)
deliberation - khorhurtagtsoutiun, voroshoum, vujir (խորՀրդակցութիւն, որոշում, վճիռ)
delicate - papoug, nourp, kunkoush (փափուկ, նուրբ, քնքուշ)
delicatessen - hamatamk, hamegh

oudelikner (համադամք, համեղ ուտելիքներ)
delicatessen (deli) - anousheghenner, hamatamk (անուշեղէններ, համադամք)
delicious - hamegh, kaghtsuraham, hianali (համեղ, քաղցրահամ, հիանալի)
delight - hiatsunel, hianal, hajouyk, uzmaylank (հիացնել, հիանալ, հաճոյք, զմայլանք)
delightful - hajeli, uzmayleli (հաճելի, զմայլելի)
delinquency - hantsank, bardazantsoutiun (յանցանք, պարտազանցութիւն)
delinquent - hantsavor, bardazants, charakordz (յանցաւոր, պարտազանց, չարագործ)
delirium tremens - zarantsank (զառանցանք)
deliver - hantsnel, pazhnel, azadil, purgel (յանձնել, բաժնել, ազատիլ, փրկել)
delivery - hantsnoum, pashkhoum, azadoum, dughaperk (յանձնում, բաշխում, ազատում, տղաբերք)
delivery system - usbasargoutian gerb (սպասարկութեան կերպ)
dell - tsorag, hovid, khoroch (ձորակ, հովիտ, խոռոչ)
delta - kedaperan (գետաբերան)
delude - moloretsunel, khapel (մոլորեցնել, խաբել)
deluge - churheghegh, deghadarap, voghoghel (ջրհեղեղ, տեղատարափ, ողողել)
delusion - badrank, tsunork, khapgank (պատրանք, ցնորք, խաբկանք)
deluvial - hegheghayin, hortahos (հեղեղային, յորդահոս)
delve - beghel, pundurdel, porel, pos, khorsh (պեղել, փնտռտել, փորել, փոս, խորշ)
demagog, demagogue - ampokhavar, zhoghovurtavar (ամբոխավար, ժողովրդավար)
demagogy - ampokhavaroutiun (ամբոխավարութիւն)
demand - khunturel, bahanchel, khunturank, bahanch (խնդրել, պահանջել, խնդրանք, պահանջ)
demarcate - sahmanakudzel, voroshel (սահմանագծել, որոշել)
demarcation - sahmanakudzoum, sahmanakidz (սահմանագծում, սահմանագիծ)
demean - nuvasdanal, usdornanal, zichanil, varmounk (նուաստանալ, ստորնանալ, զիջանիլ, վարմունք)
demeanor - untatsk, varmounk, gentsagh (ընթացք, վարմունք, կենցաղ)
dement - khentetsunel (խենթեցնել)
dementation - himaroutiun, khelakaroutiun (յիմարութիւն, խելագարութիւն)
demerit - hantsank, sukhal, meghk, anarzhanik (յանցանք, սխալ, մեղք, անարժանիք)
demi - ges (կէս)
demilitarize - abarazmaganatsunel (ապառազմականացնել)
demission - hurazharoum, hurazharagan, angoum (հրաժարում, հրաժարական, անկում)
demit - hurazharil, lukel, toghoul (հրաժարիլ, լքել, թողուլ)
demobilization - zoratsuroum (զօրացրում)
demobilize - zoratsurvel, zinartsagel (զօրացրուել, զինարձակել)
democracy - zhoghovurtavaroutiun (ժողովրդավարութիւն)
democrat - zhoghovurtavar (ժողովրդավար)
democratic - ramgavaragan (ռամկավարական)
demographic - 1hoghovurtakuragan (ժողովրդագրական)
demography - zhoghovurtakuroutiun (ժողովրդագրութիւն)
demolish - kantel, gordzanel, averel (քանդել, կործանել, աւերել)
demolition - kantoum, gordzanoum, dabaloum (քանդում, կործանում, տապալում)
demon - sadana, tev (սատանայ, դեւ)

demonstrate - abatsoutsel, tsoutsnel, haydnel (ապացուցել, ցուցնել, յայտնել)
demonstration - abatsouyts, tsoutsaturoutiun, tsouyts (ապացոյց, ցուցադրութիւն, ցոյց)
demonstrative - tsousagan, tsoutsaturagan (ցուցական, ցուցադրական)
demonstrator - tsoutsaturogh (ցուցադրող)
demoralize - paroyalukel, anparoyatsunel, vuhadetsunel (բարոյալքել, անբարոյացնել, վհատեցնել)
demulce - amokel, meghmel, gagoughtsunel (ամոքել, մեղմել, կակուղցնել)
demur - varanil, oushanal, gasgadzil, varanoum (վարանիլ, ուշանալ, կասկածիլ, վարանում)
demure - bargeshd, lourch, uzkon, lurchanal (պարկեշտ, լուրջ, զգօն, լրջանալ)
den - khoroch, vorch, khutsig, orchanal (խոռոչ, որջ, խցիկ, որջանալ)
denationalize - abazkaynatsunel (ապազգայնացնել)
denaturalize - anpunagan tartsunel, hubadagazurgel (անբնական դարձնել, հպատակազրկել)
denature - aylapokhel, aylantagel, anpunagan tartsunel (այլափոխել, այլանդակել, անբնական դարձնել)
denegate - ouranal (ուրանալ)
denegation - ouratsoum (ուրացում)
denial - herkoum, zhukhdoum, ouratsoum, merzhoum (հերքում, ժխտում, ուրացում, մերժում)
denier - ouratsogh (ուրացող)
denigrate - sevtsunogh, charakhosogh (սեւցնող, չարախօսող)
denominate - anvanel, gochel, horchorchel (անուանել, կոչել, յորջորջել)
denomination - anvanoum, horchorchoum (անուանում, յորջորջում)
denominator - haydarar, pazhanarar (յայտարար, բաժանարար)
denotate - nushanagel (նշանակել)
denotation - nushanagoum (նշանակում)
denote - nushel, nushanagel, tzoutsnel, haydnel (նշել, նշանակել, ցուցնել, յայտնել)
denounce - imatsunel, aztararel, madnanushel, madnel (իմացնել, ազդարարել, մատնանշել, մատնել)
dense - khid, hodz, tantsur (խիտ, հոծ, թանձր)
densimeter - khudachap (խտաչափ)
density - khudoutiun, tantsuroutiun (խտութիւն, թանձրութիւն)
dent - agra, pos, khoroch, nushan, adamnavorel (ակռայ, փոս, խոռոչ, նշան, ատամնաւորել)
dental - adamnayin (ատամնային)
dentelle - zhaniag (ժանեակ)
dentifrice - adamnategh, adamnakhius (ատամնադեղ, ատամնախիւս)
dentist - adamnapouyzh (ատամնաբոյժ)
dentistry - adamnapouzhoutiun (ատամնաբուժութիւն)
dentize - agra hanel (ակռայ հանել)
denture - adamnashar, geghdz agra (ատամնաշար, կեղծ ակռայ)
denudate, denude - mergatsunel (մերկացնել)
denudation - mergatsoum (մերկացում)
denunciation - patsahaydoum, meghaturoum, madnoum (բացայայտում, մեղադրում, մատնում)
deny - ouranal, herkel, zhukhdel, merzhel (ուրանալ, հերքել, ժխտել, մերժել)
deodorant - hodahan, abanokhogh, kesh hoderu makrogh (հոտահան, ապանեխող, գէշ հոտերը մաքրող)
depart - megnil, heranal, toghoul, megnoum (մեկնիլ, հեռանալ, թողուլ, մեկնում)
department - bashdonadoun, pazhanmounk, jiugh, nahank (պաշտօնատուն, բաժանմունք, ճիւղ, նահանգ)
departure - megnoum, pazhanoum, lukoum (մեկնում, բաժանում, լքում)

depend - *gakhoum ounenal, gakhvadz ullal, vusdahil* (կախում ունենալ, կախուած ըլլալ, վստահիլ)
dependence - *gakhoum, yentagayoutiun, hubadagoutiun* (կախում, ենթակայութիւն, հպատակութիւն)
dependent - *gakhial, yentaga, hubadag* (կախեալ, ենթակայ, հպատակ)
deplete - *barbel, ouzhadel, usbarel* (պարպել, ուժատել, սպառել)
deplorable - *voghpali, voghormeli, arkahadeli* (ողբալի, ողորմելի, արգահատելի)
deploration - *voghp* (ողբ)
deplore - *voghpal, apsosal, tsavil, lal* (ողբալ, ափսոսալ, ցաւիլ, լալ)
deploy - *suprel, panal, daradzel, barzel* (սփռել, բանալ, տարածել, պարզել)
deplume - *pedradel, mergatsunel* (փետրատել, մերկացնել)
deponent - *vuga, vugayogh* (վկայ, վկայող)
depopulate - *amayatsunel, barbel, anmartapunag tartsunel* (ամայացնել, պարպել, անմարդաբնակ դարձնել)
depopulation - *anmartatsoum, amayatsoum, barboum* (անմարդացում, ամայացում, պարպում)
deport - *deghapokhel, aksorel, darakurel, vudarel* (տեղափոխել, աքսորել, տարագրել, վտարել)
deportation - *deghahanoutiun, aksor, vudaroum* (տեղահանութիւն, աքսոր, վտարում)
deposal - *bashdonangoutiun, kahazurgoum* (պաշտօնանկութիւն, գահազրկում)
depose - *bashdonazurgel, kahazurgel, heratsunel* (պաշտօնազրկել, գահազրկել, հեռացնել)
deposit - *zedeghel, avant tunel, gankhavujar, bahesd* (զետեղել, աւանդ դնել, կանխավճար, պահեստ)
deposition - *goudagoum, shunorhazugoum, vugayoutiun* (կուտակում, շնորհազրկում, վկայութիւն)
depot - *muteranots, ushdemaran, zoranots, gayan* (մթերանոց, շտեմարան, զօրանոց, կայան)
depravation - *abaganoutiun, yeghdzoum, vadtaratsoum* (ապականութիւն, եղծում, վատթարացում)
deprave - *anparoyatsunel, pujatsunel, abaganel* (անբարոյացնել, փճացնել, ապականել)
depravity - *abaganoutiun, vadtaratsoum* (ապականութիւն, վատթարացում)
deprecate - *baghadil, khunturel, aghersel* (պաղատիլ, խնդրել, աղերսել)
depreciate - *arzhekazurgel, nusematsunel* (արժէքազրկել, նսեմացնել)
depreciation - *arzhekazurgoum, angoum, nusematsoum* (արժէքազրկում, անկում, նսեմացում)
depredate - *goghobdel, koghnal, tallel* (կողոպտել, գողնալ, թալլել)
depredation - *goghoboud, avar, kantoum* (կողոպուտ, աւար, քանդում)
deprehend - *hangardzagi purnel, nushmarel, kudnel* (յանկարծակի բռնել, նշմարել, գտնել)
depress - *junshel, ungjel, vuhadetsunel* (ճնշել, ընկճել, վհատեցնել)
depressed - *ungjuvadz, kerhoknadz housahad* (ընկճուած, գերյոգնած, յուսահատ)
depression - *housalukoum, junshuvadzoutiun, angoum* (յուսալքում, ճնշուածութիւն, անկում)
deprivation - *zurgoum, gorousd* (զրկում, կորուստ)
deprive - *zurgel, goghobdel, bashdonazurgel* (զրկել, կողոպտել, պաշտօնազրկել)
depth - *khoroutiun, antount, khork* (խորութիւն, անդունդ, խորք)
deputation - *badkamavoroutiun, badviragoutiun* (պատգամաւորութիւն, պատուիրակութիւն)
depute - *liazorel, garkel, undurel* (լիազօրել, կարգել, ընտրել)
deputy - *yerespokhan, badvirag, pokhanort, badkamavor* (երեսփոխան, պատուիրակ, փոխանորդ, պատգամաւոր)
deracinate - *armadakhulel, pena-*

chinch unel (արմատախլել, բնաջինջ ընել)
derange - khankarel, kharnagel, deghen hanel (խանգարել, խառնակել, տեղէն հանել)
derangement - khankaroum, angarkoutiun (խանգարում, անկարգութիւն)
derelict - ander, lukial, gorsuvadz (անտէր, լքեալ, կորսուած)
dereliction - lekoum, teratsoum (լքում, թերացում)
deride - dzaghrel, heknel (ծաղրել, հեգնել)
derision - heknank, dzaghrank (հեգնանք, ծաղրանք)
derison - dzaghur, gadag (ծաղր, կատակ)
derivation - dzakoum, usgizp, jiughavoroum, adzantsoum (ծագում, սկիզբ, ճիւղաւորում,ածանցում)
derive - usdanal, pukhetsunel, veradzel, azdantsel (ստանալ, բխեցնել, վերածել, ածանցել)
derm - mort, taghant, mashg (մորթ, թաղանթ, մաշկ)
dermatologist - mortapan (մորթաբան)
dermatology - mortapanoutiun (մորթաբանութիւն)
derogate - popokhel-orenku, nusemanal, zichanil, nusem (փոփոխել՝ օրէնքը, նսեմանալ, զիջանիլ, նսեմ)
derogation - nusematsoum, popokhoum (նսեմացում, փոփոխում)
derrick - pernaparts, navtahan (բեռնաբարձ, նաւթահան)
descend - ichnel, tsadznal, dzakil, seril (իջնել, ցածնալ, ծագիլ սերիլ)
descendant - ichnogh, serogh, se-rount, dzunount (իջնող, սերող, սերունդ, ծնունդ)
descension - angoum, vayrechk, khonarhoum (անկում, վայրէջք, խոնարհում)
descent - echk, zarivayr, khonarhoum, gaberd (էջք, զառիվայր, խոնարհում, կապերտ)
describe - nugarakurel, badgerel, kudzakurel (նկարագրել, պատկերել, գծագրել)
description - nugarakuroutiun, badgeratsoum (նկարագրութիւն, պատկերացում)
descry - zunnel, tidel, haydnel, haydnoutiun (զննել, դիտել, յայտնել, յայտնութիւն)
desecrate - bughdzel, surpabughdzel, abaganel (պղծել, սրբապղծել, ապականել)
desert - anabad, anpunag, vasdag, toghoul, tasalukel (անապատ, անբնակ, վաստակ, թողուլ, դասալքել)
desertion - lukoum, tasalukoum, housahadoutiun (լքում, դասալքում, յուսահատութիւն)
deserve - arzhananal (արժանանալ)
desiccate - tsamketsunel, chortsunel (ցամքեցնել, չորցնել)
desiderate - tsangal, papakil, denchal (ցանկալ, փափաքիլ, տենչալ)
desideration - papak, tsangoutiun (փափաք, ցանկութիւն)
design - kudzel, kudzakurel, ourvakudzel, kudzakroutiun (գծել, գծագրել, ուրուագծել, գծագրութիւն)
designate - voroshel, anvanel, nushanagel (որոշել, անուանել, նշանակել)
designation - nushanagoum, garkoum, unduroutiun (նշանակում, կարգում, ընտրութիւն)
designer - kudzakurich, nakhakudzogh, tavatir (գծագրիչ, նախագծող, դաւադիր)
desinformation - abadeghedaduvoutiun, sukhal deghegoutiun (ապատեղեկատուութիւն, սխալ տեղեկութիւն)
desirable - papakeli, tsangali, paghtsali (փափաքելի, ցանկալի, բաղձալի)
desire - papakil, tsangal, papak, tsangoutiun, ights (փափաքիլ, ցանկալ, փափաք, ցանկութիւն, իղձ)
desist - hurazharil, tatril, tatretsu-

ne, yed genal (հրաժարիլ, դադրիլ, դադրեցնել, ետ կենալ)
desistance - hurazharoum, tataroum (հրաժարում, դադարում)
desk - kuraseghan, nusdaran, ambion, pem (գրասեղան, նստարան, ամպիոն, բեմ)
desktop publishing - hamagarkichayin huradaragoutiun (համակարգիչային հրատարակութիւն)
desolate - anpunag, amayi, amayatsunel, lukel (անբնակ, ամայի, ամայացնել, լքել)
desolation - amayatsoum, lukvadzoutiun, housalukoutiun (ամայացում, լքուածութիւն, յուսալքութիւն)
despair - housahadil, vuhadil, housahadoutiun (յուսահատիլ, վհատիլ, յուսահատութիւն)
desperate - anhouys, housahad, housagudour (անյոյս, յուսահատ, յուսակտուր)
desperation - housahadoutiun, vuhadoutiun (յուսահատութիւն, վհատութիւն)
despise - arhamarhel, anarkel, adel (արհամարհել, անարգել, ատել)
despite - hagarag, charoutiun, ken, nakhadink, nakhadel (հակառակ, չարութիւն, քէն, նախատինք, նախատել)
despoil - koghnal, goghobdel, zurgel (գողնալ, կողոպտել, զրկել)
despoilment - goghoboud, talan (կողոպուտ, թալան)
despot - purnagal, inknishkhan (բռնակալ, ինքնիշխան)
despotism - purnagaloutiun, purnabedoutiun (բռնակալութիւն, բռնապետութիւն)
dess - gouyd, tez (կոյտ, դէզ)
dessert - aghanter, kaghtsureghen (աղանդեր, քաղցրեղէն)
destinate - sahmanel, hadgatsunel, sahmanial (սահմանել, յատկացնել, սահմանեալ)
destination - nubadagaged, tirakh, nubadag, vakhjan (նպատակակէտ, թիրախ, նպատակ, վախճան)
destine - sahmanel, vujrel, garkel (սահմանել, վճռել, կարգել)
destiny - jagadakir, pakhd (ճակատագիր, բախտ)
destitute - lukial, aghkad, zourg (լքեալ, աղքատ, զուրկ)
destitution - chukavoroutiun, zurgank (չքաւորութիւն, զրկանք)
destroy - gordzanel, kantel, averel (կործանել, քանդել, աւերել)
destroyer - khordungets, gordzanich (խորտընկէց, կործանիչ)
destruction - kantoum, gordzanoum, punachunchoum (քանդում, կործանում, բնաջնջում)
desultory - angab, gutsgudour, vosdosdoun (անկապ, կցկտուր, ոստոստուն)
detach - anchadel, pazhnel, zadel, oughargel (անջատել, բաժնել, զատել, ուղարկել)
detached - anchad, zad, pazhan, pazhanvadz (անջատ, զատ, բաժան, բաժանուած)
detachment - anchadoum, pazhanoum, chogad (անջատում, բաժանում, ջոկատ)
detail - manramasnoutiun, manramasnel (մանրամասնութիւն, մանրամասնել)
detain - bahel, arkilel, pandargel (պահել, արգիլել, բանտարկել)
detect - haydnel, kudnel, khouzargel (յայտնել, գտնել, խուզարկել)
detective - khouzargou, hedakhouyz, kunnich, vosdigan (խուզարկու, հետախոյզ, քննիչ, ոստիկան)
detector - koghazerdzogh, yerevan hanogh, timazerdzogh (քօղազերծող, երեւան հանող, դիմազերծող)
detente - meghmatsoum, hankisd (մեղմացում, հանգիստ)
detention - arkiloum, kuravoum, tserpagaloum (արգիլում, գրաւում, ձերբակալում)
deter - gasetsunel, getsunel, darhamozel (կասեցնել, կեցնել, տարհամոզել)
deterge - makrel, luval (մաքրել, լուալ)
detergent - aghdategh, aghdahanogh,

luvatskategh (աղտաղեղ, աղտահանող, լուացքաղեղ)
deteriorate - vadtaranal, vadtaratsunel, keshnal (վատթարանալ, վատթարացնել, գէշնալ)
deterioration - vadtaratsoum, abaganoutiun (վատթարացում, ապականութիւն)
determination - vujragamoutiun, voroshoum (վճռականութիւն, որոշում)
determine - voroshel, sahmanel, hasdadel, usdibel (որոշել, սահմանել, հաստատել, ստիպել)
deterrent - arkilogh, ahapegogh (արգիլող, ահաբեկող)
detersion - makroum, surpoum (մաքրում, սրբում)
detest - adel, zuzvil, khorshil (ատել, զզուիլ, խորշիլ)
detestable - adeli, zuzveli, karsheli (ատելի, զզուելի, գարշելի)
detestation - adeloutiun, zuzvank (ատելութիւն, զզուանք)
dethrone - kahazurgel, dabalel (գահազրկել, տապալել)
detonate - baytetsunel, baytil (պայթեցնել, պայթիլ)
detort - kheghatiurel, aghavaghel (խեղաթիւրել, աղաւաղել)
detortion - kheghatiuroum, aghavaghoum (խեղաթիւրում, աղաւաղում)
detour - tartsuvadzk, sheghoum, khodoroum (դարձուածք, շեղում, խոտորում)
detract - arzhezurgel, nusematsunel, pampasel (արժէզրկել, նսեմացնել, բամբասել)
detraction - charakhosoutiun, pampasank (չարախօսութիւն, բամբասանք)
detractor - charakhos, pampasogh, vargapegogh (չարախօս, բամբասող, վարկաբեկող)
detriment - vunas, gorousd (վնաս, կորուստ)
detrition - mashoum, kaykayoum (մաշում, քայքայում)
devalorization - arzhegorousd (արժէկորուստ)
devaluation - arzhekazurgoum, angoum (արժէքազրկում, անկում)
devastate - averel, kantel, gordzanel, amayatsunel (աւերել, քանդել, կործանել, ամայացնել)
devastation - amayatsoum, aver, kantoum, gordzanoum (ամայացում, աւեր, քանդում, կործանում)
develop - zarkanal, zarkatsunel, badgerahanel, haydadzel (զարգանալ, զարգացնել, պատկերահանել, յայտածել)
developing - lousahanoum, badgerahanoum (լուսահանում, պատկերահանում)
development - zarkatsoum, aj, daradzoum, yerevagoum (զարգացում, աճ, տարածում, երեւակում)
devest - mergatsunel, yed arnel, pedel, gorsuvil (մերկացնել, ետ առնել, փետել, կորսուիլ)
deviate - sheghil, tekil, moloril, khodoril (շեղիլ, թեքիլ, մոլորիլ, խոտորիլ)
deviation - sheghoum, moloroum, tekoum (շեղում, մոլորում, թեքում)
device - hunark, michots, ourvakidz, nushanapan (հնարք, միջոց, ուրուագիծ, նշանաբան)
devil - sadana, tev, suriga (սատանայ, դեւ, սրիկայ)
devise - hunarel, khorhil, gudagel, zharankoutiun, gudag (հնարել, խորհիլ, կտակել, ժառանգութիւն, կտակ)
deviser - hunarogh, kiudarar (հնարող, գիւտարար)
devisor - gudagogh, gudagarar (կտակող, կտակարար)
devoid - barab, tadarg, zourg, barbel, vertsunel (պարապ, դատարկ, զուրկ, պարպել, վերցնել)
devolve - pokhantsel, hantsnel, kulorel (փոխանցել, յանձնել, գլորել)
devote - nuvirel, undzayel, anidzel, nuvirial (նուիրել, ընծայել, անիծել, նուիրեալ)
devoted - nuvirial, antsnazoh (նուիրեալ, անձնազոհ)

devotee - asdvadzavakh, parebashd, chermerant (աստուածավախ, բարեպաշտ, ջերմեռանդ)
devotion - nuviroum, parebashdoutiun (նուիրում, բարեպաշտութիւն)
devour - lapel, puzukdel, kishadel (լափել, բզքտել, գիշատել)
devout - parebashd, chermerant (բարեպաշտ, ջերմեռանդ)
dew - tsogh, shagh, tsoghel, terchel (ցօղ, շաղ, ցօղել, թրջել)
dewy - tsoghod, shaghod, tsoghabad (ցօղոտ, շաղոտ, ցօղապատ)
diabetes - shakarakhd (շաքարախտ)
diabets - shakarakhd (շաքարախտ)
diabolic - sadanayagan, ankout (սատանայական, անգութ)
diadem - tak, busag, takaturel (թագ, պսակ, թագադրել)
diagnose - akhdajanachel, akhdoroshel (ախտաճանաչել, ախտորոշել)
diagnosis - akhdajanachoum, akhdoroshoum (ախտաճանաչում, ախտորոշում)
diagnostic - akhdatsouyts, akhdakidoutiun (ախտացոյց, ախտագիտութիւն)
diagonal - duramangiun, angiunakidz, sheghagi (տրամանկիւն, անկիւնագիծ, շեղակի)
diagram - ourvakidz, tsev (ուրուագիծ, ձեւ)
dial - zhamatsoutsag, heratsaynaganch, ganchel (ժամացուցակ, հեռաձայնականչ, կանչել)
dialect - parpar, kavaraparpar (բարբառ, գաւառաբարբառ)
dialectic(s) - duramapanoutiun, panaguriv (տրամաբանութիւն, բանակռիւ)
dialog, dialogue - yergkhosoutiun, zurouyts, khosagtsil (երկխօսութիւն, զրոյց, խօսակցիլ)
diameter - duramakids, dramachap (տրամագիծ, տրամաչափ)
diamond - atamant, shoghagun (ադամանդ, շողակն)
diapason - tsaynashar, tsaynadou, nertashnagoutiun (ձայնաշար, ձայնատու, ներդաշնակութիւն)
diaper - khantsarour, antserots, khantsarourel (խանձարուր, անձեռոց, խանձարուրել)
diaphragm - usdodzani, michnamashg, taghant (ստոծանի, միջնամաշկ, թաղանթ)
diarrhea - porharoutiun, porkushouk (փորհարութիւն, փորքշուք)
diary - orakir, tseradedur, oragan (օրագիր, ձեռատետր, օրական)
diaspora - uspiurk, kaghtashkharh (սփիւռք, գաղթաշխարհ)
diatribe - barsavakir, kunnatadoutiun (պարսաւագիր, քննադատութիւն)
dibble - souzil, hagil, dzagel, hoghaporich (սուզիլ, հակիլ, ծակել, հողափորիչ)
dickens - sadana, tev, shoudig (սատանայ, դեւ, շուտիկ)
dictate - telaturel, hurahankel (թելադրել, հրահանգել)
dictator - purnagal, purnabed, menader (բռնակալ, բռնապետ, մենատէր)
dictatorship - purnagaloutiun (բռնակալութիւն)
diction - asoutiun, arokanoutiun (ասութիւն, առոգանութիւն)
dictionary - pararan, parkirk (բառարան, բառգիրք)
dictum - aradz, asouyt, asatsvadz, vujir (առած, ասոյթ, ասացուած, վճիռ)
die - mernil, mahanal, nardanish, (մեռնիլ, մահանալ, նարտանիշ)
dies - daramayr, gunkots, turoshmadubel (տառամայր, կնքոց, դրոշմատպել)
diet - sununtaganon, bahetsoghoutiun sagavageroutiun (սննդականոն, պահեցողութիւն, սակաւակերութիւն)
dietary - sununtaganon, sunounti veraperial (սննդականոն, սնունդի վերաբերեալ)
differ - darperil, zanazanvil (տարբերիլ, զանազանուիլ)
difference - darperoutiun, zanazanoutiun, zanazanel (տարբերութիւն,

գանազանութիւն, գանազանել)
different - darper, zanazan (տարբեր, զանազան)
differential - darperagich (տարբերալիչ)
differentiate - darperel, darperil, zadoroshel (տարբերել, տարբերիլ, զատորոշել)
difficult - tuzhvar, dzanur, khisd (դժուար, ծանր, խիստ)
difficulty - tuzhvaroutiun (դժուարութիւն)
diffidence - amuchgodoutiun,yergchodoutiun, daragouys (ամչկոտութիւն, երկչոտութիւն, տարակոյս)
diffident - amuchgod, yergchod, anvusdah, hamesd (ամչկոտ, երկչոտ, անվստահ, համեստ)
difform - dutsev, dukegh, aylantag (տձեւ, տգեղ, այլանդակ)
diffuse - suprel, daradzel, dzavalel (սփռել, տարածել, ծաւալել)
diffusion - suproum, daradzoum, tsurvoum (սփռում, տարածում, ցրւում)
dig - porel, beghel, khotel (փորել, պեղել, խոթել)
digest - marsel, haletsunel, yiuratsunel (մարսել, հալեցնել, իւրացնել)
digestion - marsoghoutiun, yiouratsoum (մարսողութիւն, իւրացում)
digestive - marsoghagan, tiuramars (մարսողական, դիւրամարս)
digit - mad, madnachap (մատ, մատնաչափ)
digital - madi, madnayin (մատի, մատնային)
digitate - madnanushel (մատնանշել)
dignify - badvel, partsuratsunel (պատուել, բարձրացնել)
dignitary - asdijanavor, badvagal (աստիճանաւոր, պատուակալ)
dignity - arzhanabadvoutiun, medzoutiun, shouk (արժանապատուութիւն, մեծութիւն, շուք)
digress - sheghil, khodoril, zardoughil (շեղիլ, խոտորիլ, զարտուղիլ)
dike - khuram, toump, badnesh, khuramadel (խրամ, թումբ, պատնէշ, խրամատել)
dilapidate - avrel, gordzanel, vadnel, muskhel (աւրել, կործանել, վատնել, մսխել)
dilatation - untlaynoum, dzavaloum, daradzoum (ընդլայնում, ծաւալում, տարածում)
dilate - untlaynel, dzavalel, untartsagel (ընդլայնել, ծաւալել, ընդարձակել)
dilatory - tantagh, habaghgod (դանդաղ, յապաղկոտ)
dilemma - yergundurank, pokhunderoutiun (երկընտրանք, փոխընտրութիւն)
dilettant, dilettante - kegharvesdaser (գեղարուեստասէր)
diligence - chanasiroutiun, pouyt (ջանասիրութիւն, փոյթ)
dilute - loudzel, churakharnel, nosratsunel, meghmel (լուծել, ջրախառնել, նօսրացնել, մեղմել)
dim - aghod, mout, murayl, mutaknel (աղօտ, մութ, մռայլ, մթագնել)
dime - dasnots, dasu cent (տասնոց, տասը սենթ)
dimension - daradzoutiun, dzaval (տարածութիւն, ծաւալ)
diminish - nevazetsunel, bagsetsunel, buzdigtsunel, bagsil (նուազեցնել, պակսեցնել, պզտիկցնել, պակսիլ)
diminution - nevazoum, bagasoum, pokratsoum, zeghch (նուազում, պակասում, փոքրացում, զեղչ)
dimmer - lousajushtich (լուսաճշդիչ)
dimple - aydaposig, posignal (այտափոսիկ, փոսիկնալ)
din - aghmoug, aghaghag, tuntatsunel (աղմուկ, աղաղակ, թնդացնել)
dine - jashel, unturel, oudel (ճաշել, ընթրել, ուտել)
diner - jashogh, unturogh (ճաշող, ընթրող)
diner-dansant - jashabar (ճաշապար)
ding - hunchetsunel, borodakhosel, tuntiun (հնչեցնել, պոռոտախօսել, թնդիւն)
dinge - juzmuvadzk, juzmel, aghdodel (ճզմուածք, ճզմել, աղտոտել)

dining hall - *jashasurah* (ճաշասրահ)
dining room - *jashaseniag* (ճաշասենեակ)
dinner - *unturik, jash* (ընթրիք, ճաշ)
dinner-party - *jashgerouyt, hatsgerouyt* (ճաշկերոյթ, հացկերոյթ)
dinosaur - *hoyamoghez, vayri moghez* (հոյամողէզ, վայրի մողէզ)
dint - *harvadz, verk, khotsel* (հարուած, վէրք, խոցել)
diocesan - *temagan, temagal* (թեմական, թեմակալ)
diocese - *tem, vijag, ator* (թեմ, վիճակ, աթոռ)
dip - *tatkhel, unughmil, souzvil, mukhel* (թաթխել, ընկղմիլ, սուզուիլ, մխել)
diphteria - *mashgakhd* (մաշկախտ)
diphtheria - *geghdzamashg* (կեղծամաշկ)
diphtong - *yergtsayn, yergparpar* (երկձայն, երկբարբառ)
diploma - *vugayagan* (վկայական)
diplomacy - *tivanakidoutiun* (դիւանագիտութիւն)
diplomat - *tivanaked, varbedorti* (դիւանագէտ, վարպետորդի)
dipper - *souzag, sherep, souzanav* (սուզակ, շերեփ, սուզանաւ)
dire - *sarsapeli, sosgali, charakoushag* (սարսափելի, սոսկալի, չարագուշակ)
direct - *oughigh, oughghagi, shidag, oughghel, arachnortel* (ուղիղ, ուղղակի, շիտակ, ուղղել, առաջնորդել)
direction - *oughghoutiun, dunorenoutiun, gheg, goghm* (ուղղութիւն, տնօրէնութիւն, ղեկ, կողմ)
directive - *tsoutsmounk, arachnortogh, oughghich* (ցուցմունք, առաջնորդող, ուղղիչ)
directly - *oughghagi, oughigh, anmichabes, isgouyn* (ուղղակի, ուղիղ, անմիջապէս, իսկոյն)
director - *dunoren, desouch, ghegavar* (տնօրէն, տեսուչ, ղեկավար)
directory - *hastseakirk, hastsearan, oughetsouyts* (հասցէագիրք, հասցէարան, ուղեցոյց)
directress - *dunorenouhi, deschouhi* (տնօրէնուհի, տեսչուհի)
dirge - *maherk, voghp, hokehankisd* (մահերգ, ողբ, հոգեհանգիստ)
dirt - *aghp, geghd, aghdodoutiun, tsekh, dighm, aghdodel* (աղբ, կեղտ, աղտոտութիւն, ձեխ, տիղմ, աղտոտել)
dirty - *aghdod, geghdod, usdorin* (աղտոտ, կեղտոտ, ստորին)
disability - *angaroghoutiun* (անկարողութիւն)
disable - *angarogh, angarogh tartsunel, dugaratsunel* (անկարող, անկարող դարձնել, տկարացնել)
disabuse - *oughghel, shudgel, achkeru panal* (ուղղել, շտկել, աչքերը բանալ)
disaccord - *anhamatsayn, anhamatsaynoutiun* (անհամաձայն, անհամաձայնութիւն)
disadvantage - *annubasd, gorousd, vunas* (աննպաստ, կորուստ, վնաս)
disaffect - *tuzhkohetsunel, baghetsunel, siradel* (դժգոհեցնել, պաղեցնել, սիրատել)
disaffection - *tuzhkohoutiun, angarkoutiun* (դժգոհութիւն, անկարգութիւն)
disaffirm - *zhukhdel, herkel* (ժխտել, հերքել)
disagree - *chuhamatsaynil, chuharmaril* (չհամաձայնիլ, չյարմարիլ)
disagreeable - *anhajo, anakhorzh, duhaj, anhajeli* (անհաճոյ, անախորժ, տհաճ, անհաճելի)
disallow - *merzhel, chuhajil, chuhavnil* (մերժել, չհաճիլ, չհաւնիլ)
disannul - *vochunchatsunel, chunchel* (ոչնչացնել, ջնջել)
disappear - *anhedanal, anhaydanal, chukanal* (անհետանալ, անյայտանալ, չքանալ)
disappoint - *housakhapel, hiastapel* (յուսախաբել, հիասթափել)
disappointed - *housakhapvadz, hiastapvadz* (յուսախաբուած, հիասթափուած)

disappointment - housakhapoutiun (յուսախաբութիւն)
disapproval - anhavanoutiun (անհաւանութիւն)
disapprove - chuhavanil, andesel, merzhel (չհաւանիլ, անտեսել, մերժել)
disarm - abazinel, zinatapel (ապազինել, զինաթափել)
disarmament - zinatapoutiun, abazinoum (զինաթափութիւն, ապազինում)
disarrange - khankarel, kharnagel (խանգարել, խառնակել)
disarrangement - khankaroum, kharnagoum (խանգարում, խառնակում)
disarray - angarkoutiun, iraran-tsoum (անկարգութիւն, իրարանցում)
disaster - aghed, argadz, portsank, gordzanoum (աղէտ, արկած, փորձանք, կործանում)
disastrous - aghidali, gordzanarar (աղիտալի, կործանարար)
disavow - herkel, ouranal, merzhel, ankidanal (հերքել, ուրանալ, մերժել, անգիտանալ)
disband - artsagel, zoratsurvel, jampel (արձակել, զօրացրուել, ճամբել)
disbelieve - chuhavadal, yergmudil (չհաւատալ, երկմտիլ)
disburse - vujarel, hadoutsanel, dzakhsel (վճարել, հատուցանել, ծախսել)
disbursement - vujaroum (վճարում)
discard - nedel, shuburdel (նետել, շպրտել)
discern - zadoroshel, zanazanel, nushmarel (զատորոշել, զանազանել, նշմարել)
discharge - pernatapel, barbel, artsagel, guragel (բեռնաթափել, պարպել, արձակել, կրակել)
disciple - ashagerd, hedevogh, arakial (աշակերտ, հետեւող, առաքեալ)
discipline - garkabahoutiun, gark ganon, gurtoutiun, badizh (կարգապահութիւն, կարգ կանոն, կրթութիւն, պատիժ)
disclaim - hurazharil, merzhel, chuntounil (հրաժարիլ, մերժել, չընդունիլ)
disclose - haydnaperel, panal, yerevan hanel (յայտնաբերել, բանալ, երեւան հանել)
disclosure - haydnaperoum, tursevoroum (յայտնաբերում, դրսեւորում)
discolor - kounadel, duzhkounel, kounazurgel (գունատել, տժգունել, գունազրկել)
discomfit - khapanel, shupotetsunel, neghel, chakhchakhel (խափանել, շփոթեցնել, նեղել, ջախջախել)
discomfort - neghel, anhankusdatsunel, anhankusdoutiun (նեղել, անհանգստացնել, անհանգստութիւն)
disconcert - shupotetsunel, tsakhoghtsunel, khankarel (շփոթեցնել, ձախողցնել, խանգարել)
disconsolate - anmukhitar, anuspop, dukhour (անմխիթար, անսփոփ, տխուր)
discontent - tuzhkoh, tuzhkohoutiun, tuzhkohil (դժգոհ, դժգոհութիւն, դժգոհիլ)
discontinue - unthadel, tatretsunel, tatril, genal (ընդհատել, դադրեցնել, դադրիլ, կենալ)
discord - anhamatsaynoutiun, chumiapanil (անհամաձայնութիւն, չմիաբանիլ)
discordance - anhamatsaynoutiun (անհամաձայնութիւն)
discount - zeghch, zeghchel (զեղչ, զեղչել)
discourage - vuhadetsunel, housalukel (վհատեցնել, յուսալքել)
discourse - jar, khosagtsoutiun, jarel (ճառ, խօսակցութիւն, ճառել)
discover - haydnaperel, hunarel, kudnel (յայտնաբերել, հնարել, գտնել)
discovery - haydnaperoum, kiud (յայտնաբերում, գիւտ)
discredit - vargapegel, anvusdahoutiun, vargapegoum (վարկաբեկել, անվստահութիւն, վարկաբեկում)
discreet - khohem, uzkouysh, khela-

tsi (խոհեմ, զգոյշ, խելացի)
discrepancy - anhamatsaynoutiun, hagasoutiun (անհամաձայնութիւն, հակասութիւն)
discrepant - angayoun, hagasogh (անկայուն, հակասող)
discrete - anchad, zad, vorosh (անջատ, զատ, որոշ)
discretion - khohemoutiun, uzkoushavoroutiun (խոհեմութիւն, զգուշաւորութիւն)
discriminate - zadoroshel, zanazanel, khudir tunel (զատորոշել, զանազանել, խտիր դնել)
discrimination - khudraganoutiun, zanazanoum (խտրականութիւն, զանազանում)
discrown - takazurgel (թագազրկել)
discrupt - jeghkel, gudrel, khuzel, puzukduvadz (ճեղքել, կտրել, խզել, բզքտուած)
discruption - khuzoum, kaykayoum, badaroum (խզում, քայքայում, պատառում)
discuss - vijapanil, vijil, kunnargel (վիճաբանիլ, վիճիլ, քննարկել)
discussion - vijapanoutiun, kunnoum, houzoum (վիճաբանութիւն, քննում, յուզում)
disdain - arhamarhel, arhamarhank, andesoum (արհամարհել, արհամարհանք, անտեսում)
disease - hivantoutiun, akhd, hivantatsunel (հիւանդութիւն, ախտ, հիւանդացնել)
disembark - naven ichnel, pernatapel (նաւէն իջնել, բեռնաթափել)
disembarkation - pernatapoum, navahanoum (բեռնաթափում, նաւահանում)
disenchant - hiastapel, badranatapel (հիասթափել, պատրանաթափել)
disengage - azadel, artsagel, anchadel, anchadvil (ազատել, արձակել, անջատել, անջատուիլ)
disfigure - gerbaranapokhel, dukeghtsunel, aylapokhel (կերպարանափոխել, տգեղցնել, այլափոխել)
disgorge - puskhel, veratartsunel, tsaydel (փսխել, վերադարձնել, ցայտել)
disgrace - shunorhazurgel, anbadvel, shunurhazurgoum (շնորհազրկել, անպատուել, շնորհազրկում)
disguise - dzubduvil, dzubdel, dzubdoum (ծպտուիլ, ծպտել, ծպտում)
disgust - zuzvetsunel, buzhkank, zuzvank, noghgank (զզուեցնել, պշկանք, զզուանք, նողկանք)
dish - bunag, aman, usgavarag, bunagi mech tunel (պնակ, աման, սկաւառակ, պնակի մէջ դնել)
dishabille - hanvil, merganal, tetev hakousd (հանուիլ, մերկանալ, թեթեւ հագուստ)
disharmony - annertashnagoutiun (աններդաշնակութիւն)
dishearten - housahadetsunel, vuhadetsunel, housalukel (յուսահատեցնել, վհատեցնել, յուսալքել)
disherit - zharankazurgel (ժառանգազրկել)
dishonest - anbargeshd, anbadiv, khartakh (անպարկեշտ, անպատիւ, խարդախ)
dishono(u)r - anbadvel, anarkel, anbadvoutiun (անպատուել, անարգել, անպատուութիւն)
dishwasher - aman luvatsogh, khadoudig (աման լուացող, խատուտիկ)
disinfect - haganekhel, aghdahanel (հականեխել, աղտահանել)
disinfection - haganekhoum (հականեխում)
disinherit - zharankazurgel (ժառանգազրկել)
disintegrate - masnadel, manradel, kaykayel (մասնատել, մանրատել, քայքայել)
disinterested - anshahakhuntir, anachar (անշահախնդիր, անաչառ)
disinthrall - azadakurel, azadel (ազատագրել, ազատել)
disinthrallment - azadakuroum (ազատագրում)
disjoin - anchadel, pazhnel, zadel (անջատել, բաժնել, զատել)
disjoint - angab, anchad, masnadel (անկապ, անջատ, մասնատել)

disk, disc - usgavarag, usgoudegh (սկաւառակ, սկուտեղ)
diskette - usgavarag (սկաւառակ)
dislike - chusirel, adel, khorshil, adeloutiun (չսիրել, ատել, խորշիլ, ատելութիւն)
dislocate - deghapokhel, khakhdel (տեղափոխել, խախտել)
dislocation - deghapoghoum, deghahanoutiun, khakhdoum (տեղափոխում, տեղահանութիւն, խախտում)
dislodge - deghen hanel, heratsunel (տեղէն հանել, հեռացնել)
dislodgement - deghahanoum, vudaroum (տեղահանում, վտարում)
disloyal - anhavadarim, nenk (անհաւատարիմ, նենգ)
dismal - dukhour, durdoum, charakoushag (տխուր, տրտում, չարագուշակ)
dismantle - kantel, gordzanel, abazinel (քանդել, կործանել, ապազինել)
dismarry - amousnaloudzel (ամուսնալուծել)
dismask - timagazerdzel, timagu hanel (դիմակազերծել, դիմակը հանել)
dismay - ahapegel, sarsap, sosgoum (ահաբեկել, սարսափ, սոսկում)
dismember - antamahadel, masnadel (անդամահատել, մասնատել)
dismemberment - antamahadoutiun, hoshodoum (անդամահատութիւն, յօշոտում)
dismiss - artsagel, vanel, vurundel (արձակել, վանել, վռնտել)
dismissal - bashdonangoutiun, vudaroum, artsagoum (պաշտօնանկութիւն, վտարում, արձակում)
disobedience - anhunazantoutiun (անհնազանդութիւն)
disobedient - anhunazant (անհնազանդ)
disobey - anhunazantil, chansal (անհնազանդիլ, չանսալ)
disorder - angarkoutiun, kharnagoutiun, khankarel (անկարգութիւն, խառնակութիւն, խանգարել)
disorganize - gazmaloudzel, khankarel (կազմալուծել, խանգարել)
disown - ouranal, merzhel, zhukhdel (ուրանալ, մերժել, ժխտել)
dispand - daradzel, suprel (տարածել, սփռել)
dispansion - dzavaloum, daradzoum (ծաւալում, տարածում)
disparage - anarkel, nusematsunel (անարգել, նսեմացնել)
disparate - anhavasar, anchad (անհաւասար, անջատ)
disparition - anhedatsoum, anerevoutatsoum (անհետացում, աներեւութացում)
disparity - anhavasaroutiun, anhamachapoutiun (անհաւասարութիւն, անհամաչափութիւն)
dispatch - oughargel, arakel, arakoum, herakir (ուղարկել, առաքել, առաքում, հեռագիր)
dispensable - pashkheli, touyladureli (բաշխելի, թոյլատրելի)
dispensary - tarmanadoun, pouzharan (դարմանատուն, բուժարան)
dispense - pashkhel, madagararel, pazhnel (բաշխել, մատակարարել, բաժնել)
dispenser - pashkhich, madagarar (բաշխիչ, մատակարար)
disperse - tsurvel, daradzel (ցրուել, տարածել)
dispersion - tsurvoum, suproum (ցրւում, սփռում)
displace - deghapokhel, heratsunel (տեղափոխել, հեռացնել)
displacement - deghapokhoutiun, deghahanoutiun (տեղափոխութիւն, տեղահանութիւն)
display (n) - tsoutsaturoutiun, tsoutsaseghan, tsoutsadaghdag (ցուցադրութիւն, ցուցասեղան, ցուցատախտակ)
display (v) - tsoutsaturel, purel, dzaradzel (ցուցադրել, փռել, տարածել)
displease - vushdatsunel, tuzhkohetsunel (վշտացնել, դժգոհեցնել)
displeasure - anakhorzhoutiun, duhajoutiun (անախորժութիւն, տհա–

ճութիւն)
disport - uzpostsunel, khaghal, uzposank, khagh (զբօսցնել, խաղալ, զբօսանք, խաղ)
disposal - deghavoroum, garkaturoutiun, dunorinoutiun (տեղաւորում, կարգադրութիւն, տնօրինութիւն)
dispose - garkaturel, dunorinel, garkavorel, duramaturel (կարգադրել, տնօրինել, կարգաւորել, տրամադրել)
disposition - duramaturoutiun, midoum, hozharoutiun (տրամադրութիւն, միտում, յօժարութիւն)
dispost - deghahanel, bashdonazurgel (տեղահանել, պաշտօնազրկել)
dispraise - nakhadel, barsavel, nakhadink (նախատել, պարսաւել, նախատինք)
disprize - usdorakunahadel (ստորագնահատել)
disproof - herkoum (հերքում)
disproportion - anhamachapoutiun, anhamemadoutiun (անհամաչափութիւն, անհեմատութիւն)
disprove - herkel, churel, zhukhdel (հերքել, ջրել, ժխտել)
dispute - vijil, vijapanil, vej (վիճիլ, վիճաբանիլ, վէճ)
disqualification - voragazurgoum (որակազրկում)
disqualify - voragazurgel, anarzhan haydararel (որակազրկել, անարժան յայտարարել)
disquiet - mudahokel, houzel, anhankusdoutiun (մտահոգել, յուզել, անհանգստութիւն)
disregard - andesel, arhamarhel, andesoum (անտեսել, արհամարհել, անտեսում)
disreputable - anbadiv, vadahampav (անպատիւ, վատահամբաւ)
disrepute - anbadvoutiun (անպատուութիւն)
disrobe - mergatsunel, merganal, hanvil (մերկացնել, մերկանալ, հանուիլ)
dissect - antamahadel (անդամահատել)
disseminate - sermanel, tsanel, suprel (սերմանել, ցանել, սփռել)
dissent - daragardzik ullal, anhamatsaynoutiun (տարակարծիք ըլլալ, անհամաձայնութիւն)
dissentient - anhamatsayn, daragardzik, aylakhoh (անհամաձայն, տարակարծիք, այլախոհ)
dissertation - avardajar, ousoumnasiroutiun (աւարտաճառ, ուսումնասիրութիւն)
disserver - pazhnel, anchadel (բաժնել, անջատել)
dissident - aylakhoh, daragardzik, darper (այլախոհ, տարակարծիք, տարբեր)
dissimulate - geghdzel, tsevatsunel, taktsunel (կեղծել, ձեւացնել, թաքցնել)
dissimulation - koghargoum, taktsunoum, geghdzik (քօղարկում, թաքցնում, կեղծիք)
dissipate - tsurvel, paradel, chunchel (ցրուել, փարատել, ջնջել)
dissipation - vadnoum, muskhoum, tsopoutiun (վատնում, մսխում, ցոփութիւն)
dissociate - pazhnel, anchadel, kagel (բաժնել, անջատել, քակել)
dissolute - anarag, meghg, tsop (անառակ, մեղկ, ցոփ)
dissolution - loudzoum, haloum, tsopoutiun (լուծում, հալում, ցոփութիւն)
dissolve - loudzel, haletsunel, chunchel (լուծել, հալեցնել, ջնջել)
dissonant - annertashnag, kharnatsayn (աններդաշնակ, խառնաձայն)
dissuade - darhamozel, shurchel (տարհամոզել, շրջել)
distance - heravoroutiun, michots, anchurbed (հեռաւորութիւն, միջոց, անջրպետ)
distant - herou, heraga, dardam (հեռու, հեռակայ, տարտամ)
distend - ouril, ourchil, hubardanal, untlaynil (ուռիլ, ուռչիլ, հպարտանալ, ընդլայնիլ)
dister - aksorel, darakurel (աքսորել, տարագրել)
distil, distill - zudel, toretsunel,

gatgutil, kamel (կտել, Թորեցնել, կաթկթիլ, քամել)
distiller - torich, zudich, oghehan (Թորիչ, զտիչ, օղեհան)
distillery - zudaran, toranots (զտարան, Թորանոց)
distinct - vorosh, husdag, zad (որոշ, յստակ, զատ)
distinction - khudroutiun, zanazanoutiun, kunahadank (խտրութիւն, զանազանութիւն, գնահատանք)
distinguish - zanazanel, voroshel, zadel (զանազանել, որոշել, զատել)
distort - tsevapokhel, volorel, dzamadzurel, dzamadzour (ձեւափոխել, ոլորել, ծամածռել, ծամածուռ)
distortion - dzuroutiun, kalaroum, voloroum, aghavaghoum (ծռութիւն, գալարում, ոլորում, աղաւաղում)
distract - tsurvel, sheghel, heratsunel, uzpaghtsunel (ցրուել, շեղել, հեռացնել, զբաղցնել)
distraction - shupotoutiun, tsurvadzoutiun, uzposank (շփոթութիւն, ցրուածութիւն, զբօսանք)
distrain - unchazurgel, purnakuravel, junshel, daknabil (ընչազրկել, բռնագրաւել, ճնշել, տագնապիլ)
distraint - purnakuravoum, kuravoum (բռնագրաւում, գրաւում)
distress - vishd, neghoutiun, daknab (վիշտ, նեղութիւն, տագնապ)
distribute - pazhnel, tsurvel, pashkhel (բաժնել, ցրուել, բաշխել)
distribution - tsurvoum, pazhanoum, pashkhoum (ցրւում, բաժանում, բաշխում)
distributor - tsurvogh, pazhnogh (ցրուող, բաժնող)
district - shurchan, kavar, shurchannerou pazhnel (շրջան, գաւառ, շրջաններու բաժնել)
distrust - gasgadzil, yergmudil, anvusdahoutiun (կասկածիլ, երկմտիլ, անվստահութիւն)
disturb - khankarel, anhankusdatsunel, khurovel, vurtovel (խանգարել, անհանգստացնել, խռովել, վրդովել)
disturber - khankarogh, khurovarar, aghmugarar (խանգարող, խռովարար, աղմկարար)
disunion - anmioutiun, pazhanoum, yergpeghgoum (անմիութիւն, բաժանում, երկփեղկում)
disunite - pazhnel, anchadel (բաժնել, անջատել)
disunity - anmiapanoutiun (անմիաբանութիւն)
disvaluation - arzhekazurgoum, angoum (արժէքազրկում, անկում)
ditch - khuramadel, khuram, arou, kedag, pos (խրամատել, խրամ, առու, գետակ, փոս)
diuretic - mizaper (միզաբեր)
diurnal - tseregayin, aroria, amenria (ցերեկային, առօրեայ, ամէնօրեայ)
divagate - taparil, moloril, sheghil, zarantsel (Թափառիլ, մոլորիլ, շեղիլ, զառանցել)
divagation - taparoum, moloroum, zarantsank, hortoum (Թափառում, մոլորում, զառանցանք, յորդում)
divan - pazmots, divan, tahlij (բազմոց, տիւան, դահլիճ)
divaricate - jiughavoril, daradzvil (ճիւղաւորիլ, տարածուիլ)
dive - souzil, souzel, mukhurjil, souzoum, vad bantog (սուզիլ, սուզել, մխրճիլ, սուզում, վատ պանդոկ)
diverge - zanazanil, darperil, daradzuvil, suprel (զանազանիլ, տարբերիլ, տարածուիլ, սփռել)
divergence - daragardzoutiun, anhamatsaynoutiun (տարակարծութիւն, անհամաձայնութիւն)
divers - aylevayl (այլեւայլ)
diverse - zanazan, aylazan, darper (զանազան, այլազան, տարբեր)
diversify - aylagerbel, aylapokhel, zanazanel, besbisel (այլակերպել, այլափոխել, զանազանել, պէսպիսել)
diversity - pazmazanoutiun (բազմազանութիւն)
divert - uzpostsunel, khodorel, untashku pokhel (զբօսցնել, խոտո–

րել, ընթացքը փոխել)
divertise - zuvarjatsunel, zuvarjanal, uzposnoul (զուարճացնել, զուարճանալ, զբօսնուլ)
divest - mergatsunel, geghvel, goghobdel (մերկացնել, կեղուել, կողոպտել)
divide - pazhnel, anchadel, yergbaragel, pazhnuvil (բաժնել, անջատել, երկպառակել, բաժնուիլ)
divided - pazhnuvadz, anchad (բաժնուած, անջատ)
dividend - shahapazhin, pazhaneli (շահաբաժին, բաժանելի)
divider - pazhnogh, pazhanarar (բաժնող, բաժանարար)
divination - koushagoutiun (գուշակութիւն)
divine - koushagel, asdvadzayin, hurashali (գուշակել, աստուածային, հրաշալի)
diving - souzogh, souzich (սուզող, սուզիչ)
divinify - asdvadzatsunel (աստուածացնել)
divining - koushagogh (գուշակող)
divinity - asdvadzoutiun, asdvadz, (աստուածութիւն, Աստուած)
divinize - asdvadzatsunel (աստուածացնել)
divisible - pazhaneli, pazhanagan (բաժանելի, բաժանական)
division - pazhanoum, anchadoum, pazhanmounk, zorapazhin (բաժանում, անջատում, բաժանմունք, զօրաբաժին)
divisor - pazhanarar (բաժանարար)
divorce - amousnaloudzoum, pazhanoum, amousnaloudzel (ամուսնալուծում, բաժանում, ամուսնալուծել)
divulgate - hurabaragvadz (հրապարակուած)
divulgation - hurabaragoum, daradzoum (հրապարակում, տարածում)
divulge - hurabaragel, hurchagel, daradzel (հրապարակել, հռչակել, տարածել)
dizz - abshetsunel, kulkhou budouyd dal (ապշեցնել, գլխու պտոյտ տալ)
dizziness - kulkhou budouyd (գլխու պտոյտ)
dizzy - kulkhabudouyd ounetsogh, shupot, kuloukhu tarnal (գլխապտոյտ ունեցող, շփոթ, գլուխը դառնալ)
dizzyness - kulkhabudouyd (գլխապտոյտ)
do - unel, gadarel, verchatsunel (ընել, կատարել, վերջացնել)
docile - hulou, hunazant, tiurundel (հլու, հնազանդ, դիւրընտել)
dock - navagayk, navahankisd, bochu gudrel (նաւակայք, նաւահանգիստ, պոչը կտրել)
docker - navahankisdi kordzavor (նաւահանգիստի գործաւոր)
doctor - puzhishg, pouzhel, masnakidagan didghos (բժիշկ, բուժել, մասնագիտական տիտղոս)
doctress - puzhushgouhi (բժշկուհի)
doctrine - vartabedoutiun, usguzpounk (վարդապետութիւն, սկզբունք)
document - pasdatought, vaverakir (փաստաթուղթ, վաւերագիր)
documentary - vaverakuragan (վաւերագրական)
documentation - pasdakuroutiun, vaverakuroutiun (փաստագրութիւն, վաւերագրութիւն)
dodge - khousapil, pakhil, khoramangoutiun, pakhousd (խուսափիլ, փախիլ, խորամանկութիւն, փախուստ)
dodger - khoramang, jarbig, khousapogh (խորամանկ, ճարպիկ, խուսափող)
doff - hanel, mergatsunel, megti nedel (հանել, մերկացնել, մէկդի նետել)
dog - shoun, shunig, gart, jang (շուն, շնիկ, կարթ, ճանկ)
dogma - havadalik, vartabedoutiun, aghant (հաւատալիք, վարդապետութիւն, աղանդ)
dogmatic - vartabedagan, aghantavor (վարդապետական, աղանդաւոր)
doings - kordzer, arark (գործեր,

արարք)
dole - nubasd, oknoutiun, pazhin, nubasd dal, vishd (նպաստ, օգնութիւն, բաժին, նպաստ տալ, վիշտ)
doll - boubrig (պուպրիկ)
dollar - dolar (տոլար)
dolly - boubrig, luvadzki tag, tagov dzedzel (պուպրիկ, լուացքի թակ, թակով ծեծել)
dolor - tsav, vishd, gusgidz (ցաւ, վիշտ, կսկիծ)
dolorous - tsavali, dukhour, vushdali (ցաւալի, տխուր, վշտալի)
dolphin - tulpin, kharuskhagal (դլփին, խարսխակալ)
dolt - aboush, anmid, himaroutiun unel (ապուշ, անմիտ, յիմարութիւն ընել)
domain - dirabedoutiun, galvadz, hogh, punakavar (տիրապետութիւն, կալուած, Հող, բնագաւառ)
dome - kumpet, gamar, dajar, kumpetadzadzgel (գմբէթ, կամար, տաճար, գմբէթածածկել)
domestic - undani, arduni, dzara (ընտանի, առտնի, ծառայ)
domicile - punagaran, doun, punagetsunel (բնակարան, տուն, բնակեցնել)
domiciliate - punagetsunel, undanetsunel (բնակեցնել, ընտանեցնել)
dominant - dirogh, ishkhogh, kulkhavor (տիրող, իշխող, գլխաւոր)
dominate - ishkhel, direl, dirabedel (իշխել, տիրել, տիրապետել)
domination - dirabedoutiun, ishkhanoutiun, ishkhoum (տիրապետութիւն, իշխանութիւն, իշխում)
domineer - ishkhel, diragalel, purnanal, korozanal (իշխել, տիրակալել, բռնանալ, գոռոզանալ)
dominion - kerishkhanoutiun, dirabedoutiun (գերիշխանութիւն, տիրապետութիւն)
don - baron, der, choch (պարոն, տէր, ջոջ)
donate - nuvirel, dal, tsonel (նուիրել, տալ, ձօնել)
donation - nuver, nuviradououtiun (նուէր, նուիրատուութիւն)
donator - nuviradou (նուիրատու)
done - gadaradz, yeghadz, lumuntsadz, yepadz (կատարած, եղած, լմնցած, եփած)
donkey - esh, avanag, dukhmar (էշ, աւանակ, տխմար)
donor - nuviradou, nuvirogh (նուիրատու, նուիրող)
doom - tadavujir, jagadakir, tadasdan, tadabardel (դատավճիռ, ճակատագիր, դատաստան, դատապարտել)
door - tour, antsk, moudk (դուռ, անցք, մուտք)
doorkeeper - turnaban (դռնապան)
doorstep - santukhamad, turan asdijan, sem (սանդուխամատ, դրան աստիճան, սեմ)
doorstop - turnagal, arkelag (դռնակալ, արգելակ)
dormant - kunatsogh, nunchogh, nirhogh, ansharzh (քնացող, ննջող, նիրհող, անշարժ)
dormitory - nuncharan, nunchasurah (ննջարան, ննջասրահ)
dorp - kiughag (գիւղակ)
dose - chap, teghachap, kanag (չափ, դեղաչափ, քանակ)
dossier - tughtadzurar, henag (թղթածրար, յենակ)
dot - ged, pidz, ozhid, gedaturel (կէտ, բիծ, օժիտ, կէտադրել)
dotage - zaramadzoutiun, dughayamudoutiun (զառամածութիւն, տղայամտութիւն)
dotty - gidavor, dugaramid, dugar (կիտաւոր, տկարամիտ, տկար)
douane - maksadoun (մաքսատուն)
double - gurgin, gurgnagi, zouyk, gurgunel (կրկին, կրկնակի, զոյգ, կրկնել)
doublet - gurgnorinag (կրկնօրինակ)
double-dealer - khapepa, yergeres (խաբեբայ, երկերես)
double-faced - yergeres, geghdzavor (երկերես, կեղծաւոր)
double-minded - popokhamid, yergmid (փոփոխամիտ, երկմիտ)
doubt - gasgadzil, varanil, gasgadz, daragouys (կասկածիլ, վարանիլ,

կասկած, տարակոյս)
douche - churtsan, tsuntsough, churtsoghel (ջրցան, ցնցուղ, ջրցօղել)
dough - khumor, hays (խմոր, Հայս)
doughty - kach, khizakh, gudrij, houzhgou (քաջ, խիզախ, կտրիճ, Հուժկու)
dove - aghavni, dadrag (աղաւնի, տատրակ)
down - varu, nerkev, dagu, angoum, aghvamaz, dabalel (վարը, ներքեւ, տակը, անկում, աղուամազ, տապալել)
down payment - gankhavujar (կանխավճար)
downstairs - usdornaharg, varu (ստորնայարկ, վարը)
downtown - kaghakamech, getronagan shouga, aravduravayr (քաղաքամէջ, կեդրոնական շուկայ, առեւտրավայր)
downy - aghvamaz, purtod, pedralits, khoramang (աղուամազ, բրդոտ, փետրալից, խորամանկ)
down-hill - zarivayr, zaritap (զառիվայր, զառիթափ)
dowry - ozhid, nuver (օժիտ, նուէր)
dowse - ungughmel, mukhurjel, dzedzel, abdag (ընկղմել, մխրճել, ծեծել, ապտակ)
doxologize - parapanel, orhnerkel (փառաբանել, օրՀներգել)
doxology - orhnerk, parapanoutiun (օրՀներգ, փառաբանութիւն)
doxy - bujrouhi, sirouhi, poz (պչրուՀի, սիրուՀի, բոզ)
doyen - avakerets, yeritsakouyn, garkerets (աւագերէց, երիցագոյն, կարգերէց)
doze - murapel, murap, ninch (մրափել, մրափ, նինջ)
dozen - yergvetsiag, yergodasniag (երկվեցեակ, երկոտասնեակ)
doziness - kunodoutiun, tumroutiun (քնոտութիւն, թմրութիւն)
dozy - kunod, murapoun (քնոտ, մրափուն)
drab - korshakouyn, tantsur lat, bornig (գորշագոյն, թանձր լաթ, պոռնիկ)
draff - aveltsoug, tird, dagank (աւելցուկ, դիրտ, տականք)
draft - kashoum, ourvakidz, mourhag, pokhkir, kudzel (քաշում, ուրուագիծ, մուրՀակ, փոխգիր, գծել)
draftsman - kudzakurich, orenustir (գծագրիչ, օրէնսդիր)
drag - kashel, kashgurdel, kashgurdevil, vodnagab (քաշել, քաշկռտել, քաշկռտուիլ, ոտնակապ)
draggle - kashkushel, tsekhodel, tsekhodil (քաշքշել, ցեխոտել, ցեխոտիլ
dragon - vishab, vort mu (վիշապ, որդ մը)
dragoon - haladzel, harusdaharel, hedzelazor (Հալածել, ՀարստաՀարել, Հեծելազօր)
drain - tsamketsunel, chortsunel, kamel, goyoughi, poo (ցամքեցնել, չորցնել, քամել, կոյուղի, փոս)
drama - taderakhagh (թատերախաղ)
dramatic - taderagan, shindzou (թատերական, շինծու)
dramatize - pemaganatsunel, nergayatsunel (բեմականացնել, ներկայացնել)
dramaturge - taderakir, tadrerkag (թատերագիր, թատրերգակ)
dramaturgy - tadrerkoutiun, taderakuroutiun (թատրերգութիւն, թատերագրութիւն)
drape - varakourel, latazartel, dzaghrel (վարագուրել, լաթազարդել, ծաղրել)
draper - gerbasavajar, gudavakordz (կերպասավաճառ, կտաւագործ)
drapery - gerbaseghen, gerbasakordzoutiun (կերպասեղէն, կերպասագործութիւն)
draught - kashel, havakel, ourvakudzel, kashoum, oumb (քաշել, Հաւաքել, ուրուագծել, քաշում, ումպ)
draughtsman, draftsman - kudzakurich, ourvakudzogh, khaghakar (գծագրիչ, ուրուագծող, խաղաքար)
draw - kashel, kudzel, hanoum, vijagahanoutiun (քաշել, գծել, Հանում, վիճակաՀանութիւն)

drawee - pokhuntounogh, vujarogh-pokhkiri (փոխընդունող, վճարող՝ փոխգիրի)
drawer - kudzogh, pokhkir kashogh, tartsakurogh, kuzrots (գծող, փոխգիր քաշող, դարձագրող, գզրոց)
drawing - kudzakroutiun, vijagahanoutiun, kashoum (գծագրութիւն, վիճակահանութիւն, քաշում)
drawing-room - hiuraseniag, nusdaseniag (հիւրասենեակ, նստասենեակ)
drawl - gumgumal, dzamdzumel, gumgumank (կմկմալ, ծամծմել, կմկմանք)
drawn - yergatazerdz, kashvadz, hanvadz (երկաթազերծ, քաշուած, հանուած)
dray - sayl, pernagark, usgiurapouyn (սայլ, բեռնակառք, սկիւռաբոյն)
dread - sarsapil, zarhouril, sosgal, sarsap, yergiugh (սարսափիլ, զարհուրիլ, սոսկալ, սարսափ, երկիւղ)
dream - yerazel, yeraz, anourch (երազել, երազ, անուրջ)
dreamer - yerazogh, mudadzgod (երազող, մտածկոտ)
dream-book - yerazahan (երազահան)
dreary - dukhour, murayl, daknabali (տխուր, մռայլ, տագնապալի)
dreg - murour, tird (մրուր, դիրտ)
drench - voghoghel, turchel, umbeli, loudzoghagan (ողողել, թրջել, ըմպելի, լուծողական)
dress - hakvil, haktsunel, hakousd (հագուիլ, հագցնել, հագուստ)
dressing - hakousd, zartarank, hamemounk (հագուստ, զարդարանք, համեմունք)
dressmaker - tertsagouhi, garouhi (դերձակուհի, կարուհի)
dribble - gatil, gatgutil, lortsounkodil, gatgutoum (կաթիլ, կաթկթիլ, լորձունքոտիլ, կաթկթում)
dried - chortsadz (չորցած)
drier, dryer - chortsunogh, tsamketsunogh (չորցնող, ցամքեցնող)
drift - kushel, kushvil, dzupal, mughoum, hosank, dzupank (քշել, քշուիլ, ծփալ, մղում, հոսանք, ծփանք)
drill - dzagel, marzel, tsanel, guttel, dzagich, shaghap (ծակել, մարզել, ցանել, կրթել, ծակիչ, շաղափ)
drink - khumel, umbel, harpil (խմել, ըմպել, հարբիլ)
drinker - khumogh, harpetsogh (խմող, հարբեցող)
drip - gatil, gatgutil, gatetsunel, gatgutoum (կաթիլ, կաթկթիլ, կաթեցնել, կաթկթում)
drive - kushel, varel, kushvil, shurchakayoutiun (քշել, վարել, քշուիլ, շրջագայութիւն)
drivel - lortsnodil, zarantsel, lortsounk (լորձնոտիլ, զառանցել, լորձունք)
driver - varort, sharzhavar, mekenavar (վարորդ, շարժավար, մեքենավար)
driveway - garoughi, antsk (կառուղի, անցք)
driving - varortagan, sharzhamough (վարորդական, շարժամուղ)
driving license - varortakir (վարորդագիր)
driving school - mekenavaroutian tubrots (մեքենավարութեան դպրոց)
driving-belt - kodegab, sharzhapog (գօտեկապ, շարժափոկ)
drizzle - maghel, antsurevel, parag antsurev (մաղել, անձրեւել, բարակ անձրեւ)
droll - darorinag, dzidzaghasharzh (տարօրինակ, ծիծաղաշարժ)
drollery - dzidzaghelioutiun, kheghgadagoutiun (ծիծաղելիութիւն, խեղկատակութիւն)
droop - toshnil, toulnal, nevaghil, khonarhil, toshnoum (թօշնիլ, թուլնալ, նուաղիլ, խոնարհիլ, թօշնում)
drop - gatil, shit, gatetsunel (կաթիլ, շիթ, կաթեցնել)

drop out - nahanchel, anhedanal, chumudtsunel (նահանջել, անհետանալ, չմտցնել)
dross - aveltsouk, dagank, tep (աւելցուք, տականք, թեփ)
drought - yerashd, dzarav, chorou-tiun (երաշտ, ծարաւ, չորութիւն)
drove - nakhir, hod (նախիր, հօտ)
drover - khashnaradz, hoviv (խաշնարած, հովիւ)
drown - kheghtuvil, kheghtel, vogho-ghel (խեղդուիլ, խեղդել, ողողել)
drowse - nirhel, murapel, murap (նիրհել, մրափել, մրափ)
drowsy - kunod, tantsuramid (քնոտ, թանձրամիտ)
drug - tegh, teghorayk, pouzhaniu-ter, tumretsoutsich (դեղ, դեղորայք, բուժանիւթեր, թմրեցուցիչ)
druggist - teghakordz (դեղագործ)
drugstore - teghakordzi khanout (դեղագործի խանութ)
drum - tumpoug, tumpgaharel (թմբուկ, թմբկահարել)
drummer - tumpgahar (թմբկահար)
drunk - kinov, harpadz, khumadz (գինով, հարբած, խմած)
drupe - mirk, miagoriz budough (միրգ, միակորիզ պտուղ)
dry - chor, tsamak, chornal, chor-tsunel (չոր, ցամաք, չորնալ, չորցնել)
dryer - see: drier (տե՛ս՝ drier)
dryness - choroutiun (չորութիւն)
dual - zouyk, yergiag, yergou had (զոյգ, երկեակ, երկու հատ)
dualism - yergououtiun, yergabash-doutiun (երկուութիւն, երկապաշտութիւն)
dubious - anusdouyk, gasgadzeli, varanogh (անստոյգ, կասկածելի, վարանող)
dubitate - gasgadzil, daragousil (կասկածիլ, տարակուսիլ)
duchess - tuksouhi (դքսուհի)
duchy - tuksoutiun (դքսութիւն)
duck - pat, souzvil, mukhurjil, sou-zoum (բադ, սուզուիլ, մխրճիլ, սուզում)
duckler - souzogh, pokroki, usdor (սուզող, փոքրոգի, ստոր)
duckling - patig, souzoum (բադիկ, սուզում)
dudder - aghmugel, shupotetsunel, perezag (աղմկել, շփոթեցնել, փերեզակ)
dude - bujnamol, bujnaser (պճնամոլ, պճնասէր)
dudgeon - tashouyn, adeloutiun, zay-rouyt (դաշոյն, ատելութիւն, զայրոյթ)
due - vujareli, bardk, zhamged, badshaj, dal (վճարելի, պարտք, ժամկէտ, պատշաճ, տալ)
duebill - bardamourhag (պարտամուրհակ)
duel - menamard, menamardil (մենամարտ, մենամարտիլ)
duet - zoukerk, zoukanuvak (զուգերգ, զուգանուագ)
duke - touks (դուքս)
dulcify - anoushtsunel, kaghtsura-tsunel (անուշցնել, քաղցրացնել)
dull - putamid, aboush, putatsunel, putanal (բթամիտ, ապուշ, բթացնել, բթանալ)
dullard - putamid, aboush (բթամիտ, ապուշ)
duly - ganonavorabes, jishd, zhama-nagin (կանոնաւորապէս, ճիշդ, ժամանակին)
dumb - hamur, mounch, luretsunel (համր, մունջ, լռեցնել)
dummy - antsayn, mounch, shindzou (անձայն, մունջ, շինծու)
dump - nedel, tapel, vunasov dza-khel, aghpanots (նետել, թափել, վնասով ծախել, աղբանոց)
dunce - aboush, putamid (ապուշ, բթամիտ)
dune - avazagouyd, avazatoump (աւազակոյտ, աւազաթումբ)
dung - turik, aghp, barardaniut, dzurdel (թրիք, աղբ, պարարտանիւթ, ծրտել)
dungeon - zundan, nugough, pand, zundanel (զնդան, նկուղ, բանտ, զնդանել)
duo - zoukerk (զուգերգ)
dupe - khapvadz, tiurahavan,

aboush, khapel (խաբուած, դիւրաՀաւան, ապուշ, խաբել)
duplex - yerggoghm, yerghargani, gurgunagi, yergdzal (երկկողմ, երկյարկանի, կրկնակի, երկծալ)
duplicate - gurgnadib, badjen, badjenahanel, gurgnabadgel (կրկնատիպ, պատճէն, պատճէնաՀանել, կրկնապատկել)
duplication - gurgnoum, gurgnoutiun, badjenahanoum (կրկնում, կրկնութիւն, պատճէնաՀանում)
duplicator - gurgnorinagogh, badjenahan (կրկնօրինակող, պատճէնաՀան)
duplicity - yergtimoutiun, geghdzik, khartakhoutiun (երկդիմութիւն, կեղծիք, խարդախութիւն)
durability - devaganoutiun, amroutiun (տեւականութիւն, ամրութիւն)
durable - munayoun, devagan, amour, timatsgoun (մնայուն, տեւական, ամուր, դիմացկուն)
durance - devoghoutiun, pandargoutiun (տեւողութիւն, բանտարկութիւն)
duration - devoghoutiun (տեւողութիւն)
dure - dogal, devel, gardzur, khisd, dogoun (տոկալ, տեւել, կարծր, խիստ, տոկուն)
duress - iravazurgoum, pand, purnoutiun (իրաւազրկում, բանտ, բռնութիւն)
during - michotsin, aden, minch (միջոցին, ատեն, մինչ)
durity - gardzuroutiun, khusdoutiun (կարծրութիւն, խստութիւն)
dush - mukhdel, mukhdoum, zoravor harvadz (մխտել, մխտում, զօրաւոր Հարուած)
dusk - verchalouys, gisamout, mutunnal (վերջալոյս, կիսամութ, մթննալ)
dust - poshi, hogh, poshodel, khapel (փոշի, Հող, փոշոտել, խաբել)
dutch - holandatsi, holandagan (Հոլանտացի, Հոլանտական)
duty - bardaganoutiun, bardk, bashdon, harg, maks (պարտականութիւն, պարտք, պաշտօն, Հարկ, մաքս)
duty free - maksazerdz, hargazerdz (մաքսազերծ, Հարկազերծ)
dwarf - kajaj, tuzoug (գաճաճ, թզուկ)
dwell - punagil, genal, punagoum (բնակիլ, կենալ, բնակում)
dweller - punagich, punagogh, getsogh (բնակիչ, բնակող, կեցող)
dwelling - punagaran, punagoutiun (բնակարան, բնակութիւն)
dwindle - bagsil, nuvazil, pokranal, hadnil (պակսիլ, նուազիլ, փոքրանալ, Հատնիլ)
dwine - halil, usbaril, nuvaghil (Հալիլ, սպառիլ, նուաղիլ)
dye - nerg, kouyn, nergel (ներկ, գոյն, ներկել)
dyer - nergarar (ներկարար)
dying - mernogh, mahatsogh, mahatsoum, mah (մեռնող, մաՀացող, մաՀացում, մաՀ)
dynamic - ouzhagan, zoroutenagan (ուժական, զօրութենական)
dynamite - ouzhanag, baytoutsig, agan (ուժանակ, պայթուցիկ, ական)
dynamo - yelekduralits, ouzhardaturich (ելեքտրալից, ուժարտադրիչ)
dynasty - kahadohm, arkayatsegh, harusdoutiun (գաՀատոՀմ, արքայացեղ, Հարստութիւն)
dysentery - tanchk, porkushouk (թանչք, փորքշուք)
dyspepsia - anmarsoghoutiun, tuzhvaramarsoutiun (անմարսողութիւն, դժուարամարսութիւն)
dysuria, dysury - tuzhvaramizoutiun, mizarkeloutiun (դժուարամիզութիւն, միզարգելութիւն)

E

each - yiurakanchiur, amen meg (իւրաքանչիւր, ամէն մէկ)
each other - irar, irarou (իրար, իրարու)
eager - sour, zoravor, antsgalits, khisd, suramid (սուր, զօրաւոր, անձկալից, խիստ, սրամիտ)
eagle - ardziv (արծիւ)
eaglet - ardzuvig (արծուիկ)
eagre - gohag, alik, hortsank (կոհակ, ալիք, յորձանք)
ear - lusel, hergel, hasg gabel, aganch, lusoghoutiun (լսել, հերկել, հասկ կապել, ականջ, լսողութիւն)
ear wax - aganchageghd (ականջակեղտ)
early - ganoukh, vagh, shoudov, nakhgin (կանուխ, վաղ, շուտով, նախկին)
earn - shahil, vasdugil, usdanal, arzhananal (շահիլ, վաստկիլ, ստանալ, արժանանալ)
earnest - lourch, chermerant, iraganoutiun, kurav (լուրջ, ջերմեռանդ, իրականութիւն, գրաւ)
earning - shah, vasdag, shahouyt (շահ, վաստակ, շահոյթ)
earphone - aganchapogh, lusoghapogh (ականջափող, լսողափող)
earring - ogh, kint, aganchogh (օղ, գինդ, ականջօղ)
earth - yergir, yergurakount, ashkharh, taghel (երկիր, երկրագունդ, աշխարհ, թաղել)
earthquake - yergrasharzh, kednasharzh, tsuntsoum (երկրաշարժ, գետնաշարժ, ցնցում)
ease - hankisd, antorroutiun, hantardetsunel (հանգիստ, անդորրութիւն, հանդարտեցնել)
easily - tiurav, heshdoren (դիւրաւ, հեշտօրէն)
east - arevelk (արեւելք)
Easter - zadig (Զատիկ)
eastern - arevelian, arevelktsi (արեւելեան, արեւելքցի)
easy - tiurin, heshd, hankisd (դիւրին, հեշտ, հանգիստ)
eat - oudel, usbarel, vadnel (ուտել, սպառել, վատնել)
eater - oudogh, ants, peran (ուտող, անձ, բերան)
ebb - deghadououtiun, kashvil, deghi dal (տեղատուութիւն, քաշուիլ, տեղի տալ)
ebullience, ebullition - yeratsoum, bortgoum (եռացում, պոռթկում)
ebullient - yeratsogh, yeroun, pourun (եռացող, եռուն, բուռն
eccentric - darorinag, ardasovor, ardagetron (տարօրինակ, արտասովոր, արտակեդրոն)
eccentricity - darorinagoutiun, ardarotsoutiun (տարօրինակութիւն, արտառոցութիւն)
ecclesiastic - yegeghetsagan, guronavor (եկեղեցական, կրօնաւոր)
echelon - asdijan, santukhamad (աստիճան, սանդխամատ)
echo - artsakank, artsakankel (արձագանգ, արձագանգել)
eclectic - unduragan, unduroghagan (ընտրական, ընտրողական)
eclipse - khavaroum lousni, khavarel, dzadzgel (խաւարում լուսնի, խաւարել, ծածկել)
ecology - punabahbanoum (բնապահպանում)
economic - dundesagan, khunayoghagan (տնտեսական, խնայողական)
economics - dundesakidoutiun (տնտեսագիտութիւն)
economist - dundesaked, khunayogh (տնտեսագէտ, խնայող)
economize - dundesel, khunayel

(տնտեսել, խնայել)
economy - dundesoutiun, dundesakidoutiun, khunayoghoutiun, (տնտեսութիւն, տնտեսագիտութիւն, խնայողութիւն)
ecstasy - veratsoum, uzmaylank, hokeuzmaylil (վերացում, զմայլանք, հոգեզմայլիլ)
ecumenical - unthanragan, diyezeragan (ընդհանրական, տիեզերական)
ecurie - akhor (ախոր)
eddy - churabudouyd, hortsanoud, budoudgil (ջրապտոյտ, յորձանուտ, պտուտկիլ)
Eden - yetem, turakhd (Եդեմ, դրախտ)
edge - dzayr, yezerk, surel, yezerel (ծայր, եզերք, սրել, եզերել)
edict - hurovardag, huraman, huramanakir (հրովարտակ, հրաման, հրամանագիր)
edification - shinoutiun, shenk, shinararoutiun (շինութիւն, շէնք, շինարարութիւն)
edifice - shenk, garoutsvadzk (շէնք, կառուցուածք)
edify - shinel, gerdel, garoutsanel, paregurtel (շինել, կերտել, կառուցանել, բարեկրթել)
edit - huradaragel, khumpakurel, tasavorel (հրատարակել, խմբագրել, դասաւորել)
editing - verakhumpakroum, hamaturoum filmi (վերախմբագրում, համադրում ֆիլմի)
edition - huradaragoutiun (հրատարակութիւն)
editor - khumpakir, huradaragich (խմբագիր, հրատարակիչ)
editorial - khumpakragan, arachnortogh hotvadz (խմբագրական, առաջնորդող յօդուած)
editorship - khumpakuroutiun, huradaragchoutiun (խմբագրութիւն, հրատարակչութիւն)
educate - tasdiaragel, gurtel (դաստիարակել, կրթել)
education - tasdiaragoutiun, gurtoutiun, ousoutsoum (դաստիարակութիւն, կրթութիւն, ուսուցում)
educator - tasdiarag, ousoutsich, mangavarzh (դաստիարակ, ուսուցիչ, մանկավարժ)
educe - ardaperel, patsahaydel (արտաբերել, բացայայտել)
efface - chunchel, makrel, avrel, yeghdzanel (ջնջել, մաքրել, աւրել, եղծանել)
effect - artiunk, hedevank, kordz, iraganatsunel (արդիւնք, հետեւանք, գործ, իրականացնել)
effective - aztou, aztetsig, iragan, zoravor, i zorou (ազդու, ազդեցիկ, իրական, զօրաւոր, ի զօրու)
effectuate - kordzaturel, gadarel, badjarel (գործադրել, կատարել, պատճառել)
effeminate - ganatsianal, meghganal, ganatsi, touyl (կանացիանալ, մեղկանալ, կանացի, թոյլ)
effeminize - ikaganatsunel, meghgatsunel (իգականացնել, մեղկացնել)
effervesce - bughbuchal, yeral, porpokil (պղպջալ, եռալ, բորբոքիլ)
effervescent - porpokoun, yeroun, yeratsogh (բորբոքուն, եռուն, եռացող)
efficacious - artiunaved, aztou, zoravor (արդիւնաւէտ, ազդու, զօրաւոր)
efficience - garoghoutiun, adagoutiun (կարողութիւն, ատակութիւն)
efficiency - artunavedoutiun (արդիւնաւէտութիւն)
efficient - garogh, adag, aztogh, nerkordzogh (կարող, ատակ, ազդող, ներգործող)
effigiate - numantsunel, badgerel, vortekurel (նմանցնել, պատկերել, որդեգրել)
effigy - temk, badger, numanoutiun (դէմք, պատկեր, նմանութիւն)
efflate - puchel, ouretsunel (փչել, ուռեցնել)
effluence - ardahosoum, heghoum, zeghoum (արտահոսում, հեղում, զեղում)
effluent - ardahosogh, ardadzor (արտահոսող, արտածոր)
effort - jik, chank, pouyt, juknil

(ճիգ, ջանք, փոյթ, ճգնիլ)
effront - abahovtsunel, yerashkhavorel (ապահովցնել, երաշխաւորել)
effrontery - anamotoutiun, lurpoutiun (անամօթութիւն, լրբութիւն)
effuge - shoghal, ardatsolal (շողալ, արտացոլալ)
effulgence - baydzaroutiun, paylk (պայծառութիւն, փայլք)
effusion - heghoum, ardahosoum, zeghoum (հեղում, արտահոսում, զեղում)
egal - havasar, nouyn, numan (հաւասար, նոյն, նման)
egality - havasaroutiun (հաւասարութիւն)
egg - havgit, tsou (հաւկիթ, ձու)
eggplant - sumpoug (սմբուկ)
ego - yes, antsnaganoutiun (ես, անձնականութիւն)
egoism, egotism - yesasiroutiun, antsnabashdoutiun (եսասիրութիւն, անձնապաշտութիւն)
egoist, egotist - yesaser, antsnaser (եսասէր, անձնասէր)
egress - yelk, megnoum, antsk, megnil (ելք, մեկնում, անցք, մեկնիլ)
Egypt - yekibdos (Եգիպտոս)
egyptian - yekibdatsi, yekibderen, yekibdagan (եգիպտացի, եգիպտերէն, եգիպտական)
eight - outu (ութը)
eighteen - dasnuout (տասնութ)
eighty - outsoun (ութսուն)
either - ays gam ayn, megu gam miusu, yergouken megu (այս կամ այն, մէկը կամ միւսը, երկուքէն մէկը)
ejaculate - tsaydetsunel, zhaytketsunel (ցայտեցնել, ժայթքեցնել)
ejaculation - ardatoroum, tsaydoum, zhaytkoum (արտաթորում, ցայտում, ժայթքում)
eject - vurundel, vudarel, ardaksel, barbel (վռնտել, վտարել, արտաքսել, պարպել)
ejection - barboum, vudaroum, ardahanoum (պարպում, վտարում, արտահանում)
elaborate - mushagel, mushagvadz, ashkhadasirvadz (մշակել, մշակուած, աշխատասիրուած)
elaboration - mushagoum, gazmavoroum, gadarelakordzoum (մշակում, կազմաւորում, կատարելագործում)
elan - khoyank, tap, sulatsk, yerant, khant (խոյանք, թափ, սլացք, եռանդ, խանդ)
elapse - sahil, antsnil (սահիլ, անցնիլ)
elastic - aratsukagan, jugoun (առաձգական, ճկուն)
elate - hubard, koh, hubardatsunel, khantavarel (հպարտ, գոհ, հպարտացնել, խանդավառել)
elbow - armoug, angiun, mushdel, hurel (արմուկ, անկիւն, մշտել, հրել)
elder - yeritsakouyn, dzerouni, darikod (երիցագոյն, ծերունի, տարիքոտ)
elect - undurel, koueargel, undurial (ընտրել, քուէարկել, ընտրեալ)
election - unduroutiun, koueargoutiun (ընտրութիւն, քուէարկութիւն)
elector - undurogh, kuveargogh (ընտրող, քուէարկող)
electric, electrical - yelegduragan (ելեկտրական)
electrician - yelegduraked (ելեկտրագէտ)
electricity - yelegduraganoutiun (ելեկտրականութիւն)
electrify - yelegduraganatsunel (ելեկտրականացնել)
electrode - yelegduraper, yelegdurasayr (ելեկտրաբեր, ելեկտրասայր)
electromagnet - yelegduramaknis (ելեկտրամագնիս)
electrotype - yelegduradib (ելեկտրատիպ)
elegance - vayelchoutiun, shukeghoutiun (վայելչութիւն, շքեղութիւն)
elegant - vayelouch, keghagazm, nurpakegh (վայելուչ, գեղակազմ, նրբագեղ)
elegy - yeghererk, maherkoutiun (եղերերգ, մահերգութիւն)

element - dar, niut, darerk, nakhakidelik (տարր, նիւթ, տարերք, նախագիտելիք)
elementary - nakhnagan, darragan, nakhagurtagan (նախնական, տարրական, նախակրթական)
elephant - pigh (փիղ)
elevate - vertsunel, partsuratsunel, aznuvatsunel, gurtel (վերցնել, բարձրացնել, ազնուացնել, կրթել)
elevation - partsuratsoum, medzoutiun, partsounk, badiv (բարձրացում, մեծութիւն, բարձունք, պատիւ)
elevator - verelag, veramparts (վերելակ, վերամբարձ)
eleven - dasunmeg (տասնմէկ)
eleventh - dasunmegerort (տասնմէկերորդ)
elf - tuzoug, barig, voki, tunjugel (թզուկ, պարիկ, ոգի, թնճկել)
elicit - haydnaperel (յայտնաբերել)
elicitation - haydnaperoum (յայտնաբերում)
elide - gurjadel, habavel, peganel (կրճատել, յապաւել, բեկանել)
eliminate - hanel, vudarel, chunchel, chezokatsunel (հանել, վտարել, ջնջել, չէզոքացնել)
elimination - ardaksoum, vudaroum (արտաքսում, վտարում)
elision - gurjadoum, habavoum (կրճատում, յապաւում)
elite - undurani (ընտրանի)
elk - yeghcherou (եղջերու)
ellipse - havgutakidz, tsuvadzir (հաւկթագիծ, ձուածիր)
ellipsis - terad, zeghchoum-pari (թերատ, զեղչում՝ բառի)
elocution - berjakhosoutiun, jardasanoutiun (պերճախօսութիւն, ճարտասանութիւն)
eloquence - berjakhosoutiun (պերճախօսութիւն)
eloquent - berjakhos, jardasan (պերճախօս, ճարտասան)
else - ourish, ayl, patsi, yete voch (ուրիշ, այլ, բացի, եթէ ոչ)
elsewhere - aylour, ayl degh (այլուր, այլ տեղ)
elucidate - lousapanel, baydzaratsunel, husdagatsunel (լուսաբանել, պայծառացնել, յստակցնել)
elucidation - lousapanoutiun (լուսաբանութիւն)
elude - khousapil, burdzil (խուսափիլ, պրծիլ)
elusion - pakhousd, badruvag, nenkoutiun (փախուստ, պատրուակ, նենգութիւն)
elutriate - khakhdel, deghen hanel (խախտել, տեղէն հանել)
emaciate - niharnal, nihartsunel, hiudzil, mashil (նիհարնալ, նիհարցնել, հիւծիլ, մաշիլ)
emanate - pukhil, ardahosil, dzakil (բխիլ, արտահոսիլ, ծագիլ)
emanation - ardahosoum, pukhoum (արտահոսում, բխում)
emancipate - azadakurel, azadel (ազատագրել, ազատել)
emancipation - azadakuroum, azadoum (ազատագրում, ազատում)
emasculate - ikatsunel, nerkiniatsunel, nerkini, meghg (իգացնել, ներքինիացնել, ներքինի, մեղկ)
embale - pagel, gabel, hagel (փակել, կապել, հակել)
emball - kurgel (գրկել)
embalm - uzmursel (զմռսել)
embargo - purnakuravoum, navarkel, shurchapagoum (բռնագրաւում, նաւարգել, շրջափակում)
embark - nav tunel, nav mudnel, pertsunel, pernavorel (նաւ դնել, նաւ մտնել, բեռցնել, բեռնաւորել)
embarkation - navamoudk, navaroutiun (նաւամուտք, նաւառութիւն)
embarrass - shupotetsunel, khankarel, tezhvaratsunel (շփոթեցնել, խանգարել, դժուարացնել)
embassade, ambassade - tesbanoutiun, tesbanadoun (դեսպանութիւն, դեսպանատուն)
embassador - tesban (դեսպան)
embassy - tesbanoutiun, tesbanadoun (դեսպանութիւն, դեսպանատուն)
embellish - keghetsgatsunel, zartarel, bujnel (գեղեցկացնել, զարդարել, պճնել)

emblem - khorhurtanish, khorhurtanushan, nushan (խորհրդանիշ, խորհրդանշան, նշան)
embody - marmunavorel, tsevagerbel, gazmel (մարմնաւորել, ձեւակերպել, կազմել)
emboss - partsurakantagel, ouretsunel (բարձրաքանդակել, ուռեցնել)
embossing - partsurakantagoum, ouretsoum, tsutsoum (բարձրաքանդակում, ուռեցում, ցցում)
embrace - kurgel, voghchakourel, seghmel, hampourel (գրկել, ողջագուրել, սեղմել, համբուրել)
embroider - aseghnakordzel, aseghnakordz (ասեղնագործել, ասեղնագործ)
embroidery - aseghnakordzoutiun (ասեղնագործութիւն)
embroil - kharnel, khankarel, shupotel (խառնել, խանգարել, շփոթել)
embroilment - kharnashupotoutiun (խառնաշփոթութիւն)
embrotel - bornugatsunel, pozatsunel (պոռնկացնել, բոզացնել)
embryo - saghm, saghmunayin (սաղմ, սաղմնային)
emend - oughghel, parepokhel, shudgel, surpakrel (ուղղել, բարեփոխել, շտկել, սրբագրել)
emendation - parepokhoum, surpakroum (բարեփոխում, սրբագրում)
emerald, emerand - zumroukhd (զմրուխտ)
emerge - yerevil, haydnuvil, tours yellel (երեւիլ, յայտնուիլ, դուրս ելլել)
emergency - ushdab, usdiboghaganoutiun, arak oknoutiun (շտապ,ստիպողականութիւն, արագ օգնութիւն)
emigrant - kaghtogh, kaghtagan (գաղթող, գաղթական)
emigrate - kaghtel, deghapokhvil, kaghtetsunel (գաղթել, տեղափոխուիլ, գաղթեցնել)
emigration - kaght, kaghtaganoutiun, ardakaght (գաղթ, գաղթականութիւն, արտագաղթ)
emigrator - kaghtagan (գաղթական)
eminence - vusemoutiun, medzoutiun, partsounk (վսեմութիւն, մեծութիւն, բարձունք)
eminent - partsur, vusem, nushanavor, hurchagavor (բարձր, վսեմ, նշանաւոր, հռչակաւոր)
emir - ishkhan (իշխան)
emissary - kordzagal, badvirag, hedazodogh, lurdes (գործակալ, պատուիրակ, հետազօտող, լրտես)
emission - artsagoum, tsaynasuproum, suproum, ardahosoum (արձակում, ձայնասփռում, սփռում, արտահոսում)
emit - artsagel, suprel, shurchaperoutian tunel (արձակել, սփռել, շրջաբերութեան դնել)
emoloyee - bashdonia (պաշտօնեայ)
emolument - vartsk, vartsaduroutiun, yegamoud, vasdag (վարձք, վարձատրութիւն, եկամուտ, վաստակ)
emotion - houzoum, vurtovoum, khurovk (յուզում, վրդովում, խռովք)
emotional - houzich, uzkatsagan (յուզիչ, զգացական)
empale - kounadel, barusbel, tsutsabadel, amratsunel (գունատել, պարսպել, ցցապատել, ամրացնել)
emperor - gaysur (կայսր)
emphasis - sheshd, ouzhkunoutiun, untkudzoum (շեշտ, ուժգնութիւն, ընդգծում)
emphasize - sheshdel, hunchel, untkudzel (շեշտել, հնչել, ընդգծել)
emphysema - shuncharoutiun anhankusdoutiun (շնչառութեան անհանգստութիւն)
empire - gaysroutiun (կայսրութիւն)
emplace - deghavorel, zedeghel (տեղաւորել, զետեղել)
employ - kordzadzel, dzarayetsunel, uzpaghoum, kordz (գործածել, ծառայեցնել, զբաղում, գործ)
employee - bashdonia, kordzavor (պաշտօնեայ, գործաւոր)
employer - kordzader, kordzadou (գործատէր, գործատու)
employment - bashdon, kordz, uzpaghoum (պաշտօն, գործ, զբաղում)
empoison - tounavorel (թունաւորել)

empoisonment - *tounavoroum* (*թունաւորում*)
emporium - *vararadeghi, vajaragetron, vajaranots* (*վաճառատեղի, վաճառակեդրոն, վաճառանոց*)
empower - *ardonel, liazorel, iravasoutiun dal* (*արտօնել, լիազօրել, իրաւասութիւն տալ*)
empress - *gaysrouhi* (*կայսրուհի*)
empty - *barab, tadarg, tapour, barbel, tadargel* (*պարապ, դատարկ, թափուր, պարպել, դատարկել*)
emulate - *murtsil, murtsagtsil, hedamudil, paradench* (*մրցիլ, մրցակցիլ, հետամտիլ, փառատենչ*)
emulation - *hedamudoutiun, murtsoum, nakhants* (*հետամտութիւն, մրցում, նախանձ*)
emulator - *hedamoud, akhoyan* (*հետամուտ, ախոյեան*)
emulsion - *sermnagat, git* (*սերմնակաթ, կիթ*)
enable - *zoratsunel, garogh tartsunel, touyladurel* (*զօրացնել, կարող դարձնել, թոյլատրել*)
enact - *sahmanel, orenk antsunel, hasdadel* (*սահմանել, օրէնք անցնել, հաստատել*)
enamel - *chunarag, paylanerg, chunaragel* (*ջնարակ, փայլաներկ, ջնարակել*)
enamor - *siraharil, dochoril* (*սիրահարիլ, տոչորիլ*)
encage - *vantagel* (*վանդակել*)
encamp - *panagil, panagetsunel* (*բանակիլ, բանակեցնել*)
encampment - *panagoum, panagadegh* (*բանակում, բանակատեղ*)
enceinte - *hughi* (*յղի*)
enchain - *shughtayel, gabel* (*շղթայել, կապել*)
enchant - *gakhartel, tiutel, humayel* (*կախարդել, դիւթել, հմայել*)
enchantment - *gakhartank, tiutank, humayk* (*կախարդանք, դիւթանք, հմայք*)
encircle - *oghagel, shurchapagel, shurchabadel* (*օղակել, շրջափակել, շրջապատել*)
encirclement - *oghagoum, shurchapagoum, shurchabadoum* (*օղակում, շրջափակում, շրջապատում*)
enclose - *nerpagel, gutsel, badel, shurchapagel* (*ներփակել, կցել, պատել, շրջափակել*)
enclosed - *nerpagial* (*ներփակեալ*)
enclosure - *pagoum, shurchapag, tsangabad* (*փակում, շրջափակ, ցանկապատ*)
encombrance - *arkelk, khapanoum* (*արգելք, խափանում*)
encomium, encomion - *kovesd, nerpogh* (*գովեստ, ներբող*)
encompass - *shurchabadel, shurchanagel, barpagel* (*շրջապատել, շրջանակել, պարփակել*)
encore - *gurgin, verusdin, tartsial* (*կրկին, վերստին, դարձեալ*)
encounter - *pakhil, untharil, jagadil, pakhoum, hantiboum* (*բախիլ, ընդհարիլ, ճակատիլ, բախում, հանդիպում*)
encourage - *kachalerel, khurakhousel, surdabuntel, oknel* (*քաջալերել, խրախուսել, սրտապնդել, օգնել*)
encouragement - *kachalerank, khurakouys* (*քաջալերանք, խրախոյս*)
encroach - *nerkhouzhel, hapushdagel, shortel* (*ներխուժել, յափշտակել, շորթել*)
encumber - *khapanel, arkilel, kotsel* (*խափանել, արգիլել, գոցել*)
encyclopedia - *hanrakidaran* (*հանրագիտարան*)
end - *verch, dzayr, vakhjan, avard, avardel* (*վերջ, ծայր, վախճան, աւարտ, աւարտել*)
endanger - *vudankel* (*վտանգել*)
endear - *sirtsunel* (*սիրցնել*)
endearment - *kourkourank, khantaghadank* (*գուրգուրանք, խանդաղատանք*)
endeavour - *chanal, juknil, portsel, chank, jik* (*ջանալ, ճգնիլ, փորձել, ջանք, ճիգ*)
endless - *anverch, anvakhjan, anezur, ansahman* (*անվերջ, անվախճան, անեզր, անսահման*)
endocrine - *nerknahos keghts*

(ներքնահոս գեղձ)
endoderm - nerknamashg, nerkin mashg (ներքնամաշկ, ներքին մաշկ)
endogamy - neramousnoutiun, voch odar amousnoutiun (ներամուսնութիւն, ոչ օտար ամուսնութիւն)
endoplast - goriz (կորիզ)
endorse - pokhantsakurel, hedakurel (փոխանցագրել, յետագրել)
endorsee - pokhantsagal (փոխանցակալ)
endorsement - pokhantsoum, pokhantsakuroum, hasdadoum (փոխանցում, փոխանցագրում, հաստատում)
endorser - pokhantsokurogh (փոխանցագրող)
endosement - pokhantsakuroum (փոխանցագրում)
endow - ozhdel, barkevel, dal (օժտել, պարգեւել, տալ)
endowment - nuver, barkev, hasoutavoroum (նուէր, պարգեւ, հասութաւորում)
endue - shunorhel, dal, barkevel (շնորհել, տալ, պարգեւել)
endurance - hamperadaroutiun, dogounoutiun (համբերատարութիւն, տոկունութիւն)
endure - dogal, danil, gurel, devel, sharounagel (տոկալ, տանիլ, կրել, տեւել, շարունակել)
enemy - tushnami, hagaragort (թշնամի, հակառակորդ)
energetic - gorovi, yerantoun, ouzhegh (կորովի, եռանդուն, ուժեղ)
energy - ouzh, ouzhaganoutiun, yerant, zoroutiun (ոյժ, ուժականութիւթ, եռանդ, զօրութիւն)
enervate - dugaratsunel, chuladel, dugar, anouzh (տկարացնել, ջլատել, տկար, անույժ)
enervation - ouzhatapoutiun, chuladoum (ուժաթափութիւն, ջլատում)
enfeeble - dugaratsunel, ouzhatapel (տկարացնել, ուժաթափել)
enforce - zoratsunel, junshel, usdibel, zoranal (զօրացնել, ճնշել, ստիպել, զօրանալ)
enforcement - zoratsoum, junshoum, bardaturank (զօրացում, ճնշում, պարտադրանք)
engage - khosdanal, usdantsunel, vartsel, nushanel (խոստանալ, ստանձնել, վարձել, նշանել)
engagement - khoskgab, khosdoum, hantsnaroutiun, guriv (խօսքկապ, խոստում, յանձնառութիւն, կռիւ)
engender - dzunanil, arachatsunel, ardaturel (ծնանիլ, առաջացնել, արտադրել)
engine - sharzhich, sharzhag, ouzh ardaturogh mekena (շարժիչ, շարժակ, ոյժ արտադրող մեքենայ)
engineer - jardaraked, yergurachap, mekenaked, nakhakudzel (ճարտարագէտ, երկրաչափ, մեքենագէտ, նախագծել)
engineering - yerachapoutiun (երկրաչափութիւն)
England - anklia (Անգլիա)
english - ankliatsi, ankleren, ankliagan (անգլիացի, անգլերէն, անգլիական)
engorge - lapel, gullel, laplizel (լափել, կլլել, լափլիզել)
engraft - badvasdel (պատուաստել)
engrave - porakurel, turoshmel, kantagel (փորագրել, դրոշմել, քանդակել)
engravement - porakuroutiun, kantag (փորագրութիւն, քանդակ)
engraver - porakurich (փորագրիչ)
engross - medztsunel, khoshortsunel (մեծցնել, խոշորցնել)
engulf - gullel, lapel (կլլել, լափել)
enhance - partsuratsunel, aveltsunel, zoratsunel (բարձրացնել, աւելցնել, զօրացնել)
enhancement - partsuratsoum, ajoum (բարձրացում, աճում)
enigma - areghdzuvadz, haneloug (առեղծուած, հանելուկ)
enjail - pandargel (բանտարկել)
enjoin - bardaturel, badvirel, huramayel (պարտադրել, պատուիրել, հրամայել)
enjoy - hurjuvil, vayelel, zuvarjanal

(հրճուիլ, վայելել, զուարճանալ)
enjoyment - zuvarjoutiun, vayelk, hajouyk (զուարճութիւն, վայելք, հաճոյք)
enlarge - layntsunel, medztsunel, medznal, untartsagel (լայնցնել, մեծնալ, մեծցնել, ընդարձակել)
enlighten - lousavorel, lousapanel (լուսաւորել, լուսաբանել)
enlightener - lousavorich, lousavorogh (լուսաւորիչ, լուսաւորող)
enlist - zinvorakurel, artsanakurel, havakel (զինուորագրել, արձանագրել, հաւաքել)
enlistment - zinvorakuroutiun, artsanakuroutiun (զինուորագրութիւն, արձանագրութիւն)
enlock - gughbel, pagel, gabel (կղպել, փակել, կապել)
enmity - tushnamoutiun, vokh, adeloutiun (թշնամութիւն, ոխ, ատելութիւն)
ennoble - aznuvatsunel, aznuvaganatsunel (ազնուացնել, ազնուականացնել)
ennui - tsantsurouyt, daghdoug (ձանձրոյթ, տաղտուկ)
enormity - sasdgoutiun, ahaknoutiun, noghgalioutiun (սաստկութիւն, ահագնութիւն, նողկալիութիւն)
enormous - husga, vitkhari, anchap (հսկայ, վիթխարի, անչափ)
enough - pavagan, pavarar, herik (բաւական, բաւարար, հերիք)
enrage - gadghetsunel, zayratsunel (կատղեցնել, զայրացնել)
enregister - artsanakurel (արձանագրել)
enrich - harusdatsunel, jokhatsunel (հարստացնել, ճոխացնել)
enrichment - harusdatsoum, barardatsoum (հարստացում, պարարտացում)
enroachment - voduntsukoutiun (ոտնձգութիւն)
enrobe - haktsunel, uzkesdavorel (հագցնել, զգեստաւորել)
enroll - artsanakurel, zinvorakurel, pattel (արձանագրել, զինուորագրել, փաթթել)
enrollement - artsanakuroutiun, zinvorakuroutiun, bulloum (արձանագրութիւն, զինուորագրութիւն, պլլում)
ensamble - orinag, numouysh (օրինակ, նմոյշ)
ensanguine - ariunodel (արիւնոտել)
ensemble - miasin, ampoghchoutiun, khoump, hamouyt (միասին, ամբողջութիւն, խումբ, համոյթ)
enshelter - badusbarel, bahel (պատսպարել, պահել)
enshrine - bahel, bahbanel, kourkoural (պահել, պահպանել, գուրգուրալ)
enshroud - dzadzgel, koghargel, badankel (ծածկել, քողարկել, պատանքել)
ensign - nushan, khorhurtanushan, turoshag, nushanazartel (նշան, խորհրդանշան, դրօշակ, նշանազարդել)
enslave - usdurgatsunel, kerel, hubadagetsunel (ստրկացնել, գերել, հպատակեցնել)
ensue - hedevil, hedabuntel (հետեւիլ, հետապնդել)
ensure - abahovel, vusdahetsunel (ապահովել, վստահեցնել)
entangle - kharnagel, shupotetsunel, kharnushdugel (խառնել, շփոթեցնել, խառնշտկել)
enter - mudnel, tapantsel, mudtsunel, nerkhouzhel (մտնել, թափանցել, մտցնել, ներխուժել)
entering - moudk (մուտք)
enterprise - tsernarg, nakhatsernoutiun, tsernargel (ձեռնարկ, նախաձեռնութիւն, ձեռնարկել)
entertain - hiurasirel, hiurungalel, zuvarjatsunel (հիւրասիրել, հիւրընկալել, զուարճացնել)
entertainer - uzpostsunogh, zuvarjatsunogh (զբօսցնող, զուարճացնող)
entertainment - hiurasiroutiun, zuvarjoutiun (հիւրասիրութիւն, զուարճութիւն)
enthrone - kahagalel (գահակալել)
enthronement - kahagaloutioun (գա-

Հակալութիւն)
enthusiasm - khantavaroutiun, khant (խանդավառութիւն, խանդ)
enthusiat - khantavar (խանդավառ)
enthusiatic - khantavar, shenshogh (խանդավառ, շէնշող)
entice - hurabourel, kaytagghetsunel (Հրապուրել, գայթակղեցնել)
enticement - hurabouyr, hapushdagoum (Հրապոյր, յափշտակում)
entire - ampoghch, polor, povantag (ամբողջ, բոլոր, բովանդակ)
entitle - anvanel, vernakurel, gochel (անուանել, վերնագրել, կոչել)
entity - eoutiun (էութիւն)
entomb - taghel, kerezmanel (թաղել, գերեզմանել)
entombment - taghoum (թաղում)
entrails - aghikner, porodik (աղիքներ, փորոտիք)
entrance - moudk, tour, hurabourel (մուտք, դուռ, Հրապուրել)
entreat - aghachel, khunturel, baghadil, hamozel (աղաչել, խնդրել, պաղատիլ, Համոզել)
entreaty - aghers, baghadank (աղերս, պաղատանք)
entree - moudk, tour, usgizp (մուտք, դուռ, սկիզբ)
entry - moudk, nakhatour, antsk, artsanakuroutiun, dourk (մուտք, նախադուռ, անցք, արձանագրութիւն, տուրք)
entr'acte - michnarar, untmichoum (միջնարար, ընդմիջում)
enumerate - hamrel, tuvel, tevargel, hashvel (Համրել, թուել, թուարկել, Հաշուել)
enumeration - tevargoum (թուարկում)
Enunciation - haydnoutiun, ardahunchoum, ardasanoutiun (Յայտնութիւն, արտաՀնչում, արտասանութիւն)
enuresis - mizartsagoum (միզարձակում)
envelop - dzurarel, pattel (ծրարել, փաթթել)
envelope - dzurar, baharan (ծրար, պաՀարան)
envenom - tounavorel (թունաւորել)
envious - nakhantsod (նախանձոտ)
environ - shurchabadel (շրջապատել)
environment - michavayr, shurchabad (միջավայր, շրջապատ)
envoy - badvirag, badkamavor (պատուիրակ, պատգամաւոր)
envy - nakhants, adeloutiun, nakhantsil (նախանձ, ատելութիւն, նախանձիլ)
enwrap - pattel, dzurarel (փաթթել, ծրարել)
enwrapment - dzuraroum (ծրարում)
epaulet - ousnots, ousatir (ուսնոց, ուսադիր)
ephemeric - miorya, vaghantsoug, arorya, michad mu (միօրեայ, վաղանցուկ, առօրեայ, միջատ մը)
ephemeris - orakuroutiun, asdeghatsouyts, oramichad (օրագրութիւն, աստեղացոյց, օրամիջատ)
epic - tiutsaznerkagan, viberkagan (դիւցազներգական, վիպերգական)
epicede - maherk (մաՀերգ)
epicenter - hamagetron, yergurasharzhi getron (Համակեդրոն, երկրաշարժի կեդրոն)
epigram - verdaroutiun, barsavank (վերտառութիւն, պարսաւանք)
epigraph - punapan, mechperoum, artsanakir, vernakir (բնաբան, մէջբերում, արձանագիր, վերնագիր)
epilepsy - lousnodoutiun (լուսնոտութիւն)
epileptic - lousnod (լուսնոտ)
epilogue - verchapan, yezragatsoutiun (վերջաբան, եզրակացութիւն)
Epiphany - haydnoutiun, asdvadzahaydnoutiun (Յայտնութիւն, Աստուածայայտնութիւն)
episcopaly, episcopate - yebisgobosoutiun (եպիսկոպոսութիւն)
episode - turvak, tebk, michateb (դրուագ, դէպք, միջադէպ)
epistle - namag, tought, kir, tughtagtsil (Նամակ, թուղթ, գիր, թղթակցիլ)
epitaph - dabanakir, tampanakir, tampanakurel (տապանագիր, դամ-

բանագիր, դամբանագրել)
epoch - tarashurchan, zhamanag, tarakuloukh, shurchan (դարաշրջան, ժամանակ, դարագլուխ, շրջան)
epopee - tiutsaznerkoutiun (դիւցազներգութիւն)
equable - havasar, miorinag, hamachap (հաւասար, միօրինակ, համաչափ)
equal - havasar, numan, havasaril, pokharinel (հաւասար, նման, հաւասարիլ, փոխարինել)
equality - havasaroutiun (հաւասարութիւն)
equalize - havasaretsunel (հաւասարեցնել)
equate - havasaretsunel (հաւասարեցնել)
equation - havasaroutiun, havasaroum (հաւասարութիւն, հաւասարում)
equator - hasaragadz (հասարակած)
equidistant - zoukaher (զուգահեռ)
equilateral - havasaragoghm (հաւասարակողմ)
equilibrist - larakhaghats, ajbarar (լարախաղաց, աճպարար)
equip - gazmel, ozhdel, sarkavorel, usbarazinel (կազմել, օժտել, սարքաւորել, սպառազինել)
equipage - antsnagazm, khumpag, gazmadz, usbas (անձնակազմ, խմբակ, կազմած, սպաս)
equipment - gazmadz, sarkavoroum, usbarazinoum (կազմած, սարքաւորում, սպառազինում)
equitable - artar, oughghamid, anachar, artaraser (արդար, ուղղամիտ, անաչառ, արդարասէր)
equity - artaratadoutiun, oughghamudoutiun, iravounk (արդարադատութիւն, ուղղամտութիւն, իրաւունք)
equivalence - hamarzhekoutiun, hamazoroutiun (համարժէքութիւն, համազօրութիւն)
equivalent - hamarzhek, hamazor, havasar (համարժէք, համազօր, հաւասար)
equivoque - yergtimoutiun, parakhagh (երկդիմութիւն, բառախաղ)
era - tarashurchan, zhamanagashurchan (դարաշրջան, ժամանակաշրջան)
eradiate - jarakaytel (ճառագայթել)
eradiation - jarakaytoum (ճառագայթում)
eradicate - armadakhulel, gordzanel, vochunchatsunel (արմատախիլել, կործանել, ոչնչացնել)
erase - surpel, makrel, avrel, kertel (սրբել, մաքրել, աւրել, քերթել)
eraser - surpich, redin (սրբիչ, ռետին)
erasion - chunchoum, kerdzoum (ջնջում, քերծում)
ere - nakhabes, nakhkan, arach (նախապէս, նախքան, առաջ)
erect - himnel, garoutsel, oughigh, gankoun (հիմնել, կառուցել, ուղիղ, կանգուն)
erection - garoutsoum, shenk, hasdadoutiun (կառուցում, շէնք, հաստատութիւն)
eremite - juknavor, vanagan (ճգնաւոր, վանական)
Erevan - yerevan (Երեւան)
erogenous - durpadzin, durpaser (տռփածին, տռփասէր)
eros - siro durpank, serayin tsangoutiun (սիրոյ տռփանք, սեռային ցանկութիւն)
erotic - darpalits, durpagan, sirayin (տառփալից, տռփական, սիրային)
eroticism - serayin kurkuroutiun, tsangoutiun (սեռային գրգռութիւն, ցանկութիւն)
erotism - durpaganoutiun, sirerkoutiun (տռփականութիւն, սիրերգութիւն)
erotomania - durpamoloutiun (տռփամոլութիւն)
err - sukhalil, khodoril (սխալիլ, խոտորիլ)
errant - taparogh, taparashurchig, moloradz (թափառող, թափառաշրջիկ, մոլորած)
errata, erratum - vuribag, sukhal (վրիպակ, սխալ)
error - sukhal, hantsank, vuriboum

(սխալ, յանցանք, վրիպում)
erudite - humoud, nerhoun (Հմուտ, ներՀուն)
erupt - zhaytkel, huratsaydel (ժայթքել, Հրացայտել)
eruption - zhaytkoum, porpokoum, bortgoum (ժայթքում, բորբոքում, պոռթկում)
escalator - yelaran, sharzhasantoukh (ելարան, շարժասանդուխ)
escape - pakhchil, burdzil, lukel, pakhousd, azadoum (փախչիլ, պրծիլ, լքել, փախուստ, ազատում)
eschew - khousapil, uzkoushanal, khorshil (խուսափիլ, զգուշանալ, խորշիլ)
escort - oughegits, bahagakhoump, ungeragtsil, bashdbanel (ուղեկից, պաՀակախումբ, ընկերակցիլ, պաշտպանել)
escrow - nakhabaymanatoughk, avantatought (նախապայմանաթուղթ, աւանդաթուղթ)
esofagus - geragrapogh (կերակրափող)
especial - masnavor, hadoug (մասնաւոր, յատուկ)
espionage - lurdesoutiun (լրտեսութիւն)
esplanade - hartakedin, tashdavayr, dapasdan (Հարթագետին, դաշտավայր, տափաստան
espouse - amousnanal, untounil, usdantsunel (ամուսնանալ, ընդունիլ, ստանձնել)
esprit - hoki, voki, khelk, midk, imasd (Հոգի, ոգի, խելք, միտք, իմաստ)
espy - tidel, zunnel, nushmarel, lurdesel, lurdes (դիտել, զննել, նշմարել, լրտեսել, լրտես)
esquisse - ouvakidz (ուրուագիծ)
essay - ports, portsakuroutiun, agnarg, portsel, kunnel (փորձ, փորձագրութիւն, ակնարկ, փորձել, քննել)
essayist - portsakir (փորձագիր)
essence - eoutiun, hiut, pourmounk, khungel (էութիւն, Հիւթ, բուրմունք, խնկել)
essential - eagan, himnagan, isgagan (էական, Հիմնական, իսկական)
establish - hasdadel, garoutsel, himnel, amrabuntel (Հաստատել, կառուցել, Հիմնել, ամրապնդել)
established - hasdadvadz, himnuvadz (Հաստատուած, Հիմնուած)
establishment - hasdadoutiun, himnarg, himnaturoum (Հաստատութիւն, Հիմնարկ, Հիմնադրում)
estate - bedoutiun, galvadz, tirk, asdijan, hasdadel (պետութիւն, կալուած, դիրք, աստիճան, Հաստատել)
estate planning - galvadzayin dzurakroum (կալուածային ծրագրում)
esteem - kunahadel, arzhevorel, hark, badiv (գնաՀատել, արժեւորել, յարգ, պատիւ)
esthetic - keghakidagan (գեղագիտական)
esthetics - keghakidoutiun (գեղագիտութիւն)
estimable - harkeli, badvarzhan, kunahadeli (յարգելի, պատուարժան, գնաՀատելի)
estimate - kunahadel, hashvel, nakhahashiv, kunahadoum (գնաՀատել, Հաշուել, նախաՀաշիւ, գնաՀատում)
estimation - kunahadoum, hashvargoum (գնաՀատում, Հաշուարկում)
estimator - kunahadogh (գնաՀատող)
estop - getsunel, gasetsunel (կեցնել, կասեցնել)
estrade - pem, partsuravantag (բեմ, բարձրավանդակ)
estrange - odaratsunel, heratsunel (օտարացնել, Հեռացնել)
estrangement - odaratsoum, oudzatsoum (օտարացում, ուծացում)
estuary - kedaperan, kedakhorsh (գետաբերան, գետախորշ)
etch - porakurel, kerdzel, zhandakurel (փորագրել, քերծել, ժանտագրել)
etching - porakraduboutiun (փորագրատպութիւն)
eternal - havidenagan, haverzhagan, anvakhjan (յաւիտենական, յաւեր-

ժական, անվախճան)
eternify - haverzhatsunel, anmahatsunel (յաւերժացնել, անմահացնել)
eternity - haverzhoutiun, havidenaganoutiun (յաւերժութիւն, յաւիտենականութիւն)
ether - yeter, mutnolord (եթեր, մթնոլորտ)
ethic, ethical - paroyagan, paroyakidagan (բարոյական, բարոյագիտական)
ethics - paroyakidoutiun (բարոյագիտութիւն)
ethnic - tseghayin (ցեղային)
ethnographic - azkaguragan (ազգակրական)
ethology - paroyakhosoutiun (բարոյախօսութիւն)
etiology - badjarakidoutiun (պատճառագիտութիւն)
etiquette - varvelagerb, gentsaghakidoutiun (վարուելակերպ, կենցաղագիտութիւն)
etude - ousoum, varzhoutiun (ուսում, վարժութիւն)
etymology - usdoukapanoutiun (ստուգաբանութիւն)
eulogize - kovel, nerpoghel (գովել, ներբողել)
eulogy - kovesd, nerpogh, turvadik (գովեստ, ներբող, դրուատիք)
eunuch - nerkini (ներքինի)
eureka - kuda (գտա՜յ)
Europe - yevroba (Եւրոպա)
european - yevrobatsi, yevrobagan (եւրոպացի, եւրոպական)
euthanasia - heshdamahoutiun, kutamahoutiun (հեշտամահութիւն, գթամահութիւն)
evacuate - barbel, tadargel (պարպել, դատարկել)
evacuation - barboum, tadargoum, puskhouk (պարպում, դատարկում, փախուստ)
evade - pakhchil, kouys dal, burdzil (փախչիլ, խոյս տալ, պրծիլ)
evaluate - arzhevorel, kunahadel (արժեւորել, գնահատել)
evaluation - arzhevoroum, kunahadoum (արժեւորում, գնահատում)
Evangel - avedaran (Աւետարան)
evangelic, evangelical - avedaranagan (աւետարանական)
evangelism - avedaranchoutiun (աւետարանչութիւն)
evangelist - avedaranich (աւետարանիչ)
evangelize - avedaranel (աւետարանել)
evantilate - hovaharel, vijil (հովահարել, վիճիլ)
evaporate - shokiatsunel, chortsunel, shokianal, tsuntil (շոգիացնել, չորցնել, շոգիանալ, ցնդիլ)
evaporation - shokiatsoum, tsuntoum (շոգիացում, ցնդում)
evasion - pakhousd, khouys, hunark (փախուստ, խոյս, հնարք)
evasive - khousapoghagan, khapousig, pakhusdagan (խուսափողական, խաբուսիկ, փախստական)
eve - yerego, irigoun, nakhadonag (երեկոյ, իրիկուն, նախատօնակ)
even - hart, havasar, zouyk, nouynisg, hartel (հարթ, հաւասար, զոյգ, նոյնիսկ, հարթել)
evening - yerego, irigoun (երեկոյ, իրիկուն)
event - tebk, badahar, vakhjan, yegheloutiun (դէպք, պատահար, վախճան, եղելութիւն)
eventful - badahmounkov, tibvadzov (պատահմունքով, դիպուածով)
eventual - badahagan, tibvadzagan (պատահական, դիպուածական)
ever - yerpek, mishd, sharounag (երբեք, միշտ, շարունակ)
evergreen - mushdatalar, mushdaganach (մշտադալար, մշտականաչ)
everlasting - havidenagan, anverch, anmeroug (յաւիտենական, անվերջ, անմեռուկ)
evermore - devabes, untmishd (տեւապէս, ընդմիշտ)
everse - dabalel, shurchel, gordzanel (տապալել, շրջել, կործանել)
eversion - shurchoum, gordzanoum (շրջում, կործանում)
evert - shurchel, dabalel (շրջել,

տապալել)
every - yiurakanchiur, amen (իւրաքանչիւր, ամէն)
everybody - amen mart, amenku (ամէն մարդ, ամէնքը)
everyday - amenoria, aroria, amen or (ամէնօրեայ, առօրեայ, ամէն օր)
everyone - amen megu (ամէն մէկը)
everything - amen inch, amen pan (ամէն ինչ, ամէն բան)
everywhere - amen degh (ամէն տեղ)
evict - tadazurgel, iravazurgel, vudarel (դատազրկել, իրաւազրկել, վտարել)
eviction - iravazurgoum, vudaroum (իրաւազրկում, վտարում)
evidence - abatsouyts, vugayoutiun, abatsoutsel (ապացոյց, վկայութիւն, ապացուցել)
evident - haydni, vorosh, patsahayd, husdag (յայտնի, որոշ, բացայայտ, յստակ)
evil - charik, keshoutiun, kesh, hori, vunas (չարիք, գէշութիւն, գէշ, յոռի, վնաս)
evince - haydnel, abatsoutsel, tsoutsaperel (յայտնել, ապացուցել, ցուցաբերել)
evitate - khousapil, pakhchil, uzkoushanal (խուսափիլ, փախչիլ, զգուշանալ)
evocate - vokegochel, artuntsunel (ոգեկոչել, արթնցնել)
evocation - vokegochoum (ոգեկոչում)
evoke - vokegochel, haroutsanel, tadu ayl adian danil (ոգեկոչել, յարուցանել, դատը այլ ատեան տանիլ)
evolution - heghashurchoum, pareshurchoum, holovouyt (յեղաշրջում, բարեշրջում, Հոլովոյթ)
evolve - zarkanal, artsagel, suprel, panal, barzel (զարգանալ, արձակել, սփռել, բանալ, պարզել)
evulsion - khuloum, yiuratsoum, gorzoum (խլում, իւրացում, կորզում)
ex - tours, nakhgin (դուրս, նախկին)
exact - jisht, oughigh, jushkurid (ճիշդ, ուղիղ, ճշգրիտ)
exactitude - jushtoutiun, jushkurdoutiun, usdoukoutiun (ճշդութիւն, ճշգրտութիւն, ստուգութիւն)
exactly - jushkurdoren, anvureb (ճշգրտօրէն, անվրէպ)
exaggerate - chapazantsel (չափազանցել)
exaggeration - chapazantsoutiun (չափազանցութիւն)
exalt - partsuratsunel, kovel, medzarel, parapanel (բարձրացնել, գովել, մեծարել, փառաբանել)
exaltation - medzaroum, kovapanoum (մեծարում, գովաբանում)
examination - kunnoutiun, zunnoum, hartsouports (քննութիւն, զննում, Հարցափորձ)
examine - kunnel, zunnel, hartsunel (քննել, զննել, Հարցնել)
examiner - kunnich, kunnogh (քննիչ, քննող)
example - orinag, numouysh, dibar (օրինակ, նմոյշ, տիպար)
exanimate - angentan, meradz, angentanatsunel (անկենդան, մեռած, անկենդանացնել)
exasperate - zayratsunel, chughaynatsunel, kurkurel (զայրացնել, ջղայնացնել, գրգռել)
exasperation - zayratsoum, zayrouyt, kurkuroum (զայրացում, զայրոյթ, գրգռում)
excavate - beghel, porel, dzagel (պեղել, փորել, ծակել)
excavation - beghoum, poroum (պեղում, փորում)
excavator - hoghapor (Հողափոր)
exceed - kerazantsel, kerazantsil, chapen antsunil (գերազանցել, գերազանցիլ, չափէն անցնիլ)
excel - kerazantsel, kulel, antsunil (գերազանցել, գլել, անցնիլ)
excellence - vusemoutiun, medzoutiun, kerazantsoutiun (վսեմութիւն, մեծութիւն, գերազանցութիւն)
excellent - uskancheli, hoyagab, kerazants, hiyanali (սքանչելի, Հոյակապ, գերազանց, Հիանալի)

excelsior - kerundir, vusem (գերըն-տիր, վսեմ)
excentric - ardagetron, darorinag (արտակեդրոն, տարօրինակ)
except - patsarel, arargel, patsi (բացառել, առարկել, բացի)
exception - patsaroutiun, arargoutiun (բացառութիւն, առարկութիւն)
exceptional - patsarig, ardagark (բացառիկ, արտակարգ)
excess - chapazantsoutiun, shurayloutiun, avelort (չափազանցութիւն, շռայլութիւն, աւելորդ)
excessive - chapazants, dzayrahegh (չափազանց, ծայրայեղ)
exchange - pokhanagel, pokhanagoutiun, loumayapokhoutiun (փոխանակել, փոխանակութիւն, լումայափոխութիւն)
excise - maks, shahadourk (մաքս, շահատուրք)
excitation - kurkuroum, kurkuroutiun, kurkir (գրգռում, գրգռութիւն, գրգիռ)
excite - kurkurel, houzel, turtel (գրգռել, յուզել, դրդել)
excitement - kurkuroum, kurkir, houzoum (գրգռում, գրգիռ, յուզում)
exclaim - patsakanchel, kochel, aghaghagel (բացականչել, գոչել, աղաղակել)
exclamation - patsakanchoutiun, kochoum, aghaghag (բացականչութիւն, գոչում, աղաղակ)
exclude - vudarel, ardaksel, merzhel (վտարել, արտաքսել, մերժել)
exclusion - ardaksoum, vudaroum (արտաքսում, վտարում)
exclusive - yiurahadoug, sepagan, miag, daramerzh (իւրայատուկ, սեփական, միակ, տարամերժ)
exclusivity - menashunorh, arantsshunorhoum, sepaganoutiun (մենաշնորհ, առանձնաշնորհում, սեփականութիւն)
excogitate - khorhil, khogal, hunarel (խորհիլ, խոկալ, հնարել)
excommunicate - panaturel, ardaksel (բանադրել, արտաքսել)
excommunication - panatrank, nuzovk (բանադրանք, նզովք)
excoriate - kertel, sugurtel (քերթել, սկրթել)
excoriation - kertouk, sugurtouk (քերթուք, սկրթուք)
excrement - gughgughank, aghp (կղկղանք, աղբ)
excrete - gughgughel, ardaksel (կղկղել, արտաքսել)
exculpate - artaratsunel, anbard hanel (արդարացնել, անպարտ հանել)
excurse - jamportel, bududil, shurchakayil (ճամբորդել, պտըտիլ, շրջագայիլ)
excursion - shurchabudouyd, shurchakayoutiun (շրջապտոյտ, շրջագայութիւն)
excuse (n) - neroum, artaratsoum, badurvag, chukmeghank (ներում, արդարացում, պատրուակ, չքմեղանք)
excuse (v) - nerel, artaratsunel, neroghoutiun khunturel (ներել, արդարացնել, ներողութիւն խնդրել)
execrable - zuzveli, karsheli, buzhkali (զզուելի, գարշելի, պժգալի)
execrate - anidzel, nuzovel, buzhkal, zuzvil (անիծել, նզովել, պժգալ, զզուիլ)
execration - karshank, zuzvank, anidzoum (գարշանք, զզուանք, անիծում)
execute - kordzaturel, girargel, kulkhadel (գործադրել, կիրարկել, գլխատել)
execution - kordzaturoum, gadaroum, kulkhadoum (գործադրում, կատարում, գլխատում)
executive - kordzatir (գործադիր)
executor - kordzaturogh, khunamagal, gudagagadar (գործադրող, խնամակալ, կտակակատար)
exemplar - orinag, numoush, badjen (օրինակ, նմոյշ, պատճէն)
exemplary - orinageli, dibar, orinag (օրինակելի, տիպար, օրինակ)
exempt - zerdz, azad, nerel, purgel

(զերծ, ազատ, ներել, փրկել)
exequy - taghoum, houghargavoroutiun (թաղում, յուղարկաւորութիւն)
exercise (n) - varzhoutiun, hurahank, marzhank, ports (վարժութիւն, հրահանգ, մարզանք, փորձ)
exercise (v) - marzel, marzuvil, gadarel, portsel (մարզել, մարզուիլ, կատարել, փորձել)
exercise book - dedrag, portsadedur (տետրակ, փորձատետր)
exestuate - yeral, porpokil (եռալ, բորբոքիլ)
exhalation - ardashunchoum, tsuntoum, pouroum (արտաշնչում, ցնդում, բուրում)
exhale - ardashunchel, shokianal, tsuntil (արտաշնչել, շոգիանալ, ցնդիլ)
exhaust - ouzhasbaril, ardaksich, ouzhasbar, barbel (ուժասպառիչ, արտաքսիչ, ուժասպառ, պարպել)
exhaustion - ouzhasbaroum, ouzhatapoutiun, hiudzoum (ուժասպառում, ուժաթափութիւն, հիւծում)
exhibit - tsoutsaturel, nergayatsunel, tsoutsanumouysh (ցուցադրել, ներկայացնել, ցուցանմոյշ)
exhibition - tsoutsaturoutiun, tsoutsahantes (ցուցադրութիւն, ցուցահանդէս)
exhibitionist - tsoutsamol, bujnamol (ցուցամոլ, պճնամոլ)
exhibitor - tsoutsaturogh (ցուցադրող)
exhilarate - ashkhouzhatsunel, zuvartatsunel, ourakhatsunel (աշխուժացնել, զուարթացնել, ուրախացնել)
exhort - khuradel, hortorel, hamozel (խրատել, յորդորել, համոզել)
exigence, exigency - bahanch, usdiboghaganoutiun, harg (պահանջ, ստիպողականութիւն, հարկ)
exigent - bahanchgod, usdiboghagan (պահանջկոտ, ստիպողական)
exile - aksorel, darakurel, aksor, darakir (աքսորել, տարագրել, աքսոր, տարագիր)
exist - koyoutiun ounenal, ko ullal, abril, kudnuvil (գոյութիւն ունենալ, գոյ ըլլալ, ապրիլ, գտնուիլ)
existence - koyoutiun, gyank, argayoutiun (գոյութիւն, կեանք, առկայութիւն)
exit - yelk, megnoum, vakhjan (ելք, մեկնում, վախճան)
exonerate - artaratsunel, anmeghatsunel, chukmeghel (արդարացնել, անմեղացնել, չքմեղել)
exoneration - artarastoum, chukmeghank (արդարացում, չքմեղանք)
exorbitant - aylantag, ardarots, anchap (այլանդակ, արտառոց, անչափ)
exotic - odar, odarerguria, darashkharhig (օտար, օտարերկրեայ, տարաշխարհիկ)
expand - daradzel, medztsunel, dzavalil, untlaynil (տարածել, մեծցնել, ծաւալիլ, ընդլայնիլ)
expanse - daradzoutiun, michots (տարածութիւն, միջոց)
expansion - untartsagoum, daradzoum, dzavaloum (ընդարձակում, տարածում, ծաւալում)
expansive - untartsag, daradzagan (ընդարձակ, տարածական)
expatriate - hayreniken hanel, aksorel, darakurel (հայրենիքէն հանել, աքսորել, տարագրել)
expatriation - darakuroutiun, ardakaghtoum (տարագրութիւն, արտագաղթում)
expect - agungalel, usbasel, housal (ակնկալել, սպասել, յուսալ)
expectation - agungaloutiun, houys, usbasoum (ակնկալութիւն, յոյս, սպասում)
expectorant - khoukhaper (խուխաբեր)
expectorate - khukhal, khoukh teknel (խխալ, խուխ թքնել)
expedient - badshaj, harmar, shahaved, michots (պատշաճ, յարմար, շահաւէտ, միջոց)
expedite - oughargel, ghurgel, arakel, arak (ուղարկել, ղրկել, առաքել, արագ)

expedition - *arakoum, hughoum, arshav, arshavakhoump* (առաքում, յղում, արշաւ, արշաւախումբ)

expel - *vudarel, ardaksel, vurundel* (վտարել, արտաքսել, վռնտել)

expend - *dzakhsel, usbarel, vadnel, muskhel* (ծախսել, սպառել, վատնել, մսխել)

expense - *dzakhs, vadnoum, arzhek* (ծախս, վատնում, արժէք)

expensive - *sough, tang, medzadzakhs* (սուղ, թանկ, մեծածախս)

experience - *portsaroutiun, ports, humdoutiun* (փորձառութիւն, փորձ, հմտութիւն)

experienced - *portsarou, humoud* (փորձառու, հմուտ)

experiment - *ports, kidaports, portsargel* (փորձ, գիտափորձ, փորձարկել)

experimentation - *portsargoum, portsargoutiun* (փորձարկում, փորձարկութիւն)

expert - *masnaked, portsarou, humoud, varbed* (մասնագէտ, փորձառու, հմուտ, վարպետ)

expertise - *kunnel, portsakidoutiun* (քննել, փորձագիտութիւն)

expiate - *kavel, meghku chunchel* (քաւել, մեղքը ջնջել)

expilate - *avararel, goghobdel* (աւարառել, կողոպտել)

expilation - *avararoutiun, goghoboud* (աւարառութիւն, կողոպուտ)

expiration - *ardashunchoum, zhamged, vakhjan* (արտաշնչում, ժամկէտ, վախճան)

expire - *ardashunchel, hokin puchel, mernil, verchanal* (արտաշնչել, հոգին փչել, մեռնիլ, վերջանալ)

explain - *patsadurel, lousapanel, barzel* (բացատրել, լուսաբանել, պարզել)

explanation - *patsaduroutiun, megnoutiun* (բացատրութիւն, մեկնութիւն)

explication - *patsaduroutiun, megnoutiun* (բացատրութիւն, մեկնութիւն)

explicit - *patsahayd, vorosh, husdag* (բացայայտ, որոշ, յստակ)

explode - *baytil, bortgal, baytetsunel* (պայթիլ, պոռթկալ, պայթեցնել)

exploit - *shahakordzel, okdakordzel, kachakordzoutiun* (շահագործել, օգտագործել, քաջագործութիւն)

exploitation - *shahakordzoum, charashahoutiun* (շահագործում, չարաշահութիւն)

explorate - *hedazodel, yergurakhouzel* (հետազօտել, երկրախուզել)

exploration - *hedazodoutiun, yergurakhouzoutiun* (հետազօտութիւն, երկրախուզութիւն)

explorator - *yergurakhouyz, khouzargou* (երկրախոյզ, խուզարկու)

explore - *hedazodel, ousoumnasirel* (հետազօտել, ուսումնասիրել)

explorer - *hedakhouyz, yergurakhouyz* (հետախոյզ, երկրախոյզ)

explosion - *baytoum, baytiun, bortgoum* (պայթում, պայթիւն, պոռթկում)

explosive - *baytoutsig* (պայթուցիկ)

exponent - *megnapan, megnich, tsoutsargou, haydarar* (մեկնաբան, մեկնիչ, ցուցարկու, յայտարար)

export - *ardadzel, daradzoum* (տարածել, տարածում)

exportation - *ardadzoum, ardahanoum* (արտածում, արտահանում)

expose - *tsoutsaturel, barzel, koghazerdzel* (ցուցադրել, պարզել, քօղազերծել)

exposition - *tsoutsahantes, tsoutsaturoutiun* (ցուցահանդէս, ցուցադրութիւն)

exposure - *tsoutsaturoutiun, haydnoutiun, mergatsoum* (ցուցադրութիւն, յայտնութիւն, մերկացում)

expound - *patsadurel, megnel, barzel* (բացատրել, մեկնել, պարզել)

express (n) - *sourhantag, jebuntats, ushdab arakoum* (սուրհանդակ, ճեպընթաց, շտապ առաքում)

express (v) - *ardahaydel, barzel, nergayatsunel, ghurgel* (արտայայտել, պարզել, ներկայացնել, ղրկել)

express mail - arak tughtadar (արագ Թղթատար)
expression - ardahaydoutiun (արտայայտութիւն)
expressive - ardahaydich, hadganushagan (արտայայտիչ, յատկանշական)
expressman - sourhantag, jebavar (սուրհանդակ, ճեպավար)
expressway - jeboughi (ճեպուղի)
exprobrate - meghaturel, bakharagel (մեղադրել, պախարակել)
expropriate - sepaganazurgel, galvadzazurgel (սեփականազրկել, կալուածազրկել)
expropriation - sepaganazurgoum (սեփականազրկում)
expulse - ardaksel, vudarel (արտաքսել, վտարել)
expulsion - ardaksoum, vudaroum (արտաքսում, վտարում)
expunction - chunchoum (ջնջում)
expunge - chunchel (ջնջել)
expurgate - zudel, makrel, surpakurel (զտել, մաքրել, սրբագրել)
expurge - zudel, makrel, surpakurel (զտել, մաքրել, սրբագրել)
exquire - kunnel (քննել)
exquisite - undir, keghetsig, nourp, bujnaser (ընտիր, գեղեցիկ, նուրբ, պճնասէր)
exsanguinate - ariunodel, ariunu kamel (արիւնոտել, արիւնը քամել)
exscribe - untorinagel (ընդօրինակել)
exscript - orinag, artsanakuroutiun (օրինակ, արձանագրութիւն)
extant - koyadevogh (գոյատեւող)
extempore - hanbadrasdits (յանպատրաստից)
extend - daradzel, untartsagel, layntsunel (տարածել, ընդարձակել, լայնցնել)
extended - daradzvadz, yergaratsukvadz (տարածուած, երկարաձգուած)
extense - untartsag, dzavaloun (ընդարձակ, ծաւալուն)
extension - daradzoum, untartsagoum, dzavaloum (տարածում, ընդարձակում, ծաւալում)
extensive - laynadaradz, untartsag (լայնատարած, ընդարձակ)
extent - dzaval, daradzoutiun, bardakurav (ծաւալ, տարածութիւն, պարտագրաւ)
extenuate - dugaratsunel, ouzhasbarel, nuvaghil (տկարացնել, ուժասպառել, նուաղիլ)
exterior - ardakin, toursi, odar (արտաքին, դուրսի, օտար)
exterminate - punachunchel, ardaksel (բնաջնջել, արտաքսել)
extermination - punachunchoum, anjidoum (բնաջնջում, անջիտում))
extern - ardakin, tseregotig (արտաքին, ցերեկօթիկ)
external - ardakin, odar, toursi (արտաքին, օտար, դուրսի)
externat - tseregotig tubrots (ցերեկօթիկ դպրոց)
extill - gatetsunel (կաթեցնել)
extinct - maradz, meradz, mahatsadz (մարած, մեռած, մահացած)
extinction - nuvaghoum, shichoum, mah, usbaroum (նուաղում, շիջում, մահ, սպառում)
extinguish - marel, chunchel, anhaydatsunel, vujarel (մարել, ջնջել, անյայտացնել, վճարել)
extinguisher - marogh, guragamarich (մարող, կրակամարիչ)
extirpate - armadakhulel, anjidel, punachunchel (արմատախլել, անճիտել, բնաջնջել)
extol - kovel, parapanel (գովել, փառաբանել)
extort - khulel, hapushdagel, gorzel (խլել, յափշտակել, կորզել)
extortion - hapushdagoutiun, gorzoum (յափշտակութիւն, կորզում)
extra - ardasovor, patsarig, ardagark (արտասովոր, բացառիկ, արտակարգ)
extract - hanel, kaghel, ardahanel kamoug, ardahanoum (հանել, քաղել, արտահանել, քամուկ, արտահանում)
extraction - ardahanoum, khuloum, dzaghgakagh, dohm (արտահանում,

խլում, ծաղկաքաղ, տոհմ)
extraordinary - darorinag, ardagark, ansovor (տարօրինակ, արտասովոր, անսովոր)
extravagance, cy - shurayloutiun, aylantagoutiun (շռայլութիւն, այլանդակութիւն)
extravagant - shurayl, aylantag (շռայլ, այլանդակ)
extravagate - taparil, sulukdal (թափառիլ, սլքտալ)
extreme - dzayrakouyn, dzayrahegh, verchin, hedin (ծայրագոյն, ծայրայեղ, վերջին, յետին)
extremist - dzayraheghagan (ծայրայեղական)
extremity - dzayr, dzayramas, yezur, verch, dzayraheghoutiun (ծայր, ծայրամաս, եզր, վերջ, ծայրայեղութիւն)
extrude - ardaksel, tours hanel, mughel (արտաքսել, դուրս հանել, մղել)
extrusion - ardaksoum, ardamughoum (արտաքսում, արտամղում)
exude - kurdenil, kurduntsunel (քրտնիլ, քրտնցնել)
exult - tsundzal, khaydal, hurjuvil (ցնծալ, խայտալ, հրճուիլ)
eye - achk, agun, desoghoutiun (աչք, ակն, տեսողութիւն)
eyeball - agnakount (ակնագունդ)
eyebeam - nayvadzk (նայուածք)
eyebrow - honk, ardevanounk (յօնք, արտեւանունք)
eyeglass - agnots (ակնոց)
eyelash - tartich (թարթիչ)
eyeless - achazourg, anach (աչազուրկ, անաչ)
eyelid - gob (կոպ)
eyesight - desoghoutiun (տեսողութիւն)
eyewash - artsounk (արցունք)
eyewitness - aganades, vuga (ականատես, վկայ)

fable - arag, arasbel, hekiat, aragapanel (առակ, առասպել, հեքիաթ, առակաբանել)
fabler - aragakir (առակագիր)
fabric - shinvadzk, hiusk, shenk (շինուածք, հիւսք, շէնք)
fabricant - kordzaranader (գործարանատէր)
fabricate - gazmel, shinel, hunarel, geghdzel (կազմել, շինել, հնարել, կեղծել)
fabrication - garoutsoum, gazmoum, horinoum (կառուցում, կազմում, յօրինում)
fabricator - gerdich, hunarogh (կերտիչ, հնարող)
fabulist - aragakir (առակագիր)
fabulous - arasbelagan, shindzou (առասպելական, շինծու)
facade - daneres, jagad (տաներես, ճակատ)
face - temk, yeres, jagadil, nayil, timakuravel (դէմք, երես, ճակատիլ, նայիլ, դիմագրաւել)
facete - gadagakhos, suramid, badrasdapan (կատակախօս, սրամիտ, պատրաստաբան)
facile - tiurin, anhok, hajoyagadar (դիւրին, անհոգ, հաճոյակատար)
facilitate - tiuratsunel, heshdatsunel (դիւրացնել, հեշտացնել)
facility - tiuroutiun, heshdoutiun (դիւրութիւն, հեշտութիւն)
facing - yeresabadoum, ardadzadzk, asdar (երեսապատում, արտածածք,

ստար)
facsimile - nemanakir, nemanakurel (նմանագիր, նմանագրել)
fact - iroghoutiun, pasd, arark (իրողութիւն, փաստ, արարք)
faction - hadvadz, khoump, baragdoum (հատուած, խումբ, պառակտում)
factious - hadvadzagan (հատուածական)
factitious - arvesdagan, shindzou (արուեստական, շինծու)
facto - iraganabes (իրականապէս)
factor - aztag, michnort, kordzagal (ազդակ, միջնորդ, գործակալ)
factory - kordzaran, kordzadoun, ardaturavayr (գործարան, գործատուն, արտադրավայր)
factum - gudag, gudagi irakordzoum (կտակ, կտակի իրագործում)
faculty - garoghoutiun, tsirk, gajar, ousoumnaran (կարողութիւն, ձիրք, կաճառ, ուսումնարան)
fad - kumayk, darorinagoutiun (քմայք, տարօրինակութիւն)
fade - duzhkounil, kounadil, khamril, dugar, anham (տժգունիլ, գունատիլ, խամրիլ, տկար, անհամ)
fadless - antaram (անթառամ)
fag - hoknetsunel, ashkhadtsunel, duknil, hiudzoum (յոգնեցնել, աշխատցնել, տքնիլ, հիւծում)
fage - severel, nayil, agnaseveroum (սեւեռել, նայիլ, ակնասեւեռում)
fagot - khourts, durtsag (խուրձ, տրցակ)
faience - hakhjabagi (յախճապակի)
fail - tsakhoghil, usbaril, gorsuntsunel, vuriboum (ձախողիլ, սպառիլ, կորսնցնել, վրիպում)
failance - vuriboum, sukhal (վրիպում, սխալ)
failure - tsakhoghoutiun, anhachoghoutiun, sunangoutiun (ձախողութիւն, անյաջողութիւն, սնանկութիւն)
fain - ourakh, koh, hozharagam (ուրախ, գոհ, յօժարակամ)
faineant - tadargabord, dzouyl, ankordz (դատարկապորտ, ծոյլ, անգործ)
faint - anzor, dugar, nuvaghil (անզօր, տկար, նուաղիլ)
fainting - nevaghoum (նուաղում)
fair - donavajar, tsoutsahantes, keghetsig, hianali (տօնավաճառ, ցուցահանդէս, գեղեցիկ, հիանալի)
fairy - haverzhahars, barig, peri (յաւերժահարս, պարիկ, փերի)
faith - havadk, havadarmoutiun, tavanank (հաւատք, հաւատարմութիւն, դաւանանք)
faithful - havadarim, vusdaheli, bargeshd (հաւատարիմ, վստահելի, պարկեշտ)
fake - khapeoutiun, geghdzik, geghdzel , khapel (խաբէութիւն, կեղծիք, կեղծել, խաբել)
faker - khapepa, khartakh (խաբեբայ, խարդախ)
fakir - mouratsig guronavor, huntiq Juknavor (մուրացիկ կրօնաւոր, հնդիկ ճգնաւոր)
falcon - paze (բազէ)
fall - iynal, tapil, gordzanil, angoum, gordzanoum (իյնալ, թափիլ, կործանիլ, անկում, կործանում)
fallacious - khapeagan, soud, sudahot (խաբէական, սուտ, ստայօդ)
fallacy - khapeoutiun, sudoutiun, badrank (խաբէութիւն, ստութիւն, պատրանք)
fallen - ingadz, ichadz, avervadz, nuvajial (ինկած, իջած, աւերուած, նուաճեալ)
false - sukhal, soud, geghdz, khartakh, shindzou (սխալ, սուտ, կեղծ, խարդախ, շինծու)
falsify - geghdzel, nenkel, khartakhel, sudel (կեղծել, նենգել, խարդախել, ստել)
falsity - geghdzik, sudoutiun (կեղծիք, ստութիւն)
fame - hampav, hurchag, hurchagel (համբաւ, հռչակ, հռչակել)
familiar - undanegan, muderim, dzanot, modig (ընտանեկան, մտերիմ, ծանօթ, մօտիկ)
familiarize - undanetsunel, dzanotatsunel, mudermatsunel (ընտա-

նեցնել, ծանօթացնել, մտերմացնել)

family - undanik, kertasdan, tsegh, khoump (ընտանիք, գերդաստան, ցեղ, խումբ)

family medicine - undanegan, undanegan puzhushgoutiun, puzhishg (ընտանեկան, ընտանեկան բժշկութիւն, բժիշկ)

famine - sov, anotoutiun (սով, անօթութիւն)

famous - hurchagavor, nushanavor, haydni, anvani (հռչակաւոր, նշանաւոր, յայտնի, անուանի)

fan - hovahar, hovaharel, molerant, sirogh (հովահար, հովահարել, մոլեռանդ, սիրող)

fanatic - molerant, guronamol (մոլեռանդ, կրօնամոլ)

fanaticism - molerantoutiun (մոլեռանդութիւն)

fancier - yerazgod, moli, kidag (երազկոտ, մոլի, գիտակ)

fanciful - kumaykod, darorinag, yerazoun (քմայքոտ, տարօրինակ, երազուն)

fancy - yerevagayel, yerevagayoutiun, kumahajouyk (երեւակայել, երեւակայութիւն, քմահաճոյք)

fane - hoghmatsouyts, dajar, aghotadeghi (հողմացոյց, տաճար, աղօթատեղի)

fanfare - nuvakakhoump, poghherakhoump (նուագախումբ, փողերախումբ)

fang - zhanik, jang, jangel, puzukdel (ժանիք, ճանկ, ճանկել, բզքտել)

fantastic - darorinag, yerevagayagan, ardarots (տարօրինակ, երեւակայական, արտառոց)

fantasy - kumahajouyk, yerevagayoutiun, kumayk (քմահաճոյք, երեւակայութիւն, քմայք)

far - herou, heravor, heroun, khozi tsak (հեռու, հեռաւոր, հեռուն, խոզի ձագ)

Far East - dzayrakouyn arevelk (Ծայրագոյն Արեւելք)

far sighted - herades (հեռատես)

faraway - heravor (հեռաւոր)

farce - zaveshdakhagh, kheghgadagoutiun, litsk (զաւեշտախաղ, խեղկատակութիւն, լիցք)

farceur - hudbid, kheghgadag (հտպիտ, խեղկատակ)

fare - yertal, jamportel, janabarhadzakhs, oudelik (երթալ, ճամբորդել, ճանապարհածախս, ուտելիք)

farewell - hurazheshd, megnoum, voghchert (հրաժեշտ, մեկնում, ողջերթ)

farm - akarag, dourk, vartsel, mushagel (ագարակ, տուրք, վարձել, մշակել)

farmer - akaragader, hoghakordz (ագարակատէր, հողագործ)

farming - hoghakordzoutiun, yergurakordzoutiun (հողագործութիւն, երկրագործութիւն)

farrago - kharnourt, kharnaran (խառնուրդ, խառնարան)

farrier - baydar, tarpin, tsiapouyzh (պայտար, դարբին, ձիաբոյժ)

farther - aveli herou, aveli, antin (աւելի հեռու, աւելի, անդին)

fascinate - humayel, tiutel, hurabourel (հմայել, դիւթել, հրապուրել)

fashion - noratsevoutiun, sovorouyt, tsev, noratsevel (նորաձեւութիւն, սովորոյթ, ձեւ, նորաձեւել)

fast - arak, shoud, amour, zekh, dzom bahel (արագ, շուտ, ամուր, զեխ, ծոմ պահել)

fasten - amratsunel, gabel, seghmel (ամրացնել, կապել, սեղմել)

fastener - amratsunogh, gabogh, seghmich (ամրացնող, կապող, սեղմիչ)

faster - dzomabah (ծոմապահ)

fastidious - tuzhvarahaj, pudzakhuntir (դժուարահաճ, բծախնդիր)

fasting - dzomabahoutiun (ծոմապահութիւն)

fastness - amroutiun, amrots, havadarmoutiun (ամրութիւն, ամրոց, հաւատարմութիւն)

fat - jarb, yiugh, ker, jarbod (ճարպ, իւղ, գէր, ճարպոտ)

fatal - jagadakuragan, aghidali,

mahatsou (ճակատագրական, աղիտալի, մահացու)
fatalism - jagadakurabashdoutiun (ճակատագրապաշտութիւն)
fatalist - jagadakurabashd (ճակատագրապաշտ)
fatality - tuzhpakhdoutiun, mah (դժբախտութիւն, մահ)
fate - jagadakir, pakhd, aghed, mah, nakhoroshel (ճակատագիր, բախտ, աղէտ, մահ, նախորոշել)
fateful - jagadakuragan (ճակատագրական)
father (n) - hayr, nakhahayr, yegeghetsagan (հայր, նախահայր, եկեղեցական)
father (v) - hayranal, vortekurel (հայրանալ, որդեգրել)
fatherhood - hayroutiun (հայրութիւն)
fatherland - hayrenik (հայրենիք)
fatherless - anhayr, hayrazourg (անհայր, հայրազուրկ)
fathom - khorachapel, umpurnel (խորաչափել, ըմբռնել)
fatigue - hoknoutiun, khonchenk, hoknetsunel (յոգնութիւն, խոնջէնք, յոգնեցնել)
fatness - kiroutiun, barardoutiun (գիրութիւն, պարարտութիւն)
fatten - kirnal, barardatsunel (գիրնալ, պարարտացնել)
fatty - jarbod (ճարպոտ)
fatuity - aboushoutiun, himaroutiun, anmudoutiun (ապուշութիւն, յիմարութիւն, անմտութիւն)
fatuous - aboush, himar, anmid (ապուշ, յիմար, անմիտ)
faucet - dzorag (ծորակ)
fault - sukhal, teroutiun, hantsank, sukhalil (սխալ, թերութիւն, յանցանք, սխալիլ)
favor - shunorh, parik, nubasd, oknel, nubasdel (շնորհ, բարիք, նպաստ, օգնել, նպաստել)
favorable - nubasdavor, parehaj, badeh (նպաստաւոր, բարեհաճ, պատեհ)
fax - herabadjen, heradib (հեռապատճէն, հեռատիպ)
fealty - havadarmoutiun, hunazantoutiun (հաւատարմութիւն, հնազանդութիւն)
fear - vakh, yergiugh, vakhnal (վախ, երկիւղ, վախնալ)
fearful - vakhgod, sosgali, sarsapeli (վախկոտ, սոսկալի, սարսափելի)
feast - khunjouyk, khurakhjank, donel, donakhumpel (խնճոյք, խրախճանք, տօնել, տօնախմբել)
feastday - paradon (փառատօն)
feat - kachakordzoutiun, arark (քաջագործութիւն, արարք)
feather - pedour, pedravorel, pedrazartel (փետուր, փետրաւորել, փետրազարդել)
feather duster - pedravel (փետրաւել)
feature - timakidz, gerbar, tsev (դիմագիծ, կերպար, ձեւ)
featured - pedrazart, kulkhavor (փետրազարդ, գլխաւոր)
featureless - angerbaran, anpedour (անկերպարան, անփետուր)
February - pedurvar (Փետրուար)
feces, faeces - gughgughank, murour (կղկղանք, մրուր)
fecund - arkavant, peghmnavor, perri (արգաւանդ, բեղմնաւոր, բերրի)
fecundate - arkasavorel, peghmnavorel (արգասաւորել, բեղմնաւորել)
fecundation - arkasavoroum, peghmnavoroum (արգասաւորում, բեղմնաւորում)
fecundity - arkasaperoutiun, peghmnavoroutiun (արգասաբերութիւն, բեղմնաւորութիւն)
federal - tashnagtsayin (դաշնակցային)
federate - tashnagtsil, hamakhumpel, tashnagits (դաշնակցիլ, համախմբել, դաշնակից)
federation - tashnagtsoutiun (դաշնակցութիւն)
federative - tashnagtsayin, miatsial (դաշնակցային, միացեալ)
fee - dzakhk, kin, vartsk, usdatsvadzk, vujarel (ծախք, արժէք, վարձք, ստացուածք, վճարել)
feeble - dugar, vadaroghch, touyl

(տկար, վատառողջ, թոյլ)
feed - geragrel, sunoutsanel, gushdanal, sunount, ger (կերակրել, սնուցանել, կշտանալ, սնունդ, կեր)
feeder - oudogh, sunoutsich, madagarar, dzudzag (ուտող, սնուցիչ, մատակարար, ծծակ)
feeding - sunoutsoum, geragour (սնուցում, կերակուր)
feel - uzkal, uzkatsvil, tsernel (զգալ, զգացուիլ, ձեռնել)
feeler - uzkatsogh, shoshapogh (զգացող, շօշափող)
feeling - uzkayarank, uzkaynoutiun, uzkayoun (զգայարանք, զգայնութիւն, զգայուն)
feet - vodker (ոտքեր)
feign - geghdzel, tsevatsunel (կեղծել, ձեւացնել)
feint - geghdz, shindzou, hartsagoum tsevatsunel (կեղծ, շինծու, յարձակում ձեւացնել)
felicitate - shunorhavorel, khuntagtsil (շնորհաւորել, խնդակցիլ)
felicitation - shunorhavoroutiun, khuntagtsoutiun (շնորհաւորութիւն, խնդակցութիւն)
felicity - hurjuvank, yerchangoutiun (հրճուանք, երջանկութիւն)
fell - gadaghi, vayrak, moushdag, lerg pulour (կատաղի, վայրագ, մուշտակ, լերկ բլուր)
fellness - vayrakoutiun (վայրագութիւն)
fellow - unger, bashdonagits, anhad, ungeragtsil (ընկեր, պաշտօնակից, անհատ, ընկերակցիլ)
felon - vojrakordz, charakordz, yeghernakordz (ոճրագործ, չարագործ, եղեռնագործ)
felony - hantsakordzoutiun (յանցագործութիւն)
female - ikagan, ek, gin (իգական, էգ, կին)
feminine - ikagan, ganatsi, meghm (իգական, կանացի, մեղմ)
fence (n) - tsangabad, barisb, badnesh, souseramard (ցանկապատ, պարիսպ, պատնէշ, սուսերամարտ)
fence (v) - tsangabadel, shurchapagel, souseramardil (ցանկապատել, շրջափակել, սուսերամարտիլ)
fencing - tsangabadoum, surakhagh, panavej (ցանկապատում, սրախաղ, բանավէճ)
fend - bashdbanvil, hokadarel (պաշտպանուիլ, հոգատարել)
feracious - budghaper, arkasaper (պտղաբեր, արգասաբեր)
feracity - arkasaperoutiun (արգասաբերութիւն)
ferm - akarag (ագարակ)
ferment - magartel, magart, khumor, (մակարդել, մակարդ, խմոր)
fermentation - khumoroum, porpokoum, houyz (խմորում, բորբոքում, յոյզ)
ferocious - gadaghi, vayreni (կատաղի, վայրենի)
ferry - navag, lasdanav, kedants, antsaran (նաւակ, լաստանաւ, գետանց, անցարան)
ferry boat - lasdanav, kedanav (լաստանաւ, գետանաւ)
fertile - pareper, budghaper, arkasaper, peghoun (բարեբեր, պտղաբեր, արգասաբեր, բեղուն)
fertility - arkasaperoutiun (արգասաբերութիւն)
fertilization - barardatsoum, arkasaperoum, pareperoutiun (պարարտացում, արգասաբերում, բարեբերութիւն)
fertilize - barardatsunel, arkasavorel (պարարտացնել, արգասաւորել)
fertilizer - barardaniut, barardatsoutsich (պարարտանիւթ, պարարտացուցիչ)
fervent - cherm, yerantoun, pourun, khantavar (ջերմ, եռանդուն, բուռն, խանդավառ)
fervor - chermoutiun, yerant, khant (ջերմութիւն, եռանդ, խանդ)
fester - tarakhodil, porpokil, tarakhodoum, balar (թարախոտիլ, բորբոքիլ, թարախոտում, պալար)
festinate - habjeb, shoudov, arak (հապճեպ, շուտով, արագ)
festination - ajabarank (աճապարանք)

festival - paradon, donahantes, khurakhjank (փառատօն, տօնահանդէս, խրախճանք)
festivity - donakhunpoutiun, khurakhjank, don (տօնախմբութիւն, խրախճանք, տօն)
festoon - turasank, dzaghgahius, turasankel (դրասանգ, ծաղկահիւս, դրասանգել)
fetch - perel, hastsunel, hunark, varbedoutiun (բերել, հասցնել, հնարք, վարպետութիւն)
fetich, fetish - gourk, houroutk, sunodik (կուռք, յուռութք, սնոտիք)
fetish - sunodi, anhimun, avelortabashdagan ararga (սնոտի, անհիմն- աւելորդապաշտական առարկայ)
fetishism - avelortabashdoutiun (աւելորդապաշտութիւն)
fetter - shughtayel, vodnagabel, arkilel, gabank, gab (շղթայել, ոտնակապել, արգիլել, կապանք, կապ)
fettle - norokel, harmartsunel, badrasdel, norokoum (նորոգել, յարմարցնել, պատրաստել, նորոգում)
fetus - saghm (սաղմ)
feudal - avadagan, galvadzadiragan (աւատական, կալուածատիրական)
feudalism - avadaganoutiun, avadabedoutiun (աւատականութիւն, աւատապետութիւն)
fever - cherm, dent, chermakhd, toghatsunel (ջերմ, տենդ, ջերմախտ, դողացնել)
few - kich, sagav, nuvaz (քիչ, սակաւ, նուազ)
fewer - aveli kich, aveli nuvaz (աւելի քիչ, աւելի նուազ)
fez - fes, kulkharg (ֆէս, գլխարկ)
fiance' - nushanadz, pesatsou (նշանած, փեսացու)
fiancee - nushanadz, harsuntsou (նշանած, հարսնցու)
fiasco - tsakhoghoutiun (ձախողութիւն)
fiat - huraman, vujir (հրաման, վճիռ)
fib - sudel, soud, arasbel (ստել, սուտ, առասպել)
fiber - manratel (մանրաթել)
fiber, fibre - manratel, telig, neart, chigh (մանրաթել, թելիկ, նեարդ, ջիղ)
fibre - neart, manratel (նեարդ, մանրաթել)
fickle - popokhagan, angayoun, heghheghoug (փոփոխական, անկայուն, յեղյեղուկ)
fiction - arasbel, geghdzik, veb, vibakuroutiun (առասպել, կեղծիք, վէպ, վիպագրութիւն)
fictious, fictitious - geghdz, shindzou, medadzadzin (կեղծ, շինծու, մտածածին)
fictive - geghdz, shindzou, soud (կեղծ, շինծու, սուտ)
ficus - tuzeni (թզենի)
fiddle - choutag, choutag nuvakel (ջութակ, ջութակ նուագել)
fidelity - havadarmoutiun, oughghamudoutiun (հաւատարմութիւն, ուղղամտութիւն)
fidget - sharzhil, irar antsunil, vurtovil, anhankisd (շարժիլ, իրար անցնիլ, վրդովիլ, անհանգիստ)
fiduciary - khunamagal, hokadar, avantabah, havadarim (խնամակալ, հոգատար, աւանդապահ, հաւատարիմ)
fie - pouh, amot (բու~հ, ամօթ)
fief - avad, usdatsvadzk, galvadz (աւատ, ստացուածք, կալուած)
field - tashd, tashdakedin, razmatashd, ard (դաշտ, դաշտագետին, ռազմադաշտ, արտ)
field-marshal - marachakhd (մարաջախտ)
fiend - sadana, tev, charakordz, tushnami (սատանայ, դեւ, չարագործ, թշնամի)
fierce - vayrak, gadaghi, vayreni, duhaj (վայրագ, կատաղի, վայրենի, տհաճ)
fiery - guragod, hureghen, pourun, dakariun (կրակոտ, հրեղէն, բուռն, տաքարիւն)
fifteen - dasunhink (տասնհինգ)
fifth - hinkerort (հինգերորդ)
fifty - hisoun (յիսուն)

fig - touz, tuzeni (թուզ, թզենի)
fight - guriv, baderazm, jagadamard, gurvil (կռիւ, պատերազմ, ճակատամարտ, կռուիլ)
fighter - mardig, gurvogh, razmig (մարտիկ, կռուող, ռազմիկ)
figment - geghdzik, hunark, arasbel (կեղծիք, հնարք, առասպել)
figurative - aylapanagan, khorhurtavor (այլաբանական, խորհրդաւոր)
figure (n) - temk, yeres, gerbarank, badger, tsev, nushan (դէմք, երես, կերպարանք, պատկեր, ձեւ, նշան)
figure (v) - badgerel, nergayanal, nergayatsunel, nugadel (պատկերել, ներկայանալ, ներկայացնել, նկատել)
filament - manratel, telig (մանրաթել, թելիկ)
filch - koghnal, shortel (գողնալ, շորթել)
filcher - kusagahad (քսակահատ)
file - tughtadzurar, gark, khardots, sharel, garkavorel (թղթածրար, կարգ, խարտոց, շարել, կարգաւորել)
filial - vortiagan, masnajiugh (որդիական, մասնաճիւղ)
filiate - vortekurel (որդեգրել)
filibuster - dzovahen, helouzag, koghnal (ծովահէն, յելուզակ, գողնալ)
fill - letsunel, gushdatsunel, kirnal, goushd, letsoun (լեցնել, կշտացնել, գիրնալ, կուշտ, լեցուն)
fillet - zartakidz, varsagal, mazgab (զարդագիծ, վարսակալ, մազկապ)
fillip - madnazarg, khutan, khutanel, tsaydetsunel (մատնազարկ, խթան, խթանել, ցայտեցնել)
film - sharzhabadger, yeriz, mashg, taghant (շարժապատկեր, երիզ, մաշկ, թաղանդ)
film director - pematurich (բեմադրիչ)
filter - zudich, kamots, zudel, kamel (զտիչ, քամոց, զտել, քամել)
filth - aghd, aghp, geghd, munatsoug, aghdod niut (աղտ, աղբ, կեղտ, մնացուկ, աղտոտ նիւթ)
filtrate - zudel, kamel, zudots (զտել, քամել, զտոց)
filtration - kamoum, zudoum, muzoum (քամում, զտում, մզում)
fin - loghag, loghatev, tevaharel, gugurdel, pazhnel (լողակ, լողաթեւ, թեւահարել, կտրտել, բաժնել)
final - verchin, verchnagan, avardagan, vujragan (վերջին, վերջնական, աւարտական, վճռական)
finance - yelevmoud, yegamoud, dundesoutiun, dundesel (ելեւմուտ, եկամուտ, տնտեսութիւն, տնտեսել)
financial - yelevmudagan, dundesagan, turamagan (ելեւմտական, տնտեսական, դրամական)
financier - yelevmedaked, dundesaked (ելեւմտագէտ, տնտեսագէտ)
financing - finansavoroum, niutagan hokatsoum (ֆինանսաւորում, նիւթական հոգացում)
find - kudnel, haydnakordzel, imanal, degheganal (գտնել, յայտնագործել, իմանալ, տեղեկանալ)
finder - kudnogh, hunarich (գտնող, հնարիչ)
finding - kiud, haydnakordzoum, tadavujir (գիւտ, յայտնագործում, դատավճիռ)
fine (a) - nourp, undir, doukank, nurpatsunel (նուրբ, ընտիր, տուգանք, նրբացնել)
fine (v) - doukank, dourk, doukanel (տուգանք, տուրք, տուգանել)
finger - mad, madnachap, tubil, koghnal, nuvakel (մատ, մատնաչափ, դպիլ, գողնալ, նուագել)
finger print - madnadib, madnaturoshm, madnahedk (մատնատիպ, մատնադրոշմ, մատնահետք)
finical - pudzakhuntir, nurpajashag, kumahaj (բծախնդիր, նրբաճաշակ, քմահաճ)
finish - verchatsunel, lumunnal, hughgel, avardoum, payl (վերջացնել, լմննալ, յղկել, աւարտում, փայլ)
Finland - finlanda (Ֆինլանտա)
fire - gurag, pots, hurteh, guragel (կրակ, բոց, հրդեհ, կրակել)

firefan - pukots (փքոց)
firefly - gaydzorig (կայծոռիկ)
fireman - hurshech (Հրշէջ)
fireplace - guragaran (կրակարան)
fireside - vararan, undanik, ojakh (վառարան, ընտանիք, օճախ)
firestone - gaydzkar (կայծքար)
firework - hurakhaghoutiun (Հրախաղութիւն)
firm - amour, bint, vajaradoun hasdadel (ամուր, պինդ, վաճառատուն, Հաստատել)
firmament - yergnagamar, yergink (երկնակամար, երկինք)
firman - hurovardag (Հրովարտակ)
first - arachin, usgizpu, kulkhavor (առաջին, սկիզբը, գլխաւոր)
first aid - arachin oknoutiun (առաջին օգնութիւն)
firth - dzovakhorsh, kedaperan (ծովախորշ, գետաբերան)
fiscal - yelevmudagan, kantsayin, kantsabah (ելեւմտական, գանձային, գանձապաՀ)
fiscal year - hargadari (Հարկատարի)
fish - tsoug, tsoug purnel, vorsal (ձուկ, ձուկ բռնել, որսալ)
fisher, fisherman - tsugnors (ձկնորս)
fishery, fishing - tsugnorsoutiun (ձկնորսութիւն)
fishhook - gart (կարթ)
fish-monger - tsugnavajar (ձկնավաճառ)
fission - pazhanoum, jeghkoum, hertsoum (բաժանում, ճեղքում, Հերձում)
fissure - jeghk, jeghkuvadz, jeghkel, hertsel (ճեղք, ճեղքուած, ճեղքել, Հերձել)
fist - purountsk, group, gurpaharel (բռունցք, կռուփ, կռփաՀարել)
fit (a) - harmar, vayelouch, aroghch, badshaj, gatvadz (յարմար, վայելուչ, առողջ, պատշաճ, կաթուած)
fit (b) - harmaril, harmartsunel, badshajil, badrasdel (յարմարիլ, յարմարցնել, պատշաճիլ, պատրաստել)
fitful - yereroun, anhasdad, heghheghoug (երերուն, անՀաստատ, յեղյեղուկ)
fitness - harmaroutiun, aroghchoutiun, vayelchoutiun (յարմարութիւն, առողջութիւն, վայելչութիւն)
fitting - harmaretsoum, gazmadzk, sarkavoroum (յարմարեցում, կազմածք, սարքաւորում)
five - hink (Հինգ)
fix - amratsunel, hasdadel, hasdadvil, buntanal (ամրացնել, Հաստատել, Հաստատուիլ, պնդանալ)
fixation - hasdadoum, severoum (Հաստատում, սեւեռում)
fixative - amratsunogh, hasdadogh (ամրացնող, Հաստատող)
fixture - garasik, sark (կարասիք, սարք)
fizzle - soulel, sukhalil, vuribil sukhalmounk (սուլել, սխալիլ, վրիպիլ, սխալմունք)
flabby - gagough, touyl, toulamort (կակուղ, թոյլ, թուլամորթ)
flabel - hovahar (ՀովաՀար)
flaccid - touyl, dugar, taramadz (թոյլ, տկար, թառամած)
flacker - turchudil (թռչտիլ)
flag - turoshag, turosh, dzadzanil, toulnal, toultsunel (դրօշակ, դրօշ, ծածանիլ, թուլնալ, թուլցնել)
flagbearer, flagman - turoshagagir (դրօշակակիր)
flagellate - mudragel, kharazanel (մտրակել, խարազանել)
flagitious - anuzkam, anarag (անզգամ, անառակ)
flagon - survag (սրուակ)
flagrance - anuzkamoutiun, gizoum, porpokoum (անզգամութիւն, կիզում, բորբոքում)
flagrant - haydni, patsahayd, sarsapeli, potsagez (յայտնի, բացայայտ, սարսափելի, բոցակէզ)
flagrate - ayrel (այրել)
flagstone - salakar (սալաքար)
flair - hodaroutiun (Հոտառութիւն)
flake - tep, tsiuni patil, tepodil,

tepodel (թեփ, ձիւնի թափիլ, թեփոտիլ, թեփոտել)
flame - pots, gurag, yerant, purungil, potsavaril (բոց, կրակ, եռանդ, բռնկիլ, բոցավառիլ)
flanel - asviag (ասուեակ)
flange - gogh, yezur, oghezur, yezerel (կող, եզր, ողեզր, եզերել)
flank - goghmu, tigounku, zisd, goghen harvadzel (կողմը, թիկունքը, զիստ, կողէն հարուածել)
flap - kughantsk, tev, dzayr, meghm zarnel, tapaharel (քղանցք, թեւ, ծայր, մեղմ զարնել, թափահարել)
flare - potsavaril, paylil, pots, payl (բոցավառիլ, փայլիլ, բոց, փայլ)
flash - paylil, potsavaril, payl, purungoum (փայլիլ, բոցավառիլ, փայլ, բռնկում)
flasher - paylogh, tsoutsaser, gachaghag (փայլող, ցուցասէր, կաչաղակ)
flashlight - tsernalamp (ձեռնալամբ)
flask - survag, toranot, dapag shish (սրուակ, թորանոթ, տափակ շիշ)
flat - daparag, hart, tashdavayr, miorinag (տափարակ, հարթ, դաշտավայր, միօրինակ)
flatten - hartel, dapagtsunel, dapagnal (հարթել, տափակցնել, տափակնալ)
flatter - shoghokortel, kovapanel, hartich (շողոքորթել, գովաբանել, հարթիչ)
flatterer - shoghokort (շողոքորթ)
flatulence - pukodoutiun, pouk (փքոտութիւն, փուք)
flaunt - daradzil, sunabardzil, hubardanal, tsouyts (տարածիլ, սնապարծիլ, հպարտանալ, ցոյց)
flautist - surunkahar (սրնգահար)
flauto - surink (սրինգ)
flavor - pouyr, pourmounk, ham, hamemel (բոյր, բուրմունք, համ, համեմել)
flaw - jeghk, teroutiun, jeghkel, godrel (ճեղք, թերութիւն, ճեղքել, կոտրել)
flawless - gadarial, ampoghchagan (կատարեալ, ամբողջական)
flay - kertel, mortazerdzel, talanel (քերթել, մորթազերծել, թալանել)
fleck - pidz, bisag, pudzavorel (բիծ, պիսակ, բծաւորել)
fledge - pedrazartel, pedravor (փետրազարդել, փետրաւոր)
flee - pakhchil, khousapil, abasdanil (փախչիլ, խուսափիլ, ապաստանիլ)
fleece - mazakhav, pourt, khouzel (մազախաւ, բուրդ, խուզել)
fleer - dzaghrel, dzidzaghil, dzaghur, heknank (ծաղրել, ծիծաղիլ, ծաղր, հեգնանք)
fleet - navadorm, navakhoump, navargel, sulanal (նաւատորմ, նաւախումբ, նաւարկել, սլանալ)
fleme - vanel (վանել)
flesh - mis, marmin, martgoutiun, korov, mis gertsunel (միս, մարմին, մարդկութիւն, գորով, միս կերցնել)
flete - dzupal, loghal (ծփալ, լողալ)
flex - dzurel, tekel (ծռել, թեքել)
flexibility - jugounoutiun, harmaretsoum (ճկունութիւն, յարմարեցում)
flexible - jugoun, tiuratek (ճկուն, դիւրաթեք)
flexion - tekoum, dzaloum, goroutiun (թեքում, ծալում, կորութիւն)
flick - totvel, tetev mudragel (թոթուել, թեթեւ մտրակել)
flicker - tevaharel, dzadzanil, bulbulatsoum (թեւահարել, ծածանիլ, պլպլացում)
flier, flyer - turoutsig, turchogh, pakhchogh (թռուցիկ, թռչող, փախչող)
flight - turichk, savarnoum, pakhousd, yeram (թռիչք, սաւառնում, փախուստ, երամ)
flimsy - tiurapeg, dugar, sunamid, tughtaturam (դիւրաբեկ, տկար, սնամէջ, թղթադրամ)
flinch - nahanchel, ungurgil, vuhadil, ungurgoum (նահանջել, ընկրկիլ, վհատիլ, ընկրկում)
flinders - pushourk, pegorner (փշուրք, բեկորներ)

fling - *shuburdel, nedel, akatsel, shuburdoum* (շպրտել, նետել, աքացել, շպրտում)
flint - *gaydzkar* (կայծքար)
flippant - *shadakhos, lezvani, tetevamid* (շատախօս, լեզուանի, թեթեւամիտ)
flipper - *loghag, loghatev* (լողակ, լողաթեւ)
flirt - *hajoyakhagh, sirvudouk, tarbasoum, sirapanil* (հաճոյախաղ, սիրուըտուք, դարպասում, սիրաբանիլ)
flit - *turchudil, jakhrel, chuvel, kaghtel, arak* (թռչտիլ, ճախրել, ճուել, գաղթել, արագ)
flix - *aghvamaz, moushdag* (աղուամազ, մուշտակ)
float - *dzupal, dadanil, loghal, lasd, dzupank* (ծփալ, տատանիլ, լողալ, լաստ, ծփանք)
flock - *hod, yeram, khoump, pounch, khurnuvil* (հօտ, երամ, խումբ, փունջ, խռնուիլ)
floe - *sarnagouyd, sarnatashd* (սառնակոյտ, սառնադաշտ)
flog - *mudragel, kanaharel, dzedzel* (մտրակել, գանահարել, ծեծել)
flood - *heghoug, voghoghoum, voghoghel* (հեղուկ, ողողում, ողողել)
floor - *hadag, dakhdagamadz, harg, hadagel* (յատակ, տախտակամած, յարկ, յատակել)
flop - *tevapakhoum, abdag, shurumpatsunel* (թեւաբախում, ապտակ, շրմփացնել)
florescent - *dzaghgalits, dzaghgial* (ծաղկալից, ծաղկեալ)
florid - *dzaghgoun, dzaghgazart* (ծաղկուն, ծաղկազարդ)
florist - *dzaghgavajar, dzaghgapouydz* (ծաղկավաճառ, ծաղկաբոյծ)
flotation - *dzupoum, dzupank* (ծփում, ծփանք)
flounce - *tsadgurdouk, tsadgurdel* (ցատկռտուք, ցատկռտել)
flour - *aliur, aliurodel* (ալիւր, ալիւրոտել)
flourish - *zart, bajoujank, dzaghgil, parkavajil* (զարդ, պաճուճանք, ծաղկիլ, բարգաւաճիլ)
flout - *dzaghrank, dzaghrel, anarkel* (ծաղրանք, ծաղրել, անարգել)
flow - *hosank, hosil, voghoghel* (հոսանք, հոսիլ, ողողել)
flower - *dzaghig, dzaghgil, puttil* (ծաղիկ, ծաղկիլ, փթթիլ)
flowerbed - *dzaghganots, dzaghgatoump* (ծաղկանոց, ծաղկաթումբ)
flowerpot - *dzaghgaman* (ծաղկաման)
flowing - *sahoun, arad, hort* (սահուն, առատ, յորդ)
flu - *bagharoutiun* (պաղարութիւն)
fluctuate - *dadanil, dzupal, varanil* (տատանիլ, ծփալ, վարանիլ)
fluctuation - *dzadzanoum, yereroum* (ծածանում, երերում)
flue - *dzukhnelouyz, otantsk* (ծխնելոյզ, օդանցք)
fluency - *sahounoutiun, tiurahavanoutiun* (սահունութիւն, դիւրահաւանութիւն)
fluent - *sahoun, tiurasah* (սահուն, դիւրասահ)
fluff - *aghvamaz* (աղուամազ)
fluid - *heghoug, hosaniut, hosoun* (հեղուկ, հոսանիւթ, հոսուն)
flurry - *tsiunahov, houzel, khurovel* (ձիւնահով, յուզել, խռովել)
flush - *tsaydel, khouzhel, tsaydoum, baydzar, garmir* (ցայտել, խուժել, ցայտում, պայծառ, կարմիր)
fluster - *kurkurel, shupotetsunel, houzmounk, irarantsoum* (գրգռել, շփոթեցնել, յուզմունք, իրարանցում)
flute - *surink, surunkaharel* (սրինգ, սրնգահարել)
flutist - *surunkahar* (սրնգահար)
flutter - *yereroum, turturoum, houzoum, turtural, dzupal* (երերում, թրթռում, յուզում, թրթռալ, ծփալ)
flux - *hosank, hosetsunel, halel* (հոսանք, հոսեցնել, հալել)
fluxion - *hosoum, haloum, tsaydoum, dzoroum* (հոսում, հալում, ցայտում, ծորում)

fly - turchil, savarnil, sulanal, janj, (թռչիլ, սաւառնիլ, սլանալ, ճանճ)
flyer - turoutsig, dzanoutsatought, aztakir, aztatought (թռուցիկ, ծանուցաթուղթ, ազդագիր, ազդաթուղթ)
flying - turchogh, turichk (թռչող, թռիչք)
foam - purpour, purpural, zayranal (փրփուր, փրփրալ, զայրանալ)
fob - kurbanag, khapel (գրպանակ, խաբել)
focus - gizaged, vararan (կիզակէտ, վառարան)
fodder - ger, jarag, gertsunel (կեր, ճարակ, կերցնել)
foe - tushnami, vosokh (թշնամի, ոսոխ)
fog - mushoush, marakhough, musoushel, aghodel (մշուշ, մառախուղ, մշուշել, աղօտել)
foggy - mushoushod, aghod (մշուշոտ, աղօտ)
fogy - hunamid, khisd bahbanoghagan, dzeroug (Հնամիտ, խիստ պաՀպանողական, ծերուկ)
foil - chakhchakhel, haghtel, nurpatitegh, souser (ջախջախել, յաղթել, նրբաթիթեղ, սուսեր)
foist - sahetsunel, nenkel, khapel (սաՀեցնել, նենգել, խաբել)
fold - dzalel, pattel, dzalk (ծալել, փաթթել, ծալք)
folder - dzalich, dzalamekena, tughtadzal (ծալիչ, ծալամեքենայ, թղթածալ)
folding - dzaloum (ծալում)
folio - gisatert, miadzal tert, ech (կիսաթերթ, միածալ թերթ, էջ)
folk - zhoghovourt, martig, ampokh (ժողովուրդ, մարդիկ, ամբոխ)
folk dance - zhoghovurtagan bar (ժողովրդական պար)
folk song - zhoghovurtagan yerk (ժողովրդական երգ)
folklore - avantaveb, zhoghovurtayin parker (աւանդավէպ, ժողովրդային բարքեր)
follow - hedevil, hedabuntel, numanil, orinagel (Հետեւիլ, Հետապնդել, նմանիլ, օրինակել)
folly - khentoutiun, himaroutiun (խենդութիւն, յիմարութիւն)
foment - khunamel, dadzel, sunoutsanel, daktsunel (խնամել, տածել, սնուցանել, տաքցնել)
fomentation - kurkuroum, ardzardzoum (գրգռում, արծարծում)
fond - him, hadag, khork, turamakuloukh, kourkoural (Հիմ, յատակ, խորք, դրամագլուխ, գուրգուրալ)
fondle - shoyel, kukvel, paypayel, paghakushel (շոյել, գգուել, փայփայել, փաղաքշել)
font - tsouladar, daradesag, avazan, mugurdaran (ձուլատառ, տառատեսակ, աւազան, մկրտարան)
food - sunount, oudelik, geragour (սնունդ, ուտելիք, կերակուր)
fool - aboush, himar, dukhmar (ապուշ, յիմար, տխմար)
foolish - aboush, khent, animasd (ապուշ, խենդ, անիմաստ)
foot - vodk, vodnachap, hadag, usdorod, bududil (ոտք, ոտնաչափ, յատակ, ստորոտ, պտըտիլ)
football - vodnakuntag, kuntakhagh (ոտնագնդակ, գնդախաղ)
foothill - pulradag, pulouri usdorodu (բլրատակ, բլուրի ստորոտը)
foothold - megnaged, gurvan (մեկնակէտ, կռուան)
footing - henaged, gurvan, netsoug, khariskh (յենակէտ, կռուան, նեցուկ, խարիսխ)
footnote - dzanotakuroutiun, doghadag (ծանօթագրութիւն, տողատակ)
footpath - mayt, vodnoughi (մայթ, ոտնուղի)
footprint - vodnahedk, vodnadegh (ոտնաՀետք, ոտնատեղ)
footstep - kayl, kaylapokh, vodnatsayn, hedk (քայլ, քայլափոխ, ոտնաձայն, Հետք)
footwear - vodnaman, goshig (ոտնաման, կօշիկ)
fop - tsoutsamol, bujnaser, tetevsolig (ցուցամոլ, պճնասէր, թեթեւսոլիկ)
for - hamar, badjarov, nugadmamp,

pokhanag, tebi (Համար, պատճառով, նկատմամբ, փոխանակ, դէպի)
forage - khodakagh, nakhiri ger, ger havakel (խոտաքաղ, նախիրի կեր, կեր հաւաքել)
foray - asbadagel, goghobdel, asbadagoutiun (ասպատակել, կողոպտել, ասպատակութիւն)
forbear - nakhnik, uzkoushanal, arkilel, merzhel (նախնիք, զգուշանալ, արգիլել, մերժել)
forbearance - hamperoutiun, hamperadaroutiun (Համբերութիւն, Համբերատարութիւն)
forbid - arkilel, merzhel, anidzel (արգիլել, մերժել, անիծել)
force - ouzh, zoroutiun, zork, usdibel, purnanal (ույժ, զօրութիւն, զօրք, ստիպել, բռնանալ)
forced - bardaturvadz, purni, ouzhkin (պարտադրուած, բռնի, ուժգին)
forceps - ouneli, pokur aktsan (ունելի, փոքր աքցան)
forcing - usdiboum, purnatadoum (ստիպում, բռնադատում)
ford - houn, hosank, dzandzaghoud (Հուն, Հոսանք, ծանծաղուտ)
fore - usgizpu, arachin, nakhgin (սկիզբը, առաջին, նախկին)
forearm - nakhapazoug, nakhazinel (նախաբազուկ, նախազինել)
forebode - gankhakoushagel (կանխագուշակել)
forebodement - gankhazkatsoum (կանխազգացում)
forecast - nakhadesoutiun, nakhadesel, dzurakurel (նախատեսութիւն, նախատեսել, ծրագրել)
foreclose - gankhoroshel, kotsel, pagel, arkilel (կանխորոշել, գոցել, փակել, արգիլել)
foreclosure - khapanoum, kuravazurgoum, arkelapagoum (խափանում, գրաւազրկում, արգելափակում)
forefather - nakhahayr, bab (նախաՀայր, պապ)
forefinger - tsoutsamad (ցուցամատ)
forego - toghoul, hurazharil (Թողուլ, Հրաժարիլ)
forehead - jagad (ճակատ)
foreign - odar, odaragan, ardakin (օտար, օտարական, արտաքին)
foreign currency - daraturam, odar turam (տարադրամ, օտար դրամ)
foreigner - odaragan, odarazki (օտարական, օտարազգի)
foreman - veragatsou, varbed, kulkhavor, dasnabed (վերակացու, վարպետ, գլխաւոր, տասնապետ)
forenoon - aravod, gesore arach (առաւօտ, կէսօրէ առաջ)
foresee - nakhadesel, koushagel (նախատեսել, գուշակել)
forest - andar (անտառ)
forestall - gankhel, khapanel (կանխել, խափանել)
forester - andarabah, andarapunag (անտառապաՀ, անտառաբնակ)
forestry - andaramushagoutiun (անտառամշակութիւն)
foretell - nakhahaydunel, nakhabes usel (նախայայտնել, նախապէս ըսել)
forever - mishd, havidyan, munayoun (միշտ, յաւիտեան, մնայուն)
forewarn - nakhazkoushatsunel, aztararel (նախազգուշացնել, ազդարարել)
forewit - khohemoutiun, uzkoushavoroutiun (խոՀեմութիւն, զգուշաւորութիւն)
foreword - nakhapan, harachapan (նախաբան, յառաջաբան)
forfeit - doukank, gorsuntsunel (տուգանք, կորսնցնել)
forfend - arkilel (արգիլել)
forge - tarpnots, hunots, tarpnel, geghdzel (դարբնոց, Հնոց, դարբնել, կեղծել)
forgeman - tarpin (դարբին)
forger - tarpnogh, geghdzarar, turamanenk (դարբնող, կեղծարար, դրամանենգ)
forgery - tarpnoum, khartakhoutiun (դարբնում, խարդախութիւն)
forget - mornal (մոռնալ)
forget-me-not - anmoroug (անմո-

ռուկ)
forgive - nerel, shunorhel (ներել, շնորհել)
forgiveness - neroghamudoutiun (ներողամտութիւն)
forgo - toghoul, pakhtsunel, hurazharil (թողուլ, փախցնել, հրաժարիլ)
forhail - neghel (նեղել)
fork - badarakagh, yergjughil (պատառաքաղ, երկճղիլ)
forlorn - lukial, ander, anoknagan (լքեալ, անտէր, անօգնական)
form - tsev, gerbarank, burag, doms, gazmel, horinel (ձեւ, կերպարանք, պրակ, տոմս, կազմել, յօրինել)
formal - tsevagan, bashdonagan (ձեւական, պաշտօնական)
formalism - tsevabashdoutiun, dzisaganoutiun (ձեւապաշտութիւն, ծիսականութիւն)
formality - tsevagerboutiun (ձեւակերպութիւն)
format - tsev, kirki chap (ձեւ, գիրքի չափ)
formation - gazmoutiun, tsevavoroum, gazm (կազմութիւն, ձեւաւորում, կազմ)
former - nakhgin, arachva, gazmogh, ararich (նախկին, առաջուայ, կազմող, արարիչ)
formidable - ahavor, sosgali, ahegh (ահաւոր, սոսկալի, ահեղ)
formula - panatsev, daraz, teghakir (բանաձեւ, տարազ, դեղագիր)
formulate - panatsevel, tsevagerbel (բանաձեւել, ձեւակերպել)
fornicate - bornuganal, gamaratsev (պոռնկանալ, կամարաձեւ)
fornication - bornugoutiun, shunoutiun, gurabashdoutiun (պոռնկութիւն, շնութիւն, կռապաշտութիւն)
forsake - lukel, toghoul, andesel (լքել, թողուլ, անտեսել)
forswear - ouranal, soud yertnoul (ուրանալ, սուտ երդնուլ)
fort - amrots, pert (ամրոց, բերդ)
forte - zoravor, ouzhkin, hasdadoun (զօրաւոր, ուժգին, հաստատուն)
forth - harach, tebi arach, antin, antsk (յառաջ, դէպի առաջ, անդին, անցք)
forthcoming - kalik, modaloud, yerevtsogh (գալիք, մօտալուտ, երեւցող)
forthwith - anmichabes, isgouyn (անմիջապէս, իսկոյն)
fortification - amroutiun (ամրութիւն)
fortify - amratsunel, zoratsunel (ամրացնել, զօրացնել)
fortitude - zoroutiun, dogounoutiun (զօրութիւն, տոկունութիւն)
fortress - amrots, pert, michnapert (ամրոց, բերդ, միջնաբերդ)
fortuity - tebk, tibvadz, badahmounk (դէպք, դիպուած, պատահմունք)
fortune - pakhd, harusdoutiun, inchk (բախտ, հարստութիւն, ինչք)
fortuneteller - pakhdakoushag (բախտագուշակ)
forty - karasoun (քառասուն)
forum - hurabarag, havakavayr, vajaranots, adyan (հրապարակ, հաւաքավայր, վաճառանոց, ատեան)
forward - tebi arach, archevi masu, oughargel, pokhantsel (դէպի առաջ, առջեւի մասը, ուղարկել, փոխանցել)
forwarder - arakogh, ghurgogh (առաքող, ղրկող)
forwarding - arakoum, oughargoum (առաքում, ուղարկում)
fosse - khuram, pos (խրամ, փոս)
fossil - puradzo, hanadzo (բրածոյ, հանածոյ)
fossor - merelatagh (մեռելաթաղ)
foster - geragrel, sunoutsanel, khunamel, oknel (կերակրել, սնուցանել, խնամել, օգնել)
foster mother - usdundou (ստնտու)
foul - aghdod, karsheli, aborini khagh, aghdodel (աղտոտ, գարշելի, ապօրինի խաղ, աղտոտել)
found - himnel, hasdadel, tsoulel, haletsunel (հիմնել, հաստատել, ձուլել, հալեցնել)
foundation - himnarg, hasdadoutiun, him (հիմնարկ, հաստատութիւն,

Հիմ)

founder - himnatir, tsoulogh, pulvil, ungughmil, khordagil (Հիմնադիր, ձուլող, փլուիլ, ընկղմիլ, խորտակիլ)

founding - tsouloum (ձուլում)

foundry - tsoularan, tsoulvadzk (ձուլարան, ձուլուածք)

fount - aghpiur, ag, tsouladark (աղբիւր, ակ, ձուլատառք)

fountain - aghpiur, shadurvan, avazan (աղբիւր, շատրուան, աւազան)

fountain-pen - inknahos kurich (ինքնաՀոս գրիչ)

four - chors (չորս)

fourteen - dasnuchors (տասնչորս)

fourth - chorrort (չորրորդ)

fowl - medz turchoun, hav, sak ... (մեծ թռչուն, Հաւ, սագ...)

fox - aghves, khoramang, kinovtsunel, tutvetsunel (աղուէս, խորամանկ, գինովցնել, թթուեցնել)

foxy - khoramang, aghvesanuman, tutou (խորամանկ, աղուեսանման, թթու)

foyer - uzposasurah, jemasurah (զբօսասրաՀ, ճեմասրաՀ)

fozy - gagough, meghg (կակուղ, մեղկ)

fracas - aghmoug, zhukhor, vej, khordagoum (աղմուկ, ժխոր, վէճ, խորտակում)

fraction - godorag, pazhin, pushrank, khumpavoroum (կոտորակ, բաժին, փշրանք, խմբաւորում)

fractious - khozhor, gurkod, kumahaj, char (խոժոռ, կրքոտ, քմաՀաճ, չար)

fracture - godurvadzk, pegoum, godrel, chartuvil (կոտրուածք, բեկում, կոտրել, ջարդուիլ)

fragile - tiurapeg, pukhroun, nourp, dugar (դիւրաբեկ, փխրուն, նուրբ, տկար)

fragility - tiurapegoutiun, dugaroutiun (դիւրաբեկութիւն, տկարութիւն)

fragment - gudor, pegor, nushkhar (կտոր, փեկոր, նշխար)

fragrance - pouyr, pourmounk, anoushahodoutiun (բոյր, բուրմունք, անուշաՀոտութիւն)

frail - tiurapeg, touyl, angayoun, dugar (դիւրաբեկ, թոյլ, անկայուն, տկար)

frame - shurchanag, tsev, shurchanagel, gazmel (շրջանակ, ձեւ, շրջանակել, կազմել)

framing - shurchanagoum, gazmoum, gazmoutiun, tsev (շրջանակում, կազմում, կազմութիւն, ձեւ)

franc - furank, furansagan turam (ֆրանք, ֆրանսական դրամ)

France - furansa (Ֆրանսա)

franchise - arantsnashunorhoum, ardonoutiun, artsagel (առանձնաշնորՀում, արտօնութիւն, արձակել)

franc-tireur - artsagazen (արձակազէն)

frangible - tiurapeg, nourp, pukhroun (դիւրաբեկ, նուրբ, փխրուն)

frank - tsuri, arants dzakhki, angeghdz, azad (ձրի, առանց ծախքի, անկեղծ, ազատ)

fraternal - yeghpayragan (եղբայրական)

fraternity - yeghpayroutiun, yeghpayragtsoutiun (եղբայրութիւն, եղբայրակցութիւն)

fraternize - yeghpayranal, yeghpayratsunel (եղբայրանալ, եղբայրացնել)

fraud - khartakhoutiun, nenkoutiun (խարդախութիւն, նենգութիւն)

fraught - pernavor, letsoun (բեռնաւոր, լեցուն)

fray - vej, guriv, zhukhor, vakhtsunel (վէճ, կռիւ, ժխոր, վախցնել)

frazzle - mashetsunel, mashoum (մաշեցնել, մաշում)

freak - kumayk, kumadzin, aylantag, khaydel (քմայք, քմածին, այլանդակ, խայտել)

freckle - bisag, pidz, mortapidz, khayd, bisagodel (պիսակ, բիծ, մորթաբիծ, խայտ, պիսակոտել)

free - azad, tsuri, anvujar, azadel, artsagel (ազատ, ձրի, անվճար, ազատել, արձակել)

free estimate - tsuri kunahadoum (ձրի գնահատում)
freedom - azadoutiun, angakhoutiun (ազատութիւն, անկախութիւն)
freehold - galvadzk, usdatzvadzk (կալուածք, ստացուածք)
freeholder - galvadzader (կալուածատէր)
freelance - azad kordzogh, mudadzogh, vartsgan (ազատ գործող, մտածող, վարձկան)
freemason - azad vormnatir, mason (ազատ որմնադիր, մասոն)
freethinker - azadakhoh, azad mudadzogh (ազատախոհ, ազատ մտածող)
freeway - azadoughi (ազատուղի)
freeze - saretsunel, saril, musil (սառեցնել, սառիլ, մսիլ)
freezer - sarnaran, saroutsich (սառնարան, սառուցիչ)
freight - per, pokhatravarts, navakin, pernavorel (բեռ, փոխադրավարձ, նաւագին, բեռնաւորել)
french - furansatsi, furanseren, furansagan (ֆրանսացի, ֆրանսերէն, ֆրանսական)
frenzy - gadaghoutiun, moleknoutiun, tsasoum (կատաղութիւն, մոլեգնութիւն, ցասում)
frequency - hajakhaganoutiun, hajakhagioutiun (յաճախականութիւն, յաճախակիութիւն)
frequent - hajakhagi, gurgnuvogh, hajakhel (յաճախակի, կրկնուող, յաճախել)
fresco - vormnanugar, vormnanugarchoutiun, vormanugarel (որմնանկար, որմնանկարչութիւն, որմնանկարել)
fresh - tarm, talar, zov, nor (թարմ, դալար, զով, նոր)
freshen - tarmatsunel, zovatsunel, anoushtsunel, norokel (թարմացնել, զովացնել, անուշցնել, նորոգել)
freshet - aradoutiun, hortoutiun, hegheghad (առատութիւն, յորդութիւն, հեղեղատ)
freshman - norundza, gurdser ousanogh (նորընծայ, կրտսեր ուսանող)
fret - mashetsunel, houzel, vushdatsunel, hiusazartk (մաշեցնել, յուզել, վշտացնել, հիւսազարդք)
fretful - surdnegh, tuzhvarahaj, khozhor (սրտնեղ, դժուարահաճ, խոժոր)
friable - pukhroun, tiurapeg (փխրուն, դիւրաբեկ)
friar - vanagan, gousaguron, miapan (վանական, կուսակրօն, միաբան)
friary - vank, menasdan, miapanoutiun (վանք, մենաստան, միաբանութիւն)
friction - shupoum (շփում)
Friday - ourpat (Ուրբաթ)
fridge - kusel, mashetsunel (քսել, մաշեցնել)
friend - paregam, unger, muderim (բարեկամ, ընկեր, մտերիմ)
friendship - paregamoutiun, ungeroutiun (բարեկամութիւն, ընկերութիւն)
frieze - zartakantag, kantag, kodezart, dzobavorel (զարդաքանդակ, քանդակ, գօտեզարդ, ծոպաւորել)
frigate - mardanav (մարտանաւ)
fright - vakh, sosgoum, ah, yergiugh (վախ, սոսկում, ահ, երկիւղ)
frighten - vakhtsunel, sarsapetsunel (վախցնել, սարսափեցնել)
frigid - tsourd, bagh, angarogh, andarper (ցուրտ, պաղ, անկարող, անտարբեր)
frigidity - tsurdoutiun, sarnoutiun, baghoutiun (ցրտութիւն, սառնութիւն, պաղութիւն)
frigorific - saretsoutsich, tsurdatsoutsich (սառեցուցիչ, ցրտացուցիչ)
frill - toghtoghal, potel, potadzalk (ղողղողալ, փոթել, փոթածալք)
fringe - dzob, dzayr, yezerk (ծոպ, ծայր, եզերք)
frisk - vosdiun, tsadgoum, khaydank, tsadgurdel (ոստիւն, ցատկում, խայտանք, ցատկռտել)
frisky - zuvart, gaydar (զուարթ, կայտառ)
fritter - manrel, pushrel, gudor,

pushour (մանրել, փշրել, կտոր, փշուր)
frivolous - tetevsolig, anlourch, sunodi, tadarg (թեթեւսոլիկ, անլուրջ, սնոտի, դատարկ)
frizz, friz - kankurel, khobobel, kankour (գանգրել, խոպոպել, գանգուր)
frizzle - kankurel, dabgel, khorovel (գանգրել, տապկել, խորովել)
fro - antin, yed, megti, herou (անդին, ետ, մէկդի, հեռու)
frock - pajgon, sukem, uzkesd (բաճկոն, սքեմ, զգեստ)
frog - kord (գորտ)
frolic - ourakh, zevart, ourakhoutiun, khaydal, tsundzal (ուրախ, զուարթ, ուրախութիւն, խայտալ, ցնծալ)
from - ... e, ... en (... է, ... էն)
front - jagad, temk, yeres, jagadil, timaturel (ճակատ, դէմք, երես, ճակատիլ, դիմադրել)
frontier - sahman, sahmanakidz, sahmanakuloukh (սահման, սահմանագիծ, սահմանագլուխ)
frost - saretsunel, sarnamanik, saroutsoum (սառեցնել, սառնամանիք, սառուցում)
frost-bite - tsurdaharoutiun (ցրտահարութիւն)
froth - purpuril, purpour, bughbuchag (փրփրիլ, փրփուր, պղպջակ)
froward - hamar, tek, tazhan (յամառ, դեգ, դաժան)
frown - burusdoum, gunjir, gunjurel (պռստում, կնճիռ, կնճռել)
frowzy - muklodadz, karshahod, aghdod (մգլոտած, գարշահոտ, աղտոտ)
frozen - saradz (սառած)
fructify - budghaperel, arkasavorel (պտղաբերել, արգասաւորել)
frugal - khunayogh, dundesogh (խնայող, տնտեսող)
fruit - budough, mirk, budghaperel (պտուղ, միրգ, պտղաբերել)
fruiterer - budghavajar (պտղավաճառ)
fruitful - budghaper, budghali, shahaper (պտղաբեր, պտղալի, շահաբեր)
fruition - budghaperoutiun, artiunavoroum, vayelk (պտղաբերութիւն, արդիւնաւորում, վայելք)
fruitless - anbudough, abartiun (անպտուղ, ապարդիւն)
frump - pampasel, nakhadel, pampasogh, barav (բամբասել, նախատել, բամբասող, պառաւ)
frustrate - khapanel, chunchel, vochunchatsunel, i zour (խափանել, ջնջել, ոչնչացնել, ի զուր)
fry - dabgel, khorovel, yeral, dabguvadz pan, tsugnig (տապկել, խորովել, եռալ, տապկուած բան, ձկնիկ)
frying pan - dabag (տապակ)
fudge - dourmanouysh, soud, arasbel, geghdzel (տուրմանոյշ, սուտ, առասպել, կեղծել)
fuel - varelaniut, potsavarel (վառելանիւթ, բոցավառել)
fugitive - pakhusdagan, taparagan, vudaranti (փախստական, թափառական, վտարանդի)
fulcrum - netsoug, henag, henaran, henaged (նեցուկ, յենակ, յենարան, յենակէտ)
fulfil, fulfill - ampoghchatsunel, iraganatsunel, gadarel (ամբողջացնել, իրականացնել, կատարել)
full - letsoun, arad, ampoghch, li, liadagar, shadnal (լեցուն, առատ, ամբողջ, լի, լիակատար, շատնալ)
fulltime - liazham, munayoun, luriv zhamanagov (լիաժամ, մնայուն, լրիւ ժամանակով)
fully - ampoghchovin, liovin, luriv (ամբողջովին, լիովին, լրիւ)
fulmigate - vorodal, shantel, payladagel, usbarnal (որոտալ, շանթել, փայլատակել, սպառնալ)
fulmine - shantel, vorodal, artsagel (շանթել, որոտալ, արձակել)
fulsome - zuzveli, daghdugali, chapazants, goshd (զզուելի, տաղտկալի, չափազանց, կոշտ)
fumble - kharkhapel, shoshapel, pundurdel (խարխափել, շօշափել,

փնտռտել)

fume - *dzukhel, mukhal, dzoukh, moukh* (ծխել, մխալ, ծուխ, մուխ)

fumigate - *haganekhel, anoushahodel, khungargel* (հականեխել, անուշահոտել, խնկարկել)

fun - *zuvarjoutiun, gadag, khagh* (զուարճութիւն, կատակ, խաղ)

funambulist - *larakhaghats* (լարախաղաց)

function - *bashdon, ter, kordz* (պաշտօն, դեր, գործ)

functionary - *bashdonadar, bashdonia* (պաշտօնատար, պաշտօնեայ)

fund - *himnaturam, hadgatsoum* (հիմնադրամ, յատկացում)

fundamental - *himnagan, arachnahert, eagan* (հիմնական, առաջնահերթ, էական)

funeral - *taghoum, houghargavoroutiun* (թաղում, յուղարկաւորութիւն)

fungus - *soung* (սունկ)

funk - *sarsap, kesh hod, karshahodoutiun, sosgal* (սարսափ, գէշ հոտ, գարշահոտութիւն, սոսկալ)

funnel - *tsakar, dzukhnelouyz* (ձագար, ծխնելոյզ)

funny - *zuvarjali, hajeli, dzidzaghasharzh* (զուարճալի, հաճելի, ծիծաղաշարժ)

fur - *moushdag, mort, moushdagel* (մուշտակ, մորթ, մուշտակել)

furbish - *hughgel, payletsunel, makrel* (յղկել, փայլեցնել, մաքրել)

furdle - *dzalel, kaaaalarel* (ծալել, գալարել)

furious - *gadaghi, sasdig, anzousb* (կատաղի, սաստիկ, անզուսպ)

furl - *dzadzgel, ampopel, pattel* (ծածկել, ամփոփել, փաթթել)

furnace - *pour, hunots, dancharan* (փուռ, հնոց, տանջարան)

furnish - *haytaytel, gahavorel, sarkel* (հայթայթել, կահաւորել, սարքել)

furniture - *gahouyk, gah garasi, gazmadzk* (կահոյք, կահ կարասի, կազմածք)

furrier - *moushdagakordz, moushdagavajar* (մուշտակագործ, մուշտակավաճառ)

furrow - *agos, gunjir, khorshom, agosel, khuramel* (ակօս, կնճիռ, խորշոմ, ակօսել, խրամել)

furry - *moushdagavor, moushdage, moushdaganuman* (մուշտակաւոր, մուշտակէ, մուշտականման)

further - *aveli herou, aveli, oknel* (աւելի հեռու, աւելի, օգնել)

furthermore - *nayev, patsi, tartsial, yevus* (նաեւ, բացի, դարձեալ, եւս)

furtive - *kaghdakoghi, takoun* (գաղտագողի, թաքուն)

fury - *gadaghoutiun, tsasoum, moleknoutiun* (կատաղութիւն, ցասում, մոլեգնութիւն)

fuse - *halil, loudzvil, haletsunel* (հալիլ, լուծուիլ, հալեցնել)

fusee - *hurtir, gaydzhan huratsan* (հրթիռ, կայծհան հրացան)

fusil - *huratsan, tetev huratsan* (հրացան, թեթեւ հրացան)

fusillade - *huratsanatsukoutiun, kuntagaharel* (հրացանաձգութիւն, գնդակահարել)

fusion - *tsouloum, haloum, miakharnoum* (ձուլում, հալում, միախառնում)

fuss - *aghmoug, irarantsoum, tsantsuratsunel* (աղմուկ, իրարանցում, ձանձրացնել)

futile - *anokoud, anbed, pouj* (անօգուտ, անպէտ, փուճ)

future - *abaka, kalik, abarni* (ապագայ, գալիք, ապառնի)

futurist - *abakayabashd* (ապագայապաշտ)

fuzz - *aghvamaz, dzuvad, poshianal* (աղուամազ, ծուատ, փոշիանալ)

fyke, fike - *neghvil, mudmudouk* (նեղուիլ, մտմտուք)

G

gab - *shadakhosel, shadakhosoutiun, tsoghager (շատախօսել, շատախօսութիւն, ձողակեռ)*

gabber - *shadakhos, sudakhos (շատախօս, ստախօս)*

gabble - *shaghaguradel, murtmurtal, shaghagurank (շաղակրատել, մրթմրթալ, շաղակրանք)*

gabbler - *shaghagurad, murtmurtatsogh (շաղակրատ, մրթմրթացող)*

gabel - *vartsk, dourk, maks (վարձք, տուրք, մաքս)*

gabeler - *hargahavak, maksahavak (հարկահաւաք, մաքսահաւաք)*

gaby - *dukhmar, aboush, anmid (տխմար, ապուշ, անմիտ)*

gadabout - *taparashurchig (թափառաշրջիկ)*

gadder - *tadargabord (դատարկապորտ)*

gadget - *hunark, harmarank, jardaroutiun (հնարք, յարմարանք, ճարտարութիւն)*

gaff - *gartatsogh, jang , ger, gartatsoghel (կարթաձող, ճանկ, կեռ, կարթաձողել)*

gaffe - *ankhohemoutiun, tsakhaveroutiun, sukhal (անխոհեմութիւն, ձախաւերութիւն, սխալ)*

gag - *luretsunel, gashgantel, peranagab, gadag (լռեցնել, կաշկանդել, բերանակապ, կատակ)*

gage - *kurav, yerashkhik, yerashkhavorel (գրաւ, երաշխիք, երաշխաւորել)*

gaiety - *ourakhoutiun, zuvartoutiun (ուրախութիւն, զուարթութիւն)*

gain - *shahil, vasdugil, haghtel, shah, vasdag, okoud (շահիլ, վաստկիլ, յաղթել, շահ, վաստակ, օգուտ)*

gait - *kalvadzk, untatsk (քալուածք, ընթացք)*

gala - *hantisoutiun, donahantes, khurakhjank (հանդիսութիւն, տօնահանդէս, խրախճանք)*

galaxy - *hartkogh, dzir gatin (յարդգող, ծիր կաթին)*

gale - *murrig, kami, potorig (մրրիկ, քամի, փոթորիկ)*

gall - *kertel, kerel, mashetsunel, jangurduvadzk, maghts (քերթել, քերել, մաշեցնել, ճանկռտուածք, մաղձ)*

gallant - *gunamedzar, gunahajo, vayelouch, oughghamid (կնամեծար, կնահաճոյ, վայելուչ, ուղղամիտ)*

gallantry - *gunamedzaroutiun, paregurtoutiun (կնամեծարութիւն, բարեկրթութիւն)*

gallery - *badgerasurah, tsoutsasurah, michantsk (պատկերասրահ, ցուցասրահ, միջանցք)*

galley - *magouyg, tianav, daragal, sharots (մակոյկ, թիանաւ, տառակալ, շարոց)*

gallon - *galon, heghougachap (կալոն, հեղուկաչափ)*

gallows - *gakhaghan (կախաղան)*

galoot - *aghmugarar, medzakhos (աղմկարար, մեծախօս)*

galosh - *gurgnagoshig, vernamouyg (կրկնակօշիկ, վերնամոյկ)*

galp - *horanchel, gaghgantsel (յօրանջել, կաղկանձել)*

galvanize - *yelegdurazodzel, yelegduratsunel (ելեկտրազօծել, ելեկտըրացնել)*

gamble - *pakhdakhagh, pakhdakhagh khaghal (բախտախաղ, բախտախաղ խաղալ)*

gambler - *tughtamol, khaghamol (թղթամոլ, խաղամոլ)*

gambol - *tsadgel, vosdosdel, vosdoum (ցատկել, ոստոստել, ոստում)*

game - khagh, murtsoum, murtsakhagh (խաղ, մրցում, մրցախաղ)
gamin - suriga, lagod, usdahag (սրիկայ, լակոտ, ստահակ)
gammon - khapel, geghdzel, soud, khapeoutiun, khozaboukhd (խաբել, կեղծել, սուտ, խաբէութիւն, խոզապուխտ)
gamy - kach, khizakh, vorsaham, hamemvadz (քաջ, խիզախ, որսահամ, համեմուած)
gang - khumpag, avazagakhoump, hurosagakhoump (խմբակ, աւազախումբ, հրոսակախումբ)
gangrene - pudaghd, pudoutiun, pudil (փտախտ, փտութիւն, փտիլ)
gangster - charakordz, avazag, anoren (չարագործ, աւազակ, անօրէն)
gangway - antsk, navamoudk (անցք, նաւամուտք)
gaol - pand, zundan, arkelaran, pandargel (բանտ, զնտան, արգելարան, բանտարկել)
gap - jeghk, patsvadzk, jeghkel (ճեղք, բացուածք, ճեղքել)
gape - horanchel, horanchoum, perani patsvadzk (յօրանջել, յօրանջում, բերանի բացուածք)
garage - garadoun (կառատուն)
garb - hakousd, daraz, haktsunel (հագուստ, տարազ, հագցնել)
garbage - aghp, aveltsoug, porodik, porodiku makrel (աղբ, աւելցուկ, փորոտիք, փորոտիքը մաքրել)
garbage disposal - aghpadar sark (աղբատար սարք)
garble - gudurdel, hoshodel, maghel, aveltsoug (կտրտել, յօշոտել, մաղել, աւելցուկ)
garbler - gudurdogh, anchadogh, maghogh (կտրտող, անջատող, մաղող)
garden - bardez, mushagel (պարտէզ, մշակել)
gardener - bardizban (պարտիզպան)
gardening - bardizbanoutiun (պարտիզպանութիւն)
gardrobe - hantertsaran, arantsnaran, ardaknots (հանդերձարան, առանձնարան, արտաքնոց)
gargle - sosortel, gargar unel (սոսորդել, կարկառ ընել)
garland - dzaghgakagh, dzaghgebusag, dzaghgazartel (ծաղկաքաղ, ծաղկեպսակ, ծաղկազարդել)
garlic - sukhdor (սխտոր)
garment - badmoujan, hakousd (պատմուճան, հագուստ)
garner - ushdemaran, amparel (շտեմարան, ամբարել)
garnet - soudag, nurnakar (սուտակ, նռնաքար)
garnish - zart, bajoujank, zartarel, gahavorel (զարդ, պաճուճանք, զարդարել, կահաւորել)
garnishment - zartarant, zart (զարդարանք, զարդ)
garnison - bashar, muterk, bahagazork (պաշար, մթերք, պահակազօրք)
garniture - zartarank, garasik (զարդարանք, կարասիք)
garrison - bahagazork, zoranots, bahagazorel (պահակազօրք, զօրանոց, պահակազօրել)
garrulous - shadakhos, shaghagrad (շատախօս, շաղակրատ)
garter - dzungagab (ծնկակապ)
gas, gasoline - benzin, varelagaz (պենզին, վառելակազ)
gasconate - sunabardzoutiun, bardzenal, hokhordal (սնապարծութիւն, պարծենալ, յոխորտալ)
gash - khotsel, khor viravorel, khor verk, imasdoun (խոցել, խոր վիրաւորել, խոր վէրք, իմաստուն)
gaslight - gazi louys, badrouyk (կազի լոյս, պատրոյգ)
gasp - shuncharkeloutiun, hevk, heval (շնչարգելութիւն, հեւք, հեւալ)
gastric - usdamoksayin (ստամոքսային)
gastronome - shadager, vorguramol, vorovaynaser (շատակեր, որկրամոլ, որովայնասէր)
gastronomy - vorovaynamoloutiun (որովայնամոլութիւն)
gate - tarbas, tour, moudk (դարպաս, դուռ, մուտք)
gateway - garatour, pagamoudk, tu-

rantsk (կառադուռ, բակամուտք, դռանցք)

gather - havakel, havakvil, zhoghvel (Հաւաքել, Հաւաքուիլ, ժողվել)

gathering - havakoum, zhoghov, havakouyt (Հաւաքում, ժողով, Հաւաքոյթ)

gauche - tsakhlig, anjarag, goshd (ձախլիկ, անճարակ, կոշտ)

gaudy - bujnaser, bujnod, don, khurakhjank (պճնասէր, պճնոտ, տօն, խրախճանք)

gauge - chapel, jushtel, chapag, churachap (չափել, ճշդել, չափակ, ջրաչափ)

gauger - chapogh, chapich (չափող, չափիչ)

gaunt - nihar, vudid, hivantgakh (նիհար, վտիտ, Հիւանդկախ)

gauntlet - kordzi tsernots, tatban, tserunabah (գործի ձեռնոց, Թաթպան, ձեռնապահ)

gauze - shugharsh, kogh (շղարշ, քօղ)

gay - ourakh, zuvart, bujnazart, miaseragan (ուրախ, զուարթ, պճնազարդ, միասեռական)

gayety, gaiety - zuvartoutiun, tsundzoutiun (զուարթութիւն, ցնծութիւն)

gaze - abshadz nayil, achku severel, agnaseveroum (ապշած նայիլ, աչքը սեւեռել, ակնասեւեռում)

gazelle - vit, aydziam, yeghnig (վիթ, այծեամ, եղնիկ)

gazette - lurakir, tert, huradaragel (լրագիր, Թերթ, Հրատարակել)

gear (n) - gazmadzk mekanayi, akoutsich, geraniv (կազմածք մեքենայի, ագուցիչ, կեռանիւ)

gear (v) - akoutsel, tampel, adamnavorel, zartarel (ագուցել, Թամբել, ատամնաւորել, զարդարել)

geck - dzaghrel, arhamarhel, heknank, arhamarhank (ծաղրել, արՀամարՀել, Հեգնանք, արՀամարՀանք)

gelatin - vosgurahiut, tontogh, madznid (ոսկրաՀիւԹ, դոնդող, մածնիտ)

gem - kohar, koharazartel (գոՀար, գոՀարազարդել)

geminate - gurgnag, zouyk, gurgnabadgel (կրկնակ, զոյգ, կրկնապատկել)

gemma - poghpoch, budoug (բողբոջ, պտուկ)

gendarme - vosdigan, kaghakabah (ոստիկան, քաղաքապաՀ)

gendarmery - vosdiganoutiun (ոստիկանութիւն)

gender - ser, desag, dzunanil (սեռ, տեսակ, ծնանիլ)

general - zoravar, unthanour, sovoragan, kulkhavor (զօրավար, ընդՀանուր, սովորական, գլխաւոր)

general medicine - unthanour puzhushgoutiun (ընդՀանուր բժշկութիւն)

generality - unthanroutiun (ընդՀանրութիւն)

generalize - unthanratsunel (ընդՀանրացնել)

generate - dzunil, ardaturel (ծնիլ, արտադրել)

generation - dzunount, serount, azk, ardaturoutiun (ծնունդ, սերունդ, ազգ, արտադրութիւն)

generator - ardaturch, dzunich, dzunogh (արտադրիչ, ծնիչ, ծնող)

generic - unthanragan, seri hadoug (ընդՀանրական, սեռի յատուկ)

generosity - vehantsnoutiun, aradatsernoutiun (վեՀանձնութիւն, առատաձեռնութիւն)

generous - aradatsern, vehantsun, medzahoki (առատաձեռն, վեՀանձն, մեծաՀոգի)

genesis - dzakoum, dzunount, kirk dzununtots (ծագում, ծնունդ, Գիրք Ծննդոց)

genetic - dzununtagan, usguzpunagan (ծննդական, սկզբնական)

genetics - zharankagan (ժառանգական)

genitals - dzununtagan kordzaranner (ծննդական գործարաններ)

genius - daghantavor, hanjar, ozhduvadzoutiun (տաղանդաւոր, Հանճար, օժտուածութիւն)

genocide - tseghasbanoutiun (ցեղասպանութիւն)
genre - voj, tsev, gerb, desag, ser (ոճ, ձեւ, կերպ, տեսակ, սեռ)
genteel - azniv, girt, shunorhali, kaghakavar (ազնիւ, կիրթ, շնորհալի, քաղաքավար)
gentile - hetanos (հեթանոս)
gentle - azniv, paregirt, meghm, hez, aznuvatsunel (ազնիւ, բարեկիրթ, մեղմ, հեզ, ազնուացնել)
gentleman - aznuvagan, vehoki, paregirt (ազնուական, վեհոգի, բարեկիրթ)
genuine - iragan, isgagan, poun, ankhartakh (իրական, իսկական, բուն, անխարդախ)
geographer - ashkharhakuraked (աշխարհագրագէտ)
geography - ashkharhakuroutiun (աշխարհագրութիւն)
geologer - yergurapan (երկրաբան)
geologist - yergurapan (երկրաբան)
geology - yergurapanoutiun (երկրաբանութիւն)
geometer - yergurachap (երկրաչափ)
geometry - yergurachapoutiun (երկրաչափութիւն)
geopolitics - ashkharhakaghakaganoutiun (աշխարհաքաղաքականութիւն)
Georgia - vurasdan, georgia (Վրաստան, Ճորճիա)
georgian - vuratsi, vuratseren, vuratsagan (վրացի, վրացերէն, վրացական)
geosphere - yergurakount, mutnolord (երկրագունդ, մթնոլորտ)
gerant - pokhanort, kordzavar, hokapartsou (փոխանորդ, գործավար, հոգաբարձու)
germ - serm, dzil, budoug, usgizp, untsiughel (սերմ, ծիլ, պտուկ, սկիզբ, ընձիւղել)
german - azkagits, harazad (ազգակից, հարազատ)
german (I) - kermanatsi, kermaneren, kermanagan (գերմանացի, գերմաներէն, գերմանական)
german (II) - azkagits, harazad (ազգակից, հարազատ)
Germany - kermania (Գերմանիա)
germicide - manreasban (մանրէասպան)
germinate - dzulil, poghpochil, ajetsunel (ծլիլ, բողբոջիլ, աճեցնել)
gerund - terpay, payanoun (դերբայ, բայանուն)
gest - arark, sharzhoutsev, verapeproject (արարք, շարժուձեւ, վերաբերում)
gestation - hughoutiun (յղութիւն)
gesture - sharzhoutsev, sharzhelagerb (շարժուձեւ, շարժելակերպ)
get - usdanal, ounenal, haytaytel, shahil, hasnil (ստանալ, ունենալ, հայթայթել, շահիլ, հասնիլ)
get back - veratarnal (վերադառնալ)
get fat - kirnal (գիրնալ)
get hungry - anotenal (անօթենալ)
get out - tours yellel (դուրս ելլել)
get ready - badrasduvil (պատրաստուիլ)
get up - artunnal, vodki yellel (արթննալ, ոտքի ելլել)
geyser - chermoug, chermaghpiur (ջերմուկ, ջերմաղբիւր)
ghastly - sosgali, sarsapeli, ahreli (սոսկալի, սարսափելի, ահռելի)
ghetto - arantsnatagh, hureagan tagh (առանձնաթաղ, հրէական թաղ)
ghost - voki, ourvagan, usdver (ոգի, ուրուական, ստուեր)
giant - husga, vitkhari, didan (հսկայ, վիթխարի, տիտան)
gibbet - gakhaghan, gakhel (կախաղան, կախել)
gibe - dzaghrel, heknel, hantimanel, dzagur, heknank (ծաղրել, հեգնել, հանդիմանել, ծաղր, հեգնանք)
giber - yerkidzogh, heknogh (երգիծող, հեգնող)
gift - nuver, undza, shunorh, dalhant, ozhdel (նուէր, ընծայ, շնորհ, տաղանդ, օժտել)
gigantic - husga, vitkhari (հսկայ, վիթխարի)
gild - vosgezodzel, vosgechurel (ոսկեզօծել, ոսկեջրել)

gilden - vosgezodz (ոսկեզօծ)
gill - tsugnaganch, buchrouhi, sirouhi (ձկնականջ, պչրուհի, սիրուհի)
gilt - vosgezodzoutiun, vosgezodz, turam (ոսկեզօծութիւն, ոսկեզօծ, դրամ)
gimmick - hunaramudoutiun, kaghdunik pakhtanivi (հնարամտութիւն, գաղտնիք բախտանիւի)
ginger - gojabughbegh, pouysi mu gudzou armadu (կոճապղպեղ, բոյսի մը կծու արմատը)
gipsy, gypsy - kunchou, taparagan (գնչու, թափառական)
giraffe - untsoughd (ընձուղտ)
girasol - arevadzaghig (արեւածաղիկ)
gird (n) - dzaghur, heknank, heknel (ծաղր, հեգնանք, հեգնել)
gird (v) - kodegabel, kodebuntel, shurchabadel (գօտեկապել, գօտեպնդել, շրջապատել)
girdle - kodi, gamar, pattel, polorel (գօտի, կամար, փաթթել, բոլորել)
girl - aghchig, oryort (աղջիկ, օրիորդ)
girl friend - ungerouhi, sirouhi (ընկերուհի, սիրուհի)
girlhood - aghchigoutiun (աղջկութիւն)
girth - shurchagab, shurchanagachap, shurchagabel (շրջակապ, շրջանակաչափ, շրջակապել)
gist - himnaged, eoutiun (հիմնակէտ, էութիւն)
give - dal, nuvirel, hantsnel, barkevel, lukel (տալ, նուիրել, յանձնել, պարգեւել, լքել)
glaciate - saril, saretsunel (սառիլ, սառեցնել)
glacier - sartsatashd, sarnagouyd (սառցադաշտ, սառնակոյտ)
glad - ourakh, zevart, koh, ourakhatsunel (ուրախ, զուարթ, գոհ, ուրախացնել)
glade - patsasdan, patsad (բացաստան, բացատ)
gladiator - souseramardig, gurgesamardig (սուսերամարտիկ, կրկէսամարտիկ)
gladsome - ourakhali, tsundzakin (ուրախալի, ցնծագին)
glamour - ardakin payl- berjoutiun, achki badrank (արտաքին փայլ-պերճութիւն, աչքի պատրանք)
glamour, glamor - humayk, tovchank, hurabouyr (հմայք, թովչանք, հրապոյր)
glance - nayvadzk, agnarg, paylil, shoghal, agnargel (նայուածք, ակնարկ, փայլիլ, շողալ, ակնարկել)
gland - keghts, suvini got (գեղձ, սուինի կոթ)
glare - paylil, shoghal, shulatsunel, payloun, shulatsoum (փայլիլ, շողալ, շլացնել, փայլուն, շլացում)
glass - abagi, kavat, agnots, tsolatsunel, payletsunel (ապակի, գաւաթ, ակնոց, ցոլացնել, փայլեցնել)
glass maker - abagekordz (ապակեգործ)
glass work - abagekordzoutiun (ապակեգործութիւն)
glaze - chunarag, payl, chunaragel, abagebadel (ջնարակ, փայլ, ջնարակել, ապակեպատել)
glazy - payloun, voghorg, abagepayl (փայլուն, ողորկ, ապակեփայլ)
gleam - jarakayt, shogh, louys, tzolanal, jarakaytel (ճառագայթ, շող, լոյս, ցոլանալ, ճառագայթել)
glean - hasgakagh, kaghel, havakel (հասկաքաղ, քաղել, հաւաքել)
glebe - yegeghetsabadgan hogh, ard (եկեղեցապատկան հող, արտ)
glee - ourakhoutiun, zuvartoutiun, tsundzoutiun (ուրախութիւն, զուարթութիւն, ցնծութիւն)
gleek - gadagel, zuvarjanal, humayich agnarg, gadag (կատակել, զուարճանալ, հմայիչ ակնարկ, կատակ)
glen - hovid, tsor (հովիտ, ձոր)
glib - jardarakhos, shadakhos, sahoun, voghorg (ճարտարախօս, շատախօս, սահուն, ողորկ)
glide - sahoum, sahil, hosil, antsunil (սահում, սահիլ, հոսիլ, անցնիլ)
glim - louys, lamp, mom, achk (լոյս, լամբ, մոմ, աչք)

glimmer - bulbulal, nushmarvil, bulbulatsoum (պլպլալ, նշմարուիլ, պլպլացում)
glimpse - agnarg, nushouyl, nushmarel (ակնարկ, նշոյլ, նշմարել)
glint - tsolk, payl, paylpulil (ցոլք, փայլ, փայլփլիլ)
glisten - shoghal, bulbulal, payladagel (շողալ, պլպլալ, փայլատակել)
glitter - paylil, shoghal, payl, sogh (փայլիլ, շողալ, փայլ, շող)
gloaming - verchalouys, irignamoud, mutunshagh (վերջալոյս, իրիկնամուտ, մթնշաղ)
gloat - charsurdoutyamp nayil (չարսրտութեամբ նայիլ)
globe - kount, yergurakount (գունդ, երկրագունդ)
globose - kuntatsev, poloratsev (գնդաձեւ, բոլորաձեւ)
globule - aryan kuntig, hadig (արեան գնդիկ, հատիկ)
gloom - mutoutiun, khavar, takgidz, mutnel, dukhretsunel (մթութիւն, խաւար, թախիծ, մթնել, տխրեցընել)
gloria - orhnerk, parapanoutiun (օրհներգ, փառաբանութիւն)
glorification - parapanoum, paravoroum (փառաբանում, փառաւորում)
glorify - parapanel, orhnel, kovel (փառաբանել, օրհնել, գովել)
glorious - paravor, shukegh, hiyanali (փառաւոր, շքեղ, հիանալի)
glory - park, badiv, bardzank, hampav (փառք, պատիւ, պարծանք, համբաւ)
gloss - payl, shukeghoutiun, payletsunel, hughgel (փայլ, շքեղութիւն, փայլեցնել, յղկել)
glossary - paratsang, masnakidagan parkirk (բառացանկ, մասնագիտական բառգիրք)
glossy - payloun, shoghshoghoun (փայլուն, շողշողուն)
glove - tsernots (ձեռնոց)
glow - chermoutiun, dot, dab, garmuril, ayril (ջերմութիւն, տօթ, տապ, կարմրիլ, այրիլ)
gloze - paghakushel, shoghokortel, kudznil, paghakushank (փաղաքշել, շողոքորթել, քծնիլ, փաղաքշանք)
glucose - kaghtsutouts, khaghoghi shakar (քաղցրուց, խաղողի շաքար)
glue - sosints, sosuntsel, pagtsunel (սոսինձ, սոսնձել, փակցնել)
glum - murayl, khozhor, anduramatirm, dukhril, khozhoril (մռայլ, խոժոռ, անտրամադիր, տխրիլ, խոժոռիլ)
glut - gullel, lapel, kerhaketsoum, aradoutiun (կլլել, լափել, գերյագում, առատութիւն)
glutinate - sosuntsel (սոսնձել)
glutton - shadager, vorguramol, dzagachk (շատակեր, որկրամոլ, ծակաչք)
gluttony - shadageroutiun, vorguramoloutiun (շատակերութիւն, որկրամոլութիւն)
glycogen - shakaradzin (շաքարածին)
gnar, gnarr, gnarl - durdunchal, murmural, kurtmunchel, hankouyts (տրտնջալ, մրմռալ, քրթմնջել, հանգոյց)
gnash - gurjurdel- adraneru, dzamadzurel- temku (կրճտել– ակռաները, ծամածռել– դէմքը)
gnat - muzhegh, muzhghoug (մժեղ, մժղուկ)
go - yertal, kalel, megnil, pazhnel, masnagtsil (երթալ, քալել, մեկնիլ, բաժնել, մասնակցիլ)
goad - khutan, khutanel (խթան, խթանել)
goal - pert-foutboli, nushanaged, tirakh, nubadag (բերդ՝ ֆութպոլի, նշանակէտ, թիրախ, նպատակ)
goal keeper - pertabah, tarbasabah (բերդապահ, դարպասապահ)
goat - aydz (այծ)
gobbet - badar, gudor, lapel (պատառ, կտոր, լափել)
gobble - lapel, gullel (լափել, կլլել)
goblet - kavat, pazhag, umbamag, sugih) գաւաթ, բաժակ, ըմպամակ, սկիհ)
God - asdvadz (Աստուած)

godbox - madour (մատուռ)
godchild - san (սան)
goddaughter - sanouhi (սանուհի)
goddess - titsouhi, chasdvadzouhi (դիցուհի, չաստուածուհի)
godfather - gunkahayr (կնքահայր)
godless - anasduvadz (անաստուած)
godmother - gunkamayr (կնքամայր)
godparent - gunkahayr, gunkamayr (կնքահայր, կնքամայր)
going - megnoum, yert, arga, kordzogh, untatsig (մեկնում, երթ, առկայ, գործող, ընթացիկ)
gold - vosgi, harusdoutiun (ոսկի, հարստութիւն)
golden - vosgeghen, vosgia, vosgekouyn (ոսկեղէն, ոսկեայ, ոսկեգոյն)
golden age - vosgetar (ոսկեդար)
goldfoil - vosgetert (ոսկեթերթ)
goldsmith - vosgerich (ոսկերիչ)
golf - kavazanov kuntakhagh, golf, golf khaghal (գաւազանով գնդախաղ, կոլֆ, կոլֆ խաղալ)
goliard - mimos, hudbid (միմոս, հտպիտ)
gong - dzundzgha (ծնծղայ)
good - lav, lavorag, pari, azniv, arakini (լաւ, լաւորակ, բարի, ազնիւ, առաքինի)
good afternoon - parev, pari irignabah, pari yedink (բարեւ, բարի իրիկնապահ, բարի ետինք)
good day - pari or, parev (բարի օր, բարեւ)
good evening - ari irigoun (բարի իրիկուն)
Good Friday - avak ourpat (Աւագ Ուրբաթ)
good morning - pari louys (բարի լոյս)
good night - kisher pari (գիշեր բարի)
goodbye, goodby - munak parov, yertak parov (մնաք բարով, երթաք բարով)
goodluck - pari hachoghoutiun (բարի յաջողութիւն)
goodness - lavoutiun, shnorhk, paroutiun (լաւութիւն, շնորհք, բարութիւն)
goods - abrank, inchk, ardaturank, usdatsvadzk (ապրանք, ինչք, արտադրանք, ստացուածք)
goodwife - dandigin (տանտիկին)
goodwill - paryatsagamoutiun, hamagurank (բարեացակամութիւն, համակրանք)
goose - sak, miamid, dukhmar (սագ, միամիտ, տխմար)
goosery - sakaran, havnots, aboushoutiun (սագարան, հաւնոց, ապուշութիւն)
gorge - gogort, girj, antsk, gullel (կոկորդ, կիրճ, անցք, կլլել)
gorgeous - hoyagab, hiyanali, shukegh (հոյակապ, հիանալի, շքեղ)
gorget - vuznots, maniag (վզնոց, մանեակ)
gorilla - martagabig (մարդակապիկ)
gormand, gourmand - shadager, vorguramol (շատակեր, որկրամոլ)
gormandize - lapel, hadtsunel (լափել, հատցնել)
Gospel - avedaran (Աւետարան)
gossip - shadakhosoutiun, pampasank, shadakhosel (շատախօսութիւն, բամբասանք, շատախօսել)
gossiper - shadakhos, pampasogh (շատախօս, բամբասող)
gourd - tutoum (դդում)
gourmet - kimkaser, nurpager (գիմքասէր, նրբակեր)
gout - gatil, jashag, hotadab (կաթիլ, ճաշակ, յօդատապ)
govern - garavarel, ghegavarel, direl, ishkhel (կառավարել, ղեկավարել, տիրել, իշխել)
government - garavaroutiun, ishkhanoutiun (կառավարութիւն, իշխանութիւն)
governor - garavarich, nahankabed, gousagal (կառավարիչ, նահանգապետ, կուսակալ)
gowk - gugou, barzamid, aboush (կկու, պարզամիտ, ապուշ)
gown - uzkesd, badmoujan-tadavori, barekod, tignots (զգեստ, պատմուճան՝ դատաւորի, պարեգօտ, թիկնոց)
grab - hapushdagel, khulel, gogho-

boud, hapushdagoum (յափշտակել, խլել, կողոպուտ, յափշտակում)
grace - shunorh, kuravchoutiun, bujnel, zartarel (շնորհ, գրաւչութիւն, պճնել, զարդարել)
graceful - shunorhali, nazeli, paretsev (շնորհալի, նազելի, բարեձեւ)
gracious - shunorhazart, pareshunorh, kutasird (շնորհազարդ, բարեշնորհ, գթասիրտ)
gradate - asdijanavorel (աստիճանաւորել)
gradation - asdijanavoroum, tasavoroum (աստիճանաւորում, դասաւորում)
grade - asdijan, tasaran, gark, asdijanavorel (աստիճան, դասարան, կարգ, աստիճանաւորել)
gradual - asdijanagan (աստիճանական)
gradually - asdijanapar (աստիճանաբար)
graduate - shurchanavard, untatsavard, avardel (շրջանաւարտ, ընթացաւարտ, աւարտել)
graduation - shurchanavardoutiun, asdijanavoroum (շրջանաւարտութիւն, աստիճանաւորում)
graff - kerezman (գերեզման)
graffiti - badi vura dukegh kuroutiunner (պատի վրայ տգեղ գրութիւններ)
graft - badvasd, gashark, badvasdel, gasharel (պատուաստ, կաշառք, պատուաստել, կաշառել)
grail - sugih, aghotakirk mu (սկիհ, աղօթագիրք մը)
grain - tsoren, hatsahadig, hadig, manrahadel (ցորեն, հացահատիկ, հատիկ, մանրահատել)
gram, gramme - guram (կրամ)
gramercy - medz shunorhagaloutiun (մեծ շնորհակալութիւն)
grammar - keraganoutiun (քերականութիւն)
grammarian - keraganaked (քերականագէտ)
gramophone - tsaynakir (ձայնագիր)
granary - ushdemaran, ampar (շտեմարան, ամբար)
grand - medz, untartsag, yereveli, partsur, veh (մեծ, ընդարձակ, երեւելի, բարձր, վեհ)
grandchild - tornig, tor (թոռնիկ, թոռ)
grandeur - medzoutiun, vusemoutiun (մեծութիւն, վսեմութիւն)
grandfather - medz hayr, bab, babig (մեծ հայր, պապ, պապիկ)
grandiose - paravor, hoyagab, medzghi (փառաւոր, հոյակապ, մեծղի)
grandmother - medz mayr, mamig, mam (մեծ մայր, մամիկ, մամ)
granite - vortsakar, guranid (որձաքար, կրանիտ)
grant - shunorhel, nuvirel, dal, shunorhk, never (շնորհել, նուիրել, տալ, շնորհք, նուէր)
granulate - manrel, aghal (մանրել, աղալ)
granulation - manrahadoutiun, hadavoroum (մանրահատութիւն, հատաւորում)
granule - hadig (հատիկ)
grape - khaghogh, voghgouyz (խաղող, ողկոյզ)
grape-vine - vortadoung (որթատունկ)
graphic - kudzakragan, nugarchagan (գծագրական, նկարչական)
graphic arts - gerbarvesd (կերպարուեստ)
graphite - kurchakar, ourvakar (գրչաքար, ուրուաքար)
graphologist - tserakraked (ձեռագրագէտ)
graphology - tserakrakidoutiun (ձեռագրագիտութիւն)
grapple - jang, jangel, kodemardil, pattuvil (ճանկ, ճանկել, գօտեմարտիլ, փաթթուիլ)
grasp - seghmoum, umpurnoum, seghmel, khulel, umpurnel (սեղմում, ըմբռնում, սեղմել, խլել, ըմբռնել)
grass - khod, markakedin (խոտ, մարգագետին)
grass-hopper - marakh (մարախ)
grate - gasgara, vantagel, kurkurel,

zayratsunel (կասկարայ, վանդակել, գրգռել, պայրացնել)
grateful - yerakhdaked, shunorhabard, hajeli (երախտագէտ, շնորհապարտ, հաճելի)
gratification - kohounagoutiun, barkev, hadoutsoum (գոհունակութիւն, պարգեւ, հատուցում)
gratify - kohatsunel, hajoyatsunel, shunorhel (գոհացնել, հաճոյացնել, շնորհել)
gratis - tsuri, tsurioren, anvujar (ձրի, ձրիօրէն, անվճար)
gratitude - yerakhdakidoutiun, shunorhabardoutiun (երախտագիտութիւն, շնորհապարտութիւն)
gratuitous - tsuri, anvujar, anhimun (ձրի, անվճար, անհիմն)
gratuity - nuver, barkevaturam (նուէր, պարգեւադրամ)
gratulate - shunorhavorel (շնորհաւորել)
gratulation - shunorhavoroum (շնորհաւորում)
grave (a) - lourch, dzanur, garevor, murayl (լուրջ, ծանր, կարեւոր, մռայլ)
grave (n) - kerezman (գերեզման)
grave (v) - porakurel, kantagel, porel (փորագրել, քանդակել, փորել)
gravel - khij, khujakar, mizakar, khijov dzadzgel (խիճ, խճաքար, միզաքար, խիճով ծածկել)
gravelstone - khujakar (խճաքար)
graver - porakurich, kantagakordz (փորագրիչ, քանդակագործ)
gravestone - kerezmanakar, dabanakar (գերեզմանաքար, տապանաքար)
graveyard - kerezmanadoun (գերեզմանատուն)
gravid - hughi (յղի)
gravitate - dzanranal, tsukdil, hagil (ծանրանալ, ձգտիլ, հակիլ)
gravity - dzanroutiun, lurchoutiun, tsukoghoutiun (ծանրութիւն, լրջութիւն, ձգողութիւն)
gravure - porakuroutiun, kantag (փորագրութիւն, քանդակ)
graze - aradzil, aradzel, aradzoum, jarag (արածիլ, արածել, արածում, ճարակ)
grease - jarb, yiugh, gashark, yiughodel, gasharel (ճարպ, իւղ, կաշառք, իւղոտել, կաշառել)
great - medz, husga, untartsag, daradzoun, hiyanali (մեծ, հսկայ, ընդարձակ, տարածուն, հիանալի)
Greece - hounasdan (Յունաստան)
greek - houyn, hounaren, hounagan (յոյն, յունարէն, յունական)
green - ganach, talar, tarm (կանաչ, դալար, թարմ)
green light - antsoumi louys (անցումի լոյս)
greet - voghchounel, parevel, timavorel (ողջունել, բարեւել, դիմաւորել)
grenade - tsernaroump, nurnag (ձեռնառումբ, նռնակ)
grenadier - rumpatsik, nurnagavor (ռմբաձիգ, նռնակաւոր)
grey, gray - korsh, mokhrakouyn (գորշ, մոխրագոյն)
greyhound, grayhound - vorsashoun, yergaravodk shoun, parag (որսաշուն, երկարոտք շուն, բարակ)
griddle - dabag (տապակ)
gride - gudrel, dzagel, jarjadoum (կտրել, ծակել, ճարճատում)
gridiron - gasgara (կասկարայ)
grief - vishd, gusgidz, tsav, aghed (վիշտ, կսկիծ, ցաւ, աղէտ)
grievance - vishd, tsav, darabank, viravorank (վիշտ, ցաւ, տառապանք, վիրաւորանք)
grieve - vushdanal, vushdatsunel, neghel, darabetsunel (վշտանալ, վշտացնել, նեղել, տառապեցնել)
grill - gasgara, khorovel, shampurel, khorovil, danchel (կասկարայ, խորովել, շամփրել, խորովիլ, տանջել)
grillade - khorovadz, khorovoum (խորոված, խորովում)
grim - tazhan, khozhor, sosgali (դաժան, խոժոր, սոսկալի)
grimace - dzamadzuroutiun, dzamadzurel, dzurmurgel (ծամածռու-

թիւն, ծամածռել, ծռմռկել)
grime - mour, aghd, geghd, aghdodel, murodel (մուր, աղտ, կեղտ, աղտոտել, մրոտել)
grin - kumdzidzagh, heknazhubid, zhubid-agra tsoutsunelov (քմծիծաղ, հեգնաժպիտ, ժպիտ՝ ակռայ ցուցնելով)
grind - aghal, manrel, pushrel, hughgel, aghatsoum (աղալ, մանրել, փշրել, յղկել, աղացում)
grinding-mill - chaghatsk (ջաղացք)
grind-stone - aghatsakar, hesanakar (աղացաքար, յեսանաքար)
grip - seghmel, purnel, seghmoum, purnuvadzk, got (սեղմել, բռնել, սեղմում, բռնուածք, կոթ)
gripe - seghmel, neghel, seghmoum, tsav, khit, got (սեղմել, նեղել, սեղմում, ցաւ, խիթ, կոթ)
grippe - chermakharun harpoukh (ջերմախառն հարբուխ)
gripsack - oughebayousag (ուղեպայուսակ)
grisly - sosgali, ahargou, anhajo (սոսկալի, ահարկու, անհաճոյ)
grist - aliurtsou, baren, tsoren, bashar (ալիւրցու, պարէն, ցորեն, պաշար)
grit - khij, avaz, tsavar, kachoutiun, gujurdel, aghal (խիճ, աւազ, ձաւար, քաջութիւն, կճրտել, աւազ)
grizzle - mokhrakouyn, korsh, korshanal, durdunchal (մոխրագոյն, գորշ, գորշանալ, տրտնջալ)
grizzled - alekharn (ալեխառն)
groan - voghpal, hedzel, dukal, dukots, harach (ողբալ, հեծել, տքալ, տնքոց, հառաչ)
grocer - nubaravajar (նպարավաճառ)
groom - tsiaban, usbasavor, pesatsou, pesa, tsi khunamel (ձիապան, սպասաւոր, փեսացու, փեսայ, ձի խնամել)
groove - agos, khorsh, churantsk, jeghkel (ակօս, խորշ, ջրանցք, ճեղքել)
grope - voronel, shoshapel, kharkhapel (որոնել, շօշափել, խարխափել)
gross - medz, dzavaloun, khoshor, 12 yergvetsiag (մեծ, ծաւալուն, խոշոր, 12 երկվեցեակ)
grot, grotto - karayr, karantsav (քարայր, քարանցաւ)
grotesque - aylantag, goshd, ardarots, dzidzagheli (այլանդակ, կոշտ, արտառոց, ծիծաղելի)
ground - kedin, hogh, tsamak, hoghamas (գետին, հող, ցամաք, հողամաս)
ground floor - kednaharg (գետնայարկ)
group - khoump, khumpel, khumpavorvil, tasagarkel (խումբ, խմբել, խմբաւորուիլ, դասակարգել)
grout - shaghakh, dzep, murour, tird (շաղախ, ծեփ, մրուր, դիրտ)
grove - bourag, andarag (պուրակ, անտառակ)
grovel - soghal, kudznil, nuvasdanal (սողալ, քծնիլ, նուաստանալ)
grow - ajil, medznal, dzulil, pousnil (աճիլ, մեծնալ, ծլիլ, բուսնիլ)
growl - koral, murunchel, murmural, korots, murmurots (գոռալ, մռնչել, մռմռալ, գոռոց, մռմռոց)
growth - ajoum, zarkatsoum, dzakoum, arpounk (աճում, զարգացում, ծագում, արբունք)
grub - turtour, vort, baren, sunount, porel, juknil (թրթուր, որդ, պարէն, սնունդ, փորել, ճգնիլ)
grubby - aghdod, geghdod, punti (աղտոտ, կեղտոտ, փնթի)
grudge - nakhantsil, tuzhgamagil, vokh, nakhantz (նախանձիլ, դժկամակիլ, ոխ, նախանձ)
gruel - malez, khavidz, tanabour (մալէզ, խաւիծ, թանապուր)
gruesome - sosgali, ahavor (սոսկալի, ահաւոր)
gruff - goshd, khisd, tazhan (կոշտ, խիստ, դաժան)
grum - khurbod, anhajo, gobid (խռպոտ, անհաճոյ, կոպիտ)
grumble - durdunchal, kankadil, durdounch, kankad (տրտնջալ, գանգատիլ, տրտունջ, գանգատ)

guarantee - yerashkhavoroutiun, abahovoutiun, yerashkhavorel (երաշխաւորութիւն, ապահովութիւն, երաշխաւորել)
guard - bahbanel, bashdbanel, bahag, hugoghoutiun (պահպանել, պաշտպանել, պահակ, հսկողութիւն)
guardian - bahaban, bashdban, veragatsou (պահապան, պաշտպան, վերակացու)
guardianship - khunamagaloutiun (խնամակալութիւն)
guerdon - vartsadurel, vartsaduroutiun, vartsk (վարձատրել, վարձատրութիւն, վարձք)
guerilla - artsagazen, hurosag, fedayi (արձակազէն, հրոսակ, ֆետայի)
guess - koushagel, gurahel, yentaturel, gurahoum (գուշակել, կրահել, ենթադրել, կրահում)
guest - hiur, aytselou, hiurasirel (հիւր, այցելու, հիւրասիրել)
guest-house - hiuranots (հիւրանոց)
guffaw - kurkich, kah kah, kurkuchal (քրքիջ, քահ քահ, քրքջալ)
guidance - arachnortoutiun, oughghoutiun (առաջնորդութիւն, ուղղութիւն)
guide - arachnortel, oughghel, arachnort, oughekirk (առաջնորդել, ուղղել, առաջնորդ, ուղեգիրք)
guidebook - oughekirk, deghegakirk, oughetsouyts (ուղեգիրք, տեղեկագիրք, ուղեցոյց)
guideline - oughekidz, oughenushan (ուղեգիծ, ուղենշան)
guild - arhesdagits, arvesdagtsoutiun, zhoghovasurah (արհեստակից, արուեստակցութիւն, ժողովասրահ)
guile - khoramangoutiun, nenkoutiun (խորամանկութիւն, նենգութիւն)
guillotine - garapnad, kulkhadel (կառափնատ, գլխատել)
guilt - hantsank, meghk (յանցանք, մեղք)
guilty - hantsavor, meghavor (յանցաւոր, մեղաւոր)
guise - dzubdil, timag, tsev, gerbarank, yerevouyt (ծպտիլ, դիմակ, ձեւ, կերպարանք, երեւոյթ)
guitar - gitar (կիթառ)
gulf - dzovakhorsh, dzots, antount (ծովախորշ, ծոց, անդունդ)
gull - khapel, nenkel, moloretsunel, nenkoutiun (խաբել, նենգել, մոլորեցնել, նենգութիւն)
gulp - lapel, goul dal, oumb, lapoum (լափել, կուլ տալ, ումպ, լափում)
gum - lind, khezh, redin, pagtsunel (լինտ, խէժ, ռետին, փակցնել)
gump - putamid, aboush (բթամիտ, ապուշ)
gun - adurjanag, huratsan, tuntanot, vorsi yertal (ատրճանակ, հրացան, թնդանօթ, որսի երթալ)
gunshot - huratsanazarg, zinaharvadz (հրացանազարկ, զինահարուած)
gunsmith - zinakordz, huratsanakordz (զինագործ, հրացանագործ)
gunsmithing - zinakordzoutiun (զինագործութիւն)
gurgle - gargach, gargachel, kulkulal (կարկաչ, կարկաչել, գլգլալ)
gurry - ghughgughank (կղկղանք)
gush - tsaydoum, heghegh, tsaydil, hortil, tsaydetsunel (ցայտում, հեղեղ, ցայտիլ, յորդիլ, ցայտեցնել)
gust - ham, kimk, hamaroutiun, hangardzahov, jashagel (համ, քիմք, համառութիւն, յանկարծահով, ճաշակել)
gut - aghik, porodik, goghobdel (աղիք, փորոտիք, կողոպտել)
guttle - gullel, lapel (կլլել, լափել)
guy - arakasdagal, ardarots hakousd, dzidzagheli mart (առագաստակալ, արտառոց հագուստ, ծիծաղելի մարդ)
gymnasium - marzaran (մարզարան)
gymnast - marzich, marzousouyts (մարզիչ, մարզուսոյց)
gymnastic - marmunamarzoutiun (մարմնամարզութիւն)
gynecologist - gunakhdapan, mangaparts (կնախտաբան, մանկաբարձ)
gynecology - gunakhdapanoutiun

(կնախտաբանութիւն)
gypsy - kunchou, posha (գնչու, բոշայ)
gyre - tavaloum, oghag, shurchanag, tavalil (թաւալում, օղակ, շրջանակ, թաւալիլ)
gyve - shughtayel, vodnagab, gabank (շղթայել, ոտնակապ, կապանք)

H

haberdash - manravajaroutiun unel (մանրավաճառութիւն ընել)
haberdasher - manravajar, perezag (մանրավաճառ, փերեզակ)
habiliment - hakousd, uzkesdeghen (հագուստ, զգեստեղէն)
habilitate - harmartsunel, sarkel, harmar (յարմարցնել, սարքել, յարմար)
hability - garoghoutiun, untounagoutiun (կարողութիւն, ընդունակութիւն)
habit - sovoroutiun, hakousd, haktsunel, punagetsunel (սովորութիւն, հագուստ, հագցնել, բնակեցնել)
habitable - punageli (բնակելի)
habitant - punagich (բնակիչ)
habitat - punagavayr, abreladeghi (բնակավայր, ապրելատեղի)
habitation - punagoutiun, doun, punagaran (բնակութիւն, տուն, բնակարան)
habitual - sovoragan (սովորական)
habituate - varzhetsunel, undelatsunel (վարժեցնել, ընտելացնել)
habitude - sovoroutiun, ounagoutiun (սովորութիւն, ունակութիւն)
hachure - usdverakidz, usdverakudzel (ստուերագիծ, ստուերագծել)
haematuria - ariunamizoutiun (արիւմիզութիւն)
haemorrhage - ariunahosoutiun (արիւնահոսութիւն)
haffle - gagazel, murtmurtal, pakhousd dal (կակազել, մրթմրթալ, փախուստ տալ)
hag - vuhoug, barav, chadoug (վհուկ, պառաւ, ջատուկ)
haggard - pazeyi tsak, vayri, dugar, vudid (բազէի ձագ, վայրի, տկար, վտիտ)
haggle - sagargel, gudradel, vijil, sagargoutiun (սակարկել, կտրատել, վիճիլ, սակարկութիւն)
hail - gargoud, voghchouyn, voghchounel, tsaynel (կարկուտ, ողջիւն, ողջունել, ձայնել)
hair - maz, her, kes, vars (մազ, հեր, գէս, վարս)
hairbrush - mazi khozanag (մազի խոզանակ)
hairdresser - saprich, varsahartar (սափրիչ, վարսայարդար)
hairpin - dzamagal, zartasegh (ծամակալ, զարդասեղ)
hairstyle - mazatsev, mazavoj, mazahartarank (մազաձեւ, մազաոճ, մազայարդարանք)
hairstylist - mazahartar (մազայարդար)
hairy - mazod, tavamaz (մազոտ, թաւամազ)
halcyon - tsugungoul, algion, hantard (ձկնկուլ, ալկիոն, հանդարտ)
hale - aroghch, gaydar, kalel, danil (առողջ, կայտառ, քաշել, տանիլ)
half - ges, gisachap (կէս, կիսաչափ)
half and half - ges ar ges, masamp, touyl, dugar (կէս առ կէս, մասամբ, թոյլ, տկար)
halftime - gisakhagh, gisazham, ges or (կիսախաղ, կիսաժամ, կէս օր)
halftone - gisamouyn, gisasduver (կիսամոյն, կիսաստուեր)
hall - surah, tahlij (սրահ, դահլիճ)
halleluyah, halleluiah - alelouya, park hor (ալէլուիա, փառք Հօր)

hallow - orhnel, surpatsunel, bashdel (օրհնել, սրբացնել, պաշտել)
hallucinate - zarantsel, moloril (զառանցել, մոլորիլ)
hallucination - zarantsank, khapgank (զառանցանք, խաբկանք)
hallucinator - zarantsogh, badranakhap, mudamolor (զառանցող, պատրանախաբ, մտամոլոր)
hall-mark - arzhechap vosgii, gunkel, turoshmel (արժեչափ ոսկիի, կնքել, դրոշմել)
halo - lousabusag, lousabusagel (լուսապսակ, լուսապսակել)
halt - gats, getsir, getsunel (կաց, կեցիր, կեցնել)
halter - sants, arasan, kheghtagab, gabel, gakhel (սանձ, առասան, խեղդակապ, կապել, կախել)
halve - gisel (կիսել)
ham - khozaboukhd, zisd (խոզապուխտ, զիստ)
hamlet - kiughag (գիւղակ)
hammer - mourj, guran, tarpunel (մուրճ, կռան, դարբնել)
hammersmith - tarpin (դարբին)
hammer-head - murjakuloukh, verin khorakir (մրճագլուխ, վերին խորագիր)
hammock - gakhoran, jojk (կախորան, ճօճք)
hamper - goghov, sagar, zampiugh (կողով, սակառ, զամբիւղ)
hand - tserk, tat, sulak, dal, hantsnel, antsunel (ձեռք, թաթ, սլաք, տալ, յանձնել, անցնել)
handart - tserarvesd (ձեռարուեստ)
handbag - tserabayousag, dobrag (ձեռապայուսակ, տոպրակ)
handball - tserakuntag, tserakuntakhagh (ձեռագնդակ, ձեռագնդախաղ)
handbill - turoutsig, dzanoutsoum (թռուցիկ, ծանուցում)
handbook - tserakirk, deghegakirk (ձեռագիրք, տեղեկագիրք)
handcuff - tsernagab, tsernagabel (ձեռնակապ, ձեռնակապել)
handicap - hashmantam, angarogh tarnal, tsiarshav (հաշմանդամ, անկարող դառնալ, ձիարշաւ)
handicraft - arhesd, tserarhesd, varbedoutiun (արհեստ, ձեռարհեստ, վարպետութիւն)
handiwork - tserakordz (ձեռագործ)
handkerchief - tashginag (թաշկինակ)
handle - tsernel, tubchil, shoshapel, got, purnag (ձեռնել, դպչիլ, շօշափել, կոթ, բռնակ
handmade - tseragerd (ձեռակերտ)
handmaid -
handmaid - usbasouhi (սպասուհի)
handrail - pazrik (բազրիք)
handshake - tseraseghmoum (ձեռասեղմում)
handsome - keghetsig, keghahasag, vayelouch (գեղեցիկ, գեղահասակ, վայելուչ)
handwriting - tserakir (ձեռագիր)
handy - artserun, madcheli, varbed (առձեռն, մատչելի, վարպետ)
handyman - jarbig, varbed, arhesdavor (ճարպիկ, վարպետ, արհեստաւոր)
handywork - tserakordz (ձեռագործ)
hang - gakhel, dadanil, gakhvil, gakhoum (կախել, տատանիլ, կախուիլ, կախում)
hangar - otanavashenk, otanavadoun (օդանաւաշէնք, օդանաւատուն)
hanger - gakhich, ger, tahij (կախիչ, կեռ, դահիճ
hanging - gakhoum, gakhelu (կախում, կախելը)
hangman - kakhogh, tahij (կախող, դահիճ)
hanker - denchal, paghtsal, yerazel (տենչալ, բաղձալ, երազել)
hap - pakhd, badahar, badahil, hantibil (բախտ, պատահար, պատահիլ, հանդիպիլ)
happen - badahil, deghi ounenal (պատահիլ, տեղի ունենալ)
happening - hantisoutiun (հանդիսութիւն)
happiness - yerchangoutiun, yeranoutiun (երջանկութիւն, երանութիւն)
happy - yerchanig, ourakh, pakhda-

vor (երջանիկ, ուրախ, բախտաւոր)
harangue - jar, jarakhosoutiun, jarakhosel (ճառ, ճառախօսութիւն, ճառախօսել)
harass - neghel, darabetsunel, anhankusdatsunel (նեղել, տառապեցնել, անհանգստացնել)
harassment - neghoutiun, mudahokoutiun, hoknoutiun (նեղութիւն, մտահոգութիւն, յոգնութիւն)
harbinger - sourhantag, garabed, avedel (սուրհանդակ, կարապետ, աւետել)
harbor - navahankisd, abasdanil, untounil (նաւահանգիստ, ապաստանիլ, ընդունիլ)
harborage - navagayan, abasdanaran (նաւակայան, ապաստանարան)
hard - gardzur, bint, amour, khisd (կարծր, պինդ, ամուր, խիստ)
hardcover - latagazm, gardzuragazm (լաթակազմ, կարծրակազմ)
harden - gardzuratsunel, khusdatsunel, buntanal (կարծրացնել, խստացնել, պնդանալ)
hardihood - kachoutiun, arioutiun, hantuknoutiun (քաջութիւն, արիութիւն, յանդգնութիւն)
hardiness - dogounoutiun, kachoutiun (տոկունութիւն, քաջութիւն)
hardly - haziv, tuzhvaroutiamp (հազիւ, դժուարութեամբ)
hardness - gardzuroutiun, buntoutiun, tuzhvaroutiun (կարծրութիւն, պնդութիւն, դժուարութիւն)
hardship - khusdoutiun, zurgank, dazhank (խստութիւն, զրկանք, տաժանք)
hardware - yergateghenk, medaghanotk (երկաթեղէնք, մետաղանօթք)
hare - nabasdag (նապաստակ)
harem - gananots (կանանոց)
haricot - loupia (լուբիա)
hark - lusel, mudig unel (լսել, մտիկ ընել)
harlequin - hudbid, mimos. kheghgadag (հտպիտ, միմոս, խեղկատակ)
harlot - poz, bornig, hanragin (բոզ, պոռնիկ, հանրակին)
harlotry - pozoutiun (բոզութիւն)
harm - vunas, gorousd, charik (վնաս, կորուստ, չարիք)
harmonic - nertashnag, yerazhushdagan (ներդաշնակ, երաժշտական)
harmonica - tsernatashnag (ձեռնադաշնակ)
harmonize - nertashnagel, hamatsaynetsunel (ներդաշնակել, համաձայնեցնել)
harmony - nertashnagoutiun, hamatsaynoutiun (ներդաշնակութիւն, համաձայնութիւն)
harp - davigh, davigh nuvakel (տաւիղ, տաւիղ նուագել)
harrow - dapan, tsakan, dapanel, viravorel (տափան, ցաքան, տափանել, վիրաւորել)
harry - goghobdel, kantel, averel (կողոպտել, քանդել, աւերել)
harsh - khurbod, goshd, anhajo, gobid (խրպոտ, կոշտ, անհաճոյ, կոպիտ)
hart - yeghcherou (եղջերու)
harvest - hountsk, perk, huntsel (հունձք, բերք, հնձել)
harvester - huntsogh (հնձող)
hash - manruvadz mis, hosh, manrel, hoshel, gudurdel (մանրուած միս, յօշ, մանրել, յօշել, կտրտել)
haste - ajabarank, ushdab, ajabarel (աճապարանք, շտապ, աճապարել)
hasten - ajabarel, arakatsunel, poutatsunel (աճապարել, արագացնել, փութացնել)
hasty - arak, poutgod, dakariun (արագ, փութկոտ, տաքարիւն)
hat - kulkharg, kutag (գլխարկ, գդակ)
hatch - tukhsel, hunarel, toukhs, tukhsoum (թխսել, հնարել, թուխս, թխսում)
hatchet - gatsin, dabarig (կացին, տապարիկ)
hate - adel, adeloutiun, vokh (ատել, ատելութիւն, ոխ)
hatter - kulkhargavajar, kulkhalgakordz (գլխարկավաճառ, գլխարկագործ)
haught - medzamid, koroz, hubard (մեծամիտ, գոռոզ, հպարտ)

haughtiness - *medzamudoutiun, korozoutiun* (մեծամտութիւն, գոռոզութիւն)
haul - *kashel, tartsunel, pokhel, kashvil, kashoum* (քաշել, դարձնել, փոխել, քաշուիլ, քաշում)
haunch - *aztur, zisd* (ազդր, զիստ)
haunt - *hajakhel, hajakh aytselel, hajakhavayr* (յաճախել, յաճախ այցելել, յաճախավայր)
hauteur - *partsuroutiun, medzamudoutiun* (բարձրութիւն, մեծամտութիւն)
have - *ounenal, usdanal, arnel, bardil* (ունենալ, ստանալ, առնել, պարտիլ)
haven - *navahankisd, abasdanaran, dzots, abasdanil* (նաւահանգիստ, ապաստանարան, ծոց, ապաստանիլ)
havoc - *kantoum, gordzanoum, aver, kantel* (քանդում, կործանում, աւեր, քանդել)
haw - *gumgumal, gagazel* (կմկմալ, կակազել)
hawk - *paze, hazalov khoukh hanel* (բազէ, հազալով խուխ հանել)
hawthorn - *khodapouys* (խոտաբոյս)
hay - *hart, chor khod, khod huntsel* (յարդ, չոր խոտ, խոտ հնձել)
hazard - *tibvadz, pakhd, tebk, vudank, vudankel* (դիպուած, բախտ, դէպք, վտանգ, վտանգել)
hazardous - *vudankavor, argadzalits* (վտանգաւոր, արկածալից)
haze - *mushoush, mek, marakhough, mushoushabadel* (մշուշ, մէգ, մառախուղ, մշուշապատել)
hazy - *mushoushod, aghod, mikabad* (մշուշոտ, աղօտ, միգապատ)
he - *an, ink, ayr, arou martu* (ան, ինք, այր, արու մարդը)
head - *kuloukh, oughegh, bed, kulkhavor, kulkhavorel* (գլուխ, ուղեղ, պետ, գլխաւոր, գլխաւորել)
headache - *kulkhatsav* (գլխացաւ)
headband - *kulkhagab* (գլխակապ)
heading - *vernakir, khorakir, magakir, didghos* (վերնագիր, խորագիր, մակագիր, տիտղոս)
headland - *hurvantan* (Հրուանդան)
headline - *vernakir, khorakir, vernadogh* (վերնագիր, խորագիր, վերնատող)
headphone - *ungalouch, lusapogh, aganchagal* (ընկալուչ, լսափող, ականջակալ)
headquarters - *usbayagouyd, panagadeghi, getronadeghi* (սպայակոյտ, բանակատեղի, կեդրոնատեղի)
headsman - *tahij, kulkhadogh, vartsgan* (դաՀիճ, գլխատող, վարձկան)
headstrong - *vujragam, hamar, bintkuloukh* (վճռակամ, յամառ, պինդգլուխ)
headwater - *agounk, kedaghpiur* (ակունք, գետաղբիւր)
headway - *harachtimoutiun, arachkhaghatsoum* (յառաջդիմութիւն, առաջխաղացում)
heady - *anzoush, gamagor, habjeb, harpetsunogh oghi* (անզուսպ, կամակոր, Հապճեպ, Հարբեցնող՝ օղի)
head-dress - *kulkhanots, kulkhazart* (գլխանոց, գլխազարդ)
heal - *pouzhel, puzhushgel, pouzhvil, aroghchanal* (բուժել, բժշկել, բուժուիլ, առողջանալ)
healer - *pouzhogh, aroghchatsunogh* (բուժող, առողջացնող)
healing - *pouzhich, aroghcharar* (բուժիչ, առողջարար)
health - *aroghchoutiun* (առողջութիւն)
healthiness - *aroghchoutiun* (առողջութիւն)
healthy - *aroghch, kacharoghch, arouyk* (առողջ, քաջառողջ, առոյգ)
heap - *tez, gouyd, tizel* (դէզ, կոյտ, դիզել)
hear - *lusel, imanal, oungunturel, ansal* (լսել, իմանալ, ունկնդրել, անսալ)
hearer - *lusogh, ounguntir* (լսող, ունկնդիր)
hearing - *ounguntouroutiun, luselik, tadavaroutiun* (ունկնդրութիւն, լսելիք, դատավարութիւն)
hearken - *mudig unel, lusel, ansal* (մտիկ ընել, լսել, անսալ)

hearphone - lusapogh, aganchapogh ungalouch (լուսափող, ականջափող, ընկալուչ)
hearse - merelagark, tiagark (մեռելակառք, դիակառք)
heart - sird, gourdzk, kachoutiun (սիրտ, կուրծք, քաջութիւն)
heart attack - surdi daknab, gatvadz (սրտի տագնապ, կաթուած)
heart broken - vushdapeg, surdapeg (վշտաբեկ, սրտաբեկ)
heart problem - surdi anhankusdoutiun (սրտի անհանգստութիւն)
heart surgery - surdi virahadoutiun (սրտի վիրահատութիւն)
heart valve - pagan, surdi peghg, pultag (փական, սրտի փեղկ, բլթակ)
hearten - kachalerel, vokevorel (քաջալերել, ոգեւորել)
hearth - guragaran, vararan, ojakh (կրակարան, վառարան, օճախ)
hearty - surdants, angeghdz, surdapoukh, cherm (սրտանց, անկեղծ, սրտաբուխ, ջերմ)
heat - dakoutiun, chermoutiun, daktsunel (տաքութիւն, ջերմութիւն, տաքցնել)
heated - daktsadz (տաքցած)
heater - vararan, cheroutsich (վառարան, ջեռուցիչ)
heath - dapasdan, hartavayr, tsakh (տափաստան, հարթավայր, ցախ)
heathen - hetanos, anguron, guragabashd (հեթանոս, անկրօն, կրակապաշտ)
heating - daktsunogh, cheroutsich, cheroutsoum (տաքցնող, ջեռուցիչ, ջեռուցում)
heave - vertsunel, partsuratsunel, heval, partsratsoum (վերցնել, բարձրացնել, հեւալ, բարձրացում)
heaven - yergink, yeter, turakhd, arkayoutiun (երկինք, եթեր, դրախտ, արքայութիւն)
heavy - dzanur, junshogh, tuzhvar, lourch (ծանր, ճնշող, դժուար, լուրջ)
heavy-weight - dzanragushir, dzanramarmin, dzanrakash (ծանրակշիռ, ծանրամարմին, ծանրաքաշ)
hebrew - huria, yeprayeren, hureagan (հրեայ, եբրայերէն, հրէական)
hecatomb - godoradz, ariunaheghoutiun (կոտորած, արիւնահեղութիւն)
hectare - hegdar, hariuragal (հեկտար, հարիւրակալ)
hectic - tokakhdavor, hiudzakhdavor (թոքախտաւոր, հիւծախտաւոր)
hector - sunabardz, bardzengod, bardzenal, kurkurel (սնապարծ, պարծենկոտ, պարծենալ, գրգռել)
hedge - tsangabad, arkelk, tsangabadel (ցանկապատ, արգելք, ցանկապատել)
hedgehog - vozni (ոզնի)
hedonist - heshdaser, hajoyabashd (հեշտասէր, հաճոյապաշտ)
heed - oushaturoutiun, khunamk, zunnel, hokadaroutiun (ուշադրութիւն, խնամք, զննել, հոգատարութիւն)
heedful - oushatir, artoun, shurchahayiats (ուշադիր, արթուն, շրջահայեաց)
heel - dzuril, hagil, guroung, nerpan, karshabar (ծռիլ, հակիլ, կրունկ, ներբան, գարշապար)
heft - gushir, dzanroutiun, partsuratsunel (կշիռ, ծանրութիւն, բարձրացնել)
hegemony - kerishkhanoutiun, dirabedoutiun (գերիշխանութիւն, տիրապետութիւն)
heifer - hort, yerinch (հորթ, երինջ)
height - partsuroutiun, hasag, asdijan, kakat (բարձրութիւն, հասակ, աստիճան, գագաթ)
heighten - partsuratsunel, partsuranal, shadtsunel (բարձրացնել, բարձրանալ, շատցնել)
heinous - adeli, zuzveli, sosgali, hureshayin (ատելի, զզուելի, սոսկալի, հրէշային)
heir - zharank, zharankort, zharankel (ժառանգ, ժառանգորդ, ժառանգել)
heirdom - zharankoutiun (ժառան-

գութիւն)
helicopter - oughghatir, inknatir (ուղղաթիռ, ինքնաթիռ)
heliograph - arevakir, arevanugar, arevakurel (արեւագիր, արեւանկար, արեւագրել)
hell - tuzhokhk, kehen, dardaros (դժոխք, գեհեն, տարտարոս)
hellenic - hellenagan, hounagan (Հելլենական, յունական)
hello - parev, voghchiun (բարեւ, ողջոյն)
helm - gheg, ghegavarel (ղեկ, ղեկավարել)
helmet - saghavard (սաղաւարտ)
help - oknel, ozhantagel, oknoutiun (օգնել, օժանդակել, օգնութիւն)
helpless - anoknagan (անօգնական)
helve - got, purnag (կոթ, բռնակ)
hemisphere - gisakount (կիսագունդ)
hemorrhage - ariunahosoutiun (արիւնահոսութիւն)
hemorrhoids - toutk, surpani ariunod ouretsk (թութք, սրբանի արիւնոտ ուռեցք)
hen - hav, turchnazki (հաւ, թռչնազգի)
hence - hedevapar, ousdi (հետեւաբար, ուստի)
henceforth - aylyevus, aysouhedev (այլեւս, այսուհետեւ)
henchman - dzara, gamagadar, tignabah (ծառայ, կամակատար, թիկնապահ)
hencoop - havnots, havapoun (հաւնոց, հաւաբուն)
henna - hina (հինայ)
her - ir, iru, an, anor - for woman (իր, իրը, ան, անոր – իգական)
herald - sourhantag, panper, mounedig, aztararel (սուրհանդակ, բանբեր, մունետիկ, ազդարարել)
heraldry - panperoutiun, zhinanushani kudzarvesd (բանբերութիւն, զինանշանի գծարուեստ)
herb - khod, talar, pouys (խոտ, դալար, բոյս)
herd - hod, nakhir, khoump, havakel (հօտ, նախիր, խումբ, հաւաքել)
herdsman - hoviv, khashnaradz (հովիւ, խաշնարած)
here - hos, aysdegh (հոս, այստեղ)
here after - asgits yedk, aysouhedev (ասկից ետք, այսուհետեւ)
here and there - hos yev hon (հոս եւ հոն)
hereabout - ays degher, ays goghmeru (այս տեղեր, այս կողմերը)
hereafter - asgits yedk, hedakayin (ասկից ետք, հետագային)
hereby - asov, ays badjarov (ասով, այս պատճառով)
hereditary - zharankagan (ժառանգական)
heredity - zharankoutiun (ժառանգութիւն)
herein - asor, aysdegh (ասոր, այստեղ)
hereof - ays, asgits, ouremun (այս, ասկից, ուրեմն)
heresy - heredigosoutiun (հերետիկոսութիւն)
heretofore - minchev hima, asgits arach (մինչեւ հիմա, ասկից առաջ)
hereupon - asgits yedk, asor vura (ասկից ետք, ասոր վրայ)
herewith - asov (ասով)
heritage - zharankoutiun (ժառանգութիւն)
hermaphrodite - vortsevek, arouek (որձեւէգ, արուէգ)
hermetic - amrapag, antapants (ամրափակ, անթափանց)
hermit - juknavor, menagiats (ճգնաւոր, մենակեաց)
hermitage - juknaran (ճգնարան)
hernia - aghetapoutiun, ichvadzk (աղեթափութիւն, իջուածք)
hero - heros, tiutsazun (հերոս, դիւցազն)
heroic - herosagan, tiutsaznagan (հերոսական, դիւցազնական)
heroine - herosouhi, tiutsaznouhi (հերոսուհի, դիւցազնուհի)
heroism - herosoutiun, tiutsaznoutiun (հերոսութիւն, դիւցազնութիւն)
herself - inkniren, inkzink, inkun isg (ինքնիրեն, ինքզինք, ինքն

խսկ)
hesitate - *varanil, dadamsil* (վարանիլ, տատամսիլ)
hesitation - *varanoum, dadamsoum* (վարանում, տատամսում)
hew - *dashel, gopel, manrel* (տաշել, կոփել, մանրել)
hexagon - *vetsangiun* (վեցանկիւն)
hiation - *horanchoum* (յօրանջում)
hibernate - *tsumerel* (ձմեռել)
hiccup, hiccough - *tsukurdal, tsukurdots* (ձգուտալ, ձգուտոց)
hidden - *bahvadz, takoun, kaghdni* (պահուած, թագուն, գաղտնի)
hide - *bahel, bahvil, dzadzgel, mort, mashg* (պահել, պահուիլ, ծածկել, մորթ, մաշկ)
hie - *ajabarel, ajabarank* (աճապարել, աճապարանք)
hierarchy - *nevirabedoutiun, tasagarkoutiun* (նուիրապետութիւն, դասակարգութիւն)
hieroglyph - *mehenakir* (մեհենագիր)
high - *partsur, veh, verin, yereveli, loroz, yergink* (բարձր, վեհ, վերին, երեւելի, գոռոզ, երկինք)
high frequency - *hajakhoutiun, garjalik* (յաճախութիւն, կարճալիք)
high pressure - *kerjunshoum, dzanur junshoum* (գերճնշում, ծանր ճնշում)
high school - *partsurakouyn varzharan* (բարձրագոյն վարժարան)
highland - *lernatashd, partsuravantag* (լեռնադաշտ, բարձրավանդակ)
highlife - *aznevagan, partsur tas* (ազնուական, բարձր դաս)
highlight - *himnaharts, garevor ged, untkudzel* (հիմնահարց, կարեւոր կէտ, ընդգծել)
highlighting - *untkudzoum, sheshdoum* (ընդգծում, շեշտում)
highness - *partsuroutiun, partsounk, vusemoutiun* (բարձրութիւն, բարձունք, վսեմութիւն)
hight - *huramayel, anvanel, gochvil, hantsunel* (հրամայել, անուանել, կոչուիլ, յանձնել)
highway - *mayroughi* (մայրուղի)
hijack, highjack - *otanav arevankel, pakhtsunel, koghnal* (օդանաւ առեւանգել, փախցնել, գողնալ)
hijacker - *otahen, otanav purnakuravogh* (օդահէն, օդանաւ բռնագրաւող)
hike - *nedel, nedvil, kashgurdoukov yertal, nedvadzk* (նետել, նետուիլ, քաշկռտուքով երթալ, նետուածք)
hilarious - *zuvart, ourakh* (զուարթ, ուրախ)
hill - *pulour, partsuravantag* (բլուր, բարձրավանդակ)
hilt - *got, purnag* (կոթ, բռնակ)
him - *zink, zayn - for man* (զինք, զայն – արական)
himself - *inku, inkzink, inkun iren* (ինքը, ինքզինք, ինքն իրեն)
hind - *yeghnig, shinagan, akarag ashkhadogh* (եղնիկ, շինական, ագարակ աշխատող)
hinder - *arkilel, khapanel, yedevi* (արգիլել, խափանել, ետեւի)
hindou - *huntig* (հնդիկ)
hinge - *dzukhni, henag, gabel, gutsel* (ծխնի, յենակ, կապել, կցել)
hink - *keranti* (գերանդի)
hinny - *chori, vurunchel* (ջորի, վրնջել)
hint - *agnarg, agnargel, telaturel* (ակնարկ, ակնարկել, թելադրել)
hip - *zisd, aztur, yerank* (զիստ, ազդր, երանք)
hippodrome - *tsiarshavaran, tsiartsagaran* (ձիարշաւարան, ձիարձակարան)
hips -
hire - *vartsel, gasharel, vartsoum* (վարձել, կաշառել, վարձում)
hireling - *vartsgan, vartsvor* (վարձկան, վաձուոր)
hirondelle - *dzidzernag* (ծիծեռնակ)
his - *anor, iru - for man* (անոր, իրը – արական)
hiss - *soulel, fushshal, sharachel, souloum, fushshots* (սուլել, ֆշշալ, շառաչել, սուլում, ֆշշոց)
hist - *hush, luroutiun* (հը˜շ, լռութի˜ն)
historian - *badmapan, badmakir, badmich* (պատմաբան, պատմագիր,

պատմիչ)
historic - badmagan, garevor (պատմական, կարեւոր)
historiography - badmakuroutiun (պատմագրութիւն)
history - badmoutiun (պատմութիւն)
hit - zarnel, harvadzel, tubchil, tubtsunel, harvadz (զարնել, հարուածել, դպչիլ, դպցնել, հարուած)
hitch - purnuvil, burgel, miatsunel, gabel, gab, hankouyts (բռնուիլ, պրկել, միացնել, կապել, կապ, հանգոյց)
hive - petag, meghvanots, muterel, khumpuvil (փեթակ, մեղուանոց, մթերել, խմբուիլ)
hives - churdzaghig, gabouyd haz, kervudouk (ջրծաղիկ, կապոյտ հազ, քերուըտուք)
hoar - yeghiam, tsogh, aleher, jermag, dzeroutiun (եղեամ, ցող, ալեհեր, ճերմակ, ծերութիւն)
hoard - muterk, tez, bashar, kants, muterel, bahel (մթերք, դէզ, պաշար, գանձ, մթերել, պահել)
hoarse - khurbod, gerger, anakhorzh tsayn (խռպոտ, կերկեր, անախորժ ձայն)
hoax - khapeoutiun, gadag, khapel, gadagel, khaghtsunel (խաբէութիւն, կատակ, խաբել, կատակել, խաղցնել)
hobble - gaghal, gaghalov kalel, gaghoutiun (կաղալ, կաղալով քալել, կաղութիւն)
hobbly - khordouporđ (խորտուբորտ)
hobby - nakhasiroutiun, kumahajouyk, murtsatsi (նախասիրութիւն, քմահաճոյք, մրցածի)
hobgoblin - ourvagan, jivagh, char voki (ուրուական, ճիւաղ, չար ոգի)
hock - gart, jermag kini, gartadel (կարթ, ճերմակ գինի, կարթատել)
hockey - joganakhagh (ճոկանախաղ)
hocus - tumretsunel, himaratsunel, khapel, khapepa (թմրեցնել, յիմարացնել, խաբել, խաբեբայ)
hoe - purich, porel, beghel (բրիչ, փորել, պեղել)
hog - khoz, aghdod ants (խոզ, աղտոտ անձ)
hoist - vertsunel, ver kashel, partsuratsoum, verhan (վերցնել, վեր քաշել, բարձրացում, վերհան)
hold - purnel, kuravel, barounagel, kuravoum, galank (բռնել, գրաւել, պարունակել, գրաւում, կալանք)
holding - purnoum, kuravoum, vartsagaloutiun (բռնում, գրաւում, վարձակալութիւն)
holdup - getsir, usbase (կեցի՛ր, սպասէ՛)
hole - dzag, pos, jeghk, dzagel (ծակ, փոս, ճեղք, ծակել)
holiday - don, donagan or, artsagourt (տօն, տօնական օր, արձակուրդ)
holiness - surpoutiun, surpaznoutiun (սրբութիւն, սրբազնութիւն)
Holland - Holanda (Հոլանտա)
hollow - pos, khoroch, tsor, tadarg, dzagel, porel (փոս, խոռոչ, ձոր, դատարկ, ծակել, փորել)
holly - gaghniyi dzar, pusharmav (կաղնիի ծառ, փշարմաւ)
holocaust - voghchagizoum, hamaynachart (ողջակիզում, համայնաջարդ)
holt - bourag, andarapulour, vorch (պուրակ, անտառաբլուր, որջ)
holy - sourp, surpazan, nuviragan (սուրբ, սրբազան, նուիրական)
Holy Bible - sourp kirk, asdvadzashounch (Սուրբ Գիրք, Աստուածաշունչ)
Holy Cross - sourp khach (Սուրբ Խաչ)
homage - harkank, medzarank, badiv, medzarel (յարգանք, մեծարանք, պատիւ, մեծարել)
home - doun, punagaran, hayrenik, yergir (տուն, բնակարան, հայրենիք, երկիր)
homecoming - dountarts (տունդարձ)
homeland - hayrenik (հայրենիք)
homeless - andoun, dunazourg, anotevan (անտուն, տնազուրկ, անօթեւան)
homely - anbajouyj, undanegan

(անպաճոյճ, ընտանեկան)
homemade - ardunin, dounu shinvadz, deghagan (արտնին, տունը շինուած, տեղական)
homeopathy - numanapouzhoutiun (նմանաբուժութիւն)
homesick - hayrenagarod, dunapaghtsoutiun (Հայրենակարօտ, տնաբաղձութիւն)
homestead - galvadzadoun, punagaran, dzununtadeghi (կալուածատուն, բնակարան, ծննդատեղի)
homicide - martasban, martasbanoutiun (մարդասպան, մարդասպանութիւն)
homilist - karozel, jarakhos, pempasats (քարոզել, ճառախօս, բեմբասաց)
homily - karoz, khurad, jar, pempasatsoutiun (քարոզ, խրատ, ճառ, բեմբասացութիւն)
homogeneous - miadar, hamaser, hamadesag (միատարր, Համասեռ, Համատեսակ)
homologue - hamanuman, hamabadaskhan, hamatir (Համանման, Համապատասխան, Համադիր)
homonym - hamanoun, nouynatsayn (Համանուն, նոյնաձայն)
homosexual - miaseragan, arvaked (միասեռական, արուագէտ)
hone - voghpal, garodil, surel, surakar, yiughakar (ողբալ, կարօտիլ, սրել, սրաքար, իւղաքար)
honest - bargeshd, badvavor, shidag, artar (պարկեշտ, պատուաւոր, շիտակ, արդար)
honey - meghur, anoush, sirelis, anoushtsunel, kukvel (մեղր, անուշ, սիրելիս, անուշցնել, գգուել)
honeymoon - meghralousin (մեղրալուսին)
honor - badiv, park, hampav, badvel, medzarel (պատիւ, փառք, Համբաւ, պատուել, մեծարել)
honorable, honourable - harkeli, badvarzhan, badvavor (յարգելի, պատուարժան, պատուաւոր)
honorary - badvo, badvagal, badvakin, barkevavu jar (պատուոյ, պատուակալ, պատուագին, պարգեւավճառ)
honorific - badvaper, harkalits, badvagal (պատուաբեր, յարգալից, պատուակալ)
hood - veghar, kulkhanots, vegharel, dzadzgel, kotsel (վեղար, գլխանոց, վեղարել, ծածկել, գոցել)
hoodlum - tadargabord, charakordz, khoulikan (դատարկապորտ, չարագործ, խուլիգան)
hoof - sumpag, gujghag, taparil, akatsel (սմբակ, կճղակ, Թափառիլ, ագացել)
hook - gakhich, ger, gart, mankagh, jangel, purnel (կախիչ, կեռ, կարթ, մանգաղ, ճանկել, բռնել)
hookah - gulgulag (կլկլակ)
hooker - tsugnorsanav, gartogh, kuntag purnogh (ձկնորսանաւ, կարթող, գնդակ բռնող)
hooligan - charakordz, khoulikan, anarag (չարագործ, խուլիգան, անառակ)
hoop - kodi, shurchanag, shurchanagel, jich, juchal (գօտի, շրջանակ, շրջանակել, ճիչ, ճչալ)
hoopoe - hobob (յոպոպ)
hoot - gurinch, aghaghag, gurunchel, koral (կռինչ, աղաղակ, կռնչել, գոռալ)
hop - vosdosdel, turchgodel, tsadgurdel, vosdoum (ոստոստել, Թռչկոտել, ցատկռտել, ոստում)
hope - housal, agungalel, houys (յուսալ, ակնկալել, յոյս)
hopeful - housalits, housadou, khosdumnalits (յուսալից, յուսատու, խոստմնալից)
hopeless - anhouys, housahad, jarahad (անյոյս, յուսաՀատ, ճարաՀատ)
horde - horta, hurosagakhoump (Հորդայ, Հրոսակախումբ)
horizon - horizon, volord, desatashd (Հորիզոն, ոլորտ, տեսադաշտ)
horizontal - horizonagan (Հորիզոնական)
hormone - keghtsaniut (գեղձանիւթ)
horn - godosh, yeghchiur, juchag-

inknasharzhi (կոտոշ, եղջիւր, ճչակ՝ ինքնաշարժի)
horned - yeghchiuravor (եղջիւրաւոր)
hornet - ishameghou (իշամեղու)
horny - yeghcherayin, yeghcheratsev, gadzur (եղջերային, եղջերաձեւ, կարծր)
horoscope - koushagakirk, asdghakhoushagoutiun (գուշակագիրք, աստղագուշակութիւն)
horrible - sarsapeli, sosgali, ahreli, ahavor (սարսափելի, սոսկալի, ահռելի, ահաւոր)
horrid - ahreli, noghgali, ahavor, goshd (ահռելի, նողկալի, ահաւոր, կոշտ)
horrific - sosgali, sarsapeli, ahargou (սոսկալի, սարսափելի, ահարկու)
horrify - sosgatsunel, tsuntsel, sarsapetsunel (սոսկացնել, ցնցել, սարսափեցնել)
horror - sosgoum, sarsap, ahoutogh (սոսկում, սարսափ, ահուդող)
horse - tsi, yerivar, tsi hedznel (ձի, երիվար, ձի հեծնել)
horseman - tsiavor, hedzial (ձիաւոր, հեծեալ)
horseshoe - bayd (պայտ)
horticulture - bardizbanoutiun, bardizakidoutiun (պարտիզպանութիւն, պարտիզագիտութիւն)
hosanna - ovsanna, orhnoutiun (ովսաննա, օրհնութիւն)
hose - hurtehi khoghovag, negh vardik, koulba (հրդեհի խողովակ, նեղ վարտիք, գուլպայ)
hospice - hiuradoun, vanadoun, aghkadanots (հիւրատուն, վանատուն, աղքատանոց)
hospitable - hiuraser, hiurungal, asbunchagan (հիւրասէր, հիւրընկալ, ասպնջական)
hospital - hivantanots (հիւանդանոց)
hospitality - hiurasiroutiun, hiurungaloutiun (հիւրասիրութիւն, հիւրընկալութիւն)
hospitalize - hivantanots tunel (հիւանդանոց դնել)
host - hiurungal, dander, ampokh, nushkhar (հիւրընկալ, տանտէր, ամբոխ, նշխար)
hostage - badant, keri (պատանդ, գերի)
hostel - ichevan, otevan, hankusdaran (իջեւան, օթեւան, հանգստարան)
hostess - hiurungalouhi, dandirouhi (հիւրընկալուհի, տանտիրուհի)
hostility - tushnamoutiun, hagaragoutiun (թշնամութիւն, հակառակութիւն)
hosting - guriv, untharoum, zoragoch, zorahantes (կռիւ, ընդհարում, զօրակոչ, զօրահանդէս)
hot - dak, cherm, guragod, gizich, gudzou, ayrogh (տաք, ջերմ, կրակոտ, կիզիչ, կծու, այրող)
hot dog - dak yershig (տաք երշիկ)
hotel - bantog, otevan, hiuranots (պանդոկ, օթեւան, հիւրանոց)
hothead - dakkuloukh (տաքգլուխ)
hotness - dakoutiun, guragodoutiun (տաքութիւն, կրակոտութիւն)
hot-blooded - dakariun, guragod, gurkod, tiurakurkir (տաքարիւն, կրակոտ, կրքոտ, դիւրագրգիռ)
hound - vorsashoun, parag (որսաշուն, բարակ)
hour - zham, bah, zhamanag (ժամ, պահ, ժամանակ)
house - doun, punagaran, punagil, abasdanil (տուն, բնակարան, բնակիլ, ապաստանիլ)
household - ardunin, dunagan, dunetsik (արտնին, տնական, տնեցիք)
housekeeper - dandigin, dunabah (տանտիկին, տնապահ)
housekeeping - dandignoutiun, dunabahoutiun (տանտիկնութիւն, տնապահութիւն)
housemaid - usbasouhi, dzara (սպասուհի, ծառայ)
housewares - garasik, dan kouyker (կարասիք, տան գոյքեր)
housewife - dandigin, dandirouhi (տանտիկին, տանտիրուհի)
housing - punagoum, badusbaroum, abaven, tsiou dzadzgots (բնակում,

պատսպարում, ապաւէն, ձիու ծածկոց)
hovel - khurjit, hiughag, dzadzg, badusbarel (խրճիթ, Հիւղակ, ծածկ, պատսպարել)
hover - savarnil, turchudil, dadanil (սաւառնիլ, Թռչտիլ, տատանիլ)
how - inchbes, inchou, inch, inch tsevov (ի՞նչպէս, ի՞նչու, ի՞նչ, ի՞նչ ձեւով)
how do you do - inchbes ek (ի՞նչպէս էք)
how far - vorchap herou (ո՞րչափ Հեռու)
how many - kani had (քանի՞ Հատ)
how much - vorchap, kani (որչափ, քանի՞)
however - sagayn, payts, kone, teyev, vorkan al (սակայն, բայց, գոնէ, Թէեւ, որքան ալ)
howl - vornal, borchudal, vornots, borchudouk (ոռնալ, պոռչտալ, ոռնոց, պոռչտուք)
howsoever - vorchap al, inch al ulla (որչափ ալ, ինչ ալ ըլլայ)
hub - yerakhagal, nushanagaged (երախակալ, Նշանակակէտ)
hubbub - aghaghag, zhukhor, vaynasoun (աղաղակ, ժխոր, վայնասուն)
huckster - manravajar, perezag, khapepa, perezagel (մանրավաճառ, փերեզակ, խաբեբայ, փերեզակել)
hue - kouyn, yerank, jich, aghaghag (գոյն, երանգ, ճիչ, աղաղակ)
hue and cry - koroum-kochoum (գոռում-գոչում)
huff - surtoghil, zayranal, korozanal, zayrouyt (սրդողիլ, զայրանալ, գոռոզանալ, զայրոյթ)
hug - kurgel, seghmel, voghchakourel (գրկել, սեղմել, ողջագուրել)
huge - husga, vitkhari, khoshor (Հսկայ, վիԹխարի, խոշոր)
hugger - dzadzgel, bahvudil, seghmogh, kurgogh (ծածկել, պաՀուըտիլ, սեղմող, գրկող)
hugger-mugger - kaghdakoghi, dzadzgamudoutiun (գաղտագողի, ծածկամտուԹիւն)
hum - puzzal, murmural, puzziun, murmounch (բզզալ, մռմռալ, բզզիւն, մրմունջ)
human - martgayin (մարդկային)
humane - martaser, pari, azniv (մարդասէր, բարի, ազնիւ)
humanism - martgaynoutiun, martasiroutiun (մարդկայնուԹիւն, մարդասիրուԹիւն)
humanitarian - martgaynagan, martasiragan (մարդկայնական, մարդասիրական)
humanity - martgoutiun, martasiroutiun (մարդկուԹիւն, մարդասիրուԹիւն)
humanize - martgaynatsunel, martatsunel, aznuvatsunel (մարդկայնացնել, մարդացնել, ազնուացնել)
humankind - martgoutiun (մարդկուԹիւն)
humble - khonarh, hamesd, khonarhetsunel (խոնարՀ, Համեստ, խոնարՀեցնել)
humbug - khapepayoutiun, geghdzik, khapepa, khapel (խաբեբայուԹիւն, կեղծիք, խաբեբայ, խաբել)
humid - khonav (խոնաւ)
humidity - khonavoutiun (խոնաւուԹիւն)
humify - khonavtsunel, turchel, damdatsunel (խոնաւցնել, Թրջել, տամկացնել)
humiliate - nuvasdatsunel, khonarhetsunel, amuchtsunel (Նուաստացնել, խոնարՀեցնել, ամչցնել)
humiliation - nevasdatsoum, ungjoum, usdornatsoum (Նուաստացում, ընկճում, ստորնացում)
humility - hezoutiun, khonarhoutiun (ՀեզուԹիւն, խոնարՀուԹիւն)
humor - zuvartakhohoutiun, heknank, hiut (զուարԹախոՀուԹիւն, Հեգնանք, ՀիւԹ)
humorist - yerkidzapan, gadagakhos (երգիծաբան, կատակախօս)
hump - gouz, sabad, sabadel, goranal (կուզ, սապատ, սապատել, կորանալ)
hunch - gouz, sabad, sabadel, hurmushdugel (կուզ, սապատ, սապա-

տել, Հրմշտկել)
hundred - hariur (Հարիւր)
hundredfold - hariurabadig (Հարիւրապատիկ)
hungarian - hounkaratsi, hounkareren, hounkaragan (Հունգարացի, Հունգարերէն, Հունգարական)
Hungary - hounkaria (Հունգարիա)
hunger - anotoutiun, kaghts, dench, anotenal (անօթութիւն, քաղց, տենչ, անօթենալ)
hungry - anoti, kaghtsadz, sovadz (անօթի, քաղցած, սոված)
hunk - zankuvadz, khoshor, gudor, abahov, lav, hart (զանգուած, խոշոր, կտոր, ապահով, լաւ, Հարթ)
hunker - bahbanoghagan, hedatem, guguzil (պահպանողական, յետադէմ, կկզիլ)
hunt - vors, vorsortoutiun, vorsal, haladzel (որս, որսորդութիւն, որսալ, Հալածել)
hunter - vorsort, vorsi tsi (որսորդ, որսի ձի)
hunting - vorsortoutiun (որսորդութիւն)
hurl - artsagel, nedel, artsagoum (արձակել, նետել, արձակում)
hurly-burly - irarantsoum, zhukhor (իրարանցում, ժխոր)
hurra - houra, getstse, dzapaharel (Հուռա, կեցցէ՛, ծափահարել)
hurricane - voloramurrig, potorig (ոլորամրրիկ, փոթորիկ)
hurry - ajabarel, ushdabel, ajabarank (աճապարել, շտապել, աճապարանք)
hurst - bourag, andarabad, avazoudk (պուրակ, անտառապատ, աւազուտք)
hurt - vunasel, viravorel, vushdatsunel, verk, vunas (վնասել, վիրաւորել, վշտացնել, վէրք, վնաս)
hurtful - vunasagar (վնասակար)
hurtle - zarnuvil, tubchil, pakhil, harvadz, pakhoum (զարնուիլ, դպչիլ, բախիլ, Հարուած, բախում)
husband - amousin, erig, ayr (ամուսին, էրիկ, այր)
husbandman - mushag, hoghakordz (մշակ, Հողագործ)
husbandry - hoghakordzoutiun (Հողագործութիւն)
hush - lurel, luretsunel, hantardetsunel, luroutiun (լռել, լռեցնել, Հանդարտեցնել, լռութիւն)
husk - geghev, badij, geghevel (կեղեւ, պատիճ, կեղեւել)
husky - khurbod, geghevod (խռպոտ, կեղեւոտ)
hussy - anbadiv gin (անպատիւ կին)
hustle - ajabarel, hurel, hurmushdugel (աճապարել, Հրել, Հրմշտկել)
hut - dunag, khurjit, hiugh (տնակ, խրճիթ, Հիւղ)
hutch - sundoug, argugh, vantag, dagar, argughel (սնտուկ, արկղ, վանդակ, տակառ, արկղել)
hyacinth - hagint, sumpoul (յակինթ, սմբուլ)
hydraulic - churapashkhagan (ջրաբաշխական)
hydraulics - churapashghoutiun (ջրաբաշխութիւն)
hydrogen - churadzin (ջրածին)
hyena - poreni (բորենի)
hygiene - aroghchabahoutiun (առողջապահութիւն)
hymen - gousataghant (կուսաթաղանդ)
hymn - orhnerk, koverk, parapanel, koverkel (օրՀներգ, գովերգ, փառաբանել, գովերգել)
hype - uzkednel, uzkednoum (զգետնել, զգետնում)
hyperbole - chapazantsoutiun, anturatsik (չափազանցութիւն, անդրաձիգ)
hyphen - zotakidz, kudzig, zotakudzel (զօդագիծ, գծիկ, զօդագծել)
hypnosis - kunakhd, hibnos (քնախտ, Հիպնոս)
hypnotherapy - hibnosapouzhoum (Հիպնոսաբուժում)
hypnotism - kunadzoutiun, kunaperoutiun (քնածութիւն, քնաբերութիւն)
hypnotist - kunadzou, hiubnosatsogh, kunatsogh (քնածու, Հիւպնոսացող, քնացող)

hypnotize - *kunadzel, hiubnosatsunel* (քնածել, Հիւպնոսացնել)
hypocrisy - *geghdzavoroutiun* (կեղծաւորութիւն)
hypocrite - *geghdzavor* (կեղծաւոր)
hypothecate - *kuravi tunel* (գրաւի դնել)
hypothesis - *vargadz, yentatroutiun* (վարկած, ենթադրութիւն)
hysteria - *chughakaroutiun, arkantakheght* (ջղագարութիւն, արգանդախեղդ)
hysteritis - *arkantadab* (արգանդատապ)

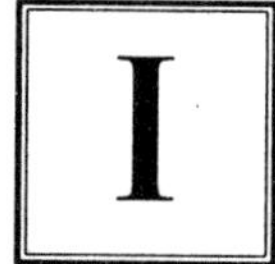

Iberian Peninsula - *iberagan teraghughzi* (Իպերական Թերակղզի)
ice - *sar, sarouyts, saretsunel, sartsabadel* (սառ, սառոյց, սառեցնել, սառցապատել)
ice cream - *baghbaghag* (պաղպաղակ)
iceberg - *sarnaler, sarnagouyd* (սառնալեռ, սառնակոյտ)
iceman - *baghbaghagavajar* (պաղպաղակավաճառ)
iceness - *sarnoutiun* (սառնութիւն)
icon - *surpanugar, badger* (սրբանկար, պատկեր)
icy - *sartsabad, sarouytse* (սառցապատ, սառոյցէ)
idea - *kaghapar, midk, gardzik, mudabadger* (գաղափար, միտք, կարծիք, մտապատկեր)
ideal - *ideal, mudadibar, deslagan, yerevagayagan* (իտէալ, մտատիպար, տեսլական, երեւակայական)
idealism - *kaghaparabashdoutiun* (գաղափարապաշտութիւն)
idealist - *kaghaparabashd, idealabashd* (գաղափարապաշտ, իտէալապաշտ)
idealogic - *kaghaparakhosagan* (գաղափարախօսական)
identic - *nouyn, miyevnouyn, nouynaman, nouynorinag* (նոյն, միեւնոյն, նոյնանման, նոյնօրինակ)
identification - *usdoukoum, nouynatsoum, inknoutian hasdadoum* (ստուգում, նոյնացում, ինքնութեան հաստատում)
identify - *usdoukel, janchnal, inknoutiunu hasdadel* (ստուգել, ճանչնալ, ինքնութիւնը հաստատել)
identity - *inknoutiun, nouynoutiun* (ինքնութիւն, նոյնութիւն)
ideogram - *kaghaparakir, nushanakir* (գաղափարագիր, նշանագիր)
ideology - *kaghaparakhosoutiun* (գաղափարախօսութիւն)
idiocy - *dukhmaroutiun, aboushoutiun* (տխմարութիւն, ապուշութիւն)
idiom - *parpar, lezou, khosvadzk, kavaraparpar* (բարբառ, լեզու, խօսուածք, գաւառաբարբառ)
idiomatic - *hadgapanagan, parparayin* (յատկաբանական, բարբառային)
idiot - *dukhmar, aboush, himar* (տխմար, ապուշ, յիմար)
idiotism - *himaroutiun* (յիմարութիւն)
idiotize - *himaranal* (յիմարանալ)
idle - *dzouyl, ankordz, barab, anshah* (ծոյլ, անգործ, պարապ, անշահ)
idol - *gourk, bashdamounki ararga* (կուռք, պաշտամունքի առարկայ)
idolater - *gurabashd, yergurbakou, bashdogh* (կռապաշտ, երկրպագու, պաշտող)
idolatry - *gurabashdoutiun, bashdoum* (կռապաշտութիւն, պաշտում)
idolize - *yergurbakel, asdvadzatsunel, gourk bashdel* (երկրպագել, աստուածացնել, կուռք պաշտել)

idyll, idyl - *hoverkoutiun, sirerkoutiun* (Հովուերգութիւն, սիրերգութիւն)
if - *yete, te vor* (եթէ, թէ որ)
ignite - *varel, purungil, ayril, potsavaril* (վառել, բռնկիլ, այրիլ, բոցավառիլ)
ignition - *varoum, gizoum, inknasharzhi hurargoutiun* (վառում, կիզում, ինքնաշարժի հրարկութիւն)
ignoble - *anark, anbadiv, usdor, tsadz, kurehig* (անարգ, անպատիւ, ստոր, ցած, գռեհիկ)
ignominious - *khaydarag, amotali* (խայտառակ, ամօթալի)
ignominy - *anbadvoutiun, khaydaragoutiun* (անպատուութիւն, խայտառակութիւն)
ignorance - *dukidoutiun, ankidoutiun* (տգիտութիւն, անգիտութիւն)
ignorant - *duked, andeghiag, ankidag* (տգէտ, անտեղեակ, անգիտակ)
ignore - *ankidanal, chukidnal, andesel* (անգիտանալ, չգիտնալ, անտեսել)
ilk - *nouyn, miyevnouyn, iurakanchiur* (նոյն, միեւնոյն, իւրաքանչիւր)
ill - *hivant, vunas, charik, anbidan, vad* (հիւանդ, վնաս, չարիք, անպիտան, վատ)
illegal - *aborini, aboren, hagaorinagan* (ապօրինի, ապօրէն, հակաօրինական)
illegible - *anunternli, chugartatsvogh* (անընթեռնլի, չկարդացուող)
illegitimate - *aborini, khort, anorinagan, aborinadzin* (ապօրինի, խորթ, անօրինական, ապօրինածին)
illiberal - *neghmid, hedamunats, gudzdzi, zhulad* (նեղմիտ, յետամնաց, կծծի, ժլատ)
illicit - *aborini, arkilvadz* (ապօրինի, արգիլուած)
illimited - *ansahman, anverch* (անսահման, անվերջ)
illiterate - *anous, ankuraked* (անուս, անգրագէտ)
illness - *hivantoutiun, dugaroutiun* (հիւանդութիւն, տկարութիւն)
illogical - *anduramapanagan* (անտրամաբանական)
illuminate - *lousavorel, lousazartel, lousapanel* (լուսաւորել, լուսազարդել, լուսաբանել)
illumination - *lousavoroum, huravaroutiun* (լուսաւորում, հրավառութիւն)
illuminator - *lousavorich* (լուսաւորիչ)
illumine - *lousavorel, lousazartel* (լուսաւորել, լուսազարդել)
illure - *humayel, hurabourel, khapel* (հմայել, հրապուրել, խաբել)
illusion - *badrank, khapgank, yerazank, tsunork* (պատրանք, խաբկանք, երազանք, ցնորք)
illusionist - *tsunorades, yerazades* (ցնորատես, երազատես)
illustrate - *badgerazartel, lousapanel, nushanavor* (պատկերազարդել, լուսաբանել, նշանաւոր)
illustration - *badgerazartoum, badger, nugar, lousapanoum* (պատկերազարդում, պատկեր, նկար, լուսաբանում)
illustrator - *badgerazartogh, lousapanogh* (պատկերազարդող, լուսաբանող)
image - *nugar, badger, nugarel, badgerel* (նկար, պատկեր, նկարել, պատկերել)
imaginable - *yerevagayeli* (երեւակայելի)
imaginary - *yerevagayagan, tsunoragan* (երեւակայական, ցնորական)
imagination - *yerevagayoutiun, mudabadger, tsunork* (երեւակայութիւն, մտապատկեր, ցնորք)
imagine - *yerevagayel, hunarel, badgeratsunel* (երեւակայել, հնարել, պատկերացնել)
imbank - *toump shinel* (թումբ շինել)
imbecile - *aboush, dukhmar, dugaramid* (ապուշ, տխմար, տկարամիտ)
imbibe - *dzudzel, tatkhel, turchel* (ծծել, թաթխել, թրջել)
imbitter - *dukhretsunel, tarnatsunel*

(տխրեցնել, զառնացնել)
imborder - yezerel (եզերել)
imbosk - dzadzgel, taktsunel, takchil (ծածկել, թաքցնել, թաքչիլ)
imbosom - voghchakourel, kurgel, kourkoural (ողջագուրել, գրկել, գուրգուրալ)
imbound - sahmanapagel (սահմանափակել)
imbrue - turchel, tatakhel, kounavorel, pudzavorel (թրջել, թաթախել, գունաւորել, բծաւորել)
imbue - letsnel, nergel, dokorel, haketsunel (լեցնել, ներկել, տոգորել, յագեցնել)
imitable - numaneli, hedeveli (նմանելի, հետեւելի)
imitate - numanil, orinagel, geghdzel, hedevil (նմանիլ, օրինակել, կեղծել, հետեւիլ)
imitation - numanoutiun, hedevoghoutiun, untorinagoum (նմանութիւն, հետեւողութիւն, ընդօրինակում)
imitator - numanogh, hedevogh, untorinagogh (նմանող, հետեւող, ընդօրինակող)
immaculate - anarad, anpidz, sourp, makour (անարատ, անբիծ, սուրբ, մաքուր)
immanent - nerkin, anpazhan, nerhadoug, munayoun (ներքին, անբաժան, ներյատուկ, մնայուն)
immask - dzadzgel, timagel (ծածկել, դիմակել)
immature - duhas, khag, terhas (տհաս, խակ, դեռհաս)
immediate - anmichagan, oughghagi, anhabagh (անմիջական, ուղղակի, անյապաղ)
immediately - anmichabes, shoudov, isgouyn (անմիջապէս, շուտով, իսկոյն)
immemorial - vaghemi, anhishadag, hunakouyn (վաղեմի, անյիշատակ, հնագոյն)
immense - ansahman, anhoun, anchap (անսահման, անհուն, անչափ)
immensity - anhounoutiun, ansahmanoutiun (անհունութիւն, անսահմանութիւն)
immerge - tatkhel, mukhurjel, souzil (թաթխել, մխրճել, սուզիլ)
immerse - ungughmel, mukherjel, churasouzel (ընկղմել, մխրճել, ջրասուզել)
immigrant - kaghtagan, noreg (գաղթական, նորեկ)
immigrate - kaghtel, kaghtagan kal, bantukhdanal (գաղթել, գաղթական գալ, պանդխտանալ)
immigration - nerkaght, kaghtaganoutiun, bantukhdoutiun (ներգաղթ, գաղթականութիւն, պանդխտութիւն)
imminent - modaloud, modig, verahas (մօտալուտ, մօտիկ, վերահաս)
imminution - nuvazoum (նուազում)
immobile - ansharzh (անշարժ)
immobility - ansharzhoutiun (անշարժութիւն)
immobilize - ansharzhatsunel (անշարժացնել)
immoderate - chapazants, dzayrahegh, anzousb (չափազանց, ծայրայեղ, անզուսպ)
immodest - anhamesd, anbargeshd (անհամեստ, անպարկեշտ)
immolate - zohaperel, zohel (զոհաբերել, զոհել)
immolation - zohaperoutiun, zoh (զոհաբերութիւն, զոհ)
immoral - anparoyagan, anbargeshd, anarag (անբարոյական, անպարկեշտ, անառակ)
immortal - anmah, haverzhagan, anants (անմահ, յաւերժական, անանց)
immortality - anmahoutiun, haverzhoutiun (անմահութիւն, յաւերժութիւն)
immortalize - anmahatsunel, haverzhatsunel (անմահացնել, յաւերժացնել)
immune - akhdamerzh, varagazerdz (ախտամերժ, վարակազերծ)
immunity - anvaragelioutiun (անվարակելիութիւն)
immunization - badvasdoum, akhdazerdzel (պատուաստել, ախտազերծել)

immunize - akhdazerdzel, varagazerdzel (ախտազերծել, վարակազերծել)
immure - badel, shurchapagel, pandargel (պատել, շրջափակել, բանտարկել)
immutable - anpopokh, anpopokheli, ansasan (անփոփոխ, անփոփոխելի, անսասան)
immute - pokhel, popokhel (փոխել, փոփոխել)
imp - sadanayi tsak, tev, voki, charajuji (սատանայի ձագ, դեւ, ոգի, չարաճճի)
impact - harvadz, pakhoum, zarg, seghmel, tukhmel (հարուած, բախում, զարկ, սեղմել, թխմել)
impair - dugaratsunel, bagsetsunel, nuvazoum, vunas (տկարացնել, պակսեցնել, նուազում, վնաս)
impale - dzagel, khotsel, shampurel tsutsaharel (ծակել, խոցել, շամփրել, ցցահարել)
impalpable - anshoshapeli, anhubeli (անշօշափելի, անհպելի)
impalsy - antamaloudzel, chuladel, mertsunel (անդամալուծել, ջլատել, մեռցնել)
impart - haghortel, dal, shunorhel, undzayel (հաղորդել, տալ, շնորհել, ընծայել)
impartial - angoghmnagal, anachar (անկողմնակալ, անաչառ)
impass - pagoughi, anel jampa (փակուղի, անել ճամբայ)
impassable - anantsaneli (անանցանելի)
impatience - anhamperoutiun (անհամբերութիւն)
impatient - anhamper, anhantard (անհամբեր, անհանդարտ)
impeach - ampasdanel, vargapegel, meghatrel, gasgadzil (ամբաստանել, վարկաբեկել, մեղադրել, կասկածիլ)
impeachment - meghatrank, ampasdanoum (մեղադրանք, ամբաստանում)
impeccable - anteri, gadarial, anmeghanchagan (անթերի, կատարեալ, անմեղանչական)
impecunious - chukavor, aghkad, turam chounetsogh (չքաւոր, աղքատ, դրամ չունեցող)
impede - khapanel, khankarel, arkilel (խափանել, խանգարել, արգիլել)
impediment - arkelk, khochuntod, tuzhvaroutiun (արգելք, խոչընդոտ, դժուարութիւն)
impel - mughel, turtel, usdibel, kushel, varel (մղել, դրդել, ստիպել, քշել, վարել)
impend - vuran gakhvil, jojel, usbarnal (վրան կախուիլ, ճօճել, սպառնալ)
impendence - usbarnalik, modaloud vudank (սպառնալիք, մօտալուտ վտանգ)
impendent - usbarnatsogh, verahas, modaloud (սպառնացող, վերահաս, մօտալուտ)
impending - modaloud, usbarnagan (մօտալուտ, սպառնական)
impenetrable - antapants, anantsaneli, khorimats (անթափանց, անանցանելի, խորիմաց)
imperative - huramayagan, usdiboghagan, bardavorich (հրամայական, ստիպողական, պարտաւորիչ)
imperator - gaysur (կայսր)
imperfect - angadar, teri, bagasavor (անկատար, թերի, պակասաւոր)
imperial - gayseragan, arkayagan, vusem, pokur morouk (կայսերական, արքայական, վսեմ, փոքր մօրուք)
imperialism - gayserabashdoutiun (կայսերապաշտութիւն)
imperialist - gayserabashd, gayseragan (կայսերապաշտ, կայսերական)
imperil - vudankel, vudanki yentargel (վտանգել, վտանգի ենթարկել)
imperious - ishkhanagan, diragan, medzashouk, koroz (իշխանական, տիրական, մեծաշուք, գոռոզ)
imperishable - angoruncheli, anants, mushdunchenagan (անկորնչելի, անանց, մշտնջենական)

impermeable - antapants, anchurantsig, antsurevanots (անթափանց, անջրանցիկ, անձրեւանոց)
impersonal - anantsnagan, anachar, timagazourg, antem (անանձնական, անաչառ, դիմակազուրկ, անդէմ)
impersonate - antsnavorel, marmnavorel, nergayatsunel (անձնաւորել, մարմնաւորել, ներկայացնել)
impertinence - aneresoutiun, lurpoutiun, gobdoutiun (աներեսութիւն, լրբութիւն, կոպտութիւն)
impertinent - aneres, lirp, anbadgar (աներես, լիրբ, անպատկառ)
imperturbable - ankhurov, anvurtov, anshupot (անխռով, անվրդով, անշփոթ)
impervious - antapantseli, anantsaneli (անթափանցելի, անանցանելի)
impetuous - ouzhkin, suruntats, pourun, anzousb (ուժգին, սրընթաց, բուռն, անզուսպ)
impiety - anhavadoutiun, anguronoutiun (անհաւատութիւն, անկրօնութիւն)
impious - anguron, amparishd (անկրօն, ամբարիշտ)
implant - dungel, mudtsunel, nermoudzel (տնկել, մտցնել, ներմուծել)
implantation - dungoum, armadavoroum (տնկում, արմատաւորում)
implement - kordzik, bidouyk, sark (գործիք, պիտոյք, սարք)
implicate - shaghel, kharnel, gunjurodel (շաղել, խառնել, կնճռոտել)
implicit - dzadzoug, lurelyayn, takoun (ծածուկ, լռելեայն, թաքուն)
imploration - aghersank, khunturank, haytsoum (աղերսանք, խնդրանք, հայցում)
implore - aghersel, khunturel, haytsel (աղերսել, խնդրել, հայցել)
imply - agnargel, hasgutsunel, nushanagel (ակնարկել, հասկցնել, նշանակել)
impolite - angirt, ankaghakavar (անկիրթ, անքաղաքավար)
imponderable - angushreli, angushir (անկշռելի, անկշիռ)
import - neradzel, mudtsunel, nermoudzoum (ներածել, մտցնել, ներմուծում)
importance - garevoroutiun (կարեւորութիւն)
important - garevor, lourch, dzanur, aztetsig (կարեւոր, լուրջ, ծանր, ազդեցիկ)
importation - neradzoum (ներածում)
importunate - tsantsurali, aneres, gubchoun, daghdugali (ձանձրալի, աներես, կպչուն, տաղտկալի)
importune - tsantsuratsunel, neghel, daghdugatsunel (ձանձրացնել, նեղել, տաղտկացնել)
impose - bardaturel, hargaturel, pernavorel (պարտադրել, հարկադրել, բեռնաւորել)
imposer - hargaturogh (հարկադրող)
imposing - bardatrogh, badgareli, dubavorich (պարտադրող, պատկառելի, տպաւորիչ)
imposition - harg, dourk, tsernatroutiun, echaturoum (հարկ, տուրք, ձեռնադրութիւն, էջադրում)
impossible - angareli, anhunarin (անկարելի, անհնարին)
impost - harg, maksadourk, maks tunel (հարկ, մաքսատուրք, մաքս դնել)
impostor - khapepa, khachakogh (խաբեբայ, խաչագող)
imposture - khapeoutiun, nenkoutiun (խաբէութիւն, նենգութիւն)
impotence - angaroghoutiun, amloutiun (անկարողութիւն, ամլութիւն)
impotent - angarogh, amoul, dugar, anzor (անկարող, ամուլ, տկար, անզօր)
impound - arkilapagel (արգիլափակել)
impoverish - aghkadatsunel, dugaratsunel (աղքատացնել, տկարացնել)
impraticable - ankordznagan, anirakordzeli (անգործնական, անիրագործելի)
imprecate - anidzel, nuzovel (անիծել, նզովել)
impregnable - anmadcheli, anarig (անմատչելի, անառիկ)

impregnate - *hughianal, peghmunavorel, hughanal, hughi* (յղիանալ, բեղմնաւորել, յղանալ, յղի)

impregnation - *hughoutiun, peghmunavoroum, hughatsoum* (յղութիւն, բեղմնաւորում, յղացում)

impresario - *taderabed, taderavar, tsernargou* (թատերապետ, թատերավար, ձեռնարկու)

impress - *dubavorel, turoshmel, dubel, aztel, turoshm* (տպաւորել, դրոշմել, տպել, ազդել, դրոշմ)

impression - *dubavoroutiun, dubakroutiun, dubakanag, hedk* (տպաւորութիւն, տպագրութիւն, տպաքանակ, հետք)

imprest - *gankhavujar, gankhavarts* (կանխավճառ, կանխավարձ)

imprint - *dubel, gunkel, turoshmel, gunik, hedk* (տպել, կնքել, դրոշմել, կնիք, հետք)

imprison - *pandargel, pandel* (բանտարկել, բանտել)

imprisonment - *pandargoutiun* (բանտարկութիւն)

improbable - *anhavanagan* (անհաւանական)

improbity - *anoughghamudoutiun, anaznououtiun* (անուղղամտութիւն, անազնուութիւն

impromptu - *hanbadrasdits yerk, hanbadrasdits* (յանպատրաստից երգ, յանպատրաստից)

improper - *anharmar, andeghi, anvayel, sukhal* (անյարմար, անտեղի, անվայել, սխալ)

improve - *paregarkel, parvokel, zarkatsunel* (բարեկարգել, բարւոքել, զարգացնել)

improvement - *parelavoum, lavatsoum* (բարելաւում, լաւացում)

improvident - *ankhohem, anhok, anuzkouysh* (անխոհեմ, անհոգ, անզգոյշ)

improvisation - *hangardzapanoutiun, badrasdapanoutiun* (յանկարծաբանութիւն, պատրաստաբանութիւն)

improvisator - *hangardzapan, hangardzerkag* (յանկարծաբան, յանկարծերգակ)

improvise - *hangardzapanel, hanbadrasdits horinel* (յանկարծաբանել, յանպատրաստից յօրինել)

imprudent - *ankhohem, anuzkouysh, ankhorhourt* (անխոհեմ, անզգոյշ, անխորհուրդ)

impudence - *anamotoutiun, anbadgaroutiun, lurpoutiun* (անամօթութիւն, անպատկառութիւն, լրբութիւն)

impudent - *aneres, lirp, anbargeshd* (աներես, լիրբ, անպարկեշտ)

impuissance - *angaroghoutiun, anzoroutiun* (անկարողութիւն, անզօրութիւն)

impulse - *mughoum, turtoum, zarg* (մղում, դրդում, զարկ)

impulsive - *mughich, turtich, khutanogh* (մղիչ, դրդիչ, խթանող)

impure - *anmakour, geghdod, abaganel* (անմաքուր, կեղտոտ, ապականել)

imputation - *verakuroum, meghaturank, khudzpudzoum* (վերագրում, մեղադրանք, խծբծում)

impute - *meghatrel, verakrel, hashvekurel* (մեղադրել, վերագրել, հաշուեգրել)

in - *mech, ners, nersu* (մէջ, ներս, ներսը)

inability - *angaroughoutiun, anuntounagoutiun* (անկարողութիւն, անընդունակութիւն)

inaccessible - *anmadcheli, anmertsenali, anhubeli* (անմատչելի, անմերձենալի, անհպելի)

inaccurate - *sukhal, anjishd* (սխալ, անճիշդ)

inaction - *ankordzouneoutiun, ankordzoutiun* (անգործունէութիւն, անգործութիւն)

inactive - *ankordzounia, ankordz, ankordzon* (անգործունեայ, անգործ, անգործօն)

inactivity - *ankordzouneoutiun* (անգործունէութիւն)

inadequate - *teri, angadar, anadag* (թերի, անկատար, անատակ)

inadmissible - *anuntouneli, anhantourzheli* (անընդունելի, անհան-

դուրժելի)
inadvertence - anuzkoushoutiun, anhokoutiun (անզգուշութիւն, անհոգութիւն)
inalterable - anaylayl, anpopokhagan (անայլայլ, անփոփոխական)
inane - tadarg, annubadag, animasd, sunamech (դատարկ, աննպատակ, անիմաստ, սնամէջ)
inanimate - angentan, anshounch, angiank (անկենդան, անշունչ, անկեանք)
inanimation - angentanoutiun (անկենդանութիւն)
inanity - tadargoutiun, anmudoutiun (դատարկութիւն, անմտութիւն)
inapplicable - ankordzadzeli, angirargeli, anharmar (անգործածելի, անկիրարկելի, անյարմար)
inappreciation - terakunahadoum (թերագնահատում)
inappropriate - anbadshaj, anharmar (անպատշաճ, անյարմար)
inapt - anuntounag, angarogh, anjarag (անընդունակ, անկարող, անճարակ)
inasmuch - kani vor, nugadelov vor, vorovhedev (քանի որ, նկատելով որ, որովհետեւ)
inattention - anoushatroutiun (անուշադրութիւն)
inattentive - anoushatir, tsurvadz (անուշադիր, ցրուած)
inaudible - anluseli, antsayn (անլսելի, անձայն)
inaugurate - patsoum gadarel, odzel, usgusil (բացում կատարել, օծել, սկսիլ)
inauguration - patsoum, odzoum (բացում, օծում)
inborn - punadzin, punadour, punagan, untodzin (բնածին, բնատուր, բնական, ընդոծին)
inbound - arduni, sahmanen ners (առտնին, սահմանէն ներս)
incalculable - anhashveli, anhamar, anhashiv (անհաշուելի, անհամար, անհաշիւ)
incandesce - shiganal, shigatsunel (շիկանալ, շիկացնել)
incandescence - hurashegoutiun, shigatsoum (հրաշէկութիւն, շիկացում)
incandescent - hurasheg, huraporp, shigatsadz (հրաշէկ, հրաբորբ, շիկացած)
incantation - tiutank, tovchoutiun, gakhartank (դիւթանք, թովչութիւն, կախարդանք)
incapability - angaroghoutiun, anuntounagoutiun (անկարողութիւն, անընդունակութիւն)
incapable - angarogh, anuntounag, anjarag (անկարող, անընդունակ, անճարակ)
incapacity - angaroughoutiun, anjaragoutiun (անկարողութիւն, անճարակութիւն)
incarcerate - pandargel, arkelapagel (բանտարկել, արգելափակել)
incarn - marmunavorel, marmunavoril (մարմնաւորել, մարմնաւորիլ)
incarnate - marmunatsunel, martatsunel, marmunavor (մարմնացընել, մարդացնել, մարմնաւոր)
incarnation - marteghoutiun, marmunavoroum (մարդեղութիւն, մարմնաւորում)
incend - potsavarel, ardzardzel (բոցավառել, արծարծել)
incendiary - hurtsik, hurtehogh, khurovarar (հրձիգ, հրդեհող, խռովարար)
incense - khungargel, koverkel, porpokel, khoung, kovesd (խնկարկել, գովերգել, բորբոքել, խունկ, գովեստ))
incentive - kurkurich, mughich, turtich, kachalerich (գրգռիչ, մղիչ, դրդիչ, քաջալերիչ)
inception - usgizp, nakhatsernoutiun (սկիզբ, նախաձեռնութիւն)
incertitude - anoroshoutiun, dardamoutiun (անորոշութիւն, տարտամութիւն)
incessant - antatar, anunthad (անդադար, անընդհատ)
incest - azkabughdzoutiun, ariunabughdzoutiun (ազգապղծութիւն, արիւնապղծութիւն)

inch - madnachap, gughzyag (մատնաչափ, կղզեակ)
incidence - badahar, tebk, untkurgoum, angoum (պատահար, դէպք, ընդգրկում, անկում)
incident - tebk, badahmounk, michateb, tibvadz (դէպք, պատահմունք, միջադէպ, դիպուած)
incinerate - mokhratsunel, ajiunatsunel, ayrel (մոխրացնել, աճիւնացնել, այրել)
incipience - usgizp, usguzpnavoroutiun (սկիզբ, սկզբնաւորութիւն)
incipient - usgusvogh, noradzak, norahasdad (սկսուող, նորածագ, նորահաստատ)
incise - jeghkel, gudrel, porakurel (ճեղքել, կտրել, փորագրել)
incite - kurkurel, turtel, khutanel (գրգռել, դրդել, խթանել)
incitement - khurakouys, kurkuroum, turtoum (խրախոյս, գրգռում, դրդում)
inclination - khonarhoum, tekoum, hagoum, hozharoutiun (խոնարհում, թեքում, հակում, յօժարութիւն)
incline - khonarhil, hagil, dzuril, midil (խոնարհիլ, հակիլ, ծռիլ, միտիլ)
inclose - see – տե՛ս (enclose)
inclosure - see – տե՛ս (enclosure)
include - povantagel, barounagel (բովանդակել, պարունակել)
including - nerarial, nerpag (ներառեալ, ներփակ)
inclusion - nerpagoum, neraroutiun (ներփակում, ներառութիւն)
incognito - andzanot, kaghdni, dzubdial (անծանօթ, գաղտնի, ծպտեալ)
incoherent - angab, angabagits, anharir (անկապ, անկապակից, անյարիր)
income - yegamoud, hasouyt, moudk (եկամուտ, հասոյթ, մուտք)
income tax - yegamudaharg, yegamoudi dourk (եկամտահարկ, եկամուտի տուրք)
incoming - zhamanoum, moudk, yegamoud, norahas (ժամանում, մուտք, եկամպուտ, նորահաս)
incommode - anhankusdatsunel, neghel, neghoutiun (անհանգստացնել, նեղել, նեղութիւն)
incommodity - neghoutiun, anharmaroutiun (նեղութիւն, անյարմարութիւն)
incomparable - anpaghtadeli, annuman (անբաղդատելի, աննման)
incompatible - anhashd, anmiapaneli, nerhag (անհաշտ, անմիաբանելի, ներհակ)
incompetence - angaroghoutiun, anadagoutiun (անկարողութիւն, անատակութիւն)
incompetent - angarogh, anhumoud, antsernhas (անկարող, անհմուտ, անձեռնհաս)
incomplete - angadar, teri, anavard (անկատար, թերի, անաւարտ)
incomprehensible - anhasgunali, animanali (անհասկնալի, անիմանալի)
incomprehension - anhasgatsoghoutiun (անհասկացողութիւն)
inconceivable - anumpurneli, animanali, anhas (անըմբռնելի, անիմանալի, անհաս)
inconnu - andzanot (անծանօթ)
inconsiderable - annugadeli, angarevor, annushan, chunchin (աննկատելի, անկարեւոր, աննշան, չնչին)
inconsiderate - anpapganugad, ankhohem (անփափկանկատ, անխոհեմ)
inconsistence - angayounoutiun, angabagtsoutiun (անկայունութիւն, անկապակցութիւն)
inconsistent - angayoun, anhasdad, popokhamid (անկայուն, անհաստատ, փոփոխամիտ)
inconsolable - anmukhitar, anmukhitareli, anuspopeli (անմխիթար, անմխիթարելի, անսփոփելի)
inconstant - angayoun, popokhagan (անկայուն, փոփոխական)
incontestable - anvijeli, anherkeli (անվիճելի, անհերքելի)
inconvenient - anharmar, anbadshaj, anbadeh (անյարմար, անպատշաճ, անպատեհ)
incorporate - miavorel, miatsunel, miakharnel, miatsoulel (միաւորել,

միացնել, միախառնել, միաձուլել)
incorporation - mioutiun, gazmagerboutiun, miavoroum (միութիւն, կազմակերպութիւն, միաւորում)
incorrect - sukhal, anjinsht, tiur (սխալ, անճիշդ, թիւր)
incorrigible - ansurpakreli, anoughgha (անսրբագրելի, անուղղայ)
incorrupt - anarad, anpidz, angashar (անարատ, անբիծ, անկաշառ)
increase - aveltsunel, ajil, shadtsunel, aj, haveloum (աւելցնել, աճիլ, շատցնել, աճ, յաւելում)
incredible - anhavadali, anhavanagan (անհաւատալի, անհաւանական)
increment - aj, haveloum, untlaynoum (աճ, յաւելում, ընդլայնում)
incroyable - anhavadali, darorinag (անհաւատալի, տարօրինակ)
incrustation - geghev, badian, khav, turvakoum (կեղեւ, պատեան, խաւ, դրուագում)
incubate - tukhsel, pazmatsunel (թխսել, բազմացնել)
inculcate - mudaturoshmel, dubavorel (մտադրոշմել, տպաւորել)
incur - yentarguvil, gurel (ենթարկուիլ, կրել)
incurable - anpouzheli, antarman (անբուժելի, անդարման)
incursion - arshavank, asbadagoutiun, hartsagoum (արշաւանք, ասպատակութիւն, յարձակում)
indebt - bardavorel (պարտաւորել)
indebted - bardagan, bardavorial, yerakhdabard (պարտական, պարտաւորեալ, երախտապարտ)
indecent - anbargeshd, anmakour, anvayel, anbadiv (անպարկեշտ, անմաքուր, անվայել, անպատիւ)
indecision - anoroshoutiun, yergmudoutiun, varanoum (անորոշութիւն, երկմտութիւն, վարանում)
indeed - artarev, anshoushd, isgabes (արդարեւ, անշուշտ, իսկապէս)
indefatigable - chuhoknogh, ankhonch (չյոգնող, անխոնջ)
indefinite - anorosh, dardam, ansahman (անորոշ, տարտամ, անսահման)
indelible - anchuncheli, chavruvogh, anmoranali (անջնջելի, չաւրուող, անմոռանալի)
indelicate - anpapganugad, goshd, annurpanugad (անփափկանկատ, կոշտ, աննրբանկատ)
indemnify - hadoutsanel, vunasu vujarel (հատուցանել, վնասը վճարել)
indemnity - ashkhadanki hadoutsoum, vunasouts hadoutsoum (աշխատանքի հատուցում, վնասուց հատուցում)
indent (n) - abusburank, huraman, bayman, bardatoukhd (ապսպրանք, հրաման, պայման, պարտաթուղթ)
indent (v) - adamnavorel, abusburel, doghu nersen sharel (ատամնաւորել, ապսպրել, տողը ներսէն շարել)
independence - angakhoutiun, inknavaroutiun (անկախութիւն, ինքնավարութիւն)
independent - angakh, inknavar, azad (անկախ, ինքնավար, ազատ)
indescribable - annugarakreli (աննկարագրելի)
indeterminate - anorosh, dardam, choroshvadz (անորոշ, տարտամ, չորոշուած)
indetermination - anoroshoutiun, varanoum (անորոշութիւն, վարանում)
index - tsoutsag, tsang, povantagoutiun, tsoutsagakrel (ցուցակ, ցանկ, բովանդակութիւն, ցուցակագրել)
India - huntgasdan (Հնդկաստան)
indian - huntig, huntgagan (Հնդիկ, Հնդկական)
indicate - tsoutsnel, nushel, madnanushel, haydnel (ցուցնել, նշել, մատնանշել, յայտնել)
indication - madnanushoum, nushoum, tsoutsmounk (մատնանշում, նշում, ցուցմունք)
indicator - tsoutsnogh, tsoutsag, madnich (ցուցնող, ցուցակ, մատնիչ)
indice - tsoutsag, tsang, tsouts-

mounk, nushan (ցուցակ, ցանկ, ցուցմունք, նշան)
indict - ampasdanel, meghaturel (ամբաստանել, մեղադրել)
indictor - ampasdanich (ամպաստանիչ)
indifference - andarperoutiun, anuzkayoutiun (անտարբերութիւն, անզգայութիւն)
indifferent - andarper, anuzka (անտարբեր, անզգայ)
indigence - aghkadoutiun, chukavoroutiun (աղքատութիւն, չքաւորութիւն)
indigene - deghatsi, punig (տեղացի, բնիկ)
indigenous - deghagan, punig, punagan (տեղական, բնիկ, բնական)
indigent - aghkad, chukavor, garikavor (աղքատ, չքաւոր, կարիքաւոր)
indigestible - anmarseli, tuzhvaramars (անմարսելի, դժուարամարս)
indigestion - anmarsoghoutiun, tuzhvaramarsoutiun (անմարսողութիւն, դժուարամարսութիւն)
indignant - zayratsadz, vurtovadz (զայրացած, վրդոված)
indignation - zayrouyt, tsasoum (զայրոյթ, ցասում)
indignity - arhamarhank, viravorank (արհամարհանք, վիրաւորանք)
indigo - leghag (լեղակ)
indirect - anoughghagi, sheghagi, goghmunagi (անուղղակի, շեղակի, կողմնակի)
indiscreet - ankhohem, ankhorhourt (անխոհեմ, անխորհուրդ)
indiscretion - ankhohemoutiun, anuzkoushoutiun (անխոհեմութիւն, անզգուշութիւն)
indiscriminate - ankhudir, kharnag, shupot (անխտիր, խառնակ, շփոթ)
indiscrimination - ankhudraganoutiun (անխտրականութիւն)
indispensable - anhurazheshd, hargavor (անհրաժեշտ, հարկաւոր)
indispose - anhankusdatsunel, neghatsunel (անհանգստացնել, նեղացնել)
indisposition - anduramatroutiun, anhankusdoutiun (անտրամադրութիւն, անհանգստութիւն)
indisputable - anvijeli, patsorosh (անվիճելի, բացորոշ)
indissoluble - anlouydz, anloudzeli, ankagdeli (անլոյծ, անլուծելի, անքակտելի)
indite - sharatrel, yergasirel, kertel (շարադրել, երկասիրել, քերթել)
individual - anhadagan, ourouyn, anhad, ants (անհատական, ուրոյն, անհատ, անձ)
individualism - anhadabashdoutiun, anhadaganoutiun (անհատապաշտութիւն, անհատականութիւն)
individuality - anhadaganoutiun, inknourounoutiun (անհատականութիւն, ինքնուրոյնութիւն)
indivisible - anpazhaneli (անբաժանելի)
indoctrinate - ousoutsanel, vartabedel (ուսուցանել, վարդապետել)
indolence - toulamortoutiun, anhokoutiun (թուլամորթութիւն, անհոգութիւն)
indolent - anuzka, anpouyt, anhok, andarper, toulamort (անզգայ, անփոյթ, անհոգ, անտարբեր, թուլամորթ)
indomitable - anbardeli, annuvajeli, anhaghteli (անպարտելի, աննուաճելի, անյաղթելի)
indoor - nersi, ardunin, nersu (ներսի, առտնին, ներսը)
indorse - see - տե՛ս (endorse)
indorsee - pokhantsagal (փոխանցակալ)
indorser - pokhantsakurogh (փոխանցագրող)
Indo-European - hunt-yevrobagan (Հնդ-եւրոպական)
indubitable - angasgadz, angasgadzeli, vusdah (անկասկած, անկասկածելի, վստահ)
induce - badjarel, mughel, turtel, khutanel (պատճառել, մղել, դրդել, խթանել)
induct - deghavorel, bashdoni nushanagel, nusdetsunel (տեղաւորել, պաշտօնի նշանակել, նստեցնել)

induction - neradzoutiun, bashdoni gochelu, magadzoutiun (ներածութիւն, պաշտօնի կոչելը, մակածութիւն)
indue - haknil, haktsunel, ozhdel, dal, barkevel (Հագնիլ, Հագցնել, օժտել, տալ, պարգեւել)
indulge - touyladurel, hantourzhel, shunorhel (Թոյլատրել, Հանդուրժել, շնորՀել)
indulgence - neroghamudoutiun, hantourzhoghoutiun, shunorh (ներողամտութիւն, Հանդուրժողութիւն, շնորՀ)
indulgent - neroghamid, paremid, zichogh (ներողամիտ, բարեմիտ, զիջող)
indurate - gardzuranal, gardzuratsunel, buntatsunel, gardzur (կարծրանալ, կարծրացնել, պնդացնել, կարծր)
induration - gardzuratsoum, buntatsoum (կարծրացում, պնդացում)
industrial - jardararvesdagan, arhesdaked, artiunaperogh (ճարտարարուեստական, արՀեստագէտ, արդիւնաբերող)
industrialize - jardararvesdaganatsunel, artiunaperel (ճարտարարուեստականացնել, արդիւնաբերել)
industry - jardararvesd, artiunaperoutiun (ճարտարարուեստ, արդիւնաբերութիւն)
indwell - nerpunagil, abril (ներբնակիլ, ապրիլ)
indweller - punagich, nerpunag (բնակիչ, ներբնակ)
inebriate - kinovtsunel, kinov (գինովցնել, գինով)
inedited - andib, chudubvadz (անտիպ, չտպուած)
ineffective - anaztetsig, anzor, abartiun (անազդեցիկ, անզօր, ապարդիւն)
ineffectual - anzor, dugar, amoul, anaztetsig (անզօր, տկար, ամուլ, անազդեցիկ)
inefficacy - anzoroutiun, anaztetsoutiun (անզօրութիւն, անազդեցութիւն)
inefficient - anzor, angarogh, anadag (անզօր, անկարող, անատակ)
inelegant - anshunorh, anvayelouch (անշնորՀ, անվայելուչ)
ineligible - anundureli (անընտրելի)
inept - angarogh, anuntounag, anadag (անկարող, անընդունակ, անատակ)
inequal - anhavasar, anhart (անՀաւասար, անՀարթ)
inequitable - anartar (անարդար)
inequity - anartaroutiun (անարդարութիւն)
inert - ansharzh, ankordz, dzouyl (անշարժ, անգործ, ծոյլ)
inertia - ansharzhoutiun, angentanoutiun (անշարժութիւն, անկենդանութիւն)
inestimable - ankunahadeli, ankin, angushreli (անգնաՀատելի, անգին, անկշռելի)
inevitable - ankhousapeli (անխուսափելի)
inexact - anjisht, sukhal, anhavasdi (անճիշդ, սխալ, անՀաւաստի)
inexcusable - annereli, anartaranali (աններելի, անարդարանալի)
inexpedient - anharmar, anzhamanag, anbadeh (անյարմար, անժամանակ, անպատեՀ)
inexpensive - azhan, azhanakin (աժան, աժանագին)
inexperienced - anports, anvarzh, khag (անփորձ, անվարժ, խակ)
inexpert - anhumoud, anked, andeghiag, anports (անՀմուտ, անգէտ, անտեղեակ, անփորձ)
infallible - ansukhalagan, anvureb (անսխալական, անվրէպ)
infamous - vadahampav, anbadiv (վատաՀամբաւ, անպատիւ)
infamy - anbadvoutiun, khaydaragoutiun (անպատուութիւն, խայտառակութիւն)
infancy - mangoutiun, yerekhayoutiun (մանկութիւն, երեխայութիւն)
infant - manoug, yerekha, dugha (մանուկ, երեխայ, տղայ)
infantile - mangagan, dughayagan (մանկական, տղայական)

infantry - hedevagazork, hedevag (հետեւակազօրք, հետեւակ)
infarction - buntoutiun, khutsoum (պնդութիւն, խցում)
infatigable - chuhoknogh, ankhoncheli (չյոգնող, անխոնջելի)
infatuate - khelku arnel, humayel, himaratsunel (խելքը առնել, հմայել, յիմարացնել)
infect - varagel, abaganel, nekhel (վարակել, ապականել, նեխել)
infection - varagoum, abaganoutiun (վարակում, ապականութիւն)
infectious - varagich, darapokhig, abaganich (վարակիչ, տարափոխիկ, ապականիչ)
infecund - amoul, anbudough (ամուլ, անպտուղ)
infecundity - amloutiun (ամլութիւն)
infer - yezragatsunel, hedevtsunel (եզրակացնել, հետեւցնել)
inference - yezragatsoutiun, hedevoutiun (եզրակացութիւն, հետեւութիւն)
inferior - usdorin, usdoratas, kesh, nerkevi (ստորին, ստորադաս, գէշ, ներքեւի)
inferiority - usdornoutiun, usdoratasoutiun (ստորնութիւն, ստորադասութիւն)
infernal - tuzhokhayin, sadanayagan, tivayin (դժոխային, սատանայական, դիւային)
infertile - anbudough, amoul (անպտուղ, ամուլ)
infertility - amloutiun, anpeghmunavoroutiun (ամլութիւն, անբեղմնաւորութիւն)
infest - vukhdal, anhankusdatsunel, neghel (վխտալ, անհանգստացնել, նեղել)
infidel - anhavadarim, anhavad (անհաւատարիմ, անհաւատ)
infidelity - anhavadarmoutiun (անհաւատարմութիւն)
infilter - kamel, zudel, muzel (քամել, զտել, մզել)
infiltrate - tapantsel, suburtil, kamvil, dzudzvil (թափանցել, սպրդիլ, քամուիլ, ծծուիլ)
infiltration - tapantsoum, nertapantsoum, suburtoum (թափանցում, ներթափանցում, սպրդում)
infinite - anhoun, ansahman, anezur, anorosh (անհուն, անսահման, անեզր, անորոշ)
infinitive - anerevouyt, anorosh (աներեւոյթ, անորոշ)
infinitude - anhounoutiun, anvakhjanoutiun (անհունութիւն, անվախճանութիւն)
infinity - anhounoutiun, vavidenaganoutiun (անհունութիւն, յաւիտենականութիւն)
infirm - dugar, hivantod, touyl, angar, anhasdad (տկար, հիւանդոտ, թոյլ, տկար, անհաստատ)
infirmary - tarmanadoun, hivantanots, angelanots (դարմանատուն, հիւանդանոց, անկելանոց)
inflame - varel, potsavarel, varil, kurkurel (վառել, բոցավառել, վառիլ, գրգռել)
inflammable - tiuravar, purungeli (դիւրավառ, բռնկելի)
inflammation - potsavaroutiun, varoum, porpokoum (բոցավառութիւն, վառում, բորբոքում)
inflate - ouretsunel, puchel, kineru partsuratsunel, ouradz (ուռեցնել փչել, գիները բարձրացնել, ուռած)
inflation - sughaj, turami angoum, untlaynoum, ouroutsoum (սղաճ, դրամի անկում, ընդլայնում, ուռուցում)
inflect - dzurel, tekel, khonarhel, holovel (ծռել, թեքել, խոնարհել, հոլովել)
inflection - tekoum, goroutiun, khonarhoum, holovoum (թեքում, կորութիւն, խոնարհում, հոլովում)
inflexible - chudzurogh, ankhordageli, amour, ansasan (չծռող, անխորտակելի, ամուր, անսասան)
inflict - badjarel, yentargel, vunas hastsunel (պատճառել, ենթարկել, վնաս հասցնել)
influence - aztetsoutiun, aztel, nerkordzel (ազդեցութիւն, ազդել, ներգործել)

influenza - chermakharun harpoukh (ջերմախառն հարբուխ)
inform - deghegatsunel, imatsunel, haghortel (տեղեկացնել, իմացնել, հաղորդել)
informal - anbashdon, arants bashdonaganoutian, barz (անպաշտօն, առանց պաշտօնականութեան, պարզ)
informatics - deghegakuragank (տեղեկագրականք)
information - deghegoutiun, haghortoum, lour (տեղեկութիւն, հաղորդում, լուր)
informed - deghiag, kidag, irazeg, angazm, dutsev (տեղեակ, գիտակ, իրազեկ, անկազմ, տձեւ)
informer - deghegadou, luradou, madnich (տեղեկատու, լրատու, մատնիչ)
infortunate - tuzhpakhd, anpakhd (դժբախտ, անբախտ)
infortune - tuzhpakhdoutiun (դժբախտութիւն)
infraction - orinazantsoutiun, khakhdoum (օրինազանցութիւն, խախտում)
infractor - orinazants (օրինազանց)
infringe - peganel, khakhdel, purnaparel, turzhel (բեկանել, խախտել, բռնաբարել, դրժել)
infuse - nerargel, mudtsunel, tapel (ներարկել, մտցնել, թափել)
infusion - nerargoum, surusgoum, nermoudzoum, tourm (ներարկում, սրսկում, ներմուծում, թուրմ)
ingenious - suramid, jardar, hunaraked, hanjaregh (սրամիտ, ճարտար, հնարագէտ, հանճարեղ)
ingenue - barzamid, miamid aghchig (պարզամիտ, միամիտ աղջիկ)
ingenuity - hunaramudoutiun, suramudoutiun, oushimoutiun (հնարամտութիւն, սրամտութիւն, ուշիմութիւն)
ingenuous - barzamid, angeghdz, anmegh, oughigh (պարզամիտ, անկեղծ, անմեղ, ուղիղ)
ingest - sunount arnel (սնունդ առնել)
ingestion - nermoudzoum, nerarоutiun (ներմուծում, ներառութիւն)
inglulf - gullel, goul dal (կլլել, կուլ տալ)
inglut - gullel (կլլել)
ingrate - aberakhd (ապերախտ)
ingratitude - aberakhdoutiun (ապերախտութիւն)
ingredient - paghatradar, niut բաղադրատարր, նիւթ)
inhabit - punagil (բնակիլ)
inhabitant - punagich, punagogh (բնակիչ, բնակող)
inhabitation - punagoutiun (բնակութիւն)
inhale - nershunchel, shounch arnel, dzudzel (ներշնչել, շունչ առնել, ծծել)
inharmony - annertashnagoutiun (աններդաշնակութիւն)
inherit - zharankel, usdanal (ժառանգել, ստանալ)
inheritance - zharankoutiun, zharankoum (ժառանգութիւն, ժառանգում)
inhibit - arkilel, zusbel, junshel, gasetsunel (արգիլել, զսպել, ճնշել, կասեցնել)
inhibition - arkiloum, arkelk, zusboum (արգիլում, արգելք, զսպում)
inhospitable - anhiurungal, anhiuraser (անհիւրընկալ, անհիւրասէր)
inhospitality - anhiurungaloutiun (անհիւրընկալութիւն)
inhuman - anmartgayin, dumarti, ankout (անմարդկային, տմարդի, անգութ)
inhumate - taghel (թաղել)
inhumation - taghoum (թաղում)
inimical - tushnamagan, anpareatsagam (թշնամական, անբարեացակամ)
inimitable - annuman, anzoukagan, angurgneli, hurashali (աննման, անզուգական, անկրկնելի, հրաշալի)
inion - sunar (սնար)
iniquitous - aboren, anartar, aborini (ապօրէն, անարդար, ապօրինի)
initial - usguzpunagan, usguzpuna-

dar, arachin (սկզբնական, սկզբնատառ, առաջին)
initiate - usgusil, nakhatsernel, noravarzh, usgusnag (սկսիլ, նախաձեռնել, նորավարժ, սկսնակ)
initiative - nakhatsernoutiun (նախաձեռնութիւն)
inject - nerargel, surusgel, nermoudzel (ներարկել, սրսկել, ներմուծել)
injection - nerargoum, surusgoum (ներարկում, սրսկում)
injudicious - anmid, ankhorhourt, ankhohem (անմիտ, անխորհուրդ, անխոհեմ)
injunction - huramanakir, vujir, voroshoum, huraman (հրամանագիր, վճիռ, որոշում, հրաման)
injure - viravorel, vunasel, nakhadel, anarkel (վիրաւորել, վնասել, նախատել, անարգել)
injurious - nakhadagan, viravoragan (նախատական, վիրաւորական)
injury - nakhadink, vunas, gorousd (նախատինք, վնաս, կորուստ)
injustice - anartaroutiun (անարդարութիւն)
ink - melan, tanak (մելան, թանաք)
inkling - agnarg, agnargoutiun, nushmar (ակնարկ, ակնարկութիւն, նշմար)
inland - nerknamas, nerkin, michnakavar (ներքնամաս, ներքին, միջնագաւառ)
inlay - zotel, gutsel, turvakel, zedeghel (զօդել, կցել, դրուագել, զետեղել)
inlet - moudk, antsk, nurpantsk, neghouts (մուտք, անցք, նրբանցք, նեղուց)
inmate - punagagits, punagich (բնակակից, բնակիչ)
inn - otevan, pokur bantog (օթեւան, փոքր պանդոկ)
innate - punadzin, punadour, untodzin (բնածին, բնատուր, ընդոծին)
inner - nerkin, nersi, khorakouyn (ներքին, ներսի, խորագոյն)
innocence - anmeghoutiun, barzamudoutiun (անմեղութիւն, պարզամտութիւն)
innocent - anmegh, miamid, barzamid (անմեղ, միամիտ, պարզամիտ)
innocuous - anvunas, anmegh (անվնաս, անմեղ)
innovate - norararel, verapokhel (նորարարել, վերափոխել)
innovation - norararoutiun, noramoudzoutiun (նորարարութիւն, նորամուծութիւն)
innovator - norarar (նորարար)
innumerous - antiv, anhamar (անթիւ, անհամար)
inoculate - badvasdel, pokhantsel (պատուաստել, փոխանցել)
inoculation - badvasd, varagoum (պատուաստ, վարակում)
inodorate - anhod (անհոտ)
inodorous - anhod (անհոտ)
inoffensive - anvunas, anmegh (անվնաս, անմեղ)
inofficial - anbashdonagan, voch bashdonagan (անպաշտօնական, ոչ պաշտօնական)
inopportune - anzhamanag, anbadeh, darazham (անժամանակ, անպատեհ, տարաժամ)
inordinate - anchap, angark, kharnashupot (անչափ, անկարգ, խառնաշփոթ)
input - nerturoum, moudzoum, moudzel, mechu tunel (ներդրում, մուծում, մուծել, մէջը դնել)
inquest - tadakunnoutiun, hartsakunnoum (դատաքննութիւն, հարցաքննում)
inquietude - medahokoutiun, neghoutiun (մտահոգութիւն, նեղութիւն)
inquire - hartsakunnel, degheganal (հարցաքննել, տեղեկանալ)
inquirer - hartsakunnich (հարցաքննիչ)
inquiry - hartsakunnoutiun, hartsouports (հարցաքննութիւն, հարցափորձ)
inquisition - hartsakunnoutiun, havadakunnoutiun (հարցաքննութիւն, հաւատաքննութիւն)
inquisitor - hartsakunnich, havada-

kunnich (հարցաքննիչ, հաւատաքննիչ)
inroad - arshavank, nerkhouzhoum, asbadagel(արշաւանք, ներխուժում, ասպատակել)
inrush - nerkhouzhel, nerkhouzhoum (ներխուժել, ներխուժում)
insane - khent, himar, khelakar (խենդ, յիմար, խելագար)
insaniate - himaratsunel, khentatsunel (յիմարացնել, խենդացնել)
insanitary - haga-aroghchabahagan, vadaroghch (հակա-առողջապահական, վատառողջ)
insanity - khentoutiun, himaroutiun (խենդութիւն, յիմարութիւն)
insatiable - anhak, angoushd, vorguramol (անյագ, անկուշտ, որկրամոլ)
inscribe - porakurel, kantagel, turoshmel, magakurel (փորագրել, քանդակել, դրոշմել, մակագրել)
inscription - artsanakuroutiun, magakuroutiun, tson (արձանագրութիւն, մակագրութիւն, ձօն)
inscrutable - ankunneli, anhasgunali, khorhurtavor (անքննելի, անհասկնալի, խորհրդաւոր)
insect - michad, juji (միջատ, ճճի)
insecticide - michadasban (միջատասպան)
insecure - anabahov, anvusdaheli (անապահով, անվստահելի)
insecurity - anabahovoutiun, anvusdahelioutiun (անապահովութիւն, անվստահելիութիւն)
inseminate - tsanel, sermanel (ցանել, սերմանել)
insensate - anuzka, himar, anmid (անզգայ, յիմար, անմիտ)
insensible - anuzka, andarper, uzkayazirg, anuzkali (անզգայ, անտարբեր, զգայազիրկ, անզգալի)
inseparable - anpazhaneli, anpazhan (անբաժանելի, անբաժան)
insert - mudtsunel, zedeghel, deghaturel, gutsel, nertir (մտցնել, զետեղել, տեղադրել, կցել, ներդիր)
insertion - deghavoroum, zedeghoum, gutsoum (տեղաւորում, զետեղում, կցում)
inset - gutsvadzk, nertir, nertunel, zotel (կցուածք, ներդիր, ներդնել, զօդել)
inside - nersu, nerknagoghm, nerkin (ներսը, ներքնակողմ, ներքին)
insider - nersen yeghogh, voch tursetsi, antam (ներսէն եղող, ոչ դրսեցի, անդամ)
insidious - nenk, tavajan, kaghdakoghi (նենգ, դաւաճան, գաղտագողի)
insight - khoradesoutiun, khoratapantsoutiun (խորատեսութիւն, խորաթափանցութիւն)
insignia - badvanushanner, shukanushanner (պատուանշաններ, շքանշաններ)
insignificant - annushan, animasd, angarevor (աննշան, անիմաստ, անկարեւոր)
insinuate - soghosgil, agnargel, hasgutsunel, sermanel (սողոսկիլ, ակնարկել, հասկցնել, սերմանել)
insinuation - soghosgoum, suburtoum, zurbardoum, agnarg (սողոսկում, սպրդում, զրպարտում, ակնարկ)
insipid - anham, anli, anjashag (անհամ, անլի, անճաշակ)
insist - buntel, hamaril (պնդել, յամառիլ)
insistence - buntoum, hamaroutiun, takhantsank (պնդում, յամառութիւն, թախանձանք)
insolence - ampardavanoutiun, lurpoutiun (ամբարտաւանութիւն, լրբութիւն)
insolent - ampardavan, lugdi, anbadgar, lirp (ամբարտաւան, լկտի, անպատկառ, լիրբ)
insoluble - anloudzeli, anlouydz, ankagdeli, tuzhvarahal (անլուծելի, անլոյծ, անքակտելի, դժուարահալ)
insolvency - sunangoutiun (սնանկութիւն)
insolvent - sunang, sunangatsadz, anvujarounag (սնանկ, սնանկացած, անվճարունակ)
insomnia - ankunoutiun, kunadoutiun (անքնութիւն, քնատութիւն)
inspect - kunnel, zunnel, tidel

(քննել, զննել, դիտել)
inspection - usdoukoum, zunnoum, kunnoutiun, veragatsoutiun (ստուգում, զննում, քննութիւն, վերակացութիւն)
inspector - kunnich, veradesouch, verakunnich (քննիչ, վերատեսուչ, վերաքննիչ)
inspiration - nershunchoum, shuncharoutiun (ներշնչում, շնչառութիւն)
inspire - sunchel, nershunchel, vokevorel, aztel (շնչել, ներշնչել, ոգեւորել, ազդել)
inspirit - khantavarel, vokevorel, gentanatsunel (խանդավառել, ոգեւորել, կենդանացնել)
instability - angayounoutiun (անկայունութիւն)
install - deghavorel, zedeghel, hasdadel, tunel (տեղաւորել, զետեղել, հաստատել, դնել)
installation - zedeghoum, hasdadoum, sarkavoroum (զետեղում, հաստատում, սարքաւորում)
installment - deghavoroum, masnavujar (տեղաւորում, մասնավճար)
instance - orinag, arit, usdiboum, aghers (օրինակ, առիթ, ստիպում, աղերս)
instant - aguntard, bah, isgouyn, usdiboghagan (ակնթարթ, պահ, իսկոյն, ստիպողական)
instantaneous - vayrgenagan, hangardzagan (վայրկենական, յանկարծական)
instead - pokhanag, pokharen, deghu (փոխարէն, փոխանակ, տեղը)
instigate - kurkurel, turtel, harachatsunel, hurahrel (գրգռել, դրդել, յառաջացնել, հրահրել)
instigation - kurkuroum, turtoum (գրգռում, դրդում)
instigator - kurkurich, turtogh, telaturogh (գրգռիչ, դրդող, թելադրող)
instill - gatetsunel, toretsunel, hosetsunel (կաթեցնել, թորեցնել, հոսեցնել)
instillation - gatetsoum (կաթեցում)
instinct - punazt, mughoum, hagoum (բնազդ, մղում, հակում)
instinctive - punaztagan (բնազդական)
institute - himnarg, ousoumnaran, himnel, hasdadel (հիմնարկ, ուսումնարան, հիմնել, հաստատել)
institution - himnargoutiun, hasdadoutiun (հիմնարկութիւն, հաստատութիւն)
instruct - ousoutsanel, gurtel, hurahankel, marzel (ուսուցանել, կրթել, հրահանգել, մարզել)
instruction - ousoutsoum, gurtoutiun, hurahank, tsoutsmounk (ուսուցում, կրթութիւն, հրահանգ, ցուցմունք)
instructor - ousoutsich, hurahankich, tasdiarag (ուսուցիչ, հրահանգիչ, դաստիարակ)
instrument - kordzik, nuvakaran, michots, bashdonakir (գործիք, նուագարան, միջոց, պաշտօնագիր)
instrumental - kordzikayin (գործիքային)
instrumentation - nuvakadzoutiun, kordzikavoroum (նուագածութիւն, գործիքաւորում)
insubordinate - anhunazant, umpost, angarkabah (անհնազանդ, ըմբոստ, անկարգապահ)
insuccess - anhachoghoutiun (անյաջողութիւն)
insufficient - anpavarar, anpavaganachap (անբաւարար, անբաւականաչափ)
insular - gughziapunag, arantsnatsadz (կղզիաբնակ, առանձնացած)
insulate - anchadel, megousatsunel, gughziatsunel (անջատել, մեկուսացնել, կղզիացնել)
insulation - anchadoum, megousatsoum, gughziatsoum (անջատում, մեկուսացում, կղզիացում)
insult - nakhadel, viravorel, anarkel, nakhadink (նախատել, վիրաւորել, անարգել, նախատինք)
insupportable - andaneli, anhantourzheli (անտանելի, անհանդուրժելի)
insurance - abahovakuroutiun (ապահովագրութիւն)

insurance policy - *abahovakir* (ապահովագիր)
insure - *abahovakurel, abahovel, vusdahetsunel* (ապահովագրել, ապահովել, վստահեցնել)
insured - *abahovakurial* (ապահովագրեալ)
insurmountable - *anbardeli, anhaghtahareli* (անպարտելի, անյաղթահարելի)
insurrection - *abusdampoutiun, khurovoutiun* (ապստամբութիւն, խռովութիւն)
intact - *anaghard, aneghdz, anvunas, antsernmukheli* (անաղարտ, անեղծ, անվնաս, անձեռնմխելի)
intake - *nertoghoum, ners arnelu, norakir zinvor* (ներթողում, ներս առնելը, նորագիր զինուոր)
intangible - *anhubeli, anshoshapeli* (անհպելի, անշօշափելի)
integer - *ampoghch, ampoghchagan tiv* (ամբողջ, ամբողջական թիւ)
integral - *ampoghchagan, luriv* (ամբողջական, լրիւ)
integrate - *ampoghchatsunel, luratsunel, miatsunel* (ամբողջացնել, լրացնել, միացնել)
integration - *ampoghchatsoum, miatsoum, tsouloum* (ամբողջացում, միացում, ձուլում)
integrity - *ampoghchoutiun, gadareloutiun, lioutiun* (ամբողջութիւն, կատարելութիւն, լիութիւն)
intellect - *midk, khelk, imatsoutiun* (միտք, խելք, իմացութիւն)
intellectual - *mudavoragan, mudayin, mudavor, imatsagan* (մտաւորական, մտային, մտաւոր, իմացական)
intelligence - *midk, khelk, khelatsoutiun, oushimoutiun* (միտք, խելք, խելացութիւն, ուշիմութիւն)
intelligent - *khelatsi, oushim, khohagan* (խելացի, ուշիմ, խոհական)
intelligentsia - *mudavoraganoutiun* (մտաւորականութիւն)
intemperate - *anzhouzhgal, anzousb, angark* (անժուժկալ, անզուսպ, անկարգ)
intend - *mudaturel, dzurakurel, voroshel, nubadagaturel* (մտադրել, ծրագրել, որոշել, նպատակադրել)
intendant - *veragatsou, desouch, hokapartsou* (վերակացու, տեսուչ, հոգաբարձու)
intense - *sasdig, ouzhkin, pourun, khid* (սաստիկ, ուժին, բուռն, խիտ)
intensify - *sasdgastsunel, ouzheghatsunel* (սաստկացնել, ուժեղացնել)
intensity - *sasdgoutiun, ouzhkunoutiun* (սաստկութիւն, ուժգնութիւն)
intensive - *sasdig, nerouzh, pourun, ouzhkin, ouzhegh* (սաստիկ, ներուժ, բուռն, ուժգին, ուժեղ)
intent - *mudatir, tsukdoum, nubadag,* (մտադիր, ձգտում, նպատակ)
intention - *mudaturoutiun, nubadag, midoum, tsukdoum* (մտադրութիւն, նպատակ, միտում, ձգտում)
intentional - *tidoumnavor, tidavorial, tidmamp* (դիտումնաւոր, դիտաւորեալ, դիտմամբ)
inter - *taghel, kerezmanel, hoghin hantsunel* (թաղել, գերեզմանել, հողին յանձնել)
interact - *michnarar, untmichoum, pokhaztel* (միջնարար, ընդմիջում, փոխազդել)
intercede - *michamudel, michnortel, parekhosel, anchadel* (միջամտել, միջնորդել, բարեխօսել, անջատել)
intercept - *khapanel, jampan gudrel, anchadel, unthadel* (խափանել, ճամբան կտրել, անջատել, ընդհատել)
interception - *untmichoum, khapanoum, hadoum* (ընդմիջում, խափանում, հատում)
intercession - *michnortoutiun, parekhosoutiun* (միջնորդութիւն, բարեխօսութիւն)
interchange - *pokhanagel, pokharinel, pokhanagoum* (փոխանակել, փոխարինել, փոխանակում)
intercommunicate - *pokhharaperil, haghortagtsil* (փոխյարաբերիլ, հաղորդակցիլ)
intercommunication - *pokhharaperoutiun, haghortagtsoutiun* (փոխյա–

բարեբրութիւն, Հաղորդակցութիւն)
interconnect - gabvil, gabagtsil, haghortagtsil (կապուիլ, կապակցիլ, Հաղորդակցիլ)
intercourse - haraperoutiun, haghortagtsoutiun (յարաբերութիւն, Հաղորդակցութիւն)
interdict - arkilel, tatretsunel, arkelk, arkiloum (արգիլել, դադրեցնել, արգելք, արգիլում)
interdiction - arkiloum, arkelk, panaturoum, gakhagayoum (արգիլում, արգելք, բանադրում, կախակայում)
interest - hedakurkurel, shahakurkurel, shah, dogos, okoud (Հետաքրքրել, շաՀագրգռել, շաՀ, տոկոս, օգուտ)
interested - hedakurkurvadz, shahakurkurvadz (Հետաքրքրուած, շաՀագրգռուած)
interesting - hedakurkir, hedakurkuragan (Հետաքրքիր, Հետաքրքրական)
interfere - michamudel, michnortel, kharnuvil, untharil (միջամտել, միջնորդել, խառնուիլ, ընդՀարիլ)
interference - michamudoutiun, khochuntod, irarakharnoum (միջամտութիւն, խոչընդոտ, իրարախառնում)
interflow - miakharnuvil, nerhosil, miakharnoum (միախառնուիլ, ներՀոսիլ, միախառնում)
interim - zhamanagamichots, zhamanagavor (ժամանակամիջոց, ժամանակաւոր)
interior - nerkin, nerknamas, nersu, nerashkharh (ներքին, ներքնամաս, ներսը, ներաշխարՀ)
interject - untmichel, unthadel, khoski mech mudnel (ընդմիջել, ընդՀատել, խօսքի մէջ մտնել)
interjection - tsaynargoutiun, patsakanchoutiun (ձայնարկութիւն, բացագանչութիւն)
interlace - miahiusel, untelouzel, akoutsel (միաՀիւսել, ընդելուզել, ագուցել)
interline - doghamech, patsad, doghamichel (տողամէջ, բացատ, տողամիջել)
interlock - irerahiusel, miagtsil (իրերաՀիւսել, միակցիլ)
interlocution - khosagtsoutiun, zurouyts (խօսակցութիւն, զրոյց)
interlocutor - khosagits, zuroutsagits (խօսակից, զրուցակից)
interlude - michnakhagh, michnarar, untmichoum (միջնախաղ, միջնարար, ընդմիջում)
intermarriage - kharnamousnoutiun, michamousnoutiun (խառնամուսնութիւն, միջամուսնութիւն)
intermarry - khunamagtsil, azkagtsil (խնամակցիլ, ազգակցիլ)
intermeddle - michamudel, kharnuvil (միջամտել, խառնուիլ)
intermediary - michnort, michangial (միջնորդ, միջանկեալ)
intermediate (a) - michev, michag, michangial, michnagark (միջեւ, միջակ, միջանկեալ, միջնակարգ)
intermediate (v) - michamudel, michnortel (միջամտել, միջնորդել)
intermediation - michamudoutiun michnortoutiun (միջամտութիւն, միջնորդութիւն)
intermediator - michnort (միջնորդ)
interment - taghoum, kerezmanoum (թաղում, գերեզմանում)
intermezzo - untmichoum (ընդմիջում)
interminable - anverchanali, anvakhjan, anusbar (անվերջանալի, անվախճան, անսպառ)
intermingle - kharnuvil, kharnel, miakharnel, shupvil (խառնուիլ, խառնել, միախառնել, շփուիլ)
intermission - michnarar, tatar, untmichoum, michots (միջնարար, դադար, ընդմիջում, միջոց)
intermit - untmichel, unthadel, unthadvil (ընդմիջել, ընդՀատել, ընդՀատուիլ)
intermittence - unthadoum. tatar (ընդՀատում, դադար)
intermittent - unthadvogh, untmichvogh (ընդՀատուող, ընդմիջուող)
intermix - miakharnel, miakharnuvil,

mianal (միախառնել, միախառնուիլ, միանալ)
intern, interne - nerkin, kisherotig, arkelapagel (ներքին, գիշերօթիկ, արգելափակել)
internal - nerkin, arduni, undanegan (ներքին, առտնի, ընտանեկան)
internal medicine - nerkin hivantoutiun (ներքին հիւանդութիւն)
international - michazkayin (միջազգային)
international money order - michazkayin pokhantsadomus (միջազգային փոխանցատոմս)
internationalize - michazkaynatsunel (միջազգայնացնել)
internship - nerkin puzhushgi asdijan, varzhoghoutian (ներքին բժիշկի աստիճան, վարժողութիւն)
interpellate - hartsabuntel, hartsakunnel (հարցապնդել, հարցաքննել)
interpellation - hartsabuntoum (հարցապնդում)
interphone - michheratsayn (միջհեռաձայն)
interpolate - punakiru pokhel, khartakhel, yeghdzanel (բնագիրը փոխել, խարդախել, եղծանել)
interpose - michamudel, mechdeghu genal, michaturel (միջամտել, մէջտեղը կենալ, միջադրել)
interposition - michamudoutiun, michaturoutiun (միջամտութիւն, միջադրութիւն)
interpret - megnapanel, lousapanel, tarkmanel (մեկնաբանել, լուսաբանել, թարգմանել)
interpretation - megnapanoutiun, megnoutiun (մեկնաբանութիւն, մեկնութիւն)
interpreter - megnapan, megnich, tarkman (մեկնաբան, մեկնիչ, թարգման))
interrelation - pokh-haraperoutiun (փոխ-յարաբերութիւն)
interrogate - hartsunel, hartsakunnel, hartsaportsel (հարցնել, հարցաքննել, հարցափորձել)
interrogation - hartsoum, hartsakunnoutiun, hartsabuntoum (հարցում, հարցաքննութիւն, հարցապնդում)
interrupt - unthadel, michamudel, untmichel (ընդհատել, միջամտել, ընդմիջել)
interruption - unthadoum, untmichoum, tatar (ընդհատում, ընդմիջում, դադար)
intersect - michhadel, hadel, khachatsevel, zirar gudrel (միջհատել, հատել, խաչաձեւել, զիրար կտրել)
intersection - khachmeroug, michhadoum (խաչմերուկ, միջհատում)
interstate - michnahankayin (միջնահանգային)
interval - zhamanagamichots, michots, michnarar (ժամանակամիջոց, միջոց, միջնարար)
intervene - michamudel, michnortel, kharnuvil (միջամտել, միջնորդել, խառնուիլ)
intervention - michamudoutiun, michnortoutiun (միջամտութիւն, միջնորդութիւն)
interview - desakhosil, hartsazurouyts, hartsazuroutsel (տեսախօսիլ, հարցազրոյց, հարցազրուցել)
interviewer - desakhos, zuroutsagits (տեսախօս, զրուցակից)
interviewing - desakhosoutiun (տեսախօսութիւն)
interweave - irerahiusel, miakharnel (իրերահիւսել, միախառնել)
intestate - angudag (անկտակ)
intestine - aghik, porodik, nerkin (աղիք, փորոտիք, ներքին)
inthrall - kerel, usdergatsunel (գերել, ստրկացնել)
intimacy - mudermoutiun (մտերմութիւն)
intimate - muderim, modig, serd, deghegatsunel (մտերիմ, մօտիկ, սերտ, տեղեկացնել)
intimidate - vakhtsunel, sarsapetsunel (վախցնել, սարսափեցնել)
intimidation - sosgatsoum, sarsapetsunoum, vakhaztetsoutiun (սոսկացում, սարսափեցում, վախազդեցութիւն)

intimity - mudermoutiun, modigoutiun (մտերմութիւն, մօտիկութիւն)
into - nersu, mech, tebi, ar (ներսը, մէջ, դէպի, առ)
intolerable - anhantourzheli, andaneli (անհանդուրժելի, անտանելի)
intolerance - anhantourzhoghoutiun, anneroghoutiun (անհանդուրժողութիւն, աններողութիւն)
intolerant - anhantourzhogh, annerogh, neghmid (անհանդուրժող, աններող, նեղմիտ)
intomb - taghel, kerezmanel (թաղել, գերեզմանել)
intonate - yeghanagavorel, yelevechel-tsayni, vorodal (եղանակաւորել, ելեւէջել՝ ձայնի, որոտալ)
intoxicate - tounavorel, kinovtsunel (թունաւորել, գինովցնել)
intoxication - tounavoroum, kinovoutiun (թունաւորում, գինովութիւն)
intractable - anoughgha, anhunazant, anhagagushreli (անուղղայ, անհնազանդ, անհակակշռելի)
intrench - khuramadel, badneshel (խրամատել, պատնէշել)
intrepid - anvakh, kach, anveher (անվախ, քաջ, անվեհեր)
intricate - gunjurod, part, kharnag, gunjurodel (կնճռոտ, բարդ, խառնակ, կնճռոտել)
intrigue - tavel, tavaturel, niutel, tav, satrank (դաւել, դաւադրել, նիւթել, դաւ, սադրանք)
intrinsic - harazad, iragan, poun, nerkin (հարազատ, իրական, բուն, ներքին)
introduce - mudtsunel, nergayatsunel, dzanotatsunel (մտցնել, ներկայացնել, ծանօթացնել)
introduction - nermoudzoum, neradzoutiun, harachapan (ներմուծում, ներածութիւն, յառաջաբան)
introvert - nerhayil, inknakunnoutiun (ներհայիլ, ինքնաքննութիւն)
intrude - inknagoch, inknamoud, nerkhouzhel, purni mudnel (ինքնակոչ, ինքնամուտ, ներխուժել, բռնի մտնել)
intrusion - nerkhouzhoum, suburtoum (ներխուժում, սպրդում)
intuition - nakhazkatsoum, haydnadesoutiun (նախազգացում, յայտնատեսութիւն)
intuitive - baydzarades, haydnades (պայծառատես, յայտնատես)
inundate - voghoghel, hegheghel (ողողել, հեղեղել)
inure - sorvetsunel, varzhetsunel, gopel (սորվեցնել, վարժեցնել, կոփել)
invade - arshavel, nerkhouzhel, asbadagel, hartsagil (արշաւել, ներխուժել, ասպատակել, յարձակիլ)
invader - hartsagogh, arshavogh, nerkhouzhogh (յարձակող, արշաւող, ներխուժող)
invalid - hashmantam, angarogh, anvaver, anzor (հաշմանդամ, անկարող, անվաւեր, անզօր)
invalidate - orinazurgel, anvaver tartsunel (օրինազրկել, անվաւեր դարձնել)
invaluable - ankin, ankunahadeli, tangakin (անգին, անգնահատելի, թանկագին)
invariable - anpopokheli, anpopokh, hasdadoun (անփոփոխելի, անփոփոխ, հաստատուն)
invasion - arshavank, nerkhouzhoum (արշաւանք, ներխուժում)
inveigh - hartsagil, hayhoyel, borchudal, loudank (յարձակիլ, հայհոյել, պոռչտալ, լուտանք)
inveigle - moloretsunel, kaytagghetsunel, khapel (մոլորեցնել, գայթակղեցնել, խաբել)
inveil - koghargel (քօղարկել)
invent - hunarel, hughanal, kudnel (հնարել, յղանալ, գտնել)
invention - kiud, hunark, haydnakordzoutiun (գիւտ, հնարք, յայտնագործութիւն)
inventory - tsoutsag, bahesdatsoutsag, tsoutsagakurel (ցուցակ, հեստացուցակ, ցուցակագրել)
inverse - hagarag, nerhag, shurchoun, khodor, hagodnia (հակառակ, ներհակ, շրջուն, խոտոր, հակոտնեայ)

inversion - shurchoum, hagatartsoutiun, shurchuvadzoutiun (շրջում, հակադարձութիւն, շրջուածութիւն)
invert - shurchel, pokhel, tartsunel (շրջել, փոխել, դարձնել)
invertebrate - anoghnahar, popokhamid (անողնայար, փոփոխամիտ)
invest - nertunel turam, dogosi dal, haktsunel, basharel (ներդնել՝ դրամ, տոկոսի տալ, հագցնել, պաշարել)
investigate - hedazodel, khouzargel, kunnel (հետազօտել, խուզարկել, քննել)
investigation - hedazodoutiun, kunnoum, khouzargoutiun (հետազօտութիւն, քննում, խուզարկութիւն)
investigator - hedazodogh, ousoumnasirogh (հետազօտող, ուսումնասիրող)
investiture - douchoutiun, shunorhoum, bashdon dalu (տուչութիւն, շնորհում, պաշտօն տալը)
investment - nerturoum, shahargoum, basharoum, hakousd (ներդրում, շահարկում, պաշարում, հագուստ)
investor - nermoudzogh, shahargou (ներմուծող, շահարկու)
inveterate - hintsadz, armadatsadz, hamar, moli (հինցած, արմատացած, յամառ, մոլի)
invidious - adeli, viravoragan, nakhantsod (ատելի, վիրաւորական, նախանձոտ)
invigorate - kodebuntel, zoratsunel, khurakhousel (գօտեպնդել, զօրացնել, խրախուսել)
invincible - anhaght, anhaghteli, anbardeli (անյաղթ, անյաղթելի, անպարտելի)
inviolate - anarad, makour, anpasir, anvunas (անարատ, մաքուր, անբասիր, անվնաս)
invisible - andesaneli, annushmareli, dzadzoug (անտեսանելի, աննշմարելի, ծածուկ)
invitation - huraver, huravirakir, khunjouyk (հրաւէր, հրաւիրագիր, խնճոյք)
invite - huravirel, ganchel, turtel, mughel (հրաւիրել, կանչել, դրդել, մղել)
invocate - aghersel, khunturel (աղերսել, խնդրել)
invocation - aghers, khunturank, baghadank, aghotk (աղերս, խնդրանք, պաղատանք, աղօթք)
invoice - hashvetsouyts, hashvetsoutsag, hashvakurel (հաշուեցոյց, հաշուեցուցակ, հաշուագրել)
invoke - ganchel, haytsel, aghersel, khunturel, baghadil (կանչել, հայցել, աղերսել, խնդրել, պաղատիլ)
involuntary - agama, anhozhar (ակամայ, անյօժար)
involve - michamukh ullal, kharnuvil, nerkashel, barpagel (միջամուխ ըլլալ, խառնուիլ, ներքաշել, պարփակել)
involved - part, nerkhuradz (բարդ, ներխրած)
involvement - michamukhoum, mechu kharnuvilu, khuroum (միջամխում, մէջը խառնուիլը, խրում)
invulnerable - ankhotseli, anviravoreli (անխոցելի, անվիրաւորելի)
inward - nerkin, nersi, hokegan, mudavor (ներքին, ներսի, հոգեկան, մտաւոր)
inwards - nerkousd, tebi ners, porodik, aghik (ներքուստ, դէպի ներս, փորոտիք, աղիք)
Iran - iran, barsgasdan (Իրան, Պարսկաստան)
iranian - irantsi, barsig, barsgeren, barsgagan (իրանցի, պարսիկ, պարսկերէն, պարսկական)
Iraq - irak (Իրաք)
iraqian - iraktsi, irakeren, irakian (իրաքցի, իրաքերէն, իրաքեան)
ire - pargoutiun, zayrouyt, tsasoum (բարկութիւն, զայրոյթ, ցասում)
ireful - pargatsod, tsasdog (բարկացոտ, ցասկոտ)
Ireland - irlanda (Իրլանտա)
iris - dziadzan, dzirani kodi, hirig (ծիածան, ծիրանի գօտի, հիրիկ)
irish - irlandatsi, irlanderen, irlandagan (իրլանտացի, իրլանտերէն, իրլանտական)

irk - tsantsuratsunel, pargatsunel, hoknetsunel (ձանձրացնել, բարկացնել, յոգնեցնել)
iron - yergat, artoug, artougel, shughtayel (երկաթ, արդուկ, արդուկել, շղթայել)
Iron Age - yergate tar (Երկաթէ Դար)
Iron Curtain - yergate varakouyr (Երկաթէ Վարագոյր)
ironic, al - heknagan, dzaghragan (Հեգնական, ծաղրական)
ironsmith - yergatakordz (երկաթագործ)
ironware - yergateghenk (երկաթեղէնք)
ironworks - tarpunots, yergatatsoularan (դարբնոց, երկաթաձուլարան)
irony - yergatia, heknank, dzaghur (երկաթեայ, Հեգնանք, ծաղր)
irradiate - jarakaytel, shoghshoghal, lousavorel (ճառագայթել, շողշողալ, լուսաւորել)
irradiation - jarakaytoum, lousavoroum (ճառագայթում, լուսաւորում)
irrationel - anduramapanagan, anpan, ankhelk, animasd (անտրամաբանական, անբան, անխելք, անիմաստ)
irreconcilable - anhashd, anhashdeli, anhamatsayn (անհաշտ, անհաշտելի, անհամաձայն)
irrecoverable - anpouzheli, antarmaneli, ankudaneli (անբուժելի, անդարմանելի, անգտանելի)
irrefutable - anherkeli (անհերքելի)
irregular - anganon, zardoughi, aborini (անկանոն, զարտուղի, ապօրինի)
irreligion - anguronoutiun (անկրօնութիւն)
irremediable - anpouzheli, antarmaneli (անբուժելի, անդարմանելի)
irremissible - annereli, ankaveli (աններելի, անքաւելի)
irremovable - ansharzh, anturtuveli, hasdadoun (անշարժ, անդրդուելի, Հաստատուն)
irreparable - anoughgheli, annorokeli, antarmaneli (անուղղելի, աննորոգելի, անդարմանելի)
irreplaceable - anpokharineli (անփոխարինելի)
irreproachable - anpasir, anteri, anmeghatreli (անբասիր, անթերի, անմեղադրելի)
irresistible - antimatureli (անդիմադրելի)
irresolute - dadanogh, yergmid, anvujragan, varanod (տատանող, երկմիտ, անվճռական, վարանոտ)
irrespirable - anshuncheli (անշնչելի)
irresponsibility - anbadaskhanaduvoutiun (անպատասխանատուութիւն)
irresponsible - anbadaskhanadou, anvusdaheli (անպատասխանատու, անվստահելի)
irretrievable - anoughgheli, antarmaneli, anhadoutsaneli (անուղղելի, անդարմանելի, անհատուցանելի)
irreverent - anbadgar, lirp, anharkeli, anamot (անպատկառ, լիրբ, անյարգելի, անամօթ)
irreversible - antarnali, anpeganeli, antarts, anshurcheli (անդառնալի, անբեկանելի, անդարձ, անշրջելի)
irrevocable - anpokheli, antarts, antarnali (անփոխելի, անդարձ, անդառնալի)
irrigate - churel, vorokel, voghoghel (ջրել, ոռոգել, ողողել)
irrigation - vorokoum, churapashkhoutiun, surusgoum (ոռոգում, ջրաբաշխութիւն, սրսկում)
irritate - kurkurel, pargatsunel, zayratsunel (գրգռել, բարկացնել, զայրացնել)
irritation - zayrouyt, pargoutiun, kurkuroum (զայրոյթ, բարկութիւն, գրգռում)
irruptiun - khouzhoum, arshavank, kuroh, voghoghoum (խուժում, արշաւանք, գրոհ, ողողում)
is - e (է)
islam - islam, mahmedagan (իսլամ, մահմետական)
islamism - islamoutiun, mahmedaga-

noutiun (խուլամութիւն, մահմեռակնութիւն)
island - gughzi, gughziatsunel (կղզի, կղզիացնել)
isle - gughzi, gughziag (կղզի, կղզեակ)
isolate - gughziatsunel, megousatsunel, anchadel, zadel (կղզիացնել, մեկուսացնել, անջատել, զատել)
isolation - megousatsoum, gughziatsoum, arantsnatsoum (մեկուսացում, կղզիացում, առանձնացում)
Israel - israyel (Իսրայէլ)
issue (n) - yelk, hunark, hedevank, huradaragoutiun (ելք, հնարք, հետեւանք, հրատարակութիւն)
issue (v) - yellel, dzakil, seril, pukhil, artsagel (ելլել, ծագիլ, սերիլ, բխիլ, արձակել)
issuer - huradaragich, tours hanogh (հրատարակիչ, դուրս հանող)
isthmus - baranots, neghouts (պարանոց, նեղուց)
it - an, aniga, zayn (ան, անիկա, զայն)
italian - idalatsi, idaleren, idalagan (իտալացի, իտալերէն, իտալական)
italic - sheghakir (շեղագիր)
Italy - idalia (Իտալիա)
itch - kervudouk, kos, tsangoutiun, kervudil (քերուըտուք, քոս, ցանկութիւն, քերուըտիլ)
item - niut, ararga, mas, nayev, tsoutsagakurel (նիւթ, առարկայ, մաս, նաեւ, ցուցակագրել)
iterate - gurgnel, yergurortel (կրկնել, երկրորդել)
itinerary - yertoughi, oughekuroutiun, oughekirk, jampa (երթուղի, ուղեգրութիւն, ուղեգիրք, ճամբայ)
itinerate - shurchil, bududil, jamportel (շրջիլ, պտըտիլ, ճամբորդել)
its - anor, ir (անոր, իր)
itself - inknin, inkniren, nouyninkun, inkzink (ինքնին, ինքնիրեն, նոյնինքն, ինքզինք)
ivory - pughosgur (փղոսկր)
ivy - paghegh (բաղեղ)
izzard - usgizpen minchev verch Z kiru, karaydzi desag (սկիզբէն մինչեւ վերջ Z գիրը, քարայծի տեսակ)

jab - khotel, tanagodzel, mukhel, akatsi, khots, verk (խոթել, դանակոծել, մխել, աքացի, խոց, վէրք)
jabber - shadakhosel, murtmurtal, gagazel, shadakhosoutiun (շատախօսել, մրթմրթալ, շատախօսութիւն)
jacinth - hagint (հակինթ)
jack (n) - guroung, tukhtakhaghi dughan, navou turosh (կռունկ, թղթախաղի տղան, նաւու դրօշ)
jack (v) - vertsunel, partsuratsunel, vorsal (վերցնել, բարձրացնել, որսալ)
jackal - shunakayl, kaylashoun (շնագայլ, գայլաշուն)
jacket - pajgonag, garj pajgon (բաճկոնակ, կարճ բաճկոն)
jackpot - pakhdakhaghi medz nuveru (բախտախաղի մեծ նուէրը)
jack-in-the-box - khaghadoupen tours tsadgogh khaghalik (խաղատուփէն դուրս ցատկող խաղալիք)
jaculate - nedel, artsagel, sulatsunel (նետել, արձակել, սլացնել)
jade - hasmugakar, dugar tsi, poz, hoknil, gukil (յասմկաքար, տկար ձի, բոզ, յոգնիլ, կքիլ)
jag - sour gudurduvadzk, adamnavorel, hertsodel (սուր կտրտուածք, ատամնաւորել, հերձոտել)
jagged - adamnavor, hertsod

(ատամնաւոր, Հերձոտ)
jaguar - hovaz, vakragouz (յովազ, վագրակուզ)
jail - pand, zundan, pandargel (բանտ, զնտան, բանտարկել)
jailbird - pandargial, hantsakordz (բանտարկեալ, յանցագործ)
jailer - pandabah, pandabed (բանտապահ, բանտապետ)
jalousie - sherdapeghg (շերտափեղկ)
jam - budghanoush, ampokh, khurnoum, seghmel, juzmel (պտղանուշ, ամբոխ, խռնում, սեղմել, ճզմել)
jamb - goghapayd - turan-badouhani (կողափայտ՝ դրան-պատուհանի)
jamboree - usgaoudahavak, khunjouyk (սկաուտահաւաք, խնճոյք)
jangle - vijil, aghmugel, vej, panaguriv, aghmoug (վիճիլ, աղմկել, վէճ, բանակռիւ, աղմուկ)
janitor - turnaban, paraban, bahag (դռնապան, բարապան, պահակ)
January - hounvar (Յունուար)
Japan - japon, chunarag, chunaragel (Ճափոն, ջնարակ, ջնարակել)
japanese - japontsi, japoneren, japonagan (Ճափոնցի, Ճափոներէն, Ճափոնական)
jape - gadag, dzaghur, gadagel (կատակ, ծաղր, կատակել)
jar - sapor, garas, jurinch, jurunchel, vijil, gurvil (սափոր, կարաս, ճռինչ, ճռնչել, վիճիլ, կռուիլ)
jargon - parpar, ramgeren, kaghdnalezou (բարբառ, ռամկերէն, գաղտնալեզու)
jasey - geghdzam (կեղծամ)
jasmine - hasmig (յասմիկ)
jaundice - teghnakhd, taloug, nakhants, talgaharel (դեղնախտ, դալուկ, նախանձ, դալկահարել)
jaunt - uzposabudouyd, uzposabududil, shurchakayil (զբօսապտոյտ, զբօսապտըտիլ, ջրջագայիլ)
jauntiness - zuvarjoutiun, anhokoutiun, inknakohoutiun (զուարճութիւն, անհոգութիւն, ինքնագոհութիւն)
jaunty - zuvart, anhok, inknakoh, tsoutsamol (զուարթ, անհոգ, ինքնագոհ, ցուցամոլ)
jaw - guzag, dzynod, dzamelik, shadakhosel (կզակ, ծնօտ, ծամելիք, շատախօսել)
jay - andzegh, jay, shadakhos (անծեղ, Ճայ, շատախօս)
jaywalker - anoushatir kalogh (անուշադիր քալող)
jazz - jaz, ramerk, aghmugararoutiun (Ճազ, ռամերգ, աղմկարարութիւն)
jealous - nakhantsod, gasgadzod, nakhantsakhuntir (նախանձոտ, կասկածոտ, նախանձախնդիր)
jealousy - nakhantz, gasgadzamudoutiun (նախանձ, կասկածամտութիւն)
jeep - jip, amerigian zinvoragan inknasharzh (Ճիփ, ամերիկեան զինուորական ինքնաշարժ)
jeer - dzaghrel, heknel, dzaghur (ծաղրել, հեգնել, ծաղր)
Jehovah - yehova (Եհովա)
jejune - anoti, hiudzadz, barab, tadarg, chor (անօթի, հիւծած, պարապ, դատարկ, չոր)
jelly - madznid, sarnakhouys, tontogh, madznil (մածնիտ, սառնախոյս, դոնդող, մածնիլ)
jeopardize - vudankel (վտանգել)
jeopardy - vudank (վտանգ)
jerk - tsuntsoum, tsaydk, aboukhd, tsuntsel, tsuntsuvil (ցնցում, ցայտք, ապուխտ, ցնցել, ցնցուիլ)
Jerusalem - yerousaghem (Երուսաղէմ)
jest - gadag, dzaghur, gadagel (կատակ, ծաղր, կատակել)
jestbook - zaveshdakirk, gadagakirk (զուեշտագիրք, կատակագիրք)
jesuit - hisousian, zhezvitagan (յիսուսեան, ժեզուիթական)
Jesus - hisous (Յիսուս)
jet - tsaydk, shadurvan, inknatir, nedvil, tsaydel (ցայտք, շատրուան, ինքնաթիռ, նետուիլ, ցայտել)
jetty - navamadouyts, toump, ampardag (նաւամատոյց, թումբ, ամբարտակ)

jew - huria, yeprayetsi (Հրեայ, եբրայեցի)
jewel - kohar, agun, koharazartel (գոհար, ակն, գոհարազարդել)
jeweler, jeweller - koharavajar, vosgerich (գոհարավաճառ, ոսկերիչ)
jewelery, jewellery - kohareghenk, vosgerchoutiun (գոհարեղէնք, ոսկերչութիւն)
jewess - hureouhi, huria gin (Հրէուհի, Հրեայ կին)
jewish - hureagan, yeprayagan (Հրէական, եբրայական)
jib - yerangiun arakasd, pernaparts mekenayi tev (եռանկիւն առագաստ, բեռնաբարձ մեքենայի թեւ)
jibe, gibe - hamatsaynil (Համաձայնիլ)
jiffy - vayrgian, robe, aguntard (վայրկեան, ռոպէ, ակնթարթ)
jig - barerkel, gadagel, khapel, ashkhouzh bar (պարերգել, կատակել, խաբել, աշխոյժ պար)
jiggle (n) - hunchiun, hankerou nertashnagoutiun, shachiun (Հնչիւն, յանգերու ներդաշնակութիւն, շաչիւն)
jiggle (v) - hunchel, ghoghanchel, zunkal, hankavorel (Հնչել, ղօղանջել, զնգալ, յագաւորել)
jill - keghouhi, sirouhi, gin (գեղուհի, սիրուհի, կին)
jillflirt - tetevsolig gin (թեթեւսոլիկ կին)
jilt - bujrouhi, hurabourel, khapel, tsukel (պչրուհի, Հրապուրել, խաբել, ձգել)
jingle - hunchel, zunkal, zunkots (Հնչել, զնգալ, զնգոց)
job (I) - kordz, uzpaghoum, ashkhadank, ashkhadil (գործ, զբաղում, աշխատանք, աշխատիլ)
job (II) - mukhoum, harvadz, mushdoum, dzagel, vartsel (մխում, Հարուած, մշտում, ծակել, վարձել)
jobber - arnogh-dzakhogh, michnort (առնող-ծախող, միջնորդ)
jobless - ankordz, kordzazourg (անգործ, գործազուրկ)
jockey - tsiavarzh, varbed tsiavor, khapel, gorzel (ձիավարժ, վարպետ ձիաւոր, խաբել, կորզել)
jocose - gadagakhos, zuvarjapan (կատակախօս, զուարճաբան)
jocular - zuvarjali, gadagaser, gadagayin (զուարճալի, կատակասէր, կատակային)
jocund - zuvart, ourakh, hajoyalits, touregan (զուարթ, ուրախ, Հաճոյալից, զուրեկան)
jog - hurel, mushdel, sharzhel, hurots, mughoum (Հրել, մշտել, շարժել, Հրոց, մղում)
jogger - tantagh vazogh, mushdogh (դանդաղ վազող, մշտող)
jogging - tantagh vazk, usgizpu tunel, mushdoum, tsuntsoum (դանդաղ վազք, սկիզբը դնել, մշտում, ցնցում)
joggle - tsuntsel, hurel, totvel, netsoug, hankouyts (ցնցել, Հրել, թօթուել, նեցուկ, Հանգոյց)
join - miatsunel, gabel, mianal, gutsel, miatsoum (միացնել, կապել, միանալ, կցել, միացում)
joint - gab, gutsvadzk, zisd, hot, miatsunel, gutsel (կապ, կցուածք, զիստ, յօդ, միացնել, կցել)
jointly - miasnapar (միասնաբար)
jointure - gutsoum, ayri gunoch tsukvadz zharank (կցում, այրի կնոջ ձգուած ժառանգ)
joint-venture - hamadegh tsernargoutiun (Համատեղ ձեռնարկութիւն)
joist - keran, hedzan, martag, hedzanel (գերան, Հեծան, մարդակ, Հեծանել)
joke - gadag, zevarjalik, surakhosoutiun, gadagel (կատակ, զուարճալիք, սրախօսութիւն, կատակել)
joker - gadagapan, tukhdakhaghi zoravor kardu (կատակաբան, թղթախաղի զօրաւոր քարտը)
jolly - ourakh, zuvart, vayelouch, zuvarjatsunel (ուրախ, զուարթ, վայելուչ, զուարճացնել)
jolt - tsuntsel, tsuntsoum, hurots (ցնցել, ցնցում, Հրոց)

Jordan - hortanan (Յորդանան)
jostle - hurel, hurmushdugel, khurnil (Հրել, Հրմշտկել, խռնիլ)
jostlement - hurmushdugoum, khurnoum (Հրմշտկում, խռնում)
jot - garj notakuroutiun, notakurel (կարճ նօթագրութիւն, նօթագրել)
journal - lurakir, tert, oradedur, orakuroutiun, orhashiv (օրագիր, թերթ, օրատետր, օրագրութիւն, օրհաշիւ))
journalism - lurakroutiun, orakroutiun (լրագրութիւն, օրագրութիւն)
journalist - lurakrogh, khumpakir, orakrogh (լրագրող, խմբագիր, օրագրող)
journalistic - lurakragan, tertayin (լրագրական, թերթային)
journey - oughevoroutiun, jamportoutiun, jamportel (ուղեւորութիւն, ճամբորդութիւն, ճամբորդել)
journeyman - panvor, kordzavor, oravartsov ashkhadogh (բանուոր, գործաւոր, օրավարձով աշխատող)
joust - nizagamard, nizagakhagh (Նիզակամարտ, Նիզակախաղ)
jovial - ourakh, zuvart, martamod (ուրախ, զուարթ, մարդամօտ)
jowl - ayd, toush, guzag (այտ, թուշ, կզակ)
joy - ourakhanal, tsundzal, hurjuvank, ourakhoutiun (ուրախանալ, ցնծալ, Հրճուանք, ուրախութիւն)
joyful - tsundzalits, ourakh, zuvart (ցնծալից, ուրախ, զուարթ)
joyless - dukhour, durdoum, takhdzod (տխուր, տրտում, թախծոտ)
joyous - ourakhali, shen, pergurali (ուրախալի, շէն, բերկրալի)
Jubilate - garmir giragi, tsundzal, hurjuvil (Կարմիր Կիրակի, ցնծալ, Հրճուիլ)
jubilee - hopelyan, hisnamyag, donagadaroutiun (յոբելեան, յիսնամեակ, տօնակատարութիւն)
jucundity - hajelioutiun (Հաճելիութիւն)
Judaism - movsisaganoutiun (Մովսիսականութիւն)
Judas - houta (Յուդայ)
judge - tadavor, tadel, vujrel (դատաւոր, դատել, վճռել)
judgement - vujir, tadavujir, tadoghoutiun (վճիռ, դատավճիռ, դատողութիւն)
judicial - tadagan, orinagan, adenagan (դատական, օրինական, ատենական)
judicious - oughghamid, khohagan, voghchamid, duramapanagan (ուղղամիտ, խոհական, ողջամիտ, տրամաբանական)
jug - gouzh, sapor, pand, khashel, khorovel (կուժ, սափոր, բանտ, խաշել, խորովել)
juggle - ajbararoutiun, khapeoutiun, khapel (աճպարարութիւն, խաբէութիւն, խաբել)
juggler - ajbarar, tsernadzou, khapepa, khartakh (աճպարար, ձեռնածու, խաբեբայ, խարդախ)
jugulate - mortel, gogortu gudrel (մորթել, կոկորդը կտրել)
juice - budghachour, pancharahuit, kamoug (պտղաջուր, բանջարաՀիւթ, քամուկ)
juicing - kamoug, kamoum, huitahanoum (քամուկ, քամում, Հիւթահանում)
juicing recipe - kamougnerou paghatratsang (քամուկներու բաղադրացանկ)
juicing regimen - kamougnerou sununtaganon (քամուկներու սննդականոն)
juicy - hiutegh, huitali, hamegh, churod, tats (Հիւթեղ, Հիւթալի, Համեղ, ջրոտ, թաց)
jukebox - yerkadoup, yerkargugh, yerazhshdadoup (երգատուփ, երգարկղ, երաժշտատուփ)
July - houlis (Յուլիս)
jumble - kharnagouyd, kharnel, kharnagel (խառնակոյտ, խառնել, խառնակել)
jumbo - medz, husga, vitkhari (մեծ, Հսկայ, վիթխարի)
jump - tsadgel, vosdnoul, ver turchil, tsadgoum, vosdoum (ցատկել, ոստնուլ, վեր թռչիլ, ցատկում,

ոստում)
jumper - tsadgogh, vosdosdogh, kar dzagogh kordzik (ցատկող, ոստոստող, քար ծակող գործիք)
jumpy - chughayin, chughakurkir, tiurakurkir (ջղային, ջղագրգիռ, դիւրագրգիռ)
junction - miatsoum, gab, zot, gutsvadzk, hot (միացում, կապ, զօդ, կցուածք, յօդ)
juncture - miatsoum, gutsvadzk, hotavoroum (միացում, կցուածք, յօդաւորում)
June - hounis (Յունիս)
jungle - matsaroud, andar (մացառուտ, անտառ)
junior - gurdser, badani (կրտսեր, պատանի)
junk - aveltsoug, tapon, tapvelik munatsort (աւելցուկ, թափօն, թափուելիք մնացորդ)
junk mail - tapvelik angarevor namagani (թափուլիք անկարեւոր նամականի)
junket - gatnabour, khunjouyk, khunjouyk sarkel (կաթնապուր, խնճոյք, խնճոյք սարքել)
jurant - yertvial vuga (երդուեալ վկայ)
jurisdiction - artaratadoutiun, iravasoutiun, adyan (արդարադատութիւն, իրաւասութիւն, ատեան)
jurisprudence - orenuskidoutiun, iravakidoutiun (օրէնսգիտութիւն, իրաւագիտութիւն)
jurist - iravapan, orenusked (իրաւաբան, օրէնսգէտ)
juror - yertvial tadavor, kunnich (երդուեալ դատաւոր, քննիչ)
jury - tadagazm, kunnazhoghov, kunnich hantsnakhoump (դատակազմ, քննաժողով, քննիչ յանձնախումբ)
juryman - yertvial tadavor (երդուեալ դատաւոր)
just - jisht, oughigh, irav, artar (ճիշդ, ուղիղ, իրաւ, արդար)
justice - artaroutiun, iravounk, iravasoutiun, adyan (արդարութիւն, իրաւունք, իրաւասութիւն, ատեան)
justifiable - artaranali, artaratsvogh (արդարանալի, արդարացող)
justification - artaratsoum, chukmeghank, shudgoum (արդարացում, չքմեղանք, շտկում)
justify - artaratsunel, bashdbanel, nerel (արդարացնել, պաշտպանել, ներել)
justle - untharil, pakhil, hurel, untharoum, pakhoum (ընդհարիլ, բախիլ, հրել, ընդհարում, բախում)
justness - jushtoutiun, shidagoutiun, artaroutiun (ճշդութիւն, շիտակութիւն, արդարութիւն)
jut - tsutsvadzk, tours tsutsvil (ցցուածք, դուրս ցցուիլ)
juvenescence - badanegoutiun, deghayoutiun (պատանեկութիւն, տղայութիւն)
juvenile - badani, terahas, badanegan (պատանի, դեռահաս, պատանեկան)
juxtapose - zoukaturel, kovu tunel, haraturel (զուգադրել, քովը դնել, յարադրել)
juxtaposition - zoukaturoum, kov kovi kalu (զուգադրում, քով քովի գալը)

kail - vayri gaghamp, gaghampabour (վայրի կաղամբ, կաղամբապուր)
kaiser - gaysur (կայսր)
kaleidoscope - hayelatsouyts, keghatidag, keghatsoutsag (հայելացոյց, գեղադիտակ, գեղացուցակ)
kangaroo - akevaz, kangarou

(ագեվազ, քանկարու)
keck - sirdkharnouk, vordzal (սիրտխառնուք, որձալ)
keel - baghetsunel, kharnel, purpouru hanel, vodnapayd (պաղեցնել, խառնել, փրփուրը հանել, ոտնափայտ)
keelman - navavar (նաւավար)
keen - sour, dzagogh, hadou, khisd, sasdig, suramid (սուր, ծակող, հատու, խիստ, սաստիկ, սրամիտ)
keep - bahel, bahbanel, khunamel, hok, khunamk, amrots (պահել, պահպանել, խնամել, հոգ, խնամք, ամրոց)
keeper - bahogh, bahag, husgogh, bahaban, khunamagal (պահող, պահակ, հսկող, պահապան, խնամակալ)
keeping - bahbanoutiun, hokadaroutiun, khunamadaroutiun (պահպանութիւն, հոգատարութիւն, խնամատարութիւն)
keg - dagarig, pokur dagar (տակառիկ, փոքր տակառ)
kelp - dzovakhod, aghpouys (ծովախոտ, աղբոյս)
ken - kidnal, imanal, hasgunal, kidelik, humdoutiun (գիտնալ, իմանալ, հասկնալ, գիտելիք, հմտութիւն)
kennel - shunapouyn, vohmag, vorchanal, dzuvaril (շնաբոյն, վոհմակ, որջանալ, ծուարիլ)
kent - hovivi kavazan (հովիւի գաւազան)
kermes - vortan garmir, vort mu (որդան կարմիր, որդ մը)
kermis, kermess, kirmess - donavajar, donahantes (տօնավաճառ, տօնահանդէս)
kernel - michoug, goriz, hadig, gorizanal (միջուկ, կորիզ, հատիկ, կորիզանալ)
kerosene, kerosine - kariugh, navt, gubratsiut (քարիւղ, նաւթ, կպրաձիւթ)
kestrel - hoghmavar, turchoun mu (հողմավար, թռչուն մը)
ketch - yerggaym arakasdanav (երկկայմ առագաստանաւ)
ketchup - tatsan, sungaghtsan (թացան, սնկաղցան)
kettle - teyaman, yerots, san (թէյաման, եռոց, սան)
key - panali, gughbank, tsaynanish, gughbel, larel (բանալի, կղպանք, ձայնանիշ, կղպել, լարել)
keyboard - usdeghnashar, pagagal (ստեղնաշար, փակակալ)
keyhole - paganadzag, panaliyi dzag (փականածակ, բանալիի ծակ)
keyline - nakhakidz, shurchakidz (նախագիծ, շրջագիծ)
keynote - khulkhavor, eagan tsaynanish (գլխաւոր, էական ձայնանիշ)
keystone - michnakar, anguinakar (միջնաքար, անկիւնաքար)
khaki - toukh, tukhakouyn (թուխ, թխագոյն)
khan - ishkhan, otevan (իշխան, օթեւան)
kick - gits, akatsi, akatsel (կից, աքացի, աքացել)
kicker - akatsogh, zarnogh, nedogh, merzhogh (աքացող, զարնող, նետող, մերժող)
kid - oul, dugheg, yerekha, dzunanil, oul perel (ուլ, տղեկ, երեխայ, ծնանիլ, ուլ բերել)
kidnap - arevankel, hapushdagel (առեւանգել, յափշտակել)
kidnapper - arevankogh, hapushdagich (առեւանգող, յափշտակիչ)
kidney - yerigamounk, kharnuvadzk (երիկամունք, խառնուածք)
kidneybean - pagla (բակլայ)
kill - usbannel, mertsunel, usbanoutiun (սպաննել, մեռցնել, սպանութիւն)
killer - martasban, usbannogh, vojrakordz (մարդասպան, սպաննող, ոճրագործ)
killing - mahatsou, usbanoutiun, khuntalen mertsunogh (մահացու, սպանութիւն, խնդալէն մեռցնող)
kiln - hunots, turdzots, gurapour, chortsunel, turdzel (հնոց, թրծոց, կրափուռ, չորցնել, թրծել
kilo - hazar (հազար)

kilogram, kilogramme - hazar guram, kilogram (Հազար կրամ, քիլօկրամ)
kilometer - hazar metur (Հազար մեթր)
kilowatt - hazar yelekduraouzh (Հազար ելեքտրաոյժ)
kin - azkagan, azkagits, khunami, harazad (ազգական, ազգակից, խնամի, Հարազատ)
kind - desag, gerb, azniv, pareser, pari, hamesd (տեսակ, կերպ, ազնիւ, բարեսէր, բարի, Համեստ)
kindergarten - mangabardez (մանկապարտէզ)
kindergartner - mangabardizbanouhi (մանկապարտիզպանուհի)
kindle - varel, porpokel, kurkurel, dzunil (վառել, բորբոքել, գրգռել, ծնիլ)
kindly - azniv, kunkoush, kaghtsur, aznuvoren, meghm (ազնիւ, քնքուշ, քաղցր, ազնուօրէն, մեղմ)
kindness - aznuvoutiun, siraliroutiun (ազնուութիւն, սիրալիրութիւն)
kindred - azkaganoutiun, azkaganner, azkagitsner (ազգականութիւն, ազգականներ, ազգակիցներ)
king - takavor, arka, vehabed, takavorel (Թագաւոր, արքայ, վեհապետ, Թագաւորել)
kingdom - takavoroutiun (Թագաւորութիւն)
kink - tunjoug, hankouyts, tunjougil (Թնճուկ, Հանգոյց, Թնճուկիլ)
kinship - azkagtsoutiun, numanoutiun (ազգակցութիւն, նմանութիւն)
kinsman - azkagan, ariunagits, azkagits (ազգական, արիւնակից, ազգակից)
kinswoman - azkaganouhi (ազգականուհի)
kiosk - gurbag, daghavar, pats khurjit (կրպակ, տաղաւար, բաց խրճիթ)
kiss - hampouyr, hampourel, hampourvil (Համբոյր, Համբուրել, Համբուրուիլ)
kist - argugh, takagh (արկղ, դագաղ)
kitchen - khohanots (խոՀանոց)
kitchen garden - pancharanots (բանջարանոց)
kitchen maid - khohararouhi (խոՀարարուՀի)
kitchener - khoharar (խոՀարար)
kite - ourour, hapushdagich turchoun, tsin, turoutsig (ուրուր, յափշտակիչ Թռչուն, ցին, Թռուցիկ)
kith - azkagan, chanchuvor (ազգական, ճանչուոր)
kitten - gadvouig, tsugnil, tsak perel (կատուիկ, ձկնիլ, ձագ բերել)
kitty - pisig, gadou (փիսիկ, կատու)
kiver - dzadzgel, dzadzgots (ծածկել, ծածկոց)
knack - jarbigoutiun, hunark, khaghalik, geghdzel (ճարպիկութիւն, Հնարք, խաղալիք, կեղծել)
knap - manrel, pushrel, godrel (մանրել, փշրել, կոտրել)
knapsack - barg, dobrag, makhagh (պարկ, տոպրակ, մախաղ)
knave - khapepa, suriga, nenkamid (խաբեբայ, սրիկայ, նենգամիտ)
knavery - nenkamudoutiun, khapepayoutiun (նենգամտութիւն, խաբեբայութիւն)
knead - shaghel, kharnel, jumlel (շաղել, խառնել, ճմլել)
knee - dzoung, dzunratir aghersel (ծունկ, ծնրադիր աղերսել)
kneel - dzunratrel, dzoungi kal (ծնրադրել, ծունկի գալ)
kneepan - dzungosgur (ծնկոսկր)
knell - mahazank, mahazankel, gochnagel (ՄաՀազանգ, ՄաՀազանգել, կոչնակել)
knick-knack - manur zartarank, khaghalik (մանր զարդարանք, խաղալիք)
knife - tanag, uzmeli, tashouyn, tanagel, tanagodel (դանակ, զմելի, դաշոյն, դանակել, դանակոտել)
knight - asbed, jadragi tsiavor, asbed garkel (ասպետ, ճատրակի ձիաւոր, ասպետ կարգել)
knighthood - asbedoutiun (ասպետութիւն)

knit - hiusel, gabel, hankoutsel, miatsunel, hiusvadzk (Հիւսել, կապել, Հանգուցել, միացնել, Հիւսուածք)
knob - gudzig, kound, ouretsk, purnag (կծիկ, գունտ, ուռեցք, բռնակ)
knock - zarnel, zarnuvil, harvadzel, zarg, harvadz (զարնել, զարնուիլ, Հարուածել, զարկ, Հարուած)
knockout - zarnelov uzkayazirg tartsunel (զարնելով զգայազիրկ դարձնել)
knoll - ghoghanchel, gochnagel, mahazank, hoghagouyd (ղօղանջել, կոչնակել, մաՀազանգ, Հողակոյտ)
knot - hankouyts, zartagab, gunjir, gab, mioutiun (Հանգոյց, զարդակապ, կնճիռ, կապ, միութիւն)
know - kidnal, janchunal, imanal, hishel (գիտնալ, ճանչնալ, իմանալ, յիշել)
knowing - oushim, khoramang, kidag, humdoutiun (ուշիմ, խորամանկ, գիտակ, Հմտութիւն)
knowledge - kidelik, kidoutiun, humdoutiun, dzanotoutiun (գիտելիք, գիտութիւն, Հմտութիւն, ծանօթութիւն)
known - dzanot, haydni (ծանօթ, յայտնի)
kodak - lousanugari pokur mekena (լուսանկարի փոքր մեքենայ)
Koran - kouran (Գուրան)
korean - koreatsi, koreyeren, koreagan (քորէացի, քորէերէն, քորէական)

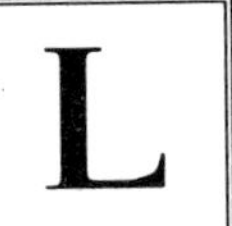

lab - largo տե'ս (laboratory)
label - bidag, bidagel (պիտակ, պիտակել)
labeled - bidagvadz (պիտակուած)
labial - shurtnayin (շրթնային)
labile - sahoun, angayoun (սաՀուն, անկայուն)
labor - ashkhadank, kordzavor, ashkhadil, hergel (աշխատանք, գործաւոր, աշխատիլ, Հերկել)
laboratory - darraloudzaran, punaloudzaran (տարրալուծարան, բնալուծարան)
laborer - ashkhadavor, kordzavor, mushag (աշխատաւոր, գործաւոր, մշակ)
laborious - ashkhadaser, tuzhvar, dazhaneli (աշխատասէր, դժուար, տաժանելի)
laborless - ankordz, anashkhad, anvasdag (անգործ, անաշխատ, անվաստակ)
labyrinth - anel, pavigh, lapiurintos, (անել, բաւիղ, լաբիւրինթոս)
lac - gunkakhezh (կնքախէժ)
lace - zhaniag, yeriz, hiusag, hiusel, yerizel (ժանեակ, երիզ, Հիւսակ, Հիւսել, երիզել)
lacerate - badrel, puzugdel, viravorel, charcharel (պատռել, բզկտել, վիրաւորել, չարչարել)
lachrymal - ardasvali, ardasvaper, ardasouki (արտասուալի, արտասուաբեր, արտասուքի)
lachrymose - lalgan, ardasvalits

(լալկան, արտասուալից)
lack - bagas, garod, patsagayoutiun, chupavararel (պակաս, կարօտ, բացակայութիւն, չբաւարարել)
lackey - laj, usbasavor, varnots, usdor, kudznil (լաճ, սպասաւոր, վարնոց, ստոր, քծնիլ)
laconic - garj, gudroug, lagonagan (կարճ, կտրուկ, լակոնական)
lacquer - chunarag, gunkamom, chunaragel (ջնարակ, կնքամոմ, ջնարակել)
lactation - tietsoum, gatundououtiun, dzidz dalu (դիեցում, կաթնտուութիւն, ծիծ տալը)
lactose - gatnashakar (կաթնաշաքար)
lacuna - baraboutiun, pats degh, bagas-pan (պարապութիւն, բաց տեղ, պակաս՝բան)
lad - manch, laj, yerekha, dugha (մանչ, լաճ, երեխայ, տղայ)
ladder - santoukh, yelaran (սանդուխ, ելարան)
lade - pernavorel, pertsunel (բեռնաւորել, բեռցնել)
laden - pernavorvadz, letsoun, jokh, gukadz (բեռնաւորուած, լեցուն, ճոխ, կքած)
lading - pernavoroum, navapernoum (բեռնաւորում, նաւաբեռնում)
ladle - sherep, medz tukal, sherepahanel (շերեփ, մեծ դգալ, շերեփահանել)
lady - digin, dirouhi, dandigin (տիկին, տիրուհի, տանտիկին)
ladylike - ganatsi, gunanuman, paretsev, vayelouch (կանացի, կնանման, բարեձեւ, վայելուչ)
lag - oushatsoum, tantagh, hedin, verchin, oushanal (ուշացում, դանդաղ, յետին, վերջին, ուշանալ)
laggard - tantagh, dzanrasharzh (դանդաղ, ծանրաշարժ)
lagoon - dzovalij, lujag (ծովալիճ, լճակ)
laic - ashkharhagan (աշխարհական)
lair - vorch, pouyn, takusdots (որջ, բոյն, թաքստոց)
laity - ashkharhagan tas (աշխարհական դաս)
lake - lij (լիճ)
lakelet - lujag (լճակ)
lam - dzedzel, khupel, tagel (ծեծել, խփել, թակել)
lamb - karnoug, kar, kar dzunanil (գառնուկ, գառ, գառ ծնանիլ)
lame - gagh, hashmantam, angarogh, hashmel (կաղ, հաշմանդամ, անկարող, հաշմել)
lament - voghpal, gusgudzal, sukal, voghp, gusgidz, godz (ողբալ, կսկծալ, սգալ, ողբ, կսկիծ, կոծ)
lamentable - voghpali, tsavali, (ողբալի, ցաւալի)
lamentation - voghp, godz, lats (ողբ, կոծ, լաց)
laminate - tertavorel, parag sherdel, tertabadel (թերթաւորել, բարակ շերտել, թերթապատել)
laminated - tertavor, sherdavor, sherdabadvadz (թերթաւոր, շերտաւոր, շերտապատուած)
laminating - tertabadoum, khavargoum (թերթապատում, խաւարկում)
lamination - sherdavoroum, tertagazmoutiun (շերտաւորում, թերթակազմութիւն)
lamp - lamp, gantegh, labder, jurak (լամբ, կանթեղ, լապտեր, ճրագ)
lamplight - jurakalouys (ճրագալոյս)
lampoon - barsavakir, khudzpidz, yerkidzel (պարսաւագիր, խծբիծ, երգիծել)
lampshade - lousampop (լուսամփոփ)
lance - nizag, dek, nizagel (նիզակ, տէգ, նիզակել)
lancer - nizagahar, nizagavor (նիզակահար, նիզակաւոր)
lancet - nushturag, pokur tanag (նշդրակ, փոքր դանակ)
lancinate - nizagel, khotsel, badurel (նիզակել, խոցել, պատռել)
land - yergir, hogh, galvadz, tsamakel, hasnil (երկիր, հող, կալուած, ցամաքել, հասնիլ)
landing - tsamakahanoum, tsamakogh (ցամաքահանում, ցամաքող)
landlord - hoghader, galvadzader,

dander (հողատէր, կալուածատէր, տանտէր)
landman - tsamakapunag, hoghader (ցամաքաբնակ, հողատէր)
landmark - sahmanakar, tsamakanushan (սահմանաքար, ցամաքանշան)
landowner - hoghader, galvadzader (հողատէր, կալուածատէր)
landscape - punabadger, punanugar, tashdanugar (բնապատկեր, բնանկար, դաշտանկար)
lane - nurpoughi, antsk, arahed, nurpantsk, jamperiz (նրբուղի, անցք, արահետ, նրբանցք, ճամբեբիզ)
language - lezou, khosvadzk, parpar (լեզու, խօսուածք, բարբառ)
languid - touyl, dugar, nuvaghoun (թոյլ, տկար, նուաղուն)
languish - nuvaghil, hiudzil, dugaranal, nuvaghetsnel (նուաղիլ, հիւծիլ, տկարանալ, նուաղեցնել)
languor - nuvaghoum, touloutiun, dugaroutiun (նուաղում, թուլութիւն, տկարութիւն)
laniate - puzukdel, badurdel (բզքտել, պատռտել)
laniation - puzukdoum, badurdoum (բզքտում, պատռտում)
lank - nihar, vudid, nurpamarmin, niharnal, nihartsunel (նիհար, վտիտ, նրբամարմին, նիհարնալ, նիհարցնել)
lantern - labder, gantegh, lousamoud (լապտեր, կանթեղ, լուսամուտ)
lap - pesh, kirg, lapoum, lapel, pattel, veradzalel (փէշ, գիրկ, լափում, լափել, փաթթել, վերածալել)
lapidary - koharaked, agnakordz, vimakir (գոհարագէտ, ակնագործ, վիմագիր)
lapidate - kargodzel (քարկոծել)
lapidify - karatsunel, karanal (քարացնել, քարանալ)
lapse - antsk, sukhalmounk, saytakoum, antsnil, iynal (անցք, սխալմունք, սայթաքում, անցնիլ, իյնալ)
larceny - koghoutiun (գողութիւն)
lard - khozajarb (խոզաճարպ)
lare - ousoum, kidoutiun, ger, geragurel (ուսում, գիտութիւն, կեր, կեր, կերակրել)
large - layn, untartsag, medz, khoshor, arad (լայն, ընդարձակ, մեծ, խոշոր, առատ)
lark - ardouyd, zuvarjoutiun, gadagel (արտոյտ, զուարճութիւն, կատակել)
larva - turtour, sherepoug (թրթուր, շերեփուկ)
laryngophone - hakakatsayn, khurchapoghatsayn (հագագաձայն, խռչափոխաձայն)
larynx - gogort (կոկորդ)
lascivious - tsangaser, vavashod, heshdaser (ցանկասէր, վավաշոտ, հեշտասէր)
laser - jarakaytartsag, shoghartsag (ճառագայթարձակ, շողարձակ)
lash - mudragel, kharazanel, mudrag, kharazan, tartich (մտրակել, խարազանել, մտրակ, խարազան, թարթիչ)
lass - aghchig, aghchunag, sirouhi (աղջիկ, աղջնակ, սիրուհի)
lassitude - hoknoutiun, khonchenk (յոգնութիւն, խոնջէնք)
last - verchin, hedin, verchabes, gaghabar, devel (վերջին, յետին, վերջապէս, կաղապար, տեւել)
lasting - devagan, munayoun (տեւական, մնայուն)
lastly - verchabes (վերջապէս)
latch - gughbank, pagan, nik, gughbel, pagel (կղպանք, փական, նիգ, կղպել, փակել)
latchet - goshgagab (կօշկակապ)
late - oush, nakhgin, verchin, meradz (ուշ, նախկին, վերջին, մեռած)
latency - taknoutiun, kaghdunioutiun (թաքնութիւն, գաղտնիութիւն)
latent - kaghdni, dzadzoug, takoun (գաղտնի, ծածուկ, թաքուն)
lateral - goghmnagi, kovundi (կողմնակի, քովնտի)
latest - verchnakouyn, amenaverchin

(վերջնագոյն, ամենավերջին)
latex - pousagat (բուսակաթ)
lathe - jakharag, sanduragal (ճախարակ, սանտրակալ)
lather - purpour, purpuretsunel, ojarel (փրփուր, փրփրեցնել, օճառել)
latin - ladin, ladineren, ladinagan (լատին, լատիներէն, լատինական)
latitude - laynoutiun, laynk, daradzoutiun (լայնութիւն, լայնք, տարածութիւն)
latrate - hachel (հաչել)
latration - hachoum (հաչում)
latter - verchin, hedin, verchinu (վերջին, յետին, վերջինը)
lattice - vantag, vantagamadz, vantagel, vantagabadel (վանդակ, վանդակամած, վանդակել, վանդակապատել)
laud - kovk, kovesd, orhnerk, kovel, orhnel (գովք, գովեստ, օրհներգ, գովել, օրհնել)
laudation - kovesd, kovapanoutiun (գովեստ, գովաբանութիւն)
laugh - khuntouk, dzidzagh, khuntal (խնդուք, ծիծաղ, խնդալ)
laughter - khuntouk, dzidzagh, kurkich (խնդուք, ծիծաղ, քրքիջ)
launch - artsagel, dzov ichetsunel, shokemagouyg (արձակել, ծով իջեցնել, շոգեմակոյկ)
launder - luval, artougel (լուալ, արդուկել)
launderer - luvatsarar (լուացարար)
laundering - luvatsararoutiun (լուացարարութիւն)
laundress - luvatsararouhi (լուացարարուհի)
laundry - luvatsaran, luvatskadoun (լուացարան, լուացքատուն)
laura - menasdan (մենաստան)
laureate - tapnegir, busagavor, tapnebusagel (դափնեկիր, պսակաւոր, դափնեպսակել)
laurel - tapni, tapnedzar (դափնի, դափնեծառ)
lava - hurahosk, huraheghoug, lava (հրահոսք, հրահեղուկ, լաւա)
lavabo, lavatory - luvatsaran, ardaknots, jemish (լուացարան, արտաքնոց, ճեմիշ)
lave - luval, luvatsvil, loknal (լուալ, լուացուիլ, լողնալ)
lavender - housam, levatsoug, anoushapouyr pouys mu (հուսամ, լուացուկ, անուշաբոյր բոյս մը)
lavish - shurayl, muskhogh, muskhel, vadnel (շռայլ, մսխող, մսխել, վատնել)
law - orenk, ganon, iravakidoutiun (օրէնք, կանոն, իրաւագիտութիւն)
law maker - orenustir (orenustir)
lawful - orinavor, orinagan (օրինաւոր, օրինական)
lawmaker - oresnustir (օրէնսդիր)
lawn - mark, talarik, marmant, markakedin (մարգ, դալարիք, մարմանդ, մարգագետին)
lawsuit - tad, tadavaroutiun (դատ, դատավարութիւն)
lawyer - iravapan, pasdapan, orenusked (իրաւաբան, փաստաբան, օրէնսգէտ)
law-court - tadasurah, tadaran (դատասրահ, դատարան)
lax - touyl, gagough, toulamort, anpouyt (թոյլ, կակուղ, թուլամորթ, անփոյթ)
laxation - touloutiun, toulatsunoum (թուլութիւն, թուլացնում)
laxative - loudzoghagan, toulatsoutsich (լուծողական, թուլացուցիչ)
lay (n) - ashkharhagan, markakedin, oukhd, havadk, yerk (աշխարհական, մարգագետին, ուխտ, հաւատք, երգ)
lay (v) - tunel, deghavorel, hasdadel, adzel, purel (դնել, տեղաւորել, հաստատել, ածել, փռել)
layer - adzogh, hiusogh, zedeghogh, khav (ածող, հիւսող, զետեղող, խաւ)
layette - noradzini shor (նորածինի շոր)
layland - khoban yergir, anmushag hoghamas (խոպան երկիր, անմշակ հողամաս)
layman - ashkharhagan (աշխարհական)

layoff - *kordzatatar, kordzazurgoum, ashkhadatatar* (գործադադար, գործազրկում, աշխատադադար)
layout - *echatroum, hadagakidz, hadagakudzel* (էջադրում, յատակագիծ, յատակագծել)
lazar - *porod* (բորոտ)
laze - *dzoulanal* (ծուլանալ)
laziness - *dzouloutiun* (ծուլութիւն)
lazy - *dzouyl* (ծոյլ)
lea - *markakedin, arodavayr* (մարգագետին, արօտավայր)
lead (n) - *gabar, arachnortoutiun, khorachap, doghanchad* (կապար, առաջնորդութիւն, խորաչափ, տողանջատ)
lead (v) - *arachnortel, varel, oughghel, ghegavarel* (առաջնորդել, վարել, ուղղել, ղեկավարել)
leader - *arachnort, ghegavar* (առաջնորդ, ղեկավար)
leadership - *arachnortoutiun* (առաջնորդութիւն)
leading - *arachnortogh, ghegavar* (առաջնորդող, ղեկավար)
leaf - *derev, saghart, tert, peghg* (տերեւ, սաղարթ, թերթ, փեղկ)
leaflet - *turoutsig, tertig, dzanoutsatert* (թռուցիկ, թերթիկ, ծանուցաթերթ)
leafy - *derevod, saghartakhid* (տերեւոտ, սաղարթախիտ)
league - *miutiun, liga, parsakh, tashnagtsil* (միութիւն, լիկա, փարսախ, դաշնակցիլ)
leak - *dzag, jeghk, gatil, ardadzorel, muzil* (ծակ, ճեղք, կաթիլ, արտածորել, մզիլ)
leal - *havadarim* (հաւատարիմ)
lean - *anjarb, nihar, anarzhek tserakir, dzuril, hagil* (անճարպ, նիհար, անարժէք ձեռագիր, ծռիլ, հակիլ)
leap - *tsadgel, tsadgurdel, vosdnoul, vosdoum* (ցատկել, ցատկռտել, ոստնուլ, ոստում)
learn - *sorvil, ousanil, serdel* (սորվիլ, ուսանիլ, սերտել)
learned - *ousial, zarkatsadz, kachahumoud* (ուսեալ, զարգացած, քաջահմուտ)
learner - *sorvogh, ousanogh, ashagerd* (սորվող, ուսանող, աշակերտ)
learning - *ousoum, ousmounk, humdoutiun* (ուսում, ուսմունք, հմտութիւն)
lease - *vartsel, vartsou dal, vartsakir* (վարձել, վարձու տալ, վարձագիր)
lease holder - *vartsagal, vartsvor* (վարձակալ, վարձուոր)
leasing - *vartsoum* (վարձում)
least - *nuvazakouyn, pokrakouyn* (նուազագոյն, փոքրագոյն)
leather - *gashi* (կաշի)
leave - *tsukel, toghoul, ardonoutiun, artsagourt* (ձգել, թողուլ, արտօնութիւն, արձակուրդ)
leaven - *tutkhumor, khumor, khumorel* (թթխմոր, խմոր, խմորել)
leavings - *munatsortner, aveltsouk, dagank* (մնացորդներ, աւելցուք, տականք)
lebanese - *lipanantsi, lipananian* (լիբանանցի, լիբանանեան)
Lebanon - *lipanan* (Լիբանան)
lech - *luzel* (լզել)
lectern - *kurkagal, kuraseghan* (գրքակալ, գրասեղան)
lecture - *tasakhosoutiun, jar, tasakhosel* (դասախօսութիւն, ճառ, դասախօսել)
lecturer - *tasakhos, panakhos, karozich* (դասախօս, բանախօս, քարոզիչ)
lectureship - *karozchoutiun* (քարոզչութիւն)
ledge - *dzayr, yezur, khout, hankerag* (ծայր, եզր, խութ, հանքերակ)
ledger - *hashvededur, mayr domar, dabanakar* (հաշուետետր, մայր տոմար, տապանաքար)
lee - *hagahov, abasdaran* (հակահով, ապաստարան)
leech - *duzroug, ariunarpou* (տզրուկ, արիւնարբու)
leer - *vavashod nayvadzk, goghmunagi nayil* (վաւաշոտ նայուածք, կողմնակի նայիլ)

lees - tird, murour, aveltsouk (դիրտ, մրուր, աւելցուք)
left - tsakh (ձախ)
leg - surounk, seghani vodk, vazel (սրունք, սեղանի ոտք, վազել)
legacy - zharankoutiun, gudag (ժառանգութիւն, կտակ)
legal - orinagan, iravagan, vaveragan (օրինական, իրաւական, վաւերական)
legalize - orinaganatsunel, vaveratsunel (օրինականացնել, վաւերացնել)
legate - badvirag, nergayatsoutsich, pokhanort, gudagel (պատուիրակ, ներկայացուցիչ, փոխանորդ, կտակել)
legation - badviragoutiun, tesbanoutiun (պատուիրակութիւն, դեսպանութիւն)
legator - gudagarar (կտակարար)
legend - arasbel, avantoutiun, avantaveb, vark surpots (առասպել, աւանդութիւն, աւանդավէպ, վարք սրբոց)
legendary - arasbelagan (առասպելական)
legerity - tetevoutiun (թեթեւութիւն)
legibility - unternelioutiun (ընթեռնելիութիւն)
legible - unternli, gartatsvelik (ընթեռնլի, կարդացուելիք)
legion - lekeon, zorakount, zorakhoump (լեգէոն, զօրագունդ, զօրախումբ)
legislate - orenusturel (օրէնսդրել)
legislation - orenusturoutiun (օրէնսդրութիւն)
legislative - orenusturagan, orenustir (օրէնսդրական, օրէնսդիր)
legislator - orenustir, orenuskurogh (օրէնսդիր, օրէնսգրող)
legislature - orenusturoutiun, orenustir marmin (օրէնսդրութիւն, օրէնսդիր մարմին)
legist - orenusked, iravaked (օրէնսգէտ, իրաւագէտ)
legitimacy - orinaganoutiun, orinavoroutiun (օրինականութիւն, օրինաւորութիւն)
legitimate - orinagan, vaveragan, orinaganatsunel (օրինական, վաւերական, օրինականացնել)
legitimation - orinaganatsoum, vortekuroum (օրինականացում, որդեգրում)
legitimize - orinaganatsunel (օրինականացնել)
legman - lurahaghort, deghegakurogh (լրահաղորդ, տեղեկագրող)
legume - panchareghen, ganacheghen (բանջարեղէն, կանաչեղէն)
leisure - hankusdi zham, zhamants, badehoutiun (հանգստի ժամ, ժամանց, պատեհութիւն)
lemon - lemon, gidron (լեմոն, կիտրոն)
lemonade - lemonachour, osharag (լեմոնաջուր, օշարակ)
lemur - aghvesagabig, gisagabig (աղուեսակապիկ, կիսակապիկ)
lend - pokh dal, haytaytel, duramaturel, untserel (փոխ տալ, հայթայթել, տրամադրել, ընձեռել)
lender - pokhadou, pokh duvogh, untserogh (փոխատու, փող տուող, ընձեռող)
length - yergaynk, daradzoutiun, michots, devoghoutiun (երկայնք, տարածութիւն, միջոց, տեւողութիւն)
lengthen - yergarel, yerguntsunel, daradzel (երկարել, երկնցնել, տարածել)
lengthwise - yergaynagi, yergaynkov (երկայնակի, երկայնքով)
lenience - meghmoutiun, kutoutiun, neroghamudoutiun (մեղմութիւն, գթութիւն, ներողամտութիւն)
lenient - neroghamid, meghm, hez, kutasird, zichogh (ներողամիտ, մեղմ, հեզ, գթասիրտ, զիջող)
lenity - meghmoutiun, kutasurdoutiun (մեղմութիւն, գթասրտութիւն)
lens - desabagi, vosbniag, manratsouyts (տեսապակի, ոսպնեակ, մանրացոյց)
Lent - medz bahk (Մեծ Պահք)
lentil - vosb, vosbuniag (ոսպ, ոսպնեակ)

lentous - gubchoun, madzoutsig (կպչուն, մածուցիկ)
leonine - ariudzagerb, ariudzanuman (առիւծակերպ, առիւծանման)
leopard - untsariudz (ընձառիւծ)
leper - porod (բորոտ)
leprosy - porodoutiun (բորոտութիւն)
lerturn -
lesbian - miaseragan-gin (միասեռական-կին)
lesion - vunasvadzk, verk, khots (վնասուածք, վէրք, խոց)
less - bagas, nuvaz, kich, pokur (պակաս, նուազ, քիչ, փոքր)
lessee - vartsagal, vartsuvor, vargagal (վարձակալ, վարձուոր, վարկակալ)
lessen - bagsil, nuvazil, bagsetsunel, nuvazetsunel (պակսիլ, նուազիլ, պակսեցնել, նուազեցնել)
lesson - tas, tasakhosoutiun, ousoutsanel, khuradel (դաս, դասախօսութիւն, ուսուցանել, խրատել)
lessor - vartsadou, vartsou duvogh, dander (վարձատու, վարձու տուող, տանտէր)
lest - koutse, chulla te (գուցէ, չըլլայ թէ)
let - tsukel, toghoul, ardonel, vartsou dal (ձգել, թողուլ, արտօնել, վարձու տալ)
lethal - mahatsou, maharit, aghedaper (մահացու, մահառիթ, աղէտաբեր)
lethargy - kunadoutiun, kunakhd, anuzkayoutiun (քնատութիւն, քնախտ, անզգայութիւն)
letraset - pokhantsadar, pokhatradar, gubchoun dar (փոխանցատառ, փոխադրատառ, կպչուն տառ)
letter - kir, dar, namag (գիր, տառ, նամակ)
letter box - posdargugh (փոստարկղ)
letter card - patsig, pats namag (բացիկ, բաց նամակ)
letter of credit - vargakir (վարկագիր)
letter paper - namagatought (նամակաթուղթ)
letterbox - namagadoup (նամակատուփ)
lettered - ousial, gurtial, kuraked (ուսեալ, կրթեալ, գրագէտ)
letterfit - daramichots (տառամիջոց)
letterhead - namagakuloukh (նամակագլուխ)
lettering - turoshmoum, duboum, kurakudzoutiun (դրոշմում, տպում, գրագծութիւն)
letterpress - daradib, dubakir տառատիպ, տպագիր)
letterwriter - namagakir (նամակագիր)
lettuce - hazar (Հազար)
leukemia - aryan kaghtsgegh (արեան քաղցկեղ)
levant - bardke pakhchil, chuvel (պարտքէ փախչիլ, չուել)
Levant - arevelk, arevelian yergirner (Արեւելք, արեւելեան երկիրներ)
levee - arevadzak, arduva untouneloutiun, ampardag (արեւածագ, առտուայ ընդունելութիւն, ամբարտակ)
level - magartad, asdijan, mageres, hart, hartel (մակարդակ, աստիճան, մակերես, Հարթ, Հարթել)
lever - ludzag (լծակ)
levigate - hughgel, manrel, poshiatsunel, hughguvadz (յղկել, մանրել, փոշիացնել, յղկուած)
levigation - hughgoum (յղկում)
levir - dakur (տագր)
levity - tetevamudoutiun, tetevsoligoutiun (թեթեւամտութիւն, թեթեւսոլիկութիւն)
levy - zorahavak, hargahavak, dourk kantsel (զօրահաւաք, Հարկահաւաք, տուրք գանձել)
lewd - tsop, vavashod, anbargeshd, anarag, lubirsh (ցոփ, վաւաշոտ, անպարկեշտ, անառակ, լպիրշ)
lexicographer - pararanakir (բառարանագիր)
lexicon - parabashar, pararan, parakirk (բառապաշար, բառարան,

բառագիրք)
liability - hantsnaroutiun, badaskhanaduvoutiun, bardk (յանձնառութիւն, պատասխանատուութիւն, պարտք)
liable - bardavor, badaskhanadou, yentaga (պարտաւոր, պատասխանատու, ենթակայ)
liaison - gabagtsoutiun, gab, haraperoutiun (կապակցութիւն, կապ, յարաբերութիւն)
liar - sudakhos, soudasan (ստախօս, սուտասան)
libation - kinetson, tsonoum, kinarpouk (գինեձօն, ձօնում, գինարբուք)
libel - zurbardoutiun, barsavakir, zurbardel, (զրպարտութիւն, պարսաւագիր, զրպարտել)
libeller - zurbardich, barsavogh (զրպարտիչ, պարսաւող)
liberal - azadagan, azadamid, aradatserun (ազատական, ազատամիտ, առատաձեռն)
liberalism - azadakhohoutiun (ազատախոհութիւն)
liberation - azadakroum, azadoum, artsagoum (ազատագրում, ազատում, արձակում)
liberator - azadarar, purgogh, azadakurogh (ազատարար, փրկող, ազատագրող)
libertine - azadamid, santsartsag, anarag, anparo (ազատամիտ, սանձարձակ, անառակ, անբարոյ)
liberty - azadoutiun, ardonoutiun, menashunorh (ազատութիւն, արտօնութիւն, մենաշնորհ)
librarian - kurataranabed, kurataranavar, kurabah (գրադարանապետ, գրադարանավար, գրապահ)
library - kurataran, kuradoun (գրադարան, գրատուն)
librate - jojel, jojetsunel (ճօճել, ճօճեցնել)
libretto - taderadedur, yerashdadedur (Թատերատետր, երաշտատետր)
lice - vochilner (ոջիլներ) pl.-յգ. louse-ի — (ոջիլ-ի)
license - ardonakir, ardonoutiun, ardonel, touyladurel (արտօնագիր, արտօնութիւն, արտօնել, Թոյլատրել)
licensed - ardonial, ardonakurial (արտօնեալ, արտօնագրեալ)
licensee - ardonader (արտօնատէր)
licentious - anarag, anparo, zeghkh, lugdi (անառակ, անբարոյ, զեղխ, լկտի)
lich - tiag, merial (դիակ, մեռեալ)
lick - luzel, lapel, lagel, lizoum, harvadz, dzedz (լզել, լափել, լակել, լիզում, հարուած, ծեծ)
lid - gaparich, khoup, gob (կափարիչ, խուփ, կոպ)
lie - soud, geghdzik, sudel, bargil, yergunnal (սուտ, կեղծիք, ստել, պառկիլ, երկննալ)
lief - hajeli, sireli, sirov, gamovin, siragan (հաճելի, սիրելի, սիրով, կամովին, սիրական)
liege - vehabed, avadabed, der, avadarou, hubadag (վեհապետ, աւատապետ, տէր, աւատառու, հպատակ)
lien - arnelik, orinagan bahanch (առնելիք, օրինական պահանջ)
lieu - degh, vayr, pokhanag (տեղ, վայր, փոխանակ)
lieutenant - deghagal, deghabah, pokhanort (տեղակալ, տեղապահ, փոխանորդ)
life - gyank, gentanoutiun, hoki, mart (կեանք, կենդանութիւն, հոգի, մարդ)
life guard - tignabah (Թիկնապահ)
life insurance - gyanki abahovakuroutiun (կեանքի ապահովագրութիւն)
lifebelt - purgakodi, purgoutian kodi (փրկագօտի, փրկութեան գօտի)
lifeboat - purganav (փրկանաւ)
lifeful - gensalits, ashkhouyzh (կենսալից, աշխոյժ)
lifeguard - bahaban, tignabah, bahag (պահապան, Թիկնապահ, պահակ)
lifeless - anshounch, angentan, meradz (անշունչ, անկենդան, մեռած)

lifeline - azadarar chouan-navi (ազատարար չուան՝ նաւի)
lifesaver - purgarar, bahaban, gensabah (փրկարար, պահապան, կենսապահ)
lifestyle - abrelagerb, abrelavoj, abrelatsev (ապրելակերպ, ապրելաոճ, ապրելաձեւ)
lifetime - tsugianus (ցկեանս)
lifetime - giank, gianki devoghoutiun (կեանք, կեանքի տեւողութիւն)
lift - verelag, yelaran, yellel, vertsunel, koghnal (վերելակ, ելարան, ելլել, վերցնել, գողնալ)
lifting - partsuratsunogh, ver hanogh (բարձրացնող, վեր հանող)
ligament - hotagab, neartagab (յօդակապ, նեարդակապ)
ligate - gabel, viragabel (կապել, վիրակապել)
ligation - gab, gaboum, zotoum (կապ, կապում, զօդում)
ligature - viragab, gab, gutsadar, viragabel, gabel (վիրակապ, կապ, կցատառ, վիրակապել, կապել)
light - louys, tsereg, tetev, varil, varel, lousavorel (լոյս, ցերեկ, թեթեւ, վառիլ, վառել, լուսաւորել)
lighten - lousavorel, payletsunel,tetevtsunel, paylil (լուսաւորել, փայլեցնել, թեթեւցնել, փայլիլ)
lighthouse - paros (փարոս)
lightness - lousavoroutiun, tetevoutiun, patsoutiun (լուսաւորութիւն, թեթեւութիւն, բացութիւն)
lightning - gaydzag, paylag, lousadagoum (կայծակ, փայլակ, լուսատակում)
lightsome - lousavor, payloun, zuvart (լուսաւոր, փայլուն, զուարթ)
lighty - lousavor, tetevagi, anhok (լուսաւոր, թեթեւակի, անհոգ)
likable - hajeli, sireli, hurabourich (հաճելի, սիրելի, հրապուրիչ)
like (n) - numan, nouyn, nouynorinag, havasar (նման, նոյն, նոյնօրինակ, հաւասար)
like (v) - sirel, hamagril, havnil, akhorzhil (սիրել, համակրիլ, հաւնիլ, ախորժիլ)
likelihood - havanaganoutiun, gareli-outiun, numanoutiun (հաւանականութիւն, կարելիութիւն, նմանութիւն
likely - havanagan, gareli, harmar (հաւանական, կարելի, յարմար)
liken - numantsunel, hamemadel, paghtadel (նմանցնել, համեմատել, բաղդատել)
likeness - numanoutiun, nouynoutiun, desil, badger (նմանութիւն, նոյնութիւն, տեսիլ, պատկեր)
likewise - numanabes, nouynbes, nayev (նմանապէս, նոյնպէս, նաեւ)
liking - hamagrank, nakhunduroutiun (համակրանք, նախընտրութիւն)
lilac - yeghrevani, pats manishagakouyn (եղրեւանի, բաց մանիշակագոյն)
lily - shoushan (շուշան)
limb - dzayr, marmuni dzayramas, antamahadel (ծայր, մարմնի ծայրամաս, անդամահատել)
limber - jugoun, tiurasharzh, gagough, jugounatsunel (ճկուն, դիւրաշարժ, կակուղ, ճկունացնել)
limbo - pand, arkelaran, kavaran (բանտ, արգելարան, քաւարան)
lime - gir, pour, loreni, gurachurel, girel (կիր, բուռ, լորենի, կրաջրել, կիրել)
limelight - guralouys (կրալոյս)
limestone - gurakar (կրաքար)
limit - sahman, yezur, sahmanapagel, sahmanel (սահման, եզր, սահմանափակել, սահմանել)
limitation - sahmanapagoum, iravasoutian jushtoum (սահմանափակում, իրաւասութեան ճշդում)
limited - sahmanapag, negh, chapavor (սահմանափակ, նեղ, չափաւոր)
limn - nugarel, kudzakurel, keghazartel, badgerazartel (նկարել, գծագրել, գեղազարդել, պատկերազարդել)
limousine - berjagark (պերճակառք)
limp - gagough, jugoun, saytakoum, gaghal, saytakil (կակուղ, ճկուն, սայթաքում, կաղալ, սայթաքիլ)
limpid - husdag, vujid, baydzar

(յստակ, վճիռ, պայծառ)

linage, lineage - seruntagits, sharavigh, doghakanag, doghavarts (սերնդակից, շառաւիղ, տողաքանակ, տողավարձ)

linden - lori, loreni, tumpi (լորի, լորենի, թմփի)

line (n) - kidz, dogh, baran, shark, garasiun, sahman (գիծ, տող, պարան, շարք, կառասիւն, սահման)

line (v) - kudzel, sharel, doghel, untkudzel (գծել, շարել, տողել, ընդգծել)

lineage - suruntagits, sharavigh, zarm (սերնդակից, շառաւիղ, զարմ)

lineament - ourvakidz, nakhakidz, timakidz (ուրուագիծ, նախագիծ, դիմագիծ)

lineman - kudzahusgich (գծահսկիչ)

linen - gudav, gerbaseghen, jermageghen (կտաւ, կերպասեղէն, ճերմակեղէն)

liner - nav - nouyn kudzov katsogh, doghahashvogh khumpakir (նաւ՝ նոյն գծով գացող, տողահաշուող խմբագիր)

linger - oushanal, habaghil, dundunal, tantaghil (ուշանալ, յապաղիլ, տնտնալ, դանդաղիլ)

lingerie - gudaveghen, ganatsi jermageghen (կտաւեղէն, կանացի ճերմակեղէն)

lingo - lezou, parpar (լեզու, բարբառ)

lingual - lezvayin, lezvagan (լեզուային, լեզուական)

linguist - lezvapan, lezvaked (լեզուաբան, լեզուագէտ)

linguistic - lezvapanagan, lezvakidagan (լեզուաբանական, լեզուագիտական)

linguistics - lezvapanoutiun, lezvakidoutiun (լեզուաբանութիւն, լեզուագիտութիւն)

lining - asdar, nerkin gudav, gudavabadoum (աստառ, ներքին կտաւ, կտաւապատում)

link - ogh, oghag, zot, gab, zotoum, oghagel, gabel (օղ, օղակ, զօղ, կապ, զօղում, օղակել, կապել)

links - golfi khaghavayr (կոլֆի խաղավայր)

linoleum - gudavag, momlate dzadzgots (կտաւակ, մոմլաթէ ծածկոց)

linotype - doghashar, doghadib (տողաշար, տողատիպ)

linseed - gudavad, gudavi serm (կտաւատ, կտաւի սերմ)

lint - dzuvad, voush, kutani gudor (ծուատ, վուշ, քթանի կտոր)

lintel - jagadakar (ճակատաքար)

lion - ariudz (առիւծ)

lip - shurtounk, shourt, dzayr, hampourel, shurtnel (շրթունք, շուրթ, ծայր, համբուրել, շրթնել)

lipa - jarb (ճարպ)

lipstick - shurtnanergi tsubig (շրթնաներկի ցպիկ)

liquid - heghoug, churod, hosoun, dzoran, sahoun (հեղուկ, ջրոտ, հոսուն, ծորան, սահուն)

liquidate - hashvehartarel, loudzarki yentargel (հաշուեյարդարել, լուծարքի ենթարկել)

liquidation - hashvehartar, loudzark (հաշուեյարդար, լուծարք)

liquidator - loudzarki yentargogh (լուծարքի ենթարկող)

liquor - khumichk, umbelik, vokelits umbeli (խմիչք, ըմպելիք, ոգելից ըմպելի)

lisp - totovel, gagazel, totovank (թոթովել, կակազել, թոթովանք)

list (I) - tsang, tsoutsag, tsoutsagakurel, artsanakurvil (ցանկ, ցուցակ, ցուցակագրել, արձանագրուիլ)

list (II) - dzayr, kudzazart, murtsaran, papak, yerizel, papakil (ծայր, գծազարդ, մրցարան, փափաք, երիզել)

listen - lusel, mudig unel, oungunturel, ansal (լսել, մտիկ ընել, ունկնդրել, անսալ)

listener - lusogh, ounguntir (լսող, ունկնդիր)

listless - anhok, andarper, anoushatir (անհոգ, անտարբեր, անուշադիր)

literacy - kurakidoutiun, kurajanachoutiun (գրագիտութիւն, գրաճանաչութիւն)
literal - paratsi, par ar par, daratsi, jushkurid (բառացի, բառ առ բառ, տառացի, ճշգրիտ)
literary - kuragan (գրական)
literate - kurogh, ousial, gartatsadz (գրող, ուսեալ, կարդացած)
literature - kuraganoutiun, tubroutiun (գրականութիւն, դպրութիւն)
lith - mas, jiugh, antam (մաս, ճիւղ, անդամ)
lithany - der voghormia, orhnaghotk (Տէր ողորմեա, օրհնաղօթք)
lithe - jugoun, tiuratek, gagough (ճկուն, դիւրաթեք, կակուղ)
lithograph - vimakurel, karakurel, vimakir (վիմագրել, քարագրել, վիմագիր)
lithographer - vimakurogh, vimakurich (վիմագրող, վիմագրիչ)
lithography - vimakuroutiun, vimaduboutiun (վիմագրութիւն, վիմատպութիւն)
Lithuania - litvania (Լիթուանիա)
lithuanian - litvanatsi, litvaneren (լիթուանացի, լիթուաներէն)
litigate - tadavijil, tad panal (դատավիճիլ, դատ բանալ)
litigation - tadavaroutiun, tad, vej (դատավարութիւն, դատ, վէճ)
litter - aghp, geghd, kahavorag, geghdodel, aghp nedel (աղբ, կեղտ, գահաւորակ, կեղտոտել, աղբ նետել)
littering - aghdodoum, geghdodoum (աղտոտում, կեղտոտում)
littery - aghdeghoutiun, kharnagouyd (աղտեղութիւն, խառնակոյտ)
little - pokur, buzdig, kich, sagav (փոքր, պզտիկ, քիչ, սակաւ)
littoral - dzovap, dzovezerk, dzovezeria, dzovapnia (ծովափ, ծովեզերք, ծովեզերեայ, ծովափնեայ)
liturgy - bashdamounk, badarakamadouyts, dzisakirk (պաշտամունք, պատարագամատոյց, ծիսագիրք)
live - abril, punagil, sunanil, gentani, voghch, yeroun (ապրիլ, բնակիլ, սնանիլ, կենդանի, ողջ, եռուն)
livelihood - abrelamichots, sunount, abrousd (ապրելամիջոց, սնունդ, ապրուստ)
lively - gensounag, ashkhouyzh, gaydar, dakariun (կենսունակ, աշխոյժ, կայտառ, տաքարիւն)
liver - leart, abrogh, punagogh (լեարդ, ապրող, բնակող)
livery - hantsnoum, pokhantsakir, toshag, usbasazkesd (յանձնում, փոխանցագիր, Թոշակ, սպասազգեստ)
livid - gabdorag, gabdakouyn, kounad (կապտորակ, կապտագոյն, գունատ)
living - abrogh, gentani, abrousd, baren (ապրող, կենդանի, ապրուստ, պարէն)
living trusts - gentani varger (կենդանի վարկեր)
living will - megou gentanoutian durvadz gudag, pokhantsakir (մէկու կենդանութեան տրուած կտակ, փոխանցագիր)
livingroom - nusdaseniag, hiuraseniag (նստասենեակ, հիւրասենեակ)
lizard - moghez, khulez (մողէզ, խլէզ)
load - per, dzanroutiun, litsk, pernavorel, pertsunel (բեռ, ծանրութիւն, լիցք, բեռնաւորել, բեռցնել)
loaded - pertsuvadz, pernavorvadz (բեռցուած, բեռնաւորուած)
loader - pertsunogh, pernavorogh (բեռցնող, բեռնաւորող)
loading - pernavoroum, partsoum, litsk, per (բեռնաւորում, բարձում, լիցք, բեռ)
loaf - nugan, hats, sulukdal, dzoulanal, taparil (նկան, հաց, սլքտալ, ծուլանալ, Թափառիլ)
loam - gavahogh, avazagav, (կաւահող, աւազակաւ)
loan - pokharoutiun, pokhadevoutiun, pokh, pokh dal (փոխառութիւն, փոխատուութիւն, փոխ, փոխ տալ)
loath - anduramatir, tuzhgamag, agama, tuzhgam (անտրամադիր, դժկամակ, ակամայ, դժկամ)

loathe - adel, noghgal, karshil (ատել, նողկալ, գարշիլ)
loathsome - zuzveli, karsheli, buzhkali (զզուելի, գարշելի, պժգալի)
loathy - zuzveli, noghgali (զզուելի, նողկալի)
lob - aboush, putamid, anshunorhk nedel, tsukel (ապուշ, բթամիտ, անշնորհք նետել, ձգել)
lobby - nakhasurah, michantsk, aztel kaghakagan martots (նախասրահ, միջանցք, ազդել քաղաքական մարդոց)
lobbyest - khohurtarani vera aztogh (խորհրդարանի վրայ ազդող)
lobbyist - nakhasurahnerou mech panagtsogh, aztogh (նախասրահներու մէջ բանակցող, ազդող)
lobe - pultag, aganchapultag (բլթակ, ականջաբլթակ)
lobster - khetskedin (խեցգետին)
local - deghagan, deghayin (տեղական, տեղային)
locality - degh, vayr, tirk (տեղ, վայր, դիրք)
localize - deghavorel, sahmanapagel, megousatsunel (տեղաւորել, սահմանափակել, մեկուսացնել)
locate - deghavorel, punagetsunel, zedeghel, deghu kudnel (տեղաւորել, բնակեցնել, զետեղել, տեղը գտնել)
location - vayr, degh, tirk, zedeghoum, deghavoroum (վայր, տեղ, դիրք, զետեղում, տեղաւորում)
loch - lij, lujag, dzovakhorsh, dzots (լիճ, լճակ, ծովախորշ, ծոց)
lock - gughbank, pagank, kankour, gughbel, pagel (կղպանք, փականք, գանգուր, կղպել, փակել)
lock up - kordzi avardazham, pagaran, pand (գործի աւարտաժամ, փակարան, բանտ)
locker - argugh, pagogh, gughbogh (արկղ, փակող, կղպող)
lockout - pagoum, megousatsoum, pagel (փակում, մեկուսացում, փակել)
locksmith - gughbankakordz, paganakordz (կղպանքագործ, փականագործ)
locomotive - vayrasharzh, shokesharzh, sharzhagan (վայրաշարժ, շոգեշարժ, շարժական)
locus - degh, vayr, tirk (տեղ, վայր, դիրք)
locust - marakh, yeghchereni (մարախ, եղջերենի)
locution - asatzvadzk, khosvadzk, jar, tartsuvadzk (ասացուածք, խօսուածք, ճառ, դարձուածք)
lodge (n) (I) - abaranki turan dunag, Masonagan surah, otevan (ապարանքի դրան տնակ, Մասոնական սրահ, օթեւան)
lodge (n) (II) - dunag, khurjit, hiughag, otiag, zhoghovadeghi (տնակ, խրճիթ, հիւղակ, օթեակ, ժողովատեղի)
lodge (v) (I) - otevanel, kisherel, vartsel, deghavorel (օթեւանել, գիշերել, վարձել, տեղաւորել)
lodge (v) (II) - deghavorel, deghaturel, otevan dal, vartsel (տեղաւորել, տեղադրել, օթեւան տալ, վարձել)
lodger - vartsagal, vartsvor (վարձակալ, վարձուոր)
lodging - ichevan, otevan, punagaran, hiuranots (իջեւան, օթեւան, բնակարան, հիւրանոց)
lodgment - otevanoum, punagoum, abasdaran (օթեւանում, բնակում, ապաստարան)
loft - vernaharg, vernadoun, ver nedel (վերնայարկ, վերնատուն, վեր նետել)
log - gojgh, keran, poun, oughechap, payd gudrel (կոճղ, գերան, բուն, ուղեչափ, փայտ կտրել)
logarithm - dibahamar, nushanagatsouyts (տիպահամար, նշանակացոյց)
loge - oteag (օթեակ)
logger - paydahad, gojghavajar (փայտահատ, կոճղավաճառ)
loggerhead - aboush, tantsuramid, dukhmar (ապուշ, թանձրամիտ, տխմար)
loggia - daghavar, badgerasurah

(տաղաւար, պատկերասրահ)
logic - duramapanoutiun (տրամաբանութիւն)
logical - duramapanagan, duramapanogh (տրամաբանական, տրամաբանող)
logo - magnish, vajaranish (մակնիշ, վաճառանիշ)
logotype - khumpadar (խմբատառ)
loin - yerigamounk, mechk (երիկամունք, մէջք)
loiter - dundunal, tantaghil, zhamavajar ullal (տնտնալ, դանդաղիլ, ժամավաճառ ըլլալ)
loiterer - dzouyl, tantagh, dundunatsogh (ծոյլ, դանդաղ, տնտնացող)
loll - yergaril, ungoghmanil, dzouloren bargil, dzouyl (երկարիլ, ընկողմանիլ, ծուլօրէն պառկիլ, ծոյլ)
lone - arantsin, megousi, menagiats, amouri (առանձին, մեկուսի, մենակեաց, ամուրի)
lonely - arantsin, megousi, menavor, miaynag, dukhour (առանձին, մեկուսի, մենաւոր, միայնակ, տխուր)
long - yergar, yergayn, herou, garodil, denchal (երկար, երկայն, հեռու, կարօտիլ, տենչալ)
longing - garod, ights, papak, tsangoutiun (կարօտ, իղձ, փափաք, ցանկութիւն)
longitude - yergaynoutiun (երկայնութիւն)
long-armed - yergarapazoug (երկաբաբազուկ)
long-lived - yergaragiats, yergaradev (երկարակեաց, երկարատեւ)
long-sighted - herades (հեռատես)
long-standing - hin, vaghemi (հին, վաղեմի)
long-term - yergaradev bayman, yergarashounch (երկարատեւ պայման, երկարաշունչ)
looby - aboush, anmid, himar (ապուշ, անմիտ, յիմար)
loofah - usbounk, lif (սպունգ, լիֆ)
look - nayil, tidel, zunnel, husgel, nayvadzk, agnarg (նայիլ, դիտել, զննել, հսկել, նայուածք, ակնարկ)
looker - nayogh, tidogh, tidort (նայող, դիտող, դիտորդ)
looking glass - hayeli (հայելի)
lookout - tours nayil, husgel, bahagoutiun (դուրս նայիլ, հսկել, պահակութիւն)
lookout point - tidaged (դիտակէտ)
loon - usdahag, aboush, souzanav (ստահակ, ապուշ, սուզանաւ)
loop - oghag, hankouyts, oghagel, purnetsunel (օղակ, հանգոյց, օղակել, բռնեցնել)
loose - azad, touyl, artsag, yelk, azad tsukel (ազատ, թոյլ, արձակ, ելք, ազատ ձգել)
loosen - toultsunel, kagel, artsagel (թուլցնել, քակել, արձակել)
looseness - touloutiun, anaragoutiun, tsopoutiun (թուլութիւն, անառակութիւն, ցոփութիւն)
loosest - amenatouyl, amenen azad, anhagagushreli (ամենաթոյլ, ամէնէն ազատ, անհակակշռելի)
loot - avar, goghoboud, avarel, goghobdel, tallel (աւար, կողոպուտ, աւարել, կողոպտել, թալլել)
lop - jiugheru gudrel, dzayradel, hodel, gudurvadz jiugh (ճիւղերը կտրել, ծայրատել, յօտել, կտրուած ճիւղ)
lope - tsadgel, gakavel, barel, tsaydoum, vosdiun (ցատկել, կաքաւել, պարել, ցայտում, ոստիւն)
loquacious - shadakhos, zuroutsaser (շատախօս, զրուցասէր)
loquacity - shadakhosoutiun (շատախօսութիւն)
lord - der, ishkhan, sebouh, arka, asduvadz (տէր, իշխան, սեպուհ, արքայ, Աստուած)
lore - ousmounk, kidoutiun, imasdoutiun (ուսմունք, գիտութիւն, իմաստութիւն)
lorry - pernagark, pernasayl (բեռնակառք, բեռնասայլ)
lose - gorsuntsunel, vunasel, darvil (կորսնցնել, վնասել, տարուիլ)
loser - gorsuntsunogh (կորսնցնող)
loss - gorousd, vunas, mah (կորուստ, վնաս, մահ)
lost - gorsuvadz (կորսուած)

lot - vijag, pakhd, kuve, kanag, pazhin, hoghamas (վիճակ, բախտ, քուէ, քանակ, բաժին, հողամաս)
lotion - odzanelik, levatsoum (օծանելիք, լուացում)
lottery - vijagahanoutiun (վիճակահանութիւն)
lotto - vijagakhagh (վիճակախաղ)
loud - partsuratsayn, ouzhkin, aghmugalits, aghmugod (բարձրաձայն, ուժգին, աղմկալից, աղմկոտ)
loudspeaker - partsurakhos (բարձրախօս)
lough - lij, lujag, dzovakhorsh (լիճ, լճակ, ծովախորշ)
lounge - hankusdaseniag, sulukdal, tekeril (հանգստասենեակ, սլքտալ, ղեգերիլ)
louse - vochil, vochlodil (ոջիլ, ոջլոտիլ)
lousy - vochlod, aghdod, zuzveli (ոջլոտ, աղտոտ, զզուելի)
lout - hagil, khonarhil, goshd, gobid հակիլ, խոնարհիլ, կոշտ, կոպիտ, միմոս)
louver, louvre - lousamoud (լուսամուտ)
lovable - sireli, siroun, hurabourich (սիրելի, սիրուն, հրապուրիչ)
love - ser, siraharoutiun, kout, sirel, denchal (սէր, սիրահարութիւն, գութ, սիրել, տենչալ)
loveless - anser, anhurabouyr (անսէր, անհրապոյր)
lovely - sireli, siroun, hurabourich (սիրելի, սիրուն, հրապուրիչ)
lover - sirogh, sirahar, siregan (սիրող, սիրահար, սիրեկան)
love-making - sirel, hampourel, kukvel, shoyel, haraperil (սիրել, համբուրել, գգուել, շոյել, յարաբերիլ)
low (I) - var, tsadz, usdorin, tsadztsunel, ichetsunel (վար, ցած, ստորին, ցածցնել, իջեցնել)
low (II) - parachel, parachiun (բառաչել, բառաչիւն)
lower - tsadztsunel, ichetsunel, ichnel, tsadznal (ցածցնել, իջեցնել, իջնել, ցածնալ)
lower case - varnargugh, pokradar (վարնարկղ, փոքրատառ)
lowland - aghkad-usdorin kavar, tashdavayr (աղքատ–ստորին գաւառ, դաշտավայր)
lowlihood - aghkadoutiun (աղքատութիւն)
lowly - usdorin, khonarh, hamesd (ստորին, խոնարհ, համեստ)
lowness - tsadzoutiun (ցածութիւն)
loyal - havadarim, oughghamid, orinabah (հաւատարիմ, ուղղամիտ, օրինապահ)
loyalty - havadarmoutiun, orinabahoutiun (հաւատարմութիւն, օրինապահութիւն)
lozenge - sheghangiun (շեղանկիւն)
lubber - goshd, gobid, putamid (կոշտ, կոպիտ, բթամիտ)
lubric - sahoun, luburdzoun, tsop (սահուն, լպրծուն, ցոփ)
lubricate - yiughel, yiughodel, luburdzel (իւղել, իւղոտել, լպրծել)
lubrication - yiughodoum (իւղոտում)
lucent - baydzar, payloun (պայծառ, փայլուն)
lucid - baydzar, husdag, lousamid, husdagades (պայծառ, յստակ, լուսամիտ, յստակատես)
lucidity - baydzaroutiun, husdagadesoutiun (պայծառութիւն, յստակատեսութիւն)
lucifer - lousaper, arousiag, sadana (լուսաբեր, Արուսեակ, սատանայ)
luck - pakhd, jagadakir, hachoghoutiun (բախտ, ճակատագիր, յաջողութիւն)
luckless - anpakhd, tuzhpakhd (անբախտ, դժբախտ)
lucky - pakhdavor, parepakhd, hachoghag (բախտաւոր, բարեբախտ, յաջողակ)
lucrative - shahaper, shahaved, yegamoudaper (շահաբեր, շահաւէտ, եկամուտաբեր)
lucre - shah, okoud, shahouyt (շահ, օգուտ, շահոյթ)
lucubrate - kisheru louysov ashkhadil (գիշերը լոյսով աշխատիլ)
ludicrous - dzidzagheli, zuvarjali

(ծիծաղելի, զուաճալի)
lug - kashel, kashkushel, kashgurdel, purnag, got (քաշել, քաշքշել, քաշկռտել, բռնակ, կոթ)
luggage - ougheper, jampargugh, per (ուղեբեռ, ճամբարկղ, բեռ)
lugger - buzdig arakasdanav (պզտիկ առագաստանաւ)
lugubrious - sukavor, durdoum, dukhour, sukali (սգաւոր, տրտում, տխուր, սգալի)
lukewarm - kaghch, gisadak, andarper (գաղջ, կիսատաք, անտարբեր)
lull - hantardetsunel, yerkov kunatsunel, khaghagh bah (հանդարտեցնել, երգով քնացնել, խաղաղ պահ)
lullaby - ororerk, ororк, ororotsi yerk (օրօրերգ, օրօրք, օրօրոցի երգ)
lumbago - mechkatsav (մէջքացաւ)
lumber - dakhdag, adaghts, tizel, letsunel, gudrel (տախտակ, ատաղձ, դիզել, լեցնել, կտրել)
lumberman - paydahad, adaghtsakordz (փայտահատ, ատաղձագործ)
luminary - lousadou (լուսատու)
luminate - lousavorel (լուսաւորել)
luminosity - lousavoroutiun (լուսաւորութիւն)
luminous - lousavor, payloun, baydzar, shoghshoghoun (լուսաւոր, փայլուն, պայծառ, շողշողուն)
lump - zankuvadz, kount, ouretsk, gouyd (զանգուած, գունդ, ուռեցք, կոյտ)
luna - lousin (լուսին)
lunacy - lousnodoutiun, khelakaroutiun (լուսնոտութիւն, խելագարութիւն)
lunar - lousnayin (լուսնային)
lunar landing - lousnechk (լուսնէջք)
lunch, luncheon - michnajash, gesorva nakhajash, nakhunturel (միջնաճաշ, կէսօրուայ նախաճաշ, նախընթրել)
lune - gisalousin, mahig, mahigatsev (կիսալուսին, մահիկ, մահիկաձեւ)
lung - tok (թոք)
lung fever - tokadab (թոքատապ)
lunge - suraharvadz, suraharvadzel (սրահարուած, սրահարուածել)
lurch - dadanil, tavalil, souzvil, tavaloum (տատանիլ, թաւալիլ, սուզուիլ, թաւալում)
lure - hurabouyr, badrank, hurabourel (հրապոյր, պատրանք, հրապուրել)
lurid - duzhkouyn, dumouyn, kounad, dukhour (տժգոյն, տմոյն, գունատ, տխուր)
lurk - bahvudil, bahvil, taranagal usbasel, takchil (պահուըտիլ, պահուիլ, դարանակալ սպասել, թաքչիլ)
luscious - kaghtsur, anoushaham (քաղցր, անուշահամ)
lush - hiutegh, vokelits umbeli, khumel, gondzel (հիւթեղ, ոգելից ըմպելի, խմել, կոնծել)
lust - durpank, denchank, tsangoutiun (տռփանք, տենչանք, ցանկութիւն)
luster, lustre - chah, paylk, hampav, payletsunel (ջահ, փայլք, համբաւ, փայլեցնել)
lustful - durpod, vavashod, gurkod (տռփոտ, վաւաշոտ, կրքոտ)
lustral - orhnial, surpatsadz (օրհնեալ, սրբացած)
lustrate - payletsunel, luval, surpel (փայլեցնել, լուալ, սրբել)
lustrous - payloun, baydzar, shoghshoghoun (փայլուն, պայծառ, շողշողուն)
lute - vin, dzep, vinadzel, dzepov kotsel (վին, ծեփ, վինածել, ծեփով գոցել)
Lutheran - louteragan (Լութերական)
luxate - khakhdel, vosgurakhakhdel (խախտել, ոսկրախախտել)
luxuriate - ourjanal, vayelel, heshdanal (ուռճանալ, վայելել, հեշտանալ)
luxurious - shukegh, partam, jokh, zekh, vavashod (շքեղ, փարթամ, ճոխ, զեխ, վաւաշոտ)
luxury - shukeghoutiun, berjank, jokhoutiun (շքեղութիւն, պերճանք,

ճոխութիւն)
lye - mokhrachour, gizachour (մոխրաջուր, կիզաջուր)
lying - sudogh, sudelu, bargogh, bargilu (ստող, ստելը, պառկող, պառկիլը)
lymph - avish, ag (աւիշ, ակ)
lynch - poghodel, charcharelov usbannel, mortel (փողոտել, չարչարելով սպաննել, մորթել)
lynx - lousan (լուսան)
lyre - kunar (քնար)
lyreman - jubour (ճպուռ)
lyric - kunaragan, kunarerkagan (քնարական, քնարերգական)
lyrism - kunarerkoutiun (քնարերգութիւն)
lyrist - kunarahar, kunarerkag, kunarerkou (քնարահար, քնարերգակ, քնարերգու)

ma - mama, mayrig (մամա, մայրիկ)
Mac, Mc., M' - vorti (որդի) - (scottish - սկովտական)
macaroni - hayseriz, tutmaj, kharnourt, bujnaser (հայսերիզ, դդմաճ, խառնուրդ, պճնասէր)
macaroon - macaroniov-noushov-shakarov shinvadz khumoreghen (մաքարոնիով-նուշով-շաքարով շինուած խմորեղէն)
mace - kavazan, magan, lakh (գաւազան, մական, լախտ)
macer - kavazanagir - takavori (գաւազանակիր՝ թագաւորի)
macerate - turchel, gagoughtsunel, dugaratsunel (թրջել, կակուղցնել, տկարացնել)
machiavelism - nenkoutiun, badehabashdoutiun, geghdzik (նենգութիւն, պատեհապաշտութիւն, կեղծիք)
machination - mekenayoutiun, tav, satrank (մեքենայութիւն, դաւ, սադրանք)
machine - mekena, kordzik, gazmadz (մեքենայ, գործիք, կազմած)
machine gun - kuntatsir (գնդացիր)
machinery - mekenaner, mekenaganoutiun, sarkavoroum (մեքենաներ, մեքենականութիւն, սարքաւորում)
machinist - mekenakordz, mekenaked, mekenavar (մեքենագործ, մեքենագէտ, մեքենավար)
mackintosh - anchurantsig verargou (անջրանցիկ վերարկու)
macro - medz, layn, khoshor, yergayn (մեծ, լայն, խոշոր, երկայն)
macrobiotic - yergaragiats (երկարակեաց)
macrocosm - hamadiyezerk (համատիեզերք)
macrometer - yergaynachap (երկայնաչափ)
mad - himar, ankhelk, gadghadz, himaratsunel, khentenal (յիմար, անխելք, կատղած, յիմարացնել, խենդենալ)
madam, madame - digin, dandigin, dirouhi (տիկին, տանտիկին, տիրուհի)
madcap - khizagh, argadzaser, hakhourun, hantoukun (խիզախ, արկածասէր, յախուռն, յանդուգն)
madden - khentatsunel, khentanal, gadghetsunel (խենդացնել, խենդանալ, կատղեցնել)
made - urav, shinets, shinvadz, shindzou, geghdz (ըրաւ, շինեց, շինուած, շինծու, կեղծ)
madefaction - damgoutiun, damgatsoum (տամկութիւն, տամկացում)
mademoiselle - oriort (օրիորդ)
madge - pou, andzegh (բու, անծեղ)
madhouse - khentanots, himaranots

(խենդանոց, յիմարանոց)
madid - tats, damoug (Թաց, տամուկ)
madman - khent, himar (խենդ, յիմար)
madness - himaroutiun, anmudoutiun, gadaghoutiun (յիմարութիւն, անմտութիւն, կատաղութիւն)
madrigal - sirerk (սիրերգ)
mad-headed - khent, vayreni (խենդ, վայրենի)
maffle - gagazel (կակազել)
mafia, maffia - kaghduni gazmagerboutiun, mafia (գաղտնի կազմակերպութիւն, մաֆիա)
magazine - barperatert, ushdemaran, muteranots, zinaran (պարբերաթերթ, շտեմարան, մթերանոց, զինարան)
mage - mok (մոգ)
magenta - posorakouyn, garmurakouyn nerg (բոսորագոյն, կարմրագոյն ներկ)
maggot - turtour, vort, kumayk (Թրթուր, որդ, քմայք)
magic - mokoutiun, gakhartoutiun (մոգութիւն, կախարդութիւն)
magical - mokagan, gakhartagan, humayich (մոգական, կախարդական, հմայիչ)
magician - gakhart, mok, vuhoug (կախարդ, մոգ, վհուկ)
magister - makisduros, varbed (մագիստրոս, վարպետ)
magisterial - tadagan, ishkhanagan, huramayagan (դատական, իշխանական, հրամայական)
magistral - vartabedagan, ishkhanagan, teghakuragan (վարդապետական, իշխանական, դեղագրական)
magistrate - tadavor, adenagal, ishkhan (դատաւոր, ատենակալ, իշխան)
magnanimity - vehantsnoutiun, medzahokioutiun (վեհանձնութիւն, մեծահոգիութիւն)
magnanimous - vehantsun, vehoki, medzhoki (վեհանձն, վեհոգի, մեծահոգի)
magnate - medzaharousd, choch, yereveli, aztetsig (մեծահարուստ, ջոջ, երեւելի, ազդեցիկ)
magnet - maknis (մագնիս)
magnetic, magnetical - maknisagan, kashoghagan (մագնիսական, քաշողական)
magnetism - maknisaganoutiun, kashoghaganoutiun, hurabouyr (մագնիսականութիւն, քաշողականութիւն, հրապոյր)
magnetize - maknisatsunel, kashel, hurabourel (մագնիսացնել, քաշել, հրապուրել)
magnific, al - uskancheli, hoyagab, shukegh (սքանչելի, հոյակապ, շքեղ)
magnificence - shukeghoutiun, berjoutiun (շքեղութիւն, պերճութիւն)
magnificent - uskancheli, hoyagab, shukegh, medzashouk (սքանչելի, հոյակապ, շքեղ, մեծաշուք)
magnify - paravorel, khoshoratsunel, chapazantsel (փառաւորել, խոշորացնել, չափազանցել)
magnifying glass - khoshoratsouyts (խոշորացոյց)
magnitude - medzoutiun - asdghi, dzaval, vehoutiun (մեծութիւն՝ աստղի, ծաւալ, վեհութիւն)
magpie - andzegh, gachaghag (անձեղ, կաչաղակ)
magyar - hounkaratsi, hounkareren, hounkaragan (հունգարացի, հունգարերէն, հունգարական)
mahometan -
maid - aghchig, gouys, usbasouhi (աղջիկ, կոյս, սպասուհի)
maiden - gouys, oriort, aghchig, gousagan (կոյս, օրիորդ, աղջիկ, կուսական)
maiden name - aghchugoutian maganounu (աղջկութեան մականունը)
maidhood - gousoutiun, anpudzoutiun (կուսութիւն, անբծութիւն)
mail (I) - namag, tughtadar, tughdaper, namag ghurgel (նամակ, Թղթատար, Թղթաբեր, նամակ ղրկել)
mail (II) - zurah, verd, zurahavorel (զրահ, վերտ, զրահաւորել)

mail order - namagabadver, namagov abusburank (նամակապատուէր, նամակով ապսպրանք)
mailbox - namagadoup (նամակատուփ)
mailing - arakoum (առաքում)
maillot - loghazkesd (լողազգեստ)
mailman - namagapashkh (նամակաբաշխ)
maim - hashmel, gudrel, dzayradel, kheghel (հաշմել, կտրել, ծայրատել, խեղել)
main - kulkhavor, poun, himnagan, medz, untartsag (գլխաւոր, բուն, հիմնական, մեծ, ընդարձակ)
main street - kulkhavor poghots (գլխաւոր փողոց)
mainland - mayr tsamak (մայր ցամաք)
mainly - kulkhavorabes, manavant, medz masamp (գլխաւորապէս, մանաւանդ, մեծ մասամբ)
maintain - bahel, bahbanel, bashdbanel, geragrel, buntel (պահել, պահպանել, պաշտպանել, կերակրել, պնդել)
maintainable - bahbaneli, bashdbaneli, chadakoveli (պահպանելի, պաշտպանելի, ջատագովելի)
maintenance - bahbanoutiun, oknoutiun, netsoug, abrousd (պահպանութիւն, օգնութիւն, նեցուկ, ապրուստ)
maize - yekibdatsoren, lazoud (եգիպտացորեն, լազուտ)
majestic - veh, vehapar, vusem, medzashouk (վեհ, վեհափառ, վսեմ, մեծաշուք)
majesty - vehoutiun, vusemoutiun, vehaparoutiun (վեհութիւն, վսեմութիւն, վեհափառութիւն)
major - avak, yerets, medzakouyn, hazarabed (աւագ, երէց, մեծագոյն, հազարապետ)
majorate - ajetsunel, medztsunel (աճեցնել, մեծցնել)
majority - medzamasnoutiun, chapahasoutiun, arpounk (մեծամասնութիւն, չափահասութիւն, արբունք)
majuscule - kulkhakir, medzadar (գլխագիր, մեծատառ)
make (n) - gazmoutiun, shinvadzk, kordz, tsev, gerduvadzk (կազմութիւն, շինուածք, գործ, ձեւ, կազմուածք)
make (v) - shinel, unel, gazmel, gadarel, shahil, tsevel (շինել, ընել, կազմել, կատարել, շահիլ, ձեւել)
maker - shinogh, horinogh, usdeghdzich, ararich (շինող, յօրինող, ստեղծիչ, արարիչ)
make-ready - badrasd, badrasd dubakroutian (պատրաստ, պատրաստ տպագրութեան)
make-up - miatsunel, shubarvil, timahartaroum, echgab (միացնել, շպարուիլ, դիմայարդարում, էջկապ)
maladroit - anjarag, tsakhaver, tsakhort (անճարակ, ձախաւեր, ձախորդ)
malady - hivantoutiun, akhd, dugaroutiun (հիւանդութիւն, ախտ, տկարութիւն)
malaise - anhankusdoutiun, neghoutiun (անհանգստութիւն, նեղութիւն)
malapert - angirt, hamartsag, lirp, gobid (անկիրթ, համարձակ, լիրբ, կոպիտ)
malaria - chermakhd, jahjadent, morakhd (ջերմախտ, ճահճատենդ, մօրախտ)
malcontent - tuzhkoh, duhaj (դժգոհ, տհաճ)
male - arou, ayr, dughamart, arnagan (արու, այր, տղամարդ, առնական)
maledicency - charakhosoutiun, nuzovk (չարախօսութիւն, նզովք)
maledict - anidzial, zuzveli (անիծեալ, զզուելի)
malediction - anedzk, nuzovk (անէծք, նզովք)
malefaction - charakordzoutiun, vojir (չարագործութիւն, ոճիր)
malefactor - charakordz, vojrakordz (չարագործ, ոճրագործ)
maleficence - jarakordzoutiun

(ճարագործութիւն)
maleficent - charakordz (չարագործ)
malevolence - charagamoutiun, charamudoutiun (չարակամութիւն, չարամտութիւն)
malformation - dutsevoutiun, aylantagoutiun (տձեւութիւն, այլանդակութիւն)
malice - charoutiun, charagamoutiun, nenkoutiun (չարութիւն, չարակամութիւն, նենգութիւն)
malicious - char, charagam, nenkamid (չար, չարակամ, նենգամիտ)
malign - char, nenkamid, charakhosel, zurbardel (չար, նենգամիտ, չարախօսել, զրպարտել)
malignant - charamid, char, charorag, mahaper (չարամիտ, չար, չարօրակ, մահաբեր)
maligner - charakhos, zurbardogh (չարախօս, զրպարտող)
malignity - charoutiun, charamudoutiun, keshoutiun (չարութիւն, չարամտութիւն, գէշութիւն)
malinger - hivant tsevanal, geghdzel (հիւանդ ձեւանալ, կեղծել)
malingerer - hivant tsevatsunogh, kordzakhouys (հիւանդ ձեւացնող, գործախոյս)
mall - jemavayr, kots shouga, khaghavayr, tag, tagel (ճեմավայր, գոց շուկայ, խաղավայր, թակ, թակել)
malleable - jugoun, gagough, guraneli, harmarogh (ճկուն, կակուղ, կռանելի, յարմարող)
mallet - tag, payde mourj (թակ, փայտէ մուրճ)
malnutrition - vad sunount, anpavarar sununtaroutiun (վատ սնունդ, անբաւարար սննդառութիւն)
malodorous - karshahod (գարշահոտ)
malodour - karshahodoutiun (գարշահոտութիւն)
malpractice - aborini kordz, sukhal tarmanoum (ապօրինի գործ, սխալ դարմանում)
malt - gasg, gasgia, makruvadz hadig, dzamel, gasgel (կասկ, կասկեայ, մաքրուած հատիկ, ծամել, կասկել)
maltreat - neghel, charcharel, kesh veraperil (նեղել, չարչարել, գէշ վերաբերիլ)
maltreatment - kesh veraperoum, khoshdankoum (գէշ վերաբերում, խոշտանգում)
maltworn - khuman, kinov (խման, գինով)
mama, mamma - mama, mayrig (a child's word for mother) - (մամա, մայրիկ - մայր բառը՝ մանուկի կողմէ)
mamma - dzidz, usdink (ծիծ, ստինք)
mammal - usdunavor, gatundou (ստնաւոր, կաթնտու)
mammalia - usdunavorner, gatnasounner (ստնաւորներ, կաթնասուններ)
mammifer - usdnavor, gatundou (ստնաւոր, կաթնտու)
mammography - gurdzki nugaroum (կրծքի նկարում)
mammon - mamona, harusdoutiun, turam (մամոնայ, հարստութիւն, դրամ)
mammoplasty - gurdzki kordzoghoutiun (կրծքի գործողութիւն)
mammoth - nakhapigh, mamout, vitkhari (նախափիղ, մամութ, վիթխարի)
mammy - mama, mayrig, sevamort usbasouhi (մամա, մայրիկ, սեւամորթ սպասուհի)
man - mart, ayr, martgoutiun, amratsunel, zinel (մարդ, այր, մարդկութիւն, ամրացնել, զինել)
manacle - tsernagabel, shughtayel, tsernagab (ձեռնակապել, շղթայել, ձեռնակապ)
manage - garavarel, ghegavarel, varel, dunorinel (կառավարել, ղեկավարել, վարել, տնօրինել))
management - ghegavaroutiun, varchoutiun, deschoutiun (ղեկավարութիւն, վարչութիւն, տեսչութիւն)
manager - varich, desouch, dundes, veragatsou, dunoren (վարիչ, տե–

սուչ, տնտես, վերակացու, տնօրէն)
mandarine - mandarin, nouma, chin bashdonia (մանտարին, նուռմայ, չին պաշտօնեայ)
mandatary - huramanagadar, hantsnagadar, badvirag (հրամանակատար, յանձնակատար, պատուիրակ)
mandate - hokadaroutiun, hantsnarakir, hurahank (հոգատարութիւն, յանձնարարագիր, հրահանգ)
mandator - hurahankich, hantsnagadar, badvirag (հրահանգիչ, յանձնակատար, պատուիրակ)
mandolin, mandoline - mandolin, viniag, gitarig (մանտոլին, վինեակ, կիթառիկ)
manducate - dzamel, oudel (ծամել, ուտել)
mane - pash (բաշ)
manequin - gaghabar, orinag (կաղապար, օրինակ)
maneuver, manoeuver - razmaports, hunark, tav, marzel, varel (ռազմափորձ, հնարք, դաւ, մարզել, վարել)
manful - arnagan, kach, vujragan (առնական, քաջ, վճռական)
manganese - mankan, archnakar (մանգան, արջնաքար)
mange - kos, kosoutiun (քոս, քոսութիւն)
manger - musour (մսուր)
mangle - hoshodel, artougel, mamlag, momlots (յօշոտել, արդուկել, մամլակ, մամլոց)
mango - mank, mankeniyi budough (մանգ, մանգենիի պտուղ)
manhood - chapahasoutiun, arnaganoutiun, ayroutiun (չափահասութիւն, առնականութիւն, այրութիւն)
mania - khelakaroutiun, mudakaroutiun, moleknoutiun (խելագարութիւն, մտագարութիւն, մոլեգնութիւն)
maniac - moli, khent, khelakar, himar, gadaghi (մոլի, խենդ, խելագար, յիմար, կատաղի)
manicure - tserakhunam, tserahartaroum, tserapouyzh (ձեռախնամ, ձեռայարդարում, ձեռաբոյժ)
manicurist - tserakhunamogh, tserapouyzh (ձեռախնամող, ձեռաբոյժ)
manifest (I) - vajaratsang, pernakir (վաճառացանկ, բեռնագիր)
manifest (II) - haydararoutiun, patsahayd, hurabaragel (յայտարարութիւն, բացայայտ, հրապարակել)
manifesto - haydararoutiun, haydararakir (յայտարարութիւն, յայտարարագիր)
manifold - pazmadzal, pazmabadig, pazmakurel, pazmatsunel (բազմածալ, բազմապատիկ, բազմագրել, բազմացնել)
manikin - martabadger, martoug, kajaj (մարդապատկեր, մարդուկ, գաճաճ)
manipulate - ghegavarel, jabigoren varvil, khartakhel (ղեկավարել, ճարպիկօրէն վարուիլ, խարդախել)
manipulation - tseravaroum, mekenayoutiun, aghavaghoun (ձեռավարում, մեքենայութիւն, աղաւաղում)
mankind - martgoutiun, martig, ayr (մարդկութիւն, մարդիկ, այր)
manna - manana (մանանայ)
mannequin - martabadger, darazatsouyts, khurdvilag (մարդապատկեր, տարազացոյց, խրտուիլակ)
manner - tsev, gerb, yeghanag, voj, vark, untatsk (ձեւ, կերպ, եղանակ, ոճ, վարք, ընթացք)
mannerly - girt, kaghakavary, shunorhali (կիրթ, քաղաքավարի, շնորհալի)
mannish - martavayel, martanuman, arnagan, ayraser (մարդավայել, մարդանման, առնական, այրասէր)
manoeuvre - see - տե՛ս (maneuver)
manor - galvadz, avadahogh, punagaran, punagoutiun (կալուած, աւատահող, բնակարան, բնակութիւն)
manqueller - martasban (մարդասպան)
mansion - abarank, tughiag, avadadoun, punagil (ապարանք, դղեակ, աւատատուն, բնակիլ)

mantle - verargou, tignots, dzadzgel, badel, dzadzguvil (վերարկու, թիկնոց, ծածկել, պատել, ծածկուիլ)
manual - tserayin, artsern kirk, tseravarzhoutiun (ձեռային, առձեռն գիրք, ձեռավարժութիւն)
manufactory - kordzaran, arhesdanots (գործարան, արհեստանոց)
manufacture - jardararvesd, tserarvesd, ardaturel (ճարտարարուեստ, ձեռարուեստ, արտադրել)
manure - aghp, barardaniut, barardatsunel (աղբ, պարարտանիւթ, պարարտացնել)
manus - tserk (ձեռք)
manuscript - tserakir, kurchakir (ձեռագիր, գրչագիր)
many - shad, pazmativ, shader, ampokh, zhoghovourt (շատ, բազմաթիւ, շատեր, ամբոխ, ժողովուրդ)
many-sided - pazmagoghmani, pazmeres (բազմակողմանի, բազմերես)
map - kardes, ashkharhatsouyts, kardisakudzel (քարտէս, աշխարհացոյց, քարտիսագծել)
maple - tughki, tughkeni (ղղքի, ղղքենի – ծառ մը)
mar - avrel, pujatsunel, abaganel, murodel (աւրել, փճացնել, ապականել, մրոտել)
marasmus - hiudzoum, haloumash (հիւծում, հալումաշ)
maraud - goghobdel, avararel, asbadagoutiun (կողոպտել, աւարառել, ասպատակութիւն)
marauder - avazag, avararou, asbadag (աւազակ, աւարառու, ասպատակ)
marble - marmar, marmaria, gouj, karekuntag, marmarel (մարմար, մարմարեայ, կուճ, քարեգնդակ, մարմարել)
March - mard (Մարտ)
march - yert, kalvadzk, kaylerk, kalel, kaletsunel (երթ, քալուածք, քայլերգ, քալել, քալեցնել)
margin - lousantsk, sahman, yezur, lousantsakurel (լուսանցք, սահման, եզր, լուսանցագրել)
marginal - lousantski, yezerki (լուսանցքի, եզերքի)
margrave - marzbed, markiz (մարզպետ, մարքիզ)
marguerite - markardadzaghig, yeritsoug (մարգարտածաղիկ, երիցուկ)
marine - dzovayin, dzovayin ouzh, navadormigh (ծովային, ծովային ոյժ, նաւատորմիղ)
mariner - navasdi, navaz (նաւաստի, նաւազ)
marionette - khamajig, godzig (խամաճիկ, կոծիկ)
marital - amousnagan, ayragan (ամուսնական, այրական)
maritime - dzovayin, dzovezeria, navayin (ծովային, ծովեզերեայ, նաւային)
mark (n) - nushan, gunik, ged, nish, hedk, nubadag, mark (նշան, կնիք, նիշ, կէտ, հետք, նպատակ, գերմ. մարք)
mark (v) - turoshmel, sheshdel, nushanagel, nushanakurel (դրոշմել, շեշտել, նշանակել, նշանագրել)
marker - turoshmich, kudzich, nushanagich (դրոշմիչ, գծիչ, նշանակիչ)
market - shouga, vajaradeghi, hurabarag (շուկայ, վաճառատեղի, հրապարակ)
marksman - nushanarou, nushanatsik (նշանառու, նշանաձիգ)
markup - kunaaj, kini haveloum (գնաաճ, գինի յաւելում)
marmalade - kaghtsuraveni, pantag (քաղցրաւենի, բանդակ)
marmoreal - marmare, marmaria (մարմարէ, մարմարեայ)
maroon - shakanagakouyn, aksorel (շագանակագոյն, աքսորել)
marquis - markiz, marzbed, medzamid (մարքիզ, մարզպետ, մեծամիտ)
marriage - amousnoutiun, harsanik, busagaturoutiun, busag (ամուսնութիւն, հարսանիք, պսակադրութիւն, պսակ)

married - amousnatsadz, garkuvadz, amousnagan (ամուսնացած, կարգուած, ամուսնական)
marron - shakanag, shakanagakouyn (շագանակ, շագանակագոյն)
marrow - dzoudz, vosguradzoudz, voghnadzoudz (ծուծ, ոսկրածուծ, ողնածուծ)
marry - amousnanal, amousnatsunel, busagel, garkel (ամուսնանալ, ամուսնացնել, պսակել, կարգել)
Mars - hurad (Հրատ)
marsh - jahij (ճահիճ)
marshal - marachakhd, panagabed, sharel, tasavorel (մարաջախտ, բանակապետ, շարել, դասաւորել)
mart - shouga, vajaradeghi, vajaranots (շուկայ, վաճառատեղի, վաճառանոց)
marteking - arevdour, kunoum (առեւտուր, գնում)
marten - gouz, samouyr (կուզ, սամոյր)
martial - baderazmagan, razmagan, zinvoragan (պատերազմական, ռազմական, զինուորական)
martyr - nahadag, mardiros, nahadagel, danchel (նահատակ, մարտիրոս, նահատակել, տանջել)
martyrization - nahadagoum, khoshdankoum (նահատակում, խոշտանգում)
martyrize - mardirosatsunel, khoshdankel (մարտիրոսացնել, խոշտանգել)
marvel - uskanchelik, hurashalik, hianal, uskanchanal (սքանչելիք, հրաշալիք, հիանալ, սքանչանալ)
marvelous - uskancheli, hurashali, hianali (սքանչելի, հրաշալի, հիանալի)
masculine - aragan, arnagan, arou, ari, kach (արական, առնական, արու, արի, քաջ)
mash - kharnourt, tunjoug, kharnel, shaghel, juzmel (խառնուրդ, թնճուկ, խառնել, շաղել, ճզմել)
mask (n) - timag, dzadzgouyt, kogh, timagahantes, geghdzik (դիմակ, ծածկոյթ, քօղ, դիմակահանդէս, կեղծիք)
mask (v) - timagel, dzadzgel, dzubdil, koghargel (դիմակել, ծածկել, ծպտիլ, քօղարկել)
masked - timagavor, dzubdial (դիմակաւոր, ծպտեալ)
masker - timagavor, dzubdial, shupotel, abshetsunel (դիմակաւոր, ծպտեալ, շփոթել, ապշեցնել)
maskery - timagahantes, timagavoroutiun (դիմակահանդէս, դիմակաւորութիւն)
masking tape - gubchoun dzadzgeriz (կպչուն ծածկերիզ)
mason - vormnatir, azad vormnatir, mason, bad hiusel (որմնադիր, ազատ որմնադիր, մասոն, պատ հիւսել)
masonic - masonagan (մասոնական)
masonry - vormashinoutiun, masonaganoutiun (որմաշինութիւն, մասոնականութիւն)
masquerade - timagahantes, timagakhagh, geghdzik (դիմակահանդէս, դիմակախաղ, կեղծիք)
mass (n) - badarak, zhamerkoutiun, zankuvadz, ampokh, gouyd (պատարագ, ժամերգութիւն, զանգուած, ամբոխ, կոյտ)
mass (v) - havakel, khumpel, goudagel, badarakel (հաւաքել, խմբել, կուտակել, պատարագել)
mass media - zhoghovurtayin zankuvadz (ժողովրդային զանգուած)
mass meeting - hanrayin zhoghov (հանրային ժողով)
massacre - chart, godoradz, usbant, chartel, godorel (ջարդ, կոտորած, սպանդ, ջարդել, կոտորել)
massage - martsoum, martsel, shupel (մարձում, մարձել, շփել)
masser - badarakich (պատարագիչ)
masseur - martsogh, shupogh (մարձող, շփող)
massive - husga, vitkhari, medzamarmin, khoshor, hodz (հսկայ, վիթխարի, մեծամարմին, խոշոր, հոծ)
mast - gaym, alehavak, gaymel (կայմ, ալեհաւաք, կայմել)

master (n) - varbed, bed, ousoutsich, dander, kordzader (վարպետ, պետ, ուսուցիչ, տանտէր, գործատէր)
master (v) - dirabedel, yentargel, diranal, ghegavarel (տիրապետել, ենթարկել, տիրանալ, ղեկավարել)
master of ceremonies - kulkhavor hantisavar (գլխաւոր Հանդիսավար)
masterpiece - kuloukh kordzots (գլուխ գործոց)
mastic - dzamon, tsiut (ծամոն, ձիւթ)
masticate - dzamel, dzaskel (ծամել, ծասքել)
mastication - dzamoum (ծամում)
mastiff - kampur (գամփռ)
masturbate - kichoutiun unel, sermu tapel (գիջութիւն ընել, սերմը թափել)
masturbation - kichoutiun, sermnahosoutiun (գիջութիւն, սերմնաՀոսութիւն)
mat - khusir, pusiat, vodnakhusir, khusirabadel (խսիր, փսիաթ, ոտնախսիր, խսիրապատել)
mat, matt - anpayl, aghod (անփայլ, աղօտ)
matador - tsulamardig, tsulasban, avak khaghakard (ցլամարտիկ, ցլասպան, աւագ խաղաքարտ)
match (n) - murtsoum, loutsgi, havasar, unger, amol (մրցում, լուցկի, Հաւասար, ընկեր, ամոլ)
match (v) - murtsil, havasaretsunel, busagel, harmaril (մրցիլ, Հաւասարեցնել, պսակել, յարմարիլ)
matchbox - loutsgedoup (լուցկետուփ)
matchless - annuman, anzoukagan, yezagi (աննման, անզուգական, եզակի)
mate (n) - unger, goghagits, amousin, gin, genagits (ընկեր, կողակից, ամուսին, կին, կենակից)
mate (v) - ungeranal, amousnanal, zoukvil, miatsunel (ընկերանալ, ամուսնանալ, զուգուիլ, միացնել)
matelot - navaz, navasdi (նաւազ, նաւաստի)
material - niutagan, niuteghen, eagan, niut, adaghts (նիւթական, նիւթեղէն, էական, նիւթ, ատաղձ)
materialism - niutabashdoutiun (նիւթապաշտութիւն)
materialist - nioutabashd (նիւթապաշտ)
materialize - niutaganatsunel, irakordzel, iragananal (նիւթականացնել, իրագործել, իրականանալ)
materiel - niout, adaghts, ararganer, razmamuterk (նիւթ, ատաղձ, առարկաներ, ռազմամթերք)
maternal - mayragan, mayreni (մայրական, մայրենի)
maternity - mayroutiun (մայրութիւն)
mathematician - ousoghaked, matematigos, chapaked (ուսողագէտ, մաթեմաթիկոս, չափագէտ)
mathematics - ousoghoutiun, matematik (ուսողութիւն, մաթեմաթիք)
matinee - tseregouyt (ցերեկոյթ)
matricide - mayrasbanoutiun, mayrasban (մայրասպանութիւն, մայրասպան)
matriculate - artsanakurvil, hamalusaran artsanakurel (արձանագրուիլ, Համալսարան արձանագրել)
matrimony - amousnoutiun, busag, tughtakhagh mu (ամուսնութիւն, պսակ, թղթախաղ մը)
matrix - arkant, mayr hogh, mayradar, darazatsouyts (արգանդ, մայր Հող, մայրատառ, տարազացոյց)
matron - dandigin, deschouhi, dundesouhi (տանտիկին, տեսչուՀի, տնտեսուՀի)
matter - niut, eoutiun, khuntir, tarakh, nushanagel (նիւթ, էութիւն, խնդիր, թարախ, նշանակել)
matting - khusir, pusiat, miahiusoum (խսիր, փսիաթ, միաՀիւսում)
mattress - angoghin, mahij (անկողին, մաՀիճ)
maturate - hasountsunel, hasounnal, tarakhodetsunel (Հասունցնել, Հասուննալ, թարախոտեցնել)
maturation - hasounoutiun, hasouna-

tsoum, tarakhodoum (հասունութիւն, հասունացում, թարախոտում)
mature (a) - chapahas, hasoun, hasountsadz, luratsadz (չափահաս, հասուն, հասունցած, լրացած)
mature (v) - hasountsunel, hasounnal, ajil, luranal (հասունցնել, հասուննալ, աճիլ, լրանալ)
maturity - hasounoutiun, chapahasoutiun, vujarman or (հասունութիւն, չափահասութիւն, վճարման օր)
maudlin - tiurahouyz, lalgan, tiurazkats, harpadz (դիւրայոյզ, լալկան, դիւրազգաց, հարբած)
maul - tag, lakhd, dzedzel, khoshdankel (թակ, լախտ, ծեծել, խոշտանգել)
maund - kurtmunchel, murmural, moural (քրթմնջել, մրմռալ, մուռալ)
maunder - mouratsgan (մուրացկան)
maunderer - kurtmunchogh, murmuratsogh (քրթմնջող, մրմռացող)
mausoleum - tamparan, shirim (դամբարան, շիրիմ)
mauve - manishagakouyn, pats dzirani kouyn (մանիշակագոյն, բաց ծիրանի գոյն)
mawkish - anham, kanetsunogh, anakhorzh, noghgali (անհամ, գանեցնող, անախորժ, նողկալի)
maxim - aradz, asatsvadzk, imasdoun khosk (առած, ասացուածք, իմաստուն խօսք)
maximize - aveltsunel, medztsunel aravelakouynus (աւելցնել, մեծցնել առաւելագոյնս)
may - garenal, touyladurel, ardonel, terevus (կարենալ, թոյլատրել, արտօնել, թերեւս)
May - mayis (Մայիս)
maybe - terevus, koutse, havanapar (թերեւս, գուցէ, հաւանաբար)
mayonnaise - tsouakhouys, mayonez (ձուախիւս, մայոնէզ)
mayor - kaghakabed, taghabed (քաղաքապետ, թաղապետ)
mayoralty - kaghakabedoutiun, kaghakabedaran (քաղաքապետութիւն, քաղաքապետարան)
maze (n) - shuvaroum, anel, lapiurintos (շուարում, անել, լաբիւրինթոս)
maze (v) - shupotetsunel, abshetsunel, abshil, shuvaril (շփոթեցնել, ապշեցնել, ապշիլ, շուարիլ)
ma'am, madam - digin (տիկին)
me - zis, indzi (զիս, ինծի)
meadow - markakedin, mark (մարգագետին, մարգ)
meagre - nihar, vudid, jughjim, vadouj (նիհար, վտիտ, ճղճիմ, վատուժ)
meal - hatsahadigi aliur, geragour, aghal, manrel (հացահատիկի ալիւր, կերակուր, աղալ, մանրել)
mean (a) - michag, tsadz, vad, usdorin, anark, nouyn (միջակ, ցած, վատ, ստորին, անարգ, նոյն)
mean (n) - michin, michots, michag, mechdegh, michink, kanag (միջին, միջոց, միջակ, մէջտեղ, միջինք, քանակ)
mean (v) - nushanagel, mudaturel, dzurakurel, nakhadesel (նշանակել, մտադրել, ծրագրել, նախատեսել)
meander - volork, volorabudouyd volorel, taparil (ոլորք, ոլորապտոյտ, ոլորել, թափառիլ)
meaning - imasd, nushanagoutiun, nubadag (իմաստ, նշանակութիւն, նպատակ)
meanness - tsadzoutiun, usdornoutiun, vadoutiun (ցածութիւն, ստորնութիւն, վատութիւն)
meantime - miazhamanag, nouyn aden (միաժամանակ, նոյն ատեն)
meanwhile - see - տե՛ս (meantime)
measles - harsanit, garmurakhd (հարսանիթ, կարմրախտ)
measure - chap, gushir, kanag, sahman, chapel, kunahadel (չափ, կշիռ, քանակ, սահման, չափել, գնահատել)
measurement - chaparoutiun, chapakuroutiun (չափառութիւն, չափագրութիւն)
meat - mis, oudelik, geragour, ge-

ragrel (միս, ուտելիք, կերակուր, կերակրել)
meatus - tsuntsough, antsk (ցնցուղ, անցք)
mechanic - mekenakordz, mekenavar, arhesdavor, mekenagan (մեքենագործ, մեքենավար, արհեստաւոր, մեքենական)
mechanician - mekenaked, mekenavar (մեքենագէտ, մեքենավար)
mechanics - mekenakidoutiun (մեքենագիտութիւն)
mechanism - mekenaganoutiun, shinvadzk, horinvadzk (մեքենականութիւն, շինուածք, յօրինուածք)
mechanist - mekenakordz, mekenavar, mekenaked (մեքենագործ, մեքենավար, մեքենագէտ)
mechanize - mekenatsunel, mekenayatsunel (մեքենացնել, մեքենայացնել)
medal - medagh, medal, badvanushan, shukanushan (մետաղ, մետալ, պատուանշան, շքանշան)
medallion - medalion, houshaturam, shukaturam (մետալիոն, յուշադրամ, շքադրամ)
meddle - kharnuvil, michamudel (խառնուիլ, միջամտել)
media - haghortamichots, michin, michnortagan (հաղորդամիջոց, միջին, միջնորդական)
mediacy - michnortoutiun, hashdararoutiun, michinoutiun (միջնորդութիւն, հաշտարարութիւն, միջինութիւն)
mediate - michnortel, michamudel, michin, michnort (միջնորդել, միջամտել, միջին, միջնորդ)
mediation - michnortoutiun, michamudoutiun (միջնորդութիւն, միջամտութիւն)
mediator - michnort, hashdarar, parekhos (միջնորդ, հաշտարար, բարեխօս)
medical - puzhushgagan, pouzhagan, pouzhich (բժշկական, բուժական, բուժիչ)
medical outreach - puzhushgagan nakhakhunamk (բժշկական նախախնամք)
medicament - tegh (դեղ)
medicate - teghel, pouzhel, tarmanel (դեղել, բուժել, դարմանել)
medication - pouzhoum, tarmanoum (բուժում, դարմանում)
medicine - puzhushgoutiun, tegh, tarman, pouzhel (բժշկութիւն, դեղ, դարման, բուժել)
mediocre - michag, michin, chapavor (միջակ, միջին, չափաւոր)
mediocrity - michagoutiun (միջակութիւն)
meditate - khorhil, khogal, mudadzel (խորհիլ, խոկալ, մտածել)
meditation - khoh, khogoum, mudadzoutiun, mudakhohoutiun (խոհ, խոկում, մտածութիւն, մտախոհութիւն)
Mediterranean - micherguragan dzov, micherguria (Միջերկրական ծով, միջերկրեայ)
medium - michag, michin, chapavor, michots, shurchabad (միջակ, միջին, չափաւոր, միջոց, շրջապատ)
medley - kharnourt, kharnijaghanj, kharnel (խառնուրդ, խառնիճաղանճ, խառնել)
meed - vartsaduroutiun, vartsk, nuver, vartsadurel (վարձատրութիւն, վարձք, նուէր, վարձատրել)
meek - hez, meghm, khonarh (հեզ, մեղմ, խոնարհ)
meet - hantibil, desnuvil, havakvil, zhoghov (հանդիպիլ, տեսնուիլ, հաւաքուիլ, ժողով)
meeting - zhoghov, hantiboum, murtsoum, aghotazhoghov (ժողով, հանդիպում, մրցում, աղօթաժողով)
megalomania - medzamoloutiun (մեծամոլութիւն)
megaphone - partsurakhos, khosapogh (բարձրախօս, խօսափող)
megrim - kulkhatsav, kumayk (գլխացաւ, քմայք)
melancholia - melamaghtsodoutiun, durdmoutiun (մելամաղձոտութիւն, տրտմութիւն)
melancholic - melamaghtsod, dur-

doum, takhdzod (մելամաղձոտ, տրտում, թախծոտ)
melancoly - melamaghtsodoutiun, durdmoutiun, takhdzoujiun (մելամաղձոտութիւն, տրտմութիւն, թախծութիւն)
melange - kharnourt (խառնուրդ)
meliorate - parelavel, parvokel, amokel (բարելաւել, բարւոքել, ամոքել)
melioration - parelavoum, parvokoum (բարելաւում, բարւոքում)
mellow (a) - papoug, gagough, hasoun, hiutegh, tarm (փափուկ, կակուղ, հասուն, հիւթեղ, թարմ)
mellow (v) - gagoughtsunel, anoushtsunel, hasounnal (կակուղցնել, անուշցնել, հասուննալ)
melodious - kaghtsurahunchiun, kaghtsuranuvak (քաղցրահնչիւն, քաղցրանուագ)
melodrama - taderanuvak, nuvakakhagh (թատերանուագ, նուագախաղ)
melody - megheti, yeghanag, khaghtsurerk (մեղեդի, եղանակ, քաղցրերգ)
melon - sekh (սեխ)
melt - haletsunel, gagoughtsunel, tsouluvil (հալեցնել, կակուղցնել, ձուլուիլ)
member - antam, mas, antamagits (անդամ, մաս, անդամակից)
membership - antamagtsoutiun, antamagitsner (անդամակցութիւն, անդամակիցներ)
membership card - antamakard (անդամաքարտ)
membrane - mashg, taghant (մաշկ, թաղանդ)
memento - housharar, hishadag (յուշարար, յիշատակ)
memoir - hishoghoutiun, houshakuroutiun, housh, hishadag (յիշողութիւն, յուշագրութիւն, յուշ, յիշատակ)
memorable - hishadageli, hisharzhan, anmoranali (յիշատակելի, յիշարժան, անմոռանալի)
memorandum - houshakir, hishadagakir, housharan (յուշագիր, յիշատակագիր, յուշարան)
memorial - hishadagaran, houshartsan, houshamadyan (յիշատակարան, յուշարձան, յուշամատեան)
memorial cross - khachkar (խաչքար)
memorial day - houshadon (յուշատօն)
memorize - kots sorvil, hishel, hishadagel, haverzhatsunel (գոց սորվիլ, յիշել, յիշատակել, յաւերժացնել)
memory - hishoghoutiun, housh, hampav (յիշողութիւն, յուշ, համբաւ)
men - marter, martig (մարդեր, մարդիկ)
menace - usbarnalik, sasd, usbarnal (սպառնալիք, սաստ, սպառնալ)
menage - dundesoutiun, douni kordz (տնտեսութիւն, տունի գործ)
mend - norokel, gargudel, shudgel, parvokel (նորոգել, կարկտել, շտկել, բարւոքել)
mendacious - sudakhos, soud, khapeagan, geghdz (ստախօս, սուտ, խաբէական, կեղծ)
mendicancy - mouratsganoutiun (մուրացկանութիւն)
mendicant - mouratsgan, mouratsig (մուրացկան, մուրացիկ)
mendicity - mouratsganoutiun (մուրացկանութիւն)
menial - dzarayagan, dzara, usbasavor (ծառայական, ծառայ, սպասաւոր)
meningitis - ougheghadab, kheladab (ուղեղատապ, խելատապ)
menopause - tashdanatatar (դաշտանադադար)
menses - tashdan, amsahosoutiun (դաշտան, ամսահոսութիւն)
menstruate - tashdan ounenal, amsahosil (դաշտան ունենալ, ամսահոսիլ)
mensual - amsagan (ամսական)
mensurate - chapel (չափել)
mensuration - chapoum (չափում)
mental - mudayin, mudavor, imatsagan, guzagayin (մտային, մտաւոր,

իմացական, կզակային)
mentality - mudaynoutiun, midk (մտայնութիւն, միտք)
mention - hishadagoutiun, hishoum, hishadagel, hishel (յիշատակութիւն, յիշում, յիշատակել, յիշել)
mentor - arachnort, khorhurtadou, mendor, tasdiarag (առաջնորդ, խորհրդատու, մենտոր, դաստիարակ)
menu - jashatsoutsag (ճաշացուցակ)
meow, meou - mulavel, mulaviun - gadoui tsayn (մլաւել, մլաւիւն - կատուի ձայն)
mephitis - nekhoutiun, jandahodoutiun (նեխութիւն, ժանտահոտութիւն)
mercantile - arevduragan, vajaraganagan (առեւտրանական, վաճառականական)
mercenary - vartsgan, vartsuvadz, shahaser (վարձկան, վարձուած, շահասէր)
mercer - gerbasavajar (կերպասավաճառ)
mercery - gerbasavajaroutiun (կերպասավաճառութիւն)
merchandise - abrank, vajark, arevdour, aroudzakhel (ապրանք, վաճառք, առեւտուր, առուծախել)
merchant - vajaragan, arevduragan (վաճառական, առեւտրական)
merchantable - vajareli, tiuravajar (վաճառելի, դիւրավաճառ)
merciful - parekout, voghormadz, kutadz (բարեգութ, ողորմած, գթած)
mercifulness - voghormadzoutiun (ողորմածութիւն)
mercury - suntig, payladzou (սնդիկ, Փայլածու)
mercy - kout, oghormadzoutiun, neroghoutiun (գութ, ողորմածութիւն, ներողութիւն)
mere - lujag, sahman, barz, sosg, pazhnel, sahmanel (լճակ, սահման, պարզ, սոսկ, բաժնել, սահմանել)
merely - barzabes, miayn, log (պարզապէս, միայն, լոկ)
merge - tsoulel, tsoulvil, mukhurjuvil, ungughmil (ձուլել, ձուլուիլ, մխրճուիլ, ընկղմիլ)
merger - miatsoum, tsouloum (միացում, ձուլում)
meridian - michore, gesor, gesorva, kakatnaged (միջօրէ, կէսօր, կէսօրուայ, գագաթնակէտ)
merit - arzhanik, arzhek, vasdag, arzhananal (արժանիք, արժէք, վաստակ, արժանանալ)
meritorious - arzhani, arzhanavor (արժանի, արժանաւոր)
mermaid - dzovanoush, churahars (ծովանոյշ, ջրահարս)
merman - houshgabarig, churoki, arasbelagan voki (յուշկապարիկ, ջրոգի, առասպելական ոգի)
merriment - tsundzoutiun, khuntoutiun, zuvarjoutiun (ցնծութիւն, խնդութիւն, զուարճութիւն)
merry - ourakh, zuvart, pergurali (ուրախ, զուարթ, բերկրալի)
mesa - sarahart, lernatashd (սարահարթ, լեռնադաշտ)
mesel - porod (բորոտ)
mesh - varsahiusk, ourgan, ourgamel, tagartel (վարսահիւսք, ուռկան, ուռկանել, թակարդել)
mess - jash, oudelik, kharnagoutiun, jashel, sunvil (ճաշ, ուտելիք, խառնակութիւն, ճաշել, սնուիլ)
message - badkam, badkamakir, avedis, lour (պատգամ, պատգամագիր, աւետիս, լուր)
messenger - luraper, luradar, badkamaper, sourhantag (լրաբեր, լրատար, պատգամաբեր, սուրհանդակ)
Messiah - krisdos, odzial, mesia (Քրիստոս, Օծեալ, Մեսիա)
messieurs, messrs. - diyark, baronner (տեարք, պարոններ)
messmate - seghanagits, jashunger-panagi (սեղանակից, ճաշընկեր՝ բանակի)
messuage - abarank (ապարանք)
metabolism - pokhargoutiun, niutapokhaganoutiun (փոխարկութիւն, նիւթափոխանակութիւն)
metabolize - pokhargel (փոխարկել)

metal - medagh, niut (մետաղ, նիւթ)
metallic - medaghe, medaghia (մետաղէ, մետաղեայ)
metallize, metalize - medaghabadel, medaghatsunel (մետաղապատել, մետաղացնել)
metallurgia - medaghakidoutiun, medaghapanoutiun (մետաղագիտութիւն, մետաղաբանութիւն)
metallurgy - medaghakordzoutiun, medaghapanoutiun (մետաղագործութիւն, մետաղաբանութիւն)
metamorphose - gerbaranapokhel, pokhagerbel (կերպարանափոխել, փոխակերպել)
metamorphosis - aylagerboum, gerbaranapokhoutiun (այլակերպում, կերպարանափոխութիւն)
metaphor - pokhaperoutiun (փոխաբերութիւն)
metaphysician - punazantsaked (բնազանցագէտ)
metaphysics - punazantsoutiun (բնազանցութիւն)
mete - sahman, sahmanakar, chap, chapel, voroshel (սահման, սահմանաքար, չափ, չափել, որոշել)
meteor - oterevouyt, asoub, yergnakar (օդերեւոյթ, ասուպ, երկնաքար)
meteorologist - oterevoutapan (օդերեւութաբան)
meteorology - oterevoutapanoutiun (օդերեւութաբանութիւն)
meter - metur, chapatsouyts (մեթր, չափացոյց)
method - metod, michots, yeghanag, gerb, hamagark (մեթոտ, միջոց, եղանակ, կերպ, համակարգ)
methodic - ganonavor, hamagarkuvadz, garkavorial (կանոնաւոր, համակարգուած, կարգաւորեալ)
methodist - metodagan, khusdaguron (մեթոտական, խստակրօն)
meticulous - pudzakhuntir, khughjamid, parekhighj (բծախնդիր, խղճամիտ, բարեխիղճ)
metier - arhesd, kordz, uzpaghoum (արհեստ, գործ, զբաղում)
metif, metis - kharnadzin (խառնածին)
metro - yentoughi, usdorkednia kunadzk (ենթուղի, ստորգետնեայ գնացք)
metropolis - mayrakaghak, vosdan (մայրաքաղաք, ոստան)
metropolitan - mayrakaghakatsi, arkebisgobosaran, arkebisgobos (մայրաքաղաքացի, արքեպիսկոպոսարան, արքեպիսկոս)
mettle - yerant, voki, kachoutiun, huzoroutiun (եռանդ, ոգի, քաջութիւն, հզօրութիւն)
mew - jay, pazevantag, mulaviun, mulavel, vantagel (ճայ, բազեվանդակ, մլաւիւն, մլաւել, վանդակել)
mewl - juchal, juval, mulavel (ճչալ, ճուալ, մլաւել)
mexican - meksigatsi, meksigagan (մեքսիկացի, մեքսիկական)
Mexico - meksiga (Մեքսիկա)
mezzo - michin, ges, michag (միջին, կէս, միջակ)
miaow, miaou - mulavel, mulaviun (մլաւել, մլաւիւն)
mica - tertakar, paylar (թերթաքար, փայլար)
mickeymouse - dzaghramugnig (ծաղրամկնիկ)
micro - tsaynapogh (ձայնափող)
microbe - manre, mikrob (մանրէ, միքրոպ)
microbicide - manreasban (մանրէասպան)
microcomputer - manragarkich (մանրակարգիչ)
microfilm - manrazhabaven, manrafilm (մանրաժապաւէն, մանրաֆիլմ)
microphone - manrakhos, manratsayn (մանրախօս, մանրաձայն)
microscope - manratidag, manratsouyts (մանրադիտակ, մանրացոյց)
microwave - manracherots, manralik (մանրաջերոց, մանրալիք)
microwave oven - cherots, manralikov pour (ջերոց, մանրալիքով բուռ)
mid - michin, mechdeghi (միջին,

մէջտեղի)
midday - gesor, gesorva (կէսօր, կէսօրուայ)
midden - aghpagouyd (աղբակոյտ)
middle - mechdegh, getron, mechdeghi, michag, michin (մէջտեղ, կեդրոն, մէջտեղի, միջակ, միջին)
Middle East - michin arevelk (Միջին Արեւելք)
middleman - michnort, kordzagadar (միջնորդ, գործակատար)
middling - michin, michag, chapavor (միջին, միջակ, չափաւոր)
midland - michnashkharh, michnakavar, micherguria (միջնաշխարհ, միջնագաւառ, միջերկրեայ)
Midlent - michink (Միջինք)
midnight - ges kisher, ges kishervan (կէս գիշեր, կէս գիշերուան)
midst - mechdegh, michev, getron, mechdeghu (մէջտեղ, միջեւ, կեդրոն, մէջտեղը)
midwife - mangaparts, tayiag, tayiagel (մանկաբարձ, դայեակ, դայեակել)
mien - gerbarank, temk, yerevouyt, varmounk (կերպարանք, դէմք, երեւոյթ, վարմունք)
miff - kuzhdoutiun, kuzhduvil, surtoghetsunel (գժտութիւն, գժտուիլ, սրդողեցնել)
might - zoroutiun, ouzh, huzoroutiun (զօրութիւն, ոյժ, հզօրութիւն)
mightily - hozorabes, zoravor gerbov, ouzhkunoren (հզօրապէս, զօրաւոր կերպով, ուժգնօրէն)
mighty - houzhgou, zoravor, huzor, garogh (հուժկու, զօրաւոր, հզօր, կարող)
migraine - kulkhatsav (գլխացաւ)
migrate - kaghtel, chuvel, ardakaghtel (գաղթել, չուել, արտագաղթել)
migration - kaght, kaghtoum, chou (գաղթ, գաղթում, չու)
migrator - kaghtogh, chuvogh, taparagan (գաղթող, չուող, թափառական)
milch - gatnadou, gutan gov (կաթնատու, կթան կով)
mild - kaghtsur, anoush, meghm, papoug, hez (քաղցր, անոյշ, մեղմ, փափուկ, հեզ)
mile - mughon (մղոն)
mileage - mughonachap, mughonakin, ougheturam (մղոնաչափ, մղոնագին, ուղեդրամ)
milestone - mughonakar (մղոնաքար)
militant - mardunchogh, razmig, zinvorial (մարտնչող, ռազմիկ, զինուորեալ)
militarism - razmaganoutiun, zinvorabashdoutiun (ռազմականութիւն, զինուորապաշտութիւն)
military - zork, panag, zinvoragan, razmagan (զօրք, բանակ, զինուորական, ռազմական)
militate - gurvil, baderazmil, mardunchil (կռուիլ, պատերազմիլ, մարտնչիլ)
militia - kaghakazork, bahagazor (քաղաքազօրք, պահակազօր)
milk - gat, gutel, gutvil (կաթ, կթել, կթուիլ)
milkmaid - gatnavajarouhi (կաթնավաճառուհի)
milkman - gatnavajar (կաթնավաճառ)
milky - gatnod, gate, gatnorag, ambamadz (կաթնոտ, կաթէ, կաթնորակ, ամպամած)
mill - chaghats, churaghats, aghal, manrel, pushrel (ջաղաց, ջրաղաց, աղալ, մանրել, փշրել)
millboard - khavakard (խաւաքարտ)
millenary - hazaramiag, hazaramia (հազարամեակ, հազարամեայ)
miller - chaghatsban, tsets (ջաղացպան, ցեց)
millet - goreg (կորեկ)
milliard - yergilion (երկիլիոն)
milling machine - medagh surogh kordzik (մետաղ սրող գործիք)
million - milion (միլիոն)
millionaire - milionader, medzaharousd (միլիոնատէր, մեծահարուստ)
millstone - chaghats, tsoren aghalou kare kordzik (ջաղաց, ցորեն աղալու քարէ գործիք)
milt - paydzagh, tsugungit, tsugun-

gutel (փայծաղ, ձկնկիթ, ձկնկթել)
mime - zaveshdakhagh, hudbid, munchgadagel (զաւեշտախաղ, Հտպիտ, մնջկատակել)
mimeograph - pazmakurogh mekena (բազմագրող մեքենայ)
mimer - mimos, hudbid (միմոս, Հտպիտ)
mimic - timakhagh, mimosoutiun, numanetsunel, gabgel (դիմախաղ, միմոսութիւն, նմանեցնել, կապկել)
minaret - minare (մինարէ)
mince - manrel, godurduvil, dzekdzekil, godurdouk (մանրել, կոտրտուիլ, ծեքծեքիլ, կոտրտուք)
mind - midk, khelk, hishoghoutiun, mudadzel, khorhil (միտք, խելք, յիշողութիւն, մտածել, խորՀիլ)
minded - hozhar, duramatir, duramaturvadz, hagamed (յօժար, տրամադիր, տրամադրուած, Հակամէտ)
mine (I) - imus, im (իմս, իմ)
mine (II) - agan, hank, kednapor, aganel, porel (ական, Հանք, գետնափոր, ականել, փորել)
mineral - hankaniut, hankayin, hanadzo (Հանքանիւթ, Հանքային, Հանածոյ)
mineralogy - hankapanoutiun, hankakidoutiun (Հանքաբանութիւն, Հանքագիտութիւն)
mingle - kharnel, paghaturel, kharnuvil, miyanal (խառնել, բաղադրել, խառնուիլ, միանալ)
miniature - manranugar, manranunugarchoutiun (մանրանկար, մանրանկարչութիւն)
minify - buzdigtsunel, terkunahadel, nuvasdatsunel (պզտիկցնել, թերգնաՀատել, նուաստացնել)
minim - pokrakouyn, chunchin, heghougachap (փոքրագոյն, չնչին, Հեղուկաչափ)
minimarket - khanout, pokur vajaradoun (խանութ, փոքր վաճառատուն)
minimize - pokratsunel, nuvazetsunel (փոքրացնել, նուազեցնել)
minimum - nuvazakouyn, pokrakouyn (նուազագոյն, փոքրագոյն)
minion - siroun, nourp, koghdurig, manradar (սիրուն, նուրբ, գողտրիկ, մանրատառ)
minister (n) - nakharar, bashdonia, karozich, yerets (նախարար, պաշտօնեայ, քարոզիչ, երէց)
minister (v) - dunorinel, oknel, dzarayel, dal, karozel (տնօրինել, օգնել, ծառայել, տալ, քարոզել)
ministry - nakhararoutiun, bashdoneoutiun, karozchoutiun (նախարարութիւն, պաշտօնէութիւն, քարոզչութիւն)
mink - churaghves, churakis (ջրաղուէս, ջրաքիս)
minor - gurdser, pokur, anchapahas (կրտսեր, փոքր, անչափաՀաս)
minority - pokramasnoutiun, anchapahasoutiun (փոքրամասնութիւն, անչափաՀասութիւն)
minster - mayr dajar, mayr yegeghetsi, vanki yegeghetsi (մայր տաճար, մայր եկեղեցի, վանքի եկեղեցի)
minstrel - ashough, kousan, yerazhishd, shurchoun yerkich (աշուղ, գուսան, երաժիշտ, շրջուն երգիչ)
mint - ananoukh, pogheranots, turamahadel, hunarel (անանուխ, փողերանոց, դրամաՀատել, Հնարել)
minus - nuvaz, bagas (նուազ, պակաս)
minuscule - pokradar, manradar, manur ararga (փոքրատառ, մանրատառ, մանր առարկայ)
minute - vayrgian, chunchin, punakir, sevakurel (վայրկեան, չնչին, բնագիր, սեւագրել)
minutia - nourp manroukner, sunodik (նուրբ մանրուքներ, սնոտիք)
minx - lirp, bornig, churaghves (լիրբ, պոռնիկ, ջրաղուէս)
miracle - hurashk, uskanchelik, hurashalik (Հրաշք, սքանչելիք, Հրաշալիք)
miraculous - hurashali, uskancheli, hiyanali (Հրաշալի, սքանչելի, Հիանալի)
mirage - gurgnerevouyt, khapgank,

badrank (կրկներեւոյթ, խաբկանք, պատրանք)
mire - jahij, dighm, bighdz, tsekhodel, bughdzel (ճահիճ, տիղմ, պիղծ, ցեխոտել, պղծել)
mirror - hayeli, dib, orinag, ardatsolel (Հայելի, տիպ, օրինակ, արտացոլել)
mirth - tsundzoutiun, hurjuvank, ourakhoutiun, khunjouyk (ցնծութիւն, Հրճուանք, ուրախութիւն, խնճոյք)
misadventure - tsakhoghank, tuzhpakhdoutiun, portsank (ձախողանք, դժբախտութիւն, փորձանք)
misanthrope - martadiats (մարդատեաց)
misapplication - zeghdzoum, charashahoum (զեղծում, չարաշաՀում)
misapply - sukhal kordzadzel, charashahel (սխալ գործածել, չարաշաՀել)
misapprehend - sukhal hasgunal (սխալ Հասկնալ)
misapprehension - tiurimatsoutiun (թիւրիմացութիւն)
misbecome - chuvaylel, chuharmaril (չվայլել, չյարմարիլ)
misbehave - kesh varmounk ounenal (գէշ վարմունք ունենալ)
misbehavior - ankaghakavaroutiun, kesh untatsk (անքաղաքավարութիւն, գէշ ընթացք)
misbelief - sukhal havadk, moloroutiun (սխալ Հաւատք, մոլորութիւն)
misbeliever - terahavad, hertsvadzogh, heredigos (թերաՀաւատ, Հերձուածող, Հերետիկոս)
miscalculate - sukhal hashvel, sukhalil (սխալ Հաշուել, սխալիլ)
miscarriage - vuriboum, vizhoum, namagi chuhasnilu (վրիպում, վիժում, նամակի չՀասնիլը)
miscarry - moloril, vizhil (մոլորիլ, վիժիլ)
miscellanea - zhoghovadzo (ժողովածոյ)
miscellaneous - zanazan, kharun, aylevayl, pazmazan (զանազան, խառն, այլեւայլ, բազմազան)
miscellany - kharnourt, havakadzo (խառնուրդ, Հաւաքածոյ)
mischance - tuzhpakhdoutiun, aghed, argadz, portsank (դժբախտութիւն, աղէտ, արկած, փորձանք)
mischief - charoutiun, vunas, neghoutiun (չարութիւն, վնաս, նեղութիւն)
mischievous - charakordz, char, charamid (չարագործ, չար, չարամիտ)
misconduct - kesh varmounk, sukhal untatsk, kesh ghegavarel (գէշ վարմունք, սխալ ընթացք, գէշ ղեկավարել)
miscount - sukhal hashvel, sukhalil (սխալ Հաշուել, սխալիլ)
miscreant - anhavad, aylaguron, ankhighj, charakordz (անՀաւատ, այլակրօն, անխիղճ, չարագործ)
miscreate - aborini, shindzou, yeriurvadz, kesh usdeghdzel (ապօրինի, շինծու, յերիւրուած, գէշ ստեղծել)
misdate - sukhal tuvagan, sukhal tuvagan tunel (սխալ թուական, սխալ թուական դնել)
misdeal - sukhal gudrel, pazhnel, sukhal pazhanoum (սխալ կտրել, բաժնել, սխալ բաժանում)
misdeed - charik, charakordzoutiun, hantsank (չարիք, չարագործութիւն, յանցանք)
misdemeanor - hantsank, meghk, kesh vark (յանցանք, մեղք, գէշ վարք)
misdirect - moloretsunel, sheghel (մոլորեցնել, շեղել)
misdoing - charakordzoutiun, charik, hantsank (չարագործութիւն, չարիք, յանձանք)
misdoubt - gasgadzil, chuvusdahil (կասկածիլ, չվստաՀիլ)
miser - gudzdzi, akah, zhulad (կծծի, ագաՀ, ժլատ)
miserable - tushvar, voghormeli, kheghj (թշուառ, ողորմելի, խեղճ)
misery - tushvaroutiun, chukavoroutiun, keghjoutiun (թշուառութիւն, չքաւորութիւն, խեղճութիւն)
misestimate - terkunahadel

(թերգնահատել)
misfit - anharmaroutiun, chuharmarogh hakousd (անյարմարութիւն, չյարմարող հագուստ)
misfortune - tuzhpakhdoutiun, tsakhortoutiun, tushpakhdanal (դժբախտութիւն, ձախորդութիւն, դժբախտանալ)
misgive - vakhtsunel, gasgadzil, nakhazkoushatsunel (վախցնել, կասկածիլ, նախազգուշացնել)
misgovern - kesh garavarel (գէշ կառավարել)
misguide - sukhal arachnortel, moloretsunel, sukhaletsunel (սխալ առաջնորդել, մոլորեցնել, սխալեցնել)
mishandle - kesh varvil, kesh kordzadzel (գէշ վարուիլ, գէշ գործածել)
misinform - sukhal deghegoutiun dal, abagoghmnoroshel (սխալ տեղեկութիւն տալ, ապակողմնորոշել)
misjudge - sukhal tadel, sukhalvil (սխալ դատել, սխալուիլ)
mislay - sukhal degh tunel, turadz deghu mornal (սխալ տեղ դնել, դրած տեղը մոռնալ)
mislead - sukhal arachnortel, moloretsunel (սխալ առաջնորդել, մոլորեցնել)
mislike - chusirel, khurdchil (չսիրել, խրտչիլ)
mismanage - vad ghegavarel, annourp varvil (վատ ղեկավարել, աննուրբ վարուիլ)
misogynist - gunadiats (կնատեաց)
misplace - sukhal degh tunel (սխալ տեղ դնել)
misprint - sukhal dubakurel, vuribag (սխալ տպագրել, վրիպակ)
mispronounce - sukhal hunchel (սխալ հնչել)
misrepresent - sukhal nergayatsunel, charapokhel (սխալ ներկայացնել, չարափոխել)
Miss - oryort (օրիորդ)
miss (I) - oryort, keghetsgouhi (օրիորդ, գեղեցկուհի)
miss (II) - vuriboum, chukoyoutiun, gorousd, patsagayoutiun (վրիպում, չգոյութիւն, կորուստ, բացակայութիւն)
miss (v) - vuribil, chuhasnil, bagsil, garodnal, pakhtsunel (վրիպիլ, չհասնիլ, պակսիլ, կարօտնալ, փախցնել)
missile - hurtir, ardungets (հրթիռ, արտընկէց)
missing - patsaga, bagas, gorsuvadz (բացակայ, պակաս, կորսուած)
mission - arakeloutiun, badkamavoroutiun, gochoum, ter (առաքելութիւն, պատգամաւորութիւն, կոչում, դեր)
missionary - karozich, arakial, misionaroutiun (քարոզիչ, առաքեալ, միսիոնարութիւն)
missive - namag, badkam, ougherts (նամակ, պատգամ, ուղերձ)
missy - aghchunag, nazeli, gousagan (աղջնակ, նազելի, կուսական)
mist - mushoush, mek, marakhough, meshoushabadel (մշուշ, մէգ, մառախուղ, մշուշապատել)
mistake - sukhal, vuribag, sukhalil, shupotil (սխալ, վրիպակ, սխալիլ, շփոթիլ)
mister - baron, der, arhesd, desag, bedk, okdagar ullal (պարոն, տէր, արհեստ, տեսակ, պէտք, օգտակար ըլլալ)
mistime - anzhamanag, voch adenin (անժամանակ, ոչատենին)
mistranslate - sukhal tarkmanel (սխալ թարգմանել)
mistreat - neghel, charcharel, kesh veraperil (նեղել, չարչարել, գէշ վերաբերիլ)
mistress - sirouhi, homanouhi (սիրուհի, հոմանուհի)
mistrust - anvusdahoutiun, gasgadz, gasgadzil (անվստահութիւն, կասկած, կասկածիլ)
mistrustful - gasgadzeli, anvusdaheli, gasgadzod (կասկածելի, անվստահելի, կասկածոտ)
misty - mushoushod, mikabad, aghod (մշուշոտ, միգապատ, աղօտ)
misunderstand - sukhal hasgunal,

sukhal umpurnel (սխալ Հասկնալ, սխալ ըմբռնել)
misuse - charachar kordzadzel, sukhal okdakordzel (չարաչար գործածել, սխալ օգտագործել)
mite - tsets, pokur michad, louma, masnig, boud (ցեց, փոքր միջատ, լումայ, մասնիկ, պուտ)
miter, mitre - tak, khouyr, takaturel (Թագ, խոյր, Թագադրել)
mitigate - meghmatsunel, tetevtsunel, hantardetsunel (մեղմացնել, Թեթեւցնել, Հանդարտեցնել)
mitigation - meghmatsoum, tetevatsoum, amokoum (մեղմացում, Թեթեւացում, ամոքում)
mitrailleuse - arakaharvadz, pokur khordungets (արագահարուած, փոքր խորտընկեց)
mitral - takatsev, kouyratsev (Թագաձեւ, խոյրաձեւ)
mitral valve - surdi takatsev turnag (սրտի Թագաձեւ դռնակ)
mittimus - pandargoutian huramanakir (բանտարկուԹեան Հրամանագիր)
mix - kharnel, miatsunel, kharnuvil, mianal (խառնել, միացնել, խառնուիլ, միանալ)
mixed - kharun, kharnuvadz, miakharun (խառն, խառնուած, միախառն)
mixer - kharnich, harich (խառնիչ, Հարիչ)
mixture - kharnourt, teghakharnoum, paghatroutiun (խառնուրդ, դեղախառնում, բաղադրուԹիւն)
mizzle - tsoghantsurev, nurpantsurevel (ցօղանձրեւ, նրբանձրեւել)
mnemonic - hishoghagan (յիշողական)
mnemonics - houshakidoutiun, hishoghoutian arvesd (յուշագիտուԹիւն, յիշողուԹեան արուեստ)
moan - voghp, hedzedzank, voghpal, hedzel (ողբ, Հեծեծանք, ողբալ, Հեծել)
moat - khuram, pos, khuramel (խրամ, փոս, խրամել)
moate - dzurdel (ծրտել)
mob - ampokh, khouzhan, khurnuvil, khouzhel, khurovel (ամբոխ, խուժան, խռնուիլ, խուժել, խռովել)
mobile - sharzhagan, sharzhoun, anhasdad, tiurasharzh (շարժական, շարժուն, անՀաստատ, դիւրաշարժ)
mobility - sharzhaganoutiun, sharzhounoutiun, arakoutiun (շարժականուԹիւն, շարժունուԹիւն, արագուԹիւն)
mobilization - zorahavak, zorasharzh (զօրաՀաւաք, զօրաշարժ)
mobilize - zorasharzhel, zork havakel (զօրաշարժել, զօրք Հաւաքել)
mock - dzaghrel, heknel, geghdzel, dzaghrank, heknank (ծաղրել, Հեգնել, կեղծել, ծաղրանք, Հեգնանք)
mocker - dzaghrogh, heknogh, khapepa (ծաղրող, Հեգնող, խաբեբայ)
mockery - dzaghur, dzaghrank, heknoutiun (ծաղր, ծաղրանք, ՀեգնուԹիւն)
modality - tsevaganoutiun, hankamank, gerbaroutiun (ձեւականուԹիւն, Հանգամանք, կերպարուԹիւն)
mode - noratsevoutiun, norouyt, yeghanag, tsev, daraz (նորաձեւուԹիւն, նորոյԹ, եղանակ, ձեւ, տարազ)
model - orinag, gaghabar, nakhadib, manragerd, tsevel (օրինակ, կաղապար, նախատիպ, մանրակերտ, ձեւել)
modeling, modelling - tsevoum, gaghabaroum (ձեւում, կաղապարում)
modelize - orinagel, gaghabarel (օրինակել, կաղապարել)
moderate - chapavorel, meghmatsunel, chapavor, meghm (չափաւորել, մեղմացնել, չափաւոր, մեղմ)
moderation - chapavoroutiun, meghmoutiun, meghmatsoum (չափաւորուԹիւն, մեղմուԹիւն, մեղմացում)
moderator - hantardetsoutsich, chapavorich, michnort (Հանդարտեցուցիչ, չափաւորիչ, միջնորդ)

modern - nor, arti, nerga, zhamanagagits (նոր, արդի, ներկայ, ժամանակակից)
modernism - artiaganoutiun, nor voj, artiamudoutiun (արդիականութիւն, նոր ոճ, արդիամտութիւն)
modernization - artiaganatsoum, ayzhmeatsoum (արդիականացում, այժմէացում)
modernize - artiaganatsunel, artiatsunel (արդիականացնել, արդիացնել)
modest - hamesd, bargeshd, barz, amotkhadz (համեստ, պարկեշտ, պարզ, ամօթխած)
modesty - hamesdoutiun, barzoutiun, amotkhadzoutiun (համեստութիւն, պարզութիւն, ամօթխածութիւն)
modification - parepokhoutiun, popokhoutiun (բարեփոխութիւն, փոփոխութիւն)
modifier - parepokhich, yeghanagavorich (բարեփոխիչ, եղանակաւորիչ)
modify - parepokhel, popokhel, tsevapokhel (բարեփոխել, փոփոխել, ձեւափոխել)
modish - noratsev, norouyt, artiatsevagan (նորաձեւ, նորոյթ, արդիաձեւական)
modist - noratsevaked, tertsagouhi, noroutavajar (նորաձեւագէտ, դերձակուհի, նորութավաճառ)
modulate - ganonavorel, yeghanagavorel, shudgel (կանոնաւորել, եղանակաւորել, շտկել)
modulation - yeghanagavoroum, yelevech, popokhoum, volorag (եղանակաւորում, ելեւէջ, փոփոխում, ոլորակ)
modulator - yeghanagavorich, tsaynargou (եղանակաւորիչ, ձայնարկու)
module - dibar, chap, hamemadachap (տիպար, չափ, համեմատաչափ)
modus - gerb, yeghanag, baymanagerb (կերպ, եղանակ, պայմանակերպ)
modus vivendi - abrelagerb (ապրելակերպ)
mohair - aydzagerbas, ankora aydzimaz (այծակերպաս, անգորա այծիմազ)
Mohammed - mouhammed (Մուհամմէտ)
mohammedan - mahmedagan, islam (մահմետական, իսլամ)
Mohammedism - mahmedaganoutiun, islamoutiun (Մահմետականութիւն, Իսլամութիւն)
moider - duknil, neghel, tsantsuratsunel (տքնիլ, նեղել, ձանձրացնել)
moiety - ges, gisamas, goghagits (կէս, կիսամաս, կողակից)
moil - duknil, dzanur ashkhadil, aghdodil, aghd (տքնիլ, ծանր աշխատիլ, աղտոտիլ, աղտ)
moist - tats, khonav, antsurevod (թաց, խոնաւ, անձրեւոտ)
moisten - khonavtsunel, turchel, gagoughtsunel (խոնաւցնել, թրջել, կակուղցնել)
moisture - khonavoutiun, tatsoutiun, damgoutiun (խոնաւութիւն, թացութիւն, տամկութիւն)
molar - aghorik, medz agra, zhanik (աղօրիք, մեծ ակռայ, ժանիք)
mold, mould - gaghabar, orinag, pousahogh, gaghabarel, muklodel (կաղապար, օրինակ, բուսահող, կաղապարել, մքլոտել)
molder, moulder - tsoulogh, gaghabarogh, pushrel, poshianal (ձուլող, կաղապարող, փշրել, փոշիանալ)
molding, moulding - gaghabaroum, tsouloum, tsouladzo (կաղապարում, ձուլում, ձուլածոյ)
mole - khulourt, bisag, godzidz, arkanti mis, toump (խլուրդ, պիսակ, կոծիծ, արգանդի միս, թումբ)
molecular - masnigayin (մասնիկային)
molecule - masnig, hiulenerou khoump (մասնիկ, հիւլէներու խումբ)
molest - charcharel, neghel, anhankusdatsunel, khankarel (չարչարել, նեղել, անհանգստացնել, խանգարել)

molestation - neghoum, neghoutiun badjarelu (նեղում, նեղութիւն պատճառելը)
moll - poz, bornig, darpouhi (բոզ, պոռնիկ, տարփուհի)
mollify - meghmel, gagoughtsunel, hantardetsunel (մեղմել, կակուղցնել, հանդարտեցնել)
mollusc, mollusk - gagghamort (կակղամորթ)
molten - tsouladzo, tapdzou, haladz (ձուլածոյ, թափծու, հալած)
moment - vayrgian, bah, zhamanag, arit, aguntard (վայրկեան, պահ, ժամանակ, առիթ, ակնթարթ)
momentary - vayrgenagan, garjadev (վայրկենական, կարճատեւ)
momentous - lourch, dzanragushir, khisd garevor (լուրջ, ծանրակշիռ, խիստ կարեւոր)
momentum - tap, tapuntats, mugoum, sharzhatap (թափ, թափընթաց, մղում, շարժաթափ)
monarch - miyabed, inknagal, arka, gaysur (միապետ, ինքնակալ, արքայ, կայսր)
monarchy - miyabedoutiun, takavoroutiun (միապետութիւն, թագաւորութիւն)
monastery - vank, menasdan, ghugheranots (վանք, մենաստան, կղերանոց)
monastic - vanagan, apegha vanki (վանական, աբեղայ վանքի)
monasticism - vanaganoutiun (վանականութիւն)
Monday - yergoushapti (Երկուշաբթի)
monetary - turamagan, turamayin (դրամական, դրամային)
money - turam, harusdoutiun, pogh, usdag (դրամ, հարստութիւն, փող, ստակ)
money box - kantsadoup, kantsanag (գանձատուփ, գանձանակ)
money lender - vashkharou (վաշխառու)
money maker - turamamol, turam tizogh (դրամամոլ, դրամ դիզող)
money market - sagaran (սակարան)
money order - vujarakir, michazkayin pokhkir (վճարագիր, միջազգային փոխգիր)
money-lendering - turamagan pokhaduvoutiun (դրամական փոխատուութիւն)
monger - vajarogh, dzakhogh (վաճառող, ծախող)
monition - aztararoutiun, hurahank, khurad (ազդարարութիւն, հրահանգ, խրատ)
monitor - khuradadou, aztararogh, aztanav, tasadou (խրատատու, ազդարարող, ազդանաւ, դասատու)
monk - vanagan, apegha, gousaguron (վանական, աբեղայ, կուսակրօն)
monkey - gabig, gabgel, dzaghrel (կապիկ, կապկել, ծաղրել)
monocarp - miabudough (միապտուղ)
monochrome - miakouyn (միագոյն)
monograph - menakir (մենագիր)
monolith - menakar, siunatsev hishadagaran (մենաքար, սիւնաձեւ յիշատակարան)
monologue - menakhosoutiun (մենախօսութիւն)
monopolize - menadirel, menashunorh tartsunel (մենատիրել, մենաշնորհ դարձնել)
monopoly - menadiroutiun, menashunorh (մենատիրութիւն, մենաշնորհ)
monosyllabe - miavang par (միավանկ՝ բառ)
monotone - miorinagoutiun, miabaghaghoutiun (միօրինակութիւն, միապաղաղութիւն)
monotonous - miorinag, miagerb, tsantsuranali (միօրինակ, միակերպ, ձանձրանալի)
monotype - miadar, miadib, meg ar meg sharogh (միատառ, միատիպ, մէկ առ մէկ շարող)
monseigneur - kerabaydzar, der, ishkhan (գերապայծառ, տէր, իշխան)
monsieur - baron (պարոն)
monster - huresh, aylantag, vitkhari, huresh tartsunel (հրէշ, այ-

լանդակ, վիթխարի, հրէշ դարձնել)
monstrous - hureshayin, jivaghayin, sosgali (հրէշային, ճիւաղային, սոսկալի)
montage - tasavoroum, garkavoroum sharzhanugari (դասաւորում, կարգաւորում շարժանկարի)
month - amis (ամիս)
monthly - amsatert, amsoria, miamsia, amsagan (ամսաթերթ, ամսօրեայ, միամսեայ, ամսական)
monument - gotogh, houshartsan, hishadagaran, houshagotogh (կոթող, յուշարձան, յիշատակարան, յուշակոթող)
monumental - gotoghagan, hoyagab, husgayagan (կոթողական, հոյակապ, հսկայական)
moo - parachel, parach, govi tsayn (բառաչել, բառաչ, կովի ձայն)
mood - duramatroutiun, vijag, gerb, yeghanag-payi (տրամադրութիւն, վիճակ, կերպ, եղանակ՝ բայի)
moody - zayratsgod, anduramatir, tuzhgam, gurkod (զայրացկոտ, անտրամադիր, դժկամ, կրքոտ)
moon - lousin, lousunga (լուսին, լուսնկայ)
mooncalf - pakhoug, aboush, miamid (բախուկ, ապուշ, միամիտ)
moonlight - lousni louys, lousunga (լուսնի լոյս, լուսնկայ)
moonstruck - lousnod, lousnahar, khelakar (լուսնոտ, լուսնահար, խելագար)
moor - jahij, tsekh, dighm, kharuskhel, mavridanatsi (ճահիճ, ցեխ, տիղմ, խարսխել, մաւրիտանացի)
mooring - kharuskhoum, baranov gaboum (խարսխում, պարանով կապում)
moorish - khapshig, jahjayin (խափշիկ, ճահճային)
moot - vijil, vijapanil, khorhurtazhoghov (վիճիլ, վիճաբանիլ, խորհրդաժողով)
mop - kedni surpich, latavel, tsamketsunel (գետնի սրբիչ, լաթաւել, ցամքեցնել)
mope - megousanal, melamaghtsodil, toulnal, aboushnal (մեկուսանալ, մելամաղձոտիլ, թուլնալ, ապուշնալ)
mopish - melamaghtsod, takhdzod (մելամաղձոտ, թախծոտ)
moquette - tavshakork, gaberd (թաւշագորգ, կապերտ)
moral - paroyagan, paroyalits, arakini (բարոյական, բարոյալից, առաքինի)
morale - paroyagan vijag (բարոյական վիճակ)
moralist - paroyaked, paroyakhos (բարոյագէտ, բարոյախօս)
morality - paroyaganoutiun (բարոյականութիւն)
moralize - paroyakhosel (բարոյախօսել)
morals - paroyakidoutiun (բարոյագիտութիւն)
morass - jahij, jakhjakhoud (ճահիճ, ճախճախուտ)
moratorium - vujaroumi hedatsukoum (վճարումի յետաձգում)
morbid - akhdavor, hivantod, hivantakin (ախտաւոր, հիւանդոտ, հիւանդագին)
mordant - khadznogh, khadzan, gujogh, gudzou, khisd (խածնող, խածան, կճող, կծու, խիստ)
more - aveli, yevus, shad, al, avelort, medzakouyn (աւելի, եւս, շատ, ալ, աւելորդ, մեծագոյն)
more or less - kurete, aveli gam bagas (գրեթէ, աւելի կամ պակաս)
morello - pal, gerasi tutvadz desagu (բալ, կեռասի թթուած տեսակը)
moreover - asge zad, patsi ayt, numanabes, tartsial (ասկէ զատ, բացի այդ, նմանապէս, դարձեալ)
morgue - tiaran, mereladoun (դիարան, մեռելատուն)
moribund - mahamerts (մահամերձ)
morn - aravod, ayk (առաւօտ, այգ)
morning - aravod, ardou, arduvan, lousapats (առաւօտ, առտու, առտուան, լուսաբաց)
morose - dukhour, anzhubid, murayl (տխուր, անժպիտ, մռայլ)
morphology - gazmakhosoutiun, tse-

vapanoutiun (կազմախօսութիւն, ճեւաբանութիւն)
morpion - vochil (ոջիլ)
morrow - vaghu, hachort oru, aravod (վաղը, յաջորդ օրը, առաւօտ)
morsel - badar, sherd, mas (պատառ, շերտ, մաս)
mortal - mahatsou, mahganatsou, mahaper (մահացու, մահկանացու, մահաբեր)
mortality - mahatsoutiun, mahatsoum (մահացութիւն, մահացում)
mortar - sant, gir, gurashaghakh, shaghakhel (սանդ, կիր, կրաշաղախ, շաղախել)
mortgage - kurav, kuravakir, galvadzakurav, kuravakurel (գրաւ, գրաւագիր, կալուածագրաւ, գրաւագրել)
mortgagee - kuravagal, kuravarou (գրաւակալ, գրաւառու)
mortgager - kuravadou, kuravatir (գրաւատու, գրաւադիր)
mortify - mahanal, mertsunel, mernil, junshel, zusbel (մահանալ, մեռցնել, մեռնիլ, ճնշել, զսպել)
mortuary - mereladoun, kerezmanadoun, mereladourk (մեռելատուն, գերեզմանատուն, մեռելատուրք)
morus - tuteni, tout (թթենի, թութ)
mosaic - khujanugar, khujanugarchoutiun (խճանկար, խճանկարչութիւն)
Mosaism - movsisaganoutiun (Մովսիսականութիւն)
moslem - mahmedagan, islam (մահմետական, իսլամ)
moslemism - mahmedaganoutiun, islamoutiun (մահմետականութիւն, իսլամութիւն)
mosque - muzgit (մզկիթ)
mosquito - muzhegh, muzhghoug (մժեղ, մժղուկ)
moss - mamour, jakhjakhoudk, mamrabadel (մամուռ, ճախճախուտք, մամռապատել)
most - amenen, amenamedz, medzakouyn, medzabes (ամէնէն, ամենամեծ, մեծագոյն, մեծապէս)
mostly - kulkhavorabes, medz masamp (գլխաւորապէս, մեծ մասամբ)
mot - surakhosoutiun (սրախօսութիւն)
mote - poshi, hiule, shiugh, masnig, zhoghov (փոշի, հիւլէ, շիւղ, մասնիկ, ժողով)
motel - buzdig bantog, ichevan (պզտիկ պանդոկ, իջեւան)
motet - saghmoserkoutiun, megheti (սաղմոսերգութիւն, մեղեդի)
moth - tsets, oudij, tsaykatiter (ցեց, ուտիճ, ցայգաթիթեռ)
mother - mayr, dzunogh, aghpiur, badjar, mayranal (մայր, ծնող, աղբիւր, պատճառ, մայրանալ)
mother tongue - mayreni lezou (մայրենի լեզու)
motherhood - mayroutiun (մայրութիւն)
motherland - mayreni yergir (մայրենի երկիր)
motherless - vorp, anmayr (որբ, անմայր)
mother-in-law - zokanch, gesour (զոքանչ, կեսուր)
motif - punapan, niut, sharzharit, punazart (բնաբան, նիւթ, շարժառիթ, բնազարդ)
motile - sharzhoun, sharzhounag, sharzhagan (շարժուն, շարժունակ, շարժական)
motion - sharzhoum, untatsk, aracharg, arachargel (շարժում, ընթացք, առաջարկ, առաջարկել)
motion picture - sharzhabadger, cinema, film (շարժապատկեր, սինեմա, ֆիլմ)
motivate - sharzhel, turtel, mughel (շարժել, դրդել, մղել)
motivation - badjarapanoutiun (պատճառաբանութիւն)
motive - sharzharit, badjar, sharzhich, turtogh (շարժառիթ, պատճառ, շարժիչ, դրդող)
motley - nakhshoun, khaydapughed, yerpnerank (նախշուն, խայտաբղէտ, երբներանգ)
motor - sharzhag, sharzhich, ouzhaniv (շարժակ, շարժիչ, ուժանիւ)

motorboat - shokemagouyg (շոգեմակոյկ)
motorcar - inknasharzh gark (ինքնաշարժ կառք)
motorcycle - sharzhaniv (շարժանիւ)
motorist - sharzhavar, varort (շարժավար, վարորդ)
mottle - pidz, bisag, pudzavorel, kounazartel, vedvidel (բիծ, պիսակ, բծաւորել, գունազարդել, վէտվիտել)
mottled - pudzavor, bisagavor, gedgidavor (բծաւոր, պիսակաւոր, կէտկիտաւոր)
motto - nushanapan, punapan, magakir (նշանաբան, բնաբան, մակագիր)
mould - see - տե՛ս (mold)
mound - toump, ampardag, hoghabadnesh, tsangabadel (Թումբ, ամբարտակ, հողապատնէշ, ցանկապատել)
mount (n) - ler, sar, hedznelou tsi, himnaturam, ouretsk (լեռ, սար, հեծնելու ձի, հիմնադրամ, ուռեցք)
mount (v) - partsuranal, yellel, vertsunel, hedznel (բարձրանալ, ելլել, վերցնել, հեծնել)
mountain - ler, sar (լեռ, սար)
mountaineer - lernapunag, leruntsi, lernagan (լեռնաբնակ, լեռնցի, լեռնական)
mountainous - lernayin, lernod, husga (լեռնային, լեռնոտ, հսկայ)
mountebank - shadakhos, khapepa, soud puzhishg (շատախօս, խաբեբայ, սուտ բժիշկ)
mourn - sukal, voghpal, harachel, souk haknil (սգալ, ողբալ, հառաչել, սուգ հագնիլ)
mourner - sukavor, sukagir, voghpatsogh (սգաւոր, սգակիր, ողբացող)
mournful - voghpali, sukali, vushdali (ողբալի, սգալի, վշտալի)
mourning - souk, voghp, godz, sukauzkesd (սուգ, ողբ, կոծ, սգազգեստ)
mouse - moug, mugnig, moug purnelvorsal (մուկ, մկնիկ, մուկ բռնել՝ որսալ)
moussiline - shugharsh (շղարշ)
moustache, mustache - bekh (պեխ)
mouth - peran, antsk, usel, khosil, lapel, hampourvil (բերան, անցք, ըսել, խօսիլ, լափել, համբուրուիլ)
mouther - lapogh, partsurakhos (լափող, բարձրախօս)
movable - sharzhagan, pokhatreli, tiurasharzh (շարժական, փոխադրելի, դիւրաշարժ)
move (n) - sharzhoum, pokhaturoutiun (շարժում, փոխադրութիւն)
move (v) - sharzhel, pokhaturel, sharzhil, deghapokhvil (շարժել, փոխադրել, շարժիլ, տեղափոխուիլ)
movement - sharzhoum, deghasharzh, yelevech, houzoum (շարժում, տեղաշարժ, ելեւէջ, յուզում)
mover - sharzhogh, nakhatsernogh, arachargogh (շարժող, նախաձեռնող, առաջարկող)
movie - sharzhanugar, sharzhabadger, cinema (շարժանկար, շարժապատկեր, սինեմա)
mow - tez, ushdemaran, marak, huntsel, godorel (դէզ, շտեմարան, մարագ, հնձել, կոտորել)
mower - huntsogh, kaghogh, chartogh (հնձող, քաղող, ջարդող)
mowing - huntsoum, kaghoum (հնձում, քաղում)
Mrs. - digin, dirouhi, ousoutschouhi (տիկին, տիրուհի, ուսուցչուհի)
Mr. - baron, der (պարոն, տէր)
much - shad, pazoum, ardagark (շատ, բազում, արտակարգ)
mucilage - khezh, houyz, pousahouyz (խէժ, հոյզ, բուսահոյզ)
muck - aghp, aghd, turik, dighm, aghdodel (աղբ, աղտ, Թրիք, տիղմ, աղտոտել)
mucker - aghdod, goshd mart (աղտոտ, կոշտ մարդ)
mucous - khulinkod, lortsnavor (խլինքոտ, լորձնաւոր)
mucus - khulink, lortsnahiut (խլինք, լորձնահիւԹ)
mud - tsekh, gav, dighm, tsekhodel, aghdodel (ցեխ, կաւ, տիղմ, ցեխոտել, աղտոտել)

muddle (n) - shupotoutiun, bughdoroutiun, shupotetsunel (շփոթութիւն, պղտորութիւն, շփոթեցնել)
muddle (v) - tumretsunel, kharnagel, shupotel, shupotil (թմրեցնել, խառնակել, շփոթել, շփոթիլ)
muddler - kharnagogh, bughdorogh (խառնակող, պղտորող)
muddy - tsekhod, bughdor, kharnag, tsekhodel, bughdorel (ցեխոտ, պղտոր, խառնակ, ցեխոտել, պղտորել)
muddy headed - tantsuramid, aboush (թանձրամիտ, ապուշ)
muff - tsernamoushdag, aboush, vuribetsunel, kharkhapel (ձեռնամուշտակ, ապուշ, վրիպեցնել, խարխափել)
muffle - dzadzgel, pattel, tsaynameghmel, dzadzgots (ծածկել, փաթթել, ձայնամեղմել, ծածկոց)
muffler - vuzgab, vuznots, tsaynameghmich, pattots (վզկապ, վզնոց, ձայնամեղմիչ, փաթթոց)
mug - kavat, umbag, peran, dzamadzurel temku (գաւաթ, ըմպակ, բերան, ծամածռել դէմքը)
muggy - khonav, dak, kheghtich ot (խոնաւ, տաք, խեղդիչ օդ)
muhammadan - mahmedagan (մահմետական)
mulatto - kharnadzin (խառնածին)
mulberry - tout, tutakouyn (թութ, թթագոյն)
mulch - tsankadzadzg, tsankadzadzgel (ցանքածածկ, ցանքածածկել)
mulct - doukank, doukankel, badzhel (տուգանք, տուգանքել, պատժել)
mule - chori, hoghatap (ջորի, հողաթափ)
muleteer - choreban (ջորեպան)
muliebrity - gunoutiun, ganatsioutiun (կնութիւն, կանացիութիւն)
mull (n) - suntous, teratsoum, kutakhodi doup, aghp (սնդուս, թերացում, գթախոտի տուփ, աղբ)
mull (v) - hamemel, daktsunel, kharnel, manrel, mudadzel (համեմել, տաքցնել, խառնել, մանրել, մտածել)
mullet - arkayatsoug, garmuroug, gepagh (արքայաձուկ, կարմրուկ, կեփաղ)
mulligrubs - khit, poratsav, gakheresoutiun (խիթ, փորացաւ, կախերեսութիւն)
mullock - aveltsoug, avelortk (աւելցուկ, աւելորդք)
multangular - pazmangiun (բազմանկիւն)
multicolor - pazmakouyn, kouynuzkouyn (բազմագոյն, գոյնզգոյն)
multifaced - pazmeres, geghdzavor (բազմերես, կեղծաւոր)
multifaith - pazmahavad (բազմահաւատ)
multifold - pazmadzal, pazmabadig (բազմածալ, բազմապատիկ)
multiform - pazmatsev (բազմաձեւ)
multilateral - pazmagoghmani (բազմակողմանի)
multilingual - pazmalezou (բազմալեզու)
multimillionaire - pazmamilionader, medzaharousd (բազմամիլիոնատէր, մեծահարուստ)
multiple - pazmabadig, pazmagoghmnagi (բազմապատիկ, բազմակողմնակի)
multiplex - pazmabadig, pazmadar (բազմապատիկ, բազմատարր)
multiplicand - pazmabadgeli (բազմապատկելի)
multiplication - pazmabadgoum, pazmabadgoutiun (բազմապատկում, բազմապատկութիւն)
multiplicity - pazmazanoutiun, shadoutiun, partoutiun (բազմազանութիւն, շատութիւն, բարդութիւն)
multiplier - pazmabadgich, pazmabadgogh (բազմապատկիչ, բազմապատկող)
multiply - pazmabadgel, pazmatsunel, pazmanal, shadnal (բազմապատկել, բազմացնել, բազմանալ, շատնալ)
multitude - pazmoutiun, shadoutiun, ampokh (բազմութիւն, շատութիւն, ամբոխ)
multitudinous - pazmativ, pazmaka-

nag, pazmadzaval (բազմաթիւ, բազմաքանակ, բազմածաւալ)
mum - *lour, ankhos, luroutiun, lure, karechour, mama* (լուռ, անխօս, լռութիւն, լռէ, քարեճուր, մամա)
mumble - *murmural, dzamdzumel, murtmurtots* (մռմռալ, ծամծմել, մրթմրթոց)
mummer - *kheghgadag, timagavor, mimos, ankhos* (խեղկատակ, դիմակաւոր, միմոս, անխօս)
mummery - *timagakhagh, kheghgadagoutiun, mimosoutiun* (դիմակախաղ, խեղկատակութիւն, միմոսութիւն)
mummify - *momiatsunel, chortsunel* (մոմիացնել, չորցնել)
mummy - *momia, uzmursuvadz, chortsuvadz* (մոմիա, զմռսուած, չորցուած)
mump - *murmural, kurtmunchel, khapel, khapelov moural* (մռմռալ, քրթմնջել, խաբել, խաբելով մուրալ)
munch - *liaperan dzamel, tsaynov oudel* (լիաբերան ծամել, ձայնով ուտել)
mundane - *ashkharhig, ashkharhayin* (աշխարհիկ, աշխարհային)
mundanity - *ashkharhaynoutiun* (աշխարհայնութիւն)
mundification - *makroum* (մաքրում)
mundify - *makurel* (մաքրել)
municipal - *kaghakabedagan, taghabedagan* (քաղաքապետական, թաղապետական)
municipality - *kaghakabedoutiun, taghabedoutiun* (քաղաքապետութիւն, թաղապետութիւն)
munificence - *paresurdoutiun, aradatsernoutiun* (բարեսրտութիւն, առատաձեռնութիւն)
munificent - *aradatserun, pareser* (առատաձեռն, բարեսէր)
muniment - *amrots, amroutiun, bashdonatought* (ամրոց, ամրութիւն, պաշտօնաթուղթ)
munite - *amratsunel, zoratsunel* (ամրացնել, զօրացնել)
munition - *razmamuterk, razmaniut, muteranots, zinel* (ռազմամթերք, ռազմանիւթ, մթերանոց, զինել)
mural - *badi, vormnayin* (պատի, որմնային)
mural painting - *vormnanugar* (որմնանկար)
murder - *martasbanoutiun, usbanoutiun, usbannel* (մարդասպանութիւն, սպանութիւն, սպաննել)
murderer - *martasban, vojrakordz* (մարդասպան, ոճրագործ)
murderous - *mahaper, usbanich, ariunarpou* (մահաբեր, սպանիչ, արիւնարբու)
murk - *mout, khavar, murayl* (մութ, խաւար, մռայլ)
murmur (n) - *murmounch, gargach, durdounch, khushshots* (մրմունջ, կարկաչ, տրտունջ, խշշոց)
murmur (v) - *murmunchel, gargachel, khushshal, durdunchal* (մրմնջել, կարկաչել, խշշալ, տրտնջալ)
murphy - *kednakhuntsor* (գետնախնձոր)
muscle - *mugan, tunter* (մկան, ջնջեր)
muscle cramp - *mugani burgoum* (մկանի պրկում)
muscular - *muganayin, muganoud, tunterod, ouzhegh* (մկանային, մկանուտ, ջնջերոտ, ուժեղ)
muse - *mousa, veratsoum, khoh, yerazel, khogal,* (մուսա, վերացում, խոհ, երազել, խոկալ)
museum - *tankaran* (թանգարան)
mushroom - *soung, soung havakel* (սունկ, սունկ հաւաքել)
music - *yerazhushdoutiun, nuvak* (երաժշտութիւն, նուագ)
music hall - *nuvakasurah, yerazhshdasurah, nuvakadoun* (նուագասրահ, երաժշտասրահ, նուագատուն)
musical - *yerazhushdagan* (երաժշտական)
musical box - *yerazhshdadoup* (երաժշտատուփ)
musician - *yerazhishd, yerkahan, nevakogh* (երաժիշտ, երգահան, նուագող)

musk - moushg, mushgiugh, mushdadoungh (մուշկ, մշկիւղ, մշտատունկ)
muslin - pehez, marmash, nourp gudav (բեհեզ, մարմաշ, նուրբ կտաւ)
musquito - muzhegh (մժեղ)
muss - irarantsoum, kharnagoutiun, kharnushdugel (իրարանցում, խառնակութիւն, խառնշտկել)
mussal - chah (ջահ)
mussel - tsugnaganch (ձկնականջ)
mussulman - mahmedagan, islam (մահմետական, իսլամ)
must - bardil, bardavorvil, usdibvil, murkachour (պարտիլ, պարտաւորուիլ, ստիպուիլ, մրգաջուր)
mustard - mananekh, khius (մանանեխ, խիւս)
muster - zorahavak, zoragoch, havakel, zhoghvuvil (զորահաւաք, զորակոչ, հաւաքել, ժողվուիլ)
musty - muklodadz, porposadz, oteg, tutvadz (մգլոտած, բորբոսած, օթեկ, թթուած)
mutable - popokhagan, anhasdad, angayoun, heghheghoug (փոփոխական, անհաստատ, անկայուն, յեղյեղուկ)
mutation - popokhoum, popokhoutiun (փոփոխում, փոփոխութիւն)
mute - hamur, lour, antsayn, luretsunel, nedel, dzurdel (համր, լուռ, անձայն, լռեցնել, նետել, ծրտել)
mutilate - hashmel, antamahadel, gurjadel, kheghel (հաշմել, անդամահատել, կրճատել, խեղել)
mutilation - hashmoum, gurjadoum, kheghoum (հաշմում, կրճատում, խեղում)
mutineer - abusdamp, khurovarar (ապստամբ, խռովարար)
mutinous - abusdamp, umpost, khurovarar, ansasd (ապստամբ, ըմբոստ, խռովարար, անսաստ)
mutiny - abusdampoutiun, khurovoutiun, abusdampil (ապստամբութիւն, խռովութիւն, ապստամբիլ)
mutism - hamroutiun (համրութիւն)
mutter - durdunchal, kurtmunchel, durdounch, kankad (տրտնջալ, քրթմնջել, տրտունջ, գանգատ)
mutual - pokhatarts, yergousdek (փոխադարձ, երկուստեք)
mutuation - pokharoutiun, pokhanagoutiun (փոխառութիւն, փոխանակութիւն)
mux - aghd, geghd, kharnushdugel (աղտ, կեղտ, խառնշտկել)
muzzle - tounch, tsuroug, pernagab, pernagabel (դունչ, ցռուկ, բերնակապ, բերնակապել)
muzzy - mudatsir, aboushtsadz (մտացիր, ապուշցած)
my - im (իմ)
myalgia - muganatsav (մկանացաւ)
myology - muganapanoutiun (մկանաբանութիւն)
myope - garjades (կարճատես)
myopia, myopy - garjadesoutiun (կարճատեսութիւն)
myriad - piuravor, antiv, anhashiv (բիւրաւոր, անթիւ, անհաշիւ)
myrrh - uzmours (զմուռս)
myrtle - murdi, murdeni (մրտի, մրտենի)
myself - yes inkus, inkus, antsamp, inkzinkus (ես ինքս, ինքս, անձամբ, ինքզինքս)
mysterious - khorhurtavor, anumpurneli, anhasgunali (խորհրդաւոր, անըմբռնելի, անհասկնալի)
mystery - khorhourt, areghdzuvadz, kaghdnik (խորհուրդ, առեղծուած, գաղտնիք)
mystic - khorhurtavor, aylapanagan, kaghduni (խորհրդաւոր, այլաբանական, գաղտնի)
mysticism - khorhurtabashdoutiun (խորհրդապաշտութիւն)
mystify - khorhurtavorel, abshetsunel, khapel (խորհրդաւորել, ապշեցնել, խաբել)
myth - arasbel, zurouyts, titsaveb (առասպել, զրոյց, դիցավէպ)
mythological - titsapanagan, arasbelagan (դիցաբանական, առասպելական)
mythology - titsapanoutiun (դիցա-

բանութիւն)

nab - hangardz purnel, tserpagalel (յանկարծ բռնել, ձերբակալել)
nabob - huntig ishkhan, medzaharousd (Հնդիկ իշխան, մեծահարուստ)
nacre - sadaf, kaghdagour (սատաֆ, գաղտակուր)
nadir - souzaged, usdornaged (սուզակէտ, ստորնակէտ)
nag - pokur tsi, homani, tsantsuratsunel, neghel (փոքր ձի, հոմանի, ձանձրացնել, նեղել)
naiad - kederou haverzhahars (գետերու յաւերժահարս)
naif, naive - miamid, barzamid (միամիտ, պարզամիտ)
nail - yeghounk, kam, jiran, pever, kamel, amurtsunel (եղունգ, գամ, ճիրան, բեւեր, գամել, ամրցնել)
nailer - kamogh (գամող)
naivete, naivety - miamudoutiun, barzamudoutiun (միամտութիւն, պարզամտութիւն)
naked - merg, anzen, anbashdban, pats, agnerev (մերկ, անզէն, անպաշտպան, բաց, ակներեւ)
namby-pamby - godurdouk, nazank, geghdz (կոտրտուք, նազանք, կեղծ)
name - anoun, hampav, anvanel, gochel, hishel (անուն, համբաւ, անուանել, կոչել, յիշել)
nameless - ananoun, andzanot, anhayd, anbadmeli (անանուն, անծանօթ, անյայտ, անպատմելի)
namely - aysinkun, usel gouzem (այսինքն, ըսել կ'ուզեմ)
namesake - anvanagits (անուանակից)
nap - murap, tetev koun, aghvamaz, murapel (մրափ, թեթեւ քուն, աղուամազ, մրափել)
nape - dzodzrag (ծոծրակ)
naphtalene - navtayin, hankayin niut mu (նաւթային, Հանքային նիւթ մը)
naphtha - navt, chuzudvadz kariugh (նաւթ, չզտուած քարիւղ)
napkin - tseralat, tserasurpich, seghani antserots (ձեռալաթ, ձեռասրբիչ, սեղանի անձեռոց)
nappiness - kunodoutiun, purtod, tavamaz (քնոտութիւն, բրդոտ, թաւամազ)
nappy - kunod, murapod, tavod (քնոտ, մրափոտ, թաւոտ)
narcissism - nargizaganoutiun, serapunazt (նարկիզականութիւն, սերաբնազդ)
narcissus - nargiz, narkes (նարկիզ, նարգէս)
narcosis - tumroutiun, anuzkayatsoum (թմրութիւն, անզգայացում)
narcotic - tumrategh, tumretsoutsich, kunaper (թմրադեղ, թմրեցուցիչ, քնաբեր)
nard - nartos (նարդոս)
nargile, narghileh - gulgulag (կլկլակ)
narrate - badmel, vibel (պատմել, վիպել)
narration - badmoutiun, badoum, veb (պատմութիւն, պատում, վէպ)
narrative - badmoghagan, badmogh, vibagan, zurouyts (պատմողական, պատմող, վիպական, զրոյց)
narrator - badmich (պատմիչ)
narrow - negh, seghm, seghmel, neghnal, neghtsunel (նեղ, սեղմ, սեղմել, նեղնալ, նեղցնել)
narthex - kavit (գաւիթ)
nasal - runkayin, kutayin, kiti (ռնգային, քթային, քիթի)
nascent - teradzin, noradzak, terahas, terapouys (դեռածին, նորա-

ծաղ, գեռաՀաս, գեռաբոյս)
nasty - aghdod, geghdod, zuzveli, buzhkali (աղտոտ, կեղտոտ, զզուելի, պժգալի)
natal - dzununtagan, dzununtian, punig, hayreni (ծննդական, ծննդեան, բնիկ, Հայրենի)
natation - logh, loghatsoum, loghortoutiun (լող, լողացում, լողորդութիւն)
nates - hedouyk, nusdadegh (յետոյք, նստատեղ)
nation - azk, zhoghovourt (ազգ, ժողովուրդ)
national - azkayin, azkaynagan (ազգային, ազգայնական)
nationalism - azkaynaganoutiun (ազգայնականութիւն)
nationalist - azkaynagan, azkaynamol (ազգայնական, ազգայնամոլ)
nationality - azkoutiun, azkaynaganoutiun, hubadagoutiun (ազգութիւն, ազգայնականութիւն, Հպատակութիւն)
nationalize - azkaynatsunel, bedaganatsunel (ազգայնացնել, պետականացնել)
nationwide - hamazkayin, hamazhoghovurtagan (Համազգային, Համաժողովրդական)
native - punig, punadzin, deghatsi, dzununtian, poun (բնիկ, բնածին, տեղացի, ծննդեան, բուն)
nativity - dzunount, dzununtaganoutiun (ծնունդ, ծննդականութիւն)
natter - shadakhosel, kurtmunchel, arargel (շատախօսել, քրթմնջել, առարկել)
natty - gogig, jashagavor, makour, bujnazart (կոկիկ, ճաշակաւոր, մաքուր, պճնազարդ)
natural - punagan, iragan, punadzin, anbajouyj (բնական, իրական, բնածին, անպաճոյճ)
naturalism - punaganoutiun, punabashdoutiun (բնականութիւն, բնապաշտութիւն)
naturalist - punaked, punakhouyz, punabashd (բնագէտ, բնախոյզ, բնապաշտ)
naturalization - kaghakatsiatsoum, hubadagoutiun (քաղաքացիացում, Հպատակութիւն)
naturalize - kaghakatsiatsunel, hubadagakurel (քաղաքացիացնել, Հպատակագրել)
nature - punoutiun, punavoroutiun, eoutiun, diyezerk (բնութիւն, բնաւորութիւն, էութիւն, տիեզերք)
naught - vochinch, vochunchoutiun, zero, anbed (ոչինչ, ոչնչութիւն, զէրօ, անպէտ)
naughty - char, charajuji, anbidan, anbargeshd (չար, չարաճճի, անպիտան, անպարկեշտ)
nausea - surdkharnouk, zuzvank, buzhkank, dzovakhd (սրտխառնուք, զզուանք, պժգանք, ծովախտ)
nauseate - surdkharnouk uzkal, kanil, karshil, noghgal (սրտխառնուք զգալ, գանիլ, գարշիլ, նողկալ)
nautical - navayin, dzovayin, navasdiagan, navakidagan (նաւային, ծովային, նաւաստիական, նաւագիտական)
naval - navayin, dzovayin (նաւային, ծովային)
nave - michaniv, antsk yegeghetsii turnen khoran (միջանիւ, անցք եկեղեցիի դռնէն՝խորան)
navel - bord, voryeve pani getronu (պորտ, որեւէ բանի կեդրոնը)
navigable - navargeli (նաւարկելի)
navigate - navargel, navavarel (նաւարկել, նաւավարել)
navigation - navargoutiun, navakunatsoutiun (նաւարկութիւն, նաւագնացութիւն)
navigator - navavar, navargogh, dzovakunats, dzovakhouyz (նաւավար, նաւարկող, ծովագնաց, ծովախոյզ)
navy - navadorm, navadormigh, dzovouzh (նաւատորմ, նաւատորմիղ, ծովուժ)
nawab - garavarich, pokharka, yerespokhan (կառավարիչ, փոխարքայ, երեսփոխան)
nay - voch, che, voch miayn ayt, ange zad (ոչ, չէ, ոչ միայն այդ,

անկէ գատ)
nazarene - nazovretsi, Nazaret kaghaki punagich (Նազովրեցի, Նազարէթ քաղաքի բնակիչ)
Nazarite - nazovretsi, oukhdial israyelatsi (Նազովրեցի, Ուխտեալ Իսրայէլացի)
naze - kuloukh, hurvartan (գլուխ, հրուանդան)
nazi - natsi, fashist (Նացի, ֆաշիստ)
near - mod, modig, mertsavor, modetsunel, modenal (մօտ, մօտիկ, մերձաւոր, մօտեցնել, մօտենալ)
nearly - modavorabes, kurete (մօտաւորապէս, գրեթէ)
neat - gogig, makour, husdag, vayelouch, archar (կոկիկ, մաքուր, յստակ, վայելուչ, արջառ)
neb - tounch, gudouts, tsuroug, kit (դունչ, կտուց, ցռուկ, քիթ)
nebula - mikamadz, achki mek, ambamadz (միգամած, աչքի մէգ, ամպամած)
nebulous - mikabad, ambamadz (միգապատ, ամպամած)
necessarily - anhurazheshdoren, ankhousapelioren, hargatrapar (անհրաժեշտօրէն, անխուսափելիօրէն, հարկադրաբար)
necessary - anhurazheshd, garevor, eagan (անհրաժեշտ, կարեւոր, էական)
necessitate - hargaturel, usdibel, hargavorel (հարկադրել, ստիպել, հարկաւորել)
necessitous - chukavor, aghkad, garikavor (չքաւոր, աղքատ, կարիքաւոր)
necessity - anhurazheshdoutiun, garik, bedk, harg (անհրաժեշտութիւն, կարիք, պէտք, հարկ)
neck - viz, baranots, jid (վիզ, պարանոց, ճիտ)
neckcloth - vuzgab, poghgab (վզկապ, փողկապ)
necklace - maniag, kayr (մանեակ, քայռ)
necktie - poghgab (փողկապ)
necrology - mahazt, mahatsoutsag, tampanagan (մահազդ, մահացուցակ, դամբանական)
necromancy - gakhartoutiun, merelahumayoutiun (կախարդութիւն, մեռելահմայութիւն)
nectar - negdar, meghrahiut (Նեկտար, մեղրահիւթ)
nectarine - negdarateghts (Նեկտարադեղձ)
need - garik, bedk, aghkadoutiun, bedk ounenal, ouzel (կարիք, պէտք, աղքատութիւն, պէտք ունենալ, ուզել)
needful - bidani, anhurazheshd, garevor (պիտանի, անհրաժեշտ, կարեւոր)
needle - asegh, sulak (ասեղ, սլաք)
needless - anbedk, angarevor, anokoud (անպէտք, անկարեւոր, անօգուտ)
needlewoman - garouhi, tertsagouhi (կարուհի, դերձակուհի)
needlework - aseghnakordzoutiun (ասեղնագործութիւն)
needs - anhurazheshdoutiun (անհրաժեշտութիւն)
needy - garikavor, aghkad, garod (կարիքաւոր, աղքատ, կարօտ)
nefarious - bighdz, usdor, karsheli, kazanayin (պիղծ, ստոր, գարշելի, գազանային)
negation - zhukhdoum, herkoum, ouratsoum (ժխտում, հերքում, ուրացում)
negative - zhukhdagan, patsasagan, merzhogh, zhukhdanugar (ժխտական, բացասական, մերժող, ժխտանկար)
neglect - andesel, arhamarhel, anhokoutiun, arhamarhank (անտեսել, արհամարհել, անհոգութիւն, արհամարհանք)
negligence - anhokoutiun, anpoutoutiun, ankhunamoutiun (անհոգութիւն, անփութութիւն, անխնամութիւն)
negociate - panagtsil, pokhantsel, vajarel (բանակցիլ, փոխանցել, վաճառել)
negotiable - panagtseli, pokhantseli,

vajareli (բանակցելի, փոխանցելի, վաճառելի)
negotiation - panagtsoutiun, michnortoutiun, arevdour (բանակցութիւն, միջնորդութիւն, առեւտուր)
negotiator - panakunats, michnort (բանագնաց, միջնորդ)
negress - sevamortouhi (սեւամորթուհի)
negro - sevamort, khapshig, aprigetsi (սեւամորթ, խափշիկ, ափրիկեցի)
neigh - vurunchel, khurkhunchel, vurunchiun (վրնջել, խրխնջել, վրնջիւն)
neighbour - turatsi, harevan, modig (դրացի, հարեւան, մօտիկ)
neighbourhood - turatsnoutiun, harevanoutiun (դրացնութիւն, հարեւանութիւն)
neither - voch meg, voch megu, voch ays voch ayn (ոչ մէկ, ոչ մէկը, ոչ այս ոչ այն)
nenuphar - harsnamad, churashoushan, nounoufar (հարսնամատ, ջրաշուշան, նունուֆար)
neologism - norapanoutiun (նորաբանութիւն)
neologist - norapan, norabashd (նորաբան, նորապաշտ)
neology - norapanoutiun, norasiroutiun (նորաբանութիւն, նորասիրութիւն)
neophyte - norahavad, norundza, noradoung, hampag (նորահաւատ, նորընծայ, նորատունկ, համբակ)
nephew - yeghpororti, kerorti (եղբօրորդի, քեռորդի)
nerve - chigh, ouzh, zoroutiun, ouzh dal, kachalerel (ջիղ, ոյժ, զօրութիւն, ոյժ տալ, քաջալերել)
nervous - chughayin, chughoud, gorovi, tiurakurkir (ջղային, ջղուտ, կորովի, դիւրագրգիռ)
nervous breakdown - chughakhankaroum (ջղախանգարում)
nervous system - chughayin turoutiun (ջղային դրութիւն)
nervy - chughoud, zoravor, inknavusdah (ջղուտ, զօրաւոր, ինքնավստահ)
nest - pouyn, vorch, abasdanaran, pouyn shinel (բոյն, որջ, ապաստանարան, բոյն շինել)
nestle - pouyn shinel, deghavorvil, nusdil, pattuvil (բոյն շինիլ, տեղաւորուիլ, նստիլ, թափփուիլ)
nestling - joudig, turchnig, tsakoug (ճուտիկ, թռչնիկ, ձագուկ)
net (I) - tsants, ourgan, ourganov vorsal, hiusel (ցանց, ուռկան, ուռկանով որսալ, հիւսել)
net (II) - zoud, zoud yegamoud, makour, ankharun (զուտ, զուտ եկամուտ, մաքուր, անխառն)
net profit - zoud shah (զուտ շահ)
nether - tsadz, vari, usdorin (ցած, վարի, ստորին)
netherlander - holandatsi (հոլանտացի)
nettle - yeghij, kurkurel, khaytel, zayratsunel (եղինձ, գրգռել, խայթել, զայրացնել)
network - tsants, ashkhadatsants, khumpavoroum, oghahiusk (ցանց, աշխատացանց, խմբաւորում, օղահիւսք)
neuralgia - chughatsav (ջղացաւ)
neurasthenia - chughatouloutiun (ջղաթուլութիւն)
neuritis - chughadab (ջղատապ)
neurology - chughapanoutiun (ջղաբանութիւն)
neurosis - chughakaroujiun, chulakhd (ջղագարութիւն, ջլախտ)
neuter - chezok, angousagtsagan, angoghmnagal (չէզոք, անկուսակցական, անկողմնակալ)
neutral - chezok, angoghmnagal, andarper (չէզոք, անկողմնակալ, անտարբեր)
neutralize - chezokatsunel, megousatsunel, hagagushrel (չէզոքացնել, մեկուսացնել, հակակշռել)
never - yerpek, punav, amenevin (երբեք, բնաւ, ամենեւին)
new - nor, arti, ayzhmeagan, tarm, anports (նոր, արդի, այժմէական, թարմ, անփորձ)
New Year - nor dari, amanor (Նոր

Տարի, Ամանոր)
newborn - noradzin, nor dzunadz (Նորածին, Նոր ծնած)
newish - noreg, pavagan nor (Նորեկ, բաւական նոր)
newly - vercherus, ter nor, noren (վերջերս, դեռ նոր, նորէն)
newlywed - norabusag (Նորապսակ)
news - lour, verjin deghegoutiun (լուր, վերջին տեղեկութիւն)
news agency - luradou kordzagaloutiun (լրատու գործակալութիւն)
news stand - lurakuri gurbag (լրագիրի կրպակ)
news weekly - shapatatert, shapatalour (շաբաթաթերթ, շաբաթալուր)
newsboy - tertavajar dugha, lurakravajar (թերթավաճառ տղայ, լրագրավաճառ)
newscast - lurapashkh gayan (լրաբաշխ կայան)
newscaster - tsaynasuproumi khosnag (ձայնասփռումի խօսնակ)
newsletter - luradou, barperatert, shurchaperagan (լրատու, պարբերաթերթ, շրջաբերական)
newsman - tertavajar, lurakravajar (թերթավաճառ, լրագրավաճառ)
newsmonger - luravajar, luradar, pampasogh (լրավաճառ, լրատար, բամբասող)
newspaper - tert, lurakir (թերթ, լրագիր)
newsprint - lurakratought (լրագրաթուղթ)
newsreel - khosoun zhabaven (խօսուն ժապաւէն)
newsy - lurashad, lourerov letsoun (լրաշատ, լուրերով լեցուն)
new-model - noratsevel (Նորաձեւել)
next - hachort, hedaka, kalik, kovi (յաջորդ, հետագայ, գալիք, քովի)
next week - hachort shapat (յաջորդ շաբաթ)
nib - kurchadzayr, sour dzayr, surel (գրչածայր, սուր ծայր, սրել)
nibble - khadzkhudzel, meghm gurdzel (խածխծել, մեղմ կրծել)
niblick - magan, golfi kavazan (մական, կոլֆի գաւազան)
nice - aghvor, siroun, nourp, koghdurig, hajeli (աղուոր, սիրուն, նուրբ, գողտրիկ, հաճելի)
nicety - nurpoutiun, aghvoroutiun, papgoutiun (Նրբութիւն, աղուորութիւն, փափկութիւն)
niche - khorsh, patsad, vormnakhorzh (խորշ, բացատ, որմնախորշ)
nick - nushan, hashvepayd, zhamged, nushel, nushan unel (Նշան, հաշուեփայտ, ժամկէտ, Նշել, Նշան ընել)
nickel - nikel, nikelabadel (Նիքել, Նիքելապատել)
nickname - dzaghranoun, paghakshagan anoun, dzaghranoun dal (ծաղրանուն, փաղաքշական անուն, ծաղրանուն տալ)
nicotine - dzukhakhodid, dzukhakhodi tounavor iughu (ծխախոտիտ, ծխախոտի թունաւոր իւղը)
nictate - tartel, kuttel, agnargel (թարթել, քթթել, ակնարկել)
nidificate - pouyn shinel (բոյն շինել)
niece - yeghpor gam kuroch aghchig (եղբօր կամ քրոջ աղջիկ)
niggard - gudzdzi, akah, zhulad (կծծի, ագահ, ժլատ)
nigger - see - տե՛ս (nigro)
nigh - mod, modig, gits, kurete (մօտ, մօտիկ, կից, գրեթէ)
night - kisher, yerego, mout, khavar (գիշեր, երեկոյ, մութ, խաւար)
night clothes - kisherazkesd, kisheranots (գիշերազգեստ, գիշերանոց)
night club - gabela, kinedoun (կապելայ, գինետուն)
night light - meghm louys nuncharani (մեղմ լոյս ննջարանի)
night mare - mughtsavanch, vakhtsunogh yeraz (մղձաւանջ, վախցնող երազ)
night school - kisherayin tubrots (գիշերային դպրոց)
nightingale - sokhag (սոխակ)
nightly - kishervan, kisherayin, amen kisher (գիշերուան, գիշերա-

յին, ամէն գիշեր)
nigro - khapshig, sevamort (խափշիկ, սեւամորթ)
nihilism - vochunchabashdoutiun (ոչնչապաշտութիւն)
nil - vochinch, anarzhek (ոչինչ, անարժէք)
nill - chouzel, merzhel (չուզել, մերժել)
nimble - arakasharzh, jugoun, badrasdapan (արագաշարժ, ճկուն, պատրաստաբան)
nimbus - lousabusag, payl, antsurevaper amb (լուսապսակ, փայլ, անձրեւաբեր ամպ)
nine - inu (ինը)
nineteen - dasnuinu (տասնինը)
nineteenth - dasnunnerort (տասնիններորդ)
ninetieth - innusounerort (իննսուներորդ)
ninety - innusoun (իննսուն)
ninny - aboush, dugaramid, dukhmar, khent (ապուշ, տկարամիտ, տխմար, խենդ)
nip - gusmit, khayt, oumb, boud, gusmetel, khaytel (կսմիթ, խայթ, ումպ, պուտ, կսմթել, խայթել)
nipper - gusmutogh, gudzogh, aktsan (կսմթող, կծող, աքցան)
nipple - dzidz, budoug, gurdzkabudoug, dzudzag gati shishi (ծիծ, պտուկ, կրծքապտուկ, ծծակ կաթի շիշի)
Nippon - Japon, japonagan (Ճաբոն, ճաբոնական)
Nirvana - nirvana, yeranoutiun (Նիրվանա, երանութիւն)
nisi - yete voch (եթէ ոչ)
niter, nitre - porag (բորակ)
nitrate - poragad (բորակատ)
nitric - poragadzin barounagogh (բորակածին պարունակող)
nitrogen - poragadzin (բորակածին)
nix - churabarig, merzhel, ouranal (ջրապարիկ, մերժել, ուրանալ)
no - voch, che, punav, voch vok, voch meg (ոչ, չէ, բնաւ, ոչ ոք, ոչ մէկ)
Noah's ark - noyan daban (Նոյեան տապան)
nob - yereveli, aznuvagan, choch (երեւելի, ազնուական, ջոջ)
nobble - tsioun vunasel, khapel, gasharel (ձիուն վնասել, խաբել, կաշառել)
nobbler - khapepa, khachakogh (խաբեբայ, խաչագող)
nobby - vayelouch, shukegh, berjashouk, bujnaser (վայելուչ, շքեղ, պերճաշուք, պճնասէր)
nobility - aznuvaganoutioun, vusemoutiun (ազնուականութիւն, վսեմութիւն)
noble - aznuvagan, azniv, veh, medzahoki, vusem (ազնուական, ազնիւ, վեհ, մեծահոգի, վսեմ)
nobleman - aznuvagan (ազնուական)
nobleness - aznuvaganoutiun (ազնուականութիւն)
nobody - voch vok (ոչ ոք)
noctambulist - kunashurchig, kisherashurchig (քնաշրջիկ, գիշերաշրջիկ)
nocturn - tsaykerk, kisherek, tsaykanuvak, tsaykabadger (ցայգերգ, գիշերերգ, ցայգանուագ, ցայգապատկեր)
nod - dzuril, parevel, murapel, kulkov nushan unel (ծռիլ, բարեւել, մրափել, գլխով նշան ընել)
noddle - kuloukh-heknankov, tutoum (գլուխ-հեգնանքով, դդում)
noddy - aboush, anmid, putamid, tutoum (ապուշ, անմիտ, բթամիտ, դդում)
node - gab, hankouyts, oghag, zartagab (կապ, հանգոյց, օղակ, զարդակապ)
nodule - goshgorag, manur ouretsk, pokur hankouyts (կոշկոռակ, մանր ուռեցք, փոքր հանգոյց)
noise - aghmoug, zhukhor, tsayn, aghmugel, haydnel (աղմուկ, ժխոր, ձայն, աղմկել, յայտնել)
noiseless - antsayn, anaghmoug (անձայն, անաղմուկ)
noisome - anakhorzh, anhajo, vadaroghch, vunasagar (անախորժ, անհաճոյ, վատառողջ, վնասակար)

noisy - aghmugod, aghmugali, aghmugarar (աղմկոտ, աղմկալի, աղմկարար)
nomad - vachgadun, vuranapunag, taparagan (վաչկատուն, վրանաբնակ, Թափառական)
nomenclature - anvanagochoutiun, paratsang (անուանակոչութիւն, բառացանկ)
nominal - anvanagan, baymanagan (անուանական, պայմանական)
nominate - nushanagel, anvanel, gochel (նշանակել, անուանել, կոչել)
nomination - nushanagoum, anvanoum, garkoum - bashdoni (նշանակում, անուանում, կարգում՝ պաշտօնի)
nominative - anvanagan, oughghagan holov (անուանական, ուղղական հոլով)
nominator - nushanagogh, anvanogh, garkogh (նշանակող, անուանող, կարգող)
nominee - nushanagial, tegnadzou, anvanial, garkial (նշանակեալ, Թեկնածու, անուանեալ, կարգեալ)
non - voch (ոչ)
non fat - voch jabayin, iugh chubarounagogh (ոչ ճարպային, իւղ չպարունակող)
non profit - dourkazerdz noch shahaper (տուրքազերծ, ոչ շահաբեր)
nonage - anchapahasoutiun (անչափահասութիւն)
nonchalance - andarperoutiun, baghoutiun (անտարբերութիւն, պաղութիւն)
nonchalant - anhok, anpouyt, andarper, bagh (անհոգ, անփոյթ, անտարբեր, պաղ)
none - voch vok, voch meg, voch meg pan (ոչ ոք, ոչ մէկ, ոչ մէկ բան)
none dairy - voch gatnayin, gat chubarounagogh (ոչ կաթնային, կաթ չպարունակող)
nonentity - vochunchoutiun, ankoyoutiun, aneoutiun (ոչնչութիւն, անգոյութիւն, անէութիւն)
nonexistent - anko (անգոյ)
nonpareil - anzoukagan, annuman (անզուգական, աննման)
nonplus - khochuntod, varanoum, shupotel, neghel (խոչընդոտ, վարանում, շփոԹել, նեղել)
nonsense - animasd, anhetetoutiun, anmudoutiun (անիմաստ, անհեԹեԹութիւն, անմտութիւն)
nonstop - arants gankari, arants tatari (առանց կանգառի, առանց դադարի)
non-addictive - voch moloutiamp (ոչ մոլուԹեամբ)
non-resident - chupunagogh, voch deghatsi (չբնակող, ոչ տեղացի)
noodle - himar, aboush, anmid (յիմար, ապուշ, անմիտ)
nook - angiun, arantsnaran, takusdots, dzovakhorsh (անկիւն, առանձնարան, Թաքստոց, ծովախորշ)
noon - gesor, michore (կէսօր, միջօրէ)
nooning - gesorel, gesorin jashel, hankusdanal (կէսօրել, կէսօրին ճաշել, հանգստանալ)
noontide - michore, gesorvan (միջօրէ, կէսօրուան)
noose - kheghtagab, oghabaran, kheghtagabel, purnel (խեղդակապ, օղապարան, խեղդակապել, բռնել)
nor - voch al (ոչ ալ)
nordic - usgandinavian, hiusisayin (սկանտինաւեան, հիւսիսային)
norm - dibar, orinag, numoush, chapanish (տիպար, օրինակ, նմոյշ, չափանիշ)
normal - punagan, ganonavor, orinavor, oughghahayiats (բնական, կանոնաւոր, օրինաւոր, ուղղահայեաց)
normal school - ousoutschanots (ուսուցչանոց)
normality - punaganoutiun (բնականութիւն)
normalize - punaganatsunel, punagan tartsunel, ganonavorel (բնականացնել, բնական դարձնել, կանոնաւորել)
north - hiusis, hiusisagoghm (հիւսիս, հիւսիսակողմ)
North America - hiusisayin ameriga

(Հիւսիսային Ամերիկա)
North Pole - hiusisayin pever (Հիւսիսային Բեւեռ)
northeast - hiusis arevelk, hiusus arevelian (Հիւսիս-Արեւելք, Հիւսիս արեւելեան)
northern - hiusisayin, hiusisagoghm (Հիւսիսային, Հիւսիսակողմ)
northerner - hiusisapunag (Հիւսիսաբնակ)
northward - tebi hiusis (դէպի Հիւսիս)
northwest - hiusis arevmoudk (Հիւսիս արեւմուտք)
norwegian - norvegiatsi, norvegren, norvegian (Նորվեկիացի, Նորվեկերէն, Նորվեկեան)
nose (n) - kit, hododelik, tsuroug, poghadzayr, gunjit (քիթ, Հոտոտելիք, ցռուկ, փողածայր, կնճիթ)
nose (v) - hododel, hodvedal, khunchel, kitu khotel (Հոտոտել, Հոտուըտալ, խնչել, քիթը խոթել)
nostalgia - hayrenadenchoutiun, garod, garodakhd (Հայրենատենչութիւն, կարօտ, կարօտախտ)
nostril - rounk, kutadzag (ռունգ, քթածակ)
nostrum - kaghduni tegh, soud puzhishgi tegh, geghdz dzurakir (գաղտնի դեղ, սուտ բժիշկի դեղ, կեղծ ծրագիր)
nosy - medzakit, kitu khotogh, hedakurkir ants (մեծաքիթ, քիթը խոթող, Հետաքրքիր անձ)
not - voch, che (ոչ, չէ)
not at all - punav, voch yerpek (բնաւ, ոչ երբեք)
notability - yerevelioutiun, nushanavor mart (երեւելիութիւն, նշանաւոր մարդ)
notable - nushanavor, yereveli, hampavavor (նշանաւոր, երեւելի, Համբաւաւոր)
notarize - vaveratsunel, hasdadel (վաւերացնել, Հաստատել)
notary - nodar, vaverakurogh, mourhagakir (Նոտար, վաւերագրող, մուրՀակագիր)
notation - notakuroutiun, nushanakuroutiun (Նօթագրութիւն, նշանագրութիւն)
notch - nish, khaz, gudadz, girj, nushel, gudrel, gidel (նիշ, խազ, կտած, կիրճ, նշել, կտրել, կիտել)
note (n) - nushan, tsaynanish, not, khaz, deghegakir, hampav (նշան, ձայնանիշ, նօթ, խազ, տեղեկագիր, Համբաւ)
note (v) - notakurel, nugadel, houshakurel, tidel (նօթագրել, նկատել, յուշագրել, դիտել)
notebook - houshadedur, tseradedur, dzotsadedur (յուշատետր, ձեռատետր, ծոցատետր)
noted - nushanavor, hurchagavor, yereveli, nushvadz (նշանաւոր, Հռչակաւոր, երեւելի, նշուած)
noter - nugadogh, tidogh, notakurogh (նկատող, դիտող, նօթագրող)
nothing - vochinch, voch meg pan (ոչինչ, ոչ մէկ բան)
notice - azt, aztakir, deghegakir, aztararel, haydnel (ազդ, ազդագիր, տեղեկագիր, ազդարարել, յայտնել)
notice of payment - vujarazt (վճարազդ)
notification - nugadaroutiun, azt, zegouyts (նկատառութիւն, ազդ, զեկոյց)
notify - zegoutsel, imatsunel, deghegatsunel, nushel (զեկուցել, իմացնել, տեղեկացնել, նշել)
notion - kaghapar, dzanotoutiun, umpurnoum, gardzik (գաղափար, ծանօթութիւն, ըմբռնում, կարծիք)
notorious - hanradzanot, vadahampav, dukhrahurchag (Հանրածանօթ, վատաՀամբաւ, տխրաՀռչակ)
notwithstanding - tebed, teyev, aysouhanterts, chunayadz (թէպէտ, թէեւ, այսուՀանդերձ, չնայած)
nougat - huroushag (Հրուշակ)
nought - see - տե'ս (naught)
noun - anoun, koyagan (անուն, գոյական)
nourish - sunoutsanel, geragrel, tiyetsunel, ajetsunel (սնուցանել, կերակրել, դիեցնել, աճեցնել)

nourishment - sunoutsoum, geragroum, sunount, oudesd (սնուցում, կերակրում, սնունդ, ուտեստ)
novel - noraveb, vibag, nor, darorinag, norahunar (նորավէպ, վիպակ, նոր, տարօրինակ, նորահնար)
novelist - vibasan (վիպասան)
novelize, novelise - vibakurel, vebi veradzel (վիպագրել, վէպի վերածել)
novelty - noroutiun, norouyt, noratsevoutiun (նորութիւն, նորոյթ, նորաձեւութիւն)
November - noyemper (Նոյեմբեր)
novice - norundza, noreg, noreloug, usgusnag, anports (նորընծայ, նորեկ, նորելուկ, սկսնակ, անփորձ)
novitiate, noviciate - norundzayaran, norundzayoutiun, norundza (նորընծայարան, նորընծայութիւն, նորընծայ)
now - hima, ayzhm, nergayis (հիմա, այժմ, ներկայիս)
nowadays - ays oreroun, ays orerus (այս օրերուն, այս օրերս)
noway - yerpek, punav, amenevin, voch meg gerbov (երբեք, բնաւ, ամենեւին, ոչ մէկ կերպով)
nowhere - voch meg degh (ոչ մէկ տեղ)
noxious - vunasagar, vadaroghch (վնասակար, վատառողջ)
nozzle - dzorag, khoghovagadzayr, poghadzayr, tsuroug (ծորակ, խողովակածայր, փողածայր, ցռուկ)
nuance - nurperank, nurpoutiun, yerank (նրբերանգ, նրբութիւն, երանգ)
nub - jeghk, kount, goshgor, himnagan gedu (ճեղք, գունդ, կոշկոռ, հիմնական կէտը)
nubile - harsuntsou (հարսնցու)
nucha - dzodzrag (ծոծրակ)
nuclear - gorizayin, michougayin (կորիզային, միջուկային)
nuclear bomb - atomagan roump (աթոմական ռումբ)
nuclear medicine - michougapouzhoutiun (միջուկաբուժութիւն)
nucleus - goriz, michoug (կորիզ, միջուկ)
nudation - mergatsoum (մերկացում)
nude - merg, holani, anzart (մերկ, հոլանի, անզարդ)
nudge - mushdel, tuntel, armougov tubil, mushdoum (մշտել, դնդել, արմուկով դպիլ, մշտում)
nudism - mergabashdoutiun(մերկապաշտութիւն)
nudist - mergabashd (մերկապաշտ)
nudity - mergoutiun (մերկութիւն)
nugatory - annushan, anzor, chunchin, anarzhek (աննշան, անզօր, չնչին, անարժէք)
nugget - tsouyl vosgi (ձոյլ ոսկի)
nuisance - tsantsuroutiun, anakhorzhoutiun, tsav (ձանձրութիւն, անախորժութիւն, ցաւ)
null - anvaver, anzor, anouzh (անվաւեր, անզօր, անուժ)
nullification - chunchoum, vochunchatsoum (ջնջում, ոչնչացում)
nullify - chunchel, anvaver tartsunel, pujatsunel (ջնջել, անվաւեր դարձնել, փճացնել
nullity - vochunchoutiun, anvaveroutiun, anzoroutiun (ոչնչութիւն, անվաւերութիւն, անզօրութիւն)
numb - tumradz, anuzka, tumretsunel, anuskayatsunel (թմրած, անզգայ, թմրեցնել, անզգայացնել)
number - tiv, kanag, tuvanushan, tuvel, hashvel, hamrel (թիւ, քանակ, թուանշան, թուել, հաշուել, համրել)
numberer - hashvogh, tuvogh (հաշուող, թուող)
numberless - anhamar, antiv (անհամար, անթիւ)
numbness - tumroutiun, anuzkayoutiun (թմրութիւն, անզգայութիւն)
numerable - tuveli, hashveli (թուելի, հաշուելի)
numeral - tiv, tuvanushan, tuvayin, tuvagan (թիւ, թուանշան, թուային, թուական)
numerate - hamrel, hashvel (համրել, հաշուել)
numerator - tuvakurogh, tuvargou, hamarich (թուագրող, թուարկու,

Համարիչ)

numeric - tuvagan, tuvayin (Թուական, Թուային)

numerous - pazmativ, shad, usdvar (բազմաթիւ, շատ, ստուար)

numismatic - turamakidagan (դրամագիտական)

numismatics - turamakidoutiun (դրամագիտութիւն)

numskull - aboush, anmid, pakhoug (ապուշ, անմիտ, փախուկ)

nun - mayrabed, miantsnouhi, gouys (մայրապետ, միանձնուհի, կոյս)

nuncio - nuvirag, babagan badvirag (նուիրակ, պապական պատուիրակ)

nunhood, nunship - mayrabedoutiun (մայրապետութիւն)

nunnery - gousanots, gousavank (կուսանոց, կուսավանք)

nuptial - amousnagan, harsanegan (ամուսնական, Հարսանեկան)

nuptials harsanik (Հարսանիք)

nurse (n) - hivantabahouhi, pouzhkouyr, tayiag, usdundou (Հիւանդապահուհի, բուժքոյր, դայեակ, ստնտու)

nurse (v) - tiyetsunel, sunoutsanel, gat dal, khunamel (դիեցնել, սնուցանել, կաթ տալ, խնամել)

nursechild - dzudzmanoug, vortekir (ծծմանուկ, որդեգիր)

nursemaid - usbasouhi, tayiag (սպասուհի, դայեակ)

nursery - manganots, mangaran, poudzaran (մանկանոց, մանկարան, բուծարան)

nursing - hivantabahoutiun, tiyetsoum (Հիւանդապահութիւն, դիեցում)

nursing home - aghkadanots, dzeranots (աղքատանոց, ծերանոց)

nursling - mangig, yerekha (մանկիկ, երեխայ)

nurture (n) - khunamk, tiyetsoum, sunount, gurtoutiun (խնամք, դիեցում, սնունդ, կրթութիւն)

nurture (v) - sunoutsanel, medztsunel, gurtel, khunamel (սնուցանել, մեծցնել, կրթել, խնամել)

nut - ungouyz, gaghin, ungouyz havakel (ընկոյզ, կաղին, ընկոյզ Հաւաքել)

nutation - yereroum, jojoum, vayrahagoum (երերում, ճօճում, վայրաՀակում)

nutmeg - mushgungouyz (մշկընկոյզ)

nutrient - sununtarar, sunoutsich (սննդարար, սնուցիչ)

nutriment - sunount, oudelik, geragour (սնունդ, ուտելիք, կերակուր)

nutrition - sununtaroutiun, geragroum, sunoutsoum (սննդառութիւն, կերակրում, սնուցում)

nutritionist - sununtaked, sunounti masnaked (սննդագէտ, սնունդի մասնագէտ)

nutritious - sununtarar, sunoutsich (սննդարար, սնուցիչ)

nuts - khent, himar, pakhoug (խենդ, յիմար, փախուկ)

nuzzle - pouyn shinel, kitu khotel, hodvudal, sunoutsanel (բոյն շինել, քիթը խոթել, Հոտուըտալ, սնուցանել)

nycturia - kisheramizoutiun (գիշերամիզութիւն)

nymph - haverzhahars, keghouhi (յաւերժահարս, գեղուհի)

nymphomania - sirakhd, vavashodoutiun, harsnemoloutiun (սիրախտ, վաւաշոտութիւն, Հարսնեմոլութիւն)

oaf - manoug, anmid, khegh yerekha, tantsuramid (մանուկ, անմիտ, խեղ երեխայ, Թանձրամիտ)

oak - gaghni, gaghnepayd (կաղնի, կաղնեփայտ)
oaken - gaghnia, gaghnepaydia (կաղնեայ, կաղնեփայտեայ)
oar - ti, tiag, tiavarel (թի, թիակ, թիավարել)
oarsman - tiavar (թիավար)
oarsmanship - tiavaroutiun (թիավարութիւն)
oasis - ovasis (ովասիս)
oat - varsag (վարսակ)
oatcake - varsagapulit (վարսակաբլիթ)
oath - yertoum, hayhoyank (երդում, հայհոյանք)
oatmeal - varsagaliur (վարսակալիւր)
obduracy - khusdasurdoutiun, gamagoroutiun (խստասրտութիւն, կամակորութիւն)
obdurate - khusdasird, hamar, gamagor, anhoki (խստասիրտ, յամառ, կամակոր, անհոգի)
obedience - hunazantoutiun, hubadagoutiun (հնազանդութիւն, հպատակութիւն)
obedient - hunazant, hulou (հնազանդ, հլու)
obeisance - medzarank, harkank, khonarhoutiun (մեծարանք, յարգանք, խոնարհութիւն)
obelisk - gotogh, kargotogh, khachanish (կոթող, քարկոթող, խաչանիշ)
obese - ker, musod, marmunegh (գէր, մսոտ, մարմնեղ)
obesity - kiroutiun, jarbodoutiun (գիրութիւն, ճարպոտութիւն)
obey - hunazantil, hubadagil (հնազանդիլ, հպատակիլ)
obfuscade - mutuntsunel, mutakunel, aghodel, shupotetsunel (մթնցնել, մթագնել, աղօտել, շփոթեցնել)
obfuscation - mutaknoum, shuvaretsoum, mutoutiun (մթագնում, շուարեցում, մթութիւն)
obit - mah, houghargavoroutiun, hokehankisd (մահ, յուղարկաւորութիւն, հոգեհանգիստ)
obituary - mahazt, mahakouyzh, mahakhosagan, tampanagan (մահազդ, մահագոյժ, մահախօսական, դամբանական)
object - ararga, ir, nubadag, arargel, hagajarel (առարկայ, իր, նպատակ, առարկել, հակաճառել)
objection - arargoutiun, hagajaroutiun, poghok (առարկութիւն, հակաճառութիւն, բողոք)
objectionable - arargeli, tadabardeli, duhaj (առարկելի, դատապարտելի, տհաճ)
objective - arargayagan, iragan, anachar (առարկայական, իրական, անաչառ)
objectivism - arargayabashdoutiun, arargayatsoum (առարկայապաշտութիւն, առարկայացում)
objector - arargogh, unttimatsogh (առարկող, ընդդիմացող)
objurgate - hantimanel, gushdampel (յանդիմանել, կշտամբել)
objurgation - hantimanoutiun, gushdampank (յանդիմանութիւն, կշտամբանք)
oblation - nuviroum, madoutsoum, zoh, tson (նուիրում, մատուցում, զոհ, ձօն)
obligate - bardaturel, bardavoretsunel (պարտադրել, պարտաւորեցնել)
obligation - bardavoroutiun, bardk, bardatought (պարտաւորութիւն, պարտք, պարտաթուղթ)
obligatory - bardavorich, hargaturogh, usdiboghagan (պարտաւորիչ, հարկադրող, ստիպողական)
oblige - usdibel, bardavorel, hargaturel, purnatadel (ստիպել, պարտաւորել, հարկադրել, բռնադատել)
obligee - bahanchader, yerakhdavor (պահանջատէր, երախտաւոր)
obliging - badrasdagam, shunorhadou, gamagadar, azniv (պատրաստակամ, շնորհատու, կամակատար, ազնիւ)
obligor - bardader, bardavor, yerakhdaked (պարտատէր, պարտաւոր, երախտագէտ)
oblique - shegh, tek, goghmnagi, sheghagi, sheghil (շեղ, թեք,

կողմնակի, շեղակի, շեղիլ)
obliterate - avrel, chunchel, surpel, anhedatsunel (աւրել, ջնջել, սրբել, անհետացնել)
obliteration - chunchoum, anhedatsnoum, vochunchatsnoum (ջնջում, անհետացնում, ոչնչացնում)
oblivion - moratsoum, moratsoutiun (մոռացում, մոռացութիւն)
oblivious - moratsgod, mortsunogh (մոռացկոտ, մոռցնող)
obliviousness - moratsgodoutiun (մոռացկոտութիւն)
oblong - yergaratsev (երկարաձեւ)
obloquy - meghatrank, pampasank, viravorank (մեղադրանք, բամբասանք, վիրաւորանք)
obnoxious - anhajeli, anpaghtsali, meghatreli, adeli (անհաճելի, անբաղձալի, մեղադրելի, ատելի)
oboe - partsurasurink, surapogh (բարձրասուրինգ, սրափող)
oboist - surunkahar (սրնգահար)
obscene - bighdz, lugdi, anbargeshd, tsop, kaneli (պիղծ, լկտի, անպարկեշտ, ցոփ, գանելի)
obscurant - khavarich, lousadyats, mutaknogh (խաւարիչ, լուսատեաց, մթագնող)
obscuration - khavaroum, khavaretsunoum (խաւարում, խաւարեցնում)
obscure (n) - mout, khavar, khurtin, anorosh, dzadzoug (մութ, խաւար, խրթին, անորոշ, ծածուկ)
obscure (v) - mutuntsunel, khavarel, khurtnatsunel, nusematsunel (մթնցնել, խաւարել, խրթնացնել, նսեմացնել)
obscurity - mutoutiun, khurtnoutiun, khavar (մթութիւն, խրթնութիւն, խաւար)
obsecrate - aghachel, aghersel, haytsel, baghadil (աղաչել, աղերսել, հայցել, պաղատիլ)
obsecration - aghachank, aghersank, baghadank (աղաչանք, աղերսանք, պաղատանք)
obsequious - kudznogh, shoghokort, khungargogh, nuvasd (քծնող, շողոքորթ, խնկարկող, նուաստ)
obsequy - houghargavoroutiun, taghman dzes (յուղարկաւորութիւն, թաղման ծէս)
observant - oushatir, tidogh, ansatsogh (ուշադիր, դիտող, անսացող)
observation - tidoghoutiun, zunnoum, husgoum, tidargoutiun (դիտողութիւն, զննում, հսկում, դիտարկութիւն)
observatory - asdghatidaran, tidaran (աստղադիտարան, դիտարան)
observe - nugadel, tidel, kunnel, zunnel, husgel, bahel (նկատել, դիտել, քննել, զննել, հսկել, պահել)
observer - tidogh, nugadogh, zunnogh (դիտող, նկատող, զննող)
obsess - mudalulgel, mudabasharel, neghel, hedabuntel (մտալլկել, մտապաշարել, նեղել, հետապնդել)
obsession - mudaseveroum, hajakhank, daknab, basharoum (մտասեւեռում, յաճախանք, տագնապ, պաշարում)
obsolescence - ankordzadzoutiun (անգործածութիւն)
obsolete - hintsadz, ankordznagan (հինցած, անգործնական)
obstacle - arkelk, khochuntod, tuzhvaroutiun (արգելք, խոչընդոտ, դժուարութիւն)
obstetrician - mangaparts (մանկաբարձ)
obstetrics - mangapartsoutiun (մանկաբարձութիւն)
obstinacy - hamaroutiun, hasdadagamoutiun (յամառութիւն, հաստատակամութիւն)
obstinate - hamar, buntakuloukh (յամառ, պնդագլուխ)
obstreperous - aghmugarar, medzatsayn, anzousb (աղմկարար, մեծաձայն, անզուսպ)
obstruct - kotsel, pagel, khapanel, khutsel, arkilel (գոցել, փակել, խափանել, խցել, արգիլել)
obstruction - khutsoum, khochuntod, khapanararoutiun (խցում, խոչընդոտ, խափանարարութիւն)

obstructist - khapanarar (խափանարար)
obstructive - arkelich, khapanogh, khankarich (արգելիչ, խափանող, խանգարիչ)
obstruent - khapanogh, khapanarar (խափանող, խափանարար)
obtain - usdanal, tserk tsukel, haytaytel, jarel (ստանալ, ձեռք ձգել, Հայթայթել, ճարել)
obtainable - usdanali, madcheli, hasaneli, hunaravor (ստանալի, մատչելի, Հասանելի, Հնարաւոր)
obtrude - usdibel, bardaturel, mudtsunel, kitu khotel (ստիպել, պարտադրել, մտցնել, քիթը խոթել)
obtrusion - michamukhoutiun, inknagochoutiun (միջամխութիւն, ինքնակոչութիւն)
obtrusive - aneres, gubchan, inknagoch, kuloukh tsavtsunogh (աներես, կպչան, ինքնակոչ, գլուխ ցաւցնող)
obtuse - pout, putadzayr, putamid (բութ, բթածայր, բթամիտ)
obverse - hagatir, toursi, yeresi, yeres turami (Հակադիր, դուրսի, երեսի, երես դրամի)
obvert - tartsunel, shurchel (դարձնել, շրջել)
obviate - gankhel, arkilel, khapanel (կանխել, արգիլել, խափանել)
obviation - arkelk, michamudoutiun (արգելք, միջամտութիւն)
obvious - desaneli, agnerev, patsahayd, haydni, barz (տեսանելի, ակներեւ, բացայայտ, յայտնի, պարզ)
obviously - patsahaydoren, haydnoren (բացայայտօրէն, յայտնօրէն)
occasion - arit, badehoutiun, badjar, tebk, baraka (առիթ, պատեհութիւն, պատճառ, դէպք, պարագայ)
occasional - badahagan, barakayagan (պատաՀական, պարագայական)
Occident - arevmoudk (Արեւմուտք)
occidental - arevmudian (արեւմըտեան)
occlude - pagel, kotsel, khutsel (փակել, գոցել, խցել)
occult - kaghduni, takoun, dzadzoug dzadzgel (գաղտնի, թաքուն, ծածուկ, ծածկել)
occupancy - kuravouadzoutiun, kuravoum, aroum (գրաւուածութիւն, գրաւում, առում)
occupant - punagich, kuravogh, zhamanagavor der (բնակիչ, գրաւող, ժամանակաւոր տէր)
occupation - kuravoum, diratsoum, uzpaghoum, kordz (գրաւում, տիրացում, զբաղում, գործ)
occupier - kuravogh, punagogh, vartsagal (գրաւող, բնակող, վարձակալ)
occupy - kuravel, direl, diranal, usdanal, uzpaghetsunel (գրաւել, տիրել, տիրանալ, ստանալ, զբաղեցնել)
occur - badahil, hantibil, ullal, hishel, mudke antsunel (պատաՀիլ, Հանդիպիլ, ըլլալ, յիշել, մտքէ անցնել)
occurence - tibvadz, tebk, badahar, antsk (դիպուած, դէպք, պատաՀար, անցք)
ocean - ovgianos, anhounoutiun (ովկիանոս, անՀունութիւն)
ochlocracy - khouzhanavaroutiun (խուժանավարութիւն)
octagon - outangiun (ութանկիւն)
octant - outniag, outerort (ութնեակ, ութերորդ)
octave - outiag, outorek (ութեակ, ութօրէք)
octennial - outamia (ութամեայ)
October - hogdemper (Հոկտեմբեր)
ocular - achki, desoghagan, agnabagi (աչքի, տեսողական, ակնապակի)
oculist - agnapouyzh (ակնաբոյժ)
odalisque, odalisk - harj, haremi gin (Հարճ, Հարեմի կին)
odd - anzouyk, gojad, aylantag, anhetet, ansovor (անզոյգ, կոճատ, այլանդակ, անՀեթեթ, անսովոր)
odd pricing - anzouykov kin dal (անզոյգով գին տալ) 99 cents, ոչ 1 $ կամ 100 cents.
oddity - darorinagoutiun, anzoukoutiun (տարօրինակութիւն, անզու-

գուԹիւն)

odds - darperoutiun, anhavasaroutiun (տարբերուԹիւն, անհաւասարուԹիւն)

ode - dagh, dagherk, koverk, nerpogh, keghon (տաղ, տաղերգ, գովերգ, ներբող, գեղօն)

odeon, odeum - yerazhushdasurah, lusaran panasdeghdzoutian (երաժշտասրահ, լսարան բանաստեղծուԹեան)

odious - adeli, karsheli, zuzveli (ատելի, գարշելի, զզուելի)

odium - adeloutiun, karshank, gushdampank (ատելուԹիւն, գարշանք, կշտամբանք)

odontology - adamnapanoputiun, adamnakhosoutiun (ատամնաբանուԹիւն, ատամնախօսուԹիւն)

odor - hod, pouyr, pouroum (հոտ, բոյր, բուրում)

odorant - hodaved, pouroumnaved, anoushahod (հոտաւէտ, բուրումնաւէտ, անուշահոտ)

odoriferous - hodaved, pouraved, anoushahod (հոտաւէտ, բուրաւէտ, անուշահոտ)

odorless - anhod (անհոտ)

odorous - hodaved, anoushapouyr pouroumnalits (հոտաւէտ, անուշաբոյր, բուրումնալից)

Odyssey - votisagan (Ոդիսական)

of - vura, masin, vasun, deghu (վրայ, մասին, վասն, տեղը)

off - herou, vurayen, herouen, megti, antin (հեռու, վրայէն, հեռուէն, մէկդի, անդին)

off and on - aysbes aynbes, asang anang, badahapar (այսպէս այնպէս, ասանկ անանկ, պատահաբար)

off day - don, donagan or, artsagourt (տօն, տօնական օր, արձակուրդ)

off duty - hankisdi or (հանգիստի օր)

offal - aveltsouk, aghp, taptupoug, murour, dagank (աւելցուք, աղբ, ԹափԹփուկ, մրուր, տականք)

offend - anarkel, viravorel, anbadvel, tushnamanal (անարգել, վիրաւորել, անպատուել, Թշնամանալ)

offense - anarkank, viravorank, nakhadink (անարգանք, վիրաւորանք, նախատինք)

offensive - hartsagoum, kuroh, hartsagoghagan, nakhadagan (յարձակում, գրոհ, յարձակողական, նախատական)

offer - aracharg, arachargel, nuvirel, huramtsunel, dal (առաջարկ, առաջարկել, նուիրել, հրամցնել, տալ)

offerable - madoutsaneli, nouireli (մատուցանելի, նուիրելի)

offerer - arachargogh, madoutsanogh, portsogh, nuvirogh (առաջարկող, մատուցանող, փորձող, նուիրող)

offerhand - shoud, vagh, anbadrasdits, anvakh (շուտ, վաղ, անպատրաստից, անվախ)

offering - arachargoutiun, nuver, voghchagez, zoh (առաջարկուԹիւն, նուէր, ողջակէզ, զոհ)

offertory - surpasatsoutiun, nuvirerkoutiun (սրբասացուԹիւն, նուիրերգուԹիւն)

offhand - hanbadrasdits, hangardz, isgouyn, gobid (յանպատրաստից, յանկարծ, իսկոյն, կոպիտ)

office - kuraseniag, dzes, himnarg, varchoutiun, bashdon (գրասենեակ, ծէս, հիմնարկ, վարչուԹիւն, պաշտօն)

office boy - kuraseniagi dugha, tughtadar (գրասենեակի տղայ, Թղթատար)

officer - bashdonia, usba, usba garkel, usbayargel (պաշտօնեայ, սպայ, սպայ կարգել, սպայարկել)

official - bashdonagan, bashdonadar, bashdonia (պաշտօնական, պաշտօնատար, պաշտօնեայ)

officialize - bashdonaganatsunel (պաշտօնականացնել)

officiate - badarakel, bashdonavarel (պատարագել, պաշտօնավարել)

officious - anbashdon, hajoyagadar, michamudogh (անպաշտօն, հաճո-

յակատար, միջամտող)
offing - dzovamech, dzovoun patseru (ծովամէջ, ծովուն բացերը)
offish - martakhouys, amuchgod, inknampop (մարդախոյս, ամչկոտ, ինքնամփոփ)
offset (n) - untsiugh, poghpoch, usgoudeghov dubakroutiun (ընձիւղ, բողբոջ, սկուտեղով տպագրութիւն)
offset (v) - havasaragushrel, hashivu kotsel, pokharinel (հաւասարակշռել, հաշիւը գոցել, փոխարինել)
offset printing - pazmadib dubakuroutiun (բազմատիպ տպագրութիւն)
offshoot - sharavigh, jiugh, untsiugh (շառաւիղ, ճիւղ, ընձիւղ)
offside - sahmanazants tirk (սահմանազանց դիրք)
offspring - zavag, serount, yerekhaner (զաւակ, սերունդ, երեխաներ)
often - hajakh, hajakhagi, pazmitsus, shad ankam (յաճախ, յաճախակի, բազմիցս, շատ անգամ)
ogle - siravar nayvadzk, goghmunagi nayil (սիրավառ նայուածք, կողմնակի նայիլ)
ogre - martager, jivagh (մարդակեր, ճիւաղ)
oh - oh (ո~հ)
oil - yiugh, tset, yiughel, yiughodel (իւղ, ձէթ, իւղել, իւղոտել)
oil change - iughapokhoum (իւղափոխում)
oil cloth - momlat (մոմլաթ)
oil color - yiughanerg (իւղաներկ)
oil filter - iughazudich (իւղազտիչ)
oil gas - kariugh (քարիւղ)
oil painting - yiughanugarchoutiun (իւղանկարչութիւն)
oil tanker - yiughadar nav (իւղատար նաւ)
oilcan - yiughaman (իւղաման)
oiler - yiughavajar, yiughakordz, yiughaman (իւղավաճառ, իւղագործ, իւղաման)
oilfield - navtahor, navtahank (նաւթահոր, նաւթահանք)
oily - yiughod, yiughayin, kudznogh, luburdzoun (իւղոտ, իւղային, քծնող, լպրծուն)
ointment - odzanelik (օծանելիք)
oitment - odzanelik, morti kuselik yiugh (օծանելիք, մորթի քսելիք իւղ)
old - dzer, hin, darikod, darets, barav, portsarou (ծեր, հին, տարիքոտ, տարեց, պառաւ, փորձառու)
Old Testament - hin gudagaran (Հին Կտակարան)
Old World - hin ashkharh (Հին Աշխարհ)
olden - hin, vaghemi, arachva (հին, վաղեմի, առաջուայ)
oldness - hunoutiun, dzeroutiun (հնութիւն, ծերութիւն)
oldster - dzerouni, barav (ծերունի, պառաւ)
oleaginous - yiughod, yiughayin, yiughaper (իւղոտ, իւղային, իւղաբեր)
oleander - tapnevart (դափնեվարդ)
olfaction - hodaroutiun (հոտառութիւն)
oligarchy - sagavabedoutiun, khumpishkhanoutiun (սակաւապետութիւն, խմբիշխանութիւն)
olive - tsiteni, tsitabodough, tsitakouyn (ձիթենի, ձիթապտուղ, ձիթագոյն)
olive oil - tsitayiugh, tset (ձիթաիւղ, ձէթ)
Olympiad - karamia shurchan voghimbiagani (քառամեայ շրջան ողիմպիականի)
Olympian - voghimbiagan, veh, uskancheli yergnayin (ողոմպիական, վեհ, սքանչելի, երկնային)
Olympic - voghimbiagan (ողիմպիական)
Olympic Games - voghimbiagan khagher (ողիմպիական խաղեր)
ominous - charakouzh, charakoushag, usbarnalits (չարագոյժ, չարագուշակ, սպառնալից)
omission - zantsaroutiun, anhokoutiun, teratsoum (զանցառութիւն,

անհոգութիւն, թերացում)
omit - andes toghoul, zants arnel, chunugadel, andesel (անտես թողուլ, զանց առնել, չնկատել, անտեսել)
omnibus - hanragark (Հանրակառք)
omnifarious - pazmadesag (բազմատեսակ)
omnipotence - amenazoroutiun (ամենազօրութիւն)
omnipotent - amenazor, amenagarogh (ամենազօր, ամենակարող)
omnipresent - amenourek (ամենուրեք)
omniscient - amenaked, hamaynaked (ամենագէտ, համայնագէտ)
omnivorous - amenager (ամենակեր)
omoplate - tignosgur, ousosgur (թիկնոսկր, ուսոսկր)
on - vura, vurayen, masin, tebi, usd, goghm (վրայ, վրայէն, մասին, դէպի, ըստ, կողմ)
onanism - kichoutiun (գիջութիւն)
once - adenok, ankam mu, miankam, meg ankam (ատենօք, անգամ մը, միանգամ, մէկ անգամ)
one - meg, miag, megu, meg had, nouyn, vok (մէկ, միակ, մէկը, մէկ հատ, նոյն, ոք)
oneirocritic - yerazahan, yerazatsouyts (երազահան, երազացոյց)
oneiromancy - yerazakoushagoutiun (երազագուշակութիւն)
oneness - minagoutiun, arantsnoutiun (մինակութիւն, առանձնութիւն)
onerous - dzanraperun, dzanur, tuzhvarin (ծանրաբեռն, ծանր, դժուարին)
oneself - inkzink, inkun (ինքզինք, ինքն)
onesided - miagoghmani, miagoghm (միակողմանի, միակողմ)
onion - sokh (սոխ)
onionskin - parag, tapantsig tought (բարակ, թափանցիկ թուղթ)
only - miag, miayn, mimiayn, arantsin, menag (միակ, միայն, միմիայն, առանձին, մենակ)
onset - hartsagoum, khouzhoum, kuroh, arshavank (յարձակում, խուժում, գրոհ, արշաւանք)
onto - vuran, tebi (վրան, դէպի)
ontology - eapanoutiun (էաբանութիւն)
onus - per, badaskhanaduvoutiun, dzanroutiun (բեռ, պատասխանատուութիւն, ծանրութիւն)
onward, onwards - harach, arachatem, tebi arach (յառաջ, առաջադէմ, դէպի առաջ)
onyx - yeghunknakar (եղնգնաքար)
ooze - dighm, dzoroum, dzoril, gatgutil, muzil (տիղմ, ծորում, ծորիլ, կաթկթիլ, մզիլ)
opacity - antapantsoutiun (անթափանցութիւն)
opal - arevakar, arevagun (արեւաքար, արեւակն)
opaque - antapants, aghod, anlouys, tantsuramid (անթափանց, աղօտ, անլոյս, թանձրամիտ)
open (a) - pats, patsvadz, haydni, angeghdz, merg (բաց, բացուած, յայտնի, անկեղծ, մերկ)
open (v) - panal, artsagel, barzel, haydnel, patsvil (բանալ, արձակել, պարզել, յայտնել, բացուիլ)
open account - pats hashiv, vusdahelioutiun (բաց հաշիւ, վստահելիութիւն)
open air - patsotia (բացօթեայ)
open handed - aradatserun, tserku pats (առատաձեռն, ձեռքը բաց)
open heart surgery - surdi pats kordzoghoutiun (սրտի բաց գործողութիւն)
open hearted - surdapats, sirdu pats, angeghdz (սրտաբաց, սիրտը բաց, անկեղծ)
open house - huraver aytsi, pats doun-vajarki hamar (հրաւէր այցի, բաց տուն՝ վաճառքի համար)
open housing - pats doun vartselou gam kunelou (բաց տուն վարձելու կամ գնելու)
open minded - pats midk, oushim, khelatsi (բաց միտք, ուշիմ, խելացի)
open mouthed - patsperan, peranapats, shadager, abshahar (բացբե-

րան, բերանբաց, շատակեր, ապ-շահար)

opening - patsoum, usgizp, dzag, patsvadzk (բացում, սկիզբ, ծակ, բացուածք)

openly - patsoren, hurabaragov, patsahaydoren (բացորէն, հրապարակով, բացայայտօրէն)

opera - yerkahagh, taderanuvak, opera (երգախաղ, թատերանուագ, օփերա)

opera house - operayi taderasurah (օփերայի թատերասրահ)

operate - kordzel, nerkordzel, virahadel, gudrel, hanel (գործել, ներգործել, վիրահատել, կտրել, հանել)

operation - kordzoghoutiun, virahadoutiun, kordzarnoutiun (գործողութիւն, վիրահատութիւն, գործառնութիւն)

operative - kordzogh, aztetsig, aztou, iravagan, kordzavor (գործող, ազդեցիկ, ազդու, իրական, գործաւոր)

operator - virapouyzh, herakhosavar, sharzhanugarich (վիրաբոյժ, հեռախօսավար, շարժանկարիչ)

operetta - zaveshderkoutiun, taderanuvak, operet (զաւեշտերգութիւն, թատերանուագ, օփերէթ)

ophthalmia - achatsav, agnaporp (աչացաւ, ակնաբորբ)

ophthalmologist - agnapouyzh, achki puzhishg (ակնաբոյժ, աչքի բժիշկ)

ophthalmology - agnapouzhoutiun (ակնաբուժութիւն)

opiate - kunategh, tumrategh, tumretsoutsich (քնադեղ, թմրադեղ, թմրեցուցիչ)

opine - gardzel, gardzik haydnel (կարծել, կարծիք յայտնել)

opinion - gardzik, midk, kaghapar, hamaroum (կարծիք, միտք, գաղափար, համարում)

opinionated, opinionative - buntakuloukh, hamar, hasdadagam (պնդագլուխ, յամառ, հաստատակամ)

opium - afion (աֆիոն)

oppilate - khurnel, khapanel (խռնել, խափանել)

oppometer - desachap (տեսաչափ)

opponent - hagaragort, unttimatir, daragardzik, hagatir (հակառակորդ, ընդդիմադիր, տարակարծիք, հակադիր)

opportune - badeh, harmar, parebadeh, nubasdavor (պատեհ, յարմար, բարեպատեհ, նպաստաւոր)

opportunity - badehoutiun, arit (պատեհութիւն, առիթ)

oppose - unttimanal, hagaragil, timaturel, arkilel (ընդդիմանալ, հակառակիլ, դիմադրել, արգիլել)

opposite - hagarag, hagatir, unttimatir, nerhag (հակառակ, հակադիր, ընդդիմադիր, ներհակ)

opposition - unttimoutiun, hagatroutiun, arkelk (ընդդիմութիւն, հակադրութիւն, արգելք)

oppress - junshel, ungjel, neghel, harusdaharel (ճնշել, ընկճել, նեղել, հարստահարել)

oppression - junshoum, geghekoum, zurgank (ճնշում, կեղեքում, զրկանք)

oppressor - junshogh, geghekich, harusdaharogh (ճնշող, կեղեքիչ, հարստահարող)

opprobrious - nakhadagan, viravoragan, amotali, khaydarag (նախատական, վիրաւորական, ամօթալի, խայտառակ)

opprobrium - anarkank, nakhadink, khaydaragoutiun (անարգանք, նախատինք, խայտառակութիւն)

optic - desoghagan, achki hadoug (տեսողական, աչքի յատուկ)

optical - desoghagan, achki (տեսողական, աչքի)

optician - agnotsavajar, agnotsakordz, agnaked (ակնոցավաճառ, ակնոցագործ, ակնագէտ)

optics - desakidoutiun, lousakidoutiun (տեսագիտութիւն, լուսագիտութիւն)

optimism - lavadesoutiun (լաւատեսութիւն)

optimist - *lavades, paredes* (լաւատես, բարետես)
optimum - *amenanubasdavor* (ամենանպաստաւոր)
option - *nakhunduroutiun, unduroutiun, gamk* (նախընտրութիւն, ընտրութիւն, կամք)
optional - *gamavor, anbardatir, undureli* (կամաւոր, անպարտադիր, ընտրելի)
optometer - *desoghachap* (տեսողաչափ)
optometrist - *desachapov ach kunnogh* (տեսաչափով աչք քննող)
optometry - *desoghachapoutiun* (տեսողաչափութիւն)
opulence - *partamoutiun, harusdoutiun* (փարթամութիւն, հարստութիւն)
opulent - *partam, jokh, berj, arad, harousd* (փարթամ, ճոխ, պերճ, առատ, հարուստ)
or - *gam, yev gam, gam te* (կամ, եւ կամ, կամ թէ)
oracle - *badkam, badkamakhos, markare, badkamadeghi* (պատգամ, պատգամախօս, մարգարէ, պատգամատեղի)
oral - *peranatsi, ankir, panavor* (բերանացի, անգիր, բանաւոր)
orally - *peranatsioren, panavor gerbov* (բերանացիօրէն, բանաւոր կերպով)
orange - *narinch, naruncheni, narurchakouyn* (նարինջ, նարնջենի, նարնջագոյն)
orangeade - *narunchachour, narinchi osharag* (նարնջաջուր, նարինջի օշարակ)
orang-outang - *martagabig, orangoutan* (մարդակապիկ, օրանկութան)
orate - *jarakhosel* (ճառախօսել)
oration - *jarakhosoutiun, adenapanoutiun* (ճառախօսութիւն, ատենաբանութիւն)
orator - *jarakhos, huredor, adenakhos, jardasan* (ճառախօս, հռետոր, ատենախօս, ճարտասան)
oratorio - *aghoterkoutiun, maghterk, nuvakakhagh* (աղօթերգութիւն, մաղթերգ, նուագախաղ)
oratory - *aghotaran, madour, berjakhosoutiun* (աղօթարան, մատուռ, պերճախօսութիւն)
orb - *yergnakount, dzir, aniv, poloragel, poloril* (երկնագունդ, ծիր, անիւ, բոլորակել, բոլորիլ)
orbicular - *kuntatsev, gulor, kount, poloragatsev* (գնդաձեւ, կլոր, գունդ, բոլորակաձեւ)
orbit - *oughedzir, shurchan, shavigh, agnagabij* (ուղեծիր, շրջան, շաւիղ, ակնակապիճ)
orchard - *murkasdan, budghasdan* (մրգաստան, պտղաստան)
orchestra - *nuvakakhoump, yerazhushdakhoump* (նուագախումբ, երաժշտախումբ)
orchestration - *kordzikavoroum* (գործիքաւորում)
orchid - *tsuvadzaghig, kholorts* (ձուածաղիկ, խոլորձ)
ordain - *garkel, tsernaturel, sahmanel, vujrel* (կարգել, ձեռնադրել, սահմանել, վճռել)
order (n) - *gark, ganon, tas, asdijan, badver, huraman* (կարգ, կանոն, դաս, աստիճան, պատուէր, հրաման)
order (v) - *abusburel, huramayel, dunorinel, tasavorel* (ապսպրել, հրամայել, տնօրինել, դասաւորել)
orderer - *abusburogh, badvirogh* (ապսպրող, պատուիրող)
orderly - *ganonavor, garkabah, bardajanach* (կանոնաւոր, կարգապահ, պարտաճանաչ)
ordinal - *tasagan tiv* (դասական թիւ)
ordinance - *vujir, huramanakir, sovoroutiun, dzes* (վճիռ, հրամանագիր, սովորութիւն, ծէս)
ordinary - *sovoragan, hasarag, ganonavor* (սովորական, հասարակ, կանոնաւոր)
ordination - *tsernaturoutiun, garkoum, garkaturoutiun* (ձեռնադրութիւն, կարգում, կարգադրութիւն)
ordnance - *huredani, tuntanot, razmazen* (հրետանի, թնդանօթ, ռազ-

մաղէն)

ordure - aghp, aghdeghoutiun, aveltsouk, gughgughank (աղբ, աղտեղութիւն, աւելցուք, կղկղանք)

ore - hankaniut, hankamedagh (Հանքանիւթ, Հանքամետաղ)

organ - kordzaran marmuni, yerkehon, bashdonatert (գործարան մարմնի, երգեհոն, պաշտօնաթերթ)

organdie - pehez, marmash (բեհեզ, մարմաշ)

organic, al - kordzaranavor, kordzaranayin, organagan (գործարանաւոր, գործարանային, օրկանական)

organism - gazmuvadzk, gazm, horinvadzk (կազմուածք, կազմ, յօրինուածք)

organist - yerkehonahar (երգեհոնահար)

organization - gazm, gazmagerboutiun, gazmoutiun (կազմ, կազմակերպութիւն, կազմութիւն)

organize - gazmel, gazmagerbel, gazmavorel, garkaturel (կազմել, կազմակերպել, կազմաւորել, կարգադրել)

organizer - gazmagerbogh, gazmagerbich (կազմակերպող, կազմակերպիչ)

organon - kidagan hedazodoutiun (գիտական Հետազօտութիւն)

orgasm - durpank, serayin kurkir, heshdahosoutiun (տռփանք, սեռային գրգիռ, Հեշտահոսութիւն)

orgy - shuvaydank, lugdi hajouyk, kinarpouk (շուայտանք, լկտի Հաճոյք, գինարբուք)

oriel - kots badushkam (գոց պատշգամ)

Orient - arevelk (Արեւելք)

orient - arachnortel, goghmnoroshvil, dzakogh (առաջնորդել, կողմնորոշուիլ, ծագող)

oriental - arevelian, arevelktsi (արեւելեան, արեւելքցի)

orientalism - arevelakidoutiun (արեւելագիտութիւն)

orientate - goghmnoroshvil, tirku jushtel (կողմնորոշուիլ, դիրքը ճշդել)

orientation - goghmnoroshoum, oughghoutiun, areveloum (կողմնորոշում, ուղղութիւն, արեւելում)

orifice - antsk, moudk, dzag, patsvadzk, peran (անցք, մուտք, ծակ, բացուածք, բերան)

origin - usgizp, dzakoum, dzunount, aghpiur, armad (սկիզբ, ծագում, ծնունդ, աղբիւր, արմատ)

original - inknadib, iurahadoug, punakir, nakhadib (ինքնատիպ, իւրայատուկ, բնագիր, նախատիպ)

originality - inknaduboutiun, darorinagoutiun (ինքնատպութիւն, տարօրինակութիւն)

originate - dzunount dal, koyatsunel, koyanal, arachanal (ծնունդ տալ, գոյացնել, գոյանալ, առաջանալ)

origination - dzakoum, dzunount, usgizp (ծագում, ծնունդ, սկիզբ)

originator - usdeghdzogh, hunarich, usguzpnabadjar (ստեղծող, Հնարիչ, սկզբնապատճառ)

orison - aghotk, maghtank, aghers (աղօթք, մաղթանք, աղերս)

ornament - zart, zartarank, shukanushan, zartarel, bujnel (զարդ, զարդարանք, շքանշան, զարդարել, պճնել)

ornamentation - zartaroum, bujnoum, zartarank (զարդարում, պճնում, զարդարանք)

ornate - zartaroun, bujnial, keghazart (զարդարուն, պճնեալ, գեղազարդ)

ornithology - turchnapanoutiun (Թռչնաբանութիւն)

orphan - vorp, vorpatsunel (որբ, որբացնել)

orphanage - vorpanots, vorpoutiun (որբանոց, որբութիւն)

orthodox - oughghapar, oughghahavad, oughigh (ուղղափառ, ուղղաՀաւատ, ուղիղ)

Orthodoxy - oughghaparoutiun (Ուղղափառութիւն)

orthodoxy - oughghaparoutiun (ուղ–

ղափառութիւն)
orthoepic - oughghakhos, oughghahunchiun (ուղղախօս, ուղղահնչիւն)
orthoepy - oughghakhosoutiun (ուղղախօսութիւն)
orthogon - oughghangiun (ուղղանկիւն)
orthographer, orthographist - oughghakir, parakir (ուղղագիր, բառագիր)
orthography - oughghakuroutiun (ուղղագրութիւն)
orthology - oughghakhosoutiun (ուղղախօսութիւն)
orthopedy - mangapouzhoutiun (մանկաբուժութիւն)
oscillate - jojil, dadanil, turtural (ճօճիլ, տատանիլ, թրթռալ)
oscillation - jojoum, dadanoum (ճօճում, տատանում)
oscitate - horanchel (յօրանջել)
oscitation - horanchoum (յօրանջում)
osculate - hubil, shoshapel, hampourel (հպիլ, շօշափել, համբուրել)
osculation - huboum, shoshapoum, hampouroum (հպում, շօշափում, համբուրում)
osier - churouri, oureni (ջրուռի, ուռենի)
osmanli - osmantsi (օսմանցի)
osseous - vosgurod, vosgure, vosgurayin (ոսկրոտ, ոսկրէ, ոսկրային)
ossification - vosguratsoum (ոսկրացում)
ossify - vosguranal, vosguratsunel, gardzuranal (ոսկրանալ, ոսկրացնել, կարծրանալ)
ossuary - vosguragouyd, shirim, kerezman (ոսկրակոյտ, շիրիմ, գերեզման)
ostensible - tsoutsamolagan, tsoutsagan, vorosh, haydni (ցուցամոլական, ցուցական, որոշ, յայտնի)
ostentation - tsoutsamoloutiun (ցուցամոլութիւն)
ostentatious - tsoutsamol, tsoutsaser (ցուցամոլ, ցուցասէր)
osteoclasis - vosgurapegoutiun (ոսկրաբեկութիւն)
osteocope - vosguratsav (ոսկրացաւ)
osteopath - vosgurapouyzh, pegapouyzh (ոսկրաբոյժ, բեկաբոյժ)
osteopathy - vosgurapouzhoutiun, pegapouzhoutiun (ոսկրաբուժութիւն, բեկաբուժութիւն)
ostier - akhoraban, tsiaban (ախոռապան, ձիապան)
ostracism - ardaksoum, vudaroum, khetsevujir (արտաքսում, վտարում, խեցեվճիռ)
ostracize - ardaksel, vudarel, khetsevujrel (արտաքսել, վտարել, խեցեվճռել)
ostrich - chaylam (ջայլամ)
other - mius, miusu, ourish, ayl, hagarag (միւս, միւսը, ուրիշ, այլ, հակառակ)
otherwhere - ayl degh, aylour (այլ տեղ, այլուր)
otherwise - aylabes, darper, yete voch, hagarag barakayin (այլապէս, տարբեր, եթէ ոչ, հակառակ պարագային)
otiose - ankordz, dzouyl, touyl (անգործ, ծոյլ, թոյլ)
ottar - varti yiough (վարդի իւղ)
otter - churasamouyr (ջրասամոյր)
ottoman - osmanian, osmantsi, tourk (օսմանեան, օսմանցի, թուրք)
oubliette - virab, anhoush pand (վիրապ, անյուշ բանտ)
ought - bedk er, vayel er, vochunchoutiun (պէտք էր, վայել էր, ոչնչութիւն)
ounce - oungi, aouns, hovazig (ունկի, աունս, յովազիկ)
our - mer (մեր)
ours - meru, merinu (մերը, մերինը)
ourself, ourselves - menk, menk mezi (մենք, մենք մեզի)
ousel - sariag, gernekh (սարեակ, կեռնեխ)
oust - vudarel, tours hanel, heratsunel, kushel, nedel (վտարել, դուրս հանել, հեռացնել, քշել, նետել)
out - tours, toursu, megti, megnadz, gorir, heratsir (դուրս, դուրսը, մէկդի, մեկնած, կորիր, հեռացիր)

out and out - liagadar, gadaryal (լիակատար, կատարեալ)
outact - kergadarel, kerazantsel (գերկատարել, գերազանցել)
outbalance - keragushrel (գերակշռել)
outbid - kinu aveltsunel (գինը աւելցնել)
outbreak - bortgoum, baytiun, khulurdoum (պոռթկում, պայթիւն, խլրտում)
outburst - zhaytkoum, bortgoum (ժայթքում, պոռթկում)
outcast - vudaranti, darakir, andoun (վտարանդի, տարագիր, անտուն)
outclass - kerazantsel, keragushrel (գերազանցել, գերակշռել)
outcome - artiunk, hedevank, yelk, hasouyt (արդիւնք, հետեւանք, ելք, հասոյթ)
outcry - jich, aghaghag, kochoum (ճիչ, աղաղակ, գոչում)
outdare - hantuknil, khizakhel (յանդգնիլ, խիզախել)
outdated - hintsadz, zhamanagu antsadz (հինցած, ժամանակը անցած)
outdo - kerazantsel, antsnil (գերազանցել, անցնիլ)
outdoor - patzotia, dounen tours (բացօթեայ, տունէն դուրս)
outdoors - toursu, pats otin mech (դուրսը, բաց օդին մէջ)
outer - toursi, ardakin (դուրսի, արտաքին)
outface - timakuravel (դիմագրաւել)
outfall - kedaperan, usgizp, agounk (գետաբերան, սկիզբ, ակունք)
outfield - ardatashd (արտադաշտ)
outfit - hantertsank, bidouyk, gazmadzk (Հանդերձանք, պիտոյք, կազմածք)
outfitter - badrasdi hakousd dzakhogh, marzagan kouyker (պատրաստի Հագուստ ծախող, մարզական գոյքեր)
outflow - ardahosk, yelk (արտահոսք, ելք)
outgo - arach antsnil, kerazantsel, megnil (առաջ անցնիլ, գերազանցել, մեկնիլ)
outgoing - megnoum, megnogh, yelk, dzaghk (մեկնում, մեկնող, ելք, ծախք)
outgrow - kerajil, aveli medznal (գերաճիլ, աւելի մեծնալ)
outgrowth - keraj, untsiough, ouretsk, artiounk (գերաճ, ընձիւղ, ուռեցք, արդիւնք)
outguard - ardabahag, harachabah (արտապաՀակ, յառաջապաՀ)
outing - ardakunatsoutiun, budouyd, yelk (արտագնացութիւն, պտոյտ, ելք)
outlander - odaragan (օտարական)
outlandish - odarerguria, odar, darorinag (օտարերկրեայ, օտար, տարօրինակ)
outlaw - kogh, orinazants, iravazourg, orinazurgel (գող, օրինազանց, իրաւազուրկ, օրինազրկել)
outlay - dzakhs, yelk, vadnoum (ծախս, ելք, վատնում)
outlearn - kerousanil (գերուսանիլ)
outlet - yelk, antsk, jampa, dzag, patsvadzk, shouga (ելք, անցք, ճամբայ, ծակ, բացուածք, շուկայ)
outline - ourvakidz, dzurakir, nakhakidz, ourvakudzel (ուրուագիծ, ծրագիր, նախագիծ, ուրուագծել)
outlive - verabril, voghch munal (վերապրիլ, ողջ մնալ)
outlook - heranugar, desaran, mudahorizon, tidaran (Հեռանկար, տեսարան, մտաՀորիզոն, դիտարան)
outlying - heravor, toursi, ardakin, anchad (Հեռաւոր, դուրսի, արտաքին, անջատ)
outmeasure - chapu antsunel (չափը անցնել)
outmost - verchin, hedin, dzayri (վերջին, յետին, ծայրի)
outnumber - tivov kerazantsel, tivu antsnil (թիւով գերազանցել, թիւը անցնիլ)
outpatient - toursi hivant (դուրսի Հիւանդ)
outpost - panagi harachatirk (բանակի յառաջադիրք)
outpour - zeghoum, zeghil, tapil,

heghoul (գեղում, գեղիլ, Թափիլ, Հեղուլ)
output - ardatrank, ardahanel, tours hanel (արտադրանք, արտահանել, դուրս Հանել)
outrage - nakhadink, tushnamank, loudank, nakhadel (նախատինք, Թշնամանք, լուտանք, նախատել)
outrageous - gadaghi, molekin, vayrak (կատաղի, մոլեգին, վայրագ)
outrank - kerazantsel (գերազանցել)
outreach - arach antsunil, hasnil (առաջ անցնիլ, Հասնիլ)
outride - arak tsiavarel, archeven yertal (արագ ձիավարել, առջեւէն երԹալ)
outright - anmichabes, isgouyn, liagadar, oughghagi (անմիջապէս, իսկոյն, լիակատար, ուղղակի)
outrun - vazelov antsnil, kerevazel (վազելով անցնիլ, գերեվազել)
outsell - shad dzakhel, sough dzakhel (շատ ծախել, սուղ ծախել)
outset - usgizp, usguzpnavoroutiun (սկիզբ, սկզբնաւորուԹիւն)
outshine - ardapaylil, shoghshoghal (արտափայլիլ, շողշողալ)
outside - toursi, ardakin, dzayrakouyn, patsotia (դուրսի, արտաքին, ծայրագոյն, բացօԹեայ)
outsider - tursetsi, odar, ardakin (դրսեցի, օտար, արտաքին)
outskirt - arvartsan, yezerk, dzayr, dzayramas, sahman (արուարձան, եզերք, ծայր, ծայրամաս, սաՀման)
outspread - dzavaloum, daradzel, daradzvil (ծաւալում, տարածել, տարածուիլ)
outstand - tsutsvil, unttimanal, aragakh-anvujar munal (ցցուիլ, ընդդիմանալ, առկախ–անվճար մնալ)
outstanding - yereveli, agnarou, tsutsoun, oushakurav (երեւելի, ակնառու, ցցուն, ուշագրաւ)
outstare - achku vakhtsunel, amuchtsunel (աչքը վախցնել, ամչցնել)
outstretch - daradzel, yerguntsunel (տարածել, երկնցնել)
outvie - kerazantsel, haghtel (գերազանցել, յաղԹել)
outvote - kuveov haghtel (քուէով յաղԹել)
outwall - barisb, ardakin bad (պարիսպ, արտաքին պատ)
outward - ardakin, toursi, agunhayd (արտաքին, դուրսի, ակնյայտ)
outwear - mashetsunel, yergar timanal (մաշեցնել, երկար դիմանալ)
outweigh - keragushrel, dzanur gushrel (գերակշռել, ծանր կշռել)
outwit - khapel, nenkel (խաբել, նենգել)
outwork - aveli ashkhadil, hoknil, badnesh (աւելի աշխատիլ, յոգնիլ, պատնէշ)
ouzel - sariag (սարեակ)
oval - havgutatsev, tsouatsev (ՀաւկԹաձեւ, ձուաձեւ)
ovarium - tsouaran (ձուարան)
ovation - khantavar tsouyts, khantavaroutiun, dzapoghchouyn (խանդավառ ցոյց, խանդավառուԹիւն, ծափողջոյն)
oven - pour, vararan, ojakh, hunots (փուռ, վառարան, օճախ, Հնոց)
over - vura, vurayen, aveli, toursi, verchatsadz (վրայ, վրայէն, աւելի, դուրսի, վերջացած)
overact - kerakhaghal, chapazantsel (գերախաղալ, չափազանցել)
overall - verargou, vernazkesd (վերարկու, վերնազգեստ)
overawe - ahapegel, vakhtsunel, vakhov ungjel (աՀաբեկել, վախցնել, վախով ընկճել)
overbalance - keragushrel, chapu antsnil (գերակշռել, չափը անցնիլ)
overbear - haghtel, ungjel, nuvajel (յաղԹել, ընկճել, նուաճել)
overbearing - haghtogh, diragalogh, koroz, ampardavan (յաղԹող, տիրակալող, գոռոզ, ամբարտաւան)
overburden - dzanrapernel (ծանրաբեռնել)
overcast - ambodel, veradzadzgel, badel, mutatsunel (ամպոտել, վերածածկել, պատել, մԹացնել)
overcharge - dzanrapernel, partsur kin tunel (ծանրաբեռնել, բարձր

գին դնել)
overcloud - ambodil (ամպոտիլ)
overcoat - verargou, tignots (վերարկու, Թիկնոց)
overcome - haghtel, nuvajel, hamagel (յաղԹել, նուաճել, Համակել)
overdo - chapazantsel, shad ashkhadil, aveli yepel (չափազանցել, շատ աշխատիլ, աւելի եփել)
overdose - kerteghakanag, kerteghachap, shad tegh dal (գերդեղաքանակ, գերդեղաչափ, շատ դեղ տալ)
overdraft - hashvebard, aveliov kashvadz koumar (Հաշուեպարտք, աւելիով քաշուած գումար)
overdraw - chapazantsel, sahmanvadzen aveli turam kashel (չափազանցել, սաՀմանուածէն աւելի դրամ քաշել)
overdress - chapazants haktsunel (չափազանց Հագցնել)
overdue - oushatsadz vujaroum, habaghial (ուշացած վճարում, յապաղեալ)
overeat - shad oudel (շատ ուտել)
overestimate - kerakunahadel (գերագնաՀատել)
overflow - hortil, voghoghel, heghegh, voghoghoum (յորդիլ, ողողել, Հեղեղ, ողողում)
overgrow - kerajil, dzadzgel (գերաճիլ, ծածկել)
overgrown - kirtsadz, kerajadz khodov dzadzguvadz (գիրցած, գերաճած, խոտով ծածկուած)
overhand - dirabedoutiun, verin ouzh, gurgnagi gar (տիրապետութիւն, վերին ոյժ, կրկնակի կար)
overhang - gakhvil, toursu tsutsvil, dzadzg (կախուիլ, դուրսը ցցուիլ, ծածկ)
overhaul - kunnel, kashel, shudgel, hasnil, norokoutiun (քննել, քաշել, շտկել, Հասնիլ, նորոգուԹիւն)
overhead - partsru, kulkhe ver, verev (բարձրը, գլխէ վեր, վերեւ)
overhear - aganchu hasnil, lusel, verahasou ullal (ականջը Հասնիլ, լսել, վերաՀասու ըլլալ)
overheat - kerdakoutiun, shad daktsunel (գերտաքուԹիւն, շատ տաքցնել)
overissue - havelativ, shad huradaragel (յաւելաԹիւ, շատ Հրատարակել)
overjoy - yerchangatsunel, shad ourakhatsunel (երջանկացնել, շատ ուրախացնել)
overland - tsamaken, tsamakov, tsamakakunats (ցամաքէն, ցամաքով, ցամաքագնաց)
overlap - veradzalel (վերածալել)
overlay - veradzadzgel, kotsel, badel, dzadzgich (վերածածկել, գոցել, պատել, ծածկիչ)
overleap - vurayen tsadgel, antsunil (վրայէն ցատկել, անցնիլ)
overlie - vuran bargil, kheghtel (վրան պառկիլ, խեղդել)
overlimit - sahmanazants (սաՀմանազանց)
overload - dzanrapernel, dzanrapernoum (ծանրաբեռնել, ծանրաբեռնում)
overlook - veranayil, husgel, veren nayil, verahusgel (վերանայիլ, Հսկել, վերէն նայիլ, վերաՀսկել)
overmatch - kerazantsel, nouajel, kerazantsogh (գերազանցել, նուաճել, գերազանցող)
overnice - pudzakhuntir, nurpaser (բծախնդիր, նրբասէր)
overnight - ampoghch kisheru, nakhort yerego, kisherel (ամբողջ գիշերը, նախորդ երեկոյ, գիշերել)
overpay - shad vujarel (շատ վճարել)
overpower - kerouzh, haghtaharel, nuvajel (գերուժ, յաղԹաՀարել, նուաճել)
overpraise - kerakovel, kerakovoum (գերագովել, գերագովում)
overpress - kerjunshel, kerjunshoum, ung joum (գերճնշել, գերճնշում, ընկճում)
overproduce - kerardaturel (գերարտադրել)
overproduction - kerardaturoutiun (գերարտադրուԹիւն)

overrate - kerakunahadel (գերագնահատել)
overrule - ishkhel, direl, dirabedel (իշխել, տիրել, տիրապետել)
overrun - vurayen vazel, voghoghel, daradzvil, asbadagel (վրայէն վազել, ողողել, տարածուիլ, ասպատակել)
oversea - anturdzovian, odar (անդրծովեան, օտար)
overseas - dzoven antin, yergure tours (ծովէն անդին, երկրէ դուրս)
oversee - veranayil, husgel, tidel (վերանայիլ, հսկել, դիտել)
overseer - verahusgich, veradesouch (վերահսկիչ, վերատեսուչ)
oversell - shad dzakhel, sough dzakhel (շատ ծախել, սուղ ծախել)
overset - shurchel, dabalel, shurchoum, dabaloum (շրջել, տապալել, շրջում, տապալում)
overshadow - usdveradzadzgel, nusematsunel, bashdbanel (ստուերածածկել, նսեմացնել, պաշտպանել)
overshoe - gurgnagoshig (կրկնակօշիկ)
overshoot - vuribil, vurayen antsunil (վրիպիլ, վրայէն անցնիլ)
oversight - veranayoum, andesoum, vuriboum, sukhalank (վերանայում, անտեսում, վրիպում, սխալանք)
oversize - anchap, chapen medz (անչափ, չափէն մեծ)
oversleep - yergar kunanal, oush artunnal (երկար քնանալ, ուշ արթննալ)
overspend - vadnel, shad dzakhsel, muskhel, usbarel (վատնել, շատ ծախսել, մսխել, սպառել)
overspread - dzadzgel (ծածկել)
overstate - chapazantsel, sheshdel (չափազանցել, շեշտել)
overstatement - chapazantsoutiun (չափազանցութիւն)
overstay - yergar munal, shad genal (երկար մնալ, շատ կենալ)
overstep - sahmanu antsunil (սահմանը անցնիլ)
overstrain - kerlaroum, kerlarel, kerhoknetsunel (գերլարում, գերլարել, գերյոգնեցնել)
overt - pats, patsahayd, haydni (բաց, բացայայտ, յայտնի)
overtake - antsunil, verahasnil, purnel (անցնիլ, վերահասնիլ, բռնել)
overtax - havelial dourk, dourkov junshel (յաւելեալ տուրք, տուրքով ճնշել)
overthrow - dabalel, gordzanel, dabaloum (տապալել, կործանել, տապալում)
overtime - havelazham, ardazhami, zhamen yedk (յաւելաժամ, արտաժամ, ժամէն ետք)
overture - aracharg, nakherkank, patsoum (առաջարկ, նախերգանք, բացում)
overturn - shurchel, dabalel, shurchoum, dabaloum (շրջել, տապալել, շրջում, տապալում)
overweeing - inknahavan, ampardavan, medzamid (ինքնահաւան, ամբարտաւան, մեծամիտ)
overweigh - keragushrel, dzanur gushrel (գերակշռել, ծանր կշռել)
overweight - keragushroutiun, ker, keragushrel (գերակշռութիւն, գէր, գերակշռել)
overwork - kerashkhadank, kerashkhadil (գերաշխատանք, գերաշխատիլ)
ovum - tsou, tsuvig, serm, saghm (ձու, ձուիկ, սերմ, սաղմ)
owe - bardil, bardagan ullal (պարտիլ, պարտական ըլլալ)
owel - havasar (հաւասար)
owelty - havasaroutiun (հաւասարութիւն)
owing - bardagan, bardavor (պարտական, պարտաւոր)
owl - pou, maksanenkoutiun unel (բու, մաքսանենգութիւն ընել)
owler - maksanenk (մաքսանենգ)
own - usdanal, diranal, ounenal, sepagan, antsnagan (ստանալ, տիրանալ, ունենալ, սեփական, անձնական)
owner - der, sepaganader (տէր, սեփականատէր)
ownership - sepaganoutiun (սեփա-

կանութիւն)
ox - yez (եզ)
oxhead - hasd kuloukh (Հաստ գլուխ)
oxidation - tutvasdznoutiun, zhankodoum (թթուածնութիւն, ժանգոտում)
oxide - tutvadzunad, tutvit, zhank (թթուածնատ, թթուիդ, ժանգ)
oxidize - tutvadzunel, tutvargel (թթուածնել, թթուարկել)
oxslip - karnanadzaghig (գարնանածաղիկ)
oxter - anout (անութ)
oxygen - tutvadzin (թթուածին)
oxygenate - tutvadznel (թթուածնել)
oxygon - sour yerangiun (սուր եռանկիւն)
oyer - ounguntouroutiun, kunnoutiun (ունկնդրութիւն, քննութիւն)
oyez - lusetsek, mudig urek (լսեցէք, մտիկ ըրէք)
oyster - vosdure (ոստրէ)
ozone - ozon (օզոն)
ozostomia - perni kesh hod (բերնի գէշ Հոտ)
o'clock - zham (ժամ)
O.K. - shad lav, sirov, hamatsayn yem (շատ լաւ, սիրով, Համաձայն եմ)

P

pabulum - sunount, oudesd, varelaniut (սնունդ, ուտեստ, վարելանիւթ)
pacable - meghmeli, hantardetsuneli (մեղմելի, Հանդարտեցնելի)
pace - kayl, kalvadzk, kaylachap, kunantsk, jemel (քայլ, քալուածք, քայլաչափ, գնանցք, ճեմել)
pacemaker - surdi ashkhadanku nertashnagogh kordzik (սրտի աշխատանքը ներդաշնակող գործիք)
pacer - hamrakunats, shororakunats (Համրագնաց, շորորագնաց)
pachyderm - tantsuramort (թանձրամորթ)
pacific - khaghagh, khaghagharar, khaghaghaser (խաղաղ, խաղաղարար, խաղաղասէր)
Pacific Ocean - khaghaghagan ovgianos (Խաղաղական Ովկիանոս)
pacification - khaghaghetsoum, hantardetsoum (խաղաղեցում, Հանդարտեցում)
pacificator - khaghararar, hashdarar (խաղարարար, Հաշտարար)
pacifier - khaghaghich, hantardetsoutsich (խաղաղիչ, Հանդարտեցուցիչ)
pacifist - khaghaghaser, khaghaghabashd (խաղաղասէր, խաղաղապաշտ)
pacify - khaghaghetsunel, hantardetsunel (խաղաղեցնել, Հանդարտեցնել)
pack (n) - dzurar, gabots, per, dzukhadoup, khaghatought (ծրար, կապոց, բեռ, ծխատուփ, խաղաթուղթ)
pack (v) - dzurarel, gabel, pattel, goudagel, khurnel (ծրարել, կապել, փաթթել, կուտակել, խռնել)
pack saddle - hamed (Համետ)
package - dzurar, gabots, dzuraroum, gaboghchek (ծրար, կապոց, ծրարում, կապողչէք)
packer - dzurarogh, pattogh (ծրարող, փաթթող)
packet - gabots, pokur dzurar, dzurarel (կապոց, փոքր ծրար, ծրարել)
packhouse - muteranots (մթերանոց)
packing - dzuraroum, gabots, dzuraravartsk (ծրարում, կապոց, ծրարավարձք)

packman - perezag, manravajar (փերեզակ, մանրավաճառ)
pact - tashink, baymanakir, oukhd, hamatsaynoutiun (դաշինք, պայմանագիր, ուխտ, համաձայնութիւն)
pad (n) - partsig, dzudzoun tought, tughtadzurar, gunkagal (բարձիկ, ծծուն թուղթ, թղթածրար, կնքակալ)
pad (v) - kalel, vodkov jamportel, goghobdel, partsel (քալել, ոտքով ճամբորդել, կողոպտել, բարձել)
padding - litsk, letsnoum, lutsaniut, khutsan, khudzoudz (լիցք, լեցնում, լցանիւթ, խցան, խծուծ)
paddle - tiavarel, kushel, tiargel, ti, tiag, tevjag (թիավարել, քշել, թիարկել, թի, թիակ, թեւճակ)
paddock - arod, hoghamas, vormapag, totosh, kord (արօտ, հողամաս, որմափակ, դօդօշ, գործ)
padlock - gabank, pagank, gughbel (կապանք, փականք, կղպել)
paean - tsundzerk, haghterk (ցնծերգ, յաղթերգ)
paediatrics, pediatrics - mangadadzoutiun, mangapouzhoutiun (մանկատածութիւն, մանկաբուժութիւն)
pagan - hetanos, gurabashd (հեթանոս, կռապաշտ)
paganish - hetanosagan (հեթանոսական)
paganism - hetanosoutiun (հեթանոսութիւն)
paganize - hetanosatsunel, hetanosanal (հեթանոսացնել, հեթանոսանալ)
page - ech, yeres, mangulavig, echakurel, tuvakurel (էջ, երես, մանկլաւիկ, էջագրել, թուագրել)
pageant - keghahantes, shukert, nergayatsoum, tsouyts (գեղահանդէս, շքերթ, ներկայացում, ցոյց)
pageantry - shukatsouyts, keghahantisoutiun (շքացոյց, գեղահանդիսութիւն)
pager - ungalouch heratsayni, haghortich (ընկալուչ հեռաձայնի, հաղորդիչ)
paginate - echakurel, tuvakurel (էջագրել, թուագրել)
pagination - echakuroutiun, echahamar (էջագրութիւն, էջահամար)
pagoda - guradoun (կռատուն)
paid - vujarvadz (վճարուած)
pail - touyl, gonk (դոյլ, կոնք)
pain - tsav, vishd, neghoutiun, tsavtsunel, danchel (ցաւ, վիշտ, նեղութիւն, ցաւցնել, տանջել)
painful - tsavod, tsavali, junshogh, danchalits (ցաւոտ, ցաւալի, ճնշող, տանջալից)
painim - gurabash, hetanos, anhavad (կռապաշտ, հեթանոս, անհաւատ)
painless - antsav, anvishd (անցաւ, անվիշտ)
paint - nugarel, kudzel, nergel, shubarel, nerg, kouyn (նկարել, գծել, ներկել, շպարել, ներկ, գոյն)
paintbrush - vurtsin (վրձին)
painted - nerguvadz, kounavor (ներկուած, գունաւոր)
painter - nugarich, keghanugarich, nergarar, navachuvan (նկարիչ, գեղանկարիչ, ներկարար, նաւաչուան)
painting - nugar, keghanugar, keghanugarchoutiun (նկար, գեղանկար, գեղանկարչութիւն)
pair - zouyk, gurgnag, amol, zoukavorel, zoukvil (զոյգ, կրկնակ, ամոլ, զուգաւորել, զուգուիլ)
pal - kordzagits, unger, muderim, mudermanal (գործակից, ընկեր, մտերիմ, մտերմանալ)
palace - balad, abarank (պալատ, ապարանք)
paladin - pakhdakhuntir asbed, kach (բախտախնդիր ասպետ, քաջ)
palate - kimk, jashag, hamaroutiun (քիմք, ճաշակ, համառութիւն)
palatine - baladagan, baladi, arkayagomus (պալատական, պալատի, արքայակոմս)
palaver - paghakshank, shoghokortoutiun, shoghokortel (փաղաքշանք, շողոքորթութիւն, շողոքորթել)
pale (a) - kounad, teghnadz, duzh-

kounil, kounadil (գունատ, դեղնած, տժգունիլ, գունատիլ)
pale (n) - tsits, tsogh, sahman, tsutsabad, tsangabadel (ցից, ձող, սահման, ցցապատ, ցանկապատել)
palelot - vernazkesd (վերնազգեստ)
paleness - kounadoutiun, duzhkounoutiun (գունատութիւն, տժգունութիւն)
paleograph, palaeograph - hunakir, hintserakir (հնագիր, հին ձեռագիր)
paleologist - hunapan, hunakhos (հնաբան, հնախօս)
paleology - hunapanoutiun (հնաբանութիւն)
Palestine - baghesdin (Պաղեստին)
palette - nergabunag, yerankabunag, kounagal (ներկապնակ, երանգապնակ, գունակալ)
palfrey - nuzhouyk, yerivar (նժոյգ, երիվար)
palimpsest - makaghat, gurgnakir (մագաղաթ, կրկնագիր)
paling - tsangabad, pagaran (ցանկապատ, փակարան)
palinode - gurgnerk, veragochoum (կրկներգ, վերակոչում)
palisade - tsutsabadnesh, jaghabad, tsoghabadel (ցցապատնէշ, ճաղապատ, ձողապատել)
pall (n) - dzadzgots takaghi, dzadzgots sugihi, dzadzgouyt (ծածկոց դագաղի, ծածկոց սկիհի, ծածկոյթ)
pall (v) - dzadzgel, haktsunel, hapranal, anhamanal (ծածկել, հագցնել, յափրանալ, անհամանալ)
pallbearer - sukagir, takaghagir (սգակիր, դագաղակիր)
pallet - khushdiag, hartangoghin, anot, kordzik (խշտեակ, յարդանկողին, անօթ, գործիք)
palliate - badurvagel, amokel, meghmel, uspopel (պատրուակել, ամոքել, մեղմել, սփոփել)
palliation - amokoum, meghmatsoum, koghargoum (ամոքում, մեղմացում, քօղարկում)
palliative - amokich, uspopich, meghmatsunogh tegh (ամոքիչ, սփոփիչ, մեղմացնող դեղ)
pallid - kounad, duzhkouyn, merelakouyn, taloug (գունատ, տժգոյն, մեռելագոյն, դալուկ)
pallidness - kounadoutiun, duzhkounoutiun (գունատութիւն, տժգունութիւն)
palm - ap, tiz, armaveni, api mech bahel, ajbararel (ափ, թիզ, ափի մէջ պահել, աճպարարել)
palm reading - tserk gartal (ձեռք կարդալ)
Palm Sunday - dzaghgazart (Ծաղկազարդ)
palmer - khapepa, khaghaturouzh, oukhdavor (խաբեբայ, խաղադրուժ, ուխտաւոր)
palmist - tsernahuma (ձեռնահմայ)
palmistry - tsernahumayoutiun (ձեռնահմայութիւն)
palpable - shoshapeli, uzkali, haydni (շօշափելի, զգալի, յայտնի)
palpate - shoshapel (շօշափել)
palpation - shoshapoum (շօշափում)
palpitant - papakhoun, tupurdoun (բաբախուն, թփրտուն)
palpitate - papakhel, duropel, toghal (բաբախել, տրոփել, դողալ)
palpitation - papakhoum, duropoum, togh (բաբախում, տրոփում, դող)
palsied - antamalouydz, hashmantam (անդամալոյծ, հաշմանդամ)
palsy - gatvadz, antamaloudzoutiun, antamaloudzel (կաթուած, անդամալուծութիւն, անդամալուծել)
palter - geghdzel, kutin khuntal (կեղծել, քթին խնդալ)
paltry - chunchin, anbed, kutsouts, tsadz (չնչին, անպէտ, գձուձ, ցած)
paludal - jahjayin (ճահճային)
palustral - jakhjakhoud, moroud (ճախճախուտ, մորուտ)
pamper - hapratsunel, shad gertsunel, yeres dal (յափրացնել, շատ կերցնել, երես տալ)
pamphlet - kurkouyg, dedrag, barsavadedur (գրքոյկ, տետրակ, պարսաւատետր)
pan - dabag, dzap, khantsagal, ha-

letsunel, kourayel (տապակ, ծախ, խանձակալ, Հալեցնել, քուրայել)
panacea - amenapouyzh, hamaynategh (ամենաբույժ, Համայնադեղ)
panache - pedrapounch (փետրափունջ)
pancake - dabagapulit, tsitapulit, otanavi oughigh echk (տապակաբլիթ, ձիթաբլիթ, օդանաւի ուղիղ էջք)
panchromatic - mahakounagan, pazmakounayin (Համագունական, բազմագունային)
pancreas - sharouyr, usdamoksakeghts (շարոյր, ստամոքսագեղձ)
pandemic - hamajarag (Համաճարակ)
pandemonium - tivaran, tuzhokhk, kharnashupotoutiun (դիւարան, դժոխք, խառնաշփոթութիւն)
pander - gavad, michnort, gavadoutiun unel (կաւատ, միջնորդ, կաւատութիւն ընել)
pane - abagia peghg, lousamoudi abagi, tevag (ապակեայ փեղկ, լուսամուտի ապակի, թեւակ)
panegerize - kovel, nerpoghel, turvadel (գովել, ներբողել, դրուատել)
panegyric - nerpoghagan, kovk (ներբողական, գովք)
panegyrist - kovasan, turvadogh (գովասան, դրուատող)
panegyrize - nerpoghel, kovel (ներբողել, գովել)
panel - shurchanagial dakhdag, yertevialner, dakhdagel (շրջանակեալ տախտակ, երդուեալներ, տախտակել)
panelling - yeresabadoum, paydia vormnadzadzg (երեսապատում, փայտեայ որմնածածկ)
pang - antsgoutiun, vishd, tsav, hokevark (անձկութիւն, վիշտ, ցաւ, Հոգեվարք)
panic - khoujab, hangardzavakh, sarsap (խուճապ, յանկարծավախ, սարսափ)
pannier - goghov, sagar, zampiugh (կողով, սակառ, զամփիւղ)
panning - hamaynabadger, hamadesaran (Համայնապատկեր, Համատեսարան)
panoply - usbarazinoutiun, zinashar (սպառազինութիւն, զինաշար)
panorama - hamaynabadger, hamabadger (Համայնապատկեր, Համապատկեր)
panoramic - hamadesil, hamaynagan, poloradesil (Համատեսիլ, Համայնական, բոլորատեսիլ)
pansexualism - hamaseraganoutiun (Համասեռականութիւն)
pansy - khogadzaghig, hir, ikaganatsadz mart (խոկածաղիկ, Հիր, իգականացած մարդ)
pant - heval, hevatsoum, hevk, surdi duropoum (Հեւալ, Հեւացում, Հեւք, սրտի տրոփում)
pantaloon - hudbid, kheghgadag (Հտպիտ, խեղկատակ)
pantaloons - negh dapad (նեղ տաբատ)
pantheism - hamasdvadzoutiun (Համաստուածութիւն)
Pantheon - banteon, dajar, mehian, titsaran (Պանթէոն, տաճար, մեհեան, դիցարան)
panther - hovaz (յովազ)
pantograph - hamakir, hamakurogh, badger orinagelou kordzik (Համագիր, Համագրող, պատկեր օրինակելու գործիք)
pantography - hamakuroutiun (Համագրութիւն)
pantomine - munchgadag, munchgadagoutiun, hamrakhagh (մնջկատակ, մնջկատակութիւն, Համրախաղ)
pantry - maran, muteranots, ushdemaran (մառան, մթերանոց, շտեմարան
pants - dapad (տաբատ)
panzer - zurahabad (զրաՀապատ)
pap - dzidz, usdink, budoug, hatsabour, sunount (ծիծ, ստինք, պտուկ, Հացապուր, սնունդ)
papa - hayrig, hayr (Հայրիկ, Հայր)
papacy - baboutiun, babaganoutiun (պապութիւն, պապականութիւն)
papal - babagan, babi (պապական,

պապի)

paper - tought, tert, lurakir, hotvadz, tughtadzurarel (Թուղթ, Թերթ, Լրագիր, յօղուած, Թղթածրարել)

paper cutter - gudrich (կտրիչ)

paper money - tughtaturam (Թղթադրամ)

paper war - kurchabaykar (գրչապայքար)

paper work - toughti kordz, toughti tasavoroum (Թուղթի գործ, Թուղթի դասաւորում)

paperback - tughtagazm (Թղթակազմ)

paperboard - khavakard (խաւաքարտ)

paperclip - tughtagal (Թղթակալ)

papers - vaveratoughter, toughter (վաւերաԹուղԹեր, ԹուղԹեր)

papism - babaganoutiun (պապականուԹիւն)

papist - babagan (պապական)

papule - pushdig (բշտիկ)

papyrus - babiros, burdatought (պապիրոս, պրտաԹուղԹ)

par - hamarzhek, havasarakin, havasaroutiun (Համարժէք, Հաւասարագին, ՀաւասարուԹիւն)

parable - arag, aylapanoutiun (առակ, այլաբանուԹիւն)

parabola - zoukort, haragits, gabagits (զուգորդ, յարակից, կապակից)

parabolic - pokhaperagan, aylapanagan, aragayin (փոխաբերական, այլաբանական, առակային)

parachute - angarkel, bahbanag (անկարգել, պահպանակ)

parachutist - angarkelavor (անկարգելաւոր)

paraclete - sourp hoki, mukhitarich, parekhos (Սուրբ Հոգի, մխիԹարիչ, բարեխօս)

parade - shukatsouyts, doghantsk, tapor, doghantsel (շքացոյց, տողանցք, Թափօր, տողանցել)

paradigm - orinag, numouysh, haratsouyts (օրինակ, Նմոյշ, յարացոյց)

paradise - turakhd, yetem, arkayoutiun (դրախտ, եդեմ, արքայուԹիւն)

parados - badnesh (պատնէշ)

paradox - darorinag, ardasovor, darumpurnoum (տարօրինակ, արտասովոր, տարըմբռնում)

paraffin - momaniut, yiugh (մոմանիւԹ, իւղ)

paragon - dibar, orinag, hamemadel (տիպար, օրինակ, Համեմատել)

paragraph - barperoutiun, hadvadz, hadvadzel (պարբերուԹիւն, Հատուած, Հատուածել)

paraleipsis - habavoum, zantsaroutiun (յապաւում, զանցառուԹիւն)

parallel - zoukaheragan, zoukaherakidz, havasaril (զուգաՀեռական, զուգաՀեռագիծ, Հաւասարիլ)

parallelism - zoukaheraganoutiun (զուգաՀեռականուԹիւն)

paralysis - antamaloudzoutiun (անդամալուծուԹիւն)

paralytic - antamalouydz, antamaloudzagan (անդամալոյծ, անդամալուծական)

paralyzation - antamaloudzoum (անդամալուծում)

paralyze - antamaloudzel, chuladel (անդամալուծել, ջլատել)

parameter - harachap, magachap (յարաչափ, մակաչափ)

paramount - kerakouyn, vehakouyn, partsurakouyn (գերագոյն, վեհագոյն, բարձրագոյն)

paramour - harj, homani, homanouhi, sirouhi (Հարճ, Հոմանի, ՀոմանուՀի, սիրուՀի)

paranoia - khelakaroutiun (խելագարուԹիւն)

paranoiac - khelakar (խելագար)

parapet - yezrabad, hoghabadnesh, jaghashar (եզրապատ, Հողապատնէշ, ճաղաշար)

paraph - hamarod usdorakuroutiun, nakhausdorakurel (Համառօտ ստորագրուԹիւն, Նախաստորագրել)

paraphernalia - gunochakouyk, artouzartk, gunochayin (կնոջագոյք, արդուզարդք, կնոջային)

paraphrase - verabadmoum, parapokhoum, barzapanel (վերապատմում, բառափոխում, պարզաբանել)
parasite - magapouydz, tsuriager, bunagalez (մակաբոյծ, ճրիակեր, պնակալէզ)
parasol - hovanots, arevanots (հովանոց, արեւանոց)
paratyphoid - aghedab (աղետապ)
parboil - terkhashel, kich mu yepel, gisepel (թերխաշել, քիչ մը եփել, կիսեփել)
parcel - dzurar, hoghasherd, mas, pazhnel, dzurarel (ծրար, հողաշերտ, մաս, բաժնել, ծրարել)
parcel post - tughtadarov arakvadz dzurar (թղթատարով առաքուած ծրար)
parch - chortsunel, khantsel, khantsil (չորցնել, խանձել, խանձիլ)
parched - chortsadz, khantsuvadz, ayradz (չորցած, խանձուած, այրած)
parchment - makaghat (մագաղաթ)
pardon - nerel, neroghoutiun khunturel, neroum (ներել, ներողութիւն խնդրել, ներում)
pardonable - nereli (ներելի)
pare - geghvel, makrel, gurjadel, gopel, kerdzel (կեղուել, մաքրել, կրճատել, կոփել, քերծել)
paregoric - meghmatsoutsich, meghmich, tsavamok (մեղմացուցիչ, մեղմիչ, ցաւամոք)
parent - dzunoghk, hayr, mayr, aghpiur, badjar (ծնողք, հայր, մայր, աղբիւր, պատճառ)
parentage - azkaganoutiun, khunamoutiun, dohm (ազգականութիւն, խնամութիւն, տոհմ)
parental - dzunoghagan, azkagtsagan (ծնողական, ազգակցական)
parenthesis - pagakidz, michangial khosk (փակագիծ, միջանկեալ խօսք)
paresis - antamaloudzoutiun (անդամալուծութիւն)
parget - dzedzel, dzep (ծեփել, ծեփ)
Paris - pariz (Փարիզ)
parish - tem, dzoukh, zhoghovurtabedoutiun (թեմ, ծուխ, ժողովրդապետութիւն)
parishioner - temagan, dzukhagan, temi antam (թեմական, ծխական, թեմի անդամ)
parity - havasaroutiun, numanoutiun, hankidoutiun (հաւասարութիւն, նմանութիւն, հանգիտութիւն)
park - uzposavayr, hanrayin bardez, getsunel, pagel (զբօսավայր, հանրային պարտէզ, կեցնել, փակել)
parking lot - garadegh, inknasharzhi gankar, gayan (կառատեղ, ինքնաշարժի կանգառ, կայան)
parlance - khoselavoj, khoselatsev, khosagtsoutiun (խօսելաոճ, խօսելաձեւ, խօսակցութիւն)
parley - panagtsoutiun, khorhurtagtsoutiun, panagtsil (բանակցութիւն, խորհրդակցութիւն, բանակցիլ)
parliament - khorhurtaran (խորհրդարան)
parliamentary - khorhurtaranagan (խորհրդարանական)
parlor - khosaran, nusdaseniag, hiuranots (խօսարան, նստասենեակ, հիւրանոց)
parlous - vudankavor, hantoukun (վտանգաւոր, յանդուգն)
parochial - temagan, neghmid, sahmanapag (թեմական, նեղմիտ, սահմանափակ)
parody - gabgoum, dzaghrerkoutiun, dzaghrerkel (կապկում, ծաղրերգութիւն, ծաղրերգել)
parole - khosdoum, badvo khosk, antsakhos zinvori (խոստում, պատուոյ խօսք, անցախօս զինուորի)
paronomasia - parakhagh, haratsaynoutiun (բառախաղ, յարաձայնութիւն)
paronym - nouynahunchiun, haranoun (նոյնահնչիւն, յարանուն)
paroxysm - zayrouyt, noba, sasdig porpokoum (զայրոյթ, նոպայ, սաստիկ բորբոքում)
parquet - kednaharg, kednasurah, dakhdagamadzel (գետնայարկ,

գետնասրահ, տախտակամածել)

parricide - dzunoghasban, hayrasban, mayrasban (ծնողասպան, հայրասպան, մայրասպան)

parrock - markasdan (մարգաստան)

parrot - toutag, toutagel (թութակ, թութակել)

parry - khouys dal, uzkoushanal, arkilel, khapanoum (խոյս տալ, զգուշանալ, արգիլել, խափանում)

parse - verloudzel, loudzel (վերլուծել, լուծել)

parsimonious - gudzdzi, akah, zhulad (կծծի, ագահ, ժլատ)

parsimony - gudzdzioutiun, zhuladoutiun, khunayoghoutiun (կծծիութիւն, ժլատութիւն, խնայողութիւն)

parsley - azadkegh (ազատքեղ)

parson - dzukhader, kahana, zhoghovurtabed (ծխատէր, քահանայ, ժողովրդապետ)

parsonage - yeritsadoun (երիցատուն)

part - mas, gudor, pazhin, shah, goghm, pazhnel, anchadel (մաս, կտոր, բաժին, շահ, կողմ, բաժնել, անջատել)

partake - masnagits ullal, masnagtsil, haghortil (մասնակից ըլլալ, մասնակցիլ, հաղորդիլ)

partaker - masnagtsogh, masnagits, gutsort (մասնակցող, մասնակից, կցորդ)

parter - pazhnogh, zadogh, zadvogh (բաժնող, զատող, զատուող)

parterre - kednaharg tadroni, pourasdan, dzaghganots (գետնայարկ թատրոնի, բուրաստան, ծաղկանոց)

partial - masnagi, voch luriv, acharou, goghmnagal (մասնակի, ոչ լրիւ, աչառու, կողմնակալ)

partiality - goghmnagaloutiun, acharoutiun (կողմնակալութիւն, աչառութիւն)

partially - masnagioren, goghmnagaloren (մասնակիօրէն, կողմնակալօրէն)

partible - pazhaneli, zadeli, pazhanagan (բաժանելի, զատելի, բաժանական)

participant - masnagits, masnagtsogh, haghort (մասնակից, մասնակցող, հաղորդ)

participate - masnagtsil, haghort ullal, mas gazmel (մասնակցիլ, հաղորդ ըլլալ, մաս կազմել)

participation - masnagtsoutiun, mas gazmelu (մասնակցութիւն, մաս կազմելը)

participle - terpay, untouneloutiun (դերբայ, ընդունելութիւն)

particle - masnig, gudor (մասնիկ, կտոր)

particular - masnavor, hadoug, iurahadoug, ourouyn (մասնաւոր, յատուկ, իւրայատուկ, ուրոյն)

particularity - masnahadgoutiun, arantsnahadgoutiun (մասնայատկութիւն, առանձնայատկութիւն)

particularization - masnavoroum, manramasnoum (մասնաւորում, մանրամասնում)

particularize - masnavorel, manramasnel (մասնաւորել, մանրամասնել)

particularly - masnavorapar, hadgapes (մասնաւորաբար, յատկապէս)

partisan - goghmnagits, gousagits, hamakhoh, fedayi (կողմնակից, կուսակից, համախոհ, ֆետայի)

partition - pazhanoum, anchadoum, michnabad, pazhnel (բաժանում, անջատում, միջնապատ, բաժնել)

partly - masamp, vorosh chapov (մասամբ, որոշ չափով)

partner - unger, kordzagits, khaghenger, goghagits (ընկեր, գործակից, խաղընկեր, կողակից)

partnership - ungeragtsoutiun, pazhnegtsoutiun (ընկերակցութիւն, բաժնեկցութիւն)

partridge - gakav (կաքաւ)

parturient - dzununtagan, dughaperki mod, peghmnavor (ծննդական, տղաբերքի մօտ, բեղմնաւոր)

parturition - dughaperk, dzununtaperoutiun (տղաբերք, ծննդաբերութիւն)

party - gousagtsoutiun, goghm, ha-

vakouyt, gousagits (կուսակցութիւն, կողմ, Հաւաքոյթ, կուսակից)
parvenu - noreloug harousd, chudes (Նորելուկ Հարուստ, չտես)
pasquin - zaveshd, yerkidzank, yerkidzakir (զաւեշտ, երգիծանք, երգիծագիր)
pasquinade - yerkidzapanoutiun (երգիծաբանութիւն)
pass - antsnil, yertal, pokhantsel, antsk, moudk (անցնիլ, երթալ, փոխանցել, անցք, մուտք)
pass away - mernil, anhedanal (մեռնիլ, անհետանալ)
passable - untouneli, michag, chapavor (ընդունելի, միջակ, չափաւոր)
passage - antsk, nurpantsk, antsoum, hadvadz, badahar (անցք, Նրբանցք, անցում, Հատուած, պատաՀար)
passbook - antsadedur, hashvededur (անցատետր, Հաշուետետր)
passenger - jamport, oughevor, antsort (ճամբորդ, ուղեւոր, անցորդ)
passer, passer-by - antsort, jamport (անցորդ, ճամբորդ)
passeriformes - jun jghazki (ճնճղազգի)
passing - antsunogh, antsunoum, khisd, kerazants, arzhamia (անցնող, անցնում, խիստ, գերազանց, արժամեայ)
passion - girk, darpank, yerant, houzoum, charcharank (կիրք, տարփանք, եռանդ, յուզում, չարչարանք)
passionate - gurkod, siraharvadz, guragod, cherm (կրքոտ, սիրաՀարուած, կրակոտ, ջերմ)
Passiontide - medz bahots verchin yergou shapatneru (Մեծ ՊաՀոց վերջին երկու շաբաթները)
Passion-Week - avak shapat (Աւագ Շաբաթ)
passive - guravoragan, ankordzounia, hulou, andarper (կրաւորական, անգործունեայ, Հլու, անտարբեր)
passivity - guravoraganoutiun, andarperoutiun (կրաւորականութիւն, անտարբերութիւն)
Passover - basek, yelits don (Պասեք, Ելից Տօն)
passport - antsakir (անցագիր)
password - dzadzgapar, nushanapar, khaghdnakhosk, antsapar (ծածկաբառ, Նշանաբառ, գաղտնախօսք, անցաբառ)
pass-partout - hamapanali, nugari shurchanag, shurchanagel (Համաբանալի, Նկարի շրջանակ, շրջանակել)
past - antsial, antsadz, hin, nakhgin (անցեալ, անցած, Հին, Նախկին)
pasta - geragouri khumoreghenner (կերակուրի խմորեղէններ)
paste - khumor, zankuvadz, sosints, sosuntsel, pagtsunel (խմոր, զանգուած, սոսինձ, սոսնձել, փակցնել)
paste up - echagazmoum (էջակազմում)
pasteboard - khavakard (խաւաքարտ)
pastel - nergamadid, yerpnamadid, lurchanerg (Ներկամատիտ, երփնամատիտ, լրջաներկ)
pasteurize - vunasagar manreneru usbannel (վնասակար մանրէները սպաննել)
pastil - hodaved shakarahad, pourahad (Հոտաւէտ շաքարաՀատ, բուրաՀատ)
pastime - zhamants, uzposank (ժամանց, զբօսանք)
pastor - hoviv, karozich, badveli (Հովիւ, քարոզիչ, պատուելի)
pastoral - hovvagan (Հովուական)
pastorate - hovvoutiun, karozchoutiun (Հովուութիւն, քարոզչութիւն)
pastry - dzagh, anousheghen, khumoreghen (ծաղ, անուշեղէն, խմորեղէն)
pasturage - arod, arodavayr, arodadegh, aradzetsoum (արօտ, արօտավայր, արօրատեղ, արածեցում)
pasture - arod, ger, jarag, khod, aradzil, aradzel (արօտ, կեր, ճարակ, խոտ, արածիլ, արածել)
pasty - khumorayin, khumoranuman, gargantag (խմորային, խմո–

բանման, կարկանդակ)

pat - shoyel, shoyank, gudor garaki, sherd, jisht (շոյել, շոյանք, կտոր՝ կարագի, շերտ, ճիշդ)

patch - gargudan, gudor, hoghi mas. gargudnel, norokel (կարկտան, կտոր, Հողի մաս, կարկտնել, նորոգել)

pate - kuloukh, khelabad (գլուխ, խելապատ)

patent - menashunorh, ardonakir, haydni, ardonakurel (մենաշնորհ, արտօնագիր, յայտնի, արտօնագրել)

patentee - ardonader, menashunorhyal (արտօնատէր, մենաշնորհեալ)

pater - hayr (Հայր)

paternal - hayragan, horenagan, hayreni (Հայրական, Հօրենական, Հայրենի)

paternity - hayroutiun (Հայրութիւն)

Paternoster - hayr mer, derounagan aghotk (Հայր Մեր, Տէրունական Աղօթք)

path - arahed, jampa, shavigh, untatsk (արահետ, ճամբայ, շաւիղ, ընթացք)

pathetic - surdahouyz, surdasharzh, hokekhurov, houzich (սրտայոյզ, սրտաշարժ, Հոգեխռով, յուզիչ)

pathetical - houzich, voghormeli (յուզիչ, ողորմելի)

pathfinder - hedakhouyz (Հետախոյզ)

pathogenesis - akhdadzunoutiun (ախտածնութիւն)

pathologic - akhdapanagan (ախտաբանական)

pathologist - akhdapan (ախտաբան)

pathology - akhdapanoutiun (ախտաբանութիւն)

pathos - houzelou shunorh, khoroung uzkatsoum (յուզելու շնորհ, խորունկ զգացում)

pathway - arahed, gadzan, nurpoughi (արահետ, կածան, նրբուղի)

patience - hamperoutiun, haradevoutiun (Համբերութիւն, յարատեւութիւն)

patient - hamperogh, hamperadar, hivant (Համբերող, Համբերատար, Հիւանդ)

patiently - hamperoutiamp, hantardoutiamp (Համբերութեամբ, Հանդարտութեամբ)

patio - nerknakavit, nersi pag (ներքնագաւիթ, ներսի բակ)

patois - kavaraparpar, ramgaparpar (գաւառաբարբառ, ռամկաբարբառ)

patriarcal - badriarkagan (պատրիարքական)

patriarch - badriark, nahabed, azkabed (պատրիարք, նաՀապետ, ազգապետ)

patriarchate - badriarkoutiun, badriarkaran (պատրիարքութիւն, պատրիարքարան)

patriarchy - badriarkoutiun (պատրիարքութիւն)

patrician - aznuvagan, aznuvazarm, badrigian (ազնուական, ազնուազարմ, պատրիկեան)

patricide - hayrasban (Հայրասպան)

patrimonial - yegeghetsabadgan, horenagan zharank (եկեղեցապատկան, Հօրենական ժառանգ)

patrimony - yegeghetsabadgan galvadz, horenagan zharank (եկեղեցապատկան կալուած, Հօրենական ժառանգ)

patriot - hayrenaser, azkaser (Հայրենասէր, ազգասէր)

patriotic - hayrenasiragan, azkasiragan (Հայրենասիրական, ազգասիրական)

patriotism - hayrenasiroutiun (Հայրենասիրութիւն)

patrol - bahag, bahagashurchig, bahagashurchil (պաՀակ, պաՀակաշրջիկ, պաՀակաշրջիլ)

patron - der, bashban, kordzader, khunamagal (տէր, պաշտպան, գործատէր, խնամակալ)

patronage - hovanavoroutiun, khunamagaloutiun (Հովանաւորութիւն, խնամակալութիւն)

patroness - bashdbanouhi, kordzadirouhi (պաշտպանուՀի, գործատիրուՀի)

patronize - hovanavorel, bashdbanel,

oknel (հովանաւորել, պաշտպանել, օգնել)
patroon - dander, hoghader (տանտէր, հողատէր)
patten - paydamoujag, payde vodnaman, sandal (փայտամուճակ, փայտէ ոտնաման, սանտալ)
patter - duropel, meghm zarnel, totovel, duropoum (տրոփել, մեղմ զարնել, թոթովել, տրոփում)
pattern - gaghabar, numouysh, nakhadib, orinagel (կաղապար, նմոյշ, նախատիպ, օրինակել)
paucity - kichoutiun, sagavoutiun (քիչութիւն, սակաւութիւն)
paunch - por, vorovayn, usdamoks (փոր, որովայն, ստամոքս)
pauper - mouratsgan, aghkad, chukavor, kheghj (մուրացկան, աղքատ, չքաւոր, խեղճ)
pauperism - chukavoroutiun, aghkadoutiun (չքաւորութիւն, աղքատութիւն)
pauperize - aghkadatsunel (աղքատացնել)
pause - tatar, michots, luroutiun, genal, gank arnel (դադար, միջոց, լռութիւն, կենալ, կանգ առնել)
pave - salahadagel, salargel, hartel, hadagel (սալայատակել, սալարկել, հարթել, յատակել)
pavement - mayt, salahadag, salargoum (մայթ, սալայատակ, սալարկում)
pavilion - daghavar, vuran, dzadzg, khoran, vuranadzadzgel (տաղաւար, վրան, ծածկ, խորան, վրանածածկել)
paving - salargoum, salarg (սալարկում, սալարկ)
paw - tat, jiran, jang, jangel, porel, tatel (թաթ, ճիրան, ճանկ, ճանկել, փորել, թաթել)
pawl - sughotsatsev aniv (սղոցաձեւ անիւ)
pawn - kurav, avant, kurav tunel, vudankel (գրաւ, աւանդ, գրաւ դնել, վտանգել)
pawnor - kuravadou (գրաւատու)
pax - voghchouyn, hampouyr, hashdoutiun (ողջոյն, համբոյր, հաշտութիւն)
pay - vujarel, hadoutsanel, dal, vujaroum (վճարել, հատուցանել, տալ, վճարում)
payable - vujareli (վճարելի)
paycheck - ashkhadachek, ashkhadavarts (աշխատաչէք, աշխատավարձ)
payday - vujarman or (վճարման օր)
payee - kantsogh, vujararou (գանձող, վճարառու)
payer - vujarogh, hadoutsanogh (վճարող, հատուցանող)
paymaster - kantsabah (գանձապահ)
payment - vujaroum, hadoutsoum, badizh (վճարում, հատուցում, պատիժ)
payoff - hadoputsanel, hashivu makrel, garkaturel (հատուցանել, հաշիւը մաքրել, կարգադրել)
payout - kagel, toultsunel, vujarel (քակել, թուլցնել, վճարել)
payroll - ashkhadavarts, vujaratsouyts (աշխատավարձ, վճարացոյց)
pay-per-view - vujarovi tidel- heradesilen (վճարովի դիտել՝հեռատեսիլէն)
pea - volor, siser (ոլոռ, սիսեռ)
peace - khaghaghoutiun, hantardoutiun, hashdoutiun (խաղաղութիւն, հանդարտութիւն, հաշտութիւն)
peaceful - khaghaghaser, hantard, khaghagh (խաղաղասէր, հանդարտ, խաղաղ)
peacefully - khaghaghoren, hantardoren, meghmoren (խաղաղօրէն, հանդարտօրէն, մեղմօրէն)
peacemaker - hashdarar (հաշտարար)
peach - teghts, teghtseni, madnel, ampasdanel (դեղձ, դեղձենի, մատնել, ամբաստանել)
peacock - siramark, tsoutsamol (սիրամարգ, ցուցամոլ)
peak - kakat, gadar, sar, tsutsvil, partsuranal, dungel (գագաթ, կատար, սար, ցցուիլ, բարձրանալ,

տնկել)
peal - vorodoum, ghoghanch, tuntiun, vorodal, tuntal (որոտում, ղօղանջ, թնդիւն, որոտալ, թնդալ)
pean - haghterk (յաղթերգ)
peanut - kednabisdag (գետնապիստակ)
pear - dants (տանձ)
pearl - markarid, sadap (մարգարիտ, սատափ)
pearly - markardia, markardapayl (մարգարտեայ, մարգարտափայլ)
peasant - kiughatsi, keghchoug, shinagan (գիւղացի, գեղջուկ, շինական)
peasantry - kiughatsioutiun (գիւղացիութիւն)
peat - gizahogh, hoghadzoukh, turik (կիզահող, հողածուխ, թրիք)
pebble - khij, manrakhij, gobij, vosbunabagi, khujel (խիճ, մանրախիճ, կոպիճ, ոսպնապակի, խճել)
peccable - meghanchagan (մեղանչական)
peccancy - meghk, meghavoroutiun (մեղք, մեղաւորութիւն)
peccant - meghanchogh, meghavor, hantsavor, vad, char (մեղանչող, մեղաւոր, յանցաւոր, վատ, չար)
peccary - varaz, andarakhoz (վարազ, անտառախոզ)
peccavi - megha (մեղայ)
pecentor - tubrbed, yerazhushdabed (դպրապետ, երաժշտապետ)
peck - tez, gouyd, pazmoutiun, gudtsel, porel (դէզ, կոյտ, բազմութիւն, կտցել, փորել)
pecker - gudtsogh, purich, paydpor (կտցող, բրիչ, փայտփոր)
pecktoral - gourdski, gurdskayin, lanchayin (կուրծքի, կրծքային, լանջային)
peculate - shortel, iuratsunel, koghnal (շորթել, իւրացնել, գողնալ)
peculation - youratsoum, gorzoum, koghoutiun (իւրացում, կորզում, գողութիւն)
peculator - iuratsunogh, gorzogh, kogh (իւրացնող, կորզող, գող)
peculiar - masnavor, hadoug, sepagan, ourouyn (մասնաւոր, յատուկ, սեփական, ուրոյն)
peculiarity - arantsnahadgoutiun (առանձնայատկութիւն)
peculiarize - masnavorel (մասնաւորել)
pecuniarily - turamabes, turamaganoren (դրամապէս, դրամականօրէն)
pecuniary - turamagan, usdagi (դրամական, ստակի)
pedagog, pedagogue - mangavarzh, vardzabed, (մանկավարժ, վարժապետ)
pedagogic - mangavarzhagan (մանկավարժական)
pedagogics - mangavarzhoutiun (մանկավարժութիւն)
pedagogy - mangavarzhoutiun (մանկավարժութիւն)
pedal - vodki, vodnag, vodnagal (ոտքի, ոտնակ, ոտնակալ)
pedant - imasdag, sopesd, sunabardz (իմաստակ, սոփեստ, սնապարծ)
pedantry - imasdagoutiun (իմաստակութիւն)
peddle - perezagel, shurchelov dzakhel (փերեզակել, շրջելով ծախել)
peddler - perezag, shurchoun manravajar (փերեզակ, շրջուն մանրավաճառ)
peddlery - perezagoutiun, perezeghenk (փերեզակութիւն, փերեզեղէնք)
peddling - perezagoutiun (փերեզակութիւն)
pedestal - bavdantan, himk, khariskh, vodk (պատուանդան, հիմք, խարիսխ, ոտք)
pedestrian - hediodun, vodkov (հետիոտն, ոտքով)
pediatric - mangapouzhagan (մանկաբուժական)
pediatrician - mangapouyzh (մանկաբոյժ)
pediatrics - mangapouzhoutiun (մանկաբուժութիւն)
pedicure - vodnatarman, vodnapouzhoutiun (ոտնադարման, ոտնաբու–

բուժութիւն)
pedometer - kaylachap, oughechap (քայլաչափ, ուղեչափ)
peel - geghev, mashg, geghvel, kertel, hanel (կեղեւ, մաշկ, կեղուել, քերթել, հանել)
peeler - geghvogh, goghobdich, vosdigan (կեղուող, կողոպտիչ, ոստիկան)
peep - yerevnal, jurvoghjel, yerevoum, jurvoghiun (երեւնալ, ճռուողել, երեւում, ճռուողիւն
peeper - noradzin, achk, lurdes, kaghdakoghi tidogh (նորածին, աչք, լրտես, գաղտագողի դիտող)
peer - yerevnal, lurdesel, havasar, zouyk, aznuvagan (երեւնալ, լրտեսել, հաւասար, զոյգ, ազնուական)
peerage - aznuvaganoutiun (ազնուականութիւն)
peeress - aznuvaganouhi, lordouhi (ազնուականուհի, լորտուհի)
peerless - anzoukagan, annuman, aznuvagan (անզուգական, աննման, ազնուական)
peevish - tazhan, andaneli, gurvarar (դաժան, անտանելի, կռուարար)
peg - seb, tsits, amratsunel, hasdadel, haradevel (սեպ, ցից, ամրացնել, հաստատել, յարատեւել)
pegging - amratsunel, gayounatsunel (ամրացնել, կայունացնել)
pelf - turam, shah, vasdag, harusdoutiun (դրամ, շահ, վաստակ, հարստութիւն)
pelican - havalousun, yergaragudouts turchoun (հաւալուսն, երկարակտուց թռչուն)
pell - gashi, mort, makaghat (կաշի, մորթ, մագաղաթ)
pellet - gudzig, kuntag, teghahad (կծիկ, գնդակ, դեղահատ)
pellicle - mashg, taghant, kulkhou tep (մաշկ, թաղանդ, գլխու թեփ)
pellucid - tapantsig, chinch, husdag (թափանցիկ, ջինջ, յստակ)
pell-mell - kharnikhourun, dagnouvura (խառնիխուռն, տակնուվրայ)
pelt - mort, gashi, zarnuvadzk, zarnel, kargodzel (մորթ, կաշի, զարնուածք, զարնել, քարկոծել)
peltry - moushdageghenk, morteghenner (մուշտակեղէնք, մորթեղէններ)
pelvis - gonk, vorovaynagonk (կոնք, որովայնակոնք)
pen - kurich, dzayr, pedrakurich, kurel, sharaturel (գրիչ, ծայր, փետրագրիչ, գրել, շարադրել)
pen name - kurchanoun, dzadzganoun (գրչանուն, ծածկանուն)
pen stock - kurchadoup (գրչատուփ)
penal - badzhagan (պատժական)
penalize - badzhel, doukanel (պատժել, տուգանել)
penalty - badizh, doukank (պատիժ, տուգանք)
penance - abashkharoutiun, zughchoum (ապաշխարութիւն, զղջում)
pence - peniner (փեններ) pl. of penny. Յգ. penny–ի:
pencil - madid, kurich, vurtsin, kudzel, nugarel (մատիտ, գրիչ, վրձին, գծել, նկարել)
pendant - gakhazart, ogh, chah, kint (կախազարդ, օղ, ջահ, գինդ)
pendent - argakh, gakh, chuloudzvadz (առկախ, կախ, չլուծուած)
pending - argakh, anorosh, dardam, michotsin, aden (առկախ, անորոշ, տարտամ, միջոցին, ատեն)
pendulous - jojoun, yereroun, dadanogh (ճօճուն, երերուն, տատանող)
pendulum - jojanag (ճօճանակ)
penetrable - tapantseli, tapantsig (թափանցելի, թափանցիկ)
penetrate - tapantsel, antsnil, aztel, hasgunal (թափանցել, անցնիլ, ազդել, հասկնալ)
penetration - tapantsoum, suramudoutiun, jeghkoum (թափանցում, սրամտութիւն, ճեղքում)
penguin - dzovasak, tevad turchoun (ծովասագ, թեւատ թռչուն)
penholder - kurchadoup, kurchagal, got (գրչատուփ, գրչակալ, կոթ)
peninsula - teragughzi (թերակղզի)
penis - arnantam, varots (առնանդամ, վարոց)
penitence - abashkharoutiun, zugh-

choum, abashav (ապաշխարութիւն, զղջում, ապաշաւ)
penitent - abashkharogh, zughchatsogh (ապաշխարող, զղջացող)
penitentiary - khosdovanadoun, abashkharhadoun (խոստովանատուն, ապաշխարատուն)
penknife - uzmeli (զմելի)
penman - keghakir, kurakir, madenakir (գեղագիր, գրագիր, մատենագիր)
penmanship - kheghakuroutiun (գեղագրութիւն)
penniless - chukavor, aghkad, angoudi (չքաւոր, աղքատ, անկուտի)
penniwise - khunayogh, gudzdzi (խնայող, կծծի)
penny - peni, sent (փենի, սենթ) - (pl. pennies, pence)
pensile - argakh, gakh, jojoun (առկախ, կախ, ճօճուն)
pension - gensatoshag, hadoutsoum, nubasd (կենսաթոշակ, հատուցում, նպաստ)
pensionary - toshagarou, hankusdian gochvadz (թոշակառու, հանգստեան կոչուած)
pensioner - toshagarou, toshagavor (թոշակառու, թոշակաւոր)
pensive - khohoun, mudakhoh, mudazpagh, dukhour (խոհուն, մտախոհ, մտազբաղ, տխուր)
pent - pagvadz, kotsvadz (փակուած, գոցուած)
Pentecost - hokekaloust, bendegosde (Հոգեգալուստ, Պենտեկոստէ)
penthouse - paydadzadzk, gakhdzadzk, vormahets (փայտածածք, կախածածք, որմայեց)
pentroof - sheghertik (շեղերդիք)
penult, penultimate - verchunter (վերջընթեր)
penumbra - gisasdver, terasdver (կիսաստուեր, թերաստուեր)
penurious - guddzi, kheghjoug, chukavor (կծծի, խեղճուկ, չքաւոր)
penury - aghkadoutiun, chukavoroutiun (աղքատութիւն, չքաւորութիւն)
people - zhoghovourt, martig, punagetsunel, pazmatsunel (ժողովուրդ, մարդիկ, բնակեցնել, բազմացնել)
pep - ouzh, arioutiun (ույժ, արիութիւն)
pepper - bughbegh, bughbeghel, harvadzel (պղպեղ, պղպեղել, հարուածել)
peppermint - ananoukh, ananoukhi yough (անանուխ, անանուխի իւղ)
peppery - bughbeghod, gudzou (պղպեղոտ, կծու)
peptic - marsoghagan, marsetsoutsich (մարսողական, մարսեցուցիչ)
per - ar, michots, yourakanchiur (առ, միջոց, իւրաքանչիւր)
peradventure - terevus, koutse, badahapar (թերեւս, գուցէ, պատահաբար)
perambulate - shurchil, shurchakayil, khouzargel (շրջիլ, շրջագայիլ, խուզարկել)
perambulation - shurchakayoutiun, aytseloutiun (շրջագայութիւն, այցելութիւն)
perambulator - shurchogh, mangasaylag (շրջող, մանկասայլակ)
perceivable - hasgunali, imanali, uzkali (հասկնալի, իմանալի, զգալի)
perceive - nushmarel, desnel, imanal, uzkal (նշմարել, տեսնել, իմանալ, զգալ)
perceiver - nushmarogh, hasgutsogh (նշմարող, հասկցող)
percentage - ar hariur (առ հարիւր)
perceptible - nushmareli, imanali, umpurneli (նշմարելի, իմանալի, ըմբռնելի)
perception - nushmaroum, umpurnoum, ungaloum (նշմարում, ըմբռնում, ընկալում)
perch - tsoghatsoug, tsogh, tar, taril (ձողաձուկ, ձող, թառ, թառիլ)
perchance - terevus, tibvadzov, badahmamp (թերեւս, դիպուածով, պատահմամբ)
percher - tarogh (թառող)
percipience - imatsoum, umpurnoghoutiun (իմացում, ըմբռնողութիւն)

percolate - zudel, kamel, zudvil, kamvil (զտել, քամել, զտուիլ, քամուիլ)
percolation - zudoum, kamoum (զտում, քամում)
percolator - kamots, kamich, zudots (քամոց, քամիչ, զտոց)
percuss - ouzhov zarnel (ուժով զարնել)
percussion - harvadz, pakhoum, untharoum, tsuntsoum (Հարուած, բախում, ընդՀարում, ցնցում)
perdition - gorousd, gordzanoum, averoum, tadabardoutiun (կորուստ, կործանում, աւերում, դատապարտութիւն)
peregrinate - bantukhdanal, odar yergirner taparil (պանդխտանալ, օտար երկիրներ Թափառիլ)
peregrination - bantukhdoutiun, odaroutiun (պանդխտութիւն, օտարութիւն)
peregrinator - bantoukhd, oughevor, darakunats (պանդուխտ, ուղեւոր, տարագնաց)
peregrine - odar (օտար)
peremptorily - patsartsagabes, vujraganoren (բացարձակապէս, վճռականօրէն)
peremptory - vujragan, anvijeli, anarargeli (վճռական, անվիճելի, անառարկելի)
perennial - daregan, devagan, mushdadev, chuchortsogh (տարեկան, տեւական, մշտատեւ, չչորցող)
perfect - gadarial, anteri, luman, luratsunel, gadarel (կատարեալ, անԹերի, լման, լրացնել, կատարել)
perfect binding - tughtagazm (Թղթակազմ)
perfection - gadareloutiun, anterioutiun (կատարելութիւն, անԹերիութիւն)
perfectionist - gadarelabashd, kerpudzakhuntir (կատարելապաշտ, գերբծախնդիր)
perfectly - gadarelabes, liovin, ampoghchovin (կատարելապէս, լիովին, ամբողջովին)
perfectness - gadareloutiun, anterioutiun (կատարելութիւն, անԹերիութիւն)
perfidious - nenkavor, tavajan, oukhdaturouzh (նենգաւոր, դաւաճան, ուխտադրուժ)
perfidiousness - nenkoutiun, anhavadarmoutiun (նենգութիւն, անՀաւատարմութիւն)
perfidy - nenkoutiun, khartakhoutiun, tav (նենգութիւն, խարդախութիւն, դաւ)
perforate - dzagel (ծակել)
perforation - dzagoum, dzagvadzk, dzag (ծակում, ծակուածք, ծակ)
perforator - dzagich, horadich (ծակիչ, Հորատիչ)
perforce - purni, usdiboghapar (բռնի, ստիպողաբար)
perform - gadarel, nergayatsunel, khaghal, unel (կատարել, ներկայացնել, խաղալ, ընել)
performance - nergayatsoum, gadaroum, kordzaturoutiun, ter (ներկայացում, կատարում, գործադրութիւն, դեր)
performer - gadarogh, terasan, teragadar (կատարող, դերասան, դերակատար)
performing - irakordzoum (իրագործում)
perfume - pourmounk, pouyr, anoushahodoutiun (բուրմունք, բոյր, անուշաՀոտութիւն)
perfumer - hodavajar, pouyravajar, pouroumnakordz (Հոտավաճառ, բոյրավաճառ, բուրումնագործ)
perfumery - pouravajaradoun, hodeghen, anoushavajaroutiun (բուրավաճառատուն, Հոտեղէն, անուշավաճառութիւն)
perfunctorily - anpoutoren, andarperoutiamp (անփուԹօրէն, անտարբերուԹեամբ)
perfunctoriness - anpoutoutiun (անփուԹութիւն)
perfunctory - anpouyt, anhok, andarper (անփոյԹ, անՀոգ, անտարբեր)
perfuse - surusgel, dzavalel, suprel,

tsoghel, liatsunel (սրսկել, ծաւալել, սփռել, ցօղել, լիացնել)

perfusion - surusgoum, voghoghoum, hamagoum (սրսկում, ողողում, Համակում)

pergola - sarpina, pousadzadzg badushkam (սարփինայ, բուսածածկ պատշգամ)

perhaps - terevus, koutse, havanapar (Թերեւս, գուցէ, Հաւանաբար)

pericarp - budghabadian, bargouj (պտղապատեան, պարկուճ)

peril - vudank, vunas, gorousd, vudankel (վտանգ, վնաս, կորուստ, վտանգել)

perilous - vudankavor, gorusdaper, portsanavor (վտանգաւոր, կորստաբեր, փորձանաւոր)

perimeter - shurchakidz, shurchabad, barakidz (շրջապատ, շրջագիծ, պարագիծ)

period - shurchan, bah, tashdan, verchaged (շրջան, պաՀ, դաշտան, վերջակէտ)

periodic - barperagan (պարբերական)

periodical - barperatert (պարբերաԹերԹ)

periphery - shurchabad, shurchagayk, arvartzan (շրջապատ, շրջակայք, արուարձան)

periphrasis - shurchapanoutiun, khoski tartsuvadzk (շրջաբանուԹիւն, խօսքի դարձուածք)

periscope - shurchatidag, shurchades, tidag untdzoviayi (շրջադիտակ, շրջատես, դիտակ ընդծովեայի)

perish - gorsuvil, gordzanil, pujanal, mernil (կորսուիլ, կործանիլ, փճանալ, մեռնիլ)

perishable - pujatsogh, avruvogh, gorusdagan, antsavor (փճացող, աւրուող, կորստական, անցաւոր)

periwig - geghdzam, geghdzam haktsunel (կեղծամ, կեղծամ Հագցնել)

perjure - turzhel, soud yertnoul (դրժել, սուտ երդնուլ)

perjured - khosdoumnaturouzh, yertoumnazants (խոստումնադրուժ, երդումնազանց)

perjurer - turzhogh, soud yertoum unogh (դրժող, սուտ երդում ընող)

perjury - yertumnazantsoutiun, soud yertoum (երդմնազանցուԹիւն, սուտ երդում)

perk - hubard, sek, gaydar, korozanal, sikal (Հպարտ, սէգ, կայտառ, գոռոզանալ, սիգալ)

perky - tsoutsamol, koroz, hantoukun, gaydar (ցուցամոլ, գոռոզ, յանդուգն, կայտառ)

permanence - devaganoutiun (տեւականուԹիւն)

permanency - devaganoutiun, mushdaganoutiun (տեւականուԹիւն, մշտականուԹիւն)

permanent - devagan, munayoun, anpopokh, mushdadev (տեւական, մնայուն, անփոփոխ, մշտատեւ)

permanently - devaganoren (տեւականօրէն)

permeable - tapantsig, tapantseli (Թափանցիկ, Թափանցելի)

permeate - tapantsel, antsnil, dzavalel, haketsunel (Թափանցել, անցնիլ, ծաւալել, յագեցնել)

permeation - tapantsoum, ners mudnelu (Թափանցում, ներս մտնելը)

permission - ardonoutiun, touyldououtiun, huraman (արտօնուԹիւն, ԹոյլտուուԹիւն, Հրաման)

permit - ardonel, toghoul, touyladurel, shunorhel, nerel (արտօնել, Թողուլ, Թոյլատրել, շնորՀել, ներել)

permittance - touylduvoutiun, huraman (ԹոյլտուուԹիւն, Հրաման)

permitter - touyladurogh, ardonogh (Թոյլատրող, արտօնող)

permutable - pokhanageli (փոխանակելի)

permutation - pokhanagoutiun, popokhoum (փոխանակուԹիւն, փոփոխում)

permute - pokhanagel (փոխանակել)

pernicious - vunasagar, vudankavor, charamid (վնասակար, վտանգաւոր, չարամիտ)

perorate - verjapanel (վերջաբանել)

peroration - verjapan jari (վերջաբան ճառի)
perpendicular - oughghahayiats (ուղղահայեաց)
perpetrate - kordzel-vojir, gadarel, kordzaturel (գործել՝ոճիր, կատարել, գործադրել)
perpetration - charakordzoutiun (չարագործութիւն)
perpetrator - charakordz (չարագործ)
perpetual - haradev, mushdadev, havidenagan, haverzhagan (յարատեւ, մշտատեւ, յաւիտենական, յաւերժական)
perpetuate - haverzhatsunel, anmahatsunel (յաւերժացնել, անմահացնել)
perpetuation - haverzhatsoum, mushdadevoutiun (յաւերժացում, մշտատեւութիւն)
perpetuity - mushdunchenaganoutiun, haverzhoutiun (մշտնջենականութիւն, յաւերժութիւն)
perplex - shuvaretsunel, abshetsunel, partatsunel, shupotel (շուարեցնել, ապշեցնել, բարդացնել, շփոթել)
perplexity - shupotoutiun, dadamsoum, varank (շփոթութիւն, տատամսում, վարանք)
perquisite - havelavarts, havelian hasouyt (յաւելավարձ, յաւելեալ հասոյթ)
perquisition - pundurdouk, khouzargoutiun (փնտռտուք, խուզարկութիւն)
perry - dantsoghi, dantsachour (տանձօղի, տանձաջուր)
persecute - haladzel, neghel, charcharel, hedabuntel (հալածել, նեղել, չարչարել, հետապնդել)
persecution - haladzank, haladzoum, neghoutiun (հալածանք, հալածում, նեղութիւն)
persecutor - haladzogh, haladzich, hedabuntogh (հալածող, հալածիչ, հետապնդող)
perseverance - haradevoutiun (յարատեւութիւն)
persevere - haradevel, sharounagel, buntel, timanal (յարատեւել, շարունակել, պնդել, դիմանալ)
Persia - barsgasdan (Պարսկաստան)
persian - barsig, barsgeren, barsgagan (պարսիկ, պարսկերէն, պարսկական)
persiflage - heknoutiun, shaghaguradoum (հեգնութիւն, շաղակրատում)
persist - devel, haradevel, dogal, sharounagel (տեւել, յարատեւել, տոկալ, շարունակել)
persistence, cy - haradevoutiun, dogounoutiun (յարատեւութիւն, տոկունութիւն)
persistent - haradevogh, dogoun, devagan, munayoun (յարատեւող, տոկուն, տեւական, մնայուն)
person - ants, antsnavoroutiun, vomun, eag, temk (անձ, անձնաւորութիւն, ոմն, էակ, դէմք)
personage - antsnavoroutiun, ants (անձնաւորութիւն, անձ)
personal - antsnagan, anhadagan (անձնական, անհատական)
personality - antsnavoroutiun, anhadaganoutiun (անձնաւորութիւն, անհատականութիւն)
personalize - antsnavorel (անձնաւորել)
personally - antsnabes, anhadapar, antsamp (անձնապէս, անհատաբար, անձամբ)
personate - antsunavorel, teragadarel, khaghal, geghdzel (անձնաւորել, դերակատարել, խաղալ, կեղծել)
personification - antsnaganatsoum, marmnatsoum (անձնականացում, մարմնացում)
personify - antsnavorel, marmunatsunel (անձնաւորել, մարմնացնել)
personnel - antsnagazm, bashdoneoutiun (անձնակազմ, պաշտօնէութիւն)
perspective - heranugar, heraged, herabadger, houys (հեռանկար, հեռակէտ, հեռապատկեր, յոյս)
perspicacious - surades, husdaga-

des, suramid, gorovi (սրատես, յստակատես, սրամիտ, կորովի)
perspicacity - suradesoutiun, khoratapantsoutiun (սրատեսութիւն, խորաթափանցութիւն)
perspicuity - husdagoutiun, suradesoutiun (յստակութիւն, սրատեսութիւն)
perspicuous - baydzar, husdag, vorosh, agnerev (պայծառ, յստակ, որոշ, ակներեւ)
perspiration - kurdink, kurdunoum (քրտինք, քրտնում)
perspire - kurdunil, kurduntsunel (քրտնիլ, քրտնցնել)
persuade - hamozel, havadatsunel, havnetsunel (Համոզել, Հաւատացնել, Հաւնեցնել)
persuasion - hamozoum, havadk (Համոզում, Հաւատք)
persuasive - hamozich, vusdaheli (Համոզիչ, վստահելի)
pert - hantoukun, gobid, lirp (յանդուգն, կոպիտ, լիրբ)
pertain - veraperil, badganil (վերաբերիլ, պատկանիլ)
pertinacious - hamar, buntajagad, hasdad (յամառ, պնդաճակատ, Հաստատ)
pertinence, cy - badshajoutiun, harmaroutiun (պատշաճութիւն, յարմարութիւն)
pertinent - badshaj, harmar, vayelouch, deghin (պատշաճ, յարմար, վայելուչ, տեղին)
pertinently - badshajoren (պատշաճօրէն)
pertly - gobdoren, lurporen (կոպտօրէն, լրբօրէն)
pertness - lurpoutiun, gobdoutiun (լրբութիւն, կոպտութիւն)
perturb - khankarel, khurovel, vakhtsunel, mudahokel (խանգարել, խռովել, վախցնել, մտաՀոգել)
perturbation - kharnagoutiun, khurovoutiun (խառնակութիւն, խռովութիւն)
pertusion - dzagodoutiun (ծակոտութիւն)
peruke - geghdzam (կեղծամ)
perusal - untertsoum, verdzanoum, verloudzoum (ընթերցում, վերծանում, վերլուծում)
pervade - tapantsel, daradzvil, diranal (թափանցել, տարածուիլ, տիրանալ)
pervasion - tapantsoum, khoratsoum (թափանցում, խորացում)
pervasive - tapantsogh, antsnogh (թափանցող, անցնող)
perverse - khatarvadz, aylaseradz, gamagor, char (խաթարուած, այլասերած, կամակոր, չար)
perversion - sheghoum, khodouroum, kheghatiuroum, aylaseroum (շեղում, խոտորում, խեղաթիւրում, այլասերում)
perversive - kheghatiurich (խեղաթիւրիչ)
pervert - moloretsunel, aghavaghel, moloradz, ouratsogh (մոլորեցնել, աղաւաղել, մոլորած, ուրացող)
pervious - tapantseli, tiuramoud (թափանցելի, դիւրամուտ)
perviousness - tapantselioutiun (թափանցելիութիւն)
pessimism - horedesoutiun (յոռետեսութիւն)
pessimist - horedes (յոռետես)
pest - zhandakhd, hamajarag, aghed (ժանտախտ, Համաճարակ, աղէտ)
pester - charcharel, neghel, tsantsuratsunel (չարչարել, նեղել, ձանձրացնել)
pestiferous - vunasaper, mahatsou, zhandaper (վնասաբեր, մաՀացու, ժանտաբեր)
pestilence - zhandakhd, hamajarag, zhandamah (ժանտախտ, Համաճարակ, ժանտամաՀ)
pestle - santagot, tag, manratsunel, pushrel (սանդղակոթ, թակ, մանրացնել, փշրել)
pet - sireli, undani gentali, kukvel, shoyel (սիրելի, ընտանի կենդանի, գգուել, շոյել)
petal - dzaghgaderev, dzaghgatert (ծաղկատերեւ, ծաղկաթերթ)
peter - usbaril, halil, khonchil (սպառիլ, Հալիլ, խոնջիլ)

petition - khunturank, aghachank, khunturel, aghachel (խնդրանք, աղաչանք, խնդրել, աղաչել)
petitioner - khunturargou, aghersogh (խնդրարկու, աղերսող)
petrel - murrugahav (մրրկահաւ)
petrifaction, petrification - karatsoum (քարացում)
petrify - karanal, karatsunel, abshetsunel (քարանալ, քարացնել, ապշեցնել)
petrol - kariugh (քարիւղ)
petroleum - naft, kariugh (նաֆթ, քարիւղ)
petrous - karod, karanuman, katayin (քարոտ, քարանման, քարային)
petticoat - vudavag, gisazkesd ganants (վտաւակ, կիսազգեստ կանանց)
pettifog - kashkushel, kheghi pasdapanoutiun unel (քաշքշել, խեղճ փաստաբանութիւն ընել)
pettifogger - kashkushogh, imasdag, kheghj pasdapan (քաշքշող, իմաստակ, խեղճ փաստաբան)
pettiness - tsadzoutiun, pokroutiun, nuvasdoutiun (ցածութիւն, փոքրութիւն, նուաստութիւն)
pettish - khozhor, tiurakurkir, tek (խոժոռ, դիւրագրգիռ, դէգ)
pettishness - tuzhvarahajoutiun, surdneghoutiun (դժուարահաճութիւն, սրտնեղութիւն)
petto - gourdzk, dzots (կուրծք, ծոց)
petty - chunchin, manur, usdorin, pouj, tsadz (չնչին, մանր, ստորին, փուճ, ցած)
petulance, cy - tiurakurkuroutiun, tsasgodoutiun, tap (դիւրագրգռութիւն, ցասկոտութիւն, թափ)
petulant - khozhor, tiurakurkir, sasdig, pourun (խոժոռ, դիւրագրգիռ, սաստիկ, բուռն)
pew - nusdaran yegeghetsiyi (նստարան եկեղեցիի)
pewee, peewee - janjors, gudtsar, hobob (ճանճորս, կտցար, յոպոպ)
pewit, peewit - hobob, gudtsar, janjors (յոպոպ, կտցար, ճանճորս)
pewter - anak, anakeghen (անագ, անագեղէն)
pewterer - anakakordz (անագագործ)
phalanges - paghankner, khoumper, vashder (փաղանգներ, խումբեր, վաշտեր)
phalanx - paghank, khoump, vashd փաղանգ, խումբ, վաշտ
phallus - arnantam, varots (առնանդամ, վարոց)
phanerite - desaneli, haydni (տեսանելի, յայտնի)
phantasm - ourvagan, tsunork, desil (ուրուական, ցնորք, տեսիլ)
phantasmagoria - tsunoradesilk, ourvadesilk (ցնորատեսիլք, ուրուատեսիլք)
phantom - voki, ourvagan, tsunork (ոգի, ուրուական, ցնորք)
pharaoh - paravon (փարաւոն)
pharisaism - parisetsioutiun (փարիսեցիութիւն)
pharisee - parisetsi (փարիսեցի)
pharmaceutical - teghakordzagan, teghakidagan (դեղագործական, դեղագիտական)
pharmaceutics - teghakordzoutiun, teghakidoutiun (դեղագործութիւն, դեղագիտութիւն)
pharmaceutist, pharmacist - teghakordz (դեղագործ)
pharmacology - teghakidoutiun, teghapanoutiun (դեղագիտութիւն, դեղաբանութիւն)
pharmacy - tegharan, teghadoun, teghakordzoutiun (դեղարան, դեղատուն, դեղագործութիւն)
pharos - paros, lousashdarag (փարոս, լուսաշտարակ)
pharynx - gogort, pogh (կոկորդ, փող)
phase - poul, asdijan, yerevouyt, tsev, gerbarank (փուլ, աստիճան, երեւոյթ, ձեւ, կերպարանք)
phasel - loupia (լուբիա)
pheasant - pasian (փասիան)
phenomena - yerevouytner (երեւոյթներ) - pl.–յգ. phenomenon-ի

phenomenal - yerevoutagan, zarmanali, uskancheli (երեւութական, զարմանալի, սքանչելի)
phenomenon - yerevouyt, desil, uskanchelik (երեւոյթ, տեսիլ, սքանչելիք)
phial - survag, shish (սրուակ, շիշ)
philander - sirapanil, kudznil, tarbasel, godurduvil (սիրաբանիլ, քծնիլ, դարպասել, կոտրտուիլ)
philanderer - gunamol, kudznogh (կնամոլ, քծնող)
philanthropic - martasiragan (մարդասիրական)
philanthropy - martasiroutiun, paresiroutiun (մարդասիրութիւն, բարեսիրութիւն)
philatelist - turoshmatought havakogh (դրոշմաթուղթ հաւաքող)
philately - turoshmahavakoum (դրոշմահաւաքում)
philharmonic - yerazhushdaser, yerashuzhdasiragan (երաժշտասէր, երաժշտասիրական)
philharmony - yerazhushdasiroutiun (երաժշտասիրութիւն)
philologer, philologist - panaser, lezvapan (բանասէր, լեզուաբան)
philologic - panasiragan, lezvakidagan (բանասիրական, լեզուագիտական)
philologize - panasirel (բանասիրել)
philology - panasiroutiun, lezvapanoutiun (բանասիրութիւն, լեզուաբանութիւն)
philomath - ousoumnaser (ուսումնասէր)
philomathy - ousoumnasiroutiun (ուսումնասիրութիւն)
philosopher - pilisopa, imasdaser (փիլիսոփայ, իմաստասէր)
philosophic - pilisopayagan, imasdasiragan (փիլիսոփայական, իմաստասիրական)
philosophist - imasdag, geghdz pilisopa (իմաստակ, կեղծ փիլիսոփայ)
philosophize - pilisopayel, imasdasirel (փիլիսոփայել, իմաստասիրել)
philosophy - pilisopayoutiun, imasdasiroutiun (փիլիսոփայութիւն, իմաստասիրութիւն)
phlegm - khoukh, khulink, baghariunoutiun (խուխ, խլինք, պաղարիւնութիւն)
phlegmatic - baghariun, andarper, sarnariun (պաղարիւն, անտարբեր, սառնարիւն)
phoenix, phenix - piunig, armavahav, anmahoutiun (փիւնիկ, արմաւահաւ, անմահութիւն)
phonation - tsaynargoutiun, tsaynaduvoutiun (ձայնարկութիւն, ձայնատուութիւն)
phone - tsayn, heratsayn, heratsaynel (ձայն, հեռաձայն, հեռաձայնել)
phonetic - tsaynagan, tsayni (ձայնական, ձայնի)
phonetics - hunchiunapanoutiun, tsaynakidoutiun (հնչիւնաբանութիւն, ձայնագիտութիւն)
phonic - tsaynagan, hunchagan, hunchiunayin (ձայնական, հնչական, հնչիւնային)
phonogram - tsaynakidz, sughakrakir (ձայնագիծ, սղագրագիր)
phonograph - tsaynakir (ձայնագիր)
phonographer - tsaynakurich (ձայնագրիչ)
phonography - tsaynakuroutiun (ձայնագրութիւն)
phosphate - lousadzunad, fosfat (լուսածնատ, ֆոսֆաթ)
phosphor - pospor, lousaper (փոսփոր, լուսաբեր)
phosphorate - lousadzunel (լուսածնել)
phosphorescent - lousapayl, posporapayl (լուսափայլ, փոսփորափայլ)
phosphorous - lousadzin, lousadznayin, posporayin (լուսածին, լուսածնային, փոսփորային)
photo - lousanugar (լուսանկար)
photo shop - lousanugarchadoun (լուսանկարչատուն)
photocopier - lousadubogh, lousadib mekena (լուսատպող, լուսատիպ մեքենայ)
photocopy - lousabadjen, lousadib,

lousadubel (լուսապատճէն, լուսատիպ, լուսատպել)
photogenic - *lousakegh, keghatem, lousanugarchagan timakidz* (լուսագեղ, գեղադէմ, լուսանկարչական դիմագիծ)
photograph - *lousanugar, lousanugarel* (լուսանկար, լուսանկարել)
photographer - *lousanugarich* (լուսանկարիչ)
photography - *lousanugarchoutiun* (լուսանկարչութիւն)
photogravure - *lousakuroutiun, lousaporakuroutiun* (լուսագրութիւն, լուսափորագրութիւն)
photolithography - *lousavimakuroutiun* (լուսավիմագրութիւն)
photometer - *lousachap* (լուսաչափ)
photoplay - *badgerakhagh* (պատկերախաղ)
phototelegraphy - *lousaherakir* (լուսահեռագիր)
phototherapy - *lousapouzhoutiun* (լուսաբուժութիւն)
phototypesetter - *lousadib* (լուսատիպ)
phototypsetter - *lousadib* (լուսատիպ)
phrase - *nakhatasoutiun, voj, khosk, ardahaydel* (նախադասութիւն, ոճ, խօսք, բանահիւսել)
phraseology - *asatsvadzk, vojapanoutiun* (ասացուածք, ոճաբանութիւն)
phrenetic - *vayrak, khent, kelatsunor* (վայրագ, խենդ, խելացնոր)
phrenitis - *ougheghadab, kangadab* (ուղեղատապ, գանկատապ)
phrenologist - *kangapan* (գանկաբան)
phrenology - *kangapanoutiun* (գանկաբանութիւն)
phthisic, al - *tokakhdavor, huidzakhdavor* (թոքախտաւոր, հիւծախտաւոր)
phthisis - *tokaghgt, huidzakhd* (թոքախտ, հիւծախտ)
phut - *baytiun* (պայթիւն)
physic - *puzhushgoutiun, tegh, pouzhel, puzhushgel* (բժշկութիւն, դեղ, բուժել, բժշկել)
physical - *marmunagan, nuitagan, punakidagan* (մարմնական, նիւթական, բնագիտական)
physically - *marmunabes, fizikabes* (մարմնապէս, ֆիզիքապէս)
physician - *puzhishg* (բժիշկ)
physics - *punakidoutiun* (բնագիտութիւն)
physiognomist - *timajanach, temki megnapan* (դիմաճանաչ, դէմքի մեկնաբան)
physiognomy - *timakidz, gerbarank, timakidoutiun* (դիմագիծ, կերպարանք, դիմագիտութիւն)
physiologer, physiologist - *punakhos* (բնախօս)
physiologic - *punakhosagan* (բնախօսական)
physiology - *punakhosoutiun, martagazmoutiun* (բնախօսութիւն, մարդակազմութիւն)
physique - *punagazmoutiun* (բնակազմութիւն)
pianist - *tashnagahar* (դաշնակահար)
piano - *tashnag, tashnamour, meghm tashnagaharoutiun* (դաշնակ, դաշնակահար, մեղմ դաշնակահարութիւն)
piaster - *tahegan* (դահեկան)
piazza - *hurabarag* (հրապարակ)
pica - *andzegh, gachaghag, 12 ged darachap, aghotakirk* (անծեղ, կաչաղակ, 12 կէտ տառաչափ, աղօթագիրք)
picaroon - *argadzakhuntir, avazag, dzovahen* (արկածախնդիր, աւազակ, ծովահէն)
pick - *purich, gudtsel, dzagel, kaghel, undurel* (բրիչ, կտցել, ծակել, քաղել, ընտրել)
picked - *undir, zadvadz, sour, suradzayr, pushod tsoug* (ընտիր, զատուած, սուր, սրածայր, փշոտ ձուկ)
picker - *havakogh, kaghogh, vertsunogh* (հաւաքող, քաղող, վերցնող)
picket - *tsits, tsogh, tsangabadel* (ցից, ձող, ցանկապատել)

picking - havakoum, kaghoum, vertsunoum, jurakagh (հաւաքում, քաղում, վերցնում, ճրաքաղ)
pickle - tutvash, aghchour, anarag, aghel, aghchurel (թթուաշ, աղջիւր, անառակ, աղել, աղջրել)
pickles - tutvash, aghtsan-panchareghеni (թթուած, աղցան՝ բանջարեղէնի)
pickpocket - kusagahad, kogh (քսակահատ, գող)
picnic - tashdakunatsoutiun, uzposakhunjouyk (դաշտագնացութիւն, զբօսախնճոյք)
picnicking - hatsgerouyt ounenal, uzposakhunjouykin jashel (հացկերոյթ ունենալ, զբօսախնճոյքին ճաշել)
pictorial - nugarazart, badgerazart (նկարազարդ, պատկերազարդ)
picture - badger, nugar, timanugar, nugarel, badgerel (պատկեր, նկար, դիմանկար, նկարել, պատկերել)
picture hanger - negaragal (նկարակալ)
picturesque - nugarakegh, nugarchagan, keghadesil (նկարագեղ, նկարչական, գեղատեսիլ)
pie - dzagh, musadzagh, gargantag, gachaghag (ծաղ, մսածաղ, կարկանդակ, կաչաղակ)
piebald - kouynuzkouyn, pazmerank, kharun (գոյնզգոյն, բազմերանգ, խառն)
piece - gudor, mas, pazhin, yerg, norokel, miatsunel (կտոր, մաս, բաժին, երկ, նորոգել, միացնել)
piecemeal - gudor gudor, asdijanapar, mas ar mas (կտոր կտոր, աստիճանաբար, մաս առ մաս)
piecer - gargudnogh, miatsunogh (կարկտնող, միացնող)
piecework - kordz kuloukh vujaroum (գործ գլուխ՝ վճարում)
pier - karap, gamaragal (քարափ, կամարակալ)
pierce - dzagel, mukhvil, tapantsel, mudnel (ծակել, մխուիլ, թափանցել, մտնել)
piety - parebashdoutiun, asdvadzavakhoutiun (բարեպաշտութիւն, աստուածավախութիւն)
pifler - shortel, koghnal. turtsunel (շորթել, գողնալ, թռցնել)
pig - khoz, khojgor, tsuknil, dabuldugil (խոզ, խոճկոր, ձգնիլ, տապլտկիլ)
pigeon - aghavni, miamid (աղաւնի, միամիտ)
piggen - sherep (շերեփ)
piggery, pigsty - khozanots (խոզանոց)
pigiron - chuzudvadz medagh (չզտուած մետաղ)
pigment - nerg, kouyn, kounaniut, kounadar (ներկ, գոյն, գունանիւթ, գունատարր)
pigmy, pygmy - kajaj, tuzoug (գաճաճ, թզուկ)
pike - dek, suvin, kaylatsoug, maksadoun kaghaki (տէգ, սուին, գայլաձուկ, մաքսատուն քաղաքի)
pile - tez, gouyd, garouyts, tsits, lousar, tizel (դէզ, կոյտ, կառոյց, ցից, լուսար, դիզել)
piled - tav, tavoud, guranvadz yergat (թաւ, թաւուտ, կռուանուած երկաթ)
pileous - mazod (մազոտ)
pilgrim - oukhdakunats, oukhdavor, oughevor, bantoukhd (ուխտագնաց, ուխտաւոր, ուղեւոր, պանդուխտ)
pilgrimage - oukhdakunatsoutiun, bantukhdoutiun (ուխտագնացութիւն, պանդխտութիւն)
pill - teghahad, geghev, geghvel, goghobdel (դեղահատ, կեղեւ, կեղուել, կողոպտել)
pillage - goghoboud, avar, goghobdel, tallel (կողոպուտ, աւար, կողոպտել, թալլել)
pillar - siun, netsoug, henaran (սիւն, նեցուկ, յենարան)
pillar-box - posdargugh (փոստարկղ)
pillory - anarkanki siun, nushavag, nushavagel (անարգանքի սիւն, նշաւակ, նշաւակել)
pillow - parts, kuloukhu partsi tunel (բարձ, գլուխը բարձի դնել)

pillow-slip - *partseres, partsi vura tunel* (բարրձերես, բարձի վրայ դնել)

pilose, pilous - *mazod, tavamaz* (մազոտ, թաւամազ)

pilosity - *mazodoutiun, tavoutiun* (մազոտութիւն, թաւութիւն)

pilot (n) - *otachu, otanavort, navavar, arachnort* (օդաչու, օդանաւորդ, նաւավար, առաջնորդ)

pilot (v) - *otanav varel, navavarel, arachnortel* (օդանաւ վարել, նաւավարել, առաջնորդել)

pilotage - *otanavavaroum, navavaroum* (օդանաւավարում, նաւավարում)

pimp (n) - *pozapouydz, pozaradz, gavad, gin haytaytogh* (բոզաբոյծ, բոզարած, կաւատ, կին հայթայթող)

pimp (v) - *gavadoutiun unel, anparoyoutian michnortel* (կաւատութիւն ընել, անբարոյութեան միջնորդել)

pimple - *pushdig, buzoug, shoud* (բշտիկ, պզուկ, շուտ)

pimpled, pimply - *balaraliz, pushdignerov li, shoudavor* (պալարալից, բշտիկներով լի, շուտաւոր)

pin - *kuntasegh, seb, kam, kuntaseghel* (գնդասեղ, սեպ, գամ, գնդասեղել)

pincase - *aseghaman* (ասեղաման)

pincers, pinchers - *aktsan, ouneli* (աքցան, ունելի)

pinch - *gusmit, gusmutel, seghmel, juzmel* (կսմիթ, կսմթել, սեղմել, ճզմել)

pincushion - *pokur aseghaman* (փոքր ասեղաման)

pine - *shoji, mayri, nuvaghil, halil, hiudzil* (շոճի, մայրի, նուաղիլ, հալիլ, հիւծիլ)

pineapple - *ananas, arkayakhuntsor* (անանաս, արքայախնձոր)

pinefold - *parakh, kom, pagaran* (փարախ, գոմ, փակարան)

ping - *shachiun, soulots kuntagi, shachel* (շաչիւն, սուլոց գնդակի, շաչել)

ping-pong - *seghani kuntakhagh, ping-pong* (սեղանի գնդախաղ, փինկ-փոնկ)

pinhole - *pokur patsvadzk* (փոքր բացուածք)

pinion - *tev, tevadzayr, pedour, tevadel, tevagabel* (թեւ, թեւածայր, փետուր, թեւատել, թեւակապել)

pink - *vartakouyn, shahokram, meghag, dibar, dzagdzugel* (վարդագոյն, շահոքրամ, մեղակ, տիպար, ծակծկել)

pinnace - *navag* (նաւակ)

pinnacle - *ashdarag, kakat, gadar* (աշտարակ, գագաթ, կատար)

pinnate, pinnated - *pedravor, pedratsev* (փետրաւոր, փետրաձեւ)

pint - *heghougacha - 1/8 gallon* (հեղուկաչափ – 1/8 կալոն)

pinup - *kuntaseghvadz-pagtsuvadz vormazt* (գնդասեղուած–փակցուած որմազդ)

pin-money - *gunoch hakousdi hamar durvadz turam* (կնոջ հագուստի համար տրուած դրամ)

pioneer - *rahvira, arachnort, yergrakhouyz, arachnortel* (ռահվիրայ, առաջնորդ, երկրախոյզ, առաջնորդել)

pious - *asdvadzavakh, parebashd, guronaser* (աստուածավախ, բարեպաշտ, կրօնասէր)

pip - *goud, goriz, ged, juval, jurvoghel* (կուտ, կորիզ, կէտ, ճուալ, ճռուողել)

pipe - *khoghovag, dzukhamorj, surink, surink nuvakel* (խողովակ, ծխամորճ, սրինգ, սրինգ նուագել)

pipeline - *naftadar, churadar, khoghovagashar* (նաւթատար, ջրատար, խողովակաշար)

pipkin - *budoug, gave aman* (պտուկ, կաւէ աման)

piquant - *gudzou, khaytogh, sour* (կծու, խայթող, սուր)

pique - *kuzhdoutiun, zayrouyt, zayratsunel, kurkurel* (գժտութիւն, զայրոյթ, զայրացնել, գրգռել)

piracy - *dzovahenoutiun, panakoghoutiun* (ծովահէնութիւն, բանա–

գողութիւն)
pirate - dzovahen, helouzag, panakogh, avazagel (ծովահէն, յելուզակ, բանագող, աւազակել)
pirating - panakoghoutiun, kurakoghoutiun (բանագողութիւն, գրագողութիւն)
piscina - khoranin gits kare avazan, tsugnaran (խորանին կից քարէ աւազան, ձկնարան)
piss - mez, mizel (մէզ, միզել)
pistachio - bisdag (պիստակ)
pistol - adurjanag, adurjanagel (ատրճանակ, ատրճանակել)
pistolet - pokur adurjanag (փոքր ատրճանակ)
piston - mukhots, sharzhagan kulan, hantsnararoutiun (մխոց, շարժական գլան, յանձնարարութիւն)
pit - pos, khuram, hor, kednavayr, porel, kurkurel (փոս, խրամ, հոր, գետնավայր, փորել, գրգռել)
pitapat - papakhoum, duropoum surdi (բաբախում, տրոփում սրտի)
pitch - tsiut, goubur, goubrabadel, panagil, nusdil (ձիւթ, կուպր, կուպրապատել, բանակիլ, նստիլ)
pitcher - artsagogh, gouzh, sapor (արձակող, կուժ, սափոր)
pitchy - goubrabad, sev, aghdod (կուպրապատ, սեւ, աղտոտ)
piteous - voghormeli, khughjali, parebashd (ողորմելի, խղճալի, բարեպաշտ)
pitfall - dzoughag, tagart, vorokayt (ծուղակ, թակարդ, որոգայթ)
pith - michoug, dzoudz pouysi, zoroutiun, ouzh (միջուկ, ծուծ բոյսի, զօրութիւն, ույժ)
pithy - michougod, ouzhegh, yerantoun (միջուկոտ, ուժեղ, եռանդուն)
pitiable - voghormeli, khughjali, kutali (ողորմելի, խղճալի, գթալի)
pitiful - voghormeli, khughjali, kutod, kutasird (ողորմելի, խղճալի, գթոտ, գթասիրտ)
pitiless - ankout, anoghorm (անգութ, անողորմ)
pity - kout, garegtsoutiun, kutal, garegtsil (գութ, կարեկցութիւն, գթալ, կարեկցիլ)
pivot - arantsk, netsoug, henag, surnag, budoudgil (առանցք, նեցուկ, յենակ, սռնակ, պտուտկիլ)
pix - masnadoup, surpadoup, tsiut (մասնատուփ, սրբատուփ, ձիւթ)
placability - tuirahashdoutiun (դիւրահաշտութիւն)
placable - meghmich, hantardetsunogh, tiurahashd (մեղմիչ, հանդարտեցուցիչ, դիւրահաշտ)
placard - aztakard, vormnakir, hurabaragel, vormakurel (ազդագիր, որմնագիր, հրապարակել, որմագրել)
placate - meghmel, sirdu arnel, shoyel (մեղմել, սիրտը առնել, շոյել)
place (n) - degh, vayr, tirk, asdijan, bashdon, hurabarag (տեղ, վայր, դիրք, աստիճան, պաշտօն, հրապարակ)
place (v) - deghavorel, hasdadel, tunel, zedeghel, garkel (տեղաւորել, հաստատել, դնել, զետեղել, կարգել)
placement - deghavoroum (տեղաւորում)
placer - deghavorogh, zedeghogh (տեղաւորող, զետեղող)
placid - hantard, khaghagh, hezatem (հանդարտ, խաղաղ, հեզադէմ)
placing - deghaturoum, deghavoroum, zedeghoum (տեղադրում, տեղաւորում, զետեղում)
plagiarism - panakoghoutiun (բանագողութիւն)
plagiarist - panakogh (բանագող)
plagiarize - panakoghel (բանագողել)
plagiary - panakoghoutiun (բանագողութիւն)
plague - zhandakhd, aghed, charik, danchel, neghel (ժանտախտ, աղէտ, չարիք, տանջել, նեղել)
plain (a) - hart, shidag, vorosh, daparag, barz, sovoragan (հարթ, շիտակ, որոշ, տափարակ, պարզ, սովորական)
plain (n) - tashd, tashdakedin, har-

tavayr (դաշտ, դաշտագետին, Հարթավայր)
plain (v) - hartel, daparagtsunel, barzel, tsavil (Հարթել, տափարակցնել, պարզել, ցաւիլ)
plainly - barzoren (պարզօրէն)
plainness - barzoutiun (պարզութիւն)
plainsman - tashdapunag (դաշտաբընակ)
plaint - durdounch, kankad, poghok, voghp (տրտունջ, գանգատ, բողոք, ողբ)
plaintiff - kankadogh, tad patsogh, tadakhaz (գանգատող, դատ բացող, դատախազ)
plaintive - voghpatsogh, kankadogh, takhdzod (ողբացող, գանգատող, թախծոտ)
plait - dzalk, hiusk, dzalel, huisel (ծալք, Հիւսք, ծալել, Հիւսել)
plan (n) - dzurakir, hadagakidz, kardes, ourvakidz (ծրագիր, յատակագիծ, քարտէս, ուրուագիծ)
plan (v) - dzurakurel, kudzakurel, tsevel (ծրագրել, գծագրել, ձեւել)
planch - dakhdagel (տախտակել)
planchette - seghan, daghdagi gudor (սեղան, տախտակի կտոր)
plane - hart, mageres, magartag, otanav, hartel (Հարթ, մակերես, մակարդակ, օդանաւ, Հարթել)
planet - molorag (մոլորակ)
planetarium - moloragatsouyts (մոլորակացոյց)
planetary - moloragayin (մոլորակային)
planish - dapagtsunel, harel, voghorgel (տափակցնել, Հարթել, ողորկել)
planisphere - hartakount (Հարթագունդ)
plank - hasd dakhdag, kaghakagan haydakir, dakhdagel (Հաստ տախտակ, քաղաքական յայտագիր, տախտակել)
planking - dakhdagoum, dakhdagabadoum (տախտակում, տախտակապատում)
planner - dzurakurogh (ծրագրող)
planometer - hartachap (Հարթաչափ)
plant - pouys, doung, toup, gazmadzk, tsanel, dungel (բոյս, տունկ, թուփ, կազմածք, ցանել, տնկել)
plantation - dungoum, dungakordzoutiun, kaghout (տնկում, տնկագործութիւն, գաղութ)
planter - dungogh, mushag, kaghtagan (տնկող, մշակ, գաղթական)
plaque - houshadakhdag, usgavarag, shukanushan (յուշատախտակ, սկաւառակ, շքանշան)
plash - churagouyd, tsaydoug, tsaydil, miahiusel (ջրակոյտ, ցայտուկ, ցայտիլ, միաՀիւսել)
plashy - churod, tsekhod, jahjod, deghmoud, dzupatsogh (ջրոտ, ցեխոտ, ճաՀճոտ, տղմուտ, ծփացող)
plasm - gensaniut, mayr gaghabar (կենսանիւթ, մայր կաղապար)
plasma - nakhaniut, avshahiut, shijoug, churariun (նախանիւթ, աւշաՀիւթ, շիճուկ, ջրարիւն)
Plaster - saghmosaran, kirk Saghmosats (Սաղմոսարան, Գիրք Սաղմոսաց)
plaster - tegheriz, kaj, dzep, dzepel, dzadzgel, kajel (դեղերիզ, գաճ, ծեփ, ծեփել, ծածկել, գաճել)
plastic - gerbungal, tsevungal, jugoun, keghakidagan (կերպընկալ, ձեւընկալ, ճկուն, գեղագիտական)
plastic surgery - keghakidagan virahadoutiun (գեղագիտական վիրաՀատութիւն)
plasticity - gerbungaloutiun, tsevaroutiun (կերպընկալութիւն, ձեւառութիւն)
plastics - gerbarvesd (կերպարուեստ)
plat - hoghasherd, hoghamas, arderou pazhnel (Հողաշերտ, Հողամաս, արտերու բաժնել)
plate (n) - bunag, apse, dakhdag, titegh, murtsanag (պնակ, ափսէ, տախտակ, թիթեղ, մրցանակ)
plate (v) - vosgezodzel, ardzatabadel, guranel, titeghel (ոսկեզօծել,

արծաթապատել, կոանել, թիթեղել)
plateau - partsuravantag, lernatashd, sarahart (բարձրավանդակ, լեռնադաշտ, սարահարթ)
platemaking - medaghadibi badrasdoutiun (մետաղատիպի պատրաստութիւն)
platform - ambion, pem, dakhdagamadz, oughekidz, dzurakir (ամպիոն, բեմ, տախտակամած, ուղեգիծ, ծրագիր)
plating - vosgezodzoum, ardzatabadoum (ոսկեզօծում, արծաթապատում)
platinum - lusnosgi (լսնոսկի)
platitude - dapagoutiun, anhamoutiun, dapag khosk (տափակութիւն, անհամութիւն, տափակ խօսք)
platitudinize - dapagapanel, dapag khosker usel (տափակաբանել, տափակ խօսքեր ըսել)
platonic - bughadonagan, makour, mudavor (պղատոնական, մաքուր, մտաւոր)
platonism - bughadonaganoutiun (պղատոնականութիւն)
platoon - chogad, vashd, koumardag (ջոկատ, վաշտ, գումարտակ)
platter - usgoudegh, khoroung bunag, huisogh (սկուտեղ, խորունկ պնակ, հիւսող)
plaudit - dzap, dzapaharoutiun, kovesd, kunahadank (ծափ, ծափահարութիւն, գովեստ, գնահատանք)
plausible - untouneli, havaneli (ընդունելի, հաւանելի)
play (n) - khagh, gadag, tadron, nuvakadzoutiun (խաղ, կատակ, թատրոն, նուագածութիւն)
play (v) - khaghal, khaghtsunel, nuvakel, nergayatsunel (խաղալ, խաղցնել, նուագել, ներկայացնել)
playback - hedsanuvak, yedeven lusvogh nuvak (յետսանուագ, ետեւէն լսուող նուագ)
playbill - nergayatsman haydakir (ներկայացման յայտագիր)
playcard - khaghatought (խաղաթուղթ)
playday - artsagourt, khaghi or (արձակուրդ, խաղի օր)
player - khaghtsogh, terasan, nuvakogh (խաղցող, դերասան, նուագող)
playfellow - khaghunger (խաղընկեր)
playful - gaydar, ourakh, khaghaser (կայտառ, ուրախ, խաղասէր)
playgoer - tadronakunats, tadronaser (թատրոնագնաց, թատրոնասէր)
playground - khaghavayr (խաղավայր)
playhouse - tadron, khaghadoun (թատրոն, խաղատուն)
playing card - khaghatought (խաղաթուղթ)
playmate - khaghunger, khaghagits (խաղընկեր, խաղակից)
plaything - khaghalik (խաղալիք)
playtime - uzposank, khaghazham (զբօսանք, խաղաժամ)
playwriter, playwright - taderakir (թատերագիր)
play-off - vujragan verjin khagh (վճռական վերջին խաղ)
plaza - hurabarag, shouga (հրապարակ, շուկայ)
plea - artaratsoum, abatsouyts, aghers, tad (արդարացում, ապացոյց, աղերս, դատ)
pleach - huisel (հիւսել)
plead - tad varel, bashdbanel, artaratsunel, chadakovel (դատ վարել, պաշտպանել, արդարացնել, ջատագովել)
pleader - bashdban, pasdapan (պաշտպան, փաստաբան)
pleadings - tad (դատ)
pleasance - hajouyk, zuvarjoutiun (հաճոյք, զուարճութիւն)
pleasant - hajeli, akhorzheli, zuvart, siroun (հաճելի, ախորժելի, զուարթ, սիրուն)
pleasantry - gadag, dzaghrank, zuvarjakhosoutiun (կատակ, ծաղրանք, զուարճախօսութիւն)
please - hajetsunel, kohatsunel, akhorzhil, hajil, sirel (հաճեցնել, գոհացնել, ախորժիլ, հաճիլ, սիրել)
pleasing - hajeli, hajo (հաճելի,

Հաճոյ)

pleasure - hajouyk, uzposank, hajetsunel, hajouyk uzkal (Հաճոյք, զբօսանք, Հաճեցնել, Հաճոյք ըզգալ)

pleat - pot, dzalk, dzaldzalel (փոթ, ծալք, ծալծալել)

plebeian - ramig, hasarag, khouzhan (ռամիկ, Հասարակ, խուժան)

plebiscite - hanrakuve (Հանրաքուէ)

pledge - kurav, kuravagan, yerashkhik, kurav tunel (գրաւ, գրաւական, երաշխիք, գրաւ դնել)

pledgee - kuravarou, khosdumnarou (գրաւառու, խոստմնառու)

pledgor, pledger - khosdumnadou, kuravadou (խոստմնատու, գրաւատու)

pleiades - hamasdeghoutiun (Համաստեղութիւն)

plenary - luman, liagadar, gadarial (լման, լիակատար, կատարեալ)

plenipotent - liazor (լիազօր)

plenipotentiary - liazor-tesban (լիազօր դեսպան)

plenitude - ampoghchoutiun, letsounoutiun, aradoutiun (ամբողջութիւն, լեցունութիւն, առատութիւն)

plenteous, plentiful - liarad, liouli, aradaper (լիառատ, լիուլի, առատաբեր)

plenty - arad, jokh, shad, aradoutiun, hortoutiun (առատ, ճոխ, շատ, առատութիւն, յորդութիւն)

pleonasm - avelortapanoutiun (աւելորդաբանութիւն)

pleurisy - goghadab (կողատապ)

pliability - jugounoutiun, tiuratekoutiun (ճկունութիւն, դիւրաթեքութիւն)

pliable - tiuradzal, tiuratek, jugoun, zichogh, hez (դիւրածալ, դիւրաթեք, ճկուն, զիջող, Հեզ)

pliant - dzaluvogh, jugoun, gagough (ծալուող, ճկուն, կակուղ)

plication - dzalk, dzaloum (ծալք, ծալում)

pliers - aktsan, ouneliag (աքցան, ունելեակ)

plight - kurav, yerashkhik, khosdanal, oukhdel (գրաւ, երաշխիք, խոստանալ, ուխտել)

plinth - badvantan, nerknakhariskh (պատուանդան, ներքնախարիսխ)

plod - antoul ashkhadil, duknil, dzanur kalel (անդուլ աշխատիլ, տքնիլ, ծանր քալել)

plodder - duknogh, zhurachan mart (տքնող, ժրաջան մարդ)

plot (n) - tav, tavajanoutiun, kedin, hogh, dzurakir (դաւ, դաւաճանութիւն, գետին, Հող, ծրագիր)

plot (v) - tavel, niutel, hunarel, dzurakurel (դաւել, նիւթել, Հնարել, ծրագրել)

ploughman - hoghakordz, hergogh, mushag (Հողագործ, Հերկող, մշակ)

plow, plough - aror, koutan, hergel, agosel, varel (արօր, գութան, Հերկել, ակօսել, վարել)

plowable - hergeli, vareli (Հերկելի, վարելի)

plowman - herhogh, hoghakordz, mushag (Հերկող, Հողագործ, մշակ)

pluck - kashel, purtsunel, khulel, khuloum, surdodoutiun (քաշել, փրցնել, խլել, խլում, սրտոտութիւն)

plucky - kach, surdod, gorovi (քաջ, սրտոտ, կորովի)

plug - khutsan, khits, khutsanel, khutsel, kotsel (խցան, խից, խցանել, խցել, գոցել)

plum - salor, saloreni, chamich, harusdoutiun (սալոր, սալորենի, չամիչ, Հարստութիւն)

plumb - gabar, gabaralar, ough ghatsik, duramachapel (կապար, կապարալար, ուղղաձիգ, տրամաչափել)

plumber - gabarakordz, khoghovagakordz (կապարագործ, խողովակագործ)

plumbing - gabarakordzoutiun, khoghovagakordzoutiun (կապարագործութիւն, խողովակագործութիւն)

plume - pedour, pedrapounch, pedrazartel, bardzenal (փետուր, փետրափունջ, փետրազարդել, պարծենալ)

plummet - *khorachap, duramalar, dzanroutiun (խորաչափ, տրամալար, ծանրութիւն)*

plump - *kiroug, ker, gulorig, kirnal, kirtsunel (գիրուկ, գէր, կլորիկ, գիրնալ, գիրցնել)*

plumper - *ouretsunogh, puchogh (ուռեցնող, փչող)*

plumpness - *kiroutiun (գիրութիւն)*

plumpy - *kiroug (գիրուկ)*

plumule - *poghpoch, untsiugh, aghvamaz turchouni (բողբոջ, ընձիւղ, աղուամազ թռչունի)*

plumy - *pedrod, pedrazart (փետրոտ, փետրազարդ)*

plunder - *goghobdel, hapushdagel, avarel, avar, goghoboud (կողոպտել, յափշտակել, աւարել, աւար, կողոպուտ)*

plunge - *mukhurjel, ungughmel, mukhurchoum, souzoum (մխրճել, ընկղմել, մխրճում, սուզում)*

plunger - *mukhurjogh, souzag (մխրճող, սուզակ)*

pluperfect - *keragadar (գերակատար)*

plural - *hoknagi, pazmativ (յոգնակի, բազմաթիւ)*

plurality - *shadoutiun, hoknagioutiun (շատութիւն, յոգնակիութիւն)*

plus - *aveli, aravel (աւելի, առաւել)*

pluvial - *antsurevayin (անձրեւային)*

pluviometer - *antsurevajap (անձրեւաչափ)*

pluvious - *antsurevod, antsurevayin (անձրեւոտ, անձրեւային)*

ply - *unel, juknil, barabil, dzalel, dzalk, pot (ընել, ճգնիլ, պարապիլ, ծալել, ծալք, փոթ)*

plywood - *sherdapayd, nurpadakhdag (շերտափայտ, նրբատախտակ)*

pneometer - *shunchachap (շնչաչափ)*

pneumatic - *otahan, otayin (օդահան, օդային)*

pneumatics - *otakidoutiun, gazapanoutiun (օդագիտութիւն, կազաբանութիւն)*

pneumonia - *tokadab (թոքատապ)*

poach - *havgit yepel, koghnal, danil (հաւկիթ եփել, գողնալ, տանիլ)*

pock - *dzaghgasbi, balar dzaghgakhdi (ծաղկասպի, պալար՝ ծաղկախտի)*

pocket - *kurban, kusag, barg, kurbanel, koghnal (գրպան, քսակ, պարկ, գրպանել, գողնալ)*

pocketbook - *houshadedur, dzotsadedur, tughtagal, artsern (յուշատետր, ծոցատետր, թղթակալ, առձեռն)*

pocketknife - *uzmeli (զմելի)*

pod - *badij, geghev, badian, yeram (պատիճ, կեղեւ, պատեան, երամ)*

podgy - *garj, ker, hasd (կարճ, գէր, հաստ)*

podiatrist - *vodnapouyzh (ոտնաբոյժ)*

podiatry - *vodnapouzhoutiun (ոտնաբուժութիւն)*

podium - *badushkam, badvantan (պատշգամ, պատուանդան)*

poem - *kertuvadz, panasdeghdzoutiun, vodanavor (քերթուած, բանաստեղծութիւն, ոտանաւոր)*

poesy - *panasdeghdzoutiun, kertoghoutiun (բանաստեղծութիւն, քերթողութիւն)*

poet - *panasdeghdz, kertogh (բանաստեղծ, քերթող)*

poetaster - *andaghant panasdeghdz (անտաղանդ բանաստեղծ)*

poetic, poetical - *panasdeghdzagan, kertoghagan (բանաստեղծական, քերթողական)*

poetrize - *panasdeghdzel, kertel (բանաստեղծել, քերթել)*

poetry - *panasdeghdzoutiun, kertughoutiun kertuvaddz (բանաստեղծութիւն, քերթողութիւն, քերթուած)*

poignant - *gudzou, khaytogh, dzagogh, sour (կծու, խայթող, ծակող, սուր)*

point (n) - *ged, dzayr, verchaged, tiv, asdijan, pidz (կէտ, ծայր, վերջակէտ, թիւ, աստիճան, բիծ)*

point (v) - *nushel, gedaturel, surel, madnanushel, tsoutsunel (նշել, կէտադրել, սրել, մատնանշել, ցուցնել)*

point of view - desaged (տեսակէտ)
pointed - suradzayr, sour, achkarou (սրածայր, սուր, աչքառու)
pointer - madnanushogh, sulak (մատնանշող, սլաք)
pointing - gedaturoutiun (կէտադրութիւն)
poise - dzanroutiun, gushir, hagagushrel (ծանրութիւն, կշիռ, հակակշռել)
poison - touyn, zhahur, tounavorel (թոյն, ժահր, թունաւորել)
poisoner - tounavorich (թունաւորիչ)
poisonous - tounavor, tounalits, abaganich (թունաւոր, թունալից, ապականիչ)
poke - kurban, dobrag, hurots, hurel, khotel (գրպան, տոպրակ, հրոց, հրել, խոթել)
poker - agish, guragkharnich, tughtakhagh mu-poker (ակիշ, կրակխառնիչ, թղթախաղ մը՝ փոքէր)
pokey, poky - pokur seniag daghdugali, gudzguvadz, tantagh (փոքր սենեակ՝ տաղտկալի, կծկուած, դանդաղ)
polar - peverayin, hagarag, nerhag (բեւեռային, հակառակ, ներհակ)
polariscope - peveratsouyts (բեւեռացոյց)
polarity - peveraganoutiun (բեւեռականութիւն)
polarization - peveratsoum (բեւեռացում)
polarize - pereratsunel, peveranal (բեւեռացնել, բեւեռանալ)
pole - pever, tsogh, siun, leh, siunel (բեւեռ, ձող, սիւն, լեհ, սիւնել)
polemic - panavej, hagajaroutiun, vijapanagan (բանավէճ, հակաճառութիւն, վիճաբանական)
polestar - peverasdgh, peverayin asdgh (բեւեռաստղ, բեւեռային աստղ)
police - vosdiganoutiun, gark bahbanel (ոստիկանութիւն, կարգ պահպանել)
policeman - vosdigan (ոստիկան)
police-station - vosdiganadoun (ոստիկանատուն)
policy - kaghakaganoutiun, khoramangoutiun, abahovakir (քաղաքականութիւն, խորամանկութիւն, ապահովագիր)
polio - mangagan antamaloudzoutiun (մանկական անդամալուծութիւն)
polish - payletsunel, hughgel, payl, hughgoum, nerg, leh (փայլեցնել, յղկել, փայլ, յղկում, ներկ, լեհ)
polished - payloun, payletsvadz, voghorg, paregirt, nourp (փայլուն, փայլեցուած, ողորկ, բարեկիրթ, նուրբ)
polisher - hughgogh, voghorgogh, payletsunogh (յղկող, ողորկող, փայլեցնող)
polite - kaghakavar, girt, gurtial (քաղաքավար, կիրթ, կրթեալ)
politic - kaghakagan, khoramang, khohem, tivanaked (քաղաքական, խորամանկ, խոհեմ, դիւանագէտ)
political - kaghakagan, gousagtsagan (քաղաքական, կուսակցական)
politician - kaghakaked, varchaked (քաղաքագէտ, վարչագէտ)
politics - kaghakaganoutiun, kaghakakidoutiun (քաղաքականութիւն, քաղաքագիտութիւն)
polity - bedagan oughekidz, kaghakagan uskuzpounk (պետական ուղեգիծ, քաղաքական սկզբունք)
polka - lehabar, lehanuvak (լեհապար, լեհանուագ)
poll (n) - kakat, kuloukh, undurou-tiun, unduratsang (գագաթ, գլուխ, ընտրութիւն, ընտրացանկ)
poll (v) - tsoutsagakurel, saprel, gudrel, khouzel (ցուցակագրել, սափրել, կտրել, խուզել)
pollen - peghmnaposhi (բեղմնափոշի)
poller - kuveargou, kuveyi artsnakir (քուէարկու, քուէի արձանագիր)
pollinate - poshodel, peghmnavorel (փոշոտել, բեղմնաւորել)
pollo - kuntakhagh tsiov, joganakhagh (գնդախաղ ձիով, ճոկանախաղ)
pollute - bughdzel, purnaparel, abaganel, aghdodel (պղծել, բռնաբա-

րել, ապականել, աղտոտել)
pollution - abaganoutiun, bughdzoutiun, kichoutiun (ապականութիւն, պղծութիւն, գիջութիւն)
poll-tax - kulkhaharg (գլխահարկ)
polonaise - lehagan, leheren, lehabar (լեհական, լեհերէն, լեհապար)
poltroon - vakhgod, yergchod, vad (վախկոտ, երկչոտ, վատ)
poly - shad, pazoum (շատ, բազում)
polyandry - pazmamayroutiun (բազմամայրութիւն)
polyclinic - pazmapouzharan, pazmapouzh tarmanadoun (բազմաբուժարան, բազմաբուժ դարմանատուն)
polygamist - pazmagin, pazmamousin, pazmamayr (բազմակին, բազմամուսին, բազմամայր)
polygamy - pazmagunoutiun, pazmamousnoutiun (բազմակնութիւն, բազմամուսնութիւն)
polygenous - pazmadesag, pazmaser (բազմատեսակ, բազմասեր)
polyglot - pazmalezou, pazmalezvaked (բազմալեզու, բազմալեզուագէտ)
polygon - pazmangiun (բազմանկիւն)
polygraphy - pazmakuroutiun (բազմագրութիւն)
polygyny - pazmagunoutiun (բազմակնութիւն)
polymathy - pazmakidoutiun (բազմագիտութիւն)
polyphase - pazmapoul (պազմափուլ)
polyphone, polyphonic - pazmatsayn (բազմաձայն)
polyphonic - pazmatsayn (բազմաձայն)
polyscope - pazmatidag, pazmatsouyts (բազմադիտակ, բազմացոյց)
polysyllable, polysyllabic - pazmavang (բազմավանկ)
polytechnic - pazmarvesdian (բազմարուեստեան)
polytheism - pazmasdvadzoutiun (բազմաստուածութիւն)
polytype - pazmadib (բազմատիպ)
polyvalent - pazmarzhek (բազմարժէք)
pomade - odzanelik, hodahiut, khuntsorahod (օծանելիք, հոտահիւթ, խնձորահոտ)
pomegranate - nour, nurneni (նուռ, նռնենի)
pommel - souserakount, gurpaharel, dzedzel, tagel (սուսերագունդ, կոփահարել, ծեծել, թակել)
pomp - shukeghoutiun, shouk, berjank, shukahantes (շքեղութիւն, շուք, պերճանք, շքահանդէս)
pomposity - paravoroutium , shukeghoutiun (փառաւորութիւն, շքեղութիւն)
pompous - parashouk, shukegh, inknahavan, sunapar (փառաշուք, շքեղ, ինքնահաւան, սնափառ)
pompously - paravorabes (փառաւորապէս)
pond - lujag, avazan, churampar (լճակ, աւազան, ջրամբար)
ponder - khorhil, khogal, mudadzel, gushratadel (խորհիլ, խոկալ, մտածել, կշռադատել)
ponderable - gushreli (կշռելի)
ponderance, ponderosity - dzanroutiun, gushirk (ծանրութիւն, կշիռք)
ponderer - khorhogh, gushratadogh (խորհող, կշռադատող)
ponderous - dzanur, dzanragushir, zoravor, tantagh (ծանր, ծանրակշիռ, զօրաւոր, դանդաղ)
poniard - tashiun, tashounaharel (դաշոյն, դաշունահարել)
pontiff - bab, kahanayabed (պապ, քահանայապետ)
pontific - babagan, kahanayabedagan (պապական, քահանայապետական)
ponton, pontoon - gamurchanav, navagamouch (կամրջանաւ, նաւակամուրջ)
pool (n) - avazan, lujag, churagouyd, arevdurakhoump (աւազան, լճակ, ջրակոյտ, առեւտրախումբ)
pool (v) - miatsunel, hamatsaynil, lujatsunel (միացնել, համաձայնիլ, լճացնել)

poor - aghkad, chukavor, kheghj, tushvar, garod (աղքատ, չքաւոր, խեղճ, Թշուառ, կարօտ)
poorness - aghkadoutiun, chukavoroutiun (աղքատուԹիւն, չքաւորուԹիւն)
pop (I) - shachiun, baytiun, hangardz baytil, baytetsunel (շաչիւն, պայԹիւն, յանկարծ պայԹիլ, պայԹեցնել)
pop (II) - zhoghovurtagan (popular paren) — ժողովրդական (popular բառի կրճատ ձեւը)
popcorn - pohradz-baytats yekibdatsoren, aghants (բոհրած-պայԹած եգիպտացորեն, աղանձ)
Pope - bab, kahanayabed (Պապ, քահանայապետ)
popish - babagan (պապական)
poplar - gaghamakh (կաղամախ)
poppy - khashkhash, megon (խաշխաշ, մեկոն)
populace - zhoghovourt, khouzhan, ampokh (ժողովուրդ, խուժան, ամբոխ)
popular - zhoghovurtagan, hanradzanot (ժողովրդական, ՀանրածանօԹ)
popularity - zhoghovurtaganoutiun (ժողովրդականուԹիւն)
popularize - zhoghovurtaganatsunel (ժողովրդականացնել)
populate - shentsunel, pazmatsunel (շէնցնել, բազմացնել)
population - punagchoutiun, zhoghovourt (բնակչուԹիւն, ժողովուրդ)
populist, populistic - zhoghovurtagan (ժողովրդական)
populous - pazmamart, martashad (բազմամարդ, մարդաշատ)
porcelain - hakhjabagi, jenabagi (յախճապակի, ճենապակի)
porch - kavit, moudk, siunasurah (գաւիԹ, մուտք, սիւնասրաՀ)
porcupine - vozni, khozag, khozoug (ոզնի, խոզակ, խոզուկ)
pore - dzagdig, antsk, haril, hapushdagvil (ծակտիկ, անցք, յառիլ, յափշտակուիլ)
pork - kozi mis (խոզի միս)
porker - khoz (խոզ)
pornography - bornugakuroutiun (պոռնկագրուԹիւն)
porosity - dzagodgenoutiun (ծակոտկէնուԹիւն)
porous - dzagodgen, dzagod (ծակոտկէն, ծակոտ)
porpoise - dzovakhoz, tulpin (ծովախոզ, դլբին)
porridge - tan, abour (Թան, ապուր)
port - navahankisd, tour, antsk, danil, gurel (նաւաՀանգիստ, դուռ, անցք, տանիլ, կրել)
portability - danelioutiun (տանելիուԹիւն)
portable - daneli, tiuradar, pokhatureli, artserun (տանելի, դիւրատար, փոխադրելի, առձեռն)
portage - pokhaturoutiun, guroum, danoghchek, oughekin (փոխադրուԹիւն, կրում, տանողչէք, ուղեգին)
portal - nakhamoudk, tarbas, kulvavor tour (Նախամուտք, դարպաս, գլխաւոր դուռ)
portend - gankhakoushagel, koushagel (կանխագուշակել, գուշակել)
portent - nakhanushan, charakoushag (Նախանշան, չարագուշակ)
porter - pernagir, turnaban, dzara (բեռնակիր, դռնապան, ծառայ)
porterage - pernaguroutiun, turnabanoutiun (բեռնակրուԹիւն, դռնապանուԹիւն)
portfolio - tughtagal, tughtabanag, nakhararoutiun (ԹղԹակալ, ԹղԹապանակ, ՆախարարուԹիւն)
portico - siunasurah, gamaragab surah (սիւնասրաՀ, կամարակապ սրաՀ)
portion - mas, gudor, pazhin, ozhid, pazhnel, ozhid dal (մաս, կտոր, բաժին, օժիտ, բաժնել, օժիտ տալ)
portly - shukegh, vehashouk, marmunegh, kiroug (շքեղ, վեՀաշուք, մարմնեղ, գիրուկ)
portmanteau - uzkesdagal, hantertsagal, oughebayousag (զգեստակալ, Հանդերձակալ, ուղեպայուսակ)
portrait - timanugar, badger, nugar,

gentanakir (դիմանկար, պատկեր, նկար, կենդանագիր)
portray - nugarel, badgerahanel, nugarakurel (նկարել, պատկերահանել, նկարագրել)
portuguese - portougaltsi, portougaleren, portougalian (փորթուկալցի, փորթուկալերէն, փորթուկալեան)
pose (n) - tirk, getsvadzk, gatsk, tsev (դիրք, կեցուածք, կացք, ձեւ)
pose (v) - tirk purnel, getsunel, genal, hartsouportsel (դիրք բռնել, կեցնել, կենալ, հարցուփորձել)
poser - neghogh, shupotetsunogh, arvesdargogh (նեղող, շփոթեցնող, արուեստարկող)
posit - zedeghel, deghavorel (զետեղել, տեղաւորել)
position - tirk, degh, gatsoutiun, getsvadzk, bashdon (դիրք, տեղ, կացութիւն, կեցուածք, պաշտօն)
positive - turagan, iragan, vorosh (դրական, իրական, որոշ)
positively - turaganoren, voroshabes, irabes (դրականօրէն, որոշապէս, իրապէս)
positivism - turabashdoutiun (դրապաշտութիւն)
positivist - turabashd (դրապաշտ)
possess - diranal, yiuratsunel, ounenal (տիրանալ, իւրացնել, ունենալ)
possession - usdatsvadzk, galvadzk, diratsoum, tivaharoutiun (ստացուածք, կալուածք, տիրացում, դիւահարութիւն)
possessive - usdatsagan, seragan (ստացական, սեռական)
possessor - usdatsogh, diratsogh, der (ստացող, տիրացող, տէր)
posset - kinemadzoun, magartel (գինեմածուն, մակարդել)
possibility - garelioutiun, hunaravoroutiun (կարելիութիւն, հնարաւորութիւն)
possible - gareli, hunaravor, havanagan (կարելի, հնարաւոր, հաւանական)
possibly - havanapar, terevus, koutse (հաւանաբար, թերեւս, գուցէ)
post (n) (I) - siun, tsogh, zoragayan, degh (սիւն, ձող, զօրակայան, տեղ)
post (n) (II) - namagadoun, tughtadar, bashdon, tirk (նամակատուն, թղթատար, պաշտօն, դիրք)
post (v) - pagtsunel, haydararel, oughargel, hantsunel (փակցնել, յայտարարել, ուղարկել, յանձնել)
post office - namagadoun (նամակատուն)
postage - posdadzakhs, namagakin, tughtadaradzakhs (փոստածախս, նամակագին, թղթատարածախս)
postal - tughtadaragan (թղթատարական)
postcard - patsig, patskir (բացիկ, բացգիր)
poster - vormazt, aztakir, aztanugar, dzanoutsakir (որմազդ, ազդագիր, ազդանկար, ծանուցագիր)
posterior - hedaka, yedevi, hedo, yedevu, hedouyk (հետագայ, ետեւի, յետոյ, ետեւը, յետոյք)
posterity - serount, hachortoutiun, abaka serount (սերունդ, յաջորդութիւն, ապագայ սերունդ)
postern - turnag, kaghdatour, yedevi tour (դռնակ, գաղտադուռ, ետեւի դուռ)
posthouse - namagadoun (նամակատուն)
posthumous - hedadzin, hed mahou (յետածին, յետ մահու)
postman - namagapashkh, sourhantag, tsurvich (նամակաբաշխ, սուրհանդակ, ցրուիչ)
postmark - gunkanish, namagaturoshm, gunkanushel (կնքանիշ, նամակադրոշմ, կնքանշել)
postmaster - namagadan dunoren (նամատական տնօրէն)
postpaid - gankhavujarvadz (կանխավճարուած)
postpone - hedatsukel, habaghel (յետաձգել, յապաղել)
postponement - hedatsukoum (յետաձգում)
postscript - hed kuroutiun, havelakir (յետ գրութիւն, յաւելագիր)

poststamp - *namagaturoshm* (նամակադրոշմ)
postulant - *khunturargou, tegnadzou, hedamoud* (խնդրարկու, թեկնածու, հետամուտ)
postulate - *khunturank, aracharg, kunturel, arachargel* (խնդրանք, առաջարկ, խնդրել, առաջարկել)
postulation - *khunturank, haytsoghoutiun* (խնդրանք, հայցողութիւն)
posture - *getsvadzk, tirk, tirk arnel* (կեցուածք, դիրք, դիրք առնել)
posy - *dzaghgepounch, nushanapan, houshadogh* (ծաղկեփունջ, նշանաբան, յուշատող)
pot - *aman, taghar, anot, gouzh, san* (աման, թաղար, անօթ, կուժ, սան)
pot pourri - *dzaghgepounch, kharnourt-yerki, oudeliki* (ծաղկեփունջ, խառնուրդ՝ երգի, ուտելիքի)
potable - *khumeli, umbeli* (խմելի, ըմպելի)
potation - *khumelik, kinarpouk, arpank* (խմելիք, գինարբուք, արբանք)
potato - *kednakhuntsor* (գետնախնձոր)
potency - *garoghoutiun, zoroutiun, aztetsoutiun* (կարողութիւն, զօրութիւն, ազդեցութիւն)
potent - *garogh, aztetsig, huzor, zoregh, zoravor* (կարող, ազդեցիկ, հզօր, զօրեղ, զօրաւոր)
potentate - *vehabed, ishkhan, bed* (վեհապետ, իշխան, պետ)
potential - *nerzor, zoroutenagan, nerouzh* (ներզօր, զօրութենական, ներոյժ)
potentiality - *garoghaganoutiun, garelioutiun* (կարողականութիւն, կարելիութիւն)
potion - *khumelik, teghachour, oumb* (խմելիք, դեղաջուր, ումպ)
potluck - *anbadrasdits jash* (անպատրաստից ճաշ)
pottage - *abour, pancharachour* (ապուր, բանջարաջուր)
potter - *puroud, gavakordz, tantaghil, dundunal* (բրուտ, կաւագործ, դանդաղիլ, տնտնալ)
pottery - *gaveghen, gavakordzaran, puroudanots* (կաւեղէն, կաւագործարան, բրուտանոց)
pouch - *gashebarg, dobrag, pamposhdaman, kurbanel* (կաշեպարկ, տոպրակ, փամփուշտաման, գրպանել)
poult - *variag, joud, havoug* (վարեակ, ճուտ, հաւուկ)
poulterer - *havavajar* (հաւավաճառ)
poultry - *haveghen, havk* (հաւեղէն, հաւք)
poultry house - *havnots* (հաւնոց)
pounce - *chunarag, adzkhaposhi, poshi tsanel, jangel* (ջնարակ, ածխափոշի, փոշի ցանել, ճանկել)
pound - *libra, vosgi, manrel, dzedzel, pushrel* (լիպրա, ոսկի, մանրել, ծեծել, փշրել)
pour - *vaztsunel, tapel, letsunel, hosil, tapil* (վազցնել, թափել, լեցնել, հոսիլ, թափիլ)
pourer - *tapogh, barbogh* (թափող, պարպող)
pourparler - *panagtsoutiun* (բանակցութիւն)
pout - *gakheresoutiun, khozhoril, neghanal, vaiag* (կախերեսութիւն, խոժոռիլ, նեղանալ, վարեակ)
pouter - *gakheres, khozhoratem* (կախերես, խոժոռադէմ)
poverty - *aghkadoutiun, chukavoroutiun, kheghjoutiun* (աղքատութիւն, չքաւորութիւն, խեղճութիւն)
powder - *poshi, varot, poshianal, poshi tsanel* (փոշի, վառօդ, փոշիանալ, փոշի ցանել)
power - *garoghoutiun, ouzh, ishkhanoutiun, zoroutiun* (կարողութիւն, ոյժ, իշխանութիւն, զօրութիւն)
powerful - *garogh, ouzhegh, huzor, zoregh, aztetsig* (կարող, ուժեղ, հզօր, զօրեղ, ազդեցիկ)
powerless - *angarogh, anzor, anouzh* (անկարող, անզօր, անոյժ)
pox - *balar, pushdig, furangakhd* (պալար, բշտիկ, ֆրանկախտ)
practicable - *kordzatureli, irakor-*

dzeli (գործադրելի, իրագործելի)
practical - kordznagan, okdagar, iragan (գործնական, օգտակար, իրական)
practice (n) - varzhoutiun, giraroutiun, sovorouyt, marzank (վարժութիւն, կիրառութիւն, սովորոյթ, մարզանք)
practice (v) - kordzaturel, girargel, unel, gadarel (գործադրել, կիրարկել, ընել, կատարել)
practitioner - portsarou, masnaked, girargogh puzhishg (փորձառու, մասնագէտ, կիրարկող՝ բժիշկ)
pragmatic, al - kordznagan, kordzounia, tsernerets, hantoukun (գործնական, գործունեայ, ձեռներէց, յանդուգն)
pragmatism - kordznabashdoutiun (գործնապաշտութիւն)
prairie - arodavayr, markakedin (արօտավայր, մարգագետին)
praise - kovel, kovapanel, kovesd, orhnoutiun (գովել, գովաբանել, գովեստ, օրհնութիւն)
praiser - koverkogh, turvadogh, parapanich (գովերգող, դրուատող, փառաբանիչ)
prance - tsadgurdel, khaydal, gaydural, tsadgoum (ցատկռտել, խայտալ, կայտռալ, ցատկում)
prank - bujnil, bujnel, zartarel, zuvarjoutiun, zaveshd (պճնիլ, պճնել, զարդարել, զուարճութիւն, զաւեշտ)
prankish - gaydar, charajuji (կայտառ, չարաճճի)
prate - shaghaguradel, shadakhosel, shadakhosoutiun (շաղակրատել, շատախօսել, շատախօսութիւն)
prater - shaghagrad (շաղակրատ)
prattle - totovel, shadakhosel, totovank, gagazoum (թոթովել, շատախօսել, թոթովանք, կակազում)
pray - aghotel, khunturel, aghachel, aghersel (աղօթել, խնդրել, աղաչել, աղերսել)
prayer - aghotk, aghersakir, aghotogh, khunturargou (աղօթք, աղերսագիր, աղօթող, խնդրարկու)
prayer book - aghotakirk (աղօթագիրք)
prayerful - aghotaser, chertmerant (աղօթասէր, ջերմեռանդ)
preach - karozel, avedaranel, khuradel (քարոզել, աւետարանել, խրատել)
preacher - karozich (քարոզիչ)
preadmonish - nakazkoushatsunel, aztararel (նախազգուշացնել, ազդարարել)
preadmonition - nakhazkoushoutiun, aztararoutiun (նախազգուշութիւն, ազդարարութիւն)
preamble - nakhapan, neradzagan, nakherkank (նախաբան, ներածական, նախերգանք)
preambulatory - nakhuntats (նախընթաց)
prearrange - arachouts garkaturel (առաջուց կարգադրել)
prebend - hasouyt, toshag (հասոյթ, թոշակ)
precarious - badahagan, anhasdad, anusdouyk, ourishe gakhial (պատահական, անհաստատ, անստոյգ, ուրիշէ կախեալ)
precaution - nakhazkoushoutiun, nakhazkoushatsunel (նախազգուշութիւն, նախազգուշացնել)
precautious - uzkouysh, khohem (զգոյշ, խոհեմ)
precede - gankhel, nakhuntanal, nakhortel (կանխել, նախընթանալ, նախորդել)
precedent - nakhort, nakhuntats, nakhateb (նախորդ, նախընթաց, նախադէպ)
preceding - nakhuntats, archi, nakhgin, nakhort (նախընթաց, առջի, նախկին, նախորդ)
precept - ganon, badviran, hurahank (կանոն, պատուիրան, հրահանգ)
preceptor - hurahankogh, dajarabed, ousoutsich (հրահանգող, տաճարապետ, ուսուցիչ)
precession - gankhoum (կանխում)
precinct - shurchabad, hoghamas, tem, sahman (շրջապատ, հողամաս, թեմ, սահման)

precious - tangarzhek, tangakin, ankin, badvagan (թանկարժէք, թանկագին, անգին, պատուական)
precipice - vih, antount, kahavezh, khorkhorad (վիհ, անդունդ, գահավէժ, խորխորատ)
precipitance - kahavizhoum (գահավիժում)
precipitant - kahavizhogh, souzvogh, uzdabogh (գահավիժող, սուզուող, շտապող)
precipitate - kahavizhil, nedvil, arakatsunel, dighm, tird (գահավիժիլ, նետուիլ, արագացնել, տիղմ, դիրտ)
precipitation - angoum, kahavizhoum, ajabarank (անկում, գահավիժում, աճապարանք)
precise - husdag, jishd, jushkurid, vorosh, patsahayd (յստակ, ճիշդ, ճշգրիտ, որոշ, բացայայտ)
precision - jushkurdoutiun, jushdoutiun, husdagoutiun (ճշգրտութիւն, ճշդութիւն, յստակութիւն)
preclude - arkilel, khapanel, pagel (արգիլել, խափանել, փակել)
preclusion - arkiloum, khapanoum, merzhoum (արգիլում, խափանում, մերժում)
precocious - gankhahas, vaghahas, vaghazham (կանխահաս, վաղահաս, վաղաժամ)
precociousness - gankhahasoutiun, vaghahasoutiun (կանխահասութիւն, վաղահասութիւն)
precognition - nakhajanachoum (նախաճանաչում)
preconceit - gankhahughatsoum (կանխայղացում)
preconceive - nakhahughanal, ganghamudadzel (նախայղանալ, կանխամտածել)
preconception - nakhahughatsoum, gankhamudadzoum (նախայղացում, կանխամտածում)
preconcert - nakhahamatsaynil, nakhatsaynoutiun (նախահամաձայնիլ, նախահամաձայնութիւն)
preconsent - gankhahavanoutiun (կանխահաւանութիւն)
preconsign - nakhasahmanel, gankhahantsunel (նախասահմանել, կանխայանձնել)
precursor - sourhantag, rahvira, garabed, harachuntats (սուրհանդակ, ռահվիրայ, կարապետ, յառաջընթաց)
predaceous, predacious - hapushdagich, kishadich, avararou (յափշտակիչ, գիշատիչ, աւարառու)
predate - gankhatuvel (կանխաթուել)
predecessor - nakhort, nakhgin, nakhahayr (նախորդ, նախկին, նախահայր)
predestination - nakhasahmanoum (նախասահմանում)
predestinator - nakhasahmanogh (նախասահմանող)
predestine - nakhasahmanel, nakhoroshel (նախասահմանել, նախորոշել)
predicament - anakhorzhoutiun, tuzhvar gatsoutiun (անախորժութիւն, դժուար կացութիւն)
predicate - hasdadel, usel, usdorokeli (հաստատել, ըսել, ստորոգելի)
predication - hasdadoum, usdorokoum (հաստատում, ստորոգում)
predict - koushagel, markareanal, gankhakoushagel (գուշակել, մարգարէանալ, կանխագուշակել)
prediction - koushagoutiun, markareoutiun (գուշակութիւն, մարգարէութիւն)
predilection - goghmunagtsoutiun, nakhasiroutiun (կողմնակցութիւն, նախասիրութիւն)
predispose - nakhaduramaturel (նախատրամադրել)
predisposed - nakhaduramatruvadz (նախատրամադրուած)
predisposition - nakhaduramaturoutiun (նախատրամադրութիւն)
predominance, predominancy - keragayoutiun, keragushroutiun (գերակայութիւն, գերակշռութիւն)
predominant - keragushir, keragushrogh, dirogh, ishkhogh (գերակշիռ, գերակշռող, տիրող, իշխող)

predominate - keragushrel, kerishkhel, ishkhel, direl (գերակշռել, գերիշխել, իշխել, տիրել)
predomination - keragayoutiun, keragushroutiun, araveloutiun (գերակայութիւն, գերակշռութիւն, առաւելութիւն)
predoom - nakhavujrel (նախավճռել)
preelect - nakhundurel (նախընտրել)
preelection - nakhunduroutiun (նախընտրութիւն)
preeminence - nakhabadvoutiun, kerabadvoutiun (նախապատուութիւն, գերապատուութիւն)
preeminence - kerabadvoutiun, nakhabadvoutiun (գերապատուութիւն, նախապատուութիւն)
preeminent - nakhabadiv, kerundir, keragushir, kerazants (նախապատիւ, գերընտիր, գերակշիռ, գերազանց)
preexamination - nakhakunnoutiun (նախաքննութիւն)
preexamine - nakhakunnel (նախաքննել)
preexistence - nakhakoyoutiun (նախագոյութիւն)
preexistent - nakhako (նախագոյ)
prefabricate - nakhagaroutsel, nakhabadrasdel (նախակառուցել, նախապատրաստել)
preface - nakhapan, neradzagan, harachapan kurel (նախաբան, ներածական, յառաջաբան գրել)
prefatory - neradzagan (ներածական)
prefect - gousagal, nahankabed, veradesouch (կուսակալ, նահանգապետ, վերատեսուչ)
prefecture - gousagaloutiun (կուսակալութիւն)
prefer - nakhundurel, nakhabadvel, nakhasirel (նախընտրել, նախապատուել, նախասիրել)
preferable - nakhundureli, nakhamedzar (նախընտրելի, նախամեծար)
preferably - nakhundurapar, nakhasirapar (նախընտրաբար, նախասիրաբար)
preference - nakhunduroutiun, nakhamedzaroutiun (նախընտրութիւն, նախամեծարութիւն)
preferential - nakhamedzar, nakhatas (նախամեծար, նախադաս)
preferment - nakhamedzaroum (նախամեծարում)
preferrer - nakhamedzarogh (նախամեծարող)
prefigure - nakhabadgerel (նախապատկերել)
prefix - nakhamasnig, nakhadzants, nakhaturel, nakhatasel (նախամասնիկ, նախածանց, նախադրել, նախադասել)
pregnancy - hughoutiun, peghmnavoroutiun (յղութիւն, բեղմնաւորութիւն)
pregnant - hughi, peghnavor, arkasavor (յղի, բեղմնաւոր, արգասաւոր)
prehensible - umperneli (ըմբռնելի)
prehension - umpurnoum (ըմբռնում)
prehistoric - nakhabadmagan (նախապատմական)
prehistory - nakhabadmoutiun (նախապատմութիւն)
prejudge - nakhatadel, gankhavujrel (նախադատել, կանխավճռել)
prejudice - nakhabasharel, nakhabasharoum (նախապաշարել, նախապաշարում)
prelacy - arachnortoutiun, yebisgobosoutiun (առաջնորդութիւն, եպիսկոպոսութիւն)
prelate - arachnort, yebisgobos, medzavor (առաջնորդ, եպիսկոպոս, մեծաւոր)
prelect - panakhosel, hurabaragav gartal (բանախօսել, հրապարակաւ կարդալ)
prelection - panakhosoutiun (բանախօսութիւն)
preliminary - nakhnagan, nakhapan, nakhabadrasdagan (նախնական, նախաբան, նախապատրաստական)
prelude - nakherkank, neradzoutiun, nakherkel (նախերգանք, ներածութիւն, նախերգել)
premature - gankhahas, vaghahas (կանխահաս, վաղահաս)

prematurity - gankhahasoutiun (կանխահասութիւն)
premeditate - gankhamudadzel (կանխամտածել)
premeditation - gankhamudadzoum (կանխամտածում)
premier - arachin, kulkhavor, hunakouyn (առաջին, գլխաւոր, հնագոյն)
premiere - arachin nergayatsoum, avak terasanouhi (առաջին ներկայացում, աւագ դերասանուհի)
premise - harachaturel, aracharg (առաջադրել, առաջարկ)
premium - pazhnekin, nakhakin, abahovakin, nuvirapazhin (բաժնեգին, նախագին, ապահովագին, նուիրաբաժին)
premogenitor - nakhahayr (նախահայր)
premonish - nakhazkoushatsunel (նախազգուշացնել)
premonition - nakhaztararoutiun (նախազդարարութիւն)
prenomen - nakhanoun, poun anoun (նախանուն, բուն անուն)
prenuptial - nakhamousnagan (նախամուսնական)
preoccupation - nakhazpaghoum, mudahokoutiun, hok (մտազբաղում, մտահոգութիւն, հոգ)
preoccupy - mudahokel, nakhakuravel, nakhabasharel (մտահոգել, նախագրաւել, նախապաշարել)
preordination - nakhavujroum (նախավճռում)
prepaid - gankhavujarvadz, nakhabes vujarvadz (կանխավճարուած, նախապէս վճարուած)
preparation - badrasdoutiun, nakhabadrasdoutiun (պատրաստութիւն, նախապատրաստութիւն)
preparative - nakhabadrasdagan (նախապատրաստական)
preparatory - nakhabadrasdagan (նախապատրաստական)
prepare - badrasdel, badrasduvil, gazmel, hantertsel (պատրաստել, պատրաստուիլ, կազմել, հանդերձել)
prepared - badrasd, badrasduvadz (պատրաստ, պատրաստուած)
preparedness - badrasdagamoutiun (պատրաստակամութիւն)
preparer - badrasdogh (պատրաստող)
prepay - gankhavujarel (կանխավճարել)
prepayment - gankhavujar (կանխավճար)
prepense - gankhamudadzel, gankhamudadzvadz (կանխամտածել, կանխամտածուած)
preponderance - keragushroutiun, keragayoutiun (գերակշռութիւն, գերակայութիւն)
preponderant - keragushir, keragushrogh (գերակշիռ, գերակշռող)
preponderate - keragushrel, dzanragushrel (գերակշռել, ծանրակշռել)
preposition - nakhatroutiun, nakhtir (նախադրութիւն, նախդիր)
prepossess - nakhakuravel, nakhabasharel, direl (նախագրաւել, նախապաշարել, տիրել)
prepossessing - kuravich, hamagreli, hajeli (գրաւիչ, համակրելի, հաճելի)
prepossession - nakhakuravoum, nakhadiroutiun (նախագրաւում, նախատիրութիւն)
prepossessor - nakhakuravogh, nakhadirogh (նախագրաւող, նախատիրող)
preposterous - animasd, aylantag, anmid, ankhorhourt (անիմաստ, այլանդակ, անմիտ, անխորհուրդ)
prepress - nakhadubakuroutiun (նախատպագրութիւն)
prepricing - nakhajushtial kin (նախաճշդեալ գին)
preprint - nakhdib, gankhadib (նախատիպ, կանխատիպ)
preprinted - nakhabes dubvadz (նախապէս տպուած)
prerecord - gankhartsanakuroutiun (կանխարձանագրութիւն)
prerogative - arantsnashunorhoum, ardonoutiun (առանձնաշնորհում,

արտօնութիւն)
presage - nakhanushan, nakhazkatsoum, gankhakoushagel (նախանըշան, նախազգացում, նախագուշակել)
presager - gankhakoushagogh (կանխագուշակող)
presbytarian - yeritsagan (երիցական)
presbyter - yerets, kahana, hoviv (երէց, քահանայ, հովիւ)
presbytery - yeritsadoun, zhoghovurtabedoutiun (երիցատուն, ժողովրդապետութիւն)
preschool - nakhabadrasdagan tubrots (նախապատրաստական դպրոց)
prescience - nakhakidoutiun (նախագիտութիւն)
prescore - gankhanushan, gankhanish, nakhatsayn (կանխանշան, կանխանիշ, նախաձայն)
prescribe - teghakurel, badvirel, sahmanel (դեղագրել, պատուիրել, սահմանել)
prescript - badvirvadz, huramayvadz, badver (պատուիրուած, հրամայուած, պատուէր)
prescription - teghakir, badver (դեղագիր, պատուէր)
presence - nergayoutiun, gerbarank, getsvadzk, yerevouyt (ներկայութիւն, կերպարանք, կեցուածք, երեւոյթ)
present (n) - nerga, arti, badrasd, anmichagan (ներկայ, արդի, պատրաստ, անմիջական)
present (v) - nergayatsunel, nuvirel, dal, tsoutsunel (ներկայացնել, նուիրել, տալ, ցուցնել)
presentable - nergayanali, vayelouch (ներկայանալի, վայելուչ)
presentation - nergayatsoum, hantes, undzayoum (ներկայացում, հանդէս, ընծայում)
presenter - nergayatsunogh (ներկայացնող)
presentiment - nakhazkatsoum, charakoushagoutiun (նախազգացում, չարագուշակութիւն)
presently - anmichabes, shoudov, nergayis (անմիջապէս, շուտով, ներկայիս)
presentment - nergayatsoum, madoutsoum (ներկայացում, մատուցում)
preservable - baheli, bahadzo (պահելի, պահածոյ)
preservation - bahbanoutiun, abahovoutiun (պահպանութիւն, ապահովութիւն)
preservative - nakharkelich, bahbanag, nakhategh, (նախարգելիչ, պահպանակ, նախադեղ)
preserve - bahbanel, bahel, bahadzo, kaghtsuraveni (պահպանել, պահել, պահածոյ, քաղցրաւենի)
preside - nakhakahel, adenabedel, verahusgel (նախագահել, ատենապետել, վերահսկել)
presidency, presidentship - nakhakahoutiun (նախագահութիւն)
president - nakhakah, adenabed (նախագահ, ատենապետ)
presidential - nakhakahagan (նախագահական)
presider - nakhakahogh, verahusgogh (նախագահող, վերահսկիչ)
press (n) - dubaran, mamoul, lurakroutiun, ajabarank (տպարան, մամուլ, լրագրութիւն, աճապարանք)
press (v) - dubel, artougel, seghmel, junshel, jumlel (տպել, արդուկել, սեղմել, ճնշել, ճմլել)
press conferenc - mamlo asoulis (մամլոյ ասուլիս)
press release - mamlo lousapanoum, patsahaydoum (մամլոյ լուսաբանում, բացայայտում)
pressing - junshoum, usdiboghagan, anhedatsukeli (ճնշում, ստիպողական, անյետաձգելի)
pressman - dubogh, dubakrich, lurakurogh, mamlavar (տպող, տպագրիչ, լրագրող, մամլավար)
pressroom - dubaran, dubakradoun (տպարան, տպագրատուն)
pressure - junshoum, usdiboum, dubvadzk (ճնշում, ստիպում, տպուածք)
presswork - dubakuroutiun (տպագրութիւն)

prestige - humayk, hampav, varg, badrank (հմայք, համբաւ, վարկ, պատրանք)
presto - junshep, shoudapouyt (ճնշեփ, շուտափոյթ)
presume - yentaturel, hamarel, gardzel, untounil (ենթադրել, համարել, կարծել, ընդունիլ)
presumption - yentaturoutiun, gardzik, medzamudoutiun (ենթադրութիւն, կարծիք, մեծամտութիւն)
presumptuous - inknahavan, medzamid, havagnod, hantoukun (ինքնահաւան, մեծամիտ, յաւակնոտ, յանդուգն)
pretend - havagnil, tsevatsunel, bahanchel, geghdzel (յաւակնիլ, ձեւացնել, պահանջել, կեղծել)
pretender - havagnort, tegnadzou (յաւակնորդ, թեկնածու)
pretense, pretence - badruvag, havagnoutiun, geghdzoum (պատրուակ, յաւակնութիւն, կեղծիք)
pretension - havagnoutiun, bahanch, hedamudoutiun (յաւակնութիւն, պահանջ, հետամտութիւն)
pretentious - havagnod, medzamid (յաւակնոտ, մեծամիտ)
pretext - badruvag, badjarank, timag, geghdzik (պատրուակ, պատճառանք, դիմակ, կեղծիք)
pretty - keghetsig, siroun, kuravich, vayelouch, kunkoush (գեղեցիկ, սիրուն, գրաւիչ, վայելուչ, քնքուշ)
prevail - ishkhel, direl, haghtel (իշխել, տիրել, յաղթել)
prevalence - kerishkhoum, aztetsoutiun, zoroutiun (գերիշխում, ազդեցութիւն, զօրութիւն)
prevalent - dirogh, kerishkhogh, keragushir, aztetsig (տիրող, գերիշխող, գերակշիռ, ազդեցիկ)
prevent - arkilel, gankhel, khapanel, gasetsunel (արգիլել, կանխել, խափանել, կասեցնել)
preventer - arkologh, khapanogh (արգիլող, խափանող)
prevention - gankhoum, khapanoum, arkelk (կանխում, խափանում, արգելք)
preventive - gankharkelich, nakhazkoushagan (կանխարգելիչ, նախազգուշական)
preview - nakhatsoutsatroutiun, gankhadesoutiun (նախացուցադրութիւն, կանխատեսութիւն)
previous - nakhuntats, nakhgin, nakhort (նախընթաց, նախկին, նախորդ)
previously - nakhabes, nakhorok, gankhabes (նախապէս, նախօրօք, կանխապէս)
previse - gankhakoushagel, nakhadesel (կանխազգուշակել, նախատեսել)
prevision - nakhadesoutiun, koushagoutiun (նախատեսութիւն, գուշակութիւն)
prey - avar, goghoboud, ger, vors, jarag, zoh (աւար, կողոպուտ, կեր, որս, ճարակ, զոհ)
preyer - avararou, hapushdagich, kishadich (աւարառու, յափշտակիչ, գիշատիչ)
pre-eminent - kerabadiv, nakhabadiv, nushanavor (գերապատիւ, նախապատիւ, նշանաւոր)
price - kin, arzhek, vartsk, kunahadel, kin gudrel (գին, արժէք, վարձք, գնահատել, գին կտրել)
price list - sagatsouyts, kunatsoutsag (սակացոյց, գնացուցակ)
priceless - ankin, ankunahadeli (անգին, անգնահատելի)
prick - khutan, khaytots, dzag, khotel, khaytel, dzagel (խթան, խայթոց, ծակ, խոթել, խայթել, ծակել)
pricker - khaytogh, gudzogh, khutan (խայթող, կծող, խթան)
prickle - poush, khayt, khaytel, gujel (փուշ, խայթ, խայթել, կճել)
prickliness - pushodoutiun (փշոտութիւն)
pride - hubardoutiun, medzamudoutiun, hubardanal (հպարտութիւն, մեծամտութիւն, հպարտանալ)
prideful - hubard, medzamid, arhamarhod (հպարտ, մեծամիտ, արհամարհոտ)

prier - hedekurkir, lurdesogh (հետաքրքիր, լրտեսող)
priest - kahana, derder, yerets, kourm (քահանայ, տէրտէր, երէց, քուրմ)
priesthood - kahanayoutiun (քահանայութիւն)
prig - sagargel, azhantsunel, shortel, kogh, havagnort (սակարկել, աժանցնել, շորթել, գող, յաւակնորդ)
priggish - medzamid, inknahavan, havagnod (մեծամիտ, ինքնահաւան, յաւակնոտ)
prim - setevet, tsevaser, godurduvogh, setevetel (սեթեւեթ, ձեւասէր, կոտրտուող, սեթեւեթել)
prima - arachin, kulkhavor (առաջին, գլխաւոր)
prima donna - nakherkchouhi, khulkhavor yerkchouhi (նախերգչուհի, գլխաւոր երգչուհի)
primacy - arachnoutiun, arkebisgobosoutiun (առաջնութիւն, արքեպիսկոպոսութիւն)
primal - kulkhavor, usguzpunagan, arachin (գլխաւոր, սկզբնական, առաջին)
primarily - nakh yev arach (նախ եւ առաջ)
primary - nakhnagan, usguzpnagan, nakhagurtaran (նախնական, սկզբնական, նախակրթարան)
primary school - dzaghgots, nakhazhoghov (ծաղկոց, նախաժողով)
primate - yebisgobosabed, arachnort (եպիսկոպոսապետ, առաջնորդ)
prime (a) - arachin, darragan, usguzpunagan, yereveli (առաջին, տարրական, սկզբնական, երեւելի)
prime (n) - aravod, ayk, arshalouys, dzakoum, mangoutiun (առաւօտ, այգ, արշալոյս, ծագում, մանկութիւն)
prime (v) - letsunel, nakhamarzel, dal (լեցնել, նախամարզել, տալ)
prime minister - varchabed, nakhararabed (վարչապետ, նախարարապետ)
prime time - nakhazham, usguzpunazham (նախաժամ, սկզբնաժամ)
primer - ayppenaran, aghotakirk, khantsargou (այբբենարան, աղօթագիրք, խանձարկու)
primeval - nakhatarian, nakhnagan (նախադարեան, նախնական)
primitive - nakhnagan, nakhatarian, hin, darragan (նախնական, նախադարեան, հին, տարրական)
primly - nazankov, godurdouelov (նազանքով, կոտրտուելով)
primness - nazank, tsevasiroutiun (նազանք, ձեւասիրութիւն)
primogeniture - antrangoutiun, yeritsoutiun (անդրանկութիւն, երիցութիւն)
primordial - nakhnagan, usguzpunagan, nakhamedzar (նախնական, սկզբնական, նախամեծար)
primrose - karnanadzaghig (գարնանածաղիկ)
prince - ishkhan, arkayorti (իշխան, արքայորդի)
princedom - ishkhanoutiun (իշխանութիւն)
princely - ishkhanavayel, ishkhanagan, ishkhanagerb (իշխանավայել, իշխանական, իշխանակերպ)
princess - ishkhanouhi, arkayatousdur (իշխանուհի, արքայադուստր)
principal - kulkhavor, himnagan, desouch, mayr koumar (գլխաւոր, հիմնական, տեսուչ, մայր գումար)
principality - ishkhanoutiun, ishkhanabedoutiun (իշխանութիւն, իշխանապետութիւն)
principally - kulkhavorabes, manavant, aravelapar (գլխաւորապէս, մանաւանդ, առաւելաբար)
principle - usguzpounk, himnaged, orenk, ganon, dar (սկզբունք, հիմնակէտ, օրէնք, կանոն, տարր)
prink - bujnuvil, zartarvil, bujnel (պճնուիլ, զարդարուիլ, պճնել)
prinkle - poush, khayt, khaytel, gujel, dzagel (փուշ, խայթ, խայթել, կճել, ծակել)
prinkly-heat - kurdinkkhash (քրտինքխաշ)
print (n) - turoshm, dib, hedk, du-

bakroutiun, porakuroutiun (դրոշմ, տիպ, հետք, տպագրութիւն, փորագրութիւն)
print (v) - dubel, dubakurel, turoshmel, huradaragel (տպել, տպագրել, դրոշմել, հրատարակել)
printer - dubogh, dubakurich, dubich (տպող, տպագրիչ, տպիչ)
printing - dubakuroutiun, duboum (տպագրութիւն, տպում)
printing press - dubakurich, dubakramekena (տպագրիչ, տպագրամեքենայ)
printing shop - dubakuradoun (տպագրատուն)
prior - nakhgin, nakhuntats, usguzpunagan, vanahayr (նախկին, նախընթաց, սկզբնական, վանահայր)
prioress - vanamayr, medzavorouhi (վանամայր, մեծաւորուհի)
priority - nakhabadvoutiun, arachnoutiun (նախապատուութիւն, առաջնութիւն)
priory - vank, vanadoun, menasdan (վանք, վանատուն, մենաստան)
prism - burismag, hadvadzagoghm (պրիսմակ, հատուածակողմ)
prison - pand, pandargoutiun, pandargel (բանտ, բանտարկութիւն, բանտարկել)
prisoner - pandargyal, keri (բանտարկեալ, գերի)
pristine - nakhgin, nakhni, hin, vaghemi (նախկին, նախնի, հին, վաղեմի)
privacy - arantsnoutiun, menoutiun, mudermoutiun (առանձնութիւն, մենութիւն, մտերմութիւն)
private - antsnagan, masnavor, arantsnahadoug, kaghduni (անձնական, մասնաւոր, առանձնայատուկ, գաղտնի)
privation - zurgank, garik, garod, bashdonazurgoum (զրկանք, կարիք, կարօտ, պաշտօնազրկում)
privative - zurgogh, patsasagan, zhukhdogh (զրկող, բացասական, ժխտող)
privilege - arantsnashunorhoum, ardonoutiun, menashunorhel (առանձնաշնորհում, արտօնութիւն, մենաշնորհել)
privity - kaghdnik, antsnagan, satrank, dzununtagank (գաղտնիք, անձնական, սաղրանք, ծննդականք)
privy - arantsin, masnavor, kaghdni (առանձին, մասնաւոր, գաղտնի)
prize (n) - murtsanag, barkev, vijagahanoutiun, avar (մրցանակ, պարգեւ, վիճակահանութիւն, աւար)
prize (v) - kunahadel, kin gudrel ludzagov sharzhel (գնահատել, գին կտրել, լծակով շարժել)
probability - havanaganoutiun (հաւանականութիւն)
probable - havanagan (հաւանական)
probably - havanapar (հաւանաբար)
probate - gudagi vaveratsoum, vaveratsial gudag (կտակի վաւերացում, վաւերացեալ կտակ)
probation - tad, tadakunnoutiun, abatsouyts, tsoutsoum (դատ, դատաքննութիւն, ապացոյց, ցուցում)
probator - tadakunnich, kunnich (դատաքննիչ, քննիչ)
probe - kunnel, virachapel, zunnel, virachap (քննել, վիրաչափել, զննել, վիրաչափ)
probity - oughghamudoutiun, artaramudoutiun (ուղղամտութիւն, արդարամտութիւն)
problem - khuntir, harts, areghdzuvadz (խնդիր, հարց, առեղծուած)
problematic - khunturagan, hartsagan, vijeli, anorosh (խնդրական, հարցական, վիճելի, անորոշ)
procedure - untatsk, kordzelagerb, tadavaroutiun, varmounk (ընթացք, գործելակերպ, դատավարութիւն, վարմունք)
proceed - usgusil, varel, tserk arnel, tad varel (սկսիլ, վարել, ձեռք առնել, դատ վարել)
proceeding - untatsk, kordzargoutiun, tadavaroutiun (ընթացք, գործարկութիւն, դատավարութիւն)
proceeds - hasouyt, yegamoud, artiunk (հասոյթ, եկամուտ, արդիւնք)
process - untatsk, gerb, kordzun-

tats, tadavaroutiun (ընթացք, կերպ, գործընթաց, դատավարութիւն)
procession - untastk, kunatsk, tapor, dzakoum (ընթացք, գնացք, թափոր, ծագում)
processioner - hantisagan, tapori masnagtogh (հանդիսական, թափորի մասնակցող)
proclaim - hurchagel, haydararel, huradaragel (հռչակել, յայտարարել, հրատարակել)
proclamation - hurchagoum, haydararoutiun (հռչակում, յայտարարութիւն)
proclivity - hagoum, midoum, badrasdagamoutiun (հակում, միտում, պատրաստակամութիւն)
proconsul - pokh hiubados (փոխ հիւպատոս)
procrastinate - hedatsukel, habaghel, oushatsunel (յետաձգել, յապաղել, ուշացնել)
procrastination - hedatsukoum, tsuktsukoum (յետաձգում, ձգձգում)
procreant - artiuanaper, budghaper, dzunich (արդիւնաբեր, պտղաբեր, ծնիչ)
procreate - dzunanil, ardaturel (ծնանիլ, արտադրել)
procreation - vortedzunoutiun, dzununtakordzoutiun (որդեծնութիւն, ծննդագործութիւն)
procreative - dzununtagan, dzunanich, ardaturich (ծննդական, ծնանիչ, արտադրիչ)
proctive - hagamed, hoshar (հակամէտ, յօժար)
proctor - veragatsou, pokhanort (վերակացու, փոխանորդ)
procumbent - kednadaradz, kednamadz (գետնատարած, գետնամած)
procuration - pokhanortoutiun, pokhanortakir, haytaytoum (փոխանորդութիւն, փոխանորդագիր, հայթայթում)
procurator - kordzagadar, pokhanort (գործակատար, փոխանորդ)
procure - haytaytel, jarel, kudnel, gavadoutiun unel (հայթայթել, ճարել, գտնել, կաւատութիւն ընել)
procurement - haytaytoum (հայթայթում)
procurer - haytaytogh, jarogh, gavad (հայթայթող, ճարող, կաւատ)
procuress - gavadouhi, gin haytaytogh (կաւատուհի, կին հայթայթող)
prod - khutan, heriun, khutanel, mukhdel, dzagel (խթան, հերիւն, խթանել, մխտել, ծակել)
prodigal - shurayl, muskhogh, anarag (շռայլ, մսխող, անառակ)
prodigality - shurayloutiun, vadnoum, muskhoum (շռայլութիւն, վատնում, մսխում)
prodigious - uskancheli, zarmanali, abshetsoutsich (սքանչելի, զարմանալի, ապշեցուցիչ)
prodigy - hurashk, zarmanalik, uskanchelik (հրաշք, զարմանալիք, սքանչելիք)
produce (n) - ardaturank, artiunk (արտադրանք, արդիւնք)
produce (v) - ardaturel, dzunanil, koyatsunel, pematurel (արտադրել, ծնանիլ, գոյացնել, բեմադրել)
producer - ardaturogh, pematurogh, dzunogh (արտադրող, բեմադրող, ծնող)
product - ardaturoutiun, perk, artiunk, hasouyt (արտադրութիւն, բերք, արդիւնք, հասոյթ)
production - ardaturoutiun, ardaperoutiun (արտադրութիւն, արտաբերութիւն)
productive - artiunaper, arkasaper, ardaturogh (արդիւնաբեր, արգասաբեր, արտադրող)
productivity - artiunaperoutiun, ardaturoghaganoutiun (արդիւնաբերութիւն, արտադրողականութիւն)
proem - nakhapan, neradzoutiun (նախաբան, ներածութիւն)
proface - pari kalousd, pari ulla (բարի գալուստ, բարի ըլլայ)
profane (a) - bighdz, ansourp, ashkharhig, anmakour (պիղծ, անսուրբ, աշխարհիկ, անմաքուր)
profane (v) - bughdzel, abaganel,

yeghdzel, yeghdzanel (պղծել, ապականել, եղծել, եղծանել)
profaner - bughdzogh, abaganogh, surpabighdz, hayhoyich (պղծող, ապականող, սրբապիղծ, հայհոյիչ)
profanity - surpabughdzoutiun, hayhoyoutiun (սրբապղծութիւն, հայհոյութիւն)
profess - khosdovanil, tavanil, haydararel, ardahaydel (խոստովանիլ, դաւանիլ, յայտարարել, արտայայտել)
profession - masnakidoutiun, uzpaghoum, gochoum, tavanank (մասնագիտութիւն, զբաղում, կոչում, դաւանանք)
professional - masnaked, arhesdakidagan, arvesdavarzh (մասնագէտ, արհեստագիտական, արուեստավարժ)
professionalism - arhesdakidoutiun, arvesdavarzhoutiun (արհեստագիտութիւն, արուեստավարժութիւն)
professor - ousoutschabed, tasakhos, khosdovanogh (ուսուցչապետ, դասախօս, խոստովանող)
professorship - ousoutschoutiun, varzhabedoutiun (ուսուցչութիւն, վարժապետութիւն)
proffer - undzayel, dal, arachargel, undza, aracharg (ընծայել, տալ, առաջարկել, ընծայ, առաջարկ)
proficience, cy - humdoutiun, portsakidoutiun, adagoutiun (հմտութիւն, փորձագիտութիւն, ատակութիւն)
proficient - humoud, adag, portsaked, masnaked (հմուտ, ատակ, փորձագէտ, մասնագէտ)
profile - gisatemk, ourvakidz, shurchakidz, ourvakudzel (կիսադէմք, ուրուագիծ, շրջագիծ, ուրուագծել)
profit - shah, okoud, hasouyt, shahil, shahetsunel (շահ, օգուտ, հասոյթ, շահիլ, շահեցնել)
profitability - shahavedoutiun (շահաւէտութիւն)
profitable - shahaper, vajarashah, okdagar, tserundou (շահաբեր, վաճառաշահ, օգտակար, ձեռնտու)
profligacy - tsopoutiun, anparoyoutiun (ցոփութիւն, անբարոյութիւն)
profligate - tsop, anparo, anarag (ցոփ, անբարոյ, անառակ)
proforma invoice - nakhahashvetsouyts (նախահաշուեցոյց)
profound - khor, khoroung, khorimats, khoratapants (խոր, խորունկ, խորիմաց, խորաթափանց)
profuse - aradatserun, shurayl, liarad (առատաձեռն, շռայլ, լիառատ)
profusion - aradatsernoutiun, shurayloutiun, muskhoum (առատաձեռնութիւն, շռայլութիւն, մսխում)
prog - mouralov shurchil, koghnal, shurchig mouradzgan (մուրալով շրջիլ, գողնալ, շրջիկ մուրացկան)
progenitor - nakhahayr, bab (նախահայր, պապ)
progenitress - nakhamayr (նախամայր)
progeny - serount, sharavigh, hednortner (սերունդ, շառաւիղ, յետնորդներ)
prognosis - akhdajanachoum, nakhimatsoutiun (ախտաճանաչում, նախիմացութիւն)
prognostic - nakhanushan, akhdanushan, akhdakoushag (նախանշան, ախտանշան, ախտագուշակ)
program, programme - haydakir, dzurakir (յայտագիր, ծրագիր)
programming - haydakuroum, dzurakuroum (յայտագրում, ծրագրում)
progress - harachtimoutiun, ajoum, harachanal, harachtimel (յառաջդիմութիւն, աճում, յառաջանալ, յառաջդիմել)
progressist - harachtimagan (յառաջդիմական)
progressive - harachtimagan, harachatem, ajogh (յառաջդիմական, յառաջադէմ, աճող)
prohibit - arkilel, khapanel (արգիլել, խափանել)
prohibition - arkiloum, khapanoum, arkelk (արգիլում, խափանում, արգելք)
project (n) - nakhakidz, dzurakir, midk, khorhourt (նախագիծ, ծրա-

գիր, միտք, խորհուրդ)

project (v) - nakhakudzel, dzurakurel, artsagel, nedel (նախագծել, ծրագրել, արձակել, նետել)

projectile - hurtir, artsagvadz roump (հրթիռ, արձակուած ռումբ)

projection - tsaydoum, lousartsagoum, nakhakudzoum (ցայտում, լուսարձակում, նախագծում)

projector - lousartsag, dzurakurogh, nakhakudzogh (լուսարձակ, ծրագրող, նախագծող))

prolepsis - gankhoum, gankharoutiun (կանխում, կանխառութիւն)

proletarian - unchazourg ashkhadavor, aghkad (ընչազուրկ աշխատաւոր, աղքատ)

proletariate - ashkhadavoroutiun, panvoroutiun (աշխատաւորութիւն, բանուորութիւն)

prolix - tsantsuranali, yergarapan, shadakhos (ձանձրանալի, երկարաբան, շատախօս)

prologue - harachapan, nakhapan, nakherkank (յառաջաբան, նախաբան, նախերգանք)

prolong - yergarel, yergaratsukel, oushatsunel, habaghel (երկարել, երկարաձգել, ուշացնել, յապաղել)

prolongation - yergaratsoum, yergaratsukoum (երկարացում, երկարաձգում)

promenade (n) - budouyd, shurchakayoutiun, jemavayr (պտոյտ, շրջագայութիւն, ճեմավայր)

promenade (v) - bududil, shurchakayil (պտըտիլ, շրջագայիլ)

prominence, prominency - yereveliоutiun, tsutsvadzk, partsounk (երեւելիութիւն, ցցուածք, բարձունք)

prominent - yereveli, tsutsoun (երեւելի, ցցուն)

promiscuity - kharnuvadzoutiun, kharnagoutiun (խառնուածութիւն, խառնակութիւն)

promiscuous - kharun, kharnag, aylaser, aylazan (խառն, խառնակ, այլասեռ, այլազան)

promise - khosdanal, housaturel, khosdoum, khosk (խոստանալ, յուսադրել, խոստում, խօսք)

promisee - khosdoumnarou, khosdatsial (խոստումնառու, խոստացեալ)

promising - housadou, housalits, khosdoumnalits (յուսատու, յուսալից, խոստումնալից)

promisor - khosdatsogh, hantsnarou (խոստացող, յանձնառու)

promontory - hurvantan, saravant (հրուանդան, սարաւանդ)

promote - partsuratsunel, harachatsunel, kachalerel (բարձրացնել, յառաջացնել, քաջալերել)

promoter - kachalerogh, nubasdogh, turtich (քաջալերող, նպաստող, դրդիչ)

promotion - partsuratsoum, harachatsoum, asdijanavoroum (բարձրացում, յառաջացում, աստիճանաւորում)

promotive - khurakhousich, housalits (խրախուսիչ, յուսալից)

prompt (a) - arak, shoud, ushdab, jisht, badrasd (արագ, շուտ, շտապ, ճիշդ, պատրաստ)

prompt (v) - poutatsunel, houshel, turtel, mughel (փութացնել, յուշել, դրդել, մղել)

prompter - housharar, poutatsunogh (յուշարար, փութացնող)

promptitude - arakoutiun, poutgodoutiun, jushtabahoutiun (արագութիւն, փութկոտութիւն, ճշդապահութիւն)

promptly - poutov, shoudov, arakoren (փութով, շուտով, արագօրէն)

promulgate - hurabaragel, haydararel (հրապարակել, յայտարարել)

promulgation - hurabaragoum, huradaragoum (հրապարակում, հրատարակում)

promulgator - haydararogh (յայտարարող)

promulge - huradaragel, sorvetsunel (հրատարակել, սորվեցնել)

promulger - huradaragogh (հրատարակող)

prone - kulkhivayr, hagial, dzuradz, hagamed (գլխիվայր, հակեալ, ծռած, հակամէտ)

prong - zhanik, adam kordziki, dzagel (ժանիք, ատամ գործիքի, ծակել)
pronominal - teranvanagan, timavor (դերանուանական, դիմաւոր)
pronoun - teranoun (դերանուն)
pronounce - ardasanel, hunchel, arokanel (արտասանել, հնչել, առոգանել)
pronounceable - ardasaneli (արտասանելի)
pronouncement - bashdonagan haydararoutiun (պաշտօնական յայտարարութիւն)
pronunciation - hunchoum, ardasanoutiun (հնչում, արտասանութիւն)
proof - abatsouyts, pasd, ports, antapantsig (ապացոյց, փաստ, փորձ, անթափանցիկ)
proof-reader - surpakurogh, portseru gartatsogh (սրբագրող, փորձերը կարդացող)
proof-reading - surpakuroum (սրբագրում)
prop - netsoug, henag, netsoug tunel (նեցուկ, յենակ, նեցուկ դնել)
propaganda - karozchoutiun, kaghapari daradzoum (քարոզչութիւն, գաղափարի տարածում)
propagandist - kaghaparadaradz, karozich (գաղափարատարած, քարոզիչ)
propagate - shadtsunel, pazmatsunel, daradzel, ajil (շատցնել, բազմացնել, տարածել, աճիլ)
propagation - daradzoum, dzavaloum, seroum, ajoum (տարածում, ծաւալում, սերում, աճում)
propel - hurel, kushel, arach mughel, khutanel (հրել, քշել, առաջ մղել, խթանել)
propeller - sharzhich, mughich budoudag (շարժիչ, մղիչ պտուտակ)
propend - tsukdil, midil (ձգտիլ, միտիլ)
propense - hagamed, hozharamid (հակամէտ, յօժարամիտ)
propension - hagamidoutiun (հակամիտութիւն)
propensity - hagoum, midoum, hozharoutiun (հակում, միտում, յօժարութիւն)
proper - hadoug, sepagan, harmar, jisht, vayelouch (յատուկ, սեփական, յարմար, ճիշդ, վայելուչ)
properly - badshajoren, shunorhkov (պատշաճօրէն, շնորհքով)
property - sepaganoputiun, galvadz, inchk, ounetsvadzk (սեփականութիւն, կալուած, ինչք, ունեցուածք)
prophecy - markareoutiun, koushagoutiun (մարգարէութիւն, գուշակութիւն)
prophesier - markareatsogh (մարգարէացող)
prophesy - markareanal, koushagel (մարգարէանալ, գուշակել)
prophet - markare, koushag (մարգարէ, գուշակ)
prophylactic - gankhazkoushagan, gankharkelich tegh (կանխազգուշական, կանխարգելիչ դեղ)
propine - oukhdel, khosdanal, genats khumel (ուխտել, խոստանալ, կենաց խմել)
propinquity - modigoutiun, mertsavoroutiun, azkaganoutiun (մօտիկութիւն, մերձաւորութիւն, ազգականութիւն)
propitiate - paghakushel, meghmel, khaghaghetsunel (փաղաքշել, մեղմել, խաղաղեցնել)
propitiation - hantardoum, khaghaghoum, hashdoutiun (հանդարտում, խաղաղում, հաշտութիւն)
propitiator - hashdarar, kavich (հաշտարար, քաւիչ)
propitious - nubasdavor, hashd, badeh, harmar (նպաստաւոր, հաշտ, պատեհ, յարմար)
propoganda - karozchoutiun, dzavaloum, daradzoum (քարոզչութիւն, ծաւալում, տարածում)
proportion - hamemadoutiun, paghtadoputiun, hamemadel (համեմատութիւն, բաղդատութիւն, համեմատել)
proportional - hamemadagan, badshaj (համեմատական, պատշաճ)
proportionate - hamemadel, badsha-

jetsunel (համեմատել, պատշաճեցնել)
proposal - aracharg, arachargoutiun (առաջարկ, առաջարկութիւն)
propose - arachargel, nergayatsunel, tserku khunturel (առաջարկել, ներկայացնել, ձեռքը խնդրել)
proposition - arachargoutiun, khoskgab, nakhatasoutiun (առաջարկութիւն, խօսքկապ, նախադասութիւն)
propound - arachargel, arachaturel (առաջարկել, առաջադրել)
proprietary - menashunorhyal, sepaganoutian iravounk (մենաշնորհեալ, սեփականութեան իրաւունք)
proprietor - der, galvadzader, sepaganader (տէր, կալուածատէր, սեփականատէր)
propriety - badshajoutiun, harmaroutiun, vayelchoutiun (պատշաճութիւն, յարմարութիւն, վայելչութիւն)
propulsion - mughoum, harach mughoum, huroum (մղում, յառաջ մղում, հրում)
prorogation - yergaratsukoum, hedatsukoum (երկարաձգում, յետաձգում)
prorogue - yergaratsukel, hedatsukel, tatretsunel (երկարաձգել, յետաձգել, դադրեցնել)
prosaic - artsagounag, hasarag, anshouk (արձակունակ, հասարակ, անշուք)
proscenium - tadroni nakhapem (Թատրոնի նախաբեմ)
proscribe - iravazurgel, darakurel, vurundel, arkilel (իրաւազրկել, տարագրել, վռնտել, արգիլել)
proscription - iravazurgoum, arkiloum, aksor (իրաւազրկում, արգիլում, աքսոր)
prose - artsag, artsagakuroutiun, dapag, artsagakurel (արձակ, արձակագրութիւն, տափակ, արձակագրել)
prosecutable - tadabardeli, hedabunteli (դատապարտելի, հետապնդելի)
prosecute - hedabuntel, hedamudil, tadi kashel, ampasdanel (հետապնդել, հետամտիլ, դատի քաշել, ամբաստանել)
prosecution - tadavaroutiun, hedabuntoum (դատավարութիւն, հետապնդում)
prosecutor - tadakhaz, hedabuntogh (դատախազ, հետապնդող)
proselyte - noratarts, norahavad, havadapokhel (նորադարձ, նորահաւատ, հաւատափոխել)
proselytism - martorsortouiun, havadapoghoutiun (մարդորսորդութիւն, հաւատափոխութիւն)
proser - artsagakir, hedevag kurogh (արձակագիր, հետեւակ գրող)
prosign - nakhanushan, nakhapar (նախանշան, նախաբառ)
prosiness - jabaghoutiun (ճապաղութիւն)
prosody - daghachapoutiun, arokanoutiun (տաղաչափութիւն, առոգանութիւն)
prospect - heranugar, houys, desaran, kunnel, voronel (հեռանկար, յոյս, տեսարան, քննել, որոնել)
prospection - nakhadesoutiun, voronoum (նախատեսութիւն, որոնում)
prospective - heranugar, kalik, abaka, usbasvogh (հեռանկար, գալիք, ապագայ, սպասուող)
prospector - khouzargogh (խուզարկող)
prospectus - dzanoutsakir, zegoutsakir, deghegakir (ծանուցագիր, զեկուցագիր, տեղեկագիր)
prosper - parkavajil, dzaghgil, hachoghil, hachoghtsunel (բարգաւաճիլ, ծաղկիլ, յաջողիլ, յաջողցնել)
prosperity - parkavajoum, paregetsoutiun, dzaghgoum (բարգաւաճում, բարեկեցութիւն, ծաղկում)
prosperous - parkavaj, dzaghgoun, ajogh, hachoghag (բարգաւաճ, ծաղկուն, աճող, յաջողակ)
prostate - shakanagakeghts, harachakeghts (շագանակագեղձ, յառաջագեղձ)
prostitute - poz, bornig, bornugatsunel, bornugil (բոզ, պոռնիկ,

պոռնկացնել, պոռնկիլ)

prostitution - pornugoutiun, pozoutiun (պոռնկութիւն, բոզութիւն)

prostitutor - bornugatsogh, shunatsogh (պոռնկացող, շնացող)

prostrate (a) - kednadaradz, purvadz, khonarhadz (գետնատարած, փռուած, խոնարհած)

prostrate (v) - khonarhetsunel, uzkednel, yergurbakel, dabalel (խոնարհեցնել, զգետնել, երկրպագել, տապալել)

prostration - yergurbakoutiun, uzkednoum, ouzhasbaroum (երկրպագութիւն, զգետնում, ուժասպառում)

protect - bashdbanel, hovanavorel, bahbanel (պաշտպանել, հովանաւորել, պահպանել)

protection - bashdbanoutiun, hovani, tigounk (պաշտպանութիւն, հովանի, թիկունք)

protector - bashdban, hovanavor, khunamagal, hokadar (պաշտպան, հովանաւոր, խնամակալ, հոգատար)

protectorate - khunamagaloutiun (խնամակալութիւն)

protein - punasbid (բնասպիտ)

protest - poghok, poghokel, arargel, poghokakurel (բողոք, բողոքել, առարկել, բողոքագրել)

protestant - poghokagan, poghokogh (բողոքական, բողոքող)

Protestantism - poghokaganoutiun (Բողոքականութիւն)

protestation - poghok, arargoutiun, poghokakir (բողոք, առարկութիւն, բողոքագիր)

protocol - bashdonagan araroghagark, artsanakuroutiun (պաշտօնական արարողակարգ, արձանագրութիւն)

protomartyr - nakhavuga, nakhamardiros (նախավկայ, նախամարտիրոս)

protoplasm - nakhaniut, nakhakhumor (նախանիւթ, նախախմոր)

prototype - nakhadib, nakhabadger, usguzpnadib (նախատիպ, նախապատկեր, սկզբնատիպ)

protract - yergarel, yergaratsukel, habaghel (երկարել, երկարաձգել, յապաղել)

protraction - yergaratsukoum, habaghoum, tsuktsukoum (երկարաձգում, յապաղում, ձգձգում)

protractor - habaghogh, oushatsogh, angiunachap (յապաղող, ուշացող, անկիւնաչափ)

protrude - yerguntsunel, tours tsutsel, yergaril (երկնցնել, դուրս ցցել, երկարիլ)

protuberant - tsutsvadz, ouradz, ouroutsig (ցցուած, ուռած, ուռուցիկ)

proturberance - ouretsk, our, ardouyts, tsutsvadzk (ուռեցք, ուռ, արտոյց, ցցուածք)

proud - hubard, koroz, ampardavan, inknahavan (հպարտ, գոռոզ, ամբարտաւան, ինքնահաւան)

prove - abatsoutsel, pasdel, hasdadel, usdoukel (ապացուցնել, փաստել, հաստատել, ստուգել)

provenance - dzakoum, aghpiur, usgizp (ծագում, աղբիւր, սկիզբ)

provender - hart, khodajarag (յարդ, խոտաճարակ)

proverb - arag, asatsvadz (առակ, ասացուած)

proverbial - aragayin, hanrahayd, arag tartsadz (առակային, հանրայայտ, առակ դարձած)

provide - haytaytel, jarel, abahovel, madagararel, hokal (հայթայթել, ճարել, ապահովել, մատակարարել, հոգալ)

provided - yete, miayn te, baymanav vor, hashvi arnelov (եթէ, միայն թէ, պայմանաւ որ, հաշուի առնելով)

providence - nakhakhnamoutiun, heradesoutiun (նախախնամութիւն, հեռատեսութիւն)

provident - khohem, nakhakhunam, nakhades (խոհեմ, նախախնամ, նախատես)

providential - nakhakhnamagan, parepakhd (նախախնամական, բարեբախտ)

provider - nakhadesogh, haytaytogh, hokatsogh (նախատեսող, հայթայթող, հոգացող)
province - kavar, nahank, dzayramas (գաւառ, նահանգ, ծայրամաս)
provincial - kavarayin, kavaragan, keghchoug, barz (գաւառային, գաւառական, գեղջուկ, պարզ)
provision - nakhabadrasdoum, muteroum, bashar, haytaytel (նախապատրաստում, մթերում, պաշար, հայթայթել)
provisional - zhamanagavor, arzhamia, nakhnagan (ժամանակաւոր, առժամեայ, նախնական)
proviso - verabahoutiun, masnavor bayman, tashink (վերապահութիւն, մասնաւոր պայման, դաշինք)
provisor - veradesouch, veragatsou, varich (վերատեսուչ, վերակացու, վարիչ)
provocation - kurkuroutiun, kurkuroum, turtoum (գրգռութիւն, գրգռում, դրդում)
provocative - kurkurich, zayratsoutsich, khutanogh (գրգռիչ, զայրացուցիչ, խթանող)
provoke - kurkurel, zayratsunel, pargatsunel, turtel (գրգռել, զայրացնել, բարկացնել, դրդել)
provost - veradesouch, dunoren, kaghakabed (վերատեսուչ, տնօրէն, քաղաքապետ)
prow - tsuroug, harachamas navou (ցռուկ, յառաջամաս նաւու)
prowess - kachakordzoutiun, arioutiun, gudrijoutiun (քաջագործութիւն, արիութիւն, կտրիճութիւն)
prowl - vorsi modenal, taparil, sulukdal, avarel (որսի մօտենալ, թափառիլ, սլքտալ, աւարել)
proximate - anmichagan, mertsavor, modig (անմիջական, մերձաւոր, մօտիկ)
proximity - modigoutiun, turatsnoutiun (մօտիկութիւն, դրացնութիւն)
proxy - pokhanortoutiun, pokhanortakir, pokhanort (փոխանորդութիւն, փոխանորդագիր, փոխանորդ)
prude - soud bargeshd, bargeshd tsevatsogh gin (սուտ պարկեշտ, պարկեշտ ձեւացող կին)
prudence - uzkoushoutiun, khohemoutiun, imasdoutiun (զգուշութիւն, խոհեմութիւն, իմաստութիւն)
prudent - khohem, khohagan, imasdoun, shurchahayats (խոհեմ, խոհական, իմաստուն, շրջահայեաց)
prudential - uzkoushavor, khohagan, khorhurtagan (զգուշաւոր, խոհական, խորհրդական)
prudently - khohemapar, uzkoushoutiamp (խոհեմաբար, զգուշութեամբ)
prudery - amotkhadzoutiun (ամօթխածութիւն)
prune - hodel, tsevavorel jiugheru, chortsuvadz salor (յոտել, ձեւաւորել ճիւղերը, չորցուած սալոր)
prurient - tsangaser, marmachoun (ցանկասէր, մարմաջուն)
pry - lurdesel, hedazodel, khouzargel, kunnel, ludzag (լրտեսել, հետազօտել, խուզարկել, քննել, լծակ)
prying - khouzargou, hartsaser, hedazodich (խուզարկու, հարցասէր, հետազօտիչ)
psalm - saghmos, hokevor yerk (Սաղմոս, հոգեւոր երգ)
psalmist - saghmoserkou, saghmosakir, tubir (Սաղմոսերգու, Սաղմոսագիր, դպիր)
pseudonym - geghdzanoun, dzadzganoun (կեղծանուն, ծածկանուն)
psychiatrist - hokepouzh (հոգեբոյժ)
psychiatry - hokepouzhoutiun (հոգեբուժութիւն)
psychic - hokegan, hokepouzhagan, mudayin (հոգեկան, հեգեբուժական, մտային)
psychism - vokeganoutiun (ոգեկանութիւն)
psychologic, al - hokepanagan (հոգեբանական)
psychologist - hokepan (հոգեբան)
psychology - hokepanoutiun (հոգեբանութիւն)
psychomancy - vokehumahoutiun (ոգեհմայութիւն)

psychosis – *mudavijag, hokevijag* (մտավիճակ, հոգեվիճակ)
psychotherapy – *hokepouzhoutiun, mudapouzhoutiun* (հոգեբուժութիւն, մտաբուժութիւն)
pubcaster – *hanrayin khosnag* (հանրային խօսնակ)
puberty – *arpounk, chapahasoutiun* (արբունք, չափահասութիւն)
pubescent – *chapahas, aghvamazia* (չափահաս, աղուամազեայ)
public – *hanroutiun, zhoghovourt, hanrayin, hasaragats* (հանրութիւն, ժողովուրդ, հանրային, հասարակաց)
public access – *hanramadcheli* (հանրամատչելի)
public enemy – *hanroutian tushnami, hasaragats vudank* (հանրութեան թշնամի, հասարակաց վտանգ)
public house – *kinedoun, bantog* (գինետուն, պանդոկ)
public library – *hanrayin kurataran* (հանրային գրադարան)
public opinion – *hanrayin gardzik* (հանրային կարծիք)
public school – *bedagan varzharan, hanrayin tubrots* (պետական վարժարան, հանրային դպրոց)
public servant – *bedagan bashdonia* (պետական պաշտօնեայ)
public service – *hanrayin usbasargoutiun* (հանրային սպասարկութիւն)
publican – *hargahavak, hargahan, kineban, bantogabed* (հարկահաւաք, հարկահան, գինեպան, պանդոկապետ)
publication – *huradaragoutiun* (հրատարակութիւն)
publicist – *hurabaragakir* (հրապարակագիր)
publicity – *kovast, dzanoudzakir, azt, haydararoutiun* (գովազդ, ծանուցագիր, ազդ, յայտարարութիւն)
publicly – *hurabaragov* (հրապարակով)
publish – *huradaragel, hurabaragel, hurchagel* (հրատարակել, հրապարակել, հռչակել)
publisher – *huradaragich* (հրատարակիչ)
publishing house – *huradaragchadoun, huradaragchagan* (հրատարակչատուն, հրատարակչական)
publishment – *huradaragoutiun, huradaragoum* (հրատարակութիւն, հրատարակում)
puck – *char voki, charajuji* (չար ոգի, չարաճճի)
pucker – *gunjir, khorshom, gunjuril, khoshomil, gudzgil* (կնճիռ, խորշոմ, կնճռիլ, խորշոմիլ, կծկիլ)
pudder – *zhukhoril, aghmugel, khankarel, zhkhor, aghmoug* (ժխորիլ, աղմկել, խանգարել, ժխոր, աղմուկ)
pudding – *kaghtsur tukhvadzk, gargantag mu, yershig* (քաղցր թխուածք, կարկանդակ մը, երշիկ)
puddle – *churaqouyd, tsekh, tsekhodel, aghdodel, dzepel* (ջրակոյտ, ձեխ, ձեխոտել, աղտոտել, ծեփել)
pudency – *amotkhadzoutiun* (ամօթխածութիւն)
pudicity – *hamesdoutiun, uzkasdoutiun* (համեստութիւն, զգաստութիւն)
puerile – *dughayagan, mangagan, yerekhayagan* (տղայական, մանկական, երեխայական)
puerility – *dughayoutiun* (տղայութիւն)
puff – *puchoum, tetev shounch, oti hosank, puchel* (փչում, թեթեւ շունչ, օդի հոսանք, փչել)
puffer – *puchogh, borodakhos, medzapan* (փչող, պոռոտախօս, մեծաբան)
puffery – *pukourouyts, jorom, kovasank* (փքուռոյց, ճոռոմ, գովասանք)
puffy – *ouradz, ouroutsig, koroz, borodakhos* (ուռած, ուռուցիկ, գոռոզ, պոռոտախօս)
pug – *gabig, shunig, dapag kit, kharnel, dzepel* (կապիկ, շնիկ, տափակ քիթ, խառնել, ծեփել)
pugilism – *gurpamardoutiun, puruntskamard* (կռփամարտութիւն,

բռնցքամարտ)
pugilist - gurpamardig, puruntskamardig (կռփամարտիկ, բռնցքամարտիկ)
pugnacious - gurvaser, gurvazan (կռուասէր, կռուազան)
pugnacity - gurvazanoutiun (կռուազանութիւն)
puisne - gurdser, usdoratas (կտրսեր, ստորադաս)
puissance - zoroutiun, ouzh, ishkhanoutiun (զօրութիւն, ոյժ, իշխանութիւն)
puissant - zoravor, ouzhegh, huzor, garogh, dogoun (զօրաւոր, ուժեղ, հզօր, կարող, տոկուն)
puke - puskhel, puskhouk (փսխել, փսխուք)
pulchritude - vayelchoutiun, shunorh (վայելչութիւն, շնորհ)
pule - juchal, lal, hegegal (ճչալ, լալ, հեկեկալ)
puler - lalgan (լալկան)
pull (n) - jik, baykar, chank, tiargoutiun, dogatsoum (ճիգ, պայքար, ջանք, թիարկութիւն, տոկացում)
pull (v) - kashel, hanel, vertsunel, havakel, kashgurdel (քաշել, հանել, վերցնել, հաւաքել, քաշկռտել)
puller - tiavar, kashogh (թիավար, քաշող)
pullet - variag (վառեակ)
pulley - jakharag (ճախարակ)
pullman - nunchagark, shukeghagark (ննջակառք, շքեղակառք)
pullover - vernasvag, pourte vernazkesd (վերնաստակ, բուրդէ վերնազգեստ)
pulmonary - tokayin (թոքային)
pulp - khius, budghamichoug, dzoudzu hanel (խիւս, պտղամիջուկ, ծուծը հանել)
pulpit - ambion, pem, khoran, karozchoutiun (ամպիոն, բեմ, խորան, քարոզչութիւն)
pulpy - gagough, papoug, musoud (կակուղ, փափուկ, մսոտ)
pulsate - duropel, papakhel, turtural (տրոփել, բաբախել, թրթռալ)
pulsatile - papaghoun (բաբախուն)
pulsation - papakhoum, duropoum, zarg (բաբախում, տրոփում, զարկ)
pulsative - papakhoun (բաբախուն)
pulsatory - duropoun, papakhich (տրոփուն, բաբախիչ)
pulse - zargerag, surdi papakhoum, duropel, papakhel (զարկերակ, սրտի բաբախում, տրոփել, բաբախել)
pulverization - poshiatsoum, pushroum, gordzanoum (փոշիացում, փշրում, կործանում)
pulverize - poshiatsunel, pushrel, poshianal (փոշիացնել, փշրել, փոշիանալ)
pulverous - poshod, poshiod, pushroun, pukhroun (փոշոտ, փոշիոտ, փշրուն, փխրուն)
pulverulent - poshelits, pushroun, pushreli, poshiod (փոշելից, փըշրուն, փշրելի, փոշիոտ)
puma - gadvariudz (կատուառիւծ)
pummel, pommel - (gurpaharel, khupel, purountskov dzedzel (կռփահարել, խփել, բռունցքով ծեծել)
pump - mughag, churhan, otamough, churhanel, kashel (մղակ, ջրհան, օդամուղ, ջրհանել, քաշել)
pumper - churhan (ջրհան)
pumpkin - tutoum, tutmeni (դդում, դդմենի)
pun - parakhagh, parakhagh unel (բառախաղ, բառախաղ ընել)
punch - puruntskaharvadz, chermoghi, harvadzel, dzedzel (բռնցքահարուած, ջերմօղի, հարուածել, ծեծել)
puncher - dzagich (ծակիչ)
punchy - garj yev kiroug (կարճ եւ գիրուկ)
punctilious - pudzakhuntir, nurpanugad (բծախնդիր, նրբանկատ)
punctual - jushtabah, jushkurid (ճշդապահ, ճշգրիտ)
punctuality - jushtabahoutiun, jushkurdoutiun (ճշդապահութիւն, ճշգրտութիւն)
punctuate - gedaturel (կէտադրել)
punctuation - gedaturoutiun (կէտադրութիւն)

punctuator - gedaturogh (կէտադրող)
punctulate - gedgidavor, bisagavor (կէտկիտաւոր, պիսակաւոր)
puncture - khaytuvadzk, anivi dzagoum, khaytel, dzagel (խայթուածք, անիւի ծակում, խայթել, ծակել)
pungence - gudzououtiun, khaytoghoutiun (կծուութիւն, խայթողութիւն)
pungent - khaytogh, dzagogh, ayrogh, gudzou (խայթող, ծակող, այրող, կծու)
punic - gargetonagan, piunigyan, anvusdaheli, tavajan (կարկեդոնական, փիւնիկեան, անվստահելի, դաւաճան)
puniness - vochunchutiun (ոչնչութիւն)
punish - badjel, dzedzel (պատժել, ծեծել)
punisher - badzhogh (պատժող)
punishment - badizh, badzhoum, dzedz (պատիժ, պատժում, ծեծ)
punk - anarzhek, angarevor, nekhadz, bornig (անարժէք, անկարեւոր, նեխած, պոռնիկ)
puny - vochinch, chunchin, kheghj, dugar, pokrig (ոչինչ, չնչին, խեղճ, տկար, փոքրիկ)
pup - lagod, kotot, tsugnil, tsak perel (լակոտ, քոթոթ, ձկնիլ, ձագ բերել)
pupil - ashagerd, san, pip (աշակերտ, սան, բիբ)
pupilage, pupillage - ashagerdoutiun, anchapahasoutiun (աշակերտութիւն, անչափահասութիւն)
puppet - khamajig, boubrig (խամաճիկ, պուպրիկ)
puppy - lagod, shan tsak, inknahavan, tetevsolig (լակոտ, շան ձագ, ինքնահաւան, թեթեւսոլիկ)
pur - murmural, munchel, munchoum (մրմռալ, մունջել, մնջում)
purchase - kunel, arnel, kunoum (գնել, առնել, գնում)
purchaser - kunogh, kunort, hajakhort (գնող, գնորդ, յաճախորդ)
pure - makour, husdag, anarad, vujid, zoud, barz (մաքուր, յստակ, անարատ, վճիտ, զուտ, պարզ)
purfle - aseghnakordzel, zartarel, nugaragerdel (ասեղնագործել, զարդարել, նկարակերտել)
purgation - kavoum, surpoum, makroum (քաւում, սրբում, մաքրում)
purgatory - kavaran, makrogh, kavogh (քաւարան, մաքրող, քաւող)
purge (n) - loudzoghagan, makroum, zudoum (լուծողական, մաքրում, զտում)
purge (v) - kavel, surpel, makrel, makruvil, zudil (քաւել, սրբել, մաքրել, մաքրուիլ, զտիլ)
purger - makrogh, artaratsunogh (մաքրող, արդարացնող)
purification - makroum, zudoum, makrakordzoum (մաքրում, զտում, մաքրագործում)
purifier - zudich, makrich (զտիչ, մաքրիչ)
purify - makrel, zudel, surpel, kavel, makruvil (մաքրել, զտել, սրբել, քաւել, մաքրուիլ)
puritan - makraguron, khusdagiats, khusdaguron (մաքրակրօն, խստակեաց, խստակրօն)
purity - makroutiun, husdagoutiun, anmeghoutiun (մաքրութիւն, յստակութիւն, անմեղութիւն)
purl - aseghnakordz, dzoperiz, yezerazartel, gargachel (ասեղնագործ, ծոփերիզ, եզերազարդել, կարկաչել)
purlieu - shurchagayk, arvartsan (շրջակայք, արուարձան)
purloin - shortel, koghnal, hapushdagel (շորթել, գողնալ, յափշտակել)
purple - dziranekouyn, gayseragan, dziranekouyn nergel (ծիրանեգոյն, կայսերական, ծիրանեգոյն ներկել)
purport - nubadag, imasd, midk, nushanagel, imasd dal (նպատակ, իմաստ, միտք, նշանակել, իմաստ տալ)
purpose - mudaturoutiun, nubadag, arachaturel, voroshel (մտադրութիւն, նպատակ, առաջադրել, որո-

շել)
purpose (n) - nubadag, mudaturoutiun, midoum, dzurakir (նպատակ, մտադրութիւն, միտում, ծրագիր)
purpose (v) - arachaturel, voroshel, nushanagel (առաջադրել, որոշել, նշանակել)
purposeful - vujragam (վճռակամ)
purposeless - annubadag, andzurakir (աննպատակ, անծրագիր)
purposely - tidmamp, midoumnavor (դիտմամբ, միտումնաւոր)
purr - murmural, murmurouk (մռմռալ, մռմռուք)
purse - kusag, turamabanag, barg, kusagel (քսակ, դրամապանակ, պարկ, քսակել)
purser - kantsabed (գանձապետ)
pursuance - hedabuntoum, hedevoum, hedevank (Հետապնդում, Հետեւում, Հետեւանք)
pursuant - hamemad, hedevogh, ipur, usd, numan (Համեմատ, Հետեւող, իբր, ըստ, նման)
pursue - hedabuntel, haladzel, hedevil, tad panal (Հետապնդել, Հալածել, Հետեւիլ, դատ բանալ)
pursuit - hedabuntoum, hedamudoutiun, uzpaghoum (Հետապնդում, Հետամտութիւն, զբաղում)
pursuivant - sourhantag, luradar (սուրՀանդակ, լրատար)
pursy - ouradz, hapratsadz, garj ou ker (ուռած, յափրացած, կարճ ու գեր)
purulence - tarakhodoutiun (Թարախոտութիւն)
purulent - tarakhod (Թարախոտ)
purvey - madagararel, haytaytel, hokal (մատակարարել, ՀայԹայԹել, Հոգալ)
purveyance - amparoum, madagararoum, muteroum (ամբարում, մատակարարում, մԹերում)
purveyor - haytaytogh, madagararogh, muterogh (ՀայԹայԹող, մատակարարող, մԹերող)
pus - tarakh, sharav (Թարախ, շարաւ)
push (n) - huroum, mughoum, junshoum, jik, usdiboum (Հրում, մղում, մխում, ճնշում, ճիգ, ըստիպում)
push (v) - hurel, mukhel, kushel, junshel, usdibel (Հրել, մխել, քշել, ճնշել, ստիպել)
push button - gojag yelekduragan (կոճակ ելեքտրական)
pusher - hurogh, mukhdogh, mughich (Հրող, մխտող, մղիչ)
pushing, pushful - hurogh, tsernerets, hantuknoutiun (Հրող, ձեռներէց, յանդգնութիւն)
pusillanimity - vakhgodoutiun, vadasurdoutiun (վախկոտութիւն, վատասրտութիւն)
pusillanimous - vakhgod, yergchod, vadasird (վախկոտ, երկչոտ, վատասիրտ)
puss, pussy - pisig, piso, gadouig, (փիսիկ, փիսոյ, կատուիկ)
pustulate - balaril, balaretsunel, tarakhod verki veradzvil (պալարիլ, պալարեցնել, Թարախոտ վէրքի վերածուիլ)
put - tunel, hasdadel, deghavorel, nedel, garkel (դնել, Հաստատել, տեղաւորել, նետել, կարգել)
put away - khunayel, havakel (խնայել, Հաւաքել)
put back - tartsunel, yed dal (դարձնել, ետ տալ)
put by - muterel, bahel (մԹերել, պաՀել)
put down - dabalel, ichetsunel (տապալել, իջեցնել)
put forth - daradzel, yerguntsunel, larel (տարածել, երկնցնել, լարել)
put forward - arachargel, arach kushel (առաջարկել, առաջ քշել)
put off - jampel, heratsunel, hedatsukel, tsuktsukoum (ճամբել, Հեռացնել, յետաձգել, ձգձգում)
put on - haknil, kinu aveltsunel (Հագնիլ, գինը աւելցնել)
put out - tours hanel, tours kushel (դուրս Հանել, դուրս քշել)
put over - hachoghtsunel, vera tunel (յաջողցնել, վրայ դնել)
put together - paghtadel, hamemadel

(բաղդատել, համեմատել)
put up - otevanil, punagil (օթեւանիլ, բնակիլ)
putative - gardzetsial, yentaturial (կարծեցեալ, ենթադրեալ)
putid - nekhadz, tsadz, anarzhek (նեխած, ցած, անարժէք)
putrefaction - pudoutiun, nekhoum (փտութիւն, նեխում)
putrefy - pudil, nekhil, kaykayvil, pudetsunel (փտիլ, նեխիլ, քայքայուիլ, փտեցնել)
putrid - pudadz, abaganadz, nekhadz (փտած, ապականած, նեխած)
putridity - pudoutiun, nekhadzoutiun, abaganoutiun (փտութիւն, նեխածութիւն, ապականութիւն)
putty - khumor, dzepan, madzig, khumorel, pagtsunel (խմոր, ծեփան, մածիկ, խմորել, փակցնել)
puzzle (n) - areghdzuvadz, haneloug, hanelougakhagh, varank (առեղծուած, հանելուկ, հանելուկախաղ, վարանք)
puzzle (v) - shuvaretsunel, shupotil, hanelougu loudzel (շուարեցնել, շփոթիլ, հանելուկը լուծել)
puzzler - shupotetsunogh, abshetsunogh, haneloug loudzogh (շփոթեցնող, ապշեցնող, հանելուկ լուծող)
puzzling - shupotetsunogh, haneloug (շփոթեցնող, հանելուկ)
pye - gachaghag (կաչաղակ)
pygmy, pigmy - kajaj, garjoug, aprigian tuzoug tsegh (գաճաճ, կարճուկ, ափրիկեան թզուկ ցեղ)
pyjamas - kisheranots (գիշերանոց)
pyorrhea -
pyorrhea, pyorrhoea - lindaghd (լինտախտ)
pyramid - pourk (բուրգ)
pyramidal - purkatsev, purkanuman (բրգաձեւ, բրգանման)
pyre - kharouyg, paydagouyd (խարոյկ, փայտակոյտ)
pyrite - hurakar (հրաքար)
pyrogenic - chermadzin (ջերմածին)
pyrolatry - gurabashdoutiun (կրապաշտութիւն)
pyrrhonism - usgebdigoutiun, gasgadzamudoutiun (սկեպտիկութիւն, կասկածամտութիւն)
pyrrhonist - usgebdig, gasgadzamid, terahavad (սկեպտիկ, կասկածամիտ, թերահաւատ)
python - varazots, khoshor antouyn ots, khoushag (վարազօձ, խոշոր անթոյն օձ, գուշակ)
pythoness - koushagouhi, chadoug (գուշակուհի, ջատուկ)
pythonist - koushag, badkamakhos (գուշակ, պատգամախօս)
pyx - surpadoup, haghortoutian doup (սրբատուփ, հաղորդութեան տուփ)
pyxis - koharadoup (գոհարատուփ)

quack - gurinch, soud puzhishg, shaghaguradel, gurunchel (կռինչ, սուտ բժիշկ, շաղակրատել, կռնչել)
quackery - shaghagradoutiun, soud puzhushgoutiun (շաղակրատութիւն, սուտ բժշկութիւն)
quad - karangiun, kariag, pand, michots (քառանկիւն, քառեակ, բանտ, միջոց)
Quadragesima - karasnortats, medz bahk (Քառասնորդաց, Մեծ Պահք)
quadrangle - karangiun (քառանկիւն)
quadrant - kariag, poloragi karortu (քառեակ, բոլորակի քառորդը)
quadrate - karagousi, harmar, jisht, harmaril (քառակուսի, յարմար,

ճիշդ, յարմարիլ)

quadratic - karagousi, karangiun (քառակուսի, քառանկիւն)

quadrature - karortoutiun, karort heravoroutiun (քառորդութիւն, քառորդ հեռաւորութիւն)

quadrennial - karamia (քառամեայ)

quadricycle - karaniv hedzaniv (քառանիւ հեծանիւ)

quadrigeminal, inous - karabadig, karamas (քառապատիկ, քառամաս)

quadrilateral - karagoghm, karagoghmani (քառակողմ, քառակողմանի)

quadriliteral - karadar, chors kirov (քառատառ, չորս գիրով)

quadrille - karabar, khumpabar, karanuvak (քառապար, խմբապար, քառանուագ)

quadrillion - karilion (քառիլիոն)

quadripartite - chorekpazhin, chors masov (չորեքբաժին, չորս մասով)

quadrisyllable - karavang (քառավանկ)

quadruped - chorkodani, chors vodkov (չորքոտանի, չորս ոտքով)

quadruple - karabadig, karabadgel (քառապատիկ, քառապատկել)

quadruplex - karabadig (քառապատիկ)

quadruplicate - karabadig, karabadgel (քառապատիկ, քառապատկել)

quadruplication - karabadgoum (քառապատկում)

quaff - gondzel, jungel, khumel (կոնծել, ճնկել, խմել)

quaffer - gondzogh, khumogh (կոնծող, խմող)

quag - jahij (ճահիճ)

quaggy - jakhjakhoud, moroud (ճախճախուտ, մօրուտ)

quail - vuhadil, ungjil, loramarki (վհատիլ, ընկճիլ, լորամարգի)

quaint - ardasovor, ardagark, nazeli, hunatarian (արտասովոր, արտակարգ, նազելի, հնադարեան)

quake - sarsil, yereral, sharzhil, togh, sarsour (սարսիլ, երերալ, շարժիլ, դող, սարսուռ)

quaker - yereratsogh, yereragan, poghokagan aghant (երերացող, երերական, բողոքական աղանդ)

qualification - voragoum, anvanoum, harmaroutiun, parepokhoum (որակում, անուանում, յարմարութիւն, բարեփոխում)

qualified - voragial, parepokhial, harmar (որակեալ, բարեփոխեալ, յարմար)

qualifier - voragich, voragogh (որակիչ, որակող)

qualify - voragel, gochel, kunahadel, parepokhel (որակել, կոչել, գնահատել, բարեփոխել)

qualitative - voragagan (որակական)

quality - vorag, hadgoutiun, paremasnoutiun, tsirk (որակ, յատկութիւն, բարեմասնութիւն, ձիրք)

qualm - nuvaghoum, sirdkharnouk, khughji khayt (նուաղում, սիրտխառնուք, խղճի խայթ)

quandary - gunjir, varanoum, daragouys (կնճիռ, վարանում, տարակոյս)

quantitative - kanagagan (քանակական)

quantity - kanag, kanagoutiun, chap, shadoutiun (քանակ, քանակութիւն, չափ, շատութիւն)

quantum - kanag, koumar, ampoghchoutiun (քանակ, գումար, ամբողջութիւն)

quarantine - karasounk, karasniag, arkelanots, makranots (քառասունք, քառասնեակ, արգելանոց, մաքրանոց)

quarrel - vej, guriv, panavej, baykar, vijil, gurvil (վէճ, կռիւ, բանավէճ, պայքար, վիճիլ, կռուիլ)

quarreler - gurvogh, vijogh (կռուող, վիճող)

quarrelsome - gurvaser, vijaser, gurvazan (կռուասէր, վիճասէր, կռուազան)

quarrier - karakordz (քարագործ)

quarry - karahank, vorsagouyd, kar godrel-hanel (քարահանք, որսակոյտ, քար կոտրել-հանել)

quarryman - karahan, karahad, karagop (քարահան, քարահատ, քա-

րակոփ)
quart - 1/4 galon, karag (1/4 կալոն, քառակ)
quarter (n) - karort, kariag, punagaran, tagh, zoranots (քառորդ, քառեակ, բնակարան, թաղ, զօրանոց)
quarter (v) - karortel, pazhnel, panagetsunel, deghavorel (քառորդել, բաժնել, բանակեցնել, տեղաւորել)
quarterly - yeramsia (եռամսեայ)
quartet - kariag (քառեակ)
quarto - karortu, karadzal (քառորդը, քառածալ)
quartz - vortsakar, gardzurakar, kavarz (որձաքար, կարծրաքար, գաւարզ)
quash - chunchel, dabalel, nuvajel (ջնջել, տապալել, նուաճել)
quasi - gardzes te, kurete, iprev te, koktses (կարծես թէ, գրեթէ, իբրեւ թէ, գոգցես)
quassation - tsuntsoum (ցնցում)
quaternate - kariag, chorsagan (քառեակ, չորսական)
quatrain - kariag, karadoun (քառեակ, քառատուն)
quaver - toghtochal, taylaylel, jurvoghel, taylayl (դողդոջալ, դայլայլել, ճռուողել, դայլայլ)
quay - karap (քարափ)
quayage - karapi dourk (քարափի տուրք)
queachy - khakhoud, yereroun (խախուտ, երերուն)
quean - lugdi gin, anparo aghchig (լկտի կին, անբարոյ աղջիկ)
queasy - tuirazkats, hivatakin, pudzakhuntir (դիւրազգաց, հիւանդագին, բծախնդիր)
queen - takouhi, arkayagin (թագուհի, արքայակին)
queen mother - mayr takouhi (մայր թագուհի)
queer - aylantag, darorinag, ardarots, geghdz turam (այլանդակ, տարօրինակ, արտառոց, կեղծ դրամ)
quell - nuvajel, juzmel, ungjel, zusbel, kheghtel (նուաճել, ճզմել, ընկճել, զսպել, խեղդել)
quench - marel, antsunel, haketsunel, chunchel (մարել, անցընել, յագեցնել, ջնջել)
quenchless - anmar, mushdavar, anshech, anhak (անմար, մշտավառ, անշէջ, անյագ)
querist - hartsaser (հարցասէր)
querulous - kankadogh, durdunchogh, tuzhkoh, gurvazan (գանգատող, տրտնջող, դժգոհ, կռուազան)
query - hartsoum, daragouys, hartsuman nushan, hartsunel (հարցում, տարակոյս, հարցման նշան, հարցնել)
quest - khuntir, harts, pundurdouk, pundurel (խնդիր, հարց, փնտռտուք, փնտռել)
question - hartsoum, harts, hartsaportsel, hartsakunnel (հարցում, հարց, հարցափորձել, հարցաքննել)
question mark - hartsuman nushan (հարցման նշան)
questionable - vijeli, gasgadzeli, anusdouyk (վիճելի, կասկածելի, անստոյգ)
questioner - hartsaser, hartsakunnich, kunnogh (հարցասէր, հարցաքննիչ, քննող)
questionless - angasgadz, anvijeli (անկասկած, անվիճելի)
questionnaire - hartsaran, hartsatert (հարցարան, հարցաթերթ)
queue - boch, shark, hert, boch purnel, herti usbasel (պոչ, շարք, հերթ, պոչ բռնել, հերթի սպասել)
quib - yerkidzank, yerkidzapanoutiun (երգիծանք, երգիծաբանութիւն)
quibble - khousapank, pakhousd, parakhagh, khousapil (խուսափանք, փախուստ, բառախաղ, խուսափիլ)
quick - arak, jarbig, varvuroun, gentani, arakatsunel (արագ, ճարպիկ, վառվռուն, կենդանի, արագացնել)
quicken - gentanatsunel, arakatsunel, vokevorel (կենդանացնել, արագացնել, ոգեւորել)
quickly - shoudov, arakoren, arak

(շուտով, արագօրէն, արագ)
quickness - arakoutiun, ashkhouyzh, suramudoutiun (արագութիւն, աշխոյժ, սրամտութիւն)
quicksand - avazoudk (աւազուտք)
quicksilver - suntig (սնդիկ)
quid - dzamon, dzukhadzamon (ծամոն, ծխածամոն)
quiddity - pudzakhunturoutiun, eoutiun (բծախնդրութիւն, էութիւն)
quidnunc - hedakurkir, pampasogh, panked (հետաքրքիր, բամբասող, բանգէտ)
quiescence - antsaynoutiun, luroutiun, antorroutiun (անձայնութիւն, լռութիւն, անդորրութիւն)
quiescent - antsayn, lour, hamur, antor, hantard (անձայն, լուռ, համր, անդորր, հանդարտ)
quiet (a) - hantard, khaghagh, hez, lurig, meghm, hankisd (հանդարտ, խաղաղ, հեզ, լռիկ, մեղմ, հանգիստ)
quiet (v) - hantardil, hantardetsunel, lurel, luretsunel (հանդարտիլ, հանդարտեցնել, լռել, լռեցնել)
quieten - hantardetsunel, meghmatsunel, luretsunel (հանդարտեցնել, մեղմացնել, լռեցնել)
quieter - hantardetsunogh (հանդարտեցնող)
quietly - hantardoren, lurig (հանդարտօրէն, լռիկ)
quietness - hantardoutiun, antorroutiun, khaghaghoutiun (հանդարտութիւն, անդորրութիւն, խաղաղութիւն)
quietude - hantardoutiun, hankisd (հանդարտութիւն, հանգիստ)
quietus - hadoutsakir, antorrakir, hankisd, mah (հատուցագիր, անդորրագիր, հանգիստ, մահ)
quill - pedour, kurich, makok, voznii poush, pattel (փետուր, գրիչ, մագոգ, ոզնիի փուշ, փաթթել)
quilt - vermag, shoullel, gutsel (վերմակ, շուլլել, կցել)
quince - sergevil (սերկեւիլ)
quinquennial - hunkamia (հնգամեայ)
quinsy - gogortatsav, gogorti porpokoum (կոկորդացաւ, կոկորդի բորբոքում)
quintet - hunkiag (հնգեակ)
quip - yerkidzank, dzagur, gadag, dzaghrel (երգիծանք, ծաղր, կատակ, ծաղրել)
quirt - mudrag (մտրակ)
quit - tsukel, megnil, hurazharil, azadvadz, zerdz (ձգել, մեկնիլ, հրաժարիլ, ազատուած, զերծ)
quitch - molakhod (մոլախոտ)
quite - luriv, ampoghchovin, gadarelabes (լրիւ, ամբողջովին, կատարելապէս)
quitter - khousapogh, housahadogh (խուսափող, յուսահատող)
quiver - toghal, sarsural, sarsuratsoum, gabarj (դողալ, սարսռալ, սարսռացում, կապարճ)
quixotic - donkishodian, azniv, ankordznagan (տոնքիշոտեան, ազնիւ, անգործնական)
quiz - harts, kunnoutiun, areghdzuvadz, hartsouportsel (հարց, քննութիւն, առեղծուած, հարցափորձել)
quo warranto - iravagan huramanakir (իրաւական հրամանագիր)
quod - karangiun, pand (քառանկիւն, բանտ)
quorum - orinavor tiv zhoghovi (օրինաւոր թիւ ժողովի)
quota - mas, pazhin, antsnapazhin (մաս, բաժին, անձնաբաժին)
quotation - mechperoum, kunatsoutsag, arzhekin (մէջբերում, գնացուցակ, արժեգին)
quotation marks - chagerd (չակերտ)
quote - mechperel, hishel, vugayel, kin dal (մէջբերել, յիշել, վկայել, գին տալ)
quotidian - amenoria, oragan, aroria (ամէնօրեայ, օրական, առօրեայ)
quotient - kanort, tsoutsanish (քանորդ, ցուցանիշ)
quotum - pazhin, hamemadoutiun (բաժին, համեմատութիւն)

R

rabbet - porvadzk, agosig, porel, akoutsel (փորուածք, ակօսիկ, փորել, ագուցել)
rabbi, rabbin - rappi, huria vartabed, der im (ռաբբի, Հրեայ վարդապետ, Տէր իմ)
rabbit - jakar, pokur nabasdag, jakar vorsal (ճագար, փոքր նապաստակ, ճագար որսալ)
rabble - ampokh, khouzhan, pazmoutiun (ամբոխ, խուժան, բազմութիւն)
rabid - gadaghi, molekin, gadghadz (կատաղի, մոլեգին, կատղած)
rabidity - gadaghoutiun, moleknoutiun (կատաղութիւն, մոլեգնութիւն)
rabies - gadaghoutiun, gadaghakhd (կատաղութիւն, կատաղախտ)
rabious - gadghadz, moleknadz, tsasgod (կատղած, մոլեգնած, ցասկոտ)
raca - pouj (փուճ)
raccoon, racoon - churarch, mugnere (ջրարջ, մկներէ)
race (n) - tsegh, azk, dohm, desag, vazk, murtsavazk (ցեղ, ազգ, տոհմ, տեսակ, վազք, մրցավազք)
race (v) - arshavel, vazel, murtsil, vaztsunel (արշաւել, վազել, մրցիլ, վազցնել)
racer - arshavogh, murtsogh, arshavatsi (արշաւող, մրցող, արշաւացի)
rachis - voghnahar (ողնահար)
racial - tseghayin (ցեղային)
racialism - tseghaguronoutiun (ցեղակրօնութիւն)
racism - tseghabashdoutiun (ցեղապաշտութիւն)
racist - tseghabashd (ցեղապաշտ)
rack (n) - burgots, dancharan, voloran, musour, gakhich (պրկոց, տանջարան, ոլորան, մսուր, կախիչ)
rack (v) - burgel, danchel, larel, turchel, kamel (պրկել, տանջել, լարել, թրջել, քամել)
racket, racquet (n) - tag, kuntagahar, moujag, zhukhor, aghmoug (Թակ, գնդակահար, մուճակ, ժխոր, աղմուկ)
racket, racquet (v) - aghmugel, zhukhorel, tughurtel (աղմկել, ժխորել, դղրդել)
racketeer - geghekich, avazag (կեղեքիչ, աւազակ)
racketeering - geghekoum, gorzoum, avazagoutiun (կեղեքում, կորզում, աւազակութիւն)
rackrent - dzanur varts (ծանր վարձ)
raconteur - badmogh, badmaser (պատմող, պատմասէր)
racy - gudzou, leghi, zoravor ham (կծու, լեղի, զօրաւոր համ)
radar - radar, herades gayan (ռատար, Հեռատես կայան)
raddle - tsangabad, hiusel (ցանկապատ, Հիւսել)
radial - jajanchayin, jarakaytayin (ճաճանչային, ճառագայթային)
radiance, radiancy - lousapayloutiun, baydzaroutiun (լուսափայլութիւն, պայծառութիւն)
radiant - payloun, shoghshoghoun, lousapayl (փայլուն, շողշողուն, լուսափայլ)
radiate - jarakaytel, paylil, shoghal (ճառագայթել, փայլիլ, շողալ)
radiathon - nubasdahavak, turamahavak tsaynaspiurov (նպաստահաւաք, դրամահաւաք ձայնասփիւռով)
radiation - jarakaytoum, shoghar-

tsagoum, shogh (ճառագայթում, շողարձակում, շող)
radiator - chermartsag, yelekdura-chermots, lolartsag (ջերմարձակ, ելեքտրաջերմոց, գոլարձակ)
radical - armadagan, kulkhavor, himnagan, armad (արմատական, գլխաւոր, Հիմնական, արմատ)
radicalism - armadaganoutiun (արմատականութիւն)
radio - tsaynaspiur (ձայնասփիւռ)
radioactive - shoghakordzon (շողագործօն)
radiogram - radioyi ungalouch mekena (ռատիոյի ընկալուչ մեքենայ)
radiograph - shoghakir, surdakir (շողագիր, սրտագիր)
radiography - shoghanugaroum, shoghanugar, surdakuroutiun (շողանկարում, շողանկար, սրտագրութիւն)
radiology - shoghakidoutiun (շողագիտութիւն)
radioscopy - shoghakunnoutiun, tsolanugaroum (շողաքննութիւն, ցոլանկարում)
radio-active - shoghartsag, shoghakordzon (շողարձակ, շողագործօն)
radio-activity - shoghartsagoum (շողարձակում)
radish - poghg (բողկ)
radium - shoghartsagogh niut, jarakaytogh, radiom (շողարձակող նիւթ, ճառագայթող, ռատիոմ)
radius - sharavigh, dzughosgurig, jajanch (շառաւիղ, ծղոսկրիկ, ճաճանչ)
radix - armad, dzakoum, usdoukapar (արմատ, ծագում, ստուգաբառ)
raff - kharnagouyd, taptupouk, ampokh, khouzhan (խառնակոյտ, թափթփուք, ամբոխ, խուժան)
raffish - ampokhayin, tsadz, pouch, anarag, tsop (ամբոխային, ցած, փուչ, անառակ, ցոփ)
raffle - vijagahanoutiun, pakhdakhagh, vijag kashel (վիճակաՀանութիւն, բախտախաղ, վիճակ քաշել)
raft - lasd, lasdapayd, lasdargel (լաստ, լաստափայտ, լաստարկել)
raftsman - lasdavar (լաստավար)
rag - kourch, lat, tsuntsodik, gobid gadag, dzaghrel (քուրջ, լաթ, ցնցոտիք, կոպիտ կատակ, ծաղրել)
rag paper - medaksatought (մետաքսաթուղթ)
rage - gadaghoutiun, zayrouyt, gadghil, zayranal (կատաղութիւն, զայրոյթ, կատղիլ, զայրանալ)
ragged - badaroun, punti, badurdazd, ankhunam (պատառուն, փնթի, պատռտած, անխնամ)
raging - gadaghoutiun, moleknoutiun, gadaghi (կատաղութիւն, մոլեգնութիւն, կատաղի)
ragstone - hesanakar (յեսանաքար)
rag-tag - ramig, khouzhan (ռամիկ, խուժան)
raid - asbadagoutiun, arshavank, arshavel, hartsagil (ասպատակութիւն, արշաւանք, արշաւել, յարձակիլ)
raider - asbadag, arshavanav, hartsagogh otanav (ասպատակ, արշաւանաւ, յարձակող օդանաւ)
rail (n) - tsogh, yergatakidz, vantagatsogh, tsangabad (ցող, երկաթագիծ, վանդակացող, ցանկապատ)
rail (v) - tsoghel, vantagel, heknel, aybanel (ցողել, վանդակել, Հեգնել, այպանել)
railer - dzaghrogh, heknogh, kunnatadogh (ծաղրող, Հեգնող, քննադատող)
railing - vantag, tsangabad, tsogh (վանդակ, ցանկապատ, ցող)
railroad, railway - yergatoughi, yergatoughakidz (երկաթուղի, երկաթուղագիծ)
raiment - hakousd, uzkesd, hanterts (Հագուստ, զգեստ, Հանդերձ)
rain - antsurev, antsurevel, deghal (անձրեւ, անձրեւել, տեղալ)
rainbow - dziadzan, dzirani kodi (ծիածան, ծիրանի գօտի)
raincoat - antsurevazkesd (անձրեւազգեստ)

rainy - antsurevod, antsurevayin, tats (անձրեւոտ, անձրեւային, թաց)
raise - vertsunel, partsuratsunel, aveltsunel, hankanagel (վերցնել, բարձրացնել, աւելցնել, հանգանակել)
raised - tsutsoun, tsutsvadzk (ցցուն, ցցուածք)
raiser - partsuratsunogh, vertsunogh (բարձրացնող, վերցնող)
raisin - chamich (չամիչ)
raising - partsuratsoum, haveloum, hankanagoutiun (բարձրացում, յաւելում, հանգանակութիւն)
rake - potsgh, durmough, kaghots, tsop, kaghotsel (փոցխ, տրմուղ, քաղոց, ցոփ, քաղոցել)
rakish - tsop, zeghkh, anarag (ցոփ, զեղխ, անառակ)
rally - havak, megdeghoum, zhoghov, murtsouyt, megdeghel (հաւաք, մէկտեղում, ժողով, մրցոյթ, մէկտեղել)
rally (n) - megdeghoum, havak, dzaghur, abakinoum (մէկտեղում, հաւաք, ծաղր, ապաքինում)
rally (v) - havakvil, hamakhumpel, dzaghrel, abakinil (հաւաքուիլ, համախմբել, ծաղրել, ապաքինիլ)
ram - khoy, shokemourj, khoyel, mukhel, khutsel (խոյ, շոգեմուրճ, խոյել, մխել, խցել)
ramble - taparoum, tekeroum, tekeril, sulukdal, taparil (թափառում, դեգերում, դեգերիլ, սլքտալ, թափառիլ)
rambler - taparogh, taparashurchig (թափառող, թափառաշրջիկ)
rambling - taparoum, tekeroum, taparig, asdantagan (թափառում, դեգերում, թափառիկ, աստանդական)
ramification - jiughavoroum, sharavigh, jiugh (ճիւղաւորում, շառաւիղ, ճիւղ)
ramify - jiughavorel, jiughavorvil (ճիւղաւորել, ճիւղաւորուիլ)
rammer - mughich, dopan, tag, harich (մղիչ, տոփան, թակ, հարիչ)
rammish - karshahod, avruvadz, muklodadz (քարշահոտ, աւրուած, մգլոտած)
ramp (n) - vosdoum, vazk, hartsagoum, pazrik, zarivayr (ոստում, վազք, յարձակում, բազրիք, զառիվայր)
ramp (v) - vosdosdel, tsadgel, makultsil, soghosgil (ոստոստել, ցատկել, մագլցիլ, սողոսկիլ)
rampage - khurovk, houzoum, gadaghil, moleknil (խռովք, յուզում, կատաղիլ, մոլեգնիլ)
rampageous - anzousb, gadaghi, moleknadz, sasdig (անզուսպ, կատաղի, մոլեգնած, սաստիկ)
rampant - zeghoun, hort, daradzvadz, gadaghi (զեղուն, յորդ, տարածուած, կատաղի)
rampart - badnesh, badvar, bashdbanoutiun, badnishel (պատնէշ, պատուար, պաշտպանութիւն, պատնիշել)
ramshackle - kharkhoul, kharkhuladz, hin (խարխուլ, խարխլած, հին)
ran - vazets (վազեց)
ranch - akarag, tsiapoudzaran, akarag mu ghegavarel (ագարակ, ձիաբուծարան, ագարակ մը ղեկավարել)
ranchero - tsiaradz, khashnapouydz (ձիարած, խաշնաբոյծ)
rancid - tutvadz, nekhadz, abaganadz, tarnaham (թթուած, նեխած, ապականած, դառնահամ)
rancidity - tutvadzoutiun, nekhadzoutiun (թթուածութիւն, նեխածութիւն)
rancor - vokh, vokhagaloutiun, charamudoutiun , ken (ոխ, ոխակալութիւն, չարամտութիւն, քէն)
rancorous - vokhagal, vokherim, charagam, anhashd (ոխակալ, ոխերիմ, չարակամ, անհաշտ)
rand - dzayr, yezur, yezrasherd (ծայր, եզր, եզրաշերտ)
random - badahmounk, tibvadz, badahagan (պատահմունք, դիպուած, պատահական)

range (n) - gark, shark, asdijan, arod, lernashughta (կարգ, շարք, աստիճան, արօտ, լեռնաշղթայ)
range (v) - tasavorel, sharel, garkaturel, zedeghvil (դասաւորել, շարել, կարգադրել, զետեղուիլ)
ranger - andarabah, taparashurchig, vorsakhouyz (անտառապահ, թափառաշրջիկ, որսախոյզ)
rank (a) - partam, perri, budghaper, tarnaham, nekhadz (փարթամ, բերրի, պտղաբեր, դառնահամ, նեխած)
rank (n) - gark, shark, dogh, zorashar, tirk, lirp (կարգ, շարք, տող, զօրաշար, դիրք, լիրբ)
rank (v) - sharel, tasel, tasavorel, tasvil, tasavorvil (շարել, դասել, դասաւորել, դասուիլ, դասաւորուիլ)
ranker - tasavorogh (դասաւորող)
rankle - tarakhil, sasdganal, porpokil, charcharel (թարախիլ, սաստկանալ, բորբոքիլ, չարչարել)
ransack - voronel, khouzargel, pundurel, goghobdel (որոնել, խուզարկել, փնտռել, կողոպտել)
ransom - purgakin, purgank, purgank vujarel, purgel (փրկագին, փրկանք, փրկանք վճարել, փրկել)
rant - medzapanel, borodakhosel, medzapan, borodakhos (մեծաբանել, պոռոտախօսել, մեծաբան, պոռոտախօս)
rap - pakhiun, zarg, harvadz, pakhel, hapushdagel (բախիւն, զարկ, հարուած, բախել, յափշտակել)
rapacious - kishadich, kishager, goghobdich, achkadzag (գիշատիչ, գիշակեր, կողոպտիչ, աչքածակ)
rape (n) - hapushdagoum, purnaparoum, arevankoum (յափշտակում, բռնաբարում, առեւանգում)
rape (v) - hapushdagel, purnaparel, arevankel, lulgel (յափշտակել, բռնաբարել, առեւանգել, լլկել)
rapid - arak, shoud, suruntats, sahank, zaritap (արագ, շուտ, սրընթաց, սահանք, զառիթափ)
rapidity - arakoutiun, suruntatsoutiun (արագութիւն, սրընթացութիւն)
rapine - goghoboud, avar, koghoutiun (կողոպուտ, աւար, գողութիւն)
rappel - tumpgaharoutiun (թմփկահարութիւն)
rapport - haraperoutiun, gabagtsoutiun (յարաբերութիւն, կապակցութիւն)
rapprochement - mertsetsoum, modigoutiun (մերձեցում, մօտիկութիւն)
rapt - khulvadz, hapushdagvadz, arevankuvadz (խլուած, յափշտակուած, առեւանգուած)
rapture - hapushdagoutiun, hiyatsoum, uzmaylank (յափշտակութիւն, հիացում, զմայլանք)
rare - hazvakiud, sagavativ, ansovor, chuknagh (հազուագիւտ, սակաւաթիւ, անսովոր, չքնաղ)
rarefaction - nosratsoum, tsantsaratsoum (նօսրացում, ցանցառացում)
rarefy - nosratsunel, nosranal, nuvazil, tsantsaril (նօսրացնել, նօսրանալ, նուազիլ, ցանցառիլ)
rarely - hazvateb, kich ankam (հազուադէպ, քիչ անգամ)
rarity - sagavoutiun, kichoutiun, anosroutiun (սակաւութիւն, քիչութիւն, անօսրութիւն)
rascal - anuzkam, suriga, khartakh, usdorin (անզգամ, սրիկայ, խարդախ, ստորին)
rase - avrel, chunchel, gordzanel (աւրել, ջնջել, կործանել)
rash - hantoukun, ankhohem, ankhorhourt, pidz morti (յանդուգն, անխոհեմ, անխորհուրդ, բիծ՝ մորթի)
rashness - ankhohemoutiun, hantuknoutiun (անխոհեմութիւն, յանդգնութիւն)
rasp - khardotsel, kusel, shupel, kerel, khardots (խարտոցել, քսել, շփել, քերել, խարտոց)
raspberry - moreni, arkayamori (մորենի, արքայամորի)
rat - arned, tasalik, kin gudrel, lukel, tavajanel (առնէտ, դասալիք, գին կտրել, լքել, դաւաճանել)
ratchet - arkelaniv, gerazhani-aniv

(արգելանիւ, կեռաժանի՝ անիւ)
rate (n) - sag, sagakin, arzhek, asdijan, untatsk (սակ, սակագին, արժէք, աստիճան, ընթացք)
rate (v) - kunahadel, sagakurel, hashvel, gushdampel (գնահատել, սակագրել, հաշուել, կշտամբել)
rath - pulrag (բլրակ)
rather - nakhundurapar, aveli, manavant, pokhanag (նախընտրաբար, աւելի, մանաւանդ, փոխանակ)
ratification - vaveratsoum, hasdadoum (վաւերացում, հաստատում)
ratifier - vaveratsunogh (վաւերացընող)
ratify - vaveratsunel, hasdadel, usdorakurel (վաւերացնել, հաստատել, ստորագրել)
rating - sagakuroum, kunahadoum, sahmanoum, asdijan (սակագրում, գնահատում, սահմանում, աստիճան)
ratio - hamemadoutiun, zoukagushir (համեմատութիւն, զուգակշիռ)
ratiocinate - duramapanel, badjarapanel (տրամաբանել, պատճառաբանել)
ratiocination - duramapanoutiun (տրամաբանութիւն)
ration - pazhin, orabahig, barenachap, orapazhin dal (բաժին, օրապահիկ, պարէնաչափ, օրաբաժին տալ)
rational - panavor, panagan, artar, iravatsi, imanali (բանաւոր, բանական, արդար, իրաւացի, իմանալի)
rationale - badjarapanoutiun (պատճառաբանութիւն)
rationalism - panabashdoutiun (բանապաշտութիւն)
rationalist - panabashd (բանապաշտ)
rationalize - panavor tartsunel, panargel (բանաւոր դարձնել, բանարկել)
rattle (n) - shachiun, tuntiun, shadakhosoutiun, aghmoug (շաչիւն, թնդիւն, շատախօսութիւն, աղմուկ)
rattle (v) - sharachel, shachel, jurunchel, aghmugel (շառաչել, շաչել, ճռնչել, աղմկել)
rattler - aghmugogh, shadakhos, tadargakhos (աղմկող, շատախօս, դատարկախօս)
raucity - khurbodoutiun (խռպոտութիւն)
raucus - khurbod, goshd, pird (խռպոտ, կոշտ, բիրտ)
ravage - gordzanoum, kantoum, aver, gordzanel, kantel (կործանում, քանդում, աւեր, կործանել, քանդել)
ravager - kantich, averich, goghobdich (քանդիչ, աւերիչ, կողոպտիչ)
rave - zarantsel, tsunoril, gadghil (զառանցել, ցնորիլ, կատղիլ)
ravel - kagel, loudzel, partanal, partatsunel (քակել, լուծել, բարդանալ, բարդացնել)
raven - akrav, goghoboud, vors, goghobdel, kishadel (ագռաւ, կողոպուտ, որս, կողոպտել, գիշատել)
ravenous - kishadich, hapushdagich, angoushd, shadager (գիշատիչ, յափշտակիչ, անկուշտ, շատակեր)
ravin - hapushdagoutiun, talan, goghoboud (յափշտակութիւն, թալան, կողոպուտ)
ravine - hegheghad, khoroung tsor (հեղեղատ, խորունկ ձոր)
ravish - hapushdagel, purnaparel, arevankel, hurabourel (յափշտակել, բռնաբարել, առեւանգել, հրապուրել)
ravisher - hapushdagogh, arevankogh, purnaparogh (յափշտակող, առեւանգող, բռնաբարող)
ravishing, ravishment - hapushdagoum, arevankoum, lulgoum (յափշտակում, առեւանգում, լլկում)
raw - houm, khag, chepadz, duhas, sugurtouk, usbi (հում, խակ, չեփած, տհաս, սկրթուք, սպի)
raw boned - nihar, vudid, vosgurod, gumakhkatsadz (նիհար, վտիտ, ոսկրոտ, կմախքացած)
raw material - houm niut (հում նիւթ)
ray - jarakayt, shogh, nushouyl, ja-

rakaytel, shoghal (ճառագայթ, շող, նշոյլ, ճառագայթել, շողալ)
raze - chunchel, avrel, kantel, kerel (ջնջել, աւրել, քանդել, քերել)
razor - adzeli, adzilel (ածելի, ածիլել)
razure - kervadzk, chunchoum, averoum, gordzanoum (քերուածք, ջնջում, աւերում, կործանում)
reabsorb - verdzudzel (վերծծել)
reach (n) - hasoghoutiun, sahman, zhamanoum, hunark (հասողութիւն, սահման, ժամանում, հնարք)
reach (v) - hasnil, hastsunel, yergaril, zhamanel, hachoghil (հասնիլ, հասցնել, երկարիլ, ժամանել, յաջողիլ)
react - hagaztel, pokhaztel, artsakankel, nerkordzel (հակազդել, փոխազդել, արձագանգել, ներգործել)
reaction - hagaztetsoutiun, unttimoutiun, timaturoutiun (հակազդեցութիւն, ընդդիմութիւն, դիմադրութիւն)
reactor - hagaztag, sharzhich, hiuleagan part (հակազդակ, շարժիչ, հիւլէական բարդ)
read - gartal, unternoul, sorvil, ousanil, serdel (կարդալ, ընթեռնուլ, սորվիլ, ուսանիլ, սերտել)
readable - unternli, gartali, heshd gartatsvogh (ընթեռնլի, կարդալի, հեշտ կարդացուող)
reader - untertsogh, gartatsogh, ousanogh, untertsaran (ընթերցող, կարդացող, ուսանող, ընթերցարան)
readily - isgouyn, anmichabes, sirov (իսկոյն, անմիջապէս, սիրով)
readiness - badrasdagamoutiun, hozharoutiun (պատրաստակամութիւն, յօժարութիւն)
reading - untertsoum, untertsanoutiun (ընթերցում, ընթերցանութիւն)
reading book - untertsaran (ընթերցարան)
reading desk - kuragal (գրակալ)
reading glass - khoshoratsouyts (խոշորացոյց)
reading room - untertsaran, untertsasurah (ընթերցարան, ընթերցասրահ)
readjust - verashudgel, verajushtel, oughghel, verasarkel (վերաշտկել, վերաճշդել, ուղղել, վերասարքել)
readjustment - verasarkoum, verashudgoum (վերասարքում, վերաշտկում)
readmission, readmittance - veruntounoum (վերընդունում)
readmit - veruntounel (վերընդունել)
readmittance - veruntouneloutiun (վերընդունելութիւն)
ready - badrasd, duramatir, hozhar, arak, artserun (պատրաստ, տրամադիր, յօժար, արագ, առձեռն)
ready made - badrasdi, voch chapi vura (պատրաստի, ոչ չափի վրայ)
reaffirm - verahasdadel (վերահաստատել)
reagent - hagaztag (հակազդակ)
real - iragan, isgagan, poun, ansharzh, rial (իրական, իսկական, բուն, անշարժ, րիալ՝ Սպանական դրամը)
real estate - ansharzh galvadz, usdatsvadzk (անշարժ կալուած, ստացուածք)
realism - irabashdoutiun (իրապաշտութիւն)
realist - irades, irabashd, kordznagan (իրատես, իրապաշտ, գործնական)
reality - iraganoutiun, iroghoutiun, jushmardoutiun (իրականութիւն, իրողութիւն, ճշմարտութիւն)
realizable - iraganali, irakordzeli (իրականալի, իրագործելի)
realization - iraganatsoum, irakordzoum, gadaroum (իրականացում, իրագործում, կատարում)
realize - irakordzel, iraganatsunel, gadarel, shahil (իրագործել, իրականացնել, կատարել, շահիլ)
really - irabes, isgabes, irok, artarev, jushmardabes (իրապէս, իսկապէս, իրօք, արդարեւ, ճշմարտապէս)
realm - takavoroutiun, bedoutiun,

yergir, galvadz (Թաղաւորութիւն, պետութիւն, երկիր, կալուած)

realtor - michnort galvadzayin arevdouri (միջնորդ կալուածային առեւտուրի)

realty - ansharzh galvadz, ansharzhoutiun (անշարժ կալուած, անշարժութիւն)

ream - gabots, dzurar toughti (կապոց, ծրար թուղթի)

reanimate - veragentanatsunel, vokevorel (վերակենդանացնել, ոգեւորել)

reannex - veragutsel, miatsunel (վերակցել, միացնել)

reap - huntsel, kaghel, havakel (հնձել, քաղել, հաւաքել)

reaper - huntsogh, huntsogh mekena (հնձող, հնձող մեքենայ)

reaping hook - mankagh (մանգաղ)

reaping machine - huntsogh mekena (հնձող մեքենայ)

reappear - vererevál, verusdin yereval (վերերեւալ, վերստին երեւալ)

reappearance - vererevoum (վերերեւում)

rear - hedsamas, yedev, medztsunel, partsuratsunel, gurtel (յետսամաս, ետեւ, մեծցնել, բարձրացնել, կրթել)

rearm - verazinel, verazinvil (վերազինել, վերազինուիլ)

rearrange - verusdin garkaturel (վերստին կարգադրել)

reascend - verusdin yellel, hedznel (վերստին ելլել, հեծնել)

reason (n) - panaganoutiun, khelk, midk, badjar (բանականութիւն, խելք, միտք, պատճառ)

reason (v) - duramapanel, badjarapanel, tadel, kunnel (տրամաբանել, պատճառաբանել, դատել, քննել)

reasonable - duramapanagan, khohem, voghchmid, chapavor (տրամաբանական, խոհեմ, ողջմիտ, չափաւոր)

reasoning - tadoghoutiun, badjarapanoutiun, arargoutiun (դատողութիւն, պատճառաբանութիւն, առարկութիւն)

reassemble - verahavakel (վերահաւաքել)

reassert - verahasdadel, vusdahetsunel (վերահաստատել, վստահեցնել)

reassertion - verahasdadoum (վերահաստատում)

reassurance - vusdahetsoum, havasdiatsoum, verabahovoum (վստահեցում, հաւաստիացում, վերապահովում)

reassure - verabahovel, havasdiatsunel, verabahovakurel (վերապահովել, հաւաստիացնել, վերապահովագրել)

reave - goghobdel, khulel, hapushdagel (կողոպտել, խլել, յափշտակել)

reaver - goghobdich, avazag, hapushdagich (կողոպտիչ, աւազակ, յափշտակիչ)

rebaptize - veramugurdel, verusdin mugurdel (վերամկրտել, վերստին մկրտել)

rebate - nuvazoum, zeghch, zeghchel, ichetsunel (նուազում, զեղչ, զեղչել, իջեցնել)

rebel - abusdamp, umposd, abusdampil, umposdanal (ապստամբ, ըմբոստ, ապստամբիլ, ըմբոստանալ)

rebellion - abusdampoutiun, umposdoutiun (ապստամբութիւն, ըմբոստութիւն)

rebellious - abusdampagan, khurovarar, umposd (ապստամբական, խռովարար, ըմբոստ)

rebind - veragazmel (վերակազմել)

rebirth - veradzunount (վերածնունդ)

rebound - veratsaydel, tsadgetsunel, vosdosdoum (վերացայտել, ցատկեցնել, ոստոստում)

rebroadcast - verasuprel, veratsoutsnel (վերասփռել, վերացուցնել)

rebuff - gudroug merzhoum, vanoum, vanel, merzhel (կտրուկ մերժում, վանում, վանել, մերժել)

rebuild - veragankunel, veragarou-

tsel (վերականգնել, վերակառուցել)
rebuilt - veraganknadz, veragagaroutsvadz (վերականգնած, վերակառուցուած)
rebuke - sasd, gushdampank, sasdel, gushdampel, hantimanel (սաստ, կշտամբանք, սաստել, կշտամբել, յանդիմանել)
rebus - nugarahaneloug, geghdzakuroutiun (նկարահանելուկ, կեղծագրութիւն)
rebut - yed hurel, vanel, herkel, soud hanel (ետ հրել, վանել, հերքել, սուտ հանել)
recalcitrant - akatsogh, ansasd, umposd (աքացող, անսաստ, ըմբոստ)
recalcitrate - akatsel, unttimanal, vanel, timaturel (աքացել, ընդդիմանալ, վանել, դիմադրել)
recall - yed arnel, hedus gochel, chunchel, bashdonazurgoum (ետ առնել, յետս կոչել, ջնջել, պաշտօնազրկում)
recant - yed arnel khosku, herkel (ետ առնել խօսքը, հերքել)
recantation - hedus gochoum, veragochoum (յետս կոչում, վերակոչում)
recapitulate - hamarodel, ampopel, yezrapagel (համառօտել, ամփոփել, եզրափակել)
recapitulation - hamarod verakagh, kaghvadz, ampopoum (համառօտ վերաքաղ, քաղուած, ամփոփում)
recapture - verakuravoum, verusdatsoum, verakuravel (վերագրաւում, վերստացում, վերագրաւել)
recast - verapokhoum, veragazmel, veratsoulel (վերափոխում, վերակազմել, վերաձուլել)
recede - ungurgil, nahanchel, kashvil (ընկրկիլ, նահանջել, քաշուիլ)
receipt - usdatsakir, ungalakir, ungalakurel (ստացագիր, ընդունագիր, ընկալագրել)
receivable - untouneli (ընդունելի)
receive - usdanal, arnel, untounil, hiurungalel (ստանալ, առնել, ընդունիլ, հիւրընկալել)
receiver - usdatsogh, untounogh, ungalouch (ստացող, ընդունող, ընկալուչ)
recency - artioutiun (արդիութիւն)
recense - veraserdel, kaghvadzk unel (վերասերտել, քաղուածք ընել)
recension - kaghvadzk, veradesoutiun, veruntertsoum (քաղուածք, վերատեսութիւն, վերընթերցում)
recent - nor, arti, ayzhmian, tarm (նոր, արդի, այժմեան, թարմ)
recently - vercherus, norerus, ter nor (վերջերս, նորերս, դեռ նոր)
receptacle - untounaran, otevan, aman, anot, badij (ընդունարան, օթեւան, աման, անօթ, պատիճ)
receptible - untouneli (ընդունելի)
reception - untouneloutiun, hiurungaloutiun, usdatsoum (ընդունելութիւն, հիւրընկալութիւն, ստացում)
receptive - untounogh, untounag, ungalogh, khelatsi (ընդունող, ընդունակ, ընկալող, խելացի)
recess - arantsnatsoum, nahanch, tatar, takusdots (առանձնացում, նահանջ, դադար, թագստոց
recession - heratsoum, ungurgoum, angoum, nahanch (հեռացում, ընկրկում, անկում, նահանջ)
recessive - hedetarts (յետադարձ)
recharge - verahartsagil, zenk letsunel, ampasdanel (վերայարձակիլ, զէնք լեցնել, ամբաստանել)
rechoose - verundurel (վերընտրել)
recipe - teghakir, jashakir, paghatratsang, gerb (դեղագիր, ճաշագիր, բաղադրացանկ, կերպ)
recipient - untounaran, untounogh, untounich, aman (ընդունարան, ընդունող, ընդունիչ, աման)
reciprocal - pokhatarts, pokhnipokh, hamarzhek (փոխադարձ, փոխնիփոխ, համարժէք)
reciprocate - pokhanagel, pokhatartsel (փոխանակել, փոխադարձել)
reciprocity - pokhatartsoutiun (փոխադարձութիւն)
recital - menahamerk, menanuvak, ardasanoum (մենահամերգ, մենանուագ, արտասանում)
recitation - ardasanoutiun, tasavan-

toutiun (արտասանութիւն, դասաւանդութիւն)
recite - ardasanel, zuroutsel, usel, khosil, tuvel (արտասանել, զրուցել, ըսել, խօսիլ, թուել)
reciter - ardasanogh, asmounkogh (արտասանող, ասմունքող)
reck - hokal, nugadi arnel, hashvi arnel, gardzel (հոգալ, նկատի առնել, հաշուի առնել, կարծել)
reckless - anhok, anuzkouysh, anpouyt (անհոգ, անզգոյշ, անփոյթ)
reckon - hashvel, tuvel, hamrel, sebel, harkel (հաշուել, թուել, համրել, սեպել, յարգել)
reckoning - hashiv, hashvoum, hashvarg, hashvetsoutsag (հաշիւ, հաշւում, հաշուարկ, հաշուեցուցակ)
reclaim - bahanchel, yed ouzel, poghokel, hergel (պահանջել, ետ ուզել, բողոքել, հերկել)
reclamation - bahanch, poghok (պահանջ, բողոք)
reclination - midoum, hagoum (միտում, հակում)
recline - hagil, henoul, gurtunil, dzuril, dzurel (հակիլ, յենուլ, կռթնիլ, ծռիլ, ծռել)
reclose - verapagel, verakotsel (վերափակել, վերագոցել)
recluse - megousatsadz, menagiats, juknavor (մեկուսացած, մենակեաց, ճգնաւոր)
reclusion - megousatsoum, juknoum, menagetsoutiun (մեկուսացում, ճգնում, մենակեցութիւն)
recognition - janachoum, untounoum, khosdovanoutiun (ճանաչում, ընդունում, խոստովանութիւն)
recognize - janchunal, imanal, untounil, hasgunal (ճանչնալ, իմանալ, ընդունիլ, հասկնալ)
recoil - ungurgoum, hedatsaydk, ungurgil, yed tsadgel (ընկրկում, յետացայտք, ընկրկիլ, ետ ցատկել)
recollect - verahavakel (վերահաւաքել)
recollection - verhishoum, verhoush, mudamperoum (վերյիշում, վերյուշ, մտամբերում)
recomfort - zoratsunel, gaztourel, surdabuntel, uspopel (զօրացնել, կազդուրել, սրտապնդել, սփոփել)
recommence - verusgusil (վերսկսիլ)
recommend - hantsnararel, hantsnel, badvirel, kovel (յանձնարարել, յանձնել, պատուիրել, գովել)
recommendable - hantsunarareli, telatureli, koveli (յանձնարարելի, թելադրելի, գովելի)
recommendation - hantsnararoutiun, badver, hantsnararagan (յանձնարարութիւն, պատուէր, յանձնարարական)
recommender - hantsnararogh (յանձնարարող)
recommit - verahantsunel (վերայանձնել)
recompense - vartsadurel, hadoutsanel, hadoutsoum, vartsk (վարձատրել, հատուցանել, յատուցում, վարձք)
recompose - verhorinel, verasharel, veragazmel (վերյօրինել, վերաշարել, վերակազմել)
recomposition - veragazmoutiun (վերակազմութիւն)
reconcilable - hashduveli, hamatsayneli, hamadegheli (հաշտուելի, համաձայնելի, համատեղելի)
reconcile - hashdetsunel, hashduvil, miapanil, hartel (հաշտեցնել, հաշտուիլ, միաբանիլ, հարթել)
reconciliation - hashdoutiun, hamatsaynoutiun, kavoutiun (հաշտութիւն, համաձայնութիւն, քաւութիւն)
recondite - khor, kaghdni, takoun, dzadzguvadz (խոր, գաղտնի, թաքուն, ծածկուած)
reconnaissance - hedazodoum, zunnoutiun, yergurakhouzoutiun (հետազօտում, զննութիւն, երկրախուզութիւն)
reconnoiter - hedazodel, hedakhouzel, shurchil, zunnel (հետազօտել, հետախուզել, շրջիլ, զննել)
reconquer - verakuravel, veradirel, veranuvajel (վերագրաւել, վերա-

տիրել, վերանուաճել)
reconquest - verakuravoum, veradiroutiun (վերագրաւում, վերատիրութիւն)
reconsider - veranayil, veranugadel, verkhorhurtadzel (վերանայիլ, վերանկատել, վերխորհրդածել)
reconsideration - veranugadoum, veranayoum (վերանկատում, վերանայում)
reconstitute - veragazmel (վերակազմել)
reconstruct - verashinel, veragaroutsel, veragankunel (վերաշինել, վերակառուցել, վերականգնել)
reconstruction - verashinoutiun, veragaroutsoum (վերաշինութիւն, վերակառուցում)
reconvene - verahavakel (վերահաւաքել)
reconvey - verapokhaturel, verahaghortel (վերափոխադրել, վերահաղորդել)
reconveyance - verapokhaturoutiun (վերափոխադրութիւն)
record - murtsanish, artsanakuroutiun (մրցանիշ, արձանագրութիւն)
record (n) - artsanakuroutiun, tsaynabunag, murtsanish (արձանագրութիւն, ձայնապնակ, մրցանիշ)
record (v) - artsanakurel, houshakurel, tsaynakurel (արձանագրել, յուշագրել, ձայնագրել)
record player - tsaynakir (ձայնագիր)
recorder - artsanakurogh, tsaynakukurogh, nodar, tadavor (արձանագրող, ձայնագրող, նոտար, դատաւոր)
recording - artsanakuroutiun (արձանագրութիւն)
recount - verahashvel, verabadmel (վերահաշուել, վերապատմել)
recoup - hadoutsanel, zeghchel, gudrel (հատուցանել, զեղչել, կտրել)
recourse - timoum, khunturank, abaven, veratarts (դիմում, խնդրանք, ապաւէն, վերադարձ)
recover - veradzadzgel, verashahil, verusdanal, pouzhvil (վերածածկել, վերաշահիլ, վերստանալ, բուժուիլ)
recovery - gaztouroum, veragankunoum, aroghchatsoum (կազդուրում, վերականգնում, առողջացում)
recreance, recreancy - vadoutiun, vakhgodoutiun, anhavadarmoutiun (վատութիւն, վախկոտութիւն, անհաւատարմութիւն)
recreant - vad, vakhgod, anhavadarim, pokroki (վատ, վախկոտ, անհաւատարիմ, փոքրոգի)
recreate - verusdeghdzel, gaztourel, zuvarjanal, vokevoril (վերստեղծել, կազդուրել, զուարճանալ, ոգեւորիլ)
recreation - uzposank, zuvarjoutiun, verusdeghdzoum (զբօսանք, զուարճութիւն, վերստեղծում)
recrement - aveltsouk, tird (աւելցուք, դիրտ)
recrudescence - sasdgatsoum, goddatsoum, ajoum (սաստկացում, կոտտացում, աճում)
recruit (n) - norazen, norakir zinvor, bahesdi zork (նորազէն, նորագիր զինուոր, պահեստի զօրք)
recruit (v) - zinvorakurel, havakel, zoranal, gaztourvil (զինուորագրել, հաւաքել, զօրանալ, կազդուրուիլ)
recruitment - zorahavak (զօրահաւաք)
rectangle - oughghangiun (ուղղանկիւն)
rectangular - oughghangunatsev (ուղղանկիւնաձեւ)
rectifiable - surpakreli, shudgeli, oughgheli (սրբագրելի, շտկելի, ուղղելի)
rectification - oughghoum, surpakuroum (ուղղում, սրբագրում)
rectify - oughghel, surpakurel, shudgel (ուղղել, սրբագրել, շտկել)
rectitude - oughghamudoutiun, shidagoutiun, bargeshdoutiun (ուղղամտութիւն, շիտակութիւն, պարկեշտութիւն)
recto - arachin yeres-terti (առաջին երես՝ թերթի)

rector - zhoghovurtabed, yerets, veradesouch, varich (ժողովրդապետ, երէց, վերատեսուչ, վարիչ)
rectorate - yeritsaran, descharan, deschoutiun (երիցարան, տեսչարան, տեսչութիւն)
rectorship - zhoghovurtabedoutiun (ժողովրդապետութիւն)
recumbent - yerguntsadz, ungoghmanadz, ansharzh (երկնցած, ընկողմանած, անշարժ)
recuperate - aroghchanal, aghegnal, gaztourvil, abakinil (առողջանալ, աղէկնալ, կազդուրուիլ, ապաքինիլ)
recuperation - abakinoum, verusdatsoum (ապաքինում, վերստացում)
recur - badahil, yed kal, veratarnal, gurgnuvil (պատահիլ, ետ գալ, վերադառնալ, կրկնուիլ)
recurrence, cy - badahaganoutiou, veratimoum, gurgnoum (պատահականութիւն, վերադիմում, կրկնում)
recurve - veradzurel (վերածռել)
recusant - merzhogh, anhamagerb, aylatavan (մերժող, անհամակերպ, այլադաւան)
recycle - veramushagoum hini, verokdakordzel (վերամշակում հինի, վերօգտագործել)
recycling - verapokhoum, vershurchanaroutiun (վերափոխում, վերշրջանառութիւն)
red - garmir, sheg (կարմիր, շէկ)
redact - khumpakurel, sharaturel (խմբագրել, շարադրել)
redaction - khumpakuroutiun, khumpakroum (խմբագրութիւն, խմբագրում)
redactor - khumpakir (խմբագիր)
redargue - tadabardel, chuhavanil (դատապարտել, չհաւանիլ)
redbreast - garmuralanch (կարմրալանջ)
redden - garmurtsunel, garmuril, shignil, sharakounil (կարմրցնել, կարմրիլ, շիկնիլ, շառագունիլ)
reddish - garmuravoun, garmurorag (կարմրաւուն, կարմրորակ
reddition - antsunaduvoutiun, verahantsunoum, hadoutsoum (անձնատուութիւն, վերայանձնում, հատուցում)
rede - khorhourt, aradz (խորհուրդ, առած)
redeem - verakunel, vujarel, hadoutsanel, kavel (վերագնել, վճարել, հատուցանել, քաւել)
redeemer - vujarogh, purgich, hadoutsanogh (վճարող, փրկիչ, հատուցանող)
redeliver - verahantsunel, verapurgel (վերայանձնել, վերափրկել)
redemand - verabahanchel, verabahanch (վերապահանջել, վերապահանջ)
redemption - verakunoum, bardavujaroum, purgoutiun (վերագնում, պարտավճարում, փրկութիւն)
redfish - garmuratsoug (կարմրաձուկ)
redhot - hurasheg, gasgarmir (հրաշէկ, կասկարմիր)
redistribute - verapashkhel, veratsurvel (վերաբաշխել, վերացրուել)
redly - garmuroutiamp (կարմրութեամբ)
redness - garmuroutiun (կարմրութիւն)
redolence - anoushahodoutiun, pourmounk, pouyr (անուշահոտութիւն, բուրմունք, բոյր)
redolent - anoushahod, pouroumnaved, hodaved (անուշահոտ, բուրումնաւէտ, հոտաւէտ)
redouble - gurgnabadgel, gurgnuvil (կրկնապատկել, կրկնուիլ)
redoubt - pertag, amrotsig, vakhnal, sosgal (բերդակ, ամրոցիկ, վախնալ, սոսկալ)
redoubtable - ahavor, sosgali, ahargou, ahegh (ահաւոր, սոսկալի, ահարկու, ահեղ)
redound - nubasdel, hortil, zeghoul, hosil, yed tarnal (նպաստել, յորդիլ, զեղուլ, հոսիլ, ետ դառնալ)
redress (n) - ougghoum, hadoutsoum, tarmanoum, oknoutiun (ուղղում, հատուցում, դարմանում, օգնութիւն)
redress (v) - oughghel, haktsunel,

tarmanel, oknel (ուղղել, Հագցնել, դարմանել, օգնել)
redskin - garmuramort, amerigatsi huntig (կարմրամորթ, ամերիկացի Հնդիկ)
reduce - nuvazetsunel, kichtsunel, veradzel, ampopel (նուազեցնել, քիչցնել, վերածել, ամփոփել)
reducement - veradzoum (վերածում)
reduction - nuvazetsoum, veradzoum, zeghch (նուազեցում, վերածում, զեղչ)
redundance - aradoutiun, shadoutiun, shadakhosoutiun (առատութիւն, շատութիւն, շատախօսութիւն)
redundant - avelort, arad, shadakhos (աւելորդ, առատ, շատախօս)
reduplicate - gurgunabadgel, gurgunel (կրկնապատկել, կրկնել)
reed - yeghek, surink, shamp, yeghekov dzadzgel (եղէգ, սրինգ, շամբ, եղէգով ծածկել)
reeden - yegheknia, yekhekov shinvadz (եղէգնեայ, եղէգէ շինուած)
reedy - yegheknoud (եղէգնուտ)
reef - kharag, vimoudk, arakasdalatu dzalel (խարակ, վիմուտք, առագաստալաթը ծալել)
reek - shoki, dzoukh, mour, mukhal (շոգի, ծուխ, մուր, մխալ)
reel - bar mu, yereroum, garzh, yereral, garzhel (պար մը, երերում, կարժ, երերալ, կարժել)
reelect - verundurel (վերընտրել)
reelection - verunduroutiun (վերընտրութիւն)
reface - veradzepel, vereresel (վերածեփել, վերերեսել)
refect - gaztourel, zoratsunel, tetev jash dal (կազդուրել, զօրացնել, թեթեւ ճաշ տալ)
refection - tetev jash, gaztouroum, (թեթեւ ճաշ, կազդուրում)
refective - gaztourich, hankusdatsoutsich (կազդուրիչ, Հանգստացուցիչ)
refectory - jashasurah, seghanadoun (ճաշասրաՀ, սեղանատուն)
refer - timel, hughel, madnanushel, agnargel (դիմել, յղել, մատնանշել, ակնարկել)
referee - iravarar (իրաւարար)
reference - vugayagochoum, verakuroum, deghegoutiun (վկայակոչում, վերագրում, տեղեկութիւն)
referendum - hanrakuve, hartsakir, (Հանրաքուէ, Հարցագիր)
refill - verusdin letsunel, pokharinel, pokhnort, bahesd (վերստին լեցնել, փոխարինել, փոխնորդ, պաՀեստ)
refinancing - verusdin turamahaytaytoum, veradundesoum (վերստին դրամաՀայթայթում, վերատնտեսում)
refine - makrel, nurpatsunel, zudel, nurpanal (մաքրել, նրբացնել, զտել, նրբանալ)
refined - hughguvadz, mushaguvadz, nourp, azniv, zoud (յղկուած, մշակուած, նուրբ, ազնիւ, զուտ)
refinement - aznuvoutiun, paregurtoutiun, papgatsoum (ազնուութիւն, բարեկրթութիւն, փափկացում)
refinery - zudaran (զտարան)
refit - veranorokel, verashudgel, veranorokoum (վերանորոգել, վերաշտկել, վերանորոգում)
reflect - tsolatsunel, ardatsolal, khogal, barsavel (ցոլացնել, արտացոլալ, խոկալ, պարսաւել)
reflection - tsolatsoum, mudadzoum, khogoum, barsav (ցոլացում, մտածում, խոկում, պարսաւ)
reflective - ardatsologh, khorhogh, anturatarts (արտացոլող, խորՀող, անդրադարձ)
reflector - anturatartsogh, tsolatsig, tsolartsag (անդրադարձող, ցոլացիկ, ցոլարձակ)
reflex - anturatarts, tsolatsoum, anturatartsunel (անդրադարձ, ցոլացում, անդրադարձնել)
reflux - hedahos, deghaduvoutiun, hagahosank, hedatarts (յետաՀոս, տեղատուութիւն, ՀակաՀոսանք, յետադարձ)
reforge - veratarpunel (վերադարբնել)
reform - parenorokel, veragazmel,

parenorokoum (բարենորոգել, վերակազմել, բարենորոգում)
reformation - parenorokoum, paregarkoutiun, veragazmoum (բարենորոգում, բարեկարգութիւն, վերակազմում)
reformer - paregarkich, veranorokich (բարեկարգիչ, վերանորոգիչ)
refound - verahimnel (վերահիմնել)
refract - peganel, godurdel, pegpegel (բեկանել, կոտրտել, բեկբեկել)
refraction - pegoum, pegpegoum (բեկում, բեկբեկում)
refractory - umpost, hamar, gamagor, chuhalogh medagh (ըմբոստ, յամառ, կամակոր, չհալող մետաղ)
refragable - herkeli (հերքելի)
refrain - gurgnerk, hangerk, zusbel, santsel (կրկներգ, յանկերգ, զսպել, սանձել)
reframe - verashurchanagel, veratsevel (վերաշրջանակել, վերաձեւել)
refresh - tarmatsunel, gaztourel, zovatsunel, uspopel (թարմացնել, կազդուրել, զովացնել, սփոփել)
refresher - zovatsoutsich, zovatsunogh, gaztourogh (զովացուցիչ, զովացնող, կազդուրող)
refreshing - zovatsoutsich, zovarar (զովացուցիչ, զովարար)
refreshment - zovatsoutsich, zovoutiun, gaztouroum (զովացուցիչ, զովութիւն, կազդուրում)
refrigerant - baghetsoutsich (պաղեցուցիչ)
refrigerate - baghetsunel, saretsunel, tsurdatsunel (պաղեցնել, սառեցնել, ցրտացնել)
refrigeration - saretsoum, baghetsoum (սառեցում, պաղեցում)
refrigerator - sarnaran (սառնարան)
refuge - abasdan, abasdanaran, abaven, abasdanil (ապաստան, ապաստանարան, ապաւէն, ապաստանիլ)
refugee - pakhusdagan, abasdanial (փախստական, ապաստանեալ)
refulgence - paylounoutiun, shoghiun (փայլունութիւն, շողիւն)
refulgent - payloun, lousapayl, lousashogh (փայլուն, լուսափայլ, լուսաշող)
refund - veratartsunel, vujarel, koumaru yed dal (վերադարձնել, վճարել, գումարը ետ տալ)
refurbish - veramakrel, payletsunel, tarmatsunel (վերամաքրել, փայլեցնել, թարմացնել)
refusable - merzheli (մերժելի)
refusal - merzhoum (մերժում)
refuse (n) - merzhuvadz, avelort, munatsougner, tird (մերժուած, աւելորդ, մնացուկներ, դիրտ)
refuse (v) - merzhel, chuntounil, chouzel, zulanal (մերժել, չընդունիլ, չուզել, զլանալ)
refuser - merzhogh (մերժող)
refutable - herkeli (հերքելի)
refutation - herkoum, merzhoum (հերքում, մերժում)
refute - herkel, churel, zhukhdel (հերքել, ջրել, ժխտել)
regain - verashahil, verusdanal, verakudnel (վերաշահիլ, վերստանալ, վերագտնել)
regal - arkayagan, arkouni, takavoragan (արքայական, արքունի, թագաւորական)
regale (n) - hiurasiroutiun, khunjouyk, geroukhoum (հիւրասիրութիւն, խնճոյք, կերուխում)
regale (v) - medzarel, hiurasirel, badvel, khunjouyk dal (մեծարել, հիւրասիրել, պատուել, խնճոյք տալ)
regard (n) - nayvadzk, nugadoum, oushaturoutiun (նայուածք, նկատում, ուշադրութիւն)
regard (v) - nayil, nugadel, harkel, veraperil (նայիլ, նկատել, յարգել, վերաբերիլ)
regardful - oushatir, uzkoushavor, hokadar (ուշադիր, զգուշաւոր, հոգատար)
regarding - nugadmamp, veraperial, masin (նկատմամբ, վերաբերեալ, մասին)
regardless - anoushatir, anhok, andarper, annugad (անուշադիր, ան-

Հող, անտարբեր, աննկատ)
regather - verazhoghvel (վերաժողվել)
regency - pokharkayoutiun, kahi khunamagaloutiun (փոխարքայութիւն, գահի խնամակալութիւն)
regenerate - veradzunil, verardaturel, veradzunial (վերածնիլ, վերարտադրել, վերածնեալ)
regeneration - veradzunount, veraganknoum (վերածնունդ, վերականգնում)
regenerator - verardaturich, veradzunich (վերարտադրիչ, վերածնիչ)
regent - ishkhan, khunamagal, pokharka (իշխան, խնամակալ, փոխարքայ)
regime - varchatsev, iravagark, sununtaganon, abrelagerb (վարչաձեւ, իրաւակարգ, սննդականոն, ապրելակերպ)
regimen - varjoutiun, garavaroutiun, sununtaganon (վարչութիւն, կառավարութիւն, սննդականոն)
regiment - zorakount, kount (զորագունդ, գունդ)
region - yerguramas, shurchan, kavar, shurchagayk (երկրամաս, շրջան, գաւառ, շրջակայք)
register - domar, artsanadedur, artsanakurogh, artsanakurel (տոմար, արձանատետր, արձանագրող, արձանագրել)
registrant - artsanakurogh, artsanakurich (արձանագրող, արձանագրիչ)
registrar - tivanabed, artsanakurogh, artsanakir (դիւանապետ, արձանագրող, արձանագիր)
registration - artsanakuroum, artsanakuroutiun, kurantzoum (արձանագրում, արձանագրութիւն, գրանցում)
registry - artsanakuroutiun, tivanadoun, tivan (արձանագրութիւն, դիւանատուն, դիւան)
regnancy - ishkhanoutiun (իշխանութիւն)
regnant - ishkhogh, ishkhan, keragushrogh (իշխող, իշխան, գերակշռող)
regorge - puskhel, tours dal, gullel (փսխել, դուրս տալ, կլլել)
regrant - verashunorhel (վերաշնորհել)
regrate - veradashel, veragopel (վերատաշել, վերակոփել)
regress - veratarts, hedatarts, verusdantsnoum (վերադարձ, յետադարձ, վերստանձնում)
regression - hedatartsoutiun, hedashurchoutiun (յետադարձութիւն, յետաշրջութիւն)
regret - zughchal, tsavil, apsosal, zughchoum, tsav, vishd (զղջալ, ցաւիլ, ափսոսալ, զղջում, ցաւ, վիշտ)
regretful - tsavali, tsavod, apsosali (ցաւալի, ցաւոտ, ափսոսալի)
regrettable - tsavali (ցաւալի)
regular - ganonavor, orinavor, hart, jisht, vanagan (կանոնաւոր, օրինաւոր, Հարթ, ճիշդ, վանական)
regularity - ganonavoroutiun, jushtoutiun (կանոնաւորութիւն, ճշդութիւն)
regularize, ise - ganonavorel (կանոնաւորել)
regularly - ganonavorabes, usd orini (կանոնաւորապէս, ըստ օրինի)
regulate - ganonavorel, garkavorel (կանոնաւորել, կարգաւորել)
regulation - ganonavoroutiun, garkavoroum, ganon (կանոնաւորութիւն, կարգաւորութիւն, կանոն)
regulator - ganonavorogh, oughghich (կանոնաւորող, ուղղիչ)
rehabilitate - verahasdadel, veragankunel, verabadvel (վերաՀաստատել, վերականգնել, վերապատուել)
rehabilitation - verahasdadoum, veragankunoum (վերաՀաստատում, վերականգնում)
rehear - veralusel (վերալսել)
rehearsal - ports, taderaports, teraports, gurgnoum (փորձ, թատերափորձ, դերափորձ, կրկնում)
rehearse - portsel, gurgnel, ardasanel, usel (փորձել, կրկնել, ար-

տասանել, ըսել)
reign - ishkhanoutiun, direl, ishkhel, takavorel (իշխանութիւն, տիրել, իշխել, թագաւորել)
reimburse - veratartsunel, verahadoutsanel, vujarel (վերադարձնել, վերահատուցանել, վճարել)
reimbursement - hadoutsoum, vujaroum (հատուցում, վճարում)
reimport - veraneradzel (վերաներածել)
rein - sants, yerasanag, gheg, santsel, zusbel, kushel (սանձ, երասանակ, ղեկ, սանձել, զսպել, քշել)
reincarnate - verusdin marmunanal, noren dzunil (վերստին մարմնանալ, նորէն ծնիլ)
reincarnation - hokepokhoutiun, veradzunount (հոգեփոխութիւն, վերածնունդ)
reinforce - veramratsunel, zoratsunel, ouzheghatsunel (վերամրացնել, զօրացնել, ուժեղացնել)
reinforcement - amratsoum, zoratsoum, zorki haytaytoum (ամրացում, զօրացում, զօրքի հայթայթում)
reins - yerigamounk, kourkourank (երիկամունք, գուրգուրանք)
reinspect - verakunnel (վերաքննել)
reinstall - verahasdadel (վերահաստատել)
reinstate - verahasdadel (վերահաստատել)
reinsurance - verabahovakuroutiun (վերապահովագրութիւն)
reinsure - gurgin abahovakurel (կրկին ապահովագրել)
reintegrate - verahasdadel, veranorokel (վերահաստատել, վերանորոգել)
reinvest - verashahargel, verashunorhel (վերաշահարկել, վերաշնորհել)
reinvigorate - veragaztourel, verazoratsunel (վերակազդուրել, վերազօրացնել)
reissue - verhuradaragel, verhuradaragoutiun (վերհրատարակել, վերհրատարակութիւն)
reiterate - gurgnel, yergurortel, veragurgunel (կրկնել, երկրորդել, վերակրկնել)
reiteration - veragurgnoutiun (վերակրկնութիւն)
reject - merzhel, chuntounil, noren nedel (մերժել, չընդունիլ, նորէն նետել)
rejection - merzhoum, puskhoum (մերժում, փսխում)
rejector - tsolatsoutsich, merzhogh (ցոլացուցիչ, մերժող)
rejoice - ourakhanal, tsundzal, hurjuvil, zuvarjatsunel (ուրախանալ, ցնծալ, հրճուիլ, զուարճացնել)
rejoicer - ourakhatsogh, tsundzatsogh (ուրախացող, ցնծացող)
rejoicing - ourakhoutiun, zuvarjoutiun, tsundzoutiun (ուրախութիւն, զուարճութիւն, ցնծութիւն)
rejoin - veramianal, veramiatsunel, haril, badaskhanel (վերամիանալ, վերամիացնել, յարիլ, պատասխանել)
rejoinder - badaskhan, arargoutiun (պատասխան, առարկութիւն)
rejoint - veragutsel, veramiatsunel (վերակցել, վերամիացնել)
rejudge - veratadel, verakunnel (վերադատել, վերաքննել)
rejunction - veramiavoroum, veragutsoum (վերամիաւորում, վերակցում)
rejuvenate - yeridasartanal, yeridasartatsunel (երիտասարդանալ, երիտասարդացնել)
rejuvenescence - verayeridasartatsoum (վերաերիտասարդացում)
rekindle - verardzardzel (վերարծարծել)
relagation - aksor, darakuroutiun, vudaroum (աքսոր, տարագրութիւն, վտարում)
relapse - veragurgnoum, yed iynalu, verangoum (վերակրկնում, ետ իյնալը, վերանկում)
relate - badmel, usel, haraperil, veraperil, badganil (պատմել, ըսել, յարաբերիլ, վերաբերիլ, պատկանիլ)

relater - badmogh (պատմող)
relation - haraperoutiun, gab, azkaganoutiun (յարաբերութիւն, կապ, ազգականութիւն)
relationship - azkagtsoutiun, khunamioutiun (ազգակցութիւն, խնամիութիւն)
relative - azkagan, veraperial, haraperagan (ազգական, վերաբերեալ, յարաբերական)
relatively - haraperapar, hamemadapar (յարաբերաբար, համեմատաբար)
relativity - azkaganoutiun, haraperoutiun (ազգականութիւն, յարաբերութիւն)
relax - meghmel, meghmatsunel, hankusdatsunel, toulnal (մեղմել, մեղմացնել, հանգստացնել, թուլնալ)
relaxation - meghmatsoum, toulatsoum, hankisd (մեղմացում, թուլացում, հանգիստ)
relay - gab, heragab, pokhargich, pokhnort tsi (կապ, հեռակապ, փոխարկիչ, փոխնորդ ձի)
release - artsagel, azadel, hanel, artsagoum, azadoum (արձակել, ազատել, հանել, արձակում, ազատում)
releasement - toghargoum, artsagoum, zerdzoum (թողարկում, արձակում, զերծում)
relegate - aksorel, darakurel, vudarel, kushel (աքսորել, տարագրել, վտարել, քշել)
relegation - vudaroum, pokhaturoum (վտարում, փոխադրում)
relent - gagoughnal, meghmanal, toulnal (կակուղնալ, մեղմանալ, թուլնալ
relentless - ankout, pird, anoghok (անգութ, բիրտ, անողոք)
relevance - harmaroutiun, badshajoutiun (յարմարութիւն, պատշաճութիւն)
relevant - badshaj, harmar, deghin (պատշաճ, յարմար, տեղին)
reliability - vusdahelioutiun (վստահելիութիւն)
reliable - vusdaheli, havadarim, usdouyk, amour (վստահելի, հաւատարիմ, ստոյգ, ամուր)
reliance - vusdahoutiun, havadk, hamaroum, abaven (վստահութիւն, հաւատք, համարում, ապաւէն)
reliant - havadarim, vusdah (հաւատարիմ, վստահ)
relic - masounk, pegor, munatsort, nushkhar, hedk (մասունք, բեկոր, մնացորդ, նշխար, հետք)
relict - ayri (այրի)
relief - oknoutiun, tarman, nubasd, kantag, yelevech (օգնութիւն, դարման, նպաստ, քանդակ, ելեւէջ)
relieve - tetevtsunel, amokel, nubasdel, pokhanortel (թեթեւցնել, ամոքել, նպաստել, փոխանորդել)
religion - guronk, tavanank, havadk (կրօնք, դաւանանք, հաւատք)
religious - guronagan, parebashd, guronavor (կրօնական, բարեպաշտ, կրօնաւոր)
relinquish - toghoul, lukel, tsukel, merzhel, hurazharil (թողուլ, լքել, ձգել, մերժել, հրաժարիլ)
relish - jashagel, umposhkhunel, vayelel, ham, jashag (ճաշակել, ըմբոշխնել, վայելել, համ, ճաշակ)
reload - verapertsunel, veraletsunel (վերաբեռցնել, վերալեցնել)
reluct - unttimanal, tuzhgamagil (ընդդիմանալ, դժկամակիլ)
reluctance - tuzhgamagoutiun (դժկամակութիւն)
reluctant - tuzhgamagogh, hagaragogh, unttimatsogh (դժկամակող, հակառակող, ընդդիմացող)
reluctantly - agamaoren, purni gerbov (ակամաօրէն, բռնի կերպով)
relumine - noren varel (նորէն վառել)
rely - vusdahil, abavinil, havadal (վստահիլ, ապաւինիլ, հաւատալ)
remain - munal, genal, devel, punagil (մնալ, կենալ, տեւել, բնակիլ)
remainder - munatsort, munatsoug (մնացորդ, մնացուկ)
remains - munatsortats, nushkhark, ajiun, tiag (մնացորդաց, նշխարք,

աճիւն, դիակ)
remake - verashinel (վերաշինել)
remand - yed ghurgel, pand oughargel, tadel (ետ ղրկել, բանտ ուղարկել, դատել)
remark - tidoghoutiun, madnanushel, nushmarel, agnargel (դիտողութիւն, մատնանշել, նշմարել, ակնարկել)
remarkable - yereveli, nushanavor, oushakurav (երեւելի, նշանաւոր, ուշագրաւ)
remarry - veramousnanal (վերամուսնանալ)
remeasure - verachapel (վերաչափել)
remediable - tarmaneli, pouzheli (դարմանալի, բուժելի)
remedial - pouzhich, pouzhogh, amokich (բուժիչ, բուժող, ամոքիչ)
remediless - antarman (անդարման)
remedy - tarman, legh, jar, hunark, puzhushgel, tarmanel (դարման, դեղ, ճար, հնարք, բժշկել, դարմանել)
remember - hishel, mudaperel, hishetsunel (յիշել, մտաբերել, յիշեցնել)
rememberer - hishogh (յիշող)
remembrance - hishoghoutiun, hishadagoutiun, hishoum (յիշողութիւն, յիշատակութիւն, յիշում)
remigrate - verakaghtel (վերագաղթել)
remigration - verakaght (վերագաղթ)
remind - hishetsunel (յիշեցնել)
reminder - hishetsunogh, housharar (յիշեցնող, յուշարար)
reminiscence - hishoghoutiun, hishadag, houshk (յիշողութիւն, յիշատակ, յուշք)
reminiscent - hishetsunogh, hishadageli (յիշեցնող, յիշատակելի)
remiss - anhok, anpouyt, touyl, tantagh, meghg (անհոգ, անփոյթ, թոյլ, դանդաղ, մեղկ)
remission - toghoum, neroum, shunorhoum, meghmoum (թողում, ներում, շնորհում, մեղմում)
remissness - touloutiun (թուլութիւն)
remit - dal, hantsunel, ghurgel, nerel, pokhantsel (տալ, յանձնել, ղրկել, ներել, փոխանցել)
remittance - vujaroum, turami pokhantsoum, arakoum (վճարում, դրամի փոխանցում, առաքում)
remitter - arakogh, hantsunogh (առաքող, յանձնող)
remnant - munatsort, aveltsouk, pegor, nushkhar (մնացորդ, աւելցուք, բեկոր, նշխար)
remodel - veratsevel, verapokhel (վերաձեւել, վերափոխել)
remodeling - parepokhoum, veratsevavoroum (բարեփոխում, վերաձեւաւորում)
remonstrance - arargoutiun, khurad (առարկութիւն, խրատ)
remonstrate - hantimanael, tidoghoutiun unel, khuradel (յանդիմանել, դիտողութիւն ընել, խրատել)
remorse - khughjmudank, zughchoum, kout, khayt (խղճմտանք, զղջում, գութ, խայթ)
remorseful - khughjahar (խղճահար)
remorseless - ankhighj, ankout (անխիղճ, անգութ)
remote - heravor, herou, angab (հեռաւոր, հեռու, անկապ)
remote control - heragab, heravar, herahusgoum (հեռակապ, հեռավար, հեռահսկում)
remotion - heratsoum (հեռացում)
removable - sharzhagan, pokhatureli, popokheli (շարժական, փոխադրելի, փոփոխելի)
removal - deghapokhoutiun, megnoum, heratsoum (տեղափոխութիւն, մեկնում, հեռացում)
remove - deghapokhel, pokhaturel, sharzhel, pokhaturvil (տեղափոխել, փոխադրել, շարժել, փոխադրուիլ)
remunerate - vartsadurel, hadoutsanel, pokharinel (վարձատրել, հատուցանել, փոխարինել)
remuneration - vartsaduroutiun, pokharinoum (վարձատրութիւն, փոխարինում)

Renaissance - veradzunount (Վերածնունդ)
renal - yerigamayin, yerigamounki (երիկամային, երիկամունքի)
renard - aghves (աղուէս)
rencounter - pakhil, hantibil, badahil, paghkhoum (բախիլ, Հանդիպիլ, պատահիլ, բաղխում)
rend - badurel, jeghkel, pazhnel, chartel, baduril (պատռել, ճեղքել, բաժնել, ջարդել, պատռիլ)
render - veratartsunel, hadoutsanel, dal, tarkumanel (վերադարձնել, Հատուցանել, տալ, Թարգմանել)
rendez-vous - zhamaturoutiun, zhamaturavayr, mianal (ժամադրութիւն, ժամադրավայր, միանալ)
rendition - antsnaduvoutiun, hantsunoum, tarkumanoutiun (անձնատուութիւն, յանձնում, Թարգմանութիւն)
renegade - ouratsogh, tasalik, havadourats, tavajan (ուրացող, դասալիք, Հաւատուրաց, դաւաճան)
renege - ouranal (ուրանալ)
renew - norokel, veranorokel, tarmatsunel, verusgusil (նորոգել, վերանորոգել, Թարմացնել, վերսկսիլ)
renewable - norokeli, norokvelik (նորոգելի, նորոգուելիք)
renewal - norokoum, veranorokoum (նորոգում, վերանորոգում)
renewer - norokich (նորոգիչ)
renitence - timatsgounoutiun (դիմացկունութիւն)
renitent - timatsgoun, dogoun (դիմացկուն, տոկուն)
renounce - hurazharil, kashvil, merzhel, chuntounil (Հրաժարիլ, քաշուիլ, մերժել, չընդունիլ)
renouncement - hurazharoum, merzhoum, ouratsoum (Հրաժարում, մերժում, ուրացում)
renovate - norokel, tarmatsunel, noratsunel (նորոգել, Թարմացնել, նորացնել)
renovation - norokoum, veragaroutsoum, tarmatsoum (նորոգում, վերակառուցում, Թարմացում)
renown - hampav, hurchag, hurchagavor tartsunel (Համբաւ, Հռչակ, Հռչակաւոր դարձնել)
renowned - anvani, hurchagavor, hampavavor (անուանի, Հռչակաւոր, Համբաւաւոր)
rent (n) - vartsk, yegamoud, jeghk, jeghkets, badruvadzk (վարձք, եկամուտ, ճեղք, ճեղքեց, պատռուածք)
rent (v) - vartsel, vartsuvil (վարձել, վարձուիլ)
rental - vartsoum, vartsakin (վարձում, վարձագին)
renter - vartsogh, vartsagal, nurpagarel (վարձող, վարձակալ, Նրբակարել)
renunciation - hurazharoum, merzhoum (Հրաժարում, մերժում)
reopen - verapanal, verapatsvil, verusgusil (վերաբանալ, վերաբացուիլ, վերսկսիլ)
reorder - verabusburel, verusdin badvirel, veragazmel (վերապսպրել, վերստին պատուիրել, վերակազմել)
reorganization - veragazmoutiun (վերակազմութիւն)
reorganize - veragazmel, veragazmuvil (վերակազմել, վերակազմուիլ)
repair - norokel, shudgel, surpakurel, norokoum (նորոգել, շտկել, սրբագրել, նորոգում)
repairable - norokeli, tarmaneli, norokvelik (նորոգելի, դարմանելի, նորոգուելիք)
repairer - norokogh (նորոգող)
repairing - norokoum, norokoutiun (նորոգում, նորոգութիւն)
repairment - norokoum, norokoutiun (նորոգում, նորոգութիւն)
reparation - norokoum, hadoutsoum, tarman, veranorokoum (նորոգում, Հատուցում, դարման, վերանորոգում)
repartee - suramid badaskhan (սրամիտ պատասխան)
repass - verantsunil, noren tarnal (վերանցնիլ, նորէն դառնալ)
repast - oudelik, geragour, jash, oudesd, hatsgerouyt (ուտելիք, կե-

րակուր, ճաշ, ուտեստ, Հացկերոյթ)
repatriate - nerkaghtel, hayrenik veratarnal, nerkaghtogh (Ներգաղթել, Հայրենիք վերադառնալ, Ներգաղթող)
repay - veravujarel, veratartsunel, hadoutsanel (վերավճարել, վերադարձնել, Հատուցանել)
repayment - veravujaroum, pokhhadoutsoum (վերավճարում, փոխՀատուցում)
repeal - vochunchatsunel, chunchel, chunchoum, veratsoum (ոչնչացնել, ջնջել, ջնջում, վերացում)
repeat - gurgnel, serdel, artsakankel, gurgnoum, ports (կրկնել, սերտել, արձագանգել, կրկնում, փորձ)
repeater - gurgnogh (կրկնող)
repel - yed mughel, hurel, vanel (ետ մղել, Հրել, վանել)
repent - zughchal, tsavil, apsosal (զղջալ, ցաւիլ, ափսոսալ)
repentance - zughchoum, apsosank, abashkharank (զղջում, ափսոսանք, ապաշխարանք)
repentant - zughchatsogh, abashkharogh (զղջացող, ապաշխարող)
repeople - verapazmatsunel (վերաբազմացնել)
repercuss - anturatartsunel, artsakankel, tsolatsunel (անդրադարձնել, արձագանգել, ցոլացնել)
repercussion - artsakank, anturatarts, tsolatsoum (արձագանգ, անդրադարձ, ցոլացում)
repertory, repertoire - tsang, tsoutsag, khaghatsang, yerkatsang (ցանկ, ցուցակ, խաղացանկ, երգացանկ)
repetition - gurgnoum, gurgnoutiun, ports (կրկնում, կրկնութիւն, փորձ)
repine - durdunchal, tuzhkohil, kankadil (տրտնջալ, դժգոՀիլ, գանգատիլ)
replace - verazedeghel, deghavorel, pokharinel (վերազետեղել, տեղաւորել, փոխարինել)
replacement - pokharinoum, verazedeghoum (փոխարինում, վերազետեղում)
replant - veradungel (վերատնկել)
replay - gurgnoum khaghi, veratsoutsaturoutiun (կրկնում խաղի, վերացուցադրութիւն)
replenish - gurgin letsunel, veraletsunel, luratsunel (կրկին լեցնել, վերալեցնել, լրացնել)
replete - letsoun, zeghoun, hort, li (լեցուն, զեղուն, յորդ, լի)
replica - gurgnorinag, gurgnadib (կրկնօրինակ, կրկնատիպ)
replicant - badaskhanogh (պատասխանող)
replication - badaskhan, gurgnoutiun (պատասխան, կրկնութիւն)
replier - badaskhanogh (պատասխանող)
reply - badaskhanel, badaskhan (պատասխանել, պատասխան)
repolish - verahughgel (վերայղկել)
report - deghegakurel, deghegatsunel, deghegakir (տեղեկագրել, տեղեկացնել, տեղեկագիր)
reporter - lurakurogh, tughtagits, luraper, deghegadou (լրագրող, թղթակից, լրաբեր, տեղեկատու)
reporting - deghegakuroutiun, deghegakir (տեղեկագրութիւն, տեղեկագիր)
reposal - hankisd, hankchilu (Հանգիստ, Հանգչիլը)
repose (n) - hankisd, tatar, koun, hantardoutiun (Հանգիստ, դադար, քուն, Հանդարտութիւն)
repose (v) - hankuchil, hankuchetsunel, genal, kunanal (Հանգչիլ, Հանգչեցնել, կենալ, քնանալ)
reposit - bargetsunel, bahel, muterel (պառկեցնել, պաՀել, մթերել)
repossess - veradiranal, verusdanal (վերատիրանալ, վերստանալ)
repossession - veradiratsoum (վերատիրացում)
reprehend - meghaturel, hantimanel, sasdel, gushdampel (մեղադրել, Հանդիմանել, սաստել, կշտամբել)
reprehensible - meghatureli, aybaneli, barsaveli (մեղադրելի, այ-

պանելի, պարսաւելի)
reprehension - hantimanoutiun, sasdoum, gushdampank (յանդիմանութիւն, սաստում, կշտամբանք)
repremand - sasdel, hantimanel, sasd, hantimanoutiun (սաստել, յանդիմանել, սաստ, յանդիմանութիւն)
represent - nergayatsunel, tsoutsunel, pokhanortel (ներկայացնել, ցուցնել, փոխանորդել)
representation - nergayatsoum, nugar, nergayatsoutschoutiun (ներկայացում, նկար, ներկայացուցչութիւն)
representative - nergayatsunogh, nergayatsoutsich, yerespokhan (ներկայացնող, ներկայացուցիչ, երեսփոխան)
representer - nergayatsoutsich, nergayatsunogh (ներկայացուցիչ, ներկայացնող)
repress - ungjel, nuvajel, junshel (ընկճել, նուաճել, ճնշել)
repression - junshoum, seghmoum, nuvajoum, zusboum (ճնշում, սեղմում, նուաճում, զսպում)
reprieve - argakhel, hedatsukel, argakhoum, hedatsukoum (առկախել, յետաձգել, առկախում, յետաձգում)
reprimand - hantimanel, hantimanoutiun (յանդիմանել, յանդիմանութիւն)
reprint - veradubel, veraduboum (վերատպել, վերատպում)
reprisal - vurizharoutiun, pokharinoum (վրիժառութիւն, փոխարինում)
reproach - hantimanel, meghaturel, meghaturank, barsav (յանդիմանել, մեղադրել, մեղադրանք, պարսաւ)
reprobate (a) - anbidan, suriga, char, anuzkam, usdor, anarag (անպիտան, սրիկայ, չար, անզգամ, ստոր, անառակ)
reprobate (v) - anarkel, barsavel, tadabardel, gushdampel (անարգել, պարսաւել, դատապարտել, կշտամբել)
reprobation - tadabardoum, merzhoum, nakhadink (դատապարտում, մերժում, նախատինք)
reproduce - verardaturel, ardadubel, untorinagel (վերարտադրել, արտատպել, ընդօրինակել)
reproducer - verardaturogh (վերարտադրող)
reproduction - verardaturoutiun, veraduboum, pazmatsoum (վերարտադրութիւն, վերատպում, բազմացում)
reproductive - verardaturich, verardaturoghagan (վերարտադրիչ, վերարտադրողական)
reproof - hantimanoutiun, nugadoghoutiun, gushdampank (յանդիմանութիւն, նկատողութիւն, կշտամբանք)
reprovable - meghatureli, hantimaneli (մեղադրելի, յանդիմանելի)
reprove - meghaturel, gushdampel, hantimanel, nakhadel (մեղադրել, կշտամբել, յանդիմանել, նախատել)
reptile - soghoun, soghatsogh, kednakarsh, usdor (սողուն, սողացող, գետնաքարշ, ստոր)
republic - hanrabedoutiun (Հանրապետութիւն)
republican - hanrabedagan (Հանրապետական)
republication - verhuradaragoutiun (վերհրատարակութիւն)
republish - verahuradaragel, veradubel (վերահրատարակել, վերատպել)
repudiate - ouranal, merzhel, hurazharil, pazhnuvil (ուրանալ, մերժել, հրաժարիլ, բաժնուիլ)
repudiation - abaharzan, gunatoghoutiun, merzhoum (ապահարզան, կնաթողութիւն, մերժում)
repugn - unttimanal, timaturel, gurvil (ընդդիմանալ, դիմադրել, կռուիլ)
repugnance - zuzvank, khorshoum, tuzhgamagoutiun (զզուանք, խորշում, դժկամակութիւն)
repugnant - zuzveli, andaneli, adeli,

hagarag (զզուելի, անտանելի, ատելի, հակառակ)

repulse - vanel, yed mughel, merzhel, vanoum, merzhoum (վանել, ետ մղել, մերժել, վանում, մերժում)

repulsion - zuzvank, vanoum, merzhoum, yed mughoum (զզուանք, վանում, մերժում, ետ մղում)

repulsive - vanoghagan, vanich, zuzvetsunogh (վանողական, վանիչ, զզուեցնող)

reputable - hampavavor, badvarzhan, yereveli (համբաւաւոր, պատուարժան, երեւելի)

reputation - hampav, hurchag, pari anoun, varg (համբաւ, հռչակ, բարի անուն, վարկ)

repute - hamarel, hashvi arnel, khorhil, varg (համարել, հաշուի առնել, խորհիլ, վարկ)

request - khuntir, khunturank, khunturel, ouzel, haytsel (խնդիր, խնդրանք, խնդրել, ուզել, հայցել)

requiem - hokehankisd (հոգեհանգիստ)

require - bahanchel, khunturel, ouzel, garodil (պահանջել, խնդրել, ուզել, կարօտիլ)

requirement - bahanch, bedk, harg, garik, anhurazheshdoutiun (պահանջ, պէտք, հարկ, կարիք, անհրաժեշտութիւն)

requirer - bahanchogh, ouzogh (պահանջող, ուզող)

requisite - anhurazheshd, hargavor, ouzvadz, bahanchuvadz (անհրաժեշտ, հարկաւոր, ուզուած, պահանջուած)

requisition - khunturank, bahanch, bahanchel, hartsakunnel (խնդրանք, պահանջ, պահանջել, հարցաքննել)

requite - hadoutsanel, pokharinel, vartsadurel (հատուցանել, փոխարինել, վարձատրել)

rerun - gurgnoum zhabaveni, veratsoutsaturoutiun (կրկնում ժապաւէնի, վերացուցադրութիւն)

resale - veravajaroum, veravajarel (վերավաճառում, վերավաճառել)

rescind - chunchel, veratsunel, gurjadel (ջնջել, վերացնել, կրճատել)

rescribe - gurgin kurel, badaskhanel (կրկին գրել, պատասխանել)

rescript - hurovardag, huramanakir, shunorhakir (հրովարտակ, հրամանագիր, շնորհագիր)

rescue - purgel, oknoutian hasnil, purgoum, azadoum (փրկել, օգնութեան հասնիլ, փրկում, ազատում)

research (n) - hedazodoum, hedakhouzoutiun, hedakhouyz (հետախուզում, հետախուզութիւն, հետախոյզ)

research (v) - hedazodel, kunnargel, khouzargel (հետազօտել, քննարկել, խուզարկել)

reseat - verazedeghel, noren nusdil (վերազետեղել, նորէն նստիլ)

reseda - siradzaghig, asdughadzaghig, yaproug (սիրածաղիկ, աստղածաղիկ, յափրուկ)

reseize - noren purnel, diranal, verakuravel (նորէն բռնել, տիրանալ, վերագրաւել)

reseizure - verakuravoum, veradiratsoum (վերագրաւում, վերատիրացում)

resell - veravajarel, arnel-dzakhel (վերավաճառել, առնել-ծախել)

resemblance - numanoutiun, nouynoutiun (նմանութիւն, նոյնութիւն)

resemble - numanil, numantsunel (նմանիլ, նմանցնել)

resent - tuzhkohil, zayranal, untvuzil, uzkatsvil (դժգոհիլ, զայրանալ, ընդվզիլ, զգացուիլ)

resentment - zayrouyt, untvuzoum, tzasoum, ken (զայրոյթ, ընդվզում, ցասում, քէն)

reservation - verabahoum, abahovoum, uzkoushoutiun (վերապահում, ապահովում, զգուշութիւն)

reserve (n) - verabahoutiun, uzkoushoutiun, bahesd (վերապահութիւն, զգուշութիւն, պահեստ)

reserve (v) - verabahel, bahel, amparel, muterel (վերապահել, պա-

Հել, ամբարել, մթերել)
reserved - verabahvadz, bahesdi, uzkoushavor, inknampop (վերապահուած, պահեստի, զգուշաւոր, ինքնամփոփ)
reservist - bahesdi zinvor (պահեստի զինուոր)
reservoir - bahesdaman, ampar, churampar, untounaran (պահեստաման, ամբար, ջրամբար, ընդունարան)
reset - verasharel, verashudgel, verashudgoum (վերաշարել, վերաշտկել, վերաշտկում)
reside - punagil, abril, munal, genal (բնակիլ, ապրիլ, մնալ, կենալ)
residence - punagaran, punagavayr, doun (բնակարան, բնակավայր, տուն)
residency - punagoutiun (բնակութիւն)
resident - punagogh, punagich, badvirag (բնակող, բնակիչ, պատուիրակ)
residential - punageli, punagoutian, dunayin (բնակելի, բնակութեան, տնային)
resider - punagogh (բնակող)
residue - munatsort, tird, murour (մնացորդ, դիրտ, մրուր)
resign - hurazharil, tsukel, lukel, verausdorakurel (հրաժարիլ, ձգել, լքել, վերաստորագրել)
resignation - hurazharoum, hurazharagan, hamagerboutiun (հրաժարում, հրաժարական, համակերպութիւն)
resigned - hunazant, khonarh, hulou, hubadag (հնազանդ, խոնարհ, հլու, հպատակ)
resigner - hurazharogh (հրաժարող)
resignment - hurazharoum, hamagerboum (հրաժարում, համակերպում)
resin - khezh, redin (խէժ, ռետին)
resist - timaturel, unttimanal, dogal, baykaril (դիմադրել, ընդդիմանալ, տոկալ, պայքարիլ)
resistance - timaturoutiun, unttimoutiun, dogounoutiun (դիմադրութիւն, ընդդիմութիւն, տոկունութիւն)
resistant - timatsgoun, timaturogh, unttimatsogh (դիմացկուն, դիմադրող, ընդդիմացող)
resoluble - loudzeli, haleli, tiurahal (լուծելի, հալելի, դիւրահալ)
resolute - vujragan, khizakh, hasdadamid, gudroug (վճռական, խիզախ, հաստատամիտ, կտրուկ)
resolution - loudzoum, vujir, voroshoum (լուծում, վճիռ, որոշում)
resolve - loudzel, haletsunel, voroshel, voroshoum, vujir (լուծել, հալեցնել, որոշել, որոշում, վճիռ)
resolved - hasdad, vujragan, hasdadamid (հաստատ, վճռական, հաստատամիտ)
resonance - hunchiun, hunchaganoutiun (հնչիւն, հնչականութիւն)
resorb - gullel (կլլել)
resort - hantibavayr, abasdan, timoum, timel, hajakhel (հանդիպավայր, ապաստան, դիմում, դիմել, յաճախել)
resound - verahunchel, artsakankel, anturatartsunel (վերահնչել, արձագանգել, անդրադարձնել)
resource - aghpiur, yegamoudi michots, hunark, ouzhaghpiur (աղբիւր, եկամուտի միջոց, հնարք, ուժաղբիւր)
resourceful - hunaramid, pazmaghpiur, hunaralits (հնարամիտ, բազմաղբիւր, հնարալից)
resources - turamagan aghpiur, harusdoutiun, inchk (դրամական աղբիւր, հարստութիւն, ինչք)
respect - harkel, medzarel, khunayel, harkank, medzarank (յարգել, մեծարել, խնայել, յարգանք, մեծարանք)
respectability - harkelioutiun, medzarelioutiun (յարգելիութիւն, մեծարելիութիւն)
respectable - harkeli, medzareli, badgareli (յարգելի, մեծարելի, պատկառելի)
respectful - harkalits, kaghakavar, harkogh, agnadzou (յարգալից, քաղաքավար, յարգող, ակնածու)
respectfully - harkankov, medzaran-

kov, agnadzankov (յարգանքով, մեծարանքով, ակնածանքով)
respective - hamabadaskhan, pokhatarts, hadoug, badganial (համապատասխան, փոխադարձ, յատուկ, պատկանեալ)
respiration - shuncharoutiun, shunchoum, shounch (շնչառութիւն, շնչում, շունչ)
respirator - shuncharou, otazudich (շնչառու, օդազտիչ)
respiratory - shuncharagan, shuncharoutian (շնչառական, շնչառութեան)
respire - shunchel, shounch arnel, hankchil (շնչել, շունչ առնել, հանգչիլ)
respite - tatar, hedatsukoum, argakhel, hedatsukel (դադար, յետաձգում, առկախել, յետաձգել)
resplendence - baydzaroutiun, shukeghoutiun, payl (պայծառութիւն, շքեղութիւն, փայլ)
resplendent - lousapayl, parahegh, shoghshoghoun (լուսափայլ, փառահեղ, շողշողուն)
respond - badaskhanel, hagaztel, badaskhan dal (պատասխանել, հակազդել, պատասխան տալ)
respondent - badaskhanogh, bashdban, tadagir (պատասխանող, պաշտպան, դատակիր)
response - badaskhan, hagaztoum (պատասխան, հակազդում)
responsibility - badaskhanaduvoutiun, bardavoroutiun (պատասխանատուութիւն, պարտաւորութիւն)
responsible - badaskhanadou, yerashkhavor (պատասխանատու, երաշխաւոր)
responsive - hamabadaskhan, badshaj, pokhasats (համապատասխան, պատշաճ, փոխասաց)
rest (n) - hankisd, tatar, hankusdaran, munatsort, mah (հանգիստ, դադար, հանգստարան, մնացորդ, մահ)
rest (v) - hankuchil, hankusdanal, munal, genal, mernil (հանգչիլ, հանգստանալ, մնալ, կենալ, մեռնիլ)
restate - verahasdadel, gugrnel (վերահաստատել, կրկնել)
restaurant - jasharan (ճաշարան)
restaurateur - jasharanabed (ճաշարանապետ)
restful - hankusdarar, hankusdatsunogh, antorraved (հանգստարար, հանգստացնող, անդորրաւէտ)
resthome - dzeranots, hankusdian doun, angelanots (ծերանոց, հանգստեան տուն, անկելանոց)
resthouse - bantog, hiuranots, otevan (պանդոկ, հիւրանոց, օթեւան)
restitute - hadoutsanel, verahasdadel, veranorokel (հատուցանել, վերահաստատել, վերանորոգել)
restitution - hadoutsoum, veraganknoum, norokoutiun (հատուցում, վերականգնում, նորոգութիւն)
restive - hamar, umpost, anhantard, kumahaj (յամառ, ըմբոստ, անհանդարտ, քմահաճ)
restless - anhantard, khurovial, anhankisd, angayoun (անհանդարտ, խռովեալ, անհանգիստ, անկայուն)
restoration - norokoutiun, veraganknoum, gaztouroum (նորոգութիւն, վերականգնում, կազդուրում)
restore - veramuterel, norokel, veragaroutsel, tarmanel (վերամթերել,նորոգել, վերակառուցել, դարմանել)
restorer - veragankunich, norokich, gaztourich (վերականգնիչ, նորոգիչ, կազդուրիչ)
restrain - chapavorel, sahmanapagel, seghmel, zusbel (չափաւորել, սահմանափակել, սեղմել, զսպել)
restrainer - zusbogh, junshogh (զսպող, ճնշող)
restraint - seghmoum, junshoum, arkelk, arkelapagoum (սեղմում, ճնշում, արգելք, արգելափակում)
restrict - sahmanapagel, seghmel, chapavorel (սահմանափակել, սեղմել, չափաւորել)
restricted - sahmanapag, negh (սահմանափակ, նեղ)
restriction - sahmanapagoum, arkelk

(սահմանափակում, արգելք)
restrictive - sahmanapagogh, sahmanapagich, zusbogh (սահմանափակող, սահմանափակիչ, զսպող)
restroom - luvatsaran, mizaran (լուացարան, միզարան)
result - artiunk, hedevank, hedevil, arach kal (արդիւնք, հետեւանք, հետեւիլ, առաջ գալ)
resume - verusgusil, ampopel, yed arnel, yed untounil (վերսկսիլ, ամփոփել, ետ առնել, ետ ընդունիլ)
resume' - ampopoum, ampop gensakuroutiun (ամփոփում, ամփոփ կենսագրութիւն)
resumption - verusgusoum, sharounagoum, veratarts (վերսկսում, շարունակում, վերադարձ)
resurge - harnel, haroutiun arnel (յառնել, յարութիւն առնել)
resurgent - veradzunvogh, haroutiun arnogh (վերածնուող, յարութիւն առնող)
resurrect - veragentanatsunel, haroutiun arnel (վերակենդանացնել, յարութիւն առնել)
resurrection - haroutiun, veragentanoutiun (յարութիւն, վերակենդանութիւն)
resuscitate - gentanatsunel, voghchuntsunel, haroutiun arnel (կենդանացնել, ողջնցնել, յարութիւն առնել)
retail - pokrakanag arevdour, manravajarel, verabadmel (փոքրաքանակ առեւտուր, մանրավաճառել, վերապատմել)
retail price - hadavajari kin (հատավաճառի գին)
retailer - hadavajar, manravajar, pokrakanag dzakhogh (հատավաճառ, մանրավաճառ, փոքրաքանակ ծախող)
retain - verabahel, bahbanel, vartsel (վերապահել, պահպանել, վարձել)
retainer - bahogh, usbasavor, gankhavujar (պահող, սպասաւոր, կանխավճար)
retaliate - hadoutsanel, pokharinel, vurej arnel (հատուցանել, փոխարինել, վրէժ առնել)
retaliation - pokhvurezh, hadoutsoum (փոխվրէժ, հատուցում)
retaliatory - pokhatarts, hagunttem, i badaskhan (փոխադարձ, հակընդդէմ, ի պատասխան)
retard - oushatsunel, oushanal, hedatsukel, arkilel (ուշացնել, ուշանալ, յետաձգել, արգիլել)
retardation - oushatsoum, habaghoum, arkelk (ուշացում, յապաղում, արգելք)
retarder - oushatsunogh (ուշացնող)
retell - gurgnel, noren usel (կրկնել, նորէն ըսել)
retention - bahoum, pandarkeloum, mizarkeloum, unpurnoum (պահում, բանտարգելում, միզարգելում, ըմբռնում)
retentive - verabah, bahogh, khelamoud, mudabah (վերապահ, պահող, խելամուտ, մտապահ)
reticence - kaghdunabahoutiun, andesoum, luroutiun (գաղտնապահութիւն, անտեսում, լռութիւն)
reticent - lour, zousb, verabah, dzadzgamid (լուռ, զուսպ, վերապահ, ծածկամիտ)
retina - achkamashg, tsantseni (աչքամաշկ, ցանցենի)
retinue - shukakhoump, hedevort (շքախումբ, հետեւորդ)
retire - kordze kashvil, toghoul, heranal, megousanal (գործէ քաշուիլ, թողուլ, հեռանալ, մեկուսանալ)
retired - bashdonatogh, kordze kashvadz (պաշտօնաթող, գործէ քաշուած)
retirement - bashdonalukoum, megousatsoum (պաշտօնալքում, մեկուսացում)
retiring - kashvogh, verabah, zousb (քաշուող, վերապահ, զուսպ)
retort - shurchel, pokhatartsel, hagajaroutiun, toranot (շրջել, փոխադարձել, հակաճառութիւն, թորանօթ)
retouch - verhuboum, surpakroum, verhubil, surpakurel (վերհպում, սրբագրում, վերհպիլ, սրբագրել)

retrace - verakudzel, hedazodel (վերագծել, հետազոտել)

retract - yed arnel, gudzgel, garjetsunel, kashvil, gudzgil (ետ առնել, կծկել, կարճեցնել, քաշուիլ, կծկիլ)

retraction - gudzgoum, ampopoum, hedus gochoum, hurazharoum (կծկում, ամփոփում, յետս կոչում, հրաժարում)

retreat - nahanch, arantsnatsoum, nahanchel, kashvil (նահանջ, առանձնացում, նահանջել, քաշուիլ)

retrench - gurjadel, khunayel, bagsetsunel, abasdanil (կրճատել, խնայել, պակսեցնել, ապաստանիլ)

retrenchment - gurjadoum, chunchoum, amratsoum (կրճատում, ջնջում, ամրացում)

retrial - verakunnoum, veranayoum (վերաքննում, վերանայում)

retribute - hadoutsanel, pokharinel (հատուցանել, փոխարինել)

retribution - hadoutsoum, vartsaduroutiun, pokharinoum (հատուցում, վարձատրութիւն, փոխարինում)

retrieval - vurusdatsoum, veratarmanoum (վերստացում, վերադարմանում)

retrieve - verakudnel, verusdanal, verashahil, tarmanel (վերագտնել, վերստանալ, վերաշահիլ, դարմանել)

retroactive - hedaztetsig (յետազդեցիկ)

retrograde - hedatarts, hedatem, hedatimel, vadtaranal (յետադարձ, յետադէմ, յետադիմել, վատթարանալ)

retrogression - hedatimoutiun, angoum (յետադիմութիւն, անկում)

retrospect - hedahayiatsk, yed nayil (յետահայեցք, ետ նայիլ)

retrospective - hedahayiats, antsiali veraperogh (յետահայեաց, անցեալի վերաբերող)

retry - veraportsel (վերափորձել)

return (n) - veratarts, hadoutsoum, pokharen, badaskhan (վերադարձ, հատուցում, փոխարէն, պատասխան)

return (v) - veratartsunel, veratarnal, badaskhanel (վերադարձնել, վերադառնալ, պատասխանել)

returnee - doun veratartsogh zinvor (տուն վերադարձող զինուոր)

reunification - veramiavoroum, veramiatsoum (վերամիաւորում, վերամիացում)

reunify - veramianal, megi veradzvil (վերամիանալ, մէկի վերածուիլ)

reunion - zhoghov, havakouyt, veramiatsoum, havakoum (ժողով, հաւաքոյթ, վերամիացում, հաւաքում)

reunite - veramiatsunel, noren mianal (վերամիացնել, նորէն միանալ)

revaluation - verakunahadoum (վերագնահատում)

reveal - haydunel, patsahaydel, panal, koghazerdzel (յայտնել, բացայայտել, բանալ, քողազերծել)

reveille - zartoutsich, aykanuvak, zartonk (զարթուցիչ, այգանուագ, զարթօնք)

revel - khurakhjank, geroukhoum, oudel khumel (խրախճանք, կերուխում, ուտել խմել)

revelation - haydnoutiun, patsahaydoum, haydnakordzoum (յայտնութիւն, բացայայտում, յայտնագործում)

revelry - geroukoum, shouaydank (կերուխում, շուայտանք)

revenge - vurezh, vurizharoutiun, vurezh arnel (վրէժ, վրիժառութիւն, վրէժ առնել)

revengeful - vokhagal, vurezhkhuntir, kinakhuntir (ոխակալ, վրէժխնդիր, քինախնդիր)

revenger - vurizharou (վրիժառու)

revenue - yegamoud, moudk, shah (եկամուտ, մուտք, շահ)

reverberate - tsolatsunel, artsakankel, ardatsolel, hunchel (ցոլացնել, արձագանգել, արտացոլել, հնչել)

reverberation - tsolatsoum, anturatartsoum, artsakank (ցոլացում, անդրադարձում, արձագանգ)

revere - harkel, medzarel, badvel

(յարգել, մեծարել, պատուել)
reverence - harkank, medzarank, agnadzank, badiv (յարգանք, մեծարանք, ակնածանք, պատիւ)
reverend - hokeshunorh, badveli, badvarzhan (Հոգեշնորհ, պատուելի, պատուարժան)
reverent - harkalits, agnadzou, medzarogh (յարգալից, ակնածու, մեծարող)
reverer - medzarogh, agnadzogh (մեծարող, ակնածող)
reverie - yerazank, tsunork, pantakoushank, anourch (երազանք, ցնորք, բանդագուշանք, անուրջ)
reversal - hagagoghm, vujrapegoum, pokhoum, chunchoum (Հակակողմ, վճռաբեկում, փոխում, ջնջում)
reverse - shurchel, dabalel, hedsagoghm, hagararts (շրջել, տապալել, յետսակողմ, Հակադարձ)
revert - shurchel, veratarnal, yed tartsunel, hedatarts (շրջել, վերադառնալ, ետ դարձնել, յետադարձ)
revet - dzadzgel, yeresabadel, hakvil, hakvetsunel (ծածկել, երեսապատել, Հագուիլ, Հագուեցնել)
revetement - yeresabadoum (երեսապատում)
review (n) - barperatert, zunnoum, zorahantes, veruntertsoum (պարբերաթերթ, զննում, զօրաՀանդէս, վերընթերցում)
review (v) - veranayil, kuratadel, shurchatidel, doghantsel (վերանայիլ, գրադատել, շրջադիտել, տողանցել)
reviewer - kuratad, kurakhos, kunnatad, verakunnich (գրադատ, գրախօս, քննադատ, վերաքննիչ)
revile - nakhadel, hayhoyel, anarkel, vargapegel (նախատել, ՀայՀոյել, անարգել, վարկաբեկել)
revisal - verakunnoutiun, veradesoutiun, veruntertsoum (վերաքննութիւն, վերատեսութիւն, վերընթերցում)
revise - verakunnel, achke antsunel (վերաքննել, աչքէ անցնել)
revision - verakunnoutiun, surpakuroutiun (վերաքննութիւն, սրբագրութիւն)
revisit - noren aytselel (Նորէն այցելել)
revisory - verusdoukich, verakunnich (վերստուգիչ, վերաքննիչ)
revival - veradzunount, veragentanatsoum, ashkhouzhatsoum (վերածնունդ, վերակենդանացում, աշխուժացում)
revive - veragentananal, norokuvil, veragentanatsunel (վերակենդանանալ, նորոգուիլ, վերակենդանացնել)
revivication - veragentanatsoum (վերակենդանացում)
revivify - veragentanatsunel (վերակենդանացնել)
revocable - hedagocheli, bashdonazurgeli, nahancheli (յետակոչելի, պաշտօնազրկելի, նաՀանջելի)
revocation - veratsoum, chunchoum, bashdonangoutiun (վերացում, ջնջում, պաշտօնանկութիւն)
revoke - hedagochel, chunchel (յետակոչել, ջնջել)
revolt (n) - abusdampoutiun, umposdoutiun, untvuzoum (ապստամբութիւն, ըմբոստութիւն, ընդվզում)
revolt (v) - abusdampil, umposdanal, abusdampetsunel (ապստամբիլ, ըմբոստանալ, ապստամբեցնել)
revolting - zuzveli, karsheli, noghgali (զզուելի, գարշելի, Նողկալի)
revolution - heghapokhoutiun, heghashurchoum, holovouyt (յեղափոխութիւն, յեղաշրջում, Հոլովոյթ)
revolutionary - heghapokhagan, heghapokhich (յեղափոխական, յեղափոխիչ)
revolutionist - heghapokhagan (յեղափոխական)
revolutionize - heghapokhaganatsunel, heghapokhel, heghashurchel (յեղափոխականացնել, յեղափոխել, յեղաշրջել)
revolve - tavalil, tarnal, kuloril, tartsunel (թաւալիլ, դառնալ, գլորիլ, դարձնել)
revolver - adurjanag (ատրճանակ)
revolving - shurchoun, shurchogh,

shurchatartsayin (շրջուն, շրջող, շրջագարձային)
revulsion - hedatarts, khodoroum, zuzvank, noghgank (յետադարձ, խոտորում, զզուանք, նողկանք)
reward - barkevaduroum, vartsadu-routiun, barkevadurel (պարգեւատրում, վարձատրութիւն, պարգեւատրել)
rewarder - vartsadurogh, vartsaha-douyts (վարձատրող, վարձահատոյց)
rewrite - ardakurel, noren kurel, verakhumpakurel (արտագրել, նորէն գրել, վերախմբագրել)
rhachis - see - տե'ս (rachis)
rhapsody - haknerkoutiun, yerka-kagh, gargadoun yerk-par (հագներգութիւն, երգաքաղ, կարկատուն երգ-բառ)
rheostat - hosanapashkh, yelektura-pokhich (հոսանաբաշխ, ելեքտրափոխիչ)
rhetoric - huredoroutiun, jardasa-noutiun (հռետորութիւն, ճարտասանութիւն)
rhetorician - jardasan (ճարտասան)
rheum - heghahiut, akhdavor ho-soum, harpoukh (հեղահիւթ, ախտաւոր հոսում, հարբուխ)
rheumatism - hotatsav (յօդացաւ)
rhinoceros - runkeghchiur (ռնգեղջիւր)
rhyme, rime - hank, hankavor voda-navor, hankavorel (յանգ, յանգաւոր ոտանաւոր, յանգաւորել)
rhythm - gushrouyt, tashnagoutiun, chap, hamachap (կշռոյթ, դաշնակութիւն, չափ, համաչափ)
rhythmic, rhythmical - gushroutavor, hamachap, chapagan (կշռութաւոր, համաչափ, չափական)
rib - goghosgur, gogh, navagogh, goghagits, gin (կողոսկր, կող, նաւակող, կողակից, կին)
ribald - anarag, krehig, hayhoya-khos, gobid, lugdi (անառակ, գռեհիկ, հայհոյախօս, կոպիտ, լկտի)
ribaldry - hayhoyakhosoutiun, lugdi-outiun, kurehig lezou (հայհոյախօսութիւն, լկտիութիւն, գռեհիկ լեզու)
ribbon - zhabaven, yeriz, yerasan, zhabavinazartel (ժապաւէն, երիզ, երասան, ժապաւինազարդել)
rice - purints (բրինձ)
rich - harousd, jokh, arad, partam, letsoun, hort (հարուստ, ճոխ, առատ, փարթամ, լեցուն, յորդ)
riches - harusdoutiun, inchk, gal-vadz (հարստութիւն, ինչք, կալուած)
richly - aradoren, jokh gerbov (առատօրէն, ճոխ կերպով)
richness - harusdoutiun, aradoutiun (հարստութիւն, առատութիւն)
rick - tez, gouyd, hartanots, tizel (դէզ, կոյտ, յարդանոց, դիզել)
rickets - vosguratek, gorakamag (ոսկրաթեք, կորաքամակ)
rickety - vosguratekoutiun (ոսկրաթեքութիւն)
rid - artsagel, azadel, purgel, tser-pazadvil (արձակել, ազատել, փրկել, ձերբազատուիլ)
riddance - purgoum, azadoum, jo-ghobroum (փրկում, ազատում, ճողոպրում)
riddle - haneloug, areghdzuvadz, maghel, loudzel (հանելուկ, առեղծուած, մաղել, լուծել)
ride - hedznel, tsiavarel, nusdil, hedzabudouyd, uzposank (հեծնել, ձիավարել, նստիլ, հեծապտոյտ, զբօսանք)
rident - khuntoun, khuntatsogh (խնդուն, խնդացող)
rider - hedzial, tsiavor, havelial gutsvadz tought (հեծեալ, ձիաւոր, յաւելեալ կցուած թուղթ)
ridge - gadar, lernashark, gurnag, agosel, gunjurel (կատար, լեռնաշարք, կռնակ, ակօսել, կնճռել)
ridged - suradzayr (սրածայր)
ridgy - agosavor (ակօսաւոր)
ridicule - dzaghrank, yerkidzank, heknank, dzaghrel, heknel (ծաղրանք, երգիծանք, հեգնանք, ծաղրել, հեգնել)
ridiculous - dzidzagheli, dzidzagha-

sharzh, aylantag (ծիծաղելի, ծիծաղաշարժ, այլանդակ)
riding - tsiavaroutiun, hedzeloughi (ձիավարութիւն, Հեծելուղի)
rife - dirabedogh, hajakhateb, dirogh, arad, jokh (տիրապետող, յաճախադէպ, տիրող, առատ, ճոխ)
riffraff - khouzhan, dagank, aveltsoug (խուժան, տականք, աւելցուկ)
rifle - goghobdel, gorzel, hapushdagel, huratsan (կողոպտել, կորզել, յափշտակել, Հրացան)
rifleman - huratsanagir (Հրացանակիր)
rifler - avazag, goghobdich, tallogh (աւազակ, կողոպտիչ, Թալլող)
rift - jeghk, patsvadzk, jeghkel, jeghkil (ճեղք, բացուածք, ճեղքել, ճեղքիլ)
rig (n) - hakvadzk, navasark, tsadgurdouk, khapeyoutiun (Հագուածք, նաւասարք, ցատկոտուք, խաբէութիւն)
rig (v) - hantertsel, hakvetsunel, bujnel, shortel (Հանդերձել, Հագուեցնել, պճնել, շորթել)
rigger - gazmogh, sarkogh (կազմող, սարքող)
rigging - hantertsank, uzkesd, navagazmadzk (Հանդերձանք, զգեստ, նաւակազմածք)
right - iravounk, jishd, ach, oughghel, shudgel (իրաւունք, ճիշդ, աջ, ուղղել, շտկել)
rightangle - oughghangiun (ուղղանկիւն)
rightaway - anmichabes, shoudov (անմիջապէս, շուտով)
righteous - artaratsi, iravatsi, arakini, asdvadzabashd (արդարացի, իրաւացի, առաքինի, աստուածապաշտ)
righteousness - artaroutiun, parebashdoutiun, iravounk (արդարութիւն, բարեպաշտութիւն, իրաւունք)
rightful - iravatsi, artaratsi, orinagan (իրաւացի, արդարացի, օրինական)
rightness - shidagoutiun, artaratsioutiun (շիտակութիւն, արդարացիութիւն)
right-hand - achagoghmian, ach goghmu kudnuvogh (աջակողմեան, աջ կողմը գտնուող)
right-handed - achlig, achatserun (աջլիկ, աջաձեռն)
rigid - gardzur, antek, khisd, goshd (կարծր, անթեք, խիստ, կոշտ)
rigidity - gardzuroutiun, khusdoutiun, antekoutiun (կարծրութիւն, խստութիւն, անթեքութիւն)
rigmarole - tsuntapanoutiun, tadargakhosoutiun (ցնդաբանութիւն, դատարկախօսութիւն)
rigor - gardzuroutiun, khusdoutiun, chermasarsour (կարծրութիւն, խստութիւն, ջերմասարսուռ)
rigorism - khusdoutiun, anacharoutiun (խստութիւն, անաչառութիւն)
rigorous - khisd, khusdabahanch, anachar, murayl (խիստ, խստապահանջ, անաչառ, մռայլ)
rile - bughdorel, houzel, khurovel, pargatsunel (պղտորել, յուզել, խռովել, բարկացնել)
rill - arvag, vudag (առուակ, վտակ)
rim - yezur, dzayr, anivazart, yezerel, yezerazartel (եզր, ծայր, անիւազարդ, եզրել, եզերազարդել)
rime - yeghiam, tsiunagargoud, saradz tsogh (եղեամ, ձիւնակարկուտ, սառած ցող)
rind - geghev, badian, mort, gujeb (կեղեւ, պատեան, մորթ, կճեպ)
ring - oghag, murtsahartag (օղակ, մրցաՀարթակ)
ring (n) - madani, murtsapem, oghag, hunchiun, zank (մատանի, մրցաբեմ, օղակ, Հնչիւն, զանգ)
ring (v) - hunchel, hunchetsunel, zankaharel, oghagel (Հնչել, Հնչեցնել, զանգաՀարել, օղակել)
ringer - zhamgoch, hunchetsunogh (ժամկոչ, Հնչեցնող)
ringleader - barakuloukh, khurovarar (պարագլուխ, խռովարար)
ringmaster - gurgesabed (կրկեսապետ)

rink - chumushgasurah (չմշկասրահ)
rinse - tzoghvel, gurgnagi luval (ցօղուել, կրկնակի լուալ)
riot - khurovoutiun, aghmoug, kinarpouk, kharnagel (խռովութիւն, աղմուկ, գինարբուք, խառնակել)
rioter - khurovarar, aghmugarar (խռովարար, աղմկարար)
rip (n) - patsvadzk, jeghk, badurvadzk, suriga (բացուածք, ճեղք, պատռուածք, սրիկայ)
rip (v) - badrel, jeghkel, pazhnel, garu kagel (պատռել, ճեղքել, բաժնել, կարը քակել)
ripe - hasoun, hasadz, khelahas, humoud, gadarial (հասուն, հասած, խելահաս, հմուտ, կատարեալ)
ripen - hasounnal, hasountsunel, gadarelakordzel (հասուննալ, հասունցնել, կատարելագործել)
ripeness - hasounoutiun (հասունութիւն)
riposte - badaskhan, hagaharvadz, hagatartsel (պատասխան, հակահարուած, հակադարձել)
ripple (n) - dzupank, dadanoum, aliag, kankuroutiun (ծփանք, տատանում, ալեակ, գանգրութիւն)
ripple (v) - dzupal, dzupatsunel, dadanil, kankurel (ծփալ, ծփացնել, տատանիլ, գանգրել)
rise (n) - partsuratsoum, dzakoum, verelk, ajoum (բարձրացում, ծագում, վերելք, աճում)
rise (v) - dzakil, yellel, partsuranal, abusdampil, ajil (ծագիլ, ելլել, բարձրանալ, ապստամբիլ, աճիլ)
riser - partsuratsunogh (բարձրացընող)
risible - dzidzagheli, dzidzaghasharzh, khuntoun (ծիծաղելի, ծիծաղաշարժ, խնդուն)
rising - yelk, verelk, dzakoum, abusdampoutioun, ajogh (ելք, վերելք, ծագում, ապստամբութիւն, աճող)
risk - vudank, vudankel, vudanki yentargel, khizakhel (վտանգ, վտանգել, վտանգի ենթարկել, խիզախել)
risker - vudankogh (վտանգող)
risky - vudankavor (վտանգաւոր)
rite - dzes, araroghoutiun, dzisagark (ծէս, արարողութիւն, ծիսակարգ)
ritual - dzisagan, donatsouyts, mashdots (ծիսական, տօնացոյց, մաշտոց)
ritually - hantisavorabes, dzesov (հանդիսաւորապէս, ծէսով)
rivage - kedap, yezur (գետափ, եզր)
rival - murtsagits, hagaragort, akhoyan, murtsil (մրցակից, հակառակորդ, ախոյեան, մրցիլ)
rivalry - murtsoutiun, murtsagtsoutiun (մրցութիւն, մրցակցութիւն)
rive - jeghkel, jeghkuvil, badrel, badurvil (ճեղքել, ճեղքուիլ, պատռել, պատռուիլ)
riven - jeghkuvadz, badurvadzk, jeghk (ճեղքուած, պատռուածք, ճեղք)
river - ked, hosank, jeghkogh (գետ, հոսանք, ճեղքող)
riverbank - kedezerk (գետեզերք)
riverhead - kedaperan (գետաբերան)
riverhorse - kedatsi (գետաձի)
rivet - pever, hotagab, kam, kamel, hasdadel (բեւեռ, յօդակապ, գամ, գամել, հաստատել)
rivulet - kedag, vudag, arvag (գետակ, վտակ, առուակ)
roach - garmuratsoug, kharagatsoug (կարմրաձուկ, խարակաձուկ)
road - jampa, garoughi, oughi, boghoda, navagayan (ճամբայ, կառուղի, ուղի, պողոտայ, նաւակայան)
roam - taparil, shurchil, tekeril, taparoum (Թափառիլ, շրջիլ, դեգերիլ, Թափառում)
roamer - taparagan, taparashurchig, tekerogh (Թափառական, Թափառաշրջիկ, դեգերող)
roar - murunchel, koral, dukal, jich, murunchiun (մռնչել, գոռալ, տքալ, ճիչ, մռնչիւն)
roarer - koratsogh, borchudogh (գոռացող, պոռչտող)

roaring - kochiun, aghaghag (գոչիւն, աղաղակ)
roast - khorovadz, khorovel, ayrel (խորոված, խորովել, այրել)
roasted - khorovadz (խորոված)
roaster - khorovots, gasgara, khorovich (խորովոց, կասկարայ, խորովիչ)
rob - koghnal, hapushdagel, goghobdel, khulel (գողնալ, յափշտակել, կողոպտել, խլել)
robber - kogh, avazag, goghobdich (գող, աւազակ, կողոպտիչ)
robbery - koghoutiun, avazagoutiun (գողութիւն, աւազակութիւն)
robe - shurchazkesd, badmoujan, haknil, haktsunel (շրջազգեստ, պատմուճան, Հագնիլ, Հագցնել)
robin - garmuralanch (կարմրալանջ)
robot - martamekena (մարդամեքենայ)
robust - houzhgou, ouzhegh, amragazm, zoravor (Հուժկու, ուժեղ, ամրակազմ, զօրաւոր)
rock - zhayr, abarazh, ororel, ororvil (ժայռ, ապառաժ, օրօրել, օրօրուիլ)
rocker - ororots (օրօրոց)
rocket - hurtir, savarnil, turchil, partsuranal (Հրթիռ, սաւառնիլ, թռչիլ, բարձրանալ)
rocky - zhayrod, abarazhod, karkarod, gardzur (ժայռոտ, ապառաժոտ, քարքարոտ, կարծր)
rod - tsogh, tsoub, jubod, kavazan, yeghek (ձող, ցուպ, ճպոտ, գաւազան, եղէգ)
rodent - gurdzogh (կրծող)
rodomont - bardzengod, sunabardz (պարծենկոտ, սնապարծ)
rodomontade - sunabardzoutiun, sunabardzil, medzakhosel (սնապարծութիւն, սնապարծիլ, մեծախօսել)
roe - oul, aydziam, yeghnig (ուլ, այծեամ, եղնիկ)
rogation - orinakidz, aghers, orhnerkoutiun (օրինագիծ, աղերս, օրՀներգութիւն)
rogue - suriga, khartakh, khapepa, avazag, mouratsig (սրիկայ, խարդախ, խաբեբայ, աւազակ, մուրացիկ)
roguery - surigayoutiun, khapepayoutiun (սրիկայութիւն, խաբեբայութիւն)
roguish - suriga, anuzkam, charajuji (սրիկայ, անզգամ, չարաճճի)
roil - bughdorel, kurkurel, vurtovel, pargatsunel (պղտորել, գրգռել, վրդովել, բարկացնել)
roister - borodakhos, gobid, ampardavan, borodal (պոռոտախօս, կոպիտ, ամբարտաւան, պոռոտալ)
roistering - aghmugararoutiun, angarkoutiun (աղմկարարութիւն, անկարգութիւն)
roke - marakhough, mushoush (մառախուղ, մշուշ)
roky - mushoushod (մշուշոտ)
role - ter, bashdon (դեր, պաշտօն)
roll (n) - tavaloum, gabots, tsang, tsoutsag, makaghat (թաւալում, կապոց, ցանկ, ցուցակ, մագաղաթ)
roll (v) - tavalil, kuloril, shurchil, pattel, koral (թաւալիլ, գլորիլ, շրջիլ, փաթթել, գոռալ)
roller - kulan, dubakulan, loghkar, logh, daban (գլան, տպագլան, լողքար, լող, տապան)
roller skate - sahnaganiv, chumushgel (սաՀնականիւ, չմշկել)
roman - hurovmeatsi, hurovmeagan, polorakir (Հռովմէացի, Հռովմէական, բոլորագիր)
romance - viberk, sirerk, viberkel, sirerkel (վիպերգ, սիրերգ, վիպերգել, սիրերգել)
romancer - vibasan (վիպասան)
romanization - ladinatsunoum, ladinatsoum (լատինացնում, լատինացում)
romantic - vibabashd, vibagan, uzkatsagan, vibayin (վիպապաշտ, վիպական, զգացական, վիպային)
romantism - vibabashdoutiun, vibaganoutiun (վիպապաշտութիւն, վիպականութիւն)
romany - kunchou, posha, kunchoueren, kunchouagan (գնչու, բոշայ, գնչուերէն, գնչուական)

romp - aghmugel, boral, aghmugakhagh, charajuji aghchig (աղմկել, պոռալ, աղմկախաղ, չարաճճի աղջիկ)
rompish - aghmugaser, aghmegalits, tetevsolig (աղմկասէր, աղմկալից, թեթեւսոլիկ)
rondel - gurgnatarts (կրկնադարձ)
rondo - gurgnerk, gurgnavor dagh (կրկներգ, կրկնաւոր տաղ)
ronish - kosod, kutsouts (քոսոտ, գձուձ)
rood - khacheloutiun, tsoghachap, ardavar (խաչելութիւն, ձողաչափ, արտավար)
roof - danik, yertik, dzadzg, danikov dzadzgel (տանիք, երդիք, ծածկ, տանիքով ծածկել)
roofless - danikazourg, andzadzg, andoun, dunang (տանիքազուրկ, անծածկ, անտուն, տնանկ)
rook - jadragi tughiag, sermnakurav, khapepa, khapel (ճատրակի ղղեակ, սերմնագրաւ, խաբեբայ, խաբել)
room - seniag, khouts, degh, vayr, punagil (սենեակ, խուց, տեղ, վայր, բնակիլ)
roommate - senegagits, unger (սենեկակից, ընկեր)
roomy - untartsag, layn, azad (ընդարձակ, լայն, ազատ)
roost - taril, hankchil, tarelou payd (թառիլ, հանգչիլ, թառելու փայտ)
rooster - akaghagh, aklor (աքաղաղ, աքլոր)
root - armad, him, badjar, armadanal, dungel (արմատ, հիմ, պատճառ, արմատանալ, տնկել)
rooted - hasdadvadz, armadatsadz (հաստատուած, արմատացած)
rope - baran, chuvan, lar, manel, huisel, gabel (պարան, չուան, լար, մանել, հիւսել, կապել)
rope dancer - larakhaghats (լարախաղաց)
roquet - kuntakhaghi mech kuntagi zarnel (գնդախաղի մէջ գնդակի զարնել)
rosary - vartasdan, dzaghganots, vartaran (վարդաստան, ծաղկանոց, վարդարան)
rose - vart, vartakouyn, dzaghgetsav, yelav (վարդ, վարդագոյն, ծաղկեցաւ, ելաւ)
rose water - vartachour (վարդաջուր)
rosemary - khungouni (խնկունի)
rosette - vartazart, vartakantag (վարդազարդ, վարդաքանդակ)
rosin - redin, khezh, redinov shupel (ռետին, խէժ, ռետինով շփել)
ross - dzari geghev (ծառի կեղեւ)
rostrum - pem, ambion, gudouts, navatsuroug (բեմ, ամպիոն, կտուց, նաւացռուկ)
rosy - vartakouyn, vartazart (վարդագոյն, վարդազարդ)
rot - pudil, nekhil, avruvil, pudetsunel, nekhoum (փտիլ, նեխիլ, աւրուիլ, փտեցնել, նեխում)
rotary, rotative - tavaloun, tartsogh (թաւալուն, դարձող)
rotate - tarnal, tavalil, tavaletsunel (դառնալ, թաւալիլ, թաւալեցնել)
rotation - tavaloum, holovoum, kuloroum, shurchanagoum (թաւալում, հոլովում, գլորում, շրջանակում)
rote - ankir, peranatsi, kots, gurgnoutiun (անգիր, բերանացի, գոց, կրկնութիւն)
rotogravure - shurchadib, tavaladib (շրջատիպ, թաւալատիպ)
rotten - pudadz, nekhadz, abaganadz (փտած, նեխած, ապականած)
rottenness - pudadzoutiun, nekhadzoutiun (փտածութիւն, նեխածութիւն)
rotter - anbed-pujatsadz mart (անպէտ–փճացած մարդ)
rotund - gulor, gulorig, ker, kuntatsev, gadarial (կլոր, կլորիկ, գէր, գնդաձեւ, կատարեալ)
rouble, ruble - roupli (ռուբլի)
roudelay - keghkeghank, gurgnerk, shurchabar (գեղգեղանք, կրկներգ, շրջապար)
roue - tsop, anarag (ցոփ, անառակ)
rouge - garmir, sunkouyr, shubar, shubarel (կարմիր, սնգոյր, շպար,

շպարել)
rough - andash, gobid, khouzhan, khordouportel (անտաշ, կոպիտ, խուժան, խորտուբորտել)
roughage - goshdoutiun, purdoutiun (կոշտութիւն, բրտութիւն)
roughen - gobdanal, purdanal, gobdatsunel, purdatsunel (կոպտանալ, բրտանալ, կոպտացնել, բրտացնել)
roughly - goshdapar, dumartoren, verivero (կոշտաբար, տմարդօրէն, վերիվերոյ)
roughness - anhartoutiun, khusdoutiun, goshdoutiun (անհարթութիւն, խստութիւն, կոշտութիւն)
roughrider - tsiavarzh, hedzelavarzh (ձիավարժ, հեծելավարժ)
roulette - pakhdaniv, pakhdakhagh mu, pokraniv, anvag (բախտանիւ, բախտախաղ մը, փոքրանիւ, անուակ)
roumanian - roumanatsi, roumaneren, roumanagan (ռումանացի, ռումաներէն, ռումանական)
round (a) - gulor, gulorag, kuntatsev, shurchan, shourch (կլոր, կլորակ, գնդաձեւ, շրջան, շուրջ)
round (v) - gulorel, gulornal, shurchabadel, polorel (կլորել, կլորնալ, շրջապատել, բոլորել)
round up - polorel, hamakhumpel, havakel, tserpagalel (բոլորել, համախմբել, հաւաքել, ձերբակալել)
roundabout - goghmunagi, shurchantsig, zardoughi (կողմնակի, շրջանցիկ, զարտուղի)
roundel - keghkeghank, gurgnerk, polorag (գեղգեղանք, կրկներգ, բոլորակ)
rounder - shurchogh, polorogh (շրջող, բոլորող)
roundness - guloroutiun, sahounoutiun (կլորութիւն, սահունութիւն)
roundtable - gulor seghan, khorhurtazhoghov (կլոր սեղան, խորհրդաժողով)
rouse - artuntsunel, artunnal, vokevorel, geroukhoum (արթնցնել, արթննալ, ոգեւորել, կերուխում)
rouser - artuntsunogh, vokevorogh, kurkurogh (արթնցնող, ոգեւորող, գրգռող)
rousing - artuntsunogh, vokevorogh, husga, hianali (արթնցնող, ոգեւորող, հսկայ, հիանալի)
roust - houzel, khurovel, artuntsunel (յուզել, խռովել, արթնցնել)
rousy - aghmugod, umposd, gurvazan (աղմկոտ, ըմբոստ, կռուազան)
rout - khouzhan, ampokh, khordagel, porel, khurgal (խուժան, ամբոխ, խորտակել, փորել, խռկալ)
route - jampa, oughi, untatsk (ճամբայ, ուղի, ընթացք)
routine - varzhoutiun, sovoroutiun, ounagoutiun, untatsig (վարժութիւն, սովորութիւն, ունակութիւն, ընթացիկ)
rove - taparil, tekeril, shurchil (թափառիլ, դեգերիլ, շրջիլ)
rover - taparashurchig, avazag, dzovahen (թափառաշրջիկ, աւազակ, ծովահէն)
row - gark, shark, tiavaroutiun, tiavarel, darvil (կարգ, շարք, թիավարում, թիավարել, տարուիլ)
rowback - verasurpakuroum, veranayoum (վերասրբագրում, վերանայում)
rowdy - gurvaser, usdahag, anarag, khoulikan (կռուասէր, ստահակ, անառակ, խուլիգան)
rowing - tiavaroutiun, tiavaroum (թիավարութիւն, թիավարում)
royal - takavoragan, arkayagan, arkouni (թագաւորական, արքայական, արքունի)
royalist - arkayaser, miabedagan, arkayagan (արքայասէր, միապետական, արքայական)
royalty - takavoroutiun, arkayadourk, heghinagi pazhin (թագաւորութիւն, արքայատուրք, հեղինակի բաժին)
rub (n) - shupoum, kusoum, makroum, gadag, khayt (շփում, քսում, մաքրում, կատակ, խայթ)
rub (v) - shupel, kusel, kerel, surpel, kusvil (շփել, քսել, քերել, սրբել, քսուիլ)

rubber - redin, surpich, shupogh, tsukakhezh, kaouchoug (ռետին, սրբիչ, շփող, ձգախէժ, քաուչուկ)
rubber cement - tsukakhezh, aratskakhezh (ձգախէժ, առաձգախէժ)
rubber stamp - gunik, gunkanushan (կնիք, կնքանշան)
rubbish - aghp, aveltsoug, nedvelik, munatsortk, dashegh (աղբ, աւելցուկ, նետուելիք, մնացորդք, տաշեղ)
rubbishy - anbedk, anbidan (անպէտք, անպիտան)
rubble - vormakar, manrakar, khij (որմաքար, մանրաքար, խիճ)
rubblestone - khij, khujakar (խիճ, խճաքար)
rubdown - martsoum, shupoum marmini hed loghalou (մարձում, շփում մարմինի յետ լողալու)
rubeola - garmuroug (կարմրուկ)
rubicund - garmurorag, garmuratem (կարմրորակ, կարմրադէմ)
ruble - roupli (ռուբլի)
rubric - khorakir, vernakir garmirov, garmurakir (խորագիր, վերնագիր կարմիրով, կարմրագիր)
rubricate - garmirov magakurel (կարմիրով մակագրել)
ruby - soudag, nurnakar, gargehan, garmurakouyn (սուտակ, նռնաքար, կարկեհան, կարմրագոյն)
ruck - dzalk, pot, khorshomel, dzaldzalel, guguzil (ծալք, փոթ, խորշոմել, ծալծալել, կկզիլ)
ructation - tsukurdoum, tsukurdots (ձգուտում, ձգուտոց)
rudd - arkayatsoug (արքայաձուկ)
rudder - gheg (ղեկ)
rudderless - angheg (անղեկ)
ruddiness - garmuroutiun (կարմրութիւն)
ruddle - garmurtsunel, garmuril (կարմրցնել, կարմրիլ)
ruddy - garmurakouyn, mortakouyn (կարմրագոյն, մորթագոյն)
rude - goshd, gobid, andash, pird (կոշտ, կոպիտ, անտաշ, բիրտ)
rudiment - nakhakidelik, darerk, nakhadar (նախագիտելիք, տարերք, նախատարր)
rudimentary - nakhnagan, usguzpunagan, darragan (նախնական, սկզբնական, տարրական)
rue - vushdanal, dukhril, voghpal, vishd, pekena (վշտանալ, տխրիլ, ողբալ, վիշտ, փեգենայ)
rueful - vushdali, voghpali, dukhour (վշտալի, ողբալի, տխուր)
ruff - pototsik, hokhordank, hokhordal, potpotel (փոթօձիք, յոխորտանք, յոխորտալ, փոթփոթել)
ruffian - anuzkam, vayrak, suriga (անզգամ, վայրագ, սրիկայ)
ruffle (n) - hokhordank, iraransoum, vej, khurovk (յոխորտանք, իրարանցում, վէճ, խռովք)
ruffle (v) - horkhordal, potpotel, dzalel, gudzgel (յոխորտալ, փոթփոթել, ծալել, կծկել)
ruffler - hokhordatsogh, sunabardz, gurvasor (յոխորտացող, սնապարծ, կռուասէր)
rufous - toukh (թուխ)
rug - gaberd, kork, taghik (կապերտ, գորգ, թաղիք)
rugby - ragbi, kuntakhagh mu (ռակպի, գնդախաղ մը)
rugged - khordoupord, anhart, gadaghi, goshd, mazod (խորտուբորտ, անհարթ, կատաղի, կոշտ, մազոտ)
ruin - gordzanoum, aver, gordzanel, averel, sunanganal (կործանում, աւեր, կործանել, աւերել, սնանկանալ)
ruination - gordzanoum, averoum (կործանում, աւերում)
ruinous - gordzanarar, khordagich, averich, khakhoud (կործանարար, խորտակիչ, աւերիչ, խախուտ)
rule (n) - orenk, gark, ganon, kanag, ishkhanoutiun (օրէնք, կարգ, կանոն, քանակ, իշխանութիւն)
rule (v) - direl, ishkhel, oughghel, kudzel, vujrel (տիրել, իշխել, ուղղել, գծել, վճռել)
ruler - dirogh, ishkhogh, kanag (տիրող, իշխող, քանակ)
ruling - ishkhogh, dirogh, vujir (իշխող, տիրող, վճիռ)

rumble - vorodoum, korots, vorodal, murunchel, murmural (որոտում, գոռոց, որոտալ, մռնչել, մռմռալ)
rumbler - murmuratsogh (մռմռացող)
ruminant - vorojatsogh, khogatsogh (որոճացող, խոկացող)
ruminate - vorojal, khogal, mudadzel (որոճալ, խոկալ, մտածել)
rumination - vorojoum, khorhurtadzoum (որոճում, խորհրդածում)
ruminator - vorojatsogh (որոճացող)
rummage - voronoum, pundurdouk, voronel, pundurel, kurkurel (որոնում, փնտռտուք, որոնել, փնտռել, քրքրել)
rummer - kavat, sugah, sugih (գաւաթ, սկահ, սկիհ)
rumor, rumour - daratsaynoutiun, zurouyts, daratsaynel (տարածայնութիւն, զրոյց, տարածայնել)
rump - gurnag, hedsamas, hedouyk, voghnadzayr, boch (կռնակ, յետսամաս, յետոյք, ողնածայր, պոչ)
rumple - jumurtgel, gunjurel, jumurtouk, gunjir, pot (ճմռթկել, կնճռել, ճմռթուք, կնճիռ, փոթ)
rumpus - khurovoutiun, vej, aghmoug, guriv (խռովութիւն, վէճ, աղմուկ, կռիւ)
run (n) - vazk, hosank, untatsk, kedag, kaght, arshav (վազք, հոսանք, ընթացք, գետակ, գաղթ, արշաւ)
run (v) - vazel, hosil, gatil, pakhchil, vaztsunel (վազել, հոսիլ, կաթիլ, փախչիլ, վազցնել)
runabout - taparagan (թափառական)
runagate - pakhusdagan, tasalik, ouratsogh (փախստական, դասալիք, ուրացող)
runaway - pakhusdagan (փախստական)
rung - santukhamad, asdijan, goghapayd, hunchets (սանդուխամատ, աստիճան, կողափայտ, հնչեց)
runlet - vudag (վտակ)
runnel - arvag (առուակ)
runner - vazogh, murtsogh, sourhantag (վազող, մրցող, սուրհանդակ)
running - vazk, vazvuzots, ardatuoutiun, vazogh, hosoun (վազք, վազվզոց, արտադրութիւն, վազող, հոսուն)
runover - harevantsi gartal, gokhgurdel, antsunil (հարեւանցի կարդալ, կոխկռտել, անցնիլ)
runt - manur gentani, kajaj, ketsouts (մանր կենդանի, ճաճաճ, գձուձ)
runty - manrig, kutsouts, jughjim (մանրիկ, գձուձ, ճղճիմ)
rupture (n) - khuzoum, kuzhdoum, jeghkoum, aghetapoutiun (խզում, ճեղքում, աղեթափութիւն)
rupture (v) - khuzel, khuzvil, khordagel, baytetsunel, baytil (խզել, խզուիլ, խորտակել, պայթեցնել, պայթիլ)
rural - kiughagan, keghchgagan, yergrakordzagan (գիւղական, գեղջկական, երկրագործական)
rural economy - kiughadundesoutiun (գիւղատնտեսութիւն)
ruse - hunark, khoramangoutiun (հնարք, խորամանկութիւն)
rush (n) - ajabarank, khoujab, khoyank, harti shiugh (աճապարանք, խուճապ, խոյանք, յարդի շիւղ)
rush (v) - ajabarel, khouzhel, khoyanal, timel (աճապարել, խուժել, խոյանալ, դիմել)
rusher - ajabarogh, hevkod (աճապարող, հեւքոտ)
rusk - hatsepig, gusgoudz, baksimad (հացեփիկ, կսկուծ, պաքսիմատ)
russet - garmurorag, shigakhuntsor, garmuralat (կարմրորակ, շիկախնձոր, կարմրալաթ)
Russia - rousia, rousasdan (Ռուսիա, Ռուսաստան)
russian - rous, rouseren, rousagan (ռուս, ռուսերէն, ռուսական)
rust - zhank, zhankodil, zhankodetsunel (ժանգ, ժանգոտիլ, ժանգոտեցնել)
rustic - kiughagan, keghchoug, gobid, goshd (գիւղական, գեղջուկ, կոպիտ, կոշտ)
rusticate - keghchganal, kiughatsia-

tsunel, kiughu aksorel (գեղջկանալ, գիւղացիացնել, գիւղը աքսորել)
rusticity - shinaganoutiun, andashoutiun, barzoutiun (շինականութիւն, անտաշութիւն, պարզութիւն)
rustiness - zhankodoutiun (ժանգոտութիւն)
rustle - khushurdots, sosapiun, khushurdal, khushshal (խշրտոց, սոսափիւն, խշրտալ, խշշալ)
rusty - zhankod, zhankodadz, muklodaz, tarnaham (ժանգոտ, ժանգոտած, մգլոտած, դառնահամ)
rut - anvahedk, anvagos, durpank, durpal, agosel (անուահետք, անուակօս, տռփանք, տռփալ, ակօսել)
rutabaca - shoghkam (շողգամ)
ruth - kout, garegtsoutiun, voghormadzoutiun (գութ, կարեկցութիւն, ողորմածութիւն)
ruthful - voghormadz (ողորմած)
ruthless - ankout, tazhan, anoghorm (անգութ, դաժան, անողորմ)
ruthlessness - ankutoutiun (անգթութիւն)
ruttish - vavashod, durpod (վաւաշոտ, տռփոտ)
rutty - durpod, vavashod, heshdaser, anvamash (տռփոտ, վաւաշոտ, հեշտասէր, անուամաշ)
rye - hajar, hatsahadig mu (հաճար, հացահատիկ մը)
rytina - dzovatsi (ծովաձի)

S

Sabbath - shapat, hankusian or (Շաբաթ, հանգստեան օր)
sable - samouyr, sevamouyn, sevargel (սամոյր, սեւամոյն, սեւարկել)
sabot - durekh, paydamoujag (տրեխ, փայտամուճակ)
sabotage - khapanararoutiun, kaghdunaveroum (խափանարարութիւն, գաղտնաւերում)
saboteur - khapanarar, vunasarar (խափանարար, վնասարար)
sabre - tour, sour, turadel, suradzel (թուր, սուր, թրատել, սրածել)
sabulous - avazod (աւազոտ)
sac - barg, dobrag (պարկ, տոպրակ)
saccarin - geghdz shakar (կեղծ շաքար)
saccharine - shakareghen, shakaraham, anoush (շաքարեղէն, շաքարահամ, անոյշ)
saccharize - shakarel (շաքարել)
sacerdotal - kahanayagan (քահանայական)
sachet - bargig, kusagig, pokur bayousag (պարկիկ, քսակիկ, փոքր պայուսակ)
sack - dobrag, barg, goghoboud, dobragel, goghobdel (տոպրակ, պարկ, կողոպուտ, տոպրակել, կողոպտել)
sackcloth - laynazkesd, khourts (լայնազգեստ, խուրձ)
sacrament - haghortoutiun, khorhourt, jashag, oukhd (հաղորդու-

թիւն, խորհուրդ, ճաշակ, ուխտ)

sacramental - *surpazan, khorhurtagan, sourp khorhourti* (սրբազան, խորհրդական, Սուրբ Խորհուրդի)

sacred - *sourp, nuviragan, surpazan, odzial* (սուրբ, նուիրական, սրբազան, օծեալ)

sacredness - *nuviraganoutiun* (նուիրականութիւն)

sacrifice - *zohoghoutiun, zoh, zohel, badarakel, nuvirel* (զոհողութիւն, զոհ, զոհել, պատարագել, նուիրել)

sacrilege - *surpabughdzoutiun* (սրբապղծութիւն)

sacrilegious - *surpabighdz, amparishd* (սրբապիղծ, ամբարիշտ)

sacrist - *zhamgoch, lousarar* (ժամկոչ, լուսարար)

sacristan - *zhamgoch, lousarar* (ժամկոչ, լուսարար)

sacristy - *avantadoun, baharan* (աւանդատուն, պահարան)

sacrosanct - *surpazan, nuviragan, antserunmukheli* (սրբազան, նուիրական, անձեռնմխելի)

sad - *dukhour, durdoum, tsavali, dzanur, vad* (տխուր, տրտում, ցաւալի, ծանր, վատ)

sadden - *durdmil, durdmetsunel, dukhretsunel* (տրտմիլ, տրտմեցնել, տխրեցնել)

saddle - *tamp, netsoug, tsiou gurnag, tampel, pertsunel* (թամբ, նեցուկ, ձիու կռնակ, թամբել, բեռցնել)

saddler - *tampakordz* (թամբագործ)

sadism - *purnamoloutiun,, anasnagan girk* (բռնամոլութիւն, անասնական կիրք)

sadly - *dukhroren, takhdzakin* (տխրօրէն, թախծագին)

sadness - *dukhroutiun, durdmoutiun* (տխրութիւն, տրտմութիւն)

safari - *vorsortagan arshav* (որսորդական արշաւ)

safe - *abahov, turamargugh, anvunas* (ապահով, դրամարկղ, անվնաս)

safeguard - *bashdbanoutiun, bahag, antsakir, bashdbanel* (պաշտպանութիւն, պահակ, անցագիր, պաշտպանել)

safely - *abahovoren, abahovabes* (ապահովօրէն, ապահովապէս)

safety - *abahovoutiun, anvudankoutiun* (ապահովութիւն, անվտանգութիւն)

safety pin - *abahovasegh* (ապահովասեղ)

saffron - *kurkoum, teghnakouyn* (քրքում, դեղնագոյն)

sag - *gukil, ungughmil, hagil, gukel, ichvadzk* (կքիլ, ընկղմիլ, հակիլ, կքել, իջուածք)

sagacious - *imasdoun, khelatsi, surades, khoratapants* (իմաստուն, խելացի, սրատես, խորաթափանց)

sagacity - *khelatsoutiun, oushimoutiun, suradesoutiun* (խելացութիւն, ուշիմութիւն, սրատեսութիւն)

sage - *imasdoun, khohem, khelok, oushim, yeghesbag* (իմաստուն, խոհեմ, խելօք, ուշիմ, եղեսպակ)

said - *usvadz, hishvadz* (ըսուած, յիշուած)

sail - *arakasd, arakasdanav, navargel* (առագաստ, առագաստանաւ, նաւարկել)

sailer - *arakasdanav* (առագաստանաւ)

sailing - *navargoutiun* (նաւարկութիւն)

sailing boat - *arakasdanav* (առագաստանաւ)

sailor - *navasdi, navaz* (նաւաստի, նաւազ)

saint - *sourp, surpatsunel* (սուրբ, սրբացնել)

sainted - *lousahoki, surpatsadz, parebashd, hankoutsial* (լուսահոգի, սրբացած, բարեպաշտ, հանգուցեալ)

sainthood - *surpoutiun, surpots tas* (սրբութիւն, սրբոց դաս)

sake - *ser, harkank, ir sirouyn, i ser, hamar* (սէր, յարգանք, իր սիրոյն, ի սէր, համար)

salaam, salam - *parev, voghchouyn* (բարեւ, ողջոյն)

salacious - *durpod, vavashod, heshdaser, anparo* (տռփոտ, վաւաշոտ, հեշտասէր, անբարոյ)

salacity - durpodoutiun, bakshodoutiun (տռփոտութիւն, պագշոտութիւն)
salad - aghtsan (աղցան)
salad oil - tsitayiugh (ձիթայիւղ)
salamander - moghez, zeroun, khulez (մողէզ, զեռուն, խլէզ)
salaried - toshagavor (թոշակաւոր)
salary - toshag, ashkhadavarts, toshag vujarel (թոշակ, աշխատավարձ, թոշակ վճարել)
sale - vajark, vajaroum, aroudzakh (վաճառք, վաճառում, առուծախ)
sale date - vajarki or (վաճառքի օր)
sales price - vajarakin, vajarman kin (վաճառագին, վաճառման գին)
salesman - vajarogh, vajarort, dzakhogh (վաճառող, վաճառորդ, ծախող)
saleswoman - vajarortouhi (վաճառորդուհի)
salience - tsaydk, tsaydounoutiun, oushakuravoutiun (ցայտք, ցայտունութիւն, ուշագրաւութիւն)
salient - tsaydoun, tsutsoun, oushakurav, vosdosdogh (ցայտուն, ցցուն, ուշագրաւ, ոստոստող)
saliferous - aghi (աղի)
saline - aghi, aghayin, aghahank (աղի, աղային, աղահանք)
salinity - aghioutiun (աղիութիւն)
saliva - lortsounk, shoghik, touk (լորձունք, շողիք, թուք)
salivate - lortsnodil, shoghik vazetsunel (լորձնոտիլ, շողիք վազեցնել)
sallow - vadaroghch, hivantakin, kounad, duzhkouyn (վատառողջ, հիւանդագին, գունատ, տժգոյն)
sally - khoyanal, tsaydel, khoyank, tsaydoum, bortgoum (խոյանալ, ցայտել, խոյանք, ցայտում, պոռթկում)
salmon - losdi-tsoug (լոստի-ձուկ)
salon - surah, untounaran, tahlij, hiurasurah (սրահ, ընդունարան, դահլիճ, հիւրասրահ)
saloon - jashaseniag, kinedoun (ճաշասենեակ, գինետուն)
salt - agh, aghaman, aghi, hamov gadag, aghel (աղ, աղաման, աղի, համով կատակ, աղել)
saltant - tsaydoun, tsaydogh, barogh (ցայտուն, ցայտող, պարող)
saltation - tsaydoum, tsadgurdouk, duropoum (ցայտում, ցատկրտուք, տրոփում)
saltcellar - aghaman (աղաման)
saltness - aghioutiun (աղիութիւն)
saltpeter, tre - aghakar, aghporag, varot (աղաքար, աղբորակ, վառօդ)
salty - aghi, aghod, aghaham (աղի, աղոտ, աղահամ)
salubrious - aroghcharar (առողջարար)
salutary - pouzhich, okdaved, purgarar, aroghcharar (բուժիչ, օգտաւէտ, փրկարար, առողջարար)
salutation - voghchiun, parev (ողջիւն, բարեւ)
salute - parev, voghchiun, parevel, voghchounel (բարեւ, ողջոյն, բարեւել, ողջունել)
saluter - voghchounogh, parevogh (ողջունող, բարեւող)
salvage - purgoum, purgakin, oknoutiun (փրկում, փրկագին, օգնութիւն)
salvation - purgoutiun, purgoum (փրկութիւն, փրկում)
salvation army - purgoutian panag (փրկութեան բանակ)
salve - usbeghani, palasan, tarmanel, purgel (սպեղանի, բալասան, դարմանել, փրկել)
salver, salvor - apse, usgoudegh, purgarar (ափսէ, սկուտեղ, փրկարար)
salvo - verabahoum, patsaroutiun, hamazarg, vorod (վերապահում, բացառութիւն, համազարկ, որոտ)
same - nouyn, mievnouyn, numan (նոյն, միեւնոյն, նման)
sameness - nouynoutiun, miorinagoutiun, numanoutiun (նոյնութիւն, միօրինակութիւն, նմանութիւն)
samovar - samavar, teyaman (սամավար, թէյաման)
sample - orinag, numouysh, gagha-

bar, numoushu portsel (օրինակ, նմոյշ, կաղապար, նմոյշը փորձել)
sanative - pouzhich, aroghcharar (բուժիչ, առողջարար)
sanatorium - pouzharan, abakinaran, aroghcharan (բուժարան, ապաքինարան, առողջարան)
sanatory - pouzhagan, pouzharar (բուժական, բուժարար)
sanctification - surpakordzoutiun (սրբագործութիւն)
sanctifier - surpakordz, surparar, sourp hoki (սրբագործ, սրբարար, Սուրբ Հոգի)
sanctify - surpakordzel, surpatsunel, nuvirakordzel (սրբագործել, սրբացնել, նուիրագործել)
sanctimonious - surpanuman, geghdz sourp (սրբանման, կեղծ սուրբ)
sanction - vaveratsoum, vaveratsunel, hasdadel (վաւերացում, վաւերացնել, հաստատել)
sanctitude - surpoutiun, nuviragaoutiun (սրբութիւն, նուիրականութիւն)
sanctity - surpoutiun (սրբութիւն)
sanctuary - surparan, surpavayr, abasdanaran (սրբարան, սրբավայր, ապաստանարան)
sanctum - surpadeghi, arantsnaran (սրբատեղի, առանձնարան)
sanctus - sourp (սուրբ)
sand - avaz, avazoudk (pl), avazel (աւազ, աւազուտք (յգ), աւազել)
sand paper - avazatought (աւազաթուղթ)
sandal - hoghatap, durekh, vodnaman (հողաթափ, տրեխ, ոտնաման)
sandpaper - avazatought (աւազաթուղթ)
sandwich - sandwich, aboukhdahats, sandwich shinel (սանտուիչ, ապուխտահաց, սանտուիչ շինել)
sane - aroghch, kacharoghch, voghchmid (առողջ, քաջառողջ, ողջմիտ)
sangfroid - baghariunoutiun, andarperoutiun (պաղարիւնութիւն, անտարբերութիւն)
sanguify - ariunel (արիւնել)
sanguinary - ariunod, ariunarpou, ariunroushd, ankout (արիւնոտ, արիւնարբու, արիւնռուշտ, անգութ)
sanguine - ariunod, ariunakouyn, yerantoun, ariunel (արիւնոտ, արիւնագոյն, եռանդուն, արիւնել)
sanguineous - ariunod, ariunakouyn (արիւնոտ, արիւնագոյն)
sanify - gensounag tartsunel (կենսունակ դարձնել)
sanitarium - aroghcharan, pouzharan (առողջարան, բուժարան)
sanitary - aroghchabahagan, aroghchagan (առողջապահական, առողջական)
sanitation - aroghchabahoutiun (առողջապահութիւն)
sanity - voghchmudoutiun (ողջմտութիւն)
Santa Claus - gaghant baba (Կաղանդ Պապա)
sap - avish, pousahiut, pos, agan, porel, aganel (աւիշ, բուսահիւթ, փոս, ական, փորել, ականել)
sapid - hamegh, hamov, akhorzhaham (համեղ, համով, ախորժահամ)
sapience - imasdoutiun, khelokoutiun (իմաստութիւն, խելօքութիւն)
sapient - khoranang, khelatsi Tavitironic, imasdoun (խորամանկ, խելացի Դաւիթ-Հեգնական, իմաստուն)
sapless - angiank, anhiut, anavish, ouzhasbar, chor (անկեանք, անհիւթ, անաւիշ, ուժասպառ, չոր)
sapling - noradoung (նորատունկ)
saponify - ojarel, ojari pokhel, ojaranal (օճառել, օճառի փոխել, օճառանալ)
sapphire - shapiugha (շափիւղայ)
sapphirine - yergnakouyn, shapiughia (երկնագոյն, շափիւղեայ)
sappy - hiutalits, avshod, terapouys, khag, mangagan (հիւթալից, աւշոտ, դեռաբոյս, խակ, մանկական)
sarcasm - tarunerkidzank, gudzou heknank (դառներգիծանք, կծու հեգնանք)
sarcastic - heknagan, tarnerkidza-

gan (Հեգնական, դառներգիծանք)
sarcenet - suntous, saten (սնդուս, սաթէն)
sarcophagous - musager (մսակեր)
sarcophagus - vimatampan, karadaban (վիմադամբան, քարատապան)
sardine - aghger-tsoug (աղկեր-ձուկ)
sardonic - purnazposig, heknagan, geghdz, shindzou (բռնազբօսիկ, Հեգնական, կեղծ, շինծու)
sark - shabig, badianel, badel (շապիկ, պատեանել, պատել)
sarment - parounag, nor jiugh (բարունակ, նոր ճիւղ)
sash - shurchanag, abagegal, kodi, gamar (շրջանակ, ապակեկալ, գօտի, կամար)
satan - sadana, tev (սատանայ, դեւ)
satanic, satanical - sadanayagan, tuzhokhayin (սատանայական, դժոխային)
satchel - bargig, tughtagal, tubrotsagan bayousag (պարկիկ, թղթակալ, դպրոցական պայուսակ)
sate - gushdatsunel, haketsunel (կշտացնել, յագեցնել)
sateen - suntous, saten (սնդուս, սաթէն)
satellite - arpaniag, gamagadar, tignabah, kordzagits (արբանեակ, կամակատար, թիկնապահ, գործակից)
satiate - haketsunel, gushdatsunel, hughpatsadz (յագեցնել, կշտացնել, յղփացած)
satiety, satiation - hakourt, haketsoum, haprank (յագուրդ, յագեցում, յափրանք)
satin - suntous (սնդուս)
satire - yerkidzank, heknoutiun, yerkidzapanoutiun (երգիծանք, Հեգնութիւն, երգիծաբանութիւն)
satiric, al - yerkidzagan, yerkidzapanagan (երգիծական, երգիծաբանական)
satirist - yerkidzapan, yerkidzakir (երգիծաբան, երգիծագիր)
satirize - yerkidzapanel, dzaghrel (երգիծաբանել, ծաղրել)
satisfaction - kohatsoum, kohounagoutiun, hadoutsoum (գոՀացում, գոՀունակութիւն, Հատուցում)
satisfactory - kohatsoutsich, hajeli (գոՀացուցիչ, Հաճելի)
satisfier - kohatsunogh, haketsunogh, gushdatsunogh (գոՀացնող, յագեցնող, կշտացնող)
satisfy - kohatsunel, pavararel, hadoutsanel, haketsunel (գոՀացնել, բաւարարել, Հատուցանել, յագեցնել)
satrab - marzban, sadrab - barsits (մարզպան, սատրապ – պարսից)
saturate - gushdatsunel, haketsunel, liatsunel (կշտացնել, յագեցնել, լիացնել)
saturated - haketsvadz (յագեցուած)
saturation - gushdatsoum, haketsoum, tatavoum (կշտացում, յագեցում, թաթաւում)
Saturday - shapat, giragnamoud (Շաբաթ, կիրակնամուտ)
sauce - hamem, hamemounk, tatsan, hamemel (Համեմ, Համեմունք, թացան, Համեմել)
saucebox - lirp, anbadgar, lugdi, anuzkam (լիրբ, անպատկառ, լկտի, անզգամ)
saucer - pazhagabunag, amanadag, amanagal (բաժակապնակ, ամանատակ, ամանակալ)
sauce-boat - tatsanaman, gatsa (թացանաման, կաթսայ)
saucy - aneres, lirp, lubirsh, sumseghoug (աներես, լիրբ, լպիրշ, սմսեղուկ)
saunter - sulukdal, taparil, jemel taparoum, uzposank (սլքտալ, թափառիլ, ճեմել, թափառում, զբօսանք)
sausage - yershig (երշիկ)
sauter - dabgel (տապկել)
savage - vayreni, vayrak, parparos, ankout (վայրենի, վայրագ, բարբարոս, անգութ)
savagery - vayrakoutiun, vayrenoutiun (վայրագութիւն, վայրենութիւն)
savant - kidoun, kidnagan (գիտուն,

գիտնական)
save - purgel, azadel, khunayel, patsi, payts (փրկել, ազատել, խնայել, բացի, բայց)
saver - khunayogh, azadogh, bahbanogh (խնայող, ազատող, պահպանող)
saving - khunayogh, dundesogh, khunayaser (խնայող, տնտեսող, խնայասէր)
savings - khunayoghoutiun, shah (խնայողութիւն, շահ)
Savior - purgich, hisous, krisdos (Փրկիչ, Յիսուս, Քրիստոս)
savior - purgich (փրկիչ)
savour, savor - ham, hod, jashag, pourel (համ, հոտ, ճաշակ, բուրել)
savoury, savory - hamegh, hamov, akhorzhaham (համեղ, համով, ախորժահամ)
saw - sughots, sughotsel, desav (սղոց, սղոցել, տեսաւ)
sawer - sughotsogh (սղոցող)
sawmill - sughotsaran (սղոցարան)
saxon - saksoniatsi, saksoneren, saksonagan (սաքսոնիացի, սաքսոներէն, սաքսոնական)
saxophone - laynasurink, saxofon (լայնասրինգ, սաքսոֆոն)
say - usel, haydunel, badmel, ardasanel (ըսել, յայտնել, պատմել, արտասանել)
saying - asatsvadzk, aradz, arag (ասացուածք, առած, առակ)
scab - usbi, verki geghev, geghdod, kos (սպի, վէրքի կեղեւ, կեղտոտ, քոս)
scabbard - souri badian (սուրի պատեան)
scabbed - kosod, anark, geghdod (քոսոտ, անարգ, կեղտոտ)
scabby - kosod, kutsouts, usbiatsadz (քոսոտ, գձուձ, սպիացած)
scabrous - anhart, goshd, khordoupord (անհարթ, կոշտ, խորտուբորտ
scaffold - gakhaghan, garapnad, lasdag, lasdagel (կախաղան, կառափնատ, լաստակ, լաստակել)
scald - ayruvadzk, gizoum, khashel-yeratsunel chourov (այրուածք, կիզում, խաշել-եռացնել ջուրով)
scale (n) - gushirk, chap, santoukh, gark, tsaynashar, tep (կշիռք, չափ, սանդուխ, կարգ, ձայնաշար, թեփ)
scale (v) - chapel, makultsil, gushrel, tepodil, tepadel (չափել, մագլցիլ, կշռել, թեփոտիլ, թեփատել)
scaled, scaly - tepod (թեփոտ)
scall - tep, kos (թեփ, քոս)
scallop - khetsi, turasankel (խեցի, դրասանգել)
scalp - kangamashg, kulkhamashg, mashgazerdzel (գանկամաշկ, գլխամաշկ, մաշկազերծել)
scaly - tepod, geghdod (թեփոտ, կեղտոտ)
scamble - taparil, vijil, makaril, gudurdel (թափառիլ, վիճիլ, մաքառիլ, կտրտել)
scambler - sulukdatsogh, bunagalez, anamot (սլքտացող, պնակալէզ, անամօթ)
scamp - suriga, anuzkam, khouys dal, pakhchil (սրիկայ, անզգամ, խոյս տալ, փախչիլ)
scamper - pakhchil, khousapil, pakhousd (փախչիլ, խուսափիլ, փախուստ)
scan - zunnel, jarakaytov kunnel, doghavangeru hamrel (զննել, ճառագայթով քննել, տողավանկերը համրել)
scandal - kaytagghoutiun, pampasank, khaydaragoutiun (գայթակղութիւն, բամբասանք, խայտառակութիւն)
scandalize - kaytagghetsunel, khaydaragel, anbadvel (գայթակղեցնել, խայտառակել, անպատուել)
scandalous - kaytagghetsoutsich, amotalits, khaydarag (գայթակղեցուցիչ, ամօթալից, խայտառակ)
scandent - makultsogh (մագլցող)
Scandinavia - uskandinavia (Սքանտինավիա)
scandinavian - uskandinaveren, uskadinavtsi, uskandinavian (սքան-

տինաւերէն, սքանտինացի, սքանտինաւեան)
scanner - zunnogh, darpaghaturogh, kouynazudich (զննող, տարբաղադրող, գոյնազտիչ)
scant - sagav, kheghjoug, aghkadig, kichnal, sagavil (սակաւ, խեղճուկ, աղքատիկ, քիչնալ, սակաւիլ)
scantness - sagavoutiun (սակաւութիւն)
scape - poun, got, tsoghoun, dzigh (բուն, կոթ, ձողուն, ծիղ)
scapegoat - kavoutian nokhaz (քաւութեան նոխազ)
scapegrace - anbidan, anshunorh, anuzkam (անպիտան, անշնորհ, անզգամ)
scapula - ousosgur (ուսոսկր)
scapulary - ourar, ousanots (ուրար, ուսանոց)
scar - usbi, pidz, verki hedk, usbianal, usbiatsunel (սպի, բիծ, վէրքի հետք, սպիանալ, սպիացնել)
scarab - puzez (բզէզ)
scaramouch - mimos, sev hudbid (միմոս, սեւ հտպիտ)
scarce - hazvakiud, sagav, nuvaz, haziv (հազուագիւտ, սակաւ, նուազ, հազիւ)
scarcely - haziv te, kich ankam (հազիւ թէ, քիչ անգամ)
scare - vakhtsunel, ahapegel, sosgoum, ah, vakh (վախցնել, ահաբեկել, սոսկում, ահ, վախ)
scarecrow - khurdvilag (խրտուիլակ)
scarf - vuznots, poghgab, shal, akoutsel, zotel, gabel (վզնոց, փողկապ, շալ, ագուցել, զօդել, կապել)
scarlet - dzirani, posor, garmurakouyn, sharakouyn (ծիրանի, բոսոր, կարմրագոյն, շառագոյն)
scath, scathe - vunas, aver, gorousd, vunasel, averel (վնաս, աւեր, կորուստ, վնասել, աւերել)
scathfull - vunasagar (վնասակար)
scathing - kantich, gordzanarar (քանդիչ, կործանարար)
scatted - tsurvadz, tsiroutsan, dardughnuvadz (ցրուած, ցիրուցան, տարտղնուած)
scatter - tsurvel, dardughnel, daradzel, tsurvil (ցրուել, տարտղնել, տարածել, ցրուիլ)
scatter-brain - mudamolor, mudatsir, anoushatir (մտամոլոր, մտացիր, անուշադիր)
scavenger - aghpahavak, aghpahan, aveladzou (աղբահաւաք, աղբահան, աւելածու)
sceance - nisd, zhoghov (նիստ, ժողով)
scenario - pematuroutiun, taderagan desaran, sharzhaveb (բեմադրութիւն, թատերական տեսարան, շարժավէպ)
scenarist - sharzhavibakir, ourvakudzakir (շարժավիպագիր, ուրուագծագիր)
scene - pem, taderapem, desaran, arar, badger (բեմ, թատերաբեմ, տեսարան, արար, պատկեր)
scenery - pemanugar, desaran, tashdanugar (բեմանկար, տեսարան, դաշտանկար)
scenic - pemagan, desaranagan, taderagan (բեմական, տեսարանական, թատերական)
scenographer - badgerakurogh, desakurogh (պատկերագրող, տեսագրող)
scenography - dateranugarchoutiun, desakuroutiun (պատկերանկարչութիւն, տեսագրութիւն)
scent - hod, hodaroutiun, pouroum, hododel (հոտ, հոտառութիւն, բուրում, հոտոտել)
scepter, sceptre - magan, arkayagan kavazan, ishkhanoutiun (մական, արքայական գաւազան, իշխանութիւն)
schedule - tsang, tsoutsag, tsangakurel, tsoutsagakurel (ցանկ, ցուցակ, ցանկագրել, ցուցակագրել)
schema - hadagakidz, tsev, badger, ourvakidz, dzurakir (յատակագիծ, ձեւ, պատկեր, ուրուագիծ, ծրագիր)
schematic - hadagakudzagan, dzurakrayin (յատակագծական, ծրագրային)

scheme - dzurakir, ourvakidz, dzurakurel, tsevel (ծրագիր, ուրուագիծ, ծրագրել, ձեւել)
schemer - mudatsevogh, nuitogh, dzurakurogh (մտածեւող, նիւթող, ծրագրող)
scheming - tav, mekenayoutiun (դաւ, մեքենայութիւն)
schism - baragdoum, hertsuvadz, yergbaragoutiun (պառակտում, հերձուած, երկպառակութիւն)
schist - hertsakar, tertakar (հերձաքար, թերթաքար)
scholar - tubrotsagan, ousoumnagan, toshagarou, tubraked (դպրոցական, ուսումնական, թոշակառու, դպրագէտ)
scholarship - gurtatoshag, ousoumnatoshag (կրթաթոշակ, ուսումնաթոշակ)
scholastic - tubrotsagan, michnatarian, varzhabedagan (դպրոցական, միջնադարեան, վարժապետական)
scholiast - megnapan, megnich (մեկնաբան, մեկնիչ)
school - tubrots, varzharan, gurtaran, sorvetsunel (դպրոց, վարժարան, կրթարան, սորվեցնել)
schooling - ousoutsoum, gurtoutiun, tubrotsatoshag (ուսուցում, կրթութիւն, դպրոցաթոշակ)
school-board - ousoumnagan khorhourt (ուսումնական խորհուրդ)
school-book - tasakirk (դասագիրք)
school-boy - ashagerd (աշակերտ)
school-girl - ashagerdouhi (աշակերտուհի)
school-master - ousoutsich, varzhabed (ուսուցիչ, վարժապետ)
school-mate - tubrotsagan unger (դպրոցական ընկեր)
school-mistress - ousoutschouhi, varzhouhi (ուսուցչուհի, վարժուհի)
school-room - tasaran, tasasurah (դասարան, դասասրահ)
school-teacher - ousoutsich, varzhabed (ուսուցիչ, վարժապետ)
school-yard - khaghatashd, tubrotsatashd (խաղադաշտ, դպրոցադաշտ)
sciatica - zusdatsav (զստացաւ)
science - kidoutiun, humdoutiun (գիտութիւն, հմտութիւն)
science-fiction - mudadzadzin kidoutiun, yerevagayoutiun (մտածածին գիտութիւն, երեւակայութիւն)
scientific - kidagan (գիտական)
scientist - kidnagan, kidoun (գիտնական, գիտուն)
scintilla - gaydz, nushouyl, shogh (կայծ, նշոյլ, շող)
scintillant - shoghshoghoun, shoghartsag (շողշողուն, շողարձակ)
scintillate - shoghshoghal, gaydzguldal (շողշողալ, կայծկլտալ)
scintillation - shoghshoghoum, payladagoum (շողշողում, փայլատակում)
scion - sharavigh, zharankort, hednort, dzil, poghpoch (շառաւիղ, ժառանգորդ, յետնորդ, ծիլ, բողբոջ)
scission - jeghkoum, gisoum, hertsoum (ճեղքում, կիսում, հերձում)
scissor - mugradel, gudrel (մկրատել, կտրել)
scissors - mugrad (մկրատ)
scissure - jeghk (ճեղք)
sclerosis - bunteragoutiun (պնդերակութիւն)
scobs - dashegh, sughotsouk, medaghi pushrank (տաշեղ, սղոցուք, մետաղի փշրանք)
scoff - dzaghur, arhamarhank, heknel, dzaghrel (ծաղր, արհամարհանք, հեգնել, ծաղրել)
scoffer - dzaghrogh, heknogh (ծաղրող, հեգնող)
scold - hantimanel, sasdel, hantimanogh, gurvazan gin (յանդիմանել, սաստել, յանդիմանող, կռուազան կին)
scolder - hantimanogh (յանդիմանող)
sconce - amrots, saghavard, momagal, kang, oughegh (ամրոց, սաղաւարտ, մոմակալ, գանկ, ուղեղ)
scoop - medz sherep, pah, barbel, hanel, porel (մեծ շերեփ, բահ,

պարպել, հանել, փորել)

scope - tidag, tidaged, nubadag, untartsagoutiun (դիտակ, դիտակէտ, նպատակ, ընդարձակութիւն)

scorch - ayrel, khargel, khandzel, gizel, varel (այրել, խարկել, խանձել, կիզել, վառել)

score (n) - hashvetsoutsag, murtsanish, kidz, kusan, khaz (հաշուեցուցակ, մրցանիշ, գիծ, քսան, խազ)

score (v) - nushanagel, shahil, paydanushel, gudrel (նշանակել, շահիլ, փայտանշել, կտրել)

scorer - nushanagogh, ged artsanagurogh (նշանակող, կէտ արձանագրող)

scorn - arhamarhank, anarkank, dzaghrank, arhamarhel (արհամարհանք, անարգանք, ծաղրանք, արհամարհել)

scorpion - garij (կարիճ)

scotch (I) - gabel, gasetsunel, viravorel, gudruvadzk, seb (կապել, կասեցնել, վիրաւորել, կտրուածք, սեպ)

scotch (II) - usgovdatsi, usgovderen, usgovdagan (սկովտացի, սկովտերէն, սկովտական)

scoundrel - tushvaragan, suriga, usdor, anuzkam (թշուառական, սրիկայ, ստոր, անզգամ)

scour - makrel, khozanagel, shupel, makroum, tanchk (մաքրել, խոզանակել, շփել, մաքրում, թանչք)

scourge - mudrag, kharazan, badizh, mudragel, kharazanel (մտրակ, խարազան, պատիժ, մտրակել, խարազանել)

scout (n) - hedakhouyz, rahvira, ted, lurdes, usgaoud (հետախոյզ, ռահվիրայ, դէտ, լրտես, սկաուտ)

scout (v) - hedakhouzel, zunnel, tidel, lurdesel (հետախուզել, զննել, դիտել, լրտեսել)

scowl - burusdel-honkeru, khozhorel, burusdoum (պռստել-յօնքերը, խոժոռել, պռստում)

scrabble - murodel, jangurdel, jangel, murodoum (մրոտել, ճանկռտել, ճանկել, մրոտում)

scrag - vudid, nihar, gumakhk, vosgurod, vizu purtsunel (վտիտ, նիհար, կմախք, ոսկրոտ, վիզը փրցնել)

scraggy - khordouporд, anhart (խորտուբորտ, անհարթ)

scramble - murtsil, makaril, hapushdagel, baykar (մրցիլ, մաքառիլ, յափշտակել, պայքար)

scrap - gudor, pushour, badar, dashegh, pushrank (կտոր, փշուր, պատառ, տաշեղ, փշրանք)

scrap book - havakadzo, dzaghgakagh (հաւաքածոյ, ծաղկաքաղ)

scrape - kerel, kertel, makrel, hanel, kertouk, gunjir (քերել, քերթել, մաքրել, հանել, քերթուք, կնճիռ)

scraping - kertouk (քերթուք)

scratch - jangel, jangurdel, kertel, murodel, jangurdouk (ճանկել, ճանկռտել, քերթել, մրոտել, ճանկռտուք)

scrawl - murodel, aghdodel, murodoum, anarzhek kurvadzk (մրոտել, աղտոտել, մրոտում, անարժէք գրուածք)

screak - jurunchel, juchal, sharachel, jurinch, jich (ճռնչել, ճչալ, շառաչել, ճռինչ, ճիչ)

scream - juchal, boral, tsaven ganchel, jich, hedzedzank (ճչալ, պոռալ, ցաւէն կանչել, ճիչ, հեծեծանք)

screamer - juchatsogh, aghaghagogh (ճչացող, աղաղակող)

screech - juchal, borchudal, boralganchel, jich (ճչալ, պոռչտալ, պոռալ-կանչել, ճիչ)

screen (n) - basdar, bahbanag, varakouyr, hurarkel, kogh (պաստառ, պահպանակ, վարագոյր, հրարգել, քող)

screen (v) - bahbanel, bahel, maghel, sharzhanugari arnel (պահպանել, պահել, մաղել, շարժանկարի առնել)

screw - budoudag, budoudagel (պտուտակ, պտուտակել)

screwdriver - budoudagatarts, budoudagich (պտուտակադարձ, պտուտակիչ)

scribble - murodel, tsapurdel, murodoum, tsapurdouk (մրոտել, ձաբռտել, մրոտում, ձաբռտուք)

scribbler - murodogh, kurchag (մրոտող, գրչակ)

scribe - kurakir, tubir, kardoughar, tsevel-gudrel, kurel (գրագիր, դպիր, քարտուղար, ձեւել-կտրել, գրել)

scrimmage - gurvudouk, hurmushdouk, vokoroum-kuntaghaghi mech (կռուըտուք, հրմշտուք, ոգորում - գնդախաղի մէջ)

scrimp - ampopel, hamarodel, ampop, garj, hamarod (ամփոփել, համառօտել, ամփոփ, կարճ, համառօտ)

scrip - pazhanortakir, garj kouroutiun, kir, tought (բաժանորդագիր, կարճ գրութիւն, գիր, թուղթ)

script - tserakir, sheghakir, pemaniut (ձեռագիր, շեղագիր, բեմանիւթ)

scriptural - asdvadzashunchagan, sourp kurots (աստուածաշնչական, սուրբ գրոց)

scripture - kurvadzk, hadvadz sourp kirken (գրուածք, հատուած Սուրբ Գիրքէն)

scrivener - nodar, kurogh (նոտար, գրող)

scroll - patouyt, gabots, zartakidz, dzurarel (փաթոյթ, կապոց, զարգիծ, ծրարել)

scrounge - shortel, iuratsunel, koghnal (շորթել, իւրացնել, գողնալ)

scrub - shupel, kerel, khozanagel, kutsouts, matsar (շփել, քերել, խոզանակել, գձուձ, մացառ)

scruff - dzodzrag (ծոծրակ)

scruple - khughjaharil, goud, pokur gudor (խղճահարիլ, կուտ, փոքր կտոր)

scrupler - khughjahar, khughjaharogh (խղճահար, խղճահարող)

scrupulosity - khughjmudoutiun, uzkoushavoroutiun (խղճմտութիւն, զգուշաւորութիւն)

scrupulous - khughjamid, manragurgid, parekhighj (խղճամիտ, մանրակրկիտ, բարեխիղճ)

scrupulousness - khughjaharoutiun, khughjmudoutiun (խղճահարութիւն, խղճմտութիւն)

scrutinize - khouzargel, hedazodel, manrazunin kunnel (խուզարկել, հետազօտել, մանրազնին քննել)

scrutiny - hedazodoutiun, usdoukoum, khorazunnoum (հետազօտութիւն, ստուգում, խորազննում)

scud - pakhchil, sulanal, kushvil, sahil, pakhousd (փախչիլ, սլանալ, քշուիլ, սահիլ, փախուստ)

scuff - sulukdal, vodkeru kuselov kalel (սլքտալ, ոտքերը քսելով քալել)

scuffle - gurvil, dzedzvil, gurvudouk, guriv (կռուիլ, ծեծուիլ, կռուըտուք, կռիւ)

scull - navagig, magouyg, tiag, tiavarel (նաւակիկ, մակոյկ, թիակ, թիավարել)

sculpt - kantagel, artsanakordzel (քանդակել, արձանագործել)

sculptor - kantagakordz, artsanakordz (քանդակագործ, արձանագործ)

sculpture (n) - kantagakordzoutiun, artsanakordzoutiun, kantag (քանդակագործութիւն, արձանագործութիւն, քանդակ)

sculpture (v) - kantagel, artsanakordzel, porakurel (քանդակել, արձանագործել, փորագրել)

scum - purpour, tird, aghd, purpuril, purpurahanel (փրփուր, դիրտ, աղտ, փրփրիլ, փրփրահանել)

scunner - kanil, kanetsunel (գանիլ, գանեցնել)

scurf - tep - mazi (թեփ՝ մազի)

scurfiness - tepodoutiun (թեփոտութիւն)

scurfy - tepod (թեփոտ)

scurrile - kheghgadag (խեղկատակ)

scurrilous, scurrile - kurehig, khaydarag, varnots, aghdod peran

(գուճհիկ, խայտառակ, վարնոց, աղտոտ բերան)
scutter - arak pakhchil (արագ փախչիլ)
scuttle - layn goghov, arak kayl, turnag, vazel, dzagel (լայն կողով, արագ քայլ, դռնակ, վազել, ծակել)
scutum - vahan (վահան)
scythe - keranti, mankagh, huntsel (գերանդի, մանգաղ, հնձել)
scytheman - huntsvor, hutsogh (հնձուոր, հնձող)
sea - dzov (ծով)
seaboard - dzovap (ծովափ)
seacoast - dzovezerk (ծովեզերք)
seafood - tsugneghen, dzovayin oudelik (ձկնեղէն, ծովային ուտելիք)
seal - pog, gunik, turoshm, gunkel, pagel, kotsel (փոկ, կնիք, դրոշմ, կնքել, փակել, գոցել)
sealer - gunkogh, turoshmahar (քնգող, դրօշմահար)
sealing-wax - gunkamom (կնքամոմ)
seam - garvadzk, gar, usbi, garel, usbiatsunel (կարուածք, կար, սպի, կարել, սպիացնել)
seamstress - garouhi, tertsagouhi (կարուհի, դերձակուհի)
seaport - navahankisd (նաւահանգիստ)
sear - khandzel, kharel, chorsunel, chortsadz, ayruvadzk (խանծել, խարել, չորցնել, չորցած, այրուածք)
search - pundurel, khouzargel, kunnel, pundurdouk, khouyz (փնտռել, խուզարկել, քննել, փնտռտուք, խոյզ)
searcher - pundurogh, khouzargou, kunnich (փնտռող, խուզարկու, քննիչ)
season (n) - yeghanag, shurchan, harmar zhamanag (եղանակ, շըրջան, յարմար ժամանակ)
season (v) - harmartsunel, varzhutsunel, hamemel, varzhuvil (յարմարցնել, վարժեցնել, համեմել, վարժուիլ)
seasonable - yeghanagavayel, harmar, badshaj, badeh (եղանակավայել, յարմար, պատշաճ, պատեհ)
seasonal - yeghanagayin (եղանակային)
seasoned - chortsadz, aghadz, hamemvadz (չորցած, աղած, համեմուած)
seasoner - hamemogh, badrasdogh, harmartsunogh (համեմող, պատրաստող, յարմարցնող)
seasoning - hamem, hamemounk (համեմ, համեմունք)
seat - ator, nusdaran, punagavayr, nusdetsunel, nusdil (աթոռ, նստարան, բնակավայր, նստեցնել, նստիլ)
seat belt - nusdakodi (նստագօտի)
seating - nusdadeghi, nusdadzadzg, nusdetsunelu (նստատեղի, նստածածկ, նստեցնելը)
sea-board - dzovezerk, dzovap (ծովեզերք, ծովափ)
sea-born - dzovadzin, dzovayin (ծովածին, ծովային)
sea-calf - pog, dzovahort (փոկ, ծովահորթ)
sea-captain - navabed (նաւապետ)
sea-coast - dzovap, dzovezur (ծովափ, ծովեզր)
sea-fight - dzovamard, navamard (ծովամարտ, նաւամարտ)
sea-man - navasdi, dzovakunats, navaz (նաւաստի, ծովագնաց, նաւազ)
sea-nymph - haverzhahars, dzovanoush (յաւերժահարս, ծովանոյշ)
sea-port - navahankisd (նաւահանգիստ)
sea-sick - dzovahar (ծովահար)
sea-sickness - dzovakhd (ծովախտ)
secant - gudrogh, hadanogh, hadich (կտրող, հատանող, հատիչ)
secede - kashvil, heranal, anchadvil, pazhnuvil (քաշուիլ, հեռանալ, անջատուիլ, բաժնուիլ)
seceder - kashvogh, anchadvogh (քաշուող, անջատուող)
secern - zadel, zanazanel, anchadel (զատել, զանազանել, անջատել)
secession - anchadoum, megnoum, pazhanoum (անջատում, մեկնում,

բաժանում)
seclude - megousanal, megousatsunel, anchadel, pazhnel (մեկուսանալ, մեկուսացնել, անջատել, բաժնել)
secluded - megousi, arantsin, megousatsadz (մեկուսի, առանձին, մեկուսացած)
seclusion - arantsnatsoum, megousatsoum, hurazharoum (առանձնացում, մեկուսացում, հրաժարում)
second - yergurort, hachort, vayrgian, bah, usdoratas (երկրորդ, յաջորդ, վայրկեան, պահ, ստորադաս)
secondary - yergrortagan, usdoratas (երկրորդական, ստորադաս)
seconder - yergurortogh, arachargogh, hasdadogh (երկրորդող, առաջարկող, հաստատող)
secondhand - hin, kordzadzvadz (հին, գործածուած)
secrecy - kaghdnioutiun, kashvadzoutiun (գաղտնիութիւն, քաշուածութիւն)
secret - kaghduni, dzadzoug, antsunagan, kaghdunik (գաղտնի, ծածուկ, անձնական, գաղտնիք)
secretariat - kardougharoutiun (քարտուղարութիւն)
secretary - kardoughar, bashdonia, kuraseghan (քարտուղար, պաշտօնեայ, գրասեղան)
secrete - bahel, dzadzgel, ardatorel (պահել, ծածկել, արտաթորել)
secretion - dzadzgoum, hiutahosoum, ardatoroum (ծածկում, հիւթահոսում, արտաթորում)
secretly - kaghdunabes (գաղտնապէս)
sect - aghant, hertsuvadz (աղանդ, հերձուած)
sectarian - aghantavor, aylatavan, neghmid, aghantavoragan (աղանդաւոր, այլադաւան, նեղմիտ, աղանդաւորական)
sectarianism - aghantavoroutiun, hertsuvadzoghoutiun (աղանդաւորութիւն, հերձուածողութիւն)
section - hadoum, hadvadz, mas, vashd (հատում, հատուած, մաս, վաշտ)
sectional - masnagi, hadvadzagan (մասնակի, հատուածական)
sector - hadvadz, hadadz, hamemadagargin (հատուած, հատած, համեմատակարգին)
secular - ashkharhig, ashkharhayin, hariuramia, taravor (աշխարհիկ, աշխարհային, հարիւրամեայ, դարաւոր)
secularization - ashkharhaganatsoum (աշխարհականացում)
secularize - ashkharhaganatsunel (աշխարհականացնել)
secure - abahov, anvudank, vusdah, vusdahatsunel, abahovel (ապահով, անվտանգ, վստահ, վստահացնել, ապահովել)
security - abahovoutiun, vusdahoutiun, anvudankoutiun (ապահովութիւն, վստահութիւն, անվտանգութիւն)
sedan - badkarag, tsernadar pazgator (պատգարակ, ձեռնատար բազկաթոռ)
sedate - hantard, khaghagh, ankhurov, anvurtov (հանդարտ, խաղաղ, անխռով, անվրդով)
sedative - meghmatsunogh, hankusdatsunogh, amokich (մեղմացնող, հանգստացնող, ամոքիչ)
sedentary - nusdoug, nusdagiats, nusdoghagan (նստուկ, նստակեաց, նստողական)
sediment - murour, tird (մրուր, դիրտ)
sedition - khurovoutiun, khurovararoutiun (խռովութիւն, խռովարարութիւն)
seduce - hurabourel, moloretsunel, khapel, bughdzel (հրապուրել, մոլորեցնել, խաբել, պղծել)
seducer - moloretsunogh, hurabourogh (մոլորեցնող, հրապուրող)
seduction - hurabouyr, hurabourank, kaytagghoum (հրապոյր, հրապուրանք, գայթակղում)
seductive - hurabourich, moloretsunogh (հրապուրիչ, մոլորեցնող)

sedulity - chanasiroutiun, ashkhadasiroutiun (ջանասիրութիւն, աշխատասիրութիւն)
sedulous - ashkhadaser, chanaser, haradevogh (աշխատասէր, ջանասէր, յարատեւող)
see - desnel, nugadel, nayil, tidel, nushmarel, tem (տեսնել, նկատել, նայիլ, դիտել, նշմարել, Թեմ)
seed - serm, hadig, zarm, aghpiur, sermanel, tsanel (սերմ, հատիկ, զարմ, աղբիւր, սերմանել, ցանել)
seeder - sermnatsan, mirki gorizahan mekena (սերմնացան, միրգի կորիզահան մեքենայ)
seediness - kounadoutiun, puntioutiun (գունատութիւն, փնթիութիւն)
seedling - sermunapouys, hounde pousadz (սերմնաբոյս, հունտէ բուսած)
seedman, seedsman - sermanogh, sermavajar (սերմանող, սերմավաճառ)
seedtime - tsank, tsanki zhamanag (ցանք, ցանքի ժամանակ)
seeing - nugadi arnelov, desnelov, kani vor (նկատի առնելով, տեսնելով, քանի որ)
seek - pundurel, voronel (փնտռել, որոնել)
seel - gourtsunel, achku garel, pagel (կուրցնել, աչքը կարել, փակել)
seem - tuvil, yerevil, tsevanal, tsevatsunel (Թուիլ, երեւիլ, ձեւանալ, ձեւացնել)
seeming - yerevtsogh, tsevatsunogh, ardakin, khapousig (երեւցող, ձեւացնող, արտաքին, խաբուսիկ)
seemly - vayel, vayelouch, badshaj (վայել, վայելուչ, պատշաճ)
seep - dzoril, hosil, muzil, kamel (ծորիլ, հոսիլ, մզիլ, քամել)
seer - desnogh, koushag, markare (տեսնող, գուշակ, մարգարէ)
seesaw - jojanots, hedzanakhagh, jojvil, dadanvil (ճօճանոց, հեծանախաղ, ճօճուիլ, տատանուիլ)
seethe - yeral, yeratsunel, yepel, yepil (եռալ, եռացնել, եփել, եփիլ)
segment - mas, hadvadz, hadamas (մաս, հատուած, հատամաս)
segregate - anchad, zad, arantsin, anchadel, anchadvil (անջատ, զատ, առանձին, անջատել, անջատուիլ)
segregation - anchadoum, zadoum, khudraganoutiun (անջատում, զատում, խտրականութիւն)
seigneur, seignior - ishkhan, baron, der (իշխան, պարոն, տէր)
seine - medz ourgan, tsants, tsoug vorsal (մեծ ուռկան, ցանց, ձուկ որսալ)
seism - yergurasharzh (երկրաշարժ)
seismic - yergurasharzhagan (երկրաշարժական)
seismograph - yergrasharzhachap (երկրաշարժաչափ)
seize - tserpagalel, purnel, kuravel, hapushdagel (ձերբակալել, բռնել, գրաւել, յափշտակել)
seizin - diroutiun, sepaganoutiun (տիրութիւն, սեփականութիւն)
seizure - kuravoum, tserpagaloutiun (գրաւում, ձերբակալութիւն)
select - undurel, zadel, voroshel, undir, patsarig (ընտրել, զատել, որոշել, ընտիր, բացառիկ)
selected - undurvadz, zadvadz, undurial (ընտրուած, զատուած, ընտրեալ)
selection - unduroutiun, chogoum, voroshoum (ընտրութիւն, ջոկում, որոշում)
selector - undurogh, zadogh (ընտրող, զատող)
self - inkun, inkun isg, antsun, sepagan (ինքն, ինքն իսկ, անձն, սեփական)
selfish - antsunaser, yesaser (անձնասէր, եսասէր)
selfishness - yesasiroutiun, yesamoloutiun (եսասիրութիւն, եսամոլութիւն)
self-abuse - kichoutiun (գիջութիւն)
self-acting - inkunakordz (ինքնագործ)
self-conceit - inkunahavanoutiun (ինքնահավանութիւն)
self-conceited - inkunahavan (ինք-

նահաւան)
self-confident - *inknavusdah, inknabasdan* (ինքնավստահ, ինքնապաստան)
self-conscious - *inkunakidagits* (ինքնագիտակից)
self-control - *inkunazusboum, baghariunoutiun* (ինքնազսպում, պարիւնութիւն)
self-defence - *inkunabashdubanoutiun* (ինքնապաշտպանութիւն)
self-denial - *antsnouratsoutiun* (անձնուրացութիւն)
self-determination - *inkunoroshoum, vujragamoutiun* (ինքնորոշում, վճռակամութիւն)
self-esteem - *inkunahamaroum, tsoutsamoloutiun* (ինքնահամարում, ցուցամոլութիւն)
self-governing - *inkunavar* (ինքնավար)
self-interest - *shahakhunturoutiun, yesasiroutiun* (շահախնդրութիւն, եսասիրութիւն)
self-love - *antsunasiroutiun* (անձնասիրութիւն)
self-respect - *inkunaharkank* (ինքնայարգանք)
self-service - *inkunasbasargoum* (ինքնասպասարկում)
self-taught - *inknous* (ինքնուս)
sell (n) - *tagart, dzoughag, khapeoutiun, tamp* (թակարդ, ծուղակ, խաբէութիւն, թամբ)
sell (v) - *dzakhel, vajarel, madnel, khapel, dzakhvil* (ծախել, վաճառել, մատնել, խաբել, ծախուիլ)
seller - *dzakhogh, vajarogh* (ծախող, վաճառող)
semaphore - *nushanadar, herakuranish* (նշանատար, հեռագրանիշ)
semblable - *numan, hamanuman* (նման, համանման)
semblance - *numanoutiun, hamanumanoutiun, yerevouyt, tsev* (նմանութիւն, համանմանութիւն, երեւոյթ, ձեւ)
semen - *serm, hound* (սերմ, հունտ)
semester - *vetsamsia, gisamia* (վեցամսեայ, կիսամեայ)
semi - *ges* (կէս)
seminal - *sermunagan, nakhnagan, darragan* (սերմնական, նախնական, տարրական)
seminar - *hamazhoghov, tasuntatsk, asoulis* (համաժողով, դասընթացք, ասուլիս)
seminarist - *zharankavor, gugherigos* (ժառանգաւոր, կղերիկոս)
seminary - *gugheranots, tubrevank, kolej, hamazhoghov* (կղերանոց, դպրեվանք, գոլէճ, համաժողով)
seminate - *tsanel, daradzel* (ցանել, տարածել)
semination - *sermanoum* (սերմանում)
semite - *semagan, Semi serount* (սեմական, Սեմի սերունդ)
semitic - *semagan* (սեմական)
semi-annual - *gisamia, vetsamsia* (կիսամեայ, վեցամսեայ)
semi-circle - *gisapolorag* (կիսաբոլորակ)
semi-colon - *michaged* (միջակէտ)
semi-lune - *gisalousin* (կիսալուսին)
semi-official - *gisabashdonagan* (կիսապաշտօնական)
sempster - *tertsag* (դերձակ)
sempstress - *tertsagouhi* (դերձակուհի)
senate - *dzeragouyd* (ծերակոյտ)
senator - *dzeragoudagan* (ծերակուտական)
send - *ghurgel, arakel, hughel, pokhantsel* (ղրկել, առաքել, յղել, փոխանցել)
sender - *ghurgogh, arakogh* (ղրկող, առաքող)
senescence - *dzeratsoum, mashoum* (ծերացում, մաշում)
senescent - *dzeratsadz, mashadz* (ծերացած, մաշած)
senile - *dzer, zaramadz, dugar* (ծեր, զառամած, տկար)
senility - *dzeroutiun* (ծերութիւն)
senior - *medz, darets, yerets, avak* (մեծ, տարեց, երէց, աւագ)
seniority - *yeritsoutiun, avakoutiun, hunoutiun* (երիցութիւն, աւագութիւն, հնութիւն)

sensation - uzkayoutiun, uskatsogoutiun, tsuntsoum (զգայութիւն, զգացողութիւն, ցնցում)
sensational - uzkayatsounts, tsuntsich (զգայացունց, ցնցիչ)
sense (n) - uzkayarank, uzkatsoum, umpurnoum, midk, imasd (զգայարանք, զգացում, ըմբռնում, միտք, իմաստ)
sense (v) - hasgunal, umpurnel, gasgadzil (հասկնալ, ըմբռնել, կասկածիլ)
senseless - animasd, anmid, anuzka (անիմաստ, անմիտ, անզգայ)
sensibility - uzkaynoutiun, tiurazkatsoutiun (զգայնութիւն, դիւրազգացութիւն)
sensible - uzkayoun, uzkaynod, kunkoush, khohem (զգայուն, զգայնոտ, քնքուշ, խոհեմ)
sensibly - uzkalabes, uzkalioren (զգալապէս, զգալիօրէն)
sensitive - uzkayoun, uzkatsagan, tiurazkats (զգայուն, զգացական, դիւրազգաց)
sensitize - uzkaynil, uzkayoun tartsunel (զգայնիլ, զգայուն դարձընել)
sensory - uzkayaran, uzkayounag, uzkatsagan (զգայարան, զգայունակ, զգացական)
sensual - uzkayagan, tsangaser, heshdaser, durpagan (զգայական, ցանկասէր, հեշտասէր, տռփական)
sensualism - heshdasiroutiun, uzkayabashdoutiun (հեշտասիրութիւն, զգայապաշտութիւն)
sensualist - heshdaser, uzkayabashd (հեշտասէր, զգայապաշտ)
sensuality - heshdasiroutiun, durpodoutiun (հեշտասիրութիւն, տռփոտութիւն)
sensualize - tsopatsunel, tsangaser tartsunel (ցոփացնել, ցանկասէր դարձնել)
sensuous - uzkaynod (զգայնոտ)
sentence - nakhatasoutiun, tadavujir, aradz, tadabardel (նախադասութիւն, դատավճիռ, առած, դատապարտել)
sententious - imasdalits, garj, aztou (իմաստալից, կարճ, ազդու)
sentience - uzkatsoghoutiun, oushimoutiun (զգացողութիւն, ուշիմութիւն)
sentient - uzkayoun, uzkatsagan, uzkatsogh, khohoun (զգայուն, զգացական, զգացող, խոհուն)
sentiment - uzkatsoum, uzkatsoghoutiun, ser, abroum (զգացում, զգացողութիւն, սէր, ապրում)
sentimental - uzkaynod, uzkayoun, uzkatsagan, tiurazkats (զգայնոտ, զգայուն, զգացական, դիւրազգաց)
sentinel - bahag, zhamabah, husgel (պահակ, ժամապահ, հսկել)
sentry - bahag, bahagoutiun (պահակ, պահակութիւն)
sentry-box - bahagakhouts, bahagadunag (պահակախուց, պահակատնակ)
separable - anchadeli, zadeli, pazhaneli (անջատելի, զատելի, բաժանելի)
separate - pazhnel, anchadel, zadel, anchadil, anchad, zad (բաժնել, անջատել, զատել, անջատիլ, անջատ, զատ)
separation - pazhanoum, anchadoum, amousnaloudzoum (բաժանում, անջատում, ամուսնալուծում)
separatist - anchadoghagan, hertsuvadzogh (անջատողական, հերձուածող)
separator - zadogh, anchadogh (զատող, անջատող)
September - sebdemper (Սեպտեմբեր)
septenary, septennial - yotnamia (եօթնամեայ)
septuble - yotnabadig, yotnabadgel (եօթնապատիկ, եօթնապատկել)
sepulcher, sepulchre - kerezman, shirim, kerezmanel, taghel (գերեզման, շիրիմ, գերեզմանել, թաղել)
sepulture - taghoum, kerezman (թաղում, գերեզման)
sequel - sharounagoutiun, hedevank,

hedevort, shark (շարունակութիւն, Հետեւանք, Հետեւորդ, շարք)
sequence - sharounagoutiun, shark, hachortoutiun (շարունակութիւն, շարք, յաջորդութիւն)
sequent - hedaka, hachort (Հետագայ, յաջորդ)
sequester, sequestrate - megousatsunel, zadel, badantel, hurazharil (մեկուսացնել, զատել, պատանդել, Հրաժարիլ)
sequestration - badantoum, zadoum (պատանդում, զատում)
seraglio - gananots, harem (կանանոց, Հարեմ)
serail - balad, garavarchadoun (պալատ, կառավարչատուն)
serenade - tsaykerk, tsaykanuvak, tsaykerkel (ցայգերգ, ցայգանուագ, ցայգերգել)
serene - husdag, chinch, baydzar, ankhurov, khaghagh (յստակ, ջինջ, պայծառ, անխռով, խաղաղ)
serenity - husdagoutiun, baydzaroutiun, barzoutiun (յստակութիւն, պայծառութիւն, պարզութիւն)
serf - usduroug, jord, kiughatsi (ստրուկ, ճորտ, գիւղացի)
serfage - usdurgoutiun (ստրկութիւն)
serfdom - jordadiroutiun, usdurgoutiun (ճորտատիրութիւն, ստրկութիւն)
sergeant, serjeant - yentasba, hisnabed, paraban (ենթասպայ, յիսնապետ, բարապան)
serial - hachortagan, sharounagvogh, barperagan (յաջորդական, շարունակուող, պարբերական)
sericeous - medaksia (մետաքսեայ)
sericulture - sheramapoudzoutiun (շերամաբուծութիւն)
series - shark, hachortaganoutiun, gark (շարք, յաջորդականութիւն, կարգ)
serigraph - medaksadib (մետաքսատիպ)
serigrapher - medaksov dubogh (մետաքսով տպող)
serigraphy - medaksaduboutiun (մետաքսատպութիւն)
serious - lourch, dzanragushir, dzanrakhoh, garevor (լուրջ, ծանրակշիռ, ծանրախոՀ, կարեւոր)
seriously - lurchoren, dzanroren (լրջօրէն, ծանրօրէն)
seriousness - lurchoutiun (լրջութիւն)
sermon - karoz, jar, khurad (քարոզ, ճառ, խրատ)
serpent - ots, izh (օձ, իժ)
serpentine - otsatsev, otsanuman, otsabudouyd, nenk (օձաձեւ, օձանման, օձապտոյտ, նենգ)
serried - khid, seghm, usdvar (խիտ, սեղմ, ստուար)
serry - seghmel, tukhmel, khurnel (սեղմել, Թխմել, խռնել)
serum - shijoug (շիճուկ)
servant - usbasavor, dzara, usbasargou, ashkhadavor (սպասաւոր, ծառայ, սպասարկու, աշխատաւոր)
serve - dzarayel, oknel, usbasargel, dal, kordzel (ծառայել, օգնել, սպասարկել, տալ, գործել)
server - dzarayogh, apse (ծառայող, ափսէ)
service - dzarayoutiun, usbasargoutiun, kordz, antserots (ծառայութիւն, սպասարկութիւն, գործ, անձեռոց)
serviceable - okdagar, bidani, kordzadzeli (օգտակար, պիտանի, գործածելի)
servient - dzarayogh, usdoratas (ծառայող, ստորադաս)
serviette - antserots, seghani tseralat (անձեռոց, սեղանի ձեռալաթ)
servile - usdurgagan, tsadz, usdurgamid, kudznogh (ստրկական, ցած, ստրկամիտ, քծնող)
servility - usdurgamudoutiun, nuvasdoutiun (ստրկամտութիւն, նուաստութիւն)
servitor - dzara, usbasargogh (ծառայ, սպասարկող)
servitude - dzarayoutiun, usdurgoutiun (ծառայութիւն, ստրկութիւն)
sesame - shoushma, sousam (շուշմայ, սուսամ)

session - nisd, nusdashurchan, zhoghov, adian (նիստ, նստաշրջան, ժողով, ատեան)
set (n) - shark, gazmadz, havakadzo, zouyk, mayramoud (շարք, կազմած, հաւաքածոյ, զոյգ, մայրամուտ)
set (v) - tunel, zedeghel, shudgel, voroshel, hasdadel (դնել, զետեղել, շտկել, որոշել, հաստատել)
set up - shudgel, deghavorel, sharel (շտկել, տեղաւորել, շարել)
settee - pazmots, yergar nusdaran (բազմոց, երկար նստարան)
setter - kurashar, sharogh, tunogh, kamogh, vorsakhouyz (գրաշար, շարող, դնող, գամող, որսախոյզ)
setting - hasdadoum, arevamoud, kurasharoutiun (հաստատում, արեւամուտ, գրաշարութիւն)
settle (n) - nusdaran, pazmots (նստարան, բազմոց)
settle (v) - hasdadel, lumuntsunel, garkaturel, hasdadvil (հաստատել, լմնցնել, կարգադրել, հաստատուիլ)
settlement - garkaturoutiun, deghavoroum, kaghout, punagaran (կարգադրութիւն, տեղաւորում, գաղութ, բնակարան)
settler - norapunag, kaghtogh, kaghtagan (նորաբնակ, գաղթող, գաղթական)
Sevan - sevan (Սեւան)
seven - yotu (եօթը)
seventeen - dasnuyotu (տասնեօթը)
seventh - yotnerort (եօթներորդ)
seventieth - yotanasounerort (եօթանասուներորդ)
seventy - yotanasoun (եօթանասուն)
sever - zadel, anchadel, pazhnel, pazhnuvil (զատել, անջատել, բաժնել, բաժնուիլ)
several - pazmativ, ayl yev ayl, vorosh, kani mu (բազմաթիւ, այլ եւ այլ, որոշ, քանի մը)
severally - arantsin, zad zad (առանձին, զատ զատ)
severe - khisd, sasdig, khozhor, tazhan, murayl (խիստ, սաստիկ, խոժոռ, դաժան, մռայլ)
severity - khusdoutiun, sasdgoutiun (խստութիւն, սաստկութիւն)
sew - garel (կարել)
sewage - goyoughi (կոյուղի)
sewer - garogh, garouhi (կարող, կարուհի)
sewing - gar (կար)
sewing machine - gari mekena (կարի մեքենայ)
sex - ser (սեռ)
sex appeal - serayin kuravchoutiun (սեռային գրաւչութիւն)
sexagenary - vatsounamia (վաթսունամեայ)
sexennial - vetsamia (վեցամեայ)
sexless - anser (անսեռ)
sextain - vetsiag, vets doghnots doun (վեցեակ, վեց տողնոց տուն)
sexton - lousarar, zhamgoch, merelatagh (լուսարար, ժամկոչ, մեռելաթաղ)
sextuple - vetsadig (վեցպատիկ)
sexual - serayin (սեռային)
sexual harassment - serayin voduntsukoutiun (սեռային ոտնձգութիւն)
sexual organs - serayin kordzaranner (սեռային գործարաններ)
sexuality - seraynoutiun, seraganoutiun (սեռայնութիւն, սեռականութիւն)
sexy - serayin, tsangaharouyts, heshdakurkir (սեռային, ցանկայարոյց, հեշտագրգիռ)
shab - kos, sugurtel, kerel (քոս, սկրթել, քերել)
shabby - tsuntsodi, mashadz, hunamash, punti (ցնցոտի, մաշած, հնամաշ, փնթի)
shackle - shughtayel, gashgantel, gabel, tsernagab (շղթայել, կաշկանդել, կապել, ձեռնակապ)
shade (n) - shouk, hovani, usduver, lousampop, ourvagan (շուք, հովանի, ստուեր, լուսամփոփ, ուրուական)
shade (v) - usduverel, dzadzgel, hovanavorel, mutakunel (ստուերել, ծածկել, հովանաւորել, մթագնել)
shadow - shouk, usduver, hovani, a-

ghod, shouk tsukel (շուք, ստուեր, Հովանի, աղօտ, շուք ձգել)
shadowy, shady - usdverod, aghod, anorosh, mushoushabad (ստուերոտ, աղօտ, անորոշ, մշուշապատ)
shaft - got, tsogh, ned, sulak, pos (կոթ, ձող, նետ, սլաք, փոս)
shag - tav maz, mazod, churakrav (թաւ մազ, մազոտ, ջրագռաւ)
shaggy - mazod, purtod, tav, goshd (մազոտ, բրդոտ, թաւ, կոշտ)
shake (n) - tsuntsoum, turturatsoum, turtir, jeghk, taylayl (ցնցում, թրթռացում, թրթիռ, ճեղք, դայլայլ)
shake (v) - tsuntsel, toghal, totvel, jojel, keghkeghel (ցնցել, դողալ, թօթուել, ճօճել, գեղգեղել)
shaken - see: shake (տե՛ս՝ shake)
shaker - tsuntsogh (ցնցող)
shaky - yereroun, dadanod, angayoun, khakhoud (երերուն, տատանոտ, անկայուն, խախուտ)
shale - badian, geghev, hertsakar, pukhrakar (պատեան, կեղեւ, Հերձաքար, փխրաքար)
shall - bidi, bedk e (պիտի, պէտք է)
shallop - navag, magouyg (նաւակ, մակոյկ)
shallow - dzandzagh, dukhmar, tetevamid, dzandzaghil (ծանծաղ, տխմար, թեթեւամիտ, ծանծաղիլ)
sham - geghdzik, khapeoutiun, khapel, tsevatsunel (կեղծիք, խաբէութիւն, խաբել, ձեւացնել)
shamble - usbantanots, kashkushvil, kedinu kusvil (սպանդանոց, քաշքշուիլ, գետինը քսուիլ)
shame - amot, khaydaragoutiun, amuchtsunel, amuchnal (ամօթ, խայտառակութիւն, ամչցնել, ամչնալ)
shamefaced - amuchgod, amotkhadz, yergchod (ամչկոտ, ամօթխած, երկչոտ)
shameful - amotali, khubnod (ամօթալի, խպնոտ)
shameless - anamot, lirp, anbadgar (անամօթ, լիրբ, անպատկառ)
shammer - khapepa, anamot (խաբեբայ, անամօթ)
shammy - karaydz, karaydzeni (քարայծ, քարայծենի)
shampoo - ojaraheghoug, martsel, shupel, kuloukhu ojarel (օճառաՀեղուկ, մարձել, շփել, գլուխը օճառել)
shampooing - martsoum, shupoum, kulkhou ojaroum (մարձում, շփում, գլխու օճառում)
shank - surounk, surunkosgur, tsoghoun, got (սրունք, սրնքոսկր, ցօղուն, կոթ)
shanty - hiughag, khurjit (Հիւղակ, խրճիթ)
shape (n) - tsev, gerbarank, daraz, gudruvadzk, hadoum (ձեւ, կերպարանք, տարազ, կտրուածք, Հատում)
shape (v) - tsevel, harmartsunel, tsevavorel, hughanal, gurtel (ձեւել, յարմարցնել, ձեւաւորել, յղանալ, կրթել)
shapeless - antsev, dutsev, angerbaran (անձեւ, տձեւ, անկերպարան)
shapely - paregazm, vayelouch, tsevavor, keghetsig (բարեկազմ, վայելուչ, ձեւաւոր, գեղեցիկ)
shard - budougi godurduvank, govou turik, dzerb (պտուկի կոտրտուանք, կովու թրիք, ծերպ)
share - pazhin, mas, pazhnetought, pazhnel, masnagtsil (բաժին, մաս, բաժնեթուղթ, բաժնել, մասնակցիլ)
shareholder - pazhneder (բաժնետէր)
sharer - masnagits, gutsort (մասնակից, կցորդ)
shark - shanatsoug, khapepa (շանաձուկ, խաբեբայ)
sharp - sour, suradzayr, hadou, gudzou, oushim (սուր, սրածայր, Հատու, կծու, ուշիմ)
sharpen - surel, surtsunel, paragnal, kurkurel, suril (սրել, սրցնել, բարակնալ, գրգռել, սրիլ)
sharper - khapepa, turamashort, varbedorti (խաբեբայ, դրամաշորթ, վարպետորդի)

sharpness - suroutiun (սրութիւն)

shatter - khordagel, pushrel, kaykayel, kaykayvil (խորտակել, փշրել, քայքայել, քայքայուիլ)

shave - adzilel, saprel, adzilvil, adziloum, saproum (ածիլել, սափրել, ածիլուիլ, ածիլում, սափրում)

shaver - saprich, adzilogh, vashkharou, geghekich (սափրիչ, ածիլող, վաշխառու, կեղեքիչ)

shaving - adziloum, dashoum (ածիլում, տաշում)

shawl - shal (շալ)

she - an, ink, gin, ek (ան, ինք, կին, էգ)

sheaf - durtsag, khourts, vora, gab, khourts gabel (տրցակ, խուրձ, որայ, կապ, խուրձ կապել)

shear - khouzel, mugradel, huntsel, khouzag, mugrad (խուզել, մկրատել, հնձել, խուզակ, մկրատ)

sheath - badian, dzadzgouyt (պատեան, ծածկոյթ)

sheathe - badianel, badel, dzadzgel (պատեանել, պատել, ծածկել)

sheathing - yeresabadoum (երեսապատում)

shed (n) - dzadzg, kom, muteranots, garadoun, otanavaran (ծածկ, գոմ, մթերանոց, կառատուն, օդանաւարան)

shed (v) - heghoul, tapil, vaztsunel, tapel, artsagel (հեղուլ, թափիլ, վազցնել, թափել, արձակել)

sheen - payl, shogh, paylil, shoghal (փայլ, շող, փայլիլ, շողալ)

sheep - vochkhar, maki, barzamid (ոչխար, մաքի, պարզամիտ)

sheepish - vakhgod, vochkharamid, amuchgod, aboush (վախկոտ, ոչխարամիտ, ամչկոտ, ապուշ)

sheer - husdag, baydzar, barz, tekvil, sheghil, heranal (յստակ, պայծառ, պարզ, թեքուիլ, շեղիլ, հեռանալ)

sheet - savan, tert, dzadzgouyt, dzadzgel, tertadel (սաւան, թերթ, ծածկոյթ, ծածկել, թերթատել)

sheeting - dzadzgots, dzadzg, savantsou gudor (ծածկոց, ծածկ, սաւանցու կտոր)

sheik, sheikh - sheikh, arap tseghabed (շէյխ, արաբ ցեղապետ)

sheld - nakhshoun (նախշուն)

shelf - tarag, kharag, khout, usdorchuria zhayr (դարակ, խարակ, խութ, ստորջրեայ ժայռ)

shell (n) - khetsi, geghev, badian, gujeb, roump, arg (խեցի, կեղեւ, պատեան, կճեպ, ռումբ, արկ)

shell (v) - geghevel, geghevu hanel-iynal, rumpagodzel (կեղեւել, կեղեւը հանել-իյնալ, ռմբակոծել)

shellac, shellack - jenachunarag, chunaragel (ճենաչնարակ, չնարակել)

shellfish - khetsemort (խեցեմորթ)

shelter - badusbaran, abasdanaran, bashdban, abasdanil (պատսպարան, ապաստանարան, պաշտպան, ապաստանիլ)

shelve - taragel, tarag shinel, dzuril, hagil (դարակել, դարակ շինել, ծռիլ, հակիլ)

shend - khankarel, avrel, nakhadel, amuchtsunel (խանգարել, աւրել, նախատել, ամչցնել)

shepherd - hoviv, karozich, kahana, aradzel, hovouel (հովիւ, քարոզիչ, քահանայ, արածել, հովուել)

shepherdess - hovvouhi, keghchgouhi (հովուհի, գեղջկուհի)

sherd - gudor, pegor (կտոր, բեկոր)

sheriff - vosdiganabed, garavarich, kiughabed, adenagal (ոստիկանապետ, կառավարիչ, գիւղապետ, ատենակալ)

shield - vahan, bashdbanoutiun, bashdbanel, badusbarel (վահան, պաշտպանութիւն, պաշտպանել, պատսպարել)

shift (n) - popokhoutiun, degha-sharzh, hert, ganants shabig (փոփոխութիւն, տեղաշարժ, հերթ, կանանց շապիկ)

shift (v) - pokhel, deghapokhel, pokharinel, pokhvil (փոխել, տեղափոխել, փոխարինել, փոխուիլ)

shifter - tartsogh, khoramang, varbedorti, pemu pokhogh (ղարձող, խորամանկ, վարպետորդի, բեմը փոխող)

shifting - popokhoutiun, deghapokhoutiun, pakhousd (փոփոխութիւն, տեղափոխութիւն, փախուստ)

shifty - sharzhoun, popokhamid, jarbig, khapepa (շարժուն, փոփոխամիտ, ճարպիկ, խաբեբայ)

shilling - shilin, ankliagan medaghaturam (շիլին, անգլիական մետաղադրամ)

shimmer - palpuloum, argaydzoum, tsolk, palpulil (փալփլում, առկայծում, ցոլք, փալփլիլ)

shine - paylil, shoghal, payletsunel, payl, shogh (փայլիլ, շողալ, փայլեցնել, փայլ, շող)

shingle - khij, tsoutsanag, parag dakhdag, maz hartarel (խիճ, ցուցանակ, բարակ տախտակ, մազ յարդարել)

shiny - payloun, shoghshoghoun, arevod, baydzar (փայլուն, շողշողուն, արեւոտ, պայծառ)

ship - nav, pernavorel, nav nusdetsunel, oughargel (նաւ, բեռնաւորել, նաւ նստեցնել, ուղարկել)

shipmate - navasdi, navou unger (նաւաստի, նաւու ընկեր)

shipment - arakoum, oughargoum, pernavoroum (առաքում, ուղարկում, բեռնաւորում)

shipped - ghurguvadz, arakvadz, pertsuvadz (ղրկուած, առաքուած, բեռցուած)

shipper - ghurgogh, arakogh, pertsunogh (ղրկող, առաքող, բեռցնող)

shipping - arakoum, navargoutiun, arevduragan navadorm (առաքում, նաւարկութիւն, առեւտրական նաւատորմ)

shipshape - ganonavor, gogig, ganonavoroutiamp (կանոնաւոր, կոկիկ, կանոնաւորութեամբ)

shipwreck - navapegoutiun, khordagoum, navapegel (նաւաբեկութիւն, խորտակում, նաւաբեկել)

shipyard - navashinaran (նաւաշինարան)

ship-master - navabed (նաւապետ)

shire - kavar, nahank, pazhanoum (գաւառ, նահանգ, բաժանում)

shirk - khousapil, pakhousd dal (խուսափիլ, փախուստ տալ)

shirt - shabig, vernashabig (շապիկ, վերնաշապիկ)

shiver - togh, sarsour, toghal, sarsural, toghatsunel (դող, սարսուռ, դողալ, սարսռալ, դողացնել)

shivery - toghtochoun, sarsuroun (դողդոջուն, սարսռուն)

shoal (I) - dzandzaghoud, avazoudk, dzandzaghil, nuvazil (ծանծաղուտ, աւազուտք, ծանծաղիլ, նուազիլ)

shoal (II) - tsugneram, pazmoutiun, khurnuvil, khumpuvil (ձկներամ, բազմութիւն, խռնուիլ, խմբուիլ)

shock (I) - tsuntsoum, zarg, harvadz, tsuntsel, zarnuvil (ցնցում, զարկ, հարուած, ցնցել, զարնուիլ)

shock (II) - khourts, tez, gouyd, tantsur maz, khourtsel (խուրձ, դէզ, կոյտ, թանձր մազ, խուրձել)

shocking - tsuntsogh, sosgali, sarsapeli, houzich (ցնցող, սոսկալի, սարսափելի, յուզիչ)

shoddy - tsadzorag, anbedk, taptupouk, anbedkoutiun (ցածորակ, անպէտք, թափթփուք, անպէտքութիւն)

shoe - goshig, vodnaman, goshig hakvil (կօշիկ, ոտնաման, կօշիկ հագուիլ)

shoe string - goshgagab (կօշկակապ)

shoe-brush - goshigi khozanag (կօշիկի խոզանակ)

shoe-horn - goshgatsik (կօշկաձիգ)

shoe-lace - goshgagab (կօշկակապ)

shoe-maker - goshgagar (կօշկակար)

shoe-making - goshgagaroutiun (կօշկակարութիւն)

shoe-repair - hunagargad, goshig norokogh (հնակարկատ, կօշիկ նորոգող)

shoe-string - goshgagab (կօշկակապ)

shoe-tree - gaghabar goshigi (կաղապար կօշիկի)

shoot (n) - guragots, barboum, hu-

ratsukoutiun, dzil (կրակոց, պարպում, հրաձգութիւն, ծիլ)
shoot (v) - guragel, artsagel, barbel, usbannel (կրակել, արձակել, պարպել, սպաննել)
shooting - huratsukoutiun, nushanaroutiun (հրաձգութիւն, նշանառութիւն)
shooting star - asoub (ասուպ)
shop - khanout, gurbag, kunoum gadarel, kunel (խանութ, կրպակ, գնում կատարել, գնել)
shopkeeper - khanoutban (խանութպան)
shopman - vajarogh, khanoutban (վաճառող, խանութպան)
shopper - kunogh, kunort, hajakhort (գնող, գնորդ, յաճախորդ)
shopping - kunoum (գնում)
shopping mall - vajaradounerou jemavayr (վաճառատուներու ճեմավայր)
shore - dzovap, dzovezur, henaran, netsoug tunel (ծովափ, ծովեզր, յենարան, նեցուկ դնել)
short - garj, hagirj, hamarod, bagas, garj dapad (կարճ, հակիրճ, համառօտ, պակաս, կարճ տաբատ)
short lived - garjagiats, vaghantsig (կարճակեաց, վաղանցիկ)
short sight - garjadesoutiun, anheradesoutiun (կարճատեսութիւն, անհեռատեսութիւն)
short sighted - garjades, anherades (կարճատես, անհեռատես)
short story - garj badmuvadzk (կարճ պատմուածք)
short term - garjadev (կարճատեւ)
short wave - garjalik (կարճալիք)
shortage - sagavoutiun, garik, anpavararoutiun (սակաւութիւն, կարիք, անբաւարարութիւն)
shortcoming - bagasoutiun, teroutiun (պակասութիւն, թերութիւն)
shorten - garjetsunel, garjunal (կարճեցնել, կարճնալ)
shortener - garjetsunogh (կարճեցնող)
shorthand - sughakuroutiun, arakakuroutiun, sughakurel (սղագրութիւն, արագագրութիւն, սղագրել)
shortly - shoudov, kich adenen, hagirj (շուտով, քիչ ատենէն, հակիրճ)
shortness - garjoutiun (կարճութիւն)
short-cut - garj jampa (կարճ ճամբայ)
shot - zargav, roump, artsagoum, harvadz, surusgoum (զարկաւ, ռումբ, յարձակում, հարուած, սրսկում)
shotgun - huratsan (հրացան)
should - bidi, bedk e, anhurazheshd e, bardim (պիտի, պէտք է, անհրաժեշտ է, պարտիմ)
shoulder - ous, tigounk, jampezur, shalgel, ousu arnel (ուս, թիկունք, ճամբեզր, շալկել, ուսը առնել)
shout - juchal, aghaghagel, dzapaharel, jich, aghaghag (ճչալ, աղաղակել, ծափահարել, ճիչ, աղաղակ)
shove - hurel, mushdel, mughel, hurmushdouk (հրել, մշտել, մղել, հրմշտուք)
shovel - ti, tiag, tiov havakel-nedel-makrel (թի, թիակ, թիով հաւաքել–նետել–մաքրել)
show (n) - tsouyts, tsoutsaturoutiun, hantes, yerevouyt (ցոյց, ցուցադրութիւն, հանդէս, երեւոյթ)
show (v) - tsoutsaturel, nergayatsunel, haydnel (ցուցադրել, ներկայացնել, յայտնել)
showcard - tsoutsakard, aztakard (ցուցաքարտ, ազդաքարտ)
showcase - tsoutsapeghg, tsutsapeghgel (ցուցափեղկ, ցուցափեղկել)
shower - deghadarap, lokank, deghal, deghatsunel (տեղատարափ, լոգանք, տեղալ, տեղացնել)
showing - tsouyts, tsoutsmounk, yerevouyt (ցոյց, ցուցմունք, երեւոյթ)
showroom - tsoutsasurah (ցուցասրահ)
showtime - hantisazham (հանդիսաժամ)
showy - payloun, tsoutsaser (փայլուն, ցուցասէր)

show-case - tsoutsanag, tsoutsasundoug, vajarataran (ցուցանակ, ցուցասնտուկ, վաճառադարան)
shred - gudor, badar, sherd, gudurdel, puzugdel (կտոր, պատառ, շերտ, կտրտել, բզկտել)
shrew - gurvaser gin, chadoug, anidzel, hayhoyel (կռուասէր կին, ճատուկ, անիծել, հայհոյել)
shrewd - suramid, artnamid, jarbig, varbed, anuzkam (սրամիտ, արթնամիտ, ճարպիկ, վարպետ, անըզգամ)
shrewish - gurvaser, sasdogh, tek (կռուասէր, սաստող, դեգ)
shrick - juchal, boral, jich, aghaghag (ճչալ, պոռալ, ճիչ, աղաղակ)
shrift - khosdovanank (խոստովանանք)
shrike - gachaghag (կաչաղակ)
shrill - zil, sour jich, juchal, soulel, mukhel (զիլ, սուր ճիչ, ճչալ, սուլել, մխել)
shrimp - dzovamarakh, garidos (ծովամարախ, կարիտոս)
shrine - masounkadoup, surparan, khoran (մասունքատուփ, սրբարան, խորան
shrink - gudzgil, ampopvil, ungurgil, gudzgoum, angoum (կծկիլ, ամփոփուիլ, ընկրկիլ, կծկում, անկում)
shrive - khosdovanil, khosdovanetsunel (խոստովանիլ, խոստովանեցնել)
shrivel - gudzguvil, khorshomil, choranal, gudzgil (կծկուիլ, խորշոմիլ, չորանալ, կծկիլ)
shroud - dzadzgouyt, badank, badankel, kotsel, dzadzgel (ծածկոյթ, պատանք, պատանքել, գոցել, ծածկել)
shrub - toup, dzarig, oghekharun osharag (թուփ, ծառիկ, ողեխառն օշարակ)
shrubbery - tavoud, andarag, tupoud (թաւուտ, անտառակ, թփուտ)
shrubby - tupalits, tupoudabad, tupayin (թփալից, թփուտապատ, թփային)
shrug - ous totvel, duhajil, totvoum (ուս թօթուել, տհաճիլ, թօթւում
shuck - ungouyzi geghev, geghvel (ընկոյզի կեղեւ, կեղուել)
shudder - sarsour, togh, sarsural, toghal, tsuntsuvil (սարսուռ, դող, սարսռալ, դողալ, ցնցուիլ)
shuffle (n) - kashgurdouk, kharnoum, hunark, khagh (քաշկռտուք, խառնում, հնարք, խաղ)
shuffle (v) - kharnel, kharnushdugel, khapel, nenkel (խառնել, խառնշտկել, խաբել, նենգել)
shun - khousapil, kashvil, pakhchil (խուսափիլ, քաշուիլ, փախչիլ)
shut - kotsel, pagel, kotsvil, pagoum, pagvadz, kots (գոցել, փակել, գոցուիլ, փակում, փակուած, գոց)
shutt off - nakhazkal, arkilel, gasetsunel, kotsel (նախազգալ, արգիլել, կասեցնել, գոցել)
shutter - kotsogh, pagogh, peghg, gaparich (գոցող, փակող, փեղկ, կափարիչ)
shuttle - gugots, makok, pokhatragark (կկոց, մաքոք, փոխադրակառք)
shy - vakhgod, yergchod, uzkoushavor (վախկոտ, երկչոտ, զգուշաւոր)
sibyl - koushagouhi, vuhoug gin (գուշակուհի, վհուկ կին)
sick - hivant, dugar (հիւանդ, տկար)
sicken - hivantanal, hivantatsunel, zuzvetsunel (հիւանդանալ, հիւանդացնել, զզուեցնել)
sickish - hivantod, noghgali (հիւանդոտ, նողկալի)
sickle - mankagh (մանգաղ)
sickly - hivantod, vadaroghch, akhdavor (հիւանդոտ, վատառողջ, ախտաւոր)
sickness - hivantoutiun, sirdkharnouk (հիւանդութիւն, սիրտխառնուք)
side - goghm, gogh, yezur, gousagtsoutiun, haril (կողմ, կող, եզր, կուսակցութիւն, յարիլ)
sider - goghmunagits, gousagits (կողմնակից, կուսակից)
sidewalk - mayt (մայթ)
sideways - goghmunagi, sheghagi,

dzour (կողմնակի, շեղակի, ծուռ)
sidewise - goghmunagi (կողմնակի)
sidle - goghmunagi, kovundi yertal (կողմնակի, քովնտի երթալ)
siege - basharoum, getronadeghi (պաշարում, կեդրոնատեղի)
siesta - murap, tseregi koun, divantor (մրափ, ցերեկի քուն, տիւանդորր)
sieve - magh, maghel (մաղ, մաղել)
sift - maghel, maghe antsunel, kunnel, zadel (մաղել, մաղէ անցնել, քննել, զատել)
sigh - harach, harachank, harachel, voghpal (հառաչ, հառաչանք, հառաչել, ողբալ)
sight - desoghoutiun, desk, desaran, achk, desnel (տեսողութիւն, տեսք, տեսարան, աչք, տեսնել)
sightless - gouyr, achazourg, andesaneli (կոյր, աչազուրկ, անտեսանելի)
sightline - goghmani louys, badahagan lour (կողմնակի լոյս, պատահական լուր)
sightly - deskov, keghetsig, desnelik (տեսքով, գեղեցիկ, տեսնելիք)
sigil - turoshm, gunik (դրոշմ, կնիք)
sign (n) - nushan, tsoutsanag, tsoutsadakhdag, desanushan (նշան, ցուցանակ, ցուցատախտակ, տեսանշան)
sign (v) - usdorakurel, vaveratsunel, turoshmel (ստորագրել, վաւերացնել, դրոշմել)
signal - nushan, aztanushan, yereveli, nushan dal (նշան, ազդանշան, երեւելի, նշան տալ)
signalize - nushel, madnanushel, nushanavorel (նշել, մատնանշել, նշանաւորել)
signatory - usdorakurogh (ստորագրող)
signature - usdorakuroutiun, nushan, gunik, turoshm (ստորագրութիւն, նշան, կնիք, դրոշմ)
signer - usdorakurogh (ստորագրող)
significance - nushanagoutiun, garevoroutiun (նշանակութիւն, կարեւորութիւն)
significant - nushanagalits, garevor nushanagali (նշանակալից, կարեւոր, նշանակալի)
signification - nushanagoutiun, midk, imasd (նշանակութիւն, միտք, իմաստ)
significator - nushanagogh (նշանակող)
signify - nushanagel, haydnel, nushel (նշանակել, յայտնել, նշել)
signor - baron, diar, der (պարոն, տիար, տէր)
silence (n) - luroutiun, hantardoutiun, hamroutiun (լռութիւն, հանդարտութիւն, համրութիւն)
silence (v) - luretsunel, hantardetsunel, hankusdatsunel (լռեցնել, հանդարտեցնել, հանգստացնել)
silent - lour, ankhos, antsayn, hantard, hamur (լուռ, անխօս, անձայն, հանդարտ, համր)
silex - gaydzkar (կայծքար)
silhouette - timasduver, usduverakidz (դիմաստուեր, ստուերագիծ)
silk - medaks, medakse (մետաքս, մետաքսէ)
silken - medaksia, medaksanuman (մետաքսեայ, մետաքսանման)
silkworm - sheram (շերամ)
sill - shem, hetsoug badouhani (շեմ, յեցուկ՝ պատուհանի)
silliness - aboushoutiun, ankhelkoutiun (ապուշութիւն, անխելքութիւն)
silly - aboush, himar, anmid (ապուշ, յիմար, անմիտ)
silt - dighm, murour, digh letsunel (տիղմ, մրուր, տիղմ լեցնել)
silva, sylva - andar, andarapanoutiun (անտառ, անտառաբանութիւն)
silvan, sylvan - andarayin, andaroud (անտառային, անտառուտ)
silver - ardzat, ardzate, ardzatia, ardzatazodzel (արծաթ, արծաթէ, արծաթեայ, արծաթազօծել)
silvern - ardzatia (արծաթեայ)
silversmith - ardzatakordz, vosgerich (արծաթագործ, ոսկերիչ)
silvery - ardzatia, payloun, jermag

(արծաթեայ, փայլուն, ճերմակ)
similar - numan, hamanuman, numanorinag (նման, համանման, նմանօրինակ)
similarity - numanoutiun, nouynoutiun (նմանութիւն, նոյնութիւն)
similarly - numanabes, nouyn tsevov (նմանապէս, նոյն ձեւով)
simile - numanapanoutiun, hamemadoutiun (նմանաբանութիւն, համեմատութիւն)
similitude - numanoutiun (նմանութիւն)
simmer - meghm yeral, bujbujal (մեղմ եռալ, պճպճալ
simper - kumdzidzaghil, inknakoh zhubdil, kumdzidzagh (քմծիծաղիլ, ինքնագոհ ժպտիլ, քմծիծաղ)
simple - barz, hasarag, anbajouyj, anzart, darragan (պարզ, հասարակ, անպաճոյճ, անզարդ, տարրական)
simplicity - barzoutiun, barzamudoutiun, angeghdzoutiun (պարզութիւն, պարզամտութիւն, անկեղծութիւն)
simplification - barzoum, tiuratsoum (պարզում, դիւրացում)
simplify - barzetsunel, barzapanel, tiuratsunel (պարզեցնել, պարզաբանել, դիւրացնել)
simply - barzabes, barzoren, voroshabes, aboushapar (պարզապէս, պարզօրէն, որոշապէս, ապուշաբար)
simulant - tsevatsunogh, geghdzogh (ձեւացնող, կեղծող)
simulate - tsevatsunel, geghdzel (ձեւացնել, կեղծել)
simulation - tsevatsunoum, geghdzoum, gabgoum (ձեւացնում, կեղծում, կապկում)
simultaneous - miazhamanag, nouynazham, hamateb (միաժամանակ, նոյնաժամ, համադէպ)
sin - meghk, meghanchoum, meghk kordzel, meghanchel (մեղք, մեղանչում, մեղք գործել, մեղանչել)
since - usgusial, i ver, kani vor, usd voroum (սկսեալ, ի վեր, քանի որ, ըստ որում)
sincere - angeghdz, surdapats, ankhartakh, annenk (անկեղծ, սրտաբաց, անխարդախ, աննենգ)
sincerity - angeghdzoutiun (անկեղծութիւն)
sinew - chigh, neart, mugan, chughabuntel, zoratsunel (ջիղ, նեարդ, մկան, ջղապնդել, զօրացնել)
sinewy - chughayin, chughoud, gorovi (ջղային, ջղուտ, կորովի)
sinful - meghavor, meghsali, hantsavor (մեղաւոր, մեղսալի, յանցաւոր)
sing - yerkel, nuvakel, saghmosel, taylaylel (երգել, նուագել, սաղմոսել, դայլայլել)
singe - khandzel, tetevoren ayrel, khandzuvadzk (խանձել, թեթեւօրէն այրել, խանձուածք)
singer - yerkich, yerkchouhi (երգիչ, երգչուհի)
singing - yerketsoghoutiun, yerleku, yerk (երգեցողութիւն, երգելը, երգ)
single - miag, amouri, arantsin, zadel, undurel (միակ, ամուրի, առանձին, զատել, ընտրել)
singleness - minagoutiun, amourioutiun (մինակութիւն, ամուրիութիւն)
single-handed - minag, anoknagan, miatser (մինակ, անօգնական, միաձեռ)
single-hearted - angeghdz, shidag, bargeshd, havadarim (անկեղծ, շիտակ, պարկեշտ, հաւատարիմ)
single-minded - oughghamid, nubadagasulats (ուղղամիտ, նպատակասլաց)
singly - anhadapar, arantsin, meg-meg (անհատաբար, առանձին, մէկ-մէկ)
singular - yezagi, arantsin, ansovor, nororinag (եզակի, առանձին, անսովոր, նորօրինակ)
singularity - yezagioutiun, arantsnahadgoutiun (եզակիութիւն, առանձնայատկութիւն)
singularly - yezagioren, medzabes, patsarig gerbov (եզակիօրէն, մեծապէս, բացառիկ կերպով)

sinister - tsakhogh, charashouk, aghidaper, charakoushag (ձախող, չարաշուք, աղիտաբեր, չարագուշակ)
sink (n) - goyoughi, dzoranots, luvatsaran, agan (կոյուղի, ծորանոց, լուացարան, ական)
sink (v) - souzel, souzvil, ungughmel, ungughmil, ichnel (սուզել, սուզուիլ, ընկղմել, ընկղմիլ, իջնել)
sinless - anmegh (անմեղ)
sinner - meghavor, meghanchogh (մեղաւոր, մեղանչող)
sinuate - volorel, tekel, dzamadzurel (ոլորել, թեքել, ծամածռել)
sinus - khorsh, khoroch, dzag, dzots (խորշ, խոռոչ, ծակ, ծոց)
sip - oumb, boud, shit, umbel, dzudzel (ումպ, պուտ, շիթ, ըմպել, ծծել)
siphon, syphon - dzudzapogh, sipon, siponov heghoug barbel (ծծափող, սիփոն, սիփոնով հեղուկ պարպել)
sir - baron, diar (պարոն, տիար)
sire - der arka, vehapar der, der im, arou gentani (տէր արքայ, վեհափառ տէր, տէր իմ, արու կենդանի)
siren - dzovahars, houshabarig, kuravich gin (ծովահարս, յուշապարիկ, գրաւիչ կին)
sirocco - khorshag, chor dak kami (խորշակ, չոր տաք քամի)
sirup, syrup - osharag, roub (օշարակ, ռուպ)
siss - soulel, souyl (սուլել, սոյլ)
sister - kouyr, mayrabed, guronouhi (քոյր, մայրապետ, կրօնուհի)
sisterhood - mayrabedoutiun, kouyroutiun (մայրապետութիւն, քոյրութիւն)
sisterly - kouyragan, kouyranuman (քոյրական, քոյրանման)
sister-in-law - keni, dal, ner (քենի, տալ, ներ)
sit - nusdil, pazmil, munal, taril, nusdetsunel (նստիլ, բազմիլ, մնալ, թառիլ, նստեցնել)
site - tirk, vayr, degh, deghamas, deghavorel (դիրք, վայր, տեղ, տեղամաս, տեղաւորել)
sithe - keranti, medz mankagh (գերանդի, մեծ մանգաղ)
sitter - nusdogh (նստող)
sitting - nusdatsouyts, nusdashurchan, nisd, nusdaran (նստացոյց, նստաշրջան, նիստ, նստարան)
sittin-groom - nusdaseniag (նստասենեակ)
situate - deghavorel, zedeghel (տեղաւորել, զետեղել)
situated - deghavorvadz, zedeghvadz, hasdadvadz (տեղաւորուած, զետեղուած, հաստատուած)
situation - tirk, bashdon, gatsoutiun, degh, vijag (դիրք, պաշտօն, կացութիւն, տեղ, վիճակ)
situationer - deghegakurogh, megnapanogh (տեղեկագրող, մեկնաբանող)
six - vets (վեց)
sixteen - dasunvets (տասնվեց)
sixteenth - dasunvetserort (տասնվեցերորդ)
sixtieth - vatsounerort (վաթսուներորդ)
sixty - vatsoun (վաթսուն)
size - chap, medzoutiun, sosints, chapel, sosuntsel (չափ, մեծութիւն, սոսինձ, չափել, սոսնձել)
sizing - sosuntsoum, sosints, chaparoutiun (սոսնձում, սոսինձ, չափառութիւն)
sizy - gubchoun, madzoutsig (կպչուն, մածուցիկ)
sizzle - soulel, shuchel, souyl (սուլել, շչել, սոյլ)
sizzling - soulots dabgotsi (սուլոց տապկոցի)
skacken - tantaghil, toulnal, meghmanal, toultsunel (դանդաղիլ, թուլնալ, մեղմանալ, թուլցնել)
skacker - kordze pakhchogh (գործէ փախչող)
skate (I) - sahnag, chumoushg, chumushgel, chumoushgov sahil (սահնակ, չմուշկ, չմշկել, չմուշկով սահիլ)

skate (II) - khaghakoumar, kurav, kuravi tunel, vudankel (խաղագումար, գրաւ, գրաւի դնել, վտանգել)
skater - keghasahort, chumushgogh (գեղասահորդ, չմշկող)
skating - keghasahk, chumoushgasahk, barasahk (գեղասահք, չմուշկասահք, պարասահք)
skating ring - sahatashd (սահադաշտ)
skeleton - gumakhk, vosgurodi (կմախք, ոսկրոտի)
skeptic - usgebdig, gasgadzod, daragousogh (սկեպտիկ, կասկածոտ, տարակուսող)
skepticism - gasgadzamudoutiun, terahavadoutiun (կասկածամտութիւն, թերահաւատութիւն)
sketch - ourvakidz, nakhakidz, dzurakir, ourvakudzel (ուրուագիծ, նախագիծ, ծրագիր, ուրուագծել)
sketchy - ourvakudzayin, mageresayin, gutsgudour (ուրուագծային, մակերեսային, կցկտուր)
skew - shegh, goghmunagi, khodor (շեղ, կողմնակի, խոտոր)
skewer - shampour, shampurel, shishu antsunel (շամփուր, շամփրել, շիշը անցնել)
ski - tahoug, tahougel (դահուկ, դահուկել)
skid - arkelag, arkelagel, sahil (արգելակ, արգելակել, սահիլ)
skier - tahougort (դահուկորդ)
skiff - magouyg, murtsamagouyg, tetev navag (մակոյկ, մրցամակոյկ, թեթեւ նաւակ)
skilful - jarbig, jardar, varbed, khelatsi, humoud (ճարպիկ, ճարտար, վարպետ, խելացի, հմուտ)
skill - varbedoutiun, humdoutiun, garoghoutiun, khelk (վարպետութիւն, հմտութիւն, կարողութիւն, խելք)
skilled - garogh, humoud, jarbig, voragavor (կարող, հմուտ, ճարպիկ, որակաւոր)
skim - purpurahanel, gatin seru arnel, seradel (փրփրահանել, կաթին սերը առնել, սերատել)
skimmilk - anser gat (անսեր կաթ)
skimming - purpuroum, purpurakaghoum, sahoum (փրփրում, փրփրաքաղում, սահում)
skimp - gurjadel, bagsetsunel, vad madagararel (կրճատել, պակսեցնել, վատ մատակարարել)
skin - mort, gashi, mashg, kertel, mortu hanel, shortel (մորթ, կաշի, մաշկ, քերթել, մորթը հանել, շորթել)
skip - vosdoum, tsadgoum, vosdosdel, tsadgurdel (ոստում, ցատկում, ոստոստել, ցատկոտել)
skipper - tsadgurdogh, barogh, navabed, khumpabed (ցատկոտող, պարող, նաւապետ, խմբապետ)
skirl - jich, juchal (ճիչ, ճչալ)
skirmish - tetev baderazm, pokur jagadamard (թեթեւ պատերազմ, փոքր ճակատամարտ)
skirr - jurinch, jurunchiun, jurunchel (ճռինչ, ճռնչիւն, ճռնչել)
skirt (n) - kughantsk, pesh, shurchazkesd, lousantsk, vudavag (քղանցք, փէշ, շրջազգեստ, լուսանցք, վտաւակ)
skirt (v) - yezerel, shurchabadel, sahmanu punagil, badel (եզերել, շրջապատել, սահմանը բնակիլ, պատել)
skit - heknank, dzaghur, gadag (հեգնանք, ծաղր, կատակ)
skittish - zhir, ashkouyzh, gamaser, khurdchogh-tsi (ժիր, աշխոյժ, կամասէր, խրտչող-ձի)
skive - kerel, hartel gashin (քերել, հարթել՝ կաշիլ)
skiwear - tsiunahakousd, sahnagadaraz (ձիւնահագուստ, սահնակատարազ)
skulk - bahvudil, taknuvil, sulukdal, kordze pakhchil (պահուըտիլ, թաքնուիլ, սլքտալ, գործէ փախչիլ)
skull - kang, kulkhosgur (գանկ, գլխոսկր)
sky - yergink, ot, yergnagamar (երկինք, օդ, երկնակամար)
skyblue - yergunakouyn, lazour (երկնագոյն, լազուր)

skygazer - yerazagan, tsunoramid (երազական, ցնորամիտ)
skylark - ardouyd (արտոյտ)
skylight - lousamoud (լուսամուտ)
skyline - horizon (Հորիզոն)
sky-scraper - yergnaker, partsuraperts shenk (երկնաքեր, բարձրաբերձ շէնք)
slab - salakar, titegh, sherdel, gudrel (սալաքար, թիթեղ, շերտել, կտրել)
slack - touyl, dzouyl, hamur, tantagh, adzkhaposhi (թոյլ, ծոյլ, յամր, դանդաղ, ածխափոշի)
slacken - tantaghil, toulnal, meghmanal, toultsunel (դանդաղիլ, թուլնալ, մեղմանալ, թուլցնել)
slake - maretsunel, meghmatsunel, maril, meghmanal (մարեցնել, մեղմացնել, մարիլ մեղմանալ)
slalom - voloravayrechk (ոլորավայրէջք)
slam - aghmougov kotsel touru, zarnel, shukhgots, sharach (աղմուկով գոցել դուռը, զարնել, շխկոց, շառաչ)
slander - pampasank, pampasel, zurbardel (բամբասանք, բամբասել, զրպարտել)
slang - ramig lezou, ramgakhosoutiun, dzaghrel (ռամիկ լեզու, ռամկախօսութիւն, ծաղրել)
slant - tekoum, tekoutiun, shegh, tekil, dzuril, hagil (թեքում, թեքութիւն, շեղ, թեքիլ, ծռիլ, Հակիլ)
slap - abdag, harvadz, abdagel (ապտակ, Հարուած, ապտակել)
slapper - abdagogh (ապտակող)
slash - gudurvadzk, gudradel, kinu godrel, mugradel (կտրուածք, կտրատել, գինը կոտրել, մկրատել)
slat - parag tsogh, dzedzel, zarnel (բարակ ձող, ծեծել, զարնել)
slate - hertsakar, hertsakarel, dzadzgel (Հերձաքար, Հերձաքարել, ծածկել)
slattern - aghdod, taptupadz gin (աղտոտ, թափթփած կին)
slaughter house - usbantanots (սպանդանոց)
slaughterer - mortogh, chartarar (մորթող, ջարդարար)
slauther - usbant, chart, chartel, mortel, usbannel (սպանդ, ջարդ, ջարդել, մորթել, սպաննել)
slav, sclav - uslav, uslaveren, uslavagan (սլաւ, սլաւերէն, սլաւական)
slave - usduroug, keri, dzara, charachar ashkhadil (ստրուկ, գերի, ծառայ, չարաչար աշխատիլ)
slaver - lortsounk, kerevajar, lortsnodil, lortsnodel (լորձունք, գերեվաճառ, լորձնոտիլ, լորձնոտել)
slavery - keroutiun (գերութիւն)
slave-trade - kerevajaroutiun (գերեվաճառութիւն)
slay - godorel, chartel, mortel, usbannel (կոտորել, ջարդել, մորթել, սպաննել)
sledge - guran, dzanur mourj (կռան, ծանր մուրճ)
sleek - voghorg, payloun-maz, hartel, gogel (ողորկ, փայլուն-մազ, Հարթել, կոկել)
sleep - kunanal, nunchel, hankchil, koun, ninch (քնանալ, ննջել, Հանգչիլ, քուն, նինջ)
sleeper - kunatsogh, nunchogh, dzouyl (քնացող, ննջող, ծոյլ)
sleepful - kunod (քնոտ)
sleepiness - kunodoutiun (քնոտութիւն)
sleeping - kunatsadz, kunatsogh, koun (քնացած, քնացող, քուն)
sleeping bag - gunabarg (քնապարկ)
sleeping car - nunchagark (ննջակառք)
sleepless - ankoun, artoun (անքուն, արթուն)
sleepwalker - kunashurchig, lousnod (քնաշրջիկ, լուսնոտ)
sleepwear - kisheranots, kisherahakousd (գիշերանոց, գիշերաՀագուստ)
sleepy - kunod, kunatatakh, kunaper (քնոտ, քնաթաթախ, քնաբեր)
sleet - tsiunakharun antsurev, manragargoud (ձիւնախառն անձրեւ, մանրակարկուտ)
sleeve - tezanik, uzkesdi tev (թե-

զանիք, զգեստի թեւ)
sleigh - sahnag, sahnagov yertal (սահնակ, սահնակով երթալ)
sleight - jarbigoutiun, ajbararoutiun (ճարպիկութիւն, աճպարարութիւն)
sleight of hand - tserki jarbigoutiun, tsernadzoutiun (ձեռքի ճարպիկութիւն, ձեռնածութիւն)
slender - nourp, parag, jugoun, paregazm, nazeli (նուրբ, բարակ, ճկուն, բարեկազմ, նազելի)
slice - sherd, badar, pazhin, sherdel, manrel (շերտ, պատառ, բաժին, շերտել, մանրել)
slide - sahatashd (սահադաշտ)
slide (n) - sahank, sahoum, sahatashd, abagebadger (սահանք, սահում, սահադաշտ, ապակեպատկեր)
slide (v) - sahil, sahetsunel, chumushgil, soghosgil (սահիլ, սահեցնել, չմշկիլ, սողոսկիլ)
sliding - sahoun, sahoug (սահուն, սահուկ)
sliding door - sahatour (սահադուռ)
slight - arhamarhel, arhamarhank, tetev, chunchin (արհամարհել, արհամարհանք, թեթեւ, չնչին)
slim - paregazm, nihar, nourp, tetev, khoramang (բարեկազմ, նիհար, նուրբ, թեթեւ, խորամանկ)
slime - dighm, goubur, tsekhodel (տիղմ, կուպր, ցեխոտել)
slimsy - tetev, dugar, touyl, khakhoud, antimatsgoun (թեթեւ, տկար, թոյլ, խախուտ, անդիմացկուն)
slimy - tsekhod, dughmod, luburdzoun (ցեխոտ, տղմոտ, լպրծուն)
sling - barsadig, lanchakodi, barsadigel, nedel, gakhel (պարսատիկ, լանջագոտի, պարսատիկել, նետել, կախել)
slink - kashvil, pakhchil, gudzgudil (քաշուիլ, փախչիլ, կծկտիլ)
slip (n) - sahoum, vuriboum, gudron, nerknazkesd - ganatsi (սահում, վրիպում, կտրօն, ներքնազգեստ՝ կանացի)
slip (v) - sahil, sahetsunel, saytakil, vizhil (սահիլ, սահեցնել, սայթաքիլ, վիժիլ)
slipper - hoghatap, moujag, arkelag (հողաթափ, մուճակ, արգելակ)
slippery - sahoun, voghorg, luburdzoun, touylperan (սահուն, ողորկ, լպրծուն, թոյլբերան)
slit - jeghkel, sherdel, jeghk (ճեղքել, շերտել, ճեղք)
slogan - mardagoch, nushanapan, hangerk (մարտակոչ, նշանաբան, յանկերգ)
slop - dighm, churagouyd, kisheranots, tapel, heghoul (տիղմ, ջրակոյտ, գիշերանոց, թափել, հեղուլ)
slope - zarivar, sheghoum, sheghetsunel, sheghil, dzuril (զառիվար, շեղում, շեղեցնել, շեղիլ, ծռիլ)
slot - agos, antsk, girj, dzag (ակօս, անցք, կիրճ, ծակ)
sloth - dzouloutiun, tantaghoutiun, hamroug (ծուլութիւն, դանդաղութիւն, յամրուկ)
slothful - dzouyl, hamrasharzh, tantaghgod (ծոյլ, յամրաշարժ, դանդաղկոտ)
slouch - anshunorh kalvadzk, taptupadz, anpouyt kalel (անշնորհ քալուածք, թափթփած, անփոյթ քալել)
slough (I) - jahij, jakhjakhoud, ungjuvadzoutiun (ճահիճ, ճախճախուտ, ընկճուածութիւն)
slough (II) - shabig-otsi, geghev -verki, shabig pokhel (շապիկ-օձի, կեղեւ-վէրքի, շապիկ փոխել)
slovak - uslovak, uslovakeren, uslovakian (սլովաք, սլովաքերէն, սլովաքեան)
sloven - punti, taptupadz, aghdod (փնթի, թափթփած, աղտոտ)
slow - tantagh, gamats, tantaghetsunel, oushatsunel (դանդաղ, կամաց, դանդաղեցնել, ուշացնել)
slow coach - putamid, tantsuramid, tantaghgod (բթամիտ, թանձրամիտ, դանդաղկոտ)
slowly - tantaghoren, gamats gamats (դանդաղօրէն, կամաց կամաց)
slowness - tantaghoutiun, dzanrasharzhoutiun (դանդաղութիւն,

ծանրաշարժութիւն)

sludge - tsegh, sarnagoutd (ցեխ, սառնակոյտ)

sludgy - tsekhod (ցեխոտ)

slug (I) - tantagh, dzouyl, tadargabord, khukhounch (դանդաղ, ծոյլ, դատարկապորտ, խխունջ)

slug (II) - purountski harvadz, huratsani kuntag, dzedzel (բռունցքի հարուած, հրացանի գնդակ, ծեծել)

sluggish - anhok, anpouyt, dzouyl, tantagh, ankordz (անհոգ, անփոյթ, ծոյլ, դանդաղ, անգործ)

sluice - sahank, churampar, hortsank, voghoghel, vorokel (սահանք, ջրամբար, յորձանք, ողողել, ոռոգել)

slum - usdorin taghamas, aghdod kaghakamas (ստորին թաղամաս, աղտոտ քաղաքամաս)

slumber - murap, tetev koun, murapel, tumril, kunanal (մրափ, թեթեւ քուն, մրափել, թմրիլ, քնանալ)

slumberer - murapogh, nirhogh (մրափող, նիրհող)

slur (n) - pidz, arad, aghd, meghaturank, khazi gab (բիծ, արատ, աղտ, մեղադրանք, խազի կապ)

slur (v) - aghdodel, khaydaragel, murodel, khazeru gutsel (աղտոտել, խայտառակել, մրոտել, խազերը կցել)

slush - churadighm, tsekh, haladz tsiun, jarb, jarbodel (ջրատիղմ, ցեխ, հալած ձիւն, ճարպ, ճարպոտել)

slushy - dughmod, tsekhod (տղմոտ, ցեխոտ)

slut - taptupadz gin, anbidan aghchig (թափթփած կին, անպիտան աղջիկ)

sluttish - taptupadz, punti, anhok, shulukhdi (թափթփած, փնթի, անհոգ, շլխտի)

sly - khoramang, charamid, sadana (խորամանկ, չարամիտ, սատանայ)

smack (n) - ham, hod, sharach, abdag, medzatsayn hampouyr (համ, հոտ, շառաչ, ապտակ, մեծաձայն համբոյր)

smack (v) - ham arnel-dal, pourel, abdagel, bachel (համ առնել–տալ, բուրել, ապտակել, պաչել)

small - buzdig, pokur, manur, kich, annushan (պզտիկ, փոքր, մանր, քիչ, աննշան)

smallpox - dzaghgagakhd (ծաղկախտ)

smarm - shoghokortel (շողոքորթել)

smarmy - shoghokortogh (շողոքորթող)

smart (n) - gusgidz, vishd, yerantoun, suramid, shukegh (կսկիծ, վիշտ, եռանդուն, սրամիտ, շքեղ)

smart (v) - gusgudzal, vushdanal, tsavil (կսկծալ, վշտանալ, ցաւիլ)

smarten - bujnuvil, zartarvil, payletsunel (պճնուիլ, զարդարուիլ, փայլեցնել)

smartness - vayelchoutiun, shukeghoutiun, ashkhouzh (վայելչութիւն, շքեղութիւն, աշխոյժ)

smash (n) - pushroum, khordagoum, aghed, sunangoutiun (փշրում, խորտակում, աղէտ, սնանկութիւն)

smash (v) - pushrel, chakhchakhel, chartel, sunanganal (փշրել, ջախջախել, ջարդել, սնանկանալ)

smatter - shaghaguradel, dukidoren khosil, ges kidag (շաղակրատել, տգիտօրէն խօսիլ, կէս գիտակ)

smatterer - imasdag, ges kidoun (իմաստակ, կէս գիտուն)

smear - arad, geghd, pidz, dzepel, kusel, aghdodel (արատ, կեղտ, բիծ, ծեփել, քսել, աղտոտել)

smell (n) - hodaroutiun, hododelik, hod, pourmounk (հոտառութիւն, հոտոտելիք, հոտ, բուրմունք)

smell (v) - hododel, hodvudal, pourel, hodil (հոտոտել, հոտուըտալ, բուրել, հոտիլ)

smeller - hodvudatsogh, hod arnogh (հոտուըտացող, հոտ առնող)

smelling - hodaroutiun, kit, hododelik (հոտառութիւն, քիթ, հոտոտելիք)

smelly - karshahod, hodadz (գարշահոտ, հոտած)

smelt - halel, haletsunel, manisha-

tsoug (հալել, հալեցնել, մանիշաձուկ)
smeltery - *tsoularan, halotsaran* (ձուլարան, հալոցարան)
smile - *zhubid, kumdzidzagh, zhubdil, khuntal, dzidzaghil* (ժպիտ, քմծիծաղ, ժպտիլ, խնդալ, ծիծաղիլ)
smirch - *geghd, arad, pidz, aghdodel, aradavorel* (կեղտ, արատ, բիծ, աղտոտել, արատաւորել)
smite - *zarnel, khupel, abdagel, mertsunel, zarnuvil* (զարնել, խփել, ապտակել, մեռցնել, զարնուիլ)
smith - *tarpin, yergatakordz, medaghakordz* (դարբին, երկաթագործ, մետաղագործ)
smithy - *tarpunots, hunots* (դարբնոց, հնոց)
smock - *pajgonag, ganats shabig, dzalkavorel* (բաճկոնակ, կանաց շապիկ, ծալքաւորել)
smog - *dzukhadzadzgouyt, mushoushakharun dzoukh* (ծխածածկոյթ, մշուշախառն ծուխ)
smoke - *moukh, dzoukh, dzukhakhod, dzukhel, mukhal* (մուխ, ծուխ, ծխախոտ, ծխել, մխալ)
smoker - *dzukhogh* (ծխող)
smoky - *dzukhalits, mukhatsogh, murodadz* (ծխալից, մխացող, մրոտած)
smolder, smoulder - *mukhalov ayril, anpots varil* (մխալով այրիլ, անբոց վառիլ)
smooth - *voghorg, hart, tiurahos, voghorgel, hartel* (ողորկ, հարթ, դիւրահոս, ողորկել, հարթել)
smoothly - *hantardoren, heshdoren, hart ou havasar* (հանդարտօրէն, հեշտօրէն, հարթ ու հաւասար)
smoothness - *hartoutiun, sahounoutiun, hezoutiun* (հարթութիւն, սահունութիւն, հեզութիւն)
smother - *kheghtel, heghtsamah unel, anshunchatsunel* (խեղդել, հեղձամահ ընել, անշնչացնել)
smudge - *murodel, sevtsunel, dzukhaharel, geghd, aghd* (մրոտել, սեւցնել, ծխահարել, մուր, կեղտ, աղտ)
smug - *bujnod, inknakoh, bujnil* (պճնոտ, ինքնագոհ, պճնիլ)
smuggle - *maksanenkel* (մաքսանենգել)
smuggler - *maksanenk* (մաքսանենգ)
smut - *mour, geghd, lugdioutiun, murodel, sevtsunel* (մուր, կեղտ, լկտիութիւն, մրոտել, սեւցնել)
smutch - *murodel, sevtsunel, mour, pidz, aghd* (մրոտել, սեւցնել, մուր, բիծ, աղտ)
smutty - *aghdod, geghdod, lugdi, anvayel, bakshod* (աղտոտ, կեղտոտ, լկտի, անվայել, պագշոտ)
snack - *tetev nakhajash, mas, pazhin, pazhnel* (թեթեւ նախաճաշ, մաս, բաժին, բաժնել)
snag - *churasouyz dzararmad, tsutsvadz agra* (ջրասոյզ ծառարմատ, ցցուած ակռայ)
snail - *khukhounch, tantagh, dzouyl* (խխունջ, դանդաղ, ծոյլ)
snake - *ots, nenkamid, kalarvil, kashkushel* (օձ, նենգամիտ, գալարուիլ, քաշքշել)
snaky - *otsatsev, otsanuman, otsalits, khoramang* (օձաձեւ, օձանըման, օձալից, խորամանկ)
snap (n) - *shachiun, jaytiun, godurvadzk, jarmant, nik* (շաչիւն, ճայթիւն, կոտրուածք, ճարմանդ, նիգ)
snap (v) - *godril, khordagvil, purtil, khadznel, jaytil* (կոտրիլ, խորտակուիլ, փրթիլ, խածնել, ճայթիլ)
snapper - *khadzan, khulogh, tsoug mu* (խածան, խլող, ձուկ մը)
snappish - *khadzan-shoun, gurvaser, zayratsgod* (խածան՝շուն, կռուասէր, զայրացկոտ)
snare - *dzoughag, tagart, vorokayt, tagartel, dzoughagel* (ծուղակ, թակարդ, որոգայթ, թակարդել, ծուղակել)
snarl (I) - *murmural, kurtmunchel, sasdel, durdounch* (մռմռալ, քրթմնջել, սաստել, տրտունջ)
snarl (II) - *tunjugel, kharnushdugel,*

tunjoug-mazi (թնճկել, խառնշտկել, թնճուկ՝ մազի)
snatch - khulel, gorzel, hapushdagel, khuloum, gorzoum (խլել, կորզել, յափշտակել, խլում, կորզում)
snatcher - khulogh, gorzogh (խլող, կորզող)
sneak - soghal, suburtil, koghnal, usdorin, kutsouts (սողալ, սպրդիլ, գողնալ, ստորին, գձուձ)
sneaker - soghatsogh, madnich, pampasogh (սողացող, մատնիչ, բամբասող)
sneaky - usdor, vakhgod, tsadz (ստոր, վախկոտ, ցած)
sneer - kumdzidzagh, dzaghur, arhamarhank, dzaghrel (քմծիծաղ, ծաղր, արհամարհանք, ծաղրել)
sneeze - purunkdal, purunkdouk (փռնգտալ, փռնգտուք)
sneezing - purunkdots (փռնգտոց)
snick - gudurvadzk, yeresants gudrel (կտրուածք, երեսանց կտրել)
snicker - kumdzidzagh, heknank, khuntouk, kumdzidzaghil (քմծիծաղ, հեգնանք, խնդուք, քմծիծաղիլ)
sniff - runkashunchoum, runkashunchel, kitu kashel (ռնգաշնչում, ռնգաշնչել, քիթը քաշել)
sniffle - gumgumal, kuten khosil, kitu kashel (կմկմալ, քթէն խօսիլ, քիթը քաշել)
snip - mugradel, gudrel, tsevel, gudruvadz, tsev (մկրատել, կտրել, ձեւել, կտրուած, ձեւ)
snipe - churagudtsar-turchounu, ankhelk, aboush (ջրակտցար՝ թռչունը, անխելք, ապուշ)
sniper - bahvudadz zinartsag, guragogh (պահուըտած զինարձակ, կրակող)
snivel - khulink, kitu vazel (խլինք, քիթը վազել)
sniveler - khulinkod, lalgan (խլինքոտ, լալկան)
snob - chudes, tsoutsamol, noroutaser (չտես, ցուցամոլ, նորութասէր)
snobbery, snobism - tsoutsamoloutiun, noroutasiroutiun (ցուցամոլութիւն, նորութասիրութիւն)
snood - mazi zhabaven (մազի ժապաւէն)
snoop - lurdesel, kitu khotel ourishi kordzin (լրտեսել, քիթը խոթել ուրիշի գործին)
snooper - lurdes (լրտես)
snooze - murap, koun, murapel (մրափ, քուն, մրափել)
snore - khurgal, khortal, khurgots (խռկալ, խորդալ, խռկոց)
snorer - khurgatsogh, khortatsogh (խրկացող, խորդացող)
snoring - khurgots (խրկոց)
snort - khurunchel, khukhunchel, khukhunchiun (խռնչել, խխնջել, խխնջիւն)
snout - tounch, murout, tsuroug, tsuroug antsunel (դունչ, մռութ, ցռուկ, ցռուկ անցնել)
snow - tsiun, tsiunel (ձիւն, ձիւնել)
snowball - tsiunakuntag, tsiunadzaghig, tsiunakuntag nedel (ձիւնագնդակ, ձիւնածաղիկ, ձիւնագնդակ նետել)
snowdrift - tsiunagouyd (ձիւնակոյտ)
snowman - tsiunamart (ձիւնամարդ)
snowshoe - tsiunagoshig (ձիւնակօշիկ)
snowy - tsiunabad, tsiunadzadzg, tsiunod, makour (ձիւնապատ, ձիւնածածկ, ձիւնոտ, մաքուր)
snow-storm - tsiunamurrig, tsiunahoghm, pouk (ձիւնամրրիկ, ձիւնահողմ, բուք)
snow-white - tsiunausbidag, tsiunapayl, jep-jermag (ձիւնասպիտակ, ձիւնափայլ, ճեփ-ճերմակ)
snub - hantimanoutiun, tsutsvadz kit, nakhadel, anarkel (յանդիմանութիւն, ցցուած քիթ, նախատել, անարգել)
snubby - gobid, arhamarhagan, ver tsutsvadz-kit (կոպիտ, արհամարհական, վեր ցցուած՝ քիթ)
snuff - kutakhod, momi kit, hodvudal, kutakhod kashel (քթախոտ, մոմի քիթ, հոտուըտալ, քթախոտ

քաշել)
snuffle - runkakhosil, kuten khosil, runkakhosoutiun (ռնգախօսիլ, քթէն խօսիլ, ռնգախօսութիւն)
snuffler - runkakhos (ռնգախօս)
snug - antor, hankusdaved, meghm, vayelouch (անդորր, Հանգստաւէտ, մեղմ, վայելուչ)
snuggle - seghmuvil, pattuvil, gubchil (սեղմուիլ, փաթթուիլ, կպչիլ)
so - aysbes, asang, ousdi, hedevapar, vorov (այսպէս, ասանկ, ուստի, Հետեւաբար, որով)
so far - arazhum, minchev hima, minchev hos (առայժմ, մինչեւ Հիմա, մինչեւ Հոս)
so then - ouremun (ուրեմն)
soak - turchel, turchuvil, dzudzel, umbel, gondzel (թրջել, թրջուիլ, ծծել, ըմպել, կոնծել)
soakage - turchoum, tatkhoum, hort antsurev, kinarpouk (թրջում, թաթխում, յորդ անձրեւ, գինարբուք)
soaked - tats, khukhoum (թաց, խխում)
soaker - turchogh, khuman, kinemol (թրջող, խման, գինեմոլ)
soap - ojar, ojarel, ojarvil (օճառ, օճառել, օճառուիլ)
soap opera - undanegan sirayin nergayatsoum (ընտանեկան սիրային ներկայացում)
soar - savarnil, partsuranal, khoyanal, turichk, khoyank (սաւառնիլ, բարձրանալ, խոյանալ, թռիչք, խոյանք)
sob - hegegal, hedzguldal, hegegank (Հեկեկալ, Հեծկլտալ, Հեկեկանք)
sober - uzkasd, zousb, bargeshd, uzkasdatsunel (զգաստ, զուսպ, պարկեշտ, զգաստացնել)
sober-minded - lurchakhoh, khohem, havasaragushruvadz (լրջախոՀ, խոՀեմ, Հաւասարակշռուած)
sobriety - uzkasdoutiun, chapavoroutiun, zhouzhgaloutiun (զգաստութիւն, չափաւորութին, ժուժկալութիւն)
sobriquet - dzaghranoun, geghdzanoun (ծաղրանուն, կեղծանուն)
soc - hargazerdzoutiun, aghalou iravounk (Հարկազերծութիւն, աղալու իրաւունք)
soccer - vodnakuntag, foutbol (ոտնագնդակ, ֆութպոլ)
sociability - martamodoutiun, ungerasiroutiun (մարդամօտութիւն, ընկերասիրութիւն)
sociable - martamod, ungeragan, ungeraser (մարդամօտ, ընկերական, ընկերասէր)
social - ungerayin, ungeragan (ընկերային, ընկերական)
socialism - ungervaroutiun (ընկերվարութիւն)
socialist - ungervaragan (ընկերվարական)
society - ungeroutiun, ungeragtsoutiun, hamaynk (ընկերութիւն, ընկերակցութիւն, Համայնք)
sociologist - ungerapan (ընկերաբան)
sociology - ungerapanoutiun (ընկեբաբանութիւն)
sock - gurgnagoshig, garj koulba, nerpan, zarnel (կրկնակօշիկ, կարճ գուլպայ, ներբան, զարնել)
socket - lousadzag, lampagal, gutsortich, momakhorsh (լուսածակ, լամբակալ, կցորդիչ, մոմախորշ)
soda - nadrachour, punadzkhad, soda (նատրաջուր, բնածխատ, սոտա)
sodomy - sotomaganoutiun (սոդոմականութիւն)
sofa - otots, pazmots (օթոց, բազմոց)
soft - gagough, papoug, meghm, hajeli, gamats (կակուղ, փափուկ, մեղմ, Հաճելի, կամաց)
soft drink - analkol khumichk (անալքոլ խմիչք)
softcover - tughtagazm, khavakardagazm (թղթակազմ, խաւաքարտակազմ)
soften - gagoughtsunel, gagoughnal, meghmatsunel, meghmanal (կակուղցնել, կակուղնալ, մեղմացնել, մեղմանալ)
softly - meghmoren, papgoren, ga-

goughoutiamp (մեղմօրէն, փափկօրէն, կակուղութեամբ)

softness - *gagghoutiun (կակղութիւն)*

software - *hamagarkichi dzurakir, haydakir (Համակարգիչի ծրագիր, յայտագիր)*

softy - *toulamort, duked, himar, touyl mart (թուլամորդ, տգէտ, յիմար, թոյլ մարդ)*

soft-hearted - *uzkayoun, papgasird, kutasird (զգայուն, փափկասիրտ, գթասիրտ)*

soggy - *churatatakh, turchuvadz (ջրաթաթախ, թրջուած)*

soil - *aghdodel, aradavorel, aghd, pidz, hogh, yergir (աղտոտել, արատաւորել, աղտ, բիծ, Հող, երկիր)*

soiree - *yeregouyt, irigoun (երեկոյթ, իրիկուն)*

sojourn - *kisherel, punagil, genal, punagoutiun (գիշերել, բնակիլ, կենալ, բնակութիւն)*

sojourner - *bantoukhd, nuzhteh, punagapokh (պանդուխտ, նժդեՀ, բնակափոխ)*

solace - *mukhitaroutiun, uspopank, mukhitarel (մխիթարութիւն, սփոփանք, մխիթարել)*

solar - *arekagnayin, arevayin (արեգակնային, արեւային)*

solar system - *arekagnayin turoutiun (արեգակնային դրութիւն)*

solarize - *arevargel, ayrel-nugaru (արեւարկել, այրել՝ նկարը)*

sold - *dzakhvadz (ծախուած)*

solder - *zot, zotaniut, zotel, pagtsunel, madzoutsel (զօդ, զօդանիւթ, զօդել, փակցնել, մածուցել)*

soldier - *zinvor, zinvoragan (զինուոր, զինուորական)*

sole (a) - *miag, arantsin, vodki dagu (միակ, առանձին, ոտքի տակը)*

sole (n) - *nerpan, karshabar, lezvatsoug, nerpanel (ներբան, քարշապար, լեզուաձուկ, ներբանել)*

solecism - *keraganagan sukhal, vuribag (քերականական սխալ, վրիպակ)*

solemn - *hantisavor, bashdonagan, medzashouk (Հանդիսաւոր, պաշտօնական, մեծաշուք)*

solemnity - *donakhumpoutiun, hantisoutiun (տօնախմբութիւն, Հանդիսութիւն)*

solemnize - *donel, donakhumpel, hurchagel (տօնել, տօնախմբել, Հռչակել)*

soleness - *minagoutiun (մինակութիւն)*

solfa - *khagherk, khagherkel (խաղերգ, խաղերգել)*

solfeggio - *khagherkoujtiun (խաղերգութիւն)*

solicit - *khunturel, bahanchel, michnortel (խնդրել, պաՀանջել, միջնորդել*

solicitation - *takhantsank, khunturank, timoum, mughoum (թախանձանք, խնդրանք, դիմում, մղում)*

solicitor - *khunturogh, khunturargou, tadakhaz, pokhanort (խնդրող, խնդրարկու, դատախազ, փոխանորդ)*

solicitous - *hokadar, hokatsogh, mudahok, takhantsogh (Հոգատար, Հոգացող, մտաՀոգ, թախանձող)*

solid - *hasdadoun, amour, dogoun, gardzur, hasdad (Հաստատուն, ամուր, տոկուն, կարծր, Հաստատ)*

solidarity - *zoragtsoutiun, miasnoutiun (զօրակցութիւն, միասնութիւն)*

solidarize - *zoragtsil (զօրակցիլ)*

solidify - *amratsunel, buntatsunel (ամրացնել, պնդացնել)*

solidity - *amroutiun, buntagazmoutiun, dogounoutiun (ամրութիւն, պնդակազմութիւն, տոկունութիւն)*

solidness - *hasdadounoutiun, buntoutiun (Հաստատունութիւն, պնդութիւն)*

soliloquize - *menakhosel (մենախօսել)*

soliloquy - *menakhosoutiun, inknakhosoutiun (մենախօսութիւն, ինքնախօսութիւն)*

solist - *menagadar, menerkag (մենակատար, մեներգակ)*

solitary - menagiats, megousi, juknavor, megousatsadz (մենակեաց, մեկուսի, ճգնաւոր, մեկուսացած)
solitude - arantsnoutiun, menagoutiun, menaran (առանձնութիւն, մենակութիւն, մենարան)
solo - menerk, menatsayn, menanuvak (մեներգ, մենաձայն, մենանուագ)
solstice - arevatarts, arevagayk (արեւադարձ, արեւակայք)
solstitial - arevatartsayin (արեւադարձային)
solubility - loudzanelioutiun (լուծանելիութիւն)
soluble - loudzeli, haleli, loudzvogh, loudzagan (լուծելի, հալելի, լուծուող, լուծական)
solute - touyl, ludzouyt (թոյլ, լուծոյթ)
solution - loudzoum, haloum, loudzouyt, vujroum, vakhjan (լուծում, հալում, լուծոյթ, վճռում, վախճան)
solvability - vujaroghoutiun, vujarelou garoghoutiun (վճարողութիւն, վճարելու կարողութիւն)
solvable - loudzeli, loudzvogh, halogh, vujareli (լուծելի, լուծուող, հալող, վճարելի)
solve - loudzel, halel, vujrel, lousapanel, patsadurel (լուծել, հալել, վճռել, լուսաբանել, բացատրել)
solvent - vujarogh, hadoutsanogh, loudzoghagan, loudzich (վճարող, հատուցանող, լուծողական, լուծիչ)
somatist - niutabashd (նիւթապաշտ)
somber, sombre - mout, mutin, khavar, murayl, dukhour (մութ, մթին, խաւար, մռայլ, տխուր)
sombrous - aghod, mutin, dukhour (աղոտ, մթին, տխուր)
some - kani mu, kich mu, mas mu, vorosh, megu, mod (քանի մը, քիչ մը, մաս մը, որոշ, մէկը, մօտ)
somebody - megu, vomun, garevor ants (մէկը, ոմն, կարեւոր անձ)
someday - or mu (օր մը)
somehow - gerbov mu, tsevov mu, amen barakayi dag (կերպով մը, ձեւով մը, ամէն պարագայի տակ)
somersault - tavaloum, tavalil (թաւալում, թաւալիլ)
something - pan mu (բան մը)
sometime - adenok, arachva, or mu, nakhgin (ատենօք, առաջուայ, օր մը, նախկին)
sometimes - yerpemun, zhamanag ar zhamanag, aden mu (երբեմն, ժամանակ առ ժամանակ, ատեն մը)
somewhat - pan mu, mas mu, pavagan, vorosh chapov (բան մը, մաս մը, բաւական, որոշ չափով)
somewhere - degh mu (տեղ մը)
somewhere else - voryeve ayl degh (որեւէ այլ տեղ)
somewhile - zhamanag mu (ժամանակ մը)
somnambulism - kunashurchigoutiun (քնաշրջիկութիւն)
somnambulist - kisherashurchig, kunashurchig, lousnod (գիշերաշրջիկ, քնաշրջիկ, լուսնոտ)
somniferous - kunaper, kunatsunogh (քնաբեր, քնացնող)
somnolence - kunodoutiun (քնոտութիւն)
somnolent - kunod, kunatatakh (քնոտ, քնաթաթախ)
son - vorti, arou zavag, dugha (որդի, արու զաւակ, տղայ)
sonance - hunchaganoutiun, huncheghoutiun, yeghanag (հնչականութիւն, հնչեղութիւն, եղանակ)
sonant - hunchoun, hunchagan (հնչուն, հնչական)
sonata - nuvakerkoutiun, hadanuvak (նուագերգութիւն, հատանուագ)
song - yerk, nuvak (երգ, նուագ)
songbook - yerkaran (երգարան)
songster - yerkich, yerkich turchoun (երգիչ, երգիչ թռչուն)
songstress - yerkchouhi (երգչուհի)
songwriter - yerkahan, yerkakir (երգահան, երգագիր)
soniferous, sonorific - tsaynadou, tsaynaper (ձայնատու, ձայնաբեր)
sonnet - hunchiag (հնչեակ)
sonny - dughas, vortis, vortiags (տղաս, որդիս, որդեակս)

sonorific - hunchagan, tsaynaper (հնչական, ձայնաբեր)
sonority - huncheghoutiun, hunchounoutiun (հնչեղութիւն, հնչունութիւն)
sonorous - hunchegh, hunchoun, hunchagan, turturoun (հնչեղ, հնչուն, հնչական, թրթռուն)
sonship - vortioutiun (որդիութիւն)
son-in-law - pesa (փեսայ)
soon - shoudov, shoud, poutov, i modo (շուտով, շուտ, փութով, ի մօտոյ)
sooner - aveli shoud (աւելի շուտ)
soot - mour, murodel (մուր, մրոտել)
sooth - hajeli, jushmardoutiun, iraganoutiun (հաճելի, ճշմարտութիւն, իրականութիւն)
soothe - meghmatsunel, hankusdatsunel, mukhitarel (մեղմացնել, հանգստացնել, մխիթարել)
soother, soothing - meghmatsoutsich, hantardetsoutsich (մեղմացուցիչ, հանդարտեցուցիչ)
soothfast - jushmarid, havadarim (ճշմարիտ, հաւատարիմ)
soothsay - koushagel, markareanal (գուշակել, մարգարէանալ)
soothsayer - koushagogh, koushag (գուշակող, գուշակ)
sootiness - murodoutiun, sevoutiun (մրոտութիւն, սեւութիւն)
sooty - murod, murodadz, aghdod, sev (մրոտ, մրոտած, աղտոտ, սեւ)
sop - hatsi tatkhuvadz badar, tatkhel, turchel (հացի թաթխուած պատառ, թաթխել, թրջել)
sophist - imasdag, sopesd (իմաստակ, սոփեստ)
sophisticate - geghdzel, nenkel, khartakhel, aghavaghel (կեղծել, նենգել, խարդախել, աղաւաղել)
sophisticated - nenkapokhvadz, kergadarelakordzuvadz (նենգափոխուած, գեր-կատարելագործուած)
sophistication - khartakhoum, chapazants gadarelakordzoum (խարդախում, չափազանց կատարելագործում)
sophistry - sopesdoutiun, imasdagoutiun (սոփեստութիւն, իմաստակութիւն)
soporose - kunaper, kunod (քնաբեր, քնոտ)
soprano - zilerkag, zilatsayn, soprano (զիլերգակ, զիլաձայն, սոփրանօ)
sorcerer - vuhoug, koushag, gakhart (վհուկ, գուշակ, կախարդ)
sorcery - gakhartoutiun, vuhougoutiun, humayoutiun (կախարդութիւն, վհուկութիւն, հմայութիւն)
sordid - punti, kutsouts, gudzdzi, akah (փնթի, գձուձ, կծծի, ագահ)
sore - tsav, gusgidz, verk, sugurtouk, tsavod, tsavov (ցաւ, կսկիծ, վէրք, սկրթուք, ցաւոտ, ցաւով)
sorely - khorabes, tsavakin, tsavov, gusgudzakin (խորապէս, ցաւագին, ցաւով, կսկծագին)
soreness - tsav, gusgidz, vishd (ցաւ, կսկիծ, վիշտ)
sorrel - sharakouyn, turtunchoug (շառագոյն, թրթնջուկ)
sorrily - tzavov, durdmakin, dukhroren, kheghjoren (ցաւով, տրտմագին, տխրօրէն, խեղճօրէն)
sorrow - tsav, dukhroutiun, vushdanal, dukhril (ցաւ, տխրութիւն, վշտանալ, տխրիլ)
sorrowful - tzavali, vushdali, tzavakin, vushdapeg (ցաւալի, վշտալի, ցաւագին, վշտաբեկ)
sorry - tzavali, dukhour, durdoum, - gu tsavim (ցաւալի, տխուր, տրտում – կը ցաւիմ)
sort - desag, tsegh, vijag, tsev, tasavorel, zadel (տեսակ, ցեղ, վիճակ, ձեւ, դասաւորել, զատել)
sortie - khoyank, otayin arshavank (խոյանք, օդային արշաւանք)
sortilege - vijagahanoutiun, vijagatsukoutiun (վիճակահանութիւն, վիճակաձգութիւն)
sot - kinemol, khuman, aboush tartsunel (գինեմոլ, խման, ապուշ դարձնել)
sotto voce - meghmatsayn (մեղմաձայն)

soubrette - nazhishd (նաժիշտ)
soul - hoki, eoutiun, ants, giank, voki, sird (Հոգի, էութիւն, անձ, կեանք, ոգի, սիրտ)
sound (I) - tsayn, hunchiun, aghmoug, hunchel, hunchetsunel (ձայն, Հնչիւն, աղմուկ, Հնչել, Հնչեցնել)
sound (II) - aroghch, voghch, zoravor, gadarial, jisht (առողջ, ողջ, զօրաւոր, կատարեալ, ճիշդ)
sound (III) - neghouts, virachap, khorachapel, kunnel (նեղուց, վիրաչափ, խորաչափել, քննել)
sounding - hunchogh, hunchagan, khorachapoutiun (Հնչող, Հնչական, խորաչափութիւն)
sound-wave - tsaynalik (ձայնալիք)
soup - abour, arkanag (ապուր, արգանակ)
soupcon - gasgadz, turtoum, touyzun kanag (կասկած, դրդում, դոյզն քանակ)
sour - tutou, khadzan, gudzou, tutvadz, tutvetsunel (թթու, խածան, կծու, թթուած, թթուեցնել)
source - aghpiur, ag, agounk, usgizp, badjar (աղբիւր, ակ, ակունք, սկիզբ, պատճառ)
souse - aghtsan, aghchour, aghchurel, khoyanal (աղցան, աղջուր, աղջրել, խոյանալ)
souter - hunagargad (Հնակարկատ)
south - harav (Հարաւ)
South America - haravayin ameriga (Հարաւային Ամերիկա)
South Pole - haravayin pever (Հարաւային Բեւեռ)
southeast - harav arevelk, harav-arevelian (Հարաւ արեւելք, Հարաւ արեւելեան)
southern - haravayin (Հարաւային)
southerner - haravayin, haravapunag (Հարաւային, Հարաւաբնակ)
southwest - harav arevmoudk, harav arevmudian (Հարաւ արեւմուտք, Հարաւ արեւմտեան)
souvenir - hishadag, housh, houshanuver (յիշատակ, յուշ, յուշանուէր)
sovereign - vehabed, kerishkhan, vosgeturam (վեհապետ, գերիշխան, ոսկեդրամ)
sovereignty - kerishkhanoutiun (գերիշխանութիւն)
soviet - khorhourt, zhoghov, soved (խորհուրդ, ժողով, սովետ)
sow - tsanel, sermanel, suprel, daradzel (ցանել, սերմանել, սփռել, տարածել)
sower - sermnatsan, tsanogh (սերմնացան, ցանող)
so-and-so - mi vomun, aysinch (մի ոմն, այսինչ)
so-called - aysbes gochvadz, ipur te, inknagoch (այսպէս կոչուած, իբր թէ, ինքնակոչ)
so-so - pavagan lav, voch lav voch kesh, daneli, michag (բաւական լաւ, ոչ լաւ ոչ գէշ, տանելի, միջակ)
space - anchurbed, michots, daradzoutiun, anchadel (անջրպետ, միջոց, տարածութիւն, անջատել)
spaceless - anverch, ansahman (անվերջ, անսաՀման)
spaceman - diyezeranavort (տիեզերանաւորդ)
spaceship - diyezeranav (տիեզերանաւ)
spacing - patsvadzk (բացուածք)
spacious - laynadaradz, untartsag, laynadzaval (լայնատարած, ընդարձակ, լայնածաւալ)
spade - pah, purich, pahov porel (բաՀ, բրիչ, բաՀով փորել)
span - tiz, tuzachap, aguntart, tizov chapel (թիզ, թզաչափ, ակնթարթ, թիզով չափել)
spangle - zanag, payloun gojag, zanagel, shoghal (զանակ, փայլուն կոճակ, զանակել, շողալ)
spanish - usbanatsi, usbaneren, usbanagan (սպանացի, սպաներէն, սպանական)
spank - abdag, dzedz, abdagel, dzedzel (ապտակ, ծեծ, ապտակել, ծեծել)
spanker - abdagogh, dzedzogh, gudrich, arakakayl (ապտակող, ծեծող,

կտրիչ, արագաքայլ)
spanner - tizov chapogh, budoudagi panali (Թիզով չափող, պտուտակի բանալի)
spar - keran, gaym, gurpamard, gaymel, gurpamardil (գերան, կայմ, կռփամարտ, կայմել, կռփամարտիլ)
spare - bahesdi, avelort, khunayogh, khunayel, bahel (պահեստի, աւելորդ, խնայող, խնայել, պահել)
spare part - bahesdamas (պահեստամաս)
sparge - surusgel (սրսկել)
sparger - surusgogh (սրսկող)
sparing - khunayogh, khunayaser, dundesogh, gudzdzi (խնայող, խնայասէր, տնտեսող, կծծի)
spark - gaydz, nushouyl, tsoutsaser, gaydzguldal, kudznil (կայծ, նշոյլ, ցուցասէր, կայծկլտալ, քծնիլ)
sparkle - gaydz, gaydzig, gaydzguldal, busbughal (կայծ, կայծիկ, կայծկլտալ, պսպղալ)
sparkler - gaydzadou, purpuratsogh (կայծատու, փրփրացող)
sparkling - paylpuloun, shoghshoghoun, purpurogh (փայլփլուն, շողշողուն, փրփրող)
sparrow - junjughoug (ճնճղուկ)
sparse - tsiroutsan, tsurvadz, tsantsar (ցիրուցան, ցրուած, ցանցառ)
spasm - muganakhutsoum, burgoum (մկանախցում, պրկում)
spate - heghegh, voghoghoum (հեղեղ, ողողում)
spatial - anchurbedayin, daradzagan, untartsag (անջրպետային, տարածական, ընդարձակ)
spatter - tsayd, tsaydoug, tsadgetsunel, tsekhodel, tsaydel (ցայտ, ցայտուկ, ցատկեցնել, ցեխոտել, ցայտել)
spatula - pahag, teghakordzi kharnich (բահակ, դեղագործի խառնիչ)
spawl - gudor, purtouj, touk (կտոր, բրթուճ, Թուք)
spawn - havgit adzel, dzurdel, dzunanil, tsou, serount (հաւկիթ ածել, ծրտել, ծնանիլ, ձու, սերունդ)
speak - khosil, usel, zuroutsel, khosagtsil (խօսիլ, ըսել, զրուցել, խօսակցիլ)
speaker - khosogh, khosnag, adenakhos, jarakhos, huredor (խօսող, խօսնակ, ատենախօս, ճառախօս, հռետոր)
speakership - adenabedoutiun (ատենապետութիւն)
speaking - ardasanoutiun, adenakhosoutiun, jar, khosogh (արտասանութիւն, ատենախօսութիւն, ճառ, խօսող)
spear - nizag, dek, dzil, dzughod, nizagel, dzayr dal (նիզակ, տէգ, ծիլ, ծղօտ, նիզակել, ծայր տալ)
spearmint - ananoukh (անանուխ)
special - masnavor, hadoug, ourouyn, vorosh (մասնաւոր, յատուկ, ուրոյն, որոշ)
specialist - masnaked (մասնագէտ)
speciality - masnakidoutiun (մասնագիտութիւն)
specialization - masnakidoutiun unel (մասնագիտութիւն ընել)
specialize - masnakidanal, masnavorel (մասնագիտանալ, մասնաւորել)
specially - masnavorapar (մասնաւորաբար)
specialty - masnakidoutiun, masnavoroutiun (մասնագիտութիւն, մասնաւորութիւն)
specific - masnahadoug, hadoug, punorosh (մասնայատուկ, յատուկ, բնորոշ)
specific gravity - desagarar gushir (տեսակարար կշիռ)
specification - manramasnoum, hadgoroshoum (մանրամասնում, յատկորոշում)
specify - masnavorel, hadganushel, manramasnel (մասնաւորել, յատկանշել, մանրամասնել)
specimen - numoush, orinag, ports (նմոյշ, օրինակ, փորձ)
specious - keghadesil, chuknagh, jushmardanuman (գեղատեսիլ, չքնաղ, ճշմարտանման)
speciously - jushmardabes, arerevouytus (ճշմարտապէս, առերեւոյԹս,

ւոյթս)
speck - arad, pidz, aradavorel (արատ, բիծ, արատաւորել)
speckle - pudzig, bisag, pudzavorel (բծիկ, պիսակ, բծաւորել)
speckled - pudzavor, bisagavor (բծաւոր, պիսակաւոր)
spectacle - desaran, taderakhagh, nergayatsoum, yerevouyt (տեսարան, թատերախաղ, ներկայացում, երեւոյթ)
spectacled - agnotsavor, agnotsov (ակնոցաւոր, ակնոցով)
spectacular - dubavorich, aztou, hoyagab, kuravich (տպաւորիչ, ազդու, հոյակապ, գրաւիչ)
spectator - hantisades, tidogh, aganades (հանդիսատես, դիտող, ականատես)
spectatress, spectatrix - hantisadesouhi, aganades gin (հանդիսատեսուհի, ականատես կին)
specter - ourvagan, tsunork, voki (ուրուական, ցնորք, ոգի)
spectrum - lousabadger, sevanugar (լուսապատկեր, սեւանկար)
specular - tsolatsug, desoghagan (ցոլացիկ, տեսողական)
speculate - mudadzel, khorhurtadzel, yentaturel, shahargel (մտածել, խորհրդածել, ենթադրել, շահարկել)
speculation - shahatidoutiun, zunnoum, hayetsoghoutiun (շահադիտութիւն, զննում, հայեցողութիւն)
speculative - hayetsoghagan, desagan, shahatidagan (հայեցողական, տեսական, շահադիտական)
speculator - shahargogh, shahated, zunnogh, tidogh (շահարկող, շահադէտ, զննող, դիտող)
speculum - hayeli, tsolatsig, zunnag (հայելի, ցոլացիկ, զննակ)
speech - jar, yelouyt, zegoutsoum, khosk, khosagtsoutiun (ճառ, ելոյթ, զեկուցում, խօսք, խօսակցութիւն)
speechless - ankhos, hamur, lour, luragyats (անխօս, համր, լուռ, լռակեաց)
speed (n) - arakoutiun, pouyt, ushdab, ajabarank (արագութիւն, փոյթ, շտապ, աճապարանք)
speed (v) - ushdabel, arakatsunel, ajabarel, poutal, vazel (շտապել, արագացնել, աճապարել, փութալ, վազել)
speedily - arakoren, poutov (արագօրէն, փութով)
speediness - arakoutiun, arakasharzhoutiun (արագութիւն, արագաշարժութիւն)
speedometer - arakachap (արագաչափ)
spell (n) - humayk, humayoutiun, garj michots, hert, gark (հմայք, հմայութիւն, կարճ միջոց, հերթ, կարգ)
spell (v) - hekel, oughghakurel, humayel, gartal, gazmel (հեգել, ուղղագրել, հմայել, կարդալ, կազմել)
spellbind - humayel, tiutel, gakhartel (հմայել, դիւթել, կախարդել)
spellbound - humayvadz, hurabourvadz, gakhartuvadz (հմայուած, հրապուրուած, կախարդուած)
speller - hekogh, hekelou tasakirk (հեգող, հեգելու դասագիրք)
spelling - hekoum, oughghakuroutiun (հեգում, ուղղագրութիւն)
spencer - garj pajgon, yergurortagan arakasdanav mu (կարճ բաճկոն, երկրորդական առագաստանաւ մը)
spend - dzakhsel, muskhel, vadnel, vadnuvil, dzakhs (ծախսել, մսխել, վատնել, վատնուիլ, ծախս)
spender - dzakhsogh, muskhogh, vadnogh (ծախսող, մսխող, վատնող)
spendthrift - shurayl, muskhogh, vadnogh (շռայլ, մսխող, վատնող)
spent - hoknadz, ouzhasbar, usbaradz, ouzhad (յոգնած, ուժասպառ, սպառած, ուժատ)
sperm - serm, saghm, sermunaheghoug, sermunahiut (սերմ, սաղմ, սերմնահեղուկ, սերմնահիւթ)
spermary - sermunaran, amortsik (սերմնարան, ամորձիք)

spew - puskhel, tours dal, puskhouk (փսխել, դուրս տալ, փսխուք)
spewer - puskhogh (փսխող)
sphere - kount, yergurakount, volord, shurchanag, gulorel (գունդ, երկրագունդ, ոլորտ, շրջանակ, կլորել)
spheric, spherical - kuntatsev, volordayin (գնդաձեւ, ոլորտային)
sphinx - usfinx (սֆինքս)
spice - hamem, hamemounk, hamemel (համեմ, համեմունք, համեմել)
spicer - hamemogh, hamemavajar (համեմող, համեմավաճառ)
spicily - hamemov, hamov-hodov (համեմով, համով-հոտով)
spick - seb, kam (սեպ, գամ)
spick and span - polorovin nor (բոլորովին նոր)
spicy - pouroumnaved, hamemod, gudzou, sour (բուրումնաւէտ, համեմոտ, կծու, սուր)
spider - sart (սարդ)
spigot - khutsan-dagari (խցան՝ տակառի)
spike - medz kam, seb, tzitz, tsutsel, peverel (մեծ գամ, սեպ, ցից, ցցել, բեւեռել)
spikenard - nartos (նարդոս)
spiky - suradzayr, sour, sebavor (սրածայր, սուր, սեպաւոր)
spill (n) - tughtakulan, payde tsits, dashegh, tsoghig, jagh (թղթագլան, փայտէ ցից, տաշեղ, ձողիկ, ճաղ)
spill (v) - tapel, nedel, tsanel, tapil, hosil, iynal (թափել, նետել, ցանել, թափիլ, հոսիլ, իյնալ)
spiller - tapogh, pazmagart arasan (թափող, բազմակարթ առասան)
spin - manel, hiusel, volorel, tavaloum, arak vazk (մանել, հիւսել, ոլորել, թաւալում, արագ վազք)
spinach - shomin, usbanakh (շոմին, սպանախ)
spinal column - voghnasiun (ողնասիւն)
spindle - il, ilig, jagh, ajil, hasag arnel (իլ, իլիկ, ճաղ, աճիլ, հասակ առնել)
spine - voghnahar, voghnashar, poush, kirki gurnag (ողնայար, ողնաշար, փուշ, գիրքի կռնակ)
spineless - anoghnahar, toulamort, vakhgod (անողնայար, թուլամորթ, վախկոտ)
spinner - manogh, hiusogh (մանող, հիւսող)
spinney - bourag, matsaroud, tupoud (պուրակ, մացառուտ, թփուտ)
spinning - voloroum, hiusk (ոլորում, հիւսք)
spinning wheel - jakharag (ճախարակ)
spinose - pushod (փշոտ)
spinster - amouri gin, manogh gin (ամուրի կին, մանող կին)
spiny - pushod, dzagogh, pushanuman (փշոտ, ծակող, փշանման)
spiral - barouratsev, volordakidz (պարուրաձեւ, ոլորտագիծ)
spire - suradzayr kakat, dzil, barouyr, bullel, pattuvil (սրածայր գագաթ, ծիլ, պարոյր, պլլել, փաթթուիլ)
spirit (n) - hoki, giank, midk, ourvagan, voki, imasd (հոգի, կեանք, միտք, ուրուական, ոգի, իմաստ)
spirit (v) - vokevorel, kachalerel, turtel, mughel (ոգեւորել, քաջալերել, դրդել, մղել)
spirited - gorovi, yerantoun, vokelits, surdod, oushim (կորովի, եռանդուն, ոգելից, սրտոտ, ուշիմ)
spiritful - khantavar, varvuroun (խանդավառ, վառվռուն)
spiritism - hokehartsoutiun, hokekhosoutiun (հոգեհարցութիւն, հոգեխօսութիւն)
spiritist - hokeharts, hokekhos, hokebashd (հոգեհարց, հոգեխօս, հոգեպաշտ)
spiritize - hokeganatsunel, anniutaganatsunel (հոգեկանացնել, աննիւթականացնել)
spiritless - anhoki, anchigh, vakhgod, dugar (անհոգի, անջիղ, վախկոտ, տկար)
spiritly - hokevorabes, mudavorabes

(Հոգեւորապէս, մտաւորապէս)
spiritness - hokevoroutiun, hokeganoutiun (Հոգեւորութիւն, Հոգեկանութիւն)
spiritous - vokeghen, makour, gorovi (ոգեղէն, մաքուր, կորովի)
spirits - duramaturoutiun, vokelits umbeli, alkol (տրամադրութիւն, ոգելից ըմպելի, ալքոլ)
spiritual - hokegan, hokeghen, nerkin, anniut, hokevor (Հոգեկան, Հոգեղէն, ներքին, աննիւթ, Հոգեւոր)
spiritualism - hokebashdoutiun (Հոգեպաշտութիւն)
spiritualist - hokebashd, hokeharts (Հոգեպաշտ, ՀոգեՀարց)
spirituous - vokelits, anniuteghen, alkolayin (ոգելից, աննիւթեղէն, ալքոլային)
spirometer - shunchachap (շնչաչափ)
spirt - see: spurt (տե՛ս՝ spurt)
spit - shampour, touk, shampurel, tuknel (շամփուր, թուք, շամփրել, թքնել)
spite - charoutiun, vokh, ken, anarkel, neghel, adel (չարութիւն, ոխ, քէն, անարգել, նեղել, ատել)
spitter - tukogh, shampurogh, pokur yeghcherou (թքող, շամփրող, փոքր եղջերու)
spittle - touk, lortsounk, shoghik (թուք, լորձունք, շողիք)
splash - dighm, tsaydouk, chourin zarnel, aghdodel (տիղմ, ցայտուք, ջուրին զարնել, աղտոտել)
splashy - tsekhod, dughmod, geghdodadz, tats (ցեխոտ, տղմոտ, կեղտոտած, թաց)
splatter - dughmodil (տղմոտիլ)
splay - hartoutiun, tekoutiun, shegh angiun, khakhdel (Հարթութիւն, թեքութիւն, շեղ անկիւն, խախտել)
spleen - paydzagh, pargoutiun, vokh, maghts (փայծաղ, բարկութիւն, ոխ, մաղձ)
spleenish - maghtsod, tiurakurkir, neghsird (մաղձոտ, դիւրագրգիռ, նեղսիրտ)
splendid - paravor, shukegh, hoyagab, lousapayl (փառաւոր, շքեղ, Հոյակապ, լուսափայլ)
splendor - shukeghoutiun, baydzaroutiun, payl (շքեղութիւն, պայծառութիւն, փայլ)
splice (n) - miahiusoum, miatsum, hankouyts, zotoum (միաՀիւսում, միացում, Հանգոյց, զօդում)
splice (v) - miatsunel, zotel, amousnatsunel, miahiusel (միացնել, զօդել, ամուսնացնել, միաՀիւսել)
splint - paydasherd, vosguragal, gudruvadz vosgoru gabel (փայտաշերտ, ոսկրակալ, կտրուած ոսկորը կապել)
split - jeghkel, badurel, baytetsunel, jeghk, hertsuvadz (ճեղքել, պատռել, պայթեցնել, ճեղք, Հերձուած)
splitter - jeghkogh, baragdogh, hertsogh, anchadogh (ճեղքող, պառակտող, Հերձող, անջատող)
splotch - pidz, arad (բիծ, արատ)
spoil (n) - goghoboud, avar, gashark, yeghdzoum (կողոպուտ, աւար, կաշառք, եղծում)
spoil (v) - goghobdel, tallel, avarel, shupatsunel, shupanal (կողոպտել, թալլել, աւարել, շփացնել, շփանալ)
spoilage - pujatsoum, pujatsadz abrank (փճացում, փճացած ապրանք)
spoiler - hapushdagich, avararou, yeghdzich, avrogh (յափշտակիչ, աւարառու, եղծիչ, աւրող)
spoke - I. khosetsav, II. jagh, anvamad, anvarkel (I. խօսեցաւ, II. ճաղ, անուամատ, անուարգել)
spoken - khosvadz, peranatsi (խօսուած, բերանացի)
spokesman - badkamaper, badvirag, panper, khosnag, huredor (պատգամաբեր, պատուիրակ, բանբեր, խօսնակ, Հռետոր)
spoliate - goghobdel, hapushdagel, avararel (կողոպտել, յափշտակել, աւարարել)
spoliation - goghoboud, avararoutiun (կողոպուտ, աւարարութիւն)
spoliator - goghobdich (կողոպտիչ)

sponge - usbounk, khuman, usbounkel (սպունգ, խման, սպունգել)
sponger - tsuriager, bunagalez, bordapouydz (ծրիակեր, պնակալէզ, պորտաբոյծ)
sponsor - yerashkhavor, khunamagal, bashdduban (երաշխաւոր, խնամակալ, պաշտպան)
sponsorship - yerashkhavoroutiun, khunamagaloutiun (երաշխաւորութիւն, խնամակալութիւն)
spontaneous - inknaperapar, anmichagan, inknapoukh (ինքնաբերաբար, անմիջական, ինքնաբուխ)
spoof - badrank, khapeoutiun, khapel, housakhapel (պատրանք, խաբէութիւն, խաբել, յուսախաբել)
spook - ourvagan, khurdvilag (ուրուական, խրտուիլակ)
spool - jakharag, gugots, magog, tertsan pattel (ճախարակ, կկոց, մակոկ, դերձան փաթթել)
spoon (I) - tukal, tukalov oudel (դգալ, դգալով ուտել)
spoon (II) - barzamid, miamid, sirapanil (պարզամիտ, միամիտ, սիրաբանիլ)
spoony - kukvaser, sirvudan, uzkayoun sirahar, aboush (գգուասէր, սիրուրտան, զգայուն սիրահար, ապուշ)
sporadic - tsantsar, anchad, badahagan, tsiroutsan (ցանցառ, անջատ, պատահական, ցիրուցան)
spore - peghmnaposhi (բեղմնափոշի)
sport (n) - marzank, marmunamarz, khagh, zhamants, dzaghur (մարզանք, մարմնամարզ, խաղ, ժամանց, ծաղր)
sport (v) - khaghal, zuvarjanal, zuvarjatsunel, dzaghrel (խաղալ, զուարճանալ, զուարճացնել, ծաղրել)
sportive - marzagan, marmunagurtagan, zuvarjaser, gaydar (մարզական, մարմնակրթական, զուաճասէր, կայտառ)
sportsman - marzig, marzaser (մարզիկ, մարզասէր)
sportwear - marzahakousd (մարզահագուստ)
spot - arad, pidz, vayr, pushdig, aradavorel, pudzodel (արատ, բիծ, վայր, բշտիկ, արատաւորել, բծոտել)
spotless - anpidz, makour, anarad (անբիծ, մաքուր, անարատ)
spotlight - lousartsag, lousaged (լուսարձակ, լուսակէտ)
spotted - aradavor, pudzavor (արատաւոր, բծաւոր)
spotter - verahusgich, usdoukich, nushogh, kudnogh (վերահսկիչ, ստուգիչ, նշող, գտնող)
spousal - harsanegan, busagi, amousnoutian (հարսանեկան, պսակի, ամուսնութեան)
spousals - harsanik (հարսանիք)
spouse - hars, pesa (հարս, փեսայ)
spout (n) - dzorag, khoghovag, peran, gudouts, pogh (ծորակ, խողովակ, բերան, կտուց, փող)
spout (v) - dzoretsunel, dzoril, hosil, vazel, tsapurdel (ծորեցնել, ծորիլ, հոսիլ, վազել, ձաբռտել)
sprag - payde netsoug, netsoug genal (փայտէ նեցուկ, նեցուկ կենալ)
sprain - hotakalar, keloum, vodku dzuril-tarnal (յօդագալար, գելում, ոտքը ծռիլ–դառնալ)
sprawl - daradzvil, kedin purvil, anshunorh bargil (տարածուիլ, գետին փռուիլ, անշնորհ պառկիլ)
spray (I) - surusgoum, churagatil, surusgich, surusgel (սրսկում, ջրակաթիլ, սրսկիչ, սրսկել)
spray (II) - jiugh, vosd, parounag (ճիւղ, ոստ, բարունակ)
spread (n) - daradzoutiun, daradzoum, patsvadzk, suprots (տարածութիւն, տարածում, բացուածք, սփռոց)
spread (v) - daradzel, panal, seghan tunel, purel (տարածել, բանալ, սեղան դնել, փռել)
spree - geroukhoum, khunjouyk (կերուխում, խնճոյք)
sprig - jughig, vosd, sharavigh, vosdazartel (ճղիկ, ոստ, շառաւիղ,

ոստազարդել)
spright - voki, ourvagan, yerevouyt (ոգի, ուրուական, երեւոյթ)
sprightly - arouyk, gaydar, zuvart, ourakh, ashkhouzh (առոյգ, կայտառ, զուարթ, ուրախ, աշխոյժ)
spring (n) - karoun, turichk, vosdiun, dzakoum, zusbanag (գարուն, թռիչք, ոստիւն, ծագում, զսպանակ)
spring (v) - tsadgel, dzakil, vosdosdel, pousnil, dzulil (ցատկել, ծագիլ, ոստոստել, բուսնիլ, ծլիլ)
springe - tagart, tagartel (թակարդ, թակարդել)
springy - aratsukagan, zusbanagavor (առաձգական, զսպանակաւոր)
sprinkle - surusgel, tsanel, suprel, surusgoum, tsoghoum (սրսկել, ցանել, սփռել, սրսկում, ցօղում)
sprinkler - tsuntsough, surusgich, shurchachurich (ցնցուղ, սրսկիչ, շրջաջրիչ)
sprint - sulatsoum, arakavazk, sulanal, arak vazel (սլացում, արագավազք, սլանալ, արագ վազել)
sprit - ourjanal, dzulil, dzil, untsiugh (ուռճանալ, ծլիլ, ծիլ, ընձիւղ)
sprite - voki, ourvagan (ոգի, ուրուական)
sprout - dzil, untsiugh, dzulil, untsiughil (ծիլ, ընձիւղ, ծլիլ, ընձիւղիլ)
spruce - bujnazart, gogig, yeghevin, bujnuvil, bujnel (պճնազարդ, կոկիկ, եղեւին, պճնուիլ, պճնել)
spry - jugoun, arakasharzh, ashkhouzh, tiuratek (ճկուն, արագաշարժ, աշխոյժ, դիւրաթեք)
spume - purpour, purpuril (փրփուր, փրփրիլ)
spumous - purpurod, purpuroun (փրփրոտ, փրփրուն)
spur - khutan, mudrag, kurkir, gadar, tanel, turtel (խթան, մտրակ, գրգիռ, կատար, խթանել, դրդել)
spurious - geghdz, anharazad, shindzou, aborini (կեղծ, անհարազատ, շինծու, ապօրինի)
spurn - arhamarhank, merzhoum, akatsel, merzhel (արհամարհանք, մերժում, աքացել, մերժել)
spurrer - khutanogh (խթանող)
spurt - tsaydil, zhaytkil, zhaytketsunel, zhaytkoum (ցայտիլ, ժայթքիլ, ժայթքեցնել, ժայթքում)
sputter - touki tsaydouk, momi fushshots, tukodel (թուքի ցայտուք, մոմի ֆշշոց, թքոտել)
spy - lurdes, hedakouyz, lurdesel, hedakhouzel (լրտես, հետախոյզ, լրտեսել, հետախուզել)
spyglass - heratidag (հեռադիտակ)
squab - ker, kiroug, anpedour, shad letsuvadz parts (գէր, գիրուկ, անփետուր, շատ լեցուած բարձ)
squabble - vej, gurvudouk, gurvudil (վէճ, կռուըտուք, կռուըտիլ)
squad - chogad, khumpag, kount (ջոկատ, խմբակ, գունդ)
squadron - hedzelakhoump, navadorm, otanavayin chogad (հեծելախումբ, նաւատորմ, օդանաւային ջոկատ)
squalid - aghdod, hodadz, geghdod (աղտոտ, հոտած, կեղտոտ)
squall - jich, potorig, borchudouk, juchal, borchudal (ճիչ, փոթորիկ, պոռչտուք, ճչալ, պոռչտալ)
squaller - aghmugogh, borchudatsogh (աղմկող, պոռչտացող)
squally - potorgalits, potorgahouyz (փոթորկալից, փոթորկայոյզ)
squalor - aghdodoutiun (աղտոտութիւն)
squander - muskhel, vadnel, shuraylel (մսխել, վատնել, շռայլել)
squanderer - muskhogh, vadnogh, shuraylogh (մսխող, վատնող, շռայլող)
square (n) - karagousi, karangiun, tsevots, hurabarag, jisht (քառակուսի, քառանկիւն, ձեւոց, հրապարակ, ճիշդ)
square (v) - karagousel, oughghel, inknirmov pazmabadgel (քառակուսել, ուղղել, ինքնիրմով բազմապատկել)

squash - juzmel, jumlel, jumloum, juzmouk budoughi (ճզմել, ճմլել, ճմլում, ճզմուք պտուղի)
squat - guguzil, bubuzil, gudzguvil, gugouz, hasdamarmin (կկզիլ, պպզիլ, կծկուիլ, կկուզ, հաստամարմին)
squatter - guguzogh, aborini hoghagal, norapunag (կկզող, ապօրինի հողակալ, նորաբնակ)
squatty - guguzoun, kiroug, gulorig (կկզուն, գիրուկ, կլորիկ)
squawk - sour jich, jurinch, juchal, borchudal, durdunchal (սուր ճիչ, ճռինչ, ճչալ, պոռչտալ, տրտնջալ)
squeak - jurrots, jurinch, jurjural, jurunchel, charakhosel (ճռռոց, ճռինչ, ճռճռալ, ճռնչել, չարախօսել)
squeal - jich, borchudouk, juchal, borchudal (ճիչ, պոռչտուք, ճչալ, պոռչտալ)
squeamish - tuzhvarahaj, tiurav sirdu kharnuvogh (դժուարահաճ, դիւրաւ սիրտը խառնուող)
squeegee - kulanag, kerots (գլանակ, քերոց)
squeeze (n) - seghmoum, junshoum, khujoghoum, ampokh (սեղմում, ճնշում, խճողում, ամբոխ)
squeeze (v) - seghmel, junshel, kamel, hurel, kamvil (սեղմել, ճնշել, քամել, հրել, քամուիլ)
squelch - juzmel, ungjel, luretsunel, khosku gudrel (ճզմել, ընկճել, լռեցնել, խօսքը կտրել)
squib - yerkidzank, barsavakir, pampoushd, dzaghrel (երգիծանք, պարսաւագիր, փամփուշտ, ծաղրել)
squint - shil, dzour nayil, gasgadzil (շիլ, ծուռ նայիլ, կասկածիլ)
squinter - shulachia, charamid (շլաչեայ, չարամիտ)
squire - zinagir, vahanagir, barunger, ungeragtsil (զինակիր, վահանակիր, պարընկեր, ընկերակցիլ)
squirm - soghal, soghosgil, makultsil, shoulluvil (սողալ, սողոսկիլ, մաքլցիլ, շուլլուիլ)
squirrel - usgiur (սկիւռ)
squirt - surusgel, zhaytketsunel, surusgich, churtsan (սրսկել, ժայթքեցնել, սրսկիչ, ջրցան)
stab - tashounel, khotsel, tashounaharoutiun, verk (դաշունել, խոցել, դաշունահարութիւն, վէրք)
stabber - tashiunaharogh, tangudogh, khotsogh (դաշիւնահարող, թանկտող, խոցող)
stability - gayounoutiun, dogounoutiun, ankhakhdoutiun (կայունութիւն, տոկունութիւն, անխախտութիւն)
stabilization - gayounatsoum (կայունացում)
stabilize - gayounatsunel, hasdadel (կայունացնել, հաստատել)
stabilizer - gayounatsunogh, gayounarar (կայունացնող, կայունարար)
stable - gayoun, dogoun, hasdadoun, akhor, akhorel (կայուն, տոկուն, հաստատուն, ախոռ, ախոռել)
stack - tez, dzukhan, gouyd, tizel, goudagel (դէզ, ծխան, կոյտ, դիզել, կուտակել)
stadium - murtsatashd, arshavaran, gurges (մրցադաշտ, արշաւարան, կրկէս)
staff - tsoub, kavazan, antsunagazm, usbayagouyd (ցուպ, գաւազան, անձնակազմ, սպայակոյտ)
stag - arou yeghcherou, amouriagan, sagarani charashah (արու եղջերու, ամուրիական, սակարանի չարաշահ)
stage - taderapem, tadron, varzhuntatsk, pematurel (թատերաբեմ, թատրոն, վարժընթացք, բեմադրել)
stager - portsarou terasan (փորձառու դերասան)
stage-play - taderakhagh (թատերախաղ)
stage-player - terasan (դերասան)
stagger - toghtughal, yereral, yerertsunel, varanil (դողդղալ, երերալ, երերցնել, վարանիլ)
stagnant - lujatsadz, ansharzh, anhos, ankordz (լճացած, անշարժ, անհոս, անգործ)

stagnate - lujanal, ansharzhanal, ankordz munal (լճանալ, անշարժանալ, անգործ մնալ)
stagnation - ansharzhoutiun, gayounoutiun, lujatsoum (անշարժութիւն, կայունութիւն, լճացում)
stagy - taderagan, arvesdagan (թատերական, արուեստական)
staid - oushim, dzanraparo, lourch (ուշիմ, ծանրաբարոյ, լուրջ)
stain - pidz, arad, geghd, pudzavorel, aradavorel (բիծ, արատ, կեղտ, բծաւորել, արատաւորել)
stainless - anpidz, anarad, makour, chujankodogh (անբիծ, անարատ, մաքուր, չժանգոտող)
stair - asdijan, santoukh, yelaran (աստիճան, սանդուխ, ելարան)
stake - tsits, kharouyg, kharouygi vura mardirosatsoum (ցից, խարոյկ, խարոյկի վրայ մարտիրոսացում)
stalactite - shutakar (շթաքար)
stale (I) - oteg, anham, avruvadz, tarmoutiunu gorsuntsunel (օթեկ, անհամ, աւրուած, թարմութիւնը կորսնցնել)
stale (II) - mez, mizel - archarnerou - tsiou (մէզ, միզել՝ արջառներու – ձիու)
stalk - tsoghoun, got, dzukhnelouyz, vorsal, sikajem kalel (ցողուն, կոթ, ծխնելոյզ, որսալ, սիգաճեմ քալել)
stall (I) - akhor, kom, musour, akhoru tunel, komel (ախոր, գոմ, մսուր, ախոռը դնել, գոմել)
stall (II) - badurvag, moloretsunel, khouys dal (պատրուակ, մոլորեցնել, խոյս տալ)
stallion - hovadag, arou tsi (յովատակ, արու ձի)
stalwart - charkash, kach, hantoukun, zoravor (չարքաշ, քաջ, յանդուգն, զօրաւոր)
stamen - tel, tertsan, arech (թել, դերձան, առէջ)
stamina - ouzh, gorov, zoroutiun, buntaniut (ոյժ, կորով, զօրութիւն, պնդանիւթ)
stammer - gagazel, totovel, gagazoum, totovank (կակազել, թոթովել, կակազում, թոթովանք)
stammerer - totov (թոթով)
stamp (I) - namagaturoshm, turoshm, gunik, turoshmel, gunkel (նամակադրոշմ, դրոշմ, կնիք, դրոշմել, կնքել)
stamp (II) - gokhgurdel, pushrel, dzedzel, topel, topiun (կոխկրտել, փշրել, ծեծել, դոփել, դոփիւն)
stampede - khoujab, kholarshav, khoujabahar pakhchil (խուճապ, խօլարշաւ, խուճապահար փախչիլ)
stamper - turoshmogh, gunkogh (դրոշմող, կնքող)
stanch - arian hosoumu tatretsunel, tatril, dogoun (արեան հոսումը դադրեցնել, դադրիլ, տոկուն)
stand (n) - tirk, gayan, pem, kuragal, seghan, daghavar (դիրք, կայան, բեմ, գրակալ, սեղան, տաղաւար)
stand (v) - gankunil, vodki genal, munal, gaynil, devel (կանգնիլ, ոտքի կենալ, մնալ, կայնիլ, տեւել)
stand by - kovu genal, bashdbanel, oknel (քովը կենալ, պաշտպանել, օգնել)
stand up - gankunadz, vodki vura, gankoun, patsahayd (կանգնած, ոտքի վրայ, կանգուն, բացայայտ)
standard - chapanich, dibar, punorinag, orinachap (չափանիշ, տիպար, բնորինակ, օրինաչափ)
standardize - miorinagatsunel, orinachapin veradzel (միօրինակացնել, օրինաչափին վերածել)
stander - getsogh (կեցող)
standing - gayoun, devagan, vodungats, gankunadz, hampav (կայուն, տեւական, ոտնկաց, կանգնած, համբաւ)
standpoint - desaged (տեսակէտ)
standstill - tataroum, lujatsoum, ansharzhoutiun (դադարում, լճացում, անշարժութիւն)
stand-by - kovu getsogh, bashdban, netsoug (քովը կեցող, պաշտպան,

նեցուկ)
staple (I) - yergatatel, amrag, ger, amragabel, buntatsunel (երկաթաթել, ամրակ, կեր, ամրակապել, պնդացնել)
staple (II) - kulkhavor ardaturank, houm niut, tel, nik (գլխաւոր արտադրանք, հում նիւթ, թել, նիգ)
star - asdgh, asdghanich, terasan, asdghazartel (աստղ, աստղանիշ, դերասան, աստղազարդել)
starch - nusha, osla, nushayel, oslayel (նշայ, օսլայ, նշայել, օսլայել)
stare - severel, haril, severoum, haroum (սեւեռել, յառիլ, սեւեռում, յառում)
starfish - dzovasdgh (ծովաստղ)
stargazer - asdghaked, asdghapashkh, mudatsir (աստղագէտ, աստղաբաշխ, մտացիր)
stark - polorovin, gadarial, patsartsag, amour, zoravor (բոլորովին, կատարեալ, բացարձակ, ամուր, զօրաւոր)
starlet - asdghig, abaka terasanouhi (աստղիկ, ապագայ դերասանուհի)
starlight - asdghapayl, asdghalouys, lousunga (աստղափայլ, աստղալոյս, լուսնկայ)
start (n) - megnoum, usgizp, tsuntsoum, sharzhoum, got (մեկնում, սկիզբ, ցնցում, շարժում, կոթ)
start (v) - usgusil, megnil, tsuntsuvil, tsuntsel, sharzhil (սկսիլ, մեկնիլ, ցնցուիլ, ցնցել, շարժիլ)
starter - usgusogh, usgusnag, megnogh, usguselou nushanadou (սկսող, սկսնակ, մեկնող, սկսելու նշանատու)
startle - tsuntsel, abshetsunel, vakhtsunel, tsuntsoum (ցնցել, ապշեցնել, վախցնել, ցնցում)
startling - sarsapeli, abshetsoutsich, sosgali, tsuntsogh (սարսափելի, ապշեցուցիչ, սոսկալի, ցնցող)
starvation - kaghts, sov, sovamahoutiun (գաղց, սով, սովամահութիւն)
starve - suvaghil, sovamah unel, sovamah ullal (սուաղիլ, սովամահ ընել, սովամահ ըլլալ)
starveling - sovahar, sovalloug, sasdig anoti (սովահար, սովալլուկ, սաստիկ անօթի)
state (n) - vijag, tirk, gatsoutiun, bedoutiun, nahank (վիճակ, դիրք, կացութիւն, պետութիւն, նահանգ)
state (v) - usel, hasdadel, haydararel, haghortel (ըսել, հաստատել, յայտարարել, հաղորդել)
statecraft - varchakidoutiun (վարչագիտութիւն)
stated - hasdadvadz, sahmanvadz, voroshvadz (հաստատուած, սահմանուած, որոշուած)
statehouse - garavaradoun, nahankayin balad (կառավարատուն, նահանգային պալատ)
stately - shukegh, vehashouk, hoyagab (շքեղ, վեհաշուք, հոյակապ)
statement - haydararoutiun, deghegakir, hashvetsouyts (յայտարարութիւն, տեղեկագիր, հաշուեցոյց)
stateroom - shukasurah, shukatahlij (շքասրահ, շքադահլիճ)
statesman - kaghakaked, tivanaked, bedagan mart (քաղաքագէտ, դիւանագէտ, պետական մարդ)
statesmanship - tivanakidoutiun (դիւանագիտութիւն)
static - gayoun, havasaragushir (կայուն, հաւասարակշիռ)
statics - gushrakidoutiun, gushrapanoutiun (կշռագիտութիւն, կշռաբանութիւն)
station (n) - gayaran, gayan, gankar, vosdiganadoun, tirk (կայարան, կայան, կանգառ, ոստիկանատուն, դիրք)
station (v) - garkel, deghavorel, bashdoni tunel, voroshel (կարգել, տեղաւորել, պաշտօնի դնել, որոշել)
station master - gayaranabed (կայարանապետ)
stationary - gayoun, ansharzh, hasdadoun, devagan (կայուն, անշարժ, հաստատուն, տեւական)
stationer - tughtavajar, kurenagan

bidouyk vajarogh (թղթավաճառ, գրենական պիտոյք վաճառող)
stationery - kurenagan bidouyk, tughtavajaroutiun (գրենական պիտոյք, թղթավաճառութիւն)
statistician - vijagakir, vijagakurogh (վիճակագիր, վիճակագրող)
statistics - vijagakuroutiun, tsoutsagakuroutiun (վիճակագրութիւն, ցուցակագրութիւն)
statuary - artsanakordzoutiun, kantagakordzoutiun (արձանագործութիւն, քանդակագործութիւն)
statue - artsan (արձան)
statuette - artsanig (արձանիկ)
stature - hasag, partsuroutiun (հասակ, բարձրութիւն)
status - vijag, turoutiun, gatsoutiun (վիճակ, դրութիւն, կացութիւն)
statute - orenk, ganon, ganonakir, ganonakuroutiun (օրէնք, կանոն, կանոնագիր, կանոնագրութիւն)
statutory - orinakurayin (օրինագրային)
staunch - orinabah, havadarim, vusdaheli, hasdad (օրինապահ, հաւատարիմ, վստահելի, հաստատ)
stave (n) - dagarasherd, tsogh, santukhamad, doun-yerki (տակառաշերտ, ձող, սանդխամատ, տուն՝ երգի)
stave (v) - jeghkel, dzagel, hedatsukel, khapanel (ճեղքել, ծակել, յետաձգել, խափանել)
stay (n) - genalu, gayk, tatar, punagoutiun, netsoug (կենալը, կայք, դադար, բնակութիւն, նեցուկ)
stay (v) - munal, genal, getsunel, usbasel, punagil, sadarel (մնալ, կենալ, կեցնել, սպասել, բնակիլ, սատարել)
stead - deghu, pokharenu (տեղը, փոխարէնը)
steadfast - amour, hasdadoun, bint (ամուր, հաստատուն, պինդ)
steadiness - hasdadamudoutiun, ankhakhdoutiun (հաստատամտութիւն, անխախտութիւն)
steady - gayoun, hasdadoun, anpokh, amour, dogoun (կայուն, հաստատուն, անփոփոխ, ամուր, տոկուն)
steak - musasherd, musagudor, tsougi sherd (մսաշերտ, մսակտոր, ձուկի շերտ)
steal - koghnal, pakhtsunel, shortel, koghoutiun (գողնալ, փախցնել, շորթել, գողութիւն)
stealth - kaghduni, dzadzoug, kaghdakoghi, koghoutiun (գաղտնի, ծածուկ, գաղտագողի, գողութիւն)
stealthiness - kaghdunik (գաղտնիք)
stealthy - kaghdunapar, koghouni, kaghdakoghi (գաղտնաբար, գողունի, գաղտագողի)
steam - shoki, kolorshi, dzoukh, shoki hanel, tsuntil (շոգի, գոլորշի, ծուխ, շոգի հանել, ցնդիլ)
steam boiler - shokegatsa (շոգեկաթսայ)
steam engine - shokegark (շոգեկառք)
steamboat - shokenavag, shokemagouyg (շոգենաւակ, շոգեմակոյկ)
steamer - shokenav, shokemekena, shokechurhan (շոգենաւ, շոգեմեքենայ, շոգեջրհան)
steamroller - logh, shokekulan (լող, շոգեգլան)
steamship - shokenav (շոգենաւ)
steamy - shokiod, shokelits, shokenuman, shokebint (շոգիոտ, շոգելից, շոգենման, շոգեպինդ)
steed - nuzhouyk, tsi (նժոյգ, ձի)
steel - boghbad, boghbadel, gardzuratsunel (պողպատ, պողպատել, կարծրացնել)
steely - boghbade, boghbadia, amour (պողպատէ, պողպատեայ, ամուր)
steep (n) - zarivar, zariver, seb, tsits, kahavezh (զառիվար, զառիվեր, սեպ, ցից, գահավէժ)
steep (v) - tatkhel, turchel, turchuvil, souzil, sebanal (թաթխել, թրջել, թրջուիլ, սուզիլ, սեպանալ)
steeple - zankagadoun, ashdarag (զանգակատուն, աշտարակ)
steeplechase - tsiarshav arkelknerov (ձիարշաւ արգելքներով)

steer - ghegavarel, oughghoutiun dal, oughghel, yeznag (ղեկավարել, ուղղութիւն տալ, ուղղել, եզնակ)
steerage - ghegasark, ghegavaroutiun, michnaharg navi (ղեկասարք, ղեկավարութիւն, միջնայարկ նաւի)
steeresman - ghegagal, ghegavar, varort (ղեկակալ, ղեկավար, վարորդ)
stell - burgel, amratsunel (պրկել, ամրացնել)
stellar - asdghayin, asdghazart, asdghanuman (աստղային, աստղազարդ, աստղանման)
stem - poun, gojgh, tsoghoun, dohm, getsunel, yed mughel (բուն, կոճղ, ցօղուն, տոհմ, կեցնել, ետ մղել)
stemmer - hosanki tem tunogh (հոսանքի դէմ դնող)
stench - karshahodoutiun, zhahur (գարշահոտութիւն, ժահր)
stencil - orinagatert, gaghabar, nugaradakhdag, nugarel (օրինակաթերթ, կաղապար, նկարատախտակ, նկարել)
stenograph - sughakir (սղագիր)
stenographer - sughakurogh (սղագրող)
stenography - sughakuroutiun (սղագրութիւն)
stent - sahmani mech bahel, zusbel, sahman, chap (սահմանի մէջ պահել, զսպել, սահման, չափ)
stentorian - partsuratsayn, voroduntosd, borjudan (բարձրաձայն, որոտնդոստ, պոռչտան)
step (n) - kayl, kaylapokh, asdijan, vodnahedk, kalvadzk (քայլ, քայլափոխ, աստիճան, ոտնահետք, քալուածք)
step (v) - kalel, yertal, gokhel, kayl nedel, vodku tunel (քալել, երթալ, կոխել, քայլ նետել, ոտքը դնել)
stepbrother - kort yeghpayr (խորթ եղբայր)
stepfather - khort hayr (խորթ հայր)
stepmother - khort mayr (խորթ մայր)
steppe - dapasdan, lernatashd (տափաստան, լեռնադաշտ)
steps - santoukh (սանդուխ)
stepsister - khort kouyr (խորթ քոյր)
stepson - khort zavag, khort dugha (խորթ զաւակ, խորթ տղայ)
stereo - dogoun, daradzoun, bint, volord, patsasdan (տոկուն, տարածուն, պինդ, ոլորտ, բացաստան)
stereograph - buntakir, hasdadakir (պնդագիր, հաստատագիր)
stereometer - daradzachap, hasdadachap (տարածաչափ, հաստատաչափ)
stereometry - daradzachapoutiun (տարածաչափութիւն)
stereophonic - volordatsayn, pazmativ goghmere lusvog (ոլորտաձայն, բազմաթիւ կողմերէ լսուող)
stereophony - daradzatsaynoutiun (տարածաձայնութիւն)
stereoscope - daradzatsouyts, dzavalatidag, dzovatidag (տարածացոյց, ծաւալադիտակ, ծովադիտակ)
stereoscopic - daradzatsoutsagan (տարածացուցական)
stereotype - buntadib, hasdadadib, buntadubel, hasdadel (պնդատիպ, հաստատատիպ, պնդատպել, հաստատել)
sterile - amoul, anbudough, anperri, manreazerdz (ամուլ, անպտուղ, անբերրի, մանրէազերծ)
sterility - amloutiun (ամլութիւն)
sterilization - amlatsoum, manreazerdzoum (ամլացում, մանրէազերծում)
sterilize - amlatsunel, manreazerdzel (ամլացնել, մանրէազերծել)
sterling - liarzhek, partsurorag, zoud, ankuliagan turam (լիարժէք, բարձրորակ, զուտ, անգլիական դրամ)
stern - khozhor, tazhan, khisd, hedsamas-navou, boch (խոժոռ, դաժան, խիստ, յետսամաս՝ նաւու, պոչ)
sternum - gurdzosgur (կրծոսկր)
sternutation - purunkdouk (փռնգտուք)

stertor - *khortoum, khurumpoum* (խորդում, խումբում)
stertorious, stertorous - *khortatsogh, khurumpatsogh* (խորդացող, խումբացող)
stethoscope - *gurdzkatidag* (կրծքադիտակ)
stew - *shokep, shokiov yepel, kurdunaran, shokekhashel* (շոգեփ, շոգիով եփել, քրտնարան, շոգեխաշել)
steward - *madoutsogh, madagarar, dundes, maranabed* (մատուցող, մատակարար, տնտես, մառանապետ)
stewardess - *madagararouhi- otanavi-navou* (մատակարարուհի՝ օդանավի-նաւու)
stick - *payd, tsoub, doghashar, khotsel, gubtsunel, sharel* (փայտ, ցուպ, տողաշար, խոցել, կպցնել, շարել)
stick (n) - *kavazan, tzoub, jubod, doghashar, jiugh* (գաւազան, ցուպ, ճպոտ, տողաշար, ճիւղ)
stick (v) - *mukhel, pagtsunel, garchil, gutsil, gubchil* (մխել, փակցնել, կառչիլ, կցիլ, կպչիլ)
sticker - *gubogh, gubchoun, bidag, poush, dadasg* (կպող, կպչուն, պիտակ, փուշ, տատասկ)
stickle - *barab degh makaril, vijil, tekeril* (պարապ տեղ մքառիլ, վիճիլ, դեգերիլ)
sticky - *gubchoun, hamar* (կպչուն, յամառ)
sticky - *gubchoun, madzoutsig, hamar* (կպչուն, մածուցիկ, յամառ)
stiff - *gardzur, dogoun, bint, hamar, pird* (կարծր, տոկուն, պինդ, յամառ, բիրտ)
stiffen - *gardzuranal, gardzuratsunel, buntatsunel* (կարծրանալ, կարծրացնել, պնդացնել)
stiffly - *khusdoren, gardzuroren* (խստօրէն, կարծրօրէն)
stiffness - *gardzuroutiun, dogounoutiun* (կարծրութիւն, տոկունութիւն)
stifle - *kheghtel-tsaynu, junshel, marel, kheghtuvil* (խեղդել՝ ձայնը, ճնշել, մարել, խեղդուիլ)
stigma - *usbi, turoshm, kharan, arad, pidz* (սպի, դրոշմ, խարան, արատ, բիծ)
stigmatization - *kharanoum* (խարանում)
stigmatize - *turoshmel, kharanel, nushanagel, anbadvel* (դրոշմել, խարանել, նշանակել, անպատուել)
stile - *hedzan, shem, tsangabadi asdijan, sulak* (հեծան, շեմ, ցանկապատի աստիճան, սլաք)
still (I) - *ansharzh, hantard, dagavin, ter, luroutiun* (անշարժ, հանդարտ, տակաւին, դեռ, լռութիւն)
still (II) - *hantardetsunel, handardil, torel, zudel* (հանդարտեցնել, հանդարտիլ, թորել, զտել)
stillborn - *mereladzin-yerakha* (մեռելածին՝ երախայ)
stillness - *hantardoutiun* (հանդարտութիւն)
stilly - *hantard, khaghagh* (հանդարտ, խաղաղ)
stilts - *vodnapayder, vodnatsouber, payde vodker* (ոտնափայտեր, ոտնացուպեր, փայտէ ոտքեր)
stimulant - *kurkurich, kurkurategh, vokelits khumick* (գրգռիչ, գրգռադեղ, ոգելից խմիչք)
stimulate - *kurkurel, khutanel, vokevorel* (գրգռել, խթանել, ոգեւորել)
stimulation - *kurkuroum, khutanoum, vokevoroutiun* (գրգռում, խթանում, ոգեւորութիւն)
stimulus - *kurkir, kurkurich, khutan, turtich* (գրգիռ, գրգռիչ, խթան, դրդիչ)
sting - *khaytots, khayt, khaytel, gujel, tsavtsunel* (խայթոց, խայթ, խայթել, կճել, ցաւցնել)
stingy - *akah, gudzdzi, zhulad* (ագահ, կծծի, ժլատ)
stink - *hodil, nekhil, karshahodoutiun, kesh hod* (հոտիլ, նեխիլ, գարշահոտութիւն, գէշ հոտ)
stinkard - *hodadz-mart* (հոտած՝ մարդ)
stinker - *hodogh, hodadz* (հոտող,

Հոտած)
stint - chap, orabahig, chapavorel, khunayel, gurjadel (չափ, օրապահիկ, չափաւորել, խնայել, կրճատել)
stipend - toshag, rojig, amsagan (Թոշակ, ռոճիկ, ամսական)
stipendiary - toshagavor, vartsgan (Թոշակաւոր, վարձկան)
stipple - gedgidel, gidanugarel (կէտկիտել, կիտանկարել)
stipulate - baymanavorel, bayman tunel (պայմանաւորել, պայման դնել)
stipulation - bayman, baymanavoroutiun, tashun (պայման, պայմանաւորութիւն, դաշն)
stir (n) - irarantsoum, aghmoug, shupotoutiun, khulurdoum (իրարանցում, աղմուկ, շփոթութիւն, խլրտում)
stir (v) - sharzhel, tsuntsel, kharnel, houzel (շարժել, ցնցել, խառնել, յուզել)
stirrer - kharnogh, kharnich (խառնող, խառնիչ)
stirring - houzich, kurkurich, sharzhoun (յուզիչ, գրգռիչ, շարժուն)
stitch - gar, garvadzk, goghi tsav, garel, hiusel (կար, կարուածք, կողի ցաւ, կարել, հիւսել)
stive - gokhel, seghmetsunel (կոխել, սեղմեցնել)
stock (n) - bashar, muterk, pazhnedoms, gojgh, nakhnik (պաշար, մԹերք, բաժնետոմս, կոճղ, նախնիք)
stock (v) - muterel, tizel, zhoghvel, letsunel (մԹերել, դիզել, ժողվել, լեցնել)
stock exchange - sagaran, muterel, abrank haytaytel (սակարան, մԹերել, ապրանք հայԹայԹել)
stock market - sagaran (սակարան)
stockade - tsutsabadnesh, tsoghapag, tsoghapagel (ցցապատնէշ, ձողափակ, ձողափակել)
stockbroker - seghanavor, michnort sagarani (սեղանաւոր, միջնորդ սակարանի)
stockholder - pazhneder (բաժնետէր)
stocking - koulba (գուլպայ)
stockish - putamid, anmid, aboush (փԹամիտ, անմիտ, ապուշ)
stocky - kiroug, garj ou ker (գիրուկ, կարճ ու գէր)
stockyard - anasnapag, anasnanots (անասնաբակ, անասնանոց)
stodge - tukhmel, khu joghel (Թխմել, խճողել)
stodgy - tuzhvaramars, dzanur, khurtin, tsantsurali (դժուարամարս, ծանր, խրԹին, ձանձրալի)
stole - ourar (ուրար)
stolid - putamid, abush, baghariun (բԹամիտ, ապուշ, պաղարիւն)
stomach - usdamoks, akhorzhag, oudel, marsel, hamperel (ստամոքս, ախորժակ, ուտել, մարսել, համբերել)
stomachic, ical - usdamoksayin, akhorzhaper (ստամոքսային, ախորժաբեր)
stomp - vodnahedk tsukel (ոտնահետք ձգել)
stone (n) - kar, vem, kohar, amortsik, goud - budoughi (քար, վէմ, գոհար, ամորձիք, կուտ՝ պտուղի)
stone (v) - kargodzel, salargel, goudu hanel (քարկոծել, սալարկել, կուտը հանել)
stoneblind - polorovin gouyr (բոլորովին կոյր)
stonecoal - adzkhakar (ածխաքար)
stonecutter - karagop (քարակոփ)
stonepit - karahank (քարահանք)
stony - karod, karkarod, karayin, ankout, tazhan (քարոտ, քարքարոտ, քարային, անգուԹ, դաժան)
stooge - ourishin usadzu gurgnogh, anmid bakharagvogh (ուրիշին ըսածը կրկնող, անմիտ պախարակուող)
stook - voranerou khourts, khourts gabel (որաներու խուրձ, խուրձ կապել)
stool - atorag, dzagator, gughgughank, gughgughel (աԹոռակ, ծակաԹոռ, կղկղանք, կղկղել)

stoop - dzuril, khonarhil, goranal, dzurel, goroutiun (ծռիլ, խոնարհիլ, կորանալ, ծռել, կորութիւն)
stop (n) - gank ar, tatar, gats, arkelk, verchaged (կանգ առ, դադար, կաց, արգելք, վերջակէտ)
stop (v) - getsunel, tataretsunel, genal, verchagedel (կեցնել, դադարեցնել, կենալ, վերջակէտել)
storage - muteroum, muteranots, bahesdanots, muteroghchek (մթերում, մթերանոց, պահեստանոց, մթերողչէք)
store (n) - bahesd, bashar, muterk, khanout, muteranots (պահեստ, պաշար, մթերք, խանութ, մթերանոց)
store (v) - muterel, havakel, amparel, tizel (մթերել, հաւաքել, ամբարել, դիզել)
stork - arakil (արագիլ)
storm - potorig, murrig, pouk, potorgil, khouzhel (փոթորիկ, մրրիկ, բուք, փոթորկիլ, խուժել)
stormy - potorgod, mururgod, molekin (փոթորկոտ, մրրկոտ, մոլեգին)
story - badmoutiun, arasbel, soud (պատմութիւն, առասպել, սուտ)
story-book - badmuvadzknerou kirk, hekiatnerou zhoghovadzou (պատմուածքներու գիրք, հեքիաթներու ժողովածու)
story-teller - hekiatasats, badmakhos, sudakhos (հեքիաթասաց, պատմախօս, ստախօս)
stout - zoravor, houzhgou, marmunegh, ker, kach (զօրաւոր, հուժկու, մարմնեղ, գէր, քաջ)
stove - chermots, vararan, daktsunel (ջերմոց, վառարան, տաքցնել)
stow - zedeghel, deghavorel, dzadzgel, taktsunel (զետեղել, տեղաւորել, ծածկել, թաքցնել)
stowage - zedeghoum, zedegharan (զետեղում, զետեղարան)
stowaway - andoms jamport (անտոմս ճամբորդ)
straddle - surounkneru patsvadzk, laynapats vodkov kalel (սրունքներու բացուածք, լայնաբաց ոտքով քալել)
strafe - badzhel, rumpagodzel, rumpagodzoum (պատժել, ռմբակոծել, ռմբակոծում)
straggle - sulukdal, taparil, khodoril, tsurvil (սլքտալ, թափառիլ, խոտորիլ, ցրուիլ)
straggler - taparagan, sulukdatsogh, hedamunats (թափառական, սլքտացող, յետամնաց)
straight - oughigh, shidag, oughghamid, angeghdz (ուղիղ, շիտակ, ուղղամիտ, անկեղծ)
straighten - shudgel, hartel, shudguvil, garki perel (շտկել, հարթել, շտկուիլ, կարգի բերել)
straightforward - oughghagi, shidag, oughigh (ուղղակի, շիտակ, ուղիղ)
straightness - shidagoutiun, oughigh ullalu (շիտակութիւն, ուղիղ ըլլալը)
straightway - anmichabes (անմիջապէս)
strain (n) - jik, burgoum, laroum, midoum, nuvak, voj (ճիգ, պրկում, լարում, միտում, նուագ, ոճ)
strain (v) - burgel, larel, vunasel, avrel, kamel (պրկել, լարել, վնասել, աւրել, քամել)
strainer - kamots, magh (քամոց, մաղ)
strait - negh, seghm, khisd, neghoutiun, girj, neghouts (նեղ, սեղմ, խիստ, նեղութիւն, կիրճ, նեղուց)
straiten - seghmel, neghel, junshel, burgel, neghatsunel (սեղմել, նեղել, ճնշել, պրկել, նեղացնել)
strand (I) - ap, dzovap, dzovezur, khuril, khuretsunel (ափ, ծովափ, ծովեզր, խրիլ, խրեցնել)
strand (II) - chuvan, arasan, sharan, pounch, hiusel, volorel (չուան, առասան, շարան, փունջ, հիւսել, ոլորել)
stranded - khuradz, ap nedvadz, gordzanadz (խրած, ափ նետուած, կործանած)
strange - odar, odarodi, andzanot, darorinag, ansovor (օտար, օտարոտի, անծանօթ, տարօրինակ, ան-

սովոր)
stranger - odar, odaragan, andzanot (օտար, օտարական, անծանօթ)
strangle - kheghtel, kheghtamah unel, junshel (խեղդել, խեղդամահ ընել, ճնշել)
strangler - kheghtogh (խեղդող)
strangulation - kheghtoum, heghtsamahoutiun, seghmoum (խեղդում, հեղձամահութիւն, սեղմում)
strangury - tuzhvaramizoutiun (դժուարամիզութիւն)
strap - yeriz, gab, kodi, gashiye sherd, gabel, surel (երիզ, կապ, գօտի, կաշիէ շերտ, կապել, սրել)
stratagem - razmahunark, khoramangoutiun (ռազմահնարք, խորամանկութիւն)
strategic - razmavaragan (ռազմավարական)
strategic, al - razmavaragan (ռազմավարական)
strategist - razmaked (ռազմագէտ)
strategy - razmavaroutiun, razmakidoutiun (ռազմավարութիւն, ռազմագիտութիւն)
stratification - sherdavoroutiun, khavatasoutiun (շերտաւորութիւն, խաւադասութիւն)
stratified - pazmakhav (բազմախաւ)
stratify - khavasharel, sherd sherd tizel, khavel (խաւաշարել, շերտ շերտ դիզել, խաւել)
straw - hart, vochinch, anarzhek pan, harte (յարդ, ոչինչ, անարժէք բան, յարդէ)
strawberry - yelag, yelageni (ելակ, ելակենի)
stray - moloril, sheghil, taparagan, gorsuvadz (մոլորիլ, շեղիլ, թափառական, կորսուած)
streak - kidz, yeriz, sherdakidz, yerizel, bisagel (գիծ, երիզ, շերտագիծ, երիզել, պիսակել)
stream (n) - ked, kedag, hosank, untatsk, oughghoutiun (գետ, գետակ, հոսանք, ընթացք, ուղղութիւն)
stream (v) - hosil, dzoril, vazel, dzupal, hosetsunel (հոսիլ, ծորիլ, վազել, ծփալ, հոսեցնել)
streamer - navaturosh, negh-yergar zhabaven, aykatsaydk (նաւադրօշ, նեղ-երկար ժապաւէն, այգացայտք)
street - poghots (փողոց)
street-car - hanragark (հանրակառք)
street-walker - bornig, poghotsayin gin (պոռնիկ, փողոցային կին)
strength - ouzh, zoroutiun, gorov, (ույժ, զօրութիւն, կորով)
strengthen - zoratsunel, amratsunel, ouzh dal, zoranal (զօրացնել, ամրացնել, ույժ տալ, զօրանալ)
strenuous - gorovi, kach, charkash, zhir, yerantoun (կորովի, քաջ, չարքաշ, ժիր, եռանդուն)
stress - hokejunshoum, laroum, kerjunshoum, sheshd, zorel (հոգեճնշում, լարում, գերճնշում, շեշտ, զօրել)
stretch (n) - daradzoutiun, tsukdoum, untatsk, michots (տարածութիւն, ձգտում, ընթացք, միջոց)
stretch (v) - yergunnal, daradzvil, patsvil, burgel, kashel (երկննալ, տարածուիլ, բացուիլ, պրկել, քաշել)
stretcher - badkarag, burgogh, kashogh (պատգարակ, պրկող, քաշող)
strew - tsanel, purel, tsurvel, suprel (ցանել, փռել, ցրուել, սփռել)
stricken - zarnuvadz, mashadz, barav, harachatsadz (զարնուած, մաշած, պառաւ, յառաջացած)
strict - khisd, negh, antsoug, jushtabah, jushkurid (խիստ, նեղ, անցուկ, ճշդապահ, ճշգրիտ)
strictly - khusdiv, khusdoutiamp (խստիւ, խստութեամբ)
strictness - khusdoutiun, jushtabahoutiun (խստութիւն, ճշդապահութիւն)
stricture - meghatrank, barsav, pagoum - mizantski (մեղադրանք, պարսաւ, փակում՝ միզանցքի)
stride - medz kayl, medzakayl kalel, yertal, tsadgel (մեծ քայլ, մեծաքայլ քալել, երթալ, ցատկել)
strife - baykar, jik, makaroum, vej

(պայքար, ճիգ, մաքրում, վէճ)
strike (n) - kordzatoul, harvadz, hartich (գործադուլ, Հարուած, Հարթիչ)
strike (v) - zarnel, harvadzel, badzhel, ichetsunel, (զարնել, Հարուածել, պատժել, իջեցնել)
striker - kordzatoulavor, kordzatogh, zarnogh (գործադուլաւոր, գործաթող, զարնող)
striking - oushakurav, hayduni, dubavorich, zarmanali (ուշագրաւ, յայտնի, տպաւորիչ, զարմանալի)
string - lar, nuvakalar, gab, baran, larel, burgel (լար, նուագալար, կապ, պարան, լարել, պրկել)
stringency - khusdoutiun, sasdgoutiun, niutagan neghoutiun (խստութիւն, սաստկութիւն, նիւթական նեղութիւն)
stringent - khusdabahanch, khisd, niutaganov daknabogh (խստապահանջ, խիստ, նիւթականով տագնապող)
string-beans - ganach loupia (կանաչ լուբիա)
strip - mergatsunel, mortu hanel, goghobdel, negh sherd (մերկացնել, մորթը Հանել, կողոպտել, նեղ շերտ)
stripe - sherd, sherdakidz, sherdavorel, dzedzel, mudragel (շերտ, շերտագիծ, շերտաւորել, ծեծել, մտրակել)
stripling - laj, terahas, badaniag (լաճ, դեռաՀաս, պատանեակ)
stripper - mergatsogh, geghevogh (մերկացող, կեղեւող)
stripping - mergatsoum, geghevoum (մերկացում, կեղեւում)
strip-tease - mergatsoum hantisadesi archev (մերկացում` Հանդիսատեսի առջեւ)
strive - juknil, makaril, baykaril (ճգնիլ, մաքրիլ, պայքարիլ)
striver - baykarogh, tsukdogh (պայքարող, ձգտող)
stroke - harvadz, gatvadz, tetev pakhoum, shupel, zarnel (Հարուած, կաթուած, թեթեւ բախում, շփել, զարնել)
stroke (I) - harvadz, gatvadz, zarg, zarnel (Հարուած, կաթուած, զարկ, զարնել)
stroke (II) - kukvank, shoyoum, shoyel, paghakushel (գգուանք, շոյում, շոյել, փաղաքշել)
stroker - shupogh, amokogh (շփող, ամոքող)
stroll - tekeroum, uzposank, tekeril, taparil, jemil (դեգերում, զբօսանք, դեգերիլ, թափառիլ, ճեմիլ)
stroller - tekerogh, uzposnogh, taparashurchig (դեգերող, զբօսնող, թափառաշրջիկ)
strong - zoravor, ouzhegh, ouzhkin, amour, timatsgoun (զօրաւոր, ուժեղ, ուժգին, ամուր, դիմացկուն)
stronghold - amrots, amroutiun (ամրոց, ամրութիւն)
strongly - ouzhov, zoroutiamp (ուժով, զօրութեամբ)
strong-box - yergatargugh, turamargugh (երկաթարկղ, դրամարկղ)
strop - surotsapog, kusots, chuvan, surel, kusel (սրոցափոկ, քսոց, չուան, սրել, քսել)
strove - see: strive (տե՛ս` strive)
struck - see: strike (տե՛ս` strike)
structural - gazmagan, usd gazmoutian, shinararagan (կազմական, ըստ կազմութեան, շինարարական)
structure - garouyts, garoutsvadzk, shenk, horinvadzk, gazm (կառոյց, կառուցուածք, շէնք, յօրինուածք, կազմ)
struggle - baykar, makaroum, jik, baykaril, makaril (պայքար, մաքրում, ճիգ, պայքարիլ, մաքրիլ)
strumpet - poz, bornig, popokhamid (բոզ, պոռնիկ, փոփոխամիտ)
strut - hubard kalvadzk, henag, sikal, netsoug genal (Հպարտ քալուածք, յենակ, սիգալ, նեցուկ կենալ)
stub - gojgh, poun, armad, armadakhil unel (կոճղ, բուն, արմատ, արմատախիլ ընել)
stubble - khozan, huntsuvadz ard,

garj gudruvadz maz (խողան, Հնձուած արտ, կարճ կտրուած մազ)
stubborn - *hamar, gardzur, buntakuloukh, pird* (յամառ, կարծր, պնդագլուխ, բիրտ)
stubbornness - *hamaroutiun, gardzuroutiun* (յամառութիւն, կարծրութիւն)
stucco - *dzep, gujadzep, dzepel* (ծեփ, կճածեփ, ծեփել)
stuck - *pagav, pagadz, pagtsuvadz* (փակաւ, փակած, փակցուած)
stud (I) - *zartagojag, jarmant, gojagazartel* (զարդակոճակ, ճարմանդ, կոճակազարդել)
stud (II) - *akhor, tsianots, tsiakhoump* (ախոր, ձիանոց, ձիախումբ)
stud farm - *tsiapoudzaran* (ձիաբուծարան)
student - *ousanogh* (ուսանող)
studio - *arvesdanots, ashkhadanots, tsoutsasurah* (արուեստանոց, աշխատանոց, ցուցասրահ)
studious - *ousoumnaser, ashkhadaser, zhurachan* (ուսումնասէր, աշխատասէր, ժրաջան)
study (n) - *ousoum, serdoghoutiun, ousoumnasiroutiun* (ուսում, սերտողութիւն, ուսումնասիրութիւն)
study (v) - *serdel, ousanil, ousoumnasirel, kunnel* (սերտել, ուսանիլ, ուսումնասիրել, քննել)
stuff - *niut, hiusgen, gudav, letsunel, tukhmel, oudel* (նիւթ, Հիւսկէն, կտաւ, լեցնել, թխմել, ուտել)
stuffy - *heghtsoutsich ot, dot, dzanur, houzhgou, khozhor* (Հեղձուցիչ՝ օդ, տօթ, ծանր, Հուժկու, խոժոռ)
stultify - *putatsunel, aboush tartsunel, chezokatsunel* (բթացնել, ապուշ դարձնել, չէզոքացնել)
stum - *kaghtsou, khaghoghachour, kaghtsouov kharnel* (քաղցու, խաղողաջուր, քաղցուով խառնել)
stumble (n) - *saytakoum, kuloroum, sahoum, angoum, gagazoum* (սայթաքում, գլորում, սաՀում, անկում, կակազում)
stumble (v) - *saytakil, moloril, kuloril, iynal, gumgumal* (սայթաքիլ, մոլորիլ, գլորիլ, իյնալ, կմկմալ)
stump - *gojgh, pegor, vodkov zarnel, undurarshav unel* (կոճղ, բեկոր, ոտքով զարնել, ընտրարշաւ ընել)
stumpy - *garjahasag, buntagazm* (կարճաՀասակ, պնդակազմ)
stun - *abshetsunel, shushmetsunel, anuzkayatsunel* (ապշեցնել, շշմեցնել, անզգայացնել)
stunk - *khaytets, khadzav* (խայթեց, խածաւ)
stunt - *aji tantaghoum, aji tataroum* (աճի դանդաղում, աճի դադարում)
stupefaction - *abshank, meds zarmank, tumroutiun, karatsoum* (ապշանք, մեծ զարմանք, թմրութիւն, քարացում)
stupefier - *tumretsunogh, abshetsunogh* (թմրեցնող, ապշեցնող)
stupefy - *tumretsunel, abshetsunel, hiyatsunel* (թմրեցնել, ապշեցնել, Հիացնել)
stupendous - *abshetsoutsich, zarmanali, uskancheli* (ապշեցուցիչ, զարմանալի, սքանչելի)
stupid - *aboush, ankhelk, dukhmar, putamid, himar* (ապուշ, անխելք, տխմար, բթամիտ, յիմար)
stupidity - *aboushoutiun, putamudoutiun, ankhelkoutiun* (ապուշութիւն, բթամտութիւն, անխելքութիւն)
stupor - *tumroutiun, abshoutiun, anuzkayoutiun* (թմրութիւն, ապշութիւն, անզգայութիւն)
stuprate - *purnaparel, lulgel* (բռնաբարել, լլկել)
sturdy - *charkash, zoravor, pird, ouzhegh, aroghch* (չարքաշ, զօրաւոր, բիրտ, ուժեղ, առողջ)
sturgeon - *tarap- tsoug mu* (թառափ- ձուկ մը)
stutter - *gagazel, totovel, gumgumal, gagazoum, totov* (կակազել, թոթովել, կմկմալ, կակազում, թոթով)
sty - *khozanots, komu tunel* (խոզանոց, գոմը դնել)

sty, stye - garig-achki (կարիկ՝ աչքի)
style - voj, gerb, yeghanag, sulak, kurich, voragel (ոճ, կերպ, եղանակ, սլաք, գրիչ, որակել)
stylish - vojavor, noratsev, vayelouch, shukegh (ոճաւոր, նորաձեւ, վայելուչ, շքեղ)
stylist - vojapan, norarar-hakousdi, zartarar (ոճաբան, նորարար՝ հագուստի, զարդարար)
stylograph - inknahos kurich (ինքնահոս գրիչ)
stylus - usdveratouyts, sulak (ստուերացոյց, սլաք)
suasion - hamozoum, hortor, khurad (համոզում, յորդոր, խրատ)
suave - meghm, hajeli, kaghtsur, kaghakavar (մեղմ, հաճելի, քաղցր, քաղաքավար)
suavity - meghmoutiun, kaghakavaroutiun (մեղմութիւն, քաղաքավարութիւն)
subaltern - usdoratas, yentasba, yergurortagan (ստորադաս, ենթասպայ, երկրորդական)
subcommittee - yentahantsunakhoump (ենթայանձնախումբ)
subconscious - yentakidagits, yentakidagtsagan (ենթագիտակից, ենթագիտակցական)
subdivide - usdorapazhanel, tartsial pazhnel (ստորաբաժանել, դարձեալ բաժնել)
subdivision - usdorapazhanoum, yentapazhanoum (ստորաբաժանում, ենթաբաժանում)
subdue - yentargel, junshel, hunazantetsunel (ենթարկել, ճնշել, հնազանդեցնել)
subject (n) - yentaga, niut, ararga, hubadag, hagamed (ենթակայ, նիւթ, առարկայ, հպատակ, հակամէտ)
subject (v) - yentargel, nuvajel, hunazantetsunel (ենթարկել, նուաճել, հնազանդեցնել)
subjection - yentargoum, hubadagetsoum, nuvajoum (ենթարկում, հպատակեցում, նուաճում)
subjective - yentagayagan, nerkin (ենթակայական, ներքին)
subjectivism - yentagayatsoum (ենթակայացում)
subjoin - gutsel, aveltsunel, harel (կցել, աւելցնել, յարել)
subjoinder - havelvadz (յաւելուած)
subjugate - ungjel, direl, nuvajel, hubadagetsunel (ընկճել, տիրել, նուաճել, հպատակեցնել)
subjugation - nuvajoum, hubadagetsoum (նուաճում, հպատակեցում)
subjunctive - usdoratasagan, yentagayagan (ստորադասական, ենթակայական)
sublease - yentavartsel, vartsagalu vartsu gou da (ենթավարձել, վարձակալը վարձու կու տայ)
sublimate - huratsuntel, veratsunel, makrazudel, vusematsunel (հրացնդել, վերացնել, մաքրազտել, վսեմացնել)
sublimation - piureghatsoum, shokiatsoum, aznuvatsoum (բիւրեղացում, շոգիացում, ազնուացում)
sublime - vusem, veh, nourp, vusemoutiun, vusematsunel (վսեմ, վեհ, նուրբ, վսեմութիւն, վսեմացնել)
subliminal - yentakidagits, yentakidagtsagan (ենթագիտակից, ենթագիտակցական)
sublimity - vusemoutiun, vehoutiun (վսեմութիւն, վեհութիւն)
submarine - untdzovia, souzanav (ընդծովեայ, սուզանաւ)
submerge - ungughmel, churasouzel, voghoghel, khotel (ընկղմել, ջրասուզել, ողողել, խոթել)
submergence - voghoghoum, souzoum, ungughmoum (ողողում, սուզում, ընկղմում)
submersion - see: submergence (տե՛ս՝ submergence)
submission - hunazantoutiun, yentargoum, hamagerboutiun (հնազանդութիւն, ենթարկում, համակերպութիւն)
submissive - hulou, hunazant (հլու, հնազանդ)
submit - hunazantil, yentarguvil, un-

tounil, hubadagil (Հնազանդիլ, ենթարկուիլ, ընդունիլ, Հպատակիլ)
subordinate - usdoratas, yentaga, usdoratasel (ստորադաս, ենթակայ, ստորադասել)
subordination - yentagayoutiun, yentargoum, usdoragarkoutiun (ենթակայութիւն, ենթարկում, ստորակարգութիւն)
subpoena - tadagoch, tadaran ganchuvadz vuga, tadagochel (դատակոչ, դատարան կանչուած վկայ, դատակոչել)
subscribe - pazhanortakurvil, usdorakurel (բաժանորդագրուիլ, ստորագրել)
subscriber - pazhanort, usdorakurogh (բաժանորդ, ստորագրող)
subscription - pazhanortakuroutiun, usdorakuroutiun (բաժանորդագրութիւն, ստորագրութիւն)
subsequent - hedaka, kalik, hachort (Հետագայ, գալիք, յաջորդ)
subserve - nubasdel, achagtsil, dzarayel, kordzik ullal (նպաստել, աջակցիլ, ծառայել, գործիք ըլլալ)
subservience - okdagaroutiun, kudznank (օգտակարութիւն, քծնանք)
subservient - nubasdogh, achagtsogh, usdurgamid (նպաստող, աջակցող, ստրկամիտ)
subside - ungughmil, nusdil, ichnel, hankuchil, hantardil (ընկղմիլ, նստիլ, իջնել, Հանգչիլ, Հանդարտիլ)
subsidiary - ozhantag, nubasd, oknagan (օժանդակ, նպաստ, օգնական)
subsidize - nubasdel, oknel, ozhantagel (նպաստել, օգնել, օժանդակել)
subsist - abril, ullal, gayanal, ko ullal (ապրիլ, ըլլալ, կայանալ, գոյ ըլլալ)
subsistence - koyoutiun, abrousd, oudesd, abrelamichots (գոյութիւն, ապրուստ, ուտեստ, ապրելամիջոց)
subsoil - yentahogh (ենթաՀող)
substance - niut, eyoutiun, isgoutiun, himk, marmin, inchk (նիւթ, էութիւն, իսկութիւն, Հիմք, մարմին, ինչք)
substantial - eyagan, himnagan, sununtarar, niutagan (էական, Հիմնական, սննդարար, նիւթական)
substantiate - koyatsunel, himnavorel, abatsoutsel (գոյացնել, Հիմնաւորել, ապացուցել)
substantive - koyagan anoun, eyagan, hasdadoun (գոյական անուն, էական, Հաստատուն)
substitute - pokharinel, pokhanortel, pokhanort, deghabah (փոխարինել, փոխանորդել, փոխանորդ, տեղապահ)
substitution - pokharinoum, pokhanagoutiun (փոխարինում, փոխանակութիւն)
substraction - hanoum (Հանում)
substrate - yentahogh, himnabadjar (ենթաՀող, Հիմնապատճառ)
substruction - himk, yentagarouyts (Հիմք, ենթակառոյց)
subterfuge - khousapoum, pakhousd, hunark, takusdots (խուսափում, փախուստ, Հնարք, թաքստոց)
subterranean - usdorerguria, unthadagia, kednapor, kaghduni (ստորերկրեայ, ընդյատակեայ, գետնափոր, գաղտնի)
subtile - nourp, suramid, jugoun, jarbig, meghm (նուրբ, սրամիտ, ճկուն, ճարպիկ, մեղմ)
subtilty - nurpoutiun, paragoutiun, jugounoutiun (նրբութիւն, բարակութիւն, ճկունութիւն)
subtract - hanel, nuvazetsunel, bagsetsunel (Հանել, նուազեցնել, պակսեցնել)
subtrahend - haneli (Հանելի)
suburb - arvartsan (արուարձան)
suburban - arvartsanapunag, kaghakamerts abrogh (արուարձանաբնակ, քաղաքամերձ ապրող)
subvention - nubasd, turamagan oknoutiun (նպաստ, դրամական օգնութիւն)
subversion - dabaloum, gordzanoum, heghashurchoum (տապալում, կործանում, յեղաշրջում)

subversive - kantich, gordzanarar, averich, kaykayich (քանդիչ, կործանարար, աւերիչ, քայքայիչ)
subvert - dabalel, gordzanel, averel, kantel (տապալել, կործանել, աւերել, քանդել)
subway - kednoughi, kednantsk, usdorerguria shokegark (գետնուղի, գետնանցք, ստորերկրեայ շոգեկառք)
succeed - hachoghil, hachortel, hedevil, pokhanortel (յաջողիլ, յաջորդել, հետեւիլ, փոխանորդել)
success - hachoghoutiun, arachtimoutiun, haghtanag (յաջողութիւն, առաջդիմութիւն, յաղթանակ)
successful - hachogh, hachoghag, pakhdavor (յաջող, յաջողակ, բախտաւոր)
succession - hachortoutiun, hachortaganoutiun (յաջորդութիւն, յաջորդականութիւն)
successive - hachortagan, hachortogh (յաջորդական, յաջորդող)
successor - hachort, hachortogh, zharankort, pokharinogh (յաջորդ, յաջորդող, ժառանգորդ, փոխարինող)
succint - hagirj, ampop, hamarod, seghm (հակիրճ, ամփոփ, համառօտ, սեղմ)
succor, succour - oknoutiun, netsoug, oknel, oknoutian hasnil (օգնութիւն, նեցուկ, օգնել, օգնութեան հասնիլ)
succulence - hiuteghoutiun (հիւթեղութիւն)
succulent - hiutegh, hamegh, hiutalits, hiutarad (հիւթեղ, համեղ, հիւթալից, հիւթառատ)
succumb - gukil, ungjuvil, barduvil, mernil (կքիլ, ընկճուիլ, պարտուիլ, մեռնիլ)
succursal - ozhantal, masnajiugh (օժանդակ, մասնաճիւղ)
such - numan, nouynbisi, iprev, bes, aysbes, aysbisi (նման, նոյնպիսի, իբրեւ, պէս, այսպէս, այսպիսի)
such as - zor orinag, aynbes inchbes (զոր օրինակ, այնպէս ինչպէս)
suck - dzudzel, kashel, gat dzudzel, dzudzoum, dzudzvadz gat (ծծել, քաշել, կաթ ծծել, ծծում, ծծուած կաթ)
sucker - dzudzogh, dzudzger, gatnager, magapouydz (ծծող, ծծկեր, կաթնակեր, մակաբոյծ)
suckle - dzudzetsunel, dzidz dal, tiyetsunel (ծծեցնել, ծիծ տալ, դիեցնել)
suckling - dzudzger, gatnager, yerakha (ծծկեր, կաթնակեր, երախայ)
sucrose - pureghashakar, budoughe hanvadz shakar (բիւրեղաշաքար, պտուղէ հանուած շաքար)
suction - dzudzoum, kashelu (ծծում, քաշելը)
sudden - hangardzagi, arak, anagungal, anusbaseli (յանկարծակի, արագ, անակնկալ, անսպասելի)
suddenly - anagungaloren, anusbaselioren (անակնկալօրէն, անսպասելիօրէն)
sudoriferous - kurdnaper (քրտնաբեր)
sudorific - kurdnetsoutsich, kurdnaper (քրտնեցուցիչ, քրտնաբեր)
suds - ojarachour (օճառաջուր)
sue - tadi kashel, hedabuntel, bahanchel, ouzel (դատի քաշել, հետապնդել, պահանջել, ուզել)
suer - khunturogh, sirapanogh (խնդրող, սիրաբանող)
suet - jarb (ճարպ)
suffer - darabil, charcharvil, danchuvil, gurel, dogal (տառապիլ, չարչարուիլ, տանջուիլ, կրել, տոկալ)
sufferance - darabank, charcharank, vishd, hamperoutiun (տառապանք, չարչարանք, վիշտ, համբերութիւն)
sufferer - darabogh (տառապող)
suffering - darabank, darabogh, vushdagir (տառապանք, տառապող, վշտակիր)
suffering - darabank, danchank (տառապանք, տանջանք)
suffice - pavel, kohatsunel, pavara-

rel, kohanal (բաւել, գոհացնել, բաւարարել, գոհանալ)
sufficiency - pavaganoutiun, adagoutiun, garoghoutiun (բաւականութիւն, ատակութիւն, կարողութիւն)
sufficient - pavaganachap, pavarar, garogh (բաւականաչափ, բաւարար, կարող)
suffix - verchadzants, hedamasnig (վերջածանց, յետամասնիկ)
sufflate - ouretsunel, puchel (ուռեցնել, փչել)
sufflation - puchoum (փչում)
suffocate - kheghtuvil, kheghtel (խեղդուիլ, խեղդել)
suffocation - kheghtoum, shunchaheghtsoutiun (խեղդում, շնչահեղձութիւն)
suffrage - kuve, tsayn, kuveargoutiun (քուէ, ձայն, քուէարկութիւն)
suffuse - daradzel, dzavalel, kusel, nergel–temku (տարածել, ծաւալել, քսել, ներկել՝ դէմքը)
suffusion - suproum, daradzoum, dzavaloum (սփռում, տարածում, ծաւալում)
sugar - shakar, shakarodil, anoushtsunel (շաքար, շաքարոտիլ, անուշցնել)
sugarcane - shakareghek (շաքարեղէգ)
sugarfree - anshakar, arants shakari (անշաքար, առանց շաքարի)
sugary - shakarod, shakaraham, shakaraser (շաքարոտ, շաքարահամ, շաքարասէր)
sugar-basin - shakaraman (շաքարաման)
suggest - telaturel, arachargel, aztel (թելադրել, առաջարկել, ազդել)
suggestion - telaturoutiun, aracharg (թելադրութիւն, առաջարկ)
suggestive - telaturagan, telaturich, khosoun (թելադրական, թելադրիչ, խօսուն)
suicide - antsnasbanoutiun, antsnasban, inknasban (անձնասպանութիւն, անձնասպան, ինքնասպան)
suit (n) - hedabuntoum, khunturank, tad, tarbas, hamazkesd (հետապնդում, խնդրանք, դատ, դարպաս, համազգեստ)
suit (v) - harmartsunel, harmaril, hakvetsunel, tad panal (յարմարեցնել, յարմարիլ, հագուեցնել, դատ բանալ)
suitable - harmar, vayelouch, badshaj (յարմար, վայելուչ, պատշաճ)
suitcase - jampargugh, tserabayousag (ճամբարկղ, ձեռապայուսակ)
suite - hedevortner, khoump, hargapazhin, hamazkesd (հետեւորդներ, խումբ, յարկաբաժին, համազգեստ)
suitor - tadakhaz, hedamoud, sirahar (դատախազ, հետամուտ, սիրահար)
suit-case - jampou bayousag (ճամբու պայուսակ)
sulk - khozhoril, yeresu gakhel, gakheresoutiun (խոժոռիլ, երեսը կախել, կախերեսութիւն)
sulky (a) - dzoureres, khozhor, murayl (ծուռերես, խոժոռ, մռայլ)
sulky (n) - arshavagark, yerganiv gark (արշաւակառք, երկանիւ կառք)
sullage - tsekh, dighm, aghdeghoutiun (ցեխ, տիղմ, աղտեղութիւն)
sullen - khozhoratem, dukhour, tazhan, gakheres (խոժոռադէմ, տխուր, դաժան, կախերես)
sully - aghdodel, aradavorel, aghdodil, aghd, arad (աղտոտել, արատաւորել, աղտոտիլ, աղտ, արատ)
sulphate - dzudzumpad (ծծմբատ)
sulphur - dzudzoump, dzudzumpoug (ծծումբ, ծծմբուկ)
sultan - soultan (սուլթան)
sultry - heghtsoutsich, dotagez, dak ou khonav (հեղձուցիչ, տօթակէզ, տաք ու խոնաւ)
sum - koumar, povantagoutiun, koumarel, ampopel (գումար, բովանդակութիւն, գումարել, ամփոփել)
summarize - ampopel (ամփոփել)
summary - ampopoum, povantagoutiun, hamarod, hagirj (ամփոփում, բովանդակութիւն, համառօտ, հա–

կիրճ)
summer - amar, vernakar, amaranots yertal (ամառ, վերնաքար, ամառանոց երթալ)
summertime - amar aden, amar yeghanag (ամառ ատեն, ամառ եղանակ)
summer-house - amaranots, amarnadoun (ամարանոց, ամառնատուն)
summit - kakat, gadar, kuloukh, dzayr, kakatnaged (գագաթ, կատար, գլուխ, ծայր, գագաթնակէտ)
summon - ganchel, aztararel, huravirel, zhoghov koumarel (կանչել, ազդարարել, հրաւիրել, ժողով գումարել)
summons - goch, gochnakir, aztaraoutiun, gochel (կոչ, կոչնագիր, ազդարարութիւն, կոչել)
sumptuous - shukegh, medzadzakhs, shurayl, jokh (շքեղ, մեծածախս, շռայլ, ճոխ)
sun - arev, arekag, louys, arevi dag genal-daknal (արեւ, արեգակ, լոյս, արեւի տակ կենալ-տաքնալ)
sunbath - arevi lokank (արեւի լոգանք)
sunbeam - arevi jarakayt (արեւի ճառագայթ)
sunbeat - arevahar (արեւահար)
sunburn - arevagizoutiun (արեւակիզութիւն)
Sunday - giragi (Կիրակի)
Sunday-school - giragnoria tubrots (կիրակնօրեայ դպրոց)
sunder - gisel, pazhnel, zadel, khuzel, zadvil (կիսել, բաժնել, զատել, խզել, զատուիլ)
sundial - arevi zhamatsouyts (արեւի ժամացոյց)
sundown - verchalouys (վերջալոյս)
sundry - zanazan, darper, desag desag, kani mu (զանազան, տարբեր, տեսակ տեսակ, քանի մը)
sunflower - arevadzaghig (արեւածաղիկ)
sunflower - arevadzaghig (արեւածաղիկ)
sung - see: sing (տե՛ս՝ sing)
sunglass - arevabagi, arevi agnots (արեւապակի, արեւի ակնոց)
sunk - see: sink (տե՛ս՝ sink)
sunken - ungughmadz, souzvadz, churasouyz (ընկղմած, սուզուած, ջրասոյզ)
sunless - arevazourg, anarev (արեւազուրկ, անարեւ)
sunlight - arevalouys (արեւալոյս)
sunny - arevod, baydzar, ourakh (արեւոտ, պայծառ, ուրախ)
sunrise - arevadzak, arevelk (արեւածագ, արեւելք)
sunset - arevnamoud (արեւնամուտ)
sunshade - arevanots (արեւանոց)
sunshine - arevalouys (արեւալոյս)
sunstroke - arevaharoutiun (արեւահարութիւն)
sunwear - arevazkesd (արեւազգեստ)
sun-bathe - arevi lokank unel (արեւի լոգանք ընել)
sun-burnt - arevagez, areven ayradz (արեւակէզ, արեւէն այրած)
sup - oumb, boud, kich kich khumel, unturel (ումպ, պուտ, քիչ քիչ խմել, ընթրել)
super - ver, ker, vura, undir, aveli (վեր, գեր, վրայ, ընտիր, աւելի)
superable - haghteli, nuvajeli (յաղթելի, նուաճելի)
superabundance - liaradoutiun (լիառատութիւն)
superabundant - hortarad, chapazants, shad letsoun (յորդառատ, չափազանց, շատ լեցուն)
superannuate - hankusdian toshagi ghurgel (հանգստեան թոշակի ղրկել)
superb - hoyagab, shukegh, uskancheli (հոյակապ, շքեղ, սքանչելի)
superficial - mageresayin, harevantsi, ardakin (մակերեսային, հարեւանցի, արտաքին)
superfine - kerazants, kerundir, nupakouyn, arachnagark (գերազանց, գերընտիր, նրբագոյն, առաջնակարգ)
superfluous - avelort, anbed (աւելորդ, անպէտ)
superhuman - kermartgayin (գերմարդկային)

superimpose - *magaturel, vuran aveltsunel, nushanagel* (մակադրել, վրան աւելցնել, նշանակել)
superintend - *verahusgel, ghegavarel* (վերահսկել, ղեկավարել)
superintendence - *verahusgoghoutiun* (վերահսկողութիւն)
superintendent - *veragatsou, husgogh, desouch, garavarich* (վերակացու, հսկող, տեսուչ, կառավարիչ)
superior - *verin, kerakouyn, partsurakouyn, medzavor* (վերին, գերագոյն, բարձրագոյն, մեծաւոր)
superiority - *keragayoutiun, medzavoroutiun* (գերակայութիւն, մեծաւորութիւն)
superlative - *keraturagan, keriver* (գերադրական, գերիվեր)
superman - *kermart* (գերմարդ)
supermarket - *medz vajaradoun, kervajaranots* (մեծ վաճառատուն, գերվաճառանոց)
supernal - *veri, verin, yergnayin* (վերի, վերին, երկնային)
supernatural - *kerpunagan, hurashali, darorinag* (գերբնական, հրաշալի, տարօրինակ)
superpose - *vuraye vura tunel, magaturel* (վրայէ վրայ դնել, մակադրել)
superposition - *magaturoutiun* (մակադրութիւն)
superscribe - *magakurel* (մակագրել)
superscription - *magakuroutiun* (մակագրութիւն)
supersede - *hachortel, deghu purnel, antsunil* (յաջորդել, տեղը բռնել, անցնիլ)
supersonic - *kertsaynayin, tsaynen arak* (գերձայնային, ձայնէն արագ)
superstar - *medz asdgh, medzahurchag terasan* (մեծ աստղ, մեծահռչակ դերասան)
superstition - *avelortabashdoutiun, nakhabasharoum* (աւելորդապաշտութիւն, նախապաշարում)
superstitious - *avelortabashd, nakhabasharial* (աւելորդապաշտ, նախապաշարեալ)
supervene - *vuran hasnil, badahil* (վրան հասնիլ, պատահիլ)
supervise - *verahusgel, nayil* (վերահսկել, նայիլ)
supervision - *verahusgoghoutiun* (վերահսկողութիւն)
supervisor - *verahusgich, veragatsou, husgich* (վերահսկիչ, վերակացու, հսկիչ)
supine - *anhok, andarper, gurnagi vura bargadz* (անհոգ, անտարբեր, կռնակի վրայ պառկած)
supper - *unturik, unturel* (ընթրիք, ընթրել)
supplant - *vodku arnel, dabalel, pokhanargel* (ոտքը առնել, տապալել, փոխանարկել)
supplanter - *pokhanargich* (փոխանարկիչ)
supple - *jugoun, tiuratek, gagough, tekel* (ճկուն, դիւրաթեք, կակուղ, թեքել)
supplement - *havelvadz, luratsoutsich, aveltsunel* (յաւելուած, լրացուցիչ, աւելցնել)
supplemental, tary - *havelvadzagan, havelial* (յաւելուածական, յաւելեալ)
suppleness - *jugounoutiun* (ճկունութիւն)
suppliant, supplicant - *aghersogh, haytsogh, aghachogh* (աղերսող, հայցող, աղաչող)
supplicate - *aghersel, haytsel, aghachel* (աղերսել, հայցել, աղաչել)
supplication - *aghachank, baghadank, aghers* (աղաչանք, պաղատանք, աղերս)
supplier - *madagararogh, haytaytich* (մատակարարող, հայթայթիչ)
supplies - *oudesdeghen, bashar, muterk, turam* (ուտեստեղէն, պաշար, մթերք, դրամ)
supply - *muterk, madoutsoum, madagararel, haytaytel* (մթերք, մատուցում, մատակարարել, հայթայ-

թել)
supply and demand - aracharg yev bahanch (առաջարկ եւ պահանջ)
support - vertsunel, gurel, hokal, netsoug, oknoutiun (վերցնել, կրել, հոգալ, նեցուկ, օգնութիւն)
supportable - daneli, hantourzheli, gureli, nereli (տանելի, հանդուժելի, կրելի, ներելի)
supporter - bashdubanogh, danogh, hokadar, zoravik (պաշտպանող, տանող, հոգատար, զօրավիգ)
suppose - yentaturel, hamarel, gardzel, sebel (ենթադրել, համարել, կարծել, սեպել)
supposition - yentatroutiun, vargadz, gardzik (ենթադրութիւն, վարկած, կարծիք)
suppository - surpanategh (սրբանադեղ)
suppress - ungjel, nuvajel, chunchel (ընկճել, նուաճել, ջնջել)
suppression - chunchoum, nuvajoum, partsoum, khapanoum (ջնջում, նուաճում, բարձում, խափանում)
suppressor - junshogh, chunchogh, zusbogh (ճնշող, ջնջող, զսպող)
suppurate - tarakhil, tarakhodil (թարախիլ, թարախոտիլ)
suppuration - tarakhoum, tarakhi hosoum, sharav (թարախում, թարախի հոսում, շարաւ)
supra - aveli, ker-, antur (prefix) աւելի, գեր-, անդր (նախաբառ)
supremacy - keragayoutiun, kerazantsoutiun (գերակայութիւն, գերազանցութիւն)
supreme - kerakouyn, verin, partsurakouyn, vusem (գերագոյն, վերին, բարձրագոյն, վսեմ)
surbase - verabadvantan, busag (վերապատուանդան, պսակ)
surcease - tatar, verj, tatretsunel, verjanal (դադար, վերջ, դադրեցնել, վերջանալ)
surcharge - dzanrapernel, gurgnaturoshmel, dzanrapernoum (ծանրաբեռնել, կրկնադրոշմել, ծանրաբեռնում)
surcoat - gurgnots, yergar verargou (կրկնոց, երկար վերարկու)
surd - anarmad, anhamachap, hamur kir (անարմատ, անհամաչափ, համր՝ գիր)
sure - vusdah, abahov, vorosh, usdouyk, havasdi (վստահ, ապահով, որոշ, ստոյգ, հաւաստի)
surely - anshoushd, angasgadz (անշուշտ, անկասկած)
surety - abahovoutiun, vusdahoutiun, yerashkhik (ապահովութիւն, վստահութիւն, երաշխիք)
suretyship - yerashkhavoroutiun (երաշխաւորութիւն)
surf - gohag, aliknerou purpour (կոհակ, ալիքներու փրփուր)
surface - mageres, yeres, mageresvouyt, mageresel (մակերես, երես, մակերեւոյթ, մակերեսել)
surfeit - hapratsunel, hapranal, hapratsoum (յափրացնել, յափրանալ, յափրացում)
surfeiter - vorguramol (որկրամոլ)
surfeiting - vorguramoloutiun (որկրամոլութիւն)
surfy - gohagod, hortsanoud (կոհակոտ, յորձանուտ)
surge - gohag, medz alik, gohaganal, ouril (կոհակ, մեծ ալիք, կոհականալ, ուռիլ)
surgeon - virapouyzh, virahad (վիրաբոյժ, վիրահատ)
surgeoncy - virapouzhoutiun (վիրաբուժութիւն)
surgery - virapouzhoutiun, virahadoutiun (վիրաբուժութիւն, վիրահատութիւն)
surgical - virapouzhagan (վիրաբուժական)
surly - khozhor, gakheres, tek (խոժոռ, կախերես, դէգ)
surmise - gasgadzil, gardzel, yentaturel, yentaturoutiun (կասկածիլ, կարծել, ենթադրել, ենթադրութիւն)
surmount - partsuranal, vuran yellel, haghtel, nuvajel (բարձրանալ, վրան ելլել, յաղթել, նուաճել)
surname - maganoun, maganvanel (մականուն, մականուանել)

surpass - *kerazantsel, kulel, zarmatsunel* (գերազանցել, գլել, զարմացնել)
surpassable - *kerazantseli* (գերազանցելի)
surpassing - *kerazantsogh, kerazants, uskancheli* (գերազանցող, գերազանց, սքանչելի)
surplus - *avelort, munatsort, aveli* (աւելորդ, մնացորդ, աւելի)
surprint - *dubel dubvadzi vura* (տպել՝ տպուածի վրայ)
surprise - *anagungal, zarmank, abshetsunel, zarmatsunel* (անակնկալ, զարմանք, ապշեցնել, զարմացնել)
surprising - *anagungal, hangardzahas, zarmanali* (անակնկալ, յանկարծահաս, զարմանալի)
surrealism - *kerirabashdoutiun* (գերիրապաշտութիւն)
surrender - *hantsnuvil, hantsnel, antsnadououtiun* (յանձնուիլ, յանձնել, անձնատուութիւն)
surreption - *kaghdakoghoutiun, nenkoutiun, khapeoutiun* (գաղտագողութիւն, նենգութիւն, խաբէութիւն)
surreptitious - *kaghdakoghi, khapebadir, nenkoutiamp* (գաղտագողի, խաբեպատիր, նենգութեամբ)
surround - *shurchabadel, badel, barpagel* (շրջապատել, պատել, պարփակել)
surrounding - *shurchaga, shurchabadogh* (շրջակայ, շրջապատող)
surroundings - *shurchagayk, michavayr* (շրջակայք, միջավայր)
surtax - *havelial dourk, havelial dourk tunel* (յաւելեալ տուրք, յաւելեալ տուրք դնել)
surtout - *tignots, vernazkesd* (Թիկնոց, վերնազգեստ)
surveillance - *husgoghoutiun* (Հսկողութիւն)
survey - *husgel, nayil, kunnel, chapel, zunnoutiun* (Հսկել, նայիլ, քննել, չափել, զննութիւն)
surveying - *ardachapoutiun, kunnoutiun* (արտաչափութիւն, քննութիւն)
surveyor - *desouch, veragatsou, kunnich, kunnachap* (տեսուչ, վերակացու, քննիչ, քննաչափ)
survival - *verabroum, haradevoum* (վերապրում, յարատեւում)
survive - *verabril, voghch munal* (վերապրիլ, ողջ մնալ)
survivor - *verabrogh* (վերապրող)
sur- - *ver, vuran, verev (prefix)* վեր, վրան, վերեւ (նախաբառ)
susceptible - *untounag, adag, tiurakurkir, hagamed* (ընդունակ, ատակ, դիւրագրգիռ, Հակամէտ)
susception - *untounoum, untouneloutiun* (ընդունում, ընդունելութիւն)
susceptive - *tiurazkats* (դիւրազգաց)
suscitate - *kurkurel, houzel* (գրգռել, յուզել)
suspect - *gasgadzil, daragousil* (կասկածիլ, տարակուսիլ)
suspend - *argakhel, gakhagayel, gakhel, unthadel* (առկախել, կախակայել, կախել, ընդՀատել)
suspender - *gakhagayogh, gakhogh, dapadagal* (կախակայող, կախող, տաբատակալ)
suspense - *anoroshoutiun, argakhoutiun, mudahokoutiun* (անորոշութիւն, առկախութիւն, մտաՀոգութիւն)
suspension - *argakhoutiun, arzhamia tataroum, unthadoum* (առկախութիւն, առժամեայ դադարում, ընդՀատում)
suspicion - *gasgadz, anvusdahoutiun* (կասկած, անվստաՀութիւն)
suspicious - *gasgadzod, gasgadzeli* (կասկածոտ, կասկածելի)
suspiral - *shunchadzag, kednachour* (շնչածակ, գետնաջուր)
suspire - *khoroungen shunchel, harachel, ah kashel* (խորունկէն շնչել, Հառաչել, ա՜Հ քաշել)
sustain - *gankoun bahel, geragurel, sunoutsanel, dogal* (կանգուն պաՀել, կերակրել, սնուցանել, տոկալ)
sustenance - *abrousd, oudesd, sunount, bahbanoutiun* (ապրուստ, ուտեստ, սնունդ, պաՀպանութիւն)
susurrus - *puspusouk, murmounch* (փսփսուք, մրմունջ)

suture - gar, garvadzk verki, garov miatsunel (կար, կարուածք՝ վէրքի, կարով միացնել)
suzerain - kerishkhan, avadabedagan (գերիշխան, աւատապետական)
suzerainty - kerishkhanoutiun (գերիշխանութիւն)
svelte - nourp, nurpagerd, tiuratek (նուրբ, նրբակերտ, դիւրաթեք)
swab - kedni surpich, surpel, makrel (գետնի սրբիչ, սրբել, մաքրել)
swaddle - khantsarour, khantsarourel, pattel (խանձարուր, խանձարուրել, փաթթել)
swag - dzurar, avar, koghon, jojoum (ծրար, աւար, գողօն, ճօճում)
swagger - dadanil, jojil, hokhordal (տատանիլ, ճօճիլ, յոխորտալ)
swaggering - sunabardzoutiun, antsnakovoutiun (սնապարծութիւն, անձնագովութիւն)
swain - keghchoug badani, sirahar hoviv (գեղջուկ պատանի, սիրահար հովիւ)
swale - tsor, hovid (ձոր, հովիտ)
swallow - dzidzernag, gogort, oumb, gullel, lapel (ծիծեռնակ, կոկորդ, ումպ, կլլել, լափել)
swamp - jahij, moroud, souzil, ungughmil (ճահիճ, մօրուտ, սուզիլ, ընկղմիլ)
swampy - jakhjakhoud, jakhjayin, moroud (ճախճախուտ, ճախճային, մօրուտ)
swan - garab (կարապ)
swap - pokhanagel, pokhanagoutiun (փոխանակել, փոխանակութիւն)
swap meet - pokhanagavayr, vajaradeghi, hantibavayr (փոխանակավայր, վաճառատեղի, հանդիպավայր)
sward - mort, markakedin, marmant, talarazartel (մարգագետին, մարմանդ, դալարազարդել)
swarm - meghvakhoump, meghvabar, kurnuvil, khumpuvil (մեղուախումբ, մեղուապար, խռնուիլ, խմբուիլ)
swart, swarth - toukh, tukhakouyn (թուխ, թխագոյն)
swash - chouri hosank, borodakhos, ouzhkin hosil (ջուրի հոսանք, պոռոտախօս, ուժգին հոսիլ)
swathe - shor, patouyt, pattel, gabel (շոր, փաթոյթ, փաթթել, կապել)
sway (n) - jojoum, gushir, aztetsoutiun, ishkhanoutiun (ճօճում, կշիռ, ազդեցութիւն, իշխանութիւն)
sway (v) - jojel, ishkhel, ghegavarel, sharzhel, hagil (ճօճել, իշխել, ղեկավարել, շարժել, հակիլ)
sweal - halil, vazel, khargel, haletsunel (հալիլ, վազել, խարկել, հալեցնել)
swear - yertunoul, vugayel, hayhoyel (երդնուլ, վկայել, հայհոյել)
swearer - yertunogh, hayhoyogh (երդնող, հայհոյող)
swearing - yertoum, hishots (երդում, հիշոց)
sweat (n) - kurdink, chank, ashkhadoutiun, khonavoutiun (քրտինք, ջանք, աշխատութիւն, խոնաւութիւն)
sweat (v) - kurdunil, duknil, ashkhadil, kurduntsunel (քրտնիլ, տքնիլ, աշխատիլ, քրտնցնել)
sweater - kurdunetsoutsich, pourte vernashabig (քրտնեցուցիչ, բուրդէ վերնաշապիկ)
swede - shouedatsi (շուէտացի)
Sweden - shoued (Շուէտ)
Swedish - shouedatsi, shouedagan (շուէտացի, շուէտական)
sweep (n) - aveladzoutiun, jojoum, dzukhani makrich (աւելածութիւն, ճօճում, ծխանի մաքրիչ)
sweep (v) - avlel, makrel, surpel, jojel, vurayen antsunil (աւլել, մաքրել, սրբել, ճօճել, վրայէն անցնիլ)
sweeper - avlogh, aveladzou (աւլող, աւելածու)
sweephead - zhamatsouytsi medz sulak (ժամացոյցի մեծ սլաք)
sweepings - avlouk, avluvadzk (աւլուք, աւլուածք)
sweepstake - tsiarshavi murtsouytu shahogh (ձիարշաւի մրցոյթը շահող)

sweepstakes - tsiarshavakurav (ձիարշաւագրաւ)
sweet - kaghtsur, anoush, anoushaham (քաղցր, անոյշ, անուշահամ)
sweeten - anoushtsunel, kaghtsuratsunel, anoushnal (անուշցնել, քաղցրացնել, անուշնալ)
sweetheart - sirouhi, sirahar (սիրուհի, սիրահար)
sweets - anousheghen (անուշեղէն)
swell - ouril, avelnal, medznal, ouretsk, gohag (ուռիլ, աւելնալ, մեծնալ, ուռեցք, կոհակ)
swelling - our, aydouts (ուռ, այտուց)
swelter - tumril, daken maril, arad kurdunil (թմրիլ, տաքէն մարիլ, առատ քրտնիլ)
swerve - sheghil, khodoril, moloril, sheghoum (շեղիլ, խոտորիլ, մոլորիլ, շեղում)
swift - arak, suruntats, shoud, karadzidzar (արագ, սրընթաց, շուտ, քարածիծառ)
swiftly - arakoren, shoudapouyt (արագօրէն, շուտափոյթ)
swig, swill - anhak khumel, gullel, meds oumb (անյագ խմել, կլլել, մեծ ումպ)
swill - goul dal, papel-khumel (կուլ տալ, լափել–խմել)
swim - loghal, dzupal, dadanil, loghatsoum (լողալ, ծփալ, տատանիլ, լողացում)
swimmer - loghort, loghatsogh (լողորդ, լողացող)
swimming - loghalu, loghalou marzank (լողալը, լողալու մարզանք)
swimming pool - loghavazan (լողաւազան)
swimmingly - tiurav, heshdoren, loghalov (դիւրաւ, հեշտօրէն, լողալով)
swimsuit - loghazkesd (լողազգեստ)
swimwear - loghahakousd (լողահագուստ)
swindle - shortel, koghnal, turamashortoutiun (շորթել, գողնալ, դրամաշորթութիւն)
swindler - turamashort, khapepa (դրամաշորթ, խաբեբայ)
swine - khoz, khozer (խոզ, խոզեր)
swing - ororvil, jojil, ororoum, jojoum, dadanoum (օրօրուիլ, ճօճիլ, օրօրում, ճօճում, տատանում)
swinge - kharazanel, mudragel, zarnel, badzhel (խարազանել, մտրակել, զարնել, պատժել)
swingle - dzedzel, dopel, dzedz (ծեծել, տոփել, ծեծ)
swinish - khozi bes, anasnagan (խոզի պէս, անասնական)
swiple - dopan, dzedz (տոփան, ծեծ)
swirl - budoudk, hortsank, budoudkil (պտոյտք, յորձանք, պտուտքիլ)
Swiss - zuvitseratsi, zuvitseragan (զուիցերիացի, զուիցերական)
switch (n) - jubod, jiugh, yelekduragan hosanki gojag (ճիպոտ, ճիւղ, ելեկտրական հոսանքի կոճակ)
switch (v) - dzedzel, turchel, pokhel, tartsunel, jubodel (ծեծել, թրջել, փոխել, դարձնել, ճիպոտել)
switzer - zuvitseriatsi (զուիցերիացի)
Switzerland - zuvitseria (Զուիցերիա)
swivel - shurchatarts ger, oghag, arantsavor tuntanot (շրջադարձ կեռ, օղակ, առանցաւոր թնդանօթ)
swoon - maril, marmuril, marmurouk (մարիլ, մարմրիլ, մարմրուք)
swoop - khoyank, khoyanal, hapushdagel (խոյանք, խոյանալ, յափշտակել)
sword - sour, tour, averadzoutiun, suradzoutiun (սուր, թուր, աւերածութիւն, սրածութիւն)
sworn - yertuvial (երդուեալ)
sycamore - zhandatuzeni, molatuzeni (ժանտաթզենի, մոլաթզենի)
sycophant - pampasogh, madnich, bunagalez, magapouydz (բամբասող, մատնիչ, պնակալէզ, մակաբոյծ)
syllabe - vang, hek, vangavorel (վանկ, հեգ, վանկաւորել)
syllabus - hamarodakuroutiun, ampopoum, tsoutsag (համառօտագրութիւն, ամփոփում, ցուցակ)

sylva, silva - andarayin, andarod, keghchoug (անտառային, անտառոտ, գեղջուկ)
symbol - khorhurtanish, khorhurtanushan, nushan, dib (խորհրդանիշ, խորհրդանշան, նշան, տիպ)
symbolic - khorhurtanushagan (խորհրդանշական)
symbolism - khorhurtabashdoutiun (խորհրդապաշտութիւն)
symbolize - khorhurtanushel, numanil (խորհրդանշել, նմանիլ)
symmetric, al - hamachap (համաչափ)
symmetry - hamachapoutiun, hamaturoutiun (համաչափութիւն, համադրութիւն)
sympathetic, al - hamagragan, hamagralits (համակրական, համակրալից)
sympathy - hamagrank, hamagroutiun (համակրանք, համակրութիւն)
sympatize - hamagril, garegtsil (համակրիլ, կարեկցիլ)
symphonic - hamerkayin, nertashnag (համերգային, ներդաշնակ)
symphony - hamanuvak, tsaynagtsoutiun, hamerk (համանուագ, ձայնակցութիւն, համերգ)
symposium - kidazhoghov, gochounk, geroukhoum, havakouyt (գիտաժողով, կոչունք, կերուխում, հաւաքոյթ)
symptom - akhdanushan (ախտանըշան)
symptomatic, al - akhdanushagan (ախտանշական)
synagogue - hureagan zhoghovaran, aghotadeghi (հրէական ժողովարան, աղօթատեղի)
synaxis - zhoghov, derounagan unturik (ժողով, տէրունական ընթրիք)
synchronism - hamazhamoutiun, zoukatiboutiun (համաժամութիւն, զուգադիպութիւն)
synchronize - amazhamil, zoukatibil, hamatibil (համաժամիլ, զուգադիպիլ, համադիպիլ)
syncopate - gutserkel, gurjadel kiru, maril (կցերգել, կրճատել՝գիրը, մարիլ)
syndrome - hamuntatsoutiun (համընթացութիւն)
synergy - hamakordzagtsoutiun (համագործակցութիւն)
synod - sinot, yegeghetsagan zhoghov, hamazhoghov (սինոդ, եկեղեցական ժողով, համաժողով)
synonym - homanish, nouynanish, hamanish, zoukanish (հոմանիշ, նոյնանիշ, համանիշ, զուգանիշ)
synonymy - homanushoutiun (հոմանշութիւն)
synopsis - ampopoum, hamatsouyts, hamadesoutiun (ամփոփում, համացոյց, համատեսութիւն)
syntax - sharatasoutiun, hamatsaynoutiun (շարադասութիւն, համաձայնութիւն)
synthesis - hamaturoutiun, hamaturouyt (համադրութիւն, համադրոյթ)
synthesize - hamaturel (համադրել)
synthetic - hamaturagan, paghaturagan, geghdz, shindzou (համադրական, բաղադրական, կեղծ, շինծու)
syphilis - furangakhd, durpakhd (ֆրանկախտ, տռփախտ)
syphilitic - furangakhdavor (ֆրանկախտաւոր)
syren - see: siren (տե՛ս՝ siren)
Syria - souria (Սուրիա)
Syriac - asoragan (ասորական)
Syrian - souriatsi, souriagan (սուրիացի, սուրիական)
syringe - nerargich, susurgoumi kordzik, sususgel (ներարկիչ, սրսկումի գործիք, սրսկել)
syrt - avazagouyd (աւազակոյտ)
syrup, sirup - osharag (օշարակ)
system - hamagark, turoutiun, metod, gerb, yeghanag (համակարգ, դրութիւն, մեթոտ, կերպ, եղանակ)
systematic - ganonavor, hamagarkuvadz (կանոնաւոր, համակարգուած)
systematical - hamagarkuvadz, ganonavor (համակարգուած, կանոնաւոր)
systematically - ganonavorabes

(կանոնաւորապէս)

systematize - ganonavorel, gark-ganoni veradzel (կանոնաւորել, կարգ-կանոնի վերածել)

systole - surdi gudzgoum, ampopoum vangi (սրտի կծկում, ամփոփում վանկի)

systyle - hamasiun dajari (Համասիւն՝ տաճարի)

syzygy - ludzagtsoutiun, ludzortoutiun, zoukortoutiun (լծակցութիւն, լծորդութիւն, զուգորդութիւն)

tab - goshgagab, bidag, yezerk, kughantsk (կօշկակապ, պիտակ, եզերք, քղանցք)

tabby - vedved, vedvidavor, payletsunel, vedvidel (վէտվէտ, վէտվիտաւոր, փայլեցնել, վէտվիտել)

tabefaction - hadnoum, vadnoum (Հատնում, վատնում)

tabefy - mashutsunel, hadtsunel (մաշեցնել, Հատցնել)

tabernacle - khoran, dabanag, surparan, dajar, daghavaril (խորան, տապանակ, սրբարան, տաճար, տաղաւարիլ)

tabes - hiudzoum, huidzakhd, haloumash (Հիւծում, Հիւծախտ, Հալումաշ)

tabid - haladz, mashadz, vudid (Հալած, մաշած, վտիտ)

tablature - vormunanugar, yerkousouyts (որմնանկար, երգուսոյց)

table (n) - seghan, dakhdag, tsang, geragour, aghiusag (սեղան, տախտակ, ցանկ, կերակուր, աղիւսակ)

table (v) - tsoutsagakurel, artsanakurel, sunoutsanel (ցուցակագրել, արձանագրել, սնուցանել)

tableau - nugar, badger, punanugar (նկար, պատկեր, բնանկար)

tablet - teghahad, tughtagal, pokur seghan, houshadedur (դեղահատ, թղթակալ, փոքր սեղան, յուշատետր)

table-book - houshamadian, hishadedur (յուշամատեան, յիշատետր)

table-cloth, -cover - suprots, seghani lat (սփռոց, սեղանի լաթ)

table-d'hote - hiuraseghan, bantogaseghan (Հիւրասեղան, պանդոկասեղան)

table-land - arodavayr, sarahart (արօտավայր, սարահարթ)

table-spoon - abouri medz tukal (ապուրի մեծ դգալ)

taboo, tabu - arkilvadz, anhubeli, arkilel (արգիլուած, անՀպելի, արգիլել)

tabor, et, ine - buzdig tumpoug, tumpugig (պզտիկ թմբուկ, թմբկիկ)

tabouret - atorag, antigounk ator (աթոռակ, անթիկունք աթոռ)

tabular - seghanatsev, harteres, tasavorial (սեղանաձեւ, Հարթերես, դասաւորեալ)

tabulate - dashel, hartatsevel, tsoutsagakurel, aghuisel (տաշել, Հարթաձեւել, ցուցակագրել, աղիւսել)

tabulation - agiusag, hartatsevoutiun (աղիւսակ, Հարթաձեւութիւն)

tacit - lurelyayn (լռելեայն)

tacitly - lurelyayn, lurig-munchig (լռելեայն, լռիկ-մնջիկ)

taciturn - sagavakhos, verabah (սակաւախօս, վերապաՀ)

tack - pokur kam, sebig, kordzelagerb, gutsel, kamel (փոքր գամ, սեպիկ, գործելակերպ, կցել, գամել)

tackle - jakharag, gazmadzk, jakharagel, tsernargel (ճախարակ, կազմածք, ճախարակել, ձեռնարկել)

tact - gentsaghakidoutiun, varvelagerb (կենցաղագիտութիւն, վա-

րուեւլակերպ)
tactful - gentsaghaked (կենցաղա-գէտ)
tactic, al - razmakidagan, varvelakidagan (ռազմագիտական, վարուեւլագիտական)
tactics - razmavaroutiun, mardakidoutiun (ռազմավարութիւն, մարտագիտութիւն)
tactile - shoshapeli, uzkali (շօշափելի, զգալի)
taction - shoshapoum, huboum (շօշափում, հպում)
tactless - anpapganugad, tsakhaver (անփափկանկատ, ձախաւեր)
taenia - yeriz (երիզ)
taffeta - gerbas (կերպաս)
tafia - shakaroghi (շաքարօղի)
tag - bidag, yerizi dzayramedagh, bidagel, gubtsunel (պիտակ, երիզի ծայրամետաղ, պիտակել, կպցնել)
tail - boch, tumag, verchamas, dzayren purnel (պոչ, դմակ, վերջամաս, ծայրէն բռնել)
tailor - tertsag, tsevel, gudrel, tertsagoutiun unel (դերձակ, ձեւել, կտրել, դերձակութիւն ընել)
tailoress - tertsagouhi, garouhi (դերձակուհի, կարուհի)
tailoring - tertsagoutiun (դերձակութիւն)
tailpiece - verchazart, zartabadger (վերջազարդ, զարդապատկեր)
taint - nergel, varagel, kounavorel, pidz, varagoum (ներկել, վարակել, գունաւորել, բիծ, վարակում)
take - arnel, purnel, vertsunel, direl, usdanal, sebel (առնել, բռնել, վերցնել, տիրել, ստանալ, սեպել)
take off - numanoutiun, dzaghranugar, vurtsunel, hanel (նմանութիւն, ծաղրանկար, վերցնել, հանել)
take-off - dzaghranugar, numanoutiun (ծաղրանկար, նմանութիւն)
taking - kuravich, varagich, kuravoum, galanoum, houzoum (գրաւիչ, վարակիչ, գրաւում, կալանում, յուզում)
tale - badmuvadzk, manraveb, arasbel, hamrank, tiv (պատմուածք, մանրավէպ, առասպել, համրանք, թիւ)
talent - daghant, tsirk, garoghoutiun (տաղանդ, ձիրք, կարողութիւն)
talented - daghantavor (տաղանդաւոր)
talisman - humayag, houroutk, puzhzhank (հմայեակ, յուռութք, բժժանք)
talk - khosil, zuroutsel, khosagtsoutiun, zurouyts (խօսիլ, զրուցել, խօսակցութիւն, զրոյց)
talkative - shadakhos, toulperan, khosoun (շատախօս, թուլբերան, խօսուն)
talker - khosogh, shadakhos, pampasogh (խօսող, շատախօս, բամբասող)
tall - yergar, partsur, partsurahasag (երկար, բարձր, բարձրահասակ)
tallow - jarb, jarbamom, jarbodel (ճարպ, ճարպամոմ, ճարպոտել)
tallowy - jarbod, jarbayin (ճարպոտ, ճարպային)
tallow-chandler - momakordz, momavajar (մոմագործ, մոմավաճառ)
tally - hashvetought, hashvepayd (հաշուեթուղթ, հաշուեփայտ)
tambour - tumpoug, aseghnakordzi shurchanag (թմբուկ, ասեղնագործի շրջանակ)
tambourine - tap, pokur tumpoug (դափ, փոքր թմբուկ)
tame - undani, undelatsadz, undanetsunel, nuvajel (ընտանի, ընտելացած, ընտանեցնել, նուաճել)
tamp - khutsel, kotsel (խցել, գոցել)
tamper - michamudel, kharnuvil (միջամտել, խառնուիլ)
tampion - khutsan, medz khits, arkelag (խցան, մեծ խից, արգելակ)
tampon - verki dzuvad, khudzoudz (վէրքի ծուատ, խծուծ)
tan - gaghnegeghev, gaghneposhi, arevagez, toukhatsunel (կաղնեկեղեւ, կաղնեփոշի, արեւակէզ, թխացնել)
tangent - shoshapakidz (շօշափա-

գիծ)
tangible - shoshapeli, hubeli, zunneli (շօշափելի, հպելի, զննելի)
tangle - gunjir, tunjoug, kharnagoutiun, tunjougil (կնճիռ, թնճուկ, խառնակութիւն, թնճուկիլ)
tangly - gun jurod, tun jugod (կնճռոտ, թնճկոտ)
tank - hurasayl, churampar, avazan, amparel (հրասայլ, ջրամբար, աւազան, ամբարել)
tankard - medz umbaman, tas, usgahag (մեծ ըմպաման, թաս, սկահակ)
tanling - arevagez, arevahar, arevatoukh (արեւակէզ, արեւահար, արեւաթուխ)
tanner - gashekordz, khaghakhort (կաշեգործ, խաղախորդ)
tannery - gashekordzaran, gashekordzoutiun (կաշեգործարան, կաշեգործութիւն)
tap - dzorag, meghm harvadz, tetev zarnel, jeghkel (ծորակ, մեղմ հարուած, թեթեւ զարնել, ճեղքել)
tape - yeriz, tsayneriz, zhabaven, zhabavenov gabel (երիզ, ձայներիզ, ժապաւէն, ժապաւէնով կապել)
taper - mom, pokur jurak, purkanal (մոմ, փոքր ճրագ, բրգանալ)
taphouse - kinedoun (գինետուն)
tapis - kork, gaberd, dzadzgots (գորգ, կապերտ, ծածկոց)
tapster - kinevajar, kinahan (գինեվաճառ, գինեհան)
tar - goubur, tsiut, navasdi, goubrel (կուպր, ձիւթ, նաւաստի, կուպրել)
tardy - oush, tantagh, habaghadz (ուշ, դանդաղ, յապաղած)
tare - vorom, molakhod, abra, abran hanel (որոմ, մոլախոտ, ապրայ, ապրան հանել)
target - tirakh, nushanaged, nushavag (թիրախ, նշանակէտ, նշաւակ)
tariff - sagakin, sag, maks, maksakin, sagakurel (սակագին, սակ, մաքս, մաքսագին, սակագրել)
tarn - lu jag, jahi j, lernali j (լճակ, ճահիճ, լեռնալիճ)
tarnish - aghodanal, mutuntsunel, aghodoutiun, pidz (աղօտանալ, մթնցնել, աղօտութիւն, բիծ)
tarry - munal, genal, hamenal, oushatsoum (մնալ, կենալ, յամենալ, ուշացում)
tarsus - bujegh, karshabar, guroung (պճեղ, գարշապար, կրունկ)
tart - tutvash, gudzou, khisd, murkahays, gargantag (թթուաշ, կծու, խիստ, մրգահայս, կարկանդակ)
tartar - tatar, kinemurour, adamnatird (թաթար, գինեմրուր, ատամնադիրտ)
Tartarus - tuzhokhk, dardaros (դժոխք, տարտարոս)
task - ashkhadank, kordz, bardk, huramayel, junshel (աշխատանք, գործ, պարտք, հրամայել, ճնշել)
tassel - dzob (ծոպ)
tastable - hamegh, jashageli (համեղ, ճաշակելի)
taste - hamdesel, jashagel, ham, jashagoum, jashag (համտեսել, ճաշակել, համ, ճաշակում, ճաշակ)
tasteful - hamegh, kaghtsuraham, jashagavor (համեղ, քաղցրահամ, ճաշակաւոր)
tasteless - anham, anakhorzh, anjashag (անհամ, անախորժ, անճաշակ)
tasty - jashagavor (ճաշակաւոր)
tatter - tsuntsodi, kourch, tsuntsodianal (ցնցոտի, քուրջ, ցնցոտիանալ)
tattle - shaghagradel, shadakhosel, shaghagradoutiun (շաղակրատել, շատախօսել, շաղակրատութիւն)
tattoo - videl, gudadzel, vedk, morti vura nugar (վիտել, կտածել, վէրք, մորթի վրայ նկար)
taunt - dzaghrel, nakhadel, nakhadink, dzaghur, gaymatsev (ծաղրել, նախատել, նախատինք, ծաղր, կայմաձեւ)
taurus - tsoul (ցուլ)
taut - bint, burguvadz, amour, tsik (պինդ, պրկուած, ամուր, ձիգ)
tauten - burgel (պրկել)
tautology - gurgnapanoutiun

(կրկնաբանութիւն)
tavern - *kinedoun, gabela, bantog* (գինետուն, կապելայ, պանդոկ)
taw - *gashekordzel, kuntagakhagh, karekuntag* (կաշեգործել, գնդակախաղ, քարեգնդակ)
tawdry - *havagnod, anjashag, sunodi* (յաւակնոտ, անճաշակ, սնոտի)
tawer - *gashekordz, mortakordz* (կաշեգործ, մորթագործ)
tax - *dourk, sag, harg, dourk tunel, dzanrapernel* (տուրք, սակ, Հարկ, տուրք դնել, ծանրաբեռնել)
tax collector, gatherer - *dourkahavak* (տուրքաՀաւաք)
tax exemption - *hargazerdzoutiun* (Հարկազերծութիւն)
tax free - *dourkazerdz, hargazerdz* (տուրքազերծ, Հարկազերծ)
tax payer - *hargadou, dourk vujarogh* (Հարկատու, տուրք վճարող)
taxable - *hargeli, dourki yentaga* (Հարկելի, տուրքի ենթակայ)
taxation - *dourk tunelu, dourki turoutiun, hargoum* (տուրք դնելը, տուրքի դրութիւն, Հարկում)
taxi - *vartsagark, inknasharzhov jamportel* (վարձակառք, ինքնաշարժով ճամբորդել)
taxi driver - *sharzhavar, garavar* (շարժավար, կառավար)
taxicab - *vartsagark, inknasharzh* (վարձակառք, ինքնաշարժ)
tea - *tey, teyajash, unturik* (թէյ, թէյաճաշ, ընթրիք)
teach - *ousoutsanel, sorvetsunel, tas dal, gurtel* (ուսուցանել, սորվեցնել, դաս տալ, կրթել)
teachable - *ousoutsaneli, hulou* (ուսուցանելի, Հլու)
teacher - *ousoutsich, varzhabed* (ուսուցիչ, վարժապետ)
teaching - *ousoutsoum, ousoutschoutiun* (ուսուցում, ուսուցչութիւն)
teacup - *teyi kavat* (թէյի գաւաթ)
team - *khaghakhoump, ludzvadz gentaniner, ludzel* (խաղախումբ, լծուած կենդանիներ, լծել)
teamster - *garaban, khumpabed, barakuloukh* (կառապան, խմբապետ, պարագլուխ)
teamwork - *khumpayin ashkhadank hamakordzagtsoutiun* (խմբային աշխատանք, Համագործակցութիւն)
teapot - *teyaman* (թէյաման)
tear (I) - *artsounk, ardasouk, lats, shit* (արցունք, արտասուք, լաց, շիթ)
tear (II) - *badurel, khuzel, puzukdel, badradzk, jeghk* (պատռել, խզել, բզքտել, պատռուածք, ճեղք)
teardrop - *ardasouk, ardasouki shit* (արտասուք, արտասուքի շիթ)
tearful - *ardasvali, lalgan* (արտասուալի, լալկան)
tearing - *gadaghi, pourun, anganon kidz* (կատաղի, բուռն, անկանոն գիծ)
tearjerker - *artsounkaper, houzich, tsuntsich* (արցունքաբեր, յուզիչ, ցնցիչ)
tearless - *anartsounk* (անարցունք)
tease - *dzuvadel, neghel, tsantsuratsunel, neghoum* (ծուատել, նեղել, ձանձրացնել, նեղում)
teaser - *gadagogh* (կատակող)
teaspoon - *teyi tukal* (թէյի դգալ)
teat - *usdink, dzidz, budoug, dzudzag* (ստինք, ծիծ, պտուկ, ծծակ)
technic, al - *arhesdakidagan* (արՀեստագիտական)
technical institute - *arhesdakidagan ousoumnaran* (արՀեստագիտական ուսումնարան)
technician - *masnaked, arhesdaked* (մասնագէտ, արՀեստագէտ)
technicolor - *pazmakouyn, kounavor, pazmakouynian* (բազմագոյն, գունաւոր, բազմագոյնեան)
technics - *kidarhesd, arhesdakidoutiun* (գիտարՀեստ, արՀեստագիտութիւն)
technique - *arhesdi humdoutiun, arvesdakidoutiun* (արՀեստի Հմտութիւն, արուեստագիտութիւն)
technologist - *arhesdaked, jardarakordz* (արՀեստագէտ, ճարտարագործ)
technology - *kiudarvesd, arvesdakidoutiun* (գիտարուեստ, արուեստա–

գիտութիւն)
techy, tetchy - tiurakurkir, tsasgod, neghsird, tek (դիւրագրգիռ, ցասկոտ, նեղսիրտ, դէգ)
tedious - tsantsuranali, daghdugali, miorinag (ձանձրանալի, տաղտկալի, միօրինակ)
tedium - daghdoug, tsantsurouyt (տաղտուկ, ձանձրոյթ)
teem - dzunanil, perel, ardaturel, vukhdal, hortil (ծնանիլ, բերել, արտադրել, վխտալ, յորդիլ)
teemer - tapogh, barbogh (թափող, պարպող)
teeming - zeghoun, budghaper (զեղուն, պտղաբեր)
teenage - anchapahas (անչափահաս)
teenager - badaniag, barman, barmanouhi (պատանեակ, պարման, պարմանուհի)
teens - terahasag (թերահասակ)
teeth - agraner (ակռաներ)
teething - adamnapousoutiun (ատամնաբուսութիւն)
teetotal - ampoghchagan, liagadar (ամբողջական, լիակատար)
teetotaler - haga-alcolagan (հակաալքոլական)
tegmen - dzadzgouyt (ծածկոյթ)
tegument - badian, taghant, dzadzgouyt (պատեան, թաղանդ, ծածկոյթ)
telecast - herasuproum, heradesili haghortoum (հեռասփռում, հեռատեսիլի հաղորդում)
telecommunication - herahaghortoum (հեռահաղորդում)
teleconference - herazurouyts (հեռազրոյց)
telegram - herakir, herakurel (հեռագիր, հեռագրել)
telegraph - herakir, herakurich (հեռագիր, հեռագրիչ)
telemarketing - heravajark, badgeravajark (հեռավաճառք, պատկերավաճառք)
telemeter - herachap (հեռաչափ)
telemetry - herachapoutiun (հեռաչափութիւն)
telepathy - herazkatsoutiun (հեռազգացութիւն)
telephone - heratsayn, herakhos, heratsaynel (հեռաձայն, հեռախօս, հեռաձայնել)
telephoto - heralousanugar (հեռալուսանկար)
telephotography - heralousanugarchoutiun (հեռալուսանկարչութիւն)
teleplay - heradesili punakir (հեռատեսիլի բնագիր)
teleprint - heradib (հեռատիպ)
teleprinter - heradubakurich (հեռատպագրիչ)
telescope - heratidag, asdghatidag, herated (հեռադիտակ, աստղադիտակ, հեռադէտ)
telescopy - heratidoutiun (հեռադիտութիւն)
telescribe - herakhosakir (հեռախօսագիր)
teleselling - vajark heradesilov gam heratsaynov (վաճառք հեռատեսիլով կամ հեռաձայնով)
telethon - heradesilov nuvirahavak (հեռատեսիլով նուիրահաւաք)
teletype - heradib (հեռատիպ)
teletype writer - herakramekena (հեռագրամեքենայ)
teletypewriter - herakramekena (հեռագրամեքենայ)
televangelist - heradesili avedaranich (հեռատեսիլի աւետարանիչ)
television - heradesil, badgeraspiur (հեռատեսիլ, պատկերասփիւռ)
telex - heradib, herakrayin haghortoum (հեռատիպ, հեռագրային հաղորդում)
tele- - herou- (prefix) - հեռու- (նախամասնիկ)
tell - usel, badmel, tuvel, imatsunel (ըսել, պատմել, թուել, իմացնել)
teller - usogh, badmogh, turamadan hashvarar, hamrogh (ըսող, պատմող, դրամատան հաշուարար, համրող)
telling - aztou, dubavorich (ազդու, տպաւորիչ)
telltale - kusou, patsperan, hamaradou, deghegadou (քսու, բացբերան, համարատու, տեղեկատու)

temerity - *hantuknoutiun, khizakhoutiun* (յանդգնութիւն, խիզախութիւն)
temper (n) - *kharnuvadzk, duramatroutiun, chapavoroutiun* (խառնուածք, տրամադրութիւն, չափաւորութիւն)
temper (v) - *parekharnel, chapavorel, gagoughtsunel* (բարեխառնել, չափաւորել, կակուղցնել)
temperament - *kharnuvadzk, punavoroutiun* (խառնուածք, բնաւորութիւն)
temperance - *chapavoroutiun, zhouzhgaloutiun* (չափաւորութիւն, ժուժկալութիւն)
temperate - *parekharun, chapavor, baghariun, michin* (բարեխառն, չափաւոր, պաղարիւն, միջին)
temperated - *parekharun, uzkasd, khohagan* (բարեխառն, զգաստ, խոհական)
temperature - *chermasdijan, parekharnoutiun* (ջերմաստիճան, բարեխառնութիւն)
temperer - *chapavorich, parekharnich* (չափաւորիչ, բարեխառնիչ)
tempest - *potorig, murrig, khurovoutiun, potergel* (փոթորիկ, մրրիկ, խռովութիւն, փոթորկել)
tempestuous - *alegodz, potorgod, gadaghi, mururgalits* (ալեկոծ, Թոփորկոտ, կատաղի, մրրկալից)
template, templet - *gaghabar, chapag, orinag, dibar* (կաղապար, չափակ, օրինակ, տիպար)
temple - *dajar, mehian, zhoghovaran, kounk* (տաճար, մեհեան, ժողովարան, քունք)
tempo - *gushrout, zhamanag, yerazhushdagan chap* (կշռոյթ, ժամանակ, երաժշտական չափ)
temporal - *zhamanagavor, antsavor, ashkharhig, kaghakagan* (ժամանակաւոր, անցաւոր, աշխարհիկ, քաղաքական)
temporarily - *arzhamabes* (առժամապէս)
temporary - *arzhamia, zhamanagavor* (առժամեայ, ժամանակաւոր)
temporization - *tsuktsukoum, adenin harmarogh* (ձգձգում, ատենին յարմարող)
temporize - *tzuktsukel, habaghel, harmaril* (ձգձգել, յապաղել, յարմարիլ)
tempt - *portsel, hurabourel* (փորձել, հրապուրել)
temptation - *portsoutiun, hurabouyr* (փորձութիւն, հրապոյր)
tempter - *portsich* (փորձիչ)
ten - *dasu* (տասը)
tenable - *baheli, bashdbaneli* (պահելի, պաշտպանելի)
tenacious - *gubchoun, pagchogh, hamar, birg* (կպչուն, փակչող, յամառ, պիրկ)
tenacity - *dogounoutiun, gubchounoutiun, burgoutiun* (տոկունութիւն, կպչունութիւն, պրկութիւն)
tenancy - *varzhagaloutiun* (վարձակալութիւն)
tenant - *vartsagal, vartsuvor, vartsel* (վարձակալ, վարձուոր, վարձել)
tend - *hokal, khunamel, bahel, husgel, midil* (հոգալ, խնամել, պահել, հսկել, միտիլ)
tendency - *midoum, tsukdoum, hagoum* (միտում, ձգտում, հակում)
tender (I) - *aracharg, doukank, aracharge l* (առաջարկ, տուգանք, առաջարկել)
tender (II) - *papoug, gagough, nourp, hokal, khunamel* (փափուկ, կակուղ, նուրբ, հոգալ, խնամել)
tenderer - *arachargogh* (առաջարկող)
tenderly - *kourkourankov* (գուրգուրանքով)
tendon - *tunter, neart, lar* (ղնդեր, նեարդ, լար)
tendril - *voloradz dzil, voloril, garchil* (ոլորած ծիլ, ոլորիլ, կառչիլ)
tenebrosity - *mutoutiun, khavar* (մթութիւն, խաւար)
tenebrous - *mout, murayl, khavar* (մութ, մռայլ, խաւար)
tenement - *vartsagaloutiun, hargapazhinnerov doun* (վարձակալու–

Թիւն, յարկաբաժիններով տուն)
tenet - havadk, gardzik, vartabedoutiun (Հաւատք, կարծիք, վարդապետութիւն)
tenfold - dasnabadig (տասնապատիկ)
tennis - tenis - kumtakhagh mu (թէնիս՝ խնդախաղ մը)
tenor (I) - veratsayn, vererkogh, tenor (վերաձայն, վերերգակ, թէնօր)
tenor (II) - untatsk, getsvadzk, nugarakir, vark (ընթացք, կեցուածք, նկարագիր, վարք)
tense - zhamanag-payi, tsukdial, birg, larvadz, tsik (ժամանակ-բայի, ձգտեալ, պիրկ, լարուած, ձիգ)
tenseness - burgoum, tsukdial vijag (պրկում, ձգտեալ վիճակ)
tension - junshoum, burgoum, laroum, burguvadzoutiun (ճնշում, պրկում, լարում, պրկուածութիւն)
tent (n) - vuran, daghavar, verki badrouyk, pilta (վրան, տաղաւար, վէրքի պատրոյգ, փիլթայ)
tent (v) - vurani dag punagil, panagil, virakhouzel (վրանի տակ բնակիլ, բանակիլ, վիրախուզել)
tentacle - shoshapoug, hubelik michadnerou (շօշափուկ, Հպելիք միջատներու)
tentation - portsoutiun (փորձութիւն)
tentative - ports, nakhaports, portsaragan, portsargou (փորձ, նախափորձ, փորձառական, փորձարկու)
tenterhooks - shad mudahok (շատ մտաՀոգ)
tenth - dasnerort, dasnort (տասներորդ, տասնորդ)
tenuity - nosroutiun, paragoutiun (նօսրութիւն, բարակութիւն)
tenuous - nosur, parag, tetev, churod (նօսր, բարակ, թեթեւ, ջրոտ)
tenure - vartsagaloutiun (վարձակալութիւն)
tepefy - kaghchatsunel, kaghchanal (գաղջացնել, գաղջանալ)
tepid - kaghch (գաղջ)
tepiness, ity - kaghchoutiun (գաղջութիւն)
tercet - yerryag, yeradogh (երրեակ, եռատող)
tergiversate - khousapil, pakhousd dal, dadamsil, pokhvil (խուսափիլ, փախուստ տալ, տատամսիլ, փոխուիլ)
term - sahman, yezur, verch, shurchan, gochel, sahmanel (սաՀման, եզր, վերջ, շրջան, կոչել, սաՀմանել)
terminal - verchagayan, dzayr, avard, dzayri (վերջակայան, ծայր, աւարտ, ծայրի
terminate - verchatsunel, avardel, verchanal, lumunnal (վերջացնել, աւարտել, վերջանալ, լմննալ)
termination - verchavoroutiun, verch, vakhjan, yezur (վերջաւորութիւն, վերջ, վախճան, եզր)
terminology - hadaapanoutiun, yezrapanoutiun (յատկաբանութիւն, եզրաբանութիւն)
terminus - verchagayan, verchakidz, vakhjan, verch (վերջակայան, վերջագիծ, վախճան, վերջ)
termite - juji, lousnamurchiun, paydort (ճճի, լուսնամրջիւն, փայտորդ)
terra - hogh, yergir (Հող, երկիր)
terrace - badushkam, danik, taradap, taradapel (պատշգամ, տանիք, դարատափ, դարատափել)
terrafirma - tsamak, hasdad kedin (ցամաք, Հաստատ գետին)
terrain - kedin, hogh, daradzoutiun (գետին, Հող, տարածութիւն)
terrapin - medz guria (մեծ կրիայ)
terrestrial - yergurayin, yergurapunag (երկրային, երկրաբնակ)
terrible - sosgali, sarsapeli, ahreli, ahavor (սոսկալի, սարսափելի, աՀռելի, աՀաւոր)
terribly - ahrelioren, ahreli gerbov (աՀռելիօրէն, աՀռելի կերպով)
terrific - ahavor, ahargou, sarsapeli (աՀաւոր, աՀարկու, սասսափելի)
terrify - sarsapetsunel, zarhouretsunel, sosgatsunel (սարսափեցնել, զարՀուրեցնել, սոսկացնել)

terrify - sarsapetsunel, zarhouretsunel, sosgatsunel (սարսափեցնել, զարհուրեցնել, սոսկացնել)

terrify - sarsapetsunel, zarhouretsunel, sosgatsunel (սարսափեցնել, զարհուրեցնել, սոսկացնել)

territorial - hoghayin, tsamakayin (Հողային, ցամաքային)

terror - sarsap, sosgoum, ah, yergiugh, ahapegoum (սարսափ, սոսկում, ահ, երկիւղ, ահաբեկում)

terrorism - ahapegchoutiun, ahapegoutiun, deror (ահաբեկչութիւն, ահաբեկութիւն, տեռոր)

terrorist - ahapegich (ահաբեկիչ)

terrorize - ahapegel, sarsapetsunel (ահաբեկել, սարսափեցնել)

terse - hagirj, gour, lagonagan (Հակիրճ, կուռ, լակոնական)

test (n) - ports, kunnoutiun, koura, halots, hagaztag (փորձ, քննութիւն, քուրայ, Հալոց, Հակազդակ)

test (v) - portsel, portsargel, kunnel, haletsunel (փորձել, փորձարկել, քննել, Հալեցնել)

testa - badian - houndi, khukhounchi (պատեան – Հունտի, խխունջի)

testacy - gudagoum (կտակում)

Testament - gudagaran, gudag, gudagakir (Կտակարան, կտակ, կտակագիր)

testate - gudagarar (կտակարար)

testicle - amortsik (ամորձիք)

testification - vugayoutiun (վկայութիւն)

testify - vugayel, hasdadel, haydararel (վկայել, Հաստատել, յայտարարել)

testimony - vugayoutiun, abatsouyts, haydararoutiun (վկայութիւն, ապացոյց, յայտարարութիւն)

testor - usdoukich (ստուգիչ)

testy - tiurakurkir, khozhor, hamar, tek (դիւրագրգիռ, խոժոռ, յամառ, դեզ)

tetanus - burgakhd, gargamakhd (պրկախտ, կարկամախտ)

tetragon - karangiun (քառանկիւն)

text - punakir, niut, punapan (բնագիր, նիւթ, բնաբան)

textbook - tasakirk (դասագիրք)

textile - hiusvadz, hiusgen, huisvadzeghen (Հիւսուած, Հիւսկէն, Հիւսուածեղէն)

textual - daratsi, punakuri hamatsayn (տառացի, բնագրի Համաձայն)

texture - hiusgen, hiusk, horinvadzk, (Հիւսկէն, Հիւսք, յօրինուածք)

than - kan, kan te (քան, քան թէ)

thank - shunorhagaloutiun, shunorhagaloutiun haydnel (շնոՀակալութիւն, շնորՀակալութիւն յայտնել)

thank God - park asdoudzo (փառք Աստուծոյ)

thank you - shunorhagal yem (շնորՀակալ եմ)

thankful - shunorhagal, yerakhdabard (շնորՀակալ, երախտապարտ)

thankless - aberakhd (ապերախտ)

thanks - shunorhagalik, shunorhagaloutiun (շնորՀակալիք, շնորՀակալութիւն)

Thanksgiving day - kohapanoutian or (ԳոՀաբանութեան օր)

that - ayt, ayn, aniga, vor, zor (այդ, այն, անիկա, որ, զոր)

thatch - hart, khozan danik dzadzgelou, danik dzadzgel (յարդ, խոզան տանիք ծածկելու, տանիք ծածկել)

thaw - tsiunahalk, halil, haletsunel (ձիւնաՀալք, Հալիլ, Հալեցնել)

the - voroshich hot- u, n (որոշիչ յօդ– ը, ն)

theater, theatre - tadron, taderasurah, taderavayr (թատրոն, թատերասրաՀ, թատերավայր)

theatrical - taderagan (թատերական)

theatricals - taderakhagh, taderagan kurvadzk (թատերախաղ, թատերական գրուածք)

thee - kez, kezi, uzkez (քեզ, քեզի, զքեզ)

theft - koghoutiun, koghon (գողութիւն, գողօն)

theine - teyin, teyamol (թէյին, թէյամոլ)

their - irents, anonts (իրենց, ա–

նոնց)
theirs - irentsu (իրենցը)
theism - asduvadzatavanoutiun (աստուածադաւանութիւն)
theist - asduvadzatavan (աստուածադաւան)
theistic, al - miasdvadzian (միաստուածեան)
them - zanonk, zirenk, irents, anonts (զանոնք, զիրենք, իրենց, անոնց)
theme - punapan, niut, sharaturoutiun, payarmad (բնաբան, նիւթ, շարադրութիւն, բայարմատ)
themselves - irenk, irenk irents, inkzinkunin (իրենք, իրենք իրենց, ինքզինքնին)
then - ayn aden, hedo, aba, ousdi, ouremun (այն ատեն, յետոյ, ապա, ուստի, ուրեմն)
thence - ange, angits, ayn zhamanag, ayt badjarov (անկէ, անկից, այն ժամանակ, այդ պատճառով)
theocracy - asdvadzabedoutiun (աստուածապետութիւն)
theologian, theologist - asduvadzapan (աստուածաբան)
theologic - asduvadzapanagan (աստուածաբանական)
theology - asduvadzapanoutiun (աստուածաբանութիւն)
theophany - asduvadzahaydnoutiun, marteghoutiun (աստուածայայտնութիւն, մարդեղութիւն)
theorem - desoutiun, pasdeli aracharg (տեսութիւն, փաստելի առաջարկ)
theorize - desoutiun gazmel (տեսութիւն կազմել)
theory - desoutiun, desapanoutiun, desagan (տեսութիւն, տեսաբանութիւն, տեսական)
therapeutic - pouzhagan, akhdapouzhagan (բուժական, ախտաբուժական)
therapeutics - akhdapouzhoutiun (ախտաբուժութիւն)
therapeutist - pouzhaked, akhdapouzh (բուժագէտ, ախտաբոյժ)
therapy - pouzhoum (բուժում)
there - hon, ayndegh, tebi hon, aha (Հոն, այնտեղ, դէպի Հոն, աՀա)
thereabouts - ayt goghmeru, modig, kurete (այդ կողմերը, մօտիկ, գրեթէ
thereby - anov, ayt michotsov (անով, այդ միջոցով)
therefore - ousdi, hedevapar (ուստի, Հետեւաբար)
therefrom - adgits, ange (ատկից, անկէ)
therein - ayndegh, anor mech, hon (այնտեղ, անոր մէջ, Հոն)
thereon - anor vura (անոր վրայ)
thereunder - anor dag (անոր տակ)
thereupon - ousdi, vorov, anmichabes yedk (ուստի, որով, անմիջապէս ետք)
therewith - miyevnouyn aden, adov (միեւնոյն ատեն, ատով)
thermal - chermugayin, chermougi (ջերմկային, ջերմուկի)
thermography - chermakuroutiun (ջերմագրութիւն)
thermometer - chermachap (ջերմաչափ)
thermos - chermabah (ջերմապաՀ)
thermoscope - chermatsouyts (ջերմացոյց)
thermostat - chermagarkich (ջերմակարգիչ)
these - asonk, zanonk (ասոնք, զանոնք)
thesis - avardajar, niut, khuntir, punapan (աւարտաճառ, նիւթ, խնդիր, բնաբան)
thew - tunter, mugan, chigh, zoroutiun (ղնդեր, մկան, ջիղ, զօրութիւն)
thewed - gorovi, chughoud (կորովի, ջղուտ)
they - anonk (անոնք)
thick - tantsur, hasd, khid, goshd, tantsuroutiun (թանձր, Հաստ, խիտ, կոշտ, թանձրութիւն)
thicken - hasdtsunel, tantsuratsunel, khudatsunel, khudanal (Հաստցնել, թանձրացնել, խտացնել, խտանալ)
thickish - hasdgeg (Հաստկէկ)
thickness - hasdoutiun, tantsuroutiun

(Հաստութիւն, Թանձրութիւն)
thick-headed - putamid, tantsuraku-loukh (բթամիտ, Թանձրագլուխ)
thief - kogh, avazag (գող, աւազակ)
thieve - koghnal (գողնալ)
thievery - koghoutiun, avazagoutiun (գողութիւն, աւազակութիւն)
thigh - zisd, aztur (զիստ, ազդր)
thimble - madnots (մատնոց)
thin (a) - parag, nihar, nourp, no-sur, tetev (բարակ, նիհար, նուրբ, նօսր, Թեթեւ)
thin (v) - paragtsunel, niharnal, nosranal, paragnal (բարակցնել, նիհարնալ, նօսրանալ, բարակնալ)
thine - kougut, kou (քուկդ, քու)
thing - pan, ir, ararga, niut (բան, իր, առարկայ, նիւԹ)
things - ararganer, kouyk, paner, i-rer, inchk (առարկաներ, գոյք, բաներ, իրեր, ինչք)
think - khorhil, mudadzel, khorhur-tadzel, gardzel (խորհիլ, մտածել, խորհրդածել, կարծել)
thinker - mudadzogh, khorhogh, i-masdoun (մտածող, խորհող, իմաստուն)
thinking - khorhourt, mudadzoum, tadoghoutiun (խորհուրդ, մտածում, դատողուԹիւն)
thinner - nosrargou, nerg gagough-tsunog (նօսրարկու, ներկ կակուղցնող)
thinness - nurpoutiun, paragoutiun (նրբուԹիւն, բարակուԹիւն)
third - yerrort (երրորդ)
thirst - dzarav, ights, dzaravil, denchal (ծարաւ, իղձ, ծարաւիլ, տենչալ)
thirsty - dzarav, dzaravadz (ծարաւ, ծարաւած)
thirteen - dasnuyerek (տասներեք)
thirteenth - dasnuyerekerort (տասներեքերորդ)
thirtieth - yeresounerort (երեսուներորդ)
thirty - yeresoun (երեսուն)
this - ays, asiga (այս, ասիկա)
thister - dzaravtsogh (ծարաւցող)
thistle - yegkan, oughghapoush, da-sg (եկքան, ուղղափուշ, տատասկ)
thither - hon, ayndegh, tebi hon, antii (հոն, այնտեղ, դէպի հոն, անդիի)
thong - pog, yergar gashi (փոկ, երկար կաշի)
thorax - gourdzk, lanchk (կուրծք, լանջք)
thorn - poush, dadasg (փուշ, տատասկ)
thorny - pushod, pushalits (փշոտ, փշալից)
thorough - luman, ampoghchabes, gadarial, povantag (լման, ամբողջապէս, կատարեալ, բովանդակ)
thoroughly - liovin, polorovin, ga-darelabes (լիովին, բոլորովին, կատարելապէս)
thorp - kiughag, dunakhoump (գիւղակ, տնախումբ)
those - anonk (անոնք)
though - teyev, tebed, tebedev (Թէեւ, Թէպէտ, Թէպէտեւ)
thought - khorhourt, midk, muda-dzoum, khorhetsav (խորհուրդ, միտք, մտածում, խորհեցաւ)
thoughtful - mudakhoh, mudadzgod, khohagan (մտախոհ, մտածկոտ, խոհական)
thoughtless - ankhorhourt, anhok (անխորհուրդ, անհոգ)
thousand - hazar (հազար)
thousandfold - hazarabadig (հազարապատիկ)
thousandth - hazarerort (հազարերորդ)
thrall - keri, usduroug (գերի, ստրուկ)
thralldom - keroutiun (գերուԹիւն)
thrash - tsorenu dzedzel, dupel, gamnel (ցորենը ծեծել, տփել, կամնել)
thread - tertsan, tel, shark, tertsan antsunel (դերձան, Թել, շարք, դերձան անցնել)
threat - usbarnalik (սպառնալիք)
threaten - usbarnal, vakhtsunel (սպառնալ, վախցնել)
three - yerek (երեք)

threefold - yerabadig (եռապատիկ)
threnody - voghperk, vogh (voghperk, voghp)
threshold - sem, moudk, usgizp (սեմ, մուտք, սկիզբ)
thrice - yeritsus, yerek ankam (երիցս, երեք անգամ)
thrift - khunayoghoutiun, dundesoutiun, dzaghgoum (խնայողութիւն, տնտեսութիւն, ծաղկում)
thriftiness - khunayoghoutiun (խնայողութիւն)
thriftless - shurayl, ankhuna, muskhogh (շռայլ, անխնայ, մսխող)
thrifty - khunayaser, khunayogh, parkavaj (խնայասէր, խնայող, բարգաւաճ)
thrill - tount, sarsour, sarsuril, aztel, aztuvil (թունդ, սարսուռ, սարսռիլ, ազդել, ազդուիլ)
thrive - hachoghil, parkavajil, harusdanal, ajil (յաջողիլ, բարգաւաճիլ, հարստանալ, աճիլ)
throat - gogort, vorgor (կոկորդ, որկոր)
throb - duropel, papakhel, zarnel, duropoum, papakhoum (տրոփել, բաբախել, զարնել, տրոփում, բաբախում)
throe - yergounk, sasdig tsav (երկունք, սաստիկ ցաւ)
thrombosis - yeragakhutsoum (երակախցում)
throne - kah, inshkhanoutiun, kah nusdetsunel (գահ, իշխանութիւն, գահ նստեցնել)
throng - ampokh, khouzhan, khurnuvil, havakuvil (ամբոխ, խուժան, խռնուիլ, հաւաքուիլ)
throttle - shunchapogh, kheghtel, seghmel, luretsunel (շնչափող, խեղդել, սեղմել, լռեցնել)
through - mechen, michotsov, meg goghmen miusu (մէջէն, միջոցով, մէկ կողմէն միւսը)
throw - nedel, tsukel, artsagel, dabalel, artsagoum (նետել, ձգել, արձակել, տապալել, արձակում)
throwaway - nedvadz haydararatert (նետուած յայտարարաթերթ)
thrum - dzob, anham nuvak, anham nuvakel (ծոպ, անհամ նուագ, անհամ նուագել)
thrush - dzudzag, dortig-turchounu (ծծակ, տորդիկ՝ թռչունը)
thrust - mukhel, khotel, mudtsunel, hurel, tashounaharoum (մխել, խոթել, մտցնել, հրել, դաշունահարում)
thud - harvadz, angoum, tapiun, tapel (հարուած, անկում, դափիւն, դափել)
thumb - putamad, pouyt, putamadov kirku aghdodel (բթամատ, բոյթ, բթամատով գիրքը աղտոտել)
thump - harvadz, pakhiun, dopiun, dopel (հարուած, բախիւն, տոփիւն, տոփել)
thunder - gaydzag, vorodoum, tuntiun, vorodal, shantel (կայծակ, որոտում, թնդիւն, որոտալ, շանթել)
thunderbolt - shant, gaydzag (շանթ, կայծակ)
thunderstruck - shantahar, abshahar, shupotadz (շանթահար, ապշահար, շփոթած)
thurible - pourvar, khungaman (բուրվառ, խնկաման)
Thursday - hinkshapti (Հինգշաբթի)
thus - aysbes, asang, ousdi, ayn gerbov (այսպէս, ասանկ, ուստի, այն կերպով)
thusfar - ayskan, minchev hos (այսքան, մինչեւ հոս)
thwack - dopel, kharazanel, dzedzel, dopiun (տոփել, խարազանել, ծեծել, տոփիւն)
thwart - gudrel, antsunil, hagaragil, sheghagi, khodornagi (կտրել, անցնիլ, հակառակիլ, շեղակի, խոտորնակի)
thy - kou, kougut (քու, քուկդ)
thyme - dzotrin, dzotor (ծոթրին, ծոթոր)
thyroid - vahanagerb-keghts (վահանակերպ՝ գեղձ)
thyself - toun inkut, toun kez (դուն ինքդ, դուն քեզ)
tiara - khouyr, tak (խոյր, թագ)

tic - tsounts- temki mugannerou, timatsounts (ցունց՝ դէմքի մկաններու, դիմացունց)
tick - varg, abarig, tik tak unel, mishd zarnel (վարկ, ապառիկ, թիք թաք ընել, միշտ զարնել)
ticket - doms, domsag, doukank, bidagel (տոմս, տոմսակ, տուգանք, պիտակել)
tickle - khudghudel, khudghudank, khudigh (խտղտել, խտղտանք, խտիղ)
tide - dzovasharzh, dzovakhaghatsk (ծովաշարժ, ծովախաղացք)
tidings - deghegoutiun, lour, dzanotoutiun (տեղեկութիւն, լուր, ծանօթութիւն)
tidy - gogig, vayelouch, gogel, bujnel (կոկիկ, վայելուչ, կոկել, պճնել)
tie - gabel, gutsel, hankoutsel, gab, hankouyts (կապել, կցել, հանգուցել, կապ, հանգոյց)
tier - gark, shark, gurdzgal, gabogh, sharel (կարգ, շարք, կրծկալ, կապող, շարել)
tiercet - yeradogh (եռատող)
tiff - oumb, pajag, ken, oumb oumb khumel, gondzel (ումպ, բաժակ, քէն, ումպ ումպ խմել, կոնծել)
tight - seghm, amour, tsik, serd, khunayogh, gogig (սեղմ, ամուր, ձիգ, սերտ, խնայող, կոկիկ)
tighten - burgel, seghmel, tsikanal (պրկել, սեղմել, ձիգանալ)
tightener - burgogh (պրկող)
tigre - vakur (վագր)
Tigris - dikris (Տիգրիս)
tile - gughmindur, salakarel, gughmindurov dzadzgel (կղմինտր, սալաքարել, կղմինտրով ծածկել)
tiler - salakordz, gughmindurov danik dzadzgogh (սալագործ, կղմինտրով տանիք ծածկող)
till - hergel, mushagel, tsanel, varel (հերկել, մշակել, ցանել, վարել)
till, until - minchev, minchev vor (մինչեւ, մինչեւ որ)
tillable - mushageli (մշակելի)
tiller - hergogh, mushagogh, untsiugh, untsiughil (հերկող, մշակող, ընձիւղ, ընձիւղիլ)
tilt (n) - vuran, dzadzgouyt, nizagi harvadz (վրան, ծածկոյթ, նիզակի հարուած)
tilt (v) - vuran larel, dzadzgel, mukhel, nizagamardil (վրան լարել, ծածկել, մխել, նիզակամարտիլ)
tilth - herg, hoghamushagoutiun, (հերկ, հողամշակութիւն)
timbal - tumpoug (թմբուկ)
timber - adaghts, dakhdag, keran, adaghtsel (ատաղձ, տախտակ, գերան, ատաղձել)
timbered - paydashen, dakhdagamadz (փայտաշէն, տախտակամած)
timbrel - tumpgig, tumpoug (թմբկիկ, թմբուկ)
time - zham, zhamanag, aden, devoghoutiun, hegh, ankam (ժամ, ժամանակ, ատեն, տեւողութիւն, հեղ, անգամ)
time out - tatar, argakhoum (դադար, առկախում)
timeless - anverch, havidenagan, anvakhjan (անվերջ, յաւիտենական, անվախճան)
timely - zhamanagin, harmar, ganoukh, jisht, tiboug (ժամանակին, յարմար, կանուխ, ճիշդ, դիպուկ)
timer - zhamabah (ժամապահ)
timetable - zhamanagatsouyts, zhamatsoutsag, tasatsoutsag (ժամանակացուցակ, ժամացուցակ, դասացուցակ)
timid - vakhgod, yergchod (վախկոտ, երկչոտ)
timidity - vakhgodoutiun, yergchodoutiun (վախկոտութիւն, երկչոտութիւն)
timing - zhamged, jushtial zham (ժամկէտ, ճշդեալ ժամ)
timorous - vakhgod, yergchod, tiuravakh (վախկոտ, երկչոտ, դիւրավախ)
tin - anak, titegh, anakel, anakazodzel (անագ, թիթեղ, անագել, անագազօծել)
tincture - nerg, kouyn, yerank, ner-

gel, yerankavorel (ներկ, գոյն, երանգ, ներկել, երանգաւորել)
tine - ger, agra (կեռ, կառայ)
tinge - yerankavorel, kounavorel, yerank, kouyn, ham (երանգաւորել, գունաւորել, երանգ, գոյն, համ)
tingle - zurunkal, hunchel, tuntal, aganchi zunkots (զրնգալ, հնչել, թնթալ, ականջի զնգոց)
tingler - tuntatsunogh (թնդացնող)
tingling - murmour, mormok, gusgidz (մրմուռ, մորմոք, կսկիծ)
tink - hunchiun, ghoghanchiun (հնչիւն, ղօղանչիւն)
tinker - aman norokogh, shurchig titeghakordz (աման նորոգող, շրջիկ թեթեղագործ)
tinkle - hunchel, ghoghanchel, hunchiun, ghoghanchiun (հնչել, ղօղանջել, հնչիւն, ղօղանչիւն)
tinman - titeghakordz (թիթեղագործ)
tinsmith - anakakordz (անագագործ)
tint - kounavorel, yerankel, yerank, pats kouyn (գունաւորել, երանգել, երանգ, բաց գոյն)
tiny - koghdurig, manrig (գողտրիկ, մանրիկ)
tip - dzayr, kit, tseratsir, nuver, hagil, nuver dal (ծայր, քիթ, ճեռաճիր, նուէր, յակիլ, նուէր տալ)
tipple - khumel, kinovnal, gondzel, khumichk (խմել, գինովնալ, կոնծել, խմիչք)
tippler - khumogh, gondzogh (խմող, կոնծող)
tipsy - kinemol, harpadz, dadanogh (գինեմոլ, հարբած, տատանող)
tirade - kashkushouk, yergaratsik kuroutiun (քաշքշուք, երկարաճիգ գրութիւն)
tirailleur - huratsanatsik (հրացանաճիգ)
tire - hoknil, hoknetsunel, kulkhazart, gurdzgal (յոգնիլ, յոգնեցնել, գլխազարդ, կրծկալ)
tired - hoknadz, daghdugali (յոգնած, տաղտկալի)
tiredness - hoknadzoutiun (յոգնածութիւն)
tireless - zhir, ankhonch, hoknil chukidtsogh (ժիր, անխոնջ, յոգնիլ չգիտցող)
tiresome - hoknetsoutsich, daghdugali (յոգնեցուցիչ, տաղտկալի)
tissue - hiusvadzeghen, hiusk, hiusgen, huisel (հիւսուածեղէն, հիւսք, հիւսկէն, հիւսել)
tit - barig, mokhrig, dzid, harvadz, pokhvurezh (պարիկ, մոխրիկ, ծիտ, հարուած, փոխվրէժ)
titbit - hamegh badar, aghvor gudor, dzaghgakagh (համեղ պատառ, աղուոր կտոր, ծաղկաքաղ)
tithe - dasanort, dasanortu vejarel dasanortel (տասանորդ, տասանորդը վճարել, տասանորդել)
titillate - khudghudel, midku khutanel (խտղտել, միտքը խթանել)
titillation - khudghudoum, khudghudank (խտղտում, խտղտանք)
title - didghos, vernakir, iravounk, anvanel, gochel (տիտղոս, վերնագիր, իրաւունք, անուանել, կոչել)
title deed - galvadzakir (կալուածագիր)
titled - didghosavor (տիտղոսաւոր)
titter - kekevel, zusbuvadz dzidzaghil, kekev (քեքեւել, զսպուած ծիծաղիլ, քեքեւ)
tittup - vosdosdel, tsadgurdel, tsadgurdouk (ոստոստել, ցատկռտել, ցատկռտուք)
titular - didghosavor, anvanagan, anvanagir (տիտղոսաւոր, անուանական, անուանակիր)
to - ar, tebi, i (առ, դէպի, ի)
toad - totosh, kordi desag (դօդօշ, գորտի տեսակ)
toady - kudznogh, shoghokort, yergeres (քծնող, շողոքորթ, երկերես)
toast (n) - hatsasherd, garmurtsuvadz hats, pazhagajar (հացաշերտ, կարմրցուած հաց, բաժակաճառ)
toast (v) - khorovel, hats garmurtsunel, genats khumel (խորովել, հաց կարմրցնել, կենաց խմել)
toaster - hatsep, hats garmurtsu-

nogh, genats khumogh (Հացեփ, Հաց կարմրցնող, կենաց խմող)
toast-master - pazhagakhos, seghanavar, seghanabed (բաժակախօս, սեղանավար, սեղանապետ)
tobacco - dzukhakhod (ծխախոտ)
tobacconist - dzukhavajar (ծխավաճառ)
tocsin - ahazank (ահազանգ)
today - aysor, nergayis (այսօր, ներկայիս)
toe - vodnamad, gujghag, vodkov tubchil (ոտնամատ, կճղակ, ոտքով դպչիլ)
toffee, taffy - roubi shakar, shakareghen (ռուպի շաքար, շաքարեղէն)
tog - hakvil (Հագուիլ)
together - miasin, miadegh (միասին, միատեղ)
toggery - hakousd, uzkesdeghen (Հագուստ, զգեստեղէն)
togs - hakousdeghenner (Հագուստեղէններ)
toil - ashkhadank, tsang, ashkhadil, juknil (աշխատանք, ցանկ, աշխատիլ, ճգնիլ)
toiler - duknogh, dzanur ashkhadogh (տքնող, ծանր աշխատող)
toilet - artouzart, zartarank, luvatsaran, ardakunots (արդուզարդ, զարդարանք, լուացարան, արտաքնոց)
token - nushan, hishadag, yerashkhik, turamanish (նշան, յիշատակ, երաշխիք, դրամանիշ)
token payment - gankhavujar (կանխավճար)
tole - hurabourel, kashel (Հրապուրել, քաշել)
tolerable - daneli, hantourzheli, touyladureli (տանելի, Հանդուրժելի, Թոյլատրելի)
tolerant - touyladou, nerogh, hamperogh, zichogh (Թոյլատու, ներող, Համբերող, զիջող)
tolerate - hantourzhel, nerel, touyladurel, zichanil (Հանդուրժել, ներել, Թոյլատրել, զիջանիլ)
toleration, tolerance - touylduvoutiun, neroghamudoutiun (Թոյլտուութիւն, ներողամտութիւն)
toll - antsadourk, mereli zank, zank hunchetsunel (անցատուրք, մեռելի զանգ, զանգ Հնչեցնել)
toll free call - anvujar heratsaynel (անվճար Հեռաձայնել)
tomahawk - amerigian huntigi gatsin, gatsinov usbannel (ամերիկեան Հնդիկի կացին, կացինով սպաննել)
tomato - lolig (լոլիկ)
tomb - kerezman, tampan, shirim, kerezmamel (գերեզման, դամբան, շիրիմ, գերեզմանել)
tombstone - dabanakar, kerezmanakar (տապանաքար, գերեզմանաքար)
tome - hador - kirki (Հատոր՝ գիրքի)
tomfool - khaydarag, aboush, mimos (խայտառակ, ապուշ, միմոս)
tomorrow - vaghu (վաղը)
ton (I) - yeghanag, voj, norouyt, noratsev daraz (եղանակ, ոճ, նորոյթ, նորաձեւ տարազ)
ton (II) - dagarachap, 1000 kilo gam 2240 pound (տակառաչափ, 1000 քիլօ կամ 2240 փաունտ)
tonality - tsaynargoutiun, kouyni asdijanoutiun (ձայնարկութիւն, գոյնի աստիճանութիւն)
tone - tsayni asdijan, yerkatsayn, nertashnagel (ձայնի աստիճան, երգաձայն, ներդաշնակել)
toner - adzkhaposhi (ածխափոշի)
tongs - ouneli (ունելի)
tongue - lezou, khosk, azk, khosil, yeghanagavorel (լեզու, խօսք, ազգ, խօսիլ, եղանակաւորել)
tongueless - anlezou, anparpar (անլեզու, անբարբառ)
tonic - tsaynagan, gaztourich (ձայնական, կազդուրիչ)
tonight, to-night - ays kisher, ays irigoun (այս գիշեր, այս իրիկուն)
tonnage - daroghoutiun, dagarachap (տարողութիւն, տակառաչափ)
tonsil - nushakeghts, nushig, dzudzag (նշագեղձ, նշիկ, ծծակ)

tonsile - khouzeli - maz (խուզելի՝ մազ)
too - khisd shad, nayev, al, yevus (խիստ շատ, նաեւ, ալ, եւս)
tool - kordzik, gazmadzk, kordzikov gudrel-shinel (գործիք, կազմածք, գործիքով կտրել-շինել)
tooth - agra, adam, adamnavorel (ակռայ, ատամ, ատամնաւորել)
toothache - agrayi tsav (ակռայի ցաւ)
toothbrush - adamnavurtsin (ատամնավրձին)
toothless - anadam (անատամ)
toothpaste - adamnakhius (ատամնախիւս)
toothpick - adamnagurgid, tsubig (ատամնակրկիտ, ցպիկ)
top (n) - kakat, kuloukh, dzayr, bed, khulkhavor, badiv (գագաթ, գլուխ, ծայր, պետ, գլխաւոր, պատիւ)
top (v) - partsuranal, dzadzgel, direl, kerazantsel (բարձրանալ, ծածկել, տիրել, գերազանցել)
topaz - dubazion, kohar (տպազիոն, գոհար)
topcoat - verargou (վերարկու)
toper - khuman, kinov (խման, գինով)
topful - lepletsoun (լեփլեցուն)
topic - vernakir, niut, punapan (վերնագիր, նիւթ, բնաբան)
topical - usd niuti, azhmeagan, deghagan (ըստ նիւթի, այժմէական, տեղական)
topographer - deghakir (տեղագիր)
topographic - deghakuragan (տեղագրական)
topography - dekhakuroutiun (տեղագրութիւն)
toponym - deghanoun (տեղանուն)
topping - kakat, vernadzayr, inknahavan (գագաթ, վերնածայր, ինքնահաւան)
topple - dabalil, var iynal, dabalel (տապալիլ, վար իյնալ, տապալել)
torch - chah (ջահ)
torchbearer - chahagir (ջահակիր)
toreador - tsulamardig (ցլամարտիկ)
torment - danchank, charcharank, darabank, danchel (տանջանք, չարչարանք, տառապանք, տանջել)
tornado - potorgahov (Թոփորկահով)
torpid - tumradz, ansharzh, anuzka, aboush, touyl (թմրած, անշարժ, անզգայ, ապուշ, թոյլ)
torpidity, torpidness - touloutiun, tumradzoutiun, aboushoutiun (թուլութիւն, թմրածութիւն, ապուշութիւն)
torpor - tumroutiun, untartsagoum, anuzkayoutiun (թմրութիւն, ընդարձակում, անզգայութիւն)
torporific - tumretsoutsich, anuzka tartsunogh (թմրեցուցիչ, անզգայ դարձնող)
torque - vuzi shughta, maniag (վզի շղթայ, մանեակ)
torrefaction - aghantsoum, pohroum, khargoum (աղանձում, բոհրում, խարկում)
torrefy - khargel, aghatsel, khantsel (խարկել, աղանձել, խանձել)
torrent - heghegh, hegheghad, hosank, hortsank, deghadarap (հեղեղ, հեղեղատ, հոսանք, յորձանք, տեղատարափ)
torrential - hegheghayin, hegheghanuman (հեղեղային, հեղեղանման)
torrid - ayretsial, gizich, khantsuvadz, chortsadz (այրեցեալ, կիզիչ, խանձուած, չորցած)
torridity, torridness - choroutiun, yerashd, yerashdoutiun (չորութիւն, երաշտ, երաշտութիւն)
torsion - kalaroum, voloroum (գալարում, ոլորում)
torso - ankuloukh artsan, angadar kordz (անգլուխ արձան, անկատար գործ)
tortoise - guria (կրիայ)
tortuous - tartstartsig, manvadzabad, otsabudouyd (դարձդարձիկ, մանուածապատ, օձապտոյտ)
torture - danchel, charcharel, danchank, charcharank (տանջել, չարչարել, տանջանք, չարչարանք)
toss - tsuntsel, ver nedel, tsuntsu-

vil, tsuntsoum (ցնցել, վեր նետել, ցնցուիլ, ցնցում)
tosspot - kinov, arpetsogh, khuman (գինով, արբեցող, խման)
tot - budulig, mangig, koumarel, koumaru kudnel (պտլիկ, մանկիկ, գումարել, գումարը գտնել)
total - luman, polor, ampoghchagan, koumaru, koumarel (լման, բոլոր, ամբողջական, գումարը, գումարել)
totalitarian - ampoghchadiragan (ամբողջատիրական)
totality - ampoghchoutiun, povantagoutiun (ամբողջութիւն, բովանդակութիւն)
totalization - ampoghchatsoum (ամբողջացում)
totalize - ampoghchatsunel, luratsunel (ամբողջացնել, լրացնել)
totally - ampoghchovin (ամբողջովին)
totter - yereral, dadanil, toghtughal (երերալ, տատանիլ, դողդղալ)
tottering - yereroum, khakhoud, toghtochoun (երերում, խախուտ, դողդոջուն)
touch (n) - huboum, shupoum, shoshapoum, houzoum (հպում, շփում, շօշափում, յուզում)
touch (v) - tubchil, hubil, shoshapel, hasnil, nuvakel (դպչիլ, հպիլ, շօշափել, հասնիլ, նուագել)
touchable - shoshapeli, hubeli (շօշափելի, հպելի)
touching - houzich, aztou, surdarouch, nugadmamp, masin (յուզիչ, ազդու, սրտառուչ, նկատմամբ, մասին)
touchy - tiurakurkir, tiurahouyz, tsasgod (դիւրագրգիռ, դիւրայոյզ, ցասկոտ)
tough - khisd, dogoun, gardzur, timatsgoun (խիստ, տոկուն, կարծր, դիմացկուն)
toughen - gardzuratsunel, khusdatsunel, gardzuranal (կարծրացնել, խստացնել, կարծրանալ)
toughness - khusdoutiun, dogounoutiun (խստութիւն, տոկունութիւն)
tour - shurchan, budouyd, shuchabudouyd, shurchan unel (շրջան, պտոյտ, շրջապտոյտ, շրջան ընել)
tourism - uzposashurchigoutiun, uzposabudouyd (զբօսաշրջիկութիւն, զբօսապտոյտ)
tourist - uzposashurchig (զբօսաշրջիկ)
tournament - murtsahantes, marzahantes, nizagakhaghoutiun (մրցահանդէս, մարզահանդէս, նիզակախաղութիւն)
tourne-vis - budoudagich, budoudagatarts (պտուտակիչ, պտուտակադարձ)
tournure - tartsuvadzk, ourvakidz, tsev, asatsvadzk (դարձուածք, ուրուագիծ, ձեւ, ասացուածք)
toushstone - portsakar (փորձաքար)
tousle - tserk nedel, kashel, anshunor purnel (ձեռք նետել, քաշել, անշնորհ բռնել)
tout - lurdesel, kaghduni tidel, tsiarshavi lurdes (լրտեսել, գաղտնի դիտել, ձիարշաւի լրտես)
tow - kashel, kashel-danil, karsh, khutsan, khudzoudz (քաշել, քաշել–տանիլ, քարշ, խցան, խծուծ)
towage, towing - garakashoum, kashel-danil, kashoghchek (կառաքաշում, քաշել–տանիլ, քաշողչէք)
toward(s) - tebi, mod, modig, nugadmamp, hanteb, hulou (դէպի, մօտ, մօտիկ, նկատմամբ, հանդէպ, հլու)
towel - antserots, tserasurpich (անձեռոց, ձեռասրբիչ)
tower - ashdarag, michnapert, partsuranal, savarnil (աշտարակ, միջնաբերդ, բարձրանալ, սաւառնիլ)
towering - partsuratsadz, sasdig, khisd, dzayrahegh (բարձրացած, սաստիկ, խիստ, ծայրայեղ)
town - kaghak (քաղաք)
town council - kaghakabedoutiun (քաղաքապետութիւն)
town house - kaghakadoun (քաղաքատուն)
townhall - kaghakabedaran (քաղաքապետարան)

townhouse - kaghakadoun (քաղաքատուն)
townline - khorakir (խորագիր)
toxic - touyn, tounavor (Թոյն, Թունաւոր)
toxication - tounavoroum (Թունաւորում)
toxicology - tounapanoutioun (Թունաբանութիւն)
toy - khaghalik, khaghal, zuvarjanal (խաղալիք, խաղալ, զուարճանալ)
trace - hedk, turoshm, nushan, hedevil, orinagel (Հետք, դրոշմ, նշան, Հետեւիլ, օրինակել)
tracer - hedakhouyz, hedakir (Հետախոյզ, Հետագիր)
trachea - shunchapogh, otapogh (շնչափող, օդափող)
track - vodnahedk, nushan, oughi, hedkeroun hedevil (ոտնաՀետք, նշան, ուղի, Հետքերուն Հետեւիլ)
tract - daradzoutiun, michots, orhnerk, guronajar (տարածութիւն, միջոց, օրՀներգ, կրօնաճառ)
tractable - hulou, ghegavareli, tiuransats, hez (Հլու, ղեկավարելի, դիւրանսաց, Հեզ)
tractor - kashogh mekena (քաշող մեքենայ)
trade - arevdour, uzpaghoum, kordz, arevdour unel (առեւտուր, զբաղում, գործ, առեւտուր ընել)
trade (n) - arevdour, vajaraganoutiun, uzpaghoum, arhesd (առեւտուր, վաճառականութիւն, զբաղում, արՀեստ)
trade (v) - arevdour unel, pokhanagel, arhesdi hedevil (առեւտուր ընել, փոխանակել, արՀեստի Հետեւիլ)
trade in - pokhanagel (փոխանակել)
trade school - arhesdits varjaran (արՀեստից վարժարան)
trademark - vajaranish, vajaraturoshm (վաճառանիշ, վաճառադրոշմ)
trader - arevduragan - ants gam nav (առեւտրական – անձ կամ նաւ)
tradesman - khanoutban (խանութպան)
tradition - avantoutiun, sovoroutiun, hantsunoum (աւանդութիւն, սովորութիւն, յանձնում)
traditional - avantagan (աւանդական)
traduce - zurbardel, charakhosel, anvanargel (զրպարտել, չարախօսել, անուանարկել)
traducer - zurbardich (զրպարտիչ)
traffic - arevdour, pokhanagoutiun, yertevegoutiun (առեւտուր, փոխանակութիւն, երթեւեկութիւն)
traffic light - aztalouys, yertevegi louys (ազդալոյս, երթեւեկի լոյս)
traffic sign - aztanushan (ազդանշան)
tragedian - voghperkag, voghperkou-teresan (ողբերգակ, ողբերգու՝ դերասան)
tragedy - voghperkoutiun, voghperk, yeghererk (ողբերգութիւն, ողբերգ, եղերերգ)
tragic, al - voghperkagan, yegheragan, aghidali (ողբերգական, եղերական, աղիտալի)
tragicomedy - voghperka-gadagerkoutiun (ողբերգա–կատակերգութիւն)
trail - hedkin hedevil, pundurel, kashel, hedk, jampa (Հետքին Հետեւիլ, փնտռել, քաշել, Հետք, ճամբայ)
trailer - kashogh, kashvogh, hedagark (քաշող, քաշուող, յետակառք)
train (n) - garakhoump, shark, tas, kughantsk (կառախումբ, շարք, դաս, քղանցք)
train (v) - gurtel, marzel, kashel, ludzel, oughghel (կրթել, մարզել, քաշել, լծել, ուղղել)
trainer - marzich, marzogh, varbed (մարզիչ, մարզող, վարպետ)
training - badrasdoutiun, marzank, gurtoutiun (պատրաստութիւն, մարզանք, կրթութիւն)
trait - hadganushagan kidz, nushanakidz, hubank (յատկանշական գիծ, նշանագիծ, Հպանք)

traitor - madnich, tavajan (մատնիչ, դաւաճան)
traject - artsagel, nedel, pokhantsel (արձակել, նետել, փոխանցել)
trajection - artsagoum, nedelu, pukhoum (արձակում, նետելը, բխում)
tralatition - pokhaperoutiun (փոխաբերութիւն)
tram - hanragark, adzkhagark, dzoughag, dashd (Հանրակառք, ածխակառք, ծուղակ, տաշտ)
trammel - vodnagab, dzoughag, arkilel, khapanel (ոտնակապ, ծուղակ, արգիլել, խափանել)
tramp - taparil, gokhgurdel, taparashurchig, taparogh (Թափառիլ, կոխկռտել, Թափառաշրջիկ, Թափառող)
trample - gokhgurdel, neghel, junshel, arhamarhel (կոխկռտել, նեղել, ճնշել, արՀամարՀել)
tramway - hanragark, kudzoughi (Հանրակառք, գծուղի)
trance - hapushdagoutiun, hiatsoum, hokeuzmayloutiun (յափշտակութիւն, Հիացում, Հոգեզմայլութիւն)
tranquil - hantard, khaghagh, ankhurov, hankisd (Հանդարտ, խաղաղ, անխռով, Հանգիստ)
tranquility - hantardoutiun, khaghaghoutiun (Հանդարտութիւն, խաղաղութիւն)
tranquilize - hantardetsunel, khaghaghetsunel (Հանդարտեցնել, խաղաղեցնել)
tranquilizer - hantardetsoutsich, amokarar (Հանդարտեցուցիչ, ամոքարար)
transact - gadarel, panagtsil, varel (կատարել, բանակցիլ, վարել)
transaction - kordzarnoutiun, kordz (գործառնութիւն, գործ)
transcend - kerazantsel, antsunil (գերազանցել, անցնիլ)
transcendence, cy - kerazantsoutiun (գերազանցութիւն)
transcendent - kerazants, keraga (գերազանց, գերակայ)
transcontinental - anturtsamakayin (անդրցամաքային)
transcribe - untorinagel, ardakurel, veradzel-yerki (ընդօրինակել, արտագրել, վերածել՝ երգի)
transcript - orinag, badjen, numanoutiun (օրինակ, պատճէն, նմանութիւն)
transcription - untorinagoutiun (ընդօրինակութիւն)
transect - sheghahadel, sheghagi gudrel (շեղաՀատել, շեղակի կտրել)
transfer - pokhantsel, deghapokhel, pokhantsoum (փոխանցել, տեղափոխել, փոխանցում)
transferable - pokhantseli, pokhatureli (փոխանցելի, փոխադրելի)
transferor, rer - pokhaturogh, pokhantsogh (փոխադրող, փոխանցող)
transfiguration - aylagerboutiun, pokhagerboutiun (այլակերպութիւն, փոխակերպութիւն)
transfigure - aylagerbel, pokhagerbel (այլակերպել, փոխակերպել)
transform - tsevapokhel, aylapokhel (ձեւափոխել, այլափոխել)
transformer - pokhargich (փոխարկիչ)
transfuse - ariun barbel-nerargel, ariunapokhel, pokharinel (արիւն պարպել–ներարկել, արիւնափոխել, փոխարինել)
transfusion - ariunapokhoutiun, untheghoum (արիւնափոխութիւն, ընդՀեղում)
transgress - meghanchel, orinazantsel, sahmanu antsunil (մեղանչել, օրինազանցել, սաՀմանը անցնիլ)
transgressor - orinazants, meghavor (օրինազանց, մեղաւոր)
tranship, transship - navapokhel (նաւափոխել)
transit - antsoughi, pokhantsoum, antsk, pokhaturoutiun (անցուղի, փոխանցում, անցք, փոխադրութիւն)
transition - antsk, antsoum, pokhantsoum, popokhoum (անցք, անցում, փոխանցում, փոփոխում)
transitory - antsavor, vaghantsig,

arzhamia (անցաւոր, վաղանցիկ, առժամեայ)
translate - tarkmanel, pokhaturel, pokantsel (Թարգմանել, փոխադրել, փոխանցել)
translation - tarkmanoutiun (Թարգմանութիւն)
translator - tarkmanich, megnich (Թարգմանիչ, մեկնիչ)
transliterate - daratartsel (տառադարձել)
transliteration - darapokhoum, daratartsoutiun (տառափոխում, տառադարձութիւն)
translocation - deghapokhoutiun (տեղափոխութիւն)
translucent - gisatapants, lousantsig (կիսաԹափանց, լուսանցիկ)
transmigrate - kaghtel, bantukhdel, hokepokhel (գաղԹել, պանդխտել, Հոգեփոխել)
transmigration - kaghtoum, bantukhdoutiun (գաղԹում, պանդխտութիւն)
transmission - pokhantsoum, sharzhahaghortich, pokhantsich (փոխացում, շարժաՀաղորդիչ, փոխանցիչ)
transmit - haghortel, pokhantsel, hastsunel (Հաղորդել, փոխանցել, Հասցնել)
transmutable - pokheli, shurcheli, aylapokheli (փոխելի, շրջելի, այլափոխելի)
transmutation - shurchoum, popokhoum, aylapokhoutiun (շրջում, փոփոխում, այլափոխութիւն)
transmute - shurchel, popokhel, aylapokhel (շրջել, փոփոխել, այլափոխել)
transom - lousamoud, turan semu (լուսամուտ, դրան սեմը)
transparency - tapantsigoutiun (Թափանցիկութիւն)
transparent - tapantsig, vujid, husdag (Թափանցիկ, վճիտ, յստակ)
transpiration - ardashunchoum, kurdunoum (արտաշնչում, քրտնում)
transpire - ardashunchel, kurdunil, tours dal, haydnuvil (արտաշնչել, քրտնիլ, դուրս տալ, յայտնուիլ)
transplant - deghapokhel - doungu, pokhaturel (տեղափոխել՝ տունկը, փոխադրել)
transplantation - ardadungoum (արտատնկում)
transport - pokhaturel, danil, darakurel, pokhaturoutiun (փոխադրել, տանիլ, տարագրել, փոխադրութիւն)
transportable - pokhatureli, daneli (փոխադրելի, տանելի)
transportation - pokhaturoutiun, darakuroutiun (փոխադրութիւն, տարագրութիւն)
transpose - deghapokhel, pokhaturel, tsaynapokhel (տեխափոխել, փոխադրել, ձայնափոխել)
transposition - deghapokhoum, pokhanagoum (տեղափոխում, փոխանակում)
transship - navapokhel, garke gark pokhaturel-pokhaturvil (Նաւափոխել, կարքէ կարք փոխադրել-փոխադրուիլ)
transshipment - navapokhoutiun (Նաւափոխութիւն)
transubstantiate - koyapokhel, ourish niuti pokhel (գոյափոխել, ուրիշ նիւԹի փոխել)
transudation - ardadzoroum (արտածորում)
transude - kurdunil, ardadzoril (քրտնիլ, արտածորիլ)
transversal - gudrogh, shegh, michahad kidz (կտրող, շեղ, միջաՀատ գիծ)
transverse - shegh, goghmunagi, khachatsev, khodornag (շեղ, կողմնակի, խաչաձեւ, խոտորնակ)
trap - tagart, dzoughag, tagartel, dzoughagu tsukel (Թակարդ, ծուղակ, Թակարդել, ծուղակը ձգել)
trapan - dzoughag, varbedoutiun, dzoughagu tsukel (ծուղակ, վարպետութիւն, ծուղակը ձգել)
trapeze - durabez, tignamugan, marzanki kordzik mu (տրապէզ, Թիկնամկան, մարզանքի գործիք մը)

trash - aveltsouk, taptupouk, hodel, makrel, nedel (աւելցուք, թափթըփուք, յոտել, մաքրել, նետել)
trasher - gamnogh, tagogh (կամնող, թակող)
trashy - anbed, pouj, anarzhek, azhan (անպէտ, փուճ, անարժէք, աժան)
travail (n) - yergounk, dughaperk, tsav, dazhank (երկունք, տղաբերք, ցաւ, տաժանք)
travail (v) - yergunel, tsav kashel, juknil, ashkhadil (երկնել, ցաւ քաշել, ճգնիլ, աշխատիլ)
travel - jamportel, antsunil, jamportoutiun (ճամբորդել, անցնիլ, ճամբորդութիւն)
traveller - jamport, oughevor (ճամբորդ, ուղեւոր)
traveller's check - turamadan pokhkir voryeve pan kunelou (դրամատան փոխգիր որեւէ բան գնելու)
traverse - mechen antsunil, gudrel antsunil, shegh, keran (մէջէն անցնիլ, կտրել անցնիլ, շեղ, գերան)
travesty - dzamadzour, dzubdial, dzubdoum, dzekel (ծամածուռ, ծպտեալ, ծպտում, ծեքել)
trawl - ourgan, ourganel (ուռկան, ուռկանել)
tray - aman, apse, dashd (աման, ափսէ, տաշտ)
treacherous - madnich, tavajan, nenk (մատնիչ, դաւաճան, նենգ)
treachery - madnoutiun, tavajanoutiun (մատնութիւն, դաւաճանութիւն)
treacle - shakari tantsur hiut, shakari tird (շաքարի թանձր հիւթ, շաքարի դիրտ)
tread - vodk tunel, gokhel, kalel, kunatsk, kayl, vodnag (ոտք դնել, կոխել, քալել, գնացք, քայլ, ոտնակ)
treadmill - vodnatarts aghorik, badzhi aghorik (ոտնադարձ աղօրիք, պատժի աղօրիք)
treadwheel - vodnaniv (ոտնանիւ)
treason - madnoutiun, tavajanoutiun (մատնութիւն, դաւաճանութիւն)
treasure - kants, ushdemaran, muterk, muterel, zhoghvel (գանձ, շտեմարան, մթերք, մթերել, ժողվել)
treasurer - kantsabah (գանձապահ)
treasury - kantsadoun, kants, kantsaran (գանձատուն, գանձ, գանձարան)
treat (n) - gochounk, khuntoutiun, hurjuvank (կոչունք, խնդութիւն, հրճուանք)
treat (v) - varvil, khunamel, tarmanel, panagtsil, khosil (վարուիլ, խնամել, դարմանել, բանակցիլ, խօսիլ)
treatise - jar, yergasiroutiun (ճառ, երկասիրութիւն)
treatment - veraperoum, varvelagerb, tarmanoum (վերաբերում, վարուելակերպ, դարմանում)
treaty - tashink, tashnakuroutiun (դաշինք, դաշնագրութիւն)
treble - yerabadig, zil tsayn, yerabadgel, yerabadguvil (եռապատիկ, զիլ ձայն, եռապատկել, եռապատկուիլ)
tree - dzar, doung, dzar hanel, gaghabarel (ծառ, տունկ, ծառ հանել, կաղապարել)
trefoil - arouyd, yereknoug, yeraderev pouys mu (առույտ, երեքնուկ, եռատերեւ բոյս մը)
trek - saylov jamportel, kaghtel, kaght, kalvadzk (սայլով ճամբորդել, գաղթել, գաղթ, քալուածք)
tremble - toghal, yereral, sarsuril, sarsour, togh (դողալ, երերալ, սարսուռիլ, սարսուռ, դող)
trembler - toghatsogh, toghtoghatsogh (դողացող, դողդողացող)
tremendous - sarsapeli, sosgali, ahargou, zarhoureli (սարսափելի, սոսկալի, ահարկու, զարհուրելի)
tremor - togh, sarsour, tsuntsoum (դող, սարսուռ, ցնցում)
tremulous - toghtochoun, toghatsogh (դողդոջուն, դողացող)
trench - agosel, khuramel, porel, agos, khuram (ակօսել, խրամել,

փորել, ակօս, խրամ)
trenchant - sour, hadou, vujragan, gudroug (սուր, հատու, վճռական, կտրուկ)
trend - tsukdoum, hagoum, midoum, tsukdil, midil (ձգտում, հակում, միտում, ձգտիլ, միտիլ)
trepid - toghtochoun (դողդոջուն)
trepidation - sosgoum, tsuntsoum (սոսկում, ցնցում)
trespass - voduntsel, meghanchel, voduntsukoutiun (ոտնձգել, մեղանչել, ոտնձգութիւն)
trespasser - hantsavor, iravazants (յանցաւոր, իրաւազանց)
tress - hiusk, khobob (հիւսք, խոպոպ)
trial - ports, portsargoutiun, tadagan kunnoutiun (փորձ, փորձառութիւն, դատական քննութիւն)
triangle - yerangiun (եռանկիւն)
tribe - tsegh, dohm, undanik, tseghakhoump (ցեղ, տոհմ, ընտանիք, ցեղախումբ)
tribulation - vishd, neghoutiun, portsank, darabank (վիշտ, նեղութիւն, փորձանք, տառապանք)
tribunal - adian, tadaran, tadavori ator (ատեան, դատարան, դատաւորի աթոռ)
tribunate - adenagaloutiun (ատենակալութիւն)
tribune - adian, pem, ambion, vernadoun, hantisapem (ատեան, բեմ, ամպիոն, վերնատուն, հանդիսաբեմ)
tributary - hargadou, hubadag, usdoratas, yentaga (հարկատու, հպատակ, ստորադաս, ենթակայ)
tribute - dourk, harg, nuver, harkanki dourk (տուրք, հարկ, նուէր, յարգանքի տուրք)
trick - khapeoutiun, nenkoutiun, hunark, khapel (խաբէութիւն, նենգութիւն, հնարք, խաբել)
trickery - nenkoutiun, ajbararoutiun (նենգութիւն, աճպարարութիւն)
trickle - hosil, gatil, gatgutoum (հոսիլ, կաթիլ, կաթկթում)
tricky - khapeagan, nenkoutiamp letsoun (խաբէական, նենգութեամբ լեցուն)
tricolor - yerakouyn (եռագոյն)
tricot - hiusag, tsantsahiusk (հիւսակ, ցանցահիւսք)
tricycle - yeraniv hedzig (եռանիւ հեծիկ)
trident - yerazhani - kordzik (եռաժանի՝ գործիք)
tried - portsuvadz, vusdaheli (փորձուած, վստահելի)
triennial - yeramia, yeramiag (եռամեայ, եռամեակ)
trier - portsogh, kunnich, portsakar (փորձող, քննիչ, փորձաքար)
trifle - chunchin, pouj, sin, sunapanil (չնչին, փուճ, սին, սնաբանիլ)
trifling - tetevamid, vochinch, sunodi (թեթեւամիտ, ոչինչ, սնոտի)
trifold - yeradzal, yeramas (եռածալ, եռամաս)
trig - gogig, vayelouch, lav, arkelag, arkelagel (կոկիկ, վայելուչ, լաւ, արգելակ, արգելակել)
trigonometer - yerangiunachap (եռանկիւնաչափ)
trigonometry - yerangiunachapoutiun (եռանկիւնաչափութիւն)
trilateral - yeragoghm (եռակողմ)
trilingual - yerek lezouyan, yerek lezou khosogh (երեք լեզուեան, երեք լեզու խօսող)
trill - keghkeghel, turturatsunel, toghtoghal, turturoum (գեղգեղել, թրթռացնել, դողդողալ, թրթռում)
trillion - yerilion (եռիլիոն)
trim - gogel, makrel, hartarel, shudgel, zart, gogig (կոկել, մաքրել, յարդարել, շտկել, զարդ, կոկիկ)
trimester - yeramsiag (եռամսեակ)
trimmer - hartarogh, hartarich (յարդարող, յարդարիչ)
trimming - hartarank, dzayrerou gydruvadzk (յարդարանք, ծայրերու կտրուածք)
trinal - yerabadig (եռապատիկ)
Trinity - yerrortoutiun (Երրորդութիւն)
trio - yeranuvak, yerrortoutiun

(եռանուագ, երրորդութիւն)
trip - budouyd, shurchan, saytakoum, saytakil, sahil (պտոյտ, շրջան, սայթաքում, սայթաքիլ, սահիլ)
tripartite - yeramas, yeragoghm (եռամաս, եռակողմ)
triple - yerabadig, yerriag, yerabadgel, yerabadguvil (եռապատիկ, երրեակ, եռապատկել, եռապատկուիլ)
triplet - yeriag, yeradogh (երրեակ, եռատող)
triplex - yerriag, yeragi (երրեակ, եռակի)
tripod - yerodani (եռոտանի)
triptych - yeradzal seghan (եռածալ սեղան)
trisful - dukhrakin (տխրագին)
triturate - manrel, pushrel, jumlel (մանրել, փշրել, ճմլել)
trituration - manroum, pushroum (մանրում, փշրում)
triumph - haghtanag, haghtoutiun, haghtanagel (յաղթանակ, յաղթութիւն, յաղթանակել)
triumphal - haghtagan, haghtanagayin (յաղթական, յաղթանակային)
triumphant - haghtogh, haghtagan (յաղթող, յաղթական)
triumpher - haghtogh, haghtagan (յաղթող, յաղթական)
triumvir - yerabed (եռապետ)
triumviral - yerabedagan (եռապետական)
trivial - vochinch, chunchin, aroria, hasarag (ոչինչ, չնչին, առօրեայ, հասարակ)
troll - gurgnerkel, garkov yerkel, hurabourel, gurgnerk (կրկներգել, կարգով երգել, հրապուրել, կրկներգ)
trombone - avakapogh (աւագափող)
troop - khoump, taderakhoump, yeram, khumpel, havakvil (խումբ, թատերախումբ, երամ, խմբել, հաւաքուիլ)
trooper - ayroutsi, tsiavor, hedzial (այրուձի, ձիաւոր, հեծեալ)
troops - zork (զօրք)
trope - pokhaperoutiun, pokhagerboutiun (փոխաբերութիւն, փոխակերպութիւն)
trophic, trophical - sununtagan (սննդական)
trophology - sununtakidoutiun (սննդագիտութիւն)
trophy - haghtanag, haghtanushan (յաղթանակ, յաղթանշան)
tropic - arevatarts (արեւադարձ)
tropical - arevatartsayin (արեւադարձային)
tropology - aylapanoutiun (այլաբանութիւն)
trot - vazk - tsiou, untosd kunatsk, soural, vazvuzel (վազք՝ ձիու, ընդոստ գնացք, սուրալ, վազվզել)
troth (n) - jushmardoutiun, havadarmoutiun, nushandouk (ճշմարտութիւն, հաւատարմութիւն, նշանտուք)
troth (v) - oukhdel, khosdanal, nushanel (ուխտել, խոստանալ, նշանել)
trotter - vodk - gentanii (ոտք՝ կենդանիի)
troubadour - ashough, kousan (աշուղ, գուսան)
trouble - neghel, vurtovel, khankarel, neghoutiun, daknab (նեղել, վրդովել, խանգարել, նեղութիւն, տագնապ)
trouble chutter - daknabalouydz (տագնապալոյծ)
troubler - neghogh, khankarogh (նեղող, խանգարող)
troublesome - neghich, tsantsuratsoutsich (նեղիչ, ձանձրացուցիչ)
trough - dashd, churortan, churpogh (տաշտ, ջրորդան, ջրփող)
trounce - dzedzel, mudragel, chekhel (ծեծել, մտրակել, չեխել)
troupe - taderakhoump, terasanakhoump (թատերախումբ, դերասանախումբ)
trousers - dapad, vardik (տաբատ, վարտիք)
trousseau - harsi ozhid, jermaghen (հարսի օժիտ, ճերմակեղէն)
trout - garmurakhayd, khaydatsoug

(կարմրախայտ, խայտաձուկ)
trow - yentaturel, havadal (ենթադրել, հաւատալ)
trowel - dzepich, dzepichov hartarel (ծեփիչ, ծեփիչով յարդարել)
truant - tubrotsapakh, dzouyl, zhamavajar (դպրոցափախ, ծոյլ, ժամավաճառ)
truce - zinatoul, zinatatar, hankisd (զինադուլ, զինադադար, հանգիստ)
truck - pernagark, pokhanagoum, pokhanagel (բեռնակառք, փոխանակում, փոխանակել)
truckage - pokhatravartsk, danoghchek (փոխադրավարձք, տանողչէք)
trucker - pernadar, pokhanagogh (բեռնատար, փոխանակող)
truckman - garaban, saylort, pokhanagich (կառապան, սայլորդ, փոխանակիչ)
truculence, cy - vayrakoutiun, parparosoutiun (վայրագութիւն, բարբարոսութիւն)
truculent - vayrak, gadaghi, parparos (վայրագ, կատաղի, բարբարոս)
trudge - hoknadz kalel, hoknadz kalvadzk (յոգնած քալել, յոգնած քալուածք)
true - iragan, jishd, shidag, jushmarid, harazad (իրական, ճիշդ, շիտակ, ճշմարիտ, հարազատ)
truffle - kednasoung, hoghadzadzg soung (գետնասունկ, հողածածկ սունկ)
truism - patzahayd jushmardoutiun (բացայայտ ճշմարտութիւն)
trull - poz, bornig, poghotsi gin (բոզ, պոռնիկ, փողոցի կին)
truly - jushmardoren, angeghdzoren, artarev (ճշմարտօրէն, անկեղծօրէն, արդարեւ)
trump - pogh, shepor, tughtakhagh mu, pogh puchel, (փող, շեփոր, թղթախաղ մը, փող փչել)
trumpery - khapeoutiun, sunodik, anarzhek (խաբէութիւն, սնոտիք, անարժէք)
trumpet - pogh, pogh puchel, parapanel (փող, փող փչել, փառաբանել)
truncate - gudradel, dzayradel, gudurdel (կտրատել, ծայրատել, կտրտել)
truncation - hadoum, dzayradoum (հատում, ծայրատում)
truncheon - lakhd, kavazan, pir, dzedzel (լախտ, գաւազան, բիր, ծեծել)
trundle - pokraniv gark, tavaloum, kulorel, tartsunel (փոքրանիւ կառք, թաւալում, գլորել, դարձնել)
trunk - gojgh, poun, puchapogh, sundoug-inknasharzhi (կոճղ, բուն, իրան, փչափող, սնտուկ՝ինքնաշարժի)
truss - dzurar, durtsag, gabots, dzurarel, shampourel (ծրար, տրցակ, կապոց, ծրարել, շամփուրել)
trust - vusdahoutiun, havadk, houys, vusdahil, havadal (վստահութիւն, հաւատք, յոյս, վստահիլ, հաւատալ)
trustee - khunamagal, hokapartsou, hokadar, khunamagalel (խնամակալ, հոգաբարձու, հոգատար, խնամակալել)
truster - vusdahogh, havadatsogh (վստահող, հաւատացող)
trustful - liavusdah, ampoghchovin vusdah (լիավստահ, ամբողջովին վստահ)
trustless - anhavadarim, anvusdaheli, khartakh (անհաւատարիմ, անվստահելի, խարդախ)
trusty - havadarim, vusdaheli, oughigh (հաւատարիմ, վստահելի, ուղիղ)
truth - jushmardoutiun, iraganoutiun, angeghdzoutiun (ճշմարտութիւն, իրականութիւն, անկեղծութիւն)
truthful - jushmardakhos, shidag, oughigh (ճշմարտախօս, շիտակ, ուղիղ)
try - portsel, chanal, juknil, zudel, halel, ports (փորձել, ջանալ, ճգնիլ, զտել, հալել, փորձ)
trying - portsich, hoknetsoutsich,

sird hadtsunogh (փորձիչ, յոգնեցուցիչ, սիրտ հատցնող)
tryout - nakhaports (նախափորձ)
tryst - zhamaturoutiun, zhamaturavayr, zhamaturvil (ժամադրութիւն, ժամադրավայր, ժամադրուիլ)
tsar, czar - tsar, rousio gaysur (ձար, Ռուսիոյ կայսր)
tub - dashd, dagarag, dagarel, dashdi mech luval (տաշտ, տակառակ, տակառել, տաշտի մէջ լուալ)
tube - khoghovag, pogh, khoghovagel (խողովակ, փող, խողովակել)
tuber - musod armad, pouysi armadi vura ouretsk (մսոտ արմատ, բոյսի արմատի վրայ ուռեցք)
tubercle - our, ouretsk, tokakhdi balar (ուռ, ուռեցք, թոքախտի պալար)
tuberculosis - tokakhd, huidzakhd, balarakhd (թոքախտ, հիւծախտ, պալարախտ)
tubular - khoghovagatsev, poghatsev (խողովակաձեւ, փողաձեւ)
tuck - tukhel, tukhmel, dzalkodel, sotdel, dzalk (թխել, թխմել, ծալքոտել, սոթտել, ծալք)
Tuesday - yerekshapti (Երեքշաբթի)
tufa - pukhrakar, hoghakar (փխրաքար, հողաքար)
tuft - vars, dzob, pounch, pounch gazmel (վարս, ծոպ, փունջ, փունջ կազմել)
tug - kashel, kashkushel, chanal, chank, tsukanav (քաշել, քաշքշել, ջանալ, ջանք, ձգանաւ)
tugger - kashogh, baran, chuvan (քաշող, պարան, չուան)
tuition - ousoutsoum, gurtatoshag, ousoumnakin (ուսուցում, կրթաթոշակ, ուսումնագին)
tulip - gagach (կակաչ)
tulle - shugharsh (շղարշ)
tumble - tavalil, kuloril, iynal, tavaloum, kuloroum (թաւալիլ, գլորիլ, իյնալ, թաւալում, գլորում)
tumbler - ajbarar, larakhaghats, tavalogh, kavat (աճպարար, լարախաղաց, թաւալող, գաւաթ)
tumbling - larakhaghoutiun (լարախաղութիւն)
tumefaction - our, ouretsk, pushdig (ուռ, ուռեցք, փշտիկ)
tumefy - ouril, ouretsunel (ուռիլ, ուռեցնել)
tumid - ouradz, ouroutsig, tsutsvadz (ուռած, ուռուցիկ, ցցուած)
tumor - our, ouretsk, aydouts, khulirt (ուռ, ուռեցք, այտուց, խլիրդ)
tumult - aghmoug, zhukhor, vulvuloug (աղմուկ, ժխոր, վլվլուկ)
tun - dagar, garas (տակառ, կարաս)
tuna - vorttsoug, pushod dants, huntgatouz (որթձուկ, փշոտ տանձ, հնդկաթուզ)
tune - nuvak, yeghanag, khaz, nuvakel, yeghanagel (նուագ, եղանակ, խազ, նուագել, եղանակել)
tunic - barekod, tignots, vudavag, badian (պարեգօտ, թիկնոց, վտաւակ, պատեան)
tunnel - paboughi, kednoughi, dzagel, kednantsk panal (փապուղի, գետնուղի, ծակել, գետնանցք բանալ)
turban - pattots, abarosh (փաթթոց, ապարօշ)
turbaned - pattotsavor (փաթթոցաւոր)
turbid - bughdor, tsekhod (պղտոր, ցեխոտ)
turbidity - bughdoroutiun (պղտորութիւն)
turbot - vahanatsoug (վահանաձուկ)
turbulence, cy - anhantardoutiun, khurovoutiun, angarkoutiun (անհանդարտութիւն, խռովութիւն, անկարգութիւն)
turbulent - aghmugarar, khurovarar, gurvaser, anhantard (աղմկարար, խռովարար, կռուասէր, անհանդարտ)
turd - tird, aghp (դիրտ, աղբ)
tureen - tanaman, khoshor aman (թանաման, խոշոր աման)
turf - tsiarshavaran, gurges, talarik, talarazartel (ձիարշաւարան, կրկէս, դալարիք, դալարազարդել)
turfy - ganachakegh, talarakegh (կանաչագեղ, դալարագեղ)

turgent - ouroutsig (ուռուցիկ)
turgescence - ouroutsigoutiun, pukatsoum (ուռուցիկութիւն, փքացում)
turgescent - ouretsogh, pukatsogh (ուռեցող, փքացող)
turk - tourk, dajig, osmantsi (Թուրք, տաճիկ, օսմանցի)
Turkey - tourkia (Թուրքիա)
turkey - huntgahav (հնդկահաւ)
turkish - turkagan, turkeren (Թրքական, Թրքերէն)
turmoil - aghmoug, guriv, dazhank, neghel, charcharel (աղմուկ, կռիւ, տաժանք, նեղել, չարչարել)
turn (n) - shurchan, tavaloum, tartsuvadzk, budouyd, hert (շրջան, Թաւալում, դարձուածք, պտոյտ, հերԹ)
turn (v) - tarnal, tartsunel, shurchil, shurchel, pokhel (դառնալ, դարձնել, շրջիլ, շրջել, փոխել)
turnabout - popokhagi (փոփոխակի)
turnaround - shourchtarts, gardzik pokhel (շուրջդարձ, կարծիք փոխել)
turnaway - artsagel, heranal (արձակել, հեռանալ)
turncoat - tasalik, oukhdazants, ouratsogh (դասալիք, ուխտազանց, ուրացող)
turndown - dzalel, merzhel (ծալել, մերժել)
turning - tarts, tartsuvadzk, jakharagakordzoutiun (դարձ, դարձուածք, ճախարակագործութիւն)
turnip - shoghkam (շողգամ)
turnkey - pandabah (բանտապահ)
turnout - yelk, oughetarts, kordzatoul (ելք, ուղեդարձ, գործադուլ)
turnover - shurchoum, verashurchoum, vajarakoumar (շրջում, վերաշրջում, վաճառագումար)
turnpike - antsatour, pazhatour (անցադուռ, բաժադուռ)
turnpoint - tartsaged (դարձակէտ)
turnscrew - budoudagatarts (պտուտակադարձ)
turnsole - arevadzaghig (արեւածաղիկ)
turntable - shurchoun dakhdag, tartsahadag (շրջուն տախտակ, դարձայատակ)
turpentine - pevegnakhezh, pevegni dzar (բեւեկնախէժ, բեւեկնի խէժ)
turpitude - khaydaragoutiun, usdornoutiun, pozoutiun (խայտառակութիւն, ստորնութիւն, բոզութիւն)
turquoise - ganachakharun gabouyd, harki kar, pirouzakar (կանաչախառն կապոյտ, յարգի քար, փիրուզաքար)
turret - pokur ashdarag, ashdaragig, manrashdarag (փոքր աշտարակ, աշտարակիկ, մանրաշտարակ)
turtle - dzovi guria, dadrag (ծովի կրիայ, տատրակ)
tussle - kodemardil, kodemard, makaroum, baykar (գօտեմարտիլ, գօտեմարտ, մաքառում, պայքար)
tutelage - khunamagaloutiun, bashdbanoutiun (խնամակալութիւն, պաշտպանութիւն)
tutelar - khunamagal, bashdban (խնամակալ, պաշտպան)
tutor (n) - khunamagal, bashdban, ousoutsich, varzhabed (խնամակալ, պաշտպան, ուսուցիչ, վարժապետ)
tutor (v) - khunamagalel, ousoutsanel, sorvetsunel (խնամակալել, ուսուցանել, սորվեցնել)
tutorial - ousoutschagan (ուսուցչական)
tuxedo - garj pajgon (կարճ բաճկոն)
twaddle - pouj khosagtsoutiun, shadakhosoutiun, shadakhosel (փուճ խօսակցութիւն, շատախօսութիւն, շատախօսել)
twain - yergou, yergiag, gurgin (երկու, երկեակ, կրկին)
twang - shachel, runkakhosel, shamrach, runkahunchiun (շաչել, ռնգախօսել, շառաչ, ռնգահնչիւն)
tweak - gusmit, gusmutel, sughmel (կսմիԹ, կսմԹել, սղմել)
tweed - parag basdar (բարակ պաստառ)
tweet - jurvoghuin, jurvoghil (ճռուողիւն, ճռուողիլ)
twelve - dasnuyergou (տասներկու)

twentieth - kusanerort (քսաներորդ)
twenty - kusan (քսան)
twice - yergou ankam, gurgin (երկու անգամ, կրկին)
twig - jiugh, vosd, dzedzel, hasgunal (ճիւղ, ոստ, ծեծել, Հասկնալ)
twilight - ayk, moutnoulouys, arshalouys, verchalouys (այգ, մութնուլոյս, արշալոյս, վերջալոյս)
twin - yergvoriag, zouyk (երկուորեակ, զոյգ)
twine - chuvan, arasan, volorel, miahiusel, pattel (չուան, առասան, ոլորել, միաՀիւսել, փաթթել)
twinge - gusmit, gusgidz, gusmutel, gusgudzetsunel (կսմիթ, կսկիծ, կսմթել, կսկծեցնել)
twinkle - shoghal, palpulil, paylil, palpulouk (շողալ, փալփլիլ, փայլիլ, փալփլուք)
twirl - tartsunel, shurchshurchel, bullouil, tartsuvadzk (դարձնել, շրջշրջել, պլլուիլ, դարձուածք)
twist - volorel, kalarel, tartsunel, bullel, bulluvil (ոլորել, գալարել, դարձնել, պլլել, պլլուիլ)
twister - dzurogh, kheghatiurogh, khapepa (ծռող, խեղաթիւրող, խաբեբայ)
twit - gushdampel, hantimanel, chekhel, gushdampank (կշտամբել, յանդիմանել, չեխել, կշտամբանք)
twitch - tsuntsoum, gudzgoum, khuloum, gorzel, khulel (ցնցում, կծկում, խլում, կորզել, խլել)
twitchy - tiurakurkir (դիւրագրգիռ)
twitch-grass - molakhod (մոլախոտ)
twitter - jurvoghiun, taylayl, jurvoghel, taylaylel (ճռուողիւն, դայլայլ, ճռուողել, դայլայլել)
two - yergou (երկու)
twofaced - yergeres, geghdzavor (երկերես, կեղծաւոր)
twofold - yergdzal, gurgin (երկծալ, կրկին)
two-edged - yergsayry, anorosh (երկսայրի, անորոշ)
two-faced - yergou goghmov, yergeres, geghdzavor (երկու կողմով, երկերես, կեղծաւոր)
two-fold - yergdzal, yergbadig (երկծալ, երկպատիկ)
tymbal - tumpoug (թմբուկ)
tympan - tumpoug, shenki jagad (թմբուկ, շէնքի ճակատ)
tympanum - aganchi tumpoug, michnaganch (ականջի թմբուկ, միջնականջ)
type (n) - dib, dibar, orinag, nakhadib, dar (տիպ, տիպար, օրինակ, նախատիպ, տառ)
type (v) - mekenakurel, sharel, kurasharel, orinagel (մեքենագրել, շարել, գրաշարել, օրինակել)
typeface - daradesag, kuradesag (տառատեսակ, գրատեսակ)
typescript - mekenakir, mekenakurvadz tserakir (մեքենագիր, մեքենագրուած ձեռագիր)
typeset - kurasharel, sharel (գրաշարել, շարել)
typesetter - kurashar (գրաշար)
typesetting - kurasharoutiun (գրաշարութիւն)
typewrite - kuramekenakurel (գրամեքենագրել)
typewriter - kuramekena, madnedib, kuramekenakurogh (գրամեքենայ, մատնետիպ, գրամեքենագրող)
typewriting - mekenakuroutiun (մեքենագրութիւն)
typhlitis - gouraghedab (կուրաղետապ)
typhoid - zhandadent, zhandacherm (ժանտատենդ, ժանտաջերմ)
typhoon - potorig, ouragan (փոթորիկ, ուրական)
typhus - zhandadent, pudzadent, tifius (ժանտատենդ, բծատենդ, թիֆիւս)
typical - dibar, yezagan, hadganushagan (տիպար, եզական, յատկանշական)
typist - kuramekenakurogh (գրամեքենագրող)
typographer - dubakurich (տպագրիչ)
typography - dubakuroutiun (տպագրութիւն)
tyrannic - purnabedagan (բռնապե–

տական)
tyrannize - *purnagalel, junshel, geghekel (բռնակալել, ճնշել, կեղեքել)*
tyranny - *purnoutiun, purnabedoutiun (բռնութիւն, բռնապետութիւն)*
tyrant - *purnagal, purnabed (բռնակալ, բռնապետ)*
tyro - *usgusnag, hampag (սկսնակ, համբակ)*
tzar, czar - *tsar, rous gaysur (ձար, ռուս կայսր)*
tzigane - *kunchou (գնչու)*

ubiquitous - *amenourek, amen degh (ամենուրեք, ամէն տեղ)*
udder - *dzidz gentaninerou (ծիծ կենդանիներու)*
udometer - *antsurevachap (անձրեւաչափ)*
ugliness - *dukeghoutiun, aylantagoutiun (տգեղութիւն, այլանդակութիւն)*
ugly - *dukegh, aylantag (տգեղ, այլանդակ)*
ulcer - *usdamoksi gegh, verk (ստամոքսի կեղ, վէրք)*
ulcerate - *verki veradzvil, gegh gabel (վէրքի վերածուիլ, կեղ կապել)*
ulterior - *hedin, yedki, verchin (յետին, ետքի, վերջին)*
ultimate - *amenaverchin, dzayrakouyn, yezrapagich (ամենավերջին, ծայրագոյն, եզրափակիչ)*
ultimatum - *verchnakir (վերջնագիր)*
ultra - *dzayrahegh, armadagan (ծայրայեղ, արմատական)*
ultramarine - *anturdzovian, lazvart (անդրծովեան, լազուարթ)*
ultrasonic - *anturtsaynayin, kertsaynayin (անդրձայնային, գերձայնային)*
ultrasound - *kertsayn (գերձայն)*
ultra-violet - *anturmanishagakouyn (անդրմանիշակագոյն)*
ululant - *vornatsogh, hachogh (ոռնացող, հաչող)*
ululate - *vornal, hachel (ոռնալ, հաչել)*
umbel - *arevanots, arevi hovamnots, hovanotsag (արեւանոց, արեւի հովանոց, հովանոցակ (բուս.)*
umbellet - *hovanotsig (հովանոցիկ)*
umber - *tukhahogh, shouk, shouk unel, toukh nergel (Թխահող, շուք, շուք ընել, Թուխ ներկել)*
umbilical cord - *bordalar (պորտալար)*
umbilicus - *bord (պորտ)*
umbra - *usdouer (ստուեր)*
umbrage - *shouk, hovani, hok, tuzhkohoutiun, gasgadz (շուք, հովանի, հոգ, դժգոհութիւն, կասկած)*
umbrella - *hovanots (հովանոց)*
umpire - *iravarar - khaghi mech, michnort, iravararel (իրաւարար՝ խաղի մէջ, միջնորդ, իրաւարարել)*
un - *prefix: opposite or reversal of the action of the verb (նախամասնիկ՝ հակասական կամ բացասական)*
unabashed - *anamot (անամօԹ)*
unable - *angarogh, anadag (անկարող, անատակ)*
unabridged - *chugurjadvadz, untartsag, liagadar (չկրճատուած, ընդարձակ, լիակատար)*
unacceptable - *anuntouneli, anhajo, anpaghtsali (անընդունելի, անհաճոյ, անբաղձալի)*
unaccomplished - *angadar, teri, gisgadar (անկատար, Թերի, կիսկատար)*
unaccountable - *anbadmeli, anhashveli, animanali (անպատմելի, ան-*

Հաշուելի, անիմանալի)
unadvised - ankhorhourt, anuzkouysh (անխորհուրդ, անզգոյշ)
unaffected - chaztuvogh, angaregir, angeghdz, barz (չազդուող, անկարեկիր, անկեղծ, պարզ)
unalterable - hasdad, anpopokheli, chavruvogh (Հաստատ, անփոփոխելի, չաւրուող)
unamiable - anparehampouyr (անբարեհամբոյր)
unanimity - miatsaynoutiun (միաձայնութիւն)
unanimous - miatsayn, hamatsayn (միաձայն, Համաձայն)
unanimously - miatsaynoutiamp (միաձայնութեամբ)
unanswerable - anbadaskhaneli, anzhukhdeli, anherkeli (անպատասխանելի, անժխտելի, անհերքելի)
unapprehensible - anumpurneli (անըմբռնելի)
unapt - angarogh, anadag, anuntounag (անկարող, անատակ, անընդունակ)
unarm - zinatapel (զինաթափել)
unarmed - zinatap, anzen (զինաթափ, անզէն)
unashamed - anamot (անամօթ)
unassuming - khonarh, hamesd, anhavagnod (խոնարհ, Համեստ, անյաւակնոտ)
unattainted - angoghmunagal, anpasir (անկողմնակալ, անբասիր)
unauthorised - chardonvadz, anvaver, chuliazorvadz (չարտօնուած, անվաւեր, չլիազօրուած)
unavoidable - ankhousapeli (անխուսափելի)
unaware - andeghiag, andzanot (անտեղեակ, անծանօթ)
unawares - anuzkoushoutiamp, hangardzagi (անզգուշութեամբ, յանկարծակի)
unbacked - anoknagan, anzoravid, anvarzh (անօգնական, անզօրավիգ, անվարժ)
unbaked - anep, chepadz (անեփ, չեփած)
unbalanced - anhavasaragushir (անՀաւասարակշիռ)
unbearable - andaneli, anhantourzheli (անտանելի, անՀանդուրժելի)
unbeat - yentasherd (ենթաշերտ)
unbeaten - anhaghteli, angokh (անյաղթելի, անկոխ)
unbecoming - anvayelouch, anharmar (անվայելուչ, անյարմար)
unbeknown - andzanot (անծանօթ)
unbelief - anhavadoutiun, usgebdigoutiun (անՀաւատութիւն, սկեպտիկութիւն)
unbeliever - anhavad, usgebdig (անՀաւատ, սկեպտիկ)
unbelt - ankodi, kodin kagel, toultsunel (անգօտի, գօտին քակել, թուլցնել)
unbend - toultsunel, artsagel (թուլցնել, արձակել)
unbiased, unbiassed - anachar, annakhabashar (անաչառ, աննախապաշարՕ
unbind - kagel, panal, artsagel, kirki goghku hanel (քակել, բանալ, արձակել, գիրքի կողքը Հանել)
unblemished - anpidz, anpasir (անբիծ, անբասիր)
unblessed, unblest - chornuvadz, anpakhd (չօրՀնուած, անբախտ)
unbodied - anmarmin (անմարմին)
unborn - chudzunadz (չծնած)
unbosom - kaghduniku panal, sirdu panal (գաղտնիքը բանալ, սիրտը բանալ)
unbounded - ansahman (անսաՀման)
unbrace - toultsunel (թուլցնել)
unbreathed - anshounch (անշունչ)
unbridle - artsagel, santsu tsukel (արձակել, սանձը ձգել)
unbuild - kantel (քանդել)
unburden - pernatapel, barbel (բեռնաթափել, պարպել)
unburied - antagh (անթաղ)
uncalled - angoch, chouzvadz (անկոչ, չուզուած)
uncanny - dardam, ansovor, khorhurtavor (տարտամ, անսովոր, խորՀրդաւոր)
uncertain - anorosh, anusdouyk,

dardam (անորոշ, անստոյգ, տարտամ)
unchain - artsagel, shughtayazerdzel (արձակել, շղթայազերծել)
unchangeable - anpopokheli (անփոփոխելի)
uncharge - pernatapel (բեռնաթափել)
uncharitable - anoghorm (անողորմ)
unchaste - anbargeshd, tsop (անպարկեշտ, ցոփ)
uncial - yergatakir, kulkhakir (երկաթագիր, գլխագիր)
uncivil - ankaghakavar, goshd (անքաղաքավար, կոշտ)
uncivilized - ankaghakagirt, vayreni, parparos (անքաղաքակիրթ, վայրենի, բարբարոս)
unclad - merg, anbajouyj (մերկ, անպաճոյճ)
unclaimed - ander, chubahanchuvadz (անտէր, չպահանջուած)
uncle - horeghpayr (հօրեղբայր)
unclean - anmakour, aghdod, bighdz (անմաքուր, աղտոտ, պիղծ)
unclose - panal (բանալ)
uncoated - anpayl, andzadzgouyt (անփայլ, անծածկոյթ)
uncomfortable - anhankisd, anhankusdaved, anhajo (անհանգիստ, անհանգստաւէտ, անհաճոյ)
uncommon - ansovor, ardasovor, hazvakiud (անսովոր, արտասովոր, հազուագիւտ)
uncompleted - angadar, anavard (անկատար, անաւարտ)
uncompromising - anzichogh, antek (անզիջող, անթեք)
unconceivable - animanali, anhasgunali (անիմանալի, անհասկնալի)
unconcern - andarperoutiun, anhokoutiun (անտարբերութիւն, անհոգութիւն)
unconditional - anverabah, arants baymani, anbayman (անվերապահ, առանց պայմանի, անպայման)
uncongeal - halil (հալիլ)
unconscious - ankidagits, andeghiag (անգիտակից, անտեղեակ)
uncontrollable - anhagagushreli, angaravareli (անհակակշռելի, անկառավարելի)
uncounted - anhamar, chuhamruvadz (անհամար, չհաշուած)
uncourteous - ankaghalavar (անքաղաքավար)
uncover - koghazerdzel, panal (քողազերծել, բանալ)
uncreate - chunchel (ջնջել)
uncrown - takazurgel (թագազրկել)
unction - odzoum, odzanelik, shunorhk (օծում, օծանելիք, շնորհք)
undated - antuvagir (անթուակիր)
undaunted - anvakh, kach, anveher (անվախ, քաջ, անվեհեր)
undecided - anvujragan, varanod (անվճռական, վարանոտ)
undeclared - chuhaydararvadz (չյայտարարուած)
undefended - anbashdban (անպաշտպան)
undeniable - anzhukhdeli, anouranali, havasdi, vorosh (անժխտելի, անուրանալի, հաւաստի, որոշ)
under - dagu, varu, nerkev, var, bagas, yentaga (տակը, վարը, ներքեւ, վար, պակաս, ենթակայ)
underact - terashkhad (թերաշխատ)
underage - anchapahas (անչափահաս)
underclothing - nerknazkesd (ներքնազգեստ)
underestimate - terakunahadel (թերագնահատել)
underestimation - terakunahadoutiun (թերագնահատութիւն)
undergo - yentarguvil, gurel, danil (ենթարկուիլ, կրել, տանիլ)
undergraduate - untatsavardtsou, ousanogh koleji (ընթացաւարտցու, ուսանող գոլէճի)
underground - unthadagia, usdorerguria, takoun (ընդյատակեայ, ստորերկրեայ, թագուն)
underlay - dagu tunel, henaran tunel (տակը դնել, յենարան դնել)
underline - untkudzel, usdorakudzel, sheshdel (ընդգծել, ստորագծել, շեշտել)
undermine - aganaharel, dagen po-

rel (ականահարել, տակէն փորել)
underprinting - *dubakroutiunu mamouli dag* (տպագրութիւնը մամուլի տակ)
underquote - *tsadz kin voroshel* (ցած գին որոշել)
underrate - *terakunahadel* (թերագնահատել)
underrun - *dagen antsunel, dubakanagu bagsetsunel* (տակէն անցնել, տպաքանակը պակսեցնել)
underscore - *usdorakudzel, usdorakidz* (ստորագծել, ստորագիծ)
undersign - *usdorakurel* (ստորագրել)
understand - *hasgunal, umpurnel* (հասկնալ, ըմբռնել)
understanding - *hasgatsoghoutiun* (հասկացողութիւն)
undertake - *tsernargel, tserk arnel, usdantsunel* (ձեռնարկել, ձեռք առնել, ստանձնել)
undertow - *yentahosank* (ենթահոսանք)
undervalue - *terakunahadel* (թերագնահատել)
undervest - *nerknashabig* (ներքնաշապիկ)
underwear - *nerknazkesd* (ներքնազգեստ)
underwood - *matsaroud* (մացառուտ)
underworld - *tuzhokhk, yentashkharh* (դժոխք, ենթաշխարհ)
underwrite - *yentakurel, usdorakurel, abahovakurel* (ենթագրել, ստորագրել, ապահովագրել)
underwriter - *abahovakurogh* (ապահովագրող)
underwriting - *abahovakuroutiun* (ապահովագրութիւն)
undesirable - *anpaghtsali* (անբաղձալի)
undetermined - *anvujragan, varanod* (անվճռական, վարանոտ)
undeveloped - *chuzarkatsadz, chumushagvadz* (չզարգացած, չմշակուած)
undirected - *anghegavar, anhurahank* (անղեկավար, անհրահանգ)
undo - *avrel, kagel, chunchel, gordzanel, khuzel* (աւրել, քակել, ջնջել, կործանել, խզել)
undoubted - *angasgadz, andaragouys* (անկասկած, անտարակոյս)
undress - *hanvetsunel, mergatsunel, hanel, dan hakousd* (հանուեցնել, մերկացնել, հանել, տան հագուստ)
undressed - *merg, arants hakousdi* (մերկ, առանց հագուստի)
undue - *aboren, anvayel, chapazantsuvadz, borod* (ապօրէն, անվայել, չափազանցուած, պոռոտ)
undulate - *dzadzanil, dzupal, dzupil, jojel* (ծածանիլ, ծփալ, ծփիլ, ճօճել)
undulation - *dzadzanoum, dzupoum, dzupank, yelevech* (ծածանում, ծփում, ծփանք, ելեւէջ)
unduly - *chapazants, anganon, anhargi* (չափազանց, անկանոն, անհարկի)
undying - *anmer, anvakhjan* (անմեռ, անվախճան)
unearth - *hoghe hanel, ardahoghel, yerevan hanel* (հողէ հանել, արտահողել, երեւան հանել)
uneasy - *anhankisd, mudahokvadz* (անհանգիստ, մտահոգուած)
unedited - *andib* (անտիպ)
unemployed - *ankordz, ankordzadzagan* (անգործ, անգործածական)
unemployment - *ankordzoutiun* (անգործութիւն)
unending - *anverchanali, antatreli* (անվերջանալի, անդադրելի)
unequal - *anhavasar, anganon* (անհաւասար, անկանոն)
unerring - *ansukhal* (անսխալ)
unessential - *angarevor, voch anhurazheshd* (անկարեւոր, ոչ անհրաժեշտ)
uneven - *anhart, anhavasar, anzouyk, khordoupord* (անհարթ, անհաւասար, անզոյգ, խորդուբորդ)
unexpected - *anagungal, hangardzagi, anhousali* (անակնկալ, յանկարծակի, անյուսալի)
unfailing - *anvureb, jisht, usdouyk* (անվրէպ, ճիշդ, ստոյգ)

unfair - anirav, anartar, anjisht (անիրաւ, անարդար, անճիշդ)
unfaith - anhavad (անհաւատ)
unfaithful - anhavadarim, anbargeshd, anvusdaheli (անհաւատարիմ, անպարկեշտ, անվստահելի)
unfasten - kagel, toultsunel, panal (քակել, թուլցնել, բանալ)
unfathomable - anchapeli, anhadag (անչափելի, անյատակ)
unfavorable - annubasd, tsakhogh (աննպաստ, ձախող)
unfeeling - anuzka, gardzurasird, tazhan (անզգայ, կարծրասիրտ, դաժան)
unfeigned - iragan, angeghdz, harazad (իրական, անկեղծ, հարազատ)
unfetter - shughtayazerdzel (շղթայազերծել)
unfilial - voch vortiagan (ոչ որդիական)
unfinished - angadar, gisavard, teri (անկատար, կիսաւարտ, թերի)
unfit - anharmar, anjarag (անյարմար, անճարակ)
unfix - toultsunel, kagel, avrel (թուլցնել, քակել, աւրել)
unfold - dzalku panal, barzel, patsadurel (ծալքը բանալ, պարզել, բացատրել)
unforgetable - anmoranali (անմոռանալի)
unformed - antsev, angerbaran (անձեւ, անկերպարան)
unfortunate - tuzhpakhd, anpakhd, tushvar (դժբախտ, անբախտ, թշուառ)
unfounded - anhimun, chuhimnavorvadz (անհիմն, չհիմնաւորուած)
unfrequent - sagavateb, kich badahogh (սակաւադէպ, քիչ պատահող)
unfriendly - voch paregamagan, anpariatsagam (ոչ բարեկամական, անբարեացակամ)
unfrock - pilonazurgel (փիլոնազրկել)
unfruitful - anbudough, amoul, anperri (անպտուղ, ամուլ, անբերրի)
unfurl - dzalku panal, daradzel, barzel, kagel (ծալքը բանալ, տարածել, պարզել, քակել)
unfurnish - chugahavorel, anshukatsunel, mergatsunel (չկահաւորել, անշքացնել, մերկացնել)
ungenerous - gudzdzi, akah (կծծի, ագահ)
unglazed - anoghorg, anpayl (անողորկ, անփայլ)
ungodly - anasduvadz, anoren (անաստուած, անօրէն)
ungovernable - angaravareli, anzousb, ansants (անկառավարելի, անզուսպ, անսանձ)
ungown - pilonazurgel (փիլոնազրկել)
ungraceful - anshunorh, dukegh, dutsev (անշնորհ, տգեղ, տձեւ)
ungrateful - aberakhd (ապերախտ)
unguent - usbeghani (սպեղանի)
unguis - yeghounk, jiran, makil (եղունգ, ճիրան, մագիլ)
ungula - sumpag, yeghounk, jang (սմբակ, եղունգ, ճանկ)
unhallow - bughdzel, surpabughdzel (պղծել, սրբապղծել)
unhappy - tuzhpakhd, aberchanig (դժբախտ, ապերջանիկ)
unhat - kulkhargu hanel (գլխարկը հանել)
unhealthy - vadaroghch, hivantod, aboroghch (վատառողջ, հիւանդոտ, ապառողջ)
unholy - ansourp, bighdz (անսուրբ, պիղծ)
unhurt - anvunas (անվնաս)
unicolor - miakouyn (միագոյն)
unification - miatsouloum (միաձուլում)
uniform - hamazkesd, miatsev, miorinag (համազգեստ, միաձեւ, միօրինակ)
uniformity - miatsevoutiun, hamorinagoutiun (միաձեւութիւն, համօրինակութիւն)
unify - miavorel, miatsunel (միաւորել, միացնել)
unilateral - miagoghmia(միակողմեայ)
uninterested - anshahakhunrir, anshahakurkir (անշահախնդիր, ան-

շահագրգիռ)
union - mioutiun, tashnagtsoutiun, amousnoutiun (միութիւն, դաշնակցութիւն, ամուսնութիւն)
unique - miag, yezagan, anzoukagan, chuknagh (միակ, եզական, անզուգական, չքնաղ)
unisex - miaser, harmar te aghchuga yev te dughou (միասեռ, յարմար թէ՛ աղջկայ եւ թէ տղու)
unisexual - miaser, meg seri badganogh (միասեռ, մէկ սեռի պատկանող)
unisexuality - miaseroutiun (միասեռութիւն)
unit - mioutiun, miavor, varganish, arantsnamas (միութիւն, միաւոր, վարկանիշ, առանձնամաս)
unite - miatsunel, miavorel, gutsel, mianal (միացնել, միաւորել, կցել, միանալ)
unity - mioutiun, nouynoutiun, gabagtsoutiun (միութիւն, նոյնութիւն, կապակցութիւն)
universal - diyezeragan, unthanragan, hamashkharhayin (տիեզերական, ընդհանրական, համաշխարհային)
universe - diyezerk, ashkharh, yergurakount (տիեզերք, աշխարհ, երկրագունդ)
university - hamalusaran (համալսարան)
unjoint - khakhdel (խախտել)
unjust - anartar, anirav (անարդար, անիրաւ)
unkind - anazniv, dumarti, goshd (անազնիւ, տմարդի, կոշտ)
unknown - andzanot (անծանօթ)
unlace - kagel, panal, toultsunel (քակել, բանալ, թուլցնել)
unlade - pernatapel (բեռնաթափել)
unlash - kagel, toultsunel (քակել, թուլցնել)
unlawful - aboren, hagaorinagan (ապօրէն, հակաօրինական)
unleaded gas - angabar benzin (անկապար պենզին)
unlearned - anous, duked (անուս, տգէտ)
unleash - gabe artsagel (կապէ արձակել)
unless - yete voch, patsi, minchev vor (եթէ ոչ, բացի, մինչեւ որ)
unlike - annuman, darper (աննման, տարբեր)
unlimited - ansahman, patsartsag (անսահման, բացարձակ)
unload - pernatapel, barbel, tetevtsunel (բեռնաթափել, պարպել, թեթեւցնել)
unlock - panal, gughbanku tartsunel (բանալ, կղպանքը դարձնել)
unloose - panal, artsagel (բանալ, արձակել)
unlovely - anhajo (անհաճոյ)
unlucky - tuzhpankhd, tsakhort, anhachogh, charapasdig (դժբախտ, ձախորդ, անյաջող, չարաբաստիկ)
unmake - avrel (աւրել)
unman - anmartatsunel (անմարդացնել)
unmarried - amouri, amousnaloudzvadz (ամուրի, ամուսնալուծուած)
unmarry - amousnaloudzvil (ամուսնալուծուիլ)
unmask - timagazerdzel (դիմակազերծել)
unmeaning - animasd (անիմաստ)
unmew - azadel, artsagel (ազատել, արձակել)
unmoral - anparoyagan, voch paroyagan (անբարոյական, ոչ բարոյական)
unnatural - anpunagan, anirabashd (անբնական, անիրապաշտ)
unnecessary - angarevor, anbed, anhargi (անկարեւոր, անպէտ, անհարկի)
unnerve - chuladel, dugaratsunel (ջլատել, տկարացնել)
unnumbered - antiv, anhamar (անթիւ, անհամար)
unoccupied - voch kuravial, anuzpagh (ոչ գրաւեալ, անզբաղ)
unopened - chupatsvadz (չբացուած)
unorganized - angazmagerb, angazm (անկազմակերպ, անկազմ)
unpack - kagel, panal-dzuraru (քակել, բանալ՝ ծրարը)

unpaid - *anvujar, tsuri* (անվճար, ձրի)
unpeople - *amayatsunel, anmartapunag tartsunel* (ամայցնել, անմարդաբնակ դարձնել)
unpitied - *ankout, ankhighj* (անգութ, անխիղճ)
unpleasant - *anhajo, anakhorzh* (անհաճոյ, անախորժ)
unpopular - *anzhoghovurtagan* (անժողովրդական)
unprecedented - *annakhuntats* (աննախընթաց)
unprejudiced - *annakhabashar, angoghmunagal* (աննախապաշար, անկողմնակալ)
unpreparation - *anbadrasdoutiun* (անպատրաստութիւն)
unpriced - *ankin* (անգին)
unprizable - *ankin, ankunahadeli* (անգին, անգնահատելի)
unprofitable - *anshah, anshahaper* (անշահ, անշահաբեր)
unqualified - *anadag, voch voragial* (անատակ, ոչ որակեալ)
unquestionable - *anvijeli, angasgadz* (անվիճելի, անկասկած)
unquiet - *anhankisd, anhantard* (անհանգիստ, անհանդարտ)
unready - *anbadrasd, tantagh* (անպատրաստ, դանդաղ)
unreal - *aniragan, tsunoragan* (անիրական, ցնորական)
unreasonable - *anpunagan, anhetet, anduramapanagan* (անբնական, անհեթեթ, անտրամաբանական)
unregenerate - *anveranorok* (անվերանորոգ)
unreliable - *anvusdaheli, anhavadarim* (անվստահելի, անհաւատարիմ)
unreserve - *anverabahoutiun, hamartsagoutiun* (անվերապահութիւն, համարձակութիւն)
unrighteous - *anirav, anartar* (անիրաւ, անարդար)
unripe - *duhas, khag* (տհաս, խակ)
unrivaled - *anmurtsagits, anzoukagan* (անմրցակից, անզուգական)
unrobe - *mergatsunel, badoujanu var arnel* (մերկացնել, պատմուճանը վար առնել)
unroll - *panal, barzel, yerevan hanel* (բանալ, պարզել, երեւան հանել)
unroof - *anertik, taniku var arnel* (աներդիք, տանիքը վար առնել)
unroot - *armaden hanel* (արմատէն հանել)
unsafe - *anabahov, vudankavor* (անապահով, վտանգաւոր)
unsafety - *anabahovoutiun* (անապահովութիւն)
unsanitary - *hagaroghch, hagaroghchagan* (հակառողջ, հակառողջական)
unsatisfactory - *ankohatsoutsich* (անգոհացուցիչ)
unsatisfied - *chukohatsogh, tuzhkoh* (չգոհացող, դժգոհ)
unsaturated - *anhakourt, angoushd* (անյագուրդ, անկուշտ)
unscrupulous - *ankhighj* (անխիղճ)
unseasonable - *anzhamanag* (անժամանակ)
unseen - *andesaneli, annushmareli* (անտեսանելի, աննշմարելի)
unsettle - *khakhdel, sharzhel* (խախտել, շարժել)
unsex - *seradel* (սեռատել)
unsight - *chudesadz* (չտեսած)
unsociable - *anungeragan, anhampouyr* (անընկերական, անհամբոյր)
unsound - *vadaroghch, anhasdad* (վատառողջ, անհաստատ)
unstable - *angayoun* (անկայուն)
unsuccessful - *anhachogh, tsakogh, tuzhpakhd* (անյաջող, ձախող, դժբախտ)
unsuitable - *anharmar* (անյարմար)
unsupportable - *andaneli, anhantourzheli* (անտանելի, անհանդուրժելի)
unswear - *yertoumu ouranal* (երդումը ուրանալ)
untangle - *tunjougu kagel* (թնճուկը քակել)
unthinking - *ankhorhourt, anmid* (անխորհուրդ, անմիտ)
unthrone - *kahazurgel* (գահազրկել)
untie - *kagel, artsagel, panal, toul-*

tsunel (քակել, արձակել, բանալ, թուլցնել)
until - *minchev, minchev vor* (մինչեւ, մինչեւ որ)
untimely - *gankhahas, anzhamanag, darazham* (կանխահաս, անժամանակ, տարաժամ)
untitled - *andidghos, voch vugayial* (անտիտղոս, ոչ վկայեալ)
unto - *tebi, minchev, i, ar* (դէպի, մինչեւ, ի, առ)
untouchable - *anhubeli* (անհպելի)
untrim - *khankarel, avrel* (խանգարել, աւրել)
untruss - *kagel, toultsunel* (քակել, թուլցնել)
untrustful - *anvusdaheli* (անվստահելի)
untruth - *soud, anjushmardoutiun* (սուտ, անճշմարտութիւն)
untruthful - *anjushmarid, sudakhos* (անճշմարիտ, ստախօս)
unused - *anvarzh, chukordzadzvadz* (անվարժ, չգործածուած)
unusual - *ansovor, hazvateb* (անսովոր, հազուադէպ)
unvarnished - *anzart, barz* (անզարդ, պարզ)
unveil - *koghazerdzel* (քօղազերծել)
unvoiced - *antsayn* (անձայն)
unwarranted - *cherashkhavorvadz, anusdouyk* (չերաշխաւորուած, անստոյգ)
unwary - *anuzkouysh, anhok, ankhohem* (անզգոյշ, անհոգ, անխոհեմ)
unweave - *panal, kagel* (բանալ, քակել)
unwilling - *anhozhar* (անյօժար)
unwind - *kagel, barzel, kagvil* (քակել, պարզել, քակուիլ)
unwisdom - *animasdoutiun, ankhelatsoutiun* (անիմաստութիւն, անխելացութիւն)
unwise - *ankhelk, anmid* (անխելք, անմիտ)
unwish - *hagaragil, chutsangal* (հակառակիլ, չցանկալ)
unwitting - *ankidag* (անգիտակ)
unworthy - *anarzhan, anarzhek, anvayel* (անարժան, անարժէք, անվայել)
unwritten - *ankir, chukurvadz* (անգիր, չգրուած)
unyoke - *artsagel, hanel, zadel* (արձակել, հանել, զատել)
up - *ver, veru, partsuru, tebi ver* (վեր, վերը, բարձրը, դէպի վեր)
upbear - *pokhaturel, danil, ver purnel* (փոխադրել, տանիլ, վեր բռնել)
upbraid - *meghaturel, aybanel, bakharagel, barsavel* (մեղադրել, այպանել, պախարակել, պարսաւել)
upcoming - *nergayatsvelik, kalik, yerevelik* (ներկայացուելիք, գալիք, երեւելիք)
update - *azhmeatsunel, tarmatsunel, verakunnel* (այժմէացնել, թարմացնել, վերաքննել)
uphill - *ver katsogh, tuzhvarin* (վեր գացող, դժուարին)
uphold - *ver hanel, ver vertsunel, bashdubanel* (վեր հանել, վեր վերցնել, պաշտպանել)
upholster - *gahavorel, zartarel, dzadzgel* (կահաւորել, զարդարել, ծածկել)
upholsterer - *gahahartar, ototsakordz* (կահայարդար, օթոցագործ)
upholstery - *gahavorank, gahahartaroum* (կահաւորանք, կահայարդարում)
upkeep - *bahbanoum* (պահպանում)
upland - *lernatashd, sarahart* (լեռնադաշտ, սարահարթ)
uplift - *partsuratsunel, ver hanel* (բարձրացնել, վեր հանել)
upmost - *amenaver* (ամենավեր)
upon - *vura* (վրայ)
upper - *aveli partsur, verin, partsurakouyn* (աւելի բարձր, վերին, բարձրագոյն)
uppercase - *vernagugh, hamagarkichi kulkhakir* (վերնարկղ, համակարգիչի գլխագիր)
uppish - *ampardavan, koroz, medzamol, sek* (ամբարտաւան, գոռոզ, մեծամոլ, սէգ)
upraise - *vertsunel, partsuratsunel* (վերցնել, բարձրացնել)

upright - oughigh, oughghatsik, gankoun, bargeshd (ուղիղ, ուղղաձիգ, կանգուն, պարկեշտ)
uprise - yellel, gankunil, partsuranal (ելլել, կանգնիլ, բարձրանալ)
uprising - partsuratsoum, verelk (բարձրացում, վերելք)
uproar - aghmoug, houzoum, ampokh (աղմուկ, յուզում, ամբոխ)
upscale - anchap, punaganen ver, partsur (անչափ, բնականէն վեր, բարձր)
upset - shurchel, dabalel, shurchil, shurchoum, irarantsoum (շրջել, տապալել, շրջիլ, շրջում, իրարանցում)
upshot - avard, artiunk, yelk, verch (աւարտ, արդիւնք, ելք, վերջ)
upside-down - kulkhivayr-shurchadz (գլխիվայր՝ շրջած)
upstairs - vernaharg, ver, veri (վերնայարկ, վեր, վերի)
upswell - ouril, partsuranal (ուռիլ, բարձրանալ)
upward - ver, tebi ver, aveli yevus վեր, դէպի վեր, աւելի եւս)
up-to-date - ayzhmeagan, nor (այժմէական, նոր)
uraemia, uremia - ariunamizoutiun (արիւնամիզութիւն)
uranium - shoghartsag medagh mu, ouraniom (շողարձակ մետաղ մը, ուրանիոմ)
urban - kaghakayin, mushagial (քաղաքային, մշակեալ)
urbane - kaghakagirt, paregirt, gentsaghaked (քաղաքակիրթ, բարեկիրթ, կենցաղագէտ)
urbanist - kaghakashinarar (քաղաքաշինարար)
urbanity - paregurtoutiun, kaghakavaroutiun (բարեկրթութիւն, քաղաքավարութիւն)
urbanization - kaghakaynatsoum (քաղաքայնացում)
urbanize - kaghakaynatsunel (քաղաքայնացնել)
uresis - hajakhamizoutiun (յաճախամիզութիւն)
ureter - mizanot, mizantsk (միզանօթ, միզանցք)
urethra - mizoug, churtap, shurpogh (միզուկ, ջրթափ, շուփող)
urge - usdibel, bardaturel, neghel (ստիպել, պարտադրել, նեղել)
urgency - usdiboum, harg, bedk (ստիպում, Հարկ, պէտք)
urgent - usdiboghagan, garevor (ստիպողական, կարեւոր)
urinal - mizaman, mizaran (միզաման, միզարան)
urinalysis - mizakunnoutiun (միզաքննութիւն)
urinate - mizel (միզել)
urination - mizoum (միզում)
urine - mez, sher (մէզ, շեռ)
urn - sapor (սափոր)
urologist - mizaked, mizapan (միզագէտ, միզաբան)
urology - mizapanoutiun (միզաբանութիւն)
us - mez, mezi, uzmez (մեզ, մեզի, զմեզ)
usage - kordzadzoutiun, sovorouyt (գործածութիւն, սովորոյթ)
usance - hasouyt, baymanazham (Հասոյթ, պայմանաժամ)
use (n) - kordzadzoutiun, giraroutiun, okoud, shah (գործածութիւն, կիրառութիւն, օգուտ, շաՀ)
use (v) - kordzadzel, girargel, panetsunel (գործածել, կիրարկել, բանեցնել)
useful - okdagar, bidani (օգտակար, պիտանի)
useless - anokoud, anshah, anbed (անօգուտ, անշաՀ, անպէտ)
user - kordzadzogh (գործածող)
usher - huramtsunogh, medzarogh, hiuramedzar (Հրամցնող, մեծարող, Հիւրամեծար)
usual - sovoragan, hasarag, kordzadzagan (սովորական, Հասարակ, գործածական)
usurer - vashkharou (վաշխառու)
usurp - hapushdagel, shortel, purnaparel (յափշտակել, շորթել, բռնաբարել)
usury - vashkharoutiun (վաշխառութիւն)

utensil - kordzik, anot, aman (գործիք, անօթ, աման)
uterine - arkantin veraperogh, arkantayin gab (արգանդին վերաբերող, արգանդային կապ)
uterus - arkant (արգանդ)
utilitarian - okdabashd (օգտապաշտ)
utility - okdagaroutiun, okoud (օգտակարութիւն, օգուտ)
utilizable - okdakordzeli (օգտագործելի)
utilize - okdakordzel (օգտագործել)
utmost - amenaverchin, dzayrakouyn (ամենավերջին, ծայրագոյն)
utopia - yerazagan, yerazaganoutiun (երազական, երազականութիւն)
utter - gadarial, polor, dzayrahegh, khosil, ardasanell (կատարեալ, բոլոր, ծայրայեղ, խօսիլ, արտասանել)
uvula - lezvag (լեզուակ)
uxorious - gunaser, gunahubadag (կնասէր, կնահպատակ)

vacancy - baraboutiun, pats degh, michots, artsagourt (պարապութիւն, բաց տեղ, միջոց, արձակուրդ)
vacant - barab, tadarg, chukuravvadz, azad (պարապ, դատարկ, չգրաւուած, ազատ)
vacate - barbel, tadargel, chunchel (պարպել, դատարկել, ջնջել)
vacation - artsagourt, tatar, tadargoum (արձակուրդ, դադար, դատարկում)
vaccinate - badvasdel (պատուաստել)
vaccination - badvasdoum (պատուաստում)
vaccinator, vaccinist - badvasdogh, badvasdich (պատուաստող, պատուաստիչ)
vaccine - badvasd (պատուաստ)
vacillate - tekeril, yereril, yergmudil, toghtughal (դեգերիլ, երերիլ, երկմտիլ, դողդղալ)
vacillation - yereroum, tekeroum, varank, yergmudoutiun (երերում, դեգերում, վարանք, երկմտութիւն)
vacuity - tadargoutiun, barab (դատարկութիւն, պարապ)
vacuous - barab, tadarg, sunamech (պարապ, դատարկ, սնամէջ)
vacuum - tadargoutiun, barab (դատարկութիւն, պարապ)
vacuum cleaner - poshegoul, poshedzudzich, otamakrich (փոշեկուլ, փոշեծծիչ, օդամաքրիչ)
vade mecum - artserun kirk, kurbani unger (առձեռն գիրք, գրպանի ընկեր)
vagabond - taparagan, taparashurchig, tadargabord (թափառական, թափառաշրջիկ, թատարկապորտ)
vagary - kumahajouyk, aylantagoutiun (քմահաճոյք, այլանդակութիւն)
vagina - ikapogh, khorobji, heshdots, antsk arkanti (իգափող, խորոպճի, հեշտոց, անցք արգանդի)
vagrancy - taparaganoutiun (թափառականութիւն)
vagrant - tadargabord, taparagan (դատարկապորտ, թափառական)
vague - anorosh, dardam, anhasdad (անորոշ, տարտամ, անհաստատ)
vail - ichetsunel, khonarhil, okduvil, tseratsir, barkev (իջեցնել, խոնարհիլ, օգտուիլ, ձեռաձիր, պարգեւ)
vain - sin, ounayn, anbudough, barab, pouj (սին, ունայն, անպտուղ, պարապ, փուճ)
vainglorious - sunabardz, sunapar, tsoutsamol, paraser (սնապարծ, սնափառ, ցուցամոլ, փառասէր)

vainly - i zour, barab degh (ի զուր, պարապ տեղ)
valance - angoghini varakouyr, dzob (անկողինի վարագոյր, ծոպ)
vale - hovid, tsor, voghchert (հովիտ, ձոր, ողջերթ)
valediction - voghchert maghtelu, hurazheshdi voghchiun (ողջերթ մաղթելը, հրաժեշտի ողջոյն)
valentine - Sourp Sarkisi oru undurvadz sirouhi, siradoms (Ս. Սարգիսի օրը ընտրուած սիրուհի, սիրատոմս)
valerian - gadvakhod (կատուախոտ)
valet - dzara, usbasavor (ծառայ, սպասաւոր)
valiancy - arioutiun, kachoutiun (արիութիւն, քաջութիւն)
valiant - kach, ari, gudrij, anveher (քաջ, արի, կտրիճ, անվեհեր)
valid - vaveragan, i zorou, arughch (վաւերական, ի զօրու, առողջ)
validate - vaveratsunel, hasdadel (վաւերացնել, հաստատել)
validation - vaveratsoum (վաւերացում)
validity - vaveraganoutiun (վաւերականութիւն)
valise - bayousag (պայուսակ)
vallation - badnesh (պատնէշ)
valley - tsor, hovid, churortan (ձոր, հովիտ, ջրորդան)
valor, valour - kachoutiun, arioutiun (քաջութիւն, արիութիւն)
valorization - kunahadoum (գնահատում)
valorize - kunahadel (գնահատել)
valorous - kach, ari, gudrij (քաջ, արի, կտրիճ)
valuable - arzhekavor (արժէքաւոր)
valuation - kunahadoutiun (գնահատութիւն)
valuator - kunahadogh (գնահատող)
value - arzhek, kin, arzhevorel, kunahadel (արժէք, գին, արժեւորել, գնահատել)
valueless - anarzhek (անարժէք)
valuer - kunahadogh, arzhevorogh (գնահատող, արժեւորող)
valve - pultag, turnag, pagan, gapouyr (բլթակ, դռնակ, փական, կափոյր)
vamose - chouel, shoudov toghoul (չուել, շուտով թողուլ)
vamp (I) - gargudnel, norokel, gargudan, moujagi yeres (կարկտնել, նորոգել, կարկտան, մուճակի երես)
vamp (II) - kaytagghetsunogh gin, kaytagghetsunel, hurabourel (գայթակղեցնող կին, գայթակղեցնել, հրապուրել)
vampire - ariunadzoudz, geghekich, haralez (արիւնածուծ, կեղեքիչ, յարալէզ)
vampirism - ariunarpoutiun (արիւնարբութիւն)
van - harachamas, razmajagad, pernagark (յառաջամաս, ռազմաճակատ, բեռնակառք)
vandal - parparos, kantich, gordzanogh, vayrenaparo (բարբարոս, քանդիչ, կործանող, վայրենաբարոյ)
vane - hoghmatsouyts, tev, pedradel (հողմացոյց, թեւ, փետրատել)
vanguard - arachabah (առաջապահ)
vanilla - hamemoug (համեմուկ)
vanish - anhedanal, chukanal, gorsuvil (անհետանալ, չքանալ, կորսուիլ)
vanity - ounaynoutiun, sunaparoutiun, baraboutiun (ունայնութիւն, սնափառութիւն, պարապութիւն)
vanquish - haghtel, nuvajel (յաղթել, նուաճել)
vantage - shah, okoud, araveloutiun (շահ, օգուտ, առաւելութիւն)
vapid - anli, anham, dugar, touyl, avruvadz (անլի, անհամ, տկար, թոյլ, աւրուած)
vapor - shoki, dzoukh, kolorshi, kolorshianal (շոգի, ծուխ, գոլորշի, գոլորշիանալ)
vaporescence - kolorshiatsoum (գոլորշիացում)
vaporing - sunabardz (սնապարծ)
vaporization - kolorshiatsoum (գոլորշիացում)
vaporize - shokiatsunel, shokianal, tsuntil (շոգիացնել, շոգիանալ,

ցնդիլ)

vapory - shokiod, shokelits (շոգիոտ, շոգելից)

variability - popokhaganoutiun (փոփոխականութիւն)

variable - popokhagan, anhasdad, tiurapopokh (փոփոխական, անհաստատ, դիւրափոփոխ)

variance - darperoutiun, popokhoum, baragdoum, vej (տարբերութիւն, փոփոխում, պառակտում, վէճ)

variant - popokhag, darperag (փոփոխակ, տարբերակ)

variate - popokhel, pokhel, darperil (փոփոխել, փոխել, տարբերիլ)

variation - popokhoutiun, popokhoum, sheghoum, besbisoutiun (փոփոխութիւն, փոփոխում, շեղում, պէսպիսութիւն)

varicose - layneragouyt, untlaynuvadz-yerag (լայներակոյթ, ընդլայնուած՝ երակ)

varied - zanazan, aylazan, nakhshoun, yerpnerank (զանազան, այլազան, նախշուն, երփներանգ)

variegate - popokhel, besbisel, kounazartel (փոփոխել, պէսպիսել, գունազարդել)

variety - aylazanoutiun, besbisoutiun, zanazanoutiun (այլազանութիւն, պէսպիսութիւն, զանազանութիւն)

variform - pazmatsev (բազմաձեւ)

variola - dzaghig, dzaghgakhd (ծաղիկ, ծաղկախտ)

variolation - badvasdoum (պատուաստում)

variole - posig, kuntig (փոսիկ, գնդիկ)

various - aylazan, pazmazan, yerpnerank (այլազան, բազմազան, երփներանգ)

varlet - usbasavor, tushvaragan, suriga (սպասաւոր, Թշուառական, սրիկայ)

varnish - chunaragel, payletsunel, chunarag, payl, shubar (ջնարակել, փայլեցնել, ջնարակ, փայլ, շպար)

vary - popokhel, zanazanel, darperil, popokhil (փոփոխել, զանազանել, տարբերիլ, փոփոխիլ)

vascular - yeragayin, anotayin, yeragavor (երակային, անօԹային, երակաւոր)

vascular surgery - yeragayin virahadoutiun (երակային վիրահատութիւն)

vase - dzaghgaman, anot, taghar (ծաղկաման, անօԹ, Թաղար)

vassal - hubadag, dzara, jord (հպատակ, ծառայ, ճորտ)

vast - untartsag, layn, daradzoun, vitkhari (ընդարձակ, լայն, տարածուն, վիԹխարի)

vat - dagar, khoshor garas, dashd (տակառ, խոշոր կարաս, տաշտ)

vatic - markareagan (մարգարէական)

Vatican - vadigan (Վատիկան)

vaticinate - markareanal, koushagel (մարգարէանալ, գուշակել)

vaticination - markareoutiun (մարգարէութիւն)

vaudeville - yerkakhagh, dzidzaghasharzh taderakhagh (երգախաղ, ծիծաղաշարժ Թատերախաղ)

vault - tsadgel, tsaydel, gamarel, gamar, maran (ցատկել, ցայտել, կամարել, կամար, մառան)

vaulter - tsadgogh, jakhrogh (ցատկող, ճախրող)

vaunt - bardzenal, sunabardzil, sunabardzoutiun (պարծենալ, սնապարծիլ, սնապարծութիւն)

veal - horti mis (հորԹի միս)

veer - tartsunel, tarnal, shurchil (դարձնել, դառնալ, շրջիլ)

vegetable - panchareghen, pouys, pousagan (բանջարեղէն, բոյս, բուսական)

vegetarian - pousager, pancharager (բուսակեր, բանջարակեր)

vegetate - ajil, sunanil, kheghj abril (աճիլ, սնանիլ, խեղճ ապրիլ)

vegetation - pousaganoutiun, ganachoutiun (բուսականութիւն, կանաչութիւն)

vehemence, cy - ouzhkunoutiun, sasdgoutiun (ուժգնութիւն, սաստկութիւն)

vehement - sasdig, ouzhkin, pourun (սաստիկ, ուժգին, բուռն)
vehicle - inknasharzh, gark, pokhatrich (ինքնաշարժ, կառք, փոխադրիչ)
veil - kogh, lachag, shugharsh, koghargel, dzadzgel (քող, լաչակ, շղարշ, քողարկել, ծածկել)
vein - yerag, zargerag, chigh-derevi (երակ, զարկերակ, ջիղ՝ տերեւի)
velation - koghargoutiun, dzadzgoum (քողարկութիւն, ծածկում)
vellicate - burgel (պրկել)
vellication - burgoum (պրկում)
vellum - parag makaghat, momatought (բարակ մագաղաթ, մոմաթուղթ)
velocity - arakoutiun (արագութիւն)
velours - tavish (թաւիշ)
velum - taghant (թաղանդ)
velure - purtod lat, basdar (բրդոտ լաթ, պաստառ)
velvet - tavish, tavshia (թաւիշ, թաւշեայ)
venal - vajareli, dzakhou, vartsgan, yeragayin (վաճառելի, ծախու, վարձկան, երակային)
venality - vartsganoutiun, gasharageroutiun (վարձկանութիւն, կաշառակերութիւն)
venatic, venatical - vorsortagan (որսորդական)
vend - dzakhel, vajarel (ծախել, վաճառել)
vendee - kunort (գնորդ)
vendetta - vurezhkhunturoutiun (վրէժխնդրութիւն)
vendible - vajareli, dzakhvelik (վաճառելի, ծախուելիք)
vendication - bashdubanoutiun, chadakovoutiun (պաշտպանութիւն, ջատագովութիւն)
vendition - vajaroum (վաճառում)
vendor - dzakhogh, vajarogh (ծախող, վաճառող)
vendue - ajourt (աճուրդ)
veneer - zartabadger, yeresabadel (զարդապատկեր, երեսապատել)
venerable - harkeli, badgareli, medzarko (յարգելի, պատկառելի, մեծարգոյ)
venerate - badvel, harkel, medzarel (պատուել, յարգել, մեծարել)
veneration - harkank, medzarank (յարգանք, մեծարանք)
venereal - veneragan, durpakhdayin (վեներական, տռփախտային)
venery - vorsortoutiun, zoukavoroutiun (որսորդութիւն, զուգաւորութիւն)
venetian - venedigian, venedigtsi (վենետիկեան, վենետիկցի)
Venezuela - venezuela (Վենեզուելա)
venge - vurezh arnel (վրէժ առնել)
vengeance - vurezhkhunturoutiun, vurizharoutiun, vokh (վրէժխնդրութիւն, վրիժառութիւն, ոխ)
vengeful - vurezhkhuntir, vurizharou (վրէժխնդիր, վրիժառու)
venial - nereli (ներելի)
venom - touyn, zhahur, tounavorel (թոյն, ժահր, թունաւորել)
venomous - tounavor, tounalits (թունաւոր, թունալից)
vent (n) - dzag, otamoud, jeghk, pakhousd, ardahosoum (ծակ, օդամուտ, ճեղք, փախուստ, արտահոսում)
vent (v) - tours dal, hosetsunel, vaztsunel, haydnel (դուրս տալ, հոսեցնել, վազցնել, յայտնել)
venter - por (փոր)
ventiduct - shunchamoud, otapogh (շնչամուտ, օդափող)
ventilate - hovaharel, otapokhel (հովահարել, օդափոխել)
ventilation - otapokhoum, hovaharoutiun (օդափոխում, հովահարութիւն)
ventilator - hovahar, otapokhich (հովահար, օդափոխիչ)
ventricle - korsh-surdi, khoroch (գործ՝ սրտի, խոռոչ)
venture (n) - hantuknoutiun, khizakh tsernarg (յանդգնութիւն, խիզախ ձեռնարկ)
venture (v) - hantuknil, khizakhel, nedvil, portsel (յանդգնիլ, խիզախել, նետուիլ, փորձել)
venturesome, venturous - argadza-

ser, hantoukun (արկածասէր, յանդուգն)
venue - mertsavayr, tapantsoum (մերձավայր, Թափանցում)
venule - manrerag (մանրերակ)
veracious - jushmardakhos, jushmardaser, jushmarid (ճշմարտախօս, ճշմարտասէր, ճշմարիտ)
veracity - jushmardoutiun, jushmardakhosoutiun (ճշմարտութիւն, ճշմարտախօսութիւն)
veranda - badushkam (պատշգամ)
verb - pay (բայ)
verbal - peranatsi (բերանացի)
verbatim - paratsi (բառացի)
verbiage - shadakhosoutiun, avelortapanoutiun (շատախօսութիւն, աւելորդաբանութիւն)
verbose - shadakos, yergarapan (շատախօս, երկարաբան)
verbosity - avelortapanoutiun (աւելորդաբանութիւն)
verdant - ganach, tarm, talar (կանաչ, Թարմ, դալար)
verdict - vujir, tadavujir (վճիռ, դատավճիռ)
verdure - ganachoutiun, khodeghen, talarik (կանաչութիւն, խոտեղէն, դալարիք)
verdurous - talarakegh (դալարագեղ)
verge - dzayr, kavazan, varots, hagil, modenal (ծայր, գաւազան, վարոց, հակիլ, մօտենալ)
verger - zhamgoch, kavazanagir (ժամկոչ, գաւազանակիր)
veridical - jushmardakhos (ճշմարտախօս)
verifiable - usdoukeli (ստուգելի)
verification - jushtoum, usdoukoum (ճշդում, ստուգում)
verify - jushtel, usdoukel, hasdadel (ճշդել, ստուգել, հաստատել)
verisimilar - jushmardanuman, havanagan (ճշմարտանման, հաւանական)
verisimilitude - jushmardanumanoutiun (ճշմարտանմանութիւն)
veritable - iragan, jushmarid, usdouyk (իրական, ճշմարիտ, ստոյգ)
verity - jushmardoutiun, iroghoutiun (ճշմարտութիւն, իրողութիւն)
vermeil - dziranekouyn, garmurategh (ծիրանեգոյն, կարմրադեղ)
vermicelli - telehays, tutmaj (Թելահայս, դդմաճ)
vermicide - vortasban, jujasban (որդասպան, ճճասպան)
vermilion - garmurategh, garmurakouyn, garmurateghel (կարմրադեղ, կարմրագոյն, կարմրադեղել)
vernacular - mayreni, dohmig-lezou (մայրենի, տոհմիկ՝ լեզու)
versant - zaritap, gogh (զառիԹափ, կող)
versatile - tiurapopokh, anhasdad, jugoun (դիւրափոփոխ, անհաստատ, ճկուն)
verse - vodanavor, panasdeghdzoutiun, daghachapoutioun (ոտանաւոր, բանաստեղծութիւն, տաղաչափութիւն)
versed - dzanot, humoud, kachadeghiag (ծանօԹ, հմուտ, քաջատեղեակ)
versicolor - pazmerank, kouynuzkouyn (բազմերանգ, գոյնզգոյն)
versification - daghachapoutiun (տաղաչափութիւն)
versify - kertel, daghachapel (քերԹել, տաղաչափել)
version - megnoutiun, tarkmanoutiun (մեկնութիւն, Թարգմանութիւն)
verso - hagagoghm, yedevu, yergurort yeresu (հակակողմ, ետեւը, երկրորդ երեսը)
versus - tem, unttem, hagarag (դէմ, ընդդէմ, հակառակ)
vert - talarik, dzaradoung, ganach (դալարիք, ծառատունկ, կանաչ)
vertebra - voghnahar, voghnosgur, voghnasiun (ողնայար, ողնոսկր, ողնասիւն)
vertebral column - voghnahar, voghnasiun (ողնահար, ողնասիւն)
vertebrate - voghnavor, voghnaharavor (ողնաւոր, ողնայարաւոր)
vertex - kakatnaged, kakatu, gadar (գագաԹնակէտ, գագաԹը, կատար)
vertical - oughghahayiats, oughghatsik (ուղղահայեաց, ուղղաձիգ)

vertiginous - kulkhatarts, kulkhou budouyd duvogh (գլխադարձ, գլխու պտոյտ տուող)
vertigo - kulkhabudouyd (գլխապտոյտ)
verve - khant, aviun (խանդ, աւիւն)
very - isgagan, jisht, poun, shad, miyevnouyn, oughigh (իսկական, ճիշդ, բուն, շատ, միեւնոյն, ուղիղ)
vesicate - kharanel (խարանել)
vesication - kharanoum (խարանում)
vesicle - pampushdig, pushdig, ouretsk (փամփշտիկ, բշտիկ, ուռեցք)
vessel - aman, anot, nav, tsuntsough (աման, անօթ, նաւ, ցնցուղ)
vest - pajgon, badmoujan, haktsunel, bujnel (բաճկոն, պատմուճան, հագցնել, պճնել)
vestiary - uzkesdeghen (զգեստեղէն)
vestibule - nakhakavit, nakhasurah, antasdag (նախագաւիթ, նախասրահ, անդաստակ)
vestige - hedk, vodnahedk, nushan (հետք, ոտնահետք, նշան)
vestment - uzkesd, hanterts (զգեստ, հանդերձ)
vestry - hantertsadoun, baharan, taghagan khorhourt (հանդերձատուն, պահարան, թաղական խորհուրդ)
vestryman - taghagan (թաղական)
vesture - hanterts, dzadzgouyt, dzadzgel, haktsunel (հանդերձ, ծածկոյթ, ծածկել, հագցնել)
vet - anasnapouyzh, anasnapouzhel (անասնաբոյժ, անասնաբուժել)
veteran - nakhgin zinvor, portsarou mart, hinavourts (նախկին զինուոր, փորձառու մարդ, հինաւուրց)
veterinarian - anasnapouyzh (անասնաբոյժ)
veterinary - anasnapouzhagan (անասնաբուժական)
veto - arkelk, merzhoum, unttimoutiun, unttinamal (արգելք, մերժում, ընդդիմութիւն, ընդդիմանալ)
vex - neghel, charcharel, neghatsunel, chughaynatsunel (նեղել, չարչարել, նեղացնել, ջղայնացնել)
vexation - neghoutiun, vurtovoum, vishd, daghdoug (նեղութիւն, վրդովում, վիշտ, տաղտուկ)
vexatious - neghich, darabetsunogh (նեղիչ, տառապեցնող)
via - jampov, vurayov, michotsov (ճամբով, վրայով, միջոցով)
viable - abrelik, abrelou garogh (ապրելիք, ապրելու կարող)
viaduct - gamaroughi, antsoughi (կամարուղի, անցուղի)
viagraph - oughekir (ուղեգիր)
viameter - oughechap (ուղեչափ)
viand - oudelik, geragour (ուտելիք, կերակուր)
vibrant - turturoun (թրթռուն)
vibrate - turtural, sharzhel, jojel, turturatsunel (թրթռալ, շարժել, ճօճել, թրթռացնել)
vibratile - turturoun (թրթռուն)
vibration - turturoum, jojoum (թրթռում, ճօճում)
vicar - deghabah, pokhanort, atoragal (տեղապահ, փոխանորդ, աթոռակալ)
vicarage - zhoghovurtabedoutiun, yeritsadoun (ժողովրդապետութիւն, երիցատուն)
vicariate - deghabahoutiun (տեղապահութիւն)
vice (I) - moloutiun, meghk, akhd, anaragoutiun (մոլութիւն, մեղք, ախտ, անառակութիւն)
vice (II) - pokhanort, pokh, deghagal, ter (փոխանորդ, փոխ, տեղակալ, դեր)
vice president - pokh nakhakah (փոխ նախագահ)
vice versa - pokhatarts, hagaragen (փոխադարձ, հակառակէն)
vicennial - kusanamia (քսանամեայ)
viceroy - pokh arka (փոխարքայ)
vicinage - mertsagayk, modaga degh (մերձակայք, մօտակայ տեղ)
vicinal - modig, modaga (մօտիկ, մօտակայ)
vicinity - shurchagayk, modoutiun, turatsnoutiun (շրջակայք, մօտութիւն, դրացնութիւն)

vicious - moli, akhdavor, ingadz, anarag, vad (մոլի, ախտաւոր, ինկած, անառակ, վատ)
vicissitude - popokhoutiun, verivayroum (փոփոխութիւն, վերիվայրում)
victim - zoh, argadzial (զոհ, արկածեալ)
victimize - zohel, zurganki madnel, khapel (զոհել, զրկանքի մատնել, խաբել)
victor - haghtogh, haghtagan (յաղթող, յաղթական)
victorious - haghtagan, haghtogh, haghtabandz (յաղթական, յաղթող, յաղթապանծ)
victory - haghtanag, haghtoutiun (յաղթանակ, յաղթութիւն)
victual - oudesdeghen, baren, oudelik, geragour (ուտեստեղէն, պարէն, ուտելիք, կերակուր)
victual - oudesdeghen (ուտեստեղէն)
video - deseriz, badgeriz (տեսերիզ, պատկերիզ)
video cassete - desadoup (տեսատուփ)
videotape - deseriz, badgeriz (տեսերիզ, պատկերիզ)
vie - murtsil, murtsagtsil, vokoril (մրցիլ, մրցակցիլ, ոգորիլ)
Vietnam - vietnam (Վիեթնամ)
view - desaran, desk, desaged, nayil, zunnel (տեսարան, տեսք, տեսակէտ, նայիլ, զննել)
viewer - tidogh, hantisades (դիտող, հանդիսատես)
viewless - andes, andesaneli (անտես, անտեսանելի)
viewpoint - desaged (տեսակէտ)
vigil - husgoum, khutoum, artoun (Հսկում, խթում, արթուն)
vigilance - husgoghoutiun, artnoutiun, uzkoushoutiun (Հսկողութիւն, արթնութիւն, զգուշութիւն)
vigilant - artoun, artnamid, oushatir, achalourch (արթուն, արթնամիտ, ուշադիր, աչալուրջ)
viginhood - gousoutiun (կուսութիւն)
vignette - zartanugar, zartakir, dubakurazart (զարդանկար, զարդագիր, տպագրազարդ)
vigor - gorov, ouzh, zoroutiun (կորով, ոյժ, զօրութիւն)
viking - dzovahen (ծովահէն)
vile - anark, tsadz, char, geghdod (անարգ, ցած, չար, կեղտոտ)
vilify - anarkel, murodel, zurbardel (անարգել, մրոտել, զրպարտել)
vilipend - anarkel, arhamarhel, var arnel (անարգել, արհամարհել, վար առնել)
vill - kiugh (գիւղ)
villa - arantsnadoun, amaranots, menadoun (առանձնատուն, ամարանոց, մենատուն)
village - avan, kiugh, kiughakaghak (աւան, գիւղ, գիւղաքաղաք)
villager - kiughapunag, kiughatsi, shinagan (գիւղաբնակ, գիւղացի, շինական)
villain - charakordz, anbidan, anuzkam, shinagan (չարագործ, անպիտան, անզգամ, շինական)
villanage, villeinage - jordoutiun, anuzkamoutiun (ճորտութիւն, անզգամութիւն)
villous, villose - tav, tavamaz, purtod, tavshia (թաւ, թաւամազ, բրդոտ, թաւշեայ)
vim - yerant, gorov (եռանդ, կորով)
vincible - haghteli, bardeli, nuvajeli (յաղթելի, պարտելի, նուաճելի)
vindicable - bashdubaneli, chadakoveli (պաշտպանելի, ջատագովելի)
vindicate - bashdubanel, chadakovel (պաշտպանել, ջատագովել)
vindictive - vurezhkuntir, kinakhuntir, vokhagal (վրէժխնդիր, քինախնդիր, ոխակալ)
vine - vortadoung, badaghij, badadoung (որթատունկ, պատաղիճ, պատատունկ)
vinegar - katsakh (քացախ)
vineyard - ayki, aykesdan (այգի, այգեստան)
vineyardist - aykeban (այգեպան)
viniculture - aykemushagoutiun (այգեմշակութիւն)
vinous - kineham, kiniod (գինեհամ, գինիոտ)

vintage - aykegoutk, khaghoghakagh (այգեկութք, խաղողաքաղ)
vintner - kinevajar (գինեվաճառ)
viol - medz yev hin choutag (մեծ եւ հին ջութակ)
viola - michag choutag mu, dzaghig-manishagi undaniken (միջակ ջութակ մը, ծաղիկ՝ մանիշակի ընտանիքէն)
violable - purnapareli (բռնաբարելի)
violate - purnaparel, bughdzel, lulgel, turzhel (բռնաբարել, պղծել, լլկել, դրժել)
violation - purnaparoum, bughdzoum, turzhoum (բռնաբարում, պղծում, դրժում)
violence - purnoutiun, sasdgoutiun, purnaparoum (բռնութիւն, սաստկութիւն, բռնաբարում)
violent - sasdig, pourun, ouzhkin, khisd, tsasgod (սաստիկ, բուռն, ուժգին, խիստ, ցասկոտ)
violet - manishag, manishagakouyn (մանիշակ, մանիշակագոյն)
violin - choutag (ջութակ)
violist - choutagahar (ջութակահար)
violoncellist - tavchoutagahar (թաւջութակահար)
violoncello - tavchoutag (թաւջութակ)
viper - izh, tounavor ots mu (իժ, թունաւոր օձ մը)
virago - arnagin, arnanuman gin (առնակին, առնանման կին)
virgin - gouys, aghchig, anarad, makour, chukordzadzvadz (կոյս, աղջիկ, անարատ, մաքուր, չգործածուած)
virginal - gousagan, aghchigoutian (կուսական, աղջիկութեան)
virginity - gousoutiun, aghchigoutiun (կուսութիւն, աղջիկութիւն)
virile - arnagan, ouzhegh, aragan (առնական, ուժեղ, արական)
virility - arnaganoutiun, ayroutiun, gorov (առնականութիւն, այրութիւն, կորով)
virtu, vertu - kegharvesdi jashag, arvesdasiroutiun (գեղարուեստի ճաշակ, արուեստասիրութիւն)
virtual - zoroutenagan, iragan (զօրութենական, իրական)
virtually - zoroutiamp, irabes (զօրութեամբ, իրապէս)
virtue - arakinoutiun, arzhanik, ouzh (առաքինութիւն, արժանիք, ոյժ))
virtuoso - arvesdaked, varbed yerazhishd, arvesdavarzh (արուեստագէտ, վարպետ երաժիշտ, արուեստավարժ)
virtuous - arakini (առաքինի)
virulence - zhahroutiun, tarakhodoutiun (ժահրութիւն, թարախոտութիւն)
virulent - tounavor, zhahrod, mahaper, pourun, sasdig (թունաւոր, ժահրոտ, մահաբեր, բուռն, սաստիկ)
virus - manre, zhahur, touyn, adeloutiun (մանրէ, ժահր, թոյն, ատելութիւն)
vis - ouzh, zoroutiun (ոյժ, զօրութիւն)
visa - antsoughakir, antsakuri vaveratsoum (անցուղագիր, անցագրի վաւերացում)
visage - temk, yeres, timakidz, gerbarank (դէմք, երես, դիմագիծ, կերպարանք)
viscera - porodik - usdamoks, sird, tok (փորոտիք – ստամոքս, սիրտ, թոք)
viscid - gubchoun, pagchoun, madzoutsig (կպչուն, փակչուն, մածուցիկ)
viscosity - gubchounoutiun, haragtsoutiun (կպչունութիւն, յարակցութիւն)
viscount - tergoms (դերկոմս)
viscountess - tergomsuhi (դերկոմսուհի)
viscous - gubchoun, madzoutsig, tantsur (կպչուն, մածուցիկ, թանձր)
visibility - desanelioutiun (տեսանելիութիւն)
visible - desaneli, nushmareli, haydni, patsahayd (տեսանելի, նշմարելի, յայտնի, բացայայտ)
visibly - haydnabes, desanelioren

(յայտնապէս, տեսանելիօրէն)
vision - desoghoutiun, mudabadger, desilk, yeraz (տեսողութիւն, մտապատկեր, տեսիլք, երազ)
visionary - yerazayin, yerevagayagan, tsunoragan (երազային, երեւակայական, ցնորական)
visit - ayts, aytseloutiun, budouyd, aytselel, kunnel (այց, այցելութիւն, պտոյտ, այցելել, քննել)
visitant - aytselou (այցելու)
visitation - aytseloutiun, badahmounk (այցելութիւն, պատահմունք)
visitor - aytselou, kunnich (այցելու, քննիչ)
visor - timabah, timag, timagel (դիմապահ, դիմակ, դիմակել)
visored - timagavor, dzubdial (դիմակաւոր, ծպտեալ)
vista - dzaroughi, desaran, heranugar, herabadger (ծառուղի, տեսարան, հեռանկար, հեռապատկեր)
visual - desaneli, desoghagan (տեսանելի, տեսողական)
visualize - mudabadgerel (մտապատկերել)
vis-a-vis - tem ar tem, tem timats, hantibagats (դէմ առ դէմ, դէմ դիմաց, հանդիպակաց)
vital - gensagan, gensadou, eagan, himnagan (կենսական, կենսատու, էական, հիմնական)
vitality - gensounagoutiun, gensaganoutiun, giank (կենսունակութիւն, կենսականութիւն, կեանք)
vitalization - gensounagoutiun, gensounagatsoum (կենսունակութիւն, կենսունակացում)
vitalize - gensounagel (կենսունակել)
vitals - gensagan organner - sird, tok, oughegh (կենսական օրգաններ – սիրտ, թոք, ուղեղ)
vitamin - gensaniut, gensahiut (կենսանիւթ, կենսահիւթ)
vitiate - avrel, khankarel, yeghdzel, abaganel (աւրել, խանգարել, եղծել, ապականել)
vitiation - abaganoutiun, yeghdzoum (ապականութիւն, եղծում)
viticulture - aykekordzoutiun (այգեգործութիւն)
vitreous - abagia, abageghen (ապակեայ, ապակեղէն)
vitric - abageghen (ապակեղէն)
vitrifacture - abagekordzoutiun (ապակեգործութիւն)
vitrify - abagi tunel (ապակի դնել)
vitriol - dzudzumpad, archasb (ծծմբատ, արջասպ)
vituperate - hantimanel, bakharagel, barsavel (յանդիմանել, պախարակել, պարսաւել)
viva - getstse (կեցցէ՛)
vivacious - varvuroun, gensahort, gaydar, gensalits (վառվռուն, կենսայորդ, կայտառ, կենսալից)
vivacity - gensounagoutiun, gaydaroutiun (կենսունակութիւն, կայտառութիւն)
vivid - ashkhouzh, gentani, gaydar, var (աշխոյժ, կենդանի, կայտառ, վառ)
vivification - gentanatsoum, gentanatsunoum (կենդանացում, կենդանացնում)
vivify - gentanatsunel, giank dal (կենդանացնել, կեանք տալ)
viviparous - gentanadzin, tsak perogh (կենդանածին, ձագ բերող)
vivisection - gentanahadoum (կենդանահատում)
vizard - timag (դիմակ)
vocable - par, khosk (բառ, խօսք)
vocabulary - paratsang, parakidoutiun, paradedur (բառացանկ, բառագիտութիւն, բառատետր)
vocal - tsaynagan, tsaynayin, tsaynavor (ձայնական, ձայնային, ձայնաւոր)
vocalism - tsaynaganoutiun (ձայնականութիւն)
vocalist - yerkich (երգիչ)
vocalize - tsaynavarzhoutiun unel, tsaynavorel (ձայնավարժութիւն ընել, ձայնաւորել)
vocation - gochoum, untounagoutiun, daghant (կոչում, ընդունակութիւն, տաղանդ)
vociferate - aghaghagel, boral, borchudal, juchal (աղաղակել, պոռալ,

պոռչտալ, ճչալ)
vociferation - aghaghag, tsaynargoutiun, ganchvurdouk (աղաղակ, ձայնարկութիւն, կանչվռտուք)
vociferous - partsurakoch, borchudan (բարձրագոչ, պոռչտան)
vodka - rousagan oghi, vodka (ռուսական օղի, վոտքա)
vogue - hurchag, hampav, norouyt (Հռչակ, Համբաւ, նորոյթ)
voice - tsayn, khosk, kuve, tsaynel, hunchel (ձայն, խօսք, քուէ, ձայնել, Հնչել)
voiceless - antsayn (անձայն)
voicing - tsaynel, tsayn dal, tsaynoum (ձայնել, ձայն տալ, ձայնում)
void - barab, zourg, pouj, tsukel, toghoul, chunchel (պարապ, զուրկ, փուճ, ձգել, թողուլ, ջնջել)
voidance - barboum, tours nedoum (պարպում, դուրս նետում)
voile - shugharsh (շղարշ)
volant - turchogh, savarnogh, souratsogh (թռչող, սաւառնող, սուրացող)
volatile - tsunteli, yeterayin, harapopokh, tetev (ցնդելի, եթերային, յարափոփոխ, թեթեւ)
volatilization - shokiatsoum (շոգիացում)
volatilize - shokiatsunel, shokianal (շոգիացնել, շոգիանալ)
volcanic - hurapukhayin (Հրաբխային)
volcano - hurapoukh (Հրաբուխ)
vole - tashdamoug (դաշտամուկ)
volitation - turchudoum (թռչտում)
volition - gamk, gametsoghoutiun (կամք, կամեցողութիւն)
volley - hamazarg, tsantsakhagh, huredanatsukoutiun (Համազարկ, ցանցախաղ, Հրետանաձգութիւն)
volt - yelegdurouzh, volt (ելեկտրոյժ, վոլթ)
volte-face - shurchtarts, yed tarts, timashurchoutiun (շրջդարձ, ետ դարձ, դիմաշրջութիւն)
voluble - tiurasah, arakakhos, shadakhosel (դիւրասաՀ, արագախօս, շատախօսել)
volume - hador, kirk, dzaval, daradzoutiun (Հատոր, գիրք, ծաւալ, տարածութիւն)
voluminous - dzavaloun, zankuvadzayin (ծաւալուն, զանգուածային)
voluntary - gamavor, inknagam, inknahojar (կամաւոր, ինքնակամ, ինքնայօժար)
volunteer - gamavor, gamavorakurvil (կամաւոր, կամաւորագրուիլ)
voluptuary - heshdaser, vavashod, zekh (Հեշտասէր, վաւաշոտ, զեխ)
voluptuous - heshdaser, tsop (Հեշտասէր, ցոփ)
vomit - puskhel, zhaytukel, puskhouk (փսխել, ժայթքել, փսխուք)
voracious - shadager, vorguramol (շատակեր, որկրամոլ)
voracity - shadageroutiun, vorguramoloutiun (շատակերութիւն, որկրամոլութիւն)
vortex - churabudouyd, hortsank (ջրապտոյտ, յորձանք)
vorticose - hortsanoud (յորձանուտ)
votary - oukhdabah, oukhdanuver (ուխտապաՀ, ուխտանուէր)
vote - kuve, kuveargoutiun, kuveargel, undurel (քուէ, քուէարկութիւն, քուէարկել, ընտրել)
voter - kuveargogh (քուէարկող)
votive - oukhdanuver, oukhdabah (ուխտանուէր, ուխտապաՀ)
vouch - vugayel, hasdadel, yerashkhavorel (վկայել, Հաստատել, երաշխաւորել)
vouchee - vugayogh, yerashkhavor (վկայող, երաշխաւոր)
voucher - vuga, vugayakir, hasdadakir, pasd (վկայ, վկայագիր, Հաստատագիր, փաստ)
vouchsafe - shunorhel, hajil, havanil, zichanil (շնորՀել, Հաճիլ, Հաւանիլ, զիջանիլ)
vow - oukhdel, yertnoul, oukhd, yertoum, khosdoum (ուխտել, երդնուլ, ուխտ, երդում, խոստում)
vowel - tsaynavor - kir (ձայնաւոր-գիր)
vower - oukhdogh, khosdatsogh

(ուխտող, խոստացող)
vox - tsayn (ձայն)
voyage - jamportoutiun, oughevoroutiun, jamportel (ճամբորդութիւն, ուղեւորութիւն, ճամբորդել)
voyager - jamport, oughevor (ճամբորդ, ուղեւոր)
vulcan - hurapoukh (Հրաբուխ)
vulcanize - dzudzumpel, dzudzumpabadel (ծծմբել, ծծմբապատել)
vulgar - ramig, ramgagan, hasarag, sovoragan, kurehig (ռամիկ, ռամկական, Հասարակ, սովորական, գռեՀիկ)
vulgarity - kurehgoutiun, hasaragatsoum (գռեՀկութիւն, Հասարակացում)
vulgarization - ramgatsoum (ռամկացում)
vulgarize - ramganal, ramgatsunel, zhoghovurtaganatsunel (ռամկանալ, ռամկացնել, ժողովրդականացնել)
vulnerability - khotselioutiun (խոցելիութիւն)
vulnerable - khotseli, viravoreli (խոցելի, վիրաւորելի)
vulnerary - virapouzhich, virategh, virakhod (վիրաբուժիչ, վիրադեղ, վիրախոտ)
vulpine - khoramang, aghvesanuman (խորամանկ, աղուէսանման)
vulture - ankugh (անգղ)
vulva - bouts, pounots (պուց, բունոց)
vying - murtsogh, tsukdogh, murtsoum (մրցող, ձգտող, մրցում) - (from - vie, vie՝ բառէն)

wabble - toghtochil, yereroum (դողդոջիլ, երերում)
wad - khourts-khodi, khourts gazmel (խուրձ՝ խոտի, խուրձ կազմել)
waddle - pati bes kalel, dadanil, jororal (բադի պէս քալել, տատանիլ, ճօրորալ)
wade - chouren antsunil, kedi hounen antsunil, houn (ջուրէն անցնիլ, գետի Հունէն անցնիլ, Հուն)
wader - houne antsunogh, partsurasurounk turchoun (Հունէ անցնող, բարձրասրունք թռչուն)
wadi, wady - tsor, chouri houn (ձոր, ջուրի Հուն)
wafer - pulit, nushkhar, nushkharov gunkel, namag pagtsunel (բլիթ, նշխար, նշխարով կնքել, նամակ փակցնել)
waffle - parag khoshor pulit, nourp kakar (բարակ խոշոր բլիթ, նուրբ քաքար)
waft - dzupal, dadanil, dzupdzupal, pouk, dadank, hov (ծփալ, տատանիլ, ծփծփալ, բուք, տատանք, Հով)
wag - jojel, tsuntsel, tsuntsuvil, suramid, gadagakhos (ճօճել, ցնցել, ցնցուիլ, սրամիտ, կատակախօս)
wage (n) - oravarts, ashkhadavarts, toshag, varts (օրավարձ, աշխատավարձ, թոշակ, վարձ)
wage (v) - kurav tunel, vudankel,

mughel, yentarguvil (գրաւ դնել, վտանգել, մղել, ենթարկուիլ)
wager - kurav, kuravagan, kuravi tunel, kuravi kal (գրաւ, գրաւական, գրաւի դնել, գրաւի գալ)
wagerer - kuravi yegogh, kuravargou (գրաւի եկող, գրաւարկու)
wages - oravarts, shapatavujar (օրավարձ, շաբաթավճար)
waggery - kheghgadagoutiun (խեղկատակութիւն)
waggish - kheghgadag, gadagakhos, gadagayin (խեղկատակ, կատակախօս, կատակային)
waggle - yereral, yerertsunel, yererank (երերալ, երերցնել, երերանք)
wagon, waggon - yergatoughii gark, pernagark, garkov danil (երկաթուղիի կառք, բեռնակառք, կառքով տանիլ)
waif - dunang, ander, gorsuvadz kouyk (տնանկ, անտէր, կորսուած գոյք)
wail - voghpal, lal, voghp, godz (ողբալ, լալ, ողբ, կոծ)
wailer - voghpatsogh (ողբացող)
wailful - voghpali (ողբալի)
wain - gark, sayl, medz arch (կառք, սայլ, Մեծ Արջ)
waist - mechk - martou (մէջք՝ մարդու)
waistcoat - pajgon (բաճկոն)
wait - usbasel, genal, munal, usbasavorel (սպասել, կենալ, մնալ, սպասաւորել)
waiter - usbasogh, usbasavor, dzara (սպասող, սպասաւոր, ծառայ)
waiting - usbasargoutiun, dzarayoutiun, usbasoum (սպասարկութիւն, ծառայութիւն, սպասում)
waiting room - usbasaran, usbasaseniag (սպասարան, սպասասենեակ)
waitress - usbasiag, seghani usbasouhi (սպասեակ, սեղանի սպասուհի)
waive - toghoul, lukel, hurazharil (թողուլ, լքել, հրաժարիլ)
wake - artunnal, artuntsunel, genal, husgoum, nakhadonag (արթննալ, արթնցնել, կենալ, հսկում, նախատօնակ)
wakeful - artoun, anninch, achalourch, husgogh (արթուն, աննինջ, աչալուրջ, հսկող)
waken - artuntsunel, artunnal, houzel (արթնցնել, արթննալ, յուզել)
waker - artuntsunogh, artuntsogh (արթնցնող, արթնցող)
wale - hedk, nushan, kidz, nerknakodi (հետք, նշան, գիծ, ներքնագօտի)
walk (n) - kalvadzk, budouyd, arahed, uzposaran (քալուածք, պտոյտ, արահետ, զբօսարան)
walk (v) - kalel, yertal, shurchil, jemel, kaletsunel (քալել, երթալ, շրջիլ, ճեմել, քալեցնել)
walkaway - tiurin kordz, haghtanag, megnil (դիւրին գործ, յաղթանակ, մեկնիլ)
walker - kalogh (քալող)
walking - kalogh, kalvadzk (քալող, քալուածք)
walkout - kordzatogh (գործաթող)
walk-a-thon - kaylarshav (քայլարշաւ)
wall - bad, vorm, barisb, bad kashel, vormel (պատ, որմ, պարիսպ, պատ քաշել, որմել)
wallet - turamabanag, tughtabanag, barg, bayousag (դրամապանակ, թղթապանակ, պարկ, պայուսակ)
wallop - yeral, dzedzel, turchel, dzedz, dzanur harvadz (եռալ, ծեծել, թրջել, ծեծ, ծանր հարուած)
wallow - dabuldugil, tavalil, tatkhuvil, tavaloum (տապլտկիլ, թաւալիլ, թաթխուիլ, տապլտկում)
wallower - dabuldugogh, dughmatatav (տապլտկող, տղմաթաթաւ)
wallpaper - vormunatought, basdar (որմնաթուղթ, պաստառ)
wall-to-wall - bade bad (պատէ պատ)
walnut - ungouyz, ungouzeni (ընկոյզ, ընկուզենի)
waltz - shurchabar, vals, surchabarel (շրջապար, վալս, շրջապարել)
wan - duzhkouyn, teghnadz, kounadil (տժգոյն, դեղնած, գունատիլ)

wand - kavazan, tsoub (գաւազան, ցուպ)
wander - taparil, moloril, khodoril (Թափառիլ, մոլորիլ, խոտորիլ)
wanderer - taparagan, taparashurchig, vudaranti (Թափառական, Թափառաշրջիկ, վտարանդի)
wandering - taparoum, taparogh (Թափառում, Թափառող)
wane - nuvazil, pokranal, iynal, nuvazoum, hadnoum (նուազիլ, փոքրանալ, իջնալ, նուազում, Հատնում)
wangle - khapel, shortel (խաբել, շորԹել)
wanness - duzhkounoutiun (տժգունուԹիւն)
want - ouzel, papakil, ughtsal, garodoutiun, bedk (ուզել, փափաքիլ, ըղձալ, կարօտուԹիւն, պէտք)
wantage - bagasoutiun, teroutiun (պակասուԹիւն, ԹերուԹիւն)
wanter - garodogh, teratsogh (կարօտող, Թերացող)
wanting - patsaga, bagas, teri, angadar (բացակայ, պակաս, Թերի, անկատար)
wanton - vayrak, lubirsh, poz, durpod, lurpanal (վայրագ, լպիրշ, բոզ, տռփոտ, լրբանալ)
war - baderazm, guriv, baderazmil, gurvil (պատերազմ, կռիւ, պատերազմիլ, կռուիլ)
warble - keghkeghel, yerkel, keghkeghank (գեղգեղել, երգել, գեղգեղանք)
ward - bashdubanel, bahel, husgel, husgoghoutiun, tirk (պաշտպանել, պահել, Հսկել, ՀսկողուԹիւն, դիրք)
warden - bahaban, bahag, pandabah (պահապան, պահակ, բանտապահ)
warder - bahogh, tsoub (պահող, ցուպ)
wardrobe - hantertsaran, hakousd (Հանդերձարան, Հագուստ)
wardship - bahbanoutiun, khunamagaloutiun (պահպանուԹիւն, խնամակալուԹիւն)
ware - uzkoushanal, uzkouysh, kidag (զգուշանալ, զգոյշ, գիտակ)
warehouse - muteranots, ampar, muterel, amparel (մԹերանոց, ամբար, մԹերել, ամբարել)
warehouseman - muterabah (մԹերապահ)
warehousing - amparoum, muteroum (ամբարում, մԹերում)
warelike - razmaser, mardagan (ռազմասէր, մարտական)
wareroom - muteranots (մԹերանոց)
warfare - baderazm, guriv, mard, baykar (պատերազմ, կռիւ, մարտ, պայքար)
warily - uzkoushoutiamp, khohemoutiamp (զգուշուԹեամբ, խոՀեմուԹեամբ)
wariness - uzkoushoutiun (զգուշուԹիւն)
warlock - gakhart, vuhoug (կախարդ, վՀուկ)
warm - dak, cherm, guragod, daktsunel, daknal (տաք, ջերմ, կրակոտ, տաքցնել, տաքնալ)
warmly - chermoren, yerantov (ջերմօրէն, եռանդով)
warmth - dakoutiun, chermoutiun, yerant (տաքուԹիւն, ջերմուԹիւն, եռանդ)
warm-blooded - dakariun (տաքարիւն)
warn - uzkoushatsunel, aztararel, khuradel (զգուշացնել, ազդարարել, խրատել)
warning - aztararoutiun, uzkoushatsoum (ազդարարուԹիւն, զգուշացում)
warp (n) - navatsik baran, chuvan, tekoum, goratsoum (նաւածիգ պարան, չուան, Թեքում, կորացում)
warp (v) - gabel, tekel, khodoretsunel, khodoril, goranal (կապել, Թեքել, խոտորեցնել, խոտորիլ, կորանալ)
warrant - yerashkhavorel, abahovel, yerashkhik, vujir (երաշխաւորել, ապաՀովել, երաշխիք, վճիռ)
warranter - yerashkhavorogh (երաշխաւորող)
warranty - yerashkhik, ardonakir, abahovoutiun (երաշխիք, արտօնա–

գիր, ապահովութիւն)

warren - *jakaranots, vorsaran, bahesdanots* (ճագարանոց, որսարան, պահեստանոց)

warrior - *razmig, zinvor, mardig* (ռազմիկ, զինուոր, մարտիկ)

warship - *mardanav, baderazmanav* (մարտանաւ, պատերազմանաւ)

wart - *morti pokur ouretsk, godzidz* (մորթի փոքր ուռեցք, կոծիծ)

wary - *uzkouysh, oushatir, shurchahayats* (զգոյշ, ուշադիր, շրջահայեաց)

was - *eyi, eyir, er* (էի, էիր, էր)

wash - *luval, luvatsvil, makrel, luvatsk, jahij* (լուալ, լուացուիլ, մաքրել, լուացք, ճահիճ)

washer - *luvatsarar, luvatski mekena* (լուացարար, լուացքի մեքենայ)

washing - *luvatsoum, luvalik, lokank* (լուացում, լուալիք, լոգանք)

washout - *usbaradz, mashadz* (սպառած, մաշած)

washstand - *luvatsaran* (լուացարան)

wasp - *bidzag, por* (պիծակ, բոռ)

waspish - *khaytogh, char, anuzkam* (խայթող, չար, անզգամ)

wassail - *geroukhoum, umbeli, paremaghtank unel* (կերուխում, ըմպելի, բարեմաղթանք ընել)

wastage - *vadnoum* (վատնում)

waste - *vadnel, usbarel, hadtsunel, vadnoum, aver* (վատնել, սպառել, հատցնել, վատնում, աւեր)

wasteful - *shurayl, averich, anarag* շռայլ, աւերիչ, անառակ)

waster, wastrel - *vadnogh, muskhogh, shurayl* (վատնող, մսխող, շռայլ)

watch (n) - *zhamatsouyts, bahbanoutiun, bahaban, ted* (ժամացոյց, պահպանութիւն, պահապան, դէտ)

watch (v) - *husgel, tidel, bahbanel, khunamel* (հսկել, դիտել, պահպանել, խնամել)

watcher - *tidogh, husgogh* (դիտող, հսկող)

watchhouse - *bahaganots, bahagadoun* (պահականոց, պահակատուն)

watchmaker - *zhamakordz* (ժամագործ)

watchman - *bahag, bahaban, husgogh* (պահակ, պահապան, հսկող)

water - *chour, churel, turchel, vorokel* (ջուր, ջրել, թրջել, որոգել)

watercan - *tsuntsough* (ցնցուղ)

watercolor - *churanerg* (ջրաներկ)

waterfall - *churvezh, churtsayd, sahank* (ջրվէժ, ջրցայտ, սահանք)

watermelon - *tsumeroug* (ձմերուկ)

watermill - *churaghats, chaghatsk* (ջրաղաց, ջաղացք)

waterproof - *anchurantsig, chouri timatsogh* (անջրանցիկ, ջուրի դիմացող)

waterski - *churasahnag* (ջրասահնակ)

watertank - *churampar* (ջրամբար)

watt - *yeledurouyzh, wat* (ելեկտրոյժ, վաթ)

wattle - *vantag, jiugh, vantag hiusel* (վանդակ, ճիւղ, վանդակ հիւսել)

wave - *alik, gohag, dzupal, yereral, dadanil* (ալիք, կոհակ, ծփալ, երերալ, տատանիլ)

waver - *varanil, yereral, dadanil, sharzhogh* (վարանիլ, երերալ, տատանիլ, շարժող)

waverer - *dadanogh, varanogh* (տատանող, վարանող)

wavering - *dadanoum, varanoum* (տատանում, վարանում)

wavy - *alegodz, dzupoun, yereroun* (ալեկոծ, ծփուն, երերուն)

wax - *meghramom, mom, gunkamom, momel, mom kusel* (մեղրամոմ, մոմ, կնքամոմ, մոմ քսել)

way - *jampa, oughi, antsk, michots* (ճամբայ, ուղի, անցք, միջոց)

wayfarer - *jamport, oughevor* (ճամբորդ, ուղեւոր)

waylay - *jampan usbasel, goghobdel* (ճամբան սպասել, կողոպտել)

waymark - *hedk, vodnahedk* (հետք, ոտնահետք)

wayside - *jampou yezerk* (ճամբու եզերք)

we - *menk* (մենք)

weak - dugar, anzor, nuvaghoun, gagough (տկար, անզօր, նուաղուն, կակուղ)
weaken - dugaratsunel, dugaranal (տկարացնել, տկարանալ)
weakness - dugaroutiun, touloutiun (տկարութիւն, թուլութիւն)
weal - hachoghoutiun, paroroutiun (յաջողութիւն, բարօրութիւն)
weald - andar, tashdavayr (անտառ, դաշտավայր)
wealth - harusdoutiun, inchk (Հարստութիւն, ինչք)
wealthiness - partamoutiun, jokhoutiun (փարթամութիւն, ճոխութիւն)
wealthy - harousd, partam (Հարուստ, փարթամ)
wean - gate gudrel, hajouyke zurgel (կաթէ կտրել, Հաճոյքէ զրկել)
weapon - zenk (զէնք)
wear - hakvil, gurel, kordzadzel, mashoum (Հագուիլ, կրել, գործածել, մաշում)
wearer - haknogh, gurogh, mashetsunogh (Հագնող, կրող, մաշեցնող)
wearful - hoknetsoutsich, daghdugali (յոգնեցուցիչ, տաղտկալի)
weariless - ankhonch (անխոնջ)
weariness - hoknoutiun, tsantsurouyt (յոգնութիւն, ձանձրոյթ)
wearing - hakvelik, hoknetsunogh (Հագուելիք, յոգնեցնող)
wearisome - daghdugali, tsantsuratsoutsich (տաղտկալի, ձանձրացուցիչ)
weary - hoknadz, ouzhasbar, tsantsuratsunel (յոգնած, ուժասպառ, ձանձրացնել)
weasand - shunchapogh (շնչափող)
weather - oti vijag, yeghanag, mutnolord (օդի վիճակ, եղանակ, մթնոլորտ)
weathercock - hoghmatsouyts (Հողմացոյց)
weave - hiusel, hiusvadzk (Հիւսել, Հիւսուածք)
weaver - choulhag, vosdaynang (ջուլՀակ, ոստայնանկ)
web - vosdayn, patet, hiusvadzk, achki aghd, huisel (ոստայն, փաթեթ, Հիւսուածք, աչքի աղտ, Հիւսել)
webster - vosdaynang (ոստայնանկ)
wed - amousnanal, busagvil, amousnatsunel (ամուսնանալ, պսակուիլ, ամուսնացնել)
wedding - harsanik, busag, amousnoutiun (Հարսանիք, պսակ, ամուսնութիւն)
wedge - seb, jeghkel, mukhel (սեպ, ճեղքել, մխել)
wedlock - harsanik (Հարսանիք)
Wednesday - chorekshapti (Չորեքշաբթի)
weed - vunasagar khod, sez, khodapouys, makrel (վնասակար խոտ, սէզ, խոտաբոյս, մաքրել)
week - shapat, yotniag (շաբաթ, եօթնեակ)
weekday - lour or, kordzi or (լուր օր, գործի օր)
weekend - shapataverch (շաբաթավերջ)
weekly - shapatatert, shapatagan (շաբաթաթերթ, շաբաթական)
ween - gardzel, yerevagayel (կարծել, երեւակայել)
weep - lal, ardasvel, voghpal (լալ, արտասուել, ողբալ)
weeper - latsogh, lalgan (լացող, լալկան)
weeping - ardasvogh, lalgan (արտասուող, լալկան)
weft - hiusvadz, vosdayn (Հիւսուած, ոստայն)
weigh - gushrel, kunnel, gushratadel, junshel (կշռել, քննել, կշռադատել, ճնշել)
weight - gushirk, dzanroutiun, ouyzh, neghoutiun (կշիռք, ծանրութիւն, ոյժ, նեղութիւն)
weighty - dzanur, dzanragushir, aztou (ծանր, ծանրակշիռ, ազդու)
weir - churarkel bad, tsugnarkel (ջրարգել, ձկնարգել)
weird - vuhoug, gakhart, pakhd, jagadakir (վՀուկ, կախարդ, բախտ, ճակատագիր)
welcome - pari kalousd, pari ye-

gadz, voghchounel (բարի գալուստ, բարի եկած, ողջունել)
welcoming - hiurungalel, sirov untounil (հիւրնկալել, սիրով ընդունիլ)
weld - zotel, miatsunel, tarpunel, zotoum (զօդել, միացնել, դարբնել, զօդում)
welfare - paroroutiun, yerchangoutiun, hachoghoutiun (բարօրութիւն, երջանկութիւն, յաջողութիւն)
welkin - yergink, yergnagamar (երկինք, երկնակամար)
well - lav, aroghch, hankisd, churhor, pukhil, yellel (լաւ, առողջ, հանգիստ, ջրհոր, փխել, ելլել)
wellborn - aznuvagan, aznuvazarm (ազնուական, ազնուազարմ)
wellbred - paregirt, kaghakavar (բարեկիրթ, քաղաքավար)
welldoer - parekordz (բարեգործ)
welt - yezur, dzayr, shourt, yezrazart, yezrel (եզր, ծայր, շուրթ, եզրազարդ, եզրել)
welter - tavalil, kuldorvil, tavaloum (թաւալիլ, գլտորուիլ, թաւալում)
wen - our, ouretsk, ardouyts (ուռ, ուռեցք, արտոյց)
wench - aghchig, usbasopuhi, poz, bornig (աղջիկ, սպասուհի, բոզ, պոռնիկ)
wend - yertal, jampa gudrel, megnil (երթալ, ճամբայ կտրել, մեկնիլ)
went - kunats (գնաց)
wept - latsav (լացաւ)
West - arevmoudk (Արեւմուտք)
western - arevmudian (արեւմտեան)
wet - tats, khonav, turchel (թաց, խոնաւ, թրջել)
wetness - tatsoutiun, damgoutiun (թացութիւն, տամկութիւն)
wetnurse - tayiag (դայեակ)
wetting - vorokoum, churoum, turchoum (որոգում, ջրում, թրջում)
whack - harvadzel, sharachov zarnel, harvadz (հարուածել, շառաչով զարնել, հարուած)
whale - ged tsoug, dupotsel, ged tsoug vorsal (կէտ ձուկ, տփոցել, կէտ ձուկ որսալ)
whang - dupel, dupots (տփել, տփոց)
wharf - navamadouyts, karap (նաւամատոյց, քարափ)
what - inch? vor? (ի՞նչ, ո՞ր)
what-so-ever - inch vor al, orveve pan vor (ինչ որ ալ, որեւէ բան որ)
wheal - khaghavard, verk, harvadzi nushan (խաւաքարտ, վէրք, հարուածի նշան)
wheat - tsoren, hatsahadig (ցորեն, հացահատիկ)
wheedle - paghakushel, hamozel, kudznil, shahil (փաղաքշել, համոզել, քծնիլ, շահիլ)
wheel - aniv, jakharag, tartsunel, tavalil (անիւ, ճախարակ, դարձնել, թաւալիլ)
wheelman - hedzanivort (հեծանիւորդ)
wheeze - hudzdziun, dzanur shouncharoutiun, hudzdzel (հծծիւն, ծանր շնչառութիւն, հծծել)
whelp - lagod, shan tsak, kotot (լակոտ, շան ձագ, քոթոթ)
when - yerp?, yerpvor (ե՞րբ, երբոր)
whence - ourge, ousgits (ուրկէ, ուսկից)
whenever - yerpvor (երբոր)
when-so-ever - yerp vor, yerpevitse, yerp vor al ulla (երբ որ, երբեւիցէ, երբ որ ալ ըլլայ)
where - our, minchter (ուր, մինչդեռ)
whereabout - our, vordeghu, vorou nugadmamp, ourdegh ullalu (ուր, որու նկատմամբ, ուրտեղ ըլլալը)
whereas - minchter, kani vor, vorovhedev (մինչդեռ, քանի որ, որովհետեւ)
whereat - inch pani hamar, inchou, inchov (ինչ բանի համար, ինչու, ինչով)
wherefore - ousdi, ouremun, inchou, badjar (ուստի, ուրեմն, ի՞նչու, պատճառ)
wherein - inchov, yerp, our (ինչով, երբ, ուր)
whereof - ourdeghen, ourdegh (ուր-

տեղէն, ուրտեղ)
whereon - inch pani, vorou vura (ի՞նչ բանի, որու վրայ)
wheresoever - our vor, tebi our vor (ուր որ, դէպի ուր որ)
whereto - voroun, our, tebi our (որուն, ուր, դէպի ուր)
whereupon - voroun vura, inch pani vura (որուն վրայ, ի՞նչ բանի վրայ)
wherever - our vor (ուր որ)
wherewith - inchov, inch panov, vorov (ինչով, ինչ բանով, որով)
whet - surel, surtsunel, kurkurel (սրել, սրցնել, գրգռել)
whether - te voch, te, artiok (թէ ոչ, թէ, արդեօք)
whetstone - hesanakar (յեսանաքար)
whetter - surogh, hesanogh (սրող, յեսանող)
whey - tan (թան)
wheyface - talgeres, tuzhkouyn temk (դալկերես, դժգոյն դէմք)
which - vor, zor, inch vor, vor megu (որ, զոր, ինչ որ, որ մէկը)
whiff - moukh, dzoukh, hosank, puchel, dzukhel (մուխ, ծուխ, հոսանք, փչել, ծխել)
whiffle - dadanil, sharzhil, anganon puchel (տատանիլ, շարժիլ, անկանոն փչել)
while - minch, minchter, michots, yerp, bah (մինչ, մինչդեռ, միջոց, երբ, պահ)
whilom - yerpemun, adenok, yerpemni (երբեմն, ատենօք, երբեմնի)
whilst - minchter, minch (մինչդեռ, մինչ)
whim - kumayk, kumahajouyk (քմայք, քմահաճոյք)
whimmy - kumaykod (քմայքոտ)
whimper - meghm lal, hedzel, hegegal (մեղմ լալ, հեծել, հեկեկալ)
whimsical - kumaykod, aylantag, khelakar (քմայքոտ, այլանդակ, խելաքար)
whine - gaghgants, hedz, gaghgantsel (կաղկանձ, հեծ, կաղկանձել)
whinny - vurunchel, khurkhunchel, vurunchiun (վրնջել, խրխնջել, վրնջիւն)
whip - kharazan, mudrag, kharazanel, mudragel (խարազան, մտրակ, խարազանել, մտրակել)
whipper-snapper - anbidan, suriga, sunabardz (անպիտան, սրիկայ, սնապարծ)
whipping - mudragoum, kharazanoum, dzedz (մտրակում, խարազանում, ծեծ)
whirl - tartsunel, budoudkel, tavalk, tartsuvadzk (դարձնել, պտուտքել, թաւալք, դարձուածք)
whirlpool - hortsank, churabudouyd (յորձանք, ջրապտոյտ)
whish - shushiun, shurshiun, shurshurshil (շշիւն, շրշիւն, շրշիլ)
whisk - khozanagel, makrel, khozanag (խոզանակել, մաքրել, խոզանակ)
whisky - armudoghi, ouiski (արմտօղի, ուիսքի)
whisper - puspusal, hudzdzel, puspusouk, hudzdziun (փսփսալ, հծծել, փսփսուք, հծծիւն)
whist - lour, antsayn, tughtakhagh mu (լուռ, անձայն, թղթախաղ մը)
whistle - soulel, souloum, soulich (սուլել, սուլում, սուլիչ)
whit - hiule, boud mu, annushan kanag, masnig (հիւլէ, պուտ մը, աննշան քանակ, մասնիկ)
white - jermag, usbidag (ճերմակ, սպիտակ)
White House - nakhakahi doun (Նախագահի Տուն)
whiten - jermugtsunel, jermugnal, jermugil (ճերմկցնել, ճերմկնալ, ճերմկիլ)
whitener - jermaftsunogh (ճերմակցնող)
whiteness - jermagoutiun, makroutiun (ճերմակութիւն, մաքրութիւն)
whitewash - guradzep, jermugtsunel, hantsanku dzadzgel (կրածեփ, ճերմկցմել, յանցանքը ծածկել)
whither - our, ourdegh, tebi our, our vor (ուր, ուրտեղ, դէպի ուր, ուր որ)
whitting - dashoyuk (տաշուք)

whittle - tanag, gudrel, dashel (դանակ, կտրել, տաշել)
whittling - dashouk (տաշուք)
whiz - vuzzal, puzzal, puzziun (վզզալ, բզզալ, բզզիւն)
who - ov, vor (ով, որ)
whoa - getsir, gank ar (կեցի՛ր, կանգ առ)
whoever - ov vor (ով որ)
whole - ampoghch, luman, gadarial (ամբողջ, լման, կատարեալ)
whole saler - medzakanag vajarogh (մեծաքանակ վաճառող)
wholeness - ampoghchoutiun (ամբողջութիւն)
wholesale - medzakanag vajark (մեծաքանակ վաճառք)
wholesale price - medzakanagi kin (մեծաքանակի գին)
wholesaler - medzakag vajarogh (մեծաքանակ վաճառող)
wholesome - aroghcharar, okdagar, bidani (առողջարար, օգտակար, պիտանի)
whole-hearted - miasird, cherm, angeghdz (միասիրտ, ջերմ, անկեղծ)
wholly - ampoghchovin, polorovin, liovin (ամբողջովին, բոլորովին, լիովին)
whom - zor (զոր) - to whom (vorou, zov (որու, զո՞վ)
whomsoever - voru vor, vor megu vor (որը որ, որ մէկը որ)
whoop - jich, kochiun, aghaghag (ճիչ, գոչիւն, աղաղակ)
whop, whap - dupel, dupotsel, dzedzel, dupots, dzedz (տփել, տփոցել, ծեծել, տփոց, ծեծ)
whore - boz, bornig, pozanal, pozatsunel (բոզ, պոռնիկ, բոզանալ, բոզացնել)
whoredom - bornugoutiun (պոռնկութիւն)
whoreson - bornugorti (պոռնկորդի)
whose - vorou, voroun, voronts (որու, որուն, որոնց)
whoso - ov vor, megu vor (ով որ, մէկը որ)
whosoever - ov vor, vor megu vor (ով որ, որ մէկը որ)
why - inchou, inchou hamar (ինչու, ինչու համար)
wick - badrouyk (պատրոյգ)
wicked - char, charakordz, anuzkam (չար, չարագործ, անզգամ)
wide - layn, untartsag, pats, daradzoutiun, herou (լայն, ընդարձակ, բաց, տարածութիւն, հեռու)
widen - layntsunel, laynnal, untartsagel, untartsagil (լայնցնել, լայննալ, ընդարձակել, ընդարձակիլ)
widow - ayri gin, ayriatsunel (այրի կին, այրիացնել)
widower - ayri mart, ginu meradz (այրի մարդ, կինը մեռած)
width - laynk, laynoutiun, patsoutiun (լայնք, լայնութիւն, բացութիւն)
wield - hagagushrel, varel, jojel, sharzhel (հակակշռել, վարել, ճօճել, շարժել)
wielder - varogh, varich (վարող, վարիչ)
wife - gin-amousnatsadz martou (կին՝ ամուսնացած մարդու)
wifehood - gunoutiun (կնութիւն)
wifely - gunavayel, vayelouch (կնավայել, վայելուչ)
wig - geghdzam (կեղծամ)
wigged - geghdzamavor (կեղծամաւոր)
wigging - hantimanoutiun (յանդիմանութիւն)
wiggle - meghmoren sharzhil, yereroum (մեղմօրէն շարժիլ, երերում)
wight - mart, eag, araradz, ants (մարդ, էակ, արարած, անձ)
wigwam - khurjit, daghavar - amerigian huntignerou (խրճիթ, տաղաւար՝ ամերիկեան հնդիկներու)
wild - vayreni, vayri, gadaghi, pird, amayi, anpunag (վայրենի, վայրի, կատաղի, բիրտ, ամայի, անբնակ)
wildbeast - vayri kazan (վայրի գազան)
wilder - shupotetsunel, shuvaretsunel (շփոթեցնել, շուարեցնել)
wilderness - amayoutiun, anabad (ամայութիւն, անապատ)

wildfire - *anshicheli gurag* (անշիջելի կրակ)
wildness - *vayrenoutiun* (վայրենութիւն)
wile - *hunark, khoramangoutiun, humayel, khapel* (Հնարք, խորամանկութիւն, Հմայել, խաբել)
wilful, willful - *tidoumnavor, hamar, gamavor* (դիտումնաւոր, յամառ, կամաւոր)
wiliness - *khoramangoutiun* (խորամանկութիւն)
will (n) - *gamk, papak, inghts, nubadag, gudag* (կամք, փափաք, իղձ, նպատակ, կտակ)
will (v) - *ouzel, gamenal, gudagel* (ուզել, կամենալ, կտակել)
willer - *gudagogh* (կտակող)
willful - *tidoumnavor, gamagor, hamar* (դիտումնաւոր, կամակոր, Համառ)
willing - *hozhar, gametsogh, badrasdagam* (յօժար, կամեցող, պատրաստակամ)
willingness - *badrasdagamoutiun* (պատրաստակամութիւն)
willow - *ouri, oureni* (ուռի, ուռենի)
willowy - *jugoun, shunorhali, yergarahasag, ourenazart* (ճկուն, շնորհալի, երկարահասակ, ուռենազարդ)
willy - *pambag makrelou mekena* (բամպակ մաքրելու մեքենայ)
wilt - *taramil, toshnil, tormil, lukhgil* (թառամիլ, թօշնիլ, թոռմիլ, լխկիլ)
wily - *khoramang, hunaramid, khapogh* (խորամանկ, Հնարամիտ, խաբող)
wimple - *lachag, kogh, lachagel* (լաչակ, քող, լաչակել)
win - *shahil, haghtel, vasdugil, usdanal* (շաՀիլ, յաղթել, վաստկիլ, ստանալ)
wince - *ungurgil, vuhadil, akatsel, ungurgoum* (ընկրկիլ, վՀատիլ, աքացել, ընկրկում)
winch - *verhan mekena, guroung* (վերՀան մեքենայ, կռունկ)
wind (I) - *hov, kami, pouk, ot, hovaharel, potorgel* (Հով, քամի, բուք, օդ, ՀովաՀարել, փոթորկել)
wind (II) - *pattel, volorel, tartsunel, bullel, garavarel* (փաթթել, ոլորել, դարձնել, պլլել, կառավարել)
windbag - *shadakhos* (շատախօս)
windfall - *hove ingadz* (Հովէ ինկած)
winding - *tartsuvadzk, otsabudouyd, larelu* (դարձուածք, օձապտոյտ, լարելը)
windjammer - *arakasdanav* (առագաստանաւ)
windlass - *pernaparts mekena, guroung* (բեռնաբարձ մեքենայ, կռունկ)
windmill - *hoghmaghats, chaghatsk* (Հողմաղաց, ջաղացք)
window - *badouhan, lousamoud* (պատուՀան, լուսամուտ)
windpipe - *shunchapogh* (շնչափող)
windstorm - *murrig* (մրրիկ)
windy - *hovod, barab, sunamech* (Հովոտ, պարապ, սնամէջ)
wind-up - *shurchabadoum, pagoum, verj* (շրջափակում, փակում, վերջ)
wine - *kini, kini khumel* (գինի, գինի խմել)
winebibber - *kinemol* (գինեմոլ)
wineglass - *kinepazhag* (գինեբաժակ)
wing - *tev, turichk, hovani, turchil, turtsunel* (թեւ, թռիչք, Հովանի, թռչիլ, թռցնել)
winged - *tevavor, tevod, arak* (թեւաւոր, թեւոտ, արագ)
wingless - *antev* (անթեւ)
wink - *aguntart, agnarg, kuttel, tartel, achk kotsel* (ակնթարթ, ակնարկ, քթթել, թարթել, աչք գոցել)
winner - *shahogh, haghtogh* (շաՀող, յաղթող)
winning - *shahogh, vasdugogh, hurabourich, shahvadz koumar* (շաՀող, վաստկող, Հրապուրիչ, շաՀուած գումար)
winnow - *tsorenu harten zadel, maghel* (ցորենը յարդէն զատել, մաղել)
winsome - *hajeli, kuravich* (Հաճելի,

գրաւիչ)
winter - tsumer, tsumerel (ձմեռ, ձմեռել)
wintery - tsumernayin, khisd tsourd (ձմեռնային, խիստ ցուրտ)
wipe - surpel, makrel, hanel, surpich, tashginag, abdag (սրբել, մաքրել, հանել, սրբիչ, թաշկինակ, ապտակ)
wire - tel, medaghalar, herakuratel, herakurel (թել, մետաղալար, հեռագրաթել, հեռագրել)
wiredraw - tel kshel, tel tsukel (թել քաշել, թել ձգել)
wireless - heraspiur, antel herakir (հեռասփիւռ, անթել հեռագիր)
wiring - telapashkhoutiun (թելաբաշխութիւն)
wiry - telanuman, telayin, bint (թելանման, թելային, պինդ)
wisdom - imasdoutiun (իմաստութիւն)
wisdom tooth - imasdoutian agra (իմաստութեան ակռայ)
wise (a) - imasdoun, khohem, khelatsi, kidoun, vuhoug (իմաստուն, խոհեմ, խելացի, գիտուն, վհուկ)
wise (n) - yeghanag, tsev, gerb (եղանակ, ձեւ, կերպ)
wisely - imasdoutiamp, khelatsoutiamp (իմաստութեամբ, խելացութեամբ)
wish - papak, ights, tsangoutiun, papakil, tsangal (փափաք, իղձ, ցանկութիւն, փափաքիլ, ցանկալ)
wisher - maghtogh (մաղթող)
wishy-washy - nihar, parag, touyl, anzor, anhedakurkir (նիհար, բարակ, թոյլ, անզօր, անհետաքրքիր)
wisp - durtsag mu khod, pokur avel, mazi khourts (տրցակ մը խոտ, փոքր աւել, մազի խուրձ)
wistful - ughtsod, mudadzgod, khohoun (ըղձոտ, մտածկոտ, խոհուն)
wit - kidnal, sorvil, midk, khelk, gadagapan (գիտնալ, սորվիլ, միտք, խելք, կատակաբան)
witch - vuhoug, gakhart gin, humayel, gakhartel (վհուկ, կախարդ կին, հմայել, կախարդել)
witch doctor - hurashakordz puzhishg, mok (հրաշագործ բժիշկ, մոգ)
witchery - mokoutiun, gakhartoutiun, tiutank (մոգութիւն, կախարդութիւն, դիւթանք)
with - hed, megdegh, miadegh (հետ, մէկտեղ, միատեղ)
withal - nayev, miankamayn, aylev (նաեւ, միանգամայն, այլեւ)
withdraw - yed kashel, heratsunel, nahanchel, kashvil (ետ քաշել, հեռացնել, նահանջել, քաշուիլ)
withdrawal - nahanch, megnoum (նահանջ, մեկնում)
withe - tiuratek, tiurin dzurog jiugh (դիւրաթեք, դիւրին ծռող ճիւղ)
wither - chornal, taramil, toshnil, chortsunel (չորնալ, թառամիլ, թոշնիլ, չորցնել)
withhold - purnel, arkilel, getsunel (բռնել, արգիլել, կեցնել)
withholder - purnogh, arkilogh (բռնող, արգիլող)
within - mechu, nersu (մէջը, ներսը)
without - patsi, arants, toursu (բացի, առանց, դուրսը)
withstand - timaturel, dogal, unttimanal, hagaragil (դիմադրել, տոկալ, ընդդիմանալ, հակառակիլ)
witless - anmid, animasd, khentoutiun (անմիտ, անիմաստ, խենթութիւն)
witness - vuga, aganades, vugayoutiun, vugayel (վկայ, ականատես, վկայութիւն, վկայել)
witticism - imasdagoutiun, anham surakhosoutiun (իմաստակութիւն, անհամ սրախօսութիւն)
wittily - suramudoren (սրամտօրէն)
wittiness - suramudoutiun, hanjar (սրամտութիւն, հանճար)
witting - dugaramid, anmid, pakhoug (տկարամիտ, անմիտ, փախուկ)
wittingly - kidagtsapar, kidnalov (գիտակցաբար, գիտնալով)
witty - suramid, oushim, yerkidzapan (սրամիտ, ուշիմ, երգիծաբան)
wive - gin arnel, amousnanal (կին

առնել, ամուսնանալ)
wives - giner (կիներ)
wizard - gakhart, koushag, vuhoug (կախարդ, գուշակ, վհուկ)
wizen - chornal, toshnil, taramil, vudid, nihar (չորնալ, Թօշնիլ, Թառամիլ, վտիտ, նիհար)
wizened - chortsadz (չորցած)
woad - lurchapouys, lurchadoung, gabdatsunogh niut (լրջաբոյս, լրջատունկ, կապտացնող նիւԹ)
wobble - yereril, toghtochel, sharzhil, yereroum (երերիլ, դողդոջել, շարժիլ, երերում)
woe - vishd, tsav, aghed, voh, avagh (վիշտ, ցաւ, աղէտ, ո՜հ, աւա՜ղ)
woeful - tzavali, dukhour, voghpali, aghidali (ցաւալի, տխուր, ողբալի, աղիտալի)
wold - patsad, andzar degh (բացատ, անձառ տեղ)
wolf - kayl, lapel, lagel (գայլ, լափել, լակել)
wolfish - kaylatsoug (գայլաձուկ)
woman - gin, gunig, gunamart (կին, կնիկ, կնամարդ)
womanhood - gunoutiun, ganatsioutiun, ganayk (կնուԹիւն, կանացիուԹիւն, կանայք)
womanish - ganatsi, ikagan (կանացի, իգական)
womb - arkant, por (արգանդ, փոր)
wonder - zarmank, hiatsoum, hurashk, uskanchelik (զարմանք, հիացում, հրաշք, սքանչելիք)
wonderful - uskancheli, zarmanali (սքանչելի, զարմանալի)
wonderland - hurashaliknerou yergir (Հրաշալիքներու երկիր)
wonderwork - hurashakordzoutiun (ՀրաշագործուԹիւն)
wondrous - zarmanali, abshetsoutsich, hianali (զարմանալի, ապշեցուցիչ, հիանալի)
wont - varzh, sovor, sovoragan, sovoroutiun (վարժ, սովոր, սովորական, սովորուԹիւն)
woo - sirapanil, tarbasel, kudznil, paghakushel (սիրաբանիլ, դարպասել, քծնիլ, փաղաքշել)
wood - payd, andar, bourag (փայտ, անտառ, պուրակ)
woodcut - paydakuroutiun, paydi vura porakuroutiun (փայտագրուԹիւն, փայտի վրայ փորագրուԹիւն)
wooden - payde, paydashen, dukegh (փայտէ, փայտաշէն, տգեղ)
woodland - dzarasdan, andar (ծառաստան, անտառ)
woodman - andarabah, paydahad (անտառապահ, փայտահատ)
woody - dzarakhid, andarod, paydayin (ծառախիտ, անտառոտ, փայտային)
wooer - sirapanogh, darpadzou (սիրաբանող, տարփածու)
woof - lat, tezanik, hiusvadzk (լաԹ, Թեզանիք, հիւսուածք)
wool - pourt (բուրդ)
woolen - purteghen, pourte shinvadz (բրդեղէն, բուրդէ շինուած)
word - par, khosk, khosdoum, khosil, ardahaydel (բառ, խօսք, խոստում, խօսիլ, արտայայտել)
word processing - paravaroum (բառավարում)
word processor - paravarich, parasarkich (բառավարիչ, բառասարքիչ)
wordbook - parakirk, pararan (բառագիրք, բառարան)
work (n) - kordz, ashkhadank, ashkhadoutiun, chank (գործ, աշխատանք, աշխատուԹիւն, ջանք)
work (v) - ashkhadil, kordzel, chanal, ashkhadtsunel (աշխատիլ, գործել, ջանալ, աշխատցնել)
workaday - amenoria, aroria-kordz (ամէնօրեայ, առօրեայ՝ գործ)
workday - kordzi or, ashkhadanki or (գործի օր, աշխատանքի օր)
worker - kordzogh, kordzavor, ashkhadavor, murchiun (գործող, գործաւոր, աշխատաւոր, մրջիւն)
workfellow - kordzagits, kordzi unger (գործակից, գործի ընկեր)
workman - kordzavor, ashkhadavor (գործաւոր, աշխատաւոր)
workshop - kordzadoun, gurbag,

ashkhadanisd, ashkhadabah (գործունեության, կրպակ, աշխատանոց, աշխատավայր)
worktable - kordzaseghan, gari seghan (գործասեղան, կարի սեղան)
world - ashkharh, yergir, diyezerk, martig (աշխարհ, երկիր, տիեզերք, մարդիկ
worldwide - hamashkharhayin, ashkharhadaradz (համաշխարհային, աշխարհատարած)
worm - vort, turtour, juji, soghosgil, suburtil (որդ, թրթուր, ճճի, սողոսկիլ, սպրդիլ)
wormwood - oshintur, leghvaham pouys (օշինդր, լեղուահամ բոյս)
wornout - mashadz, hintsadz, usbaradz (մաշած, հինցած, սպառած)
worriment - neghoutiun (նեղութիւն)
worrisome - mudahokich, neghogh (մտահոգիչ, նեղող)
worry - puzukdel, charcharel, neghel, neghoutiun (բզքտել, չարչարել, նեղել, նեղութիւն)
worse - aveli kesh (աւելի գէշ)
worsen - aveli keshtsunel (աւելի գէշցնել)
worship - bashdamounk, yergurbakoutiun, bashdel (պաշտամունք, երկրպագութիւն, պաշտել)
worst - horekouyn, vadtarakouyn, haghtel (յոռեգոյն, վատթարագոյն, յաղթել)
worsted - manadz pourt, tezan (մանած բուրդ, թեզան)
wort - pouys, khod, murmuroug karechouri (բոյս, խոտ, մրմրուկ գարեջուրի)
worth - arzhani, arzhek, hark, kin, ullal, kal (արժանի, արժէք, գին, յարգ, գին, ըլլալ, գալ)
worthiness - arzhanik, arzhanabadvoutiun (արժանիք, արժանապատուութիւն)
worthless - anarzhek, chunchin, anbidan, suriga (անարժէք, չնչին, անպիտան, սրիկայ)
worthy - arzhanavor, harkarzhan, arzhani (արժանաւոր, յարգարժան, արժանի)
would - gouzeyi, gu papakeyi, bidi ouzeyi (կ'ուզէի, կը փափաքէի, պիտի ուզէի)
wound - verk, khots, viravorel (վէրք, խոց, վիրաւորել)
wrack - gordzanoum, gorousd, vunas, navapegoutiun (կործանում, կորուստ, վնաս, նաւաբեկութիւն)
wraith - ourvagan, voki (ուրուական, ոգի)
wrangle - vej, guriv, vijil, gurvil (վէճ, կռիւ, վիճիլ, կռուիլ)
wrap - pattel, badel, dzadzgel, tetev dzadzgots (փաթթել, պատել, ծածկել, թեթեւ ծածկոց)
wrapper - dzadzgots, patouyt, tetev verargou (ծածկոց, փաթոյթ, թեթեւ վերարկու)
wrath - pargoutiun, zayrouyt, tsasoum (բարկութիւն, զայրոյթ, ցասում)
wrathful - gadaghi, molekin, zayratsadz, tsasgod (կատաղի, մոլեգին, զայրացած, ցասկոտ)
wreak - vurezh loudzel, zayrouyt tapel (վրէժ լուծել, զայրոյթ թափել)
wreath - dzaghgepounch, dzaghgebusag (ծաղկեփունջ, ծաղկեպսակ)
wreathe - hiusel, volorel, polorel-dzaghig (հիւսել, ոլորել, բոլորել՝ ծաղիկ)
wreck (n) - navapegoutiun, gordzanoum, aver (նաւաբեկութիւն, կործանում, աւեր)
wreck (v) - navapegel, gordzanel, gordzanil, khordagil (նաւաբեկել, կործանել, կործանիլ, խորտակիլ)
wreckage - navapegoutiun, navapegor, khordagoum (նաւաբեկութիւն, նաւաբեկոր, խորտակում)
wren - tsakhsarig (ցախսարիկ)
wrench - burgel, kalarel, kashel, voloroum, khuloum (պրկել, գալարել, քաշել, ոլորում, խլում)
wrest - volorel, kashgurdel, kashel, purnoutiun (ոլորել, քաշկռտել, քաշել, բռնութիւն)
wrestle - kodemardil, makaril (գօտեմարտիլ, մաքառիլ)

wrestling - kodemard, umpushamard (գօտեմարտ, ըմբշամարտ)

wretch - tushvaragan, hek, anuzkam (Թշուառական, Հէգ, անզգամ)

wretched - voghormeli, tuzhpakhd, tushvar, khughjali (ողորմելի, դժբախտ, Թշուառ, խղճալի)

wriggle - soghosgil, kalarvil, soghal (սողոսկիլ, գալարուիլ, սողալ)

wright - arhesdavor, mekenakordz (արհեստաւոր, մեքենագործ)

wring - volorel, kalarel, tartsunel, seghmel (ոլորել, գալարել, դարձնել, սեղմել)

wrinkle - gunjir, khorshom, dzalk, gunjurel (կնճիռ, խորշոմ, ծալք, կնճռել)

wrist - tasdag (դաստակ)

wristlet - tsernagab (ձեռնակապ)

writ - huraman, huramanakir, vujir (Հրաման, Հրամանագիր, վճիռ)

write - kurel, artsanakurel, heghinagel (գրել, արձանագրել, Հեղինակել)

writer - kurogh, heghinag, khumpakir (գրող, Հեղինակ, խմբագիր)

writhe - kalaril, kalarel, danchuvil, neghvil (գալարիլ, գալարել, տանջուիլ, նեղուիլ)

writing - tserakir, kuroutiun, artsanakuroutiun (ձեռագիր, գրուԹիւն, արձանագրուԹիւն)

wrong - sukhal, dzour, anjisht, aniravel, vunasel (սխալ, ծուռ, անճիշդ, անիրաւել, վնասել)

wrongful - anirav, vunasagar (անիրաւ, վնասակար)

wroth - pargatsadz, zayratsadz, tsasgod (բարկացած, զայրացած, ցասկոտ)

wrought - ashkhadtsuvadz, nurpakordz, yeghadz (աշխատցուած, նրբագործ, եղած)

wry - dzuradz, sheghadz, voloravadz (ծռած, շեղած, ոլորուած)

wynd - arahed, nurpantsk (արաՀետ, նրբանցք)

X rated - pokrerou arkilvadz sharzhabadger (փոքրերու արգիլուած շարժապատկեր)

xenial - hiuraser (Հիւրասէր)

xenon - gaz mu - kusenon (կազ մը՝ քսենոն)

Xenon - kusenon (Քսենոն)

xenophobia - odaradiatsoutiun (օտարատեացուԹիւն)

xerography - lousadubakuroutiun (լուսատպագրուԹիւն)

xerox machine - lousadib mekena, lousadubich (լուսատիպ մեքենայ, լուսատպիչ)

Xmas - sourp dzunount (Ս. Ծնունդ)

xylograph, pher - paydakir (փայտագիր)

xylography - paydakuroutiun (փայտագրուԹիւն)

xyloid - paydia, paydagerb (փայտեայ, փայտակերպ)

xylotomist - paydahad (փայտաՀատ)

xylotomy - paydahadoutiun (փայտաՀատուԹիւն)

X-ray - ke jarakayt, ke jarakaytov nugarel (Ք. ճառագայԹ, Ք. ճառագայԹով նկարել)

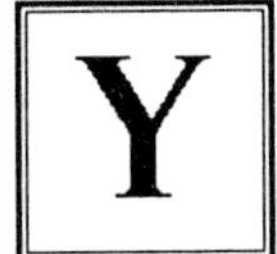

yacht - uzposanav, murtsanav (զբօսանաւ, մրցանաւ)
yachting - uzposanavov budouyd (զբօսանաւով պտոյտ)
Yahvism - yehovaganoutiun (Եհովականութիւն)
yak - tsorakhoy, khodoroug, yeghnatsi (ձորախոյ, խոտորուկ, եղնացի)
yankee - amerigatsi (ամերիկացի)
yap - gaghgantsel, vornal, hachel, vornots (կաղկանձել, ոռնալ, հաչել, ոռնոց)
yard - ankliagan gankoun, tsoghachap, pag, kavit (անգլիական կանգուն, ձողաչափ, բակ, գաւիթ)
yarn - tel, tertsan, manadz, arasbel, hekyat (թել, դերձան, մանած, առասպել, հէքեաթ)
yashmak - ganatsi kulkhou-yeresi kogh (կանացի գլխու- երեսի քօղ)
yataghan - tashouyn, yataghan (դաշոյն, եաթաղան)
yaup - jich, kochiun, juchal (ճիչ, գոչիւն, ճչալ)
yaw - navou sheghoum, sheghil, pushdig, balar (նաւու շեղում, շեղիլ, բշտիկ, պալար)
yawl - magouyg, arakasdanav, jich, juchal (մակոյկ, առագաստանաւ, ճիչ, ճչալ)
yawn - horanchel, tsangal, horanchoum, tsangoutiun (յօրանջել, ցանկալ, յօրանջում, ցանկութիւն)
year - dari, dareshurchan (տարի, տարեշրջան)
yearbook - darekirk (տարեգիրք)
yearly - daregan, miamia, darin ankam mu (տարեկան, միամեայ, տարին անգամ մը)
yearn - denchal, tsangal, garodnal, mormokil (տենչալ, ցանկալ, կարօտնալ, մորմոքիլ)
years - darik, dzeroutiun (տարիք, ծերութիւն)
yeast - tutkhumor, khumorel, magartel (թթխմոր, խմորել, մակարդել)
yeggman - suriga, avazag, yeghernakordz (սրիկայ, աւազակ, եղեռնագործ)
yell - boral, gantsel, gaghgantsel, vornal, borchudouk (պոռալ, կանչել, ոռնալ, պոռչտուք)
yellow - teghin, teghnil (դեղին, դեղնիլ)
yellowish - teghnakouyn, teghnorag (դեղնագոյն, դեղնորակ)
yelp - gaghgantsel, gaghgants (կաղկանձել, կաղկանձ)
yeoman - akaragaban, gamavor hedzelazor (ագարակապան, կամաւոր հեծելազօր)
yerk - tsuntsel, akatsel, gits dal, gits (ցնցել, աքացել, կից տալ, կից
yes - ayo (այո)
yester - yeregoua (երէկուայ)
yesterday - yereg (երէկ)
yesternight - yereg kisher (երէկ գիշեր)
yesternoon - yereg gesor (երէկ կէսօր)
yesteryear - antsial dari (անցեալ տարի)
yet - dagavin, ter (տակաւին, դեռ)
yew - keghts, garmuradzar (գեղձ, կարմրածառ)
yield (n) - ardaturoutiun, perk, hasouyt, artiunk (արտադրութիւն, բերք, հասոյթ, արդիւնք)
yield (v) - zichil, ardaturel, hantsunel, dal, poustsunel (զիջիլ, արտադրել, յանձնել, տալ, բուսցնել)
yielder - hamagerbogh, deghi duvogh (համակերպող, տեղի տուող)
yielding - hamagerboutiun, tiuratek

(Համակերպութիւն, դիւրաթեք)
yodel - *yelevechel-tsaynu* (ելեւէջել՝ ձայնը)
yogurt, yoghurt, yoghourt - *madzoun* (մածուն)
yoke - *loudz, keroutiun, zouyk, zoukel, miatsunel* (լուծ, գերութիւն, զոյգ, զուգել, միացնել)
yokefellow - *ludzagits, unger* (լծակից, ընկեր)
yokel - *hodagh, keghchoug* (Հօտաղ, գեղջուկ)
yolk - *havgiti teghnouts* (Հաւկիթի դեղնուց)
yon - *hon, ayndeghi* (Հոն, այնտեղի)
yonder - *antii, hon, ayn degh , antur* (անդիի, Հոն, այն տեղ, անդր)
yore - *zhamanagin, adenok* (ժամանակին, ատենօք)
you - *toun, kez, kezi, touk, tsez, tsezi* (դուն, քեզ, քեզի, դուք, ձեզ, ձեզի)
young - *yeridasart, anports, noradi, gurdser* (երիտասարդ, անփորձ, նորատի, կրտսեր)
younger - *gurdserakouyn, aveli yeridasart* (կրտսերագոյն, աւելի երիտասարդ)
youngish - *teradi* (դեռատի)
youngster - *manoug, manchoug, badaniag* (մանուկ, մանչուկ, պատանեակ)
your - *kou, tser* (քու, ձեր)
yours - *tser, tseru* (ձեր, ձերը)
yourself - *toun inkut, toun kezi* (դուն ինքդ, դուն քեզի)
yourselves - *touk, antsamp, touk inknerut* (դուք, անձամբ, դուք ինքներդ)
youth - *yeridasartoutiun, badanoutiun, yeridasart* (երիտասարդութիւն, պատանութիւն, երիտասարդ)
youthful - *norahas, madagh, yeridasartagan* (նորաՀաս, մատաղ, երիտասարդական)
yowl - *vornots, gaghgants, vornal* (ոռնոց, կաղկանձ, ոռնալ)
yucca - *armavashoushan* (արմաւաշուշան)
yule - *donakhumpoutiun sourp dzununti* (տօնախմբութիւն Սուրբ Ծննդի)
yule tree - *donadzar* (տօնածառ)
yuletide - *sourp dzununtian don* (Սուրբ Ծննդեան տօն)

Z

zany - *himar, hudbid, kheghgadag* (յիմար, Հտպիտ, խեղկատակ)
zeal - *nakhants, nakhantsakhuntutoutiun, yerant, pouyt* (նախանձ, նախանձախնդրութիւն, եռանդ, փոյթ)
zealless - *anpouyt, touyl, annakhants* (անփոյթ, թոյլ, աննախանձ)
zealot - *nakhantsakhuntir, khantod, yerantod* (նախանձախնդիր, խանդոտ, եռանդոտ)
zealous - *nakhantsakhuntir, khantavar, yerantod* (նախանձախնդիր, խանդավառ, եռանդոտ)
zebra - *vakratsi, vazeratsi* (վագրաձի, վազերաձի)
zend - *zend, zendagan lezou* (զենտ, զենտական լեզու)
zenith - *kakatnaged, partsuraged, zenit* (գագաթնակէտ, բարձրակէտ, զենիթ)
zephyr - *zepiur, siuk* (զեփիւռ, սիւք)
zero - *zero, zuro, vochinch* (զէրօյ, զրոյ, ոչինչ)
zest - *bobog, narinchi geghev, umposhkhnoum, geghevel* (պոպոկ, նարինջի կեղեւ, ըմբոշխնում, կեղեւել)

zigzag - otsabudouyd, dzouroumour, zigzag, dzamadzurel (օձապտոյտ, ծուռումուռ, զիկզակ, ծամածռել)
zinc - zing, zingov badel (ցինկ, ցինկով պատել)
zincographer - zingakir (ցինկագիր)
zincography - zingakuroutiun, zingi porakuroutiun (ցինկագրութիւն, ցինկի փորագրութիւն)
Zion - sion (Սիոն)
Zionism - sionaganoutiun (Սիոնականութիւն)
zip - vuzzots, kuntali soulots, vuzzal (վզզոց, գնդակի սուլոց, վզզալ)
zip code - shurchativ, oughetiv (շրջանաթիւ, ուղեթիւ)
zipper - jarmant, pagatel, pagank (ճարմանդ, փակաթել, փականք)
zippy - gorovi, gensounag (կորովի, կենսունակ)
zodiac - gentanagamar (կենդանակամար)
zonal - shurchanayin, kodiyi (շրջանային, գօտիի)
zone - kodi, shurchan, gamar (գօտի, շրջան, կամար)
zoo - gentanapanagan bardez (կենդանաբանական պարտէզ)
zooid - gentanagerb (կենդանակերպ)
zoolater - gentanabashd (կենդանապաշտ)
zoologist - gentanapan (կենդանաբան)
zoology - gentanapanoutiun (կենդանաբանութիւն)
zoon - gentani, anasoun (կենդանի, անասուն)
zoophilous - gentanaser (կենդանասէր)
zygoma - aydosguri tsutsvadzk (այտոսկրի ցցուածք)
zymase - khumor, khumorahiut (խմոր, խմորահիւթ)
zymometer - khumorachap (խմորաչափ)

THE ARMENIAN ALPHABET

Discovered in
406 A.D.
by
MESROB
MASHDOTZ

Աա Բբ Գգ Դդ Եե Զզ Էէ Ըը

Թթ Ժժ Իի Լլ Խխ Ծծ Կկ Հհ

Ձձ Ղղ Ճճ Մմ Յյ Նն Շշ Ոո Չչ

Պպ Ջջ Ռռ Սս Վվ Տտ Րր Ցց

Իւ Փփ Քք Օօ Ֆֆ